MCDOUGAL LITTELL

Passport
to **Algebra** and **Geometry**

RON LARSON

LAURIE BOSWELL

TIMOTHY D. KANOLD

LEE STIFF

McDougal Littell
A HOUGHTON MIFFLIN COMPANY
Evanston, Illinois • Boston • Dallas

About the Cover

The Passport series brings mathematics to life with many real-life applications. The cover shows a use of mathematics in space exploration. Other examples of mathematics in space exploration are shown on pages 23, 25, 435, 520, 534, 545, 553, and 593. The mathematical statements and diagrams on the cover show some of the material covered in this book—algebra, geometry, and problem solving. Look for exciting applications of these and other topics as you study mathematics this year!

ISBN: 0-395-87988-4   456789—VJM—02 01 00 99

Internet Web Site: http://www.mlmath.com

Ron Larson is a professor of mathematics at the Behrend College of Pennsylvania State University at Erie. He is the author of many well-known high school and college mathematics textbooks, including *Heath: Algebra 1*, *Geometry*, *Algebra 2*, *Precalculus*, *Precalculus with Limits,* and *Calculus*. He is a pioneer in the development of interactive textbooks, and his calculus textbook is published on CD-ROM. Dr. Larson is a member of NCTM and frequently speaks at NCTM and other professional conferences.

Laurie Boswell is a mathematics teacher at Profile Junior-Senior High School in Bethlehem, New Hampshire. She is active in NCTM and local mathematics organizations. A recipient of the 1986 Presidential Award for Excellence in Mathematics Teaching, she is also the 1992 Tandy Technology Scholar and the 1991 recipient of the Richard Balomenos Mathematics Education Service Award presented by the New Hampshire Association of Teachers of Mathematics. She is an author of *Heath Geometry* and Houghton Mifflin *Math Central*.

Timothy D. Kanold is Director of Mathematics and Science and a teacher at Adlai Stevenson High School in Lincolnshire, Illinois. A 1986 recipient of the Presidential Award for Excellence in Mathematics Teaching, he is also the 1993 recipient of the Illinois Council of Teachers of Mathematics Outstanding Leadership Award. A member of NCTM, he served on NCTM's Professional Standards for Teaching Mathematics Commission. He is an author of *Heath: Algebra 1* and *Algebra 2*.

Lee Stiff is an associate professor of mathematics education in the College of Education and Psychology of North Carolina State University at Raleigh and has taught mathematics at the high school and middle school levels. A member of NCTM, he served on the Board of Directors. He is also the 1992 recipient of the W.W. Rankin Award for Excellence in Mathematics Education presented by the North Carolina Council of Teachers of Mathematics. He is an author of *Heath: Algebra 1*, *Geometry*, *Algebra 2*, and Houghton Mifflin *Math Central*.

Reviewers and Contributors

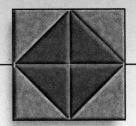

Linda Bailey
Mathematics Coordinator
Putnam City Schools
Oklahoma City, OK

David S. Bradley
Mathematics Department Chairperson
Thomas Jefferson Junior High School
Kearns, UT

John A. Carter
Mathematics Department Chairperson
West Chicago Community High School
West Chicago, IL

Anthony C. Dentino
Supervisor of Curriculum and Instruction
Brick Township School District
Brick, NJ

John Paul Fox
Mathematics Department Chairperson
Clinton Middle School
Columbus, OH

Gregory J. Fry
Mathematics Teacher
White Bear Lake High School
White Bear Lake, MN

Sue D. Garriss
Mathematics Teacher
Millbrook Senior High School
Raleigh, NC

Leigh M. Graham
Learner Support Strategist
Awtrey Middle School
Cobb County, GA

Tammie Manley-Gurley
Mathematics Teacher
Forestwood Middle School
Flower Mound, TX

Judith Jones Hall
Mathematics Department Chairperson
St. John School
Seattle, WA

Barbara Handley
Mathematics Chairperson
San Jacinto Junior High
  School
Midland, TX

Sandra A. Hinker
Mathematics Department Chairperson
Marshfield Junior High School
Marshfield, WI

Audrey M. Johnson
Mathematics Coordinator
Luke O'Toole Elementary School
Chicago, IL

Kathy Johnson
Mathematics Teacher
East Paulding Middle School
Dallas, GA

Charlene M. Kincaid
Teacher on Special Assignment
National Museum of Naval Aviation
Pensacola, FL

Betty Koleilat
Assistant Principal of Curriculum
Drew Academy
Houston, TX

Marsha W. Lilly
Secondary Mathematics Coordinator
Alief Independent School District
Alief, TX

Christine S. Losq
Mathematics Consultant
The Whole Math ™ Project
Palo Alto, CA

Veronica G. Meeks
Mathematics Teacher
Western Hills High School
Fort Worth, TX

Ileene Paul
Director of Special Education
Aldai E. Stevenson High School
Lincolnshire, IL

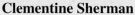

Clementine Sherman
Director
Dade County Public Schools
Miami, FL

Robyn Silbey
Mathematics Specialist
Montgomery County Public Schools
Rockville, MD

Ricardo Torres
Mathematics Teacher
M.B. Lamar Middle School
Laredo, TX

Thomas M. Tobiasen
Mathematics Supervisor
Parsippany-Troy Hills Township Schools
Parsippany, NJ

Linda Tucci
Mathematics Teacher
Rice Avenue Middle School
Girard, PA

Betsy L. Wiens
V.P. Middle Level:
Kansas Association of Teachers of Math
Washburn Rural Middle School
Topeka, KS

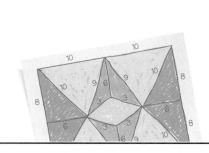

Student Review Panel

Laina Carlos
Greeneville Middle School
Greeneville, TN

Amelia Groeschel
Peet Junior High School
Conroe, TX

Kendra Hudgins
Brewer Middle School
Fort Worth, TX

Jennifer Karr
West Middle School
Holland, MI

Megan Keller
Marinette Middle School
Marinette, WI

Danny Kelly
Norton Middle School
Norton, OH

Frank Kincel, Jr.
West Scranton Intermediate
  School
Scranton, PA

Jessica Kull
Haven Middle School
Evanston, IL

Jonathan Larason
Woodbury School
Salem, NH

Rebecca Marriott
Southeastern Randolph
  Middle School
Asheboro, NC

Megan McDiffett
Wendler Middle School
Anchorage, AK

Meredith McKenna
Plymouth Community
  Intermediate School
Plymouth, MA

Gaston Prevette
Smithfield Middle School
Smithfield, NC

Gabrielle Ramos
Frederick H. Tuttle Middle
  School
South Burlington, VT

Reathie Rogers
Durham Magnet School
Durham, NC

Eric Roskens
Thayer Jay Hill Middle School
Naperville, IL

Arlie Sommer
Middleton Middle School
Middleton, ID

Kelly Swift
Anderson High School
Cincinnati, OH

Kelli VanDeusen
Irons Junior High School
Lubbock, TX

Sarah Zanoff
Forestwood Middle School
Lewisville, TX

Exploring Patterns

Applications

Race Times 5
Music 9
Designing a Garden 11
Designing a Room 13
School Supplies 19
World's Largest Flag 20
Space 23
Robotic Rover 25
Super Bowl 26
Olympic Medals 28
Architecture 35
Summer Job 36
Distance, Rate, Time 44

Assessment
Ongoing Assessment *3, 7, 11, 17, 23, 27, 33, 39*
Standardized Test Practice *5, 9, 13, 19, 25, 29, 35, 41*
Spiral Review *14, 36*
Mid-Chapter Assessment *20*   **Chapter Assessment** *46*
Problem Solving Strategies
Applying Strategies *3, 4, 12, 14, 15, 20, 27, 39, 40, 41, 46*
Interdisciplinary Features
History Connection: Hindu-Arabic Numerals *14*
Career Interview: Research Scientist *36*
Communicating About Mathematics: Where the Buffalo Roam *37*

Investigations in Algebra

CHAPTER

3

Modeling Integers

Applications

Assessment

Problem Solving Strategies

Interdisciplinary Features

Exploring the **Language** of **Algebra**

Applications

Assessment

CHAPTER 5

Exploring Data and Graphs

Applications

Assessment

CHAPTER
6

Exploring Number Theory

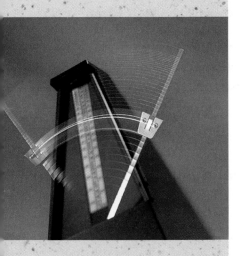

Applications

Assessment

CHAPTER 7

Rational Numbers and Percents

Applications

Assessment

Proportion, Percent, and Probability

Applications

Assessment

Problem Solving Strategies

Interdisciplinary Features

CHAPTER 9

Real Numbers and Inequalities

Applications

Assessment

Geometry Concepts and Spatial Thinking

Applications

Assessment

Congruence, Similarity, and Transformations

Applications

Miniature Golf 513
Photography 519
Pets 520
Lunar Rotation 529
Computer Animation 531
Driving in Alabama 533
Amusement Park 535
Launch Towers 539
Model Car 544
Painting 545
Fundraising 550
Space Shuttle 553

Assessment

Ongoing Assessment *513, 517, 523, 527, 531, 537, 543, 547, 553*
Standardized Test Practice *515, 520, 525, 529, 533, 539, 545, 549, 555*
Spiral Review *520, 550*
Mid-Chapter Assessment *535*   Chapter Assessment *560*

Problem Solving Strategies

Applying Strategies *515, 519, 526, 529, 553*

Interdisciplinary Features

Communicating About Mathematics: Looking at the Stars *534*
Career Interview: Robotics Engineer *550*

CHAPTER 12

Measurements in Geometry

Applications

Assessment

CHAPTER 13

Exploring Linear Equations

Applications

CHAPTER 14

Exploring Data and Polynomials

Applications

Weather 669
Chemistry 671
Social Studies 673
Indianapolis 500 674
Life Expectancy 675
Biology 679
Pet Store 685
Rainfall 687
Bridges 691
Business 697
Gardens 700
Art 705
Mosaics 707
Home Remodeling 712

Assessment
Ongoing Assessment *669, 673, 677, 683, 689, 695, 699, 705*
Standardized Test Practice *671, 675, 680, 685, 691, 697, 701, 707*
Spiral Review *680, 702*
Mid-Chapter Assessment *687*   **Chapter Assessment** *712*

Problem Solving Strategies
Applying Strategies *705, 707*

Interdisciplinary Features
Communicating About Mathematics: The Hardest 100 *686*
History Connection: Galileo *702*

Student Handbook

You can use the reference tools in the Student Handbook to help you find answers to your math questions.

ENGLISH-TO-SPANISH GLOSSARY

absolute value/valor absoluto (p. 105) Distancia entre un número y el 0 en una línea numérica. Por ejemplo: $|3| = 3$, $|-3| = 3$, $|0| = 0$.

absolute value signs/signos de valor absoluto (p. 105) Par de líneas verticales que se usan para

area/área (p. 7) Medida de la superficie cubierta por una figura. El área se mide en unidades cuadradas.

Associative Property of Addition/Propiedad asociativa de la adición (p. 67) Cambiar el

GLOSSARY

absolute value (p. 105) The distance between a number and 0 on a number line. For example, $|3| = 3$, $|-3| = 3$, $|0| = 0$.

absolute value signs (p. 105) A pair of vertical rules that are used to indicate the absolute value of a number or expression between them.

acute angle (p. 465) An angle whose measure is between 0° and 90°.

acute triangle (p. 479) A triangle with three acute angles.

add matrices (p. 683) To find the sum of two matrices by adding the corresponding entries.

add polynomials (p. 694) To find the sum of two polynomials by combining the like terms.

Addition Property of Equality (p.) Adding the same number to each side of an equation produces an equivalent equation. If $a = b$, then $a + c = b + c$.

adjacent side *See* cosine of an angle, tangent of an angle.

algebraic expression (p. 22) A collection of numbers, variables, operations, and grouping symbols. For example, 2(

algebraic model (p. 23) An expression or equation used to represent a real-life situation.

angle (p. 464) A figure formed by two rays that begin at the same point. The rays are the sides of the angle and the point is the vertex of the angle.

area (p. 7) A measure of the amount of surface covered by a figure. Area is measured in square units.

EXTRA PRACTICE

Use after Lesson 1.1, page 4

Describe a pattern for the sequence. Then list the next 3 numbers.

1. $-2, -5, -8, -11, \boxed{?}, \boxed{?}, \boxed{?}$

2. $0, 2, 5, 9, \boxed{?}, \boxed{?}, \boxed{?}$

3. $0, 1, 4, 9, \boxed{?}, \boxed{?}, \boxed{?}$

4. $99, 90, 81, 72, \boxed{?}, \boxed{?}, \boxed{?}$

Use after Lesson 1.6, page 28

The table shows the enrollments in Social Studies courses at Plainview High School for three years. Let P, W, and U represent the number of students in Psychology, World History, and U.S. History.

Class	Year		
	1994	1995	1996
Psychology	70	62	72

TOOLBOX

Problem Solving Strategies

The ability to solve problems is an important part of mathematics. When you are solving a problem, organize your work by using the following four-step problem solving plan.

Step 1	**Understand the problem.** Read the problem carefully. Decide what information you are given and what you need to find.
Step 2	**Make a plan to solve the problem.** Choose a strategy. Decide if you will use a tool such as a calculator, a graph, or a spreadsheet.
Step 3	**Carry out the plan to solve the problem.** Use the strategy and tool(s) you have chosen. Do any calculations that are needed. Answer the question that the problem asks.
Step 4	**Check to see if your solution is reasonable.** Reread the problem and see if your answer agrees with the given information.

Example 1 Raoul bought some pencils for $.25 each and some erasers for $.40 each. If he spent $2.45 in all, how many of each did he buy?

Solution *Step 1: Read and understand the problem.*
Notice that you are given the cost for each pencil, the cost for each eraser, and the total amount spent. You are asked to find the number of pencils and the number of erasers that Raoul bought.

Step 2: Choose a strategy to solve the problem.
It may appear at first that there is not enough information to solve the problem. Select the guess and check method as a problem solving strategy.

Step 3: Apply the guess and check method.
Guess how many pencils Raoul bought and see if the corresponding number of erasers is a whole number. For example, if he bought 3 pencils, then $0.25(3) + 0.4y = 2.45$; solving gives $y = 4.25$, which doesn't make sense in this situation because he cannot buy part of an eraser. By continuing to guess how many pencils he might have bought and testing each guess in the equation $0.25x + 0.40y = 2.45$, you will find that there is only one possible solution: $x = 5$ and $y = 3$. He bought 5 pencils and 3 erasers.

Step 4: Check your answer.
You can check your answer by putting the solutions into the equation and making sure that they make sense.

Problem Solving Strategies

PRACTICE AND PROBLEM SOLVING

In Exercises 1–10, use the problem solving plan to solve the problem. A problem may contain information that is not needed or may not provide enough information to be solved. If there is not enough information, write *cannot be solved*.

1. May works 40 h a week at her usual hourly rate. When she works more than 40 h in a week, she is paid 50% more for each additional hour. One week May worked 48 h and was paid $936. Find her usual hourly rate.

2. A museum charges $8 per visit to nonmembers. Members pay a $25 membership fee and then $5 per visit. How many times must a person visit the museum for a membership to be less expensive than paying for each visit?

3. The Rogers family drove 140 mi on the interstate at an average speed of 56 mi/h. Then they spent 45 min at a restaurant having lunch and putting gas in the car. Finally, they completed their trip driving 57 mi through the country at an average speed of 30 mi/h. How long did their entire trip take?

4. Student tickets and general admission tickets were sold for the school play. The total amount of money collected was $1250. If 86 more student tickets than general admission tickets were sold, how many of each type of ticket was sold?

5. A customer handed a bank teller a check for $210 and asked for equal numbers of $20 bills and $10 bills. How many of each type of bill did the customer receive?

6. A regulation swimming pool is divided into eight lanes. Each lane in the pool is 50 m long and 2.4 m wide. The water in the pool is at least 1.2 m deep. If a person swims 12 laps from one end to the other in a regulation pool, how far did the person swim altogether?

7. A bunch of bananas weighs 2.5 lb and costs $1.70. Find the cost of a bunch that weighs 3.5 lb.

8. An electrician charges a basic service fee plus a labor charge for each hour of service. A 2 h job costs $74 and a 4 h job costs $118. Find the electrician's basic service fee.

9. In the National Hockey League, a team earns 2 points for a win, 1 point for a tie, and 0 points for a loss. In a recent season, the Detroit Red Wings played 82 games and earned 131 points. How many games did they win that season?

10. Sixty-four meters of fencing was needed to enclose a square garden. What is the area of the garden?

716

742 Toolbox

Toolbox

Real-Life Applications

Look through this list for things that interest you. Then find out how they are linked to mathematics.

Animals/Pets 195, 222, 223, 226, 435, 520, 544, 555, 670, 685

Architecture/Construction 35, 175, 373, 431, 454, 463, 471, 479, 600

Art/Design 277, 304, 319, 411, 447, 461, 477, 485, 514, 519, 542, 545, 559, 560, 705

Automobiles 161, 210, 362, 401, 420, 429, 544, 589, 645, 664, 674

Banking 81, 86, 117, 256, 263, 348, 352, 384

Bicycling 95, 153, 333, 423, 441, 445, 481, 631

Business and Industry 55, 61, 83, 88, 91, 100, 130, 145, 148, 165, 185, 204, 250, 296, 389, 697

Communication 161, 189, 191, 233, 385, 387, 388, 400

Computers 184, 191, 210, 228, 343, 375, 386, 531, 533

Consumer Spending 67, 69, 82

Earning Money 36, 73, 95, 118, 165, 173, 228, 278, 331, 333, 353

Education and School 19, 89, 90, 181, 210, 225, 232, 323, 379, 382, 436, 674

Energy Resources 257, 306, 317, 347, 597

Fashion 53, 85, 221, 329, 358, 395, 523

Flowers, Plants, and Trees 11, 59, 63, 169, 182, 219, 237, 334, 441, 506, 557, 650, 700

Food 275, 277, 283, 333, 334, 339, 352, 371, 394, 454, 651

Fundraising 139, 163, 199, 424, 441, 550, 631, 653

Geography 35, 107, 122, 544, 659

Health and Fitness 70, 313, 347, 374, 443, 445, 473, 583, 635

History 41, 113, 207, 263, 327, 337

Hobbies/Models/Crafts 81, 222, 269, 365, 372, 414, 605

Mail/Postage 166, 191, 206, 353, 355, 457, 625

Meteorology 111, 364, 669, 687

Movies/Entertainment 25, 141, 180, 194, 222, 225, 239, 307, 352, 379, 441, 457

Music 9, 79, 228, 267, 278, 291, 306, 364, 384, 385, 468, 483, 588, 679

Population 171, 211, 287, 321, 406, 649

Puzzles 285, 491, 569, 651

Real Estate 216, 229, 439, 456, 671

Recreation 5, 75, 81, 90, 150, 390, 513, 525, 535

Recycling and the Environment 210, 217, 226, 231, 243, 289, 650

Retail Prices 128, 190, 352, 357, 362, 365, 379, 384, 385, 404

Science and Medicine 123, 245, 287, 291, 302, 319, 325, 375, 411, 435, 508, 529, 539, 568, 585, 639, 645, 671, 679

Shopping 14, 70, 346, 383, 394

Signs and Symbols 34, 194, 273, 474, 482

Social Studies 214, 323, 343, 345, 351, 352, 673, 678

Space Exploration 23, 25, 435, 520, 534, 545, 553, 593

Sports and Athletics 5, 26, 27, 28, 46, 69, 75, 85, 93, 107, 112, 114, 116, 117, 135, 159, 175, 194, 200, 223, 233, 249, 250, 264, 305, 311, 371, 379, 423, 626, 650, 651

Surveying/Planning 13, 428, 430, 449, 581, 583

Temperature 29, 112, 129, 185, 619, 625, 687

Travel and Vacations 5, 176, 205, 206, 216, 248, 328, 473, 629

Real Life... **R**eal Math

You may be surprised at all the ways mathematics is connected to daily life and careers.

Real Life... Real People

Real Life... Real Facts

Welcome to the Passport series

Preparing you for success in mathematics in the middle grades and beyond.

As you progress through this course you will see that:

Mathematics makes connections

In this course you will study important middle grade mathematics concepts and see how they are related. You will also find a gradual approach to understanding the underlying principles of algebra and geometry.

Mathematics is accessible

Each lesson in the *Passport* series will help you learn more about math.The interesting activities and the useful pictures, charts, graphs, and models will make it easier for you to learn.

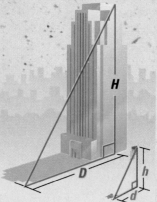

Mathematics is meaningful

Throughout each book in the series, you will explore and discover the importance of mathematics in daily life. In fact, you will find that many of the things you do, see, and hear are linked to mathematics.

Making mathematics relevant.

The Passport series emphasizes real data and real-life applications. The series also shows how to use modeling to understand concepts and solve problems.

The value of math is highlighted through the **LESSON OBJECTIVES** which will explain what you will learn, and why it is important.

ALGEBRA CONNECTION

4.1

What you should learn:

Goal 1 How to use two operations to solve a two-step equation

Goal 2 How to solve real-life problems using two-step equations

Why you should learn it:

You need to use two or more operations to solve most equations from real-life situations, such as finding how many hours you can play tennis at a club.

TOOLBOX

Solving Equations, page 751

Solving Two-Step Equations

Goal 1 USING TWO OPERATIONS

Solving an equation often requires two or more operations. Here are some guidelines that can help you decide how to start.

1. Simplify both sides of the equation (if needed).
2. Use inverse operations to isolate the variable.

Example 1 Solving an Equation

Solve $3x + 8 = 2$.

Solution

Remember that your goal is to isolate the variable.

$3x + 8 = 2$	Write original equation.
$3x + 8 - 8 = 2 - 8$	To isolate the *x*-term, subtract 8 from each side.
$3x = -6$	Simplify.
$\dfrac{3x}{3} = \dfrac{-6}{3}$	To isolate *x*, divide each side by 3.
$x = -2$	Solution: *x* is by itself.

The solution is -2.

✔**Check:** Substitute to see that $3(-2) + 8 = -6 + 8 = 2$.

Example 2 Solving an Equation

Solve $\dfrac{x}{-4} - 8 = 1$.

Solution

$\dfrac{x}{-4} - 8 = 1$	Write original equation.
$\dfrac{x}{-4} - 8 + 8 = 1 + 8$	Add 8 to each side.
$\dfrac{x}{-4} = 9$	Simplify.
$-4 \cdot \dfrac{x}{-4} = -4 \cdot 9$	Multiply each side by -4.
$x = -36$	Solution: *x* is by itself.

The solution is -36. Check this in the original equation.

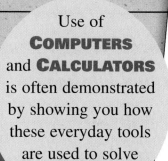

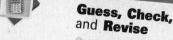

Guess, Check, and Revise

STRATEGY To solve problems successfully, y... strategies such as Making a Table, Pattern, Working Backward, Drawing a Diagram, Check, and Revise.

TOOLBOX
Problem Solving Strategies, page 744

STUDY TIP
The problem solving strategy Guess, Check, and Revise uses the steps below.

Guess a reasonable solution based on data in the problem.

Check the guess.

Revise the guess and check again. Continue until you find a solution.

Example
You have been asked to design an aquarium for the lobby of a new science museum. It will be a cube that holds 1000 gal (133.7 ft^3) of water. Give the dimensions of the aquarium.

Solution
STRATEGY **GUESS, CHECK, AND REVISE** The volume of the cube is

Volume = $(\text{Side})^3 = 133.7 \text{ ft}^3$.

To find the length of each side, find a number whose cube is 133.7.

Guess	Calculator Steps	Display	Check
5	5 ▢ 3 ▢	125	Too small
5.1	5.1 ▢ 3 ▢	132.651	Too small
5.2	5.2 ▢ 3 ▢	140.608	Too large
5.11	5.11 ▢ 3 ▢	133.43283	Too small
5.12	5.12 ▢ 3 ▢	134.21773	Too large

The cube of 5.11 and the cube of 5.12 are both close to 133.7. The cube of 5.11 is closer, so each side must be about 5.11 ft long.

Exercises

1. **GUESS, CHECK, AND REVISE** Find the dimensions of a cube whose volume is 100 ft³.

2. In the example above, suppose your clients decide to double the size of the aquarium. Discuss two meanings that this could have. Do the two meanings describe the same size aquarium?

Education	Mean Income*
9th–10th Grade, No Diploma	$20,968
High School Graduate	$27,440
Some College, No Degree	$29,441
Associate Degree	$31,097
Bachelor's Degree	$42,734
Master's Degree	$48,851
Doctorate Degree	$48,008
Professional Degree	$60,475

Airline Passengers

Delta	✈✈✈✈✈✈
American	✈✈✈✈✈✈
United	✈✈✈✈✈
USAir	✈✈✈✈✈
Southwest	✈✈✈✈

✈ = 10 million passengers

Art Store Monthly Profits

Goal 2 MODELING REAL-LIFE SITUATIONS

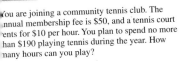

Example 3 Using a Verbal Model

You are joining a community tennis club. The annual membership fee is $50, and a tennis court rents for $10 per hour. You plan to spend no more than $190 playing tennis during the year. How many hours can you play?

Real Life... Real Facts

Tennis
There are about 240,000 tennis courts in the United States. Of these, about 10,000 are indoor courts. (Source: Tennis Industry Association)

Solution
You can use a verbal model and algebra to solve the problem.

Verbal Model

$$\text{Total spent} = \text{Annual fee} + \text{Hourly rate} \cdot \text{Hours of tennis}$$

Labels

Total spent = 190	(dollars)
Annual fee = 50	(dollars)
Hourly rate = 10	(dollars per hour)
Number of hours played = n	(hours)

Algebraic Model

$$190 = 50 + 10 \cdot n$$
$$190 - 50 = 50 + 10n - 50$$
$$140 = 10n$$
$$\frac{140}{10} = \frac{10n}{10}$$
$$14 = n$$

You can play 14 h of tennis.

✔**Check:** When you check the result, don't just check the numbers. You also need to check the units of measure.

Verbal Model

$$\text{Total spent} = \text{Annual fee} + \text{Hourly rate} \cdot \text{Hours of tennis}$$

Total spent = 50 dollars +
= 50 doll...
= 190...

REAL LIFE, REAL FACTS shows the everyday value and importance of mathematics.

ONGOI...

Write About It

Solve each equation. Show your steps. Explain how inverse operations help you decide what the next step should be.

$5x - 4 = 6$
... = 9
... 7

Mathematical **MODELING** shows you math at work in real-life situations and demonstrates the problem-solving power of mathematics.

Sales Prices of New Homes

Making mathematics easy to learn.

Throughout the Passport series, lessons and labs make even the most difficult concepts easier to understand.

Each **LESSON** has two goals: the first goal helps you to understand the math skill, the second goal shows you how the skill is applied to daily life.

Important **TERMS** are highlighted and defined clearly, making it easy to understand key math vocabulary.

2.1 The Distributive Property

What you should learn:

Goal ❶ How to use the Distributive Property

Goal ❷ How to use the Distributive Property in real life

Why you should learn it:

You can use the Distributive Property to model real life, such as ordering clothes for a clothing store.

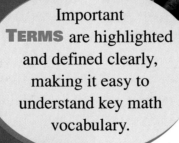

Goal ❶ USING THE DISTRIBUTIVE PROPERTY

Two algebraic expressions are **equivalent** if they have the same values when numbers are substituted for the variables.

One way to discover that two expressions are equivalent is to use algebra tiles. For instance, the tiles at the right show that $2(x + 2)$ and $2x + 4$ are equivalent.

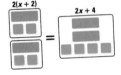

$$2(x + 2) = 2x + 4$$

Another way to show these expressions are equivalent is with the **Distributive Property**.

THE DISTRIBUTIVE PROPERTY

Let a, b, and c be numbers or variable expressions.

$$a(b + c) = ab + ac \quad \text{and} \quad ab + ac = a(b + c)$$

Example 1 Using the Distributive Property

a. $2(x + 3) = 2(x) + 2(3)$ Use the Distributive Property.

      $= 2x + 6$ Simplify.

b. $5(2) + 5(4) = 5(2 + 4)$ Use the Distributive Property.

      $= 5(6)$ Simplify.

      $= 30$ Simplify.

c. $x(x + 4) = x(x) + x(4)$ Use the Distributive Property.

      $= x^2 + 4x$ Simplify.

In part (c), notice that $x(4)$ is usually written as $4x$. This is a use of the *Commutative Property of Multiplication.*

Solving Addition Equations

Materials Needed
- algebra tiles
- pencils or pens
- paper

Part A USING ALGEBRA TILES

Algebra tiles can be used to model addition equations. Here is an example that shows how to solve the equation $x + 3 = 6$.

1 Model the equation with algebra tiles.

$x + 3 = $

2 To get the x tile by itself, remove (subtract) 3 small tiles from each side.

Isolate the x tile on one side of the equation.

3 The x tile is equal to 3 small tiles. So, the solution is $x = 3$.

$x = 3$

In Exercises 1 and 2, describe the step shown. Is the step one that you should use to solve the equation? Explain why or why not.

1.

2.

3. When you use algebra tiles to solve an addition equation, how can you tell how many tiles to rem...

Part B SOLVING ADDITION EQUATIONS

In Exercises 4 and 5, write the equation that is modeled with algebra tiles. Then use algebra tiles to solve the equation. Make a sketch of your steps. Check your solution by substituting into the original equation.

4.

5.

In Exercises 6–9, use algebra tiles to solve the equation. Draw a sketch of the steps you used.

6. $x + 7 = 11$

7. $x + 1 = 8$

8. $x + 4 = 14$

9. $x + 8 = 8$

NOW TRY THESE

In Exercises 10 and 11, write two different equations that have the indicated solution.

10.

11.

...rcises 10 and 11, h...
...ions could you ha...
...ted solution? Exp...

LESSON INVESTIGATION

Investigating Diagonals of Polygons

GROUP ACTIVITY For each polygon in the table, count how many diagonals can be drawn from a single vertex. Then count the total number of diagonals that can be drawn in the polygon. Copy and complete the table. What patterns do you see?

Type of polygon	Number of vertices	Diagonals from a single vertex	Total number of diagonals
Triangle	3	?	?
Quadrilateral	4	?	?
Pentagon	5	?	?
Hexagon	6	3	9

GOAL 2 SOLVING REAL-LIFE PROBLEMS

...e Distributive Property is usually stated with a sum involving ...y two terms. However, it also applies to sums involving three ...more terms.

$$a(b + c + d) = ab + ac + ad \qquad \text{Sum with 3 terms}$$
$$a(b + c + d + e) = ab + ac + ad + ae \qquad \text{Sum with 4 terms}$$

Example 2 Using the Distributive Property

...ou are a fashion buyer for a clothing retailer that ...s 5 stores. You are attending a fashion show and ...cide to order 10 dresses of style A, 12 dresses of ...yle B, and 15 dresses of style C for *each* of the 5 stores. Use ...e Distributive Property to find the total number of dresses you ...ill order.

REAL LIFE
Fashion

STUDY TIP

When you choose labels for a verbal model, you can use any letters as the variables. Common choices are n, x, and y. But it sometimes helps to choose a letter that reminds you of the quantity, such as T for total.

Solution

Verbal Model

$$\text{Total} = \begin{bmatrix} \text{Number} \\ \text{of stores} \end{bmatrix} \cdot \begin{bmatrix} \text{Style A} \\ \text{dresses} \end{bmatrix} + \begin{bmatrix} \text{Style B} \\ \text{dresses} \end{bmatrix} + \begin{bmatrix} \text{Style C} \\ \text{dresses} \end{bmatrix}$$

Labels

Total number of dresses $= T$
Number of stores $= 5$
Number of style A dresses $= 10$
Number of style B dresses $= 12$
Number of style C dresses $= 15$

ONGOING ASSESSMENT

Write About It

1. Use the Distributive Property to write an equivalent expression for $4(3x + 1)$.

2. Evaluate both expressions when $x = 5$. Compare the two solutions.

3. Which expression do you think is easier to evaluate? Why?

Algebraic Model

$$T = 5(10 + 12 + 15)$$
$$= 5(10) + 5(12) + 5(15)$$
$$= 50 + 60 + 75$$
$$= 185$$

You will order 185 dresses.

✔**Check:** You can check this by adding first.
$$5(10 + 12 + 15) = 5(37)$$
$$= 185$$

Providing opportunities to practice skills and to solve problems.

The Passport series helps you achieve success in each lesson and chapter, in standardized tests, and more.

GUIDED PRACTICE aids you and your teacher in assessing your understanding of each skill.

3.4 Exercises   Extra Practice,

GUIDED PRACTICE

1. Explain how to evaluate $5 - (-2)$.   2. Apply the Dis

REASONING In Exercises 3–6, decide whether the statement is true for all values of x, some values of x, or no values of x. Explain.

3. $5x - 2x - 12 = 5x + (-2x) + (-12)$ 4. The opposite of x is 0.

5. $3(x - 4) = 3x - (-12)$ 6. The opposite of x is negative.

PRACTICE AND PROBLEM SOLVING

In Exercises 7–18, find the difference. Write your conclusion as an equation.

7. $19 - 17$ 8. $5 - 9$ 9. $23 - (-8)$ 10. $2 - (-4)$

11. $-10 - 7$ 12. $-3 - 3$ 13. $-5 - (-5)$ 14. $-16 - (-8)$

15. $-5 - 5$ 16. $-16 - 8$ 17. $0 - 27$ 18. $0 - (-61)$

19. **TECHNOLOGY** Explain the difference between the ▩ key and the ▩ key on a calculator.

In Exercises 20–23, evaluate the expression when $a = 5$ and when $a = -5$.

20. $a - 1$ 21. $1 - a$ 22. $a - 6$ 23. $6 - a$

In Exercises 24–27, rewrite the expression as a sum. Then identify the terms of the expression.

24. $3x - 2x + 16$ 25. $7x - 9x - 5$ 26. $7a - 5b$ 27. $4 - 2n + 4m$

In Exercises 28–39, simplify the expression.

28. $9x - 6x - 17$ 29. $18n - 12n + 4$ 30. $-11y - (-15y) - 2$

31. $-20x - (-30x) + 10$ 32. $b - (-2b)$ 33. $3x - (-3x)$

34. $-2a - 3a - 4$ 35. $-13x - 13x - 13$ 36. $4m - 6m + 8$

37. $16y - 20y + 24$ 38. $-14x - (-10x)$ 39. $-30x - (-19x)$

40. **GEOGRAPHY** In Death Valley National Park, the highest point is Telescope Peak (11,049 ft) and the lowest point is Badwaters (-282 ft). What is the diffe— in elevation between these two

PRACTICE AND PROBLEM SOLVING gives you the opportunity to master key skills and apply them to real-world situations and problems.

CHAPTER PROJECTS

offer you a unique way to develop math skills and demonstrate your problem solving abilities.

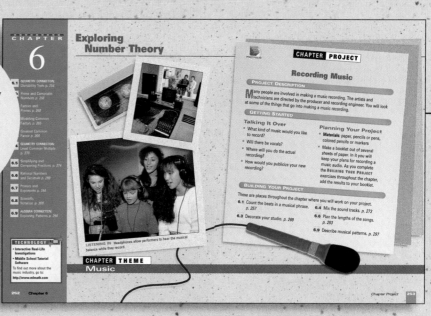

ONGOING ASSESSMENT

helps you check your progress by talking and writing about mathematics problems.

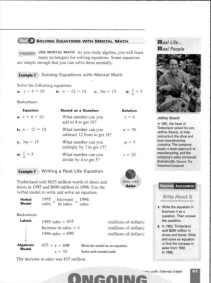

STANDARDIZED TEST PRACTICE

not only prepares you for these important tests, but also strengthens your ability to solve problems and to think critically.

COMMUNICATING ABOUT MATHEMATICS

encourages you to build your communication skills while learning about real-world applications.

Exploring Patterns

T E C H N O L O G Y

- **Interactive Real-Life Investigations**
- **Middle School Tutorial Software**

To find out more about interesting places to visit, go to:

http://www.mlmath.com

WASHINGTON, D.C. Every year, the Capitol building has over 3 million visitors.

CHAPTER THEME
Places to Visit

PORTFOLIO

CHAPTER PROJECT

Planning a Class Trip

PROJECT DESCRIPTION

Think of somewhere you would like to go with your class. For example, you could go to a park, a museum, or a zoo. Make a booklet as you plan the trip.

GETTING STARTED

Talking It Over

- What sorts of trips have you been on with your class or your school? Who chose the destinations for the trips? Why do you think these destinations were chosen?

- Who went on the field trip? What kind of transportation did you use to get there? What kinds of costs were there, such as admission fees or bus fares? Who paid them?

Planning Your Project

- **Materials:** colored paper, markers, stapler or report cover

- Choose a place in your area to visit with your class. Call, write, or visit to get brochures, hours, and admission prices.

- Write your name and the place on the booklet's cover. You will add pages as you go through this chapter. You can use pictures from the brochures to decorate your booklet.

BUILDING YOUR PROJECT

These are places throughout the chapter where you will work on your project.

1.1

Number Patterns

What you should learn:

Goal 1 How to use numbers to identify and measure objects

Goal 2 How to recognize and describe number patterns

Why you should learn it:

You use numbers in real life to measure objects such as shoes, and to identify objects such as city streets.

In Canyon, Texas, the numbered avenues run east-west. The numbered streets run north-south.

Goal 1 IDENTIFYING AND MEASURING

Mathematics is not just the study of numbers. Mathematics is also the study of how numbers are *used* in real life. For instance, ZIP codes are numbers that help locate addresses. This map shows the first digit of the ZIP codes in different regions of the United States. South Carolina is enlarged to show the first three digits.

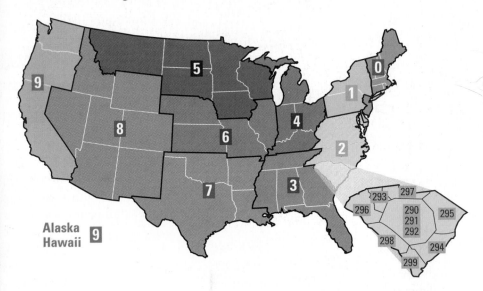

Alaska Hawaii 9

LESSON INVESTIGATION

COOPERATIVE LEARNING

Investigating Number Uses

GROUP ACTIVITY With your group, follow the steps below.

1. Make four lists of numbers that are used for identification or measurement. Each list should contain at least five numbers. For example, you might list five phone numbers, or five people's heights.

2. For each list, decide whether the numbers are used for identification or for measurement.

3. Share one of your lists with the other groups. Ask whether they can tell what the numbers identify or measure. For instance, the numbers

    10019, 20066, 60607, 75261, and 94118

    are, in order, ZIP codes for New York City, Washington, D.C., Chicago, Dallas, and San Francisco.

Goal 2 DESCRIBING NUMBER PATTERNS

Sometimes when you see numbers in real life, the numbers form a pattern. For instance, when you go into a shoe store, you might see numbers representing shoe sizes.

$6, 6\frac{1}{2}, 7, 7\frac{1}{2}, 8, 8\frac{1}{2}, 9, 9\frac{1}{2}, 10, 10\frac{1}{2}$ **Shoe sizes**

An ordered list of numbers is called a **sequence**. In the sequence above, each number is $\frac{1}{2}$ more than the previous number.

Example 1 Describing Number Patterns

STRATEGY **LOOK FOR A PATTERN** Describe a pattern for each sequence. Then use the pattern to write the next three numbers in the sequence.

a. 4, 8, 12, 16, ? , ? , ?
b. 128, 64, 32, 16, ? , ? , ?

Solution

a. One pattern for this sequence is that each number is 4 more than the previous number. The next three numbers are shown below.

4, 8, 12, 16,   20,   24,   28
         + 4   + 4   + 4

b. One pattern for this sequence is that each number is one half of the previous number. The next three numbers are shown below.

128, 64, 32, 16,   8,   4,   2
         $\times \frac{1}{2}$ $\times \frac{1}{2}$ $\times \frac{1}{2}$

TOOLBOX

Problem Solving Strategies, page 744

ONGOING ASSESSMENT

Talk About It
....

Use the rule given to find the next three numbers in the sequence.

2, 3, 5, ? , ? , ?

1. Add 1, then add 2, then add 3, and so on.

2. To get the next number, add the two previous numbers.

3. Write the next prime number.

GUIDED PRACTICE

1. **WRITING** In your own words, describe what mathematics is.

2. Give several examples of how numbers are used to identify objects.

3. Give several examples of how numbers are used to measure objects. Name some units of measure, such as centimeters or pounds.

4. Give an example of a real-life number sequence. Describe its pattern.

PRACTICE AND PROBLEM SOLVING

LOOKING FOR A PATTERN In Exercises 5–14, describe a pattern for the sequence. Then list the next three numbers.

5. 1, 3, 5, 7, ?, ?, ?

6. 80, 75, 70, 65, ?, ?, ?

7. 1, 3, 6, 10, ?, ?, ?

8. 63, 60, 56, 51, ?, ?, ?

9. $\frac{1}{2}, \frac{2}{3}, \frac{3}{4}, \frac{4}{5}$, ?, ?, ?

10. $\frac{2}{3}, \frac{4}{5}, \frac{6}{7}, \frac{8}{9}$, ?, ?, ?

11. $2, \frac{7}{2}, 5, \frac{13}{2}$, ?, ?, ?

12. 100, 81, 64, 49, ?, ?, ?

13. 2, 6, 18, 54, ?, ?, ?

14. 4096, 1024, 256, 64, ?, ?, ?

LOOKING FOR A PATTERN In Exercises 15–18, describe a pattern for the sequence. Then list the next three letters.

15. A, C, E, G, ?, ?, ?

16. Z, A, Y, B, X, C, ?, ?, ?

17. A, N, B, O, ?, ?, ?

18. A, Y, C, W, ?, ?, ?

NUMBER SENSE In Exercises 19 and 20, write the first six numbers in the sequence.

19. The first number is 50. After that, each number is 3 less than the previous number.

20. The first number is 1 and the second number is 3. After that, each number is the sum of the two previous numbers.

VISUALIZING PATTERNS In Exercises 21 and 22, draw the next three figures in the pattern.

21.
  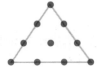

22.
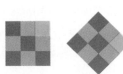

23. RACE TIMES You run a 100 m race with a time of 16 s. Your friend's time is 17 s. Who wins the race?

24. LONG JUMP In a long-jump contest, you jump 14 ft 3 in. and your friend jumps 13 ft 11 in. Who wins the contest? How much longer is the winner's jump than the loser's?

25. VACATION TRAVEL You and your family travel to an amusement park. As you near the park, you begin to see signs that state the number of miles to the park. What happens to the numbers on the signs as you get closer and closer to the park?

26. RECREATION Imagine that you are at an amusement park or at a fair. Describe several ways that numbers are used to identify things or to measure things.

Real Life...
Real People

Running By age 14, Angela T. Williams had won 15 national championships and set 6 national sprinting records.

 STANDARDIZED TEST PRACTICE

27. The seventh row of a theater has 26 seats, the sixth row has 23 seats, and the fifth row has 20 seats. If this pattern continues, how many seats does the first row have?

A 5   **B** 8   **C** 11   **D** 14

28. The first number in a sequence is 2. After that, each number is twice the previous number. What is the sixth number in the sequence?

A 12   **B** 16   **C** 32   **D** 64

 EXPLORATION AND EXTENSION

PORTFOLIO

29. BUILDING YOUR PROJECT You are planning a class trip to see a show at the science museum, but the schedule that they sent you is torn.

a. You want to see the show after 1 P.M. If the pattern in the schedule at the right continues, what is the earliest time that you can see the show? Explain your reasoning.

b. At what time will the show be over? Explain.

Schedule of Showtimes	
Start	**End**
9:00 A.M.	9:30 A.M.
9:45 A.M.	10:15 A.M.
10:30 A.M.	11:00 A.M.

30. BUILDING YOUR PROJECT If possible, find out the schedule of events at the place you have chosen for your class trip. Describe any patterns you can find in the schedule.

Number Operations

What you should learn:

Goal 1 How to use the four basic number operations

Goal 2 How to use models for multiplication

Why you should learn it:

Number operations are important in almost all real-life uses of numbers, such as multiplying to find the cost of apples.

If you buy 3 lb of apples at $1.25/lb, you can find the cost using multiplication: $3 \times 1.25 = 3.75$.

Goal 1 USING NUMBER OPERATIONS

There are four basic number operations: addition, subtraction, multiplication, and division. Each of these operations can be described verbally and symbolically.

Example 1 Finding Sums and Differences

a. Addition

Verbal Description	Symbolic Description
The **sum** of 5 and 13 is 18.	$5 + 13 = 18$

b. Subtraction

Verbal Description	Symbolic Description
The **difference** of 9 and 6 is 3.	$9 - 6 = 3$

In Example 2, notice that multiplication can be specified by the symbols $\times$, $\cdot$, or by parentheses. Division can be specified by $\div$, /, or by a fraction bar.

Example 2 Finding Products and Quotients

a. Multiplication

Verbal Description	Symbolic Description
The **product** of 3 and 5 is 15.	$3 \times 5 = 15$
	$3 \cdot 5 = 15$
	$3(5) = 15$
	$(3)(5) = 15$

The numbers 3 and 5 are **factors** of 15.

b. Division

Verbal Description	Symbolic Description
The **quotient** of 14 and 7 is 2.	$14 \div 7 = 2$
	$14 / 7 = 2$
	$\dfrac{14}{7} = 2$

The **numerator** is 14. The **denominator** is 7.

Goal 2 USING MODELS FOR MULTIPLICATION

A **model** helps you visualize or understand an actual process or object. For instance, the family tree at the right is a model that can help you understand how your cousins are related to you. Examples 3 and 4 show two different models for multiplication.

Example 3 Using an Area Model

CONNECTION
Geometry

Use an area model to represent the product of 3 and 6.

Solution

One way to do this is to draw a 3-by-6 rectangle. Count the squares to see that the area of the rectangle is 18 square units. The area of a rectangle is given by

Area = 18

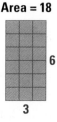
6

3

    Width × Length = Area.

So, 3 × 6 = 18.

Example 4 Using a Number Line Model

Use a number line model to represent the multiplication fact 2 × 5 = 10.

Solution

Method ❶ You can think of the product 2 × 5 as two 5's. On a number line, start at 0. Move 5 units to the right twice.

You end at 10, so 2 × 5 = 10.

Method ❷ You can also think of the product 2 × 5 as five 2's. Start at 0 and move 2 units to the right five times.

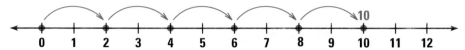

Again, you end at 10. So, 2 × 5 = 10.

GREAT-GRANDPARENTS

GRANDPARENTS

PARENTS   AUNT & UNCLE

YOU   COUSINS

ONGOING ASSESSMENT

Write About It

The diagram shows an area model.

1. What product does the model represent?

2. Draw two different number line models for the product.

1.2 Exercises

Extra Practice, page 716

GUIDED PRACTICE

1. State the four basic number operations.

2. State the symbol or symbols that represent each number operation.

3. What is a model? Describe a model that represents multiplication.

4. Describe a real-life example of a number operation.

PRACTICE AND PROBLEM SOLVING

NUMBER SENSE In Exercises 5–12, write a verbal description of the number sentence.

5. $6 \times 8 = 48$

6. $25 \div 5 = 5$

7. $3 + 14 = 17$

8. $9(7) = 63$

9. $111 - 56 = 55$

10. $12 / 4 = 3$

11. $2 \cdot 54 = 108$

12. $\frac{132}{11} = 12$

In Exercises 13–24, find the sum or difference.

13. $659 + 23$

14. $350 + 211$

15. $746 - 27$

16. $858 - 349$

17. $75 + 40 + 98$

18. $352 + 67 + 20$

19. $10.9 - 8.6$

20. $112.7 - 72.9$

21. $\frac{5}{6} + \frac{1}{6}$

22. $\frac{3}{8} + \frac{1}{8}$

23. $\frac{9}{12} - \frac{5}{12}$

24. $\frac{6}{13} - \frac{3}{13}$

 NUMBER SENSE In Exercises 25–40, find the product or quotient. You may want to use a calculator for some of the exercises.

25. 16×7

26. 21×14

27. $527 \div 31$

28. $1435 \div 35$

29. $(4.7)(8.9)$

30. $(13.2)(5.1)$

31. $(321)156$

32. $497(38)$

33. $\frac{256}{32}$

34. $\frac{1024}{64}$

35. $3 \cdot \frac{4}{6}$

36. $7 \cdot \frac{1}{8}$

37. $76.97 \div 4.3$

38. $145.2 \div 33$

39. $1977 / 15$

40. $2125 / 34$

In Exercises 41–44, write the multiplication fact that is represented by the model.

41.

42.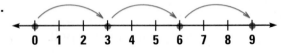

43.

44.

MUSIC In Exercises 45–48, use the graph of sales of compact discs (CDs) and cassettes.

45. How many cassettes were sold in 1990?

46. In 1995, how many more CDs were sold than cassettes?

47. How many more CDs were sold in 1995 than in 1992?

48. What do you predict will happen in future sales of CDs and cassettes?

49. Your CD storage unit holds 5 stacks of 14 CDs. How many CDs can it hold?

50. **NUMBER SENSE** Copy and complete the table. Tell whether each result is *odd* or *even*.

First number	Operation	Second number	Result
Odd	+	Even	?
Odd	+	Odd	?
Odd	•	Even	?
Odd	•	Odd	?

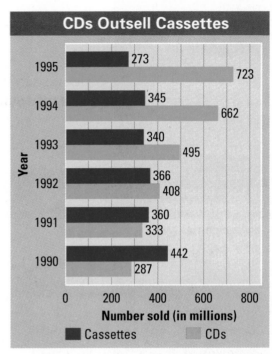

CDs Outsell Cassettes

(Source: Recording Industry Association of America)

STANDARDIZED TEST PRACTICE

51. If a human heart beats an average of 72 times per min, how many times will it beat in 1 h?

   A 72   **B** 132   **C** 4320   **D** 4325

52. You have a savings account with a $527 balance. You withdraw $58. What is the new balance in your account?

   A $585   **B** $569   **C** $479   **D** $469

EXPLORATION AND EXTENSION

PORTFOLIO

53. **BUILDING YOUR PROJECT** For your class trip, you plan to travel by van. Each van holds 7 students and an adult driver.

   a. Find out how many students there are in your class.

   b. How many vans do you need to transport your entire class? If your teacher drives one van, how many more adult drivers do you need?

Powers and Square Roots

What you should learn:

Goal How to evaluate powers

Goal How to use square roots

Why you should learn it:

You can use powers and square roots to solve real-life problems involving lengths and areas, such as designing plots for a community garden.

Goal 1 USING POWERS

The squares shown below have sides whose lengths are 1, 2, 3, and 4. The areas of the squares can be written as products, such as 3×3, or as *powers*, such as 3^2.

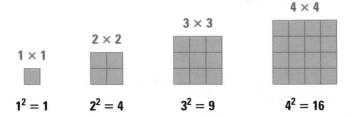

1×1 2×2 3×3 4×4

$1^2 = 1$ $2^2 = 4$ $3^2 = 9$ $4^2 = 16$

A **power** has two parts: a **base** and an **exponent**. In the power 4^2, the base is 4 and the exponent is 2.

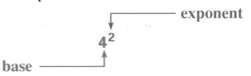

exponent

4^2

base

Example 1 Reading Powers

Power	Meaning	Verbal Description
5^2	5×5	5 to the second power, *or* 5 squared
10^3	$10 \times 10 \times 10$	10 to the third power, *or* 10 cubed
7^4	$7 \times 7 \times 7 \times 7$	7 to the fourth power

Example 2 Using a Calculator to Find Powers

Use a calculator to evaluate the power.

a. 47^2

b. 6^5

c. $(4.2)^3$

Solution

Calculator Steps	Display	Written Result
a. 47 $\boxed{x^2}$	2209.	$47^2 = 2209$
b. 6 $\boxed{y^x}$ 5 $\boxed{=}$	7776.	$6^5 = 7776$
c. 4.2 $\boxed{y^x}$ 3 $\boxed{=}$	74.088	$(4.2)^3 = 74.088$

Goal 2 USING SQUARE ROOTS

The **square root** of a number is denoted by the symbol $\sqrt{}$, which is called a **radical** or **square root symbol**. When you square the square root of a number, you obtain the original number. For instance, $\sqrt{9} = 3$ because $3^2 = 9$.

Example 3 Using a Calculator to Find Square Roots

Evaluate each square root. Round the result to the nearest hundredth.

a. $\sqrt{841}$ **b.** $\sqrt{90.25}$ **c.** $\sqrt{6}$

Solution

Calculator Steps	Display	Written Result
a. 841 $\boxed{\sqrt{x}}$	29.	$\sqrt{841} = 29$
b. 90.25 $\boxed{\sqrt{x}}$	9.5	$\sqrt{90.25} = 9.5$
c. 6 $\boxed{\sqrt{x}}$	2.4494897	$\sqrt{6} \approx 2.45$

Round to the nearest hundredth.

✔**Check:** You can check each answer by squaring the result. For instance, $(2.45)^2 = 6.0025$, which is about equal to 6.

Example 4 Designing a Garden

You are designing a community garden. You want each member to have a square plot whose area is 130 ft^2. How long should you make each side of the plot? What is the plot's perimeter?

Area = 130 ft^2

Solution

You need to find a number whose square is 130.

$$(\text{Side})^2 = 130$$
$$\text{Side} = \sqrt{130}$$

Calculator Steps	Display	Written Result
130 $\boxed{\sqrt{x}}$	11.401754	$\sqrt{130} \approx 11.4$

Each side of the plot should be about 11.4 ft long. The perimeter is the sum of the lengths of the four sides, which is $4(11.4) = 45.6$ ft.

GUIDED PRACTICE

1. Copy and complete the following sentence.
A power has two parts, a ? and an ? .

2. Write a verbal description of the number sentence $3^4 = 81$.

In Exercises 3–5, find the value of the expression.

3. $\sqrt{16}$ **4.** $\sqrt{49}$ **5.** $\sqrt{81}$

6. Write a verbal description of the number sentence $\sqrt{36} = 6$.

PRACTICE AND PROBLEM SOLVING

In Exercises 7–10, write a verbal description of the number sentence.

7. $6^4 = 1296$ **8.** $(2.9)^2 = 8.41$ **9.** $\sqrt{1.21} = 1.1$ **10.** $\sqrt{2.25} = 1.5$

TECHNOLOGY **In Exercises 11–16, write each expression as a power. Then use a calculator to find the value of the power.**

11. 12×12 **12.** $8 \times 8 \times 8 \times 8 \times 8$ **13.** $(3.4)(3.4)(3.4)$

14. $(9.7)(9.7)(9.7)(9.7)$ **15.** $3 \cdot 3 \cdot 3 \cdot 3 \cdot 3 \cdot 3$ **16.** $\dfrac{3}{5} \cdot \dfrac{3}{5} \cdot \dfrac{3}{5} \cdot \dfrac{3}{5} \cdot \dfrac{3}{5}$

TECHNOLOGY **In Exercises 17–22, use a calculator to find the value of the expression. Round the result to the nearest hundredth.**

17. $\sqrt{169}$ **18.** $\sqrt{441}$ **19.** $\sqrt{117}$

20. $\sqrt{372}$ **21.** $\sqrt{5.5}$ **22.** $\sqrt{8.26}$

GUESS, CHECK, AND REVISE **In Exercises 23–28, find the number that is represented by** △.

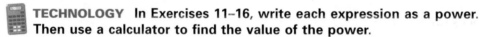

> **TOOLBOX**
> Problem Solving
> Strategies, page 744

23. $\triangle \cdot \triangle \cdot \triangle = 512$ **24.** $\triangle \cdot \triangle \cdot \triangle \cdot \triangle = 625$

25. $\triangle \cdot \triangle = 4.41$ **26.** $\triangle^3 = 42.875$

27. $\sqrt{\triangle} = 9$ **28.** $\sqrt{\triangle} = 17$

In Exercises 29–32, replace each ? with >, <, or =. (The symbol < means "is less than" and the symbol > means "is greater than.")

29. 2^3 ? 3^2 **30.** 2^4 ? 4^2 **31.** 4^3 ? 3^4 **32.** 5^2 ? 2^5

33. MAKING AN ESTIMATE Without using a calculator, predict which is greater: 10^2 or 2^{10}. Explain your reasoning.

34. **GUESS, CHECK, AND REVISE** Find the greatest power of 5 that is less than 20,000.

35. **DESIGNING A ROOM** You are designing a computer classroom. You want the classroom to be a square whose area is 506.25 ft^2.

   a. Find the length of each side of the classroom.

   b. Find the perimeter of the classroom.

   c. You want to divide the classroom into nine equal-sized square workspaces. Draw a diagram of the classroom and find the area of each workspace.

   d. Find the length of each side of one of the square workspaces. Explain the method you used.

GEOMETRY **In Exercises 36 and 37, use the cube shown. Each edge of the cube is 7 in.**

36. The surface area of a cube is the sum of the areas of the faces.

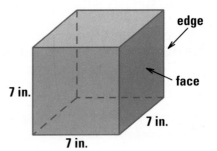

   a. How many faces does a cube have?

   b. What is the area of one face of the cube?

   c. Find the surface area of the cube. Explain how you got your answer.

37. If you double the length of each edge of the cube, does its surface area double? Explain your reasoning.

38. Which expression represents $8^3 \times 3^4$?

   (A) $8 \times 3 \times 3 \times 4$ **(B)** 24×12

   (C) $8 \times 8 \times 3 \times 3 \times 3 \times 4$ **(D)** $8 \times 8 \times 8 \times 3 \times 3 \times 3 \times 3$

39. Which of the following equals $\sqrt{125.44}$?

   (A) 10.44 **(B)** 11.2 **(C)** 11.8 **(D)** 12.544

EXPLORATION AND EXTENSION

40. The areas of parks and forests are often measured in *acres*. One acre is 4840 yd^2. Suppose a square plot of land has an area of one acre.

   a. Find the length (in yards) of each side of the plot.

   b. Find the perimeter of the plot.

SPIRAL REVIEW

In Exercises 1–4, simplify the fraction. (Toolbox, page 746)

1. $\frac{2}{4}$ **2.** $\frac{6}{3}$ **3.** $\frac{12}{8}$ **4.** $\frac{6}{20}$

In Exercises 5–8, write the fraction as a decimal. (Toolbox, page 746)

5. $\frac{1}{2}$ **6.** $\frac{1}{4}$ **7.** $\frac{3}{8}$ **8.** $\frac{2}{5}$

LOOKING FOR A PATTERN In Exercises 9–12, describe a pattern for the sequence. Then list the next three numbers. (1.1)

9. 2, 4, 6, 8, ?, ?, ?

10. 30, 27, 24, 21, ?, ?, ?

11. $\frac{1}{2}, \frac{3}{4}, \frac{5}{6}, \frac{7}{8}$, ?, ?, ?

12. 1, 6, 12, 19, ?, ?, ?

13. **SHOPPING** Suppose you buy three magazines for \$2.75 each. **(1.2)**

a. Find the total cost.

b. You pay with a ten-dollar bill. What is your change?

TECHNOLOGY In Exercises 14–16, use a calculator to find the value of the expression. Round the result to the nearest hundredth. (1.3)

14. 5^7 **15.** $(3.9)^2$ **16.** $\sqrt{22}$

HISTORY Connection

HINDU-ARABIC NUMERALS

The modern *Hindu-Arabic numerals* that we use evolved from the *West Arabic numerals* (shown below), which Arabs had been using since before 1000 A.D. These evolved from the *Indian numerals* that Hindu mathematicians in India used as early as the 6th century A.D.

Modern Hindu-Arabic 1 2 3 4 5 6 7 8 9 0

West Arabic

Indian

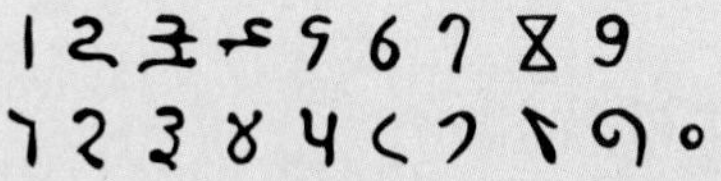

Hindu mathematicians wrote *rū* before known numbers. They wrote numbers side by side to represent addition. For multiplication, they wrote *bha* after the factors.

Hindu notation	**Modern notation**
rū 3 *rū* 5 *rū* 8	3 + 5 + 8
rū 2 *rū* 6 *bha*	2 × 6

Evaluate each expression.

1. *rū* 7 *rū* 8 *rū* 1 **2.** *rū* 5 *rū* 3 *bha* **3.** *rū* 9 *rū* 4

Guess, Check, and Revise

🔑 STRATEGY To solve problems successfully, you can use strategies such as *Making a Table, Looking for a Pattern, Working Backward, Drawing a Diagram*, and *Guess, Check, and Revise*.

TOOLBOX

Problem Solving
Strategies, page 744

STUDY TIP

The problem solving strategy *Guess, Check, and Revise* uses the steps below.

Guess a reasonable solution based on data in the problem.

⬇

Check the guess.

⬇

Revise the guess and check again. Continue until you find a solution.

Example

You have been asked to design an aquarium for the lobby of a new science museum. It will be a cube that holds 1000 gal (133.7 ft^3) of water. Give the dimensions of the aquarium.

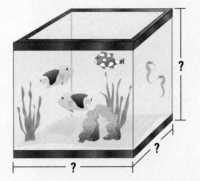

Solution

🔑 STRATEGY **GUESS, CHECK, AND REVISE** The volume of the cube is

$$\text{Volume} = (\text{Side})^3 = 133.7 \text{ ft}^3.$$

To find the length of each side, find a number whose cube is 133.7.

Guess	Calculator Steps	Display	Check
5	5 [yˣ] 3 [=]	125.	Too small
5.1	5.1 [yˣ] 3 [=]	132.651	Too small
5.2	5.2 [yˣ] 3 [=]	140.608	Too large
5.11	5.11 [yˣ] 3 [=]	133.43283	Too small
5.12	5.12 [yˣ] 3 [=]	134.21773	Too large

The cube of 5.11 and the cube of 5.12 are both close to 133.7. The cube of 5.11 is closer, so each side must be about 5.11 ft long.

Exercises

1. **GUESS, CHECK, AND REVISE** Find the dimensions of a cube whose volume is 100 ft^3.

2. In the example above, suppose your clients decide to double the size of the aquarium. Discuss two meanings that this could have. Do the two meanings describe the same size aquarium?

1.4

Order of Operations

What you should learn:

Goal 1 How to use the order of operations

Goal 2 How to simplify expressions that have grouping symbols

Why you should learn it:

Using grouping symbols and the order of operations helps you communicate with others about your mathematical ideas.

Goal 1 USING THE ORDER OF OPERATIONS

A **numerical expression** is a collection of numbers, operations, and grouping symbols such as parentheses. In order to avoid confusion about how to simplify numerical expressions, mathematicians have agreed on an **order of operations**. First priority is given to powers, second priority to multiplication and division, and third priority to addition and subtraction.

Example 1 Priority of Operations

a. $2 + 12 \div 3 = 2 + 4$ First divide.

$= 6$ Then add.

b. $4 \times 3^2 = 4 \times 9$ First evaluate the power.

$= 36$ Then multiply.

Some expressions contain two or more operations that have the same priority, such as multiplication and division, or addition and subtraction. The **Left-to-Right Rule** states that when operations have the same priority, you perform them from left to right.

Example 2 Using the Left-to-Right Rule

a. $6 \div 3 \cdot 5 = 2 \cdot 5$ Left-to-Right Rule: Divide.

$= 10$ Multiply.

b. $15 - 8 \div 4 \times 4 = 15 - 2 \times 4$ Left-to-Right Rule: Divide.

$= 15 - 8$ Multiply.

$= 7$ Subtract.

NEED TO KNOW

Some calculators use the established order of operations and some do not. Enter

3 **+** 6 **×** 2 **=**

into your calculator. If it displays 15, it uses the correct order of operations. If it displays 18, it does not.

ORDER OF OPERATIONS

When simplifying an expression, use the following order.

1. First do operations that occur within grouping symbols such as parentheses.
2. Then evaluate powers.
3. Then do multiplications and divisions from left to right.
4. Finally, do additions and subtractions from left to right.

Goal 2 USING GROUPING SYMBOLS

When you want to change the order of operations or simply want to make an expression clearer, you should use **grouping symbols**. The most common grouping symbols are parentheses ( ) and brackets [ ].

Example 3 ▸ Expressions with Grouping Symbols

Simplify each expression.

a. $(3 + 4) \cdot 2$ **b.** $8 \div [(5 \times 3) - 7]$

Solution

a. $(3 + 4) \cdot 2 = 7 \cdot 2$ **Add within parentheses.**

$\qquad\qquad = 14$ **Multiply.**

b. $8 \div [(5 \times 3) - 7] = 8 \div [15 - 7]$ **Multiply within parentheses.**

$\qquad\qquad\qquad = 8 \div 8$ **Subtract within brackets.**

$\qquad\qquad\qquad = 1$ **Divide.**

Example 4 ▸ Finding the Area of a Region

CONNECTION
Geometry

Write an expression that represents the area of the region below. Then simplify the expression.

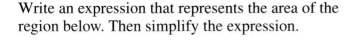

Solution

The region can be divided into two rectangles and one square.

$$\begin{array}{c}\text{Area of} \\ \text{region}\end{array} = \begin{array}{c}\text{Area of} \\ \text{rectangle}\end{array} + \begin{array}{c}\text{Area of} \\ \text{rectangle}\end{array} + \begin{array}{c}\text{Area of} \\ \text{square}\end{array}$$

$$= 2 \times 3 + 5 \times 4 + 3^2$$
$$= 6 + 20 + 9$$
$$= 35 \text{ square units}$$

1.4 Exercises

Extra Practice, page 716

GUIDED PRACTICE

1. Why is it important to learn to communicate mathematics? Give a real-life example of communicating mathematics.

2. State the established order of operations. Why is it important to have an established order of operations?

3. Evaluate the expression.

   a. $18 - 4 \times 3$ **b.** $48 \div 6 \times 3$ **c.** $12 + 4^2 - 3 \times (5 - 2)$

4. **REASONING** Copy the number sentence and insert parentheses to make it true.

   a. $4 \div 2 \times 8 + 2 = 20$ **b.** $3 \times 4 + 8 - 2 = 34$

PRACTICE AND PROBLEM SOLVING

In Exercises 5–18, simplify the expression without using a calculator.

5. $7 + 12 \div 6$

6. $12 - 3 \times 4$

7. $5 \cdot 3 + 2^2$

8. $5^2 - 8 \div 2$

9. $11 + 4 \div 2 \times 9$

10. $21 - 1 \cdot 2 \div 4$

11. $14 - 8 + 4 \cdot 2^3$

12. $3^3 - 8 \cdot 3 \div 12$

13. $(9 + 7) \div 4 \times 2$

14. $6 \div (17 - 11) \cdot 14$

15. $4 - 5(5) + 13$

16. $16 \div 4 \cdot 2 - 7$

17. $3[16 - (3 + 7) \div 5]$

18. $(6 + 32)(4 - 2)$

In Exercises 19–26, simplify the expression. You may want to use a calculator for some of the exercises.

19. $29 + 16 \div 8 \cdot 25$

20. $36 + 16 - 50 \div 25$

21. $18 \cdot 3 \div 3^3$

22. $10 + 5^3 - 25$

23. $20 - (3^2 \div 27) \cdot 2$

24. $149 - (2^8 - 40) \div 6$

25. $22 + (34 \cdot 2)^2 \div 8$

26. $85 - (4 \cdot 2)^2 - 3$

GEOMETRY In Exercises 27 and 28, write an expression that represents the area of the region. Then simplify the expression.

27.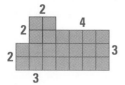

28.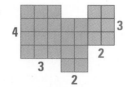

REASONING In Exercises 29–34, decide whether the number sentence is *true* or *false*. If it is false, copy it and insert parentheses to make it true.

29. $6 + 21 \div 3 = 9$

30. $6 \cdot 3 - 2 \cdot 5 = 8$

31. $6 + 3^2 \div 3 = 5$

32. $8^2 - 1 \cdot 3 - 5 = 56$

33. $7 + 7 \cdot 2 + 6 = 63$

34. $36 \div 9 - 6 \div 2 = 6$

35. SCHOOL SUPPLIES Your school bookstore's prices are shown on the sign at the right. You purchase 5 folders, 3 notebooks, and a calculator at the bookstore. Write an expression that represents your total cost. Then simplify the expression to find out how much money you spent.

BACK TO SCHOOL
SALE
FOLDER $0.50
HIGHLIGHTER $1.49
NOTEBOOK $2.25
CALCULATOR $5.99

STANDARDIZED TEST PRACTICE

36. Which one of the following number sentences is *not* true?

(A) $3 + 4 \times 8 \div 2 = 19$　　**(B)** $6 \times 3 - (5 + 9) = 4$

(C) $56 \div 8 \cdot 3 + 3 = 24$　　**(D)** $5^2 - 3^2 \times 2 = 32$

37. Choose the number that makes the following number sentence true.

$$(3 + 3)^2 + 44 \div \boxed{?} = 40$$

(A) 2　　　**(B)** 4　　　**(C)** 11　　　**(D)** 18

EXPLORATION AND EXTENSION

PORTFOLIO

38. In 1995, $2.05 billion worth of recorded country music was sold. Recorded rock music sold about twice that amount. The total amount of *all* recorded music sold in 1995 was twice the sum of country and rock. Write an expression for the total amount of all recorded music sold in 1995. Simplify the expression.

Tech Link

Investigation 1, Interactive Real-Life Investigations

39. BUILDING YOUR PROJECT Your class takes a trip to a zoo that charges $3.00 admission for adults and $1.75 for students.

a. Use the numbers of students and adults you found in Exercise 53 on page 9. Write an expression that represents the total cost of admission to the zoo. How much will it cost?

b. If possible, find out the prices for admission to the place you have chosen for your class trip. Repeat part (a) for your class trip.

Take this test as you would take a test in class. The answers to the exercises are given in the back of the book.

1. List several ways that numbers are used to describe objects. **(1.1)**

LOOKING FOR A PATTERN In Exercises 2–5, describe a pattern for the sequence. Then list the next three numbers in the sequence. **(1.1)**

2. 3, 6, 9, 12, ? , ? , ?

3. 90, 81, 72, 63, ? , ? , ?

4. 1, 4, 9, 16, ? , ? , ?

5. $\frac{1}{2}, \frac{1}{3}, \frac{1}{4}, \frac{1}{5},$? , ? , ?

In Exercises 6 and 7, draw the next three figures in the pattern. **(1.1)**

6.

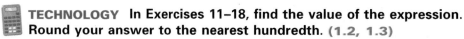

7. 1 2 3 4 5 9

In Exercises 8–10, write a verbal description of the number sentence. **(1.2, 1.3)**

8. $22 \cdot 4 = 88$

9. $4^5 = 1024$

10. $\sqrt{289} = 17$

TECHNOLOGY In Exercises 11–18, find the value of the expression. Round your answer to the nearest hundredth. **(1.2, 1.3)**

11. $12 \cdot 4$

12. $(176)(12)$

13. $\frac{369}{41}$

14. 5^8

15. $(4.3)^2$

16. $\sqrt{256}$

17. $\sqrt{795.24}$

18. $\sqrt{19}$

In Exercises 19–24, simplify the expression. **(1.4)**

19. $28 - 21 \div 7$

20. $8 \div 2 \cdot 4^2$

21. $40 + \frac{15}{3} - 6$

22. $6 + 9 \div 3 - 1$

23. $9 \times (3 + 4) - 7$

24. $48 \div [2 \cdot (12 - 4)]$

In Exercises 25–27, copy the number sentence and insert parentheses to make it true. **(1.4)**

25. $21 - 8 \times 2 = 26$

26. $24 - 20 \div 4 + 6 = 22$

27. $24 - 12 - 4 \cdot 2 = 8$

WORLD'S LARGEST FLAG Exercises 28–30 are about the American "Superflag." The flag is a rectangle that is 255 ft wide and 505 ft long. **(1.2)**

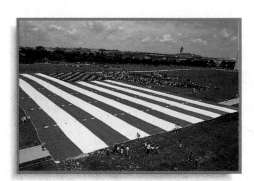

28. Find the area of the flag.

29. The flag has 13 stripes of equal width. Find the width of each stripe.

30. The blue rectangle is as wide as 7 stripes. Find the width of the blue rectangle.

GEOMETRY CONNECTION

Finding Patterns

The first four figures in a sequence are shown below. The table shows the perimeter of each figure.

Materials Needed
- graph paper
- triangular dot paper
- pencils or pens

Figure 1   Figure 2   Figure 3   Figure 4

Figure	1	2	3	4	5	6
Perimeter	4	6	8	10	12	?
Pattern	$2 + 2(1)$	$2 + 2(2)$	$2 + 2(3)$	$2 + 2(4)$	$?$ $+ 2($ $?$ $)$	?

1. Copy the table. Draw the 5th and 6th figures on graph paper, and use your drawing to complete the table.

2. Use the pattern to help you predict the perimeter of the 10th figure. Then draw the figure to check your prediction.

3. What is the perimeter of the nth figure? Explain your answer.

4. Find the perimeter of the 41st figure.

NOW TRY THESE

5. Below are the first four figures in a sequence. Draw the 5th and 6th figures on triangular dot paper.

Figure 1   Figure 2   Figure 3   Figure 4

6. Make a table similar to the one above for the sequence of figures in Exercise 5.

7. Predict the perimeter of the 9th figure. Then draw the figure to check your prediction.

8. What is the perimeter of the nth figure?

9. Find the perimeter of the 34th figure.

What you should learn:

Goal 1 How to evaluate expressions that contain variables

Goal 2 How to use formulas to model real-life situations

Why you should learn it:

Learning to use expressions with variables is a key part of learning algebra. Algebraic expressions allow you to model real-life situations, such as finding the distance traveled by a moon rover.

Variables in Expressions

Goal 1 EVALUATING EXPRESSIONS WITH VARIABLES

A **variable** is a letter that is used to represent one or more numbers. The numbers are **values of the variable**. An **algebraic expression** is a collection of numbers, variables, operations, and grouping symbols. Here are some examples.

Algebraic Expression	Verbal Description
$5n$	5 times n
$4x^2$	4 times the square of x
$2a + bc$	2 times a, plus b times c

The third expression above is a sum. The parts that are added to form the sum, $2a$ and bc, are the **terms** of the expression.

Replacing each variable in an algebraic expression by a number is called **substituting**. The number obtained after simplifying is the **value of the expression**. To evaluate an expression, use the following steps.

Write the algebraic expression. ➤ Substitute values for the variables. ➤ Simplify the numerical expression.

Example 1 Evaluating an Algebraic Expression

a. Evaluate $2n + 5$ when $n = 13$.

b. Evaluate $3x^2 - 11x$ when $x = 6$.

Solution

a. Value $= 2n + 5$ Write original expression.
$= 2(13) + 5$ Substitute 13 for n.
$= 26 + 5$ Multiply.
$= 31$ Add.

b. Value $= 3x^2 - 11x$ Write original expression.
$= 3(6^2) - 11(6)$ Substitute 6 for x.
$= 3(36) - 11(6)$ Evaluate the power.
$= 108 - 66$ Multiply.
$= 42$ Subtract.

Algebraic expressions are often used to model real-life quantities. You can translate a **verbal model** into an **algebraic model** by using labels. Algebraic models are sometimes called **formulas**.

Verbal Model	Labels	Algebraic Model
The area of a rectangle is the product of its length and its width.	A = area l = length w = width	$A = lw$
The distance traveled is the product of the rate and the time.	d = distance r = rate (or speed) t = time	$d = rt$

Example 2 **Evaluating a Formula**

Evaluate the formula $P = 2l + 2w$ when $l = 4$ and $w = 6$.

Solution

$$P = 2l + 2w \qquad \text{Write original formula.}$$
$$= 2(4) + 2(6) \qquad \text{Substitute 4 for } l \text{ and 6 for } w.$$
$$= 20 \qquad \text{Simplify.}$$

Example 3 **Finding a Distance**

REAL LIFE
Space

A rover driving on the moon's surface travels at a speed of 60 ft/min. How far will it travel in 90 min?

Solution

Begin by writing a verbal model for the situation.

Verbal Model **Distance = Rate · Time**

Labels
Distance = d (feet)
Rate = r (feet per minute)
Time = t (minutes)

Algebraic Model
$$d = rt \qquad \text{Write algebraic model.}$$
$$= (60)(90) \qquad \text{Substitute 60 for } r \text{ and 90 for } t.$$
$$= 5400 \qquad \text{Simplify.}$$

In 90 min, the rover will travel 5400 ft.

1.5 Exercises

Extra Practice, page 716

GUIDED PRACTICE

1. What is an algebraic expression? Give an example of an algebraic expression and write a verbal description of the expression.

2. **WRITING** What does it mean to *evaluate* an algebraic expression?

In Exercises 3–6, suppose you are asked to evaluate the expression $4 + n$ when $n = 3$. Identify the following.

3. The variable

4. The value of the variable

5. The expression

6. The value of the expression

In Exercises 7 and 8, evaluate the expression when $a = 5$ and $b = 3$.

7. $3a + b$

8. $(b^2 + 6) \div a$

PRACTICE AND PROBLEM SOLVING

In Exercises 9–20, evaluate the expression when $x = 4$.

9. $5 + x$

10. $32 \div x$

11. $12x$

12. $x \cdot 3x$

13. $3x^2 + 9$

14. $2x^2 \cdot 3x$

15. $(x + 3)6$

16. $(x - 2) \div 4$

17. $(9 - x)^2$

18. $(7 - x)^3$

19. $(8 - x + 8) \div x$

20. $x^2 - 3 \cdot x$

In Exercises 21–32, evaluate the expression when $a = 2$ and $b = 7$.

21. $b - a$

22. ab

23. $3b - a$

24. $5a + 2b$

25. $3a^2 \cdot b$

26. $(4b) \div (2a)$

27. $(24a - 6) \div b$

28. $b(9 - a)$

29. $(b - a)^3$

30. $(5 + b)^2 + a$

31. $(a + b) \div (b - 2a)$

32. $6(b - a) \div (3a)$

In Exercises 33–36, evaluate the expression when $x = 5$, $y = 8$, and $z = 9$.

33. $x + y - z$

34. $x + (z - y)$

35. $z \div (y - x) + z$

36. $y(z - x) + x$

In Exercises 37–40, match the verbal description with an algebraic expression.

37. The difference of a number and 8

   A. $a + 8$

38. The product of a number and 8

   B. $x - 8$

39. The quotient of a number and 8

   C. $n \div 8$

40. The sum of a number and 8

   D. $8y$

24   **Chapter 1** *Exploring Patterns*

ROBOTIC ROVER In Exercises 41 and 42, imagine that you are controlling a robotic rover to look for meteorites in Antarctica. The rover is traveling at a speed of 50 ft/min.

41. How far will the rover travel in 30 min?

42. Use the formula *time = distance ÷ rate* to find how much time it will take the rover to travel 2600 ft.

43. The expression $4x + 2$ has a value of 18. Find the value of x.

44. The expression $5n - 3$ has a value of 47. Find the value of n.

45. **GOING TO A MOVIE** You treat some friends to a movie. Tickets cost $6.00 per person, and you buy each person a bag of popcorn for $2.00. Let p represent the number of people.

   a. Write an expression for the total amount you spend.

   b. If $p = 3$, how much did you spend?

Real Life...
Real Facts

Rover Researchers in Pittsburgh directed this 1600 lb rover across a desert in South America. Robots like it will search for meteorites in Antarctica and explore the Moon.

 STANDARDIZED TEST PRACTICE

46. Sandy's family traveled 228 mi to visit an amusement park. They drove at a speed of 60 mi/h. Let t represent the amount of time the trip took. Which equation models the situation?

   A $t = 228 \cdot 60$ **B** $60 = 228t$ **C** $228 = 60t$ **D** $228 = 60 \div t$

47. If $x = 5$ and $y = 5.01$, which of the following is true?

   A $x = y$ **B** $x < y$ **C** $y < x$ **D** $x > y$

 EXPLORATION AND EXTENSION

PORTFOLIO

48. **BUILDING YOUR PROJECT** Your class goes to a state park 80 mi away. You travel 5 mi on city streets, and then 75 mi on the highway.

   a. Your average speed is 20 mi/h in the city and 50 mi/h on the highway. Use the formula *time = distance ÷ rate*. How much time will you spend traveling on city streets? How much time will you spend on the highway?

   b. Use your answers from part (a) to find the total travel time.

   c. If possible, find out the distance from your school to the place you have chosen for your class trip. Estimate how much of this distance will be driven on streets and how much will be on the highway. Find your total travel time.

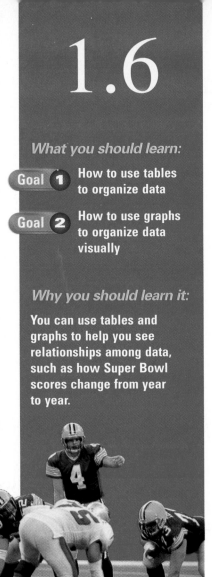

1.6

Exploring Data: **Tables** and **Graphs**

What you should learn:

Goal ❶ How to use tables to organize data

Goal ❷ How to use graphs to organize data visually

Why you should learn it:

You can use tables and graphs to help you see relationships among data, such as how Super Bowl scores change from year to year.

Goal ❶ USING TABLES TO ORGANIZE DATA

The word *data* is plural, and it means facts or numbers that describe something. A collection of data is easier to understand when it is organized in a table or graph. There is no best way to organize data, but there are many good ways.

Data for the perimeters of the rectangles below are shown underneath the figures.

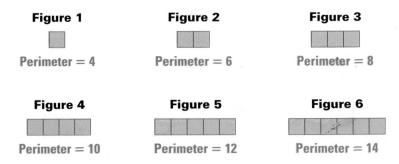

Figure 1	**Figure 2**	**Figure 3**
Perimeter = 4	Perimeter = 6	Perimeter = 8

Figure 4	**Figure 5**	**Figure 6**
Perimeter = 10	Perimeter = 12	Perimeter = 14

The pattern of the perimeters is easier to see if you organize the data in a table. Each perimeter is **2** more than the previous one.

Figure number	1	2	3	4	5	6
Perimeter	4	6	8	10	12	14

+ 2   + 2   + 2   + 2   + 2

Example 1 **Making a Table**

The winning and losing scores at the Super Bowl from 1990 through 1997 are shown below. Use a table to organize the data.
(Source: National Football League)

55 to 10 (1990)	20 to 19 (1991)	37 to 24 (1992)
52 to 17 (1993)	30 to 13 (1994)	49 to 26 (1995)
27 to 17 (1996)	35 to 21 (1997)	

Solution

One way to organize the data in a table is shown below.

Year	1990	1991	1992	1993	1994	1995	1996	1997
Winning score	55	20	37	52	30	49	27	35
Losing score	10	19	24	17	13	26	17	21

STRATEGY **USE A GRAPH** There are many ways to organize data in graphs. Two types of graphs are shown in Example 2.

Example 2 Drawing Graphs

Draw a bar graph and a line graph that represent the Super Bowl data from Example 1.

Solution

In a bar graph, the lengths of the bars represent the values of the data. Since there are two sets of data (the winning scores and the losing scores), use a *double* bar graph.

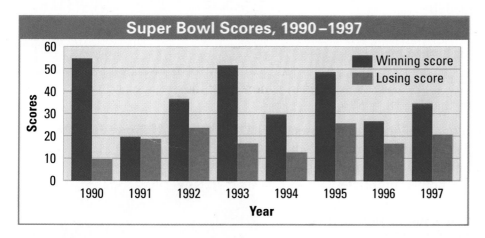

A line graph uses points to represent data. Plot the data points, and draw line segments to connect adjacent points in each set of data.

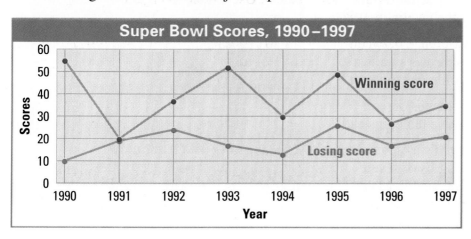

Talk About It
....

Consider the graphs in Example 2.

1. Which Super Bowl do you think was the most exciting? Why?

2. Compare the two graphs. How are they similar? How are they different?

GUIDED PRACTICE

1. Name some ways that you can organize data.

2. OPEN-ENDED PROBLEM How could you organize the following data?

a. The number of students eating school lunches each day last week

b. The number of hours each student spent studying last night

PRACTICE AND PROBLEM SOLVING

OLYMPIC MEDALS In Exercises 3–7, use the table at the right. The table gives the medal count for the top five medal winners in the 1996 Summer Olympics. Let *G*, *S*, and *B* represent the number of gold, silver, and bronze medals won by a team.

1996 Olympic Medals	Gold	Silver	Bronze
United States	44	32	25
Russia	26	21	16
Germany	20	18	27
China	16	22	12
France	15	7	15

3. Which team won 101 medals?

4. As a group, did the five teams win more gold medals, silver medals, or bronze medals?

5. For which team is it true that $G - 10 = B$?

6. For which team is it true that $B - 8 = S$?

7. Draw either a bar graph or a line graph to represent the number of gold and silver medals won by each team. Which type of graph did you choose? Explain why that type of graph is more appropriate.

JAVELIN THROW The bar graph shows the winning distances of the javelin throw in the Olympics. Use the bar graph in Exercises 8–10.

8. MAKING AN ESTIMATE How far did the men's champion throw the javelin in 1980?

9. In what year was the difference between the men's and women's throws smallest? In what year was this difference greatest?

10. What would be the advantages of representing the data with a table, instead of a graph? Explain.

11. GEOMETRY The side lengths of seven squares are 1, 2, 3, 4, 5, 6, and 7. Make a table that shows the perimeter and area of each square.

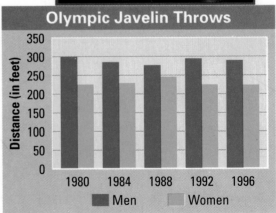

Olympic Javelin Throws

■ Men   ■ Women

In Exercises 12 and 13, use the table. The table lists the average monthly temperatures in degrees Fahrenheit for Cleveland, Ohio, and Seattle, Washington. (Source: National Oceanic and Atmospheric Administration)

Month	Jan.	Feb.	Mar.	Apr.	May	June	July	Aug.	Sept.	Oct.	Nov.	Dec.
Cleveland	25°	27°	37°	48°	58°	68°	72°	70°	64°	53°	43°	31°
Seattle	41°	44°	47°	50°	56°	61°	65°	66°	61°	54°	46°	42°

12. Represent the data with a bar graph and with a line graph.

13. **MAKING AN ESTIMATE** Estimate the average yearly temperature in Cleveland and in Seattle. Explain your reasoning.

14. **WRITING** Describe some advantages and disadvantages of organizing data with a table and with a graph.

STANDARDIZED TEST PRACTICE

15. Which of the following does *not* follow from the graph?

(A) The combined population of Lake City and Union is less than that of Franklin.

(B) The population of Troy Center is less than 10,000.

(C) Twice as many people live in Franklin as in Union.

(D) The combined population of Union and Franklin is greater than 90,000.

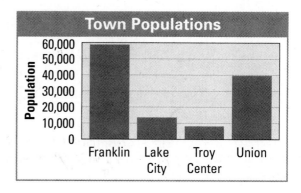

EXPLORATION AND EXTENSION

PORTFOLIO

16. **BUILDING YOUR PROJECT** The graph shows, for each weekday, the average number of students and adults that visit the place you will go on your class trip.

a. Estimate the total number of visitors on each of the five weekdays.

b. For which day of the week will you plan your trip? Explain.

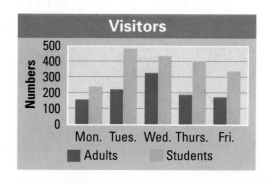

GEOMETRY CONNECTION

Patterns in Geometry

Materials Needed
• geoboard and
  rubber bands
• square dot paper
• pencils
• colored pencils

Part A FINDING AREAS OF BASIC PIECES

On the geoboard shown, square *A* has an area of 1.

1. On dot paper, draw a 1-by-1 square.
   Draw a diagonal to split it into two
   triangles. Use the drawing to find the
   area of triangle *B*.

2. Make a drawing on dot paper to find
   the area of triangle *C*.

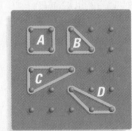

3. Copy the diagram at the right onto
   dot paper. Use it to find the area of
   triangle *D*. Explain your reasoning.

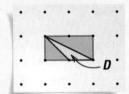

Part B FINDING AREAS OF QUADRILATERALS

4. On your geoboard, make a quadrilateral
   that has an odd number of pegs on each
   of its four sides.

5. Connect the middle peg on each of the
   sides of the large quadrilateral to form
   a small quadrilateral.

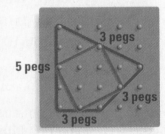

6. Draw both of the
   quadrilaterals on dot
   paper. On your drawing,
   split each quadrilateral
   into the basic pieces
   from Part A.

7. Find the area of each
   quadrilateral by adding
   up the areas of its
   pieces.

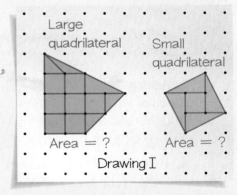

Drawing I

8. Repeat Part B of this lab three more times, until you have found the areas of four pairs of quadrilaterals.

9. Record your results in a table like the one below.

Drawing	I	II	III	IV
Area of large quadrilateral	?	?	?	?
Area of small quadrilateral	?	?	?	?

10. How is the area of each small quadrilateral related to the area of the corresponding large quadrilateral?

11. A quadrilateral has an area of 20 square units. Predict the area of the small quadrilateral that is formed when you connect the midpoints of its sides. Explain your reasoning.

NOW TRY THESE

12. Using your geoboard, make four triangles that have an odd number of pegs on each side. Connect the midpoints of the sides of each large triangle to form a small triangle.

13. Draw each large triangle and its corresponding small triangle on dot paper. Find their areas.

14. Make a table of the areas of the triangles. How is the area of each small triangle related to the area of the corresponding large triangle?

15. Suppose a triangle has an area of 20 square units. Predict the area of the corresponding small triangle. Explain your reasoning.

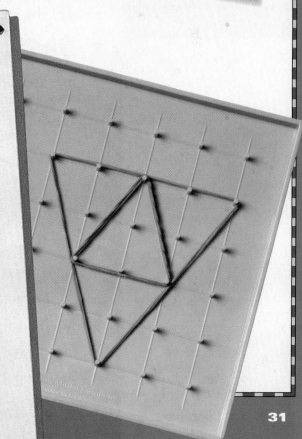

1.7

Exploring Patterns in **Geometry**

Goal 1 IDENTIFYING POLYGONS

Geometry is the study of shapes and their measures. One of the most common geometric shapes is a *polygon*.

POLYGONS

A **polygon** is a *closed* figure whose **sides** are straight line segments. Each corner of the figure is a **vertex** . (The plural is *vertices*.) The number of vertices of a polygon is the same as the number of sides. The number of sides determines the name of the polygon.

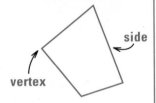

3: Triangle	4: Quadrilateral	5: Pentagon
6: Hexagon	7: Heptagon	8: Octagon
9: Nonagon	10: Decagon	n: n-gon

Example 1 Identifying Polygons

State whether the figure is a polygon. If it is, name it. If it is not, explain why not.

a.    **b.**    **c.**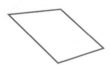

d.    **e.**    **f.**

Solution

a. This is not a polygon because it is not closed.

b. This is not a polygon because its sides are not all straight.

c. This is a polygon with 4 sides. It is a quadrilateral.

d. This is a polygon with 7 sides. It is a heptagon.

e. This is a polygon with 5 sides. It is a pentagon.

f. This is a polygon with 6 sides. It is a hexagon.

A segment that connects two vertices of a polygon and is not a side is called a **diagonal** of the polygon.

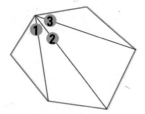

You can draw 3 diagonals from a single vertex of a hexagon.

You can draw a total of 9 different diagonals in a hexagon.

LESSON INVESTIGATION

COOPERATIVE LEARNING

Investigating Diagonals of Polygons

GROUP ACTIVITY For each polygon in the table, count how many diagonals can be drawn from a single vertex. Then count the total number of diagonals that can be drawn in the polygon. Copy and complete the table. What patterns do you see?

Type of polygon	Number of vertices	Diagonals from a single vertex	Total number of diagonals
Triangle	3	? 0	? 0
Quadrilateral	4	? 1	? 2
Pentagon	5	? 2	? 5
Hexagon	6	3	9

7
8   4   5.   14
                                    20

Example 2 Using Verbal and Algebraic Models

Use what you learned in the investigation to write a verbal model and an algebraic model for the number of diagonals in a polygon.

Verbal Model $\dfrac{\text{Total}}{\text{diagonals}} = \dfrac{\text{Number}}{\text{of vertices}} \times \dfrac{\text{Diagonals from}}{\text{a single vertex}} \div 2$

Total number of diagonals = T

Number of vertices = n

Number of diagonals from a single vertex = $n - 3$

Algebraic Model $T = n \times (n - 3) \div 2$

ONGOING **ASSESSMENT**

Write About It
· · · · · · · · · · · · · · · · · ·

Use the algebraic model from Example 2.

1. Find the total number of diagonals in a heptagon.

2. Check your answer by drawing a diagram.

GUIDED PRACTICE

1. **WRITING** In your own words, state the definition of a polygon.

In Exercises 2 and 3, use the figure at the right.

2. State the name of each polygon in the word FIFTY.

3. How many diagonals can be drawn in the I of FIFTY?

4. Give an example of a verbal model and an algebraic model.

PRACTICE AND PROBLEM SOLVING

In Exercises 5–12, decide whether the figure is a polygon. If it is, name it. If it is not, explain why not.

5.

6.

7.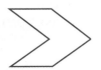

8.

9.

10.

11.

12.

GEOMETRY Use the table below to answer Exercises 13–15. The table lists the base, *b*, the height, *h*, and the area, *A*, of some triangles.

Base, b	Height, h	Base × Height	Area, A
6	4	24	12
3	2	6	3
10	5	50	25

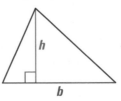

13. Write a verbal model for the area of a triangle.

14. Write an algebraic model for the area of a triangle.

15. Find the area of a triangle with a base of 16 in. and a height of 8 in.

SIGNS In Exercises 16–19, decide whether the outer edge of the sign is a polygon. If it is, name the polygon. If it is not, explain why not.

16.

17.

18.

19.

ARCHITECTURE In Exercises 20–25, use the photo of houses in Florida. Decide whether the shape outlined in the given color is a polygon. If it is, name it. If not, explain why not.

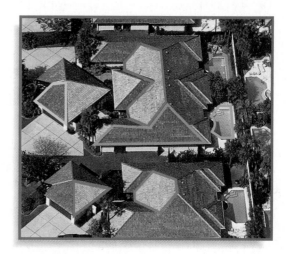

20. Yellow

21. Red

22. Orange

23. Light blue

24. Green

25. Purple

26. Use the algebraic model from Example 2 to find the number of diagonals in an octagon. Then draw a diagram to check your answer.

27. Draw a hexagon with two sides equal in measure.

28. Draw an octagon with four sides equal to one length and the remaining four sides equal to a different length.

STANDARDIZED TEST PRACTICE

29. In the polygon at the right, identify the part labeled *X*.

Ⓐ Vertex   **Ⓑ** Side

Ⓒ Diagonal   **Ⓓ** Face

EXPLORATION AND EXTENSION

30. COMMUNICATING ABOUT MATHEMATICS At the right is a map of Yellowstone National Park. (For more information about Yellowstone National Park, see page 37.)

a. Draw a polygon that approximates the boundary of the park.

b. How many sides does your polygon have? If possible, name the polygon.

c. Use the scale on the map to estimate the length (in miles) of each side of the polygon. Label each side with its estimated length.

31. COMMUNICATING ABOUT MATHEMATICS Estimate the area of Yellowstone National Park. Explain the method you used.

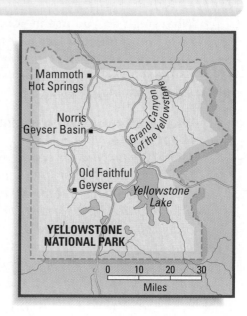

TECHNOLOGY In Exercises 1–6, perform the operation. Round the result to the nearest hundredth. (1.2, 1.3)

1. $6(14.2)$

2. $8.45 \cdot 5$

3. $\dfrac{13}{9}$

4. $\dfrac{647}{20}$

5. 7^5

6. $\sqrt{155}$

7. SUMMER JOB You earn and save $20 each week mowing lawns. (1.4)

    a. Write an expression for the amount of money you have after working for 6 weeks.

    b. Suppose you buy a bike for $50. Rewrite the expression you wrote in part (a) to reflect this information. Then simplify the expression to find out how much money you have left.

In Exercises 8–15, evaluate the expression when $x = 4$, $y = 5$, and $z = 2$. (1.5)

8. $2y$

9. $4z - x$

10. $(x + y)^2$

11. $5x(x - 4)$

12. $x + y \times z$

13. $2x \div z^2$

14. $(y - z)^2 - x$

15. $(y - x) \div z$

CAREER Interview

RESEARCH SCIENTIST

Carol Stoker is a research scientist at NASA Ames Research Center in Moffett Field, California. She spent years working in Antarctica because its environment most closely mirrors the conditions astronauts would face on the Moon and Mars.

Q What led you into this career?
My primary interest has always been anything to do with the human exploration of Mars.

Q What math do you use in your work?
I use lots of algebra, geometry, and calculus. Although I am always using computers, I must do the thinking. I need to understand the logic behind why things work.

Q What would you like to tell kids in school about math?
Math is important for coping with everyday life decisions, not just for high-tech careers. Living in Antarctica where RadioShack and Kmart are not around the corner, I must estimate and order what supplies I will need for my entire trip. If a piece of equipment breaks, I can't just call out for repairs. I must use my problem solving skills to figure out the solution on my own.

Where the Buffalo Roam

READ About It

Established in 1872, Yellowstone National Park was the first national park in the United States. Its area is 2.2 million acres, which makes it larger than the combined areas of Rhode Island and Delaware. The park has 370 miles of paved roads and approximately 1200 miles of trails.

Eighty percent of Yellowstone National Park is forest. In 1988, large fires burned much of the park—800,000 acres. Before 1988, fires of this magnitude had not occurred at the park for hundreds of years. The burned areas have already begun the natural process of regeneration.

Yellowstone National Park is famous for its geysers and hot springs; there are about 10,000 in the park. In fact, Yellowstone National Park has more geysers and hot springs than the rest of the world combined.

WRITE About It

1. How many acres of Yellowstone National Park were not touched by fire in 1988? Explain how you got your answer.

2. What is the total length of trails and paved roads in Yellowstone National Park? Express your answer in a sentence.

3. You are told that a tree has fallen across a road or a trail somewhere in the park. Do you think it is more likely that the tree was found on a paved road or on a trail? Explain your reasoning.

4. Your friend visited a park in another country which he says has 15,000 hot springs. Do you think your friend is right? Explain.

5. The state of Delaware has an area of 1.3 million acres. What can you conclude about the area of Rhode Island? Explain.

1.8

Exploring Patterns with Technology

What you should learn:

Goal 1 How to use a calculator to discover number patterns

Goal 2 How to use diagrams to discover number patterns in real-life situations

Why you should learn it:

Many real-life situations, such as setting up a carnival game, have patterns that can be described with algebraic models. Knowing the patterns can help you understand the real-life situations.

Goal 1 DISCOVERING NUMBER PATTERNS

Every number can be written as a decimal. The decimals can either terminate, repeat, or continue without repeating.

$\frac{1}{2} = 0.5$	$\frac{3}{8} = 0.375$	**Terminating decimals**
$\frac{1}{3} = 0.3333\ldots$	$\frac{5}{6} = 0.83333\ldots$	**Repeating decimals**
$\sqrt{2} = 1.41421\ldots$	$\pi = 3.14159\ldots$	**Nonrepeating decimals**

To indicate that a decimal repeats, write a bar over the repeating part. For example, $0.83333\ldots = 0.8\overline{3}$.

Example 1 Finding a Pattern for Decimals

Evaluate fractions of the form $\frac{1}{n}$ as a decimal for several values of n. What values of n produce terminating decimals?

Solution

Fraction	$\frac{1}{2}$	$\frac{1}{3}$	$\frac{1}{4}$	$\frac{1}{5}$	$\frac{1}{6}$	$\frac{1}{7}$	$\frac{1}{8}$	$\frac{1}{9}$	$\frac{1}{10}$
Decimal	0.5	$0.\overline{3}$	0.25	0.2	$0.1\overline{6}$	$0.\overline{142857}$	0.125	$0.\overline{1}$	0.1

The fraction $\frac{1}{n}$ terminates if n is a product of 2's and 5's. For instance, $10 = 2 \cdot 5$ and $8 = 2 \cdot 2 \cdot 2$, so $\frac{1}{10}$ and $\frac{1}{8}$ are terminating decimals.

Example 2 Finding a Pattern for Products

Use a calculator to find the product of 19 and the first five natural numbers. Describe the pattern in the digits.

Solution

Evaluate $19n$, when n is a natural number from 1 to 5.

n	1	2	3	4	5
$19n$	19	38	57	76	95

Each time n increases, the **tens' digit** increases by 2 and the **ones' digit** decreases by 1.

NEED TO KNOW

The whole numbers are all of the numbers in the sequence
0, 1, 2, 3, 4, 5, . . .

The natural numbers are all of the numbers in the sequence 1, 2, 3, 4, 5, . . .

Example 3 Modeling Triangular Numbers

You are in charge of a carnival booth in which people try to knock over a stack of wooden bottles with a baseball. Stacks with 1, 2, 3, and 4 rows are shown. How many bottles does an *n*-row stack have?

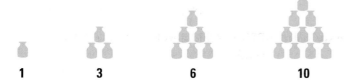

Solution

STRATEGY **DRAW A DIAGRAM** You can see the pattern more easily by simplifying the diagram.

These numbers are called *triangular numbers*. To help discover their pattern, try doubling the size of each stack.

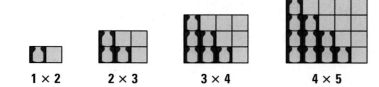

The *n*th triangular number is half the area of an *n*-by-$(n + 1)$ rectangle.

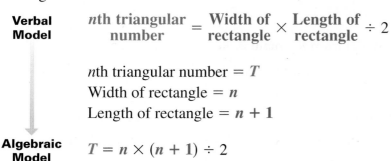

Verbal Model

$$\text{*n*th triangular number} = \text{Width of rectangle} \times \text{Length of rectangle} \div 2$$

*n*th triangular number = T
Width of rectangle = n
Length of rectangle = $n + 1$

Algebraic Model

$$T = n \times (n + 1) \div 2$$

ONGOING ASSESSMENT

Write About It
• • • • • • • • • • • • • • • • • • •

Use the algebraic model from Example 3.

1. Find the seventh triangular number.

2. Check your answer by drawing a diagram.

GUIDED PRACTICE

1. What is the smallest whole number? What is the smallest natural number?

2. 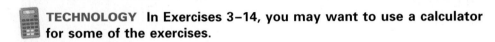 Use a calculator to write the fraction $\frac{n}{11}$ as a decimal for the values of *n* from 1 through 5. Describe any patterns you see.

PRACTICE AND PROBLEM SOLVING

TECHNOLOGY In Exercises 3–14, you may want to use a calculator for some of the exercises.

MAKING A TABLE In Exercises 3–8, make a table showing your results.

3. Find the quotient of 192 and each of the first 4 natural numbers.

4. Find the product of 75 and each of the first 9 whole numbers.

5. Evaluate the fraction $\frac{n}{3}$ as a decimal for the values of *n* from 1 through 9.

6. Calculate $\frac{n^2}{2}$ for the first 7 whole numbers.

7. Calculate $\frac{n}{n+1}$ for the first 5 natural numbers.

8. Evaluate fractions of the form $\frac{2}{n}$ as a decimal for the values of *n* from 1 through 6. What values of *n* produce repeating decimals?

In Exercises 9–11, simplify the expressions. Then write the next three numbers in the sequence and describe the pattern.

9. $8(2) + 2$, $8(23) + 3$, $8(234) + 4$, $8(2345) + 5$, ?, ?, ?

10. $\frac{5}{6} + 9\left(\frac{1}{3}\right)$, $\frac{5}{6} + 9\left(\frac{2}{3}\right)$, $\frac{5}{6} + 9\left(\frac{3}{3}\right)$, $\frac{5}{6} + 9\left(\frac{4}{3}\right)$, ?, ?, ?

11. $77(1443)$, $154(1443)$, $231(1443)$, $308(1443)$, ?, ?, ?

In Exercises 12–14, use the algebraic model from Example 3.

12. Find the eighth triangular number. Then draw a diagram to check your answer.

13. How many bottles are in a 9 row stack of bottles?

14. How many bottles are in a 20 row stack?

DRAWING A DIAGRAM Exercises 15 and 16 are about the sequence of *cubic numbers* 1, 8, 27, ... The *n*th cubic number is the volume of a cube with edges of length *n*.

15. Draw a diagram to represent the fourth cubic number. Find the number.

16. Write a verbal model and an algebraic model for the *n*th cubic number. In the algebraic model, let C stand for the *n*th cubic number.

  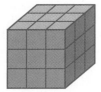

Volume = 1^3 = 1   Volume = 2^3 = 8   Volume = 3^3 = 27

STANDARDIZED TEST PRACTICE

17. The perimeter of the rectangle shown is 32 m. What is its area?

(**A**) 16 m^2 (**B**) 32 m^2

(**C**) 60 m^2 (**D**) 320 m^2

10 m

EXPLORATION AND EXTENSION

FIBONACCI SEQUENCE In Exercises 18–20, use the sequence 1, 1, 2, 3, 5, 8, 13, ... This is called the *Fibonacci Sequence* because the Italian mathematician Leonardo Fibonacci (around 1170–1240) was the first to describe it.

18. Describe the pattern of the sequence.

19. Find the next four numbers in the sequence.

20. **GROUP ACTIVITY** Each member of your group should pick two natural numbers such that the second is larger than the first. Each of you should develop a Fibonacci-like sequence from the two numbers. Find the ratios of the consecutive terms in your sequence. Record the results in a table. For example, the numbers 12 and 20 lead to the sequence 12, 20, 32, 52, . . . and the ratios in the table below. Describe the pattern of the ratios in your table. Compare your results with others in your group.

Real Life...
Real Facts

In the head of a sunflower, the number of clockwise spirals and the number of counterclockwise spirals are consecutive terms in the Fibonacci Sequence.

Term	12	20	32	52
Ratio	$\frac{20}{12} \approx 1.667$	$\frac{32}{20} = 1.6$	$\frac{52}{32} = 1.625$	$\frac{84}{52} \approx 1.615$

WHAT did you learn?   WHY did you learn it?

		WHAT did you learn?	WHY did you learn it?
Skills	1.1	Use numbers to identify and measure. Describe number patterns.	Measure objects and identify locations.
	1.2	Use the four basic number operations.	Calculate your change when buying products.
	1.3	Use powers and square roots.	Design outdoor and indoor spaces to have a given area.
	1.4	Use the order of operations to simplify expressions.	Communicate with others about mathematical ideas.
	1.5	Evaluate algebraic expressions. Use formulas to model real life.	Find the distance a vehicle travels.
	1.6	Use tables and graphs to organize data.	See how sports scores change over time.
	1.7	Identify polygons and parts of polygons.	Describe geometric shapes in nature.
	1.8	Use a calculator to explore number patterns. Use diagrams.	Understand patterns in the real world.
Strategies	1.1–1.8	Use problem solving strategies.	Solve a variety of real-life problems.
Using Data	1.1–1.8	Use tables and graphs.	Organize data and solve problems.

HOW does it fit in the bigger picture of mathematics?

You can represent patterns using geometric models, verbal models, and algebraic models. Here is an area model for the squares of numbers.

Geometric Model

Area = 1^2 Area = 2^2 Area = 3^2 Area = 4^2

Verbal Model   Area of square = (Side length)^2

Area of square = A
Side length = n

Algebraic Model $A = n^2$

VOCABULARY

- sequence (p. 3)
- sum (p. 6)
- difference (p. 6)
- product (p. 6)
- factors (p. 6)
- quotient (p. 6)
- numerator (p. 6)
- denominator (p. 6)
- model (p. 7)
- power (p. 10)
- base (p. 10)
- exponent (p. 10)

- square root (p. 11)
- radical (p. 11)
- square root symbol (p. 11)
- numerical expression (p. 16)
- order of operations (p. 16)
- Left-to-Right Rule (p. 16)
- grouping symbols (p. 17)
- variable (p. 22)
- value of the variable (p. 22)
- algebraic expression (p. 22)
- term (p. 22)

- substitute (p. 22)
- value of an expression (p. 22)
- verbal model (p. 23)
- algebraic model (p. 23)
- formula (p. 23)
- polygon (p. 32)
- side (p. 32)
- vertex (p. 32)
- diagonal (p. 33)
- whole numbers (p. 38)
- natural numbers (p. 38)

1.1 NUMBER PATTERNS

By studying the first few numbers in a sequence, you can describe a pattern and make a conjecture about the next numbers in the sequence.

Examples 4, 7, 10, 13, ? , ? , ?
16, 19, 22

Each number is 3 more than the previous number.

1, 1, 2, 3, 5, 8, ? , ? , ?
13, 21, 34

Each number is the sum of the two previous numbers.

Describe a pattern for the sequence. Then list the next two numbers.

1. 2, 4, 8, 16, ? , ?

2. 50, 43, 36, 29, ? , ?

3. 192, 96, 48, 24, ? , ?

4. 1, 5, 10, 16, ? , ?

5. 105, 90, 76, 63, ? , ?

6. 3, 10, 13, 23, 36, ? , ?

1.2 NUMBER OPERATIONS

The four basic number operations are addition, subtraction, multiplication, and division. You know several ways to represent multiplication and division.

Examples $4(3) = 4 \cdot 3 = 4 \times 3 = 12$ $10 / 2 = 10 \div 2 = \frac{10}{2} = 5$

Perform the operation.

7. $105 + 8$

8. $46 - 19$

9. $125 - 42$

10. $359 + 154 + 12$

11. $50 \cdot 6$

12. $153 \div 9$

13. $(16)4$

14. $65 / 5$

1.3 POWERS AND SQUARE ROOTS

A power has two parts: the base and the exponent. The exponent tells how many times to multiply the base by itself. For instance, $5^3 = 5 \cdot 5 \cdot 5$.

Examples **a.** Evaluate the power 6^4. **b.** Evaluate $\sqrt{640.09}$.

Solution	Calculator Steps	Display	Written Result
a.	6 $\boxed{y^x}$ 4 $\boxed{=}$	1296.	$6^4 = 1296$
b.	640.09 $\boxed{\sqrt{x}}$	25.3	$\sqrt{640.09} = 25.3$

Evaluate the expression. Round your result to the nearest hundredth.

15. 2^9 **16.** 9^5 **17.** 7^3 **18.** $(2.4)^2$

19. $\sqrt{421}$ **20.** $\sqrt{729}$ **21.** $\sqrt{2088.49}$ **22.** $\sqrt{500}$

1.4 ORDER OF OPERATIONS

When simplifying an expression, first do operations within grouping symbols. Then evaluate powers. Then do multiplication and division from left to right. Finally, do addition and subtraction from left to right.

Examples
$$8 + 3 \times 5 - 6 = 8 + 15 - 6 \qquad\qquad 72 \div (2 + 4)^2 = 72 \div 6^2$$
$$= 23 - 6 \qquad\qquad\qquad\qquad\qquad = 72 \div 36$$
$$= 17 \qquad\qquad\qquad\qquad\qquad\qquad = 2$$

Simplify the expression without using a calculator.

23. $4 + 3(3)$ **24.** $15 - 6 \times 4 \div 8$ **25.** $12 \div 3 \cdot 2 + 1$ **26.** $50 - 20 \times 2 - 1$

27. $2 + (9 - 6) \div 3$ **28.** $12 \cdot 3 - (2 + 5)$ **29.** $(16 + 2^2) \div 4$ **30.** $2[20 - (10 + 4)]$

1.5 VARIABLES IN EXPRESSIONS

To evaluate an algebraic expression, substitute values for the variables.

Examples Evaluate $3n + 4$ when $n = 25$.   Evaluate $t^2 - 5t$ when $t = 7$.
$$3n + 4 = 3(25) + 4 \qquad\qquad\qquad t^2 - 5t = (7)^2 - 5(7)$$
$$= 75 + 4 \qquad\qquad\qquad\qquad\qquad = 49 - 35$$
$$= 79 \qquad\qquad\qquad\qquad\qquad\qquad = 14$$

31. Evaluate $(8 - n)^2$ when $n = 3$.

32. Evaluate $x - 2y + z$ when $x = 3$, $y = 5$, and $z = 2$.

$3 - 10 + 2$

33. DISTANCE, RATE, TIME Use the formula *distance = rate · time*. Find the distance traveled by a car that drives for 3 h at 55 mi/h.

1.6 EXPLORING DATA: TABLES AND GRAPHS

In Exercises 34–36, use the graph at the right. The graph shows the populations in 1980 and 1995 of Arizona, Iowa, Maryland, Washington, and West Virginia.

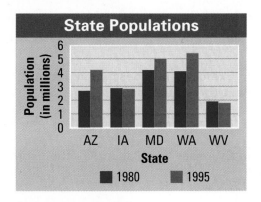

State Populations

34. In which states did the population increase between 1980 and 1995?

35. Which state had the highest population in 1980?

36. Which state had the highest population in 1995?

1.7 EXPLORING PATTERNS IN GEOMETRY

A polygon is a closed figure whose sides are straight line segments.

Examples

This is a polygon with 6 sides. It is a hexagon.

This is not a polygon because its sides are not all straight.

Is the figure a polygon? If so, name it. If not, explain why not.

37.

38.

39.

40.

1.8 EXPLORING PATTERNS WITH TECHNOLOGY

Decimals can either terminate, repeat, or continue without repeating. To show that a decimal repeats, write a bar over the repeating part. For example, $0.1111\ldots = 0.\overline{1}$.

Example Evaluate the fraction $\frac{n}{9}$ for the first five natural numbers. Describe the pattern in the digits.

Solution

n	1	2	3	4	5
$\frac{n}{9}$	$0.\overline{1}$	$0.\overline{2}$	$0.\overline{3}$	$0.\overline{4}$	$0.\overline{5}$

The value of $\frac{n}{9}$ is a repeating decimal in which each digit is the same as n.

41. Use a calculator to create a table for the product of 105 and the first 9 natural numbers. Describe any patterns in the digits.

In Exercises 1–6, evaluate the expression when $a = 8$, $b = 3$, and $c = 5$.

1. $a \cdot c$

2. b^2

3. $a / 4$

4. $3c^3$

5. $4(a + 1)^2$

6. $\sqrt{a + 1}$

In Exercises 7–9, describe a pattern for the sequence. Then list the next three numbers.

7. 15, 13, 11, 9, ?, ?, ?

8. 3, 6, 12, 24, ?, ?, ?

9. 9, 16, 25, 36, ?, ?, ?

In Exercises 10–13, simplify the expression.

10. $3 + 5 \cdot 2 + 4$

11. $10 - 4 + 5 \div 4$

12. $(6 + 2) \cdot 2 + 3^2$

13. $14 \div (9 - 2) + 2^3$

14. Calculate the product of 21 and the first 9 whole numbers. Record the results in a table. Describe any patterns in the digits.

In Exercises 15–17, state whether the figure is a polygon. If it is, name it. If not, explain why not.

15.

16.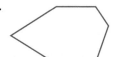

17.

In Exercises 18–20, use the bar graph.
(Source: National Basketball Association)

18. MAKING AN ESTIMATE How many games did the Indiana Pacers win?

19. Which two teams had the same number of losses?

20. Which team had the greatest difference between wins and losses?

21. PRECIOUS METALS The average prices of gold and platinum (in dollars per ounce) for the years 1990 through 1995 are shown in the table. Make a bar graph and a line graph to represent the data.

NBA Final Standings 1995–1996

Year	1990	1991	1992	1993	1994	1995
Price of gold	385	363	345	361	385	385
Price of platinum	467	371	356	370	406	430

(Source: *Statistical Abstract of the United States*)

1. Which sentence describes the sequence $1, \frac{3}{2}, 2, \frac{5}{2}, 3, \ldots$?

   A Each number is $\frac{1}{2}$ times the previous number.

   B Each number is $1\frac{1}{2}$ more than the previous number.

   C Each number is $\frac{1}{2}$ more than the previous number.

   D Each number is 1 more than the previous number.

2. Simplify $10 - 2^3 \div 2$.

   A 1   **B** 6

   C 8   **D** 10

In Questions 3 and 4, use the bar graph, which shows the number of boys and girls in your class for 4 different years.

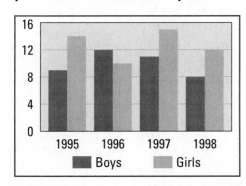

3. In which year were there more boys than girls?

   A 1995   **B** 1996

   C 1997   **D** 1998

4. In which year was your class largest?

   A 1995   **B** 1996

   C 1997   **D** 1998

5. What is the value of the next expression in the sequence $5(9), 5(98), 5(987), 5(9876), \ldots$?

   A 4,935   **B** 49,380

   C 59,256   **D** 493,825

In Questions 6 and 7, use the following information. The infield of a baseball field is a square with an area of 8100 ft². Each base is a square with a side length of 15 in.

6. What is the side length of the infield?

   A 81 ft   **B** 90 ft

   C 900 ft   **D** 2025 ft

7. What is the area of a base?

   A 30 in.^2 **B** 45 in.^2

   C 60 in.^2 **D** 225 in.^2

8. Which sentence about the figure at the right is *true*?

   A The figure is a quadrilateral.

   B The figure is not a polygon.

   C The figure is not closed.

   D The figure is a rectangle.

9. Which expression represents the following phrase? *Four times the difference of ten and three.*

   A $4(10 - 3)$ **B** $4 \cdot 10 - 3$

   C $4 \cdot 3 - 10$ **D** $10 - 3 \times 4$

10. Evaluate $x^2 - 2x$ when $x = 6$.

   A 0   **B** 24

   C 28   **D** 48

Investigations in Algebra

TECHNOLOGY

- **Interactive Real-Life Investigations**
- **Middle School Tutorial Software**

To find out more about starting your own business, go to:

http://www.mlmath.com

RETAIL Fashion Buyers must choose what clothes to buy for their store.

CHAPTER THEME
Fashion Business

CHAPTER PROJECT

Starting a Business

PROJECT DESCRIPTION

Think of a service business that you could start. For example, you can fix things, cut hair, mow lawns, teach a language, or go shopping for your neighbors. You will write a business plan to guide you through the process of starting your business.

GETTING STARTED

Talking It Over

The following questions may help you choose a service that your business can provide.

- What sorts of things must people in your community do regularly? Which of these things can you do for them?

- What do you enjoy doing? What do you do well? Who else could benefit from these things?

Planning Your Project

- **Materials:** colored paper, markers, and folder

- Choose a service your business will provide. Select a name and logo for your business.

- Make a cover for your business plan. You will add pages to the plan as you go through this chapter. When the plan is done, join the pages together to form a booklet.

BUILDING YOUR PROJECT

These are places throughout the chapter where you will work on your project.

2.1 Identify potential customers. *p. 55*

2.2 Project your earnings. *p. 59*

2.3 Choose how much to charge. *p. 63*

2.4 Plan start-up capital. *p. 69*

2.5 Plan repayment of loan. *p. 75*

2.6 Plan advertising. *p. 81*

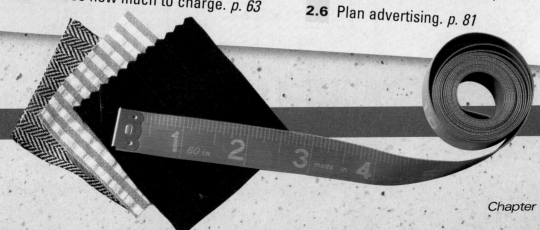

Algebraic Expressions

Algebra tiles, like those shown below, can be used to model algebraic expressions.

Materials Needed
• algebra tiles
• pencils or pens
• paper

 1

1

This 1-by-1 square tile has
an area of 1 square unit.
It represents the number 1.

 1

x

This 1-by-x rectangular tile
has an area of x square
units. It represents the variable x.

Part A MODELING EXPRESSIONS

Here are three examples of modeling algebraic expressions.

$3x + 2$ $2x + 5$ $x + 11$

1. Write the expression that is modeled by the tiles.

a.

b.

c.

In Exercises 2–7, model the expression with algebra tiles. Then, make a sketch of your model.

2. 8   **3.** $2x$

4. $3x + 9$ **5.** $2x + 5$

6. $x + 3$ **7.** $4x + 7$

8. Do the algebra tiles shown below model the expression $2x + 10$? Explain.

Two algebraic expressions are *equivalent* if they have the same values when numbers are substituted for the variables. For instance, $(x + 1 + 1)$ and $(x + 2)$ are equivalent. You can write an equation relating the two expressions.

$$x + 1 + 1 = x + 2$$

You can use algebra tiles to discover equivalent expressions. Here is an example.

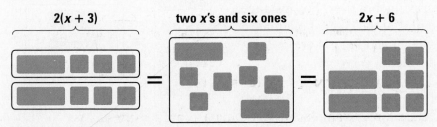

$2(x + 3)$ two x's and six ones $2x + 6$

From this, you can see that $2(x + 3) = 2x + 6$.

In Exercises 9–12, match the algebra tiles with two expressions. Write an equation relating the two expressions.

A. $4x + 2$ B. $6x + 9$ C. $4x + 4$ D. $2(3x + 1)$

E. $3(2x + 3)$ F. $2(2x + 1)$ G. $6x + 2$ H. $4(x + 1)$

9.

10.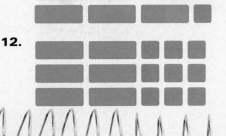

11.

12.

13. Discuss the results of Exercises 9–12. Write a statement telling how you can rewrite $n(ax + b)$ in an equivalent form.

NOW TRY THESE

In Exercises 14 and 15, sketch an algebra tile model for the expression.

14. $3x + 5$ **15.** $x + 4$

In Exercises 16–19, rewrite the expression in an equivalent form. Sketch an algebra tile model to confirm your result.

16. $3(x + 4)$ **17.** $2(3x + 5)$

18. $2x + 6$ **19.** $3x + 3$

The Distributive Property

What you should learn:

Goal 1 How to use the Distributive Property

Goal 2 How to use the Distributive Property in real life

Why you should learn it:

You can use the Distributive Property to model real life, such as ordering clothes for a clothing store.

Goal 1 USING THE DISTRIBUTIVE PROPERTY

Two algebraic expressions are **equivalent** if they have the same values when numbers are substituted for the variables.

One way to discover that two expressions are equivalent is to use algebra tiles. For instance, the tiles at the right show that $2(x + 2)$ and $2x + 4$ are equivalent.

$$2(x + 2) = 2x + 4$$

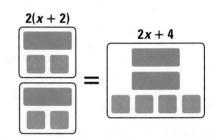

Another way to show these expressions are equivalent is with the **Distributive Property**.

THE DISTRIBUTIVE PROPERTY

Let *a*, *b*, and *c* be numbers or variable expressions.

$$a(b + c) = ab + ac \quad \text{and} \quad ab + ac = a(b + c)$$

Example 1 Using the Distributive Property

a. $2(x + 3) = 2(x) + 2(3)$ Use the Distributive Property.

$ = 2x + 6$ Simplify.

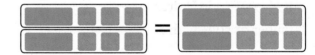

b. $5(2) + 5(4) = 5(2 + 4)$ Use the Distributive Property.

$ = 5(6)$ Simplify.

$ = 30$ Simplify.

c. $x(x + 4) = x(x) + x(4)$ Use the Distributive Property.

$ = x^2 + 4x$ Simplify.

In part (c), notice that $x(4)$ is usually written as $4x$. This is a use of the *Commutative Property of Multiplication*.

STUDY TIP

When you choose labels for a verbal model, you can use any letters as the variables. Common choices are *n*, *x*, and *y*. But it sometimes helps to choose a letter that reminds you of the quantity, such as *T* for total.

The Distributive Property is usually stated with a sum involving only two terms. However, it also applies to sums involving three or more terms.

$a(b + c + d) = ab + ac + ad$ **Sum with 3 terms**

$a(b + c + d + e) = ab + ac + ad + ae$ **Sum with 4 terms**

Example 2 Using the Distributive Property

You are a fashion buyer for a clothing retailer that has 5 stores. You are attending a fashion show and decide to order 10 dresses of style A, 12 dresses of style B, and 15 dresses of style C for *each* of the 5 stores. Use the Distributive Property to find the total number of dresses you will order.

REAL LIFE
Fashion

Solution

Verbal Model

$$\text{Total} = \frac{\text{Number}}{\text{of stores}} \cdot \left[\frac{\text{Style A}}{\text{dresses}} + \frac{\text{Style B}}{\text{dresses}} + \frac{\text{Style C}}{\text{dresses}} \right]$$

Labels

Total number of dresses $= T$

Number of stores $= 5$

Number of style A dresses $= 10$

Number of style B dresses $= 12$

Number of style C dresses $= 15$

Algebraic Model

$T = 5(10 + 12 + 15)$

$= 5(10) + 5(12) + 5(15)$

$= 50 + 60 + 75$

$= 185$

You will order 185 dresses.

✔**Check:** You can check this by adding first.

$5(10 + 12 + 15) = 5(37)$

$= 185$

ONGOING **ASSESSMENT**

Write About It

1. Use the Distributive Property to write an equivalent expression for $4(3x + 1)$.

2. Evaluate both expressions when $x = 5$. Compare the two solutions.

3. Which expression do you think is easier to evaluate? Why?

GUIDED PRACTICE

1. WRITING Copy and complete the table. Choose any value of x for the last column. How does the table show that the expressions $2(x + 2)$ and $2x + 4$ are equivalent?

	$x = 0$	$x = 1$	$x = 3$	$x = 10$	$x = ?$
$2(x + 2)$	$2(0 + 2) = 4$	$2(1 + 2) = ?$	?	?	?
$2x + 4$	$2(0) + 4 = 4$	$2(1) + 4 = ?$	?	?	?

2. Which are correct applications of the Distributive Property?

A. $2(3 + 5) = 2(3) + 5$ **B.** $4(y + 7) = 4(y) + 4(7)$

C. $16(x + 1) = 16x + 16$ **D.** $2(a + 6) = 2a + 6$

3. REASONING Is the statement true? Explain your reasoning.

a. $3(5x) \stackrel{?}{=} 15x$ **b.** $4(9x) \stackrel{?}{=} 13x$ **c.** $2(5 + 6) \stackrel{?}{=} 21$

PRACTICE AND PROBLEM SOLVING

MODELING EXPRESSIONS In Exercises 4 and 5, write the dimensions of the rectangle and an expression for its area. Then use the Distributive Property to rewrite the expression.

4.

5.

In Exercises 6–9, use the Distributive Property to write an equivalent expression. Illustrate your result with an algebra tile sketch.

6. $4(x + 2)$ **7.** $2(x + 1)$ **8.** $2(5x + 3)$ **9.** $5(2x + 3)$

ALGEBRA In Exercises 10–21, use the Distributive Property to rewrite the expression.

10. $9(8 + 7)$ **11.** $11(10 + 5)$ **12.** $4(x + 9)$ **13.** $16(z + 3)$

14. $5(y + 20)$ **15.** $8(4 + q)$ **16.** $0(x + 12)$ **17.** $a(b + 4)$

18. $r(s + t)$ **19.** $4(6 + 10 + 12)$ **20.** $3(5 + 8 + 9)$ **21.** $12(s + t + w)$

OPEN-ENDED PROBLEMS In Exercises 22–24, use a calculator to evaluate the expression two ways. Which way do you prefer? Why?

22. $3(1.21 + 5.48)$ **23.** $10(6.81 + 9.06)$ **24.** $525(11.19 + 27.60)$

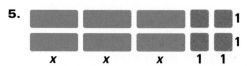

In Exercises 25 and 26, use the blue rectangle.

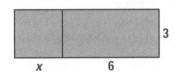

3

x   6

25. Write an expression for the area of the rectangle.

26. Rewrite your expression in Exercise 25 using the Distributive Property.

27. **BUSINESS** You own a small business that has three employees. You pay one employee $1800 a month, the second $1500 a month, and the third $1300 a month.

    a. Write a verbal model that represents how much you pay all three employees in the year.

    b. Use the model in part (a) to determine how much you pay your employees in a year.

Real Life...
Real Facts

Business

Some of the fastest growing businesses in 1996 were restaurants, trucking firms, and doctors' offices.

STANDARDIZED TEST PRACTICE

28. Mr. Wyant took his family of 4 to a baseball game. Each ticket cost $9.00. Mr. Wyant bought each person a hat for $7.95 and a T-shirt for $19.75. Which expression represents the amount of money he spent?

   Ⓐ $4 \times 9.00 + 7.95 + 19.75$ **Ⓑ** $4 + (9.00 + 7.95 + 19.75)$

   Ⓒ $4(9.00 \times 7.95 \times 19.75)$ **Ⓓ** $4(9.00 + 7.95 + 19.75)$

EXPLORATION AND EXTENSION

PORTFOLIO

29. **BUILDING YOUR PROJECT** Make a list of potential customers.

    a. How many jobs per month do you expect from each customer? Let j = the rate you will charge per job. Use the verbal model below to write an expression for your monthly earnings.

$$\text{Earnings} = \frac{\text{Rate}}{\text{per job}} \times \left[\frac{\text{Jobs for}}{\text{Customer A}} + \frac{\text{Jobs for}}{\text{Customer B}} + \cdots \right]$$

    b. You can charge by the hour instead of by the job. Let h = your hourly rate. Write an expression for your monthly earnings.

$$\text{Earnings} = \frac{\text{Hourly}}{\text{rate}} \times \left[\frac{\text{Hours for}}{\text{Customer A}} + \frac{\text{Hours for}}{\text{Customer B}} + \cdots \right]$$

2.2

Simplifying by Adding Like Terms

What you should learn:

Goal 1 How to simplify expressions by adding like terms

Goal 2 How to simplify expressions in geometry.

Why you should learn it:

Evaluating a simplified expression is usually easier than evaluating one that has not been simplified.

Goal 1 ADDING LIKE TERMS

Two or more terms in an expression are **like terms** if they have the same variables raised to the same powers.

Expression	Like Terms
$3x + x + 2$	$3x$ and x
$5y + 5 + 4$	5 and 4
$3y^2 + 4y + y^2 + y$	$3y^2$ and y^2, $4y$ and y

You can simplify an algebraic expression by **collecting like terms** and then adding them.

LESSON INVESTIGATION

COOPERATIVE LEARNING

Investigating Addition of Like Terms

GROUP ACTIVITY The expression $3x + 2x + 2$ can be modeled with algebra tiles. After collecting like tiles, you can see that there are five x's and two 1's.

| 3x | 2x | 2 |

This means the expression $5x + 2$ is equivalent to $3x + 2x + 2$.

Model each of the following with algebra tiles, collect like tiles, and write the simplified expression.

a. $2x + 3 + 4x$ **b.** $x + 2x + 3x + 5$ **c.** $4x + 3 + x$

In parts (a)–(c), compare the x-terms in the original expression with the x-term in your answer.

NEED TO KNOW

In part (b) of Example 1, you can reorder the terms of an expression. That is, $3b + 2 + 5b$ can be rewritten as $3b + 5b + 2$. This procedure is justified by the Commutative Property of Addition.

The Distributive Property can be used to **add like terms**. The rewritten algebraic expression is said to be *simplified*.

Example 1 Simplify by Adding Like Terms

a. $2x + 5x + 1 = (2 + 5)x + 1$ Distributive Property

$ = 7x + 1$ Simplify.

b. $3b + 2 + 5b = 3b + 5b + 2$ Commutative Property

$ = (3 + 5)b + 2$ Distributive Property

$ = 8b + 2$ Simplify.

Example 2 > **Simplifying Before Evaluating**

Write an expression that represents the perimeter of the triangle. Then, evaluate the perimeter when x is 1, 2, 3, 4, and 5. Organize your results in a table and in a graph. Describe the pattern.

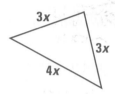

Solution

Perimeter $= 3x + 3x + 4x$ **Add the side lengths.**

        $= 10x$ **Add like terms.**

Evaluate the expression $10x$ when x is 1, 2, 3, 4, and 5. The results are organized in the table and in the graph.

x	Perimeter
1	10
2	20
3	30
4	40
5	50

Perimeters

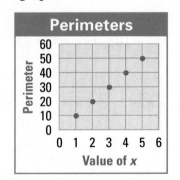

The perimeter increases by 10 each time x increases by 1.

Example 3 > **Writing an Expression**

Write an expression for the perimeter of the figure. Is the expression equivalent to the expression in Example 2?

CONNECTION
Geometry

Solution

Perimeter $= 3x + (x + 2) + 5x + (x + 2)$ **Add the side lengths.**

          $= 3x + x + 5x + x + 2 + 2$ **Reorder terms.**

          $= 10x + 4$ **Add like terms.**

This expression is not equivalent to $10x$. For each value of x, the value $10x + 4$ is 4 more than the value of $10x$.

2.2 Exercises

Extra Practice, page 717

GUIDED PRACTICE

1. **WRITING** What is meant by like terms? Give an example.

2. Give an example of adding like terms. Illustrate your example with an algebra tile sketch.

3. **WRITING** Describe in your own words the Commutative Property of Addition.

4. **WRITING** When is it helpful to add like terms?

WRITING In Exercises 5–8, can the expression be simplified? Explain.

5. $3x + x$
6. $2a + 7$
7. $2r + 5r^2$
8. $5 + 2(x + 8)$

PRACTICE AND PROBLEM SOLVING

ALGEBRA In Exercises 9–23, simplify the expression.

9. $2a + a$
10. $5b + 7b + 10$
11. $3x + 6x + 9$

12. $3a + 2b + 5a$
13. $6x + x + 2y$
14. $5 + r + 2s + 13r$

15. $p + 9q + 9 + 14p$
16. $2x + 4y + 3z + 17z$
17. $a + 2b + 2a + b + 2c$

18. $b + b^2 + 2b$
19. $x^2 + x^2$
20. $3(x + 3) + 4x$

21. $8(y + 2) + y + 4$
22. $3(a + b) + 3(b + a)$
23. $5(x + y) + 2(y + x)$

24. **OPEN-ENDED PROBLEM** Write an expression that has four terms and simplifies to $16x + 5$.

25. **REASONING** Describe the steps used to simplify $2x + 3 + 5x$.

ALGEBRA In Exercises 26–34, simplify the expression. Then evaluate when $x = 2$ and $y = 5$.

26. $2x + 3x + y$
27. $y + 4y + 8x$
28. $4(x + y) + x$

29. $3y + 2x + 6y$
30. $5x + 2(2x + y)$
31. $6x + 6y + 6x$

32. $(x + y)4 + 7x$
33. $xy + x^2 + xy$
34. $6xy + x^2 + x^2$

GEOMETRY In Exercises 35 and 36, write an expression for the perimeter of each polygon. Are the expressions equivalent? Explain.

35.
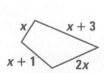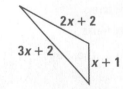

36.
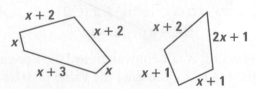

GEOMETRY In Exercises 37 and 38, write an expression for the perimeter. Find the perimeter when *x* is 1, 2, 3, 4, and 5. Organize your results in a table or bar graph. Describe the pattern as the values of *x* increase by 1.

37.

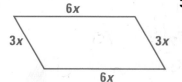

38.

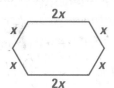

39. **LANDSCAPING** You have a landscaping job for the summer. You work for 5 hours per day Monday through Thursday. You earn $6 per hour. Write an expression that represents the number of hours you work in a week.

STANDARDIZED TEST PRACTICE

40. Simplify $6x + 2x + x + 1$.

   A $3x + 5$ **B** $8x + 1$ **C** $9x + 1$ **D** $8x + 2$

41. The graph shows the number of people who joined a certain health club during one week. The cost of joining the club is *x* dollars. Which expression represents the total amount of money received by the health club for memberships during the week?

   A 16   **B** $16x$

   C $144x$ **D** $16x^5$

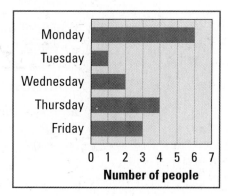

EXPLORATION AND EXTENSION

PORTFOLIO

42. **BUILDING YOUR PROJECT** Suppose you plan to work 3 h after school each Wednesday, Thursday, and Friday, and 9 h each Saturday. You will earn *x* dollars per hour.

   a. Write an expression that represents your weekly earnings.

   b. Suppose you earn $3.25 per hour. How much money will you earn each week?

Solving Equations with **Mental Math**

What you should learn:

Goal ❶ How to check that a number is a solution of an equation

Goal ❷ How to use Mental Math

Why you should learn it:

Learning how to solve equations helps you solve real-life problems.

Goal ❶ CHECKING SOLUTIONS

An **equation** states that two expressions are equivalent. Some equations, called **identities**, are true for all values of the variables they contain. Here are two examples.

$$3 + 2^2 = 7 \qquad \text{Identity: Always true}$$

$$2(x + 3) = 2x + 6 \qquad \text{Identity: True for all values of } x$$

Other equations, called **conditional equations**, are *not* true for all values of the variables they contain.

$$x + 1 = 4 \qquad \text{Conditional equation: true only for } x = 3$$

$$3x = 12 \qquad \text{Conditional equation: true only for } x = 4$$

Finding the values of a variable that make a conditional equation true is called **solving the equation**, and these values of the variable are **solutions** of the equation. Two equations are **equivalent** if they have the same solutions. You can check that a number is a solution by substituting in the original equation.

Example 1 **Checking Possible Solutions**

Which of the following are solutions of $4x - 3 = 5$?
a. $x = 2$ **b.** $x = 3$

Solution

a.
$4x - 3 = 5$	Write original equation.
$4(2) - 3 \overset{?}{=} 5$	Substitute 2 for *x*.
$8 - 3 \overset{?}{=} 5$	Simplify.
$5 = 5$	$x = 2$ is a solution.

b.
$4x - 3 = 5$	Write original equation.
$4(3) - 3 \overset{?}{=} 5$	Substitute 3 for *x*.
$12 - 3 \overset{?}{=} 5$	Simplify.
$9 \neq 5$	$x = 3$ is *not* a solution.

STUDY TIP

Throughout this course, you will learn to be a better problem solver if you develop the habit of always checking your solutions.

Example 2 **Solving an Equation**

$$3z + 9 = 3(z + 3)$$
$$3z + 9 = 3z + 9 \qquad \text{Use the Distributive Property.}$$

This equation is true for any value of z. So, this is an identity.

Goal 2 SOLVING EQUATIONS WITH MENTAL MATH

STRATEGY **USE MENTAL MATH** As you study algebra, you will learn many techniques for solving equations. Some equations are simple enough that you can solve them mentally.

Example 3 Solving Equations with Mental Math

Solve the following equations.

a. $x + 4 = 10$ **b.** $n - 12 = 18$ **c.** $3m = 15$ **d.** $\frac{s}{4} = 5$

Solution

Equation	Stated as a Question	Solution
a. $x + 4 = 10$	What number can you add to 4 to get 10?	$x = 6$
b. $n - 12 = 18$	What number can you subtract 12 from to get 18?	$n = 30$
c. $3m = 15$	What number can you multiply by 3 to get 15?	$m = 5$
d. $\frac{s}{4} = 5$	What number can you divide by 4 to get 5?	$s = 20$

Example 4 Writing a Real Life Equation

REAL LIFE
Sales

Timberland sold $655 million worth of shoes and boots in 1995 and $690 million in 1996. Use the verbal model to write and solve an equation.

Verbal Model $\dfrac{1995}{\text{sales}} + \dfrac{\text{Increase}}{\text{in sales}} = \dfrac{1996}{\text{sales}}$

Solution

Labels
1995 sales = **655**   (millions of dollars)
Increase in sales = x (millions of dollars)
1996 sales = **690**   (millions of dollars)

Algebraic Model $655 + x = 690$ Write the model as an equation.

$x = 35$ Solve with mental math.

The increase in sales was $35 million.

ONGOING ASSESSMENT

Write About It

1. Write the equation in Example 4 as a question. Then answer the question.

2. In 1992, Timberland sold $290 million in shoes and boots. Write and solve an equation to find the increase in sales from 1992 to 1996.

Extra Practice, page 718

GUIDED PRACTICE

1. Give an example of an identity.

2. Give an example of a conditional equation.

3. **WRITING** Explain how to check a solution of an equation.

PRACTICE AND PROBLEM SOLVING

WORKING BACKWARD In Exercises 4–7, match the equation with the correct solution.

> **TOOLBOX**
>
> Problem Solving Strategies, page 744

A. 2   **B.** 3   **C.** 4   **D.** 5

4. $5x + 7 = 22$ **5.** $10 - 2y = 2$ **6.** $n^2 - 4 = 21$ **7.** $20 = 5x^2$

MENTAL MATH In Exercises 8–11, write the equation as a question. Then solve it mentally.

8. $z + 8 = 14$ **9.** $7x = 42$ **10.** $y - 18 = 16$ **11.** $\dfrac{9}{x} = 3$

MENTAL MATH In Exercises 12–15, write the question as an equation. Then solve it mentally.

12. What number can you subtract from 33 to get 24?

13. What number can you add to 7 to get 19?

14. What number can you multiply by 8 to get 56?

15. What number can you divide by 9 to get 5?

MENTAL MATH In Exercises 16–19, decide whether $r = 4$ is a solution of the equation. If it isn't, use mental math to find the solution.

16. $5r = 20$ **17.** $19 - r = 15$ **18.** $24 = 8r$ **19.** $3r + r = 16$

REASONING In Exercises 20–23, decide whether the equations have the same solutions. Explain your reasoning.

20. a. $x - 15 = 8$ **21. a.** $x + 4 = 17$ **22. a.** $3x = 12$ **23. a.** $x \div 3 = 6$

  b. $15 - x = 8$ **b.** $4 + x = 17$ **b.** $\dfrac{x}{12} = 3$ **b.** $3 \div x = 6$

MENTAL MATH In Exercises 24–31, solve the equation using mental math. Check your solution.

24. $r + 11 = 14$ **25.** $20 + n = 41$ **26.** $x - 13 = 2$ **27.** $81 - y = 76$

28. $11x = 55$ **29.** $21 = 3m$ **30.** $\dfrac{x}{4} = 9$ **31.** $\dfrac{26}{y} = 2$

In Exercises 32–34, decide whether the equation is an identity. Explain.

32. $4(x + 7) = 4x + 28$ **33.** $3 + x = 10 + 3$ **34.** $9x = 72 + x$

$X - 106 = 990$

GROWING PUMPKINS **In Exercises 35–37, write an algebraic equation. Use mental math to solve the equation. Check your answer.**

35. The 1991 winner weighed 209.5 lb less than the 1994 winner. How much did the 1994 winner weigh?

36. The 1993 winner weighed 106 lb less than the 1994 winner. How much did the 1993 winner weigh?

37. The 1994 winner weighed 22 lb more than the 1995 winner. How much did the 1995 winner weigh?

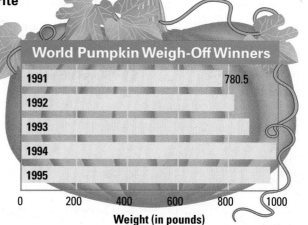

World Pumpkin Weigh-Off Winners

1991 .... 780.5
1992
1993
1994
1995

0   200   400   600   800   1000
Weight (in pounds)
(Source: Great Pumpkin Chronicle)

STANDARDIZED TEST PRACTICE

38. Which two shapes have the same perimeter for all values of x?

1.

4

4

2.

2
2
2x   2
6 4

3.

4
x   3
5 4

4.

2
1
2x   3
7   3

Ⓐ 1 and 3   Ⓑ 2 and 4   Ⓒ 2 and 3   Ⓓ 3 and 4

PORTFOLIO

EXPLORATION AND EXTENSION

BUILDING YOUR PROJECT **In Exercises 39 and 40, write an algebraic equation. Then use mental math to solve the equation. Suppose a neighbor pays you $12 to mow the lawn.**

Time · Hourly earnings = $12

39. If the job takes four hours, how much do you earn per hour?

40. If the job takes three hours, how much do you earn per hour?

41. Do you want to be paid by the job or by the hour? Why?

42. How much will you charge for your service? Use one of your expressions from Lesson 2.1 to estimate your monthly earnings.

Solving Addition Equations

Part **A** USING ALGEBRA TILES

Materials Needed
- algebra tiles
- pencils or pens
- paper

Algebra tiles can be used to model addition equations. Here is an example that shows how to solve the equation $x + 3 = 6$.

1 Model the equation with algebra tiles.

2 To get the x tile by itself, remove (subtract) 3 small tiles from each side.

Isolate the x tile on one side of the equation.

3 The x tile is equal to 3 small tiles. So, the solution is $x = 3$.

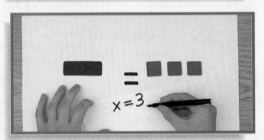

In Exercises 1 and 2, describe the step shown. Is the step one that you should use to solve the equation? Explain why or why not.

1.

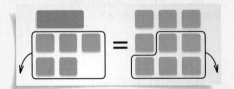

2.

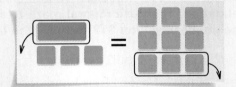

3. When you use algebra tiles to solve an addition equation, how can you tell how many tiles to remove from each side? Use your rule to draw a sketch showing how to solve the algebra tile equation in Exercise 2 correctly.

In Exercises 4 and 5, write the equation that is modeled with algebra tiles. Then use algebra tiles to solve the equation. Make a sketch of your steps. Check your solution by substituting into the original equation.

4.

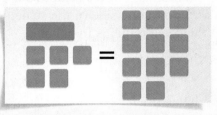

5.

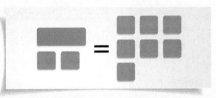

In Exercises 6–9, use algebra tiles to solve the equation. Draw a sketch of the steps you used.

6. $x + 7 = 11$

7. $x + 1 = 8$

8. $x + 4 = 14$

9. $x + 8 = 8$

NOW TRY THESE

In Exercises 10 and 11, write two different equations that have the indicated solution.

10.

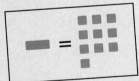

11.

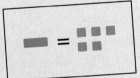

12. In Exercises 10 and 11, how many different equations could you have written that have the indicated solution? Explain your reasoning.

Solving Equations: Addition or Subtraction

What you should learn:

Goal ❶ How to use addition or subtraction to solve an equation

Goal ❷ How to use equations to solve real-life problems

Why you should learn it:

You can use addition or subtraction to solve equations that model real life situations, such as buying a book.

Goal ❶ USING ADDITION OR SUBTRACTION

One way to model and solve an equation is to use a scale. Your goal is to find the value of *x*. Whatever you do to one side of the scale, you must also do to the other so that the scale remains in balance.

Original equation:
$x - 2 = 5$

Add 2 to both sides. Scale stays in balance.

Simplify both sides. Solution is $x = 7$.

ADDITION AND SUBTRACTION PROPERTIES OF EQUALITY

Adding the same number to both sides of an equation or subtracting the same number from both sides of an equation produces an equivalent equation.

Example 1 Solving Equations

Solve the equation.

a. $x - 31 = 14$ **b.** $214 = y + 112$

Solution

a.
$$x - 31 = 14 \quad \text{Write original equation.}$$
$$x - 31 + 31 = 14 + 31 \quad \text{Add 31 to both sides.}$$
$$x = 45 \quad \text{Solution: } x \text{ is by itself.}$$

The solution is 45.

✔**Check:** You can subtract to see that $45 - 31 = 14$.

b.
$$214 = y + 112 \quad \text{Write original equation.}$$
$$214 - 112 = y + 112 - 112 \quad \text{Subtract 112 from both sides.}$$
$$102 = y \quad \text{Solution: } y \text{ is by itself.}$$

The solution is 102. Check this in the original equation.

Goal 2 MODELING REAL LIFE WITH EQUATIONS

STRATEGY **PROBLEM SOLVING** When you are modeling a real-life situation, we suggest that you use the following three steps.

| Write a verbal model. | → | Assign labels to the model. | → | Write the algebraic model. |

Example 2 Using an Equation in Real Life

REAL LIFE
Purchases

You have a $12.50 gift certificate for a bookstore. You want to buy a book that costs $14.59. How much extra money do you need?

Solution

Verbal Model	$\dfrac{\text{Gift}}{\text{certificate}} + \dfrac{\text{Extra}}{\text{money}} = \dfrac{\text{Price}}{\text{of book}}$	
Labels	Value of gift certificate = **12.50**	(dollars)
	Extra money = x	(dollars)
	Price of book = **14.59**	(dollars)

$$\text{Algebraic Model} \quad \mathbf{12.50} + x = \mathbf{14.59}$$
$$12.50 + x - 12.50 = 14.59 - 12.50$$
$$x + 12.50 - 12.50 = 14.59 - 12.50$$
$$x = 2.09$$

You need an extra $2.09.

✔**Check:** You can add to see that $12.50 + 2.09 = 14.59$.

In the 3rd step of the solution, the *Commutative Property of Addition* was used to reorder terms.

> ### PROPERTIES OF ADDITION AND MULTIPLICATION
>
> Commutative Property of Addition: $a + b = b + a$
>
> Commutative Property of Multiplication: $ab = ba$
>
> Associative Property of Addition: $a + (b + c) = (a + b) + c$
>
> Associative Property of Multiplication: $a(bc) = (ab)c$

ONGOING ASSESSMENT

Talk About It
....

1. Write a real-life problem that can be modeled by an equation. Trade problems with a partner. Use the steps shown above to solve the problem. Discuss your solutions.

2.4 Exercises

Extra Practice, page 718

GUIDED PRACTICE

1. Give an example of the Addition Property of Equality.

2. **WRITING** Explain why the equations $x + 5 = 8$ and $x = 3$ are equivalent.

WRITING In Exercises 3–6, explain how to solve the equation.

3. $x + 24 = 38$ 4. $y - 16 = 53$ 5. $152 = r + 72$ 6. $185 = s - 68$

ALGEBRA In Exercises 7–10, state the property that is demonstrated.

7. $3 \cdot (8 \cdot 4) = (3 \cdot 8) \cdot 4$ 8. $(3)(8) = (8)(3)$

9. $4 + 7 = 7 + 4$ 10. $8 + (9 + 7) = (8 + 9) + 7$

PRACTICE AND PROBLEM SOLVING

ALGEBRA In Exercises 11–14, copy and complete the solution.

11.
$$x - 34 = 52$$
$$x - 34 + \boxed{?} = 52 + \boxed{?}$$
$$x = \boxed{?}$$

12.
$$76 = y - 29$$
$$76 + \boxed{?} = y - 29 + \boxed{?}$$
$$\boxed{?} = y$$

13.
$$r + 62 = 111$$
$$r + 62 - \boxed{?} = 111 - \boxed{?}$$
$$r = \boxed{?}$$

14.
$$279 = t + 194$$
$$279 - \boxed{?} = t + 194 - \boxed{?}$$
$$\boxed{?} = t$$

ALGEBRA In Exercises 15–26, solve the equation. Then check your solution.

15. $n + 17 = 98$ 16. $m + 39 = 81$ 17. $x - 61 = 78$

18. $z - 129 = 200$ 19. $356 = y - 219$ 20. $445 = t - 193$

21. $736 = x + 598$ 22. $907 = s + 316$ 23. $n + 1.7 = 3.9$

24. $11.31 = 5.31 + y$ 25. $7.49 = m - 5.86$ 26. $q - 12.42 = 9$

27. **WRITING** Describe the steps you used to solve Exercise 20.

28. **WRITING** Describe the steps you used to solve Exercise 21.

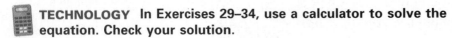 **TECHNOLOGY** In Exercises 29–34, use a calculator to solve the equation. Check your solution.

29. $r + 217.46 = 598.07$ 30. $952.70 = s + 420.38$ 31. $1.397 = x - 1.973$

32. $y - 4.85 = 13.01$ 33. $m + 1024 = 9785$ 34. $5826 = p - 2290$

COMPUTATION SENSE In Exercises 35–40, write an equation that represents the statement. Then solve the equation.

35. The sum of x and 49 is 165.

36. The sum of r and 2.4 is 7.2.

37. The difference of y and 5.8 is 12.2.

38. The difference of n and 40 is 38.

39. The answer 189 is the sum of a number and 137.

40. The answer 317 is the difference of a number and 723.

DOWNHILL SKIING In Exercises 41 and 42, use the information given below.

Vail, Colorado, is a popular Rocky Mountain ski resort. The base elevation of the resort is 8200 ft. The summit elevation is 11,250 ft.

41. How much higher is the summit than the base?

42. You are skiing on a beginners' trail. The head of the trail is 1530 ft higher than the base elevation. At what elevation does the beginners' slope start?

43. **BUYING SKIS** You buy a pair of used skis for $89.99 (including tax). You have $5.63 left. How much money did you have before buying the skis?

STANDARDIZED TEST PRACTICE

44. Which of the following equations is *not* equivalent to the others?

A $x + 7 = 28$ **B** $x - 28 = 7$ **C** $x = 28 - 7$ **D** $7 + x = 28$

45. Lisa and Ana are on a canoe expedition. The trip is 56 mi long. The first day, they canoe 18 mi. How much further do they have to canoe?

A 28 mi **B** 38 mi **C** 44 mi **D** 74 mi

EXPLORATION AND EXTENSION

PORTFOLIO

46. **BUILDING YOUR PROJECT** Start-up capital is money that you use to buy the equipment you need to start your business. For example, if you mow lawns you will need a lawn mower and if you baby-sit you might need a supply of toys. What will you need to buy to start your business? How much will it cost?

Take this test as you would take a test in class. The answers to the exercises are given in the back of the book.

ALGEBRA In Exercises 1 and 2, simplify the expression. (2.1)

1. $5(x + 3)$

2. $2(a + 2b + 4)$

GEOMETRY For Exercises 3 and 4, match the rectangle with its perimeter. (There may be more than one correct match.) (2.1)

3.

4.

A. $2x + 2y$ **B.** $2(3x + 1)$ **C.** xy

D. $3x$ **E.** $x + y$ **F.** $6x + 2$

G. $2(x + y)$ **H.** $3x + 1$ **I.** $2x + y$

5. SHOPPING For each of your 6 classes you are buying a $2.50 notebook and a $1.20 book cover. What property allows you to find your total cost by using either $6(2.50 + 1.20)$ or the expression $6(2.50) + 6(1.20)$? What is your total cost? (2.1)

ALGEBRA In Exercises 6–8, simplify the expression. (2.2)

6. $2a + 10a$

7. $2x + 8 + x$

8. $7(x + 3) + 2x$

9. Simplify $2(3x + 4) + x$. Evaluate the expression when $x = 4$. (2.2)

10. Which expressions are equivalent to $3(2x + 1) + 3x$? (2.2)

    A. $6x + 3 + 3x$ **B.** $5x + 3 + 3x$ **C.** $9x + 3$

11. GEOMETRY Write expressions for the perimeter and area of the rectangle. (2.1, 2.2)

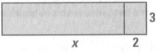

MENTAL MATH In Exercises 12–14, use mental math to solve the equation. (2.3)

12. $3x = 39$ **13.** $\dfrac{n}{4} = 20$ **14.** $\dfrac{1}{2}x = 7$

In Exercises 15 and 16, solve the equation. (2.4)

15. $x + 13 = 28$ **16.** $19 = m - 4$

FITNESS In Exercises 17 and 18, use the bar graph at the right. (2.4) (Source: The Fitness Products Council)

17. About 2 million more people run than use a treadmill. How many people run?

18. About 6 million fewer people lift weights than walk. How many people lift weights?

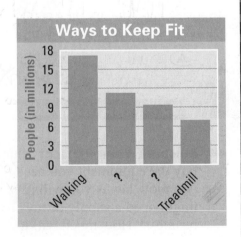

Ways to Keep Fit

LAB 2.5

COOPERATIVE LEARNING

Solving Multiplication Equations

Algebra tiles can be used to model multiplication equations. Here is an example that shows how to solve the equation $2x = 6$.

Materials Needed
- algebra tiles
- pencils or pens
- paper

1 Model the equation with algebra tiles.

2 To get an x tile by itself, divide each side into 2 groups and remove one group from each side.

3 The x tile is equal to 3 small tiles. So, the solution is $x = 3$.

In Exercises 1 and 2, describe the step shown. Is the step one that you should use to solve the equation? Explain.

1. 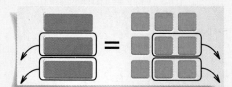   **2.**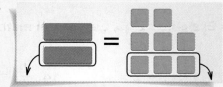

NOW TRY THESE

In Exercises 3–6, use algebra tiles to model and solve the equation. Sketch your solution.

3. $2x = 4$ **4.** $3n = 9$ **5.** $4y = 12$ **6.** $2b = 12$

7. Describe how to use algebra tiles to solve a multiplication equation. Use your rule to draw a correct sketch of Exercises 1 and 2.

2.5 Solving Equations: Multiplication or Division

What you should learn:

Goal 1 How to use multiplication or division to solve an equation

Goal 2 How to use equations to solve real-life problems

Why you should learn it:

You can use multiplication or division to find the hourly rate for baby-sitting.

Goal 1 USING MULTIPLICATION OR DIVISION

In Lesson 2.4 you learned how to use addition or subtraction to solve an equation. You can also use multiplication or division.

MULTIPLICATION AND DIVISION PROPERTIES OF EQUALITY

Multiplying both sides of an equation by the same nonzero number or dividing both sides of an equation by the same nonzero number produces an equivalent equation.

Example 1 Solving Equations

Solve.

a. $5x = 20$ **b.** $12 = \dfrac{n}{4}$

Solution

a. $5x = 20$ Write original equation.

$\dfrac{5x}{5} = \dfrac{20}{5}$ Divide both sides by 5.

$x = 4$ Solution: x is by itself.

The solution is 4.

✔**Check:** You can multiply to see that $5(4) = 20$.

b. $12 = \dfrac{n}{4}$ Write original equation.

$4 \cdot 12 = 4 \cdot \dfrac{n}{4}$ Multiply both sides by 4.

$48 = n$ Solution: n is by itself.

The solution is 48. Check this in the original equation.

In Example 1, notice that you can simplify a fraction that has a *common factor* in its numerator and denominator.

Fraction	Factor.	Divide.	Simplify.
$\dfrac{6}{4}$	$\dfrac{2 \cdot 3}{2 \cdot 2}$	$\dfrac{\cancel{2} \cdot 3}{\cancel{2} \cdot 2}$	$\dfrac{3}{2}$
$\dfrac{3x}{3}$	$\dfrac{3 \cdot x}{3}$	$\dfrac{\cancel{3} \cdot x}{\cancel{3}}$	$\dfrac{x}{1}$ or x

STUDY TIP

Here is an area model for part (b) of Example 1.

One fourth of the area is twelve. The entire area is forty-eight.

Example 2 Using an Equation in Real Life

REAL LIFE
Baby-sitting

You are baby-sitting for a neighbor. You arrive at 3:30 P.M. and leave at 8:00 P.M. Your neighbor pays you $13.50. How much did you get paid per hour?

Solution

From 3:30 to 8:00 is a total of 4.5 h.

Verbal Model	$\dfrac{\text{Total}}{\text{time}} \cdot \dfrac{\text{Hourly}}{\text{rate}} = \dfrac{\text{Total}}{\text{pay}}$	
Labels	Total time = **4.5**	(hours)
	Hourly rate = x	(dollars per hour)
	Total pay = **13.5**	(dollars)

Algebraic Model

$$4.5 \cdot x = 13.5$$
$$\frac{4.5x}{4.5} = \frac{13.5}{4.5}$$
$$x = 3$$

You got paid $3 per hour.

✔**Check:** You can multiply to see that $4.5(3) = 13.5$.

STRATEGY **UNIT ANALYSIS** When you solve real-life problems, be sure that your units of measure make sense. You can check that the units of measure in Example 2 make sense as follows.

$$4.5 \text{ hours} \cdot \frac{3 \text{ dollars}}{\text{hour}} = 13.5 \text{ dollars}$$

Example 3 Unit Analysis

a. $\dfrac{50 \text{ miles}}{\text{hour}} \cdot 3 \text{ hours} = 150 \text{ miles}$

b. $\dfrac{2.5 \text{ dollars}}{\text{pound}} \cdot 4 \text{ pounds} = 10 \text{ dollars}$

c. $\dfrac{28 \text{ miles}}{\text{gallon}} \cdot 10 \text{ gallons} = 280 \text{ miles}$

ONGOING ASSESSMENT

Write About It

For each part of Example 3, write a real-life problem that can be modeled by the equation. Then state the solution of the problem.

2.5 Exercises

Extra Practice, page 718

Extra Practice, page 718

GUIDED PRACTICE

1. **WRITING** In your own words, state the Multiplication and Division Properties of Equality.

2. Give an example of how the Multiplication Property of Equality can be used. How would you use the Division Property of Equality?

In Exercises 3 and 4, state your first step to solve the equation.

3. $6x = 54$

4. $\frac{x}{3} = 12$

5. Describe a real-life situation that can be modeled with an equation.

PRACTICE AND PROBLEM SOLVING

PROBLEM SOLVING In Exercises 6–9, write the equation as a verbal sentence. Then solve.

6. $2x = 4$

7. $3x = 21$

8. $\frac{b}{2} = 3$

9. $\frac{a}{3} = 3$

ALGEBRA In Exercises 10–29, solve the equation. Check your solution.

10. $4x = 16$

11. $12y = 144$

12. $56 = 7n$

13. $6s = 48$

14. $2z = 50$

15. $10a = 240$

16. $5x = 625$

17. $5y = 100$

18. $\frac{n}{4} = 25$

19. $\frac{m}{3} = 3$

20. $\frac{b}{20} = 2$

21. $16 = \frac{x}{4}$

22. $6.3 = 3y$

23. $5t = 6.5$

24. $4.8b = 36$

25. $9.6x = 72$

26. $\frac{z}{3.2} = 8$

27. $\frac{t}{7.4} = 6$

28. $524 = \frac{a}{1}$

29. $\frac{y}{6} = 345$

 TECHNOLOGY In Exercises 30–37, use a calculator to solve the equation. Check your answer.

30. $456x = 1368$

31. $824x = 1648$

32. $23x = 966$

33. $55x = 3025$

34. $\frac{x}{9} = 1025$

35. $\frac{x}{8} = 624$

36. $\frac{x}{136} = 17$

37. $\frac{x}{189} = 19$

GEOMETRY In Exercises 38–41, find the width of the rectangle.

38. Area = 15 ft^2

39. Area = 27 cm^2

40. Area = 38 m^2

41. Area = 48 km^2

3 ft
n

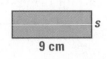
9 cm
s

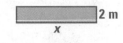
2 m
x

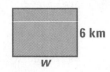
6 km
w

COMPUTATION SENSE In Exercises 42–45, write an equation that represents the sentence. Then solve the equation.

42. The number of football players, f, times 4 equals 28 players.

43. The product of the number of dancers, d, and 4 is 100 dancers.

44. The number of bicycles, b, divided by 12 equals 2 bicycles.

45. The quotient of the number of ties, t, and 6 is 10 ties.

46. **BASKETBALL** Use the diagram of the basketball court at the right. The area of the court is 4700 ft^2.

    a. Write an equation that represents the area of the court.

    b. Solve the equation to find the length.

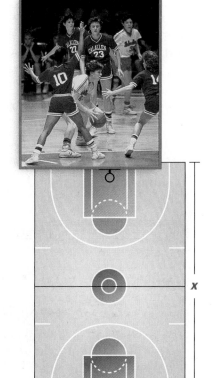

In Exercises 47 and 48, use the following information. You play on your school's basketball team. This season your team played 24 games. You averaged 15.75 points per game.

47. Write a verbal model that represents the points you scored this season.

48. Write an algebraic model that represents your total points scored this season. Solve the equation.

49. **ROLLERBLADING** You rollerblade 5 days per week. Each day you travel the same route. How many miles a day do you skate if you rollerblade a total of 20.5 mi in 5 days?

50. Karla competed in a 3.9 km race. She finished the race in 10 min. What was her average speed?

    (A) 0.39 km/h   **(B)** 3.9 km/min   **(C)** 23.4 km/h   **(D)** 39 m/h

EXPLORATION AND EXTENSION

PORTFOLIO

51. **BUILDING YOUR PROJECT** In Lesson 2.4 you estimated the start-up capital you need. If you borrow this money, how long will it take you to repay the loan? Use your estimated monthly earnings from Lesson 2.3. Assume that all of your income goes to repaying the loan and no interest is charged. Use the verbal model.

    Monthly income × Months to repay loan = Amount of loan

In Exercises 1–8, evaluate the expression when $x = 6$. (1.5)

1. $3x + 1$ **2.** $\dfrac{x}{3} + 4$ **3.** $x^2 - 8$ **4.** $\dfrac{x}{2} - 3$

5. $(x - 1) \cdot 2$ **6.** $2 \cdot (x \div 3)$ **7.** $\dfrac{1}{4} \cdot x^2$ **8.** $(x^2 - 12) \div 4$

In Exercises 9–14, simplify the expression and evaluate for $r = 4$ and $s = 5$. (1.5, 2.1, 2.2)

9. $16r + 2 - 12r$ **10.** $2r^2 + r + r^2$ **11.** $4s + 3r + 2s$

12. $3(r + s) - 2r$ **13.** $2(r^2 + s) + r^2$ **14.** $\dfrac{1}{5} + s + 3s$

15. BOOKSTORE At the bookstore, you buy a novel that costs $4.99 and 3 bookmarks that cost $1.50 each. You give the clerk a $10.00 bill. How much change should you get?

HISTORY Connection

CURRENCY

Often, in order to get things, you must find someone who is willing to trade for something you have. This process became easier in about 650 B.C., when a convenient item was created, the coin. The first known metal coin, the *stater* (meaning "standard"), was made of 0.3 ounces of gold and stamped with a lion's head. The value of the coins was based on the amount of precious metal in them.

Currency	in U.S. dollars
British pound	1.5313
Canadian dollar	0.7302
Greek drachma	0.0042
Japanese yen	0.0099
Mexican peso	0.2980
Italian lira	0.00003

Between A.D. 700 and 900, the Chinese introduced paper money. Paper money had value only because people trusted they could trade it for coins. In the Middle Ages, banks were established to help merchants establish credit to buy goods.

In our day, world trading demands that the money of one country be exchanged for the money of another. Newspapers publish the rates of exchange between currencies daily.

1. Use the chart and verbal model to determine how many British pounds you can get in exchange for 100 U.S. dollars.

2. How many U.S. dollars can you get for 100 Japanese yen?

Verbal Model $\left(\begin{array}{c}\text{Foreign currency} \\ \text{rate}\end{array}\right)\left(\begin{array}{c}\text{Number of} \\ \text{U.S. dollars}\end{array}\right) = \begin{array}{c}\text{Number of units} \\ \text{of foreign currency}\end{array}$

Charting Your Knowledge

Computer spreadsheets provide an easy method of keeping track of data, allowing you to change your information as often as you like. The data below is organized into *rows* and *columns*. Each box in the table is called a cell.

Example

Your total pay for working from 1 to 4 hours at hourly rates ranges from $4 to $6 per hour. Create a spreadsheet for your own reference.

Solution

Write the verbal model to find your salary given the number of hours you work.

Your Salary = Number of Hours Worked × Hourly Rate

After typing in column A and row 1, enter a formula into each cell to tell the computer how to calculate your wages. For example, in cell B2 you would type

$$= A2*4.00$$

$=A2+.5$
$=A2\cdot B1$

Wage Table

	A	B	C	D	E	F
1	Hours	$4.00/h	$4.50/h	$5.00/h	$5.50/h	$6.00/h
2	1.0	$4.00	$4.50	$5.00	$5.50	$6.00
3	1.5	$6.00	$6.75	$7.50	$8.25	$9.00
4	2.0	$8.00	$9.00	$10.00	$11.00	$12.00
5	2.5	$10.00	$11.25	$12.50	$13.75	$15.00
6	3.0	$12.00	$13.50	$15.00	$16.50	$18.00
7	3.5	$14.00	$15.75	$17.50	$19.25	$21.00
8	4.0	$16.00	$18.00	$20.00	$22.00	$24.00

You can now use the table to find your total pay. For instance, if you work 3.5 h at $5.00 per hour, then your total pay is $17.50.

Exercises

1. Create a spreadsheet representing the distance traveled for several different times and speeds.

2. Create a spreadsheet representing the areas of several rectangles of different widths and heights.

2.6 Modeling Verbal Expressions

What you should learn:

Goal 1 How to translate verbal phrases into algebraic expressions

Goal 2 How to model real-life situations with algebraic expressions

Why you should learn it:

To use algebra to solve real-life problems, you must translate verbal phrases into algebraic expressions.

Goal 1 TRANSLATING VERBAL EXPRESSIONS

When you translate verbal phrases into algebraic expressions, look for words that indicate a number operation.

	Verbal phrase	Algebraic expression
Addition:	The *sum* of 5 and a number Nine *more than* a number A number *plus* 2	$5 + x$ $n + 9$ $y + 2$
Subtraction:	The *difference* of 8 and a number Ten *less than* a number Twelve *minus* a number	$8 - n$ $y - 10$ $12 - x$
Multiplication:	The *product* of 3 and a number Seven *times* a number A number *multiplied* by 4	$3x$ $7y$ $4n$
Division:	The *quotient* of a number and 3	$\dfrac{x}{3}$
	Four *divided* by a number	$\dfrac{4}{n}$

Example 1 Translating Verbal Phrases

a. Three more than twice a number can be written as
$$2x + 3.$$
Label: *x* represents a number.

b. The sum of a number and 3 times another number can be written as
$$n + 3m.$$
Labels: *n* is a number, and *m* is another number.

c. One number times the sum of 2 and another number can be written as
$$x(2 + y).$$
Labels: *x* is a number, and *y* is another number.

Example 2 Translating Verbal Phrases

a. Dan ran 5 mi more than Ralph.

b. Najra bought 2 times as many books.

Solution

a. $5 + r$

b. $2b$

STUDY TIP

Order is important only for subtraction or division. For instance, "ten less than a number" is written as $y - 10$, not $10 - y$. On the other hand, "the sum of 5 and a number" can be written as $5 + x$ or $x + 5$.

Example 3 **Modeling a Real-Life Situation**

You are buying some cassettes and some compact discs. Each cassette costs $12 and each compact disc costs $15. Write an algebraic expression for the total cost. Then use the expression to find the cost of each purchase.

REAL LIFE
Music

a. 3 cassettes and 2 compact discs

b. 2 cassettes and 3 compact discs

Solution

Begin by using the problem solving plan:
(1) Write a verbal model, (2) Assign labels to the model, and (3) Write the algebraic model.

| **Verbal Model** | $\dfrac{\textbf{Cost}}{\textbf{per cassette}} \cdot \dfrac{\textbf{Number}}{\textbf{of cassettes}} + \dfrac{\textbf{Cost}}{\textbf{per disc}} \cdot \dfrac{\textbf{Number}}{\textbf{of discs}}$ |

Labels   Cost per cassette = **12**   (dollars per cassette)
       Number of cassettes = c (cassettes)
       Cost per disc = **15**   (dollars per disc)
       Number of discs = d (discs)

Algebraic Model $12 \cdot c + 15 \cdot d$

a. Use the algebraic model to find the cost of **3** cassettes and **2** discs.

Total cost	$= 12c + 15d$	Write the algebraic expression.
	$= 12(3) + 15(2)$	Substitute 3 for c and 2 for d.
	$= 36 + 30$	Multiply.
	$= 66$	Simplify.

The total cost is $66.

b. Use the algebraic model to find the cost of **2** cassettes and **3** discs.

Total cost	$= 12c + 15d$	Write the algebraic expression.
	$= 12(2) + 15(3)$	Substitute 2 for c and 3 for d.
	$= 24 + 45$	Multiply.
	$= 69$	Simplify.

The total cost is $69.

ONGOING ASSESSMENT

Write About It

1. In Example 3, suppose the total cost of buying some cassettes and compact discs is $60. Use *Guess, Check, and Revise* to find how many of each you bought. How many answers are there?

2.6 Exercises

Extra Practice, page 718

GUIDED PRACTICE

In Exercises 1–4, write the phrase as an algebraic expression.

1. The temperature, decreased by 20°

2. Five miles per hour more than the speed limit

3. One dollar plus ten cents per minute

4. Five dollars times the number of people, minus ten dollars

PRACTICE AND PROBLEM SOLVING

In Exercises 5–10, match the verbal phrase with its algebraic expression.

A. $20y$ B. $20 + n$ C. $1 + m$

D. $2s + 8$ E. $x - 6$ F. $6 - x$

5. The sum of a number and 20

6. Eight more than twice a number

7. The difference of 6 and a number

8. Six less than a number

9. The product of a number and 20

10. One more than a number

ALGEBRA In Exercises 11–20, translate the verbal phrase into an algebraic expression.

11. A number divided by 23

12. The quotient of a number and 7

13. Nine more than ten times a number

14. One plus the product of a number and two

15. Four less than five times a number

16. Eight minus the product of two and a number

17. One hundred two times a number

18. Eleven times the sum of six and a number

19. A number divided by the sum of 2 and another number

20. Ten minus the quotient of one number and another number

ALGEBRA In Exercises 21–28, write the verbal phrase as an algebraic expression.

21. Four more miles than yesterday

22. Your salary plus a bonus of $572

23. Six times as much money as your sister

24. Number of passengers times 3

25. Two less runs than the Pirates scored

26. Four years younger than your cousin

27. Number of students divided by 3

28. Half as much money as your brother

ALGEBRA In Exercises 29–31, write an algebraic expression that represents the phrase. Let _a_ represent your age now.

29. Your age eight years ago   30. Ten times your age   31. Three fourths your age

32. COLLECTORS' ITEMS You are buying some comic books and packs of baseball cards. Each comic book costs $1.50 and each pack of cards costs $1.00.

a. Write an algebraic expression representing the total cost. Let c be the number of comics and b be the number of packs of baseball cards.

b. Find the cost of 4 comic books and 2 packs of baseball cards.

33. TABLE TENNIS You and three friends are playing table tennis. The cost of renting the table tennis table is $7 for the first hour and $3 for each additional half hour.

a. Write an algebraic expression that represents the total cost. Let h be the number of additional half hours.

b. You and three friends are sharing the total cost equally. Write an expression that represents *your* cost.

c. You play for a total of 2.5 h. Find *your* cost by substituting for h.

34. CURRENCY EXCHANGE April 1, 1997, the exchange rate between U.S. currency and Canadian currency was 1.38 Canadian dollars per 1.00 U.S. dollar. Write an expression for the number of Canadian dollars you can buy with n U.S. dollars. Then complete the table.

U.S. dollars	$1	$2	$5	$10	$n	?	?	?
Canadian dollars	$1.38	$2.76	?	?	?	$8.28	$11.04	$1.38

STANDARDIZED TEST PRACTICE

35. Brenda bought 2 pairs of jeans and 3 shirts for school. Each pair of jeans cost $25 and each shirt cost $14. How much did Brenda spend?

Ⓐ $39 　　　Ⓑ $92 　　　Ⓒ $103 　　　Ⓓ $350

36. Evaluate the expression $8x - 2y$ when $x = 4$ and $y = 3.5$.

Ⓐ 5 　　　Ⓑ 20 　　　Ⓒ 25 　　　Ⓓ 60.5

EXPLORATION AND EXTENSION

37. BUILDING YOUR PROJECT Will you advertise in the newspaper? Print fliers? Write a verbal expression for your advertising costs. Assign labels and write an algebraic expression. Can you estimate the total advertising cost? If not, identify what information you need.

2.7

Real-Life Modeling with Equations

What you should learn:

Goal 1 How to translate verbal sentences into algebraic equations

Goal 2 How to model real-life situations with algebraic equations

Why you should learn it:

You can use algebraic equations to solve real-life problems.

Use algebraic equations to find the total cost of 5 bunches of radishes and 7 bunches of scallions. (*Hint:* Find the price per bunch.)

Goal 1 TRANSLATING VERBAL SENTENCES

A phrase does not usually contain a verb, but a sentence must contain a verb. As you learned in Lesson 2.6, many phrases can be modeled as algebraic expressions. You will now learn how to model sentences as algebraic equations. Here are examples of an expression and an equation.

Verbal Phrase	The cost of several cassettes at $12 each.	**Verbal Sentence**	The cost of several cassettes at $12 each is $60.

Algebraic Expression	$12x$	**Algebraic Equation**	$12x = 60$

Notice that you can solve an equation, but you cannot solve an expression. For instance, the solution of the equation $12x = 60$ is $x = 5$, but it doesn't make sense to try to "solve" the expression $12x$.

Example 1 Modeling with an Equation

The price of one television set is $283. It costs $147 less than another set. What is the price of the more expensive set?

REAL LIFE
Purchase

Solution

Verbal Model	$\dfrac{\text{Lower}}{\text{price}} = \dfrac{\text{Higher}}{\text{price}} - 147$	

| **Labels** | Lower price = **283** | (dollars) |
| | Higher price = x | (dollars) |

Algebraic Model

$$283 = x - 147$$
$$283 + 147 = x - 147 + 147$$
$$430 = x$$

The price of the more expensive set is $430.

✔**Check:** Subtract to check that $283 is $147 less than $430.

Example 2 Modeling a Real-Life Situation

You work in a clothing store and are responsible for the jeans department. To earn a bonus in November and December, you need to sell at least 1.25 times as many jeans as you sold last year during the same two months. The graph shows this year's sales. You sold exactly as many pairs of jeans needed for the bonus. How many total pairs did you sell in November and December a year ago?

REAL LIFE
Sales

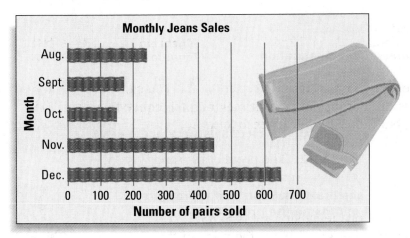

Monthly Jeans Sales

Solution

From the graph, you can estimate that the November sales this year are about 450 pairs of jeans and the December sales this year are about 650 pairs. To find the total number of pairs of jeans you sold a year ago, use the problem-solving steps shown below.

Verbal Model $1.25 \cdot \dfrac{\text{Number sold}}{\text{last year}} = \dfrac{\text{Number sold}}{\text{this year}}$

Labels Number sold last year $= n$ (pairs)

Number sold this year $= 450 + 650 = 1100$ (pairs)

Algebraic Model
$$1.25 \cdot n = 1100$$
$$\frac{1.25n}{1.25} = \frac{1100}{1.25}$$
$$n = 880$$

So, you sold a total of about 880 pairs of jeans in November and December a year ago.

ONGOING ASSESSMENT

Write About It

1. Describe a real-life problem for the verbal model below. Write the problem so that the distance is unknown.

$$\frac{\text{Distance}}{\text{Time}} = \text{Speed}$$

2. Assign labels, write the equation, and solve it. Write the solution of the problem as a sentence.

GUIDED PRACTICE

ALGEBRA In Exercises 1–4, state whether the quantity is an expression or an equation. Solve or simplify.

1. $3 + x = 19$ **2.** $5x - 3x + 6$ **3.** $2x = 18$ **4.** $\dfrac{x}{3} = 7$

In Exercises 5 and 6, write an algebraic equation that represents the verbal sentence. Name the property you can use to solve the equation.

5. The number of cars decreased by 21 is 84.

6. The cost of 10 T-shirts at x dollars each is $75.

PRACTICE AND PROBLEM SOLVING

In Exercises 7–12, match the sentence with an equation.

A. $7 = x + 5$ **B.** $\dfrac{x}{7} = 5$ **C.** $x - 7 = 5$ **D.** $7 = \dfrac{x}{5}$ **E.** $7x = 35$ **F.** $5x = 35$

7. The difference of x and 7 is 5.

8. Five times x equals thirty-five.

9. Seven is the sum of x and five.

10. Seven equals x divided by five.

11. The quotient of x and 7 is 5.

12. The product of x and 7 is 35.

ALGEBRA In Exercises 13–17, write an algebraic equation that represents the verbal sentence. Solve the equation and name the property you used.

13. The number of dogs increased by 9 is 20.

14. Sixteen equals the number of tennis shoes decreased by three.

15. The number of pencils divided by 12 is 4.

16. The cost of 3 sweaters at x dollars each is $90.75.

17. Five hours equals y miles divided by forty-five miles per hour.

In Exercises 18–23, write a verbal sentence that represents the equation.

18. $f + 15 = 33$ **19.** $90 = s - 3$ **20.** $7c = 56$

21. $\dfrac{b}{9} = 8$ **22.** $11 + a = 23$ **23.** $21 = d - 18$

ALGEBRA In Exercises 24 and 25, use a verbal model, labels, and an algebraic model to answer the question.

24. The product of a number and 38 is 912. What is the number?

25. One number is 251 more than another number. The larger number is 420. What is the smaller number?

GEOMETRY In Exercises 26 and 27, use the verbal model to write an algebraic equation. Then use the Guess, Check, and Revise method to solve the equation.

26. Perimeter = 2(Width + Length)

Perimeter
is 25 units.
w

8

27. Area = Width • Length

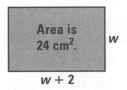

Area is
24 cm^2.
w

$w + 2$

FASHION BUSINESS In Exercises 28 and 29, use the following information.

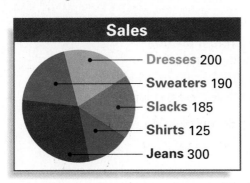

Sales

Dresses 200
Sweaters 190
Slacks 185
Shirts 125
Jeans 300

The company you work for designs a variety of clothes. Last week's sales are shown above. You expect to sell 500 more garments this week than last week.

28. In the following equation, what does n represent?
$$n = (200 + 125 + 185 + 190 + 300) + 500$$

29. How many of the 500 additional garments would you expect to be sweaters? Explain your reasoning.

30. PLAYING BASKETBALL You play basketball for your school team. Last year, your team scored a total of 560 points in 16 games.

   a. Write a verbal model that represents the average number of points your team scored per game. Assign labels and write an algebraic model.

   b. Solve the algebraic model. What is the average number of points your team scores per game?

   c. This year one of your team goals is to score an average of 5 points more per game than last year. How many total points must your team score this year?

Tech
Link

**Investigation 2,
Interactive
Real-Life
Investigations**

31. Which equation models the situation illustrated at the right? Let q equal the width of the quarter.

Ⓐ $1\frac{3}{2} + q = 2\frac{1}{2}$

Ⓑ $1\frac{3}{4} + q = 2\frac{1}{4}$

Ⓒ $1\frac{3}{8} + q = 2\frac{1}{8}$

Ⓓ $1\frac{3}{16} + q = 2\frac{1}{8}$

EXPLORATION AND EXTENSION

32. COMMUNICATING ABOUT MATHEMATICS For more information about designer jeans, see the next page. Marketing managers decide how and where their product will be advertised. An excellent advertising vehicle for jeans is fashion magazines. In fact, there can be a yearly total of 60 to 100 pages of jeans advertised in one monthly magazine.

a. Assume there are 80 pages of jeans advertised in a fashion magazine during the year. Write a verbal model for the average number of jeans advertisements in each monthly issue of a fashion magazine. Assign labels and write an equation for the model.

b. Solve the equation from part (a). How many pages of jeans advertisements are there in each issue?

SPIRAL REVIEW

In Exercises 1–4, state an operation that can be used to solve the equation. (2.4, 2.5)

1. $c + 2 = 6$ **2.** $5b = 75$ **3.** $\frac{a}{3} = 2$ **4.** $d - 4 = 10$

In Exercises 5–12, simplify the expression. (1.5)

5. $2f + 3f$ **6.** $12r - 3r$ **7.** $2(g + 3)$ **8.** $5(4t + 3)$

9. $2s + 3s + s$ **10.** $8p + 2p - p$ **11.** $4 + 3h + 2h$ **12.** $2q + 9 + 12$

In Exercises 13–20, solve the equation. (2.4, 2.5)

13. $8n = 32$ **14.** $m - 12 = 20$ **15.** $3n = 2$ **16.** $y + 6 = 10$

17. $x - 4 = 6$ **18.** $\frac{t}{8} = 2$ **19.** $y + 2 = 2$ **20.** $\frac{z}{12} = 3$

21. SAVING MONEY You want to save the same amount of money from each week's paycheck so that you can buy a bicycle that costs $130. You want to buy the bicycle in 5 weeks. How much will you have to save each week? **(2.7)**

What's in a 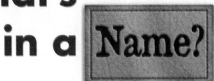 Name?

READ About It

About $7 billion worth of blue jeans are sold each year in the United States alone.

Most of the jeans sold in the U.S. cost between $8 and $15 to make, and they sell for $20 to $50. Traditional jeans have sold in America since the beginning of this century, while the more expensive designer jeans are a recent phenomenon. More expensive, fashion-oriented denims cost about $20 to make but sell in many areas for over $135. The total sales of these designer jeans account for one seventh of the jeans market.

Some people say, "The only difference between designer jeans and ordinary jeans is the label—and $100!"

WRITE About It

1. The manufacturing cost for an order of jeans was $144,000. The person who placed the order paid as little as possible to have the jeans made. Write a verbal model that can be used to estimate the number of jeans that were ordered.

2. Write a verbal model that can be used to find the total sales for traditional jeans in a year in the United States.

3. Assign labels to the models in Questions 1 and 2 and write their equations. Solve the equations and write the solutions in words.

4. The wholesale price is the amount the designer charges the retail store. One brand of designer jeans has a wholesale price of $65. Estimate the designer's profit for a pair of these jeans. Show your work.

5. Estimate the amount of profit a retail store makes on one pair of designer jeans. Show your work.

Gold Rush miners preferred their jeans with extra room in the seat because they needed to squat down to pan for gold. Today, these jeans are a fashion statement.

A Problem Solving Plan

What you should learn:

Goal 1 How to use a general problem solving plan

Goal 2 How to use other problem solving strategies

Why you should learn it:

Learning to be a general problem solver will help you in many real-life occupations.

Goal 1 USING A PROBLEM SOLVING PLAN

In Lessons 2.4 through 2.7 you studied three steps for algebraic modeling. Use these steps as part of your problem solving plan.

A GENERAL PROBLEM SOLVING PLAN

1. Decide what you need to know to answer the question. **Write a verbal model** that gives you what you need to know.

2. **Assign values to the labels** in your verbal model. If you don't know the value, use a variable, like x.

3. Use the labels to **write an algebraic model** based on your verbal model.

4. **Solve** the algebraic model.

5. **Answer** the original question.

6. **Check** that your answer is reasonable.

Example 1 Using a Problem Solving Plan

REAL LIFE
Sales

You are a sales representative. Each year your bonus is one twentieth of the amount by which you exceed your previous year's sales. Last year your sales totaled $456,000. This year your bonus was $9300. What were your sales this year?

Solution

Verbal Model

$$\frac{1}{20} \cdot \text{Amount over last year's sales} = \text{Bonus}$$

Labels

Amount over last year's sales $= x$ (dollars)

Bonus $= 9300$ (dollars)

Algebraic Model

$$\frac{1}{20} \cdot x = 9300$$

$$20 \cdot \frac{1}{20} \cdot x = 20 \cdot 9300$$

$$x = 186{,}000$$

This is *not* the answer.

You sold $186,000 more than last year.

So, your sales for this year were $456{,}000 + 186{,}000$, or $642{,}000.

STRATEGY **CHOOSE A STRATEGY** In this (and every) lesson, don't be afraid to try a variety of problem solving strategies. For instance, you might try *Guess, Check, and Revise* or *Solving a Simpler Problem.*

Example 2 **Decision Making**

It is 1995, and you have just graduated from high school. Explain how to use the table to decide whether a bachelor's degree from college is a good financial investment. (Source: U.S. Bureau of the Census)

REAL LIFE
Education

Education	Mean Income*
9th–10th Grade, No Diploma	$20,968
High School Graduate	$27,440
Some College, No Degree	$29,441
Associate Degree	$31,097
Bachelor's Degree	$42,734
Master's Degree	$48,851
Doctorate Degree	$48,008
Professional Degree	$60,475

*1995 data for males aged 25–34

Solution

This is a complicated question with many unknowns, such as the cost of college, the rate of inflation, and the actual salaries you will receive.

However, to obtain a general sense of the answer, assume that a four-year bachelor's degree will cost **$40,000**. Also assume that you will work 45 years with a high school diploma or work 41 years with a bachelor's degree.

High School Graduate $45(\textbf{\$27,440}) = \$1,234,800$

Bachelor's Degree $41(\textbf{\$42,734}) - \textbf{\$40,000} = \$1,712,094$

Although this analysis is overly simple, it still appears clear that a bachelor's degree is a good financial investment.

Real Life...
Real Facts

Back to School

After working in factories and as an assistant teacher, Maxine Waters earned a bachelor's degree in Sociology. She went on to become a United States Representative.

ONGOING ASSESSMENT

Talk About It
••••••••••••••••••••

You have just received a bachelor's degree.

1. Use the information in Example 2 to decide whether a master's degree (requiring 2 more years) is a good financial investment. Explain your reasoning.

GUIDED PRACTICE

1. Order the steps for a general problem solving plan.

A. Assign labels.   **B.** Answer the original question.

C. Solve the algebraic model.   **D.** Write a verbal model.

E. Check your solution.   **F.** Write an algebraic model.

2. **WRITING** When using the problem solving plan, what is the last step before beginning the next problem? Explain.

PRACTICE AND PROBLEM SOLVING

GRADES In Exercises 3–9, consider the following question.

Your history grade is based on 5 tests. To earn an A, you need a total of 460 points. Your first four test scores are 89, 85, 92, and 97. What is the minimum score you need on the fifth test to earn an A?

3. Write a verbal model that relates the total points needed, the number of points obtained so far, and the final test score.

4. Assign labels to the three parts of your model.

5. Use the labels to translate your verbal model into an algebraic model.

6. Solve the algebraic model.

7. Answer the question.

8. Explain why your answer is reasonable.

9. Your final test score is 98 points. Did you get an A?

HIKING In Exercises 10–15, consider the following question.

You are taking a three day hiking and camping trip. The trail is 29 mi long. On the first day you hike 8 mi. On the second day you hike 11 mi. How much farther do you need to go?

10. Write a verbal model that relates the trail length, the number of miles traveled, and the distance left to hike.

11. Assign labels to the three parts of your model.

12. Translate your verbal model into an algebraic model.

13. Solve the algebraic model.

14. Answer the question.

15. Evaluate your solution for reasonableness.

Real Life...
Real Facts

Hiking Trail

The Appalachian National Scenic Trail extends about 2000 mi from Mt. Katahdin in Maine to Springer Mountain in Georgia.

SALES MANAGER In Exercises 16–19, use the following information.

Each year you earn a base salary and a sales commission. Your commission is one twentieth of the amount of your annual sales. Your base salary is $16,500 and you sell $150,000 of merchandise this year. How much money do you make?

16. Write a verbal model that relates your sales commission, your commission rate, and your annual sales.

17. Assign labels to each part of your model.

18. Use the labels to translate your verbal model into an algebraic model.

19. Solve the model. Answer the original question. Check your answer.

PROBLEM SOLVING In Exercises 20 and 21, decide which information is necessary to solve the problem. Then solve the problem.

20. Every morning your sister gets up at 5:30 A.M. and travels 7 mi to the skating rink to practice. At 7:30 A.M., she travels 7 mi home. How many miles does she travel each week to practice?

21. Your Spanish club is selling T-shirts for $9.50. The club needs to raise $2000 for a trip. You sell 17 T-shirts and have 3 left to sell. How much money have you raised?

STANDARDIZED TEST PRACTICE

22. Which best estimates the average weight of an apple?

   A 0.6 ounces   **B** 6 ounces

   C 60 ounces   **D** 600 ounces

23. Which best estimates the length of a newborn human baby?

   A 0.5 cm   **B** 5 cm   **C** 50 cm   **D** 500 cm

EXPLORATION AND EXTENSION

REASONING In Exercises 24 and 25, decide if the answer seems reasonable. Explain your reasoning.

24. You are planning a vacation. You estimate the time it takes to drive a car from Washington, D.C., to Portland, Oregon. Your answer is 12 h.

25. Your company makes desks. You need to know the area of a desktop. Your answer is 100 ft^2.

2.9

Exploring Variables and Inequalities

What you should learn:

Goal 1 How to solve simple inequalities

Goal 2 How to use inequalities to solve real-life problems

Why you should learn it:

You can use inequalities in real life, such as describing the number of yards needed for a first down.

Goal 1 SOLVING SIMPLE INEQUALITIES

You can model some sentences better with **inequalities** than with equations. An inequality is formed when an **inequality symbol** is placed between two expressions. There are four inequality symbols.

Inequality Symbol	Meaning
$<$	is less than
$\leq$	is less than or equal to
$>$	is greater than
$\geq$	is greater than or equal to

A **solution** of an inequality is a number that produces a true statement when it is substituted for the variable in the inequality. For instance, 2 is one of the many solutions of $x < 5$, because $2 < 5$ is a true statement.

Finding all solutions of an inequality is called **solving the inequality**. This is similar to solving an equation. That is, you can add or subtract the same number from each side, or you can multiply or divide both sides by the same positive number.

The inequality $x < 5$ is read as "x is less than 5." You can also write this inequality as $5 > x$, which is read as "5 is greater than x."

Example 1 Solving Inequalities

Solve each inequality.

a. $x + 4 \leq 6$ **b.** $3x \geq 12$ **c.** $14 > x - 2$

Solution

a. $\quad x + 4 \leq 6$ Write original inequality.

$\quad x + 4 - 4 \leq 6 - 4$ Subtract 4 from each side.

$\qquad\qquad x \leq 2$ Solution of the inequality

b. $3x \geq 12$ Write original inequality.

$\quad \dfrac{3x}{3} \geq \dfrac{12}{3}$ Divide both sides by 3.

$\quad x \geq 4$ Solution of the inequality

c. $\quad 14 > x - 2$ Write original inequality.

$\quad 14 + 2 > x - 2 + 2$ Add 2 to each side.

$\qquad\quad 16 > x$ Solution of the inequality

Example 2 Modeling a Real-Life Situation

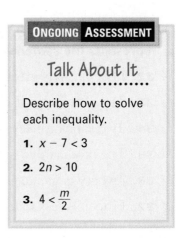

REAL LIFE
Football

In football, the team with the ball must bring the ball at least 10 yd closer to the opponent's end zone within four turns, called downs, or else the ball is given to the other team. Your team was given the ball on your 35 yd line. At the beginning of the fourth down, the ball is on your 40 yd line. How many more yards must your team gain to keep the ball?

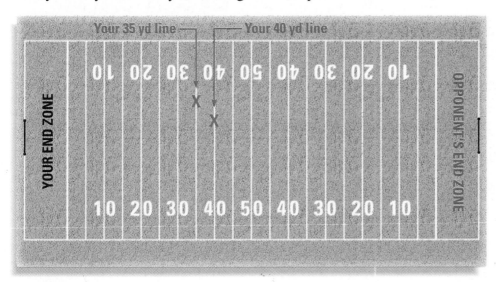

Solution

Going into its fourth down, your team has gained 5 yd. By the end of the fourth down, the team needs to have gained at least 10 yd.

Verbal Model	$\underset{\text{first 3 downs}}{\text{Yards gained in}} + \underset{\text{4th down}}{\text{Yards gained in}} \geq 10$

↓

Labels   Yards gained in first 3 downs = **5**   (yards)

Yards gained in 4th down = x (yards)

↓

Algebraic Model

$$5 + x \geq 10$$
$$5 + x - 5 \geq 10 - 5$$
$$x + 5 - 5 \geq 10 - 5$$
$$x \geq 5$$

The team must gain at least 5 yd in its fourth down.

ONGOING ASSESSMENT

Talk About It
....

Describe how to solve each inequality.

1. $x - 7 < 3$

2. $2n > 10$

3. $4 < \dfrac{m}{2}$

2.9 Exercises

Extra Practice, page 719

GUIDED PRACTICE

1. Write the four kinds of inequality symbols and their meanings.

2. **TRUE OR FALSE?** An inequality can have many solutions.

In Exercises 3–6, state whether the number is a solution of the inequality $x - 5 < 11$.

3. 11   **4.** 16   **5.** 15   **6.** 30

ALGEBRA **In Exercises 7–9, solve the inequality.**

7. $x + 4 \leq 7$ **8.** $3x \geq 10$ **9.** $9 < x - 5$

10. **PROBLEM SOLVING** State an example of an inequality used in a real-life situation.

PRACTICE AND PROBLEM SOLVING

ALGEBRA **In Exercises 11–16, state two solutions of the inequality.**

11. $x < 4$ **12.** $y \geq 12.3$ **13.** $45 < x$

14. $100 \geq a$ **15.** $t < 2\frac{1}{2}$ **16.** $y \geq 0$

ALGEBRA **In Exercises 17–31, solve the inequality.**

17. $x + 5 < 11$ **18.** $s - 4 > 9$ **19.** $7y \leq 42$

20. $22 \leq b + 22$ **21.** $16 \geq s - 3$ **22.** $56 < 14t$

23. $45 > 5m$ **24.** $n - 34 \leq 16$ **25.** $17y \geq 68$

26. $x + 3.4 > 5.8$ **27.** $y - 13.7 < 5.4$ **28.** $8.9k \geq 17.8$

29. $\frac{x}{8} \geq 11$ **30.** $\frac{x}{2} \leq 52$ **31.** $\frac{a}{2.5} \leq 4.2$

WRITING EQUATIONS **In Exercises 32–37, write an inequality that represents the sentence. Then solve the inequality.**

32. Five plus c is greater than or equal to nineteen and three tenths.

33. The difference of b and 7 is less than 24.

34. Two times x is less than forty-two.

35. The product of y and 3 is greater than 39.

36. Twenty is greater than or equal to m divided by six.

37. Fifteen is less than or equal to the quotient of x and five.

38. FREELANCING Carla earns $32 per hour as a freelance computer troubleshooter. Her salary minimum per job is $320; maximum of $4500. Write two inequalities that best represent Carla's pay per job.

WRITING In Exercises 39–44, write a sentence that represents the inequality.

39. $d + 11 < 52$

40. $f - 5 \geq 29$

41. $3h \leq 60$

42. $\dfrac{p}{36} > 2$

43. $17 > c - 31$

44. $23 \leq a + 9$

45. BIKE RACING You are a member of the "Hot Wheelers." Your team competes in a relay race with 4 other teams. The table shows the times that each team took to finish the 20 mi of rugged terrain.

Team name	Time
Hot Wheelers	69 min
Bikin' Buddies	85 min
Cruisin' Kids	76 min
Brave Bikers	71 min
Flyin' Friends	81 min

a. Which team finished first? Convert this finishing time to hours.

b. By how many minutes does the last place team need to improve its time to place first? Use verbal and algebraic models.

c. By how many minutes do the Cruisin' Kids need to improve their time to tie or beat the Brave Bikers?

d. Using the formula, $D = r \cdot t$, find the average speed of the Hot Wheelers.

STANDARDIZED TEST PRACTICE

46. Which symbol makes the following statement true?

$6x + 7x$? $10x + 3x + 1$

(A) $=$ **(B)** $<$ **(C)** $>$ **(D)** $\leq$

EXPLORATION AND EXTENSION

GEOMETRY In Exercises 47–50, decide whether the lengths could form a triangle. The *Triangle Inequality* states that the sum of the lengths of *any* two sides must be greater than the length of the third side.

47. 4 ft, 5 ft, 6 ft **48.** 2 in., 3 in., 6 in. **49.** 4 m, 6 m, 12 m **50.** 8 km, 9 km, 11 km

CHAPTER 2 *Summary*

WHAT *did you learn?*   **WHY** *did you learn it?*

Skills

2.1	Use the Distributive Property to simplify expressions.	Model real-life situations.
2.2	Simplify expressions by adding like terms.	Find earnings such as weekly salary for a job.
2.3	Use mental math to solve equations. Check equations.	Help plan for future sales.
2.4	Solve equations using addition or subtraction.	Find capital needed to start a business.
2.5	Solve equations using multiplication or division.	Find earnings such as hourly salary for baby-sitting.
2.6	Translate verbal phrases into algebraic expressions.	Write algebraic models in real-life situations.
2.7	Translate verbal sentences into algebraic equations.	Analyze your sales quota.
2.8	Use problem solving strategies.	Analyze the value of further education.
2.9	Write and solve inequalities.	Analyze real-life sports.

Strategies

| 2.1–2.9 | Use problem solving strategies. | Solve a wide variety of real-life problems. |

Using Data

| 2.9 | Use tables and graphs. | Organize and solve problems. |

HOW *does it fit in the bigger picture of mathematics?*

Mathematics uses several techniques to solve simple equations. This chapter studies three basic building blocks of algebra.

expressions   Play two different video games x number of times each; one costs 25¢ and the other costs 50¢: $0.25x + 0.50x$, or $0.75x$

equations   A whale can swim 15 mi/h faster than a squid: $w = 15 + s$

inequalities   Grandfather is at least 40 years older than me: $g \geq m + 40$

Equations and inequalities can be solved with mental math or with properties of equalities and inequalities.

VOCABULARY

- equivalent expressions (p. 52)
- Distributive Property (p. 52)
- like terms (p. 56)
- collect like terms (p. 56)
- add like terms (p. 56)
- equation (p. 60)
- identities (p. 60)
- conditional equations (p. 60)
- solving the equation (p. 60)
- solutions (of an equation) (p. 60)

- equivalent equations (p. 60)
- Commutative Property of Addition (p. 67)
- Commutative Property of Multiplication (p. 67)
- Associative Property of Addition (p. 67)
- Associative Property of Multiplication (p. 67)
- general problem solving plan (p. 88)
- inequalities (p. 92)
- inequality symbol (p. 92)
- solution (of an inequality) (p. 92)
- solving the inequality (p. 92)

2.1 THE DISTRIBUTIVE PROPERTY

Examples $5(x + 3) = 5x + 15$ $3(a + 2b + c) = 3a + 6b + 3c$

Use the Distributive Property to rewrite the expression.

1. $4(x + 2)$ **2.** $3(6z + 1)$ **3.** $2(6m + 12)$ **4.** $5(a + b)$

5. $7(d + f + 2)$ **6.** $2(3a + b + 2c)$ **7.** $5(g + 2h)$ **8.** $4(5 + y)$

2.2 SIMPLIFYING BY ADDING LIKE TERMS

Examples $\begin{aligned} 4x + 2x + 1 &= (4 + 2)x + 1 \\ &= 6x + 1 \end{aligned}$ $\begin{aligned} z + 2z + 5y + y &= (1 + 2)z + (5 + 1)y \\ &= 3z + 6y \end{aligned}$

Simplify the expressions.

9. $8w + 9w$ **10.** $3x + 4 + x$ **11.** $14 + 7v + v$

12. $16 + 5b + 3b + 9$ **13.** $5 + 6t + 9 + 2a$ **14.** $2x + 3t + x + 2t$

2.3 SOLVING EQUATIONS: MENTAL MATH

Examples
 a. $x + 6 = 11$: "What number can be added to 6 to get 11?" $x = 5$
 b. $4n = 16$: "What number can be multiplied by 4 to get 16?" $n = 4$

Solve using mental math.

15. $9 + y = 10$ **16.** $b - 11 = 11$ **17.** $6q = 12$ **18.** $10 + t = 20$

19. $\dfrac{15}{w} = 5$ **20.** $\dfrac{m}{3} = 9$ **21.** $9r = 36$ **22.** $\dfrac{24}{w} = 2$

$5w = 15$

2.4 SOLVING EQUATIONS: ADDITION OR SUBTRACTION

Examples

a. $x - 21 = 12$

$$-21 + 21 = 12 + 21$$

$$x = 33$$

b. $136 = y + 113$

$$136 - 113 = y + 113 - 113$$

$$23 = y$$

Solve the equation.

23. $m - 54 = 72$ **24.** $n + 13 = 132$ **25.** $t - 6 = 50.11$ **26.** $w + 19.95 = 20$

2.5 SOLVING EQUATIONS: MULTIPLICATION OR DIVISION

Examples

a. $6x = 42$ $\longrightarrow$ $\dfrac{6x}{6} = \dfrac{42}{6}$ $\longrightarrow$ $x = 7$

b. $11 = \dfrac{y}{3}$ $\longrightarrow$ $3 \cdot 11 = 3 \cdot \dfrac{y}{3}$ $\longrightarrow$ $33 = y$

27. $32k = 8$ **28.** $25q = 100$ **29.** $\dfrac{r}{0.7} = 1400$ **30.** $\dfrac{g}{3} = 13$

2.6 MODELING VERBAL EXPRESSIONS

Examples

a. The product of 4 and a number: $4x$

b. Quotient of x and 3: $\dfrac{x}{3}$ **Order is important in subtraction and division.**

Write the verbal phrase as an algebraic expression.

31. Your salary plus $10

32. Five times as many tapes

33. Walked 5 mi more than last week

34. Your age 5 years ago

2.7 REAL-LIFE MODELING WITH EQUATIONS

Example

The number of pens divided by 15 is 3.

$$\dfrac{p}{15} = 3 \longrightarrow 15 \cdot \dfrac{p}{15} = 15 \cdot 3 \longrightarrow p = 45 \text{ pens}$$

Use a verbal model, labels, and an algebraic model to answer the question.

35. Kathy's cat, Willie, likes to hide in the bushes around the house. The area of the house is 576 ft². Kathy walked around the house twice calling Willie's name. How far did Kathy walk?

36. How much do $2\frac{1}{4}$ lb of tomatoes cost at $1.05 per pound?

2.8 A PROBLEM SOLVING PLAN

Example
You are going to drive 540 mi. During the first 3 h you travel 170 mi. You travel 250 mi during the next 5 h. How many miles are left to travel?

Verbal Model

$$\underset{\text{for trip}}{\text{Total miles}} = \underset{\text{traveled}}{\text{Miles}} + \underset{\text{to travel}}{\text{Miles left}}$$

Labels

Total miles for trip = **540**	(miles)
Miles traveled = **170 + 250**	(miles)
Miles left to travel = t	(miles)

Algebraic Model

$540 = (170 + 250) + t$	Write the equation.
$540 = 420 + t$	Simplify.
$540 - 420 = 420 + t - 420$	Subtract 420 from each side.
$120 = t$	Simplify.

You have 120 mi left to travel.

37. One third of students in a school have a newspaper route. There are 900 students in the school. How many students in the school have a paper route?

38. You want to buy a camera. You get an allowance of $10.00 per week. The camera costs $47.00, including tax. You spend $2.50 per week and save the rest. How many weeks will it take to buy the camera?

39. Your salary is $36,000 plus $\frac{1}{100}$ of the profit your company made during the year as a bonus. This year your bonus was $1200. How much profit did your company make this year?

40. Your backyard is 60 ft by 40 ft. You want to put a fence on both long sides and one short side. How much fencing do you need?

2.9 EXPLORING VARIABLES AND INEQUALITIES

Examples

a.
$$5 + x < 13$$
$$5 + x - 5 < 13 - 5$$
$$x < 8$$

b.
$$3m > 18$$
$$\frac{3m}{3} > \frac{18}{3}$$
$$m > 6$$

41. $y - 13 < 3$

42. $z + 13 \leq 16$

43. $6k \geq 30$

44. $5g < 15$

45. $1.2 \geq 0.2t$

46. $\frac{p}{4} < 12$

47. $2.08 < v + 0.31$

48. $21 < \frac{w}{0.7}$

In Exercises 1–4, rewrite the expression.

1. $7(a + 2)$ **2.** $3(b + 2c + 3)$ **3.** $2d + 12$ **4.** $6e + 4d + 2$

ALGEBRA **In Exercises 5–8, solve the equation. Check your solution.**

5. $3x = 15$ **6.** $y - 6 = 0$ **7.** $p + 2 = 9$ **8.** $\frac{1}{4} = 3q$

ALGEBRA **In Exercises 9–12, solve the inequality. Show your work.**

9. $x - 2 > 4$ **10.** $10 \geq 3 + y$ **11.** $7 + z < 4$ **12.** $a + 9 \leq 24$

13. **GEOMETRY** Write expressions for the perimeter and area of the rectangle.

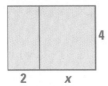

14. **BUSINESS** You are the manager of two sporting goods stores. The weekly cost to operate Store 1 is \$3500, and for Store 2 it is \$5600.

    a. Write a verbal model that represents the yearly costs of the two stores.

    b. Use part (a) to determine the yearly cost of operating both stores.

In Exercises 15–17, you buy *n* juice boxes. Each juice box costs \$.50.

15. Write an algebraic expression for the total amount you spent.

16. You spent \$3. Write an equation to find the number of juice boxes you bought.

17. Solve the equation to find how many juice boxes you bought.

In Exercises 18–20, simplify by adding like terms.

18. $3a + 6b + 2a$ **19.** $12p + 4q + 2q + 3p$ **20.** $3x + 5y + 9x + 10z$

In Exercises 21 and 22, solve the verbal sentence.

21. A number decreased by 14 is at least 36.

22. The product of a number and 12 equals 60.

In Exercises 23 and 24, write an expression for the perimeter. Find the perimeter when *x* is 1, 2, 3, and 4. Represent your results in a table.

23.

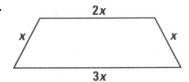

24.

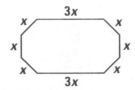

1. Which statement demonstrates the Distributive Property *incorrectly*?

   A $4(x + y + z) = 4x + 4y + 4z$

   B $3(a + 1) = 3a + 3$

   C $6(2 + m) = 8 + 6m$

   D $2(5 + 3) = 2(5) + 2(3)$

2. Find the perimeter of the figure.

   A $6x + 3$

   B $4x + 3$

   C $7 + 3x$

   D $7x + 3$

3. Which equation represents the following verbal statement? *What number can 8 be subtracted from to obtain 9?*

   A $8 - n = 9$ **B** $n - 9 = 8$

   C $n - 8 = 9$ **D** $9 - n = 8$

4. Which statement cannot represent the equation $20 + x = 35$?

   A The cake needs 35 min to bake. It has been in the oven 20 min.

   B You are on the 20th floor. You climb the stairs to the 35th.

   C You have earned $20. You earn more money for a total of $35.

   D You buy a shirt for $20 and a pair of jeans for $35.

5. Which is *not* a solution of the inequality $m - 9 \le 3$?

   A 9   **B** 12

   C 13   **D** 10

6. Solve $y - 4.2 = 5.7$.

   A $y = 1.5$ **B** $y = 1.9$

   C $y = 9.5$ **D** $y = 9.9$

7. The area of the rectangle is 63 in.^{2} Which equation do you use to find its width?

   A $9w = 63$ **B** $63w = 9$

   C $\frac{w}{63} = 9$ **D** $\frac{w}{9} = 63$

8. It takes 5 min to ride your bike to Rita's house 2 mi away. How many miles per hour did you travel?

   A 6 mi/h   **B** 22 mi/h

   C 24 mi/h   **D** 35 mi/h

9. Which phrase represents $\frac{n}{4} - 1$?

   A The quotient of n and 4, subtracted from 1

   B Four divided by a number, subtracted from 1

   C One less than the quotient of a number and 4

   D The difference of 4 divided by n, minus 1

10. A store has a 25% off sale on shoes. You buy a pair discounted by $13.75. What was the original price?

    A $38.75   **B** $41.25

    C $55.00   **D** $68.75

Modeling Integers

IN THE NEWS At Boston's Kid Company, student
reporters prepare stories for a radio show.

TECHNOLOGY

• **Interactive Real-Life
Investigations**

• **Middle School Tutorial
Software**

To find out more about sports
reporting, go to:

http://www.mlmath.com

CHAPTER THEME
Sports

CHAPTER PROJECT

Sports Reporting

You will be the sports reporter for your school newspaper. You will write an article about some aspect of sports for each edition of the paper. Use the **BUILDING YOUR PROJECT** questions to determine subjects for your articles.

GETTING STARTED

Talking It Over

- In your groups, talk about the different sports teams that are sponsored by your school.

- Which of these sports do you like to play or watch?

- How are sports scores and statistics calculated and recorded in newspaper stories?

Planning Your Project

- **Materials:** paper, pencils or pens, word processor (optional)

- Think of a name for your column. How long will each article be?

- As you answer the **BUILDING YOUR PROJECT** questions, write articles that include the results of the questions. Keep the articles that you write in your portfolio.

BUILDING YOUR PROJECT

These are places throughout the chapter where you will work on your project.

3.1 Write an article about diving. *p. 107*

3.2 Investigate some long jumpers' distances. *p. 113*

3.3 Write an article about plays in a football game. *p. 117*

3.6 Focus on scores of an athlete in the sport of your choice. *p. 135*

3.7 Report on a team fund-raising project. *p. 141*

3.1

Integers and Absolute Value

What you should learn:

Goal 1 How to model integers on a number line

Goal 2 How to find the absolute value of a number

Why you should learn it:

You can use integers to model real-life situations, such as temperatures that are below zero.

A thermometer is a vertical number line. On the Celsius scale, negative temperatures are below freezing.

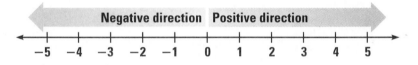 **INTEGERS AND THE NUMBER LINE**

Many real-life situations can be modeled with whole numbers. Some things, such as temperatures, are more easily modeled with an expanded set of numbers called *integers*.

INTEGERS

The following numbers are called **integers**.

$$\ldots, -3, -2, -1, \qquad 0, \qquad 1, 2, 3, \ldots$$

Negative   Zero   Positive

You can model integers on a number line.

Negative direction   **Positive direction**

$$-5 \quad -4 \quad -3 \quad -2 \quad -1 \quad 0 \quad 1 \quad 2 \quad 3 \quad 4 \quad 5$$

Here are some things you need to know about integers.

1. A negative integer such as -5 is read as "negative 5." Although the negative sign "$-$" is the same sign that is used for subtraction, it does not mean the same thing.

2. A positive integer such as 12 can be written with a positive sign as $+12$. It is more common, however, to omit the positive sign.

3. If a and b are integers, then the inequality $a < b$ means that a lies *to the left* of b on the number line.

Example 1   **Plotting Integers on the Number Line**

Draw a number line and plot the integers -6, -2, and 3.

Solution

To *plot* the integers on the number line, draw a dot at the point that represents the integer. Note that -6 is to the left of -2, which means that $-6 < -2$.

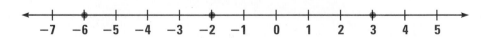

$$-7 \quad -6 \quad -5 \quad -4 \quad -3 \quad -2 \quad -1 \quad 0 \quad 1 \quad 2 \quad 3 \quad 4 \quad 5$$

The **absolute value** of a number is the distance between the number and 0. Absolute values are written with two vertical rules called **absolute value signs**.

$$|-7| = 7 \qquad \text{Absolute value of } -7 \text{ is } 7.$$

Because distance cannot be negative, the absolute value of a number cannot be negative.

Example 2 Evaluating Absolute Values

Evaluate each absolute value.

a. $|-4|$ **b.** $|3|$

Solution

a. The distance between -4 and 0 is 4. So, $|-4| = 4$.

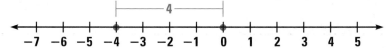

b. The distance between 3 and 0 is 3. So, $|3| = 3$.

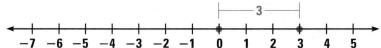

Two numbers that have the same absolute value but opposite signs are called **opposites**. For instance, -4 and 4 are opposites.

Example 3 Using Absolute Value in Real Life

The graph at the right shows the depth of a diver. Use absolute value to find the distance the diver must travel to the surface.

Solution

The depth of the diver is -18 ft. The distance the diver must travel is

$$|-18| = 18 \text{ ft.}$$

So, the diver must travel 18 ft to the surface.

ONGOING ASSESSMENT

Talk About It

Decide whether the statement is true. Explain your reasoning.

1. -6 is greater than -4.

2. Zero is the only integer that is its own opposite.

3. If $a \le b$, then $|a| \le |b|$.

3.1 Exercises   Extra Practice, page 719

GUIDED PRACTICE

In Exercises 1–6, use the following set of numbers.

$$-4, -3, -2, -1, 0, 1, 2, 3, 4$$

1. Which are integers?

2. Which are whole numbers?

3. Which are natural numbers?

4. Which is the smallest positive integer?

5. Which is the greatest negative integer?

6. Which is neither positive nor negative?

7. Give an example of two numbers that are opposites.

8. State two values of x that make $|x| = 5$ true.

9. On a horizontal number line, which direction is positive?

10. **OPEN-ENDED PROBLEM** Describe an example (other than temperature) of how negative integers are used in real life.

PRACTICE AND PROBLEM SOLVING

In Exercises 11–16, draw a number line and plot the integers.

11. $0, 4, -3$

12. $-1, 2, -6$

13. $-5, -3, 0$

14. $-4, 2, 3$

15. $-7, -8, -5$

16. $0, -2, 7$

In Exercises 17–22, compare the integers using < or >.

17. 0 ? 4

18. -2 ? 1

19. -3 ? -5

20. 4 ? -6

21. $|-1|$? -2

22. $|-14|$? $|-13|$

In Exercises 23–30, write the opposite and the absolute value of the integer.

23. 1

24. -4

25. -3

26. 3

27. 20

28. -32

29. -100

30. 144

NUMBER SENSE In Exercises 31–38, write the integer that represents the situation.

31. 250 ft below sea level

32. An elevation of 5050 ft

33. A gain of 25 yd

34. $100 deposit in a checking account

35. $17°$ below zero

36. A profit of $40

37. A loss of 15 lb

38. A gain of 6 h

In Exercises 39–44, order the integers from least to greatest.

39. $0, -6, 5, -3, 4$

40. $-1, -10, 1, -4, -6$

41. $-1, 2, -2, 0, -4$

42. $-9, -11, 11, 1, -7$

43. $6, 4, -4, -5, -2$

44. $-7, -8, -9, -6, -5$

GEOGRAPHY **In Exercises 45–50, use the number line to estimate the distance in miles between the two cities.**

45. LaSalle and Rochelle

46. LaSalle and Bloomington

47. Mendota and Bloomington

48. Decatur and LaSalle

49. Bloomington and Decatur

50. Rochelle and Decatur

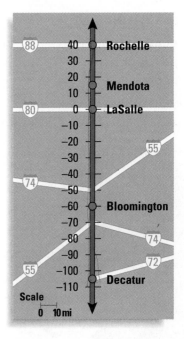

In Exercises 51–54, decide whether the statement is _true_ or _false_. In each case, explain your reasoning.

51. The absolute value of a negative integer is a positive integer.

52. The absolute value of any integer is positive.

53. The absolute value of -6 is greater than the absolute value of -4.

54. If $a \geq b$, then $|a| \geq |b|$.

STANDARDIZED TEST PRACTICE

55. Which statement is true when $x = -2$ and $y = |-2|$?

(A) $x > y$ **(B)** $x = y$ **(C)** $|x| = y$ **(D)** $|x| < y$

EXPLORATION AND EXTENSION

PORTFOLIO

56. **BUILDING YOUR PROJECT** For an article about diving, investigate the height of the diving board and the depth of the water at a local swimming pool, or ask a teacher for realistic data.

In your article, write a description of a dive. Include a diagram like the one at the right. Describe how you can use your diagram to calculate how far the diver descends.

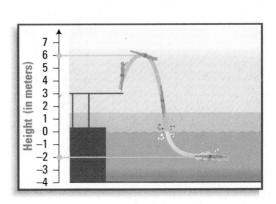

Modeling Addition

Part A ADDING NUMBERS WITH THE SAME SIGN

In this lab, you will use number counters to model integer addition. Each  counter represents positive 1. Each ⊖ counter represents negative 1.

Here are two samples of using number counters to add two integers.

Sample: Find the sum of 3 and 2.

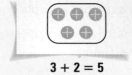

+3   +2

3 + 2 = 5

1 Choose counters to model positive 3 and positive 2.

2 Put the counters on the paper and count the total.

3 The sum of 3 and 2 is 5.

Sample: Find the sum of −4 and −3.

−4   −3

−4 + (−3) = −7

1 Choose counters to model negative 4 and negative 3.

2 Put the counters on the paper and count the total.

3 The sum of −4 and −3 is −7.

In Exercises 1–6, use number counters to find the sum. Describe how you got your solution.

1. $5 + 2$
2. $-3 + (-2)$
3. $-6 + (-3)$
4. $2 + 3 + 2$
5. $-1 + (-4)$
6. $-3 + (-5)$

7. Write a general statement about the sign of the sum of two positive integers.

8. Write a general statement about the sign of the sum of two negative integers.

Sample: Find the sum of -7 and 4.

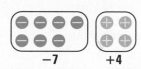

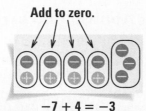

Add to zero.

$-7 + 4 = -3$

1 Choose counters to model negative 7 and positive 4.

2 Put the counters on the paper. Group pairs of positive and negative counters. Each pair has a sum of 0. Count the remaining counters.

3 The sum of -7 and 4 is -3.

Sample: Find the sum of 5 and -3.

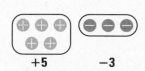

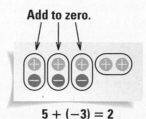

Add to zero.

$5 + (-3) = 2$

1 Choose counters to model positive 5 and negative 3.

2 Put the counters on the paper. Group pairs of positive and negative counters.

3 The sum of 5 and -3 is 2.

In Exercises 9–14, use number counters to find the sum. Draw a sketch of your solution.

9. $-2 + 5$

10. $6 + (-4)$

11. $-6 + 5$

12. $5 + (-7)$

13. $(-2) + 8$

14. $-5 + 5$

NOW TRY THESE

In Exercises 15–18, use number counters to find the sum. Draw a sketch of your solution.

15. $5 + 4$

16. $-6 + (-3)$

17. $-2 + 5$

18. $7 + (-8)$

19. Can the sum of a positive integer and a negative integer be positive? Can it be negative? How can you predict when a sum will be positive or negative?

20. Can the sum of two integers be zero? What can you say about such integers?

3.2

Adding Two Integers

What you should learn:

Goal 1 How to use absolute values to add two integers

Goal 2 How to use integer addition to solve real-life problems

Why you should learn it:

You can use integer addition to solve real-life problems, such as finding the temperature.

Goal 1 ADDING TWO INTEGERS

In this lesson, you will study rules for adding two integers.

ADDING TWO INTEGERS	
Rule	**Examples**
1. To add two integers with the *same sign*, add their absolute values and write the common sign.	$3 + 4 = 7$ $-2 + (-6) = -8$
2. To add two integers with *different signs*, subtract the smaller absolute value from the larger absolute value. Write the sign of the integer with the larger absolute value.	$-2 + 5 = 3$ $1 + (-7) = -6$
3. The sum of 0 and any integer is the integer.	$0 + (-4) = -4$
4. The sum of any two opposites is zero.	$-5 + 5 = 0$

Example 1 Adding Integers with the Same Sign

a. The sum of two positive integers is positive.

$$4 + 5 = 9$$

b. The sum of two negative integers is negative.

$$-12 + (-3) = -15$$

Example 2 Adding Integers with Different Signs

a. The sum of 5 and -8 is negative because -8 has a greater absolute value than 5.

Subtract 5 from 8.

$$5 + (-8) = -3$$

Write sign of -8.

b. The sum of 6 and -6 is zero because both integers have the same absolute value and different signs.

$$6 + (-6) = 0$$ Sum of opposites is zero.

Goal 2 SOLVING REAL-LIFE PROBLEMS

You can use integer addition to model changes in temperature.

Example 3 **Finding a Temperature**

REAL LIFE
Meteorology

The thermometers show the temperatures (in degrees Celsius) at 1 P.M., 2 P.M., and 3 P.M.

  1 P.M.

 2 P.M.

 3 P.M.

a. Use the thermometers to approximate the temperatures.

b. Write an addition equation that relates the temperatures at 1 P.M. and 2 P.M.

c. Write an equation that relates the temperatures at 2 P.M. and 3 P.M.

Solution

a. At 1 P.M. the temperature is 20°C. At 2 P.M. the temperature is 10°C. At 3 P.M. the temperature is 15°C.

b. From 1 P.M. to 2 P.M. the temperature *dropped* 10°. You can show this by adding −10° to the 1 P.M. temperature.

$$\underset{\text{temperature}}{\text{1 P.M.}} + \underset{\text{drop of }10°}{\text{Temperature}} = \underset{\text{temperature}}{\text{2 P.M.}}$$
$$20 \quad + \quad (-10) \quad = \quad 10$$

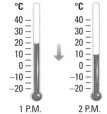
1 P.M.   2 P.M.

c. From 2 P.M. to 3 P.M. the temperature *rose* 5°. You can show this by adding 5° to the 2 P.M. temperature.

$$\underset{\text{temperature}}{\text{2 P.M.}} + \underset{\text{rise of }5°}{\text{Temperature}} = \underset{\text{temperature}}{\text{3 P.M.}}$$
$$10 \quad + \quad 5 \quad = \quad 15$$

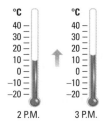
2 P.M.   3 P.M.

ONGOING ASSESSMENT

Write About It
....

Write each situation as a question. Then show how integer addition can be used to answer the question.

1. You owe your uncle $25. You pay back $15.

2. You owe your sister $15. You borrow another $15 from her.

3. You owe your mom $40. You pay back all of it.

3.2 Exercises

Extra Practice, page 719

GUIDED PRACTICE

In Exercises 1–4, find the sum.

1. $4 + 3$ **2.** $2 + (-2)$ **3.** $7 + (-5)$ **4.** $-7 + (-5)$

In Exercises 5 and 6, find a pair of integers whose sum is −1. (Use the integers labeled *a*, *b*, *c*, and *d*.)

5.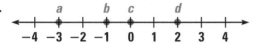

6.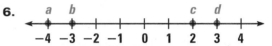

7. Look back at the four rules used in this lesson to add integers. Which rule should you use to find the sum of 8 and -11? Explain.

8. From the number line below state whether $a + b$ is negative, zero, or positive. Explain.

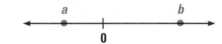

PRACTICE AND PROBLEM SOLVING

In Exercises 9–24, find the sum. Write your conclusion as an equation.

9. $11 + 15$ **10.** $-8 + (-2)$ **11.** $-13 + (-13)$ **12.** $10 + 24$

13. $10 + (-10)$ **14.** $-8 + 8$ **15.** $-13 + 13$ **16.** $24 + (-24)$

17. $13 + 0$ **18.** $-7 + 0$ **19.** $0 + 15$ **20.** $0 + (-33)$

21. $2 + (-9)$ **22.** $39 + (-21)$ **23.** $-16 + 12$ **24.** $-17 + 13$

LOOKING FOR A PATTERN In Exercises 25–28, complete the statements. Then describe the pattern.

25.
$4 + 2 = \boxed{?}$
$4 + 1 = \boxed{?}$
$4 + 0 = \boxed{?}$
$4 + (-1) = \boxed{?}$

26.
$-2 + (-2) = \boxed{?}$
$-2 + (-1) = \boxed{?}$
$-2 + 0 = \boxed{?}$
$-2 + 1 = \boxed{?}$

27.
$3 + (-5) = \boxed{?}$
$3 + (-3) = \boxed{?}$
$3 + (-1) = \boxed{?}$
$3 + 1 = \boxed{?}$

28.
$-6 + (-5) = \boxed{?}$
$-6 + (-6) = \boxed{?}$
$-6 + (-7) = \boxed{?}$
$-6 + (-8) = \boxed{?}$

In Exercises 29–32, match the equation with the real-life situation. Then solve the equation for *x* and explain what *x* represents in the problem.

A. **ELEVATOR** You enter an elevator on the 5th floor. The elevator goes down 3 floors.

B. **TEMPERATURE** The temperature is 35°F. It drops 10°F.

C. **FOOTBALL** Your team is on its own 35 yd line. You rush for a 10 yd gain.

D. **MONEY** Your sister owes you $5. She pays $3 of it back to you.

29. $-5 + 3 = x$ **30.** $5 - 3 = x$ **31.** $35 + 10 = x$ **32.** $35 + (-10) = x$

MENTAL MATH In Exercises 33–36, use mental math to solve the equation.

33. $4 + x = 7$ **34.** $6 + n = 5$ **35.** $-2 + m = -5$ **36.** $-3 + y = 0$

OPEN-ENDED PROBLEMS In Exercises 37–40, find three sets of values of x and y that make the equation true. (There are many correct answers.)

37. $x + y = 7$ **38.** $x + y = -2$ **39.** $x + y = -8$ **40.** $x + y = 10$

DINOSAURS In Exercises 41–43, find the period in which the dinosaur lived.

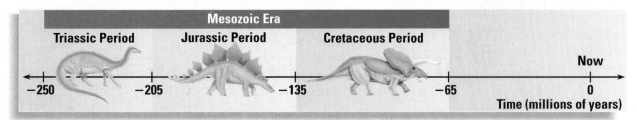

Mesozoic Era

Triassic Period   Jurassic Period   Cretaceous Period   Now

−250   −205   −135   −65   0

Time (millions of years)

41. *Stegosaurus:* 122 million years before the end of the Cretaceous Period

42. *Torosaurus:* 117 million years after the beginning of the Jurassic Period

43. *Plateosaurus:* 72 million years before the end of the Jurassic Period

STANDARDIZED TEST PRACTICE

44. Simplify $\left| -10 \right| + (-1)$.

   A -11 **B** -9 **C** 9 **D** 11

45. Simplify $\left| 5 \right| + \left| -8 \right|$.

   A -13 **B** -3 **C** 3 **D** 13

EXPLORATION AND EXTENSION

PORTFOLIO

46. BUILDING YOUR PROJECT Last season, the long jumpers on the track team averaged a distance of 15 ft per jump. In the first meet this season, Jason jumped 3 ft short of the average, Abdul jumped 2 ft over the average, Van jumped 4 ft over the average, and Maha jumped 1 ft short of the average. Write an article about the track meet. Use integer addition to find how far each athlete jumped.

3.3 Adding Three or More Integers

What you should learn:

Goal 1 How to add three or more integers

Goal 2 How to simplify expressions by adding like terms

Why you should learn it:

You can use integer addition to solve real-life problems, such as finding the total number of yards gained in football.

Goal 1 ADDING THREE OR MORE INTEGERS

You can model the addition of integers using a number line. To add a positive number, move to the *right*. To add a negative number, move to the *left*.

Example 1 Modeling Addition with a Number Line

The sum of 3, -5, and 4 can be modeled as shown below.

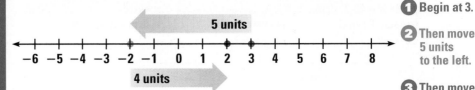

1 Begin at 3.

2 Then move 5 units to the left.

3 Then move 4 units to the right.

Because you end at **2**, it follows that $3 + (-5) + 4 = 2$

Example 2 Using a Calculator to Add Integers

You can use a calculator to find $-6 + 5 + (-7) + 1$.

To enter -6 on a scientific calculator, press 6 **+/−** .

Calculator Steps	Display	Conclusion
6 **+/−** **+** 5 **+** 7 **+/−** **+** 1 **=**	-7	The sum is -7.

Example 3 Finding the Number of Yards Gained

REAL LIFE
Football

In football, a team has four chances, called "downs," to advance the ball toward the end zone. Suppose that on its first down, your team gained 7 yd. On its second down, it lost 13 yd. On its third down, it gained 9 yd. On its fourth down, it gained 6 yd. Did your team gain at least 10 yd and thus earn another first down?

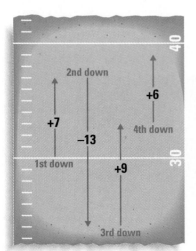

Solution

A diagram of the gains and losses is shown at the left. The total number of yards gained is

$$7 + (-13) + 9 + 6, \text{ or } 9.$$

The team did not earn a first down.

NEED TO KNOW

Coefficients of 1 and −1 are usually implied, rather than written.

The coefficient of x is 1 and the coefficient of −x is −1.

In the expression $-5x + 2x + 4$, the numbers -5 and 2 are **coefficients** of x. The terms $-5x$ and $2x$ are *like terms* because their variable parts are the same.

like terms

$$-5x + 2x + 4$$

coefficient   unlike terms

When you add like terms, you can add the coefficients.

Expression	Use Distributive Property.	Simplify.
$4n + (-6n) + 3$	$[4 + (-6)]n + 3$	$-2n + 3$
$-5x + 7x + (-3x)$	$[-5 + 7 + (-3)]x$	$-x$

Example 4   **Evaluating an Expression**

a. Simplify the expression $-15x + 40x + (-16x)$.

b. Evaluate the expression when $x = 2$.

c. Evaluate the expression when $x = 4$.

Solution

a. $-15x + 40x + (-16x) = [-15 + 40 + (-16)]x$ **Distributive Property**
$$= 9x$$ **Simplify.**

b. When $x = 2$, the expression has a value of
$$9x = 9(2) = 18.$$

c. When $x = 4$, the expression has a value of
$$9x = 9(4) = 36.$$

Example 5   **Using Coefficients of 1 or −1**

Simplify the expression $-n + 5n + 3$.

Solution

$-n + 5n + 3 = -1n + 5n + 3$ **Coefficient of −n is −1.**
$$= (-1 + 5)n + 3$$ **Use Distributive Property.**
$$= 4n + 3$$ **Simplify.**

ONGOING ASSESSMENT

Talk About It
....

Simplify each expression. How can you use mental math to combine the like terms?

1. $4x + (-2x) + 3$

2. $-6m + (-7m) + m$

3. $2y + (-y) + z$

3.3 Exercises

Extra Practice, page 719

GUIDED PRACTICE

In Exercises 1 and 2, use a number line to illustrate the movement. Then write your conclusion as an equation.

1. Begin at 4. Move 2 units to the right. Then move 6 units to the left.

2. Begin at 2. Move 5 units to the left. Then move 8 units to the right.

3. What are the terms in $-3x + 5x + 7$? Simplify the expression.

4. From the number line, state whether $a + b + c$ is negative, positive, or zero. Explain.

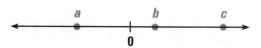

PRACTICE AND PROBLEM SOLVING

In Exercises 5–16, find the sum. Write your conclusion as an equation.

5. $4 + (-5) + 6$

6. $3 + (-9) + 13$

7. $-7 + 1 + (-8)$

8. $-6 + 2 + (-15)$

9. $-8 + 12 + (-1)$

10. $-10 + 16 + (-4)$

11. $-12 + (-4) + (-8)$

12. $-11 + (-7) + (-3)$

13. $5 + (-6) + (-13)$

14. $4 + (-8) + 9 + (-2)$

15. $-7 + (-6) + 2 + (-7)$

16. $-12 + (-4) + 20$

REASONING In Exercises 17–19, decide whether the sum is positive or negative. Explain how you can make your decision without actually finding the sum.

17. $-237 + 122 + 69$

18. $-142 + 127 + 89$

19. $-97 + 230 + (-213)$

 In Exercises 20–25, use a calculator to find the sum. Use the ⊞ or ⊟ key to enter negative numbers.

20. $-36 + 49 + (-2) + 15$

21. $-23 + 112 + (-9) + 13$

22. $19 + (-39) + (-51)$

23. $92 + (-20) + (-101)$

24. $84 + (-89) + (-40)$

25. $111 + 105 + (-99)$

GOLF In Exercises 26–28, use the table below. The table shows scores above and below par for the four rounds of a Masters golf tournament.

26. Find the total score for each player.

27. Which two players tied?

28. By how much did Tiger Woods beat Tom Kite?

Kite	+5	−3	−6	−2
Rocca	−1	−3	−2	+3
Stankowski	−4	+2	−3	+2
Watson	+3	−4	−3	0
Woods	−2	−6	−7	−3

Real Life... Real People

Tiger Woods

In 1997, at age 21, Tiger Woods became the youngest golfer to win the Masters tournament.

FOOTBALL In Exercises 29 and 30, decide whether the football team gains at least 10 yd. Explain your reasoning.

29. On its first down, the team gains 6 yd. On its second down, it loses 3 yd. On its third down, it loses 4 yd. On its fourth down, it gains 8 yd.

30. On its first down, the team gains 8 yd. On its second down, it gains 1 yd. On its third down, it loses 5 yd. On its fourth down, it gains 7 yd.

PERSONAL FINANCES In Exercises 31 and 32, use the bar graph at the right. The graph shows the amounts of money you deposited into your checking account and the amounts you withdrew from the account.

31. Find the sum of the deposits and withdrawals.

32. Suppose you had $50 in your checking account before you made your first transaction. How much money did you have in your checking account after you made your last transaction?

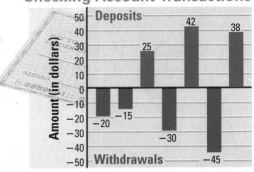

Checking Account Transactions

In Exercises 33–44, simplify the expression. Then evaluate it when $x = 2$.

33. $-x + 4x + 9$

34. $8x + (-6x) + 3$

35. $-2x + 10x + (-7x)$

36. $9x + 13x + (-10x)$

37. $13x + (-11x) + x$

38. $9x + (-x) + 2x$

39. $-3x + 2x + 26x$

40. $-4x + 9x + 6x$

41. $-7x + 8 + 17x$

42. $-8x + 10 + 12x$

43. $5x + 3 + (-8) + (-3x)$

44. $9x + 6 + (-18) + (-6x)$

STANDARDIZED TEST PRACTICE

45. Use the thermometers at the right. How much did the temperature decrease between 12:00 P.M. and 9:00 P.M.?

(**A**) 1°C   (**B**) 11°C   (**C**) 12°C   (**D**) 13°C

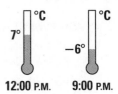

EXPLORATION AND EXTENSION

46. **BUILDING YOUR PROJECT** A football coach keeps track of the yards gained and lost by the team with integer addition. For four successive downs, he has written $7 + (-3) + (-9) + 15$. Write an article that describes the gains and losses on these four downs. Tell whether the team gained the 10 yd it needs to earn another first down.

In Exercises 1–8, evaluate the expression when $n = 3$. (1.3–1.5)

1. $6n - 12$ **2.** $n^2 - 4$ **3.** $13n + 16$ **4.** $1.2n + 1.5$

5. $6 \times (n - 1)$ **6.** $\frac{1}{4}(n \times 8)$ **7.** $n^2 \div 3$ **8.** $14 \times (n + 2) - 15$

In Exercises 9–11, complete the statement using >, <, or =. (3.1)

9. $\frac{1}{8}(32)$ **?** $\frac{1}{4}(16)$ **10.** $16 + (-8)$ **?** $10 + (-3)$ **11.** $-12 + (-2)$ **?** $-17 + 5$

12. Are the equations $x - 12 = 4$ and $x = 17$ equivalent? Explain. (2.4)

In Exercises 13–20, solve the equation. Check your solution. (2.4)

13. $x - 2 = 14$ **14.** $y + 5 = 6$ **15.** $14 + z = 34$ **16.** $a - 11 = 22$

17. $3b = 6$ **18.** $16c = 32$ **19.** $\frac{1}{2}p = 5$ **20.** $10q = \frac{1}{2}$

21. To raise money for a charity organization, you and a group of friends wash 9 cars on Thursday, 12 cars on Friday, and 16 cars on Saturday. You charge x dollars per car. Write an expression that represents the amount of money you raise. Suppose you charge $4.50 per car. How much money do you raise? (2.2)

CAREER Interview

DOWNHILL SKI COACH

Catherine Smith, certified by the Vermont Handicapped Ski and Sports Association, is the head downhill ski coach for the Vermont Special Olympics.

Q What led you into this career?
My brother has Down's syndrome and required special instruction when learning to ski.

Q What is your favorite part of your job?
Working with the athletes. Our athletes have a unique perspective—they care as much about the success of their peers as they do about their own success.

Q What math do you use in your job?
To maintain balance and stability, skiers have to learn how to position their skis at different angles in order to turn, speed, and stop. I draw a diagram of a clock in the snow and use the hand positions on the clock to describe the position of the skis.

Q What would you like to tell kids who are in school about math?
Don't get uptight about math. It's easy when you relate it to things you know and it is fun! There are a lot of uses for it and math is one of the most important skills you'll use when you get any type of job.

LAB 3.4

COOPERATIVE LEARNING

Modeling Subtraction

Materials Needed
• **number counters**
• **pencil or pen**
• **paper**

Part A SUBTRACTING NUMBERS

Sample: The difference $-5 - (-3) = -2$ can be modeled as follows.

Model for -5.   Subtract -3.   Result is -2.

In Exercises 1–3, use number counters to find the difference. Describe how you got your solution.

1. $6 - 4$ **2.** $-3 - (-2)$ **3.** $-7 - (-4)$

Part B SUBTRACTING USING ZERO PAIRS

A positive and negative counter form a *zero pair*. Adding zero pairs to a model does not change its value.

Sample: The difference $4 - 7 = -3$ can be modeled as follows.

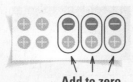 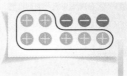 

Add to zero.

Model for 4.   Revise model for 4.   Subtract 7.   Result is -3.

4. Suppose you want to model the difference $1 - (-4) = 5$ using number counters. Show how to revise the model for 1 so that you can take away four negative counters.

NOW TRY THESE

In Exercises 5–10, use number counters to find the difference. Describe how you got your solution.

5. $5 - 7$ **6.** $2 - 9$ **7.** $-6 - (-7)$

8. $-3 - (-5)$ **9.** $-7 - 4$ **10.** $-4 - 6$

3.4

Subtracting Integers

What you should learn:

Goal 1 How to use opposites to subtract integers

Goal 2 How to simplify expressions involving subtraction

Why you should learn it:

You can use integer subtraction to simplify algebraic expressions, such as $5x - (-4x) + 3$.

Goal 1 SUBTRACTING INTEGERS

In this lesson, you will learn how to subtract integers. The number you get from subtracting one integer from another is the **difference** of the integers.

LESSON INVESTIGATION

Investigating Integer Subtraction

GROUP ACTIVITY Complete each statement. Compare the results of the two columns. Describe a rule for subtracting integers.

$5 - 1 = \boxed{?}$	$5 + (-1) = \boxed{?}$
$5 - 2 = \boxed{?}$	$5 + (-2) = \boxed{?}$
$5 - 3 = \boxed{?}$	$5 + (-3) = \boxed{?}$
$5 - 4 = \boxed{?}$	$5 + (-4) = \boxed{?}$
$5 - 5 = \boxed{?}$	$5 + (-5) = \boxed{?}$
$5 - 6 = \boxed{?}$	$5 + (-6) = \boxed{?}$
$5 - 7 = \boxed{?}$	$5 + (-7) = \boxed{?}$

You can express a subtraction problem as an addition problem if you use opposites.

SUBTRACTING INTEGERS

To subtract an integer b from an integer a, add the opposite of b to a.

$$a - b = a + (-b)$$

Example 1 Subtracting Integers

a. $5 - 7 = 5 + (-7) = -2$ **Opposite of 7 is −7.**

b. $-6 - 8 = -6 + (-8) = -14$ **Opposite of 8 is −8.**

c. $-9 - (-9) = -9 + 9 = 0$ **Opposite of −9 is 9.**

d. $-5 - (-1) = -5 + 1 = -4$ **Opposite of −1 is 1.**

e. $13 - 12 = 13 + (-12) = 1$ **Opposite of 12 is −12.**

NEED TO KNOW

The opposite of b, written as $-b$, is not necessarily negative. If b is negative, then its opposite, $-b$, is positive.

The *terms* of an algebraic expression are separated by addition, not subtraction. To identify the terms of an expression involving subtraction, you can rewrite the expression as a sum.

Example 2 Identifying Terms

Expression	Equivalent Sum	Terms
a. $2x - 4$	$2x + (-4)$	$2x$ and -4
b. $-3x - 2x + 5$	$-3x + (-2x) + 5$	$-3x$, $-2x$, and 5

The *Distributive Property*, $a(b + c) = ab + ac$, also applies to subtraction. The "subtraction form" of the property is the Distributive Property for Subtraction.

DISTRIBUTIVE PROPERTY FOR SUBTRACTION

Let a, b, and c be numbers or variable expressions.

$$a(b - c) = ab - ac \quad \text{and} \quad ab - ac = a(b - c)$$

The next example shows how this property can be used.

Example 3 Simplifying Expressions

a. Simplify the expression $11x - 2x + 3$.

b. Evaluate the expression when $x = 5$.

c. Evaluate the expression when $x = 8$.

Solution

a. $11x - 2x + 3 = (11 - 2)x + 3$ **Use the Distributive Property.**

$\qquad\qquad\qquad = 9x + 3$ **Simplify.**

b. When $x = 5$, the value of the expression is

$\qquad 9x + 3 = 9(5) + 3 = 48$.

c. When $x = 8$, the value of the expression is

$\qquad 9x + 3 = 9(8) + 3 = 75$.

ONGOING ASSESSMENT

Talk About It

1. A friend of yours says, "The weather is not bad today." Your friend's statement contains a *double negative*. How is the statement related to the mathematical equation $3 - (-4) = 7$?

GUIDED PRACTICE

1. Explain how to evaluate $5 - (-2)$.

2. Apply the Distributive Property to $r(s - t)$.

REASONING In Exercises 3–6, decide whether the statement is true for all values of x, some values of x, or no values of x. Explain.

3. $5x - 2x - 12 = 5x + (-2x) + (-12)$

4. The opposite of x is 0.

5. $3(x - 4) = 3x - (-12)$

6. The opposite of x is negative.

PRACTICE AND PROBLEM SOLVING

In Exercises 7–18, find the difference. Write your conclusion as an equation.

7. $19 - 17$

8. $5 - 9$

9. $23 - (-8)$

10. $2 - (-4)$

11. $-10 - 7$

12. $-3 - 3$

13. $-5 - (-5)$

14. $-16 - (-8)$

15. $-5 - 5$

16. $-16 - 8$

17. $0 - 27$

18. $0 - (-61)$

19. **TECHNOLOGY** Explain the difference between the ⊞ key and the ⊟ key on a calculator.

In Exercises 20–23, evaluate the expression when $a = 5$ and when $a = -5$.

20. $a - 1$

21. $1 - a$

22. $a - 6$

23. $6 - a$

In Exercises 24–27, rewrite the expression as a sum. Then identify the terms of the expression.

24. $3x - 2x + 16$

25. $7x - 9x - 5$

26. $7a - 5b$

27. $4 - 2n + 4m$

In Exercises 28–39, simplify the expression.

28. $9x - 6x - 17$

29. $18n - 12n + 4$

30. $-11y - (-15y) - 2$

31. $-20x - (-30x) + 10$

32. $b - (-2b)$

33. $3x - (-3x)$

34. $-2a - 3a - 4$

35. $-13x - 13x - 13$

36. $4m - 6m + 8$

37. $16y - 20y + 24$

38. $-14x - (-10x)$

39. $-30x - (-19x)$

40. **GEOGRAPHY** In Death Valley National Park, the highest point is Telescope Peak (11,049 ft) and the lowest point is Badwaters (-282 ft). What is the difference in elevation between these two points?

SCIENCE In Exercises 41–43, use the table, which gives the low and high surface temperatures of four planets.

	Mercury	Venus	Earth	Mars
Low	−280°F	721°F	−129°F	−220°F
High	800°F	925°F	136°F	68°F

41. Find the difference between the high temperature and the low temperature of each planet.

42. Find the difference between the low temperatures of Earth and Mars.

43. Find the difference between the high temperatures of Mercury and Venus.

NUMBER SENSE In Exercises 44–47, find values for x and y so that the statement is true. (There are many correct answers.)

44. x is positive, y is positive, and $x - y$ is positive.

45. x is positive, y is positive, and $x - y$ is negative.

46. x is negative, y is negative, and $x - y$ is negative.

47. x is negative, y is negative, and $x - y$ is positive.

In Exercises 48–51, evaluate the expression.

48. $5 - 3$ **49.** $3 - 5$ **50.** $-7 - 12$ **51.** $12 - (-7)$

52. **LOOKING FOR A PATTERN** Use the results of Exercises 48–51 to make a prediction about the values of $a - b$ and $b - a$. Test your prediction with several values of a and b.

STANDARDIZED TEST PRACTICE

53. Which number comes next in the pattern?   13, 9, 5, 1, . . .

    (A) 0   **(B)** −2   **(C)** −3   **(D)** −4

EXPLORATION AND EXTENSION

54. Find the highest and lowest temperatures ever recorded where you live. (Or, use the data in the table on the bottom of page 129.) Find the difference between the highest and lowest temperatures.

Modeling Multiplication

Materials Needed
• number counters
• pencil or pen
• paper

Sample: What is $+3$ times -2?

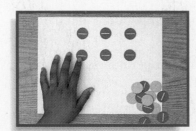

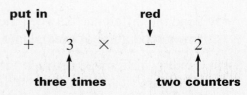

Put three models of -2 on the paper and count the total.

In Exercises 1–3, use number counters to find the product. Describe how you got your solution.

1. $2 \times (-2)$ **2.** $4 \times (-5)$ **3.** $3 \times (-5)$

Sample: What is -3 times $+2$?

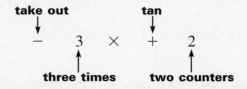

1 You need to take out 3 models of $+2$. Because there are no tan counters to take out, begin by modeling 0 with 6 pairs of red and tan counters.

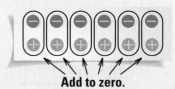

Add to zero.

2 Now take out 2 tan counters 3 times.   **3** Result is -6.

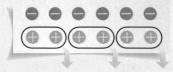 

In Exercises 4–6, use number counters to find the product. Describe how you got your solution.

4. -4×3 **5.** -3×5 **6.** -6×2

Sample: What is -3 times -2?

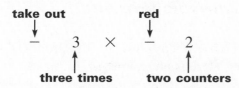

three times **two counters**

1 You need to take out 3 models of -2. Because there are no red counters to take out, begin by modeling 0 with 6 pairs of red and tan counters.

Add to zero.

2 Now take out 2 red counters 3 times.

3 Result is $+6$.

In Exercises 7–9, use number counters to find the product. Describe how you got your solution.

7. $-2 \times (-4)$ **8.** $-3 \times (-1)$ **9.** $-4 \times (-5)$

NOW TRY THESE

In Exercises 10–15, use number counters to find the product. Describe how you got your solution.

10. $3 \times (-4)$ **11.** $-2 \times (-1)$ **12.** -4×4
13. $-5 \times (-2)$ **14.** $4 \times (-3)$ **15.** -2×4

16. What can you say about the product of a negative integer and a positive integer? Can the result be positive?

17. Write a general statement about the product of two negative integers.

...find -2×4 I started with ...ht zero pairs.

...ok away four positive ...twice.

...ht negative

3.5

Multiplying Integers

What you should learn:

Goal **1** How to multiply integers

Goal **2** How to use integer multiplication to model real-life problems

Why you should learn it:

You can use integer multiplication to solve real-life problems, such as converting temperatures.

On Mount Washington in New Hampshire, temperatures have been recorded as low as $-47°F$.

Goal **1** MULTIPLYING INTEGERS

In this lesson, you will learn how to find products of one or more negative factors. Here is an example.

$$3(-3) = (-3) + (-3) + (-3) = -9$$

LESSON INVESTIGATION

COOPERATIVE LEARNING

Investigating Integer Multiplication

 GROUP ACTIVITY Use a calculator to complete the following. What patterns do you notice?

$(2)(3) =$?	$(2)(-2) =$?
$(1)(3) =$?	$(1)(-2) =$?
$(0)(3) =$?	$(0)(-2) =$?
$(-1)(3) =$?	$(-1)(-2) =$?
$(-2)(3) =$?	$(-2)(-2) =$?
$(-3)(3) =$?	$(-3)(-2) =$?

You can see from the investigation that the sign of a product depends on the signs of the numbers being multiplied.

MULTIPLYING INTEGERS

1. The product of two positive numbers is positive.

2. The product of two negative numbers is positive.

3. The product of a positive and a negative number is negative.

Example 1 Multiplying Integers

a. $4(3) = 12$ The product is positive.
b. $5(-2) = -10$ The product is negative.
c. $(-4)(6) = -24$ The product is negative.
d. $(-3)^2 = (-3)(-3) = 9$ The product is positive.

In part (d), parentheses act as grouping symbols. When there are no grouping symbols, evaluate powers before negative signs.

$$-3^2 = -3 \cdot 3 = -9 \quad -x^2 = -x \cdot x = -\left(x^2\right)$$

The rules for multiplying positive and negative integers also apply to fractions and decimals. For example, $\frac{1}{2} \cdot (-4) = -2$.

Example 2 Writing and Using a Model

To convert from a Celsius temperature to a Fahrenheit temperature, multiply the Celsius temperature by $\frac{9}{5}$ and add 32. Write an algebraic model for this relationship. Use the model to find the Fahrenheit temperature that corresponds to each Celsius temperature.

a. $-20°C$ **b.** $-30°C$ **c.** $37°C$

Solution

Verbal Model   **Fahrenheit temperature** $= \frac{9}{5} \cdot$ **Celsius temperature** $+ 32$

Labels   Fahrenheit temperature $= F$ (degrees F)
Celsius temperature $= C$ (degrees C)

Algebraic Model $F = \frac{9}{5} \cdot C + 32$

a. The Fahrenheit temperature corresponding to $-20°C$ is

$$F = \frac{9}{5}C + 32 \qquad \text{Write model.}$$
$$= \frac{9}{5}(-20) + 32 \qquad \text{Substitute } -20 \text{ for } C.$$
$$= -36 + 32 \qquad \text{Simplify.}$$
$$= -4°F. \qquad \text{Simplify.}$$

b. The Fahrenheit temperature corresponding to $-30°C$ is

$$F = \frac{9}{5}C + 32 \qquad \text{Write model.}$$
$$= \frac{9}{5}(-30) + 32 \qquad \text{Substitute } -30 \text{ for } C.$$
$$= -22°F. \qquad \text{Simplify.}$$

c. The Fahrenheit temperature corresponding to $37°C$ is

$$F = \frac{9}{5}C + 32 \qquad \text{Write model.}$$
$$= \frac{9}{5}(37) + 32 \qquad \text{Substitute } 37 \text{ for } C.$$
$$= 98.6°F. \qquad \text{Simplify.}$$

Real Life...
Real People

Peak Experience
At age 12, Taras Genet became the youngest person to reach the summit of Mount McKinley's South Peak, where temperatures can fall below $-45°C$.

ONGOING ASSESSMENT

Write About It
. . . .

To convert from Fahrenheit to Celsius, subtract 32 from the Fahrenheit temperature and multiply by $\frac{5}{9}$. Find the Celsius temperature that corresponds to each Fahrenheit temperature.

1. $-4°F$ **2.** $140°F$

In Exercises 1–3, write the sum as a product. Then simplify.

1. $(-4) + (-4) + (-4)$ **2.** $(-x) + (-x) + (-x)$ **3.** $(-8) + (-8) + (-8) + (-8)$

4. Use the number line to decide whether ab, ac, and bc are positive or negative.

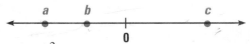

5. Which expression is equal to $(-4)(-4)$: -4^2 or $(-4)^2$?

6. REASONING If x is not zero, which expression must be positive: x^2, $2x$, or $-4x$?

In Exercises 7–14, find the product. Write your conclusion as an equation.

7. $-4 \cdot (-6)$ **8.** $-10 \cdot (-2)$ **9.** $5 \cdot (-11)$ **10.** $-8 \cdot 6$

11. $(-7)(-9)$ **12.** $(-10)(3)$ **13.** $(-1)(54)$ **14.** $(-20)(0)$

15. Is the product of three negative numbers positive or negative?

16. Is the product of four negative numbers positive or negative?

In Exercises 17–20, simplify the expression.

17. $-7 \cdot x$ **18.** $6 \cdot (-y)$ **19.** $(-14)(-a)$ **20.** $(-b)(-25)$

In Exercises 21–24, evaluate the expression when $a = 8$ and $b = -2$. Remember to evaluate powers before multiplying.

21. ab **22.** ab^2 **23.** $-b$ **24.** a^2b^3

COUPONS In Exercises 25–27, use the following information.

On a "double coupon day" at a grocery store, an item with regular price r costs only $-2c + r$ if you have a coupon with value c.

25. Suppose a bottle of juice costs $1.29 and you have a 25¢ coupon. Evaluate $-2c + r$ when $r = 1.29$ and $c = 0.25$.

26. Suppose a jar of salsa costs $2.39 and you have a 49¢ coupon. Evaluate $-2c + r$ when $r = 2.39$ and $c = 0.49$.

27. What expression can you use to calculate prices on a "triple coupon day"? Find the prices of the juice and salsa on such a day.

MENTAL MATH In Exercises 28–35, use mental math to solve the equation.

28. $2x = -4$ **29.** $3m = -9$ **30.** $-6b = 12$ **31.** $-8n = 24$

32. $-3a = 27$ **33.** $-7y = 42$ **34.** $1.5m = -3$ **35.** $-2x = -3.2$

TEMPERATURE In Exercises 36 and 37, use the following.

Temperatures are sometimes measured on the Kelvin scale.

- To convert from Fahrenheit to Celsius, subtract 32 from the Fahrenheit temperature and multiply by $\frac{5}{9}$.

- To convert from Celsius to Kelvin, add 273.15 to the Celsius temperature.

36. Write algebraic models for converting from Fahrenheit to Celsius and from Celsius to Kelvin.

37. Copy and complete the table.

Fahrenheit	Celsius	Kelvin
212°F	?	373.15K
32°F	0°C	?
−40°F	?	?

Real Life...
Real Facts

The lowest temperature recorded on Earth was 28 billionths of a degree Kelvin above absolute zero, at the Helsinki University of Technology in Finland.

GEOMETRY In Exercises 38 and 39, use the rectangle at the right. The rectangle has an area of 15 square units. The base of the rectangle rests on a number line.

38. If $a = -4$, what is b?　　**39.** If $b = -6$, what is a?

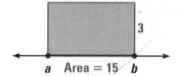

a　Area = 15　*b*

STANDARDIZED TEST PRACTICE

40. Which word best completes the sentence?
If the product of two integers is positive and the sum of the same two integers is negative, then both integers are . . .

　A even.　　**B** odd.　　**C** positive.　　**D** negative.

EXPLORATION AND EXTENSION

41. Find the highest and lowest temperatures ever recorded where you live. (Or, use the data in the table.) Convert the temperatures from degrees Fahrenheit to degrees Celsius.

City	High	Low
Bismarck, ND	109°F	−44°F
El Paso, TX	114°F	−8°F
Juneau, AK	90°F	−22°F
Phoenix, AZ	122°F	17°F

Tech Link

Investigation 3,
Interactive
Real-Life
Investigations

Take this test as you would take a test in class. The answers to the exercises are given in the back of the book.

In Exercises 1–3, draw a number line and plot the integers. (3.1)

1. $-2, 1, -4$

2. $4, -1, 0$

3. $2, -2, 0$

4. Write the opposite and the absolute value of 7. **(3.1)**

5. Write the opposite and the absolute value of -5. **(3.1)**

6. Order the integers $-2, 4, 3,$ and -3 from least to greatest. **(3.1)**

In Exercises 7–9, use mental math to solve the equation. (3.2)

7. $2 + a = 10$

8. $-5 + b = 5$

9. $3 + c = -2$

In Exercises 10–13, find the sum. Write your conclusion as an equation. (3.2)

10. $5 + (-7)$

11. $-8 + (-1)$

12. $-3 + 5$

13. $7 + (-7)$

14. BUSINESS You own an art supply business whose monthly profits and losses are shown in the graph. **(3.3)**

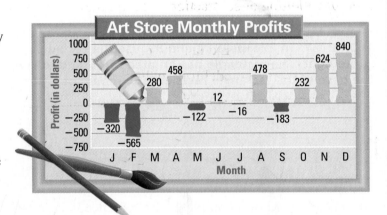

Art Store Monthly Profits

   a. Did your business have an overall profit or loss for the year?

   b. What was the amount of the overall profit or loss?

In Exercises 15 and 16, simplify the expression. Then evaluate it when $a = 6$ and $b = 2$. (3.3, 3.4)

15. $4a + 2a - 6b$

16. $7a - 2b - 3a$

In Exercises 17–22, simplify the expression. (3.3, 3.4)

17. $-3x - (-12x) + 2$

18. $-4x - (-9x) - 6$

19. $-x + 2x - (-x)$

20. $-6x - 6x - 6$

21. $12x - 6x + 12$

22. $8x - (-10x) + (-7x)$

In Exercises 23–28, find the product. (3.5)

23. $-4 \cdot 9$

24. $7 \times (-8)$

25. $(-12)(-5)$

26. $-6 \times (-3)$

27. $5 \cdot (-13)$

28. $(-3)(-1)$

MOUNTAIN photography

READ About It

It's not easy being a nature photographer! Carrying a pack that weighed almost half as much as he did, photographer James Martin started toward Mount Challenger (elevation 8200 feet) in Washington.

He hiked 4 miles from the road to Hannegan Pass (elevation 5100 feet), then down into a valley. He walked 5 miles, crossed a river, and climbed to Whatcom Pass (elevation 5200 feet).

There, Martin's path was blocked by Whatcom Peak (elevation 7600 feet). Still carrying his 70-pound pack, Martin made it up and down the mountain.

After 3 days and 20 miles of walking, he made his campsite on Mount Challenger at an elevation of 7000 feet. For all that climbing, Martin says that he got "two good images, and I'm very happy with that."

WRITE About It

1. Write a sentence comparing the elevations of Hannegan and Whatcom Passes.

2. How much higher is Whatcom Peak than Whatcom Pass? Did you use addition or subtraction to get your answer? Explain.

3. Write an equation that you could use to approximate James Martin's weight. Explain the equation and solve it.

4. Write a verbal model for the difference in elevation between Martin's campsite on Mt. Challenger and the mountain top.

3.6

Dividing Integers

What you should learn:

Goal 1 How to divide integers

Goal 2 How to use integer division to model real-life problems

Why you should learn it:

You can use integer division to solve problems involving averages, such as finding the average trial times of speed skaters.

Goal 1 DIVIDING INTEGERS

To perform division by hand, use long division as shown below. When you divide two numbers, you can check your result by multiplying.

$$\text{Divisor} \longrightarrow 4\overline{)52} \longleftarrow \text{Dividend}$$

Quotient → 13

$$\frac{52}{0}$$

Check ✓
$$4 \times 13 = 52$$

LESSON INVESTIGATION

COOPERATIVE LEARNING

Investigating Integer Division

GROUP ACTIVITY Solve each division problem. Explain how to use multiplication to check your answer. Write a general statement about the sign of the quotient of two integers.

a. $24 \div (-6)$ **b.** $-24 \div (-6)$ **c.** $(-24) \div 6$

When you divide integers, the sign of the quotient depends on the signs of the divisor and the dividend.

QUOTIENTS OF INTEGERS

1. The quotient of two positive integers is positive.
2. The quotient of two negative integers is positive.
3. The quotient of a positive and a negative integer is negative.
4. When 0 is divided by a nonzero number, the result is 0.

Example 1 Dividing Integers

a. $\dfrac{12}{-2} = -6$ **The quotient is negative.**

b. $\dfrac{-20}{4} = -5$ **The quotient is negative.**

c. $\dfrac{-36}{-6} = 6$ **The quotient is positive.**

d. $\dfrac{0}{-2} = 0$ **The quotient is zero.**

You can't divide by zero. For example, $5 \div 0$ is meaningless because you cannot divide 5 into 0 parts.

MODELING REAL-LIFE PROBLEMS

To find the **mean** (or average) of *n* numbers, add the numbers and divide the result by *n*.

Example 2 Averaging Positive Numbers

A wrestler is weighed every two weeks. His weights (in pounds) are 126, 132, 130, and 128. Find the average of these weights.

Solution

$$\text{Average} = \frac{\text{Sum of weights}}{\text{Number of weights}}$$

$$= \frac{126 + 132 + 130 + 128}{4}$$

$$= \frac{516}{4}$$

$$= 129 \text{ lb}$$

The wrestler's average weight is 129 lb.

Example 3 Averaging Positive and Negative Numbers

You are coaching your school's wrestling team. During the months of December and January, the 15 members of the team recorded the following weight gains or losses (in pounds).

$$-5, 0, -7, -3, 2, -4, -6, -1, 0, -3, -4, -4, -2, -5, -3$$

What was the average weight gain or loss per team member?

Solution

Verbal Model	$\textbf{Average gain or loss} = \dfrac{\textbf{Sum of gains and losses}}{\textbf{Number of wrestlers}}$

Labels
Average gain or loss = A (pounds)
Sum of gains and losses = -45 (pounds)
Number of wrestlers = 15

Algebraic Model
$$A = \frac{-45}{15}$$
$$= -3$$

The average weight loss was 3 lb.

ONGOING ASSESSMENT

Write About It

1. Write a list of weight changes that satisfies the following:

• Ten people are on the wrestling team.

• Four people gained, five lost, and one stayed the same.

• The average weight change was a loss of 3 lb.

GUIDED PRACTICE

In Exercises 1–4, state whether the quotient is negative or positive.

1. $216 \div 9$ **2.** $-28 \div 4$ **3.** $\dfrac{48}{-6}$ **4.** $\dfrac{-522}{-9}$

5. Explain how to check that $\dfrac{-6}{-2} = 3$.

NUMBER SENSE In Exercises 6–8, decide whether $\dfrac{a}{b}$ is positive.

6.    **7.** 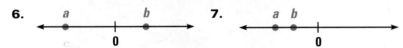   **8.**

PRACTICE AND PROBLEM SOLVING

In Exercises 9–20, evaluate the expression. Check your result by multiplying.

9. $\dfrac{54}{2}$ **10.** $\dfrac{384}{-12}$ **11.** $\dfrac{-90}{15}$ **12.** $\dfrac{-130}{26}$

13. $0 \div (-75)$ **14.** $376 \div (-8)$ **15.** $-954 \div (-18)$ **16.** $-1058 \div (-46)$

17. $1568/(-16)$ **18.** $242/(-11)$ **19.** $-1020/30$ **20.** $-3621/(-71)$

LOOKING FOR A PATTERN In Exercises 21–24, complete the statements. Then describe the pattern.

21. $-2 \div 2 = \boxed{?}$ **22.** $-1 \div (-1) = \boxed{?}$ **23.** $0 \div (-1) = \boxed{?}$ **24.** $64 \div (-32) = \boxed{?}$

$-4 \div 2 = \boxed{?}$ $-2 \div (-2) = \boxed{?}$ $0 \div (-2) = \boxed{?}$ $32 \div (-16) = \boxed{?}$

$-6 \div 2 = \boxed{?}$ $-3 \div (-3) = \boxed{?}$ $0 \div (-3) = \boxed{?}$ $16 \div (-8) = \boxed{?}$

$-8 \div 2 = \boxed{?}$ $-4 \div (-4) = \boxed{?}$ $0 \div (-4) = \boxed{?}$ $8 \div (-4) = \boxed{?}$

In Exercises 25–28, evaluate the expression when $x = -2$, $y = 3$, and $z = -4$.

25. $\dfrac{-2x}{4}$ **26.** $\dfrac{xz}{2}$ **27.** $\dfrac{xy}{z}$ **28.** $\dfrac{-yz}{x}$

MENTAL MATH In Exercises 29–32, use mental math to solve the equation.

29. $\dfrac{b}{7} = -7$ **30.** $\dfrac{z}{-8} = 5$ **31.** $\dfrac{m}{-2} = -24$ **32.** $\dfrac{81}{p} = -3$

33. **STOCK MARKET** A newspaper reports these changes in the price of a stock over four days: -1, -5, $+3$, and -9 (in eighths of a dollar). Find the average daily change.

In Exercises 34–39, find the average of the numbers.

34. 35, 38, 34, 39, 32, 38

35. 22, 19, 21, 20, 18, 22, 25

36. −4, −2, 0, 1, −3, 1, 2, −5, 3, −3

37. 3, 3, −4, 6, 2, 1, −2, −1, 2, −4, 5

38. −6, −9, −4, −2, −7, −6, −8

39. −20, −16, −12, −17, −10

SPEED SKATING In Exercises 40–42, use the following information.

In five trial runs on a 500 m track, a skater has times of 44.21 s, 45.02 s, 44.78 s, 45.10 s, and 44.13 s.

40. Find the average trial time of the skater.

41. Another skater, after five trial runs, had an average trial time of 45.07 s. What could this skater's trial times have been?

42. Is it possible that the second skater had a faster trial time than the first? Explain.

Real Life... **R**eal People

Bonnie Blair By 1994, Bonnie Blair had won 5 Olympic gold medals.

STANDARDIZED TEST PRACTICE

43. Which of the following statements is *always true*?

(**A**) The sum of a positive number and a negative number is positive.

(**B**) The difference of two negative numbers is negative.

(**C**) The product of a positive number and a negative number is positive.

(**D**) The quotient of a positive number and a negative number is negative.

EXPLORATION AND EXTENSION

PORTFOLIO

44. BUILDING YOUR PROJECT Write an article about a sport, such as gymnastics or figure skating, in which a score is assigned to each athlete.

   a. Find at least nine of an individual athlete's scores for a season, or find the scores of at least nine athletes in a competition.

   b. Calculate the mean of the scores.

   c. Subtract the mean of the scores from each score.

   d. Calculate the mean of the results from part (c). What do you find?

```
        8.9
        9.6
        9.3
        9.5
        9.7
        8.7
        8.9
        9.2
   +    9.0
   82.8 ÷ 9 = 9.2
```

In Exercises 1–8, evaluate the expression. (3.2–3.6)

1. $9 + 3$ **2.** $4 - 2$ **3.** $6 + (-3)$ **4.** $8 - (-2)$

5. $8 \times (-4)$ **6.** $(-3) \times (-5)$ **7.** $-84 \div 4$ **8.** $(-7)^2$

In Exercises 9 and 10, translate the verbal sentence into an algebraic equation. (2.7)

9. The cost of 3 burritos is $4.20.   **10.** The depth of 4 fathoms is 24 ft.

In Exercises 11–14, describe the pattern and list the next three numbers in the sequence. (1.1, 3.5, 3.6)

11. $2, -4, 8, -16, \boxed{?}, \boxed{?}, \boxed{?}, \ldots$ **12.** $-1, 3, -9, 27, \boxed{?}, \boxed{?}, \boxed{?}, \ldots$

13. $-2, 1, -\dfrac{1}{2}, \dfrac{1}{4}, \boxed{?}, \boxed{?}, \boxed{?}, \ldots$ **14.** $-78125, 15625, -3125, 625, \boxed{?}, \boxed{?}, \boxed{?}, \ldots$

In Exercises 15–20, evaluate the expression. (1.4, 3.2–3.6)

15. $3 + (-6) \times (-4)$ **16.** $-4 \times 6 \div 3$ **17.** $(3 - 6)^2$

18. $8 - (-2) \times 4$ **19.** $15 \times \left(\dfrac{3}{5} - \dfrac{2}{5}\right)$ **20.** $6.2 - 4.5 \div 1.5$

21. Write an equation to represent the limerick shown at the right. (*Hint:* A gross is a dozen dozens, and a score is 20.) **(2.6)**

A dozen, a gross, and a score,
Plus three times the square root of four,
Divided by seven,
Plus five times eleven,
Equals nine to the square and no more.

SPORTS Connection

COMPETITION SCORING

In gymnastics competitions, seven judges score each performance. The head judge eliminates the highest and lowest scores of the other six judges and averages the remaining four scores. The head judge's score is usually not used.

1. Listed in the table are the judges' scores (excluding the head judge's) for the gold, silver, and bronze medalists in an international gymnastics competition. Which gymnast won the gold?

2. OPEN-ENDED PROBLEM Suppose a gymnast finished with a final score of 9.2. What could the gymnast's scores have been?

Gymnast 1: 9.85, 9.30, 9.70, 9.65, 9.35, 9.50

Gymnast 2: 9.80, 9.60, 9.45, 9.30, 9.50, 9.25

Gymnast 3: 9.10, 9.45, 9.95, 9.70, 9.55, 9.65

Using Parentheses Keys

Most calculators have parentheses keys. These keys can help you enter complicated expressions on a calculator.

CALCULATOR TIP

If you evaluate fractions without using parentheses, you may get a wrong answer.

In part (a), the result without parentheses is −4.71429, because the calculator follows the order of operations:

$(−5 × 6) ÷ (−7) − 9$
$= −4.71429$

Example

Use a calculator to evaluate each expression.

a. $\dfrac{-5 \times 6}{-7 - 9}$

b. $\dfrac{-12}{-2 + 5 + (-6)}$

Solution

In the following steps, notice how parentheses help you tell the calculator to perform the operations in the correct order.

a. Calculator Steps

(5 +/− × 6) ÷ (7 +/− − 9) =

Display

| 1.875 |

b. Calculator Steps

12 +/− ÷ (2 +/− + 5 + 6 +/−) =

Display

| 4. |

Exercises

In Exercises 1–6, use a calculator to evaluate the expression. When appropriate, use parentheses. Round your answer to two decimal places.

1. $\dfrac{-9 \div (-6)}{8 + (-4)}$

2. $\dfrac{-8 + (-3) - (-4)}{-11 + (-3)}$

3. $\dfrac{-3 + (-4) + 2 + (-6) + (-3)}{5}$

4. $\dfrac{5 \times (-4)}{-12 \div 3}$

5. $\dfrac{-8}{(-4)2 - (-4)}$

6. $\dfrac{-2 - (-4)}{-7 \times 4 - 8}$

7. The low temperatures during a week (in degrees Celsius) were −4, −8, −1, 3, 5, 7, and 11. Use a calculator to find the average low temperature for the week. Explain how parentheses can help.

8. Explain why you would get an incorrect answer of 5 if you forgot to use parentheses when calculating part (b) of the example above.

Problem Solving Using Integers

What you should learn:

Goal 1 How to use properties of equality to solve equations involving integers

Goal 2 How to use integer operations to model real-life problems

Why you should learn it:

You can use integer operations to solve real-life problems, such as finding the profit or loss from a dance.

Goal 1 SOLVING EQUATIONS

You can use the properties of equality that you learned in Chapter 2 to solve equations that contain negative integers. For instance, to solve the equation $x - 5 = -7$, you can add 5 to each side of the equation.

Example 1 Using Addition or Subtraction

Solve the equations.

a. $x - 5 = -7$ 　　　　　　　　**b.** $-12 = n + 3$

Solution

a. 　　$x - 5 = -7$ 　　　　　　Write original equation.

　　$x - 5 + 5 = -7 + 5$ 　　　　Add 5 to each side.

　　　　　　$x = -2$ 　　　　　　Solution: x is by itself.

The solution is -2. Check this in the original equation.

b. 　　$-12 = n + 3$ 　　　　　Write original equation.

　　$-12 - 3 = n + 3 - 3$ 　　　Subtract 3 from each side.

　　　　$-15 = n$ 　　　　　　　Solution: n is by itself.

The solution is -15. Check this in the original equation.

Example 2 Using Multiplication or Division

Solve the equations.

a. $3y = -18$ 　　　　　　　　**b.** $\dfrac{m}{-2} = 15$

Solution

a. $3y = -18$ 　　　　　　　　Write original equation.

$\dfrac{3y}{3} = \dfrac{-18}{3}$ 　　　　　　Divide each side by 3.

　$y = -6$ 　　　　　　　　Solution: y is by itself.

The solution is -6. Check this in the original equation.

b. 　　$\dfrac{m}{-2} = 15$ 　　　　　Write original equation.

$-2 \cdot \dfrac{m}{-2} = -2 \cdot 15$ 　　　　Multiply each side by -2.

　　　$m = -30$ 　　　　　　Solution: m is by itself.

The solution is -30. Check this in the original equation.

Example 3 **Planning a Dance**

Your class is sponsoring a school dance. Your expenses will be $750 for a disk jockey, $75 for security, and $40 for advertisements. You will charge $6 per person.

Will your class make a profit if 125 people attend? What if 250 people attend?

Tickets for Sale

Solution

The profit is the difference between your total income (from ticket sales) and your total expenses.

Verbal Model **Profit = Ticket price · Number of people − Expenses**

Labels   Profit = P (dollars)
Ticket price = **6**   (dollars per person)
Number of people attending = n (people)
Expenses:
$750   disk jockey
$75   security
$40   advertisements
$865   **total**

Algebraic Model $P = 6 \cdot n - 865$

If 125 people attend, then the profit is

$$P = 6(125) - 865 = -115,$$

which means that your class will have a loss of $115.

If 250 people attend, then the profit is

$$P = 6(250) - 865 = 635,$$

which means that your class will have a profit of $635.

ONGOING ASSESSMENT

Write About It

Solve each equation and show your steps. For each equation, state the original operation in the equation. Then state the inverse operation used to solve the equation.

1. $-3 + m = -8$

2. $p - (-5) = 4$

3. $-3x = 21$

4. $\dfrac{y}{-5} = -100$

3.7 Exercises

Extra Practice, page 720

GUIDED PRACTICE

1. WRITING In your own words, state the four properties of equality.

In Exercises 2–5, state the property of equality that can be used to solve the equation. Then solve the equation.

2. $x - 4 = -8$ **3.** $-6 = y + 8$ **4.** $\dfrac{a}{-5} = 7$ **5.** $-5b = 35$

6. Describe a real-life situation that uses integer operations.

PRACTICE AND PROBLEM SOLVING

In Exercises 7–12, decide whether the value of the variable is a solution of the equation. If not, find the solution.

7. $x - 7 = 3; x = 10$ **8.** $t + 7 = -10; t = -17$ **9.** $9 = s + 5; s = 14$

10. $-42 = -14b; b = 3$ **11.** $\dfrac{m}{-2} = 12; m = -24$ **12.** $\dfrac{n}{-6} = -8; n = -48$

In Exercises 13–24, solve the equation. Check your solution.

13. $x + 2 = -11$ **14.** $x - 9 = 15$ **15.** $-17 = p - 13$ **16.** $q + 12 = 3$

17. $72 = -6x$ **18.** $-15t = -60$ **19.** $-5 = \dfrac{s}{-11}$ **20.** $\dfrac{c}{-6.1} = -9$

21. $\dfrac{a}{20} = -4$ **22.** $b + 5.6 = -8.4$ **23.** $y - 3.8 = 5.2$ **24.** $2 = -4z$

In Exercises 25–28, write an algebraic equation for the sentence. Then solve the equation and write your conclusion as a sentence.

25. The difference of x and 20 is -4. **26.** -10 is the sum of y and 25.

27. 51 is the product of a and -3. **28.** The quotient of t and -6 is -14.

TECHNOLOGY In Exercises 29–34, use a calculator to solve the equation. Then check the solution.

29. $-1088 = y + 129$ **30.** $m - 364 = -1980$ **31.** $-486s = 7776$

32. $-555t = -8325$ **33.** $-56 = \dfrac{p}{-23}$ **34.** $\dfrac{q}{67} = -31$

In Exercises 35–40, match the equation with its solution.

  A. 9   **B.** -13 **C.** -8 **D.** 7   **E.** -12 **F.** -16

35. $a - 4 + 9 = -8$ **36.** $t - 12 + 3 = -2$ **37.** $x + 6 - 7 = -13$

38. $-27 = 4x - 7x$ **39.** $y + 3y = -32$ **40.** $\dfrac{p}{2} = 13 - 21$

BALLOONING In Exercises 41 and 42, imagine that you are taking a hot-air balloon ride.

41. You are flying at an altitude of x ft. You descend 6891 ft to an altitude of 18,479 ft. Which of the following models can you use to determine your original altitude? Solve the correct model and use the result to determine your original altitude.

   A. $x - 6891 = 18,479$ **B.** $18,479 - x = 6891$

42. You are flying at an altitude of 19,653 ft. You descend 8905 ft, rise 9842 ft, descend 14,450 ft, and descend another 6140 ft. Write an algebraic model that represents your final altitude. What is your final altitude?

ENTERTAINMENT In Exercises 43 and 44, use the information.

Your school is sponsoring a concert. The expenses include $800 for the band, $20 for posters, $200 for refreshments, and $70 for security. The tickets cost $5 per person.

43. Use the verbal model **Profit = Income − Expenses** to write an algebraic model for the profit. Let P represent the profit and let n represent the number of tickets sold.

44. **GUESS, CHECK, AND REVISE** How many people must attend to make a profit of $250?

TOOLBOX
Problem Solving Strategies, page 744

STANDARDIZED TEST PRACTICE

45. A civic group hosted a dinner and donated the $2500 profits to charity. The expenses for hosting the dinner were $2000. If 250 people attended, how much did the civic group charge per person?

   A $2   **B** $10   **C** $15   **D** $18

46. Solve the equation $-24 + x = 12$.

   A -12 **B** 12   **C** 36   **D** 48

EXPLORATION AND EXTENSION

PORTFOLIO

47. **BUILDING YOUR PROJECT** Write an article about planning a fundraiser—such as a car wash or student dance—for a sports team at your school. Estimate your costs. Decide how much to charge for your event. How will your profits depend on the number of people who participate?

What you should learn:

Goal 1 How to plot points in a coordinate plane

Goal 2 How to use a coordinate plane to represent data graphically

Why you should learn it:

Representing data in a coordinate plane helps you discover relationships and patterns between two variables.

Exploring Patterns in the Coordinate Plane

Goal 1 PLOTTING POINTS IN A COORDINATE PLANE

A **coordinate plane** has two number lines, called **axes**, that intersect at a right angle. The axes divide the plane into four parts called **quadrants**.

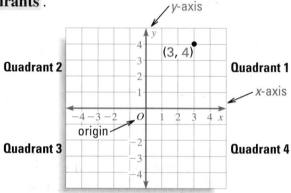

Each point in a coordinate plane can be represented by an **ordered pair** of numbers (x, y). For instance, the ordered pair $(3, 4)$ represents the point shown in the graph above.

$$(\mathbf{3}, \mathbf{4})$$

x-coordinate $\qquad$ y-coordinate

The first number is the **x-coordinate**, and the second number is the **y-coordinate**. These coordinates give the position of the point relative to the x-axis and y-axis.

Example 1 Plotting Points in a Coordinate Plane

Plot the points $A(4, 3)$, $B(4, -2)$, $C(-4, -2)$, and $D(-4, 3)$. Then find the perimeter and area of rectangle $ABCD$.

Solution

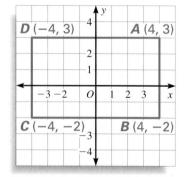

STRATEGY **DRAW A DIAGRAM** To plot the point $(4, 3)$, start at the origin. Then move 4 units to the right and 3 units up. To plot the point $(4, -2)$, start at the origin. Then move 4 units to the right and 2 units down. All four points are plotted at the left.

Rectangle $ABCD$ has a width of **8** and a height of **5**. To find the perimeter, add the lengths of the sides.

Perimeter = **5 + 8 + 5 + 8 = 26** units

To find the area, multiply the width by the height.

Area = **8 × 5 = 40** square units

An ordered pair (x, y) is a **solution** of an equation involving x and y if the equation is true when the values of x and y are substituted into the equation. Three solutions of $x + y = 4$ are shown below.

Equation	Solution	Check
$x + y = 4$	$(1, 3)$	$1 + 3 = 4$
$x + y = 4$	$(-3, 7)$	$-3 + 7 = 4$
$x + y = 4$	$(0, 4)$	$0 + 4 = 4$

Example 2 Representing Data

Make a table that shows several solutions of the equation $2 + x = y$. Then plot the corresponding points. What do you notice?

Solution

Begin by choosing an x-value, such as $x = -3$. Substitute -3 for x in the equation and simplify.

$$2 + (-3) = y$$
$$-1 = y$$

So, $(-3, -1)$ is a solution of the equation. Other solutions are shown in the table.

x	-3	-2	-1	0	1	2
y	-1	0	1	2	3	4
(x, y)	$(-3, -1)$	$(-2, 0)$	$(-1, 1)$	$(0, 2)$	$(1, 3)$	$(2, 4)$

After plotting the points in a coordinate plane, you can see that all the points lie on a line.

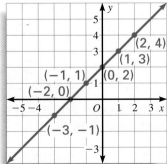

If you try finding other solution points of the equation, you will discover that they all lie on the same line.

ONGOING ASSESSMENT

Write About It

1. Make a table that shows several solutions of the equation

   $x + y = 3$.

2. Plot the corresponding points. What do you notice?

GUIDED PRACTICE

1. Explain how to draw and label a coordinate plane.

2. Explain how to decide whether an ordered pair (x, y) is a solution of an equation.

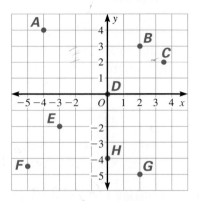

In Exercises 3–10, use the coordinate plane at the right. State the *x*- and *y*-coordinates of the point. Name the quadrant that contains the point.

3. A	**4.** B	**5.** C	**6.** D
7. E	**8.** F	**9.** G	**10.** H

PRACTICE AND PROBLEM SOLVING

In Exercises 11–16, match the ordered pair with its point in the coordinate plane. Name the quadrant that contains the point.

11. $(1, -2)$ **12.** $(-2, 1)$ **13.** $(0, -3)$

14. $\left(-\dfrac{3}{2}, -4\right)$ **15.** $(5, 0)$ **16.** $\left(\dfrac{7}{2}, 4\right)$

In Exercises 17–24, plot the points on a single coordinate plane. Name the quadrant that contains the point.

17. $A(-6, -2)$ **18.** $B(-1.5, -5)$

19. $C(3, 7)$ **20.** $D(7, 3)$

21. $E(-1, 0)$ **22.** $F(0, 4)$

23. $G(-4.25, 5)$ **24.** $H(2, -6)$

GEOMETRY **In Exercises 25 and 26, plot the points to form the vertices of a rectangle. Find the perimeter and area of rectangle *ABCD*.**

25. $A(1, 3), B(-2, 3), C(-2, -4), D(1, -4)$ **26.** $A(-4, 4), B(1, 4), C(1, -1), D(-4, -1)$

In Exercises 27–29, show that the ordered pair is a solution of the equation. Then find three other solutions.

27. $3 + x = y$; $(7, 10)$ **28.** $y - 5 = x$; $(-8, -3)$ **29.** $x + y = 6$; $(8, -2)$

LOOKING FOR A PATTERN **In Exercises 30–35, make a table that shows several solutions of the equation. Then plot the corresponding points. What do you notice?**

30. $y = 4 - x$ **31.** $-5x = y$ **32.** $2x - y = 1$

33. $\dfrac{1}{2}x + 3 = y$ **34.** $x + y = -2$ **35.** $3x - \dfrac{1}{2} = y$

REASONING In Exercises 36–39, name the quadrant that contains the point (*x, y*).

36. $x < 0$ and $x = y$

37. $x > 0$ and $y = -x$

38. $y > 0$ and $y = -x$

39. $y > 0$ and $x = y$

BUSINESS In Exercises 40–43, use the following information.

You own a clothing store. You pay $20 for a pair of jeans. The number of pairs you sell in a month depends, in part, on the price you charge customers, as shown in the demand curve at the right.

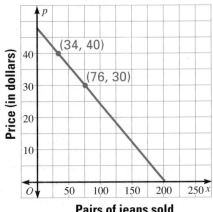

40. When the price is $30, how many pairs will you sell?

41. When the price is $40, how many pairs will you sell?

42. Your profit, if you sell *x* pairs of jeans, is given by

Profit $= px - 20x$.

What is your profit when $p = \$30$? When $p = \$40$?

43. **OPEN-ENDED PROBLEM** Can stores always make a greater profit by charging more? Explain your reasoning.

STANDARDIZED TEST PRACTICE

44. Identify point *Q* shown in the graph at the right.

(A) (4, 3)   **(B)** (4, −3)

(C) (3, 4)   **(D)** (−3, 4)

45. Which quadrant contains the point (−3, 5)?

(A) first   **(B)** second

(C) third   **(D)** fourth

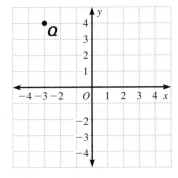

EXPLORATION AND EXTENSION

In Exercises 46 and 47, start at the given point and apply the rule to find another point. Repeat three times, each time using the new point to find another point. Plot the five points on a coordinate plane. What do you notice?

46. (0, 4); add 1 to the *x*-coordinate and subtract 1 from the *y*-coordinate.

47. (3, 1); subtract 3 from the *x*-coordinate and add 2 to the *y*-coordinate.

WHAT did you learn?

WHY did you learn it?

Skills

3.1 Plot integers on a number line. Find absolute value.

Model temperatures below zero.

3.2 Add two integers.

Find a temperature after a rise or a drop.

3.3 Add three or more integers.

Find the total yardage in a football play.

3.4 Subtract integers.

Simplify algebraic expressions with integer coefficients.

3.5 Multiply integers.

Convert between temperature scales.

3.6 Divide integers.

Calculate averages that involve positive and negative numbers.

3.7 Solve equations involving integers.

Find profit or loss.

3.8 Plot points in all quadrants.

Discover patterns in two-variable equations.

Strategies

3.1–3.8 Draw a diagram.

Plot integers on a number line to solve real-life problems.

Using Data

3.8 Use a coordinate plane.

Organize and interpret data.

HOW does it fit in the bigger picture of mathematics?

In this chapter you learned that the equation-solving techniques you studied in Chapter 2 can also be applied to equations involving integers.

Later, you will learn that the same techniques can be applied to equations with variables on both sides and to equations that contain fractions.

Rather than remembering dozens of rules for solving equations, you will learn that you only need one basic rule: *Performing the same operation to both sides of an equation produces an equivalent equation.*

Example:

Solve $m + 3 = -7$.

Solution:

$$m + 3 = -7$$

$$m + 3 - 3 = -7 - 3$$

Subtract 3 from both sides to solve.

$$m = -10$$

VOCABULARY

- integers (p. 104)
- absolute value (p. 105)
- absolute value signs (p. 105)
- opposites (p. 105)
- coefficients (p. 115)

- difference (p. 120)
- mean (p. 133)
- inverse operation (p. 138)
- coordinate plane (p. 142)
- axes (p. 142)

- quadrants (p. 142)
- ordered pair (p. 142)
- *x*-coordinate (p. 142)
- *y*-coordinate (p. 142)
- solution (p. 143)

3.1 INTEGERS AND ABSOLUTE VALUE

Example Plot the integers 4, 0, and -5.

Solution

The absolute value of a number is the distance between the number and 0. Two numbers that have the same absolute value but opposite signs are called opposites.

Examples The absolute value of $\left|-3\right|$ is 3.   The opposite of 2 is -2.

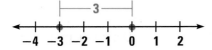

1. Draw a number line and plot the integers $2, 3, -2, -5$.

2. Find the absolute values of -8 and 5.

3. Find the opposites of 3 and -7.

Decide whether the statement is *sometimes*, *always*, or *never* true.

4. The opposite of n is negative.   **5.** The absolute value of n is $-n$.

3.2 ADDING TWO INTEGERS

To add two integers with the same sign, add their absolute values and write the common sign.

Example $6 + 7 = 13$

To add two integers with different signs, subtract the smaller absolute value from the larger absolute value and write the sign of the integer with the larger absolute value.

Example $-4 + 2 = -2$

6. Simplify $-10 + 31$.   **7.** Simplify $17 + (-16)$.

3.3 ADDING THREE OR MORE INTEGERS

You can use a number line to find the sum of three or more integers. Move to the right when adding positive numbers. Move to the left when adding negative numbers.

Example Find the sum of -3, 7, and -5.

① **Begin at -3.**
② **Move 7 units to the right.**
③ **Then move 5 units to the left.**
$-3 + 7 + (-5) = -1$

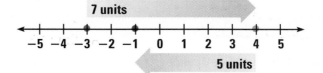

Use the following information.

You have two $250 investments. At the end of each quarter you receive a statement that shows the change in your balance.

8. Which investment earned more after 6 months?

9. Which investment earned more after 12 months?

Time (in months)	3	6	9	12
Investment 1	+$18	−$15	+$7	+$20
Investment 2	+$4	+$4	+$4	+$4

3.4 SUBTRACTING INTEGERS

To subtract integer b from integer a, add the opposite of b to a.

$$a - b = a + (-b)$$

Example $-4 - (-1) = -4 + 1$ The opposite of -1 is 1.
$$= -3$$ Add.

10. Simplify $-10 - 31$.

11. Simplify $-11 - (-12)$.

3.5 MULTIPLYING INTEGERS

When multiplying integers, use the following rules.

- The product of two positive numbers is positive.
- The product of two negative numbers is positive.
- The product of a positive number and a negative number is negative.

Example $-5 \times 8 = -40$

12. Simplify $5 \times (-9)$.

13. Simplify $-6 \times (-4)$.

3.6 DIVIDING INTEGERS

When dividing integers, use the following rules.

- The quotient of two positive numbers is positive.
- The quotient of two negative numbers is positive.
- The quotient of a positive number and a negative number is negative.

Example $14 \div (-2) = -7$

14. Simplify $-96 \div (-12)$. **15.** Simplify $-52 \div 13$.

3.7 PROBLEM SOLVING USING INTEGERS

You can use properties of equality to solve equations that contain integers.

Example

$$x + 9 = -6$$ Write original equation.
$$x + 9 - 9 = -6 - 9$$ Subtract 9 from each side.
$$x = -15$$ Solution: *x* is by itself.

Write an algebraic model for the statement. Then solve the model.

16. The difference of a number and -8 is 7. **17.** The sum of a number and -9 is -21.

18. The product of a number and 4 is -28. **19.** The quotient of a number and -15 is 3.

20. **SUBMARINES** A submarine is traveling at a depth of 1050 ft below sea level. It rises to a depth of 800 ft below sea level. Which of the following models can you use to find how many feet the submarine rose? Solve the correct model.

A. $-1050 - x = -800$ **B.** $-1050 + x = -800$ **C.** $-1050 + x = 800$

3.8 EXPLORING PATTERNS IN THE COORDINATE PLANE

Each point in a coordinate plane can be represented by an ordered pair of numbers (x, y). An ordered pair (x, y) is a solution of an equation if the equation is true when the values of x and y are substituted into it.

Example The point $(2, 5)$ is a solution of the equation $y = 3x - 1$ because $5 = 3(2) - 1$.

21. Plot the point $(-5, 1)$ and name the quadrant that contains it.

22. Is $(-3, 1)$ a solution of the equation $x - y = -2$?

23. **GEOMETRY** In a coordinate plane, plot the points $A(7, 1)$, $B(7, -5)$, $C(-1, -5)$, and $D(-1, 1)$. Find the perimeter and area of $ABCD$.

In Exercises 1 and 2, write the integer that represents the situation.

1. An altitude of 3000 ft

2. A loss of $60

In Exercises 3 and 4, write the opposite and the absolute value of the integer.

3. 120

4. -54

5. Order the integers $-4, 5, -3, 0, 2,$ and -1 from least to greatest.

6. Find the average of $-5, 3, -4, -2,$ and -7.

In Exercises 7–12, simplify.

7. $-4 + 8$

8. $-6 - (-3)$

9. $-2 \times (-5)$

10. $(-4)(-5)$

11. $\dfrac{-12}{-6}$

12. $\dfrac{36}{-9}$

In Exercises 13–15, use the graph at the right.

13. Write the coordinates of A, B, C, D, and E.

14. Which point lies in quadrant 3?

15. The points A, B, and C form three vertices of a rectangle. Write the coordinates of the fourth vertex. Find the perimeter and area of the rectangle.

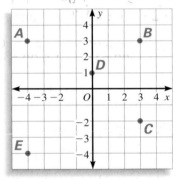

In Exercises 16–18, use mental math to solve the equation.

16. $x + 2 = -4$

17. $2x = -6$

18. $\dfrac{x}{9} = -2$

In Exercises 19 and 20, use the following information.

The low temperatures for 6 days in a row are $-7°, -3°, -6°, 3°, 0°,$ and $-2°$.

19. If the average low temperature for the week was $-2°$, what was the low temperature on the seventh day?

20. If the average low temperature for the week was $-1°$, what was the low temperature on the seventh day?

21. **BOWLING** Your bowling-league average is the sum of your scores divided by the number of games bowled. On your first night you bowled games of 128, 99, and 109. On the second night you bowled 117, 101, and 130. What was your average after the two nights?

1. Which statement is false?

   A -3 is less than -4.

   B The opposite of a positive integer is a negative integer.

   C The absolute value of a smaller negative integer is greater than the absolute value of the larger negative integer.

   D The sum of a number and its opposite is zero.

2. The temperature was $-2°F$ at 5:00 P.M. The temperature at 6:00 P.M. can be represented by the expression $-2 + (-6)$. Which statement is false?

   A The temperature fell 6°F between 5:00 P.M. and 6:00 P.M.

   B The temperature was $-8°F$ at 6:00 P.M.

   C The temperature was colder at 6:00 P.M. than at 5:00 P.M.

   D The temperature rose 6°F between 5:00 P.M. and 6:00 P.M.

3. You are watching a golf championship. After completing 15 holes, your favorite golfer had a score of -6 (6 under par). The golfer's scores for the next three holes were 2 over par, 1 under par, and 2 under par. With what score did the golfer finish?

   A -9 **B** -7

   C -3 **D** 1

4. What is the product $-5 \times 2 \times (-8)$?

   A -80 **B** -18

   C 24 **D** 80

5. Which statement is false about the expression $-14 - (-8)$?

   A The difference is a negative number.

   B The expression can be rewritten as $-14 + 8$.

   C The difference is -22.

   D A verbal phrase for the expression is "The difference of negative fourteen and negative eight."

6. Convert $-15°C$ to degrees Fahrenheit by using the following model.

   $$F = \frac{9}{5}C + 32$$

   A $-20.6°F$ **B** $-5°F$

   C $5°F$ **D** $59°F$

7. Your cousin started a small business. The profit or loss for the first four months was $-\$45$, $-\$32$, $\$70$, and $-\$25$. What is the average profit or loss for the first four months?

   A $-\$8$ **B** $-\$4.40$

   C $\$8$ **D** $\$30.50$

8. Which equation is shown below?

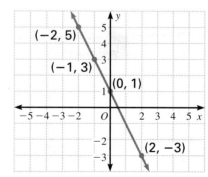

   A $y = -x + 2$ **B** $y = -2x + 1$

   C $y = x - 2$ **D** $y = \frac{1}{2}x + 1$

In Exercises 1–6, describe the pattern. Then list the next 3 numbers or letters. (1.1)

1. 20, 18, 16, 14, ?, ?, ?, . . .

2. 1, 5, 9, 13, ?, ?, ?, . . .

3. $\frac{1}{2}, \frac{3}{4}, \frac{5}{6}, \frac{7}{8}$, ?, ?, ?, . . .

4. $\frac{14}{13}, \frac{12}{11}, \frac{10}{9}, \frac{8}{7}$, ?, ?, ?, . . .

5. Z, W, T, Q, ?, ?, ?, . . .

6. A, Z, C, X, ?, ?, ?, . . .

 TECHNOLOGY In Exercises 7–15, evaluate the expression using a calculator. Round to two decimal places when necessary. (1.3, 1.4)

7. 4^8

8. $\left(\frac{3}{4}\right)^5$

9. $\sqrt{48}$

10. $\sqrt{352}$

11. $(3.8)^7$

12. $\sqrt{26.19}$

13. $150 - 60 \div 3 \cdot 4$

14. $35 \div (19 - 12) + 4^5$

15. $3^3 + (14 + 8) \cdot 12 - 11$

In Exercises 16–24, evaluate the expression. (1.4, 3.1–3.6)

16. $|-3| - |5|$

17. $-|-4| + |-3|$

18. $-5 + 12 - 9 - 13$

19. $21 - 32 - 1 + 4$

20. $(10)(-11)$

21. $\frac{-144}{-2}$

22. $(-4)(6)$

23. $2^2 + (3 - 4)^2 \cdot 9$

24. $20 - (5 - 8)^3 \div 9$

GEOMETRY In Exercises 25–28, decide whether the figure is a polygon. If it is, name it. If it is not, explain. (1.7)

25.

26.

27.

28.

In Exercises 29–40, write the expression without parentheses and combine like terms when possible. Then evaluate it when $x = 3$, $y = 4$, and $z = 6$. (1.5, 2.1, 2.2, 3.1–3.5)

29. $3(x + y + 3)$

30. $4(x + y + z + 3)$

31. $2(z + 3y)$

32. $5(z - 2x)$

33. $7x + x + z + y$

34. $9y - 2y - z - 2$

35. $4z + 6z - 9y - 25$

36. $-16 + 5x - 3x + y$

37. $6(5x - 3x + x)$

38. $3(2y + y) + 16$

39. $z(y + 2) + |-y|$

40. $|-z| + 3(y - 1)$

In Exercises 41–44, draw a number line and plot the integer. (3.1)

41. -3

42. 5

43. -4

44. 0

BICYCLING **In Exercises 45 and 46, use the following information. (1.5)**

You and a friend are riding bicycles a distance of 20 mi. You finish the ride in 80 min and your friend finishes in 85 min.

45. How fast did you travel in miles per hour?

46. How fast did your friend travel in miles per hour?

In Exercises 47–50, plot the points on one coordinate plane. (3.8)

47. $A(2, -3)$

48. $B(-1, 0)$

49. $C(-4, -5)$

50. $D(2, 4)$

In Exercises 51–66, solve the equation or inequality. (2.3–2.5, 2.9, 3.7)

51. $x + 7 = 16$

52. $y + 5 = -6$

53. $z - 8 = -16$

54. $a - 8 = 13$

55. $10b = 100$

56. $-9x = 36$

57. $\dfrac{y}{-12} = 8$

58. $\dfrac{m}{4} = 16$

59. $n + 6 < 7$

60. $p + 4 > 12$

61. $x - 2 \geq 5$

62. $y - 11 \leq 9$

63. $15c > 30$

64. $26 > 13t$

65. $\dfrac{q}{3} \leq 25$

66. $40 \leq \dfrac{s}{9}$

In Exercises 67–70, write an algebraic equation or inequality for the sentence. Then solve the equation or inequality. (2.7, 2.9, 3.7)

67. -12 is the sum of a number and 9.

68. The difference of a number and 16 is less than or equal to 20.

69. The product of 7 and a number is greater than 91.

70. Three is the quotient of a number and 4.

GEOMETRY **In Exercises 71 and 72, write the coordinates of the vertices of each figure. Then find the perimeter of each figure, and find the area of the entire shaded region. (1.4, 3.8)**

71.

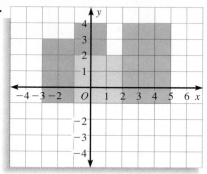

72.

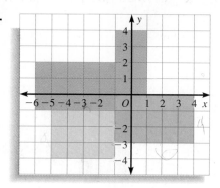

TECHNOLOGY

- **Interactive Real-Life Investigations**
- **Middle School Tutorial Software**

To find out more about ways to save energy, go to:

http://www.mlmath.com

ENERGY SOURCES Almost half of the energy used in the world comes from oil.

SAVING ENERGY Caulking windows is one way to save energy.

CHAPTER THEME
Energy Conservation

PORTFOLIO

CHAPTER PROJECT

Home Energy Savings

PROJECT DESCRIPTION

There are many ways that you can conserve energy. For example, if every household in the United States lowered its temperature in the winter by 6°F for just one day, we would save more than 570,000 barrels of oil. Make a plan for what you can do to conserve energy and save money on utilities at the same time.

GETTING STARTED

Talking It Over

- What forms of energy, such as gas, electricity, and propane, do you use every day? Do bills for these come every month, or do you pay for them as you use them?

- What things do you do that use electricity? How can you use less electricity every day?

Planning Your Project

- **Materials:** paper, pencils or pens, glue or tape

- Find out which utility companies send bills to your house every month. Try to get a sample bill from a summer month and one from a winter month.

- Make a booklet out of several pieces of paper. Write your name and a title on the cover.

BUILDING YOUR PROJECT

These are places throughout the chapter where you will work on your project.

4.1 Make a goal for saving electricity. *p. 161*

4.3 Find how much insulation you need. *p. 171*

4.5 Calculate what kind of light bulb is most economical. *p. 181*

4.6 Compare heating costs. *p. 186*

4.8 Find the cost of sealing windows. *p. 195*

LAB 4.1

COOPERATIVE LEARNING

Solving Two-Step Equations

Materials Needed
- algebra tiles
- pencil or pen
- paper

In this investigation, you will use algebra tiles to model and solve two-step equations.

Part A USING ALGEBRA TILES

Here is an example of how you can use algebra tiles to solve the equation $2x + 1 = 5$. The goal is to get one x tile by itself on one side of the equation.

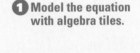

1 Model the equation with algebra tiles.

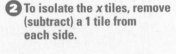

2 To isolate the x tiles, remove (subtract) a 1 tile from each side.

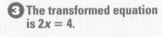

3 The transformed equation is $2x = 4$.

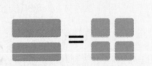

4 To isolate one x tile, divide each side into 2 groups and discard one group from each side.

5 The solution is $x = 2$.

1. Do the algebra tiles show a solution?

a. 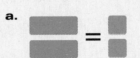 b. 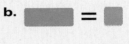 c.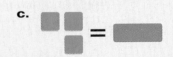

2. When you use algebra tiles to model and solve an equation, how do you know when you have found the solution?

In Exercises 3–5, use algebra tiles to solve the equation. Draw a sketch of your steps.

3. $2x + 5 = 9$ **4.** $3m + 4 = 13$ **5.** $13 = 5 + 4y$

In Part A, algebra tiles were used to solve $2x + 1 = 5$. You can write the solution steps in algebraic form.

$2x + 1 = 5$	**1** Write original equation.
$2x + 1 - 1 = 5 - 1$	**2** Subtract 1 from each side.
$2x = 4$	**3** Simplify.
$\dfrac{2x}{2} = \dfrac{4}{2}$	**4** Divide each side by 2.
$x = 2$	**5** Solution: x is by itself.

6. Translate the model below into algebra. Include a description of each step.

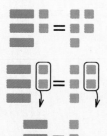

NOW TRY THESE

In Exercises 7–10, use algebra tiles to model and solve the equation. Draw a sketch of your solution. Then translate your sketch into algebra.

7. $3x + 2 = 14$

8. $15 = 2n + 1$

9. $11 = 3 + 4y$

10. $6m + 3 = 15$

11. Explain what is wrong with the solution shown below. Draw a correct algebra tile solution of the equation. How do you know that your solution is correct?

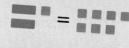
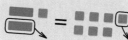
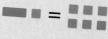
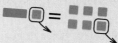

Solving Two-Step Equations

What you should learn:

Goal ❶ How to use two operations to solve a two-step equation

Goal ❷ How to solve real-life problems using two-step equations

Why you should learn it:

You need to use two or more operations to solve most equations from real-life situations, such as finding how many hours you can play tennis at a club.

Goal ❶ USING TWO OPERATIONS

Solving an equation often requires two or more operations. Here are some guidelines that can help you decide how to start.

1. Simplify both sides of the equation (if needed).

2. Use inverse operations to isolate the variable.

Example 1 **Solving an Equation**

Solve $3x + 8 = 2$.

Solution

Remember that your goal is to isolate the variable.

$3x + 8 = 2$	Write original equation.
$3x + 8 - 8 = 2 - 8$	To isolate the x-term, subtract 8 from each side.
$3x = -6$	Simplify.
$\dfrac{3x}{3} = \dfrac{-6}{3}$	To isolate x, divide each side by 3.
$x = -2$	Solution: x is by itself.

The solution is -2.

✔**Check:** Substitute to see that $3(-2) + 8 = -6 + 8 = 2$.

Example 2 **Solving an Equation**

Solve $\dfrac{x}{-4} - 8 = 1$.

Solution

$\dfrac{x}{-4} - 8 = 1$	Write original equation.
$\dfrac{x}{-4} - 8 + 8 = 1 + 8$	Add 8 to each side.
$\dfrac{x}{-4} = 9$	Simplify.
$-4 \cdot \dfrac{x}{-4} = -4 \cdot 9$	Multiply each side by -4.
$x = -36$	Solution: x is by itself.

The solution is -36. Check this in the original equation.

Example 3 > Using a Verbal Model

You are joining a community tennis club. The annual membership fee is $50, and a tennis court rents for $10 per hour. You plan to spend no more than $190 playing tennis during the year. How many hours can you play?

REAL LIFE
Monthly Dues

Solution

You can use a verbal model and algebra to solve the problem.

| **Verbal Model** | $\dfrac{\text{Total}}{\text{spent}} = \dfrac{\text{Annual}}{\text{fee}} + \dfrac{\text{Hourly}}{\text{rate}} \cdot \dfrac{\text{Hours of}}{\text{tennis}}$ |

Labels

$$\text{Total spent} = 190 \qquad\qquad \text{(dollars)}$$
$$\text{Annual fee} = 50 \qquad\qquad \text{(dollars)}$$
$$\text{Hourly rate} = 10 \qquad\qquad \text{(dollars per hour)}$$
$$\text{Number of hours played} = n \qquad\qquad \text{(hours)}$$

Algebraic Model

$$190 = 50 + 10 \cdot n$$
$$190 - 50 = 50 + 10n - 50$$
$$140 = 10n$$
$$\frac{140}{10} = \frac{10n}{10}$$
$$14 = n$$

You can play 14 h of tennis.

✔**Check:** When you check the result, don't just check the numbers. You also need to check the units of measure.

Verbal Model $\quad \dfrac{\text{Total}}{\text{spent}} = \dfrac{\text{Annual}}{\text{fee}} + \dfrac{\text{Hourly}}{\text{rate}} \cdot \dfrac{\text{Hours of}}{\text{tennis}}$

$$\text{Total spent} = 50 \text{ dollars} + \frac{10 \text{ dollars}}{\text{hour}} \cdot 14 \text{ hours}$$
$$= 50 \text{ dollars} + 140 \text{ dollars}$$
$$= 190 \text{ dollars}$$

ONGOING ASSESSMENT

Write About It
. . . .

Solve each equation. Show your steps. Explain how inverse operations help you decide what the next step should be.

1. $5x - 4 = 6$

2. $\dfrac{n}{3} + 7 = 9$

3. $13 = 3m + 7$

GUIDED PRACTICE

In Exercises 1–3, describe the first step you would use to solve the equation.

1. $3x - 4 = 2$

2. $5x + 3 = 15$

3. $-2 = 2 - 4x$

4. ERROR ANALYSIS Describe the error.

$$3x - 8 = 12$$
$$\frac{3x}{3} - 8 = \frac{12}{3}$$
$$x - 8 = 4$$
$$x = 12$$

In Exercises 5–8, match the equation with an equivalent equation.

A. $2x = -8$ **B.** $2x = 8$ **C.** $2x = -24$ **D.** $2x = 24$

5. $2x + 8 = 16$ **6.** $2x - 8 = 16$ **7.** $2x - 8 = -16$ **8.** $2x + 8 = -16$

PRACTICE AND PROBLEM SOLVING

In Exercises 9–17, solve the equation. Then check your solution.

9. $3x + 15 = 24$

10. $4x + 11 = 31$

11. $2 = 8 + 6p$

12. $4 = 14 + 5q$

13. $-2r - 4 = 22$

14. $-3s - 5 = -20$

15. $\frac{t}{2} + 6 = 10$

16. $21 = 17 + \frac{z}{3}$

17. $\frac{x}{4} - 2 = -7$

18. MODELING Sketch an algebra tile solution for the equation $3x + 4 = 7$. Use the example on page 156.

In Exercises 19–24, write the sentence as an equation. Then solve it.

19. Three times a number, plus 7, is 34.

20. Eight times a number, plus 12, is 100.

21. One fourth of a number, minus 2, is 5.

22. Half of a number, plus 13, is 30.

23. The sum of 21 and $7x$ is -14.

24. The sum of 84 and $\frac{x}{2}$ is -36.

GEOMETRY In Exercises 25 and 26, the upper line segment has the same length as the lower double line segment. Write the implied equation and solve for x.

25.

26.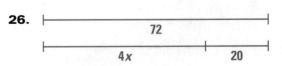

27. OPEN-ENDED PROBLEM Describe a real-life situation that can be modeled by the equation $5x - 7 = 120$.

28. PHONE RATES You are at a phone booth and need to make a long-distance call home. The call will cost 25¢ for the first minute and 15¢ for each additional minute or fraction of a minute. You have 95¢ in your pocket. How many minutes can you talk?

   a. Write a verbal model of the problem. Assign labels to each part and write an algebraic model.

   b. Answer the question. Then check your solution.

29. CAR REPAIR You are the service manager at an auto repair shop. You charge $22 per hour for labor plus the cost of any parts. A car needed $256 of new parts and the final bill for the car was $421. How long did it take to repair the car?

STANDARDIZED TEST PRACTICE

30. What is the first step to solve the equation $\frac{x}{4} - 7 = 33$?

   A Add 7.   **B** Subtract 7. **C** Multiply by 4.   **D** Subtract 33.

31. At the fair, you spend $6 for some food, then use the rest of the $20 you brought for ride tickets. You buy 56 ride tickets. How much does each of the ride tickets cost?

   A $0.48   **B** $0.35   **C** $0.25   **D** $0.20

EXPLORATION AND EXTENSION

PORTFOLIO

BUILDING YOUR PROJECT **For Exercises 32–35, use the following information.**

Most electric companies charge a basic customer service charge in addition to a rate per kilowatt hour (kW · h) of electricity that you use. Use an electric bill from home or use the bill shown.

32. What is the basic service charge? What is the rate per kilowatt hour?

33. Write a verbal model, assign labels, and write an equation that you can use to calculate the total bill if x kW · h of electricity are used.

34. If you use 490 kW · h, what will your total bill be?

35. If you do not want to pay more than $40.00 for electricity, how many kilowatt hours of electricity can you use?

Meter Number	Amount Now Due
894763	$43.51

ELECTRICITY USED THIS PERIOD

Previous Meter Reading	4310
Present Meter Reading	4799
-----	
kW·h Consumed This Period	489

COST OF ELECTRICITY

Basic Service Charge	$5.00
Energy Charge	
489 kW·h × $.078760/kW·h	$38.51

Total Charges	$43.51

Solving Multi-Step Equations

What you should learn:

Goal 1 How to use more than two operations to solve an equation

Goal 2 How to solve real-life problems using multi-step equations

Why you should learn it:

You can use multi-step equations to calculate how much you must sell to make a profit.

Goal 1 SOLVING MULTI-STEP EQUATIONS

Before using inverse operations to solve an equation, you should check to see whether one or both sides of the equation can be simplified by combining like terms.

Example 1 Simplifying First

Solve the equation $2x + 3x - 4 = 11$.

Solution

$2x + 3x - 4 = 11$	Write original equation.
$5x - 4 = 11$	Combine like terms: $2x + 3x = 5x$.
$5x - 4 + 4 = 11 + 4$	Add 4 to each side.
$5x = 15$	Simplify.
$\dfrac{5x}{5} = \dfrac{15}{5}$	Divide each side by 5.
$x = 3$	Solution: x is by itself.

The solution is 3.

✔**Check:** Substitute to see that $2(3) + 3(3) - 4 = 6 + 9 - 4 = 11$.

As you become more of an expert in solving equations, you may want to perform some of the solution steps mentally. If you do this, don't forget to check your solution.

STUDY TIP

When some people use the "expert" solver format, they say they are skipping steps. That, however, isn't really what is happening. They aren't skipping steps—they are simply doing some of the steps mentally. For instance, in Example 2, which steps were performed mentally?

Example 2 "Expert" Equation Solver Format

Solve the equation $-13 = 3n + 3 + n$.

Solution

$-13 = 3n + 3 + n$	Write original equation.
$-13 = 4n + 3$	Combine like terms.
$-16 = 4n$	Subtract 3 from each side.
$-4 = n$	Divide each side by 4.

The solution is -4.

✔**Check:** $3(-4) + 3 + (-4) = -12 + 3 + (-4) = -13$

Example 3 Modeling a Real-Life Problem

Your Spanish club is making posters to raise money. The printer charges a base fee of $270, plus $2 per poster for supplies. You sell each poster for $5. How many posters must you sell to make a $300 profit?

REAL LIFE
Poster Sales

Solution

Verbal Model	Profit = Income − Expenses	
	Profit = 5 · Number of posters − (Base fee + Supplies)	

Labels	Profit = 300	(dollars)
	Number of posters = n	(posters)
	Base fee = 270	(dollars)
	Supplies = 2 · Number of posters	(dollars)

Algebraic Model	$300 = 5n − (270 + 2n)$	Write equation.
	$300 = 5n − 270 − 2n$	Use the Distributive Property.
	$300 = 3n − 270$	Simplify.
	$570 = 3n$	Add 270 to each side.
	$190 = n$	Divide each side by 3.

You need to sell 190 posters to make a profit of $300.

....

Be sure you see how the Distributive Property is used in Example 3. Notice that it makes sense to subtract both expenses from the income.

$$\text{Income} - \text{Expenses} = \text{Income} - \frac{\text{Base}}{\text{fee}} - \frac{\text{Fee for}}{\text{Supplies}}$$

$$5n - (270 + 2n) = 5n - 270 - 2n$$

Example 4 Distributing a Negative

$$2 - (3x - 4) = 2 - 1(3x - 4)$$
$$= 2 - 1(3x) - 1(-4)$$
$$= 2 - 3x + 4$$
$$= 6 - 3x$$

It can help to rewrite − as −1.

ONGOING ASSESSMENT

Talk About It
••••••••••••••••••••

With your partner, discuss how to use the Distributive Property to simplify each expression. How can you check your answer?

1. $3m - (2m + 4)$

2. $6n - (5n - 2)$

GUIDED PRACTICE

LOGICAL REASONING In Exercises 1–3, explain each step of the solution.

1. $3x - x + 8 = -16$

$2x + 8 = -16$

$2x = -24$

$x = -12$

2. $4x + 7 - 5x = 9$

$-x + 7 = 9$

$-x = 2$

$(-1)x = 2$

$x = -2$

3. $-5 = -5x - 3x + 11$

$-5 = -8x + 11$

$-16 = -8x$

$2 = x$

PRACTICE AND PROBLEM SOLVING

In Exercises 4–6, decide whether the given value is a solution of the equation. If not, find the solution.

4. $4x - x - 5 = -8; x = 1$ **5.** $4t - 2t - 8 = 1; t = 3$ **6.** $2 = 3a - 8a + 17; a = 3$

In Exercises 7–21, solve the equation. Check your solution.

7. $2a + 3a = 15$

8. $s + 5s - 3s = 21$

9. $22 = 12t + 4t - 5t$

10. $8x + 2x - 4 = 6$

11. $6y - 3y + 2 = -16$

12. $42 = 8a - 2a + 12$

13. $6m - 2m - 6 = -60$

14. $5x - 3x + 12 = 8$

15. $n - 3n + 8 = -8$

16. $2y - 7y - 4y = 81$

17. $\frac{5}{2}x - \frac{1}{2}x - 3 = 5$

18. $\frac{3}{2}x - \frac{1}{2}x - 2 = 4$

19. $5 + 3(x + 1) = 5$

20. $4 - (x + 1) = 8$

$4 - x - 1$

21. $3p - (6p + 24) = 0$

In Exercises 22 and 23, write an equation that represents the sentence. Solve the equation.

22. The sum of $3x$ and $2x$ and $7x$ and 6 is 42.

23. Five subtracted from the difference of $4y$ and y is -29.

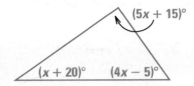

GEOMETRY In Exercises 24 and 25, use the given information to write an equation. Then solve the equation.

24. The two angles shown below are *complementary*. This means that the sum of their measures is 90°.

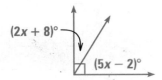

25. The sum of the measures of the angles of a triangle is 180°.

26. **PRINTING COSTS** In Example 3 on page 163, suppose the printer raises the price to $275 plus $3 per poster. How many posters do you need to sell to make a profit of $300?

27. **BUSINESS** You start a business selling bottled fruit juices. You invest $10,000 for equipment. Each bottle costs you $0.30 to make. You sell each bottle for $0.75. How many bottles must you sell to earn a profit of $2000?

28. **SUMMER JOB** You have a job mowing lawns for x dollars per lawn. The table shows the number of lawns you mowed each day during a week. That week, you earned $252. How much are you paid per lawn?

M	T	W	Th	F	S
1	2	2	1	3	5

Real Life... Real People

Tom Scott and Tom First began a fruit juice business called Nantucket Nectars. In 1996, the business sold $30 million worth of fruit juices. (Source: Nantucket Nectars)

STANDARDIZED TEST PRACTICE

29. On a class trip, Nancy Kim brings $50 to pay for museum admission. She buys an adult ticket for $3.50 and 13 student tickets. Three students arrive late so she buys 3 more student tickets. She has $18.50 left. Which equation can you use to find the cost of a student ticket?

(A) $13x + 3x = 50 - 18.50$ (B) $13x + 3.50 + 3x = 50$

(C) $50 - 13x - 3x - 3.50 = 18.50$ (D) $3x = 3.50 + 13x$

30. You are buying carpet to cover a 15 yd^2 room, a 6 yd^2 staircase, and a 30 yd^2 room. The clerk tells you that your total is $1147.50. How much did the carpet cost per square yard?

(A) $42.50   (B) $22.50   (C) $12.50   (D) $2.50

EXPLORATION AND EXTENSION

COORDINATE GEOMETRY In Exercises 31–34, complete the table showing several solutions of the equation. Write the solutions as ordered pairs. Then plot the ordered pairs in a coordinate plane. Describe the pattern. (For a sample, look at Lesson 3.8.)

x	y
−2	?
−1	?
0	?
1	?
2	?

31. $x + y = 7$

32. $2x - y = 5$

33. $-2x + y = 1$

34. $x + y = 0$

In Exercises 1–3, evaluate the expression when $a = 4$ and $b = 5$. **(3.4)**

1. $6b - 3$ **2.** $a - 2b$ **3.** $a^2 - 2b - 3$

4. Describe the steps used to solve the equation $4x - 2 = 12$. **(4.2)**

5. Plot the points $(3, 2)$ and $(-2, 4)$ in a coordinate plane. **(3.8)**

In Exercises 6–8, write the expression without parentheses. **(2.1)**

6. $4(3 + 2y)$ **7.** $4(2x - 3)$ **8.** $0.25(4m + 8)$

In Exercises 9–14, solve the equation. **(4.1, 4.2)**

9. $2y - 14 = 0$ **10.** $16a + 14 = 110$ **11.** $2.06r + 1.14r = 8.32$

12. $\frac{5}{2}x - \frac{1}{2}x = -1$ **13.** $\frac{m}{3} + 1 = 7$ **14.** $2c + 4c - c = 10$

15. **POSTAGE** You are sending invitations to friends for a party. You spend \$2.56 on stamps to mail the invitations. Each stamp costs \$.32. How many invitations are you sending? **(2.5)**

CAREER Interview

Michael A. Coca, a solar consultant and construction contractor, teaches others how to improve their homes with solar energy. He owns his own company, San Miguel Sun Dwellings.

Q What types of math do you use on your job?
In order to determine the best way to improve the heating system of a house or business, heat-load analysis must be performed. This requires estimating how many square feet of different materials will be needed and drawing a two-dimensional scaled model of the construction.

Q What led you to this career?
It was exciting to be at the beginning of a new technology. I wanted to use what I learned to help people with the basic necessities of life, particularly shelter.

Q What would you like to tell kids who are still in school?
Education is not just about learning math, English, science, and social studies. It is about learning how to live. Many of you have a vision of how you want to live when you grow up—you want to own a home, have a family, own a car, etc. In order to make that vision a reality, you must learn what it takes to get there.

Rounding Error

When you check a solution that has been rounded, the solution will make the original equation *approximately* true.

....

Example

Solve the equation $34x - 5 - 23x = 15$. Check your solution.

CALCULATOR TIP

Notice that when you use a scientific calculator to check the solution, you can skip a step. This is because scientific calculators automatically follow the order of operations.

Solution

$34x - 5 - 23x = 15$	Write original equation.
$11x - 5 = 15$	Combine like terms.
$11x - 5 + 5 = 15 + 5$	Add 5 to each side.
$11x = 20$	Simplify.
$\dfrac{11x}{11} = \dfrac{20}{11}$	Divide each side by 11.
$x \approx 1.82$	Round to 2 decimal places.

The solution is about 1.82.

✔**Check:** Check the solution in the original equation.

$34x - 5 - 23x = 15$	Write original equation.
$34(1.82) - 5 - 23(1.82) \overset{?}{=} 15$	Substitute 1.82 for x.
$61.88 - 5 - 41.86 \overset{?}{=} 15$	Use a calculator.
$15.02 \approx 15$	Approximate check

✔**Check:** You can also perform the check on a scientific calculator using the following keystrokes.

Calculator Keystrokes   **Display**

34 $\boxed{\times}$ 1.82 $\boxed{-}$ 5 $\boxed{-}$ 23 $\boxed{\times}$ 1.82 $\boxed{=}$ $\boxed{15.02}$

Exercises

In Exercises 1–9, solve the equation. Round your solution to two decimal places. Check your rounded solution in the original equation. Does it check exactly? If not, why?

1. $2x + 5x - 7 = 9$ **2.** $3y - 7 + 4y = 10$ **3.** $2n + 7n - 13 = -4$

4. $-5a + 17 + 2a = 8$ **5.** $12 = -2x + 5x - 9$ **6.** $-13 = 4y + 8y + 9$

7. $-4n - 14 - 5n = 11$ **8.** $5m + 8m - 14 = 23$ **9.** $5b - 21 - 2b = 10$

4.3

Two-Step Equations and Problem Solving

What you should learn:

Goal 1 How to solve an equation by multiplying by a reciprocal

Goal 2 How to use two-step equations to model real-life problems

Why you should learn it:

You can use two-step equations to solve real-life problems, such as finding how many plants you can buy for your garden.

Goal 1 USING RECIPROCALS

Often, there is more than one way to solve a problem. For instance, Example 1 shows two ways to solve $3x - 4 = 11$. In the second method, notice that $\frac{1}{3}$ is the *reciprocal* of 3.

Example 1 Using Two Methods

Method 1 Divide each side by the same number.

$$3x - 4 = 11 \qquad \text{Write original equation.}$$
$$3x = 15 \qquad \text{Add 4 to each side.}$$
$$\frac{3x}{3} = \frac{15}{3} \qquad \text{Divide each side by 3.}$$
$$x = 5 \qquad \text{Solution: } x \text{ is by itself.}$$

Method 2 Multiply each side by a reciprocal.

$$3x - 4 = 11 \qquad \text{Write original equation.}$$
$$3x = 15 \qquad \text{Add 4 to each side.}$$
$$\frac{1}{3} \cdot 3x = \frac{1}{3} \cdot 15 \qquad \text{Multiply each side by } \frac{1}{3}.$$
$$x = 5 \qquad \text{Solution: } x \text{ is by itself.}$$

The solution is 5. Check this in the original equation.

Example 2 Multiplying by a Reciprocal

a.
$$\frac{1}{3}x = 12 \qquad \text{Write original equation.}$$
$$3 \cdot \frac{1}{3}x = 3 \cdot 12 \qquad \text{Multiply each side by 3.}$$
$$x = 36 \qquad \text{Solution: } x \text{ is by itself.}$$

b.
$$-\frac{1}{4}t + 2 = 6 \qquad \text{Write original equation.}$$
$$-\frac{1}{4}t + 2 - 2 = 6 - 2 \qquad \text{Subtract 2 from each side.}$$
$$-\frac{1}{4}t = 4 \qquad \text{Simplify.}$$
$$-4 \cdot \left(-\frac{1}{4}t\right) = -4 \cdot 4 \qquad \text{Multiply each side by } -4.$$
$$t = -16 \qquad \text{Solution: } t \text{ is by itself.}$$

Check the solutions in the original equations.

NEED TO KNOW

When you multiply a number by its reciprocal, you obtain 1. Here are some examples.

$$5 \cdot \frac{1}{5} = 1$$

$$\left(-\frac{1}{3}\right) \cdot (-3) = 1$$

$$(-2) \cdot \left(-\frac{1}{2}\right) = 1$$

$$\frac{1}{4} \cdot 4 = 1$$

Example 3 Modeling a Real-Life Problem

You are planning to plant a small kitchen garden to grow tomatoes, peppers, and squash. Your supplies (tools and fertilizer) cost $16. Each plant costs $.60. You have $35 to spend on the garden. How many plants can you get? (The prices include sales tax.)

REAL LIFE
Gardening

Solution

You can use a verbal model and algebra to solve the problem.

Verbal Model	$\text{Total cost} = \text{Cost of supplies} + \text{Cost per plant} \times \text{Number of plants}$

Labels
Total cost $= \mathbf{35}$ (dollars)
Cost of supplies $= \mathbf{16}$ (dollars)
Cost per plant $= \mathbf{0.6}$ (dollars per plant)
Number of plants $= n$ (plants)

Algebraic Model

$$35 = 16 + 0.6n \qquad \text{Write equation.}$$
$$35 - 16 = 16 - 16 + 0.6n \qquad \text{Subtract 16 from each side.}$$
$$19 = 0.6n \qquad \text{Simplify.}$$
$$\frac{19}{0.6} = \frac{0.6n}{0.6} \qquad \text{Divide each side by 0.6.}$$
$$31.67 \approx n \qquad \text{Solution: } n \text{ is by itself.}$$

You have enough money to buy 31 plants.

....

You can solve Example 3 *without* using algebra. To do that, you can reason that after paying for the supplies, you have $19 left.

$35 - 16 = \$19$ **Money to spend on plants**

To find the number of plants, divide this amount by the cost per plant, or $.60.

$\dfrac{19}{0.6} \approx 31.67$ **Number of plants**

So why should you use algebra to solve this problem? The answer is that many real-life problems are complicated and need algebra. Practicing algebra with simpler problems will help you to develop the skills needed to solve complicated problems.

ONGOING ASSESSMENT

Talk About It
....

1. The problem in Example 3 is solved twice on this page, once with algebra and once without algebra. Discuss the similarities between the two solutions.

4.3 Exercises   Extra Practice, page 721

Extra Practice, page 721

GUIDED PRACTICE

In Exercises 1–4, find the reciprocal of the number, if possible.

1. $\dfrac{1}{3}$ **2.** $-\dfrac{1}{4}$ **3.** -5 **4.** 0

In Exercises 5 and 6, complete the solution.

5.
$$7x = -28$$
$$\boxed{?} \cdot 7x = \boxed{?} \cdot (-28)$$
$$x = \boxed{?}$$

6.
$$-\dfrac{1}{4}x = 12$$
$$\boxed{?} \cdot \left(-\dfrac{1}{4}x\right) = \boxed{?} \cdot 12$$
$$x = \boxed{?}$$

GEOMETRY **In Exercises 7 and 8, use the figure at the right. The white region has an area of 24 square units. The green region has an area of 36 square units.**

7. Find the length, x, of the rectangle.

8. Describe another method for finding x.

[figure: rectangle with white inner region, height 6, base labeled x]

PRACTICE AND PROBLEM SOLVING

In Exercises 9–12, describe two different ways to solve the equation.

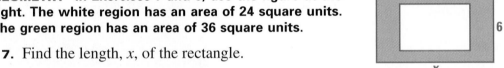

9. $\dfrac{1}{3}x = -15$ **10.** $-2x = 14$ **11.** $27 = 9n$ **12.** $-48 = -\dfrac{1}{4}y$

In Exercises 13–27, solve the equation.

13. $2y - 12 = 4$ **14.** $5n - 21 = 24$ **15.** $-\dfrac{1}{8}x + 14 = 6$

16. $-12t - 7 = -15$ **17.** $21z - 16 = 12$ **18.** $5r + 15 = 10$

19. $-\dfrac{1}{10}m - 11 = 1$ **20.** $\dfrac{1}{5}x - 3 = -2$ **21.** $-\dfrac{1}{3}y + 27 = 39$

22. $-\dfrac{1}{7}b + 2 = 1$ **23.** $\dfrac{1}{5}p - 3 = 0$ **24.** $\dfrac{2}{3}x - \dfrac{1}{3}x = 12$

25. $-11t + 16 = -6$ **26.** $0.2x + 7 = 27$ **27.** $1.25t + 2 = 6$

28. **DRAWING A DIAGRAM** A triangle has a perimeter of 30 cm. The shortest side is x cm long and the longest side is 8 cm longer than the shortest side. The third side is 1 cm shorter than the longest side.

a. Make a sketch of the triangle. Use variable expressions to label the side lengths.

b. Find the lengths of the triangle's sides.

29. POPULATION In 1996, the estimated population of Nebraska was about 169,000 less than 3 times the estimated population of Alaska. The total population of the two states was about 2,259,000. Find the estimated 1996 population of each state. (Source: U.S. Bureau of the Census)

Verbal Model

$$\text{Total Population} = \text{Population of Nebraska} + \text{Population of Alaska}$$

Labels

Population of Alaska $= A$

Population of Nebraska $\approx 3A - 169{,}000$

30. POPULATION In 1996, the estimated population of Utah was about 363,000 more than half the estimated population of Connecticut. The total population of the two states was about 5,274,000. Find the 1996 estimated population of each state. (Source: U.S. Bureau of the Census)

Real Life...
Real Facts

Alaska ranks 48th in population, but it ranks first in area. Its area is about one fifth that of the area of the lower 48 states.

STANDARDIZED TEST PRACTICE

31. Dario is twice as old as his younger brother and 6 years younger than his sister. The total of the three ages equals the age of Dario's uncle. Dario's uncle is 31. Which equation can you use to find Dario's age?

(A) $2x + x + 6 = 31$

(B) $31 + 6 = 2x + x$

(C) $\dfrac{x}{2} + 2x + 6 = 31$

(D) $31 + x = 6 + \dfrac{x}{2}$

PORTFOLIO

EXPLORATION AND EXTENSION

32. BUILDING YOUR PROJECT You can save on heating and cooling costs by using insulation. A material's ability to insulate is called its *R-value*. The R-value depends on the thickness. For example, for fiberglass, the R-value increases by about 2.2 for each additional inch of thickness.

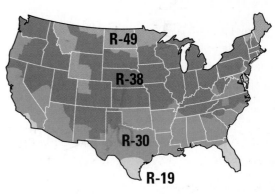

a. Check the map to see what R-value is recommended where you live.

b. Suppose your current insulation has an R-value of 12. How many inches of fiberglass should you add to your insulation?

4.4

Solving Equations: The Distributive Property

What you should learn:

Goal 1 How to use the Distributive Property to solve equations

Goal 2 How to use the Distributive Property to model and solve real-life problems

Why you should learn it:

You can use the Distributive Property in real-life situations, such as earning a sales bonus.

Goal 1 USING THE DISTRIBUTIVE PROPERTY

In Lesson 4.1, you studied guidelines for solving equations. The first guideline often uses the Distributive Property.

1. Simplify both sides of the equation (if needed).

2. Use inverse operations to isolate the variable.

Example 1 Simplifying First

Solve $5y + 2(y - 3) = 92$.

Solution

$5y + 2(y - 3) = 92$	Write original equation.
$5y + 2y - 6 = 92$	Use the Distributive Property.
$7y - 6 = 92$	Combine like terms.
$7y - 6 + 6 = 92 + 6$	Add 6 to each side.
$7y = 98$	Simplify.
$\dfrac{7y}{7} = \dfrac{98}{7}$	Divide each side by 7.
$y = 14$	Solution: y is by itself.

The solution is 14. Check this in the original equation.

Example 2 Using the Distributive Property

Solve $24 = \dfrac{1}{4}(x - 8)$.

Solution

$24 = \dfrac{1}{4}(x - 8)$	Write original equation.
$24 = \dfrac{1}{4}x - \dfrac{1}{4}(8)$	Use the Distributive Property.
$24 = \dfrac{1}{4}x - 2$	Simplify.
$26 = \dfrac{1}{4}x$	Add 2 to each side.
$104 = x$	Multiply each side by 4.

The solution is 104. Check this in the original equation.

STUDY TIP

Another way to solve the equation in Example 2 is to first multiply each side by the reciprocal of $\frac{1}{4}$.

$$24 = \frac{1}{4}(x - 8)$$

$$4 \cdot 24 = 4 \cdot \frac{1}{4}(x - 8)$$

$$96 = x - 8$$

$$96 + 8 = x - 8 + 8$$

$$104 = x$$

Example 3 Solving Real-Life Problems

You sell medical equipment. You earn a \$30,000 salary, plus a bonus. Your bonus is $\frac{1}{30}$ of the amount by which your sales exceed \$500,000. How much must you sell to earn \$40,000?

REAL LIFE
Sales Bonus

Solution

Verbal Model	$\dfrac{\text{Total}}{\text{Earnings}}$ = **Salary + Bonus**
	$\dfrac{\text{Total}}{\text{Earnings}}$ = **Salary** + $\dfrac{1}{30}$**(Total sales − 500,000)**

Labels

Total Earnings = 40,000	(dollars)
Salary = 30,000	(dollars)
Total sales = S	(dollars)

Algebraic Model

$$40,000 = 30,000 + \frac{1}{30}(S - 500,000)$$

$$40,000 - \mathbf{30,000} = 30,000 - \mathbf{30,000} + \frac{1}{30}(S - 500,000)$$

$$10,000 = \frac{1}{30}(S - 500,000)$$

$$\mathbf{30} \cdot 10,000 = \mathbf{30} \cdot \frac{1}{30}(S - 500,000)$$

$$300,000 = S - 500,000$$

$$300,000 + \mathbf{500,000} = S - 500,000 + \mathbf{500,000}$$

$$800,000 = S$$

To earn \$40,000, you must sell \$800,000 of medical equipment.

Example 4 Distributing Negative Integers

$5 - 3(x - 2) = 5 - 3x - 3(-2)$	**Use the Distributive Property.**
$= 5 - 3x - (-6)$	**Simplify.**
$= 5 - 3x + 6$	**Subtracting a number is the same as adding its opposite.**
$= 11 - 3x$	**Simplify.**

ONGOING ASSESSMENT

Write About It
• • • • • • • • • • • • • • • • • •

Solve each equation and show your steps. Next to each step, write a description of the step.

1. $3x + 3(x - 4) = 12$

2. $3 = \frac{1}{3}(3n - 6)$

3. $5p - 2(p - 7) = 21$

GUIDED PRACTICE

1. **WRITING** In your own words, describe a set of guidelines for solving an equation.

2. Explain how your guidelines can be used to solve the equation $\frac{1}{7}(x - 5) = 9$.

3. For the equation in Exercise 2, is it easier to apply the Distributive Property first or multiply both sides by the reciprocal of $\frac{1}{7}$ first? Explain.

4. Describe each step of the solution.

$$6x + 4(x - 3) = 8$$
$$6x + 4x - 12 = 8$$
$$10x - 12 = 8$$
$$10x - 12 + 12 = 8 + 12$$
$$10x = 20$$
$$\frac{10x}{10} = \frac{20}{10}$$
$$x = 2$$

PRACTICE AND PROBLEM SOLVING

In Exercises 5–7, describe the error. Then solve the equation.

5. $2(x - 2) = 4$
   $2x - 2 = 4$
   $2x = 6$
   $x = 3$

6. $5x - 7x + 5 = 3$
   $-2x + 5 = 3$
   $-2x = -2$
   $x = -1$

7. $-2x - 4x + 6 = 10$
   $-2x + 6 = 10$
   $-2x = 4$
   $x = -2$

In Exercises 8–19, solve the equation. Check your solution.

8. $x + 4(x + 6) = -1$

9. $1 = y + 3(y - 9)$

10. $3x + 2(x + 8) = 21$

11. $3(4 - s) - 5s = 52$

12. $5(2n + 3) = 65$

13. $8(4z - 7) = -56$

14. $\frac{1}{2}(x + 12) = -8$

15. $14 = \frac{1}{4}(q - 9)$

16. $-3(y + 4) = 18$

17. $2 = n - (2n + 3)$

18. $5r - 7(1 + r) = 5$

19. $6(2n - 5) = 42$

20. Solve the equation $\frac{1}{3}(x - 6) = 6$ in two ways.

   a. Use the Distributive Property first.

   b. Multiply by a reciprocal first.

   c. **OPEN-ENDED PROBLEM** Which way do you prefer? Why?

GEOMETRY **In Exercises 21–23, write an equation for the area of the rectangle. Then solve for x.**

21. Area is 63 square units.

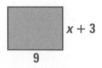
$x + 3$
9

22. Area is 48 square units.

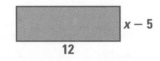
$x - 5$
12

23. Area is 35 square units

5
$2x - 1$

In Exercises 24 and 25, write an equation and solve the equation for *x*.

24. VOLLEYBALL The perimeter of a volleyball court is 177 ft.

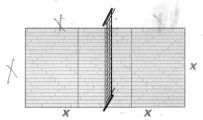

25. GEOMETRY The sum of the measures of the angles of a triangle is 180°.

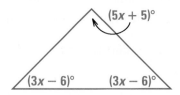

$(5x + 5)°$

$(3x - 6)°$ $(3x - 6)°$

26. CONSTRUCTION You own a house weatherproofing business. You install weather-stripping for *x* dollars per foot and insulation for $(x + 5)$ dollars per foot. This week your income came from installing 480 ft of weather-stripping and 2200 ft of insulation. Your expenses for the week are $7500.

a. Write an algebraic model that represents your income if this week's profit is $11,540.

b. How much do you charge to install insulation?

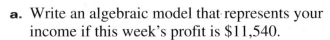

STANDARDIZED TEST PRACTICE

27. Solve the equation $510 = 2(3x + 4)$.

  A $82\frac{2}{3}$ **B** $83\frac{2}{3}$ **C** 85 **D** $167\frac{1}{3}$

28. Mr. Hill earns $300 each week plus 5% of any amount over $100 that he sells. He made $450 last week. How much did he sell?

  A $150   **B** $3000   **C** $3100   **D** $9100

EXPLORATION AND EXTENSION

29. COMMUNICATING ABOUT MATHEMATICS For information about ocean thermal energy conversion (OTEC), see page 187.

a. What is the temperature, in degrees Fahrenheit, of the cold water used by the OTEC plant? Use the formula $C = \frac{5}{9}(F - 32)$, where C = Temperature in Celsius, and F = Temperature in Fahrenheit.

b. How warm must the surface water be? Explain your reasoning.

Take this test as you would take a test in class. The answers to the exercises are given in the back of the book.

1. **DRAWING A DIAGRAM** A triangle has a perimeter of 16 cm. The longest side is p cm long and the shortest side is 4 cm shorter than the longest side. The third side is 3 cm longer than the shortest side. Sketch the triangle and find its dimensions. **(4.3)**

In Exercises 2–4, find the reciprocal. (4.3)

2. 3

3. $-\dfrac{1}{21}$

4. $-\dfrac{1}{5}$

In Exercises 5–10, solve the equation. Then check your solution. (4.1)

5. $2y - 4 = 10$

6. $4t + 16 = 0$

7. $8 - 2b = 2$

8. $\dfrac{1}{2}r + 6 = 8$

9. $6m + 5 = -1$

10. $20p - 8 = 32$

In Exercises 11–14, solve the equation. Then check your solution. (4.2, 4.4)

11. $9s + 6s - 12s = 15$

12. $10t - 7t + t = -24$

13. $19 + 12p - 17p = -1$

14. $3(n + 4) + 1 = 28$

In Exercises 15–17, write an equation that represents the verbal sentence. Then solve the equation. (4.1, 4.2)

15. The sum of $2x$ and 3 is 21.

16. The difference of $\dfrac{x}{4}$ and 3 is 1.

17. 17 is the sum of $2x$, x, and 5.

In Exercises 18 and 19, use the following information. (4.3)

TRAVEL You are in Western Samoa in the Pacific Ocean. In Apia, on Upolu Island, you see the sign at the right. The people of Apia want to add two more cities to the sign, and ask you for the distances.

18. The distance from Apia to New York City is about the distance to Honolulu plus half the distance to Nairobi, Kenya. Estimate the distance to Nairobi.

19. The distance from Apia to Nouméa is about one fourth the sum of 500 km and the distance to Austin, TX. What is the distance to Austin?

Solving Equations: Variables on Both Sides

Here is an example of how you can use algebra tiles to solve the equation $2x + 2 = x + 4$.

Materials Needed
• algebra tiles
• pencil or pen
• paper

1 Model the original equation, $2x + 2 = x + 4$.

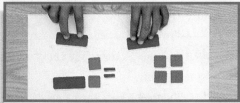

2 Remove (subtract) an *x* tile from each side so that you only have *x* tiles on one side. The new equation is $x + 2 = 4$.

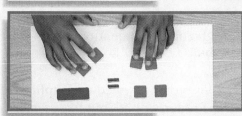

3 To isolate *x*, remove (subtract) two 1 tiles from each side. The solution is $x = 2$.

1. The algebra tile model below shows the solution of an equation. Write the equation and its solution steps. Check your result.

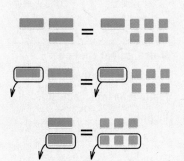

NOW TRY THESE

In Exercises 2–5, use algebra tiles to solve the equation. Draw a sketch of your solution. Then translate your sketch into algebra.

2. $4x + 3 = 3x + 5$

3. $y + 9 = 3y + 3$

4. $3n + 5 = n + 11$

5. $5m + 2 = 2m + 14$

4.5

Solving Equations: Variables on Both Sides

What you should learn:

Goal 1 How to solve equations with variables on both sides

Goal 2 How to use equations to model problems in geometry

Why you should learn it:

You can use equations with variables on both sides to compare costs, such as the costs of different kinds of light bulbs.

Goal 1 COLLECTING VARIABLES ON ONE SIDE

Some equations, such as $2x + 3 = 3x + 5$, have variables on both sides. To solve such equations, *collect like variables* on the same side. We suggest that you collect the variables on the side with the term that has the greater variable coefficient.

Example 1 Collecting Like Variables

Solve $2x + 3 = 3x + 5$.

Solution

Remember that your goal is to isolate the variable.

$2x + 3 = 3x + 5$	Write original equation.
$2x + 3 - 2x = 3x + 5 - 2x$	Subtract 2x from each side.
$3 = x + 5$	Simplify.
$3 - 5 = x + 5 - 5$	Subtract 5 from each side.
$-2 = x$	Solution: x is by itself.

The solution is -2. Check this in the original equation.

Before you can collect like variables, you may need to simplify the equation by using the Distributive Property or adding like terms.

Example 2 Simplifying First

Solve $8n - 4 = 3(2n - 8)$.

Solution

$8n - 4 = 3(2n - 8)$	Write original equation.
$8n - 4 = 6n - 24$	Use the Distributive Property.
$8n - 4 - 6n = 6n - 24 - 6n$	Subtract 6n from each side.
$2n - 4 = -24$	Simplify.
$2n - 4 + 4 = -24 + 4$	Add 4 to each side.
$2n = -20$	Simplify.
$\dfrac{2n}{2} = \dfrac{-20}{2}$	Divide each side by 2.
$n = -10$	Solution: n is by itself.

The solution is -10. Check this in the original equation.

Example 3 ▸ Comparing Perimeters

Find the value of *x* so that the rectangle and the triangle have the same perimeter.

CONNECTION
Geometry

x + 1
x + 2

x + 2 △ *x* + 3
x + 4

Solution

$$\frac{\text{Rectangle's}}{\text{perimeter}} = \frac{\text{Triangle's}}{\text{perimeter}}$$ **Write verbal model.**

$$2(x + 1) + 2(x + 2) = (x + 2) + (x + 3) + (x + 4)$$
$$2x + 2 + 2x + 4 = (x + 2) + (x + 3) + (x + 4)$$
$$4x + 6 = 3x + 9$$
$$x + 6 = 9$$
$$x = 3$$

When *x* = 3, each figure has a perimeter of 18.

Example 4 ▸ Creating an Equilateral Triangle

A triangle is **equilateral** if its sides all have the same length. Find a value of *x* so that △*ABC* is equilateral.

CONNECTION
Geometry

A
3*x* − 1 *x* + 3
B *x* + 3 *C*

Solution

$$\frac{\text{Length of}}{\text{side } AB} = \frac{\text{Length of side}}{AC \text{ or } BC}$$ **Write verbal model.**

$$3x - 1 = x + 3$$ **Write equation.**
$$2x - 1 = 3$$ **Subtract *x* from each side.**
$$2x = 4$$ **Add 1 to each side.**
$$x = 2$$ **Divide each side by 2.**

When *x* = 2, each side has a length of 5.

ONGOING ASSESSMENT

Talk About It
· ·

1. In Example 3, which values of *x* make the rectangle's perimeter larger than the triangle's perimeter?

2. Show how you can use a table to get your answer to Exercise 1.

GUIDED PRACTICE

1. **WRITING** In your own words, describe a strategy for solving an equation that has variables on both sides.

2. **LANGUAGE** The prefix *equi-* means "equal" and *lateral* means "side." Explain how these word parts are related to the term *equilateral triangle*.

In Exercises 3–6, on which side of the equation would you collect the variable terms? Why?

3. $2x - 4 = x$ 4. $4y + 10 = 6y$ 5. $x + 15 = 4x + 6$ 6. $-3x + 5 = x + 3$

PRACTICE AND PROBLEM SOLVING

In Exercises 7–18, solve the equation. Then check your solution.

7. $7x + 12 = 13x$ 8. $10x + 17 = 4x - 1$ 9. $5x - 8 = -2x + 6$

10. $-5x + 6 = x + 12$ 11. $-2x + 6 = -x$ 12. $7y = 3(5y - 8)$

13. $10(2n + 10) = 120n$ 14. $4(7 + y) = 16 - 2y$ 15. $6(x - 3) = 4(x + 3)$

16. $2(x - 9) = 3(x - 6)$ 17. $\frac{7}{2}t + 12 = 6 + \frac{5}{2}t$ 18. $-13 - \frac{1}{12}s = \frac{11}{12}s + 2$

19. One less than three times a number is equal to the same number plus 19. What is the number?

20. Four times a number plus seventeen is equal to the sum of seven times the same number and 2. What is the number?

21. **GEOMETRY** Find the value of x so that the rectangle and the triangle have the same perimeter. What is the perimeter?

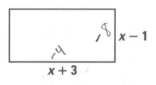
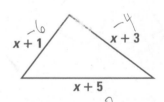

22. **GEOMETRY** Find the value of x so that the triangle is equilateral.

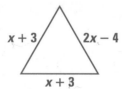

23. **GEOMETRY** Find the value of x so that the figure is a square.

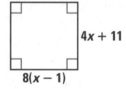

24. **MOVIES** The cost of seeing x movies at the theater is $7x$ dollars. Buying a VCR and renting x movies costs $350 + 3x$ dollars. Set the expressions equal and solve for x. What does your answer represent?

LITERATURE In Exercises 25–27, use the following information.

A Greek named Aesop told fables about animals. In one, a tortoise and a hare are in a race. The hare is far ahead and sure it will win, so it takes a nap. When it wakes up, it sees the tortoise about to cross the finish line.

25. Suppose the hare runs 50 ft/s and the tortoise runs 0.25 ft/s. When the hare wakes up, the tortoise is 1000 ft ahead. Which equation can you use to tell when the hare will catch up with the tortoise? (Let t represent time in seconds.)

    A. $0.25t = 50t + 1000$ **B.** $50t = 0.25t + 1000$

    C. $0.25t - 1000 = 50t$ **D.** $50t = 1000$

26. Solve the correct equation in Exercise 25.

27. If the tortoise is 5 ft from the finish line when the hare wakes up, who will win? Explain your reasoning.

Real Life...
Real Facts

Marathon
This sculpture of the tortoise and the hare was made for the 100th anniversary of the Boston Marathon, the oldest foot race in the United States.

STANDARDIZED TEST PRACTICE

28. Solve the equation $4t + 9 = 11t - 83$.

    A $4\frac{14}{15}$ **B** $6\frac{2}{15}$ **C** $13\frac{1}{7}$ **D** $20\frac{3}{4}$

29. Which equation has the solution -6?

    A $20(3x + 6) = -246 - x$ **B** $20(3x + 6) = 1086 - x$

    C $20(3x + 6) = 480 - x$ **D** $20(3x + 6) = 486 - x$

EXPLORATION AND EXTENSION

PORTFOLIO

BUILDING YOUR PROJECT In Exercises 30 and 31, use the table below. The bulbs in the table give the same amount of light.

30. How much does it cost to use each bulb for x hours? Use the verbal model to write an expression for each bulb. Assume that the cost of electricity is $0.08 per kW · h.

    $$\text{Total} \atop \text{cost} \approx {\text{Cost of} \atop \text{bulb}} + {\text{Cost of} \atop \text{electricity}} \cdot {\text{Power} \atop \text{needed}} \cdot x$$

	Standard light bulb	Fluorescent light bulb
Cost of bulb (dollars)	0.75	25.00
Power needed (kilowatts)	0.075	0.02

31. When is the cost of using a standard bulb the same as the cost of using a fluorescent bulb? Set the expressions from Exercise 30 equal to each other and solve for x.

4.6

Problem Solving Strategies

What you should learn:

Goal 1 How to use tables and graphs to solve real-life problems

Goal 2 How to use a general problem solving plan

Why you should learn it:

To be an efficient problem solver, you should be able to solve real-life problems in more than one way.

Goal 1 USING TABLES AND GRAPHS

There are usually many ways to solve a real-life problem. It can be helpful to use more than one method and then compare results.

Example 1 Using Tables and Graphs

A logging company is making a reforestation plan. The company has 60 mi^2 of logged land, and is logging 10 mi^2 more each year. If 16 mi^2 of new trees are planted each year, when will all of the logged land be reforested?

REAL LIFE
Reforestation

Solution

STRATEGY **MAKE A TABLE** One way to solve the problem is to use a table. For the logged area, start with 60 mi^2 and add 10 mi^2 each year. For the reforested area, start with 0 mi^2 and add 16 mi^2 each year.

Year	0 (now)	1	2	3	4	5	6	7	8	9	10
Logged area (square miles)	60	70	80	90	100	110	120	130	140	150	160
Reforested area (square miles)	0	16	32	48	64	80	96	112	128	144	160

From the table, you can see that it will take 10 years to reforest all the land that has been logged. You can make a graph to help you visualize the data in the table.

STRATEGY **USE A GRAPH**

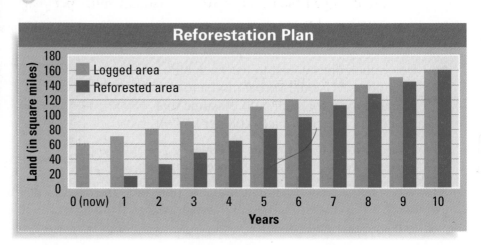

In Example 1, you saw how to solve a problem with a table and with a graph.

Example 2 shows how to use a verbal model and algebra to solve the same problem. Remember from Lesson 2.8 that the general problem solving plan has six basic steps, as shown at the right.

Problem Solving Plan

Write a verbal model.

↓

Assign labels.

↓

Write an algebraic model.

↓

Solve the algebraic model.

↓

Answer the question.

↓

Check your answer.

Example 2 Using a Problem Solving Plan

Show how to use the general problem solving plan to solve the problem in Example 1.

Solution

🔑 STRATEGY USE A VERBAL AND ALGEBRAIC MODEL

Verbal Model

$$\begin{array}{c}\text{Land}\\\text{already}\\\text{logged}\end{array} + \begin{array}{c}\text{Land}\\\text{logged}\\\text{each year}\end{array} \cdot \begin{array}{c}\text{Number}\\\text{of years}\end{array} = \begin{array}{c}\text{Land}\\\text{reforested}\\\text{each year}\end{array} \cdot \begin{array}{c}\text{Number}\\\text{of years}\end{array}$$

Labels

Land already logged = 60 (square miles)
Land logged each year = 10 (square miles per year)
Number of years = n (years)
Land reforested each year = 16 (square miles per year)

Algebraic Model

$60 + 10n = 16n$	Write equation.
$60 + 10n - 10n = 16n - 10n$	Subtract $10n$ from each side.
$60 = 6n$	Simplify.
$\dfrac{60}{6} = \dfrac{6n}{6}$	Divide each side by 6.
$10 = n$	Solution: n is by itself.

The solution is 10. So, it will take 10 years to reforest all of the logged land.

ONGOING ASSESSMENT

Write About It
· · · · · · · · · · · · · · · ·

1. Suppose you have logged 12 mi^2. You log 3 mi^2 a year and begin reforesting 5 mi^2 a year. How long will it take to reforest all of the logged land? Use two methods and compare your solutions.

Extra Practice, page 722

GUIDED PRACTICE

1. **WRITING** In your own words, describe the general problem solving plan.

ALGEBRAIC MODEL In Exercises 2–4, use the following information.

A cornstalk is 5 in. tall and a weed is 11 in. tall. The cornstalk is growing at a rate of $2\frac{1}{2}$ inches per week and the weed is growing at a rate of 1 inch per week. When will the cornstalk and the weed be the same height?

$$\begin{matrix} \text{Height of} \\ \text{cornstalk} \\ \text{now} \end{matrix} + \begin{matrix} \text{Stalk's} \\ \text{rate of} \\ \text{growth} \end{matrix} \cdot \begin{matrix} \text{Number} \\ \text{of weeks} \end{matrix} = \begin{matrix} \text{Height} \\ \text{of weed} \\ \text{now} \end{matrix} + \begin{matrix} \text{Weed's} \\ \text{rate of} \\ \text{growth} \end{matrix} \cdot \begin{matrix} \text{Number} \\ \text{of weeks} \end{matrix}$$

2. Assign labels to each part of the verbal model. Indicate the units of measure.

3. Write an algebraic model. Solve the algebraic model.

4. When will the cornstalk and the weed be the same height?

PRACTICE AND PROBLEM SOLVING

5. **INTERACTIVE CDS** You want to join an interactive CD club to buy interactive books on compact disks. Your friend says that it is more economical to buy the CDs from a bookstore. You decide to consider your options. The CD club has a membership fee of $50 and each interactive book costs $25. The bookstore charges $35 for each interactive book.

> **TOOLBOX**
> Problem Solving
> Strategies, page 744

   a. Complete the table and interpret the results.

Number of CDs	1	2	3	4	5	6	7	8	9	10
Bookstore cost ($)	?	?	?	?	?	?	?	?	?	?
CD club cost ($)	?	?	?	?	?	?	?	?	?	?

   b. How many CDs do you have to buy for the costs of both options to be the same?

   c. Is your friend correct?

   d. Show how the problem can be solved with a bar graph.

TEMPERATURE **In Exercises 6–11, use the following information.**

The temperature is 86°F in Santa Fe, New Mexico, and is decreasing at a rate of 3 degrees per hour. At the same time, the temperature is 56°F in Minot, North Dakota, and is increasing at a rate of 2 degrees per hour. When will the temperatures be the same?

6. Write a verbal model.

7. Assign labels to each part of the model.

8. Write an algebraic model.

9. Solve the algebraic model.

10. When will the temperatures be the same?

11. Describe at least one way to check your answer.

12. OPEN-ENDED PROBLEM You are considering joining one of two jazz dance clubs in your area. At Club 1, there is no membership fee and lessons cost $6.00 per hour. At Club 2, there is an annual membership fee of $30, and lessons cost $4.50 per hour. Explain how you would decide which club to join.

13. BUSINESS You own a small business that makes skateboards. You want to know how many skateboards you must sell to break even. Your costs are $1500, plus $15 in materials for each skateboard. You sell each skateboard for $32. To break even, your total cost must be equal to your total income. Use the following model to find the number of skateboards you must sell to break even.

Total cost = Total Income

$$1500 + 15 \cdot \text{Number sold} = 32 \cdot \text{Number sold}$$

STANDARDIZED TEST PRACTICE

14. For each size of egg, the table shows the weight of a dozen eggs. How much do 3 dozen large eggs weigh?

A 27 oz

B 63 oz

C 72 oz

D 864 oz

Size	Weight (oz/dozen)
Jumbo	30
Extra Large	27
Large	24
Medium	21
Small	18
Peewee	15

15. **BUILDING YOUR PROJECT** Heat is often measured in British Thermal Units (BTU). The graph shows typical costs, in dollars per million BTU, of heating a home with different energy sources.

   a. Suppose you use propane to produce three million BTU. How much more or less would you spend if you used electricity? If you used oil?

   b. What fuel do you use to heat your home? What factors, other than the cost of fuel, might influence your decision of what kind of fuel to use for heat?

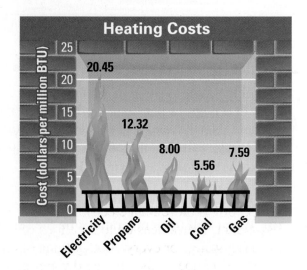

Heating Costs

SPIRAL REVIEW

In Exercises 1–8, solve the equation. (4.5)

1. $4a = 28$
2. $6 - 9x = -48$
3. $4.5r - 2 = 7$
4. $12x + 3x = 30$

5. $3a = 2 + 2a$
6. $14s - 6 = 12s$
7. $z + 2(4 - z) = 4$
8. $\frac{4}{3}p = \frac{12}{3} + \frac{2}{3}p$

In Exercises 9–12, write the verbal sentence as an algebraic equation and solve. (4.3)

9. Six times a number is 3.

10. The sum of $3x$ and 2 is $8x$.

11. $5x$ is the difference of 1 and x.

12. 2 times the sum of x and 2 is $-x$.

In Exercises 13 and 14, find the average of the numbers. (3.6)

13. 14, 24, 20, 12, 17, 22, 7, 20

14. $-2.4, 1.1, 2.7, -1.4, -0.5$

In Exercises 15–20, solve the inequality. (2.9)

15. $2x \geq 1$
16. $7y < 28$
17. $48 < 16y$

18. $3c < 21$
19. $\frac{r}{4} \geq 6$
20. $0.2p \leq 12$

21. **LOGICAL REASONING** You ask 25 families what kinds of telephones they own. Thirteen families say they own a cordless telephone and 21 say they own a regular telephone. How many families own both types of telephones? Assume every family owns at least one phone.

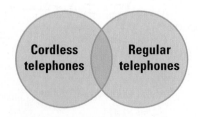

Energy from the Ocean

READ About It

Ocean thermal energy conversion (OTEC) is a way to use cold and warm seawater to make electricity. To work, the difference in temperature between the warm and cold water must be at least 36°F.

OTEC offers more than electricity. As a byproduct, it produces up to 5 gallons of drinking water for every 1000 gallons of cold seawater pumped. Also, the cold water could provide air conditioning with only one ten-thousandth of the energy that conventional air conditioners use. This water can also be used to cool the roots of plants that normally grow in colder climates so that they can thrive in hot, dry areas.

Although OTEC is one of the most environmentally friendly ways of producing electricity, it requires large amounts of seawater. A large OTEC plant would move as much water as the Colorado River. Since 1988, a small OTEC plant in Hawaii has had two pipelines pumping 11,300 gallons of warm water each minute. Other pipes pump up to 17,100 gallons per minute from a depth of 2000 feet. The water temperature at this depth is a chilly 6°C.

WRITE About It

1. Write an expression that gives the amount of cold water pumped in *m* minutes. Set this expression equal to 500,000. Explain what solving for *m* will tell you, and then solve for *m*.

2. About how many gallons of drinking water can the OTEC system in Hawaii produce each minute? Explain your reasoning.

3. If it takes 5,000,000 watts of energy to cool thousands of homes with conventional air conditioning, how much energy would it take to cool them with water from OTEC? Explain.

4. The 36°F temperature difference described above exists in regions that are within 25 degrees latitude of the equator. Use a world map to find other locations that could use the OTEC system.

In this chamber, steam from seawater turns a turbine.

After leaving the OTEC plant, the nutrient-rich seawater can be used to raise kelp, mushrooms, abalone, shrimp, lobster, and fish.

4.7

Solving Equations Using Technology

What you should learn:

Goal 1 How to round decimals while solving equations

Goal 2 How to use a table to solve problems

Why you should learn it:

Many real-life problems involve decimal amounts, such as phone rates.

This man is using a telecommunications device for the deaf to talk with someone on the telephone.

Goal 1 ROUNDING DECIMALS

COOPERATIVE LEARNING

LESSON INVESTIGATION

Investigating Round-Off Error

GROUP ACTIVITY In the following solutions, the red numbers are rounded to 2 decimal places. Which solution is more accurate? What does that tell you about rounding before the final step?

Rounding Early	Rounding at Final Step
$0.12(3.45x - 2.80) = 9.45$	$0.12(3.45x - 2.80) = 9.45$
$0.414x - 0.336 = 9.45$	$0.414x - 0.336 = 9.45$
$0.41x - 0.34 \approx 9.45$	$0.414x = 9.786$
$0.41x \approx 9.79$	$x = \dfrac{9.786}{0.414}$
$x \approx \dfrac{9.79}{0.41}$	$x \approx 23.64$
$x \approx 23.88$	

Example 1 Solving an Equation with Decimals

Solve $3.56x + 4.78 = 2.69(1.20x - 4.18)$. Round the solution to two decimal places.

Solution

$$3.56x + 4.78 = \mathbf{2.69(1.20x - 4.18)}$$
$$3.56x + 4.78 = \mathbf{3.228x - 11.2442}$$
$$3.56x + 4.78 - \mathbf{3.228x} = 3.228x - 11.2442 - \mathbf{3.228x}$$
$$0.332x + 4.78 = -11.2442$$
$$0.332x + 4.78 - \mathbf{4.78} = -11.2442 - \mathbf{4.78}$$
$$0.332x = -16.0242$$
$$\frac{0.332x}{\mathbf{0.332}} = \frac{-16.0242}{\mathbf{0.332}}$$
$$x \approx -48.27 \qquad \text{Round to 2 decimal places.}$$

The solution is about -48.27. Check this in the original equation.

Example 2 Using a Table

STRATEGY **MAKE A TABLE** You are making a long-distance call to a pen pal. The call costs $1.53 for the first minute and $.92 for each additional minute. You don't want to spend more than $10.00 on the call. How long can you talk?

Solution

| **Verbal Model** | Total cost | = | $\text{Cost of first minute}$ | + | $\text{Cost of each additional minute}$ | $\cdot$ | $\text{Number of additional minutes}$ |

Labels
Total cost = C (dollars)

Cost of first minute = **1.53**   (dollars)

Cost of each additional minute = **0.92**   (dollars per minute)

Number of additional minutes = t (minutes)

Algebraic Model $C = 1.53 + 0.92 \cdot t$

You want to find the values of t such that C is less than or equal to $10.00. One way to do this is with a table. From the table, you can see that you can talk for up to 10 min (1 min plus 9 additional minutes).

Additional minutes	Calculations	Cost
1	1.53 + 0.92(1) =	$2.45
2	1.53 + 0.92(2) =	$3.37
3	1.53 + 0.92(3) =	$4.29
4	1.53 + 0.92(4) =	$5.21
5	1.53 + 0.92(5) =	$6.13
6	1.53 + 0.92(6) =	$7.05
7	1.53 + 0.92(7) =	$7.97
8	1.53 + 0.92(8) =	$8.89
9	1.53 + 0.92(9) =	$9.81
10	1.53 + 0.92(10) =	$10.73

ONGOING ASSESSMENT

Write About It
. . . .
You don't want to spend more than the amount shown. How long can you talk? Use the equation in Example 2. (Remember that t represents the number of additional minutes, not the length of the call.)

1. $5.00

2. $16.25

3. $30.00

4.7 Exercises

Extra Practice, page 722

GUIDED PRACTICE

1. **REASONING** Which of the following solutions of $9x = 1$ are you more likely to get if you use a calculator or computer? Why?

   A. $x \approx 0.111$

   B. $x = \dfrac{1}{9}$

2. Solve the equation $0.25(3.2x + 4.1) = 7.2$. Round your answer to two decimal places.

3. Explain the difference between $x = 2.5$ and $x \approx 2.5$.

4. **MEASUREMENT SENSE** The total weight of 11 students is 1117 lb. Which is the better way to list the average weight? Why?

   A. 101.54545 lb

   B. 101.5 lb

PRACTICE AND PROBLEM SOLVING

 TECHNOLOGY In Exercises 5–21, use a calculator. Round your answer to two decimal places.

In Exercises 5 and 6, describe the error. Then write a correct solution.

5. $1.1(2.5x - 3.5) = 11.2$
   $2.8x - 3.9 = 11.2$
   $2.8x = 15.1$
   $x \approx 5.39$

6. $0.26(2.39x - 4.91) = 10.64$
   $0.62x - 1.28 = 10.64$
   $0.62x = 11.92$
   $x \approx 19.23$

In Exercises 7–19, solve the equation.

7. $3x + 12 = 17$

8. $13y + 22 = 16$

9. $29t - 17 = -86$

10. $15 - 11x = 108$

11. $6(4x - 12) = 8x + 9$

12. $13x - 22 = 2(9x + 10)$

13. $1.3y + 22.1 = 12.9$

14. $-7.4m + 36.4 = 9.5$

15. $0.15(9.85x + 3.70) = 4.65$

16. $2.16(3.47x - 8.60) = 17.59$

17. $0.19t - 1.57 = 0.46t$

18. $2.4x + 13.7 = 8.1x - 22.5$

19. $3.14x + 17.5 = 9.77x + 24.1$

20. **SALES TAX** You purchase an item. The sales tax rate is 0.06 and the total cost of the item is $6.35. Let p represent the price of the item (not including sales tax). Solve the following equation to find the price of the item.

    $p + 0.06p = 6.35$

21. **SALES TAX** You purchase an item. The sales tax rate is 0.05 and the total cost of the item is $2.61. Let p represent the price of the item (not including sales tax). Solve the following equation to find the price of the item.

    $p + 0.05p = 2.61$

POSTAGE **In Exercises 22 and 23, use the following information.**

You are mailing a letter with pictures inside to your friend. Postage costs $.32 for the first ounce and $.23 for each additional ounce. How heavy can your letter be if you have $2.00 to spend?

22. Write a verbal model for the problem.

23. Create a table similar to the one in Example 2 to solve the problem.

INTERNET PROVIDERS **In Exercises 24 and 25, use the following information. You are trying to choose between two Internet providers. Provider A charges $9.95 for the first five hours of use, and $2.95 for every hour after that. Provider B charges $4.95 for the first hour of use, and $2.50 for every hour after that.**

24. Write a verbal model and an algebraic expression for how much each company will charge if you are on-line for t hours each month.

25. To see when the companies' charges will be equal, set the expressions equal to each other and solve. Which company will be less expensive if you are on-line *more* than this many hours each month?

26. Solve the equation $0.75x + 3.22 = 6.97$.

(A) 5   **(B)** 6.07   **(C)** 10.94   **(D)** 13.59

27. Which is the best approximation for the solution of the equation $0.12x - 0.65 = 1.28$?

(A) 0.24   **(B)** 5.25   **(C)** 16.08   **(D)** 16.68

EXPLORATION AND EXTENSION

28. **PHONE RATES** You often call your cousin in another state. Which long-distance company would you choose? Explain your reasoning.

Company A charges $.48 for the first minute and $.07 for each additional minute.

Company B charges $.15 for the first minute and $.10 for each additional minute.

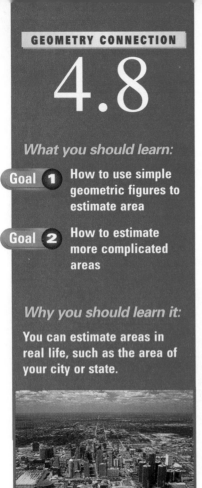

GEOMETRY CONNECTION

4.8

What you should learn:

Goal 1 How to use simple geometric figures to estimate area

Goal 2 How to estimate more complicated areas

Why you should learn it:

You can estimate areas in real life, such as the area of your city or state.

Detroit is the largest city in Michigan.

Formulas and Variables in Geometry

Goal 1 USING FORMULAS FROM GEOMETRY

You know several formulas for perimeter and area.

Perimeter of a polygon = sum of the side lengths

Area of a rectangle = (length)(width)

Area of a triangle = $\frac{1}{2}$(base)(height)

Area of a square = $(\text{side})^2$

Example 1 **Estimating an Area**

Use the map to estimate the area of Detroit, Michigan.

CONNECTION
Geometry

Solution

One way to solve this problem is to sketch a triangle whose area appears to be about the same as Detroit's area.

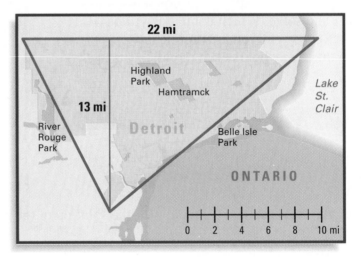

From the scale on the map, you can see that the triangle has a base of about 22 mi and a height of about 13 mi.

$$\text{Area of Detroit} \approx \text{Area of triangle}$$

$$= \frac{1}{2}(\text{base})(\text{height})$$

$$= \frac{1}{2}(22)(13)$$

$$= 143$$

The area of Detroit is about 143 mi^2.

TOOLBOX

Areas, page 754

Example 2 Modeling with Simple Shapes

STRATEGY **SOLVE A SIMPLER PROBLEM** One way to estimate the area of Texas is to divide the state into 4 regions. You can approximate each region with a rectangle or a triangle, as shown below. Use the map's scale to estimate the dimensions of each figure.

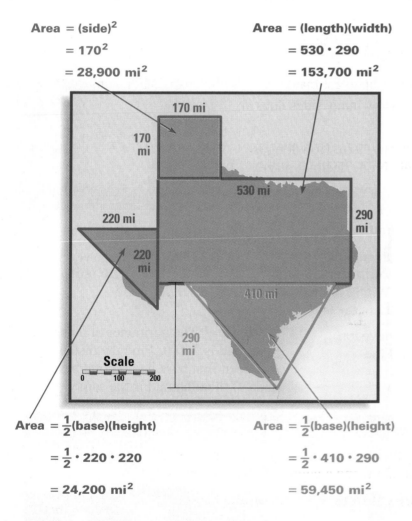

Area = (side)^2

$= 170^2$

$= 28,900$ mi^2

Area = (length)(width)

$= 530 \cdot 290$

$= 153,700$ mi^2

170 mi

170 mi

530 mi

290 mi

220 mi

220 mi

410 mi

290 mi

Scale

0   100   200

Area = $\frac{1}{2}$(base)(height)

$= \frac{1}{2} \cdot 220 \cdot 220$

$= 24,200$ mi^2

Area = $\frac{1}{2}$(base)(height)

$= \frac{1}{2} \cdot 410 \cdot 290$

$= 59,450$ mi^2

To estimate the total area of Texas, add the areas of the regions.

Total area of Texas $\approx$ **28,900 + 153,700 + 24,200 + 59,450**

$= 266,250$ mi^2

So, Texas has an area of about 266,250 mi^2. (This estimate is good. The actual area of Texas is 266,874 mi^2.)

ONGOING ASSESSMENT

Talk About It
....

1. The triangle in Example 1 gives a good estimate for the area of Detroit. (In fact, it is correct to the nearest square mile.) Do you think the triangle could be used to estimate the perimeter of Detroit? Explain.

GUIDED PRACTICE

1. **DRAWING A DIAGRAM** Write a formula used in geometry. Sketch a figure to illustrate the formula. Label the variables on the figure.

In Exercises 2–6, match the formula with the polygon. State the formula in words. (Each polygon can be used more than once.)

   A. Triangle   **B. Square**   **C. Rectangle**

   2. $A = s^2$ **3.** $P = 2l + 2w$ **4.** $A = \frac{1}{2}bh$ **5.** $P = 4s$ **6.** $A = bh$

PRACTICE AND PROBLEM SOLVING

STREET SIGNS **In Exercises 7–9, use the stop sign at the right.**

7. The sign is a *regular octagon*. How many sides does an *octagon* have?

8. The perimeter of the sign is about 99 in. How long is each side? Round your answer to one decimal place.

9. If each side were 10 in. long, what would the perimeter be?

In Exercises 10–12, solve for x and find the dimensions of the polygon.

10. **Rectangle**
    Perimeter: 36 units
    Width: x
    Length: $4x - 2$

11. **Rectangle**
    Perimeter: 58 units
    Width: $6x - 4$
    Length: $3x + 6$

12. **Square**
    Perimeter: 16 units
    Side: $x - 5$

13. **TELEVISION** The front of the television has a total area of 320 in.^{2} Find the area of the television screen.

14. **BASEBALL** The perimeter of a baseball diamond is 360 ft. Find the distance between first base and second base. Each side of the diamond is the same length.

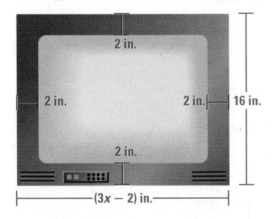

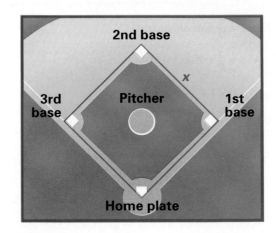

In Exercises 15–17, solve for x and find the missing dimension.

15. Pentagon
Perimeter: 90 units
Each side: $5x - 7$

16. Triangle
Area: 155 square units
Height: 10 units
Base: $3x + 10$

17. Rectangle
Area: 225 square units
Width: 9 units
Length: $2x + 9$

WILDLIFE REFUGE In Exercises 18 and 19, trace the map and estimate the area of the wildlife refuge. Explain how you got your answer.

Tech Link

Investigation 4,
Interactive
Real-Life
Investigations

18.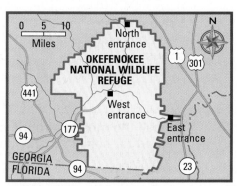

19.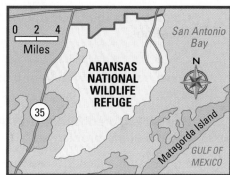

STANDARDIZED TEST PRACTICE

20. What is the perimeter of a square that has the same area as a 2 in.-by-8-in. rectangle?

   (A) 4 in.   **(B)** 16 in.

   (C) 64 in.   **(D)** Not enough information

21. Find the area of the triangle at the right.

   (A) 168 square units   **(B)** 91 square units

   (C) 90 square units   **(D)** 84 square units

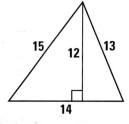

EXPLORATION AND EXTENSION

PORTFOLIO

22. BUILDING YOUR PROJECT An inexpensive way to save money on heating and air conditioning is by putting removable clear plastic film on the insides of windows to prevent drafts. The cost is $4.99 for a roll of plastic that measures 10 ft by 25 ft.

   a. How many windows are there where you live? How big are they?

   b. How much would it cost you to cover all of the windows with plastic? Explain your reasoning.

WHAT *did you learn?*	**WHY** *did you learn it?*
Skills 4.1 Solve two-step equations.	Solve real-life problems, such as comparing membership plans.
4.2 Solve multi-step equations. Use an "expert" equation-solver format.	Solve real-life problems, such as calculating profits.
4.3 Use reciprocals to solve equations.	Solve problems in real-life situations, such as gardening.
4.4 Use the Distributive Property to solve equations.	Solve problems in real-life situations, such as earning a bonus.
4.5 Solve equations with variables on both sides.	Compare costs.
4.6 Use tables, graphs, and equations to solve real-life problems.	Choose the most appropriate method for solving a real-life problem.
4.7 Solve equations involving decimals.	Solve problems involving money.
4.8 Find areas.	Estimate areas in real life.
Strategies 4.1–4.8 Use problem solving strategies, such as *Making a Table* and *Using a Graph*. Follow a general problem solving plan.	Solve a wide variety of real-life problems.

HOW *does it fit into the bigger picture of mathematics?*

As in real life, problems in mathematics can often be solved in more than one way. In this chapter, you solved problems by making tables, making graphs, and using a generalized problem solving plan to write and solve an algebraic equation. As you tackle any problem in mathematics, you should follow each of the steps at the right.

> **Read and understand the problem.**
>
> ↓
>
> **Make a plan.**
>
> ↓
>
> **Carry out the plan.**
>
> ↓
>
> **Check the solution.**

VOCABULARY

- reciprocal (p. 168)
- equilateral triangle (p. 179)

4.1 SOLVING TWO-STEP EQUATIONS

Use inverse operations to isolate the variable.

Example

$3x + 15 = 27$	Write original equation.
$3x + 15 - 15 = 27 - 15$	Subtract 15 from each side.
$3x = 12$	Simplify.
$\dfrac{3x}{3} = \dfrac{12}{3}$	Divide each side by 3.
$x = 4$	Solution: x is by itself.

Solve the equation.

1. $\dfrac{x}{2} + 12 = 20$ **2.** $5t - 4 = 21$ **3.** $7 - 5x = -3$

4.2 SOLVING MULTI-STEP EQUATIONS

Combine like terms, then isolate the variable.

Example

$3n + 4 - n = -2$	Write original equation.
$2n + 4 = -2$	Combine like terms.
$2n = -6$	Subtract 4 from each side.
$n = -3$	Divide each side by 2.

Solve the equation.

4. $7n - 2n - 1 = 29$ **5.** $s + 5s - 3s = 36$ **6.** $-31 = \dfrac{2}{3}x - 26 + \dfrac{1}{3}x$

7. $12 = 3t - t + 4$ **8.** $2y - 5y + 4 = 10$ **9.** $-12 = g + 9 - 4g$

4.3 TWO-STEP EQUATIONS AND PROBLEM SOLVING

Use reciprocals to isolate the variable.

Example

$\dfrac{1}{3}x = 8$	Write original equation.
$3 \cdot \dfrac{1}{3}x = 3 \cdot 8$	Multiply by the reciprocal of $\dfrac{1}{3}$.
$x = 24$	Solution: x is by itself.

Solve the equation.

10. $\dfrac{1}{5}x + 1 = 9$ **11.** $-2 = \dfrac{1}{2}x - 5$ **12.** $7s + 11 = 53$

4.4 USING THE DISTRIBUTIVE PROPERTY

Use the following steps to solve equations.

1 Use the Distributive Property and gather like terms to simplify the equation.

2 Use inverse operations to isolate the variable.

Example

$\frac{1}{2}(z - 10) = 7$	Write original equation.
$\frac{1}{2}z - \frac{1}{2}(10) = 7$	Use the Distributive Property.
$\frac{1}{2}z - 5 = 7$	Simplify.
$\frac{1}{2}z - 5 + 5 = 7 + 5$	Add 5 to each side.
$\frac{1}{2}z = 12$	Simplify.
$2 \cdot \frac{1}{2}z = 2 \cdot 12$	Multiply each side by 2.
$z = 24$	Solution: z is by itself.

Solve the equation.

13. $5(t - 9) = 55$ **14.** $-2(x + 1) + x = -8$ **15.** $11(m - 6) - 17 = 38$

4.5 EQUATIONS WITH VARIABLES ON BOTH SIDES

Collect the variables on the side with the term that has the greater variable coefficient.

Example

$-18t + 175 = 7t$	Write original equation.
$-18t + 18t + 175 = 7t + 18t$	Add 18t to each side.
$175 = 25t$	Simplify.
$\frac{175}{25} = \frac{25t}{25}$	Divide each side by 25.
$7 = t$	Solution: t is by itself.

Solve the equation.

16. $2x - 9 = 5x$ **17.** $6y + 39 = -7y$ **18.** $\frac{5}{2}x + 4 = \frac{1}{2}x$ **19.** $3(3 - b) = 5(2b + 7)$

20. GEOMETRY Find x so that the triangle is equilateral.

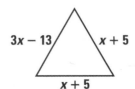

$3x - 13$ $x + 5$

$x + 5$

4.6 PROBLEM SOLVING STRATEGIES

There are usually several ways to solve real-life problems. For example, you can use tables and graphs. You can also use the general problem solving plan shown at the right.

Write a verbal model.

↓

Assign labels.

↓

Write an algebraic model.

↓

Solve the algebraic model.

↓

Answer the question.

↓

Check your answer.

21. You and your friends go canoeing on a river. The first canoe leaves at 11:00 A.M. and goes 4 mi/h. Your canoe leaves an hour later and goes 6 mi/h. When will you catch up to the first canoe? Use a table or a graph.

22. Show how to use the general problem solving plan to solve the problem in Exercise 21.

4.7 SOLVING EQUATIONS USING TECHNOLOGY

Wait until the last step to round decimals.

Example Solve $\frac{1}{8}(5x + 3) = 4$.

Solution

$$\frac{1}{8}(5x + 3) = 4$$
$$0.625x + 0.375 = 4$$
$$0.625x = 3.625$$
$$x = 5.80$$

$$\frac{1}{8}(5x + 3) = 4$$
$$0.63x + 0.38 \approx 4$$
$$0.63x \approx 3.62$$
$$x \approx 5.75$$

23. Solve $2.12(4.86y - 3.79) = 19$. Round to 2 decimal places.

24. **FUNDRAISING** Your class is selling subs to raise money for a field trip. The cost of the food to make the subs is $150. You sell each sub for $2.50. How many subs must your class sell to raise $600?

4.8 USING FORMULAS FROM GEOMETRY

Example Area of a triangle $= \frac{1}{2}$(base)(height)

$$= \frac{1}{2}(34)(26)$$
$$= 442 \text{ cm}^2$$

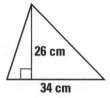

26 cm

34 cm

25. Solve for x and find the dimensions of the triangle.

Perimeter: 120 in.   Each side: $2x - 4$

In Exercises 1–8, solve the equation.

1. $4y - 2 = 18$

2. $3 - 3a = 21$

3. $12(r - 2) = 36$

4. $8x + 4 - 3x = 19$

5. $7s - 12 = s$

6. $\frac{1}{2}(x + 8) = 4$

7. $0.7x = 1.3x - 1.2$

8. $p + 2(p - 1) = 2p$

In Exercises 9 and 10, write the reciprocal of the number.

9. $-\dfrac{1}{2}$

10. 10

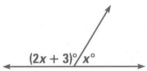 **TECHNOLOGY** In Exercises 11–13, use a calculator to solve the equation. Round your answer to two decimal places.

11. $5(3 + x) - 2x = 17$

12. $\frac{1}{7}(4x - 5) = 152$

13. $0.11(3.45x - 2.80) = 8.33$

14. The sum of the measures of the two angles at the right is $180°$. Find the measure of each angle.

$(2x + 3)° \quad x°$

SWIMMING In Exercises 15–17, use the diagram of the swimming pool. The pool is surrounded by a deck and a fence. The length of the fence is 172 ft.

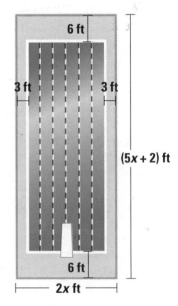

6 ft

3 ft   3 ft

$(5x + 2)$ ft

6 ft

$2x$ ft

15. Write an equation for the length of the fence and solve for x.

16. What are the dimensions of the swimming pool?

17. What is the area of the swimming pool?

In Exercises 18–20, use the following information.

When you started your homework assignment, your friend already had 6 exercises done. You can do about 2 exercises per minute. Your friend can only do 1 exercise per minute.

18. Copy and complete the table.

Minutes	0	1	2	3	4	5	6	7	8
Number of exercises you have solved	0	2	?	?	?	?	?	?	?
Number of exercises your friend has solved	6	7	?	?	?	?	?	?	?

19. How many minutes will it take you to catch up to your friend?

20. When you catch up, how many exercises will you have done?

1. The perimeter of the rectangle is 38 ft. What are the dimensions of the rectangle?

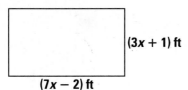

(3x + 1) ft

(7x − 2) ft

   A 8 ft by 11 ft

   B $8\frac{2}{5}$ ft by $10\frac{3}{5}$ ft

   C 7 ft by 12 ft

   D 6 ft by 13 ft

2. As a food server, you earn $5.50 per hour, plus tips. Last week you earned a total of $288. Your tips were $90. Which equation can be used to find the number of hours you worked?

   A $5.50p = 288$

   B $5.50p - 90 = 288$

   C $5.50p + 90 = 288$

   D $5.50p - 288 = 90$

3. The sum of the measures of the angles of a triangle is 180°. What is the measure of $\angle A$?

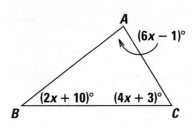

   A 14°   **B** 19°

   C 59°   **D** 83°

4. Which is the first incorrect step when solving the following equation?

   $2y - 4(y - 3) = 10$

   A Step 1 $2y - 4y \div 12 = 10$

   B Step 2 $-2y + 12 = 10$

   C Step 3 $-2y = -2$

   D Step 4 $y = 1$

For Questions 5 and 6, use the following information.

You want to join a health club for one year. Club A charges $55 per month and has no initiation fee. Club B costs $45 a month and has an initiation fee of $100.

5. At how many months do the two health club memberships have the same cost?

   A 8   **B** 9

   C 10   **D** 11

6. Which statement is false?

   A Club B is more expensive than Club A after the first 9 months of membership.

   B Club A would cost you $330 after one half of a year.

   C Club A would be less expensive for you to join.

   D Club B would cost you $145 after 1 month.

7. Which is the best approximation of the solution of the equation $-2.9n - 4.89 = 1.75(n + 14.5)$?

   A -17.81 **B** -6.51

   C -4.55 **D** -4.41

RECYCLING In 1995, the American public generated 4.3 pounds of trash per person per day, for a total of 208,000,000 tons of waste. Of this, 56,000,000 tons were recovered through recycling.

CHAPTER THEME
Recycling

TECHNOLOGY

• **Interactive Real-Life Investigations**

• **Middle School Tutorial Software**

To find out more about recycling, go to:

http://www.mlmath.com

CHAPTER PROJECT

Conducting a Recycling Survey

PROJECT DESCRIPTION

You will take a survey on the recycling habits of people in your school or in your neighborhood. You will make graphs of the results and display them on a poster.

GETTING STARTED

Talking It Over

- What questions should you ask? Below are sample questions.

  1. How many cans and bottles do you use each week? How many do you recycle?

  2. Which items do you recycle? (Check all that apply.)
     Paper___   Metal___
     Plastic___   Glass___

  3. How important do you think it is to recycle, on a scale of 1 (very) to 5 (not at all)?

Planning Your Project

- **Materials:** paper, markers, posterboard

- At least one question should ask "how many," like Question 1 at the left. At least one should let people choose from categories, like Question 2. At least one should ask for answers on a numerical scale, like Question 3.

- You will add graphs to your poster as you go through this chapter.

BUILDING YOUR PROJECT

These are places throughout the chapter where you will work on your project.

5.1 Conduct the survey. *p. 207*

5.2 Make a bar graph. *p. 211*

5.4 Choose an appropriate graph. *p. 224*

5.5 Make a misleading graph. *p. 229*

5.6 Make a line plot. *p. 234*

5.1

Exploring Pictographs and Time Lines

What you should learn:

Goal 1 How to read and make pictographs

Goal 2 How to read and make time lines

Why you should learn it:

Being able to interpret pictographs and time lines helps you read graphs that show, for example, the prices of movie tickets around the world.

Goal 1 USING PICTOGRAPHS

One of your goals in this course is to learn to use mathematics to communicate with others. In this chapter, you will learn many ways that graphs are used to communicate. For instance, Example 1 shows how a **pictograph** can be used to compare the cost of seeing a movie in different cities.

Example 1 Making a Pictograph

The price of a movie ticket in 1996 in each of several cities is shown below. Use a pictograph to represent these data. (Sources: *Fortune*, Runzheimer International)

REAL LIFE
Economics

City	Price	City	Price
London	$9.21	Mexico City	$2.52
New York	$8.50	Sydney	$9.53
Tokyo	$17.58	Toronto	$5.11

Solution

One way to represent the price of a movie ticket in the 6 cities is shown below. In this pictograph, each ticket symbol represents $3. The price of a movie ticket in each city is represented by the number of symbols in its row.

Movie Ticket Prices Around the World

London	🎟️🎟️🎟️ $9.21
New York	🎟️🎟️🎟️ $8.50
Tokyo	🎟️🎟️🎟️🎟️🎟️🎟️ $17.58
Mexico City	🎟️ $2.52
Sydney	🎟️🎟️🎟️ $9.53
Toronto	🎟️🎟️ $5.11

🎟️ = $3

Goal 2 USING TIME LINES

History books, as well as magazines and newspapers, use *time lines* to show how events are related in time. A **time line** is a graph that shows the dates of several events. Example 2 shows a time line about the history of aviation.

Example 2 › Drawing a Time Line

CONNECTION
History

The introduction dates of several types of airplanes are shown in the table. Also shown is an estimate of the total number of passengers on United States airlines during each year. Draw a time line for these data.

Year	Type of plane introduced	Total passengers
1903	First working airplane (biplane)	Not available
1906	First monoplane	Not available
1936	DC-3 transport plane	1,000,000
1942	First jet airplane in the U.S.	3,000,000
1952	First commercial jet airliner (the Comet)	25,000,000
1970	First jumbo jet (the 747)	170,000,000
1976	Concorde supersonic transport	225,000,000

Solution

One way to draw the time line is shown. Draw a number line that includes all of the years for which data are given. Draw tick marks at equally spaced intervals. Each interval should correspond to the same amount of time. In the time line below, the interval is 5 years.

A History of Air Travel

Monoplane						
Biplane	DC-3 (1 million)	U.S. jet (3 million)	Comet (25 million)	747 (170 million)	Concorde (225 million)	
1900	1920	1940	1960	1980	2000	

ONGOING ASSESSMENT

Talk About It

In 1976, there were about 215,000,000 people in the United States.

1. How does this compare with the number of air passengers in 1976?

2. Explain how there can be more passengers than people.

5.1 Exercises

Extra Practice, page 723

In Exercises 1 and 2, refer to Example 1 on page 204.

1. Use the pictograph to help you rank the cities from highest to lowest according to ticket price.

2. About how many times greater is the cost of a movie ticket in Tokyo than the cost in Mexico City?

3. Look back at Example 2 on page 205. How much did the number of air passengers increase between the first Comet and the first 747?

PRACTICE AND PROBLEM SOLVING

In Exercises 4 and 5, draw a time line that represents the set of data.

4. **POSTMASTERS** The years in which selected postmasters general took office are listed below.

   Benjamin Franklin, 1775   William T. Barry, 1829   John Wanamaker, 1889
   Frank H. Hitchcock, 1909   James A. Farley, 1933   Lawrence F. O'Brien, 1965

5. **STAMPS** Between 1975 and 1995, the cost of a first-class postage stamp increased several times.

September 14, 1975	10¢	December 31, 1975	13¢	May 29, 1978	15¢
March 22, 1981	18¢	November 1, 1981	20¢	February 17, 1985	22¢
April 3, 1988	25¢	February 3, 1991	29¢	January 1, 1995	32¢

**AIR TRAVEL In Exercises 6–9, use the pictograph.
The pictograph shows how many passengers traveled
on the five most heavily traveled U.S. airlines in 1995.**

6. How many passengers does each airplane represent?

7. About how many passengers traveled on United?

8. Estimate how many more passengers traveled on American than on USAir.

9. How would the pictograph change if each airplane represented 20 million passengers?

Airline Passengers

Delta	✈✈✈✈✈✈✈✈✈
American	✈✈✈✈✈✈✈✈
United	✈✈✈✈✈✈✈✈
USAir	✈✈✈✈✈✈
Southwest	✈✈✈✈✈·

✈ = 10 million passengers

(Source: Air Transport Association of America)

10. The table below shows the price of toothpaste in several cities in 1996. Use the data to create a pictograph.
    (Source: Runzheimer International)

City	Hong Kong	Mexico City	Munich	Paris
Price of toothpaste	$2.26	$1.33	$2.45	$3.63

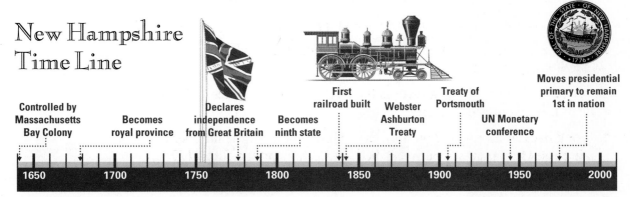

New Hampshire Time Line

Controlled by Massachusetts Bay Colony

Becomes royal province

Declares independence from Great Britain

Becomes ninth state

First railroad built

Webster Ashburton Treaty

Treaty of Portsmouth

UN Monetary conference

Moves presidential primary to remain 1st in nation

1650   1700   1750   1800   1850   1900   1950   2000

11. What is the time interval used in the time line?

12. Estimate the year in which New Hampshire's first railroad was built.

13. What event in New Hampshire's history occurred in 1776?

14. List two events that occurred in New Hampshire in the 19th century.

15. **HISTORY** Make a time line of the innovations listed below.

1793	Eli Whitney invents cotton gin.	1816	Sir David Brewster invents kaleidoscope.
1837	Samuel Morse patents telegraph.	1859	Edwin Drake drills first oil well.
1876	Alexander Bell invents telephone.	1898	Marie Curie discovers radium.
1923	Garrett Morgan patents traffic light.	1934	Wallace Carothers invents nylon.

16. Make a time line of some of the important events in your life.

STANDARDIZED TEST PRACTICE

17. Which of the following statements is true?

(A) $a + b > c$ **(B)** $a - b < d$

(C) $ab > c$ **(D)** $a \div b < d$

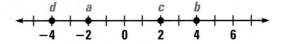

EXPLORATION AND EXTENSION

PORTFOLIO

18. **BUILDING YOUR PROJECT** Follow the guidelines on page 203 to design and conduct a survey. Survey at least 20 people. Tally the results of your survey and keep them in your portfolio. You will be using them to complete the Building Your Project exercises throughout the chapter.

Have you ever dreamed of owning your own business? That dream came true for Shiree Sanchez, who started a successful direct marketing business.

Goal 1 USING BAR GRAPHS

The three basic types of **bar graphs** are shown below. When you use a bar graph to represent real-life data, you first need to decide which type will best represent the data.

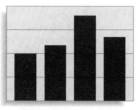

Simple bar graph

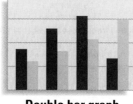

Double bar graph

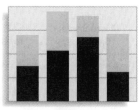

Stacked bar graph

Example 1 Drawing a Bar Graph

A survey asked 250 adults about their personal goals. The results are listed below. Represent these data with a bar graph.

Goal	Have (or had) goal	Achieved goal
Owning a home	157	109
Happy marriage	140	100
Owning a car	131	150
Having children	131	113
Being rich	113	7
Interesting job	111	60

Solution

Each category (each goal) has two pieces of data. So, you can use a double bar graph to represent the data.

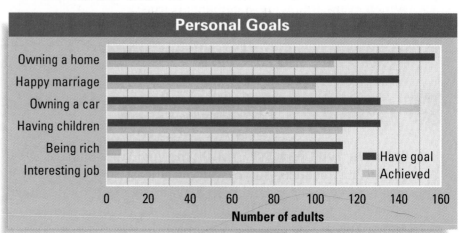

Personal Goals

Owning a home
Happy marriage
Owning a car
Having children
Being rich
Interesting job

■ Have goal
■ Achieved

0   20   40   60   80   100   120   140   160

Number of adults

A **histogram** is a bar graph in which the bars represent equally spaced intervals of numbers.

Example 2 Drawing a Histogram

REAL LIFE
Student Heights

You have taken a survey of the heights (in inches) of 30 students. Organize the data in a histogram.

$58\frac{1}{2}$, 65, 60, $61\frac{1}{2}$, $58\frac{1}{2}$, 63, $64\frac{1}{2}$, $66\frac{1}{2}$, 62, 67, 59, 68, $62\frac{1}{2}$, 68, $56\frac{1}{2}$,

59, 60, 62, $63\frac{1}{2}$, 54, $65\frac{1}{2}$, 57, 64, 65, 67, 61, $60\frac{1}{2}$, 62, $64\frac{1}{2}$, 62

Solution

Decide which intervals to use. Then make a **frequency distribution** that shows the number of events or items in each interval.

The frequency distribution at the right shows how many students' heights are in each interval.

Frequency Distribution

Interval	Tally	Total
54–55.9	I	1
56–57.9	II	2
58–59.9	IIII	4
60–61.9	IIII	5
62–63.9	IIII II	7
64–65.9	IIII I	6
66–67.9	III	3
68–69.9	II	2

Use the totals in the frequency distribution to draw a histogram. An important difference between a histogram and a bar graph is that there are no spaces between the bars in a histogram.

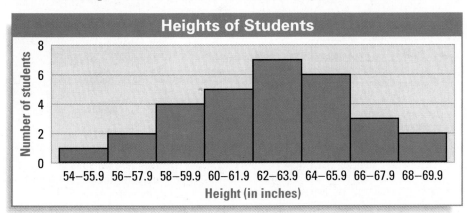

Heights of Students

Number of students — Height (in inches): 54–55.9, 56–57.9, 58–59.9, 60–61.9, 62–63.9, 64–65.9, 66–67.9, 68–69.9

ONGOING ASSESSMENT

Write About It

Use the data from Example 2.

1. Make a new histogram using the intervals 54–57.9, 58–61.9, 62–65.9, and 66–69.9.

2. Compare your new histogram to the one in Example 2. Which one gives a more detailed picture of how the data are distributed?

5.2 Exercises

Extra Practice, page 723

GUIDED PRACTICE

1. How do you make a frequency distribution from given data?

2. How is a frequency distribution used?

In Exercises 3 and 4, refer to Example 1 on page 208.

3. Which goal was achieved by the most people? by the fewest?

4. Which was the most popular goal? How many people achieved it?

PRACTICE AND PROBLEM SOLVING

5. **CARS** Out of the 10 top-selling cars in 1993, Chevrolet made 2, Ford made 3, Honda made 2, and Toyota made 1. Which type of bar graph would you use to represent these data? Explain.

Investigation 5,
Interactive
Real-Life
Investigations

6. **SCHOOLS** The table shows the fall enrollment (in millions of students) in grades K–8 for public and private schools. Represent the results with a stacked bar graph. Use one color for public schools and one for private schools. On the graph, tell what each color represents.

Type of school	1980	1985	1990	1995
Public	27.6	27.0	29.9	32.4
Private	4.0	4.2	4.1	4.4

7. **ENVIRONMENT** You record the ages of 36 volunteers cleaning a local park. Organize the data in a histogram.

```
13 17  8  9 12 13 13 16 14 10 15 14
15  9 15 10 11 16 13 11 10 17 11 12
13 10 12  9  6 14 16 11  9  9 10  7
```

8. **COMPUTERS** A survey asked 100 parents of children ages 6 to 17 the skills that they believe their children develop from using computers. Represent the results with a bar graph.

Skill	Number of parents
Word processing/typing	32
Reading	26
Mathematics	26
Hand-eye coordination	22
Writing	18
Thinking/reasoning	18
Analytical problem solving	9
Speed	2

Real Life...
Real People

Computer Whiz At 16, Minneapolis resident Trent Eisenberg runs his own computer technical support company.

POPULATION In Exercises 9–13, use the bar graph. The graph shows the projected population (in millions) of young Americans for 1995, 2000, and 2005.

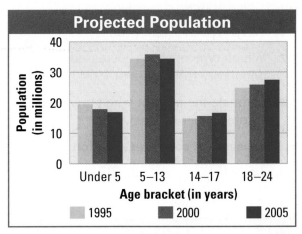

Projected Population

(Source: *Statistical Abstract of the United States*)

9. Which two age brackets have about the same population in 2005?

10. Which age bracket shows a decrease in population from 1995 to 2005?

11. Which age bracket has the smallest population in 2000?

12. Estimate the increase in 14–17 year-olds from 1995 to 2005.

13. **EVALUATING CONCLUSIONS** An analyst uses the graph to conclude that the number of 18–24 year-olds will increase from the year 2005 to the year 2010. Do you agree? Explain.

STANDARDIZED TEST PRACTICE

14. The graph shows the number of visitors to two museums for five months. During which month did the art museum have the greatest number of visitors?

   A May   **B** June

   C July   **D** August

15. What was the total number of visitors to both museums in July?

   A 3000   **B** 4000

   C 7000   **D** 10,000

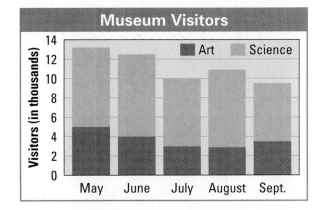

Museum Visitors

EXPLORATION AND EXTENSION

PORTFOLIO

16. **BUILDING YOUR PROJECT** Make a bar graph representing some of the results from your survey. Display the graph on your poster. From your graph, what can you conclude about the recycling habits of the people you surveyed?

In Exercises 1–3, use the graph. The graph shows the percent of Americans ages 14 to 17 who purchased each type of shoes.

(Source: *Statistical Abstract of the United States*) **(5.2)**

1. What type of graph is this?

2. Which type of shoes decreased in popularity from 1992 to 1994?

3. Estimate the percent who purchased aerobic shoes in 1993.

Shoe Purchases

Percent of 14–17 year-olds

20
15
10
5
0

Aerobic shoes | Gym shoes | Running shoes | Walking shoes

■ 1992
■ 1993
■ 1994

In Exercises 4–7, solve the equation. **(4.3–4.5)**

4. $3x + 4 = x$

5. $2(2x + 1) = 8$

6. $\frac{1}{3}(6x - 3) = 7$

7. $4t + 6t = 8t - 13$

CAREER Interview

RECYCLING ENGINEER

Stephen Morgan designs, starts up, and troubleshoots systems to recycle paper at paper mills. He ensures that the paper brought from recycling bins is made into new paper products efficiently. The job takes him all over the United States and to foreign countries.

Q What led you into this career?
When I learned about it in college, I felt it was an interesting, new, and exciting field.

Q What is your favorite part of your job?
I like to travel, and the different people I meet together with the variety of the work keeps it exciting and fun.

Q Do you use high school mathematics in your work?
Yes, I use algebra a great deal in my work, solving equations for unknown values. For example, I use it when I calculate mass balances as treated pulp is being moved from one place to another inside the mills. In addition, I also need to understand geometry when planning an installation.

Q What would you like to tell students about math?
Math is very important; it makes life easier to understand. Knowing math makes you aware of your surroundings.

Making a **Histogram**

You can use a graphing calculator to make histograms.

Example

The frequency distribution at the right shows the heights of 30 students, as discussed in Example 2 on page 209.

Use a graphing calculator to make a histogram of these data.

Interval	Tally	Total
54–55.9	I	1
56–57.9	II	2
58–59.9	IIII	4
60–61.9	⊬	5
62–63.9	⊬ II	7
64–65.9	⊬ I	6
66–67.9	III	3
68–69.9	II	2

Solution

1 Press WINDOW and set the viewing window.

Xmin = 52   Xmax = 72   Xscl = 2
Ymin = −1   Ymax = 10   Yscl = 1

2 Press STAT. Select "1: Edit" and enter the data.

3 Press 2nd STAT PLOT. Select "1: Plot 1" and the options below. Press GRAPH.

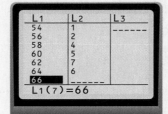

Exercises

In Exercises 1 and 2, use a graphing calculator to make a histogram.

1.

Interval	Tally	Total
33–35.9	III	3
36–38.9	⊬ II	7
39–41.9	⊬ I	6
42–44.9	⊬ I	6
45–47.9	⊬	5
48–50.9	III	3

2.

Interval	Tally	Total
10–14.9	⊬ III	8
15–19.9	⊬ II	7
20–24.9	⊬ I	6
25–29.9	III	3
30–34.9	I	1
35–39.9	IIII	4

5.3

Exploring Line Graphs

What you should learn:

Goal 1 How to use line graphs to represent data

Goal 2 How to use line graphs to explore patterns in geometry

Why you should learn it:

Line graphs can help you communicate about real-life situations, such as the numbers of female and minority members of Congress.

Student reporters talk with Carrie Meek, a United States Congresswoman from Florida.

TOOLBOX

Line Graphs, page 761

Goal 1 USING LINE GRAPHS

Line graphs are often used to show trends over intervals of time. A *simple* line graph shows changes in one quantity. A *double* line graph shows changes in two quantities.

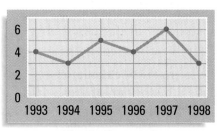

Simple line graph

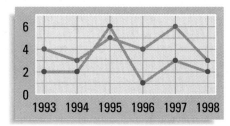

Double line graph

Example 1 Interpreting a Line Graph

The *triple* line graph below shows the numbers of female, African American, and Hispanic members of the United States House of Representatives from 1981 to 1997. (Representatives are elected for 2-year terms.) In which time intervals did the number of representatives in every group increase?

REAL LIFE
U.S. Congress

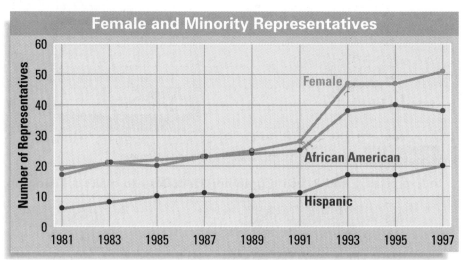

Solution

Look for time intervals in which all 3 lines increase as the lines move from left to right. This occurs four times: between 1981 and 1983, between 1985 and 1987, between 1989 and 1991, and between 1991 and 1993.

Example 2 ▶ **Finding a Geometric Pattern**

CONNECTION
Geometry

The sum of the measures of the angles of a triangle is 180°. Use this result to find the sum of the measures of the angles in the polygons below. Represent your results with a line graph. Describe the pattern of the points on the graph.

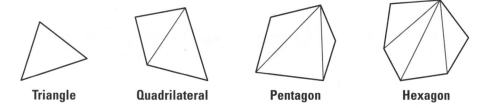

| Triangle | Quadrilateral | Pentagon | Hexagon |

Solution

The quadrilateral can be divided into 2 triangles, as shown above. This means that the sum of its angle measures is $2 \times 180°$, which equals 360°. You can find the sum of the angle measures in the pentagon and in the hexagon using the same method.

Polygon	Number of triangles	Sum of angle measures
Triangle	1	$1 \times 180° = 180°$
Quadrilateral	2	$2 \times 180° = 360°$
Pentagon	3	$3 \times 180° = 540°$
Hexagon	4	$4 \times 180° = 720°$

The results in the table are represented by the line graph below. All four of the points on the graph lie on a straight line.

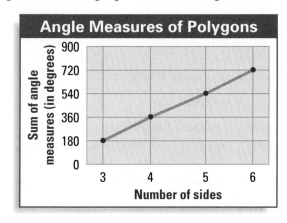

Angle Measures of Polygons

Sum of angle measures (in degrees) / Number of sides

Talk About It
. . . .

Use the graph and table in Example 2.

1. How much does the sum of the angle measures increase from a 4-sided to a 5-sided polygon?

2. How does this increase compare with the increases in the other intervals?

5.3 Exercises

Extra Practice, page 723

GUIDED PRACTICE

USING A GRAPH In Exercises 1–3, use the line graph in Example 1 on page 214.

1. Estimate the number of African American representatives in 1995.

2. Estimate the increase in female representatives from 1991 to 1993.

3. Estimate the increase in Hispanic representatives from 1981 to 1997.

PRACTICE AND PROBLEM SOLVING

BUYING A HOUSE In Exercises 4–8, use the line graph. It shows the average sales price of a new house in each region of the United States.
(Source: *Statistical Abstract of the United States*)

4. Name the units on the horizontal axis and the units on the vertical axis.

5. Four different colors are used for the data points. What does each color represent?

6. Estimate the average sales price of a new home in the Midwest in 1985 and in 1995.

7. Which region of the United States had the lowest average new home price in 1980?

8. In one of the regions of the United States, new home prices dropped during one time interval. Name the region and the years.

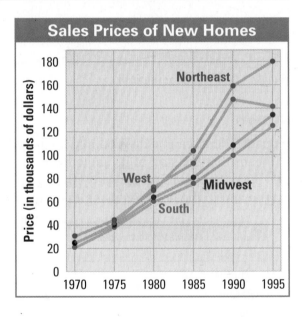

GEOMETRY In Exercises 9 and 10, use the triangles shown below.

  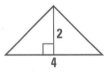 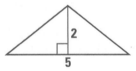

9. Create a table that lists the base, height, and area of each triangle.

10. Make a line graph showing how the base relates to the area.

11. AIRLINES The total profit or loss (in billions of dollars) for airlines in the United States is given in the table. Make a line graph for the data.

Year	1988	1989	1990	1991	1992	1993	1994	1995
Profit or loss	1.7	0.1	−3.9	−1.9	−4.8	−2.1	−0.3	2.4

COLLEGE COSTS In Exercises 12 and 13, use the table. The table lists the average annual cost (in dollars) of tuition and fees at public and private four-year colleges. (Source: U.S. Department of Education)

Year	Public	Private
1980	804	3617
1983	1148	5093
1986	1414	6658
1989	1780	8396
1992	2349	10,294
1995	2848	12,239

12. Make a line graph of the data.

13. **OPEN-ENDED PROBLEM** Are the costs for a public college increasing at a faster or slower rate than the costs for a private college? Explain your reasoning.

14. **WRITING** Describe a real-life situation that could be represented by the line graph at the right. Include the units of measure for the data, and explain how the graph could be used to answer questions about the data.

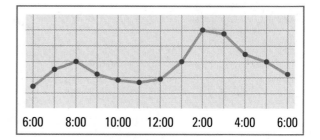

15. The line graph shows the price of a share of stock in a company over a period of five months. In which month did the price increase by more than $2.00?

(**A**) February (**B**) March

(**C**) April (**D**) May

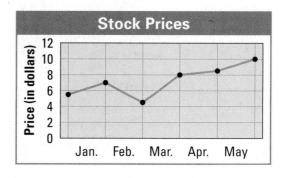

Stock Prices

EXPLORATION AND EXTENSION

In Exercises 16–18, use the table. It shows how many sheets of paper were in the recycling bins of two classrooms over the course of a week.

Day	Monday	Tuesday	Wednesday	Thursday	Friday
Ms. Dalton's class	86	72	64	66	95
Mr. Valdez's class	80	75	72	76	119

16. Make a line graph of the data.

17. Overall, which class recycled more paper?

18. **OPEN-ENDED PROBLEM** On what day was the most paper recycled? Give a possible reason for this.

LAB 5.4

COOPERATIVE LEARNING

Choosing Appropriate Graphs

Materials Needed
- graph paper
- colored pencils

Part A GRAPHING SURVEY RESULTS

In a survey, you asked 200 people what they are afraid of. The results are shown below.

Scary thing	Number of people
Snakes	81
Public speaking	51
High places	37
Mice	32
Flying on a plane	32
Spiders and insects	22

1. Represent these data with one of the three types of graphs listed below. Choose one that works well with the data.

   Pictograph   *Line Graph*   *Bar Graph*

2. If you couldn't use your first choice in Exercise 1, what would be your second choice?

3. One of the three choices in Exercise 1 is not a good way to represent these data. Tell which one, and explain why it is not appropriate.

Part B BAR GRAPHS AND LINE GRAPHS

Every 4 years, a survey asked people whether the amount that was spent on improving the nation's education system was *too little money*, *about the right amount*, or *too much money*. The percents of people who said "too little" or "about right" are shown in the table.

Year	1974	1978	1982	1986	1990	1994
Too little	54%	53%	57%	61%	74%	72%
About right	38%	35%	34%	34%	23%	22%

(Source: General Social Survey)

4. Represent these data with a bar graph and with a line graph.

5. In which graph from Exercise 4 is it easier to see how the percent that answered "about right" changed over time? Explain.

A survey was taken of people who enjoy gardening. Here are the percents of gardeners in different age groups who pursue the hobby at least 4 hours per week. (Source: *American Demographics*)

Age group of gardeners	18–29	30–44	45–59	60+
Percent who garden at least 4 h/wk	16%	19%	28%	29%

6. Represent these data with one of the four types of graphs listed below. Explain why you chose that type of graph.

   Pictograph   Histogram   Bar Graph   Time Line

7. If you couldn't use your first choice in Exercise 6, what would be your second choice?

8. Name one of the choices in Exercise 6 that is *not* an appropriate type of graph for these data. Explain why it is not appropriate.

NOW TRY THESE

In Exercises 9–11, use the following information.

In a survey, people were asked if they were members of different kinds of organizations. Below are the percents of people who were members of hobby clubs and sports clubs.

Year	1987	1989	1991	1993
Hobby club	10%	9%	11%	13%
Sports club	20%	22%	19%	20%

(Source: General Social Survey)

9. Graph these data. Use a type of graph that is appropriate to the data.

10. Name another type of graph that is also appropriate to the data. Explain why it is appropriate.

11. Name a type of graph that is not appropriate to the data. Explain.

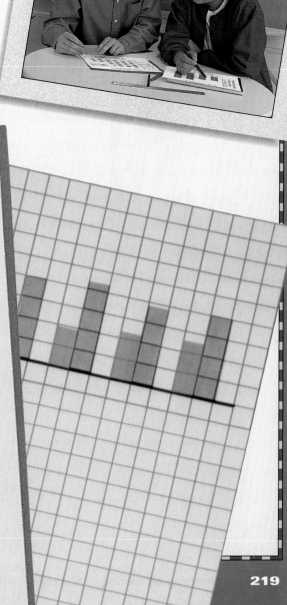

Problem Solving: Choosing an **Appropriate Graph**

What you should learn:

Goal 1 How to choose an appropriate graph to represent data

Goal 2 How to use graphs to make presentations

Why you should learn it:

Graphs can help you communicate about real-life situations, such as the numbers of miles walked each day by doctors and other professionals.

Goal 1 CHOOSING APPROPRIATE GRAPHS

Here are some guidelines that will help you decide when to use a bar graph, a line graph, and a pictograph.

GUIDELINES FOR CHOOSING A GRAPH

 Use a bar graph when the data fall into distinct categories and you want to compare totals.

 Use a line graph when the categories have a numerical order, such as a sequence of years.

 Use a pictograph instead of a bar graph when you want high visual appeal.

Example 1 Organizing Data with a Graph

You take a survey to find out how much walking people do while at work. The results are shown below.

Occupation	Distance walked per day
Mail carrier	4.4 mi
Doctor	3.5 mi
Police officer	6.8 mi
Retail salesperson	3.4 mi

Solution

You can use either a bar graph (shown below) or a pictograph.

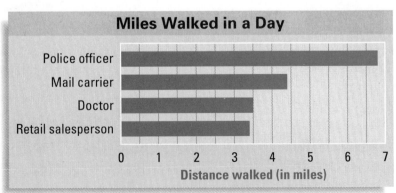

Example 2 Making a Presentation

You are a clothing designer who surveyed adults on the colors of their favorite suits for dressy occasions. You want to use the results (shown in the table below) in a presentation. Make a graph of the data.

REAL LIFE
Fashion

Clothing color	Black	Blue	Gray	Red	Brown
Number of women	727	551	223	222	102
Number of men	702	473	649	78	198

Solution

If you want high visual appeal, use a pictograph.

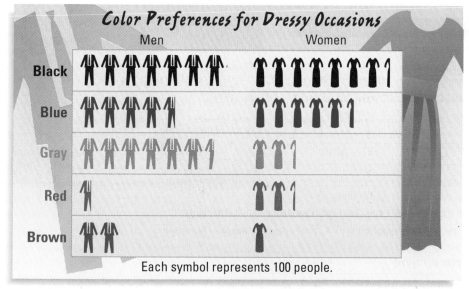

Color Preferences for Dressy Occasions

Men   Women

Black
Blue
Gray
Red
Brown

Each symbol represents 100 people.

You could also use a double bar graph or a stacked bar graph. A stacked bar graph of the same data is shown at the right.

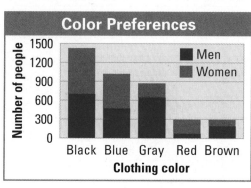

Color Preferences

Number of people

Men
Women

Black Blue Gray Red Brown
Clothing color

A line graph would not be appropriate because the categories (the clothing colors) do not have a numerical order.

ONGOING **ASSESSMENT**

Talk About It

Use the two graphs in Example 2.

1. Explain why the pictograph might be more effective than the bar graph in a presentation.

2. What are some advantages of using a bar graph instead of a pictograph?

GUIDED PRACTICE

In Exercises 1 and 2, refer to Example 1 on page 220.

1. How many more miles per day do police officers walk than mail carriers?

2. In which occupation do people walk half the distance per day that police officers do?

In Exercises 3 and 4, refer to Example 2 on page 221.

3. How many more men than women prefer to wear gray?

4. Which is the least popular suit color for women? Which is the least popular suit color for men?

PRACTICE AND PROBLEM SOLVING

In Exercises 5–7, choose a type of graph to represent the data. Explain why you chose that type, then draw the graph.

5. **HOBBIES** You survey the people in your neighborhood about hobbies they have.

Craft or hobby	Number of people
Sewing/needlecrafts	46
Candy making/cake decorating	15
Painting/drawing	14
Plastic model kits	11
Ceramics	9
Flowers	8
Model railroading	6

6. **VIDEOCASSETTE RECORDERS** A growing percentage of American households have videocassette recorders (VCRs). (Source: *Trends in Television*)

Year	1980	1984	1988	1992	1996
Percent	1	10	57	74	81

7. **CATS** You survey a group of cat owners about why they own cats.

Reason for owning a cat	Percent of owners
Someone to play with	93
Companionship	84
Help children learn responsibility	78
Someone to communicate with	62
Security	51

8. **DOGS** You take a poll of dog owners to find out what tricks their dogs know. Make a graph of the data. Explain why you used the type of graph that you did.

Trick	Number of dogs
Sit	53
Shake paw	38
Roll over	29
Speak	27
Stand on hind legs	19
Sing	8
Fetch newspaper	4

9. Make a double bar graph of the data in Example 2 on page 221. Compare your graph with the stacked bar graph in Example 2. Which is more effective at showing the differences between men's and women's preferences? Which is better for showing overall color preferences? Explain.

LITTLE LEAGUE In Exercises 10–13, use the graph below. The graph shows the number of kids playing Little League baseball from 1940 through 1995.

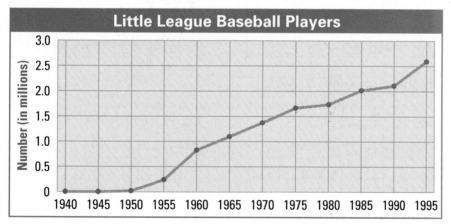

Little League Baseball Players

(Source: Little League Baseball)

10. Estimate the number of players in 1980, 1985, and 1995.

11. Estimate the total increase in the number of players from 1940 to 1995.

12. During which 5-year interval did the number of players increase the most?

13. Why is a line graph a good choice for presenting these data?

14. The line graph at the right shows a company's revenue and expenses for 6 months. In which month were the expenses the greatest?

    (A) August   **(B)** September

    (C) October   **(D)** November

15. Profit is the difference of revenue and expenses. What was the company's profit in November?

    (A) −$19,000   **(B)** −$18,000

    (C) $10,000   **(D)** $19,000

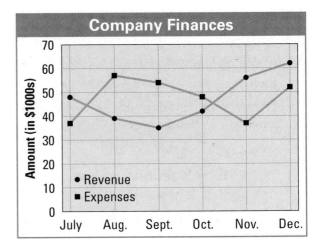

Company Finances

EXPLORATION AND EXTENSION

PORTFOLIO

16. **BUILDING YOUR PROJECT** Choose some of the data from your survey that you have not yet graphed. Make an appropriate graph of the data and display the graph on your poster. Explain why you chose the type of graph you did.

SPIRAL REVIEW

In Exercises 1–6, simplify the expression without using a calculator. (1.4)

1. $3 + 6 \times 8 \div 2$

2. $10 \cdot 7 - 2 \cdot 4$

3. $16 - 5 + 2(6)$

4. $12 \div 3 + 3 \times 2$

5. $25 + 45 \div 3^2$

6. $4 \times 2^3 - 5$

In Exercises 7–15, simplify the expression. (3.3–3.6)

7. $-4 - 2$

8. $\dfrac{15}{-3}$

9. $12 + (-2)$

10. $-6 \times (-7)$

11. $22 - (-9)$

12. $-14 + 12$

13. $6 + (-18)$

14. -11×8

15. $-3 - (-33)$

In Exercises 16–21, solve the equation. (4.3)

16. $16 + 2k = 10$

17. $5d + 11 = 76$

18. $22 = 6 - 4w$

19. $\dfrac{1}{3}a - 5 = 17$

20. $24 = 4(m - 7)$

21. $3z + 7 = 19$

22. You want to buy a bicycle that costs $112. From your part-time job, you manage to save $14 each week. Write an algebraic model and solve it to find how many weeks you have to save in order to buy the bicycle. **(2.7)**

Take this test as you would take a test in class. The answers to the exercises are given in the back of the book.

In Exercises 1–4, use the graph. It shows how much was spent to advertise various products on television networks. (5.3)

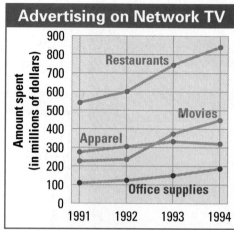

Advertising on Network TV

1. What type of graph is this?

2. Name the only product whose network advertising expenses ever decreased.

3. Which product had the greatest increase in network advertising from 1991 to 1992?

4. Which product spent about $375 million for network advertising in 1993?

5. **LITERATURE** The table lists the year of birth of several famous authors. Make a time line using this information. (5.1)

Author	Year of birth
Emily Dickinson	1830
Mark Twain	1835
Jack London	1876
John Steinbeck	1902
Alice Walker	1944

6. The table shows the price of a share of stock in each company in April, 1997. Draw a graph to represent these data. Explain your choice of graph. (5.4)

Company	Stock price
Sears, Roebuck	$49
Wal-Mart Stores	$28
J.C. Penney	$47
Kmart Corp.	$13

7. **VIDEO RENTALS** The amount Americans spent on video tape rentals is given below. Graph the data and explain why you chose that type of graph. (5.4)

1989: $4.4 trillion   1990: $5.0 trillion   1991: $5.0 trillion

1992: $5.5 trillion   1993: $6.0 trillion   1994: $6.6 trillion

In Exercises 8–11, you survey people about the reasons they doodle. The results are shown in the graph. (5.2)

8. What type of graph is this?

9. What seems to be the most common reason for doodling?

10. Estimate the number of people who doodle while they are thinking or solving problems.

11. Which reason do about 82 people give for doodling?

People Who Doodle

Problem Solving: Misleading Graphs

What you should learn:

Goal 1 How to recognize misleading pictographs and bar graphs

Goal 2 How to recognize and correct misleading line graphs

Why you should learn it:

Knowing when a graph is misleading helps you interpret information that is presented graphically in magazines and newspapers.

Goal 1 MISLEADING PICTOGRAPHS AND BAR GRAPHS

Example 1 Interpreting a Pictograph

(Source: *Statistical Abstract of the United States*)

From the scale on the vertical axis, you can tell that there were just over 15 tons of waste recycled in 1985, and about two times as much (over 30 tons) in 1990. The pictograph is misleading because the drawing of the recycling bin for 1990 has an area that is about four times the area of the 1985 bin.

Example 2 Interpreting a Bar Graph

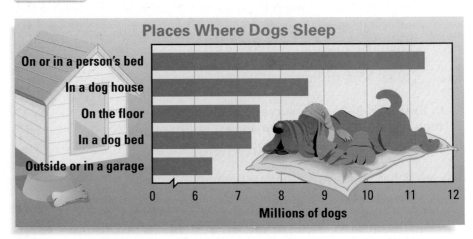

NEED TO KNOW

In Example 2, the symbol ─⋏─ indicates a break in the scale on the horizontal axis.

This graph could be misleading. The lengths of the bars make it appear that about four times as many dogs sleep on or in people's beds as sleep outside or in a garage. You can tell from the scale on the horizontal axis, however, that it is really only about twice as many.

Example 3 Interpreting Line Graphs

The line graphs below show the numbers of paperback and hardcover books sold in the United States from 1988 to 1994.

(Source: *Statistical Abstract of the United States*)

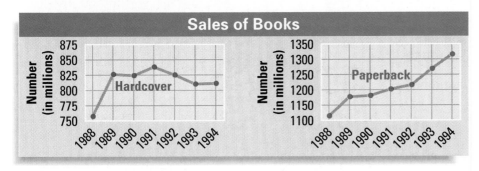

a. Explain why this graphical display could be misleading.

b. Make a graph of the data that is not misleading.

Solution

a. By using a different vertical scale for each graph, the display gives the visual impression that paperbacks and hardcovers sold about the same number of copies. By looking at the scale, however, you can tell that paperbacks actually sold many more copies than hardcovers. Also, the vertical axes do not begin at zero, so the changes from one year to the next are accentuated.

b. A better way to graph these data is to use a double line graph, as shown below. Both sets of data are graphed using the same vertical scale. Also, the vertical axis begins at zero.

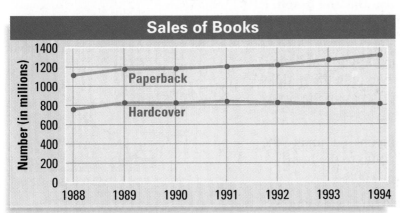

GUIDED PRACTICE

In Exercises 1 and 2, use the graph, which shows the number of junior high schools with modems in 1992 and 1995.

1. If you look only at the size of the school buildings and ignore the scale on the vertical axis, what will you conclude about the numbers of junior high schools with modems in 1992 and 1995?

2. Explain why the graph could be misleading.

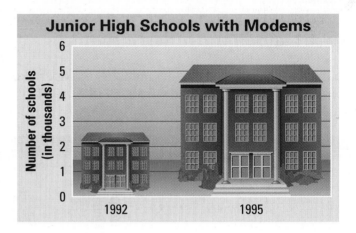

PRACTICE AND PROBLEM SOLVING

INSTRUMENTS In Exercises 3–6, use the bar graph. The graph shows the number of Americans (in millions) that play each musical instrument.
(Source: American Music Conference)

3. If you look only at the length of the bars and ignore the scale on the vertical axis, how will you think the number of drummers compares to the number of saxophone players?

4. Use the scale on the vertical axis to compare the number of drummers to the number of saxophone players.

5. Explain why this graph could be misleading.

6. Sketch a graph of the data that is not misleading.

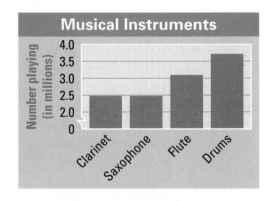

HOURLY PAY In Exercises 7–9, use the line graph. It shows the average hourly pay for factory workers from April 1994 through March 1997. (Source: *The Wall Street Journal*)

7. If you ignore the numbers on the vertical scale, how will you think the hourly pay in the middle of 1996 compares to the hourly pay in the first few months of 1995?

8. Use the scale on the vertical axis to compare the hourly pay in the middle of 1996 to the hourly pay in the first few months of 1995.

9. Explain why this graph could be misleading.

In Exercises 10 and 11, use the two graphs, which show the same data.

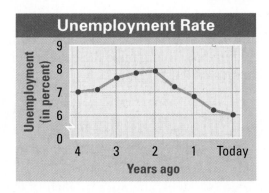

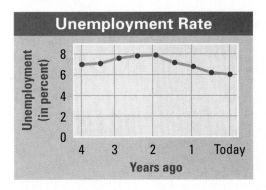

10. A candidate who has been in office for four years wants to show that the unemployment rate has decreased over that time. Which graph might this candidate use? Explain.

11. A challenger wants to show that unemployment was high during the past four years. Which graph might the challenger use? Explain.

12. **HOME PRICES** The pictograph shows the average sales price of a new one-family house in 1970 and in 1995. Explain why the graph is misleading. (Source: *Statistical Abstract of the United States*)

13. **RESEARCH** Find a misleading graph in a newspaper or magazine. Explain why it is misleading.

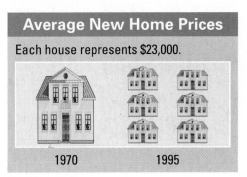

STANDARDIZED TEST PRACTICE

14. Which of these should you always do when you make a bar graph?

   (A) Break the vertical axis

   (B) Use bars that have unequal widths

   (C) Show the scale on the vertical axis

   (D) Start the vertical axis at something other than zero

PORTFOLIO

EXPLORATION AND EXTENSION

15. **BUILDING YOUR PROJECT** Choose one of the graphs that you have already made from the results of your survey. Make a misleading graph of the same data, and display it on your poster near the original graph. Explain why the new graph is misleading.

5.6

Statistics: Line Plots

What you should learn:

Goal 1 How to use line plots to organize data

Goal 2 How to use organized data to help make decisions

Why you should learn it:

Data are more useful when they are organized. For example, wildlife biologists collect and organize data such as ages of squirrels and sizes of moose.

NEED TO KNOW

Line plots are different from *line graphs*, which you studied in Lesson 5.3.

Goal 1 USING LINE PLOTS

When data from an experiment or a survey are first collected, they are usually not organized. Deciding how to organize the data is a critical part of a branch of mathematics called *statistics*.

LESSON INVESTIGATION

Organizing Data

GROUP ACTIVITY The data below list the ages of each of the squirrels in a population. Is it easy to see patterns in or make conclusions about the data in this form? With your group, discuss different ways to organize the data. Then organize the data. Is it easier to see patterns in or make conclusions about the data after they are organized? Explain.

3, 1, 1, 5, 11, 12, 5, 7, 7, 3, 2, 4, 1, 10, 11, 4, 4, 4,
1, 5, 6, 6, 7, 4, 1, 3, 2, 1, 9, 2, 12, 4, 4, 1, 8, 9,
1, 3, 3, 2, 5, 1, 3, 1, 2, 2, 1, 1, 2, 2, 1, 1, 3, 3,
1, 6, 2, 6, 1, 1, 8, 3, 2, 2, 2, 2, 5, 5, 1, 3, 8, 2

Example 1 Using a Line Plot

One way to organize the data in the investigation above is with a **line plot**. Draw a number line that includes all of the integers from 1 through 12. For each number in the list of data, place an **x** above its coordinate on the number line, as shown below.

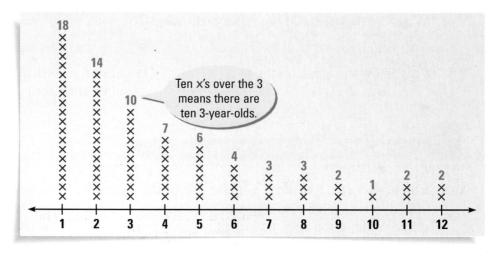

Example 2 **Interpreting a Survey**

In a survey, you ask 30 people how important it is to recycle aluminum cans. What can you conclude from the results shown?

1. *Very important.* I always recycle aluminum cans.

2. *Quite important.* I usually recycle aluminum cans.

3. *Somewhat important.* I sometimes recycle aluminum cans.

4. *Not very important.* I recycle aluminum cans only when it is convenient.

5. *Not at all important.* I never recycle aluminum cans.

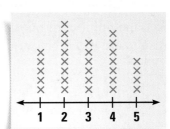

Real Life...
Real Facts

A 1994 survey asked Americans how often they sort cans, papers, and other materials for recycling. Of those surveyed, 35% said *always*, 25% said *often*, and 25% said *sometimes*.

Solution

STRATEGY **USE A GRAPH** It appears that many of the people surveyed do not feel that recycling is very important. Four people said that they never recycle aluminum cans, and another seven said they recycle cans only when it is convenient.

Example 3 **Using a Line Plot**

Each time you fill your car with gas, you divide the distance traveled (in miles) by the amount of gas used (in gallons). During the summer, you do this twelve times. The results (in miles per gallon) are shown.

$$24, \ 22, \ 20, \ 21, \ 24, \ 23, \ 22, \ 17, \ 25, \ 23, \ 21, \ 22$$

Use a line plot to organize the data. What do you observe?

Solution

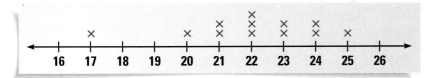

Your gas mileage is usually between 20 and 25 miles per gallon. The low mileage result might have been due to heavy traffic.

ONGOING ASSESSMENT

Write About It
....

When checking the calculations described in Example 3, you notice you wrote

306 mi ÷ 18 gal

when you should have written

396 mi ÷ 18 gal.

1. Correct the data and draw a new line plot.

GUIDED PRACTICE

1. **WRITING** In your own words, describe the meaning of *statistics*.

In Exercises 2 and 3, refer to Example 1 on page 230.

2. How many 5-year-old squirrels are there?

3. What is the relationship between number of squirrels and age?

4. Thirty students were asked the number of books each read over the summer vacation. The results are listed below. Organize the data in a line plot.

   6, 0, 3, 3, 4, 8, 5, 6, 7, 0, 5, 2, 4, 9, 2,
   7, 1, 6, 5, 2, 3, 6, 1, 1, 4, 5, 2, 4, 4, 3

PRACTICE AND PROBLEM SOLVING

ORGANIZING DATA **In Exercises 5 and 6, decide whether the data could be organized with a line plot. Explain your reasoning.**

5. The following data show the ages of 35 singers in a chorus.

Age (in years)	Number of people
12	2
13	5
14	8
15	10
16	7
17	3

6. The data show the number of cars of different ages on the road in 1994.

Age of cars	Number on road
0 years old	5,540,000
1 year old	8,201,000
2 years old	7,718,000
3 years old	7,995,000
4 years old	8,225,000
5 years old	9,126,000

(Source: American Automobile Manufacturers Association)

7. **HOMEWORK** Thirty students in a class were asked to keep track of the number of hours each spent doing homework during a specific week. The results are shown below. Organize the data in a line plot.

   9, 3, 8, 1, 6, 8, 3, 7, 10, 15, 2, 14, 15, 9, 10,
   4, 11, 7, 6, 7, 9, 5, 4, 8, 9, 5, 6, 6, 8, 12

8. **SIBLINGS** Thirty students in a class were asked the number of brothers and sisters each has. The results are shown below. Organize the data in a line plot.

   2, 1, 4, 1, 3, 0, 1, 1, 0, 2, 0, 0, 1, 2, 2,
   1, 5, 1, 0, 1, 1, 3, 0, 3, 1, 4, 1, 0, 2, 1

9. PHONE NUMBERS You take a survey of the digits in the phone numbers of ten students. You organize the data in a line plot, as shown at the right. An x is drawn over a digit every time that digit occurs in any of the phone numbers.

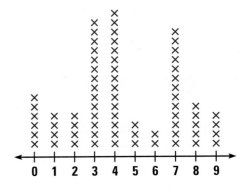

a. Which digit occurs the most in the phone numbers? Which occurs the least?

b. All the phone numbers have the same exchange (first three digits). What are the three digits in the exchange? List all six possible exchanges that have these digits.

10. JOGGING You ask 30 joggers how many miles they jog each day. You organize the data in a line plot as shown. Each x represents a person who jogs that number of miles.

a. How many people jog 5 miles a day? Find the total number of miles jogged by all who jog 5 miles a day.

b. Find the average of the number of miles that all 30 people jogged.

11. SOCCER The table shows the number of regular-season wins in 1996 for each team in Major League Soccer. Organize the data with a line plot. Your number line should go from 9 to 19. The column of x's above each number should show how many teams had that number of wins. (Source: *The World Almanac*)

Team name	Wins
Tampa Bay Mutiny	19
Washington, D.C. United	15
NY/NJ MetroStars	12
Columbus Crew	11
New England Revolution	9
Los Angeles Galaxy	15
Dallas Burn	12
Kansas City Wiz	12
San Jose Clash	12
Colorado Rapids	9

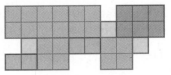

12. GEOMETRY The figure at the right is made up of ten colored squares and rectangles. Each small square is 1 unit by 1 unit.

a. Find the area of each of the squares and rectangles.

b. Use a line plot to organize the ten areas you found in part (a).

c. What is the total area of the figure?

13. Determine the difference of the largest data value and the smallest data value in the list below.

$$51, 12, 35, 67, 45, 55, 82, 15, 44, 71, 22, 17, 20, 80$$

(A) 12 **(B)** 35 **(C)** 70 **(D)** 82

EXPLORATION AND EXTENSION

PORTFOLIO

14. BUILDING YOUR PROJECT Make a line plot from some of the results of your survey. Display the line plot on your poster.

SPIRAL REVIEW

In Exercises 1–3, use the graphical display below. The graphs compare the amounts that two companies spent on advertising in the United States in 1994 and 1995. (Source: *Advertising Age*) **(5.5)**

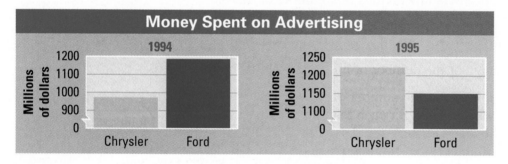

1. If you look only at the length of the bars and ignore the scale on the vertical axis, how will you think the two 1994 amounts compare?

2. From the graphical display, it appears that Ford spent more on advertising in 1994 than Chrysler spent in 1995. Why is this?

3. Explain how to represent these data with a single graph that is not misleading.

> **TOOLBOX**
>
> Adding Fractions, page 747

In Exercises 4–9, solve the equation. (4.1–4.7)

4. $5(n - 2) = 0$

5. $6r - 2 = 2r$

6. $2r + 6r = 4r - 28$

7. $2(p + 1) = -2(p + 1)$

8. $\frac{4}{5}s + 3.2 = -\frac{1}{5}s$

9. $\frac{1}{7}(x + 1) = 6$

In Exercises 10–12, use the picture at the right. The frame is 2 in. wide on all four sides. (4.8)

10. What are the inside dimensions of the picture frame?

11. What is the area of the picture inside the frame?

12. What is the area of the picture frame?

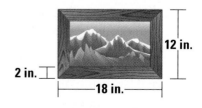

The Power of Suggestion

READ About It

A great deal of advertising is directed at the 53 million children (ages 13 and under) in the United States. Advertisers realize that children have a lot of influence on what their parents buy. One example is vacations. In a survey that asked children what aspects of vacations they influence, 66% said activities, 47% said destination, 60% said restaurants visited, 24% said selection of a hotel, and 18% said means of transportation.

Not everyone approves of child-directed advertising. How people feel about ads on children's TV programming depends on what's being sold. For instance, 3 out of 4 adults say it is okay to show commercials for toys. Only 58% of adults feel the same way about commercials for candy.

WRITE About It

Fun Family Getaways

A trip to the beach is a perfect way to enjoy the sunshine.

Young and old alike enjoy hiking in the great outdoors.

1. Make a graph to represent the data about children's influence on vacations. Explain why you chose the type of graph that you did.

2. If you choose a child at random, is the child likely to think that he or she influences the family's choice of hotel on vacations? Explain your reasoning.

3. About how many children, in millions, believe they influence the restaurants their families go to on vacations? Explain.

4. If you survey 100 adults, how many do you think will *not* approve of toy advertising on children's TV programming?

5. Write a sentence describing adult opinions about advertising candy to children.

5.7

Statistics: Scatter Plots

What you should learn:

Goal 1 How to use scatter plots to see patterns in data

Goal 2 How to use scatter plots to help make decisions

Why you should learn it:

Scatter plots can help you understand how two real-life quantities are related.

Goal 1 USING SCATTER PLOTS

A **scatter plot** is the graph of a collection of ordered pairs of numbers (x, y). If the y-coordinates tend to increase as the x-coordinates increase, then x and y have a **positive correlation**. If the y-coordinates tend to decrease as the x-coordinates increase, then x and y have a **negative correlation**. If no pattern exists between the coordinates, then x and y have **no correlation**.

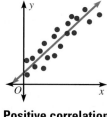
Positive correlation

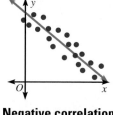
Negative correlation

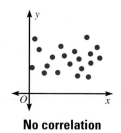
No correlation

Example 1 Drawing a Scatter Plot

The ordered pairs below show the elbow-to-fingertip and wrist measurements (in centimeters) for 14 students. Draw a scatter plot of these data. What can you conclude?

(32, 12), (42, 16), (40, 14), (39, 15), (37, 15), (41, 16), (43, 17),

(38, 14), (45, 16), (34, 14), (41, 15), (34, 13), (35, 13), (37, 14)

Solution

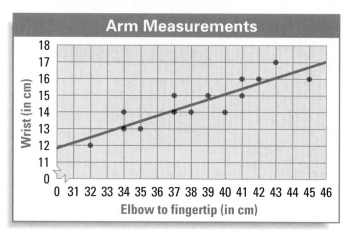

NEED TO KNOW

If there appears to be a correlation in a scatter plot, you can use a ruler to draw a line of fit. The line should show the overall pattern of the data. It does not need to pass through any of the data points.

The measurements have a positive correlation. This means that people in the group with longer forearms tend to have larger wrists. The red *line of fit* approximates the pattern of the data points.

Example 2 Interpreting a Scatter Plot

You live near Sioux Falls, South Dakota, and want to plant corn once temperatures rise above 10°C. If you assume this year will be like the one graphed below, you can use the graph to help decide when to plant.

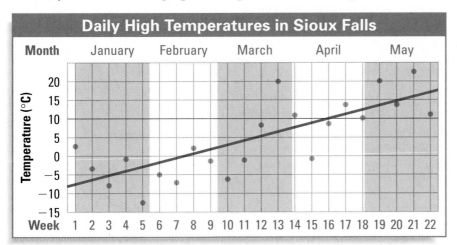

Daily High Temperatures in Sioux Falls

You can plant in late April, when temperatures are above 10°C.

Example 3 Interpreting a Line of Fit

The numbers (in millions) of black and white television sets sold in 6 different years are shown below. You can use a scatter plot to estimate the number of black and white televisions sold in 1992.

Year	1980	1982	1984	1986	1988	1990
Black and white TVs	6.7	5.7	5.1	4.0	2.6	1.4

(Source: *Trends in Television*)

A scatter plot of the data is shown at the right. Since there appears to be a correlation, you can draw a line of fit.

The line of fit appears to pass through the point (**1992, 0.5**). So, you can estimate that in 1992, there were about 0.5 million black and white televisions sold.

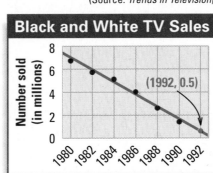

Black and White TV Sales

(1992, 0.5)

Real Life...
Real Facts

Corn In 1994, South Dakota produced a record 367,200,000 bushels of grain corn. (Source: South Dakota Department of Agriculture)

ONGOING ASSESSMENT

Talk About It

Do you think each of the following have a *positive correlation, negative correlation,* or *no correlation*?

1. Height and shoe size

2. Salary and shoe size

3. Year and winning times at Olympics

GUIDED PRACTICE

In Exercises 1–3, refer to Example 3 on page 237.

1. Do the year and the number of black and white televisions sold have a *positive correlation*, a *negative correlation*, or *no correlation*?

2. Use the line of fit to estimate the number of black and white televisions sold in 1987.

3. REASONING Is it possible that the trend represented by the line of fit has continued to the present day? Explain your reasoning.

PRACTICE AND PROBLEM SOLVING

In Exercises 4–6, tell whether *x* and *y* have a *positive correlation*, a *negative correlation*, or *no correlation*. Describe a real-life situation that the scatter plot might represent.

4.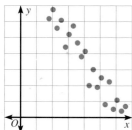

5.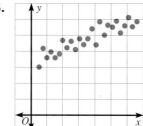

6.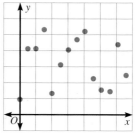

REASONING **In Exercises 7–10, tell whether the two quantities have a *positive correlation*, a *negative correlation*, or *no correlation*. Explain.**

7. A student's study time and test scores

8. The age and value of a family car

9. A student's height and test scores

10. The height and age of a pine tree

UNDERWATER DIVING **In Exercises 11–15, use the table. The table shows the pressure (in pounds per square inch) at various depths underwater.**

Depth (ft)	5	10	15	20	25	30	35
Pressure $(lb/in.^2)$	17	19	21	?	26	28	30

11. Make a scatter plot of the data.

12. How are depth and pressure related?

13. Draw a line of fit. Use it to estimate the pressure 20 ft underwater.

14. Use your line of fit to estimate the pressure at a depth of 45 ft.

15. Estimate the depth at which the pressure is 20 $lb/in.^2$

In Exercises 16–18, use the scatter plot at the right. It shows how many households had cable TV from 1982 to 1996.

16. Estimate the number of households that had cable TV in 1994.

17. Copy the scatter plot on graph paper and draw a line of fit.

18. Use the line of fit to estimate the number of households with cable TV in the year 2000.

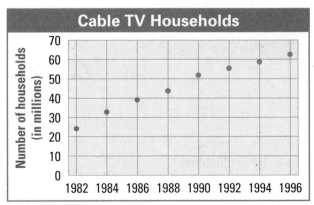

(Source: *Trends in Television*)

GEOMETRY In Exercises 19 and 20, use the figure of a rectangle below.

19. Copy and complete the table.

Length, x	1	2	3	4	5
Width, y	?	?	?	?	?
Perimeter	12	12	12	12	12

Perimeter = 12

y

x

20. Make a scatter plot of the lengths and widths. Is there a correlation? If so, what type is it?

21. **WRITING** Look back at the three examples in this lesson (on pages 236–237). In each of them, a line of fit is used to approximate the pattern of the data. Which one of the data sets is closest to fitting on a line? Which one is the farthest from fitting on a line? Explain.

STANDARDIZED TEST PRACTICE

22. Which pair of points have the same x-coordinate?

Ⓐ A and B Ⓑ A and C

Ⓒ A and D Ⓓ C and D

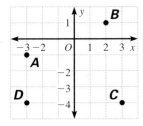

EXPLORATION AND EXTENSION

23. **COMMUNICATING ABOUT MATHEMATICS** Ask 10 people if they approve of toy advertisements on children's TV programming. Then ask if they approve of candy advertisements. How do the results of your survey compare to the information discussed on page 235?

LAB 5.8

COOPERATIVE LEARNING

Probability

Materials Needed
- **paper**
- **pencils or pens**
- **graphing calculator**

You can use a graphing calculator as shown to choose a random whole number from 0 to 4.

If you press [ENTER] 24 more times, you will get a total of 25 random numbers, such as the set of numbers below.

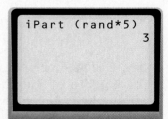

```
iPart (rand*5)
                3
```

3, 4, 2, 0, 2, 4, 2, 1, 1, 3, 0, 0, 2,

2, 1, 4, 4, 4, 2, 0, 1, 3, 3, 4, 3

Organizing these numbers in a line plot makes it easy to see how often each number occurred.

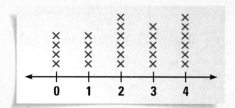

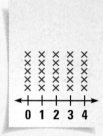

1. Do you think that one number is more likely to occur than another number? Explain your reasoning.

2. Would you be surprised if the line plot of the results looked like the one shown? Why or why not?

a.    **b.** 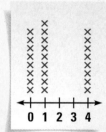   **c.**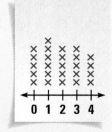

3. Suppose you perform this experiment. Predict what percent of the time each number will occur. Explain your reasoning.

4. Use a graphing calculator to generate 25 random whole numbers from 0 to 4. Organize your data in a line plot. Calculate the percent of the time that each number occurs. How do these percents compare to the prediction you made in Exercise 3?

5. Use a table like the one below to combine your data with data from three other groups. Add the numbers for all four groups and record the totals in the last column.

How many times did each number occur?

	Our group	Group A	Group B	Group C	Total
0	?	?	?	?	?
1	?	?	?	?	?
2	?	?	?	?	?
3	?	?	?	?	?
4	?	?	?	?	?

6. Use the last column of the table to calculate the percent of the time that each number occurred for all four groups combined. How do these percents compare to the percents you calculated in Exercise 4? How do they compare to the prediction you made in Exercise 3?

7. Which do you think will give you results closer to the prediction you made in Exercise 3, a small set of random numbers or a large set? Explain your reasoning.

	Barbara & Tim	Amanda & Rita	Sean & Quang	Maria & Reggie
0	4	4	6	5
1	4	5	4	6
2	6	3	6	3
3	5	6	5	
4	6	7	4	

NOW TRY THESE

8. Describe a way to conduct the experiment in this lab without a graphing calculator.

9. Suppose you generate 1000 random numbers from 0 to 9. About how many times do you think each number will occur? Explain your reasoning.

Exploring Probability

What you should learn:

Goal 1 How to calculate the probability of an event

Goal 2 How to use concepts of probability to solve real-life problems

Why you should learn it:

Many events in real life are not certain. Probability can help you determine the likelihood that such events will occur.

Goal 1 FINDING THE PROBABILITY OF AN EVENT

The **probability of an event** tells you how likely it is that the event will happen. Probability is measured on a scale from 0 to 1.

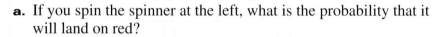

$P = 0$	$P = 0.25$	$P = 0.5$	$P = 0.75$	$P = 1$
Impossible	Not likely	Equally likely	Quite likely	Certain

When you do an experiment, the different possible results are called *outcomes*. The outcomes for which a particular event occurs are called *favorable outcomes*.

PROBABILITY OF AN EVENT

When all outcomes are equally likely, the probability that an event will occur is

$$\text{Probability of event} = \frac{\text{Number of favorable outcomes}}{\text{Total number of outcomes}}.$$

Example 1 Probability Experiments

a. If you spin the spinner at the left, what is the probability that it will land on red?

b. You have 15 pennies in your pocket. Two are Canadian, and the rest are United States pennies. If you take one penny out, what is the probability that it will be a United States penny?

Solution

a. There are 12 regions, so there are 12 possible outcomes when you spin the spinner. Since 3 of the regions are red, there are 3 favorable outcomes. The probability of landing on red is

$$P = \frac{\text{Number of red regions}}{\text{Total number of regions}} = \frac{3}{12} = 0.25.$$

This means that if you spin the spinner 100 times, it should land on a red region about 25 times.

b. You can choose any of 15 pennies, so there are 15 possible outcomes. Thirteen of these are favorable outcomes (United States pennies). The probability of getting a U.S. penny is

$$P = \frac{\text{Number of U.S. pennies}}{\text{Total number of pennies}} = \frac{13}{15} \approx 0.87.$$

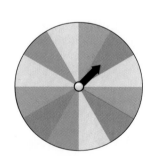

TOOLBOX

Fraction Concepts, page 746

Suppose you build the spinner from part (a) of Example 1. You spin it 100 times, and it lands on red 29 of those times. The *experimental probability* of the spinner landing on red is

$$\text{Experimental probability} = \frac{29}{100} = 0.29.$$

This is close to the *theoretical probability* of 0.25 that was calculated in the solution to Example 1. You use experimental probability when you use the results of a poll to make predictions.

NEED TO KNOW

When you take a poll, the group of people you interview is called the sample. You should only make predictions about people who are like the people in the sample.

Example 2 Conducting a Poll

You are taking a poll about water conservation. As part of the poll, you ask 600 adults how long they take in the shower. The results are shown in the table.

REAL LIFE
Conservation

Length of shower (minutes)	Number of people
1 or less	1
Between 1 and 5	111
Between 5 and 10	360
Between 10 and 15	109
Between 15 and 20	16
20 or more	3

If you ask another adult the length of time he or she takes in the shower, what is the probability that the person will answer "between 5 and 10 minutes"?

Solution

Find the experimental probability. Of the 600 people sampled, 360 answered "between 5 and 10 minutes."

$$P = \frac{\text{Number of people answering "5 to 10 minutes"}}{\text{Number of people in survey}}$$

$$= \frac{360}{600}$$

$$= 0.6$$

The probability that a person will answer "between 5 and 10 minutes" is 0.6.

ONGOING ASSESSMENT

Write About It

1. Based on the survey results in Example 2, your friend says there is a probability of 0.6 that a child will answer "between 5 and 10 minutes." Do you agree? Explain.

5.8 Exercises

GUIDED PRACTICE

1. Describe what a "probability of 0.5" means.

2. **MAKING DECISIONS** A contestant on a game show must decide between door A and door B. There is a probability of 0.4 that the prize is behind door A and a probability of 0.6 that it is behind door B. Which door should the contestant choose? Explain.

3. **MAKING DECISIONS** If the probability of rain is 0.8, decide whether you should bring an umbrella with you. Explain your answer.

4. How do you find the experimental probability of an event?

PRACTICE AND PROBLEM SOLVING

In Exercises 5–8, find the theoretical probability that the spinner at the right will land on the color.

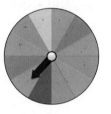

5. Green

6. Red

7. Purple

8. Blue

TOSSING A COIN In Exercises 9–12, suppose you toss a coin that is equally likely to land with heads or tails on top.

9. What is the theoretical probability that the coin will land heads up?

10. Toss a coin 30 times and record your results.

11. Divide the number of times that heads was on top by 30. The result is the experimental probability of the coin landing heads up.

12. Compare the experimental probability you found in Exercise 11 with the theoretical probability you found in Exercise 9.

EXPERIMENT In Exercises 13–16, think about the following experiment. Suppose you write each letter in the word ALABAMA on a separate scrap of paper and put them all in a bag. Without looking, you choose one.

13. What is the theoretical probability of choosing an M?

14. What is the theoretical probability of choosing an A?

15. Perform the experiment. Choose a scrap of paper from the bag, record the letter, and replace the scrap. Do this 30 times, recording how many times you draw each letter. Which did you draw most often?

16. Divide the number of times you chose an A by 30. The result is the experimental probability of choosing an A. Compare this to the theoretical probability you found in Exercise 14.

17. Copy the spinner shown. Then use the following statements to color the spinner.

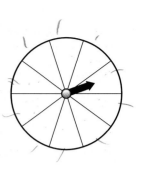

- Probability of red is 0.1
- Probability of blue is 0.4
- Probability of yellow is 0.3
- Probability of green is 0.2

18. **REASONING** Using the probabilities in Exercise 17, is there more than one way to color the spinner? If so, show another way.

MEDICINE **In Exercises 19 and 20, you take a poll to find the blood types of 200 people. You obtain the results shown in the table.**

Blood type	O^+	O^-	A^+	A^-	B^+	B^-	AB^+	AB^-
Number of people	76	14	68	12	18	4	6	2

19. From the results of your survey, what is the probability that a randomly chosen person has the given blood type?

  a. O^+ **b.** B^- **c.** A^+ or A^-

20. What is the probability that a person has a positive $(+)$ blood type?

21. **SAMPLING METHODS** To predict who will win the next election for mayor, an analyst asks residents on one street which candidate they will vote for. On that street, 60% choose candidate A and 40% choose candidate B. The analyst concludes that candidate A will win the election. Do you agree with this reasoning? Explain.

STANDARDIZED TEST PRACTICE

22. You want to color the spinner shown so that the probability of landing on blue is 0.25. How many of the regions should you color blue?

  A 1   **B** 2

  C 3   **D** 6

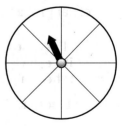

EXPLORATION AND EXTENSION

23. **EXPERIMENT** Tape a penny to a quarter using transparent tape. Toss this compound coin 30 times. Use the results to find the experimental probability of the penny landing on top. Suppose the compound coin is tossed to see who gets the ball in a sports game. Decide whether to call "penny up" or "quarter up" if you want to win the toss. Explain.

WHAT *did you learn?* **WHY** *did you learn it?*

		WHAT	WHY
Skills	5.1	Use a pictograph or a time line to represent data.	Illustrate important dates in history.
	5.2	Use a bar graph or a histogram to represent data.	Compare numerical aspects of categories.
	5.3	Use a line graph to represent data.	Illustrate the changes in real-life data over time.
	5.4	Choose appropriate graphs to represent data.	Accurately compare an aspect of different careers.
	5.5	Recognize misleading pictographs, bar graphs, and line graphs.	Correctly interpret data in newspapers and magazines.
	5.6	Use a line plot to organize data.	See the frequency of data values quickly and clearly.
	5.7	Use a scatter plot to represent data.	Describe how two real-life quantities are related.
	5.8	Find the probability of an event.	Find the likelihood that real-life events will occur.
Strategies	5.1–5.7	Use a graph.	Display real-life data effectively and appropriately.
	5.7	Look for a pattern.	Use lines of fit to estimate unknown values.
Using Data	5.1–5.8	Use tables and graphs.	Organize and interpret data to solve problems.

HOW *does it fit in the bigger picture of mathematics?*

Organizing data is part of a branch of mathematics called statistics. In this chapter, you were introduced to some basic strategies for organizing, presenting, and interpreting data. There are often many appropriate ways to represent a set of data graphically. Some graphing techniques, however, are often misleading and therefore inappropriate. For instance, you learned that breaking the scale on an axis can create false impressions.

Throughout your study of mathematics, remember that a graph can help you recognize patterns. In fact, *Using a Graph* and *Looking for a Pattern* are important problem solving strategies in almost every branch of mathematics.

VOCABULARY

- pictograph (p. 204)
- time line (p. 205)
- bar graph (p. 208)
- histogram (p. 209)

- frequency distribution (p. 209)
- line graph (p. 214)
- line plot (p. 230)
- scatter plot (p. 236)

- positive correlation (p. 236)
- negative correlation (p. 236)
- no correlation (p. 236)
- probability of an event (p. 242)

5.1 EXPLORING PICTOGRAPHS AND TIME LINES

1. Use the pictograph shown to estimate the amount of paper products in 100 pounds of trash.

2. Make a time line for the following events in automobile history.

1890	First electric car built
1908	Model T Ford car built
1948	Tubeless tires introduced
1976	Computer engine control introduced

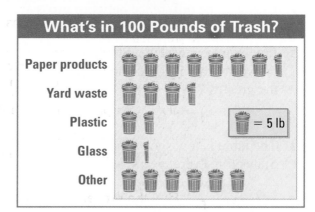

(Source: *Consumer Reports*, 1994)

5.2 EXPLORING BAR GRAPHS AND HISTOGRAMS

Examples Simple Bar Graph   Histogram

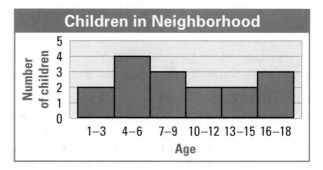

3. You survey 50 people about the pets they own: *dog, cat, bird,* or *other*. What type of bar graph will best show your results? Explain.

Use the histogram above.

4. Which age intervals have the smallest number of children?

5. Which age interval has the most children?

5.3 EXPLORING LINE GRAPHS

A simple line graph shows changes in one quantity over time. A double line graph shows changes in two quantities.

ANALYZING A COMPANY **In Exercises 6–8, use the graph at the right.**

6. Which is increasing more rapidly, gross income or profit?

7. Estimate the difference between gross income and profit in 1995.

8. In which year was the difference between gross income and profit the greatest?

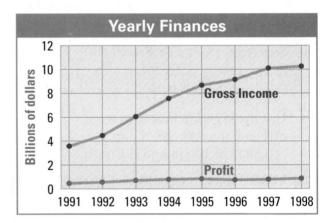

9. The table below shows the number of college students in the United States for several years. Make a line graph of these data.

Year	1970	1975	1980	1985	1990	1995
Students (in millions)	6.3	8.1	8.5	9.1	9.7	10.3

5.4 CHOOSING AN APPROPRIATE GRAPH

You should use a bar graph when the data fall into distinct categories. To show consecutive amounts of data over time, use a line graph. When you want high visual appeal, use a pictograph.

In Exercises 10 and 11, organize the data and represent your results graphically. Explain why you used the type of graph that you did.

10. **TRANSPORTATION** The table below shows how American workers traveled to work in 1990.

Mode of transportation	Car, truck, or van	Public transportation	Motorcycle or bicycle	Walked	Other	Worked at home
Percent of workers	86.5	5.3	0.6	3.9	0.7	3.0

11. The table below gives the United States population for seven years.

Year	1989	1990	1991	1992	1993	1994	1995
Population (in millions)	247	250	253	255	258	261	263

5.5 PROBLEM SOLVING: MISLEADING GRAPHS

To recognize a graph that is misleading, look at the scales on the axes.

SPORTS **Use the bar graph at the right. The graph shows what percents of running shoe buyers belong to three different age groups.**
(Source: *Statistical Abstract of the United States*)

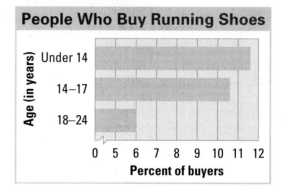

People Who Buy Running Shoes

12. Explain why this graph could be misleading.

13. Use the same data to make a graph that is not misleading.

5.6 STATISTICS: LINE PLOTS

14. In the line plot at the right, which digit occurs the most? Which digit occurs the least?

15. Organize the data below in a line plot.

   12, 16, 9, 11, 16, 3, 17, 5, 15, 13,
   12, 15, 17, 8, 14, 12, 17, 11, 7, 14

5.7 STATISTICS: SCATTER PLOTS

A scatter plot can help you decide whether a set of data has a positive correlation, a negative correlation, or no correlation.

16. The table below gives the population of Indiana for six years. Draw a scatter plot of the data. Use it to estimate the 1997 population.

Year	1990	1991	1992	1993	1994	1995
Population (in millions)	5.54	5.60	5.65	5.71	5.76	5.80

5.8 EXPLORING PROBABILITY

To find the probability of an event, divide the number of favorable outcomes by the total number of outcomes.

Find the probability that the spinner at the right will land on the given color.

17. green   18. yellow   19. red

In Exercises 1–3, use the graph. It shows how much money was spent on four types of advertising in 1995. (Source: *Statistical Abstract of the United States*)

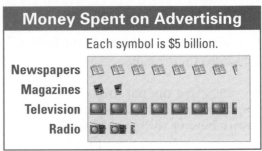

Money Spent on Advertising

Each symbol is $5 billion.

1. Name the type of graph shown.

2. On which type of advertising was the least money spent?

3. Estimate the total amount of money spent on all four types of advertising.

In Exercises 4–6, use the graph at the right. It shows the average hourly earnings of production workers for several years. (Source: U.S. Bureau of Labor Statistics)

4. Name the type of graph.

5. Without looking at the scale on the vertical axis, compare the 1990 earnings to the 1980 earnings.

6. Explain why this graph could be misleading.

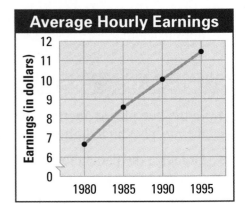

Average Hourly Earnings

7. **BASEBALL** The table lists the number of home runs in major league baseball for several years. Graph the data. Explain why you chose the type of graph you did. (Source: National Baseball Hall of Fame)

Year	1990	1991	1992	1993	1994	1995	1996
Home runs	3317	3383	3038	4030	3306	4081	4962

BUSINESS **In Exercises 8 and 9, the management of a company is keeping track of how many minutes each employee is late on a specific day. The results are shown below.**

0, 5, 7, 2, 1, 0, 0, 1, 0, 0, 2, 0, 7, 10,
0, 8, 4, 5, 0, 12, 0, 0, 3, 1, 2, 5, 6, 10

8. Organize the data in a line plot.

9. How many people arrived at work on time?

10. Create a scatter plot of the data (x, y) shown below.

   (0, 1)   (4, 6)   (3, 3)   (2, 3)   (7, 9)   (5, 7)   (6, 6)   (1, 2)

11. In Exercise 10, do x and y have a correlation? If so, what type?

12. **PROBABILITY** A box contains 12 Ping-Pong balls numbered from 1 through 12. One ball is chosen at random. What is the probability that the number on the ball is less than 4?

1. The histogram shows the times (in minutes) of people on a track team who ran a mile. Which of the statements is false?

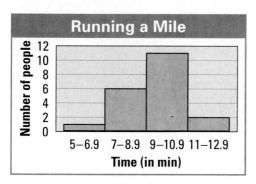

Running a Mile

A Five more people had times in the 9–10.9 min interval than the 7–8.9 min interval.

B A person whose time is 9.5 min would be in the tallest bar.

C Twenty people were timed.

D A total of nine people had times in the 9–10.9 and 11–12.9 min intervals.

2. What were your total baby-sitting earnings from 1995 through 1998?

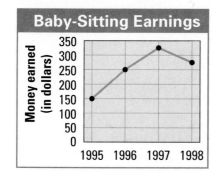

Baby-Sitting Earnings

A $950 B $975

C $1000 D $1050

For Questions 3 and 4, use the line plot, which shows the number of telephones in each of ten households.

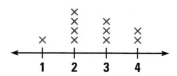

3. Which set of data is shown by the line plot?

A 1, 2, 3, 2, 4, 3, 2, 2, 4, 2

B 4, 3, 2, 2, 4, 3, 3, 4, 2, 1

C 3, 2, 2, 2, 3, 4, 1, 3, 4, 3

D 2, 3, 4, 4, 2, 1, 3, 2, 3, 2

4. If you choose one of the ten households at random, what is the probability that it will have 2 telephones?

A 0.04 B 0.2

C 0.4 D 2.5

5. Which statement is true about the scatter plot?

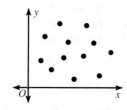

A *x* and *y* have a positive correlation.

B *x* and *y* have no correlation.

C *x* and *y* have a negative correlation.

D The pattern of the scatter plot is linear.

Exploring
Number Theory

LISTENING IN Headphones allow performers to hear the musical
balance while they record.

CHAPTER THEME
Music

TECHNOLOGY

- **Interactive Real-Life
Investigations**
- **Middle School Tutorial
Software**

To find out more about the
music industry, go to:

http://www.mlmath.com

PORTFOLIO

Recording Music

PROJECT DESCRIPTION

Many people are involved in making a music recording. The artists and technicians are directed by the producer and recording engineer. You will look at some of the things that go into making a music recording.

GETTING STARTED

Talking It Over

- What kind of music would you like to record?

- Will there be vocals?

- Where will you do the actual recording?

- How would you publicize your new recording?

Planning Your Project

- **Materials:** paper, pencils or pens, colored pencils or markers

- Make a booklet out of several sheets of paper. In it you will keep your plans for recording a music audio. As you complete the **BUILDING YOUR PROJECT** exercises throughout the chapter, add the results to your booklet.

BUILDING YOUR PROJECT

These are places throughout the chapter where you will work on your project.

6.1 Count the beats in a musical phrase. *p. 257*

6.3 Decorate your studio. *p. 269*

6.4 Mix the sound tracks. *p. 273*

6.6 Plan the lengths of the songs. *p. 283*

6.9 Describe musical patterns. *p. 297*

6.1

Divisibility Tests

What you should learn:

Goal 1 How to use divisibility tests

Goal 2 How to factor natural numbers

Why you should learn it:

You can use divisibility tests to decide how to divide a group of objects into equal parts.

If the number of glass bricks you have can be factored, then you can build a rectangular wall.

Goal 1 USING DIVISIBILITY TESTS

If one natural number divides evenly into another natural number, then the second number is **divisible** by the first. For instance, 198 is divisible by 9 because $198 \div 9 = 22$, but 198 is not divisible by 4 because 4 does not divide evenly into 198.

DIVISIBILITY TESTS

A natural number is divisible by

  2 if the number is even.

  3 if the sum of its digits is divisible by 3.

  4 if the number formed by its last 2 digits is divisible by 4.

  5 if its last digit is 0 or 5.

  6 if the number is even and divisible by 3.

  8 if the number is divisible by 4 and the result is even.

  9 if the sum of its digits is divisible by 9.

  10 if its last digit is 0.

Example 1 Using a Divisibility Test

Decide whether 534 is divisible by 2, 3, 4, 5, 6, 8, 9, and 10.

Solution

n	Is 534 divisible by n?	Reason
2	Yes	534 is even.
3	Yes	$5 + 3 + 4 = 12$, and 12 is divisible by 3.
4	No	34 is not divisible by 4.
5	No	The last digit of 534 is not 0 or 5.
6	Yes	534 is even and divisible by 3.
8	No	534 is not divisible by 4.
9	No	$5 + 3 + 4 = 12$, and 12 is not divisible by 9.
10	No	The last digit of 534 is not 0.

You can also use a calculator to decide whether one number is divisible by another. For example, 534 is not divisible by 8 because $534 \div 8 = 66.75$, which is not a whole number.

A natural number is **factored** when it is written as the product of two or more natural numbers. For instance, 28 can be factored as 4 · 7. The numbers 4 and 7 are **factors** of 28.

You can use divisibility tests to factor a number. For instance, because 39 ÷ 3 = 13, you can conclude that 39 = 3 · 13.

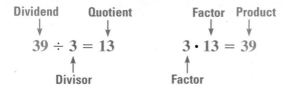

Example 2 **Finding Factors of a Number**

A rectangle has an area of 24 square units. The lengths of the sides are whole numbers.

CONNECTION
Geometry

The area is the product of length and width.

$A = l \cdot w$ **width**

length

a. Name the possible dimensions.

b. Find the factors of 24.

Solution

a. You are hunting for pairs of numbers whose product is 24. That is, you are hunting for ways to factor 24 into the product of two numbers.

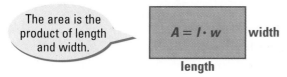

From the rectangles above, you can see that the possible side lengths are **1 by 24**, **2 by 12**, **3 by 8**, and **4 by 6**.

b. The factors of 24 are **1, 2, 3, 4, 6, 8, 12**, and **24**.

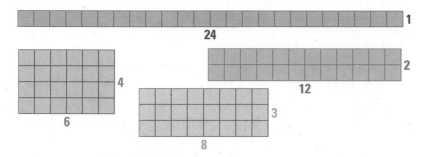

ONGOING ASSESSMENT

Talk About It
• • • • • • • • • • • • • • • • • •

List all the factors of the number. Explain your method.

1. 30

2. 31

3. 32

6.1 Exercises

Extra Practice, page 725

GUIDED PRACTICE

1. Explain what it means to say that one natural number is divisible by another natural number.

2. Decide whether 4485 is divisible by 2, 3, 4, 5, 6, 8, 9, and 10.

3. Find the factors of 36.

4. **GEOMETRY** Each of the rectangles at the right has an area of 30 square units. Explain how to use these rectangles to find the factors of 30.

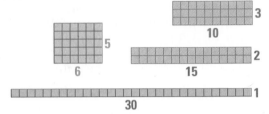

In Exercises 5–8, decide whether the statement is *true* or *false*. Explain your reasoning.

5. A number divisible by 3 is also divisible by 9.

6. A number divisible by 10 is also divisible by 2.

7. The numbers 6 and 12 are factors of 72.

8. The number 18 is a factor of 9.

PRACTICE AND PROBLEM SOLVING

In Exercises 9–16, use the divisibility tests to determine whether the number is divisible by 2, 3, 4, 5, 6, 8, 9, and 10.

9. 2160   10. 25,920   11. 192   12. 9756

13. 1234   14. 3725   15. 6859   16. 2401

17. **REASONING** Which digits will make the number 34,?21 divisible by 3?

In Exercises 18–21, find the digit that makes the number divisible by 9.

18. 39,9?8   19. 5,43?,216,789   20. 12,?51   21. 2,546,?24

22. List all natural numbers less than 200 that are divisible by 3, 4, and 5.

23. Find the smallest natural number divisible by 2, 3, 4, 5, 6, 8, and 9. Explain how you found your answer.

In Exercises 24–31, find all factors of the number.

24. 18   25. 36   26. 42   27. 45

28. 50   29. 100   30. 72   31. 96

32. **GEOMETRY** A rectangle has an area of 64 square units. The lengths of the sides are natural numbers. Find the possible dimensions.

33. **BANKING** You bring a check for $80 to a bank and ask for bills that are all the same denomination. How many ways can this be done?

CONSERVATION In Exercises 34–36, imagine you are part of a team that is planting tree seedlings.

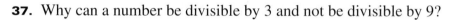

34. Your team is instructed to plant the trees in a rectangular region. You can use any rectangle, as long as its area is 1600 ft². If the side lengths (in feet) are natural numbers, what are the possible dimensions of the region?

35. Your team wants to construct a temporary fence around the seedlings. Of the dimensions in Exercise 34, which have the smallest perimeter?

36. Your team is instructed to plant 350 tree seedlings in straight rows with the same number of trees in each row. One team member wants to plant 15 rows. Is that possible? Explain why or why not.

37. Why can a number be divisible by 3 and not be divisible by 9?

38. Why is a number that is divisible by 8 also divisible by 4?

39. a. WRITING Explain why the divisibility test for 4 works.

   b. Another divisibility test for 8 is this: "A natural number is divisible by 8 if the number formed by its last 3 digits is divisible by 8." Explain why this test works.

REASONING In Exercises 40–43, suppose the numbers a and b are each divisible by 3. Tell whether each expression is also divisible by 3. Explain your reasoning.

40. $a + b$ **41.** $a - b$ **42.** ab **43.** $a \div b$

STANDARDIZED TEST PRACTICE

44. Which number is divisible by 4, 5, and 9?

   A 90   **B** 216   **C** 270   **D** 360

EXPLORATION AND EXTENSION

PORTFOLIO

45. BUILDING YOUR PROJECT You are working on the music for your recording. A section in the music contains 45 beats. The time signature is three-four, indicating that there are 3 beats per measure. Will the section be contained in a whole number of measures?

LAB 6.2

COOPERATIVE LEARNING

Prime and Composite Numbers

Materials Needed
- paper
- pencil or pen

A *prime* number is a whole number that has exactly two factors: itself and 1. A *composite* number has more than two factors. In this investigation, you will look at some patterns people have used to find prime numbers.

Part A BUILDING THE SIEVE OF ERATOSTHENES

Eratosthenes was a mathematician who lived in Alexandria, Egypt, around 230 B.C. The procedure described below is called the Sieve of Eratosthenes. Here, it is applied to the whole numbers from 2 to 30.

Write the whole numbers from 2 to 30 in order.

2 3 4 5 6 7 8 9 10 11 12 13 14 15 16 17 18 19 20 21 22 23 24 25 26 27 28 29 30

Start with 2. Keep it, and cross out every multiple of 2 after 2.

2 3 4̸ 5 6̸ 7 8̸ 9 1̸0̸ 11 1̸2̸ 13 1̸4̸ 15 1̸6̸ 17 1̸8̸ 19 2̸0̸ 21 2̸2̸ 23 2̸4̸ 25 2̸6̸ 27 2̸8̸ 29 3̸0̸

Move to the next number that is not crossed out, 3.
Keep it, and cross out every multiple of 3 after 3.

2 3 4̸ 5 6̸ 7 8̸ 9̸ 1̸0̸ 11 1̸2̸ 13 1̸4̸ 1̸5̸ 1̸6̸ 17 1̸8̸ 19 2̸0̸ 2̸1̸ 2̸2̸ 23 2̸4̸ 25 2̸6̸ 2̸7̸ 2̸8̸ 29 3̸0̸

Move to the next number that is not crossed out, 5.
Keep it, and cross out every multiple of 5 after 5.

2 3 4̸ 5 6̸ 7 8̸ 9̸ 1̸0̸ 11 1̸2̸ 13 1̸4̸ 1̸5̸ 1̸6̸ 17 1̸8̸ 19 2̸0̸ 2̸1̸ 2̸2̸ 23 2̸4̸ 2̸5̸ 2̸6̸ 2̸7̸ 2̸8̸ 29 3̸0̸

1. List the numbers that are not crossed out. What type of numbers are they?

2. Describe the next step in the Sieve of Eratosthenes. What are the numbers that are crossed out in the next step?

3. List the whole numbers from 31 to 60. Which ones are not crossed out in the Sieve of Eratosthenes? What type of numbers are they?

4. Write the whole numbers from 1 to 60 in six rows as shown below.

Row 1	1	7	13	19	25	31	37	43	49	55
Row 2	2	8	14	20	26	32	38	44	50	56
Row 3	3	9	15	21	27	33	39	45	51	57
Row 4	4	10	16	22	28	34	40	46	52	58
Row 5	5	11	17	23	29	35	41	47	53	59
Row 6	6	12	18	24	30	36	42	48	54	60

5. Which rows contain the even numbers? How many of these are prime?

6. Which rows contain the multiples of 3? How many of these are prime?

7. Circle all the prime numbers you found in Part A. What patterns do you see? Which rows are they in? Why?

NOW TRY THESE

In Exercises 8–10, use the following information: Prime numbers have no pattern. Sometimes several primes occur close together and sometimes there are long stretches of numbers with no primes.

8. Is it possible to find two consecutive numbers (other than the numbers 2 and 3) that are both prime? If so, list them. If not, explain why.

9. Is it possible to find two consecutive odd numbers that are both prime? If so, list several pairs. If not, explain why.

10. Write the numbers from 210 to 220. Are any of these numbers prime? How can you tell?

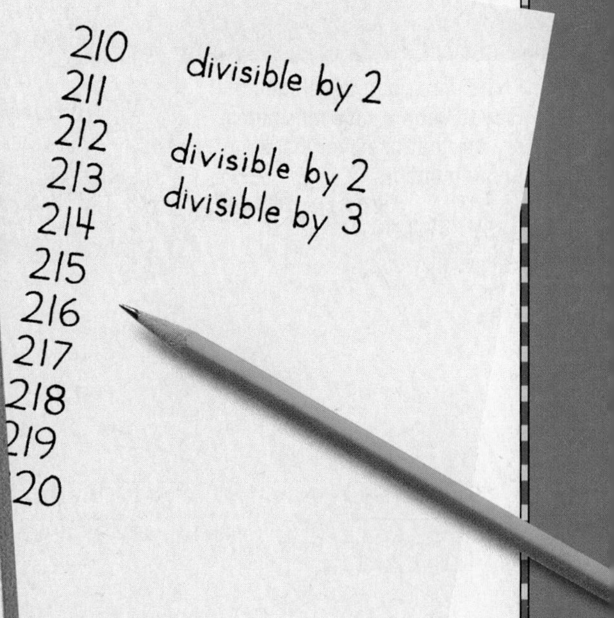

210
211 — divisible by 2
212
213 — divisible by 2
214 — divisible by 3
215
216
217
218
219
220

Phil Zimmerman developed a way to keep e-mail messages private that uses very large prime numbers.

Goal 1 CLASSIFYING PRIMES AND COMPOSITES

Natural numbers can be classified according to the number of factors they have.

PRIME AND COMPOSITE NUMBERS

1. A natural number is **prime** if it has exactly two factors, itself and 1. For instance, 2, 3, 5, and 7 are prime.
2. A natural number is **composite** if it has three or more factors. For instance, 4, 6, and 8 are composite.
3. The natural number 1 is neither prime nor composite.

You can use **tree diagrams** to factor a number until all factors are primes. Here are three tree diagrams for $30 = 2 \cdot 3 \cdot 5$.

$$
\begin{array}{ccc}
30 & 30 & 30 \\
3 \cdot 10 & 2 \cdot 15 & 5 \cdot 6 \\
3 \cdot 2 \cdot 5 & 2 \cdot 3 \cdot 5 & 5 \cdot 2 \cdot 3
\end{array}
$$

The diagrams show that there is exactly one prime factorization of a number, except for the order of the primes.

Example 1 Prime Factorization

Write the prime factorization of 42.

Solution

STRATEGY DRAW A DIAGRAM

$$
\begin{array}{l}
42 \\
6 \cdot 7 \\
2 \cdot 3 \cdot 7
\end{array}
$$

Start with 42.

Factor 42 as $6 \cdot 7$.

Factor 6 as $2 \cdot 3$.

From the tree diagram, you can see that the prime factorization of 42 is $2 \cdot 3 \cdot 7$.

Note that factors in a prime factorization are usually written in increasing order.

Goal ② FACTORING ALGEBRAIC EXPRESSIONS

TOOLBOX

Prime Factorization, page 749

Example 2 Repeated Factors

Write the prime factorization of each number.

a. 40

b. 225

Solution

a. $40 = 8 \cdot 5$

$\quad\quad = 2 \cdot 4 \cdot 5$

$\quad\quad = 2 \cdot 2 \cdot 2 \cdot 5$

$\quad\quad = 2^3 \cdot 5$

b. $225 = 5 \cdot 45$

$\quad\quad\quad = 5 \cdot 9 \cdot 5$

$\quad\quad\quad = 5 \cdot 3 \cdot 3 \cdot 5$

$\quad\quad\quad = 3^2 \cdot 5^2$

You can use the factoring technique shown above to factor negative integers and expressions involving variables. For instance, $-6ab^2$ can be written as $(-1) \cdot 2 \cdot 3 \cdot a \cdot b^2$.

Example 3 Factoring Algebraic Expressions

Factor each expression. Write the result using exponents.

a. -24

b. $63a^3$

c. $18x^2y$

Solution

a. $-24 = (-1) \cdot 2 \cdot 2 \cdot 2 \cdot 3 = (-1) \cdot 2^3 \cdot 3$

b. $63a^3 = 3 \cdot 3 \cdot 7 \cdot a \cdot a \cdot a = 3^2 \cdot 7 \cdot a^3$

c. $18x^2y = 2 \cdot 3 \cdot 3 \cdot x \cdot x \cdot y = 2 \cdot 3^2 \cdot x^2 \cdot y$

Example 4 Prime Factorization

To help a friend learn to factor, you write some factoring problems. For one, you multiply 13 and 17 to get 221. Your friend factors 221 as $3 \cdot 7 \cdot 11$. Without multiplying, how do you know your friend has made a mistake?

Solution

You know that there is exactly one prime factorization of a number. Because 221 is $13 \cdot 17$, you know that the factorization cannot be $3 \cdot 7 \cdot 11$.

ONGOING ASSESSMENT

Write About It

Write the prime factorization of each number.

1. 78

2. 308

3. 136

GUIDED PRACTICE

In Exercises 1–4, use a tree diagram to write the prime factorization of the number.

1. 18   **2.** 24   **3.** 72   **4.** 110

In Exercises 5–8, decide whether the statement is _true_ or _false_. If it is false, explain why.

5. Thirty-nine is a composite number.   **6.** Twenty-nine is a prime number.

7. The prime factorization of 45 is $3^2 \cdot 5$.   **8.** The prime factorization of 56 is $7 \cdot 8$.

PRACTICE AND PROBLEM SOLVING

In Exercises 9–12, is the number prime or composite? Explain.

9. 17   **10.** 9   **11.** 35   **12.** 27

In Exercises 13–16, write the factorization shown by the tree diagram.

13.

14.

15.
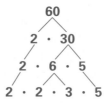

16.
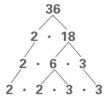

In Exercises 17–24, write the prime factorization of the number. Write your answer in exponent form.

17. 36   **18.** 63   **19.** 84   **20.** 100

21. 32   **22.** 64   **23.** 72   **24.** 90

In Exercises 25–32, write the expression in expanded form and exponent form.

25. -27 **26.** -28 **27.** $9x^3$ **28.** $125y^4$

29. $8a^3b^2$ **30.** $12p^4q$ **31.** $-45mn^3$ **32.** $-50s^2t^5$

In Exercises 33–36, evaluate the expression.

33. $2^3 \cdot 3 \cdot 5$ **34.** $2 \cdot 3^2 \cdot 13$ **35.** $-1 \cdot 3^2 \cdot 5 \cdot 13$ **36.** $-1 \cdot 2^3 \cdot 3 \cdot 7$

In Exercises 37–40, list all possible factors of the number.

37. 8   **38.** 16   **39.** 32   **40.** 64

41. NUMBER SENSE If you double an odd number, does the list of all possible factors of the number double? What if you double an even number?

42. HISTORY A famous unproven conjecture by Christian Goldbach (1690–1764) states that every even natural number except 2 is the sum of two prime numbers. Write the even numbers from 20 to 40 as the sum of two primes.

43. Twin primes are primes whose difference is 2, such as 3 and 5, 5 and 7, and 11 and 13. Write the next five twin prime pairs.

44. GEOMETRY If the lengths of the sides of a triangle are consecutive integers, could the perimeter be a prime number? Explain.

45. A class is divided into groups, with each group containing more than one student. If each group is the same size, could the number of students in the class be prime? Explain.

46. CURRENCY The table lists the U.S. paper money printed for use today. The table also lists whose portrait is on each bill. For each value, state whether the number is *prime*, *composite*, or *neither*. If the number is composite, write its prime factorization.

47. Bills larger than $100 were made until 1969. These bills included the $500, $1000, $5000, $10,000, and $100,000 dollar bills. Write the prime factorization of each bill amount.

Denomination	Portrait
$1	George Washington
$2	Thomas Jefferson
$5	Abraham Lincoln
$10	Alexander Hamilton
$20	Andrew Jackson
$50	Ulysses S. Grant
$100	Benjamin Franklin

STANDARDIZED TEST PRACTICE

48. A prime number is any natural number that . . .

A is not an even number.

B has three or more factors.

C is not divisible by 2.

D has exactly two factors, itself and 1.

EXPLORATION AND EXTENSION

In Exercises 49 and 50, copy and complete the puzzle using single digits. Each digit must be a factor of the number at the beginning of its row and column. Use each digit only once.

49.

	18	8	35
42	?	?	?
60	?	?	?
72	?	?	?

50.

	36	30	56
35	?	?	?
24	?	?	?
18	?	?	?

1. Use the divisibility tests to decide whether 612 is divisible by 2, 3, 4, 5, 6, 8, 9, and 10. **(6.1)**

2. Use a calculator to decide whether 612 is divisible by 11, 12, 13, 14, 15, 16, 17, 18, 19, and 20. **(6.1)**

In Exercises 3–6, you randomly select one letter from the word DIVISIBILITY. What is the probability that the letter is as described? (5.8)

3. S 4. I 5. D or Y 6. Not an I

In Exercises 7–10, write the prime factorization of the number. (6.2)

7. 87 8. 98 9. 76 10. 88

In Exercises 11–14, solve the equation. Show your work. (4.2, 4.4, 4.5)

11. $\frac{1}{2}(x + 2) = 4$

12. $\frac{1}{4}(r - 1) = 0$

13. $7(y + 2) = 5y$

14. $3.2 + 1.2s = -0.4s$

15. **SPORTS** Your score after 17 holes in a miniature golf tournament is 3 under par (-3). On the 18th hole, you score 2 under par (-2). Write an expression that represents your final score. What is your final score? **(3.2)**

MUSIC Connection

PYTHAGOREAN SCHOOL

Scholars in ancient Greece (600 B.C.–500 B.C.) believed that four subjects ruled their universe—music, geometry, arithmetic, and astronomy. Pythagoras, a Greek mathematician and philosopher, and his followers, found that musical sounds made by equally tight lyre strings were related to their lengths. So, starting with any note, you can go down the scale merely by changing the length of the string as shown in the chart.

When played together, strings whose lengths were in ratios made up of small integers, like 1 to 2, had a more "agreeable" sound than strings whose ratios were made up of larger integers, like 23 to 13.

- Which notes do you think are "more agreeable" to C?

- Which notes would be "less agreeable"?

Try playing the notes together to check your answers.

$2s$
$\frac{16}{9}s$
$\frac{8}{5}s$
$\frac{3}{2}s$
$\frac{4}{3}s$
$\frac{6}{5}s$
$\frac{16}{15}s$
s

C higher B A G F E D C lower

LAB 6.3

COOPERATIVE LEARNING

Modeling Common Factors

A factor of two numbers is a *common factor* of the numbers.

To find the common factors of 12 and 16, imagine a 12 ft-by-16 ft floor that is being covered with square tiles. You can't cut or overlap the tiles. If an *n* ft-by-*n* ft square tile can be used to cover the floor, then *n* is a common factor of 12 and 16.

Materials Needed
• graph paper
• pencil or pen

1. Use the following diagrams to decide whether 1, 2, 3, 4, 5, and 6 are common factors of 12 and 16.

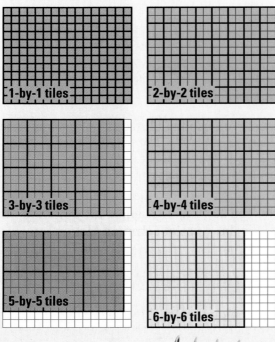

1-by-1 tiles   2-by-2 tiles

3-by-3 tiles   4-by-4 tiles

5-by-5 tiles   6-by-6 tiles

2. Are there any other common factors of 12 and 16 other than the ones you found in Exercise 1? Explain.

3. Use a tiling model to find the common factors of 9 and 12.

NOW TRY THESE

In Exercises 4–6, use a tiling model to find the common factors of the room's width and length. Which is the greatest common factor?

4. 16 ft by 20 ft   5. 14 ft by 20 ft   6. 16 ft by 18 ft

6.3

Greatest Common Factor

What you should learn:

Goal **1** How to find the greatest common factor of two numbers

Goal **2** How to find the greatest common factor of two expressions

Why you should learn it:

You can use the greatest common factor of two numbers to solve real-life problems, such as comparing frequencies of notes on a musical scale.

Goal **1** FINDING COMMON FACTORS

In this lesson, you will study common factors of two numbers.

> **GREATEST COMMON FACTOR**
>
> Let m and n be natural numbers.
>
> **1.** A number that is a factor of both m and n is a **common factor** of m and n.
>
> **2.** Of all common factors of m and n, the largest is called the **greatest common factor** (GCF).

Example 1 Finding the Greatest Common Factor

Find the greatest common factor of 16 and 20.

Solution

With small numbers, you can list all factors of each number.

Number	16	20
Factors	1, 2, **4**, 8, 16	1, 2, **4**, 5, 10, 20

From the lists, you can see that 1, 2, and 4 are common factors of 16 and 20. Of these, 4 is the greatest common factor.

Example 2 Finding the Greatest Common Factor

Find the greatest common factor of 180 and 378.

Solution

With large numbers, you can find the greatest common factor by writing the prime factorization of each.

Number	180	378
Prime Factorization	$2 \cdot 2 \cdot 3 \cdot 3 \cdot 5$	$2 \cdot 3 \cdot 3 \cdot 3 \cdot 7$

From the prime factorizations, you can see that the common prime factors are 2, 3, and 3. The greatest common factor is the product of these common prime factors.

Greatest Common Factor $= 2 \cdot 3 \cdot 3 = 18$

NEED TO KNOW

Two numbers are relatively prime if their greatest common factor is 1. For example, 8 and 15 are relatively prime.

Example 3 Using Greatest Common Factors

Every musical note has a *frequency*. The frequency is the number of air vibrations per second that create the sound. Higher notes have greater frequencies than lower notes.

REAL LIFE
Music

a. What is the greatest common factor of the three A's shown on the piano keyboard below?

b. What is the greatest common factor of the three G's?

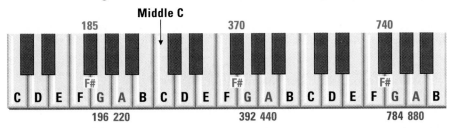

Real Life...
Real Facts

Solution

a. The three A's have frequencies of 220, 440, and 880. Because 440 and 880 are each divisible by 220, it follows that 220 is the greatest common factor of the numbers.

b. The three G's have frequencies of 196, 392, and 784. Because 392 and 784 are each divisible by 196, it follows that 196 is the greatest common factor of the numbers.

The concept of a greatest common factor also applies to algebraic expressions. For example, the greatest common factor of $18x^2$ and $12x$ is $6x$.

Example 4 Finding the GCF of Variable Expressions

Find the greatest common factor (GCF) of $3x^2y$ and $6xy^3$.

Solution

Write the prime factorization of each expression.

$$3x^2y = 3 \cdot x \cdot x \cdot y \qquad 6xy^3 = 2 \cdot 3 \cdot x \cdot y \cdot y \cdot y$$

The common prime factors are 3, x, and y. The greatest common factor is the product of the common prime factors, which is $3 \cdot x \cdot y$, or $3xy$.

ONGOING ASSESSMENT

Talk About It
· · · · · · · · · · · · · · · · ·

Decide whether the numbers are relatively prime.

1. 135 and 224

2. 135 and 225

3. 134 and 224

GUIDED PRACTICE

In Exercises 1–4, find the common factors of the two numbers. What is the greatest common factor?

1. Factors of 12: 1, 2, 3, 4, 6, 12
Factors of 18: 1, 2, 3, 6, 9, 18

2. Factors of 24: 1, 2, 3, 4, 6, 8, 12, 24
Factors of 16: 1, 2, 4, 8, 16

3. Factors of 20: 1, 2, 4, 5, 10, 20
Factors of 35: 1, 5, 7, 35

4. Factors of 39: 1, 3, 13, 39
Factors of 25: 1, 5, 25

5. Two natural numbers are relatively prime if their greatest common factor is **?** .

6. Decide whether 160 and 189 are relatively prime.

PRACTICE AND PROBLEM SOLVING

In Exercises 7–14, find the greatest common factor of the numbers.

7. 20, 32

8. 36, 54

9. 90, 210

10. 126, 216

11. 1008, 1080

12. 546, 1995

13. 128, 256

14. 255, 256

OPEN-ENDED PROBLEMS In Exercises 15–18, find two pairs of numbers that have the given greatest common factor. (There are many correct answers.)

15. 4

16. 6

17. 21

18. 18

In Exercises 19–22, decide whether the numbers are relatively prime.

19. 384, 945

20. 80, 189

21. 120, 336

22. 220, 315

GEOMETRY In Exercises 23–26, find the area and perimeter of the rectangle. Are the two measures relatively prime? Explain.

23.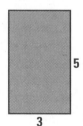
5
3

24.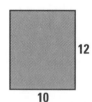
12
10

25.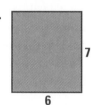
7
6

26.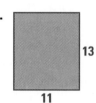
13
11

27. Find the greatest common factor of the terms in the following sequence:
6, 12, 18, 24, 30, ...

28. Find the greatest common factor of the terms in the following sequence:
8, 12, 16, 20, 24, ...

29. CRAFTS Three reeds have lengths of 39 cm, 52 cm, and 65 cm. To weave a basket, you want to cut the reeds so that the resulting pieces are all the same length. How can you make the pieces as long as possible?

39 cm
52 cm
65 cm

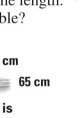

In Exercises 30 and 31, tell whether the statement is true or false.

30. The greatest common factor of $2^2 \cdot 3 \cdot 5 \cdot 19$ and $2 \cdot 3^2 \cdot 7 \cdot 19$ is 19.

31. If n and m are different primes, then they are relatively prime.

In Exercises 32–35, find the greatest common factor of the expressions.

32. $2y^2z, 8yz^2$ **33.** $3x^2y^2, 15x^2y$ **34.** $9r^2z, 21rz$ **35.** $42s^3t^4, 70s^4t^3$

STANDARDIZED TEST PRACTICE

36. What is the greatest common factor of $84x^2y$ and $96xy^2$?

Ⓐ 12   Ⓑ $12xy$ Ⓒ $12x^2y^2$ Ⓓ $12x^3y^3$

37. Which two numbers are relatively prime?

Ⓐ 13 and 52   Ⓑ 7 and 56   Ⓒ 9 and 42   Ⓓ 9 and 56

EXPLORATION AND EXTENSION

PORTFOLIO

BUILDING YOUR PROJECT You want to decorate your recording studio with famous record album covers. The rectangular region you want to decorate measures 72 in. by 63 in. The album covers measure 12 in. by 12 in.

38. Will you be able to completely cover this area with the album covers? If so, how many album covers will you use? If not, what is the largest number of album covers that will fit?

39. You have a color copier that can copy the album covers and resize them to 6 in. by 6 in., 9 in. by 9 in., or 15 in. by 15 in. Will any of these sizes completely cover the area? Explain.

6.4

What you should learn:

Goal 1 How to find the least common multiple of two numbers

Goal 2 How to use a least common multiple to solve problems in geometry

Why you should learn it:

You can use the least common multiple of two numbers to solve real-life problems, such as analyzing the movements of gears.

A technician adjusts the gears of a printing press.

Least Common Multiple

Goal 1 FINDING THE LEAST COMMON MULTIPLE

When you double, triple, or quadruple a number, you are finding *multiples* of the number.

> **LEAST COMMON MULTIPLE**
>
> A number that is a multiple of two natural numbers is a **common multiple** of them. Of all the common multiples of two numbers, the smallest is the **least common multiple** (LCM).

Example 1 Finding the Least Common Multiple

Find the least common multiple of 6 and 9.

Solution

With small numbers, you can list multiples of each number.

Number	Multiples	Common Multiples
6	6, 12, **18**, 24, 30, **36**, . . .	**18**, **36**, . . .
9	9, **18**, 27, **36**, . . .	**18**, **36**, . . .

The least common multiple is 18.

Example 2 Finding the Least Common Multiple

Find the least common multiple of 180 and 378.

Solution

With large numbers, you can find the least common multiple by writing the prime factorization of each number.

Number	Prime Factors	Common	Not Common
180	$2 \cdot 2 \cdot 3 \cdot 3 \cdot 5$	$2 \cdot 3 \cdot 3$	$2 \cdot 5$
378	$2 \cdot 3 \cdot 3 \cdot 3 \cdot 7$	$2 \cdot 3 \cdot 3$	$3 \cdot 7$

The least common multiple is the product of the common prime factors and all the prime factors that are not common.

Least Common Multiple $= 2 \cdot 3 \cdot 3 \cdot 2 \cdot 5 \cdot 3 \cdot 7 = 3780$

The least common multiple of 180 and 378 is 3780.

Example 3 Using a Least Common Multiple

You have a box of tiles, each of which is 4 in. by 6 in. Without overlapping or cutting the tiles, what is the least number of tiles you need to form a square region?

CONNECTION
Geometry

Solution

8 is a multiple of 4 but it is not a multiple of 6.

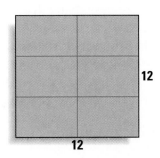

12 is a common multiple of 4 and 6.

Because 12 is a common multiple of 4 and 6, you can make a square with sides of length 12. Because it is the least common multiple, this is the *smallest* square you can make. You need 6 tiles.

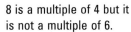

You can also find the least common multiple of algebraic expressions. For instance, the least common multiple of $6x$ and $4xy$ is $12xy$.

Example 4 Algebraic Expressions

Find the least common multiple of $10ab$ and $6b$.

Solution

Expression	Prime Factors	Common	Not Common
$10ab$	$2 \cdot 5 \cdot a \cdot b$	$2 \cdot b$	$5 \cdot a$
$6b$	$2 \cdot 3 \cdot b$	$2 \cdot b$	3

The least common multiple is the product of the common prime factors and all the prime factors that are not common.

$$2 \cdot b \cdot 5 \cdot a \cdot 3 = 30ab$$

The least common multiple of $10ab$ and $6b$ is $30ab$.

ONGOING ASSESSMENT

Write About It

Find the least common multiple of the numbers or expressions. Show your work.

1. 8 and 12

2. 15 and 24

3. $9m$ and $6mn$

GUIDED PRACTICE

In Exercises 1 and 2, find the three missing multiples of the number.

1. Multiples of 4: [?], 8, [?], 16, 20, [?]   **2.** Multiples of 6: 6, [?], 18, [?], 30, [?]

3. What is the least common multiple (LCM) of 4 and 6?

4. Describe two ways to find the least common multiple of two numbers. Which way would you use to find the least common multiple of 10 and 16? Which way would you use to find the least common multiple of 112 and 204?

In Exercises 5–7, match the number with its prime factorization. Then find the least common multiple of the three numbers.

A. $2^2 \cdot 3 \cdot 5^2$ B. $2 \cdot 3^2 \cdot 5$ C. $2^3 \cdot 5^2$

5. 200   **6.** 90   **7.** 300

8. What is the least common multiple of $2a^2b^3$ and $4ab^4$?

PRACTICE AND PROBLEM SOLVING

In Exercises 9–20, list the first several multiples of each number. Use the lists to find the least common multiple.

9. 3, 7   **10.** 7, 8   **11.** 6, 8   **12.** 3, 9

13. 8, 10   **14.** 10, 15   **15.** 10, 26   **16.** 4, 22

17. 3, 4, 18   **18.** 3, 6, 9   **19.** 5, 10, 20   **20.** 6, 9, 18

In Exercises 21–32, write the prime factorization of each expression. Use the results to find the least common multiple.

21. 90, 108   **22.** 7, 8   **23.** 125, 500   **24.** 160, 432

25. 135, 375   **26.** 225, 324   **27.** 144, 162   **28.** $16x, 32x^4$

29. $7s^2t, 49st^2$ **30.** $2x^3y, 3xy^5$ **31.** $3m^4n^4, 7m^6n^2$ **32.** $4a^6b^3, 8a^7b^5$

33. REASONING If two numbers are relatively prime, then what is their least common multiple? Give two examples.

34. REASONING If one number is a multiple of another, then what is their least common multiple? Give two examples.

In Exercises 35–38, use the results of Exercises 33 and 34 to find the least common multiple.

35. 3, 8   **36.** 8, 9   **37.** 3, 6   **38.** 8, 24

NUMBER SENSE In Exercises 39–42, find all pairs of numbers that satisfy the conditions.

39. Two prime numbers whose LCM is 35

40. Two composite numbers whose LCM is 16

41. Two square numbers whose LCM is 36

42. Two even numbers whose LCM is 12

43. **TILES** You have a box of tiles, each of which is 4 in. by 14 in. Without overlapping or cutting the tiles, what is the least number of tiles you need to form a square region? Draw a diagram and explain your answer.

44. **GEARS** The gears at the right are rotating. The large gear has 46 teeth and the small gear has 27 teeth. How many complete revolutions must each gear make for the gears to align again as shown?

45. **STOPLIGHTS** A stoplight turns red every 6 min. Another stoplight turns red every 8 min. A third stoplight turns red every 10 min. At 2:00 P.M., the three stoplights turn red at the same time. When is the next time all three stoplights turn red?

STANDARDIZED TEST PRACTICE

46. What is the least common multiple of 20 and 30?

(**A**) 10 (**B**) 60 (**C**) 120 (**D**) 600

47. What is the least common multiple of $4x^2y$ and $6xy^2$?

(**A**) $24x^2y^2$ (**B**) $12x^2y^2$ (**C**) $12xy$ (**D**) $2xy$

EXPLORATION AND EXTENSION

PORTFOLIO

48. **BUILDING YOUR PROJECT** You are recording a track that will include drums, guitars, and vocals. The drum track accents every beat. The guitar track accents every fourth beat. You know that when you mix the sounds on a computer, you will have to enhance the vocals so that they can be heard when both instruments accent the same beat. How often will you have to enhance the vocals?

Simplifying and Comparing Fractions

What you should learn:

 Goal 1 How to simplify a fraction

 Goal 2 How to compare two fractions

Why you should learn it:

Rewriting a fraction in a different form helps you decide whether one fraction is larger than another.

Some steel drums have 24 notes, with 15 notes in the outer ring and 9 notes in the center. This means that $\frac{3}{8}$ of the notes are in the center, because $\frac{9}{24} = \frac{3}{8}$.

Goal 1 SIMPLIFYING A FRACTION

Two fractions are **equivalent** if they have the same decimal form. For instance, the fractions $\frac{1}{2}$ and $\frac{2}{4}$ are equivalent because each is equal to 0.5. The following squares show that the fractions $\frac{2}{3}$, $\frac{4}{6}$, and $\frac{8}{12}$ are also equivalent.

 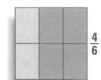 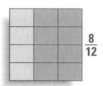

The first of these fractions, $\frac{2}{3}$, is in **simplest form**, because the numerator and denominator have no common factors. Writing a fraction in simplest form is called **simplifying** the fraction.

Example 1 Simplifying a Fraction

Simplify the fraction $\frac{12}{20}$.

Solution

To simplify the fraction, factor its numerator and denominator. Then divide the numerator and denominator by any common prime factors.

$$\frac{12}{20} = \frac{\cancel{2} \cdot \cancel{2} \cdot 3}{\cancel{2} \cdot \cancel{2} \cdot 5} = \frac{3}{5}$$

Another way to simplify a fraction is to divide the numerator and denominator by their greatest common factor.

$$\frac{12}{20} = \frac{12 \div 4}{20 \div 4} = \frac{3}{5}$$

Example 2 Simplifying a Fraction with Variables

Simplify the fraction $\frac{4x^2}{6x}$.

Solution

$$\frac{4x^2}{6x} = \frac{\cancel{2} \cdot 2 \cdot x \cdot \cancel{x}}{\cancel{2} \cdot 3 \cdot \cancel{x}} = \frac{2x}{3}$$

For fractions with like denominators, the greater fraction is the one with the greater numerator. For instance, $\frac{5}{7} > \frac{4}{7}$. In this example, 7 is called a *common denominator*.

To compare fractions with unlike denominators, rewrite them with a common denominator. A good common denominator is the least common multiple of the original denominators.

Example 3 Comparing Fractions

Which fraction is greater, $\frac{7}{12}$ or $\frac{9}{16}$?

Solution

The denominators are 12 and 16. Their least common multiple is 48. So, rewrite each fraction with a denominator of 48.

$\frac{7}{12} = \frac{7}{12} \times \frac{4}{4} = \frac{28}{48}$ **Multiply by $\frac{4}{4}$ to get a denominator of 48.**

$\frac{9}{16} = \frac{9}{16} \times \frac{3}{3} = \frac{27}{48}$ **Multiply by $\frac{3}{3}$ to get a denominator of 48.**

Now, because 28 > 27, it follows that $\frac{7}{12} > \frac{9}{16}$.

Example 4 Comparing Fractions

You ate 4 pieces of a small pizza that was cut into 6 equal pieces. Your friend ate 5 pieces of a small pizza that was cut into 8 equal pieces. Who ate more pizza?

Solution

You ate $\frac{4}{6}$ of a pizza and your friend ate $\frac{5}{8}$ of a pizza. The least common multiple of 6 and 8 is 24.

$\frac{4}{6} = \frac{4}{6} \times \frac{4}{4} = \frac{16}{24}$ **Multiply by $\frac{4}{4}$ to get a denominator of 24.**

$\frac{5}{8} = \frac{5}{8} \times \frac{3}{3} = \frac{15}{24}$ **Multiply by $\frac{3}{3}$ to get a denominator of 24.**

Because $\frac{16}{24} > \frac{15}{24}$, it follows that you ate more pizza.

ONGOING ASSESSMENT

Write About It
....

1. Draw a number line and mark it with 17 equally spaced tick marks. Label the tick marks

    $0, \frac{1}{16}, \frac{2}{16}, \frac{3}{16}, \cdots, \frac{15}{16}, 1$.

2. Use the number line to order the following fractions from least to greatest:

    $\frac{1}{2}, \frac{7}{8}, \frac{11}{16}, \frac{3}{4}, \frac{9}{16}$.

GUIDED PRACTICE

In Exercises 1–4, write a fraction that represents the portion of the region that is shaded. Then simplify the fraction.

1.

2.

3.

4.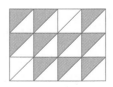

In Exercises 5 and 6, write the fraction that is shaded in each rectangle. Then rewrite the fractions with a common denominator and decide which is larger.

5.

6.

PRACTICE AND PROBLEM SOLVING

In Exercises 7–14, what is the greatest common factor of the numerator and denominator? Use your answer to simplify the fraction.

7. $\dfrac{14}{20}$

8. $\dfrac{16}{36}$

9. $\dfrac{9}{42}$

10. $\dfrac{63}{105}$

11. $\dfrac{10}{75}$

12. $\dfrac{8}{28}$

13. $\dfrac{36}{54}$

14. $\dfrac{117}{143}$

In Exercises 15–22, simplify the variable expression.

15. $\dfrac{2ab}{8b^2}$

16. $\dfrac{3x^2y}{9y}$

17. $\dfrac{25z^2}{150z^3}$

18. $\dfrac{22s^3t}{55s^3t^2}$

19. $\dfrac{6yz}{8y}$

20. $\dfrac{15x}{21x^2}$

21. $\dfrac{28p^2q^2}{42p^3q^3}$

22. $\dfrac{34m^2}{68mn}$

23. REASONING Explain how you can determine whether a fraction is in simplest form.

In Exercises 24–27, write three fractions that are equivalent to the given fraction.

24. $\dfrac{1}{2}$

25. $\dfrac{2}{5}$

26. $\dfrac{10}{22}$

27. $\dfrac{8}{18}$

In Exercises 28–35, complete the statement with <, >, or =.

28. $\dfrac{1}{7}$? $\dfrac{1}{6}$

29. $\dfrac{18}{38}$? $\dfrac{27}{57}$

30. $\dfrac{1}{12}$? $\dfrac{1}{13}$

31. $\dfrac{8}{14}$? $\dfrac{6}{13}$

32. $\dfrac{7}{8}$? $\dfrac{8}{9}$

33. $\dfrac{0}{2}$? $\dfrac{0}{100}$

34. $\dfrac{15}{39}$? $\dfrac{5}{13}$

35. $\dfrac{26}{50}$? $\dfrac{27}{51}$

PHOTOGRAPHY **In Exercise 36, use the following information.**

Shutter speed is the length of time the shutter is open. Many cameras allow a photographer to adjust the shutter speed. A slow shutter speed allows more light to expose film than a fast shutter speed does.

36. The shutter speed on your camera is $\frac{1}{250}$ of a second. You want to decrease the shutter speed. Which of the following would be appropriate: $\frac{1}{500}$ of a second or $\frac{1}{125}$ of a second? Explain.

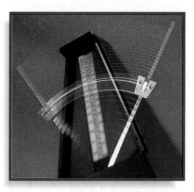

This photograph appears blurry because of the long shutter speed.

NUTRITION **In Exercises 37–40, use the bar graph at the right. It shows the numbers of servings for maintaining a balanced diet.** (Source: The World Almanac for Kids)

37. Write the servings of meat as a fraction of all servings. Simplify.

38. Write the servings of vegetables and bread as a fraction of all servings. Simplify.

39. A friend tells you that one third of the food servings should be fruits and vegetables. Compare this to the recommendation given in the graph.

40. A friend tells you that one fourth of the food servings should be from the dairy and meat groups. Compare this to the recommendation given in the graph.

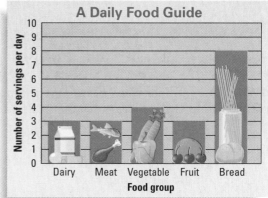

STANDARDIZED TEST PRACTICE

41. Which of the following is not equivalent to $\frac{7}{8}$?

   A $\frac{14}{16}$ **B** $\frac{17}{18}$ **C** $\frac{21}{24}$ **D** $\frac{28}{32}$

42. Which group of fractions is correctly ordered from least to greatest?

   A $\frac{1}{2}, \frac{1}{3}, \frac{1}{4}$ **B** $\frac{2}{9}, \frac{1}{3}, \frac{2}{5}$ **C** $\frac{12}{21}, \frac{4}{9}, \frac{3}{7}$ **D** $\frac{5}{8}, \frac{7}{15}, \frac{1}{2}$

43. Estimate the fraction of the circle that is *not* shaded.

   A $\frac{1}{10}$ **B** $\frac{3}{13}$ **C** $\frac{4}{7}$ **D** $\frac{5}{6}$

44. **MUSIC** A glockenspiel (shown at the right) has bars of different lengths, like the lyre strings shown on page 264. Rewrite the lyre string fractions from page 264 using a common denominator. How could you use the numerators to help you build a small glockenspiel?

45. **PAY SCALES** Which pay scale would you prefer? Explain.

    Pay scale A: $4 for each $\frac{1}{2}$ h worked

    Pay scale B: $5 for each $\frac{2}{3}$ h worked

In Exercises 1–4, evaluate the expression when *m* = 7. (1.5)

1. $m + 11$
2. $22 - m$
3. $\dfrac{84}{m}$
4. $6 \times m$

In Exercises 5–7, solve the inequality. (2.9)

5. $13 > x - 14$
6. $19 + n \le 24$
7. $7y \ge 105$

GEOMETRY **In Exercises 8–10, plot the points in the same coordinate plane. Name the quadrant that contains each point. (3.8)**

8. $A(-2, 4)$
9. $B(0, 2)$
10. $C(3, -1)$

11. The points in Exercises 8–10 all lie on a line. Find another point that lies on the same line. (3.8)

In Exercises 12–14, use the information in the advertisements below. (4.7)

12. For each music club, find the total cost of the required 15 cassettes.

13. For each music club, write an algebraic expression for the total cost of getting 15 cassettes and buying *d* more cassettes.

14. Set the expressions in Exercise 13 equal to each other and solve for *d*. Which music club would you choose? Explain.

Music Club 1

Get 8 **FREE** cassettes when you join!

Members must purchase 7 more cassettes for $13.98 each.

MUSIC CLUB 2

Club members get 9 **FREE** cassettes

Members must buy an additional 6 cassettes at $15.99 each.

Take this test as you would take a test in class. The answers to the exercises are given in the back of the book.

In Exercises 1 and 2, use the divisibility tests to decide whether the number is divisible by 2, 3, 4, 5, 6, 8, 9, and 10. (6.1)

1. 510

2. 1360

3. **TECHNOLOGY** Use a calculator to decide whether 816 is divisible by 11, 12, 13, 14, 15, 16, 17, 18, 19, or 20. **(6.1)**

4. List all the factors of the number 56. **(6.2)**

In Exercises 5–7, write the prime factorization of the number. (6.2)

5. 80

6. 44

7. 105

In Exercises 8–10, find the greatest common factor. (6.3)

8. 12, 60

9. 36, 15

10. 135, 45, 25

In Exercises 11–13, find the least common multiple. (6.4)

11. 13, 5

12. 14, 21

13. $6x, 9x^2$

In Exercises 14–16, simplify the expression. (6.5)

14. $\dfrac{5}{25}$

15. $\dfrac{45}{306}$

16. $\dfrac{8y^2}{24y}$

GEOMETRY In Exercises 17 and 18, what is the least number of tiles you need to form a square without overlapping or cutting the tiles? How is the length of the square's sides related to the lengths of the sides of the tile? **(6.4)**

17.
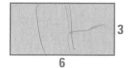
3
6

18.
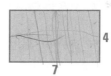
4
7

PACKING In Exercises 19 and 20, imagine that you are stacking boxes. One stack uses 6 in. boxes, and the other stack uses 14 in. boxes. **(6.4)**

19. To make two stacks of the same height, what is the least number of boxes of each size that you need?

20. In Exercise 19, is the height of each stack the least common multiple of 6 and 14 or the greatest common factor of 6 and 14?

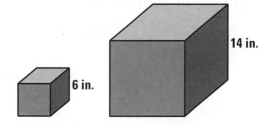
14 in.
6 in.

6.6

Rational Numbers and Decimals

What you should learn:

Goal 1 How to show that a number is rational

Goal 2 How to write a decimal as a fraction

Why you should learn it:

Knowing how to rewrite numbers in decimal form or as fractions helps you interpret results given by calculators.

Goal 1 IDENTIFYING RATIONAL NUMBERS

In this lesson, you will study properties of *rational numbers*.

RATIONAL NUMBERS

A number is **rational** if it can be written as the quotient of two integers. Numbers that cannot be written as the quotient of two integers are called **irrational**.

Rational Numbers	Irrational Numbers
$\frac{1}{2}, -\frac{3}{5}, \frac{9}{4}, \frac{5}{1}$	$\sqrt{2}, \sqrt{3}, \sqrt{5}$

Example 1 Recognizing Rational Numbers

Show that the following numbers are rational.

a. 4 **b.** 0.5 **c.** -3

Solution

To show that a number is rational, you must show that it can be written as the quotient of two integers.

a. 4 is rational because it can be written as $4 = \frac{4}{1}$.

b. 0.5 is rational because it can be written as $0.5 = \frac{1}{2}$.

c. -3 is rational because it can be written as $-3 = \frac{-3}{1}$.

....

Natural numbers $(1, 2, 3, \ldots)$, whole numbers $(0, 1, 2, \ldots)$, and integers $(\ldots, -2, -1, 0, 1, 2, \ldots)$ are examples of rational numbers.

Example 2 Showing That a Mixed Number Is Rational

Show that the mixed number $1\frac{1}{4}$ is rational.

Solution

$$1\frac{1}{4} = 1 + \frac{1}{4} = \frac{4}{4} + \frac{1}{4} = \frac{5}{4}$$

This Venn diagram shows that each natural number, whole number, and integer is a rational number.

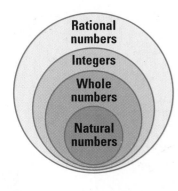

Rational numbers
Integers
Whole numbers
Natural numbers

TOOLBOX

Adding Fractions, page 747

Goal 2 WRITING DECIMALS AS FRACTIONS

Decimals can be *terminating*, *repeating*, or *nonrepeating*. In decimal form, every rational number is either terminating or repeating, and every irrational number is nonrepeating.

Number	Decimal Form	Comment
$\frac{3}{8}$	0.375	Rational, terminating
$\frac{16}{11}$	$1.454545\ldots = 1.\overline{45}$	Rational, repeating
$\sqrt{2}$	$1.414213562\ldots$	Irrational, nonrepeating

Example 3 Writing Decimals as Fractions

Write the decimal as a fraction.

a. 0.45

b. $0.090909\ldots = 0.\overline{09}$

Solution

a. This terminating decimal represents 45 hundredths, as shown in the decimal model at the right.

$$0.45 = \frac{45}{100} \qquad \text{Write as 45 hundredths.}$$

$$= \frac{5 \cdot 9}{5 \cdot 20} \qquad \text{Factor.}$$

$$= \frac{9}{20} \qquad \text{Simplify.}$$

b. To write a repeating decimal as a fraction, use the following strategy.

$$x = 0.090909\ldots \qquad \text{Let } x \text{ represent the number.}$$

$$100x = 9.090909\ldots \qquad \text{Multiply each side by 100.}$$

$$99x = 9 \qquad \text{Subtract first equation from second.}$$

$$x = \frac{9}{99} \qquad \text{Divide each side by 99.}$$

$$x = \frac{1}{11} \qquad \text{Simplify.}$$

Note that each side is multiplied by 100 because $0.090909\ldots$ has two repeating digits. For one repeating digit, multiply by 10. For three repeating digits, multiply by 1000.

ONGOING ASSESSMENT

Write About It

Write each decimal as a fraction in simplest form. Show your work and explain each step.

1. 0.375

2. $1.6666\ldots = 1.\overline{6}$

3. $0.8383\ldots = 0.\overline{83}$

4. $0.0454545\ldots = 0.0\overline{45}$

GUIDED PRACTICE

In Exercises 1–5, state whether the number is rational or irrational. If it is rational, write it as the quotient of two integers.

1. -3 **2.** $\sqrt{6}$ **3.** $2\frac{3}{5}$ **4.** 7 **5.** 0.4

In Exercises 6–9, write the decimal that is represented by the yellow portion of the grid. Then write the number as a fraction and simplify. (Each small square has an area of 0.01.)

6.   **7.**   **8.**   **9.**

10. WRITING Explain how to write a mixed number as a quotient of two integers.

PRACTICE AND PROBLEM SOLVING

In Exercises 11–18, write the number as a fraction in simplest form.

11. 5 **12.** 0.75 **13.** 0.25 **14.** -9

15. $1\frac{1}{6}$ **16.** $2\frac{2}{9}$ **17.** $-1\frac{5}{8}$ **18.** $-2\frac{4}{5}$

In Exercises 19–26, decide whether the number is rational or irrational. Then write the decimal form of the number and state whether the decimal is terminating, repeating, or nonrepeating.

19. $\frac{3}{5}$ **20.** $\frac{9}{11}$ **21.** $\sqrt{8}$ **22.** $\sqrt{9}$

23. $\frac{8}{15}$ **24.** $\frac{7}{10}$ **25.** $\frac{7}{2}$ **26.** $\frac{13}{12}$

In Exercises 27–34, write the decimal as a fraction. Simplify the result.

27. 0.8 **28.** 0.35 **29.** 0.84 **30.** 0.64

31. $0.\overline{45}$ **32.** $0.\overline{86}$ **33.** $2.\overline{3}$ **34.** $1.\overline{135}$

In Exercises 35–40, match the rational number with its decimal form.

A. 0.4 B. 3.08 C. 3.12 D. $0.2\overline{7}$ E. $0.08\overline{3}$ F. $0.\overline{296}$

35. $\frac{10}{120}$ **36.** $\frac{6}{15}$ **37.** $3\frac{3}{25}$ **38.** $\frac{5}{18}$ **39.** $\frac{8}{27}$ **40.** $3\frac{6}{75}$

In Exercises 41 and 42, describe the pattern. Then write each rational number in decimal form.

41. $\dfrac{1}{11}, \dfrac{2}{11}, \dfrac{3}{11}, \dfrac{4}{11}, \dfrac{5}{11}, \dfrac{6}{11}$

42. $\dfrac{1}{2}, \dfrac{3}{4}, \dfrac{5}{6}, \dfrac{7}{8}, \dfrac{9}{10}, \dfrac{11}{12}$

 In Exercises 43 and 44, use a calculator to simplify the expression. Write your answer as a fraction.

43. $\dfrac{2}{3} - \dfrac{1}{2}$

44. $\dfrac{2}{3} + \dfrac{1}{9}$

GEOMETRY In Exercises 45–47, find the perimeter of the figure. Write the result in fraction form, as a mixed number, and as a decimal.

45.

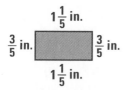

$1\frac{1}{5}$ in.

$\frac{3}{5}$ in. $\frac{3}{5}$ in.

$1\frac{1}{5}$ in.

46.

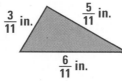

$\frac{3}{11}$ in. $\frac{5}{11}$ in.

$\frac{6}{11}$ in.

47.

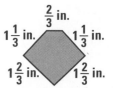

$\frac{2}{3}$ in.

$1\frac{1}{3}$ in. $1\frac{1}{3}$ in.

$1\frac{2}{3}$ in. $1\frac{2}{3}$ in.

48. SURVEYS Each fraction indicates the portion of students surveyed who chose each fruit as their favorite.

a. Write each fraction in decimal form.

b. Order the fruits from most popular to least popular.

Favorite Fruit					
Portion of Students	$\dfrac{21}{50}$	$\dfrac{13}{25}$	$\dfrac{41}{100}$	$\dfrac{9}{20}$	$\dfrac{41}{50}$

 STANDARDIZED TEST PRACTICE

49. Use the Venn diagram on page 280 to tell which statement is true.

Ⓐ All rational numbers are integers. Ⓑ All whole numbers are natural numbers.

Ⓒ All integers are whole numbers. Ⓓ All natural numbers are integers.

 EXPLORATION AND EXTENSION

PORTFOLIO

50. BUILDING YOUR PROJECT The lengths, in minutes and seconds, of the songs on your recording are 5:06, 4:20, 5:45, and 4:42.

a. Write the length of each song in minutes as a mixed fraction, using 60 as a denominator.

b. Write each fraction as a decimal.

c. Will all of the songs fit on a 20 min tape? Explain.

6.7

Powers and Exponents

What you should learn:

Goal 1 How to evaluate powers that have negative and zero exponents

Goal 2 How to multiply and divide powers

Why you should learn it:

You can multiply and divide powers to solve problems involving large or small numbers, such as the amount of food eaten in the United States.

Sand is composed of tiny pieces of rocks that vary in width from 20^{-2} in. to 12^{-1} in.

Goal 1 USING NEGATIVE AND ZERO EXPONENTS

You already know how to evaluate powers that have positive integer exponents. For instance, $2^3 = 2 \cdot 2 \cdot 2 = 8$ and $(-3)^2 = (-3) \cdot (-3) = 9$.

In this lesson, you will learn how to evaluate powers that have negative integer or zero exponents.

LESSON INVESTIGATION

Investigating Negative and Zero Exponents

GROUP ACTIVITY Use a calculator to write each power in decimal form.

| 10^3 | 10^2 | 10^1 | 10^0 | 10^{-1} | 10^{-2} | 10^{-3} |

| 2^3 | 2^2 | 2^1 | 2^0 | 2^{-1} | 2^{-2} | 2^{-3} |

Sample Keystrokes for 10^{-2}: 10 [y^x] 2 [+/-] [=]

What patterns can you discover? What does it mean to have a zero or negative exponent?

You may have discovered the following definitions.

NEGATIVE AND ZERO EXPONENTS

Let n be a positive integer and let a be a nonzero number.

$$a^{-n} = \frac{1}{a^n} \quad \text{and} \quad a^0 = 1$$

Example 1 Evaluating Powers

a. $2^{-2} = \frac{1}{2^2} = \frac{1}{4}$

b. $-3^{-2} = -\frac{1}{3^2} = -\frac{1}{9}$

c. $(-4)^{-2} = \frac{1}{(-4)^2} = \frac{1}{16}$

d. $4^0 = 1$

> Evaluate powers before multiplying.

e. $x^{-1} = \frac{1}{x^1} = \frac{1}{x}$

f. $2b^{-2} = 2(b^{-2}) = 2\left(\frac{1}{b^2}\right) = \frac{2}{b^2}$

Goal **2** MULTIPLYING AND DIVIDING POWERS

To multiply two powers with the same base, add their exponents. To divide two powers with the same base, subtract the exponent of the denominator from the exponent of the numerator.

EXPONENT RULES

1. $a^m \cdot a^n = a^{m+n}$ **2.** $\dfrac{a^m}{a^n} = a^{m-n}$

Example 2 **Multiplying and Dividing Powers**

Using Exponent Rules   **Using Factors**

a. $4^2 \cdot 4^3 = 4^{2+3} = 4^5$ $4^2 \cdot 4^3 = 4 \cdot 4 \cdot 4 \cdot 4 \cdot 4 = 4^5$

b. $\dfrac{3^3}{3^2} = 3^{3-2} = 3^1 = 3$ $\dfrac{3^3}{3^2} = \dfrac{3 \cdot 3 \cdot 3}{3 \cdot 3} = 3$

c. $2^4 \cdot 2^{-2} = 2^{4+(-2)} = 2^2$ $2^4 \cdot \dfrac{1}{2^2} = \dfrac{2 \cdot 2 \cdot 2 \cdot 2}{2 \cdot 2} = 2^2$

d. $\dfrac{5}{5^3} = 5^{1-3} = 5^{-2}$ $\dfrac{5}{5^3} = \dfrac{5}{5 \cdot 5 \cdot 5} = \dfrac{1}{5^2} = 5^{-2}$

Example 3 **Rubik's Cube Puzzles**

You have a stack of Rubik's Cube puzzles, as shown at the right. Suppose each of these contains 3^3 small cubes. How many small cubes are in the stack?

Solution

There are 3^3 small cubes in each puzzle and 3^3 puzzles in the stack.

$3^3 \cdot 3^3 = 3^{3+3}$ **Multiply powers with same base.**

$\qquad = 3^6$ **Add exponents.**

$\qquad = 729$

This means the stack has 729 small cubes.

✔**Check:** You can check this result by reasoning that if each Rubik's Cube puzzle is composed of 27 small cubes, then the stack has $27 \cdot 27$ or 729 small cubes.

ONGOING ASSESSMENT

Talk About It

Work with a partner. Simplify each expression. One of you should use exponent rules and the other should use factors. Compare your results and discuss your steps.

1. $5^3 \cdot 5^4$ **2.** $5^3 \cdot 5^{-4}$

3. $\dfrac{5^4}{5^2}$ **4.** $\dfrac{5^3}{5}$

GUIDED PRACTICE

1. **WRITING** In your own words, state the definitions for negative integer exponents and zero exponents.

In Exercises 2–5, rewrite the expression without negative or zero exponents.

2. 4^{-1}

3. 5^{-2}

4. 100^0

5. x^{-3}

6. **WRITING** In your own words, state how to multiply and divide two powers that have the same base.

In Exercises 7–10, simplify the expression, if possible.

7. $p^5 \cdot p^2$

8. $r^2 \cdot s^3$

9. $\dfrac{m^6}{n^4}$

10. $\dfrac{x^4}{x^2}$

PRACTICE AND PROBLEM SOLVING

In Exercises 11–18, simplify the expression.

11. 3^{-2}

12. -10^{-3}

13. 16^0

14. $(-9)^2$

15. t^{-4}

16. $2x^{-3}$

17. $3s^{-2}$

18. r^0

In Exercises 19–26, simplify the expression.

19. $(-6)^{-3} \cdot (-6)^5$

20. $8^0 \cdot 8^4$

21. $x^{25} \cdot x^{-10}$

22. $y^{-6} \cdot y^4$

23. $\dfrac{7^5}{7^4}$

24. $\dfrac{-9^2}{-9^4}$

25. $\dfrac{a^{12}}{a^0}$

26. $\dfrac{b^7}{b^{10}}$

 TECHNOLOGY In Exercises 27–30, use a calculator to evaluate the expression. If necessary, round the result to three decimal places.

27. $(2.5)^{-4}$

28. $(5.5)^{-2}$

29. $(5.5)^3 \cdot (5.5)^2$

30. $\dfrac{(0.5)^3}{(0.5)^6}$

MENTAL MATH In Exercises 31–34, solve the equation for n.

31. $\dfrac{2^5}{2^2} = 2^n$

32. $\left(\dfrac{1}{2}\right)^n = 1$

33. $3^{-3} \cdot 3^n = 3^3$

34. $4^{-5} = \dfrac{1}{4^n}$

35. **GUESS, CHECK, AND REVISE** Find the largest value of n such that $2^n < 100,000$.

36. **GUESS, CHECK, AND REVISE** Find the largest value of n such that $3^{-n} > 0.00001$.

In Exercises 37–40, complete the statement with <, >, or =.

37. 3^{10} **?** $3 \cdot 3^9$

38. 2^{-5} **?** 5^{-2}

39. $\dfrac{4^3}{4^2}$ **?** $\dfrac{4^2}{4^3}$

40. $\dfrac{4^{14}}{4^3}$ **?** 4^{10}

In Exercises 41 and 42, rewrite the sequence as powers of 10. Write the next three terms as powers of 10.

41. 1, 10, 100, 1000, ? , ? , ?

42. 1, 0.1, 0.01, 0.001, 0.0001, ? , ? , ?

43. GEOMETRY Suppose a Rubik's Cube puzzle contains 4^3 cubes. How many small cubes would be in a $4 \times 4 \times 4$ stack?

44. FOOD In 1994, the United States had a population of about 260 million people. In that year, Americans ate about 17 billion lb of beef. Find the average amount eaten by each American by simplifying the expression. (Source: U.S. Department of Agriculture)

$$\frac{1.7\left(10^{10}\right) \text{ lb}}{2.6\left(10^{8}\right) \text{ people}}$$

45. BIOLOGY Most cells of living organisms are about 10 micrometers wide. One micrometer is 10^{-6} m, which means that a typical cell is about $10 \cdot 10^{-6}$ m wide. Write this measurement as a power of 10.

46. LASERS A laser is a device that amplifies light. A laser beam can be focused on a point that is just $(0.05)^2$ mm wide. Write this measurement as a fraction.

STANDARDIZED TEST PRACTICE

47. POPULATION In 1997, the United States had a population of about 270 million. Which of the following expressions represents this number? (Source: U.S. Bureau of the Census)

(A) $2.7(10^6)$ **(B)** $2.7(10^7)$ **(C)** $2.7(10^8)$ **(D)** $2.7(10^9)$

EXPLORATION AND EXTENSION

48. Each small yellow cube contains $20. Each small red cube contains $10. Each small blue cube contains $5. Which of the large cubes contains the most money? Explain.

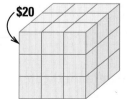
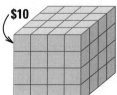
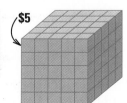

$20

$10

$5

6.8

Scientific Notation

What you should learn:

Goal 1 How to use scientific notation to represent numbers

Goal 2 How to use scientific notation to solve real-life problems

Why you should learn it:

Scientific notation is a convenient way to represent numbers whose absolute values are very small or very large.

Goal 1 WRITING SCIENTIFIC NOTATION

Many numbers in real life are very large or very small. For instance, the population of the world is about 5,600,000,000. Instead of writing this many zeros, you can write

$$5,600,000,000 = 5.6 \times 1,000,000,000 = 5.6 \times 10^9.$$

The form on the right is called **scientific notation**.

SCIENTIFIC NOTATION

A number is written in scientific notation if it has the form

$$c \times 10^n$$

where c is greater than or equal to 1 and less than 10.

Example 1 Writing Numbers in Scientific Notation

Decimal Form	Product Form	Scientific Notation
a. 3,400	3.4×1000	3.4×10^3
b. 56,000,000	$5.6 \times 10,000,000$	5.6×10^7
c. 0.00923	9.23×0.001	9.23×10^{-3}
d. 0.0000004	4×0.0000001	4×10^{-7}

In Example 1, notice that the exponent of 10 indicates the number of places the decimal point is moved. For instance, in part (a) the decimal point is moved 3 places and in part (d) the decimal point is moved 7 places.

Decimal Form	Scientific Notation
3,400.00	3.4×10^3
3 places to the left	
0.0000004	4×10^{-7}
7 places to the right	

Notice that negative exponents in scientific notation indicate very small numbers, not negative numbers.

STUDY TIP

Positive exponents correspond to large numbers and negative exponents correspond to small numbers.

1,000	10^3
100	10^2
10	10^1
1	10^0
0.1	10^{-1}
0.01	10^{-2}
0.001	10^{-3}

To multiply two numbers that are written in scientific notation, you can use the rule for multiplying powers with like bases.

Example 2 Multiplying with Scientific Notation

Find the product of (3.2×10^5) and (4×10^6).

Solution

Product $= (3.2 \times 10^5) \times (4 \times 10^6)$	Write the product.
$= 3.2 \times 4 \times 10^5 \times 10^6$	Reorder.
$= (3.2 \times 4) \times (10^5 \times 10^6)$	Regroup.
$= 12.8 \times 10^{11}$	Multiply.
$= 1.28 \times 10^{12}$	Rewrite in scientific notation.

This can also be written as 1,280,000,000,000, or 1.28 trillion.

Example 3 Multiplying with Scientific Notation

You work in a warehouse that stores recycled paper. Each sheet of paper is 4.4×10^{-3} in. thick. The paper comes in packages of 500 sheets. Each carton of paper has two stacks of 5 packages. About how tall is a stack of 10 cartons?

Solution

Verbal Model

$$\frac{\text{Height}}{\text{of stack}} = \frac{\text{Number}}{\text{of sheets}} \times \frac{\text{Thickness}}{\text{of sheet}}$$

Labels

Number of sheets $= 10(5)(500) = 25,000$ (sheets)

Thickness of sheet $= 4.4 \times 10^{-3}$ (inches per sheet)

Algebraic Model

$$\begin{aligned}
\text{Height} &= 25,000 \times (4.4 \times 10^{-3}) \\
&= (2.5 \times 10^4) \times (4.4 \times 10^{-3}) \\
&= (2.5 \times 4.4) \times (10^4 \times 10^{-3}) \\
&= 11 \times 10^1 \\
&= 110
\end{aligned}$$

The stack of 10 cartons is about 110 in. high.

**Real Life...
Real Facts**

Paper Chase

In 1994, Americans recycled an average of about 220 lb of paper per person.

ONGOING ASSESSMENT

Write About It
• • • • • • • • • • • • • • • • • • •

State whether the number is in scientific notation. If it isn't, explain why and rewrite it in scientific notation.

1. 12.4×10^{-3}

2. 3.8×10^{-2}

3. 0.05×10^4

GUIDED PRACTICE

1. Which of the following is written in scientific notation?

   A. 12.3×10^3 **B.** 1.23×10^4 **c.** 0.123×10^5

In Exercises 2 and 3, find the power of 10.

2. $350,000 = 3.5 \times 10^{?}$ **3.** $0.00943 = 9.43 \times 10^{?}$

In Exercises 4 and 5, write the number in decimal form.

4. 6.25×10^5 **5.** 8.7×10^{-6}

6. POPULATION One of the following is the approximate 1996 population of China. The other is the approximate 1996 population of Canada. Which is which? Explain your reasoning.

   A. 2.9×10^7 **B.** 1.2×10^9

PRACTICE AND PROBLEM SOLVING

In Exercises 7–14, write the number in scientific notation.

7. 5000 **8.** $643,000$ **9.** 0.00041 **10.** 0.18

11. $32,610,000$ **12.** $5,730,000,000$ **13.** 0.000000012 **14.** 0.000008

In Exercises 15–22, write the number in decimal form.

15. 5.7×10^{-3} **16.** 3.41×10^{-6} **17.** 2.50×10^4 **18.** 2.4×10^9

19. 6.2×10^{10} **20.** 8.59×10^5 **21.** 3.63×10^{-7} **22.** 5.99×10^{-1}

In Exercises 23–28, decide whether the number is in scientific notation. If it is not, rewrite the number in scientific notation.

23. 5.3×10^{-5} **24.** 0.392×10^6 **25.** 25.6×10^8

26. 3.7×10^9 **27.** 791×10^{-4} **28.** 68.8×10^3

In Exercises 29–32, evaluate the product. Write the result in scientific notation and in decimal form.

29. $\left(6.2 \times 10^2\right)\left(8 \times 10^3\right)$ **30.** $\left(4.5 \times 10^{-3}\right)\left(3.4 \times 10^5\right)$

31. $\left(0.3 \times 10^{-4}\right)\left(0.6 \times 10^{-1}\right)$ **32.** $\left(9.7 \times 10^4\right)\left(2.4 \times 10^2\right)$

NUMBER SENSE **In Exercises 33 and 34, decide which is larger. Explain.**

33. 1×10^9 or 9×10^8 **34.** 5×10^{-5} or 1×10^{-4}

35. ASTRONOMY Some stars in the Milky Way are 8×10^4 light-years from Earth. A light-year is 5.88×10^{12} mi. Write 8×10^4 light-years in miles.

In Exercises 36 and 37, write the number in scientific notation.

36. A thunderstorm cloud holds about 6,000,000,000,000 raindrops.

37. The adult human body contains about 100,000,000,000,000 cells.

38. MUSICAL INSTRUMENTS The table shows the number of people in the United States who play the six most popular instruments. Rewrite the table so that the numbers are in decimal form. (Source: American Music Conference)

Instrument	Piano	Guitar	Organ	Flute	Clarinet	Drums
Number	2.06×10^7	1.89×10^7	6.3×10^6	4×10^6	4×10^6	3×10^6

39. DENSITY Light elements such as oxygen have a smaller density than heavy elements such as iron. Write each of the following densities (in grams per cubic centimeter) in scientific notation. Then order the elements from lightest to heaviest.

Element	Density
Chlorine	0.00295
Helium	0.0001664
Hydrogen	0.00008375
Nitrogen	0.001165
Oxygen	0.001332

STANDARDIZED TEST PRACTICE

40. Find the area of the rectangle.

(A) 35.28×10^6

(B) 3.528×10^6

(C) 12.6×10^5

(D) 3.528×10^5

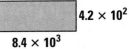

4.2 × 10²

8.4 × 10³

Not drawn to scale

EXPLORATION AND EXTENSION

41. COMMUNICATING ABOUT MATHEMATICS For information about monarch butterflies, see page 293. The monarch is only one of about 2.0×10^4 species of butterflies in the world. Write this number as a decimal.

42. The smallest butterfly is only about $\frac{3}{8}$ in. long. Write this length as a decimal and then express it in scientific notation.

Expressing Scientific Notation

With a scientific calculator, use the `EE` key to enter numbers whose absolute values are very small or very large.

CALCULATOR TIP

Some scientific calculators have an `EXP` key instead of an `EE` key.

Example 1 Entering Scientific Notation

Number	Keystrokes	Display
3.629×10^{12}	3.629 `EE` 12 `=`	3.629 12
8.75×10^{-15}	8.75 `EE` 15 `+/−` `=`	8.75 -15

With a scientific calculator, you enter the decimal portion of the number and the exponent. The base of 10 is not entered or displayed.

Example 2 Reading the Calculator Display

Perform the indicated operation.

a. $232,000 \times 1,500,000$ b. $0.003 \div 1,500,000$

Solution

a. The calculator displays 3.48 11 . Because it is understood that the base of the exponent is 10, the display means 3.48×10^{11}.

b. The calculator displays 2 -09 . The display means 2×10^{-9}.

Exercises

In Exercises 1–8, write the result of the operation.

1. $(3.6 \times 10^4)(6.3 \times 10^2)$
2. $(9.83 \times 10^{10})(5.2 \times 10^8)$
3. $(1.35 \times 10^{-3})(8.2 \times 10^{-9})$
4. $(4.7 \times 10^{-7})(2.65 \times 10^{-5})$
5. $(422,000)(135,000)$
6. $(9,364,000)(2150)$
7. $(0.014) \div (560,000)$
8. $(9.12 \times 10^{-3}) \div (2.4 \times 10)$

9. Use the power key to evaluate the expression in Exercise 8.

    9.12 `×` 10 `yˣ` 3 `+/−` `÷` 2.4 `×` 10 `=`

    What do you notice? Why is it a good idea to use the `EE` key, rather than the power key, when computing with scientific notation?

Butterfly Migration *Cycles*

READ About It

In a migrating flock of birds, the older birds have flown the route before. With a migrating flock of monarch butterflies, each butterfly is flying the route *for the first time!*

How do they know where to go? Scientists think that each monarch has an internal compass.

Each complete migration involves three generations of monarchs. The first is hatched in the Appalachian Mountains and flies to Mexico for the winter.

In Mexico, up to 4 million monarchs per acre crowd into 30 sites along a 40 mile stretch in the mountains. After the winter, this first generation flies to Texas and Louisiana, lays eggs, and dies.

When the second generation hatches, it flies north to the Great Lakes region, where it lays eggs and dies.

The third generation flies to the Appalachian Mountains, lays eggs, and dies. When these eggs hatch, they form a new generation that begins the cycle again.

WRITE About It

1. There are 43,560 ft^2 in an acre. At the winter sites, about how many monarchs are in a square foot?

2. Will the fourth generation spend the winter in Mexico? the fifth? the sixth? the seventh?

3. Which generations spend the winter in Mexico?

4. Which generations fly to the Appalachian Mountains?

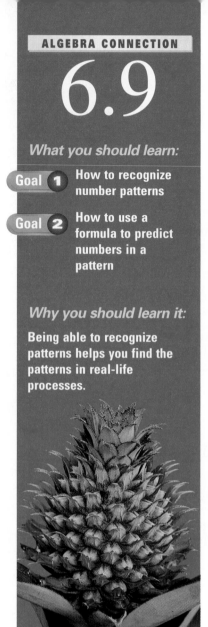

What you should learn:

Goal 1 How to recognize number patterns

Goal 2 How to use a formula to predict numbers in a pattern

Why you should learn it:

Being able to recognize patterns helps you find the patterns in real-life processes.

Fibonacci numbers appear in the spirals on a pineapple.

Exploring Patterns

Goal 1 RECOGNIZING NUMBER PATTERNS

In earlier lessons, you studied several number patterns.

Name	Numbers	Pattern
Square (1.3)	1, 4, 9, 16, 25, . . .	n^2
Cubic (1.8)	1, 8, 27, 64, 125, . . .	n^3
Triangular (1.8)	1, 3, 6, 10, 15, . . .	$\frac{1}{2}n(n + 1)$
Prime (6.2)	2, 3, 5, 7, 11, . . .	None is known.
Fibonacci (1.8)	1, 1, 2, 3, 5, . . .	Each (after 1, 1) is the sum of the two previous numbers.

For thousands of years, people have studied number patterns. Some patterns are simple, but some are very difficult. No one has been able to write a formula for the nth prime number.

Example 1 Pentagonal Numbers

The first four pentagonal numbers are shown below. Draw and calculate the next two pentagonal numbers.

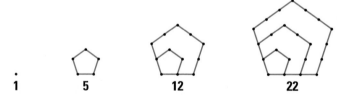

. 1   5   12   22

Solution

Each time you add a new pentagon, the number of points on each of its sides increases by 1. The pentagonal number is the total number of points. Here are the next two.

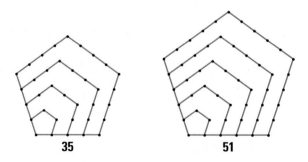

35   51

Example 2 Pentagonal Number Differences

a. For the first six pentagonal numbers, find the differences between adjacent numbers. Describe the pattern.

b. Use the pattern to find the next two pentagonal numbers.

Solution

a. The first six pentagonal numbers are 1, 5, 12, 22, 35, and 51. The differences are shown below.

Pentagonal numbers

Differences

Each difference is 3 more than the previous difference.

b. The next two differences are $16 + 3$, or **19**, and $19 + 3$, or **22**. So, the next two pentagonal numbers are 70 and 92.

$$51 \qquad 70 \qquad 92$$
$$\underset{+19}{\qquad} \underset{+22}{\qquad}$$

Example 3 Using a Formula

The formula for the nth pentagonal number is $\frac{1}{2}n(3n - 1)$. Use this formula to check the result of Example 2.

Solution

$$\text{7th number} = \frac{1}{2}n(3n - 1) \qquad\qquad \text{8th number} = \frac{1}{2}n(3n - 1)$$

$$= \frac{1}{2} \cdot 7 \cdot (3 \cdot 7 - 1) \qquad\qquad = \frac{1}{2} \cdot 8 \cdot (3 \cdot 8 - 1)$$

$$= \frac{1}{2} \cdot 7 \cdot 20 \qquad\qquad\qquad = \frac{1}{2} \cdot 8 \cdot 23$$

$$= 70 \qquad\qquad\qquad\qquad\qquad = 92$$

These results match the results of Example 2.

ONGOING ASSESSMENT

Talk About It
·····················

1. Work with a partner. Find the 9th and 10th pentagonal numbers. One of you should use the pattern described in Example 2 and the other should use the formula described in Example 3. Compare your results.

GUIDED PRACTICE

1. Complete the table.

n	1	2	3	4	5	6
$2n^2 + 1$	?	?	?	?	?	?

In Exercises 2–4, use the first 4 triangular numbers shown at the right.

2. Draw and calculate the next two triangular numbers.

3. For the first six triangular numbers, find the differences between adjacent numbers. Describe the pattern. Then use the pattern to find the next two triangular numbers.

4. The formula for the *n*th triangular number is $\frac{1}{2}n(n + 1)$. Use this formula to check the results of Exercise 3.

1

3

6

10

PRACTICE AND PROBLEM SOLVING

In Exercises 5–8, use the formula to construct a table similar to that shown in Exercise 1.

5. $n^2 + 1$ **6.** $n^2 + n$ **7.** 2^{n-1} **8.** 2^{1-n}

In Exercises 9–12, describe the pattern. Then list the next three terms in the sequence.

9. 1, 2, 4, 7, 11, ? , ? , ? , . . .   **10.** 0, 3, 8, 15, 24, ? , ? , ? , . . .

11. 15, 12, 6, −3, −15, ? , ? , ? , . . .   **12.** 2, 4, 12, 48, 240, ? , ? , ? , . . .

13. STOCK MARKET Suppose you buy a stock on Monday and its price is $4\frac{1}{8}$. On Tuesday, the price is $4\frac{1}{4}$ and on Wednesday the price is $4\frac{3}{8}$. If the pattern continues, what will the price be on Thursday?

Tech Link

Investigation 6,
Interactive
Real-Life
Investigations

FIGURATE NUMBERS **In Exercises 14 and 15, each figure represents a figurate number. Predict the next two numbers in the sequence. Then draw figures to check your predictions.**

14.

1   4   9   16

15.

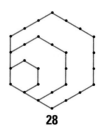

1   6   15   28

PERFECT NUMBERS In Exercises 16–20, use the following information.

A natural number is a *perfect number* if it is equal to the sum of its factors except itself. For example, 6 is a perfect number.

Factors of 6 are 1, 2, 3, 6   and   1 + 2 + 3 = 6

Every even perfect number is of the form $2^{p-1}(2^p - 1)$, where p and $2^p - 1$ are prime.

16. Verify that 28 is a perfect number.

17. Verify that 10 and 12 are not perfect numbers.

18. Evaluate 2^{p-1} and $2^p - 1$ when $p = 5$. Is $2^p - 1$ prime?

19. Evaluate $2^{p-1}(2^p - 1)$ when $p = 5$.

20. Verify that the number you found in Exercise 19 is perfect.

21. **FIBONACCI-LIKE SEQUENCE** The sequence 1, 1, 2, 4, 7, 13, 24, . . . is similar to the Fibonacci sequence. Describe the pattern. Then list the next three terms.

22. **OPEN-ENDED PROBLEM** Make up your own "Fibonacci-like" sequence.

Real Life...
Real People

George Woltman helps people on the Internet search for big primes. $2^{2,976,221} - 1$ is the largest known prime. It is 895,932 digits long.

STANDARDIZED TEST PRACTICE

23. The sum of the first n natural numbers can be determined using the formula $\frac{1}{2}n(n + 1)$. What is the sum of the first 20 natural numbers?

(A) 190   **(B)** 210   **(C)** 420   **(D)** 840

EXPLORATION AND EXTENSION

PORTFOLIO

BUILDING YOUR PROJECT In Exercises 24 and 25, use the musical phrase below.

24. Describe a pattern for the number of beats for the notes in this phrase. (Each hollow note takes 2 beats. Each filled note takes 1 beat.)

25. Describe a pattern for the position of the notes on the musical staff. How would the pattern continue?

WHAT *did you learn?*

WHY *did you learn it?*

Skills

6.1 Use divisibility tests and factor natural numbers.

Divide groups into equal parts.

6.2 Write prime factorizations. Factor algebraic expressions.

Prepare for finding greatest common factors and least common multiples.

6.3 Find the greatest common factor of two numbers or expressions.

Compare numbers, such as frequencies of notes on a musical scale.

6.4 Find the least common multiple of two numbers or expressions.

Determine how often two events will happen at the same time.

6.5 Simplify and compare fractions.

Compare fractions in real life, such as amounts of pizza.

6.6 Identify rational numbers. Write decimals as fractions.

Understand how fractions are represented by calculators.

6.7 Evaluate powers that have negative and zero exponents. Multiply and divide powers with the same base.

Solve problems with exponents, such as finding the amount of food eaten in the United States.

6.8 Use scientific notation.

Solve problems involving small and large numbers.

6.9 Recognize and describe number patterns.

Make predictions.

Strategies 6.1–6.9 Use problem-solving strategies.

Solve a wide variety of real-life problems.

Using Data 6.1–6.9 Use tables and graphs.

Organize data and solve problems.

HOW *does it fit in the bigger picture of mathematics?*

Number theory is one of the oldest branches of mathematics. In this chapter, you learned about several types of numbers, such as prime, composite, and rational numbers. You also learned that finding prime factorizations of numbers can help you calculate greatest common factors and least common multiples.

GCF = 2 · 3

24 (2   2) 5) 30
    (2   3)

LCM = 2 · 2 · 2 · 3 · 5

VOCABULARY

- divisible (p. 254)
- factored (p. 255)
- factors (p. 255)
- prime (p. 260)
- composite (p. 260)
- tree diagrams (p. 260)

- common factor (p. 266)
- greatest common factor (p. 266)
- relatively prime (p. 266)
- common multiple (p. 270)
- least common multiple (p. 270)
- equivalent (p. 274)

- simplest form (p. 274)
- simplifying (p. 274)
- rational numbers (p. 280)
- rational (p. 280)
- irrational (p. 280)
- scientific notation (p. 288)

6.1 DIVISIBILITY TESTS

To decide whether a number is divisible by another number, use the divisibility tests.

Example Decide whether 747 is divisible by 2, 3, 4, 5, 6, 8, 9, and 10.

Solution

2	No	747 is not even.
3	Yes	$7 + 4 + 7 = 18$, and 18 is divisible by 3.
4	No	47 is not divisible by 4.
5	No	The last digit is not 5 or 0.
6	No	747 is not even.
8	No	747 is not divisible by 4.
9	Yes	$7 + 4 + 7 = 18$, and 18 is divisible by 9.
10	No	The last digit is not 0.

Decide whether each number is divisible by 2, 3, 4, 5, 6, 8, 9, and 10.

1. 180 **2.** 184 **3.** 235 **4.** 336

6.2 FACTORS AND PRIMES

A number is *prime* if its only factors are 1 and itself. Numbers with 3 or more factors are *composite*.

Examples

Expression	Expanded Form	Exponent Form
48	$2 \cdot 2 \cdot 2 \cdot 2 \cdot 3$	$2^4 \cdot 3$
$42x^2$	$2 \cdot 3 \cdot 7 \cdot x \cdot x$	$2 \cdot 3 \cdot 7 \cdot x^2$
$36xy^2$	$2 \cdot 2 \cdot 3 \cdot 3 \cdot x \cdot y \cdot y$	$2^2 \cdot 3^2 \cdot x \cdot y^2$

5. Is 101 prime? If not, write its prime factorization.

6. Write the expression $27x^2$ in expanded and exponent form.

6.3 GREATEST COMMON FACTOR

To find the *greatest common factor* (GCF) of two or more numbers, write the prime factorization of each number. Multiply the common prime factors to find the greatest common factor.

Examples　Find the greatest common factor of 96 and 54.

Find the greatest common factor of 24 and 27.

Solutions　$96 = 2 \cdot 2 \cdot 2 \cdot 2 \cdot 2 \cdot 3$

$54 = 2 \cdot 3 \cdot 3 \cdot 3$

$\text{GCF} = 2 \cdot 3 = 6$

$24 = 2 \cdot 2 \cdot 2 \cdot 3$

$27 = 3 \cdot 3 \cdot 3$

$\text{GCF} = 3$

Find the greatest common factor of each pair of numbers.

7. 30 and 45　　**8.** 28 and 84　　**9.** 15 and 29　　**10.** 160 and 195

6.4 LEAST COMMON MULTIPLE

To find the *least common multiple* (LCM) of two or more numbers, write the prime factorization of each number. Then multiply the common prime factors by all the other factors.

Examples　Find the least common multiple of 14 and 24.

Find the least common multiple of 21 and 28.

Solutions　$14 = 2 \cdot 7$　$24 = 2 \cdot 2 \cdot 2 \cdot 3$

$\text{LCM} = 2 \cdot 2 \cdot 2 \cdot 3 \cdot 7 = 168$

$21 = 3 \cdot 7$　$28 = 2 \cdot 2 \cdot 7$

$\text{LCM} = 7 \cdot 2 \cdot 2 \cdot 3 = 84$

Find the least common multiple of each pair of numbers.

11. 34 and 68　　**12.** 90 and 100　　**13.** 13 and 52　　**14.** 12 and 15

6.5 SIMPLIFYING AND COMPARING FRACTIONS

To simplify a fraction, factor its numerator and denominator. Then divide the numerator and denominator by any common factors.

Examples　$\dfrac{15}{20} = \dfrac{3 \cdot \cancel{5}}{2 \cdot 2 \cdot \cancel{5}} = \dfrac{3}{4}$

$\dfrac{32y^2}{12y^3} = \dfrac{\cancel{2} \cdot \cancel{2} \cdot 2 \cdot 2 \cdot 2 \cdot \cancel{y} \cdot \cancel{y}}{\cancel{2} \cdot \cancel{2} \cdot 3 \cdot \cancel{y} \cdot \cancel{y} \cdot y} = \dfrac{8}{3y}$

Simplify the fraction.

15. $\dfrac{32}{6}$　　**16.** $\dfrac{65}{20}$　　**17.** $\dfrac{200x^2}{14x}$　　**18.** $\dfrac{48m}{64m^3}$

6.6 RATIONAL NUMBERS AND DECIMALS

Examples Show that 0.4 is rational. Write 0.33333. . . as a fraction.

Solutions $0.4 = \frac{4}{10} = \frac{2}{5}$

Let $x = 0.33333. . . .$ Then $10x = 3.33333. . . .$

$$10x - x = 3.33333. . . - 0.33333. . .$$
$$9x = 3$$
$$x = \frac{3}{9} = \frac{1}{3}$$

19. Write $\frac{7}{11}$ as a decimal.

20. Write 2.666666. . . as a fraction.

6.7 POWERS AND EXPONENTS

Use these formulas:

$$a^{-n} = \frac{1}{a^n} \qquad a^m \cdot a^n = a^{m+n} \qquad \frac{a^m}{a^n} = a^{m-n}$$

Examples $4^{-3} = \frac{1}{4^3} = \frac{1}{64}$ $x^2 \cdot x^3 = x^5$ $\frac{y^4}{y^7} = y^{4-7} = y^{-3}$

Simplify the expression.

21. $4x^{-4}$

22. $\frac{x^4}{x^{10}}$

23. $5y^2 \cdot 3y^4$

24. $\frac{15^3}{15^2}$

6.8 SCIENTIFIC NOTATION

The scientific form of a number is $c \times 10^n$, where c is between 1 and 10.

Examples
$45,000,000 = 4.5 \times 10,000,000 = 4.5 \times 10^7$ $0.00003 = 3 \times 0.00001 = 3 \times 10^{-5}$

Write the number in scientific notation.

25. 743,000

26. 0.00012

27. 1,203,000

28. 0.0407

6.9 EXPLORING PATTERNS

To recognize a number pattern, look for patterns in differences or quotients.

Example 1, 5, 13, 25, . . .

The differences are 4, 8, and 12. Differences increase by 4 each time, so
the next numbers are 25 + 16, or 41, and 41 + 20, or 61.

List the next three terms in the sequence.

29. 2, 5, 10, 17, . . . **30.** −2, 2, 6, 10, . . . **31.** 10, 9, 7, 4, . . . **32.** 2, 10, 50, 250, . . .

1. Use the divisibility tests to decide whether 1224 is divisible by 2, 3, 4, 5, 6, 8, 9, and 10.

2. **TECHNOLOGY** Decide whether 1224 is divisible by 11, 12, 13, 14, 15, 16, 17, 18, 19, and 20.

In Exercises 3 and 4, write the prime factorization of the number.

3. 120

4. 125

In Exercises 5 and 6, write the prime factorization of the expression.

5. $99ab$

6. $121x^2$

In Exercises 7 and 8, find the greatest common factor.

7. 48, 36

8. 56, 98

In Exercises 9–11, find the least common multiple.

9. 10, 35

10. 5, 18

11. 7, 10, 14

12. Simplify the fraction $\dfrac{20}{800}$.

13. Decide which fraction is larger: $\dfrac{3}{11}$ or $\dfrac{5}{22}$.

14. Write 0.65 as a fraction and simplify.

15. Simplify the expression $x^9 \cdot x^{-4}$.

In Exercises 16–19, match the scientific notation with its decimal form.

A. 0.00016   B. 0.016   C. 160   D. 16,000

16. 1.6×10^4

17. 1.6×10^{-4}

18. 1.6×10^{-2}

19. 1.6×10^2

In Exercises 20–23, describe the pattern. Then list the next three terms in the sequence.

20. 4, 5, 7, 10, . . .

21. 48, 44, 36, 24, . . .

22. 7, 21, 63, 189, . . .

23. 5, 15, 45, 135, . . .

In Exercises 24–26, use the following information.

ASTRONOMY Scientists have measured the speed of light to be about 300,000 km/s. It takes light about 500 s to travel from the sun to Earth.

24. Write the speed of light in scientific notation.

25. Write the time (in seconds) that it takes light to travel from the sun to Earth in scientific notation.

26. Use the verbal model to approximate the distance between the sun and Earth.

Distance = Speed of light · Time from sun to Earth

1. Which number is not a factor of 654?

   (A) 2   (B) 3

   (C) 6   (D) 9

2. Which of the following is an *incorrect* answer to this question: How many friends can share 20 tokens evenly to play video games if each person gets at least 4 tokens?

   (A) 2   (B) 4

   (C) 5   (D) 10

3. What is the prime factorization of 126?

   (A) $2 \cdot 3 \cdot 21$

   (B) $2 \cdot 2 \cdot 3 \cdot 11$

   (C) $2 \cdot 3 \cdot 3 \cdot 7$

   (D) $3 \cdot 6 \cdot 7$

4. Which statement is *false*?

   (A) Both 8 and 12 are divisible by 2.

   (B) The greatest common factor of 8 and 12 is 2.

   (C) The least common multiple of 8 and 12 is 24.

   (D) Both 8 and 12 are divisible by 4.

5. A group of people share a rectangular lasagna cut into 18 slices and a round cake cut into 12 slices. If everyone is served equal amounts of lasagna and equal amounts of cake, what is the largest number of people the group might contain?

   (A) 2   (B) 3

   (C) 6   (D) 12

6. Two model trains begin at the train station and travel in opposite directions on a circular track. Train 1 completes one trip in 20 s and Train 2 completes one trip in 8 s. After how many seconds will the two trains pass each other at the train station?

   (A) 4   (B) 24

   (C) 40   (D) 160

7. Which number is not equivalent to $\frac{15}{24}$?

   (A) $\frac{10}{16}$ (B) 0.625

   (C) $\frac{5}{8}$ (D) $\frac{3}{12}$

8. Simplify $5x^{-4}$.

   (A) $\frac{1}{5x^4}$ (B) $\frac{5}{x^4}$

   (C) $-5x^4$ (D) $\frac{-1}{5x^4}$

9. A lobster can lay up to 150,000 eggs at a time. Write this number in scientific notation.

   (A) 15×10^4 (B) 1.5×10^5

   (C) 1.5×10^{-5} (D) 0.15×10^{-6}

10. Simplify $(5 \times 10^{-7})(3.6 \times 10^4)$.

    (A) 1.8×10^{-4} (B) 1.8×10^{-3}

    (C) 1.8×10^{-2} (D) 18×10^{-3}

11. Find the next number in the pattern 1, 16, 81, 256, . . .

    (A) 345   (B) 625

    (C) 681   (D) 1024

LOOKING FOR A PATTERN In Exercises 1–4, describe a pattern for the sequence, then list the next three numbers or letters. (1.1)

1. 7, 14, 21, 28,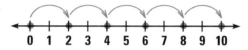

2. 5, 7, 9, 11,

3. A, C, E, G, ?, ?, ?

4. Z, W, T, Q, ?, ?, ?

In Exercises 5 and 6, write the multiplication fact represented by the model. (1.2)

5.

6.

In Exercises 7–14, use a calculator to find the value of the expression. Round the result to the nearest hundredth. (1.3, 1.4)

7. 5^7

8. $\left(\dfrac{4}{9}\right)^4$

9. $\sqrt{84}$

10. $(5^4 - 20) \div 11 + 9$

11. $\sqrt{\dfrac{5}{12}}$

12. $(6.3)^6$

13. $\sqrt{17.82}$

14. $2^5 + (24 - 6) \cdot 3$

In Exercises 15–20, simplify the expression without using a calculator. (1.4)

15. $|-8| + 17 - 13 - 5$

16. $|-6| - 9 - 4 + 21$

17. $(-5)(3)(-6)(-2)$

18. $\dfrac{-625}{-5}$

19. $43 + (7 - 2)^2 \div 5$

20. $32 - (7 - 4)^3 \cdot 3$

MENTAL MATH In Exercises 21–24, write the question as an equation. Then solve it mentally. (2.3)

21. What number can you add to 5 to get 21?

22. What number can you subtract from 17 to get 8?

23. What number can you multiply by 4 to get 32?

24. What number can you divide by 3 to get 7?

OIL PAINTING In Exercises 25–29, consider the following question. (2.8)

You are buying supplies for an oil painting course. You have to buy a palette which costs $5.70 and 8 tubes of paint which cost $2.70 each. How much money do you need to buy your supplies?

25. Write a verbal model that relates the cost of the palette, the total cost of the tubes of paint, and the total amount of money you need.

26. Assign labels to the three parts of your model.

27. Use the labels to translate your verbal model into an algebraic model.

28. Solve the algebraic model.

29. Check your answer.

In Exercises 30–35, write an algebraic equation or inequality for the verbal sentence. Then solve the equation or inequality. (2.7, 2.9, 3.7)

30. The sum of n and 16 is 3.

31. The product of y and -8 is -104.

32. The quotient of x and 5 is greater than or equal to 25.

33. The difference of x and 9 is -18.

34. The sum of z and 9 is less than -5.

35. The product of m and 7 is greater than 147.

RUNNING In Exercises 36–38, use the following information.

Julie tries to run an average of 7 mi a day for 5 days out of the week. She records her mileage in a training log. When she exceeds her goal, she records the extra miles. When she runs under her goal, she records the missed miles. If the sum of the week's numbers is greater than or equal to zero, then Julie met her goal. **(3.3)**

Day	Mon	Tue	Wed	Thu	Fri	Sat	Sun
Miles	$+1$	no run	-4	$+2$	$+3$	-1	no run

36. Add the numbers in the table. Did Julie meet her goal for the week?

37. Find the number of miles that Julie ran on each day.

38. Find the total number of miles Julie ran.

In Exercises 39–44, simplify the expression. Then evaluate it when $x = -2$, $y = 4$, and $z = 5$. (3.1–3.5)

39. $5(x + y + z)$

40. $-4(x - y + 2z)$

41. $3y - 6x + 3z - 5y$

42. $-2(4x + 3x + y)$

43. $-7 + x(z + y)$

44. $2(3z - z) - y$

LOOKING FOR A PATTERN In Exercises 45–48, complete the statements. Then describe the pattern. (3.2, 3.6)

45.
$4 + (0) = $?
$4 + (-1) = $?
$4 + (-2) = $?
$4 + (-3) = $?

46.
$5 - (-6) = $?
$6 - (-6) = $?
$7 - (-6) = $?
$8 - (-6) = $?

47.
$7 \times 21 = $?
$7 \times 18 = $?
$7 \times 15 = $?
$7 \times 12 = $?

48.
$6 \div 3 = $?
$12 \div 3 = $?
$24 \div 3 = $?
$48 \div 3 = $?

GEOMETRY In Exercises 49–52, plot the points to form the vertices of a rectangle. Find the perimeter and area of rectangle $ABCD$. (3.8)

49. $A(-2, 2)$, $B(-2, 4)$, $C(-4, 4)$, $D(-4, 2)$

50. $A(1, 1)$, $B(6, 1)$, $C(6, -2)$, $D(1, -2)$

51. $A(0, -1)$, $B(0, -4)$, $C(3, -4)$, $D(3, -1)$

52. $A(-2, 3)$, $B(-6, 3)$, $C(-6, 0)$, $D(-2, 0)$

In Exercises 53–58, solve the equation. Then check your solution.
(4.1, 4.2)

53. $6x - 17 = 7$

54. $4y + 13 = -19$

55. $-\dfrac{n}{7} + 9 = 5$

56. $8m + 3m - 2 = 9$

57. $\dfrac{3}{4}z - \dfrac{1}{4}z + 6 = 12$

58. $15t + 14 - 7t = 30$

In Exercises 59–64, solve the equation. Then check your solution.
(4.4, 4.5)

59. $10y - 27 = y$

60. $13x - 80 = 60 - 7x$

61. $3(4t + 3) = 2t$

62. $b + 6 = 2(b - 2)$

63. $2\left(4n + \dfrac{1}{2}\right) = 10n$

64. $3(y - 2) + 2 = -y$

 TECHNOLOGY In Exercises 65–68, use a calculator. Round your answer to one decimal place. (4.7)

65. $15x - 21 = -42x + 89.2$

66. $14.1(2.37y + 5.6) = 0.71y - 29.3$

67. $-7.3 + 6p = -32p + 23.8$

68. $4.62s - 18.5 = 7.23(9.78s + 3.6)$

69. **ENERGY USE** The amount of energy use differs around the world. The table gives the kilograms of coal used per person in 1990 and 1992 for selected countries. Represent the results with a bar graph. Then explain why you chose the type of bar graph you did. **(5.2)**

Country	1990	1992
Algeria	1594	1586
Brazil	810	785
Denmark	4655	4642
France	5434	5191
Israel	3268	3149
South Korea	3188	2743
Mexico	1891	1863
South Africa	2488	2608
United States	10,737	10,749
Venezuela	3214	3352

70. **RADIO STATIONS** The table shows the number of stations for each type of music in the United States in 1995. Choose a type of graph to represent the data. Explain why you chose that type, and then draw the graph. **(5.4)**

Type of music	Number of stations
Country	2613
Adult Contemporary	1655
Rock	828
Oldies	710
Top 40	318
Easy Listening	61
Classical	39

71. TELEVISIONS You conduct a survey among 20 classmates and ask each person how many television sets they have at home. The results are shown below. Organize the data in a line plot. **(5.6)**

1 2 3 1 0 5 2 4 2 2 1 2 1 3 1 4 4 1 2 2

NAVY In Exercises 72–74, use the table. The table shows the annual salary of a navy captain for the given years of service. **(5.7)**

Years of Service	14	16	18	20
Salary (in thousands of dollars)	51	59	62	64

72. Make a scatter plot of the data.

73. How are years of service and salary related?

74. Draw a line of fit. Use it to estimate the salary after 22 years of service.

PROBABILITY In Exercises 75–78, find the theoretical probability that the spinner will land on the color. **(5.8)**

75. Blue

76. Red

77. Orange

78. Green

In Exercises 79–86, use the divisibility tests to determine whether the number is divisible by 2, 3, 4, 5, 6, 8, 9, and 10. **(6.1)**

79. 12,985   **80.** 567   **81.** 1893   **82.** 4556

83. 711   **84.** 16,543   **85.** 810   **86.** 7232

In Exercises 87–92, write the prime factorization of each expression. Use the results to find the least common multiple. **(6.4)**

87. 7, 49   **88.** 4, 18   **89.** 270, 450

90. 864, 972   **91.** $6x^2y, 8xy^3$ **92.** $9a^2b, 12ab^4$

In Exercises 93–96, what is the greatest common factor of the numerator and denominator? Use your answer to simplify the fraction. **(6.5)**

93. $\dfrac{6}{48}$ **94.** $\dfrac{25}{45}$ **95.** $\dfrac{10}{15}$ **96.** $\dfrac{52}{54}$

In Exercises 97–104, simplify the expression. **(6.7)**

97. 5^0 **98.** 3^{-2} **99.** a^{-4} **100.** $\dfrac{x}{x^3}$

101. $\dfrac{8a}{10a^2}$ **102.** $4^2 \cdot 4^{-2}$ **103.** $\dfrac{3^4}{3^5}$ **104.** $\dfrac{10^0}{10^4}$

SOCCER Many people play
sports to exercise.

TECHNOLOGY

• **Interactive Real-Life
Investigations**

• **Middle School Tutorial
Software**

To find out more about health
and nutrition, go to:

http://www.mlmath.com

CHAPTER **THEME**
Health and Nutrition

PORTFOLIO

CHAPTER PROJECT

Making a Personal Health Plan

PROJECT DESCRIPTION

Exercise and good eating habits help people stay healthy. You will investigate what foods and exercises are best for you, and make your own health plan.

GETTING STARTED

Talking It Over

- There are many ways to exercise. Do you like to skate or play ball? What things do you do to exercise? How often do you exercise?

- Do you know which foods are low in fat? High in nutrition? Do you think about what sorts of snacks you eat?

Planning Your Project

- **Materials:** paper, pencils or pens, colored pencils or markers

- Make a booklet out of several sheets of paper. Write your name and "Personal Health Plan" on the cover. As you complete the **BUILDING YOUR PROJECT** exercises, add the results to your booklet.

BUILDING YOUR PROJECT

These are the places throughout the chapter where you will work on your project.

7.2 Plan your time. *p. 319*

7.4 Use exercise to burn calories. *p. 327*

7.5 Plan meals to get essential minerals. *p. 334*

7.6 Use the food pyramid to plan a balanced diet. *p. 339*

7.8 Calculate your target heart rate. *p. 347*

7.1

Addition and Subtraction of Like Fractions

What you should learn:

Goal 1 How to add like fractions

Goal 2 How to subtract like fractions

Why you should learn it:

You can use addition and subtraction of like fractions to compare measures such as the times of two runners.

Goal 1 ADDING LIKE FRACTIONS

Like fractions are fractions that have the same denominator.

Like Fractions	Unlike Fractions
$\dfrac{1}{5}$ and $\dfrac{3}{5}$	$\dfrac{1}{2}$ and $\dfrac{1}{3}$
$\dfrac{a}{c}$ and $\dfrac{b}{c}$	$\dfrac{a}{c}$ and $\dfrac{a}{d}$

ADDING LIKE FRACTIONS

To add like fractions, add the numerators and write the sum over the denominator.

Numerical Example

$$\frac{1}{5} + \frac{3}{5} = \frac{1+3}{5} = \frac{4}{5}$$

Variable Example

$$\frac{a}{c} + \frac{b}{c} = \frac{a+b}{c}$$

Example 1 Adding Like Fractions

a. $\dfrac{5}{8} + \dfrac{7}{8} = \dfrac{5+7}{8}$ Add numerators.

$= \dfrac{12}{8}$ Simplify numerator.

$= \dfrac{\cancel{4} \cdot 3}{\cancel{4} \cdot 2}$ Factor numerator and denominator.

$= \dfrac{3}{2}$ Simplify fraction.

b. $1\dfrac{2}{6} + 1\dfrac{3}{6} = \dfrac{8}{6} + \dfrac{9}{6}$ Rewrite as improper fractions.

$= \dfrac{8+9}{6}$ Add numerators.

$= \dfrac{17}{6}$ Simplify numerator.

c. $\dfrac{6x}{5} + \dfrac{4x}{5} = \dfrac{6x + 4x}{5}$ Add numerators.

$= \dfrac{10x}{5}$ Simplify numerator.

$= 2x$ Simplify.

STUDY TIP

You can use a geometric model to see why the numerical example

$\dfrac{1}{5} + \dfrac{3}{5} = \dfrac{4}{5}$ is true.

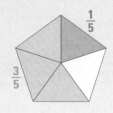

Subtracting like fractions is similar to adding them.

> ### SUBTRACTING LIKE FRACTIONS
>
> To subtract like fractions, subtract the numerators and write the difference over the denominator.
>
> | Numerical Example | Variable Example |
> |---|---|
> | $\frac{3}{5} - \frac{1}{5} = \frac{3-1}{5} = \frac{2}{5}$ | $\frac{a}{c} - \frac{b}{c} = \frac{a-b}{c}$ |

> **NEED TO KNOW**
>
> Negative fractions can be written in several ways.
>
> $-\frac{4}{5}$, $\frac{-4}{5}$, and $\frac{4}{-5}$
>
> are all equivalent.

Example 2 **Subtracting Like Fractions**

REAL LIFE
Track

You are helping two of your friends train for a track meet. You time your friends on a 100 m sprint. One friend's time is $11\frac{2}{4}$ s and the other's time is $13\frac{1}{4}$ s. How much longer did your second friend take to complete the sprint?

Solution

Difference in times = Second friend's time − First friend's time

$$\text{Difference} = 13\frac{1}{4} - 11\frac{2}{4} \qquad \text{Substitute times.}$$

$$= \frac{53}{4} - \frac{46}{4} \qquad \text{Rewrite as improper fractions.}$$

$$= \frac{53 - 46}{4} \qquad \text{Subtract numerators.}$$

$$= \frac{7}{4} \qquad \text{Simplify numerator.}$$

Your second friend took $1\frac{3}{4}$ s longer to complete the sprint.

Example 3 **Solving Equations with Fractions**

CONNECTION
Algebra

$$m + \frac{6}{4} = \frac{7}{4} \qquad \text{Original equation}$$

$$m + \frac{6}{4} - \frac{6}{4} = \frac{7}{4} - \frac{6}{4} \qquad \text{Subtract } \tfrac{6}{4} \text{ from each side.}$$

$$m = \frac{1}{4} \qquad \text{Subtract fractions.}$$

> **ONGOING ASSESSMENT**
>
> ## Write About It
>
> Add or subtract and simplify your answer. Show your work and explain your steps.
>
> 1. $\frac{5}{6} + \frac{2}{6}$
>
> 2. $\frac{5}{12} - \frac{1}{12}$
>
> 3. $\frac{2}{5} + \frac{3}{5}$

Extra Practice, page 726

MODELING In Exercises 1 and 2, write the indicated sum or difference.

1.

2.

3. WRITING In your own words, describe how to add like fractions. How is this different from subtracting fractions? Give examples.

PRACTICE AND PROBLEM SOLVING

FRACTIONS In Exercises 4–15, add or subtract. Then simplify.

4. $\dfrac{2}{6} + \dfrac{3}{6}$

5. $\dfrac{8}{12} - \dfrac{4}{12}$

6. $\dfrac{-8}{15} - \dfrac{7}{15}$

7. $\dfrac{-3}{8} + \dfrac{-7}{8}$

8. $\dfrac{-a}{5} - \dfrac{4a}{5}$

9. $\dfrac{12y}{10} - \dfrac{4y}{10}$

10. $3\dfrac{1}{2} + 1\dfrac{1}{2}$

11. $3\dfrac{2}{3} - 4\dfrac{1}{3}$

12. $\dfrac{1}{z} + \dfrac{6}{z}$

13. $\dfrac{2}{4t} - \dfrac{9}{4t}$

14. $\dfrac{4}{5b} - \dfrac{1}{5b}$

15. $\dfrac{1}{8x} + \dfrac{3}{8x} - \dfrac{7}{8x}$

ALGEBRA In Exercises 16–23, solve the equation. Then simplify.

16. $x + \dfrac{2}{3} = \dfrac{4}{3}$

17. $y - \dfrac{6}{8} = \dfrac{5}{8}$

18. $m + \dfrac{19}{5} = \dfrac{4}{5}$

19. $n - \dfrac{1}{6} = -\dfrac{9}{6}$

20. $s + \dfrac{5}{4} = -\dfrac{9}{4}$

21. $t - \dfrac{8}{11} = -\dfrac{6}{11}$

22. $3x + \dfrac{1}{2} = \dfrac{5}{2}$

23. $2z - \dfrac{8}{7} = \dfrac{6}{7}$

 TECHNOLOGY In Exercises 24–27, use a calculator to evaluate the expression as a decimal rounded to two decimal places.

24. $\dfrac{1}{7} + \dfrac{3}{7}$

25. $\dfrac{7}{6} - \dfrac{3}{6}$

26. $\dfrac{5}{9} - \dfrac{8}{9}$

27. $\dfrac{5}{16} - \dfrac{11}{16}$

PATTERNS In Exercises 28 and 29, add or subtract. Then describe the pattern and write the next three completed equations.

28. $\dfrac{1}{8} + \dfrac{2}{8} = \boxed{?}$

$\dfrac{3}{8} + \dfrac{4}{8} = \boxed{?}$

$\dfrac{5}{8} + \dfrac{6}{8} = \boxed{?}$

$\dfrac{7}{8} + \dfrac{8}{8} = \boxed{?}$

29. $\dfrac{10}{2} - \dfrac{1}{2} = \boxed{?}$

$\dfrac{-9}{2} - \dfrac{2}{2} = \boxed{?}$

$\dfrac{8}{2} - \dfrac{3}{2} = \boxed{?}$

$\dfrac{-7}{2} - \dfrac{4}{2} = \boxed{?}$

ERROR ANALYSIS In Exercises 30 and 31, describe the error. Then correct it.

30. $\dfrac{2}{5} + \dfrac{1}{5} = \dfrac{2 + 1}{5 + 5}$

$= \dfrac{3}{10}$

31. $1\dfrac{1}{3} + 2\dfrac{1}{3} = 1 + \dfrac{1}{3} + 2 + \dfrac{1}{3}$

$= 3 + \dfrac{1}{3} = 3\dfrac{1}{3}$

MODELING In Exercises 32 and 33, write the modeled sum or difference.

32.

```
  ◄──┼────┼──●──┼──┼──►
     0    1        1
          4
```

33.

```
  ◄──┼──●──┼──┼──┼──┼──●──┼──┼──►
     0                  6     1
                        8
```

34. HEALTH DRINKS Each recipe shown serves one person. You decide to combine both recipes and invite a friend over to taste your creation with you. How much of each ingredient do you use?

Huge Summer Fruit Shake
$\dfrac{1}{2}$ C mashed ripe banana
$\dfrac{1}{4}$ C instant nonfat milk powder
$\dfrac{3}{4}$ C frozen orange juice
$\dfrac{1}{3}$ C crushed ice
$\dfrac{1}{4}$ C sparkling water

Island Gulp
$\dfrac{1}{2}$ C mashed ripe banana
$\dfrac{2}{4}$ C frozen orange juice
$\dfrac{1}{4}$ C frozen pineapple juice
$\dfrac{1}{3}$ C crushed ice
$\dfrac{1}{4}$ C sparkling water

STANDARDIZED TEST PRACTICE

35. In your school's standing long jump contest, you jump $1\dfrac{7}{10}$ m on your first jump and $1\dfrac{9}{10}$ m on your second jump. How much farther did you jump on your second jump?

(A) $\dfrac{1}{10}$ m   **(B)** $\dfrac{1}{5}$ m   **(C)** $\dfrac{2}{5}$ m   **(D)** $\dfrac{36}{10}$ m

EXPLORATION AND EXTENSION

FRACTION RIDDLE Find the fraction that is described by the clues given.

36. The fraction is between 0 and 1. It is more than $\dfrac{1}{4}$. If you add $\dfrac{2}{8}$ to it, the fraction will be equivalent to $\dfrac{10}{16}$.

LAB 7.2

COOPERATIVE LEARNING

Materials Needed
• fraction strips

Adding and Subtracting Fractions

In this activity, you will use fraction strips to investigate the sum and difference of fractions with different denominators. As you work on the lab, notice the importance of the *least common multiple* of the denominators.

Part Ⓐ ADDING WITH FRACTION STRIPS

To add $\frac{2}{3}$ and $\frac{1}{6}$ with fraction strips, use the following steps.

❶ Begin with fraction strips for $\frac{2}{3}$ and $\frac{1}{6}$. To "add" the strips, place the shaded parts together.

❷ Find another fraction strip that has this length.

From this, you can conclude that $\frac{2}{3} + \frac{1}{6} = \frac{5}{6}$.

In Exercises 1–4, use fraction strips to add the fractions.

1. $\frac{2}{5} + \frac{3}{10}$ **2.** $\frac{1}{2} + \frac{1}{4}$ **3.** $\frac{1}{4} + \frac{1}{6}$ **4.** $\frac{1}{6} + \frac{3}{8}$

5. Copy the table. Then use the sums above to complete the table. What can you conclude?

Fractions	Sum	Denominators	Least common multiple of denominators
$\frac{2}{5} + \frac{3}{10}$	?	5, 10	?
$\frac{1}{2} + \frac{1}{4}$	?	2, 4	?
$\frac{1}{4} + \frac{1}{6}$	?	4, 6	?
$\frac{1}{6} + \frac{3}{8}$	?	6, 8	?

To subtract $\frac{1}{4}$ from $\frac{2}{3}$ with fraction strips, overlap the shaded parts.

Then, find another fraction strip that has the same length as the difference.

From this, you can conclude

that $\frac{2}{3} - \frac{1}{4} = \frac{5}{12}$.

6. Write the difference modeled by the fraction strips.

$\frac{1}{3}$	$\frac{1}{3}$	

	$\frac{1}{6}$				

In Exercises 7–10, use fraction strips to subtract the fractions.

7. $\frac{2}{5} - \frac{1}{10}$

8. $\frac{2}{3} - \frac{1}{4}$

9. $\frac{5}{6} - \frac{1}{4}$

10. $\frac{3}{4} - \frac{1}{6}$

11. Compare the least common multiple of the denominators in Exercises 7–10 with the denominator of the differences. What can you conclude?

NOW TRY THESE

In Exercises 12 and 13, use fraction strips to add or subtract.

12. $\frac{2}{5} + \frac{1}{2}$

13. $\frac{3}{4} - \frac{2}{3}$

14. a. What is the least common multiple of the denominators in Exercise 12?

b. Rewrite each fraction with this as the denominator.

c. Now, add the fractions. Do you get the same result as in Exercise 12?

d. Repeat parts (a) through (c) for Exercise 13.

7.2

Addition and Subtraction of Unlike Fractions

What you should learn:

Goal 1 How to add and subtract unlike fractions

Goal 2 How to add fractions in real-life situations

Why you should learn it:

You can use fractions to analyze real-life situations, such as comparing the ways electric power is produced.

This power plant in Daggett, California, uses the sun's energy to generate electricity.

Goal 1 ADD AND SUBTRACT UNLIKE FRACTIONS

The **least common denominator**, abbreviated LCD, of two fractions is the least common multiple of their denominators.

> **ADDITION AND SUBTRACTION OF UNLIKE FRACTIONS**
>
> To add or subtract unlike fractions
> 1. rewrite the fractions with a common denominator.
> 2. add or subtract the resulting like fractions.

Example 1 Add and Subtract Unlike Fractions

a. $\dfrac{5}{6} + \dfrac{3}{8} = \dfrac{5 \cdot 4}{6 \cdot 4} + \dfrac{3 \cdot 3}{8 \cdot 3}$ The LCD of 6 and 8 is 24.

$\qquad = \dfrac{20}{24} + \dfrac{9}{24}$ Rewrite as like fractions.

$\qquad = \dfrac{29}{24}$ Add like fractions.

b. $\dfrac{7}{12} - \dfrac{3}{4} = \dfrac{7}{12} - \dfrac{3 \cdot 3}{4 \cdot 3}$ The LCD of 12 and 4 is 12.

$\qquad = \dfrac{7}{12} - \dfrac{9}{12}$ Rewrite as like fractions.

$\qquad = -\dfrac{2}{12}$ Subtract like fractions.

$\qquad = -\dfrac{1}{6}$ Simplify fraction.

c. $\dfrac{2}{a} + \dfrac{3}{2} = \dfrac{2 \cdot 2}{a \cdot 2} + \dfrac{3 \cdot a}{2 \cdot a}$ The LCD of 2 and a is $2a$.

$\qquad = \dfrac{4}{2a} + \dfrac{3a}{2a}$ Rewrite as like fractions.

$\qquad = \dfrac{4 + 3a}{2a}$ Add like fractions.

d. $\dfrac{x}{4} - \dfrac{x}{5} = \dfrac{x \cdot 5}{4 \cdot 5} - \dfrac{x \cdot 4}{5 \cdot 4}$ The LCD of 5 and 4 is 20.

$\qquad = \dfrac{5x}{20} - \dfrac{4x}{20}$ Rewrite as like fractions.

$\qquad = \dfrac{x}{20}$ Subtract like fractions.

Real Life...
Real Facts

Example 2 Adding Unlike Fractions

The circle graph compares the different ways that electricity is produced in the United States. Show that the sum of the six fractions is 1. (Source: Electrical Power Annual)

REAL LIFE
Electricity

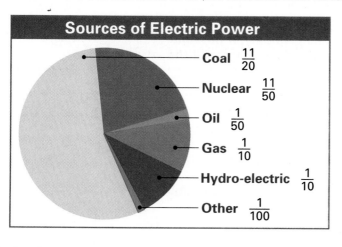

Sources of Electric Power

Coal $\frac{11}{20}$

Nuclear $\frac{11}{50}$

Oil $\frac{1}{50}$

Gas $\frac{1}{10}$

Hydro-electric $\frac{1}{10}$

Other $\frac{1}{100}$

Water Power
The Grand Coulee Dam in Washington is the largest dam in the United States. It generated 27.7 billion kW•h of electricity in 1996.

Solution

Begin by finding the least common denominator of the fractions.

Denominator	Multiples
20	20, 40, 60, 80, **100**, 120, . . .
50	50, **100**, 150, 200, . . .
10	10, 20, 30, 40, 50, 60, 70, 80, 90, **100**, 110, 120, . . .
100	**100**, 200, 300, . . .

From this list, you can see that the least common multiple is 100. So, the least common denominator is 100. Now add the fractions.

$$\frac{11}{20} + \frac{11}{50} + \frac{1}{50} + \frac{1}{10} + \frac{1}{10} + \frac{1}{100}$$

$$= \frac{11 \cdot 5}{20 \cdot 5} + \frac{11 \cdot 2}{50 \cdot 2} + \frac{1 \cdot 2}{50 \cdot 2} + \frac{1 \cdot 10}{10 \cdot 10} + \frac{1 \cdot 10}{10 \cdot 10} + \frac{1}{100}$$

$$= \frac{55}{100} + \frac{22}{100} + \frac{2}{100} + \frac{10}{100} + \frac{10}{100} + \frac{1}{100}$$

$$= \frac{55 + 22 + 2 + 10 + 10 + 1}{100}$$

$$= \frac{100}{100}$$

$$= 1 \qquad \text{You have shown that the sum of the six fractions is 1.}$$

ONGOING ASSESSMENT

Write About It

Add or subtract and simplify your answer. Show your work and explain your steps.

1. $\frac{5}{6} + \frac{2}{3}$

2. $\frac{5}{12} - \frac{1}{6}$

3. $\frac{2}{5} + \frac{3}{4}$

GUIDED PRACTICE

MODELING In Exercises 1 and 2, the area of each region is 1. Write the fraction that represents the area of each green region. Then add the fractions.

1.

2.

In Exercises 3–6, find the sum or difference. Then simplify, if possible. Explain your steps and identify the least common denominator of the fractions.

3. $\dfrac{2}{5} + \dfrac{1}{3}$

4. $\dfrac{4}{5} - \dfrac{3}{10}$

5. $\dfrac{a}{2} - \dfrac{a}{3}$

6. $\dfrac{4}{t} + \dfrac{2}{2t}$

PRACTICE AND PROBLEM SOLVING

In Exercises 7–22, find the sum or difference. Then simplify, if possible.

7. $\dfrac{1}{6} + \dfrac{7}{12}$

8. $\dfrac{2}{3} - \dfrac{3}{8}$

9. $\dfrac{-1}{2} + \dfrac{-7}{12}$

10. $\dfrac{7}{9} - \dfrac{4}{5}$

11. $\dfrac{-11}{15} + \dfrac{2}{5}$

12. $\dfrac{-3}{7} - \dfrac{1}{3}$

13. $\dfrac{-3}{10} + \dfrac{7}{8}$

14. $\dfrac{1}{2} + \dfrac{5}{6} - \dfrac{7}{9}$

15. $\dfrac{x}{3} + \dfrac{x}{6}$

16. $\dfrac{a}{8} - \dfrac{a}{12}$

17. $\dfrac{2}{x} + \dfrac{9}{10}$

18. $\dfrac{4}{a} + \dfrac{11}{15}$

19. $\dfrac{-2}{3t} - \dfrac{4}{9t}$

20. $\dfrac{-7}{s} + \dfrac{4}{2s}$

21. $\dfrac{2}{n} - \dfrac{1}{3n}$

22. $1\dfrac{2}{3} + 1\dfrac{3}{4}$

SEQUENCE In Exercises 23–26, consider the following sequence.

$$\dfrac{1}{2}, \ -\dfrac{2}{3}, \ \dfrac{3}{4}, \ -\dfrac{4}{5}, \ \dots$$

23. Describe the pattern.

24. Write the next 2 terms of the sequence.

25. Find the sum of the first 3 terms.

26. Find the sum of the first 5 terms.

GEOMETRY In Exercises 27 and 28, find the perimeter of the figure.

27.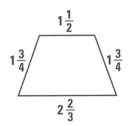

28.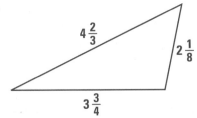

In Exercises 29–31, use the circle graph at the right. The graph shows what most influences students in grades 3–12 in their interest in science. The fractions represent portions of the student population.
(Source: Purdue University)

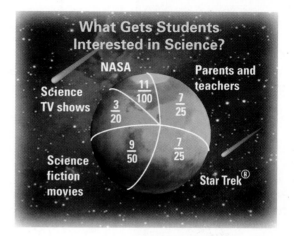

29. What portion of students are influenced most by *Star Trek* and science fiction movies?

30. Find the difference in the portions influenced by science television shows and by NASA.

31. Show that the sum of the five fractions is 1.

32. **ART** You are putting a mat on one of your paintings. The outside of the mat is $4\frac{1}{2}$ in.-by-$6\frac{1}{8}$ in. The border of the mat is $1\frac{1}{4}$ in. wide on all four sides.

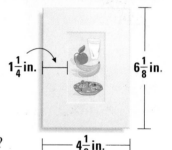

   a. What is the outside perimeter of the mat?

   b. What are the dimensions of the visible part of the painting?

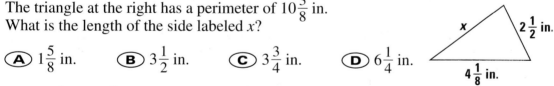

STANDARDIZED TEST PRACTICE

33. The triangle at the right has a perimeter of $10\frac{3}{8}$ in. What is the length of the side labeled x?

   A $1\frac{5}{8}$ in.   **B** $3\frac{1}{2}$ in.   **C** $3\frac{3}{4}$ in.   **D** $6\frac{1}{4}$ in.

34. Add $15\frac{4}{7} + 27\frac{6}{11}$.

   A $42\frac{9}{77}$ **B** $42\frac{68}{77}$ **C** $43\frac{9}{77}$ **D** $43\frac{68}{77}$

EXPLORATION AND EXTENSION

PORTFOLIO

BUILDING YOUR PROJECT In Exercises 35–40, estimate the fraction of a typical school day that you do each activity. The six fractions should all add up to 1.

35. Eat

36. Sleep

37. Attend school

38. Do homework

39. Personal grooming

40. Other

7.3

Exploring Fractions and **Decimals**

What you should learn:

Goal 1 How to combine fractions by writing the fractions as decimals

Goal 2 How to use addition and subtraction of decimals to solve real-life problems

Why you should learn it:

You can use addition and subtraction of decimals to solve real-life problems, such as interpreting the results of a survey.

Goal 1 ADDING AND SUBTRACTING DECIMALS

Another way to combine fractions is to rewrite them as decimals.

LESSON INVESTIGATION

COOPERATIVE LEARNING

Investigating Fraction Operations

PARTNER ACTIVITY Here are three ways to add $\frac{1}{2}$ and $\frac{1}{4}$.

Add as Fractions: $\frac{1}{2} + \frac{1}{4} = \frac{2}{4} + \frac{1}{4} = \frac{3}{4}$

Add as Decimals: $\frac{1}{2} + \frac{1}{4} = 0.50 + 0.25 = 0.75$

Add as Geometric Models:

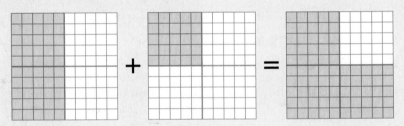

Use all three methods to evaluate the following. Discuss your results. Which method do you prefer?

1. $\frac{1}{5} + \frac{1}{2}$ **2.** $\frac{1}{4} - \frac{1}{5}$ **3.** $\frac{3}{4} + \frac{1}{10}$

Example 1 Adding and Subtracting Decimals

Evaluate the expression by first rewriting in decimal form. Then round the result to two decimal places.

Solution

a. $\frac{4}{13} + \frac{5}{8} \approx 0.308 + 0.625$ Write as rounded decimals.

$= 0.933$ Add decimals.

≈ 0.93 Round to 2 decimal places.

b. $\frac{8}{11}x - \frac{3}{7}x \approx 0.727x - 0.429x$ Write as rounded decimals.

$= 0.298x$ Subtract decimals.

$\approx 0.30x$ Round to 2 decimal places.

STUDY TIP

To avoid a round-off error, you should first round the numbers to one place more than is required in the solution. What happens if you first round the fractions to 0.31 and 0.63 in part (a) of Example 1?

Example 2 **Adding and Subtracting Decimals**

REAL LIFE
Population

This circle graph shows the age distribution of United States citizens in 1994.

a. Find the portion of U.S. citizens who are "45 to 64" or "65 and over."

b. What is the sum of all 8 fractions?

c. Use the result of part (a) to find the portion who are "18 to 24."

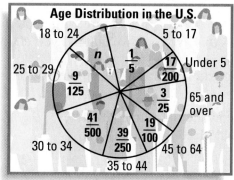

Age Distribution in the U.S.

18 to 24   5 to 17

n $\frac{1}{5}$ $\frac{17}{200}$ Under 5

25 to 29 $\frac{9}{125}$

$\frac{3}{25}$ 65 and over

$\frac{41}{500}$ $\frac{19}{100}$

30 to 34 $\frac{39}{250}$ 45 to 64

35 to 44

(Source: U.S. Bureau of the Census)

Solution

STRATEGY **USE A GRAPH**

a. Add the fractions for "45 to 64" and "65 and over."

$$\frac{19}{100} + \frac{3}{25} = 0.190 + 0.120$$
$$= 0.310$$

So, about 310 out of every 1000 people in the United States are over 45 years old.

b. The sum of all the fractions is 1. This is true of all circle graphs.

c. To find the portion who are "18 to 24," add the other five fractions with your result from part (a) and subtract the result from 1.

$$n = 1 - \left(\frac{17}{200} + \frac{1}{5} + \frac{9}{125} + \frac{41}{500} + \frac{39}{250} + 0.310\right)$$

$$= 1 - (0.085 + 0.200 + 0.072 + 0.082 + 0.156 + 0.310)$$

$$= 1 - 0.905$$

$$= 0.095$$

So, about 95 out of every 1000 people in the U.S. are between the ages of 18 and 24.

ONGOING ASSESSMENT

Write About It

Use a calculator to write the fractions as decimals. Then add or subtract the decimals. Round your results to two decimal places.

1. $\frac{3}{7} + \frac{5}{16}$

2. $\frac{12}{13} - \frac{5}{7}$

GUIDED PRACTICE

1. REASONING Explain each of the following steps.

$$\frac{7}{9} + \frac{11}{19} \approx 0.778 + 0.579$$
$$= 1.357$$
$$\approx 1.36$$

2. MODELING The sum of the fractions in the circle graph at the right is 1. Use fractions or decimals to solve for x. Which did you choose? Why?

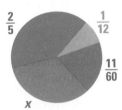

3. REASONING Which is greater: $\frac{2}{3}$ or 0.67? Explain your reasoning.

4. **TECHNOLOGY** Use a calculator to evaluate $\frac{2}{5} - \frac{10}{13}$. Round your result to two decimal places.

PRACTICE AND PROBLEM SOLVING

In Exercises 5–8, evaluate the expression.

5. $0.31 + 0.55$ **6.** $1.823 + 0.021$ **7.** $3.73 - 2.09$ **8.** $2.009 - 1.793$

MODELING In Exercises 9 and 10, write the expression represented by the model. Then use decimals or fractions to evaluate the expression.

9.

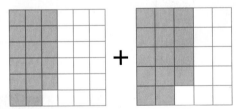

10.

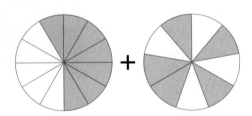

MODELING FRACTIONS In Exercises 11–14, sketch a geometric model of the fraction.

11. $\frac{11}{16}$ **12.** $\frac{24}{50}$ **13.** 0.45 **14.** 0.625

TECHNOLOGY In Exercises 15 and 16, simplify the expression by first rewriting in decimal form. Round your result to two decimal places.

15. $\frac{73}{111} + \frac{54}{109} + \frac{82}{89} - \frac{76}{127}$ **16.** $2y - \left(\frac{21}{56}y + \frac{32}{99}y + \frac{3}{25}y\right)$

17. PEACHES Hafez purchases $4\frac{1}{3}$ lb of peaches at the grocery store for $6.50. How much does one pound of peaches cost?

GOVERNMENT SPENDING In Exercises 18–20, use the circle graph, which shows how the United States federal government spent its money in 1997.

18. Find the sum of the portions for all categories other than national defense.

19. What portion was spent on national defense?

20. Find the sum of the portions spent on state and local grants and "other federal operations."

21. QUIZZES During a 10 min quiz, Anna spent $2\frac{1}{2}$ min on the first question, $\frac{3}{4}$ min on the second question, and 3 min on the third. How much time did she have to check her work?

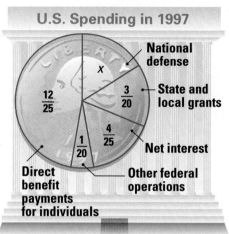

U.S. Spending in 1997

(Source: Office of Management and Budget)

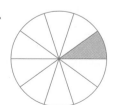

STANDARDIZED TEST PRACTICE

22. The fraction $\frac{19}{40}$ is equal to which decimal?

(**A**) 0.525 (**B**) 0.475 (**C**) 0.315 (**D**) 0.225

23. Which inequality is true?

(**A**) $\frac{13}{21} > 0.62$ (**B**) $-\frac{5}{13} > -0.38$ (**C**) $\frac{6}{17} < 0.333$ (**D**) $-\frac{9}{11} > -0.9$

EXPLORATION AND EXTENSION

AREA MODELS In Exercises 24–26, each circle has an area of 1 square unit. Write the fraction and decimal that represent the shaded part.

24.

25.

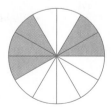

26.

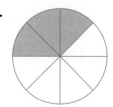

Multiplication of Rational Numbers

What you should learn:

Goal 1 How to multiply rational numbers

Goal 2 How to multiply rational numbers in real-life situations

Why you should learn it:

You can multiply rational numbers to find areas such as the area of a butterfly greenhouse.

Goal 1 MULTIPLYING RATIONAL NUMBERS

When you add or subtract fractions, you need to consider whether they have like denominators or unlike denominators. In this lesson, you will learn that the rule for multiplying fractions applies whether the denominators are like or unlike.

MULTIPLYING RATIONAL NUMBERS

To multiply two rational numbers, $\frac{a}{b}$ and $\frac{c}{d}$, multiply the numerators and multiply the denominators.

Numerical Example	Variable Example
$\frac{1}{5} \cdot \frac{3}{4} = \frac{1 \cdot 3}{5 \cdot 4} = \frac{3}{20}$	$\frac{a}{b} \cdot \frac{c}{d} = \frac{a \cdot c}{b \cdot d} = \frac{ac}{bd}$

Example 1 **Multiplying Rational Numbers**

a. $\frac{5}{8} \cdot \frac{-2}{3} = \frac{5 \cdot (-2)}{8 \cdot 3}$ **Multiply numerators and multiply denominators.**

$= \frac{-10}{24}$ **Simplify.**

$= \frac{2 \cdot (-5)}{2 \cdot 12}$ **Factor numerator and denominator.**

$= \frac{-5}{12}$ **Simplify fraction.**

b. $1\frac{2}{3} \cdot 3\frac{4}{5} = \frac{5}{3} \cdot \frac{19}{5}$ **Rewrite as improper fractions.**

$= \frac{5 \cdot 19}{3 \cdot 5}$ **Multiply numerators and multiply denominators.**

$= \frac{19}{3}$ **Simplify fraction.**

c. $\frac{6x}{5} \cdot 10 = \frac{6x}{5} \cdot \frac{10}{1}$ **Rewrite 10 as $\frac{10}{1}$.**

$= \frac{6x \cdot 10}{5 \cdot 1}$ **Multiply numerators and multiply denominators.**

$= \frac{6x \cdot 5 \cdot 2}{5}$ **Factor numerator.**

$= 12x$ **Simplify fraction.**

STUDY TIP

You can use an area model to multiply fractions.

The model shows
$\frac{1}{5} \cdot \frac{3}{4} = \frac{3}{20}$.

Example 2 Finding the Area of a Region

CONNECTION
Geometry

You are building one wall of a butterfly greenhouse. It is made of square plastic panels.

Each panel is $3\frac{1}{3}$ ft by $3\frac{1}{3}$ ft.

a. Find the height of the wall.

b. Find the width of the wall.

c. Find the area of the wall.

The Butterfly Pavilion and Insect Center in Colorado is about 80 ft wide, 90 ft long, and 16 ft high. It has between 1200 and 1500 butterflies every day.

Solution

a. The wall is 4 panels high.

$\text{Height} = 4 \cdot 3\frac{1}{3}$ **Multiply 4 times panel height.**

$\quad\quad\quad = \frac{4}{1} \cdot \frac{10}{3}$ **Rewrite $3\frac{1}{3}$ as an improper fraction.**

$\quad\quad\quad = \frac{40}{3}$ ft   **Multiply.**

b. The wall is 3 panels wide.

$\text{Width} = 3 \cdot 3\frac{1}{3}$ **Multiply 3 times panel width.**

$\quad\quad\quad = \frac{3}{1} \cdot \frac{10}{3}$ **Rewrite $3\frac{1}{3}$ as an improper fraction.**

$\quad\quad\quad = \frac{30}{3}$ **Multiply.**

$\quad\quad\quad = 10$ ft   **Simplify.**

c. To find the area, multiply the height by the width.

$\text{Area} = \text{Width} \cdot \text{Height}$ **Use the formula for area.**

$\quad\quad\quad = 10 \cdot \frac{40}{3}$ **Substitute for width and height.**

$\quad\quad\quad = \frac{400}{3}$ **Multiply.**

The wall's area is $\frac{400}{3}$, or about 133.3 ft^2.

✔**Check:** You can check these results by multiplying the width by the height. So, the area is $10 \cdot 13.33$, or 133.3 ft^2.

ONGOING ASSESSMENT

Write About It
....

Multiply the numbers. Show your work and explain each step.

1. $\frac{3}{5} \cdot \frac{10}{3}$

2. $\frac{5}{4} \cdot \frac{1}{2}$

3. $\frac{6}{7} \cdot 14$

Extra Practice, page 727

GUIDED PRACTICE

1. WRITING Explain in your own words how to multiply fractions.

In Exercises 2–5, multiply. Then simplify, if possible.

2. $\dfrac{4}{7} \cdot \dfrac{3}{5}$ **3.** $\dfrac{4}{7} \cdot \dfrac{7}{4}$ **4.** $\dfrac{5x}{9} \cdot \dfrac{2}{4}$ **5.** $1\dfrac{3}{5} \cdot 2\dfrac{1}{2}$

AREA MODELS In Exercises 6–9, the large square is 1 unit by 1 unit. Find the dimensions and area of the green region.

6.   **7.**   **8.**   **9.**

PRACTICE AND PROBLEM SOLVING

In Exercises 10–21, multiply. Then simplify, if possible.

10. $\dfrac{1}{4} \cdot \dfrac{4}{5}$ **11.** $\dfrac{-2}{3} \cdot \dfrac{8}{9}$ **12.** $\dfrac{-5}{6} \cdot \dfrac{-3}{4}$ **13.** $1\dfrac{2}{5} \cdot 2\dfrac{2}{7}$

14. $\left(1\dfrac{1}{5}\right) \cdot \left(-6\dfrac{2}{3}\right)$ **15.** $\left(-4\dfrac{1}{2}\right) \cdot \left(-2\dfrac{5}{9}\right)$ **16.** $\dfrac{2}{3} \cdot \dfrac{-4}{7} \cdot \dfrac{4}{5}$ **17.** $\dfrac{-4}{9} \cdot \dfrac{2}{3} \cdot \dfrac{-3}{8}$

18. $\dfrac{5x}{6} \cdot 12$ **19.** $7 \cdot \dfrac{8y}{3}$ **20.** $\dfrac{-13t}{20} \cdot \dfrac{-1}{2}$ **21.** $\dfrac{-5}{6} \cdot \dfrac{-6a}{15}$

GEOMETRY In Exercises 22–24, find the area of the figure.

22.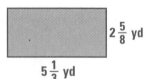

$2\dfrac{5}{8}$ yd

$5\dfrac{1}{3}$ yd

23.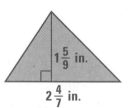

$1\dfrac{5}{9}$ in.

$2\dfrac{4}{7}$ in.

24.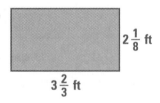

$2\dfrac{1}{8}$ ft

$3\dfrac{2}{3}$ ft

TECHNOLOGY In Exercises 25–28, use a calculator to multiply. Round your result to three decimal places.

25. $\dfrac{9}{16} \cdot \dfrac{6}{13}$ **26.** $\dfrac{17}{25} \cdot 2\dfrac{3}{4}$ **27.** $\dfrac{23}{48}(-7)$ **28.** $-\dfrac{21}{32} \cdot \dfrac{2}{5}$

In Exercises 29–32, write each decimal as a fraction. Then multiply.

29. $0.25; 0.\overline{6}$ **30.** $0.\overline{3}; 0.75$ **31.** $0.2; 0.625$ **32.** $0.375; 0.7$

DINOSAURS In Exercises 33–36, use the following information to find the length of each dinosaur.

The *Diplodocus* is the longest known dinosaur, measuring 90 ft.

33. *Allosaurus*: Length is $\frac{1}{3}$ of *Diplodocus*

34. *Stegosaurus*: Length is $\frac{2}{3}$ of *Allosaurus*

35. *Ankylosaurus*: Length is $\frac{3}{4}$ of *Stegosaurus*

36. *Tyrannosaurus*: Length is $2\frac{2}{3}$ of *Ankylosaurus*

COINS In Exercises 37–39, represent the money as a fraction of a dollar.

37.  **38.**  **39.**

> **TOOLBOX**
>
> Fraction Concepts, page 746

STANDARDIZED TEST PRACTICE

40. You are creating a design for a tree house. You want the total area of the tree house floor to be at least 54 ft². Which of the following floor designs provides such an area?

Ⓐ 8 ft × $6\frac{3}{4}$ ft   **Ⓑ** $8\frac{1}{4}$ ft × $6\frac{1}{2}$ ft   **Ⓒ** $8\frac{1}{2}$ ft × $6\frac{1}{4}$ ft   **Ⓓ** $8\frac{3}{4}$ ft × 6 ft

EXPLORATION AND EXTENSION

PORTFOLIO

41. BUILDING YOUR PROJECT Aerobic exercises strengthen the heart and lungs. The table shows energy use for various activities. Choose an activity that you enjoy from the table. If you exercise for $\frac{3}{4}$ h Tuesdays and Thursdays and for $1\frac{1}{4}$ h Saturdays and Sundays, how many calories will you burn in one week?

Activity	Approximate energy use (Cal/h)
running, cross country	575
swimming, fast crawl	450
bicycling, leisure	425
football	475
basketball	475
climbing hills, with no load	425

In Exercises 1–6, choose an operation that makes the equation true. (1.2)

1. $14 \; ? \; 7 = 2$

2. $4 \; ? \; 6 = 10$

3. $36 \; ? \; 3 = 12$

4. $13 \; ? \; 9 = 4$

5. $14 \; ? \; 2 = 28$

6. $12 \; ? \; 12 = 1$

In Exercises 7–10, solve the equation. (7.2)

7. $a + \dfrac{2}{3} = \dfrac{4}{3}$

8. $y + \dfrac{1}{4} = \dfrac{3}{4}$

9. $\dfrac{14}{9} = b - \dfrac{13}{9}$

10. $x - \dfrac{3}{10} = -\dfrac{9}{10}$

In Exercises 11–14, find the least common multiple. (6.4)

11. 2 and 7

12. 10 and 16

13. 3, 4, and 5

14. 4, 5, and 6

In Exercises 15–19, find the sum or difference. (7.2)

15. $\dfrac{1}{20} + \dfrac{1}{4}$

16. $\dfrac{2}{3} - \dfrac{1}{5}$

17. $\dfrac{99}{100} - \dfrac{6}{25}$

18. $\dfrac{4}{5} + \dfrac{6}{25}$

19. **VACATION** You have a chance to win a cruise to the Bahamas. Each letter of the word BAHAMAS is placed in a bag. If you choose the letter "A," you win. What is the probability that you will win? (5.8)

CAREER Interview

Gwenndolyn White, a nutritionist at the University of California Cooperative Extension in Berkeley, provides nutritional education to low-income families.

Q What led you to this career?
Since I liked to eat and cook, I thought home economics would be fun. While studying nutrition in college, a woman from the Cooperative Extension came to talk about what she did. It sounded interesting, and I started working for her a few years later, while pursuing graduate studies in nutrition at the same time.

Q What is your favorite part of the job?
I like showing people how to make healthy foods that taste good and don't cost a lot of money. It's not enough for food to be simply nutritious. It has to taste good, too, or people won't eat it.

Q How does math help you with your job?
I don't think about math all that much, but I use it often. For instance, in grocery stores, I show people how to compare prices and how to figure out the percentage of calories that come from fat. Math is also useful with recipes. Depending on the size of your family, you may have to increase or decrease the amounts of ingredients. That involves multiplication, division, and fractions.

Take this test as you would take a test in class. The answers to the exercises are given in the back of the book.

In Exercises 1–4, find the sum or difference and simplify, if possible. (7.1, 7.2)

1. $\dfrac{1}{11} + \dfrac{3}{11}$ **2.** $\dfrac{5}{6} - \dfrac{1}{6}$ **3.** $\dfrac{7}{10} - \dfrac{4}{25}$ **4.** $\dfrac{9}{10} - \dfrac{1}{2}$

In Exercises 5–8, find the product and simplify, if possible. (7.4)

5. $\dfrac{-4}{7} \cdot \dfrac{7}{8}$ **6.** $\dfrac{2}{3} \cdot \dfrac{3}{4} \cdot \dfrac{4}{5}$ **7.** $\dfrac{7}{10} \cdot 2$ **8.** $\dfrac{2}{5} \cdot \dfrac{-6}{5}$

ALGEBRA **In Exercises 9–12, simplify the expression by first rewriting in decimal form. Round the result to 2 decimal places.** (7.3)

9. $\dfrac{3}{8} + \dfrac{9}{17}$ **10.** $\dfrac{18}{29}x + \dfrac{35}{48}x$ **11.** $\dfrac{7}{9}y - \dfrac{7}{11}y$ **12.** $\dfrac{27}{31} - \dfrac{11}{50}$

13. **GEOMETRY** Find the perimeter and area of the rectangle. (7.2, 7.4)

$2\dfrac{2}{5}$ in.

$5\dfrac{1}{3}$ in.

14. **GEOMETRY** The large square has an area of 1. Find the area of the blue region. (7.4)

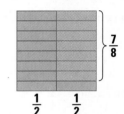

$\dfrac{7}{8}$

$\dfrac{1}{2}$ $\dfrac{1}{2}$

SHOES **In Exercises 15 and 16, use the following information.**

You are shopping for shoes and find a clearance rack with shoes that are $\dfrac{1}{3}$ to $\dfrac{1}{2}$ off the original price. The original price of the shoes is \$30. (7.3, 7.4)

15. If the shoes are $\dfrac{1}{3}$ off the original price, then the discount is $\dfrac{1}{3} \cdot 30$. What is the discount?

16. If the shoes are $\dfrac{1}{2}$ off the original price, then the discount is $\dfrac{1}{2} \cdot 30$. What is the discount? How much do you pay?

17. Which is larger: 0.72 or $\dfrac{8}{11}$? (7.3)

18. **COINS** Which of the following cannot be represented exactly with United States coins? (7.4)

   A. One fifth of \$2.85   **B.** One fourth of \$2.85   **C.** One third of \$2.85

7.5

Division of Rational Numbers

What you should learn:

Goal 1 How to divide rational numbers

Goal 2 How to use division of rational numbers to solve real-life measurement problems

Why you should learn it:

You can use division of rational numbers to find the number of horses that can be grazed on a pasture.

Goal 1 DIVIDING RATIONAL NUMBERS

Suppose you took 7 rides on a water slide in a half hour. How many rides could you take in an hour?

$$7 \text{ rides} \div \frac{1}{2} \text{ hour} = \frac{7}{1} \div \frac{1}{2} \text{ rides per hour}$$

$$= \frac{7}{1} \cdot \frac{2}{1} = 14 \text{ rides per hour}$$

Dividing by $\frac{1}{2}$ produces the same result as multiplying by 2.

DIVIDING RATIONAL NUMBERS

To divide by a fraction, multiply by its reciprocal.

Numerical Example

$$\frac{1}{5} \div \frac{3}{4} = \frac{1}{5} \cdot \frac{4}{3} = \frac{4}{15}$$

Variable Example

$$\frac{a}{b} \div \frac{c}{d} = \frac{a}{b} \cdot \frac{d}{c} = \frac{ad}{bc}$$

Example 1 Dividing Rational Numbers

a. $\frac{3}{4} \div 3 = \frac{3}{4} \cdot \frac{1}{3}$ The reciprocal of 3 is $\frac{1}{3}$.

$\qquad = \frac{3 \cdot 1}{4 \cdot 3}$ Multiply fractions.

$\qquad = \frac{1}{4}$ Simplify fraction.

b. $\frac{-2}{3} \div \frac{-4}{5} = \frac{-2}{3} \cdot \frac{5}{-4}$ The reciprocal of $\frac{-4}{5}$ is $\frac{5}{-4}$.

$\qquad = \frac{-10}{-12}$ Multiply fractions.

$\qquad = \frac{5}{6}$ Simplify fraction.

c. $2 \div 4\frac{1}{2} = 2 \div \frac{9}{2}$ Write the mixed number as an improper fraction.

$\qquad = 2 \cdot \frac{2}{9}$ The reciprocal of $\frac{9}{2}$ is $\frac{2}{9}$.

$\qquad = \frac{4}{9}$ Multiply.

d. $\frac{x}{2} \div 3 = \frac{x}{2} \cdot \frac{1}{3}$ The reciprocal of 3 is $\frac{1}{3}$.

$\qquad = \frac{x}{6}$ Multiply fractions.

Example 2 > **Multiplying and Dividing Fractions**

You own a horse ranch. Your pasture is a rectangle that is $\frac{1}{2}$ mi wide and $\frac{3}{4}$ mi long. The recommended grazing area for each horse is $\frac{3}{2}$ acres. There are 640 acres (A) in 1 mi². What is the maximum number of horses you should have in your pasture?

Solution

Your pasture has an area of $\frac{1}{2} \cdot \frac{3}{4}$, or $\frac{3}{8}$ mi².

Number of acres in your pasture $= \frac{640 \text{ acres}}{1 \text{ mi}^2} \cdot \frac{3}{8} \text{ mi}^2 = 240 \text{ acres}$

To find the maximum number of horses, divide 240 A by $\frac{3}{2}$.

$240 \text{ acres} \div \left(\frac{3}{2} \text{ acres/horses}\right) = 240 \text{ acres} \cdot \frac{2}{3} \text{ horses/acres}$

$= 240 \cdot \frac{2}{3} \text{ horses}$

$= 160 \text{ horses}$

The maximum number of horses is 160.

Example 3 > **Dividing Fractions**

You baby-sat your niece for $1\frac{2}{3}$ h. You were paid $6. Since an hourly rate is given in *dollars per hour*, you should divide money by time to find your hourly rate.

Hourly rate $= \$6 \div 1\frac{2}{3}$ h   Divide amount by time.

$= 6 \div \frac{5}{3}$ dollars per hour   Rewrite as an improper fraction.

$= 6 \cdot \frac{3}{5}$ dollars per hour   The reciprocal of $\frac{5}{3}$ is $\frac{3}{5}$.

$= \frac{18}{5}$ dollars per hour   Multiply.

$= \$3.60$ per hour   Simplify.

Real Life... Real Facts

NARHA The North American Riding for the Handicapped Association uses horseback riding as therapy for children and adults with disabilities. It provides not only increased flexibility and balance but also greater confidence and self esteem.

ONGOING ASSESSMENT

Talk About It

Describe a real-life problem that can be solved using the expression. What are the units of the answer?

1. $3\frac{1}{3}$ h $\cdot \$7\frac{1}{2}$ per hour

2. $7\frac{1}{2}$ mi $\div 1\frac{1}{2}$ mi/h

7.5 Exercises

Extra Practice, page 727

GUIDED PRACTICE

MENTAL MATH In Exercises 1–4, write the reciprocal.

1. $\dfrac{1}{5}$ **2.** $-\dfrac{2}{3}$ **3.** 7 **4.** $\dfrac{4}{t}$

ERROR ANALYSIS In Exercises 5 and 6, describe the error. Then correct it.

5. $\dfrac{5}{6} \div 3 = \dfrac{5}{6} \cdot \dfrac{3}{1}$

$= \dfrac{5 \cdot 3}{2 \cdot 3}$

$= \dfrac{5}{2}$

6. $\dfrac{-4}{3} \div \dfrac{3}{2} = \dfrac{-4}{3} \cdot \dfrac{2}{3}$

$= \dfrac{-4 \cdot 2}{3}$

$= \dfrac{-8}{3}$

In Exercises 7–10, simplify the expression.

7. $\dfrac{1}{2} \div \dfrac{5}{6}$ **8.** $6 \div \dfrac{4}{9}$ **9.** $\dfrac{n}{3} \div \dfrac{3}{2}$ **10.** $3\dfrac{1}{2} \div \dfrac{4}{x}$

PRACTICE AND PROBLEM SOLVING

MENTAL MATH In Exercises 11–14, write the reciprocal.

11. $\dfrac{1}{4}$ **12.** $\dfrac{3}{x}$ **13.** $\dfrac{7a}{5}$ **14.** $-2\dfrac{2}{3}$

ERROR ANALYSIS In Exercises 15–17, describe the error. Then correct it.

15. $-\dfrac{3}{2} \div \dfrac{3}{5} = -\dfrac{2}{3} \cdot \dfrac{3}{5}$

$= \dfrac{-2 \cdot 3}{3 \cdot 5}$

$= -\dfrac{2}{5}$

16. $8 \div 2\dfrac{1}{2} = 8 \cdot \dfrac{5}{2}$

$= \dfrac{40}{2}$

$= 20$

17. $\dfrac{1}{3} \div \dfrac{1}{3} = \dfrac{1}{3} \cdot \dfrac{1}{3}$

$= \dfrac{1}{3 \cdot 3}$

$= \dfrac{1}{9}$

ALGEBRA In Exercises 18–33, simplify the expression.

18. $\dfrac{3}{2} \div \dfrac{1}{2}$ **19.** $\dfrac{3}{2} \div \dfrac{1}{3}$ **20.** $\dfrac{3}{2} \div \dfrac{1}{4}$ **21.** $\dfrac{3}{2} \div \dfrac{1}{5}$

22. $\dfrac{3}{4} \div 2$ **23.** $3 \div \dfrac{-5}{6}$ **24.** $\dfrac{-1}{2} \div \dfrac{1}{3}$ **25.** $\dfrac{7}{4} \div \dfrac{1}{-4}$

26. $3\dfrac{1}{2} \div \dfrac{3}{4}$ **27.** $\dfrac{4}{5} \div 1\dfrac{1}{2}$ **28.** $\dfrac{x}{2} \div (-4)$ **29.** $-\dfrac{3}{5} \div \dfrac{9}{x}$

30. $6\dfrac{2}{3} \div a$ **31.** $n \div 1\dfrac{1}{4}$ **32.** $\dfrac{1}{y} \div \dfrac{4}{y}$ **33.** $\dfrac{3b}{2} \div \dfrac{9b}{5}$

MENTAL MATH In Exercises 34–37, simplify the expression.

34. $\dfrac{1}{4} \div 2$

35. $\dfrac{1}{4} \div 3$

36. $\dfrac{1}{4} \div 4$

37. $\dfrac{1}{4} \div 5$

38. PATTERNS In Exercises 34–37, write each result as a decimal, rounded to two decimal places. Describe the pattern. What happens when you divide a number by larger and larger numbers?

In Exercises 39–42, decide whether to use multiplication or division to solve the problem. Solve the problem and explain why you selected that operation.

39. BICYCLING You are riding your bike on a trail that is 11 mi long. You plan on stopping to rest every $2\dfrac{3}{4}$ mi. How many rest stops do you plan to make? Check your answer.

40. BABY-SITTING You baby-sat your neighbor's son for $3\dfrac{3}{4}$ h. You earned $12.00. What was your hourly wage?

41. PIZZA You order 3 pizzas. You think each person will eat $\dfrac{3}{8}$ of a pizza. How many people can you feed?

42. WATER PITCHER A pitcher holds $\dfrac{3}{4}$ gal of water. If each water glass holds $\dfrac{1}{16}$ gal, how many glasses can be filled?

GEOMETRY In Exercises 43–46, write an equation that allows you to solve for x. Then solve the equation.

43. Area $= \dfrac{7}{15}$

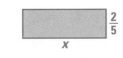

44. Area $= \dfrac{63}{4}$

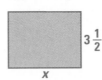

45. Area $= \dfrac{9}{8}$

46. Area $= \dfrac{3}{40}$

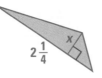

STANDARDIZED TEST PRACTICE

47. Use the restrictions for the numbers a and b below to determine which of the following statements can never be true.

a is greater than 1.

b is between 0 and 1.

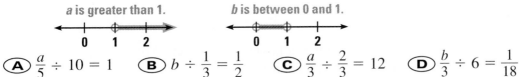

Ⓐ $\dfrac{a}{5} \div 10 = 1$ Ⓑ $b \div \dfrac{1}{3} = \dfrac{1}{2}$ Ⓒ $\dfrac{a}{3} \div \dfrac{2}{3} = 12$ Ⓓ $\dfrac{b}{3} \div 6 = \dfrac{1}{18}$

BUILDING YOUR PROJECT Two minerals that you may not get enough of in your diet are calcium and iron. The amount recommended by the USDA of each mineral is 1200 mg of calcium and 15 mg of iron. The amount contained in some foods is shown in the table below.

48. For breakfast you eat 5 oz of fortified breakfast cereal with $\frac{1}{2}$ c (4 oz) of skim milk. You drink 6 oz of orange juice with calcium added.

   a. How much iron and how much calcium did you get from each of the three foods?

   b. What fraction of the recommended amount of calcium did you consume?

   c. What fraction of the recommended amount of iron did you consume?

Food	Calcium (mg in 3.5 oz serving)	Food	Iron (mg in 3.5 oz serving)
Parmesan cheese	1360	Clams	4
Mozzarella cheese	724	Breakfast cereal (fortified)	12
Ricotta cheese	272	Tofu	2
Orange juice (calcium added)	131	Liver	7
Skim milk	70	Spinach	3

SPIRAL REVIEW

In Exercises 1–3, solve for *x* and find the dimensions of the polygon. (4.8)

1. Perimeter = 48 units   **2.** Perimeter = 50 units   **3.** Perimeter = 51 units

$x + 4$
$x + 4$

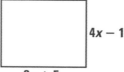
$4x - 1$
$3x + 5$

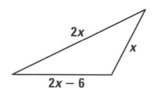
$2x$
x
$2x - 6$

In Exercises 4–7, find the sum or difference. Then simplify, if possible. (7.2)

4. $\frac{5}{6} - \frac{1}{4}$ **5.** $\frac{1}{2} + \frac{5}{9}$ **6.** $\frac{-2}{3} + \frac{4}{15}$ **7.** $\frac{-3}{10} - \frac{1}{8}$

In Exercises 8–11, multiply or divide. Then simplify, if possible. (7.4, 7.5)

8. $-2\frac{1}{4} \times 1\frac{5}{6}$ **9.** $\frac{-5}{9} \times \frac{-3}{5}$ **10.** $2 \div \frac{-3}{8}$ **11.** $3\frac{1}{3} \div 5$

12. LANDSCAPING You earn $38.00 mowing lawns on Saturday. You charge $9.50 per lawn. How many lawns did you mow? (2.7)

LAB 7.6

COOPERATIVE LEARNING

Modeling Portions of Regions

What is one fourth of 25? One way to answer this question is to draw a 5-by-5 square and shade one fourth of it. Three ways are shown below. In each case, the entire square has an area of 25 square units and the green shaded portion has an area of $6\frac{1}{4}$ square units.

Materials Needed
• graph paper or grid paper

In Exercises 1–3, copy the diagram on graph paper. Use your sketch to determine what portion of the 10-by-10 square is shaded orange.

1.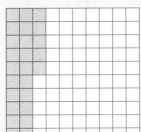

2.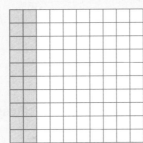

3.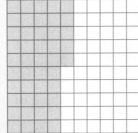

In Exercises 4 and 5, outline the rectangle on graph paper. Then shade the indicated number of unit squares. What portion of the rectangle is shaded?

4. A 4-by-10 rectangle: Shade 8 unit squares.

5. A 5-by-5 rectangle: Shade 10 unit squares.

6. Shade 12 unit squares on a piece of graph paper. Then draw a rectangle so that the shaded unit squares form one third of the rectangle.

NOW TRY THESE

7. Outline a 5-by-9 rectangle on graph paper. Then shade 9 squares. What portion of the rectangle is shaded?

8. Shade 8 unit squares on a piece of graph paper. Then draw a rectangle so that the shaded unit squares form one third of the rectangle.

Exploring Percents

What you should learn:

Goal 1 How to write portions as percents

Goal 2 How to use percents to solve real-life problems

Why you should learn it:

You can use percents to find and analyze patterns such as those found in ancient writings.

Sixty percent of the human body is made up of water.

Goal 1 WRITING PERCENTS

A **portion** is a fraction that compares the measure of part of a quantity to the measure of the whole quantity. For instance, if you own 12 T-shirts, 3 of which are black, then you can say that $\frac{3}{12}$, or $\frac{1}{4}$, of your T-shirts are black. For these portions, the denominators are 12 and 4. When the denominator is 100, the portion is called a **percent**.

PERCENT

A **percent** is a portion whose denominator is 100. The symbol % means *percent*. Here is an example.

Fraction Form	Percent Symbol Form	Verbal Form
$\frac{65}{100}$	65%	65 percent

Example 1 Comparing Percents

Which of the following has the greatest percent of its area shaded?

A.   B.   C.

Solution

A. For figure A, the portion of the region that is shaded is

$$\frac{10}{25} = \frac{10}{25} \cdot \frac{4}{4} = \frac{40}{100} = 40\%.$$

B. For figure B, the portion of the region that is shaded is

$$\frac{2}{8} = \frac{1}{4} = \frac{1}{4} \cdot \frac{25}{25} = \frac{25}{100} = 25\%.$$

C. For figure C, the portion of the region that is shaded is

$$\frac{6}{20} = \frac{6}{20} \cdot \frac{5}{5} = \frac{30}{100} = 30\%.$$

Figure A has the greatest percent of its area shaded.

Goal 2 SOLVING REAL-LIFE PROBLEMS

Example 2 ▸ Writing Percents

In the ancient Egyptian hieroglyph shown below, what percent of the symbols represent water?

REAL LIFE
Archaeology

Solution

The hieroglyph contains 15 symbols, 3 of which represent water.

$$\text{Portion} = \frac{\text{Water symbols}}{\text{Total symbols}} = \frac{3}{15} = \frac{1}{5}$$

To rewrite this portion as a percent, multiply the numerator and denominator by 20.

$$\frac{1}{5} = \frac{1}{5} \cdot \frac{20}{20} = \frac{20}{100} = 20\%$$

So, 20% of the symbols are symbols for water.

Example 3 ▸ Writing Percents

The photograph at the right shows an ancient Egyptian hieroglyph symbol for the sound *st*. To estimate the percent of the photograph that occupies the figure's ears, add a 10-by-10 grid to the drawing. The ears occupy about 7 full squares, 5 half squares, and 2 quarter squares. This is about 7 + 2.5 + 0.5 or 10 squares. So, the ears occupy about 10% of the photograph.

Real Life...
Real Facts

The Rosetta Stone
For hundreds of years, no one could decode Egyptian hieroglyphics. This stone, called the Rosetta Stone, helped solve the mystery. It contains the same message in three languages.

ONGOING ASSESSMENT

Talk About It
. . . .

Draw a geometric model for the indicated percent. Compare your model to a classmate's model. Is one easier to see than the other? Explain.

1. 25%

2. 40%

3. 75%

GUIDED PRACTICE

1. Copy and complete the table.

Fraction form	Percent symbol form	Verbal form
$\frac{24}{100}$	?	?
?	83%	?
?	?	49 percent

2. What percent of the figure is shaded?

3. Write $\frac{9}{20}$ as a percent.

4. MODELING Draw two geometric models for 60%.

PRACTICE AND PROBLEM SOLVING

In Exercises 5–8, what percent of the figure is shaded purple?

5.   **6.**   **7.**   **8.**

9. AREA MODELS Which of the following has the least percent of its area shaded yellow? Which has the greatest?

A.   **B.**   **C.**   **D.**

In Exercises 10–17, write each portion as a percent.

10. $\frac{1}{10}$ **11.** $\frac{1}{20}$ **12.** $\frac{31}{50}$ **13.** $\frac{7}{25}$

14. $\frac{24}{32}$ **15.** $\frac{18}{40}$ **16.** $\frac{45}{150}$ **17.** $\frac{180}{300}$

MODELING In Exercises 18–21, draw two geometric models for the percent.

18. 25%   **19.** 20%   **20.** 80%   **21.** 100%

PATTERNS In Exercises 22–25, find the percent of the figure that is shaded blue.

22.

23.

24.

25.

MAPPING In Exercises 26 and 27, use the map at the right. The blue regions on the map indicate water.

26. About what percent of the region shown on the map is water?

27. Explain how to use your answer to Exercise 26 to estimate the percent of the region that is *not* water.

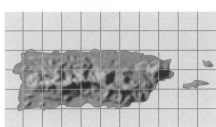

 STANDARDIZED TEST PRACTICE

28. Which model does *not* represent 25%?

PORTFOLIO **EXPLORATION AND EXTENSION**

BUILDING YOUR PROJECT In Exercises 29 and 30, use the food pyramid at the right. It gives guidelines on how many servings of different kinds of foods you should eat every day. (Source: U.S. Department of Agriculture)

29. According to the food pyramid, how many servings of vegetables should you eat each day? According to the food pyramid, about what percent of your daily diet is this? Explain.

30. How many servings of bread, cereals, and rice should you eat each day? About what percent of your daily diet is this? Explain.

Fats, Oils and Sweets
Use sparingly.

Milk and Cheese Group
2–3 servings

Meat, Fish, and Eggs Group
2–3 servings

Vegetable Group
3–5 servings

Fruit Group
2–4 servings

Bread and Cereal Group
6–11 servings

Percents, Decimals, and Fractions

What you should learn:

Goal 1 How to write percents as decimals and how to write decimals as percents

Goal 2 How to write fractions as percents and how to write percents as fractions

Why you should learn it:

Knowing how to interpret percents helps you maintain a healthy diet.

Fish are an excellent source of high-grade protein and minerals. Meat, fish, poultry, dry beans, eggs, and nuts should make up about 12% of your diet.

Goal 1 WRITING PERCENTS AS DECIMALS

In real life, percents are written in several different forms. For instance, a 35% discount at a store can be written several ways.

Percent Form	Verbal Form	Fraction Form	Decimal Form
35%	35 percent	$\frac{35}{100}$, or $\frac{7}{20}$	0.35

The first two forms are used for communication and the second two forms are used for computation.

> **PERCENTS AND DECIMALS**
>
> 1. To write a percent as a decimal, remove the percent sign from the number and divide by 100.
> 2. To write a decimal as a percent, multiply the decimal by 100%.

Example 1 Rewriting Percents as Decimals

When you are rewriting a percent in decimal form, remember that *percent* means *per hundred*.

a. $14\% = \frac{14}{100} = 0.14$

b. $0.5\% = \frac{0.5}{100} = 0.005$

c. $125\% = \frac{125}{100} = 1.25$

d. $33\frac{1}{3}\% \approx \frac{33.3}{100} = 0.333$

Example 2 Rewriting Decimals as Percents

To rewrite a decimal as a percent, multiply the decimal by 100%.

a. $0.28 = 0.28 \cdot (100\%)$
$= 28\%$

b. $0.346 = 0.346 \cdot (100\%)$
$= 34.6\%$

c. $1.045 = 1.045 \cdot (100\%)$
$= 104.5\%$

d. $0.001 = 0.001 \cdot (100\%)$
$= 0.1\%$

Often it helps to rewrite a fraction as a percent.

FRACTION FORM

1. To rewrite a fraction as a percent, rewrite the fraction in decimal form. Then, multiply by 100%.
2. To rewrite a percent in fraction form, divide by 100%. Then simplify, if possible.

Example 3 Rewriting Fractions as Percents

a. $\frac{7}{8} = 0.875 = 0.875(100\%) = 87.5\%$

b. $\frac{12}{5} = 2.4 = 2.4(100\%) = 240\%$

Example 4 Rewriting Percents as Fractions

a. $72\% = \frac{72}{100} = \frac{18}{25}$

b. $140\% = \frac{140}{100} = \frac{7}{5}$

DIFFERENT FORMS OF IMPORTANT PERCENTS

$\frac{1}{10} = 0.1 = 10\%$	$\frac{1}{8} = 0.125 = 12.5\%$	$\frac{1}{6} \approx 0.167 = 16.7\%$
$\frac{2}{10} = 0.2 = 20\%$	$\frac{1}{4} = 0.25 = 25\%$	$\frac{1}{3} \approx 0.333 = 33.3\%$
$\frac{3}{10} = 0.3 = 30\%$	$\frac{3}{8} = 0.375 = 37.5\%$	$\frac{3}{6} = 0.5 = 50\%$
$\frac{4}{10} = 0.4 = 40\%$	$\frac{1}{2} = 0.5 = 50\%$	$\frac{2}{3} \approx 0.667 = 66.7\%$
$\frac{5}{10} = 0.5 = 50\%$	$\frac{5}{8} = 0.625 = 62.5\%$	$\frac{5}{6} \approx 0.883 = 88.3\%$
$\frac{6}{10} = 0.6 = 60\%$	$\frac{3}{4} = 0.75 = 75\%$	$1 = 100\%$
$\frac{7}{10} = 0.7 = 70\%$	$\frac{7}{8} = 0.875 = 87.5\%$	$0 = 0\%$
$\frac{8}{10} = 0.8 = 80\%$		
$\frac{9}{10} = 0.9 = 90\%$		

Extra Practice, page 728

GUIDED PRACTICE

In Exercises 1–4, write each fraction as a decimal.

1. $\dfrac{3}{5}$
2. $\dfrac{5}{10}$
3. $\dfrac{4}{6}$
4. $\dfrac{1}{6}$

MODELING **In Exercises 5–8, what portion of the figure is blue? Express your answer as a percent and as a decimal.**

5.
6.
7.
8.

9. **WRITING** Explain how to rewrite a percent as a decimal. Then rewrite 48% as a decimal.

10. **WRITING** Explain how to rewrite a fraction as a percent. Then rewrite $\dfrac{5}{16}$ as a percent.

11. **WRITING** Explain how to rewrite a decimal as a percent. Then rewrite 0.045 as a percent.

12. Give a real-life example of a percent greater than 100%.

PRACTICE AND PROBLEM SOLVING

In Exercises 13–16, rewrite the percent as a decimal.

13. 36%
14. 1.44%
15. 115%
16. $14\dfrac{2}{3}\%$

In Exercises 17–20, rewrite the decimal as a percent.

17. 0.25
18. 0.826
19. 0.7
20. 1.4

In Exercises 21–28, rewrite the percent as a fraction in simplest form.

21. 52%
22. 75%
23. 6%
24. 8%
25. 160%
26. 248%
27. 102%
28. 95%

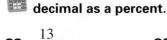 **In Exercises 29–36, rewrite the fraction as a decimal. Then rewrite the decimal as a percent.**

29. $\dfrac{13}{208}$
30. $\dfrac{52}{650}$
31. $\dfrac{78}{99}$
32. $\dfrac{375}{450}$

33. $\dfrac{104}{64}$
34. $\dfrac{429}{286}$
35. $\dfrac{180}{54}$
36. $\dfrac{357}{252}$

In Exercises 37–40, complete the statement with <, >, or =.

37. $\dfrac{3}{8}$? 3.75%　　**38.** $\dfrac{7}{16}$? 43.75%　　**39.** $\dfrac{1}{25}$? 4%　　**40.** $\dfrac{3}{50}$? 0.6%

POLLS In Exercises 41–44, match the percent with the portion of the American population that you think has the indicated characteristic.

A. Over 85 years old　　**B.** Female　　**C.** Watch television　　**D.** Under 10 years old

41. 51%　　　　　**42.** 91%　　　　　**43.** 15%　　　　　**44.** 1%

MULTIMEDIA AUDIENCES In Exercises 45–48, use the bar graph at the right.

45. Create a table showing each percent rewritten as a decimal and as a fraction in simplest form.

46. Which percent is about ten times as large as another?

47. Why is the sum greater than 100%?

48. In a sample of 250 adults, about how many access the Internet? Did you use decimals, fractions, or percents to get your answer? Why?

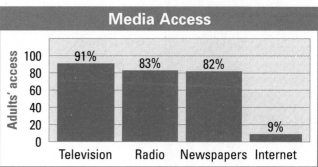

(Source: Mediamark Research)

49. What percent of the figure at the right is shaded?

(A) $\dfrac{1}{3}$%　　　(B) 30%

(C) 33%　　　(D) $33\dfrac{1}{3}$%

EXPLORATION AND EXTENSION

ESTIMATION In Exercises 50–52, estimate the percent that is represented by each part of the circle graph. Which parts are easiest to estimate? Why?

50.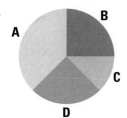

51.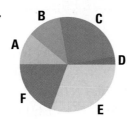

52.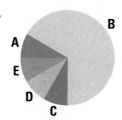

What you should learn:

Goal 1 How to find a percent of a number

Goal 2 How to use percents to solve real-life problems

Why you should learn it:

Knowing how to find a percent of a number helps you solve real-life problems, such as finding how many people voted for a presidential candidate.

In the United States, a winning candidate can get more than 50% of the electoral votes without getting more than 50% of the popular vote. This happened in 1992.

Goal 1 FINDING A PERCENT OF A NUMBER

One way to find a percent of a number is to multiply the *decimal form* of the percent by the number.

Example 1 Finding Percents of Numbers

a. Find 36% of 825.

b. Find 150% of 38.

Solution

a. Begin by writing **36%** as **0.36**. Then multiply by 825.

$$0.36 \times 825 = 297$$

Thus, 36% of 825 is 297.

b. Begin by writing **150%** as **1.5**. Then multiply by 38.

$$1.5 \times 38 = 57$$

Thus, 150% of 38 is 57.

Example 2 Finding a Percent of an Area

A 6-by-10 rectangle has 60 small squares. How many of the small squares are in 40% of the rectangle?

Solution

Method 1 One way to answer the question is to draw the rectangle and shade 40%, or $\frac{4}{10}$, of it. Then, you can count the shaded squares to discover that 40% of 60 is 24.

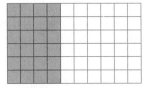

Method 2 Another way to answer the question is to rewrite **40%** as **0.4**, and multiply by 60.

$$0.4 \times 60 = 24$$

So, 40% of 60 is 24.

Example 3 Finding Percents of Numbers

Tech Link

Investigation 7,
Interactive
Real-Life
Investigations

In the 1992 election, about 104 million Americans voted. The total number of people who voted is called the *popular vote*. The percent of the popular vote received by the candidates is shown below. Create a circle graph showing the percent of votes each candidate received.

Candidate	Political party	Percent of popular vote
George Bush	Republican	37.4%
Bill Clinton	Democrat	43.0%
Ross Perot	Independent	18.9%
Other candidates	Independent	0.7%

Solution

First draw a circle. Next, draw a wedge that fills 18.9% of the circle. This will represent the popular vote for Ross Perot.

Since a circle graph is measured in degrees, each percent must be transferred into degree measures. There are 360° in the circle graph.

$$18.9\% \text{ of } 360° = 0.189 \cdot 360°$$

$$\approx 68°$$

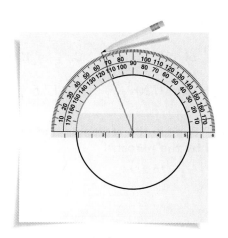

TOOLBOX

Circle Graphs, page 762

With a protractor measure the first slice of the graph. Color and label the slice. Continue this method until all candidates are represented.

$$43.0\% \text{ of } 360° = 0.430 \cdot 360°$$

$$\approx 155°$$

$$37.4\% \text{ of } 360° = 0.374 \cdot 360°$$

$$\approx 135°$$

$$0.7\% \text{ of } 360° = 0.007 \cdot 360°$$

$$\approx 2°$$

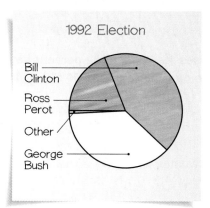

1992 Election

Bill Clinton
Ross Perot
Other
George Bush

ONGOING ASSESSMENT

Talk About It
....

1. In the 1992 presidential election, how many people voted for someone other than Bush, Clinton, or Perot? Explain.

GUIDED PRACTICE

1. Explain in your own words how to find the percent of a number.

2. Find 45% of 380.

3. **MENTAL MATH** Use mental math to evaluate the expression.

   a. 10% of 48   **b.** $33\frac{1}{3}$% of 96   **c.** 50% of 64   **d.** 200% of 23

PRACTICE AND PROBLEM SOLVING

 TECHNOLOGY In Exercises 4–11, write the percent as a decimal. Then multiply to find the percent of the number.

  4. 16% of 50   **5.** 80% of 285   **6.** 76% of 375   **7.** 340% of 5

  8. 120% of 35   **9.** 250% of 46   **10.** 0.8% of 500   **11.** 6.5% of 800

In Exercises 12–15, match the percent phrase with the fraction phrase. Then find the percent of the number.

  A. $\frac{1}{8}$ of 120   **B.** $\frac{1}{3}$ of 120   **C.** $\frac{3}{5}$ of 120   **D.** $\frac{1}{4}$ of 120

  12. 25% of 120   **13.** 60% of 120   **14.** 12.5% of 120   **15.** $33\frac{1}{3}$% of 120

MODELING In Exercises 16–18, copy the rectangle and shade the number of squares indicated by the percent.

  16. 25%   **17.** $33\frac{1}{3}$%   **18.** 45%

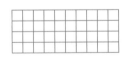

 TECHNOLOGY In Exercises 19–22, use the percent key on a calculator to find the percent of the number. Sample: 50 `%` `×` 62 `=`

  19. 96% of 25   **20.** 185% of 40

  21. 624% of 50   **22.** 1.5% of 800

23. **SHOPPING** You buy a sweater with a 35% discount. The original price of the sweater is $40.

  a. How much is the discount? That is, what is 35% of $40?

  b. How much do you have to pay for the sweater?

24.  TECHNOLOGY In a poll, high school seniors were asked how regularly they participate in sports, athletics, or exercise. Create a circle graph of these results.

Time spent exercising	Percent of high school seniors
Almost every day	45.0%
At least once a week	25.8%
Once or twice a month	12.8%
A few times a year	9.2%
Never	7.2%

WATER RESOURCES In Exercises 25–27, use the following information. Earth has about 326 million cubic miles of water. Of that, 3% is fresh water.

25. How many cubic miles of fresh water are on Earth?

26. How many cubic miles of salt water are on Earth?

27. A cubic mile of water contains about 9.5×10^{11} gal. How many gallons of fresh water are on Earth?

Real Life... Real Facts

Health

Studies show that if you exercise regularly, you will be more relaxed and be able to concentrate more easily.

STANDARDIZED TEST PRACTICE

28. In a survey of 2500 people, 750 said that they regularly drink orange juice at breakfast. What percent does this represent?

A 30%   **B** 33%   **C** 40%   **D** 45%

29. Which of the following is *not* equal to 6?

A 4% of 150   **B** $\frac{1}{2}$ of 12   **C** 75% of 8   **D** $\frac{1}{8}$ of 56

EXPLORATION AND EXTENSION

PORTFOLIO

30. BUILDING YOUR PROJECT To maintain a good aerobic workout, you need to keep your heart rate within a certain range for 15 min or more. This range varies with your age. Calculate your "target range" by substituting your age into the expressions:

Minimum heart rate per minute = $(220 - \text{your age}) \times 50\%$

Maximum heart rate per minute = $(220 - \text{your age}) \times 85\%$

Computer Banking

The interest paid in a savings account is a percent of the amount held in the account. You can use a spreadsheet or a graphing calculator to see how the account grows.

Example

You deposit $50 in a savings account that pays 6% annual interest. If you make no other deposits or withdrawals, how much will you have after one year? After six years?

Solution

Create a spreadsheet showing the balances in your untouched savings account during the first six years.

After entering column A and rows 1 and 2, you need to multiply your balance with the bank's interest rate in decimal form to find the interest you've earned. For instance, in cell B3, use this formula.

$$=0.06*C2$$

To find your new balance, add the amount the bank pays in interest to your previous balance. For instance, in cell C3, use this formula.

$$=C2+B3$$

You have $53.00 after one year and $70.93 after six years.

My Savings Account		
	A	**B**	**C**
1	Year	Interest	Balance
2	0	$0.00	$50.00
3	1	$3.00	$53.00
4	2	$3.18	$56.18
5	3	$3.37	$59.55
6	4	$3.57	$63.12
7	5	$3.79	$66.91
8	6	$4.01	$70.93

Exercises

1. You have deposited $120 in a bank that pays 7% annual interest. Create a spreadsheet showing your balances after 1, 2, 3, and 4 years.

In Exercises 2–5, use the following information to complete the table.

A formula for finding the balance A after n years is $A = P(1 + r)^n$ where P is the original deposit and r is the annual interest rate *in decimal form.*

	Deposit	Interest rate	Number of years	New balance
2.	$80.00	7%	8 years	?
3.	$500.00	6%	20 years	?
4.	$500.00	8%	10 years	?
5.	$1000.00	8%	5 years	?

Running on Empty?

READ About It

S ome people fear that the mighty Colorado River—the river that carved the Grand Canyon—is being drained dry.

Seven western states and Mexico have always depended on the river as a main water source. The Colorado River Compact assigns the states about 15 million acre-feet (abbreviated maf) each year. In addition, our treaty with Mexico guarantees them 1.5 maf of water. This was believed to overestimate the regions' demands. In reality, about $13\frac{1}{2}$ maf is pumped out of the river each year.

The map shows the approximate percentage of the total 16.5 maf that is assigned to each region and the amount each region uses.

If you spread out 15 maf of water so that it is only 1 ft deep, it would cover 15 million acres. (1 acre-foot is about 325,850 gal.)

WRITE About It

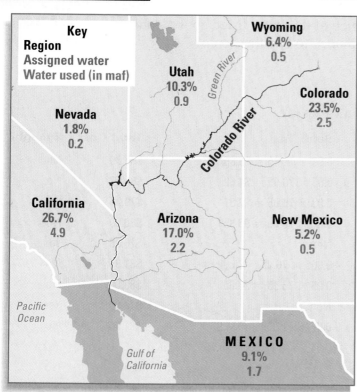

Key
Region
Assigned water
Water used (in maf)

Wyoming
6.4%
0.5

Utah
10.3%
0.9

Green River

Colorado
23.5%
2.5

Nevada
1.8%
0.2

Colorado River

California
26.7%
4.9

Arizona
17.0%
2.2

New Mexico
5.2%
0.5

Pacific Ocean

MEXICO
9.1%
1.7

Gulf of California

1. What fraction of the 16.5 maf of water assigned to the 8 regions is actually being pumped out of the Colorado River? What percent is this?

2. Order water assignment by region from least to most. Which region is assigned the least water? Which is assigned the most? Write your answers as sentences.

3. Make a table showing the amounts of water assigned to each region in both acre-feet and gallons. Does each region use all the water it is assigned? Explain.

4. Pick one region. What percent of its assigned water did this region actually use?

Problem Solving
with Percents

What you should learn:

Goal 1 How to use percents to solve real-life consumer problems

Goal 2 How to use percents to help organize data

Why you should learn it:

You can use percents to calculate the sales tax on a purchase.

Americans pay many types of taxes to federal, state, city, and local governments. These taxes are used to provide services, such as roads and health care.

Goal 1 USING PERCENTS IN REAL LIFE

Most states charge a sales tax when you purchase certain items. To find the sales tax you are being charged, change the percent to a decimal and multiply by the amount of the purchase.

Here are the sales tax rates for some western states.

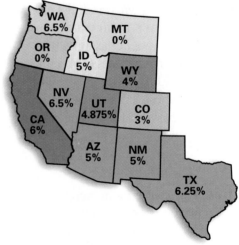

WA 6.5%	MT 0%
OR 0%	ID 5%
NV 6.5%	WY 4%
CA 6%	UT 4.875%	CO 3%
	AZ 5%	NM 5%
		TX 6.25%

Example 1 Finding Sales Tax Amounts

You have $80.75. The stereo you want to buy costs $76.95. In which of the states listed above would you have enough money to buy the stereo?

REAL LIFE
Retail

Solution

STRATEGY MAKE A LIST

State	Sales Tax	Total Cost	Enough?
Arizona	$0.05 \times 76.95 = \$3.85$	$80.80	No
California	$0.06 \times 76.95 = \$4.62$	$81.57	No
Colorado	$0.03 \times 76.95 = \$2.31$	$79.26	Yes
Idaho	$0.05 \times 76.95 = \$3.85$	$80.80	No
Montana	None	$76.95	Yes
Nevada	$0.065 \times 76.95 = \$5.00$	$81.95	No
New Mexico	$0.05 \times 76.95 = \$3.85$	$80.80	No
Oregon	None	$76.95	Yes
Texas	$0.0625 \times 76.95 = \$4.81$	$81.76	No
Utah	$0.04875 \times 76.95 = \$3.75$	$80.70	Yes
Washington	$0.065 \times 76.95 = \$5.00$	$81.95	No
Wyoming	$0.04 \times 76.95 = \$3.08$	$80.03	Yes

Goal 2 USING PERCENTS TO ORGANIZE DATA

Example 2 Organizing Data

REAL LIFE
Taking a Poll

You ask 250 people to read each common saying and state whether they believe it is true.

Saying	Number Answering True
a. Beauty is only skin deep.	205
b. Don't put all your eggs in one basket.	218
c. Look before you leap.	240
d. The early bird catches the worm.	188
e. The grass is always greener on the other side of the fence.	95
f. What's good for the goose is good for the gander.	143

To find the percent who answered true, divide the number who answered true by the total number surveyed.

a. $\frac{205}{250} = 0.82 = 82\%$ **b.** $\frac{218}{250} = 0.872 = 87.2\%$

c. $\frac{240}{250} = 0.96 = 96\%$ **d.** $\frac{188}{250} = 0.752 = 75.2\%$

e. $\frac{95}{250} = 0.38 = 38\%$ **f.** $\frac{143}{250} = 0.572 = 57.2\%$

You can organize the results in a bar graph like the one shown below.

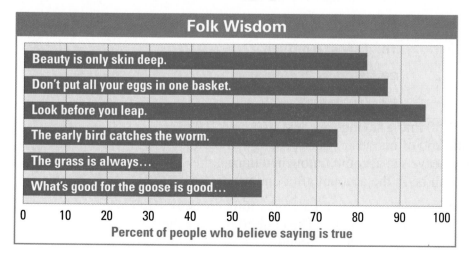

Folk Wisdom

Beauty is only skin deep.
Don't put all your eggs in one basket.
Look before you leap.
The early bird catches the worm.
The grass is always...
What's good for the goose is good...

0 10 20 30 40 50 60 70 80 90 100
Percent of people who believe saying is true

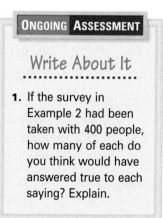

ONGOING ASSESSMENT

Write About It
. . . .

1. If the survey in Example 2 had been taken with 400 people, how many of each do you think would have answered true to each saying? Explain.

GUIDED PRACTICE

1. **SALES TAX** The sales tax on a $19.79 toaster is 5.75%. What is your total cost?

RESTAURANT BILL In Exercises 2 and 3, use the following information.

At a restaurant, the cost of the meal is $27.53. The sales tax is 5.75%.

2. What is your total cost, including the sales tax?

3. If you leave a 15% tip (of your total cost for the meal), how much do you leave for the tip?

4. **MOVIES** In a survey of 175 adults, 104 said they attend at least one movie per year. What percent does this represent?

PRACTICE AND PROBLEM SOLVING

SALES TAX In Exercises 5–8, the price of an item is given. Find the total cost of the item, including a 4% sales tax.

5. $4.65   6. $10.39   7. $50   8. $463.87

NATIONAL ORIGINS In 1990, the total population of the United States was 250 million people. In Exercises 9–22, find the percent of the population with the given ancestry. The top 14 groups are given below. (Source: Bureau of the Census)

9. German: 58 million
10. Irish: 39 million
11. English: 33 million
12. African-American: 24 million
13. Italian: 15 million
14. Mexican: 12 million
15. French: 10 million
16. Polish: 9 million
17. American Indian: 9 million
18. Dutch: 6 million
19. Scotch-Irish: 6 million
20. Scottish: 5 million
21. Swedish: 5 million
22. Norwegian: 4 million

23. **BANKING** You deposit $350 into a savings account that pays 5.75% in *simple interest*. (At the end of one year your account will earn 5.75% in interest.) If you leave the account untouched during the year, how much money will be in the account after one year?

24. **BUDGETING** A small town council must decrease operating costs by 17%. The present operating cost is $476,000. The council reduces the operating cost to $397,000. Is that enough? Explain.

PAYROLL TAXES In Exercises 25–30, use the following information.

Your gross pay for one week is $650. To find your take-home pay, subtract each of the following taxes from your gross pay: Federal income tax: 18.1%, state income tax: 2.8%, Social Security tax: 6.2%, local income tax: 1%, and Medicare tax: 1.5%.

25. What is your Federal income tax?

26. What is your state income tax?

27. What is your Social Security tax?

28. What is your local income tax?

29. What is your Medicare tax?

30. What is your take-home pay?

31. NEWSPAPER SUBSCRIBERS Your local newspaper has subscriptions for 31,500 morning papers, 10,800 evening papers, and 17,900 Sunday papers. If the total number of subscriptions increases to 72,000, how many would you expect to be for the morning paper? Did you use decimals, fractions, or percents to get your answer? Why?

STANDARDIZED TEST PRACTICE

In Exercises 32 and 33, use the following information. About 4886 million tons of coal are produced each year. The graph shows how much coal is produced by various regions. Each value listed is in millions of tons. (Source: Energy Information Administration)

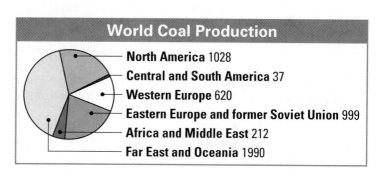

World Coal Production

- North America 1028
- Central and South America 37
- Western Europe 620
- Eastern Europe and former Soviet Union 999
- Africa and Middle East 212
- Far East and Oceania 1990

32. Which region produces about 12.5% of the world's coal?

(A) North America   (B) Africa and Middle East

(C) Western Europe   (D) Eastern Europe and former Soviet Union

33. What percent of the world's coal does North America produce?

(A) 12.5%   (B) 16%   (C) 21%   (D) 25%

EXPLORATION AND EXTENSION

34. COMMUNICATING ABOUT MATHEMATICS For more information about water resources see page 349. Lake Maryut in Egypt used to cover 66,000 acres (A), but it now covers only 16,000 A. What percent of the land once covered by Lake Maryut is now dry?

CHAPTER 7 *Summary*

WHAT *did you learn?*　　　　**WHY** *did you learn it?*

Skills

7.1 Add and subtract fractions with like denominators.

Compare real-life fractions such as running times.

7.2 Add and subtract fractions with unlike denominators.

Compare fractions in a circle graph.

7.3 Add and subtract fractions by writing decimals.

Interpret the results of a survey.

7.4 Multiply fractions.

Find areas of real-life objects such as for construction.

7.5 Divide fractions.

Find the number of horses that can graze in a pasture.

7.6 Write percents.

Find patterns in ancient writings.

7.7 Write percents in fraction and decimal form.

Recognize commonly used percents.

7.8 Find a percent of a number.

Display real-life data in a circle graph.

7.9 Use percents in real-life situations.

Compare the sales taxes in different states.

Strategies

7.1–7.9 Model operations with fractions, decimals, and percents.

Solve a variety of real-life problems.

Using Data

7.2, 7.3, 7.7, 7.8 Interpret and create circle graphs.

Organize and solve problems.

HOW *does it fit in the bigger picture of mathematics?*

Numbers can be written in several different ways. For instance, the number $\frac{1}{4}$ can be written as $\frac{2}{8}$, 0.25, $\frac{25}{100}$, or 25%. The *best* way to write a number depends on the way the number is being used.

Examples

a. If you are advertising a clothing sale, you would choose 25% as the best way to describe the discount.

b. When you calculate the discount on a purchase, it helps to use the decimal form, 0.25, or the fraction form, $\frac{1}{4}$.

VOCABULARY

- like fractions (p. 310)
- least common denominator (p. 316)
- portion (p. 336)
- percent (p. 336)

7.1 ADDING AND SUBTRACTING LIKE FRACTIONS

Examples $\dfrac{3}{4} + \dfrac{2}{4} = \dfrac{5}{4}$ $\dfrac{10}{9} - \dfrac{4}{9} = \dfrac{6}{9} = \dfrac{2}{3}$

Add or subtract the fractions.

1. $\dfrac{3}{6} + \dfrac{1}{6}$

2. $\dfrac{4}{8} + \dfrac{4}{8}$

3. $\dfrac{7}{9} + \dfrac{8}{9}$

4. $\dfrac{24}{25} - \dfrac{19}{25}$

5. $\dfrac{2w}{6} - \dfrac{w}{6}$

6. $\dfrac{12y}{7} - \dfrac{10y}{7}$

7. $1\dfrac{2}{3} - \dfrac{1}{3}$

8. $\dfrac{2}{5t} + \dfrac{3}{5t}$

7.2 ADDING AND SUBTRACTING UNLIKE FRACTIONS

Remember to first rewrite the fractions with a common denominator.

Examples $\dfrac{1}{8} + \dfrac{2}{3} = \dfrac{3}{24} + \dfrac{16}{24} = \dfrac{19}{24}$ $\dfrac{3}{4} - \dfrac{1}{3} = \dfrac{9}{12} - \dfrac{4}{12} = \dfrac{5}{12}$

Add or subtract the fractions.

9. $\dfrac{1}{6} + \dfrac{4}{9}$

10. $\dfrac{2}{8} + \dfrac{4}{5}$

11. $\dfrac{3}{2} + \dfrac{w}{3}$

12. $\dfrac{7}{8} - \dfrac{7}{9}$

13. $2\dfrac{1}{4} - 1\dfrac{1}{2}$

14. $\dfrac{4}{9} - \dfrac{2}{c}$

15. $\dfrac{a}{25} - \dfrac{a}{5}$

16. $\dfrac{m}{3} - \dfrac{m}{7}$

THE MAIL In Exercises 17 and 18, use the circle graph at the right, which shows the makeup of mail in the United States.
(Source: National Postal Museum)

17. Find the sum of the portions representing personal mail and other (newspapers, magazines, etc.).

18. Find the difference in the portions of mail that are advertising and bills.

What Makes Up Our Mail?

$\dfrac{16}{25}$ Advertising

$\dfrac{7}{100}$ Other (newspaper, magazines, etc.)

$\dfrac{11}{100}$ $\dfrac{9}{50}$

Bills

Personal mail

7.3 EXPLORING FRACTIONS AND DECIMALS

Write each fraction as a decimal. Then add or subtract the decimals.

Examples
$$\frac{4}{11} + \frac{3}{8} \approx 0.364 + 0.375$$
$$= 0.739$$
$$\approx 0.74$$

$$\frac{4x}{7} - \frac{x}{11} \approx 0.571x - 0.091x$$
$$= 0.480x$$
$$= 0.48x$$

Evaluate by first rewriting in decimal form. Round your result to two decimal places.

19. $\frac{63}{163} + \frac{32}{123}$

20. $\frac{12y}{17} + \frac{11y}{13}$

21. $\frac{12}{29} + \frac{29}{24}$

22. $\frac{45}{76} - \frac{51}{121}$

23. $\frac{187}{768} - \frac{5}{900}$

24. $\frac{k}{345} + \frac{78k}{957}$

7.4 MULTIPLICATION OF RATIONAL NUMBERS

Examples
$$\frac{3}{10} \cdot \frac{-4}{9} = \frac{-12}{90}$$
$$= -\frac{2}{15}$$

$$1\frac{2}{3} \cdot 2\frac{7}{8} = \frac{5}{3} \cdot \frac{23}{8}$$
$$= \frac{115}{24}$$

Multiply. Simplify, if possible.

25. $\frac{1}{9} \cdot \frac{3}{4}$

26. $2\frac{2}{5} \cdot 3\frac{1}{2}$

27. $\frac{11}{121} \cdot \frac{22}{33}$

28. $\frac{4x}{5} \cdot 10$

29. $\frac{2}{13} \cdot \frac{2}{3}$

30. $\frac{12h}{15} \cdot \frac{5}{3}$

7.5 DIVISION OF RATIONAL NUMBERS

Examples
$$\frac{6}{7} \div \frac{2}{7} = \frac{6}{7} \cdot \frac{7}{2}$$
$$= \frac{42}{14}$$
$$= 3$$

$$\frac{x}{5} \div 3 = \frac{x}{5} \cdot \frac{1}{3}$$
$$= \frac{x \cdot 1}{5 \cdot 3}$$
$$= \frac{x}{15}$$

Divide. Simplify, if possible.

31. $\frac{6}{7} \div \frac{1}{14}$

32. $\frac{5}{6} \div \frac{5}{3}$

33. $\frac{8}{9} \div \frac{2}{3}$

34. $4\frac{1}{2} \div 2\frac{1}{4}$

35. $\frac{6n}{5} \div \frac{2}{3}$

36. $2\frac{2}{5} \div \frac{5}{6}$

7.6 EXPLORING PERCENTS

To write a fraction as a percent, rewrite the percent as a fraction with a denominator of 100.

Example What percent of the figure is shaded green?

Solution $\frac{9}{20} = \frac{45}{100} = 45\%$

37. Write $\frac{7}{20}$ as a percent.

38. What percent of the figure is shaded red?

39. Write $\frac{6}{30}$ as a percent.

40. What percent of the figure is shaded gold?

7.7 PERCENTS, DECIMALS, AND FRACTIONS

Examples Write 17% as a decimal.   Write 64% as a fraction.

Solution $17\% = \frac{17}{100} = 0.17$ $64\% = \frac{64}{100} = \frac{16}{25}$

41. Write 6% as a decimal.

42. Write 25% as a fraction.

43. Rewrite $\frac{8}{9}$ as a percent.

44. Rewrite 0.231 as a percent.

7.8 FINDING A PERCENT OF A NUMBER

Examples 51% of 400 is   28% of 4925 is
           $0.51 \times 400 = 204$. $0.28 \times 4925 = 1379$.

45. Find 30% of 120.

46. Find $7\frac{3}{4}\%$ of 19,500.

47. Find $33\frac{1}{3}\%$ of 162.

48. Find 10% of 1500.

7.9 PROBLEM SOLVING WITH PERCENTS

49. You have $50.00 and want to buy a remote control truck for your brother that costs $47.50, plus sales tax. In which states would you have enough money to buy the truck?

Sales tax	
California: 6%	Ohio: 5%
Rhode Island: 7%	Texas: 6.25%
Utah: 4.875%	Wyoming: 4%

In Exercises 1–4, find the sum or difference and simplify.

1. $\dfrac{1}{5} + \dfrac{3}{5}$
   2. $\dfrac{11x}{12} - \dfrac{7x}{12}$
   3. $\dfrac{4}{5} + \dfrac{1}{10}$
   4. $\dfrac{11}{18} - \dfrac{2}{3}$

In Exercises 5–8, find the product or quotient and simplify.

5. $\dfrac{4}{5} \cdot \dfrac{1}{2}$
   6. $\dfrac{4}{5} \div \dfrac{1}{2}$
   7. $1\dfrac{1}{3} \cdot 1\dfrac{1}{2}$
   8. $\dfrac{5s}{6} \div \dfrac{3s}{5}$

9. AREA MODEL Find the total area of the figure below. Then find the percent of the area that is red, blue, and yellow.

10. BOOKS The graph shows types of books sold each week. If the bookstore sold 2546 books in a week, how many would you expect to be fiction?

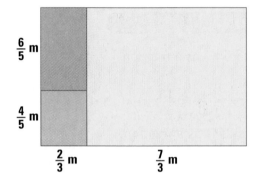

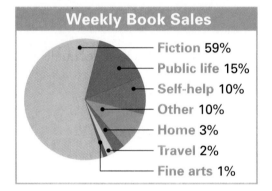

11. Write $\dfrac{10}{25}$ as a percent.

12. Write 0.365 as a percent.

13. Write 24.5% as a decimal.

14. Write 32% as a fraction and simplify.

CLOTHING In Exercises 15 and 16, use the following information.

A clearance rack has 65 shirts. Of these, 18 are T-shirts. Of the 18 T-shirts, 5 are blue and 8 are white.

15. What percent of the total number of shirts are T-shirts?

16. What percent of the total number of T-shirts are blue?

SURVEY In Exercises 17 and 18, use the following information. (Source: Impact Resources, Inc.)

A survey was taken to determine the amount of TV that American adults watch in a day.

17. Organize these results in a circle graph.

18. Of 415 American adults, how many would you expect to watch TV for 1 h or less each day?

Time spent each day	Percent of adults
1 h or less	18.4%
between 1 and 5 h	68.8%
between 5 and 10 h	10.2%
between 10 and 15 h	1.9%
over 15 h	0.7%

1. What is the perimeter of the figure shown below?

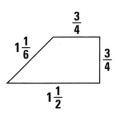

   (A) $2\frac{1}{6}$ **(B)** $2\frac{1}{2}$

   (C) $3\frac{2}{3}$ **(D)** $4\frac{1}{6}$

2. Which statement about the circle graph is false?

   (A) The value of x is 0.35.

   (B) The sum of all shaded regions is 0.65.

   (C) If 100 people were surveyed, 7 people would represent the white region.

   (D) The value of x is $\frac{7}{20}$.

3. The area of the rectangle is $\frac{1}{2}$. What is its length?

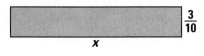

   (A) $\frac{3}{20}$ **(B)** $\frac{3}{5}$

   (C) $1\frac{2}{3}$ **(D)** $6\frac{2}{3}$

4. What is the solution of the equation

$$y + \frac{3}{5} = \frac{-12}{5}?$$

   (A) $y = -15$ **(B)** $y = -3$

   (C) $y = -\frac{9}{5}$ **(D)** $y = 3$

5. What percent of the figure is shaded?

   (A) 35%   **(B)** 55%

   (C) 60%   **(D)** 90%

For Questions 6 and 7, use the circle graph, which shows the results of a survey that asked 50 people to name their favorite type of vacation.

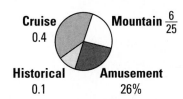

6. Which statement is false?

   (A) 24% chose mountain.

   (B) 10 people chose historical.

   (C) 50% chose cruise or historical.

   (D) 13 people chose amusement.

7. Forty percent of the people surveyed chose a cruise as their favorite. How many people is this?

   (A) 8   **(B)** 20

   (C) 40   **(D)** 125

Proportion, Percent, and Probability

TECHNOLOGY

• **Interactive Real-Life Investigations**
• **Middle School Tutorial Software**

To find out more about theater, go to:

http://www.mlmath.com

ALL THE WORLD'S A STAGE These students are rehearsing for a production of *Romeo and Juliet.*

CHAPTER THEME
Theater

PORTFOLIO

Staging a Talent Show

PROJECT DESCRIPTION

Many people can act, sing, dance, or play a musical instrument. Sometimes schools or clubs host talent shows where people can let others enjoy their accomplishments. You will plan a talent show and keep a scrapbook about the event.

GETTING STARTED

Talking It Over

- What would you do if your school were having a talent show?

- Would you perform, or would you rather work on costumes or scenery?

- What things do you think would need to be done to make a successful talent show?

Planning Your Project

- **Materials:** paper, pencils or pens, colored pencils or markers

- Make a booklet out of several sheets of paper. It will be your scrapbook.

- As you complete the **BUILDING YOUR PROJECT** exercises throughout the chapter, you will add the results to your scrapbook.

BUILDING YOUR PROJECT

These are places throughout the chapter where you will work on your project.

Exploring Rates and **Ratios**

What you should learn:

Goal 1 How to find rates

Goal 2 How to find ratios

Why you should learn it:

You can use rates and ratios to solve real-life problems, such as finding unit prices.

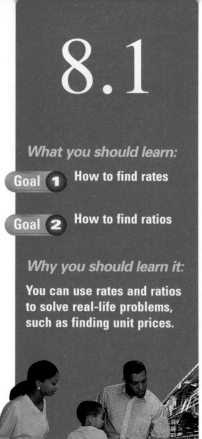

Goal 1 FINDING RATES

If two quantities *a* and *b* have different units of measure, then the **rate** of *a per b* is $\frac{a}{b}$. Here are two examples.

Quantity *a*	Quantity *b*	Rate
$21.00	3 hours	$\frac{21 \text{ dollars}}{3 \text{ hours}} = 7$ dollars per hour
240 miles	12 gallons	$\frac{240 \text{ miles}}{12 \text{ gallons}} = 20$ miles per gallon

Example 1 Finding a Rate

You drove 200 mi in 4 h. What was your average speed?

REAL LIFE
Average Speed

Solution

To find the rate, divide the distance by the time.

$$\text{Rate} = \frac{\text{Distance}}{\text{Time}} \qquad \textbf{Verbal model}$$

$$\text{Rate} = \frac{200 \text{ mi}}{4 \text{ h}} \qquad \textbf{Substitute for distance and time.}$$

$$= 50 \text{ mi/h} \qquad \textbf{Simplify.}$$

Your rate (or average speed) was 50 mi/h.

Example 2 Finding a Rate

A 16 oz box of breakfast cereal costs $2.89, and a 20 oz box costs $3.49. Which is the better buy?

REAL LIFE
Unit Price

Solution

Price	Weight	Unit Price
$2.89	16 ounces	$\frac{\$2.89}{16 \text{ ounces}} \approx 0.181$ dollars per ounce
$3.49	20 ounces	$\frac{\$3.49}{20 \text{ ounces}} \approx 0.175$ dollars per ounce

Because the larger box has the smaller unit price, it follows that it is the better buy.

If two quantities *a* and *b* have the same units of measure, then the
ratio of *a* to *b* is $\frac{a}{b}$.

Example 3 **Finding a Ratio**

To build the 8 ft robot mantis shown below, the model makers studied
a real praying mantis that was 4 in. long. What is the ratio of the
robot mantis's length to the real mantis's length?

The Creative
Presentations company
built several huge insect
robots for a traveling
museum show called
"Backyard Monsters."

Solution

To find a ratio, both quantities must have the same units of measure.
In inches, the length of the robot mantis is

$$8 \text{ ft} = 8 \text{ ft} \cdot \frac{12 \text{ in.}}{1 \text{ ft}} = 96 \text{ in.}$$

Now, find the ratio of the robot length to the real mantis length.

$$\text{Ratio} = \frac{\text{Robot length}}{\text{Mantis length}}$$

$$= \frac{96 \text{ in.}}{4 \text{ in.}} \quad \text{Both quantities have the same units.}$$

$$= \frac{24}{1}$$

The ratio of the robot mantis's length to the real mantis's length
is 24 to 1. In other words, the robot is 24 times as long as the
real mantis.

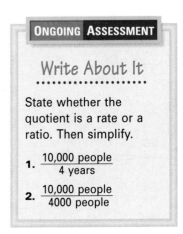

ONGOING ASSESSMENT

Write About It

State whether the
quotient is a rate or a
ratio. Then simplify.

1. $\frac{10{,}000 \text{ people}}{4 \text{ years}}$

2. $\frac{10{,}000 \text{ people}}{4000 \text{ people}}$

GUIDED PRACTICE

1. Explain the difference between a rate and a ratio. Give examples.

In Exercises 2–5, state whether the quotient is a *rate* or a *ratio*. Then simplify.

2. $\dfrac{100 \text{ mi}}{4 \text{ h}}$

3. $\dfrac{10 \text{ in.}}{4 \text{ in.}}$

4. $\dfrac{8 \text{ balloons}}{24 \text{ balloons}}$

5. $\dfrac{\$27.99}{3 \text{ lb}}$

6. You work for 12 h and get paid $60. What is your rate of pay? Include units of measure in your answer.

7. Describe six ratios that compare the colors of the nine triangles below.

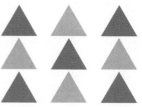

8. Which of the following measures the rate at which an automobile uses gasoline?

   A. Miles per hour

   B. Gallons per mile

   C. Miles per gallon

PRACTICE AND PROBLEM SOLVING

In Exercises 9–12, determine whether the quotient is a *rate* or a *ratio*. Then simplify.

9. $\dfrac{16 \text{ students}}{18 \text{ students}}$

10. $\dfrac{120 \text{ m}}{15 \text{ s}}$

11. $\dfrac{88 \text{ points}}{4 \text{ games}}$

12. $\dfrac{3 \text{ cars}}{5 \text{ cars}}$

In Exercises 13–16, write the verbal phrase as a *rate* or a *ratio*. Explain why the phrase is a rate or a ratio.

13. Recommended by 4 out of 5 doctors

14. Approved by 9 out of 10 inspectors

15. Traveled 1600 mi in 3 days

16. Answered 40 questions in 60 min

In Exercises 17–24, write each quotient as a ratio and simplify.

17. $\dfrac{2 \text{ ft}}{18 \text{ in.}}$

18. $\dfrac{2640 \text{ ft}}{1 \text{ mi}}$

19. $\dfrac{2 \text{ min}}{300 \text{ s}}$

20. $\dfrac{1 \text{ h}}{3600 \text{ s}}$

21. $\dfrac{640¢}{\$4}$

22. $\dfrac{2 \text{ gal}}{10 \text{ qt}}$

23. $\dfrac{200 \text{ cm}}{3 \text{ m}}$

24. $\dfrac{2 \text{ L}}{50 \text{ mL}}$

25. **CONCERT TICKETS** A concert sold out in 6 hours. Nine thousand tickets were sold for the concert. At what rate did the tickets sell?

26. **RECORD SNOWFALL** The record for snowfall in 24 h is 78 in. at Mile 47 Camp, Cooper River Division, Alaska, on February 7, 1963. At what rate did snow fall on that day?

UNIT PRICING In Exercises 27–30, decide which is the better buy. Explain your reasoning.

27. 6 apples for $1.18 or 10 apples for $1.79

28. a 12 oz box for $2.69 or an 18 oz box for $3.99

29. 2 lb, 4 oz for $7.89 or 5 lb, 2 oz for $18.89

30. six 12 oz cans for $2.69 or one half-gal bottle for $4.59

31. **BALLOONING** It took 86 h for Joe Kittinger to cross the Atlantic in his balloon, *Rosie O'Grady*. What was the average speed of the balloon if he traveled 3543 mi?

32. **MODEL RAILROAD** On an N-gauge model train set, a tank car is 3.75 in. long. An actual tank car is 50 ft long. What is the ratio of the length of the actual car to the length of the model car?

GEOMETRY In Exercises 33–36, find the ratio of the green region's perimeter to the yellow region's perimeter. Then find the ratio of the green region's area to the yellow region's area. Which ratio is greater?

Real Life... Real People

Across the Sea
Joe Kittinger was the first man to complete a solo transatlantic crossing by balloon. In September, 1984, he flew from Caribou, Maine, to Montenotte, Italy.

33. **34.** 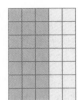 **35.** 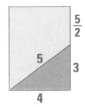 **36.**

STANDARDIZED TEST PRACTICE

37. Your soccer team finishes the regular season with a record of 20 wins and 8 losses. What is the ratio of wins to losses?

　(A) 2 to 5　　**(B)** 5 to 2　　**(C)** 5 to 7　　**(D)** 2 to 7

EXPLORATION AND EXTENSION

PORTFOLIO

38. **BUILDING YOUR PROJECT** For a musical number in the talent show, everyone will wear matching hats. A formal wear shop will rent you a hat for $5.50 for two days. A costume supplier will rent you a hat for $10.50 for five days. What is the price per day at each supplier? Which would you choose?

The Golden Ratio

Materials Needed
- paper
- compass
- pencil or pen
- ruler
- scissors

Part **A** APPROACHING THE GOLDEN RATIO

How would you describe the rectangles below? You might describe the left one as square-like. A more precise way to describe a rectangle's shape is to find the ratio of its length to its width.

$\dfrac{\text{Length}}{\text{Width}} = \dfrac{6}{5} = 1.2$ $\dfrac{\text{Length}}{\text{Width}} = \dfrac{8}{5} = 1.6$ $\dfrac{\text{Length}}{\text{Width}} = \dfrac{8}{3} \approx 2.667$

From these examples, you can see that the closer a rectangle is to being a square, the closer its length-to-width ratio is to 1.

In Exercises 1–4, use the following rectangles.

    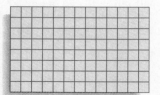

1. Find the length-to-width ratio of each rectangle.

2. Describe the pattern of the lengths and widths. Predict the lengths and widths of the next three rectangles in the pattern.

3. Use the results of Exercises 1 and 2 to complete the table.

Length	2	3	5	8	13	?	?	?
Width	1	2	3	5	8	?	?	?
Ratio	?	?	?	?	?	?	?	?

4. The *golden ratio* is the number $\dfrac{\sqrt{5}+1}{2}$. Use a calculator to round this number to three decimal places. How does the result relate to the table in Exercise 3?

The steps below show how to construct a *golden rectangle*, which is a rectangle whose length and width are in the golden ratio.

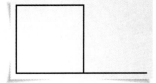

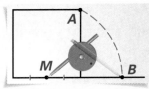

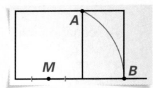

1 Draw a square and extend one side.

2 Place a compass at the midpoint of the side. Draw an arc from *A* to *B* as shown.

3 Point *B* is one corner of a golden rectangle.

5. Construct a golden rectangle. Measure its length and width to see how close your rectangle is to a golden rectangle.

6. Make a copy of your rectangle. Tear the original square from the copy, as shown below. Measure the length and width of the rectangle that remains. What can you conclude?

Large Rectangle   **Small Rectangle**

Fold and tear a square.

To answer Exercises 7–10, use this information: *When two fractions are equal, the products shown are called cross products.*

$$\frac{a}{b} = \frac{c}{d}$$

$$bc \qquad ad$$
cross products

NOW TRY THESE

In Exercises 7–9, find the cross products.

7. $\frac{2}{3} = \frac{4}{6}$ **8.** $\frac{5}{2} = \frac{20}{8}$ **9.** $\frac{6}{21} = \frac{2}{7}$

10. Write a conjecture about cross products.

11. For the two rectangles you made, write this equation. Is the equation true?

$$\frac{\text{large rectangle length}}{\text{large rectangle width}} = \frac{\text{small rectangle length}}{\text{small rectangle width}}$$

8.2

Solving Proportions

What you should learn:

Goal 1 How to solve proportions

Goal 2 How to write proportions for similar triangles

Why you should learn it:

You can use proportions to solve problems about rates, such as speeds in a canoe race.

Goal 1 SOLVING PROPORTIONS

An equation that equates two ratios is a **proportion**.

$$\frac{a}{b} = \frac{c}{d}$$

"*a* is to *b* as *c* is to *d*."

If you know three parts of a proportion, you can find the unknown part.

Example 1 Solving a Proportion

Solve the proportion: $\frac{x}{2} = \frac{3}{4}$.

Solution

$$\frac{x}{2} = \frac{3}{4} \qquad \text{Write original proportion.}$$

$$2 \cdot \frac{x}{2} = 2 \cdot \frac{3}{4} \qquad \text{Multiply each side by 2.}$$

$$x = \frac{6}{4} \qquad \text{Simplify.}$$

$$x = \frac{3}{2} \qquad \text{Solution: } x \text{ is by itself.}$$

The solution is $x = \frac{3}{2}$. Check this in the original proportion.

Example 2 Solving a Proportion

Solve the proportion: $\frac{3}{m} = \frac{5}{8}$.

Solution

To solve this proportion, you can use the *Cross Product Property*.

$$\frac{3}{m} = \frac{5}{8} \qquad \text{Write original proportion.}$$

$$3 \cdot 8 = m \cdot 5 \qquad \text{Use Cross Product Property.}$$

$$\frac{3 \cdot 8}{5} = \frac{m \cdot 5}{5} \qquad \text{Divide each side by 5.}$$

$$\frac{24}{5} = m \qquad \text{Solution: } m \text{ is by itself.}$$

The solution is $m = \frac{24}{5}$. Check this in the original proportion.

NEED TO KNOW

Cross Product Property
The cross products of a proportion are equal.

If $\frac{a}{b} = \frac{c}{d}$, then $ad = bc$.

Two triangles are **similar** if they have the same angle measures. **Similar triangles** have the same shape, but not necessarily the same size. The following triangles are similar because each has a **30° angle**, a **60° angle**, and a **90° angle**.

When two angles have the same measure, they are marked with the same symbol.

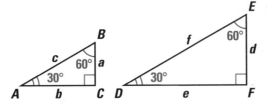

The **single** and **double** angle arcs identify corresponding angles.

If two triangles are similar, then the ratios of **corresponding sides** are equal. For the similar triangles above, you can write

$$\frac{a}{d} = \frac{b}{e} = \frac{c}{f}.$$

Example 3 **Writing a Proportion**

The triangles below are similar. Find the value of a.

CONNECTION
Geometry

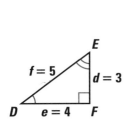 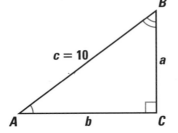

Solution

Begin by writing a proportion that involves a. Then solve the proportion.

$\dfrac{a}{d} = \dfrac{c}{f}$ **Ratios of corresponding sides are equal.**

$\dfrac{a}{3} = \dfrac{10}{5}$ **Substitute for c, d, and f.**

$3 \cdot \dfrac{a}{3} = 3 \cdot \dfrac{10}{5}$ **Multiply each side by 3.**

$a = 6$ **Solution: a is by itself.**

Note that each side of $\triangle ABC$ is twice as long as the corresponding side of $\triangle DEF$.

ONGOING ASSESSMENT

Write About It
....

Write a proportion for each statement. Solve the proportion. Did you use the Cross Product Property or another property? Why?

1. x is to 5 as 3 is to 30.

2. 4 is to n as 2 is to 15.

3. 5 is to 3 as m is to 5.

4. 4 is to 7 as 6 is to y.

8.2 Exercises

Extra Practice, page 728

GUIDED PRACTICE

1. A person paid $2000 in property tax on an $80,000 house. In the same neighborhood, another person paid $3000 tax on a $100,000 house. Is that fair? Explain how a proportion could be used to answer the question.

2. Proportions are often used to measure fairness or equity in real life. Exercise 1 gives one example. Describe some others.

In Exercises 3–6, solve the proportion. Explain how you can check your answers.

3. $\dfrac{b}{3} = \dfrac{4}{12}$ 　　　　**4.** $\dfrac{9}{x} = \dfrac{3}{5}$ 　　　　**5.** $\dfrac{2}{3} = \dfrac{m}{36}$ 　　　　**6.** $\dfrac{7}{18} = \dfrac{21}{y}$

In Exercises 7 and 8, state whether the triangles are similar. If they are, write three of the proportions that compare their sides.

7.

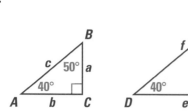

8.

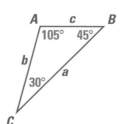

PRACTICE AND PROBLEM SOLVING

In Exercises 9–12, decide whether the proportion is true. Explain.

9. $\dfrac{1}{4} \stackrel{?}{=} \dfrac{3}{12}$ 　　**10.** $\dfrac{6}{16} \stackrel{?}{=} \dfrac{3}{7}$ 　　**11.** $\dfrac{4}{9} \stackrel{?}{=} \dfrac{16}{36}$ 　　**12.** $\dfrac{9}{7} \stackrel{?}{=} \dfrac{18}{15}$

In Exercises 13–20, solve the proportion. Check your solution.

13. $\dfrac{x}{3} = \dfrac{4}{9}$ 　　**14.** $\dfrac{y}{5} = \dfrac{8}{5}$ 　　**15.** $\dfrac{5}{7} = \dfrac{z}{2}$ 　　**16.** $\dfrac{5}{12} = \dfrac{t}{2}$

17. $\dfrac{8}{m} = \dfrac{2}{5}$ 　　**18.** $\dfrac{9}{x} = \dfrac{15}{2}$ 　　**19.** $\dfrac{2}{3} = \dfrac{12}{b}$ 　　**20.** $\dfrac{2.8}{y} = \dfrac{11}{2.5}$

In Exercises 21–26, write the sentence as a proportion. Then solve.

21. x is to 6 as 8 is to 9. 　　**22.** y is to 5 as 6 is to 17. 　　**23.** 3 is to 8 as m is to 24.

24. 2 is to 5 as 10 is to n. 　　**25.** 5 is to 6 as 12 is to s. 　　**26.** 2 is to t as 4 is to 13.

TECHNOLOGY **In Exercises 27–30, use a calculator to solve the proportion. Round your result to two decimal places.**

27. $\dfrac{14}{15} = \dfrac{x}{25}$ 　　**28.** $\dfrac{y}{32} = \dfrac{16}{27}$ 　　**29.** $\dfrac{p}{21} = \dfrac{8}{42}$ 　　**30.** $\dfrac{14}{15} = \dfrac{x}{36}$

31. CANOE RACING Two canoes competed in a 20 mi race. Canoe 1 traveled at a rate of 4 mi every 25 min. Canoe 2 traveled at a rate of 3 mi every 20 min.

   a. How many minutes did it take each canoe to complete the race? How many hours?

   b. How fast (in miles per hour) were the canoes traveling?

   c. Which canoe won the race?

GEOMETRY In Exercises 32–35, pairs of similar triangles are shown. Find the missing lengths of the sides.

32.

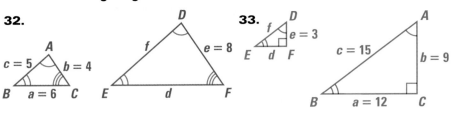

33.

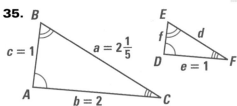

34.

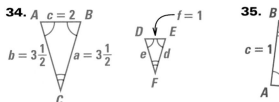

35.

36. YOGURT SALES You work for a frozen yogurt shop. You sell yogurt cones at an average rate of 170 every 3 h. The shop is open for 12 h. About how many will be sold in a day?

STANDARDIZED TEST PRACTICE

37. You can type at a rate of 26 words per minute. How long will it take you to type a report containing 1040 words?

   A 30 min   **B** 40 min   **C** 45 min   **D** 27,040 min

EXPLORATION AND EXTENSION

PORTFOLIO

38. BUILDING YOUR PROJECT For your talent show, you need a ramp from the stage to a platform 36 in. high. You have a ramp that is 56 in. long and 24 in. high. How many inches must you add to the length so that the ramp rises 36 in.?

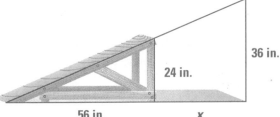

Problem Solving Using Proportions

What you should learn:

Goal **1** How to use proportions to solve real-life problems

Goal **2** How to use similar triangles to measure objects indirectly

Why you should learn it:

You can use proportions to solve real-life problems, such as finding dimensions from a scale model.

Goal **1** SOLVING REAL-LIFE PROBLEMS

Proportions are used in architecture and manufacturing to construct scale models. For instance, if you are drawing house plans that have a 1 ft-to-$\frac{1}{8}$ in. scale, then the ratio of the actual house dimensions to the dimensions on the plans is

$$\frac{1 \text{ ft}}{\frac{1}{8} \text{ in.}} = \frac{12 \text{ in.}}{\frac{1}{8} \text{ in.}} \qquad \text{Rewrite 1 ft as 12 in.}$$

$$= \frac{12 \cdot 8}{\frac{1}{8} \cdot 8} \qquad \text{Multiply numerator and denominator by 8.}$$

$$= \frac{96}{1} \qquad \text{Simplify.}$$

$$= 96. \qquad \text{Simplify.}$$

Each dimension of the actual house is 96 times as large as the corresponding dimension in the house plans.

Example 1 Finding Dimensions

You have a scale model of a Boeing 767. The model was built using a 1-to-250 scale. The wing span on the model is $7\frac{1}{2}$ in. What is the wing span of an actual 767?

REAL LIFE
Aircraft

Solution

Verbal Model	$\dfrac{\text{Model wing span}}{\text{767 wing span}} = \dfrac{1}{250}$	
Labels	Model wing span = 7.5	(inches)
	767 wing span = x	(inches)

Algebraic Model	$\dfrac{7.5}{x} = \dfrac{1}{250}$	Write a proportion.
	$7.5 \cdot 250 = x \cdot 1$	Use Cross Product Property.
	$1875 = x$	Solution: x is by itself.

The wing span of a 767 is 1875 in. To convert this measurement to feet, divide by 12 to obtain a wing span of about 156 ft.

In Lesson 8.2, you learned that the ratios of corresponding sides of similar triangles are equal. This property of similar triangles can be used to find the height of a building that cannot be measured directly.

For instance, in the drawing, the ratio of the building's height to the flagpole's height is equal to the ratio of the building's shadow to the flagpole's shadow.

$$\frac{H}{h} = \frac{D}{d}$$

Knowing the flagpole's height and the lengths of the shadows allows you to find the building's height.

Not drawn to scale

R**eal Life...** R**eal Facts**

Transco Tower
The 64-story Transco Tower, designed by Philip Johnson, has a Water Wall fountain at its base.

Example 2 **Finding the Height of a Building**

REAL LIFE
Architecture

To estimate the height of the Transco Tower in Houston, Texas, you measure its shadow to be about 55 m. The shadow of a 50 m flagpole is about 10 m. Estimate the height of the Transco Tower.

Solution

Verbal Model	$\dfrac{\textbf{Transco Tower height}}{\textbf{Flagpole height}} = \dfrac{\textbf{Transco Tower shadow}}{\textbf{Flagpole shadow}}$

Labels
Transco Tower height $= H$ (meters)
Flagpole height $= h = 50$ (meters)
Transco Tower shadow $= D = 55$ (meters)
Flagpole shadow $= d = 10$ (meters)

Algebraic Model

$$\frac{H}{h} = \frac{D}{d}$$ Write a proportion.

$$\frac{H}{50} = \frac{55}{10}$$ Substitute for *h*, *D*, and *d*.

$$H \cdot 10 = 50 \cdot 55$$ Use Cross Product Property.

$$H = 275$$ Solution: *H* is by itself.

The Transco Tower is about 275 m high.

ONGOING **ASSESSMENT**

Talk About It
. . . .

1. At noon you start working for your uncle. At 1:00 P.M., your brother starts working at the same job. At 3:00 P.M., you both finish. Your uncle pays you $16 and pays your brother $12. Is that fair? Use a proportion to decide.

GUIDED PRACTICE

In Exercises 1–4, use the following information.

A flagpole is casting a 15 ft shadow. You are 5 ft tall and cast a 3 ft shadow. What is the height of the flagpole?

1. Sketch a diagram of the given information.

2. Which of the following verbal models is correct?

A. $\dfrac{\text{Flagpole height}}{\text{Your height}} = \dfrac{\text{Your shadow}}{\text{Flagpole shadow}}$

B. $\dfrac{\text{Flagpole height}}{\text{Your height}} = \dfrac{\text{Flagpole shadow}}{\text{Your shadow}}$

3. Write an algebraic model for the problem. Let h represent the height of the flagpole.

4. Solve the algebraic model to find the height of the flagpole.

PRACTICE AND PROBLEM SOLVING

HEARTBEAT RATES   In Exercises 5–7, use the following information.

A typical heartbeat rate (or pulse) is 72 beats per minute. When you exercise, this rate increases.

5. Assume you have the typical heartbeat rate. If you take your pulse for 10 s, how many beats would you feel?

6. After jogging one-half hour, you take your pulse for 6 s. You feel 11 beats. What is your heartbeat rate in beats per minute?

7. After jumping rope for 15 min, you take your pulse for 15 s. You feel 40 beats. What is your heartbeat rate in beats per minute?

ESTIMATION   In Exercises 8 and 9, use the following information.

In 1995, about 317,600 Americans per month became teenagers.

8. About how many Americans became teenagers each day?

9. About how many Americans became teenagers in 1995?

10. ESTIMATION If you sleep 220,000 h by age 70, about how many hours will you have slept by age 30?

11. ESTIMATION If you pay $1500 in property tax for a $90,000 house, about how much would you pay for a $110,000 house?

Real Life...
Real Facts

Jumping rope is an aerobic exercise that burns calories at the same rate as jogging 5.5 mi/h.

MICROSCOPES **In Exercises 12–14, use the following information.**

An amoeba, a one-celled organism, has been magnified 100 times by a microscope and photographed. In the photo, the amoeba is 25 mm wide. What is the actual width of the amoeba?

12. Which of the following verbal models is correct?

A. $\dfrac{\text{Photo amoeba width}}{\text{Actual amoeba width}} = \dfrac{100}{1}$

B. $\dfrac{\text{Photo amoeba width}}{1\ \text{mm}} = \dfrac{\text{Actual amoeba width}}{100\ \text{mm}}$

13. Assign labels to the verbal model and write an algebraic model.

14. Solve the algebraic model to find the width of the amoeba.

15. **COMPUTERS** Computer screen displays are made of square pixels. One typical computer screen is 624 pixels high and 832 pixels wide. Another computer screen is 768 pixels high. How wide must it be to have the same proportions as the smaller screen?

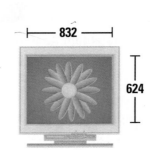

 STANDARDIZED TEST PRACTICE

16. An architectural design of a building has a 1 ft-to-$\frac{1}{4}$ in. scale.

In the design the building has a height of 16 in. How tall is the actual building?

(A) 16 ft   **(B)** 64 ft   **(C)** 192 ft   **(D)** 768 ft

 EXPLORATION AND EXTENSION

PORTFOLIO

17. **BUILDING YOUR PROJECT** The set designer for your talent show gives you a scale drawing of a room for a skit. How long does the designer want the back wall to be? How big is the sofa?

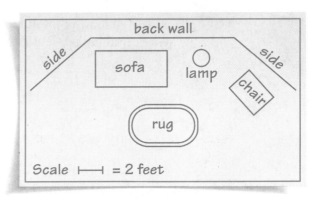

8.3 *Problem Solving Using Proportions*   **375**

What you should learn:

Goal 1 How to find what percent one number is of another

Goal 2 How to solve a percent equation

Why you should learn it:

You can use percents to describe real-life situations, such as finding the percent of field goals made out of all the attempts.

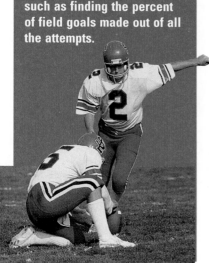

Solving Percent Equations

Goal 1 FINDING PERCENTS

In Chapter 7, you learned that percents can be written in different forms. For instance, 25% can be written as

$$25\%, \frac{25}{100}, 0.25, \text{ or } 25 \text{ percent.}$$

The most common use of percents is to compare one quantity to another. For instance, because 3 is one fourth of 12, and one fourth is 25%, you can say that 3 is 25% of 12.

THE PERCENT EQUATION

The statement "*a* is *p* percent of *b*" is equivalent to the equation

$$\frac{a}{b} = \frac{p}{100}. \qquad \textit{Percent equation}$$

In this equation, *b* is the **base** and *a* is the number that is compared to the base.

Example 1 Finding Percents

a. You got 17 points on a 20-point quiz. You can find the percent *p* that you got correct as follows.

$$\frac{17}{20} = \frac{p}{100} \qquad \textbf{Write percent equation.}$$

$$0.85 = \frac{p}{100} \qquad \textbf{Divide to obtain decimal form.}$$

$$85 = p \qquad \textbf{Solution: } p \text{ is by itself.}$$

You got 85% correct. One way to describe this is to say that *17 is 85% of 20.*

b. On a 50-point quiz, you got 48 points plus 5 bonus points. You can find the percent *p* that you got correct as follows.

$$\frac{53}{50} = \frac{p}{100} \qquad \textbf{Write percent equation.}$$

$$1.06 = \frac{p}{100} \qquad \textbf{Divide to obtain decimal form.}$$

$$106 = p \qquad \textbf{Solution: } p \text{ is by itself.}$$

You got 106% correct. One way to describe this is to say that *53 is 106% of 50.*

Example 2 **Problem Solving with Percents**

In a survey of 250 people, 82% said they prefer blue jeans to any other color of jeans. How many preferred blue jeans?

Solution

Let a represent the number who preferred blue jeans.

$$\frac{a}{250} = \frac{82}{100}$$ **Write percent equation.**

$$250 \cdot \frac{a}{250} = 250 \cdot \frac{82}{100}$$ **Multiply each side by 250.**

$$a = \frac{20,500}{100}$$ **Multiply.**

$$a = 205$$ **Solution: a is by itself.**

So, 205 people said they prefer blue jeans.

Example 3 **Problem Solving with Percents**

You paid $26.49, which is 75% of the full price, for a sweater. What is the full price?

Solution

Let b represent the full price.

$$\frac{26.49}{b} = \frac{75}{100}$$ **Write percent equation.**

$$26.49 \cdot 100 = b \cdot 75$$ **Use Cross Product Property.**

$$\frac{26.49 \cdot 100}{75} = \frac{b \cdot 75}{75}$$ **Divide each side by 75.**

$$35.32 = b$$ **Solution: b is by itself.**

The full price of the sweater is $35.32.

Summary of the Three Basic Types of Percent Problems

What is p percent of b?	a is p percent of what?	a is what percent of b?
$\dfrac{a}{b} = \dfrac{p}{100}$	$\dfrac{a}{b} = \dfrac{p}{100}$	$\dfrac{a}{b} = \dfrac{p}{100}$
Solve for a.	Solve for b.	Solve for p.

TOOLBOX

Solving Proportions, page 752

ONGOING ASSESSMENT

Talk About It
· · · · · · · · · · · · · · · · · · ·

1. A friend of yours works in a clothing store. She tells you that a quick way to find p% of b is to change p% to decimal form and multiply by b. Is she correct?

GUIDED PRACTICE

In Exercises 1 and 2, describe the strategy that was used to solve the problem.

1. Problem: What is 65% of 160?

   Solution: $\dfrac{a}{160} = \dfrac{65}{100}$

   $\dfrac{a}{160} = 0.65$

   $a = 104$

2. Problem: 50 is what percent of 40?

   Solution: $\dfrac{50}{40} = \dfrac{p}{100}$

   $1.25 = \dfrac{p}{100}$

   $125 = p$

In Exercises 3–5, identify the base. Then write and solve the percent equation.

3. 20 is what percent of 25?   **4.** What is 16% of 50?   **5.** 90 is 75% of what?

6. Is fifteen 250% of six? Explain your reasoning.

PRACTICE AND PROBLEM SOLVING

In Exercises 7–9, solve the percent equation.

7. $\dfrac{13}{25} = \dfrac{p}{100}$ **8.** $\dfrac{a}{20} = \dfrac{85}{100}$ **9.** $\dfrac{3}{b} = \dfrac{60}{100}$

In Exercises 10–19, solve the percent equation. Round your answer to two decimal places if necessary.

10. 22 is what percent of 30?   **11.** What is 33 percent of 165?

12. What is 2% of 360?   **13.** 66 is 120 percent of what number?

14. 34 is 50% of what number?   **15.** 45 is what percent of 20?

16. What is 110 percent of 110?   **17.** 6.06 is 20.2% of what number?

18. 71.5 is what percent of 90?   **19.** What is 25.5% of 270?

MENTAL MATH   In Exercises 20–23, use mental math to solve the equation.

20. 100 is 200 percent of what number?   **21.** What is 50% of 200?

22. 100 is 100% of what number?   **23.** 5 is what percent of 15?

ERROR ANALYSIS   In Exercises 24 and 25, find and correct the error.

24. Problem: 45 is what percent of 150?

   Equation: $\dfrac{150}{45} = \dfrac{p}{100}$

25. Problem: What is 24 percent of 50?

   Equation: $\dfrac{24}{50} = \dfrac{p}{100}$

26. TEST SCORES On a 35-question exam, you needed to get 90% of the questions correct to earn an A. You answered 31 questions correctly. Did you earn an A? Explain.

27. SALES TAX You buy a new home video game. You pay $54.99 for the game plus $2.75 in sales tax. What is the sales tax percent?

28. FIELD GOALS During the regular season, a field goal kicker made 75% of the field goals he attempted. He made 24 field goals. How many did he attempt?

ENTERTAINMENT **In Exercises 29 and 30, use the following information.**

When the Grammy Awards began in 1958, there were 28 categories in which to win an award. In 1993, there were 81 categories.

(Source: National Academy of Recording Arts and Sciences)

29. The number of awards given in 1958 is what percent of the number of awards given in 1993?

30. The number of awards given in 1993 is what percent of the number of awards given in 1958?

STANDARDIZED TEST PRACTICE

31. What percent of the figure at the right is shaded?

    A 16%   **B** 25%   **C** 50%   **D** 64%

32. The unshaded area is what percent of the shaded area in the figure at the right?

    A 3%   **B** 33.$\overline{3}$%   **C** 300%   **D** 400%

EXPLORATION AND EXTENSION

PORTFOLIO

33. BUILDING YOUR PROJECT There are 350 seats in the auditorium. You will sell many tickets in advance, but you want to be sure to save about 5% of the seats for people who want to buy tickets at the door. How many advance tickets can you sell?

In Exercises 1–9, solve the equation. Check your solution. (4.2, 4.4, 4.5)

1. $4(x + 2) = 12$

2. $3y = 4y - 7$

3. $a + \dfrac{5}{3} = 2a - \dfrac{1}{3}$

4. $\dfrac{1}{12}p - \dfrac{1}{12} = \dfrac{5}{12}$

5. $5 + 2(q - 3) = 0$

6. $0.2s - 5.4 = 0$

7. $1 = \dfrac{1}{2}(p - 1)$

8. $\dfrac{1}{4}x + \dfrac{1}{4}x = 3$

9. $\dfrac{1}{3}p - 2 = 2$

In Exercises 10–13, write the percent in decimal form. (7.6–7.8)

10. 52%

11. 83%

12. 146%

13. 206%

In Exercises 14–17, determine whether the quotient is a *rate* or a *ratio*. Then simplify. (8.1)

14. $\dfrac{16 \text{ yards}}{2 \text{ jumps}}$

15. $\dfrac{28 \text{ points}}{4 \text{ quarters}}$

16. $\dfrac{2 \text{ animals}}{20 \text{ animals}}$

17. $\dfrac{4 \text{ ft}}{10 \text{ s}}$

18. At a restaurant, 2 loaves of bread that are the same size are placed on your table. You eat 1 slice of the loaf of bread that is cut into 6 equal pieces. Your cousin eats 2 slices of the loaf of bread that is cut into 9 equal pieces. Who ate more bread? How much more? **(6.6, 7.2)**

Theater Arts Connection

RAKED STAGES

Many theaters use a *raked* (slanted) stage to make the action easier to see.

Sometimes raked platforms are built on stages with flat floors. You can use proportions and similar triangles to construct them.

The supports for the raked platform make a right angle with the stage, as shown in the diagram below. $\triangle ABC$ is similar to $\triangle ADE$.

[Diagram: B, 12 in., C, 48 in., E, x, D, 96 in., A]

1. Suppose $AC = 144$ in., $BC = 12$ in., and $AE = 96$ in. Use a proportion to find DE.

2. What is the ratio of AC to AE? of BC to DE? of AB to AD?

Take this test as you would take a test in class. The answers to the exercises are given in the back of the book.

In Exercises 1–4, determine whether the quotient is a *rate* or a *ratio*. Then simplify. **(8.1)**

1. $\dfrac{100 \text{ m}}{18 \text{ s}}$ **2.** $\dfrac{18 \text{ lures}}{6 \text{ fishermen}}$ **3.** $\dfrac{42 \text{ lb}}{3 \text{ lb}}$ **4.** $\dfrac{5 \text{ days}}{1 \text{ week}}$

In Exercises 5 and 6, state whether the triangles are similar. If they are, write three of the proportions that compare their sides. **(8.2)**

5.

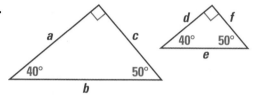 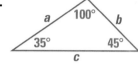

6.

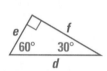

In Exercises 7–9, decide whether the proportion is true. Explain. **(8.2)**

7. $\dfrac{2}{11} \overset{?}{=} \dfrac{10}{55}$ **8.** $\dfrac{250}{350} \overset{?}{=} \dfrac{2}{3}$ **9.** $\dfrac{5}{7} \overset{?}{=} \dfrac{25}{35}$

In Exercises 10–13, solve the proportion. Check your solution. **(8.2)**

10. $\dfrac{x}{4} = \dfrac{8}{2}$ **11.** $\dfrac{3}{7} = \dfrac{a}{9}$ **12.** $\dfrac{18}{b} = \dfrac{25}{36}$ **13.** $\dfrac{y}{3} = \dfrac{10}{2}$

In Exercises 14–16, solve the percent equation. **(8.4)**

14. What is 35% of 18?   **15.** 18 is 150% of what?   **16.** 36 is what percent of 150?

17. You are visiting the Gateway Arch in St. Louis, Missouri, the tallest monument in the United States. To find out how tall the monument is, you measure the length of the shadow as 60 ft. At the same time, your own shadow is $\frac{1}{2}$ ft long. If you are $5\frac{1}{4}$ ft tall, how tall is the Gateway Arch? **(8.3)**

Tech Link

Investigation 8, Interactive Real-Life Investigations

In Exercises 18 and 19, △*ABC* is similar to △*DEF*. The lengths of the sides of △*ABC* are $a = 8$, $b = 10$, and $c = 12$. The shortest side of △*DEF* is $d = 9$. **(8.2)**

18. In △*DEF*, find the length of the longest side.

19. In △*DEF*, find the length of the third side.

Problem Solving Using Percents

Goal 1 USING A PROBLEM SOLVING PLAN

In this lesson, you will see how to use the problem solving plan (page 67) to solve real-life percent problems.

Example 1 Using a Problem Solving Plan

In a survey, parents of elementary school children were asked how many hours per week they spent helping their children with homework. Suppose 88 parents said they spent 1 to 4 h.

a. How many parents were surveyed?

b. How many said "none"?

c. How many said "5 hours or more"?

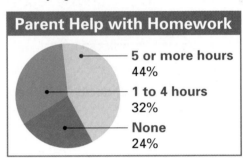

Parent Help with Homework

- 5 or more hours 44%
- 1 to 4 hours 32%
- None 24%

(Source: 20/20 Research)

Solution

a.

| Verbal Model | $\dfrac{\text{Number spending 1–4 h}}{\text{Number surveyed}} = \dfrac{\text{Percent}}{100}$ |

Labels
Number spending 1–4 h $= 88$ (people)
Number surveyed $= b$ (people)
Percent $= 32$ (percent)

Algebraic Model

$\dfrac{88}{b} = \dfrac{32}{100}$ Write percent equation.

$88 \cdot 100 = b \cdot 32$ Use Cross Product Property.

$\dfrac{88 \cdot 100}{32} = b$ Divide each side by 32.

$275 = b$ Solution: b is by itself.

So, 275 parents were surveyed.

b. To find the number who said "none," find 24% of 275.
$24\% \cdot 275 = 0.24 \cdot 275 = 66$

So, 66 parents said "none."

c. To find the number who said "5 hours or more," find 44% of 275.
$44\% \cdot 275 = 0.44 \cdot 275 = 121$

So, 121 parents said "5 hours or more."

When an item is "on sale," the difference between the regular price and the sale price is called the **discount** .

$$\text{Discount} = \text{Regular Price} - \text{Sale Price}$$

To find the **discount percent** , use the regular price as the base. For instance, if a $36 book is on sale for $27, then the discount is $9, and the discount percent is

$$\frac{\text{Discount}}{\text{Regular Price}} = \frac{9}{36}$$ **Divide discount by regular price.**

$$= 0.25$$ **Rewrite in decimal form.**

$$= 25\%.$$ **Rewrite in percent form.**

PRICES SLASHED 45% OFF

Example 2 **Finding a Discount Percent**

REAL LIFE
Shopping

Last week you bought a sweatshirt on sale for $16.80. This week you visit the store again and find that the sweatshirt is back at the regular price of $22.68.

a. A friend claims that you got a 35% discount because 22.68 − 16.80 = 5.88 and $5.88 is 35% of $16.80. Is your friend correct?

b. If not, what is the discount percent?

Solution

a. Your friend is using the sale price as the base.

$$\frac{5.88}{16.80} = 0.35 = 35\%$$

This is not correct. The regular price should be the base.

b. The discount is

$$22.68 - 16.80 = \$5.88.$$ **Subtract sale price from regular price.**

Now, use the formula for the discount percent.

$$\frac{5.88}{22.68} \approx 0.259$$ **Divide discount by regular price.**

$$= 25.9\%$$ **Write in percent form.**

The discount percent is about 25.9%.

GUIDED PRACTICE

1. **DISCOUNT** You pay $38.15 for a pair of tennis shoes. The discount was $16.35.

   a. What was the original price?

   b. Based on the original price, what is the discount percent?

2. **DISCOUNT** You are shopping for basketball shoes and see the sign at the right. Explain how you could find the original price.

PRACTICE AND PROBLEM SOLVING

MUSIC **In Exercises 3 and 4, use the following.**

You take a survey in your classroom about favorite types of music. The circle graph shows the percent of students in each type. Nine students said that country was their favorite.

3. How many students were surveyed?

4. How many students said

   a. pop?   **b.** rhythm and blues?   **c.** easy listening?

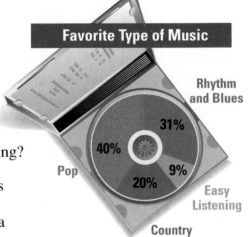

Favorite Type of Music

Rhythm and Blues 31%
Pop 40%
Country 20%
Easy Listening 9%

5. **SPANISH** In a recent year, about 410,000 Americans took a course in Spanish. This represented 41% of those who took a language course. How many took a language course? (Source: Modern Language Association)

6. **FRENCH** In the same year, 27.4% of the Americans who took a language course took a course in French. Use the result of Exercise 5 to find the number of Americans who took a course in French.

7. **BANKING** You deposit $470 into a savings account. At the end of one year, your account will earn interest at the rate of 3.5%. A shortcut for finding your new balance is

$$\text{Balance} = 470(1.035)$$

Use the Distributive Property to explain this shortcut.

8. **BANKING** In Exercise 7, suppose that you leave the money in the account for two years. You make no additional deposits or withdrawals. What is your balance at the end of two years?

RADIOS In Exercises 9–12, use the following information.

The table shows the numbers, in millions, of radios in specific locations in American households.

Location	Radios (millions)
Bedrooms	172.3
Living rooms	63.3
Kitchens	46.2
Bathrooms	14.7
Dining Rooms	13.3
Other	33.2

9. How many radios do Americans own?

10. Find the percent of radios in bedrooms.

11. Find the percent of radios in living rooms.

12. Find the percent of radios in kitchens.

13. DISCOUNT You buy a pair of in-line skates. The sign at the sporting goods store stated that the price of in-line skates had been discounted 25%. The discount was $21.40. What was the regular price of the in-line skates?

PAY PHONES In Exercises 14–16, use the following.

The circle graph shows the categories and the amounts of money that make up the yearly income for the average pay phone. Coin revenue makes up 35% of the yearly income. (Source: *USA Today*)

14. What is the yearly income for the average pay phone?

15. Describe another way to find the yearly income.

16. Find the percent of yearly income of

    a. calling and credit cards.   **b.** collect calls.   **c.** third-party calls.

Yearly Income for the Average Pay Phone

Calling cards, credit cards $1170

Coin revenue $1050

Collect calls $488

Third-party calls $292

STANDARDIZED TEST PRACTICE

17. The shaded region has an area of 50 cm². What is the area of the entire region?

    Ⓐ $16\frac{2}{3}$ cm²   Ⓑ $37\frac{1}{2}$ cm²   Ⓒ $66\frac{2}{3}$ cm²   Ⓓ 150 cm²

EXPLORATION AND EXTENSION

PORTFOLIO

18. BUILDING YOUR PROJECT You will sell advance tickets to your talent show for $3.50 each. Tickets at the door will cost $5.00 each. Design an advertising flier that mentions the discount percent for people who buy tickets in advance.

Exploring Percent of Increase or Decrease

What you should learn:

Goal 1 How to find a percent of increase

Goal 2 How to find a percent of decrease

Why you should learn it:

You can use percents to show how quantities, such as the number of computers in public schools, increase or decrease over time.

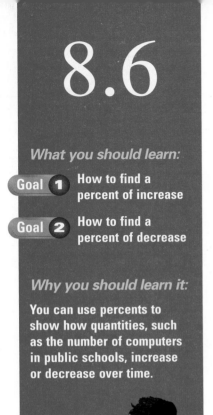

Goal 1 FINDING A PERCENT OF INCREASE

A **percent of increase** or **percent of decrease** tells how much a quantity has changed. For instance, the enrollments at Roosevelt Middle School for 1997 and 1998 are shown below.

1997 Enrollment: 400

1998 Enrollment: 420

From 1997 to 1998, the enrollment *increased* by 20 students. The percent of increase is

$$\text{Percent of increase} = \frac{20}{400} = 0.05 = 5\%.$$

PERCENT OF INCREASE OR DECREASE

The percent of change of a quantity is given by

$$\frac{\text{Actual change}}{\text{Original amount}}$$

This percent is a **percent of increase** if the quantity increased and it is a **percent of decrease** if the quantity decreased.

Example 1 Finding a Percent of Increase

REAL LIFE
Technology

There were 2.2 million computers used in public schools in 1991 and 2 million in 1990. Find the percent of increase. (Source: Market Data Retrieval)

Solution

The actual increase was 0.2 million computers. To find the percent of increase, find the ratio of 0.2 million (the increase) to 2 million.

$$\frac{\text{Number in 1991} - \text{Number in 1990}}{\text{Number in 1990}} = \frac{2.2 \text{ million} - 2 \text{ million}}{2 \text{ million}}$$

$$= \frac{0.2 \text{ million}}{2 \text{ million}}$$

$$= 0.1$$

$$= 10\%$$

The percent of increase is 10%.

Example 2 Finding a Percent of Decrease

REAL LIFE
Communication

The bar graph shows the average cost per minute of a "coast-to-coast" long distance call from 1985 through 1997. (Source: Federal Communications Commission)

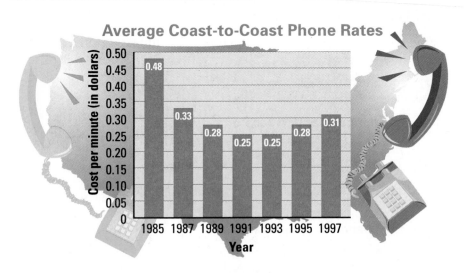

a. Find the decrease from 1985 to 1987.

b. Find the percent of decrease from 1985 to 1987.

c. During which other periods did the cost decrease?

Solution

a. From 1985 to 1987, the change was

$$1985 \text{ Cost} - 1987 \text{ Cost} = \$.48 - \$.33$$
$$= \$.15.$$

The cost decreased by $.15 per minute.

b. The percent of decrease from 1985 to 1987 was

$$\frac{\text{Decrease from } 1985 \text{ to } 1987}{1985 \text{ Cost}} = \frac{\$.15}{\$.48}$$
$$= 0.3125$$
$$= 31.25\%.$$

c. From the bar graph, you can see that the cost also decreased from 1987 to 1989 and from 1989 to 1991.

ONGOING ASSESSMENT

Write About It
••••••••••••••••••••

Use the data about long-distance costs. Find the decrease (or increase) and percent of decrease (or increase) from

1. 1989 to 1991.

2. 1993 to 1995.

3. What do you notice?

GUIDED PRACTICE

LONG DISTANCE RATES In Exercises 1 and 2, use the long-distance telephone call bar graph on page 387.

1. Find the percent of decrease in the cost per minute from 1985 to 1995.

2. Find the percent of increase in the cost per minute from 1995 to 1997.

In Exercises 3 and 4, state whether the quantities represent a percent of increase or a percent of decrease. Then find the percent.

3. Yesterday: $16.35   Today: $18.21   **4.** May: 1056 units   June: 972 units

PRACTICE AND PROBLEM SOLVING

In Exercises 5–10, decide whether the change is an _increase_ or a _decrease_ and find the percent.

5. Before: 10, After: 12   **6.** Before: 15, After: 12   **7.** Before: 75, After: 60

8. Before: 110, After: 143   **9.** Before: 90, After: 200   **10.** Before: 260, After: 160

In Exercises 11–14, decide whether the change is an _increase_ or a _decrease_ and find the percent.

11. 1994 Expenses: $171.33
1995 Expenses: $201.59

12. Regular Price: $31.99
Sale Price: $22.39

13. Beginning Balance: $521.43
End Balance: $413.68

14. Opening Price: $18.77
Closing Price: $19.17

LOOKING FOR A PATTERN In Exercises 15–18, use percents to describe the sequence's pattern. Then list the next three terms.

15. 1, 2, 4, 8, ? , ? , ?   **16.** 4096, 1024, 256, 64, ? , ? , ?

17. 15625, 3125, 625, 125, ? , ? , ?   **18.** 1, 3, 9, 27, ? , ? , ?

In Exercises 19 and 20, describe a real-life situation that involves the given increase or decrease.

19. An increase of 15%   **20.** A decrease of 30%

21. Copy and complete the table.

Original Number	New Number	Percent Change
45	72	?
45	18	?
400	?	25% increase
400	?	25% decrease

22. PROFITS The graph at the right shows the net profits (in millions of dollars) of *Reebok* from 1990 to 1996. Approximate the percent of change of net profit for each year.

Reebok's Net Profit

Net profit (in millions of dollars)

177, 235, 232, 231, 255, 210, 139
1990 1991 1992 1993 1994 1995 1996

(Source: Reebok International, Ltd.)

REASONING In Exercises 23–26, decide whether the statement is *true* or *false*. **Explain.**

23. Two times a number is a 100% increase of the number.

24. Half a number is a 50% decrease of the number.

25. A 20% decrease of 80 is 60.

26. A 25% increase of 100 is 125.

27. MANUFACTURING During August, a small company produced 32,562 units. During September, the company produced 28,894 units. Find the percent of decrease from August to September.

In Exercises 28–30, use the following information.

You are considering two job offers, each with a starting salary of $24,000. Job 1 will give you a 4% raise every year. Job 2 will give you a $1000 raise every year.

28. PROPORTIONAL RELATIONSHIP Calculate the salary for Job 1 for each of the five years following the first year.

29. NONPROPORTIONAL RELATIONSHIP Calculate the percent of increase in salary for Job 2 for each of the five years following the first year. What do you notice?

30. Suppose other aspects of the jobs are equal. Which job should you take: Job 1 or Job 2?

STANDARDIZED TEST PRACTICE

31. You receive 10 shares of stock valued at $12 per share. After one year, the stock price increases to $15 per share. What is the percent of increase in the share price of the stock?

A 3%   **B** 15%   **C** 20%   **D** 25%

32. In 1990, the population of Bridgeton was 12,000. In 2000, the town's projected population is 10,800. By what percent is Bridgeton's population expected to decrease?

A 10%   **B** 11.1%   **C** 12%   **D** 15%

33. BUILDING YOUR PROJECT Ticket prices both last year and this year were $3.50 in advance and $5.00 at the door. Last year you sold 220 tickets in advance and 30 tickets at the door. This year you sold 180 tickets in advance and 70 tickets at the door.

a. What was the percent of increase or decrease in attendance?

b. What was the percent of increase or decrease in revenue?

SPIRAL REVIEW

In Exercises 1–4, use the spinner at the right. All the divisions are the same size. (5.8)

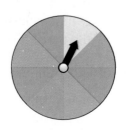

1. Find the probability that the spinner will stop on red.

2. Find the probability that the spinner will stop on blue.

3. Find the probability that the spinner will stop on green.

4. Find the probability that the spinner will stop on yellow.

In Exercises 5–8, evaluate the expression when $a = -8$ and $b = 2$. (3.1)

5. $|ab|$ **6.** $|a^2|$ **7.** $|a| - |b|$ **8.** $|a - b|$

9. On a number line, plot the integers 4, -3, -2, and 0. (3.1)

10. Order the numbers $\frac{1}{2}, \frac{1}{3}, \frac{5}{8}, \frac{3}{7}$, and $\frac{4}{9}$ from least to greatest. (6.5, 7.7)

11. What is the average of -1.02, -0.98, -1.01, -1, and -1.04? (3.6)

In Exercises 12–15, simplify the expression, if possible. Then evaluate the expression when $x = 5$ and $y = -4$. (3.3)

12. $3x + 2y + x$ **13.** $4x - 5y$ **14.** $xy - 2y$ **15.** $10x + 20y + 2x$

In Exercises 16–19, solve the percent problem. (8.4)

16. What is 35% of 80? **17.** 32 is 45% of what number?

18. 190 is what percent of 310? **19.** What is 116% of 92?

20. IN-LINE SKATES You want to buy a pair of in-line skates priced at $89.99. The sales tax is 7%. How much is the sales tax? What is the total price of the in-line skates? (7.9)

Pascal's Triangle

The pattern below is called Pascal's Triangle. It is named after the French mathematician Blaise Pascal (1623–1662).

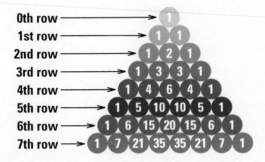

0th row ——→ 1
1st row ——→ 1 1
2nd row ——→ 1 2 1
3rd row ——→ 1 3 3 1
4th row ——→ 1 4 6 4 1
5th row ——→ 1 5 10 10 5 1
6th row ——→ 1 6 15 20 15 6 1
7th row ——→ 1 7 21 35 35 21 7 1

There are many patterns in this triangle. For instance, the first and last numbers in each row are 1. Also, every other number is the sum of the two numbers that lie directly above it. For instance, 7 is the sum of 1 and 6. You can use this pattern to write the 8th row.

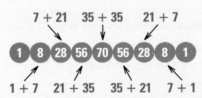

7 + 21   35 + 35   21 + 7

1 8 28 56 70 56 28 8 1

1 + 7   21 + 35   35 + 21   7 + 1

NOW TRY THESE

1. Write the 9th row of Pascal's Triangle.

2. Write the 10th row of Pascal's Triangle.

3. Find the sum of the numbers in each of rows 0 through 7. Then copy and complete the table.

Row	0	1	2	3	4	5	6	7
Sum	?	?	?	?	?	?	?	?

4. Describe the pattern in the table. Use the pattern to predict the sum of the 8th row. Then find the sum to confirm your prediction.

The Counting Principle

What you should learn:

Goal 1 How to use the Counting Principle

Goal 2 How to use Pascal's Triangle to count the number of ways an event can happen

Why you should learn it:

You can use the Counting Principle to solve real-life problems, such as finding the number of different ways of ordering items from a menu.

Goal 1 USING THE COUNTING PRINCIPLE

The math club in your school has 5 officers: 3 boys and 2 girls. You are forming a committee of two officers to visit the math club at another school. You want the committee to have a boy and a girl. How many different committees are possible?

One way to decide is to use a tree diagram.

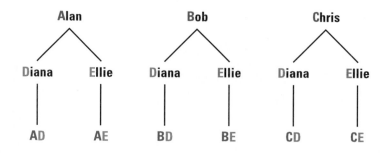

From the tree diagram, you can see that there are 6 possible committees. This is an example of the **Counting Principle**.

THE COUNTING PRINCIPLE

If one event can occur in m ways and another event can occur in n ways, then the two events can occur in mn ways.

Example 1 Using the Counting Principle

a. Use the Counting Principle to find the number of different committees in the problem above.

b. Suppose there are 4 math teachers in your school and each committee will have a math teacher, a boy, and a girl. How many committees are now possible?

TOOLBOX

Counting Methods, page 759

Solution

a. You can choose a boy in **3** ways and a girl in **2** ways.
Number of possible committees = $3 \cdot 2 = 6$

b. You can choose a math teacher in **4** ways.
Number of possible committees = $4 \cdot 3 \cdot 2 = 24$

Example 2 > Forming a Committee

After finding the number of ways that a boy and a girl can be chosen to form the committee, someone in the math club objects. The person thinks that any two of the officers should be able to be on the committee—even if the two are both boys or both girls. How many ways can you choose 2 committee members out of the 5 officers?

Solution

STRATEGY > MAKE A LIST

AB	AC	AD	AE
	BC	BD	BE
		CD	CE
			DE

There are 10 possible committees.

Another way to find the number of committees in Example 2 is to use Pascal's Triangle. (It is shown on page 391.) If you have *m* people to choose from, use the *m*th row. If you are choosing *n* people for the committee, use the $(n + 1)$st number in the row.

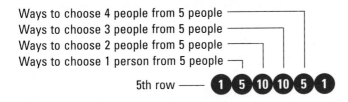

Ways to choose 4 people from 5 people
Ways to choose 3 people from 5 people
Ways to choose 2 people from 5 people
Ways to choose 1 person from 5 people
5th row ——— 1 5 10 10 5 1

Example 3 > Using Pascal's Triangle

How many 3-member committees can you choose from 8 people?

Solution

You are choosing from among 8 people. So, write the 8th row of Pascal's Triangle.

1 8 28 56 70 56 28 8 1

You are choosing 3 people, so use the 4th number in the row, which is 56. There are 56 possible committees.

ONGOING ASSESSMENT

Talk About It
. . . .

How many 2-member committees can you choose from a group of 6 people? Find the answer with each of the following. Then talk about which method you prefer.

1. Use a tree diagram or list to find all the committees.

2. Use Pascal's Triangle.

GUIDED PRACTICE

1. You have 2 pairs of jeans and 4 T-shirts. Use the Counting Principle to determine how many different outfits you can wear by choosing a pair of jeans and a T-shirt.

2. You are writing a three-digit number. The first digit must be 1 or 7, the second digit must be 3, 6, or 9, and the number must be divisible by 5. Use a tree diagram to find how many numbers are possible.

3. Your school requires that you read 3 books during the year. You can choose among 3 mystery books, 4 autobiographies, and 6 historical fiction books. How many ways can you choose one of each type of book?

4. The diagram at the right shows how many ways you can choose 2 sweaters from a group of 7 sweaters. Explain how to use Pascal's Triangle to find how many ways you can choose 2 sweaters from 7 sweaters.

PRACTICE AND PROBLEM SOLVING

5. **MENU PLANNING** The menu at the right shows the choices of side dishes that come with each dinner. You are to choose a dish from each column. Use the Counting Principle to find how many different choices you have. Then confirm your answer by listing the different choices.

6. **SHOPPING** You are buying a sweatshirt. You have a choice of a pullover, button-down, or hooded sweatshirt. Each style comes in red, white, blue, gray, green, or purple.

   a. How many different sweatshirts can you choose from?

   b. Verify your answer with a tree diagram.

7. **TRUE-FALSE TESTS** You are taking a test with 8 questions. Each question must be answered true or false. Which of the following represents the number of ways you can answer the 8 questions? Explain.

   A. $2 \cdot 2 \cdot 2 \cdot 2 \cdot 2 \cdot 2 \cdot 2 \cdot 2 = 2^8$ **B.** $2 + 2 + 2 + 2 + 2 + 2 + 2 + 2 = 8(2)$

8. **DESIGNING A WARDROBE** For your summer wardrobe, you have 3 pairs of shoes, 6 pairs of shorts, and 10 shirts. How many different outfits can you wear?

In Exercises 9–12, use the rows from Pascal's Triangle shown below to find the number of ways to choose the following.

9. Choose 3 books from 7 books.

10. Choose 4 pencils from 8 pencils.

11. Choose 5 CDs from 6 CDs.

12. Choose 3 photos from 9 photos.

STANDARDIZED TEST PRACTICE

13. The city of Greenville is forming a planning committee to organize a parade. There are 4 people in the mayor's office, 12 in the police department, 11 in the fire department, and 25 in the veterans' association. Suppose the committee must have one person from each group. Which expression can you use to determine how many different committees are possible?

Ⓐ $4 + 12 + 11 + 25$

Ⓑ $4 \cdot 12 + 11 \cdot 25$

Ⓒ $4 \cdot 12 \cdot 11 \cdot 25$

Ⓓ $(4 + 12 + 11 + 25) \div 4$

EXPLORATION AND EXTENSION

PORTFOLIO

14. **BUILDING YOUR PROJECT** There are ten groups competing in the talent show. Three of the groups will receive prizes.

a. How many ways could you choose 3 winning groups from 10 if their order does not matter?

b. Suppose there is a first, a second, and a third prize, so the order in which you choose the winning groups matters. How many ways can you choose 3 groups to win these prizes?

Beetle Mania

READ About It

A Berkeley physiologist, Rodger Kram, read that the 0.1 oz rhinoceros beetle could support 850 times its own body weight. He decided to check it out.

Kram bought lead weights at a hobby shop. In his lab, he fastened them to the beetles with a bit of Velcro. Although the beetles didn't live up to their reputation, they did manage some amazing feats.

The most Kram could get a beetle to lift was 10 oz. With this amount, however, the beetle could not move.

With trial and error, Kram found that the beetle could carry 30 times its body weight without stress for half an hour.

During this time, the beetle's oxygen consumption only increased by a factor of 4. With humans, the oxygen consumption increase is proportional to the ratio of the lifted weight to body weight.

WRITE About It

1. Write and solve the proportion to find how much weight the beetle carried on its back for half an hour. Write your proportion as a sentence.

2. If a rhinoceros beetle could really support 850 times its own body weight, how much should it have been able to lift? What percent of this weight could the beetle actually lift? Explain.

3. In proportion to a rhinoceros beetle, what is the maximum weight a 150 lb person could lift? Explain.

4. In proportion to a rhinoceros beetle, how much should a 150 lb person be able to carry without stress for half an hour? Explain.

Modeling Probability with a Computer

Because of their speed, computers are often used to model situations where many random numbers must be selected. A program that mimics a real-life experiment is called a *simulation*.

Example

You are making a long-distance telephone call to a friend. You remember the first part of your friend's number, but you forget the last two digits. If you randomly chose the digits, what is the probability that the number is correct? (The actual last two digits are 55.)

Solution

One way to answer this question is to use a computer simulation, as shown below. Each time the program is run, it selects 1000 random 2-digit numbers. The program then counts the number of times the number 55 was chosen. To test the simulation, we ran the program 100 times. The results are shown in the line plot. The exercises ask you to analyze these results.

COMPUTER TIP

In line 30 of the program below, the "RND" is a variable random number that changes for each of the 1000 trials.

```
BASIC PROGRAM
10 RANDOMIZE
20 FOR I = 1 TO 1000
30 N = FIX(100*RND)
40 IF N = 55 THEN C = C + 1
50 NEXT
60 PRINT "55 WAS CHOSEN"
   C "TIMES."
70 END
```

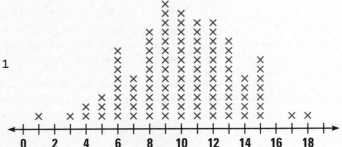

Exercises

1. For each of the 100 times the program was run, it selected 1000 numbers. How many numbers did it select altogether?

2. Use the line plot to determine how many times the program selected the correct number.

3. Use the results of Exercises 1 and 2 to find the experimental probability that the correct number is selected.

8.8

Probability and Simulations

What you should learn:

Goal 1 How to compare theoretical and experimental probabilities

Goal 2 How to find the probabilities of compound events (dependent and independent)

Why you should learn it:

You can use probability to solve real-life problems, such as finding the likelihood of various letter combinations on automobile license plates.

Goal 1 COMPARING PROBABILITIES

Example 1 Theoretical and Experimental Probabilities

Suppose you forget a friend's post office box number. You know the box number has 2 digits and both digits are multiples of 3. By choosing random digits that are multiples of 3, what is the probability that you will choose the correct box number?

a. Use the Counting Principle to find a theoretical probability.

b. Use a simulation to find an experimental probability.

Solution

a. Each digit is 3, 6, or 9.

$$\underset{\text{1st digit}}{\text{Choices for}} \cdot \underset{\text{2nd digit}}{\text{Choices for}} = 3 \cdot 3 = 9$$

Because only **1** of these **9** outcomes is correct, the theoretical probability that you will choose the correct box number is

$$\frac{\text{Number of correct outcomes}}{\text{Number of possible outcomes}} = \frac{1}{9} \approx 0.11.$$

b. To simulate choosing two digits, write 3, 6, and 9 on slips of paper and put them in two bags, as shown. Choose a slip from each bag and record the digits. Repeat until you have 50 pairs of numbers. Sample results are shown in the table.

Number	33	36	39	63	66	69	93	96	99
Frequency	8	5	5	7	4	3	6	5	7

Suppose the actual number is 39. The frequency table shows that 39 was selected 5 times out of 50. So, the experimental probability of choosing the correct box number is

$$\frac{\text{Frequency of correct outcome}}{\text{Total number of outcomes}} = \frac{5}{50} = \frac{1}{10} = 0.10.$$

In Example 1, the experimental probability does not *exactly* match the theoretical probability. However, if you repeat a simulation many times, the two numbers are likely to be very close.

Example 2 **Probability of Dependent Events**

Suppose that the digits of your friend's post office box number are multiples of 3 and are *different from each other*. What is the probability that you will choose the correct box number by guessing?

Solution

After selecting the 1st digit, there are only 2 choices left for the 2nd digit, because you cannot repeat digits.

$$\text{Choices for 1st digit} \cdot \text{Choices for 2nd digit} = 3 \cdot 2 = 6$$

Because only **1** of the **6** outcomes is correct, the probability is $\frac{1}{6}$.

In Example 2, the choice of the 2nd digit *depends on* the choice of the 1st digit, so the choices are *dependent events*. In Example 3, the color that one spinner lands on *does not depend on* the color the other lands on. The results of the spins are *independent events*.

Example 3 **Probability of Independent Events**

You spin the spinners shown at the right. What is the probability that one will land on a red region and the other will land on a blue region?

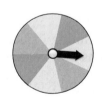

Solution

The number of ways that one spinner can land on red while the other lands on blue is

$$\underset{\text{on 1st spinner}}{\text{Number of red regions}} \cdot \underset{\text{on 2nd spinner}}{\text{Number of blue regions}} = 2 \cdot 3 = 6.$$

The total number of possible outcomes you can spin is

$$\underset{\text{on 1st spinner}}{\text{Number of regions}} \cdot \underset{\text{on 2nd spinner}}{\text{Number of regions}} = 7 \cdot 9 = 63.$$

The probability of one landing on red and the other landing on blue is

$$\frac{\text{Number of successful outcomes}}{\text{Number of possible outcomes}} = \frac{6}{63} = \frac{2}{21}.$$

NEED TO KNOW

When two or more events are combined, the result is called a *compound event*. The probability of a compound event is related to the probabilities of the events that make it up.

ONGOING ASSESSMENT

Write About It

1. Suppose a friend's post office box number has *three* digits that are multiples of 3. What is the probability of choosing it randomly if

   a. the digits can be repeated?

   b. there are no repeated digits?

2. Which part in Exercise 1 uses dependent events?

GUIDED PRACTICE

CHOOSING A COMMITTEE **In Exercises 1–4, use the following information.**

The math class in your school has five officers: 3 boys and 2 girls.
To form a committee of two officers, you select two names at random.
(The possible committees are listed on page 393.)

1. How many committees are possible?

2. What is the probability that the committee will consist of one boy and one girl?

3. What is the probability that the committee will consist of two boys?

4. What is the probability that the committee will consist of two girls?

PRACTICE AND PROBLEM SOLVING

FLIPPING COINS **In Exercises 5–7, use the following information.**

When you flip a fair coin, it lands heads up (H) about half the time and tails up (T) about half the time. Ignore the possibility that a coin might land on its edge.

5. Suppose you flip two coins. Use the Counting Principle to find the theoretical probability that both coins will land heads up (HH).

6. Suppose you flip two coins. Use the Counting Principle to find the theoretical probability that both coins will land tails up (TT).

7. **ACTING IT OUT** Flip two coins 40 times and record your results in a table that lists the frequency of each outcome: HH, HT, TH, and TT. Use your table to find the experimental probabilities of HH and TT.

TELEPHONE NUMBERS **In Exercises 8–10, suppose you forget the last two digits of a friend's telephone number but remember that they are both even.**

8. What is the probability that you will dial the correct number if you choose the last two digits randomly from the even numbers?

9. Suppose you remember that the two even digits are not the same. What is the probability that you will dial the correct number if you choose the last two digits randomly but don't repeat digits?

10. **ACTING IT OUT** How could you simulate the process of selecting two even digits randomly? How could you simulate the process of selecting two *different* even digits randomly?

> **TOOLBOX**
>
> Problem Solving
> Strategies, page 744

LICENSE PLATES **In Exercises 11–14, use the following information.**

In many states, license plates have 3 letters followed by 3 digits.

11. You try to remember the last 2 digits on a license plate. What is the probability that you will be correct if you guess the digits randomly?

12. You try to remember the first 2 letters on a license plate. What is the probability that you will be correct if you guess the letters randomly?

13. What is the probability that the first 2 letters in a license plate are a consonant followed by a vowel?

14. In some states, the letters I and O are not used on license plates because they resemble the digits 1 and 0. How do the answers to Exercises 12 and 13 change if the letters I and O are not allowed?

15. **OPEN-ENDED PROBLEM** Some states once had 3 letters and 3 digits on license plates, but switched to 4 letters and 2 digits. Why do you think this change was necessary?

SPINNERS **In Exercises 16–21, use the spinners shown. Find the probability of each compound event.**

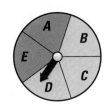

16. *C* and 6

17. *E* and 5

18. a vowel and 4

19. a vowel and an even number

20. a consonant and 2

21. a consonant and an odd number

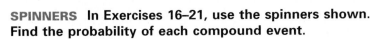

STANDARDIZED TEST PRACTICE

22. You spin the three spinners at the right. What is the probability of landing on the shaded area, the number 4, and the letter A?

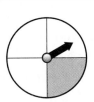 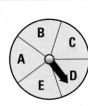

(A) $\frac{1}{120}$ (B) $\frac{37}{180}$ (C) $\frac{1}{3}$ (D) $\frac{37}{60}$

EXPLORATION AND EXTENSION

23. **COMMUNICATING ABOUT MATHEMATICS** Scientists estimate there are 12,000 species of rain forest beetles. About 10,300 have never been named. You are writing a report about rain forest beetles, and you randomly choose a species out of a list of all the named species. If a friend randomly chooses a species from the same list, what is the probability that it will match yours? (For more information about beetles, see page 396.)

WHAT did you learn?

WHY did you learn it?

Skills

8.1 Find rates and ratios.

Compare unit prices.

8.2 Write and solve proportions.

Use proportions to find unknown side lengths in similar triangles.

8.3 Solve real-life problems using proportions.

Estimate a property tax that is proportional to a house's value.

8.4 Solve a percent equation.

Use percent to calculate your score on a quiz.

8.5 Solve real-life problems using percent.

Understand how discounts are calculated. Interpret circle graphs.

8.6 Find a percent of increase or decrease.

Explain how amounts change over time, such as telephone rates.

8.7 Use the Counting Principle and Pascal's Triangle.

Find the number of ways of choosing n items from m items, such as choosing a committee.

8.8 Find probabilities of independent and dependent compound events.

Explain outcomes of flipping coins, spinning spinners, or randomly selecting numbers.

Strategies **8.1–8.8** Use problem solving strategies.

Solve a wide variety of real-life problems.

Using Data **8.1–8.8** Use tables and graphs.

Organize data and solve problems.

HOW does it fit in the bigger picture of mathematics?

When you use rational numbers to model a real-life situation, it is important to know the units of measure.

For example, if a is measured in miles and b is measured in hours, then the rate $\frac{a}{b}$ is measured in miles per hour. When a and b have the same units of measure, the ratio $\frac{a}{b}$ has no units of measure.

Percents and probabilities are examples of ratios. Knowing this can help you check the units in your answers.

Example What is 25% of 8 dollars?

Solution 25% of 8 *dollars* is $0.25 \cdot 8$ or 2 *dollars*.

VOCABULARY

- rate (p. 362)
- ratio (p. 363)
- proportion (p. 368)
- Cross Product Property (p. 368)

- similar (p. 369)
- similar triangles (p. 369)
- corresponding sides (p. 369)
- base of a percent (p. 376)

- discount (p. 383)
- discount percent (p. 383)
- percent of increase (p. 386)
- percent of decrease (p. 386)
- Counting Principle (p. 392)

8.1 EXPLORING RATES AND RATIOS

The quantity $a \div b$ is a *rate* if the two quantities have different units of measure. It is a *ratio* if the two quantities have the same units.

Examples

You ran 10 mi in 2 h. What is your average speed?

$$\text{Rate} = \frac{\text{Distance}}{\text{Time}}$$

$$= \frac{10 \text{ mi}}{2 \text{ h}}$$

$$= 5 \text{ mi/h}$$

A tree is 10 ft high and 4 ft wide. Find the ratio of its height to width.

$$\frac{\text{Tree height}}{\text{Tree width}} = \frac{10 \text{ ft}}{4 \text{ ft}}$$

$$= \frac{5}{2}$$

1. Write the phrase "Traveled 1500 mi in 2 days" as a quotient. State whether the result is a rate or a ratio.

2. Write $\dfrac{3 \text{ ft}}{24 \text{ in.}}$ as a ratio and simplify.

3. Ground beef costs $3.98 for 2 lb, and ground turkey costs $6.25 for 5 lb. Which meat is the better buy? Explain.

8.2 SOLVING PROPORTIONS

An equation of two ratios is a proportion. $\dfrac{a}{b} = \dfrac{c}{d}$

Example

$$\frac{2}{b} = \frac{3}{8}$$ Write original proportion.

$$2 \cdot 8 = b \cdot 3$$ Use Cross Product Property.

$$\frac{2 \cdot 8}{3} = \frac{b \cdot 3}{3}$$ Divide each side by 3.

$$\frac{16}{3} = b$$ Solution: *b* is by itself.

Solve the proportion. Describe your method.

4. $\dfrac{x}{4} = \dfrac{5}{8}$

5. $\dfrac{10}{3} = \dfrac{12}{t}$

6. $\dfrac{14}{s} = \dfrac{56}{9}$

7. $\dfrac{5}{7} = \dfrac{m}{16}$

8.3 PROBLEM SOLVING USING PROPORTIONS

Example The three triangles are similar. Find x.
Write a proportion comparing sides.

Solution

$\dfrac{x}{6} = \dfrac{5}{7.5}$ Write a proportion.

$x \cdot 7.5 = 6 \cdot 5$ Use the Cross Product Property.

$x = \dfrac{30}{7.5} = 4$ Solution: x is by itself.

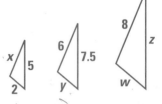

Use the similar triangles in the above example.

8. Find y.   **9.** Find z.   **10.** Find w.

8.4 SOLVING PERCENT EQUATIONS

Example 25 is what percent of 125?

Solution

$\dfrac{25}{125} = \dfrac{p}{100}$ Write percent equation.

$100 \cdot \dfrac{25}{125} = 100 \cdot \dfrac{p}{100}$ Multiply each side by 100.

$20 = p$ Solution: p is by itself.

Solve the percent equation.

11. 35 is what percent of 40?   **12.** What is 68 percent of 22?

13. 44 is 25% of what number?   **14.** 55 is what percent of 25?

8.5 PROBLEM SOLVING USING PERCENTS

Example A camera that normally sells for $45 is reduced by $9. What is the discount percent?

Solution

$\dfrac{9}{45} = \dfrac{p}{100}$ Write percent equation.

$9 \cdot 100 = 45 \cdot p$ Use the Cross Product Property.

$\dfrac{900}{45} = \dfrac{45 \cdot p}{45}$ Divide each side by 45.

$20 = p$ Solution: p is by itself.

15. DISCOUNT A sign in a store states that all baseball hats are 45% off. The regular price is $15. What is the sale price of the hat?

16. DISCOUNT A sign in a store states that all baseball hats are 45% off. The discount is $9.36. What was the regular price of the hat?

Example On Sunday, 845 people went to the zoo. On Tuesday, 169 people went. What is the percent of decrease from Sunday to Tuesday?

Solution Percent of decrease $= \dfrac{845 - 169}{845} = \dfrac{676}{845} = 0.8$

The percent of decrease is 80%.

Decide whether the two quantities represent a percent of *increase* or a percent of *decrease* and find the percent.

17. Beginning Balance: $740.20
Ending Balance: $777.21

18. Regular Price: $65.50
Sale Price: $45.85

Example How many kinds of tacos can you make if you use 3 kinds of cheese and 4 kinds of sauce?

Solution You can use the Counting Principle.
The number of possible tacos is $3 \cdot 4 = 12$.

19. You are buying a pet rabbit. You can choose from black, brown, or white, and from short-haired or long-haired. There are 5 rabbits in the pet store. Are all possible choices represented? Explain.

Example A coin is tossed. Then a cube with the colors red, blue, black, green, purple, and brown is rolled. Find the probability that the coin lands heads up and the color of the cube's side facing up starts with the letter *b*.

Solution The number of ways of getting heads and a color that begins with the letter *b* is $1 \cdot 3 = \mathbf{3}$.

The number of ways a coin can land times the number of ways the cube can land is $2 \cdot 6 = \mathbf{12}$.

So, the probability is $\dfrac{3}{12} = \dfrac{1}{4}$.

Each of the computer passwords consists of 5 letters and 3 digits. You randomly choose letters or digits to complete each password. What is the probability that you will get the correct password?

20. M L K ? P 1 2 ?

21. N ? A C ? 4 8 7

In Exercises 1–4, use the similar triangles at the right.

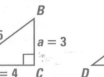
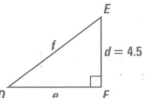
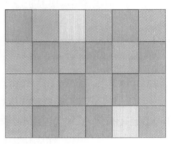

1. Find the ratio of a to d.

2. Solve for f.

3. Solve for e.

4. Find the ratio of b to e.

In Exercises 5 and 6, decide whether the change is an increase or a decrease and find the percent.

5. Before: 76   After: 95

6. Before: $15   After: $9

7. You rent a car for 5 days for $195. What is the daily rental rate?

8. What is 82% of 115?

9. 56 is what percent of 70?

In Exercises 10–13, use the rectangle at the right. Each small rectangle is the same size.

10. What percent of the large rectangle is red?

11. What percent of the large rectangle is yellow?

12. If one of the small rectangles is chosen at random, what is the probability that it will be green?

13. If one of the small rectangles is chosen at random, what is the probability that it will *not* be red?

In Exercises 14–20, use the given information.

SHADOWS A building is casting a 100 ft shadow at the same time that a 5 ft post is casting a 1 ft shadow.

14. Draw a diagram that shows the building, the post, and the two shadows.

15. Write a proportion that involves the height of the building, the height of the post, and the lengths of the two shadows.

16. Solve the proportion to find the height of the building.

COMMITTEES A two-person committee is to be chosen from 3 seventh-grade students and 3 eighth-grade students. The committee must have one student from each grade.

17. List the different committees that are possible.

18. Use the Counting Principle to confirm your list.

BIRTH RATES On an average day, about 10,500 women give birth in the United States. Of these, 217 women give birth to twins and 5 women give birth to triplets.

19. Estimate the chance of having twins.   **20.** Estimate the chance of having triplets.

1. A 5 lb bag of potatoes costs $1.99, and a 10 lb bag costs $3.89. Which statement is false?

   (A) The price per pound is a ratio.

   (B) The 10 lb bag is the better buy.

   (C) The unit price for the smaller bag is $.398/lb.

   (D) The unit price is a rate.

2. What is the missing side length of the similar triangles?

   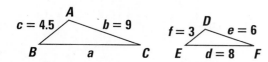

   (A) 6   (B) $6\frac{3}{4}$

   (C) 12   (D) 16

3. A model of the space vehicle Saturn 5 has a 1-to-484 scale. The height of the model is 9 in. What is the height (in feet) of the actual Saturn 5?

   (A) $30\frac{1}{4}$ ft   (B) $53\frac{7}{9}$ ft

   (C) 363 ft   (D) 4356 ft

4. Which percent equation can be used to answer the following question?

   50 is 125% of what number?

   (A) $\frac{a}{50} = \frac{125}{100}$ (B) $\frac{50}{b} = \frac{125}{1000}$

   (C) $\frac{50}{b} = \frac{125}{100}$ (D) $\frac{a}{50} = \frac{125}{1000}$

5. What is the percent of decrease?

   1997: 225   1998: 180

   (A) 20%   (B) 25%

   (C) $44.\overline{4}$%   (D) 45%

6. The circle graph shows the results of a survey that asked people to name their favorite type of food. Mexican food was the favorite of 50 people. Which statement is false?

   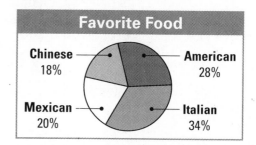

   (A) 85 people said Italian.

   (B) 250 people were surveyed.

   (C) 10 more people said American than Chinese.

   (D) 45 people said Chinese.

7. You are buying sneakers. You can choose from aerobic, walking, running, basketball, or volleyball sneakers. Each pair is available in white or black, with white, blue, red, or black laces. How many different pairs of sneakers are there?

   (A) 10   (B) 11

   (C) 24   (D) 40

8. You want to write to a friend. You don't have her ZIP code. You know that the first three digits of her ZIP code are the same as yours. What is the probability that you choose the correct ZIP code?

   (A) $\frac{1}{100}$ (B) $\frac{1}{81}$

   (C) $\frac{2}{100}$ (D) $\frac{1}{20}$

Real Numbers
and Inequalities

TECHNOLOGY

- **Interactive Real-Life
  Investigations**
- **Middle School Tutorial
  Software**

To find out more about roller
coasters, go to:

http://www.mlmath.com

THE MEAN STREAK roller coaster at Cedar Point
in Ohio was designed to have a hill that is 155 ft tall.

CHAPTER THEME
Amusement Parks

CHAPTER PROJECT

Designing a Roller Coaster

PROJECT DESCRIPTION

In 1884, the first American roller coaster was built at Coney Island in New York City. Since that time, coasters have gotten faster and more complex, often having loops, twists, and drops. You will design a coaster that has at least one loop and hill.

GETTING STARTED

Talking It Over

- Have you ever ridden a roller coaster? Was it made with wooden or metal supports? What is your favorite feature in a coaster?

- What things do you think a roller coaster designer must consider when designing a coaster?

Planning Your Project

- **Materials:** posterboard, colored pencils or markers

- Keep the results of the **BUILDING YOUR PROJECT** exercises in your portfolio. Use them to make a poster describing your roller coaster design. Be sure to label the heights and lengths of each part of the coaster.

Coney Island, 1884

BUILDING YOUR PROJECT

These are places throughout the chapter where you will work on your project.

9.1 Calculate your coaster's speed at the bottom of the first hill. *p. 413*

9.3 Calculate the length of track between supports. *p. 423*

9.5 Calculate the coaster's speed on a "teardrop" loop. *p. 436*

9.6 Decide on the height of a "teardrop" loop. *p. 441*

9.1

Exploring Square Roots

What you should learn:

Goal **1** How to solve equations whose solutions are square roots

Goal **2** How to use square roots to solve real-life problems

Why you should learn it:

You can use square roots to solve real-life problems, such as finding the time it takes an object to fall a given distance.

Goal **1** USING THE SQUARE ROOT PROPERTY

The square below has an area of 16 square units. Each side is x units long, so $x^2 = 16$.

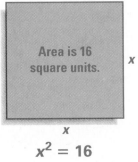

Area is 16 square units.

x

x

$$x^2 = 16$$

There are two numbers whose square is 16: -4 and 4. Because length must be positive, each side of the square has a length of 4 units.

SQUARE ROOT PROPERTY

If a is a positive number, then $x^2 = a$ has two solutions.

1. $x = -\sqrt{a}$ is a solution because $\left(-\sqrt{a}\right)^2 = a$.

2. $x = \sqrt{a}$ is a solution because $\left(\sqrt{a}\right)^2 = a$.

Example 1 Using Square Roots to Solve Equations

a. $t^2 = 25$ Write original equation.

$\quad t = -\sqrt{25}$ or $t = \sqrt{25}$ Use the Square Root Property.

$\quad t = -5 \qquad t = 5$ Simplify.

There are two solutions: $t = -5$ and $t = 5$.

✔ **Check:** Multiply to see that $(-5)^2 = 25$ and $5^2 = 25$.

b. $\quad x^2 + 2 = 9$ Write original equation.

$\quad x^2 + 2 - 2 = 9 - 2$ Subtract 2 from each side.

$\quad\quad\quad x^2 = 7$ Simplify.

$\quad\quad x = -\sqrt{7}$ or $x = \sqrt{7}$ Use the Square Root Property.

There are two solutions: $x = -\sqrt{7}$ and $x = \sqrt{7}$. Check these in the original equation.

NEED TO KNOW

The symbol $\sqrt{a}$ represents the nonnegative (positive or zero) square root of a. To represent the negative square root of a, write $-\sqrt{a}$. Remember that $a \geq 0$.

Example 2 Finding a Painting's Dimensions

REAL LIFE
Paintings

The square painting, "Falling Star," has an area of 3600 in.^{2} It was painted by Robert Orduño, a native American artist. It shows Wohpe, a Lakota legendary figure, falling from the sky. What are the dimensions of the painting?

Solution

Verbal Model Area of Square = (length of side)^2

Labels Area of square = 3600 (square inches)
Length of side = s (inches)

Algebraic Model $3600 = s^2$ Write algebraic model.
$60 = s$ Choose the positive square root.

The length of each side of the painting is 60 in.

Example 3 Finding a Falling Time

CONNECTION
Science

In a science experiment, you drop a baseball and measure how long it takes to fall 10 ft. With no air resistance, the time t (in seconds) should be the solution of $16t^2 = 10$. How long does it take the ball to fall 10 ft?

Solution

$16t^2 = 10$ Write original equation.

$t^2 = \dfrac{5}{8}$ Divide each side by 16.

$t = \sqrt{\dfrac{5}{8}}$ Choose the positive square root.

$t \approx 0.8$ Use a calculator.

With no air resistance, the ball takes about 0.8 s to fall 10 ft. Because of air resistance, the actual time is a little longer than 0.8 s.

9.1 Exercises

Extra Practice, page 730

GUIDED PRACTICE

1. Explain why $r^2 = 4$ has two solutions.

In Exercises 2–5, write the square roots of the number.

2. 49   3. 5   4. 0.25   5. $\dfrac{25}{4}$

6. Solve the equation $2x^2 = 228$.

PRACTICE AND PROBLEM SOLVING

In Exercises 7–14, write both square roots of the number.

7. 14   8. 22   9. 64   10. 169

11. 256   12. 1600   13. 0.36   14. $\dfrac{64}{9}$

In Exercises 15–22, write both solutions of the equation.

15. $t^2 = 9$ 16. $x^2 = 100$ 17. $p^2 = 22$ 18. $r^2 = 17$

19. $b^2 + 2 = 27$ 20. $y^2 - 6 = 30$ 21. $3a^2 = 243$ 22. $4s^2 = 49$

 ESTIMATION In Exercises 23–26, the small squares of the graph paper are each 1 square unit. Estimate the side lengths of the green square. Use a calculator to confirm your estimate.

23. Area of green square is 20 square units.

24. Area of green square is 56 square units.

25. Area of green square is 31 square units.

26. Area of green square is 39 square units.

In Exercises 27–30, write an algebraic equation for the sentence. Then solve the equation.

27. The positive square root of 25 is x.   28. The product of 3 and r squared is 27.

29. The sum of a squared and 6 is 15.   30. y squared is 47.

31. **FALLING OBJECTS** The time, t, in seconds it takes an object to fall when dropped can be modeled by $-16t^2 + s = 0$, where s is the height in feet from which the object is dropped. If a ball is dropped from a height of 20 ft, how long does it take before it hits the ground? Round your answer to the nearest tenth.

HORIZON **In Exercises 32 and 33, use the following information.**

On a clear day, the distance, d, in miles that you can see out to the ocean can be estimated using the equation $d^2 = \frac{3}{2}h$, where h is the height in feet of your eyes above sea level.

32. You are on an observation deck at the beach. Your eyes are 10 ft above sea level. How far can you see?

33. You climb to the top of an observation tower where your eyes are 30 ft above sea level. How far can you see?

34. The surface area of a cube is the sum of the areas of its faces. How long is each edge if the surface area is 216 cm^2?

STANDARDIZED TEST PRACTICE

35. Between which two numbers is $\sqrt{72.25}$?

    (A) 6 and 7   **(B)** 7 and 8   **(C)** 8 and 9   **(D)** None of these

36. A baseball diamond is a square with a base at each corner. The area is 8100 ft^2. What is the distance between bases?

    (A) 9 ft   **(B)** 81 ft   **(C)** 90 ft   **(D)** 2025 ft

EXPLORATION AND EXTENSION

PORTFOLIO

37. **BUILDING YOUR PROJECT** The speed of a roller coaster car at the bottom of the first hill depends on the height that it has dropped. Copy and complete the table.

Height, h (in feet)	25	50	75	100	125	150
64h	1600	3200	4800	?	?	?
Speed $\approx \sqrt{64h}$ (in ft/s)	40	57	?	?	?	?

a. Is the speed twice as fast when the hill is twice as high?

b. Choose realistic heights for the top and bottom of the first hill in your roller coaster design. What will be the speed of the coaster car at the bottom of the first hill?

9.2

The Real Number System

What you should learn:

Goal 1 How to classify real numbers as rational or irrational

Goal 2 How to represent real numbers with a number line

Why you should learn it:

Some real-life problems can be modeled only with irrational numbers.

Goal 1 CLASSIFYING REAL NUMBERS

In Lesson 6.6, you learned that a *rational number* can be written as the quotient of two integers. *Irrational numbers* are numbers that cannot be written as the quotient of two integers. Rational numbers and irrational numbers together make up the set of **real numbers**.

Number	Type	Decimal Form	Decimal Type
$\frac{3}{4}$	Rational	$\frac{3}{4} = 0.75$	Terminating
$\frac{1}{11}$	Rational	$\frac{1}{11} = 0.0909\ldots = 0.\overline{09}$	Repeating
$\sqrt{3}$	Irrational	$\sqrt{3} = 1.7320508\ldots$	Nonrepeating

Notice that the decimal form of an irrational number does not terminate and does not repeat. Example 1 describes a real-life length that is irrational.

Example 1 Irrational Lengths

You are designing a small quilt. Each piece of cloth is a right triangle. Eight of the pieces form a square that is 2 in. by 2 in.

a. How long are the sides of each piece?

b. Can these lengths be written exactly as decimals?

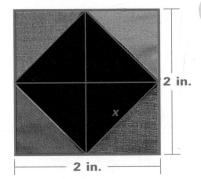

REAL LIFE
Quilting

Solution

a. The large square is formed by 8 pieces of cloth and has an area of 4 in.^{2} The black square is formed by 4 pieces of cloth. This means that the black square must have an area of 2 in.^{2}

$$\text{Area of black square} = x^2$$
$$2 = x^2$$
$$\sqrt{2} = x$$

b. Thus, each piece of cloth has side lengths of 1 in., 1 in., and $\sqrt{2}$ in. A length of 1 in. can be represented exactly as a decimal, but a length of $\sqrt{2}$ in. cannot. Rounding to two decimal places, you can approximate $\sqrt{2}$ in. as $\sqrt{2} \approx 1.41$ in.

Real numbers can be plotted on a number line.

$-\dfrac{3}{2} = -1.5 \quad -0.5 \qquad\qquad\qquad \sqrt{3} \approx 1.73 \quad \dfrac{8}{3} \approx 2.67$

Example 2 **Comparing Numbers on a Number Line**

Plot each pair of numbers on a number line. Then complete the statement with $<$, $>$, or $=$.

a. $\sqrt{\dfrac{1}{2}}$ **?** $\dfrac{1}{2}$ **b.** $\sqrt{2}$ **?** 2 **c.** $\sqrt{\dfrac{9}{4}}$ **?** $\dfrac{3}{2}$

Solution

a. Using a calculator, write the numbers as decimals and plot them.

Because $\sqrt{\dfrac{1}{2}}$ is to the right of $\dfrac{1}{2}$, it follows that $\sqrt{\dfrac{1}{2}} > \dfrac{1}{2}$.

$\dfrac{1}{2} = 0.5 \qquad \sqrt{\dfrac{1}{2}} \approx 0.71$

b. Using a calculator, write the numbers as decimals and plot them. Because $\sqrt{2}$ is to the left of 2, it follows that $\sqrt{2} < 2$.

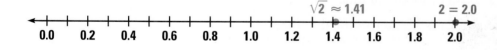

$\sqrt{2} \approx 1.41 \qquad\qquad 2 = 2.0$

c. Using a calculator, write the numbers as decimals and plot them.

Because $\sqrt{\dfrac{9}{4}}$ is at the same place as $\dfrac{3}{2}$, it follows that $\sqrt{\dfrac{9}{4}} = \dfrac{3}{2}$.

$\dfrac{3}{2} = 1.5 \qquad \sqrt{\dfrac{9}{4}} = 1.5$

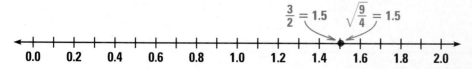

GUIDED PRACTICE

1. **WRITING** What is a rational number? Use your own words.

2. **WRITING** How is the decimal form of a rational number different from the decimal form of an irrational number?

3. State whether the number is irrational. Explain your reasoning.

   a. 0.123   **b.** $0.\overline{123}$ **c.** 0.123714356...

In Exercises 4–7, state whether the number is rational or irrational.

4. $\dfrac{8}{2}$ 5. $\sqrt{5}$ 6. $\sqrt{9}$ 7. $-\sqrt{\dfrac{16}{9}}$

8. Plot the set of numbers on a number line.

   $$\left\{0, \frac{1}{2}, -\frac{5}{3}, -2.1, \sqrt{4}, \sqrt{6}, -\sqrt{8}, 3\right\}$$

PRACTICE AND PROBLEM SOLVING

NUMBER SENSE In Exercises 9–16, tell whether the number is rational or irrational. Explain your reasoning.

9. $\dfrac{11}{5}$ 10. $\dfrac{-21}{16}$ 11. $\sqrt{10}$ 12. $-\sqrt{15}$

13. $\sqrt{1.44}$ 14. $-\sqrt{\dfrac{100}{36}}$ 15. $-\sqrt{\dfrac{3}{2}}$ 16. $\sqrt{\dfrac{9}{6}}$

LOGICAL REASONING In Exercises 17–20, complete the statement using *always*, *sometimes*, or *never*. Explain.

17. A real number is __?__ a rational number.

18. An irrational number is __?__ a real number.

19. A negative integer is __?__ an irrational number.

20. The square root of a number is __?__ an irrational number.

In Exercises 21–24, evaluate the expression when $a = 2$, $b = 4$, and $c = 9$. Is the result rational?

21. $\sqrt{a} + \sqrt{b}$ 22. $\sqrt{b} - \sqrt{c}$ 23. $\sqrt{c} \cdot \sqrt{b}$ 24. $\sqrt{c} \div \sqrt{b}$

In Exercises 25–29, match the number with its graph.

25. $\sqrt{8}$ 26. $-\sqrt{15}$ 27. 0.49   28. $\sqrt{3.8}$ 29. $-\sqrt{\dfrac{25}{16}}$

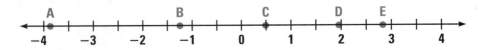

In Exercises 30–33, compare the numbers by completing the statement with <, >, or =.

30. $\sqrt{0.16}$? 0.16 **31.** -7 ? $-\sqrt{7}$ **32.** $\sqrt{2.25}$? $\dfrac{3.6}{2.4}$ **33.** $\sqrt{3}$? $\dfrac{23}{13}$

In Exercises 34–39, list the numbers in order from least to greatest.

34. $-\dfrac{1}{2}, -\dfrac{3}{4}, -\dfrac{1}{8}$

35. $-1\dfrac{1}{2}, -2\dfrac{1}{4}, -\dfrac{7}{8}$

36. $-0.5, -3.5, -2$

37. $-0.75, -0.5, -1.3$

38. $125\%, 35\%, 45\%$

39. $\dfrac{1}{2}, 0.75, 25\%$

40. TILES You are designing floor tiles that are right triangles. Eight tiles form a square as shown. Can the side lengths of the green square be written exactly as decimals? Explain.

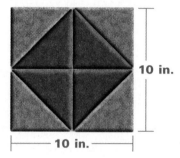

10 in.

10 in.

41. CONJECTURES The numbers 2, 7, and 65 are examples of numbers whose square roots are irrational. The numbers 1, 4, and 25 have rational square roots. Make a conjecture about numbers that have irrational square roots. List some more examples and non-examples.

STANDARDIZED TEST PRACTICE

42. Which statement is false?

(A) A rational number can be written as a quotient of two integers.

(B) The decimal form of an irrational number repeats.

(C) All real numbers are either rational or irrational.

(D) None of the above

EXPLORATION AND EXTENSION

43. VENN DIAGRAM Copy the table. Use checks to mark all the labels that describe each number. The Venn diagram can help you make your decisions.

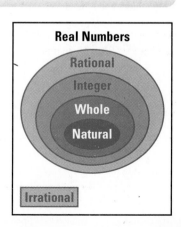

	Natural	Whole	Integer	Rational	Irrational	Real
-5			✔	✔		✔
$\dfrac{15}{12}$						
$\sqrt{7}$						
11						
0						

The Pythagorean Theorem

Materials Needed
- metric dot paper
- pencils or pens
- metric ruler

Part A EXPLORING RIGHT TRIANGLES

1 A right triangle is a triangle that has a right angle (a 90° angle). Draw a right triangle that has the dimensions shown at the right.

2 Draw a square on each leg of the triangle. Label the lengths of the sides of the squares.

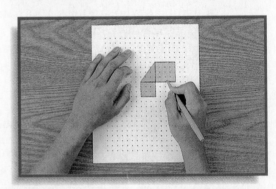

3 Use a metric ruler or a piece of dot paper to measure the length of the hypotenuse. Do you think your measurement is exact? Draw a square on the hypotenuse and label its dimensions.

1. Find the area of each square. Write an addition equation that relates the three areas.

2. Let a and b be the lengths of the legs of the triangle. Let c be the length of the hypotenuse. Write a conjecture about the values of a, b, and c.

In Exercises 3 and 4, copy the triangle and squares on metric dot paper. Measure the length of the hypotenuse. Compare the values of a^2, b^2, and c^2. Do they agree with the conjecture you wrote in Exercise 2? If not, check your calculations. Revise your conjecture if necessary.

3.

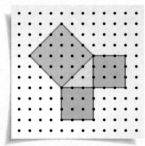

4.

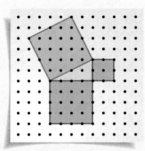

5. Repeat the above directions for several other triangles. Does your conjecture seem right?

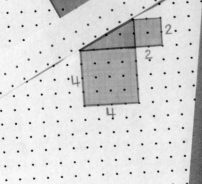

NOW TRY THESE

In Exercises 6 and 7, use the figure shown at the right.

6. Find the areas of the two blue squares. Use your conjecture from Exercises 2–5 to find the area of the red square.

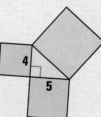

7. What is the length of the hypotenuse of the right triangle? Explain your reasoning.

8. Draw a right triangle on plain paper. Measure the lengths of its legs. Explain how to use these lengths to find the length of the hypotenuse. Then, check your result by measuring the hypotenuse.

9.3

The Pythagorean Theorem

What you should learn:

Goal 1 How to use the Pythagorean Theorem

Goal 2 How to solve a right triangle

Why you should learn it:

You can use the Pythagorean Theorem to solve real-life problems, such as finding a driving distance.

Goal 1 USING THE PYTHAGOREAN THEOREM

A right triangle is a triangle that has a **right angle** (one whose measure is 90°). The sides that form the right angle are the **legs** of the triangle, and the other side is the **hypotenuse**. The small square in the corner indicates which angle is the right angle.

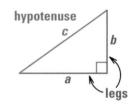

The lengths of the sides of any right triangle are related by a rule called the **Pythagorean Theorem**. This rule is named after the Greek mathematician Pythagoras (about 585–500 B.C.).

PYTHAGOREAN THEOREM

For any right triangle, the sum of the squares of the lengths of the legs, a and b, equals the square of the length of the hypotenuse, c.

$$a^2 + b^2 = c^2$$

Example 1 Finding the Length of the Hypotenuse

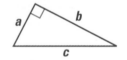

REAL LIFE
Driving

From the junction of Highways 330 and 30, you drive to Ames, Iowa. Then you turn south and drive on Highway 35 to Des Moines. How many miles of driving would you have saved if you had driven on Highways 330 and 65 to Des Moines?

Solution

The highways on the map form a right triangle.

$$a^2 + b^2 = c^2 \qquad \text{Use the Pythagorean Theorem.}$$
$$28^2 + 29^2 = c^2 \qquad \text{Substitute for } a \text{ and } b.$$
$$1625 = c^2 \qquad \text{Simplify.}$$
$$\sqrt{1625} = c \qquad \text{Choose the positive square root.}$$
$$40 \approx c \qquad \text{Use a calculator.}$$

The distance along Highways 330 and 65 is about 40 mi. You would have saved $(28 + 29) - 40 = 17$ mi.

Using the lengths of two sides of a right triangle to find the length of the third side is called **solving a right triangle**.

Example 2 **Solving a Right Triangle**

CONNECTION
Geometry

a. In the triangle at the right, $c = 10$ and $a = 6$. You can use the Pythagorean Theorem to find the length of the other leg.

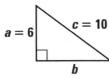

$a^2 + b^2 = c^2$ Use the Pythagorean Theorem.

$6^2 + b^2 = 10^2$ Substitute for a and c.

$36 + b^2 = 100$ Simplify.

$b^2 = 64$ Subtract 36 from each side.

$b = 8$ Choose the positive square root.

The length of the other leg is 8.

b. The triangle at the right is **isosceles**, which means that its legs are the same length. The hypotenuse has a length of 8. You can use the Pythagorean Theorem to find the length of each leg.

$d^2 + e^2 = f^2$ Use the Pythagorean Theorem.

$d^2 + d^2 = 8^2$ Substitute d for e and 8 for f.

$2d^2 = 64$ Simplify.

$d^2 = 32$ Divide each side by 2.

$d = \sqrt{32}$ Choose the positive square root.

$d \approx 5.66$ Use a calculator.

Each leg has a length of about 5.66.

....

When the lengths of the sides of a right triangle are all natural numbers, the lengths are called a **Pythagorean triple**. In part (a) of Example 2, the numbers 6, 8, and 10 are a Pythagorean triple.

NEED TO KNOW

In part (*b*) of Example 2, the legs of the right triangle are the same length. To indicate this, you can draw the same number of "tick marks" through the sides.

ONGOING ASSESSMENT

Talk About It
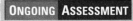

1. Find as many different Pythagorean triples as you can.

GUIDED PRACTICE

1. **DRAWING A DIAGRAM** Draw a right triangle. Label its legs m and n and its hypotenuse t. How are the legs and hypotenuse related by the Pythagorean Theorem?

2. **WRITING** Can a right triangle have an obtuse angle? Explain.

ESTIMATING In Exercises 3 and 4, a and b are the lengths of the legs of a right triangle, and c is the length of the hypotenuse. Draw the right triangle on graph paper and estimate the missing length. Then use the Pythagorean Theorem to confirm your estimate.

3. $a = 6, b = 7, c = \boxed{?}$

4. $a = 3, b = \boxed{?}, c = 5$

PRACTICE AND PROBLEM SOLVING

LOGICAL REASONING In Exercises 5–8, decide whether the statement is *sometimes*, *always*, or *never* true.

> **TOOLBOX**
>
> Triangles, page 757

5. The Pythagorean Theorem is true for an acute triangle.

6. The hypotenuse is the longest side of a right triangle.

7. The legs of a right triangle are the same length.

8. In a right triangle, if a and b are integers, then c is an integer.

In Exercises 9–14, a and b are the lengths of the legs of a right triangle, and c is the length of the hypotenuse. Find the missing length. If necessary, use a calculator and round your answer to two decimal places.

9. $a = 7, b = 11$

10. $a = 16, c = 34$

11. $b = 12, c = 15$

12. $a = 6, c = 16.16$

13. $b = 42, c = 43.17$

14. $a = 18, b = 28$

DRAWING A DIAGRAM In Exercises 15–18, if possible, draw a right triangle whose sides have the given lengths.

15. 8, 15, 17

16. 5, 12, 13

17. 9, 38, 38

18. 13, 36, 40

In Exercises 19–22, find the length of the third side. If necessary, use a calculator and round your answer to two decimal places.

19.

20.

21.

22.

VOLLEYBALL **In Exercises 23–25, use the following information.**

You are setting up a volleyball net. To keep each pole standing straight, you use two ropes and two stakes as shown at the right.

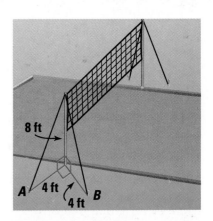

23. How long is each piece of rope?

24. What is the total amount of rope you need for both poles?

25. What is the distance between the stakes marked A and B?

26. **BICYCLING** You ride your bike to your friend's house. You usually take the back roads as shown on the map at the right. How many miles will you save if you go straight through town?

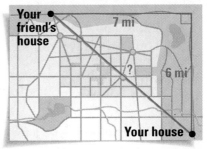

In Exercises 27 and 28, you are given the lengths of two sides of a right triangle. Draw two _different_ sizes of right triangles that have these side lengths and find the length of the third side.

27. 8, 10   **28.** 5, 6

STANDARDIZED TEST PRACTICE

29. Use the Pythagorean Theorem to find x.

  A 2 cm   **B** 4 cm

  C 10 cm   **D** 11.38 cm

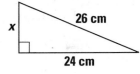

EXPLORATION AND EXTENSION

PORTFOLIO

30. **BUILDING YOUR PROJECT** Roller coasters are built using wooden or metal supports for the track. You can use the Pythagorean Theorem to estimate the length of track between supports.

  a. Suppose two supports are 10 ft apart and the coaster drops 12 ft between them. Estimate the length of track between the supports.

  b. Draw a hill for your roller coaster, including supports for the track. Show how you can use the lengths of the supports to estimate the length of a section of track.

In Exercises 1–4, find the missing length. If necessary, use a calculator and round your answer to two decimal places. (9.3)

1.

2.

3.

4.

In Exercises 5–8, solve the inequality. (2.9)

5. $x + 2 \geq 9$ **6.** $2p < 14$ **7.** $5n > 8$ **8.** $y - 7 \leq 4$

In Exercises 9–12, find the greatest common factor. (6.3)

9. 24 and 39   **10.** 88 and 60   **11.** $100x$ and $222y$ **12.** 9, 12, and 15

13. **FUNDRAISING** Your class is selling subs to raise money. You spent $400 to buy food to make the subs. The class has sold 130 subs for $2.50 each. Have you made a profit yet? Use the verbal model. (3.7)

$$\text{Profit} = \frac{\text{Sub}}{\text{Price}} \times \frac{\text{Number of}}{\text{Subs Sold}} - \text{Expenses}$$

CAREER Interview

CIVIL ENGINEER

Maribel Chavez is a civil engineer. More than 350 employees work for her as she oversees the construction and maintenance of highways and other transportation systems in the Abilene District of Texas. In 1996, Chavez received the Hispanic Engineer National Achievement Award.

Q What led you into this career?
As a little girl, I liked a TV show called "Family Affair" that had a character, Uncle Bill, who went around building bridges. I didn't know what it meant to be a civil engineer at the time, but it seemed like a pretty neat job.

Q What is your favorite part of the job?
I enjoy working with people and trying to solve their problems — like getting an overpass built at a dangerous intersection.

Q What would you like to tell kids about math?
I wasn't particularly good at math, but my teachers kept telling me I had to learn math if I wanted to build bridges. Although math may seem abstract at times, you should bear with it because you'll use math every day whether you know it or not. This is true, even if you don't go into a math- or science-related profession.

GEOMETRY CONNECTION

Plotting Irrational Numbers

There are two ways to plot an irrational number, such as $\sqrt{20}$, on a number line. One way is to write the number as a decimal. Another way is to use a *straightedge and compass construction*.

Materials Needed
- compass
- straightedge
- graph paper
- pencil

1. Draw a number line on graph paper. Draw a right triangle whose legs have lengths 2 and 4. Draw the triangle so that one of the legs lies on the number line and the hypotenuse touches zero, as shown.

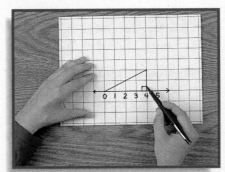

2. Using the Pythagorean Theorem, you know that the length of the hypotenuse is

$$c = \sqrt{2^2 + 4^2} = \sqrt{20}.$$

Use a compass to copy the hypotenuse's length onto the number line. From the number line, you can estimate that

$\sqrt{20} \approx 4.5$.

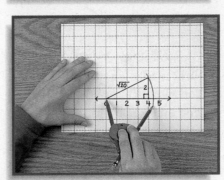

NOW TRY THESE

In Exercises 3 and 4, state the irrational number that is plotted on the number line. Estimate the number to one decimal place.

3.

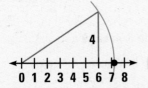

4.

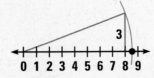

In Exercises 5–8, use a compass and straightedge to plot the number on a number line. Estimate the value of the number.

5. $\sqrt{2}$ **6.** $\sqrt{5}$ **7.** $\sqrt{8}$ **8.** $\sqrt{10}$

Problem Solving Using the Pythagorean Theorem

What you should learn:

Goal 1 How to use properties of triangles to solve real-life problems

Goal 2 How to use the Pythagorean Theorem to measure indirectly

Why you should learn it:

You can use properties of triangles to solve real-life problems, such as finding the area of a park.

Goal 1 USING PROPERTIES OF TRIANGLES

You have now studied four properties of triangles.

- **Perimeter** The perimeter of a triangle is the sum of the lengths of its sides. **(Lesson 2.2)**

- **Area** The area of a triangle is one half the product of its base and its height. **(Lesson 4.8)**

- **Similar Triangles** The ratios of corresponding sides of similar triangles are equal. **(Lesson 8.2)**

- **Pythagorean Theorem** In a right triangle, the sum of the squares of the lengths of the legs is equal to the square of the length of the hypotenuse. **(Lesson 9.3)**

In many real-life problems, you may need to use two or more of these properties to solve the problem.

Example 1 Finding Area and Perimeter

You are planning a city park, as shown at the right. You need to know the area and perimeter so you can order grass seed for the lawn and plants for a hedge. What are the area and the perimeter?

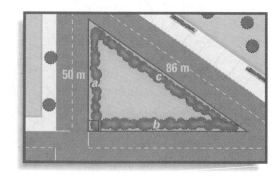

TOOLBOX

Areas, page 754

Solution

Use the Pythagorean Theorem to find the unknown length, b.

$$a^2 + b^2 = c^2 \qquad \text{Use the Pythagorean Theorem.}$$
$$50^2 + b^2 = 86^2 \qquad \text{Substitute for } a \text{ and } c.$$
$$2500 + b^2 = 7396 \qquad \text{Simplify.}$$
$$b^2 = 4896 \qquad \text{Subtract 2500 from each side.}$$
$$b = \sqrt{4896} \qquad \text{Choose the positive square root.}$$
$$b \approx 70 \qquad \text{Use a calculator.}$$

The perimeter of the park is about $50 + 86 + 70 = 206$ m. The area of the park is about

$$\text{Area} = \tfrac{1}{2}ab = \tfrac{1}{2}(50)(70) = 1750 \text{ m}^2.$$

Goal 2 INDIRECT MEASUREMENT

In Lesson 8.3, you learned how to use ratios of corresponding sides of similar triangles to indirectly measure the height of a tree or a building. The Pythagorean Theorem can also be used to measure objects indirectly.

Example 2 Using the Pythagorean Theorem

You work on a street maintenance crew for a city. Part of the street has caved in, as shown below. You don't have any ropes or tape measures that are long enough to stretch across the hole. Explain how you can measure the distance across the hole indirectly.

REAL LIFE
Street Maintenance

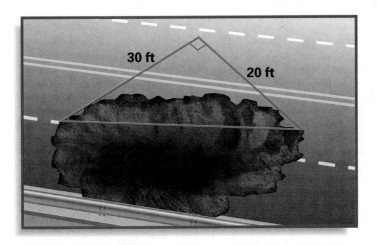

30 ft

20 ft

Solution

Here is one way to solve the problem. Mark the vertices of a right triangle whose hypotenuse is the distance across the hole. Measure the legs of the right triangle, as shown in the figure. Then use the Pythagorean Theorem to find the length of the hypotenuse.

$$a^2 + b^2 = c^2$$ Use the Pythagorean Theorem.

$$30^2 + 20^2 = c^2$$ Substitute for *a* and *b*.

$$900 + 400 = c^2$$ Simplify.

$$1300 = c^2$$ Simplify.

$$\sqrt{1300} = c$$ Choose the positive square root.

$$36 \approx c$$ Use a calculator.

The distance across the hole is about 36 ft.

ONGOING ASSESSMENT

Talk About It
· · · · · · · · · · · · · · · · · · ·

1. Measure the length and width of 2 or 3 rectangles in your classroom.

2. Decide how you can indirectly measure the length of the diagonal, and do it.

3. Use a ruler to directly measure the length of the diagonal. How do the two measures compare?

1. **DRAWING A DIAGRAM** Draw sketches to illustrate the four properties of triangles that you have studied in this course.

2. **PLAYGROUND** You are designing a neighborhood playground shaped like a right triangle. You measure one of the legs to be 45 m and the hypotenuse to be 75 m. Do you need to make any more measurements to find the perimeter and the area of the playground? Explain.

 TECHNOLOGY In Exercises 3–14, use a calculator if necessary. Round your result to two decimal places.

In Exercises 3–6, find the perimeter and area of the figure.

3.

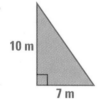

10 m

7 m

4. 11 ft

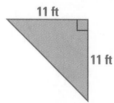

11 ft

5. 6 in.

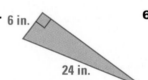

24 in.

6.

30 cm

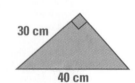

40 cm

In Exercises 7–10, find the perimeter and area of the figure.

7. 9 mi

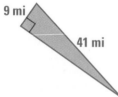

41 mi

8.

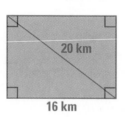

20 km

16 km

9.

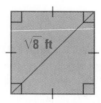

√8 ft

10.

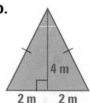

4 m

2 m   2 m

11. **CAMPING** What is the tallest that a person can be to stand in the tent?

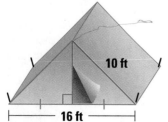

10 ft

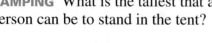

16 ft

12. The triangles below are similar. Find *a*.

10

a

15

9

13. FLYING A KITE You are flying a kite. You have let out 200 ft of string. The kite's shadow is 135 ft from you, and the sun is directly overhead. How high is the kite?

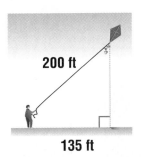

200 ft

135 ft

14. DRIVING To drive from Cleveland, OH, to Toronto, ON, you must go around two of the Great Lakes. How many miles are saved by flying directly over the lakes?

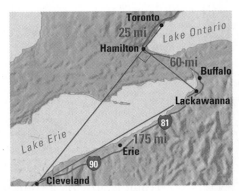

Tech Link

Investigation 9, Interactive Real-Life Investigations

STANDARDIZED TEST PRACTICE

15. The lengths of the sides of 4 triangles are listed below. Which set describes a right triangle?

    (A) 4, 4, 4   **(B)** 3, 4, 6   **(C)** 9, 12, 15   **(D)** 8, 11, 14

16. Estimate the missing side length of the triangle.

    (A) 19.7 mm   **(B)** 20.4 mm

    (C) 21 mm   **(D)** 21.7 mm

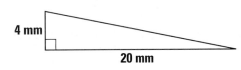

4 mm

20 mm

EXPLORATION AND EXTENSION

In Exercises 17 and 18, use the following information.

The ancient Egyptians used a rope with equally spaced knots like the one at the right. When the rope is held tight as shown, it forms a triangle.

17. For the triangle to be a right triangle, what must be true about the number of spaces on each side? Explain.

18. Which sets of lengths result in a right triangle?

    A. 4, 5, 6   **B.** 5, 12, 13

    C. 6, 8, 10   **D.** 5, 7, 9

Approximating Square Roots

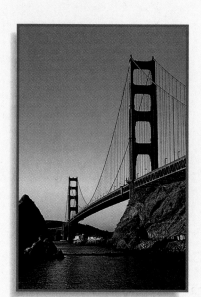

Example

You are designing a suspension bridge. To begin, you want a rough estimate for the length of the cable between points A and B on the diagram below. What is your estimate?

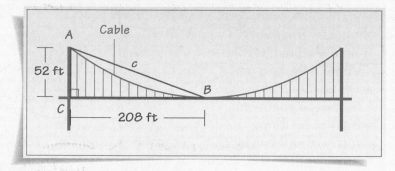

Solution

Triangle ABC is a right triangle, so you can use the Pythagorean Theorem to find the length of c.

$$c = \sqrt{52^2 + 208^2}$$ **Use the Pythagorean Theorem.**

$$= \sqrt{2704 + 43{,}264}$$ **Square the lengths of the legs.**

$$= \sqrt{45{,}968}$$ **Simplify.**

$$\approx 214.4014925 \text{ ft}$$ **Use a calculator.**

Since the length of the hypotenuse is only a rough estimate of the length of the cable, it doesn't make sense to give the answer to several decimal places.

$$214.4014925 \approx 214 \text{ ft}$$

Because the shortest distance between A and B lies on the hypotenuse, you can conclude that the cable length is greater than 214 ft.

Exercises

1. Use the diagram at the right to obtain a better estimate of the length of the cable. Show your work and explain your steps.

2. **OPEN-ENDED PROBLEM** How can you obtain an even better estimate of the length of the cable?

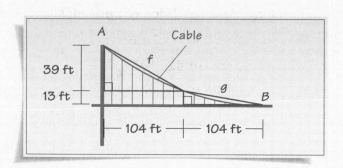

Take this test as you would take a test in class. The answers to the exercises are given in the back of the book.

In Exercises 1–4, write the square roots of the number. (9.1)

1. 16 **2.** 121 **3.** 0.49 **4.** 0.36

 In Exercises 5 and 6, how long is each side of the square? If necessary, use a calculator and round your answer to two decimal places. (9.1)

5.

Area is 33 cm².

6.

Area is 121 in.²

In Exercises 7–10, write both solutions of the equation. (9.1)

7. $x^2 = 7$ **8.** $t^2 = 49$ **9.** $s^2 + 3 = 4$ **10.** $3k^2 = 39$

In Exercises 11–14, tell whether the number is rational or irrational. Explain your reasoning. (9.2)

11. $\sqrt{250}$ **12.** $\sqrt{25}$ **13.** $\sqrt{2.5}$ **14.** $\sqrt{0.25}$

 TECHNOLOGY In Exercises 15–18, find the missing length. If necessary, use a calculator and round your answer to two decimal places. (9.3)

15.

3, h, 12

16.

13, r, 12

17.

q, 128, q

18.

s, s, 50

CARPENTRY In Exercises 19–21, use the following information. (9.4)

You are building a bookshelf in the corner of your room, as shown at the right. The walls intersect at a right angle.

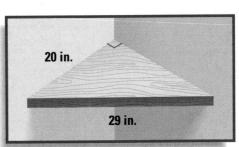

20 in.

29 in.

19. How long is the third side of the shelf?

20. What is the perimeter of the shelf?

21. What is the area of the shelf?

22. Tell whether the statement is *true* or *false*. (9.2)

$\sqrt{5}$ is rational because it can be written as $\dfrac{\sqrt{5}}{1}$.

9.5

Graphing Inequalities

What you should learn:

Goal 1 How to graph an inequality

Goal 2 How to write equivalent inequalities

Why you should learn it:

You can use inequalities to model and solve real-life problems, such as describing the weight of an ostrich.

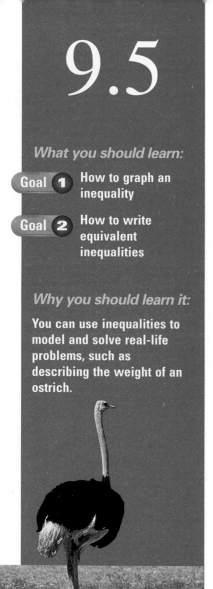

Goal 1 GRAPHING INEQUALITIES

There are four basic types of simple inequalities. Example 1 shows how to graph each type.

Example 1 Graphing Inequalities on a Number Line

Verbal Phrase	Inequality	Graph
a. All real numbers **less** than 2	$x < 2$	open — open dot at 2, shaded left
b. All real numbers **greater** than -3	$x > -3$	open — open dot at -3, shaded right
c. All real numbers **less** than or equal to -1	$x \le -1$	closed — closed dot at -1, shaded left
d. All real numbers **greater** than or equal to 0	$x \ge 0$	closed — closed dot at 0, shaded right

In Lesson 2.9, you learned to solve inequalities such as $x + 3 > 1$. Graphing the solution on a number line can help you visualize the values of x that make the inequality true.

Example 2 Solving an Inequality

Solve $x + 3 > 1$ and graph the solution.

Solution

$$x + 3 > 1 \qquad \text{Write original inequality.}$$
$$x + 3 - 3 > 1 - 3 \qquad \text{Subtract 3 from each side.}$$
$$x > -2 \qquad \text{Solution: } x \text{ is by itself.}$$

The solution is the set of all real numbers that are greater than -2. To graph this inequality, plot the number -2 with an open dot to show that -2 is not included. Then shade the part of the number line that is to the right of -2.

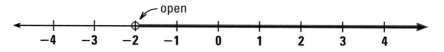

Each of the inequalities in Example 1 is written with the variable on the left. They can also be written with the variable on the right. For instance, $x < 2$ is the same as $2 > x$.

The graph of the inequality $x < 2$ is all real numbers that are less than 2.

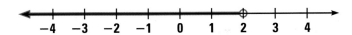

$x < 2$

The graph of the inequality $2 > x$ is all real numbers that 2 is greater than.

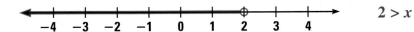

$2 > x$

To write an inequality that is equivalent to $x < 2$, move each number and letter to the other side, and reverse the inequality.

$$x < 2 \rightarrow 2 > x$$

Example 3 Writing Equivalent Inequalities

For each of the following, write an equivalent inequality. State the inequality verbally.

a. $y > -3$ **b.** $0 \le m$ **c.** $4 \ge t$

Solution

a. The inequality $y > -3$ is equivalent to $-3 < y$.

Either inequality can be written verbally as "the set of all real numbers that are greater than -3."

b. The inequality $0 \le m$ is equivalent to $m \ge 0$.

Either inequality can be written verbally as "the set of all real numbers that are greater than or equal to 0."

c. The inequality $4 \ge t$ is equivalent to $t \le 4$.

Either inequality can be written verbally as "the set of all real numbers that are less than or equal to 4."

STUDY TIP

One way to check that two inequalities are equivalent is to see that the inequality symbols "point" toward the same number or variable. For instance, in the inequalities $x < 2$ and $2 > x$, the symbols point to x.

ONGOING ASSESSMENT

Write About It

Solve the inequality. Show your work and explain your steps. Then graph your solution.

1. $3 + b \ge 5$

2. $-3 \ge x + 2$

3. $y - 4 < -8$

9.5 Exercises

In Exercises 1–4, match the inequality with its graph.

A.

B.

C.

D.

1. $x < 10$ **2.** $x \geq -4$ **3.** $x \leq -4$ **4.** $x > 10$

In Exercises 5–8, write two equivalent inequalities for the phrase.

5. All real numbers less than 15

6. All real numbers greater than or equal to 0

7. All real numbers greater than -3

8. All real numbers less than or equal to -11

In Exercises 9 and 10, solve the inequality. Then graph the solution.

9. $x + 5 < -2$ **10.** $x - 5 \geq -2$

In Exercises 11–14, graph the inequality.

11. $x \geq 1$ **12.** $x < 0$ **13.** $x > 7$ **14.** $x \leq -2$

In Exercises 15–18, write the inequality represented by the graph.

15.

16.

17.

18.

In Exercises 19–22, write the inequality given by the verbal phrase. Then graph the inequality.

19. All real numbers greater than $\sqrt{2}$

20. All real numbers less than or equal to $\sqrt{5}$

21. All real numbers less than $-\sqrt{3}$

22. All real numbers greater than or equal to $-\sqrt{6}$

In Exercises 23–28, solve the inequality. Then graph the solution.

23. $x + 3 \geq 2$ **24.** $5 > y + 2$ **25.** $13 < n - 4$

26. $t - 1 \leq 7$ **27.** $z + 7 > -2$ **28.** $15 \geq w - 4$

In Exercises 29–32, write an equivalent inequality. Then write the inequality verbally.

29. $x \leq -20$ **30.** $y > -3$ **31.** $s < 17$ **32.** $m \geq 13$

33. SOLAR CARS The *Sunraycer* set a record speed of 48.71 mi/h for solely solar-powered vehicles. Let S represent the speed of the *Sunraycer*. Which of the following best describes the car's speed? Explain your reasoning.

    A. $0 < S$ and $S < 48.71$

    B. $0 < S$ and $S \leq 48.71$

    C. $0 \leq S$ and $S < 48.71$

    D. $0 \leq S$ and $S \leq 48.71$

34. SPACE EXPLORATION The sun is about 93 million miles from Earth. In 1977, *Voyager I* was launched from Earth and moved out in the solar system (away from the sun). Let d represent the distance between *Voyager I* and the sun. Write an inequality that describes the values of d.

35. ABSOLUTE ZERO The coldest it is possible for any object to get is $-459.7°F$. Let T represent the temperature of an object. Write an inequality that describes the possible values of T.

36. BIRD WEIGHTS The largest birds are ostriches. Ostriches can weigh up to 300 lb. Let w be the weight of a bird. Write two equivalent inequalities that describe the possible values of w.

Real Life... Real People

Molly Brennan, shown here outside the Lincoln Memorial, drove the *Sunraycer* at a record speed.

In Exercises 37 and 38, match the statement with the graph that you think is the best representation. Explain your reasoning.

A.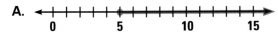

B.

37. At least 5 students attended the party.   **38.** The temperature is at least 5°.

 STANDARDIZED TEST PRACTICE

39. Which is the correct graph of $x \geq -3$?

    Ⓐ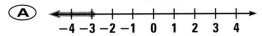

    Ⓑ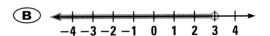

    Ⓒ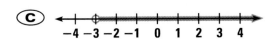

    Ⓓ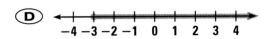

40. BUILDING YOUR PROJECT Some roller coaster loops have teardrop designs, as shown at the right. The height of the loop is h feet. Just before the loop, the car needs to have dropped at least $\frac{4}{3}h$ feet. With a drop of $\frac{4}{3}h$ feet, the car will have the following speeds.

Speed at $Y = 16\sqrt{\dfrac{h}{3}}$ ft/s

Speed at $Z = 8\sqrt{\dfrac{h}{3}}$ ft/s

a. Suppose $h = 64$ ft. Find the velocities at Y and Z.

b. Between Y and Z, how fast will the car be traveling? Use a number line to illustrate your answer.

c. Add a teardrop loop to your roller coaster design. Make sure that the height of the preceding hill is $\frac{4}{3}h$. Find the speed of your roller coaster car at the points Y and Z on the loop.

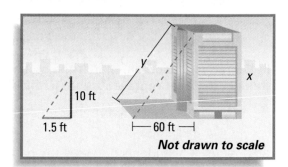

SPIRAL REVIEW

In Exercises 1–3, use the diagram at the right. (9.4)

1. Find x, the height of the building.

2. Find y, the distance from the top of the building to the end of the building's shadow.

3. Find the distance from the top of the pole to the end of its shadow.

Diagram labels: y, x, 10 ft, 1.5 ft, 60 ft, *Not drawn to scale*

In Exercises 4–7, solve the inequality. Then graph the solution. (9.5)

4. $x + 2 > 12$ **5.** $0 > x - 2$ **6.** $x - 5 \le 10$ **7.** $4 \ge x - 9$

In Exercises 8–13, write the prime factorization of the number. (6.2)

8. 70   **9.** 360   **10.** 270

11. 189   **12.** 369   **13.** 368

14. SCHOOL LUNCH In a survey of 350 students, 36% said they pack their lunch for school. How many students is this? (7.8)

READ About It

Cedar Point amusement park in Sandusky, Ohio, built its first roller coaster in 1892. That coaster was 25 ft tall and its cars traveled at a maximum speed of 10 mi/h. Since then, the park has set a world record for the number of roller coasters in one place.

SCREAM
Machines

In 1991, Cedar Point added a huge wooden roller coaster called the Mean Streak. The first hill of the Mean Streak has a vertical drop of 155 ft. The second hill has a height of 124 ft.

During a $2\frac{3}{4}$ min ride, riders cover 5427 ft of track. With its three trains that each carry 28 passengers, the Mean Streak can frighten 1600 riders in an hour.

WRITE About It

1. In the middle of the first hill, a car drops about $15\frac{1}{2}$ ft for every 12 ft of horizontal run. Find the length of track the car covers during such a $15\frac{1}{2}$ ft drop.

2. You can use the formula $v^2 = 64h$ to estimate a car's speed in feet per second, v, at the bottom of a hill of height h. Estimate the speed of a car at the bottom of the first hill of the Mean Streak. Convert your answer to miles per hour.

3. Estimate a car's speed at the bottom of the second hill. Compare your result to the speed found in Exercise 2.

4. What is the average speed of a car during the ride? Explain how you found your answer.

5. Does the Mean Streak have two trains in motion at any time? Explain your reasoning.

Solving Inequalities: Multiplying and Dividing

What you should learn:

Goal 1 How to use properties of inequalities

Goal 2 How to use multiplication and division to solve inequalities

Why you should learn it:

You can use inequalities to model and solve real-life problems, such as meeting fundraising goals.

Goal 1 USING PROPERTIES OF INEQUALITIES

In this lesson, you will learn that there is an important difference between solving an equation and solving an inequality.

LESSON INVESTIGATION

Investigating Solutions of Inequalities

GROUP ACTIVITY You can check whether a number is a solution of the inequality $-2x < 6$ by substituting the number for x.

$$-2(1) = -2 \qquad \text{1 is a solution because } -2 < 6.$$
$$-2(-4) = 8 \qquad \text{-4 is not a solution because } 8 \not< 6.$$

Use *Guess, Check, and Revise* to discover the solution of $-2x < 6$. Can you obtain your solution by dividing each side of the inequality by -2? Explain your reasoning.

In this investigation, you may have discovered that the solution of $-2x < 6$ is $x > -3$. To obtain this solution, you can divide each side of the original inequality by -2, but you must also reverse the direction of the inequality symbol.

Example 1 Solving an Inequality

$-2x < 6$ Write original inequality.

$\dfrac{-2x}{-2} > \dfrac{6}{-2}$ Divide each side by −2 and reverse inequality symbol.

$x > -3$ Solution: *x* is by itself.

PROPERTIES OF INEQUALITIES

1. Adding or subtracting the same number on each side of an inequality produces an equivalent inequality.
2. Multiplying or dividing each side of an inequality by the same *positive* number produces an equivalent inequality.
3. Multiplying or dividing each side of an inequality by the same *negative* number and *reversing the direction of the inequality symbol* produces an equivalent inequality.

Example 2 **Solving Inequalities**

a. $-\frac{1}{2}x \geq 6$ Write original inequality.

$-2 \cdot \left(-\frac{1}{2}\right)x \leq -2 \cdot 6$ Multiply each side by -2 and reverse inequality symbol.

$x \leq -12$ Solution: x is by itself.

The solution is $x \leq -12$, which is the set of all real numbers that are less than or equal to -12.

b. $12 < 3m$ Write original inequality.

$\frac{12}{3} < \frac{3m}{3}$ Divide each side by 3.

$4 < m$ Solution: m is by itself.

The solution is $4 < m$ or $m > 4$, which is the set of all real numbers that are greater than 4.

To check a solution of an inequality, substitute several numbers into the original inequality. For instance, when you check the solution in part (b) of Example 2, numbers that are greater than 4 yield true statements and numbers that are less than 4 yield false statements.

Example 3 **Solving a Real-Life Inequality**

You are a real-estate agent and earn a 5% commission for each house you sell. What range of house prices will earn you a commission of at least $4000?

REAL LIFE
Real Estate

Solution

Let H represent the price of the house. Then your commission is 5% of H, or $0.05H$.

$0.05H \geq 4000$ Commission is at least $4000.

$\frac{0.05H}{0.05} \geq \frac{4000}{0.05}$ Divide each side by 0.05.

$H \geq 80{,}000$ Solution: H is by itself.

The price of the house you sell must be at least $80,000.

ONGOING ASSESSMENT

Write About It

1. In your own words, explain how to check the solution of an inequality. How is it different from checking the solution of an equation?

GUIDED PRACTICE

In Exercises 1–4, use <, >, =, ≤, or ≥ to complete the inequality.

1. $4 > -x$

-4 **?** x

2. $-3 \geq -t$

3 **?** t

3. $3y > 15$

y **?** 5

4. $-2 \geq -\frac{1}{2}a$

4 **?** a

In Exercises 5–8, will the strategy require reversing the direction of the inequality?

5. Multiply both sides by -1.

6. Divide both sides by 4.

7. Multiply both sides by $\frac{1}{4}$.

8. Divide both sides by -5.

In Exercises 9–12, solve the inequality.

9. $4b > 24$

10. $-\frac{1}{4}x \leq 14$

11. $-5 < 0.2h$

12. $36 \geq -\frac{1}{2}f$

PRACTICE AND PROBLEM SOLVING

ERROR ANALYSIS   In Exercises 13–15, describe the error.

13.
$$1 < -0.4c$$
$$\frac{1}{0.4} > \frac{-0.4c}{-0.4}$$
$$2.5 > c$$

14.
$$\frac{1}{3}z \leq -12$$
$$3 \cdot \frac{1}{3}z \geq 3 \cdot (-12)$$
$$z \geq -36$$

15.
$$-4x > 28$$
$$\frac{-4x}{-4} > \frac{28}{-4}$$
$$x > -7$$

In Exercises 16–19, match the inequality with the graph of its solution.

A.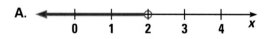

B.

C.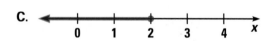

D.

16. $0.7x \leq 1.4$

17. $-1 > -\frac{1}{2}x$

18. $\frac{1}{8} \leq \frac{1}{16}x$

19. $-3x > -6$

In Exercises 20–35, solve the inequality. Then graph the solution.

20. $3m < 4$

21. $2n \geq 5$

22. $\frac{x}{2} \leq 8$

23. $\frac{y}{9} > 4$

24. $-5b \leq 35$

25. $-2a > \frac{1}{2}$

26. $-\frac{1}{2}z > 5$

27. $-\frac{1}{5}p \leq 2$

28. $-3a \leq -6$

29. $-1.2x \geq -3.6$

30. $4 < 0.8r$

31. $-5.6 \leq -1.4m$

32. $\frac{a}{6} > -2$

33. $\frac{3}{5}y \leq -6$

34. $14 > -\frac{1}{3}n$

35. $-\frac{3}{2} < -\frac{1}{4}x$

36. GARDENING You want to plant a 3 ft wide rectangular flower border in front of the school. You have enough seedlings to plant an area of at most 60 ft². How long can the border be?

37. FUNDRAISER Your softball team is selling sandwiches to raise money. You make a profit of $.75 for each sandwich sold and you need to raise at least $300.00. How many sandwiches must you sell? Write your answer as an inequality and as a sentence.

38. MOVIES The movie video you want to buy costs $26.95. You earn $3 an hour baby-sitting. How many hours must you baby-sit to earn enough money to buy the video?

39. BICYCLING Your top bicycling speed is 40 km/h. How far can you travel in 3 h?

STANDARDIZED TEST PRACTICE

40. You plan to invest some money for one year at an interest rate of 5%. What range of investment amounts will provide at least $100 in interest?

    A $x \geq \$200$ **B** $x \geq \$2000$ **C** $x \geq \$20,000$ **D** $x < \$2000$

41. Solve the inequality $\dfrac{45}{75} \leq \dfrac{n}{120}$.

    A $n \geq 72$ **B** $n \geq 200$ **C** $72 \geq n$ **D** $200 \geq n$

EXPLORATION AND EXTENSION

PORTFOLIO

42. BUILDING YOUR PROJECT You are creating a second teardrop loop for your roller coaster. The height of the hill just before the loop is 140 ft. The inequality below describes the possible values for h, the height of the loop.

$$140 \geq \frac{4}{3}h$$

a. Solve the inequality for h.

b. Choose one of the possible values for h and use it in the design of your second teardrop loop.

9.7 Solving Multi-Step Inequalities

Goal 1 SOLVING MULTI-STEP INEQUALITIES

In this lesson you will learn to solve inequalities that require two or more steps. Remember that if you multiply or divide by a negative number, you must reverse the direction of the inequality symbol.

Example 1 Solving a Multi-Step Inequality

Solve $2x + 1 \leq 4$, and graph the solution.

Solution

$2x + 1 \leq 4$	Write original inequality.
$2x + 1 - 1 \leq 4 - 1$	Subtract 1 from each side.
$2x \leq 3$	Simplify.
$\dfrac{2x}{2} \leq \dfrac{3}{2}$	Divide each side by 2.
$x \leq \dfrac{3}{2}$	Solution: x is by itself.

The solution is all real numbers that are less than or equal to $\frac{3}{2}$. A graph of the solution is shown below.

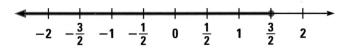

Example 2 Solving a Multi-Step Inequality

Solve $-\frac{1}{3}m - 5 > 2$.

Solution

$-\dfrac{1}{3}m - 5 > 2$	Write original inequality.
$-\dfrac{1}{3}m - 5 + 5 > 2 + 5$	Add 5 to each side.
$-\dfrac{1}{3}m > 7$	Simplify.
$(-3)\left(-\dfrac{1}{3}\right)m < (-3)(7)$	Multiply each side by −3 and reverse the inequality symbol.
$m < -21$	Solution: m is by itself.

The solution is all real numbers that are less than -21.

Example 3 Solving a Real-Life Inequality

REAL LIFE
Nutrition

You are baking a batch of 36 oatmeal chocolate chip cookies. Without the chips, the recipe has 1000 calories (Cal). You want each cookie to have less than 45 Cal. Each chocolate chip has 2.4 Cal. How many chips can you have in each cookie?

Solution

Without any chocolate chips, each cookie has $\frac{1}{36}(1000) \approx 28$ Cal.

Method **1**   Write and solve an inequality.

Verbal Model $28 + 2.4 \cdot$ Number of chips per cookie < 45

Labels   Number of chocolate chips per cookie $= n$ (chips)

Algebraic Model
$$28 + 2.4 \cdot n < 45$$
$$2.4n < 17$$
$$n < \frac{17}{2.4}$$
$$n < 7.1$$

You can use up to 7 chocolate chips per cookie.

Method **2**   Use a table or a graph. Notice that the calories exceed 45 when the number of chips is greater than 7.

Chips	Calories
0	28
1	30.4
2	32.8
3	35.2
4	37.6
5	40.0
6	42.4
7	44.8
8	47.2
9	49.6
10	52

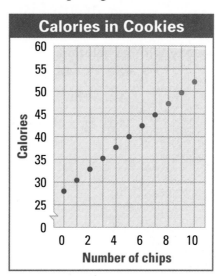

Calories in Cookies

Number of chips

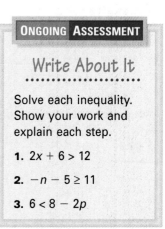

ONGOING ASSESSMENT

Write About It

Solve each inequality. Show your work and explain each step.

1. $2x + 6 > 12$

2. $-n - 5 \geq 11$

3. $6 < 8 - 2p$

GUIDED PRACTICE

REASONING In Exercises 1 and 2, solve the inequality. Explain your steps.

1. $3x - 2 \le 13$

2. $4 < -\frac{1}{5}y + 2$

3. When you solve an inequality, when should you reverse the direction of the inequality sign?

In Exercises 4 and 5, solve the inequality and graph the solution.

4. $4y - 1 > -3$

5. $-18 + 10y \ge 12$

PRACTICE AND PROBLEM SOLVING

ERROR ANALYSIS In Exercises 6–8, describe the error. Then correct it.

6.
$$-4x + 7 \ge -5$$
$$-4x + 7 - 7 \ge -5 - 7$$
$$\frac{-4x}{-4} \ge \frac{-12}{-4}$$
$$x \ge 3$$

7.
$$3(2y - 1) < -7$$
$$6y - 3 < -7$$
$$6y - 3 + 3 < -7 + 3$$
$$\left(\frac{1}{6}\right)(6y) > \left(\frac{1}{6}\right)(-4)$$
$$y > -\frac{2}{3}$$

8.
$$\frac{1}{2}x \le \frac{3}{4}x + \frac{1}{4}$$
$$\frac{1}{2}x - \frac{3}{4}x \le \frac{3}{4}x - \frac{3}{4}x + \frac{1}{4}$$
$$\frac{1}{4}x \le \frac{1}{4}$$
$$x \le 1$$

LOGICAL REASONING In Exercises 9–12, decide whether the statement is *sometimes*, *always*, or *never* true.

9. If $-5x + 9 \le -11$, then $x = 3$.

10. If $5y - 20 \ge 15$, then $y = 7$.

11. If $-15b - 12 > -3$, then $b < -\frac{3}{5}$.

12. If $4(2a - 6) < 8$, then $a < 1$.

In Exercises 13–16, match the inequality with its solution.

A. $x < -2$ **B.** $x < 2$ **C.** $x > -2$ **D.** $x > 2$

13. $2x + 13 > 9$

14. $-2x - 8 > -4$

15. $6 < 18 - 6x$

16. $16 - 10x < 4 - 4x$

In Exercises 17–25, solve the inequality.

17. $-11x + 3 < -30$

18. $\frac{1}{5}y + 12 \le 8$

19. $5a + 6 \ge -9$

20. $-9 < 2b - 13$

21. $\frac{3}{4}m \le \frac{1}{4}m + 2$

22. $-\frac{1}{5}x > \frac{4}{5}x + 3$

23. $2(x + 1) \ge -2$

24. $4x + 1 \le 2(x + 2)$

25. $-4x + 3 \ge -5x$

In Exercises 26–28, let n, $n + 1$, and $n + 2$ be consecutive integers. Write the inequality that represents the verbal sentence. Solve the inequality.

26. The sum of 2 consecutive integers is less than or equal to 7.

27. The sum of 3 consecutive integers is more than 18.

28. The sum of 3 consecutive integers is less than 20.

GEOMETRY **In Exercises 29 and 30, describe the possible values of x.**

29. The area is at least 28 cm^2.

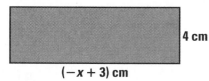

4 cm

$(-x + 3)$ cm

30. The perimeter is less than or equal to 36 ft.

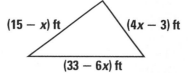

$(15 - x)$ ft $(4x - 3)$ ft

$(33 - 6x)$ ft

31. **NUTRITION** Work with a partner to plan a macaroni and cheese school lunch that is to contain at least 20 grams of protein. Without the macaroni and cheese, the lunch has 6 grams of protein. The macaroni and cheese has 2 grams of protein per ounce. What size servings of macaroni and cheese should you plan?

32. **CARNIVAL** You are going to a carnival. It costs $10 to enter and $.25 each for tickets for games and rides. You don't want to spend more than $20. Write and solve an inequality to find the number of tickets you can buy.

33. Show how you can use a table to answer Exercise 32.

34. **BICYCLING** You plan to ride your bike more than 12 mi. Your average speed is 15 mi/h. Write an inequality that represents the time (in hours) that you will ride your bike. Solve the inequality.

Real Life...
Real Facts

Antique Carousels
In a racing derby, the four horses in a row compete against each other. One of these very rare carousels is in Sandusky, Ohio.

STANDARDIZED TEST PRACTICE

35. The ordered pair, $(3, -1)$, is *not* a solution of which inequality?

   Ⓐ $4x - 5y \leq 21$ **Ⓑ** $x + y > 0$ **Ⓒ** $-2x + 4y \leq -10$ **Ⓓ** $3x - y < 10$

EXPLORATION AND EXTENSION

36. **EQUATION SENSE** In a coordinate plane, graph all ordered pairs, (x, y), for which the following is true: x and y are positive integers and $x + y \leq 8$.

Why you should learn it:

You can use the Triangle Inequality to estimate distances.

The Triangle Inequality

Goal 1 USING THE TRIANGLE INEQUALITY

In this lesson you will study the **Triangle Inequality** .

THE TRIANGLE INEQUALITY

The sum of the lengths of any two sides of a triangle is greater than the length of the third side.

$$d + e > f \qquad d + f > e \qquad e + f > d$$

Example 1 **Estimating Distances**

You have moved to a new city, and are told that your apartment is 5 mi from your school and 6 mi from the restaurant where you have a part-time job. You are also told that your apartment, school, and restaurant do not lie on a straight line. Without knowing any other information, what can you say about the distance between your school and the restaurant?

PROBLEM SOLVING STRATEGY

Solution

STRATEGY **DRAW A DIAGRAM** Begin by drawing a diagram. Because your apartment, school, and restaurant do not lie on a line, they must form the vertices of a triangle.

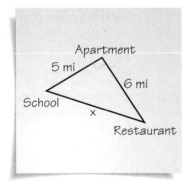

Using the Triangle Inequality, you can write the following.

$5 + x > 6$	and	$5 + 6 > x$	**Use the Triangle Inequality.**
$x > 1$		$11 > x$	**Simplify.**

The distance between the school and the restaurant is greater than 1 mi ($x > 1$) and less than 11 mi ($x < 11$).

Example 2 Checking Side Lengths

You are designing a small stained glass window. To begin, you draw a pattern and label the lengths (in inches) of each piece of glass. A friend looks at the pattern and says that there is something wrong with the measurements. How can your friend tell?

REAL LIFE
Art

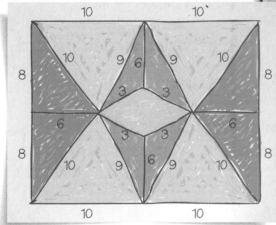

Solution

There are three different sizes of triangles in the pattern. Use the Triangle Inequality to check the side lengths of each triangle.

A 6-8-10 triangle is possible because each inequality is true.

$6 + 8 > 10$	$6 + 10 > 8$	$8 + 10 > 6$
$14 > 10$	$16 > 8$	$18 > 6$

A 9-10-10 triangle is possible because each inequality is true.

$9 + 10 > 10$	$10 + 10 > 9$
$19 > 10$	$20 > 9$

A 3-6-9 triangle is not possible because one of the inequalities is false.

~~$3 + 6 > 9$~~	$3 + 9 > 6$	$6 + 9 > 3$
~~$9 > 9$~~	$12 > 6$	$15 > 3$

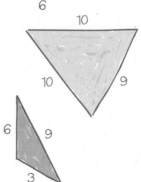

ONGOING ASSESSMENT

Talk About It
. . . .

Can the numbers be side lengths of a triangle? How can you tell?

1. 50, 10, 71

2. 60, 82, 100

3. 53, 85, 138

9.8 Exercises

Extra Practice, page 732

GUIDED PRACTICE

1. Which of the following are true statements about the lengths of the sides of the triangle at the right?

A. $s < r + t$ **B.** $r > s + t$ **C.** $r + s > t$

In Exercises 2–4, can the numbers be the side lengths of a triangle? Explain your answer with a sketch.

2. 3, 4, 6   3. 4, 6, 10   4. 5, 7, 11

In Exercises 5–7, the lengths of two sides of a triangle are given. What can you say about the length of the third side?

5. 3 ft and 5 ft   6. 9 in. and 11 in.   7. 16 cm and 20 cm

PRACTICE AND PROBLEM SOLVING

In Exercises 8–11, can the side lengths be correct? Explain.

8.   9.   10.   11.

12. Copy and complete the table.

Length of side 1	Length of side 2	Length of side 3 is greater than	Length of side 3 is less than
3 cm	8 cm	?	?
9 in.	16 in.	?	?
10 ft	21 ft	?	?
30 m	45 m	?	?
100 cm	225 cm	?	?

In Exercises 13–16, can the numbers be side lengths of a triangle?

13. $\dfrac{5}{2}, \dfrac{7}{2}, \dfrac{9}{2}$ 14. $\sqrt{2}, \sqrt{3}, \sqrt{10}$ 15. 3.25, 6.79, 10.1   16. $\dfrac{1}{8}, \dfrac{1}{4}, \dfrac{1}{2}$

VISUAL THINKING In Exercises 17 and 18, decide whether the string can be folded at the indicated points to form a triangle. Explain.

17. 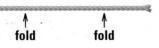   18.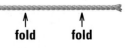

In Exercises 19–22, use the figure at the right to complete the statement.

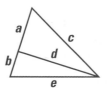

19. $b + d > $ **?**

20. $a + b + $ **?** $ > e$

21. $a < d + $ **?**

22. $b + $ **?** $ + e > c$

23. **SCISSORS** The blades on your scissors are both 3.75 in. long. The two tips of the blades and the pin that holds the scissors together can form a triangle. When a triangle is formed, how far apart can the tips of the blades be? Explain your reasoning.

24. **ENGINEERING** Engineers often use triangles to support structures that they build. After receiving the following partial blueprint design for a project, you discover that a mistake has been made. What is it?

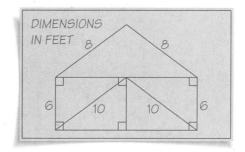

25. **NUMBER SENSE** A triangle has side lengths of 11 cm and 14 cm. The perimeter of the triangle must be between what two numbers?

STANDARDIZED TEST PRACTICE

26. Two sides of a triangle have lengths of 9 in. and 15 in. and the third side is x inches long. Which inequality must be true?

(A) $x \geq 24$ **(B)** $x < 24$ **(C)** $x \leq 23$ **(D)** $x < 6$

27. Consider the triangle shown at the right. Which number is not a possible value of x?

(A) 2.1   **(B)** 8.7

(C) 10.5   **(D)** 14.1

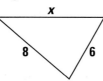

EXPLORATION AND EXTENSION

28. **COMMUNICATING ABOUT MATHEMATICS**
You are meeting a friend at the Giant Wheel. Your friend said that it takes 5 min to walk from Gemini to the Corkscrew and 2 min to walk from the Corkscrew to the Giant Wheel. How long does it take to walk from Gemini to the Giant Wheel? Explain. For more information about Cedar Point, see page 437.

WHAT *did you learn?*

WHY *did you learn it?*

Skills

9.1	Use the Square Root Property to solve equations.	Find the time it takes an object to fall.
9.2	Identify and graph real numbers on a number line.	Estimate and compare numbers from real life.
9.3	Use the Pythagorean Theorem. Solve a right triangle.	Calculate distances.
9.4	Use the Pythagorean Theorem with other formulas from geometry.	Find measurements when you don't have much information.
9.5	Solve inequalities by adding and subtracting. Graph the solutions. Write equivalent inequalities.	Solve real-life problems involving ranges of values, such as possible car speeds.
9.6	Solve inequalities by multiplying and dividing.	Solve more real-life problems involving ranges of values.
9.7	Solve multi-step inequalities.	Decide how to meet nutrition requirements.
9.8	Use the Triangle Inequality.	Estimate distances and check the side lengths of triangles.

Strategies

9.1–9.8	Use verbal and algebraic models.	Solve a wide variety of real-life problems.

Using Data

9.1–9.8	Use tables and graphs.	Organize data and solve problems.

HOW *does it fit in the bigger picture of mathematics?*

As you use math to describe new things, you may need new kinds of numbers. For example, to say how many people are in a group, you only need **whole numbers**. But to describe how much pie you ate, you probably need **rational numbers**.

Mathematicians discovered **irrational numbers** when they tried to describe the lengths of sides of triangles. As you learn more math, you will learn about **imaginary numbers** and **complex numbers**. These numbers are used to describe things in real life such as music and electricity.

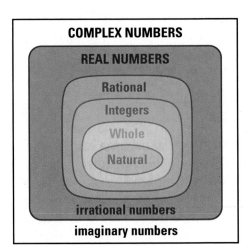

COMPLEX NUMBERS

REAL NUMBERS

Rational

Integers

Whole

Natural

irrational numbers

imaginary numbers

VOCABULARY

- **real numbers** (p. 414)
- **right angle** (p. 420)
- **legs** (p. 420)
- **hypotenuse** (p. 420)
- **Pythagorean Theorem** (p. 420)
- **solving a right triangle** (p. 421)
- **isosceles** (p. 421)
- **Pythagorean triple** (p. 421)
- **Triangle Inequality** (p. 446)

9.1 EXPLORING SQUARE ROOTS

Example

$t^2 + 4 = 20$	Write original equation.
$t^2 + 4 - 4 = 20 - 4$	Subtract 4 from each side.
$t^2 = 16$	Simplify.
$t = -\sqrt{16}$ or $t = \sqrt{16}$	Use the Square Root Property.
$t = -4$ or $t = 4$	Simplify.

Write both solutions of the equation.

1. $y^2 = 169$ **2.** $5m^2 = 605$ **3.** $s^2 + 5 = 14$ **4.** $3 + r^2 = 10$

9.2 THE REAL NUMBER SYSTEM

A real number is rational if it can be written as the quotient of two integers, and it is irrational if it cannot.

Examples   Is the number rational or irrational?

$$\frac{3}{8} = 0.375 \qquad\qquad \sqrt{6} = 2.449489743\ldots$$

Solutions

This number is rational because the decimal form of the number terminates.

This number is irrational because the decimal form of the number does not terminate or repeat.

You can plot each of these numbers on a number line.

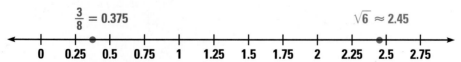

$\frac{3}{8} = 0.375$ $\sqrt{6} \approx 2.45$

0   0.25   0.5   0.75   1   1.25   1.5   1.75   2   2.25   2.5   2.75

Tell whether each number in the set is rational or irrational. Then plot the set of numbers on a number line.

5. $\left\{\frac{7}{4}, \sqrt{12}, \frac{5}{2}\right\}$ **6.** $\left\{\frac{3}{5}, 1.2, \sqrt{3}\right\}$ **7.** $\left\{\sqrt{5}, \frac{4}{3}, -2.2\right\}$ **8.** $\left\{1, \sqrt{6}, -\sqrt{2}\right\}$

9.3 THE PYTHAGOREAN THEOREM

You can use the Pythagorean Theorem, $a^2 + b^2 = c^2$, to solve a right triangle, where a and b are the lengths of the legs and c is the length of the hypotenuse.

Example

$a^2 + b^2 = c^2$	Use the Pythagorean Theorem.
$7^2 + 4^2 = c^2$	Substitute for a and b.
$65 = c^2$	Simplify.
$\sqrt{65} = c$	Choose the positive square root.
$c \approx 8.06$	Use a calculator.

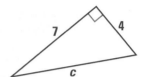

 TECHNOLOGY Find the missing length. If necessary, use a calculator and round your answer to two decimal places.

9.

7, 8

10.

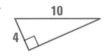
10, 4

11.

7, 3

12.

12, 14

9.4 USING THE PYTHAGOREAN THEOREM

Example You are setting up a tent, as shown at the right. What is the tallest that a person can be to stand in the tent?

Solution

$a^2 + \left(\dfrac{10}{2}\right)^2 = 7^2$	Use the Pythagorean Theorem and substitute.
$a^2 + 25 = 49$	Simplify.
$a^2 = 24$	Subtract 25 from each side.
$a \approx 4.9$	Choose the positive square root.

$a \approx 4.9$ ft $\approx$ 4 ft 11 in.

The person could be 4 ft 11 in. tall.

13. **WATER-SKIING** A professional water-skier jumps off the end of the ramp shown at the right. Estimate the height of the ramp. Give your answer to the nearest foot.

9.5 GRAPHING INEQUALITIES

Examples

Verbal Phrase	Inequality	Graph
All real numbers less than 2	$x < 2$	
All real numbers greater than or equal to -1	$x \geq -1$	

14. Graph the inequality $x \leq 4$ on a number line.

15. Write "all real numbers greater than -3" as an inequality. Then graph the inequality.

9.6–9.7 SOLVING INEQUALITIES

To solve an inequality, you must *reverse the direction of the inequality symbol* if you multiply or divide by a negative number.

Example

$-5x \leq 20$ Write original inequality.

$\dfrac{-5x}{-5} \geq \dfrac{20}{-5}$ Divide each side by -5 and reverse inequality symbol.

$x \geq -4$ Solution: *x* is by itself.

Solve the inequality. Then graph the solution.

16. $-4x - 5 \geq 3$ **17.** $-\dfrac{1}{4} < \dfrac{1}{10}x$ **18.** $6x + 7 \leq 4$ **19.** $-\dfrac{5}{8}x > -\dfrac{2}{3}$

9.8 THE TRIANGLE INEQUALITY

To use the Triangle Inequality, remember that the sum of the lengths of any two sides of a triangle is greater than the length of the third side.

Example   Can 12, 4, and 7 be the side lengths of a triangle?

Solution $12 + 4 > 7?$ $12 + 7 > 4?$ $4 + 7 > 12?$

       yes   yes   no

The triangle cannot have the given side lengths.

Decide whether a triangle can have the given side lengths.

20. 12, 2, 3   **21.** 5, 6, 9   **22.** 17, 7, 21

23. Two sides of a triangle are 5 in. and 7 in. long. What can you say about the length of the third side?

In Exercises 1–3, write both solutions of the equation.

1. $x^2 = 225$

2. $a^2 + 3 = 39$

3. $8 - s^2 = -6$

4. A square has an area of 65.61 in.^{2} What is the length of each side?

In Exercises 5–7, the lengths of two sides of a triangle are given. What can you say about the length of the third side?

5. 3 in. and 12 in.

6. 22 ft and 3 ft

7. 8 m and 15 m

In Exercises 8–11, match each number with a point on the number line.

8. $\dfrac{9}{5}$

9. $\dfrac{9}{4}$

10. $\sqrt{3}$

11. $\sqrt{0.2}$

12. **CATERING** A caterer plans to cut out 8 pastry shells from a rectangular piece of dough. The lengths of the sides of each shell are 4 in. and 9 in. What is the length of the diagonal cut?

In Exercises 13–15, solve the triangle.

13.

14.

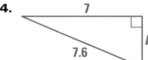

15.

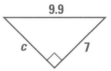

In Exercises 16–18, solve the inequality and graph the solution.

16. $-x < 2$

17. $-8r + 16 \le 8$

18. $-2p \ge 5$

HOUSE PAINTING **In Exercises 19–21, use the following information.**

You have a summer job painting houses. You begin one day by placing a 20 ft ladder as shown.

19. How far away from the house is the bottom of the ladder?

20. To improve the ladder's stability, you move it so it touches the top of the window. Now how far away from the house is the bottom?

21. For the best stability, your supervisor tells you to place the bottom of the ladder 5 ft from the house. How high will the top be?

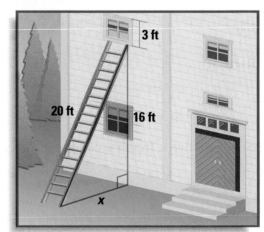

1. You are at an amusement park. You are playing a game to win tickets to trade for a stuffed animal. You have $5.50 and each game costs $.50. Which inequality can you use to find how many games you can play?

    (A) $0.5x > 5.5$ **(B)** $5.5x \geq 0.5$

    (C) $0.5x \leq 5.5$ **(D)** $5.5x < 0.5$

In Questions 2 and 3, use the following information.

You live 2 mi directly east of the post office. Your friend lives 4 mi directly south of the post office and 5.5 mi from the convenience store. Your home, your friend's home, and the convenience store do not lie in a straight line.

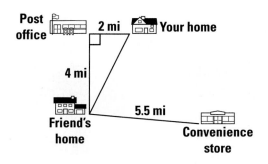

2. You ride your bike in a straight line from your home to your friend's home. How far is it?

    (A) 3.5 mi   **(B)** 4.5 mi

    (C) 6 mi   **(D)** 10 mi

3. You bike in a straight line from your home to the convenience store. Which of the following cannot be the distance you bike?

    (A) 3 mi   **(B)** 5 mi

    (C) 9.5 mi   **(D)** 10 mi

4. What is the length of the third side of the triangle?

    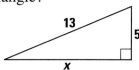

    (A) 4   **(B)** 8

    (C) 12   **(D)** 14

5. Which statement most accurately describes the graph?

    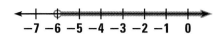

    (A) x is at least -6.

    (B) x is less than -6.

    (C) x is no more than -6.

    (D) x is greater than -6.

6. Solve the inequality $-3(x - 1) \geq -9$.

    (A) $x \geq 2$ **(B)** $x \leq 4$

    (C) $x \geq 4$ **(D)** $x \leq -4$

7. You are building a square sandbox that has an area of 16 ft^2. How long is each side?

    (A) 4 ft^2 **(B)** 4 ft

    (C) 8 ft   **(D)** 16 ft

8. Which statement about the following number is *false*?

    $$1.69$$

    (A) The number is rational.

    (B) The number is real.

    (C) The number is an integer.

    (D) The number is terminating.

In Exercises 1–4, add or subtract. Then simplify. (7.1, 7.2)

1. $\dfrac{2}{7} + \dfrac{4}{7}$ **2.** $\dfrac{16x}{4} - \dfrac{14x}{4}$ **3.** $\dfrac{1}{4} + \dfrac{1}{6}$ **4.** $\dfrac{5}{8} - \dfrac{17}{32}$

TECHNOLOGY In Exercises 5–8, simplify the expression by first rewriting in decimal form. Round your result to two decimal places. (7.3)

5. $\dfrac{64}{71} + \dfrac{57}{90}$ **6.** $\dfrac{4}{5}x - \dfrac{2}{7}x$ **7.** $2 - \left(\dfrac{3}{2} + \dfrac{7}{3} \right)$ **8.** $\dfrac{26}{9}t + \dfrac{85}{200}t$

In Exercises 9–12, simplify the expression. (7.4, 7.5)

9. $\dfrac{5}{12} \cdot \dfrac{10}{3}$ **10.** $\dfrac{5}{2} \div \dfrac{1}{5}$ **11.** $\dfrac{7n}{4} \cdot 16$ **12.** $-\dfrac{6}{10} \div \dfrac{z}{5}$

In Exercises 13–15, find the perimeter and the area of the figure.
(7.1, 7.2, 7.4)

13.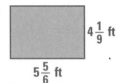
$4\frac{1}{9}$ ft

$5\frac{5}{6}$ ft

14.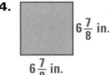
$6\frac{7}{8}$ in.

$6\frac{7}{8}$ in.

15.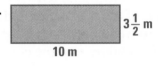
$3\frac{1}{2}$ m

10 m

In Exercises 16–19, write each portion as a percent. (7.6)

16. $\dfrac{3}{10}$ **17.** $\dfrac{18}{25}$ **18.** $\dfrac{140}{175}$ **19.** $\dfrac{300}{250}$

20. **GEOMETRY** What portion of the spinner at the right is shaded green? Express your answer as a percent and as a decimal. (7.7)

21. **SIMPLE INTEREST** You deposit $632 in a savings account that pays 4.82% in simple interest. If you make no other deposits or withdrawals, how much money is in the account after one year? (7.9)

In Exercises 22–25, tell whether the quotient is a *rate* or a *ratio*. Then simplify. (8.1)

22. $\dfrac{84 \text{ cups}}{3 \text{ min}}$ **23.** $\dfrac{5 \text{ cars}}{3 \text{ cars}}$ **24.** $\dfrac{16 \text{ ft}}{24 \text{ in.}}$ **25.** $\dfrac{63 \text{ m}}{1.5 \text{ s}}$

In Exercises 26–29, solve the proportion. Check your solution. (8.2)

26. $\dfrac{3}{18} = \dfrac{t}{30}$ **27.** $\dfrac{12}{16} = \dfrac{27}{n}$ **28.** $\dfrac{1}{m} = \dfrac{1.5}{6}$ **29.** $\dfrac{x}{55} = \dfrac{5}{8}$

30. **PROPERTY TAX** If you pay $2100 in property tax for a $105,000 house, how much property tax would you pay for a $140,000 house? (8.3)

In Exercises 31–34, solve the percent equation. Round your answer to two decimal places. (8.4)

31. 63 is what percent of 90?   **32.** What is 85% of 40?

33. What is 62.5% of 320?   **34.** 105 is 150% of what number?

MOVIES In Exercises 35–39, use the following information. (8.5)

You take a survey about favorite types of movies. The circle graph shows the results of your survey. Eighteen people said that science fiction movies were their favorite.

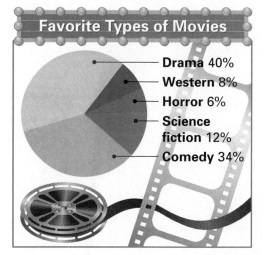

Favorite Types of Movies

Drama 40%
Western 8%
Horror 6%
Science fiction 12%
Comedy 34%

35. How many people were surveyed?

36. How many people said drama?

37. How many people said comedy?

38. How many people said western?

39. How many people said horror?

In Exercises 40 and 41, decide whether the change is an increase or a decrease and find the percent. (8.6)

40. 1995: 207,100 units
    1996: 215,025 units

41. Regular Price: $39.99
    Sale Price: $25.99

ZIP CODES In Exercises 42–44, use the following information. (8.7)

In Canada, each postal code begins with a letter, then the code alternates between numbers and letters. The letters D, F, I, O, Q, and U are never used. How many postal codes could have the given form?

42. L 2 R 1 [?] 0

43. H [?] C 4 [?] 9

44. L 2 R [?] [?] [?]

45. Plot the set of numbers on a number line. (9.2)

$$\left\{ \frac{12}{15},\ -\sqrt{3},\ -\sqrt{\frac{81}{121}},\ \sqrt{17},\ -\frac{14}{29},\ \sqrt{5.76} \right\}$$

In Exercises 46–48, solve the right triangle. (9.3)

46.

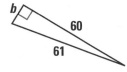

b, 60, 61

47.

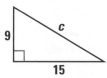

9, c, 15

48.

10, 13, a

In Exercises 49–52, solve the inequality. Then graph the solution. (9.5–9.6)

49. $a + 12 < 7$ **50.** $b - 19 \geq 15$ **51.** $-4 \geq -6m$ **52.** $-\dfrac{n}{8} > \dfrac{2}{3}$

In Exercises 53–55, decide whether the numbers can be the lengths of three sides of a triangle. (9.8)

53. 5, 9, 13 **54.** $\dfrac{1}{16}, \dfrac{1}{4}, \dfrac{3}{8}$ **55.** 4, 7, $\sqrt{7}$

Geometry Concepts and Spatial Thinking

TECHNOLOGY

- **Interactive Real-Life Investigations**
- **Middle School Tutorial Software**

To find out more about malls, go to:

http://www.mlmath.com

DESIGN This architect is working on plans for a new shopping mall.

CHAPTER THEME
Shopping Malls

CHAPTER PROJECT

Designing a Mall

PROJECT DESCRIPTION

Deciding to develop a shopping mall is a major business decision. The success of the venture will depend on the location that is selected, on the availability of other shopping places, and on the design and features of the mall itself. You will design a floor plan for one level of a shopping mall.

GETTING STARTED

Talking It Over

- Is there a shopping mall in your area? What food, entertainment, and stores does it contain? Does the mall have any unique features? What is your favorite part of the mall?

- Where will your mall be located? Discuss the site. What will make your mall unique? Discuss names for your mall.

Planning Your Project

- **Materials:** posterboard, paper, pencils or pens, colored pencils

- Write the name of your mall at the top of your poster. As you complete the **BUILDING YOUR PROJECT** exercises, keep the results in your portfolio. When you have completed the chapter, draw your plans on the poster.

BUILDING YOUR PROJECT

These are places throughout the chapter where you will work on your project.

10.2 Design the hallways. *p. 467*

10.4 Design a seating area. *p. 477*

10.5 Design a food court. *p. 482*

10.6 Plan shapes and sizes of stores. *p. 487*

10.7 Plan the layout for a department store. *p. 491*

10.1

Exploring Points, Lines, and Planes

What you should learn:

Goal 1 How to identify points, lines, and planes

Goal 2 How to describe real-life objects

Why you should learn it:

You can use geometry to describe real-life shapes such as sculptures and mazes.

Goal 1 IDENTIFYING POINTS, LINES, AND PLANES

In Chapters 10, 11, and 12, you will learn how geometry is used in real-life situations. To become skilled in geometry, you must understand both the *words* and the *properties* of geometry.

Pictured at the right are **points**, a **line**, a **plane**, a **ray**, and a **line segment**. Two line segments that are the same length are **congruent**. Notice that a line, a ray, and a line segment can be named in more than one way.

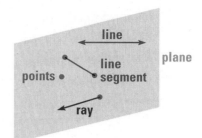

Example 1 Drawing Rays

Use the diagram at the right to draw each ray.

a. $\overrightarrow{AB}$ **b.** $\overrightarrow{CB}$ **c.** $\overrightarrow{BC}$

Solution

When rays are named, the endpoint is listed first to make it clear where the ray begins.

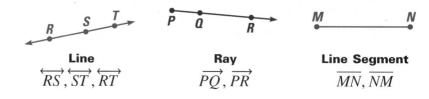

a.   b.   c.

Example 2 Finding Line Segment Lengths

STUDY TIP

In part (c) of Example 2, notice that you can write "$\overline{XY}$ is congruent to $\overline{YZ}$" as $\overline{XY} \cong \overline{YZ}$.

a. The length of $\overline{XY}$ is 3. You can write this as $XY = 3$.

b. The length of $\overline{XZ}$ is 6. You can write this as $XZ = 6$.

c. $\overline{XY}$ is congruent to $\overline{YZ}$. You can write this as $\overline{XY} \cong \overline{YZ}$.

Real Life...
Real Facts

Example 3 Identifying Objects in Planes

The outdoor sculpture at the right is in New York City. The front and the top two sides of the sculpture represent three planes.

a. Name a line segment in the same plane as $\overline{CF}$.

b. Name a point in the same plane as point A.

Solution

a. The line segment $\overline{DE}$ is in the same plane as $\overline{CF}$.

b. Point B is in the same plane as point A.

Cornfield Maze

In 1995, this maze set a record as the largest maze in the world. It was located in Shippensburg, PA.

The **intersection** of two lines is the set of points that are in both lines. Two lines are **parallel** if they are in the same plane and do not intersect. The **red arrowheads** indicate that the two lines are parallel.

Example 4 Identifying Line Segments

The walls of the maze represent lines. For example, you can imagine $\overleftrightarrow{PQ}$, which passes through points P and Q.

a. Identify a pair of parallel lines in the maze.

b. Identify a pair of intersecting lines. Name their point of intersection.

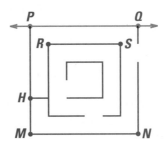

Solution

a. There are several pairs of parallel lines. For example, $\overleftrightarrow{PQ}$ is parallel to $\overleftrightarrow{MN}$, and $\overleftrightarrow{PQ}$ is parallel to $\overleftrightarrow{RS}$.

b. There are also several pairs of intersecting lines. For example, the intersection of $\overleftrightarrow{PQ}$ and $\overleftrightarrow{PM}$ is point P.

ONGOING ASSESSMENT

Write About It

In the maze in Example 4, the points H, P, and M lie on the same line.

1. Give three names for this line.

2. How many points of intersection do the lines $\overleftrightarrow{PH}$ and $\overleftrightarrow{PM}$ have?

10.1 Exercises

Extra Practice, page 732

GUIDED PRACTICE

GEOMETRY In Exercises 1–4, match the term with the figure it best describes.

A.

B.

C. [shaded parallelogram]

D. [line through P and Q with arrows]

1. Ray

2. Line Segment

3. Line

4. Plane

5. Use symbols to name each figure in Exercises 1–3.

6. Describe examples of parallel lines and intersecting lines in your classroom.

PRACTICE AND PROBLEM SOLVING

GEOMETRY In Exercises 7–15, use the diagram at the right.

7. Write four names for the line $\overleftrightarrow{CF}$.

8. Name 3 different line segments that lie on $\overleftrightarrow{AG}$.

9. Name 5 rays that have the same endpoint.

10. Name 2 lines that appear to be parallel.

11. Name 2 pairs of lines that intersect.

12. Are $\overrightarrow{EB}$ and $\overrightarrow{BE}$ the same ray? Explain.

13. Are $\overline{EJ}$ and $\overline{JE}$ the same line segment? Explain.

14. Do EB and BE represent the same length? Explain.

15. If the length of $\overline{EH}$ is $1\frac{1}{2}$, what is HB?

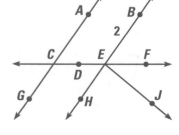

In Exercises 16–21, use the pyramid at the right.

A *pyramid* is a solid whose base is a polygon and whose other faces are triangles that share a common vertex.

16. How many planes form the pyramid's faces?

17. Name the line segments that form the pyramid's edges.

18. Name the points that form the pyramid's vertices.

19. Name four points that lie in the same plane.

20. Which line is parallel to $\overleftrightarrow{DE}$? to $\overleftrightarrow{CD}$?

21. Name four rays that have the same endpoint.

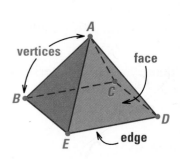

In Exercises 22–25, draw the indicated figure.

22. Three lines that do not intersect

23. Three lines that intersect in one point

24. Three lines that intersect in two points

25. Three lines that intersect in three points

ARCHITECTURE **In Exercises 26–30, use the brick building shown at the right.**

Each window in the building is 10 ft wide and 7 ft high. The front doors of the building are 10 ft wide and 10 ft high. The space between the windows is 3 ft, and the space between the windows and the edges of the building is 3 ft.

26. Describe some windows that lie in the same plane.

27. Find the length, *BD*, and width, *DF*, of the building's base.

28. Find the height, *CD*, of the building.

29. Is the base of every window parallel to the base of every other window? Explain.

30. What percent of the front of the building is glass?

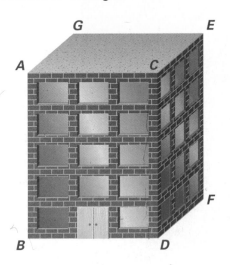

STANDARDIZED TEST PRACTICE

In Exercises 31 and 32, use the figure at the right.

31. Name a ray that begins at point *A*.

   A $\overrightarrow{DA}$ **B** $\overline{AD}$ **C** $\overrightarrow{AD}$ **D** $\overleftrightarrow{AD}$

32. Name a line in the same plane as line $\overleftrightarrow{CD}$.

   A $\overleftrightarrow{BE}$ **B** $\overleftrightarrow{FG}$

   C $\overleftrightarrow{BF}$ **D** None of the above

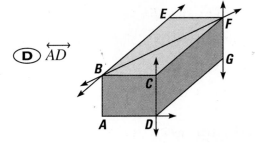

EXPLORATION AND EXTENSION

33. **LINE SEGMENTS** Suppose you are driving through Michigan on a specific route. You start at Detroit and then go to Howell, Ann Arbor, Battle Creek, Kalamazoo, Grand Rapids, Lansing, Flint, and then return to Detroit. How far will you drive?

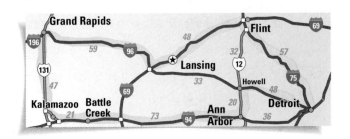

Naming, Measuring, and Drawing Angles

The mirrors in this kaleidoscope form a 30° angle.

Goal 1 MEASURING ANGLES

An **angle** consists of two rays that begin at the same point. The rays are the *sides* of the angle, and the point is the **vertex** of the angle. The angle at the right can be named ∠*BAC*, ∠*CAB*, or ∠*A*.

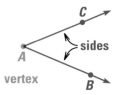

The **measure** of ∠*A* is written as *m* ∠*A*. Two angles are **congruent** if they have the same measure. A **protractor** can be used to approximate the measure of an angle.

Example 1 Measuring an Angle

❶ To measure ∠ *RST*, begin by placing the protractor's center on the angle's vertex.

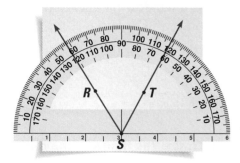

❷ Line up the protractor's 0° line with one side of the angle.

❸ Read the measure of the protractor where the other side crosses it.

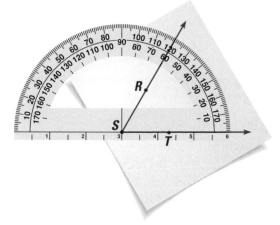

The measure of ∠*RST* is 60°, which is written as *m* ∠*RST* = 60°.

Angles are classified by their measures, as follows.

50°
A

B

110°
C

180°
D

Acute angle	**Right angle**	**Obtuse angle**	**Straight angle**
An angle that measures between 0° and 90°.	An angle that measures 90°.	An angle that measures between 90° and 180°.	An angle that measures 180°.

Example 2 **Classifying Angles**

There are three acute angles in the diagram: $\angle TSV$, $\angle VSU$, and $\angle TSU$.

There are two obtuse angles in the diagram: $\angle RST$ and $\angle RSU$.

There is one straight angle in the diagram: $\angle RSV$.

There are no right angles in the diagram.

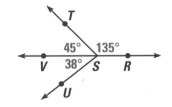

Two lines that meet at right angles are **perpendicular**. Two angles are **complementary** if the sum of their measures is 90°. Two angles are **supplementary** if the sum of their measures is 180°.

Example 3 **Measuring Supplementary Angles**

In the diagram at the right, $\angle ABC$ and $\angle CBD$ are supplementary. Find $m \angle ABC$.

CONNECTION
Algebra

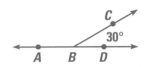

Solution

$m \angle ABC + m \angle CBD = 180°$ The angles are supplementary.

$m \angle ABC + 30° = 180°$ Substitute 30° for $m \angle CBD$.

$m \angle ABC = 150°$ Subtract 30° from each side.

The measure of $\angle ABC$ is 150°.

10.2 Exercises

Extra Practice, page 732

GUIDED PRACTICE

GEOMETRY In Exercises 1–4, use the figure at the right.

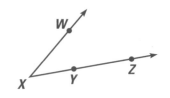

1. Name the vertex of $\angle WXZ$.

2. Name the sides of $\angle WXZ$.

3. State other names for $\angle WXZ$.

4. Which appears to have the greater measure: $\angle WXZ$ or $\angle WYZ$?

PROTRACTOR In Exercises 5–8, use a protractor to measure the angle. Is the angle *acute*, *obtuse*, *right*, or *straight*?

5.   **6.** 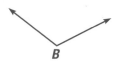   **7.** 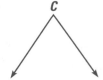   **8.**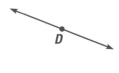

PRACTICE AND PROBLEM SOLVING

GEOMETRY In Exercises 9–13, use the figure at the right.

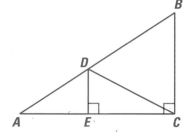

9. How many acute angles are in the figure? List them.

10. How many obtuse angles are in the figure? List them.

11. If $\angle AED$ is supplementary to $\angle CED$, then what is $m \angle AED$?

12. How many right angles are in the figure? List them.

13. Identify the vertex and sides of $\angle CDE$. Explain why you can't simply name the angle as $\angle D$.

In Exercises 14–17, use the figure at the right.

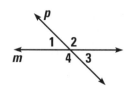

14. If $m \angle 1 = 45°$, what is $m \angle 2$?

15. Find $m \angle 3$.

16. Find $m \angle 4$.

17. What is the relationship between $\angle 1$ and $\angle 4$? Explain.

DRAWING A DIAGRAM In Exercises 18–21, use a protractor to draw the angle.

18. $30°$ **19.** $90°$ **20.** $125°$ **21.** $135°$

In Exercises 22–25, use a protractor to measure the angle.

22.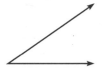

23.

24.

25.

26. WRITING In your own words, explain what it means for two angles to be congruent.

CLOCK FACES In Exercises 27–30, classify the type of angle (*acute*, *right*, *obtuse*, or *straight*) the clock hands make at the given time.

27. 6:00 P.M.   **28.** 9:00 A.M.   **29.** 4:00 A.M.   **30.** 10:00 P.M.

STANDARDIZED TEST PRACTICE

In Exercises 31 and 32, use the angles shown at the right. The angles are supplementary.

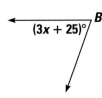
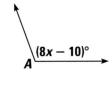

$(3x + 25)°$

$(8x − 10)°$

31. Which expression can you use to find the value of *x*?

   Ⓐ $8x − 10 + 3x + 25 = 180$ **Ⓑ** $8x − 10 + 3x + 25 = 90$

   Ⓒ $8x − 10 − 3x − 25 = 18$ **Ⓓ** $8x + 10 + 3x + 25 = 360$

32. What is the measure of each angle?

   Ⓐ $m \angle A = 65°, m \angle B = 25°$ **Ⓑ** $m \angle A = 110°, m \angle B = 70°$

   Ⓒ $m \angle A = 110°, m \angle B = 250°$ **Ⓓ** $m \angle A = 100°, m \angle B = 80°$

EXPLORATION AND EXTENSION

PORTFOLIO

33. BUILDING YOUR PROJECT
Develop a floor plan for the hallways of your mall. Be sure to include hallways that meet at angles other than 90°. How many entrances will the mall have? Measure and label each angle in your floor plan.

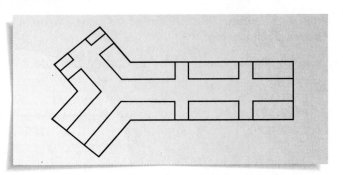

In Exercises 1–4, plot the points on a single coordinate plane. (3.8)

1. $A(3, 3)$

2. $B(3, -1)$

3. $C(-1, -1)$

4. $D(-1, 3)$

In Exercises 5–7, use the points in Exercises 1–4. (9.4, 10.1)

5. Use the points to identify parallel lines.

6. Use the points to identify perpendicular lines.

7. Find the length of $\overline{AC}$. (Round your answer to 2 decimal places.)

ESTIMATION In Exercises 8–11, without using a protractor, match the angle with its measure. (10.2)

A. 45°

B. 90°

C. 180°

D. 135°

8.

9.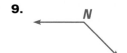

10.

11.

ALGEBRA In Exercises 12–19, find the sum or difference. Then simplify. (7.1, 7.2)

12. $\dfrac{5}{6} + \dfrac{-1}{6}$

13. $\dfrac{2}{3} + \dfrac{3}{6}$

14. $\dfrac{-3}{5} - \dfrac{1}{3}$

15. $4\dfrac{1}{2} + 1\dfrac{1}{2}$

16. $\dfrac{x}{6} + \dfrac{x}{6}$

17. $\dfrac{2}{y} - \dfrac{2}{5}$

18. $\dfrac{3}{z} - \dfrac{2}{z}$

19. $\dfrac{a}{5} - \dfrac{a}{10}$

20. MUSIC In 1994, the United States had a population of about 260 million. In that year, Americans spent \$15 billion on recorded music. Find the average amount spent by each American.

(Source: Veronis, Suhler & Associates, Inc.) **(6.8)**

Chemistry Connection

MOLECULAR SHAPES

The air that you breathe and the water you drink are made up of tiny molecules. The properties of a molecule depend largely on its shape.

Describe the shape of each molecule. Use a protractor to find the measure of the angle.

1. Water

2. Carbon Dioxide

3. Sulfur Dioxide

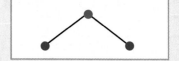

Exploring Parallel Lines

In this investigation, you will explore the angles made by two sets of parallel lines.

Materials Needed
- ruled paper
- straightedge
- colored pencils
- scissors

Step ❶ Use a pencil and straightedge to darken three lines on a piece of ruled paper. Then draw two other parallel lines, one on each side of the straightedge, as shown.

Step ❷ On another piece of paper, trace one of the quadrilaterals formed by the parallel lines. Cut it out and use it to compare the angles formed by the parallel lines. What can you conclude?

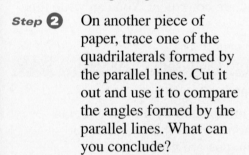

Step ❸ The five lines should form 24 angles. Use colored pencils to indicate all angles that seem congruent.

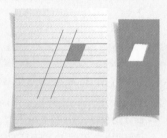

1. In the quadrilateral that you cut out, are any of the four angles congruent? How can you tell?

NOW TRY THESE

2. Draw 2 parallel lines. Then draw a third line that intersects each of the first 2 lines at a slant. How many angles are formed by the 3 lines?

3. Use colored pencils to classify the angles into congruent groups.

10.3

Exploring Parallel Lines

What you should learn:

Goal **1** How to identify angles formed when two parallel lines intersect a third line

Goal **2** How to use parallel lines to solve real-life problems

Why you should learn it:

You can use properties of parallel lines to solve real-life problems, such as measuring angles in construction projects.

Goal **1** USING A PROPERTY OF PARALLEL LINES

Angles that are formed by intersecting lines are classified as **vertical angles** and **corresponding angles** . Several examples are shown below.

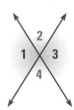 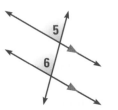

Vertical angles
∠1 and ∠3, ∠2 and ∠4

Corresponding angles
∠5 and ∠6, ∠7 and ∠8

In the diagram above, ∠2 and ∠4 are congruent. You can write this as ∠2 ≅ ∠4.

VERTICAL ANGLES AND A PROPERTY OF PARALLEL LINES

1. Vertical angles are congruent.
2. When two parallel lines are intersected by a third line, the corresponding angles are congruent. If the lines are not parallel, the corresponding angles are not congruent.

Example 1 Identifying Congruent Angles

In the diagram, identify all:

a. congruent vertical angles.

b. congruent corresponding angles.

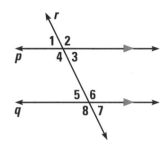

NEED TO KNOW

In Example 1, the red arrowheads indicate that line *p* and line *q* are parallel.

Solution

a. There are 4 sets of congruent vertical angles.

∠1 ≅ ∠3, ∠2 ≅ ∠4, ∠5 ≅ ∠7, and ∠6 ≅ ∠8

b. Because line *p* and line *q* are parallel, the 4 sets of corresponding angles are congruent.

∠1 ≅ ∠5, ∠2 ≅ ∠6, ∠3 ≅ ∠7, and ∠4 ≅ ∠8

Example 2 Finding Angle Measures

In the diagram at the right, $m \angle 1 = 50°$. Find the measures of the other three angles.

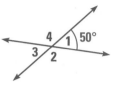

Solution

Since $\angle 1$ and $\angle 3$ are vertical angles, they are congruent and must have the same measure. Thus,

$m \angle 3 = 50°$.

Also, since $\angle 1$ and $\angle 2$ combined form a straight angle, you know that the sum of their measures is 180°. Thus,

$$m \angle 2 = 180° - m \angle 1$$
$$= 180° - 50°$$
$$= 130°.$$

Because $\angle 2$ and $\angle 4$ are vertical angles, they are congruent and you can conclude that

$m \angle 4 = 130°$.

Example 3 Identifying Congruent Angles

In the photo at the right, the lower man is sitting on a pair of cross beams. Draw a diagram of the beams and label the congruent angles.

REAL LIFE
Construction

Solution

The beams form two pairs of parallel lines, as shown at the right. By using vertical angles and a property of parallel lines, you can conclude that

$\angle 1 \cong \angle 3$.

Using similar reasoning, you can also conclude that

$\angle 2 \cong \angle 4$.

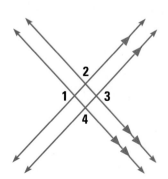

> **ONGOING ASSESSMENT**
>
> ## Write About It
> · · · · · · · · · · · · · · · ·
>
> **1.** In Example 3, explain why $\angle 1 \cong \angle 3$ and $\angle 2 \cong \angle 4$. If $m \angle 2 = 84°$, what are the measures of the other three angles? Explain your reasoning.

GUIDED PRACTICE

GEOMETRY In Exercises 1–6, use the figure at the right.

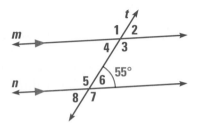

1. Which two lines are parallel?

2. Name four pairs of vertical angles.

3. Name four pairs of corresponding angles.

4. What is the measure of $\angle 2$? Explain your reasoning.

5. What is the measure of $\angle 4$? Explain your reasoning.

6. What is the measure of $\angle 8$? Explain your reasoning.

7. **REASONING** Two lines intersect to form four angles. One of the angles measures 45°. What do the other three angles measure? Explain your reasoning.

8. **DRAWING A DIAGRAM** Draw two parallel lines. Then draw a line that intersects one of the lines to form a 60° angle. Of the eight angles that are formed, how many measure 60°?

PRACTICE AND PROBLEM SOLVING

GEOMETRY In Exercises 9–15, use the figure at the right.

9. Explain why $\angle 4$ is not congruent to $\angle 8$.

10. List all angles whose measure is 65°.

11. List all angles whose measure is 75°.

12. List all angles whose measure is 115°.

13. List all angles whose measure is 105°.

14. Name two corresponding angles that have different measures.

15. Name two corresponding angles that have the same measure.

PARALLEL LINES In Exercises 16 and 17, explain why the red angles are congruent.

GEOMETRY In Exercises 18 and 19, draw the figure. List the lines that seem parallel.

16.
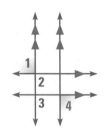

17.
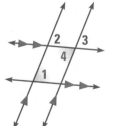

18.
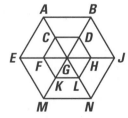

19.
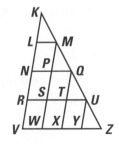

20. LOOKING FOR A PATTERN How many triangles are in the figure in Exercise 19?

WALKING **In Exercises 21–23, use the map at the right and the information below.**

You live on 4th Street, which runs parallel to 5th and 6th Streets. The route you follow from your house to your friend's house is shown on the map. The turn from 4th Street onto Cherry Street is 117° and from Lake Street onto 6th Street is 34°.

21. Draw and label a diagram of the streets.

22. Identify all of the congruent angles.

23. Find the measure of each angle.

24. GREAT BRITAIN Draw a diagram of the flag of Great Britain shown at the right. Is it true that every line segment in the flag is parallel to the top of the flag, the right side of the flag, or one of its two diagonals?

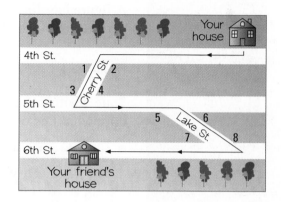

25. Use a protractor to measure several of the angles in Great Britain's flag. How many different angle measures are there? Explain your reasoning.

STANDARDIZED TEST PRACTICE

26. Which of the following statements is *false*?

(A) Any two right angles are congruent.

(B) Any two vertical angles are congruent.

(C) Any two corresponding angles are congruent.

(D) If two angles are supplementary, then their sum is 180°.

EXPLORATION AND EXTENSION

27. COMMUNICATING ABOUT MATHEMATICS Trace the floor plan of the Mall of America on page 498. Which of the hallways appear to be parallel to each other? Label all parallel lines on the floor plan.

10.4

Symmetry

What you should learn:

Goal 1 How to identify line symmetry

Goal 2 How to identify rotational symmetry

Why you should learn it:

You can use symmetry to describe real-life objects, such as in biology.

This microscopic diatom has both line symmetry and rotational symmetry.

Goal 1 **IDENTIFYING LINE SYMMETRY**

A figure has **line symmetry** if it can be divided by a line into two parts, each of which is the mirror image of the other.

Example 1 **Identifying Line Symmetry**

State whether the figure has a vertical line of symmetry or a horizontal line of symmetry.

a.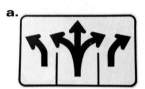
b.
c.

Solution

a. This figure has a vertical line of symmetry.

b. This figure has no line of symmetry.

c. This figure has a vertical *and* a horizontal line of symmetry.

LESSON INVESTIGATION

COOPERATIVE LEARNING

Investigating Line Symmetry

PARTNER ACTIVITY Fold a sheet of paper as shown below. Cut a design out of one or more edges of the folded paper. Predict the pattern when the paper is unfolded. Explain how symmetry can help you make the prediction.

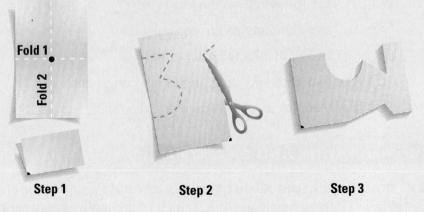

Fold 1
Fold 2

Step 1   Step 2   Step 3

A figure has **rotational symmetry** if it coincides with itself after rotating 180° or less, either clockwise or counterclockwise, about a point.

Example 2 Identifying Rotational Symmetry

Identify any rotational symmetry in the figures.

a.

b.

c.

Solution

a. This figure has rotational symmetry. It will coincide with itself after being rotated 90° or 180° in either direction.

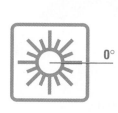 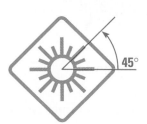 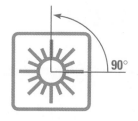

b. This figure has rotational symmetry. It will coincide with itself after being rotated 60°, 120°, or 180° in either direction.

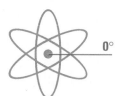 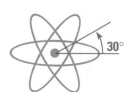 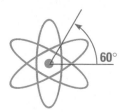

c. This figure has no rotational symmetry. (It does have a horizontal line of symmetry.)

10.4 Exercises

Extra Practice, page 733

GUIDED PRACTICE

1. Name several objects in your classroom that have symmetry.

DATA STORAGE In Exercises 2–5, identify any symmetry of the figure.

2.

3.

4.

5.

PRACTICE AND PROBLEM SOLVING

ORIGAMI In Exercises 6–9, identify any symmetry of the figure.

6.

7.

8.

9.

In Exercises 10–13, draw, if possible, a figure that has the given characteristics.

10. Exactly one line of symmetry

11. Exactly two lines of symmetry

12. Line, but not rotational, symmetry

13. Rotational, but not line, symmetry

GEOMETRY In Exercises 14–17, copy the figure. Then shade one square so that the figure has the indicated symmetry.

14. Line

15. Rotational

16. Rotational

17. Line

18. **GUESS, CHECK, AND REVISE** Can you draw a figure that has a vertical and horizontal line of symmetry but does not have rotational symmetry?

19. **GUESS, CHECK, AND REVISE** Can you draw a figure that has a vertical line of symmetry and rotational symmetry but does not have a horizontal line of symmetry?

PHOTOGRAPHY In Exercises 20–22, identify any symmetry.

20.

21.

22.

In Exercises 23–25, trace the figure and find out what word is spelled using the indicated line of symmetry. (*Hint:* You can also use a mirror to solve the problems.)

23. ⟵ BOX ⟶ 24. ⟵ DECK ⟶ 25. ⟵ OHIO ⟶

26. **OPEN-ENDED PROBLEM** List as many words as you can that have the type of symmetry used in Exercises 23–25. Try to write an entire sentence using such words.

STANDARDIZED TEST PRACTICE

27. Identify the symmetry in the figure at the right.

Ⓐ vertical line of symmetry

Ⓑ horizontal line of symmetry

Ⓒ vertical and horizontal lines of symmetry

Ⓓ rotational symmetry of 180°

EXPLORATION AND EXTENSION

PORTFOLIO

28. **BUILDING YOUR PROJECT** Malls often have central areas with benches and decorative items where shoppers can stop and rest. Design such an area in your mall. Make sure your area has at least one line of symmetry. Label features such as plants, fountains, and seating. Label all lines of symmetry.

10.5

Exploring Triangles

What you should learn:

Goal 1 How to classify triangles by their sides

Goal 2 How to classify triangles by their angles

Why you should learn it:

Triangles occur in a wide variety of real-life situations.

The sails of these sailboards are like scalene triangles.

TOOLBOX

Triangles, page 757

Goal 1 **CLASSIFY TRIANGLES BY THEIR SIDES**

In this lesson, you will learn that a triangle can be classified according to the measures of its angles or the lengths of its sides.

LESSON INVESTIGATION

Investigating Types of Triangles

PARTNER ACTIVITY Use the sheet of triangles provided by your teacher. Cut the triangles out.

Sort the triangles into two piles so that every triangle in one pile has a certain property and every triangle in the other pile does not have the property. Ask your partner to describe the property.

Reverse roles and ask your partner to sort the triangles. Try to guess your partner's property.

Find as many ways as you can to sort the triangles into two piles. Make a list of the properties you used.

Triangles are classified by their sides into three categories. For a **scalene** triangle, all sides have different lengths. For an **isosceles** triangle, at least two sides have the same length. For an **equilateral** triangle, all three sides have the same length.

Example 1 Classifying Triangles

Classify each triangle according to its sides.

Use "tick marks" to show congruent sides.

a.

b.

c.

Solution

a. $\triangle ABC$ is isosceles because it has two sides of length 5.

b. $\triangle DEF$ is equilateral because each side has a length of 6.

c. $\triangle RST$ is scalene—all three sides have different lengths.

Goal 2 IDENTIFYING TRIANGLES BY THEIR ANGLES

Triangles are classified by their angles into four categories.
A triangle is **acute** if all three angles are acute. An acute triangle is
equiangular if all three angles have the same measure. A triangle is
obtuse if one of its angles is obtuse. A triangle is **right** if one of its
angles is a right angle.

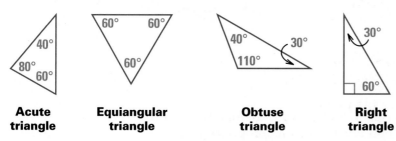

| **Acute triangle** | **Equiangular triangle** | **Obtuse triangle** | **Right triangle** |

Example 2 **Comparing Work Triangles**

REAL LIFE
Architecture

The diagrams below show three basic types of
kitchen designs. In each design, a work triangle is
formed by the sink (S), refrigerator (R), and
cooking surface (C).

Classify each work triangle as acute, obtuse, right, or equiangular.

a. In the galley kitchen, $\triangle RSC$
appears to be a right triangle.

b. In the L-shaped kitchen,
$\triangle RSC$ is an obtuse triangle.

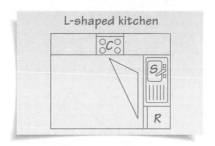

c. In the U-shaped kitchen,
$\triangle RSC$ is an acute triangle
and also appears equiangular.

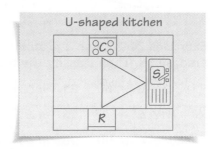

ONGOING ASSESSMENT

Write About It
. . . .

1. Classify the 3 work
triangles in Example 2
by their sides: as
isosceles, equilateral,
or *scalene.*

GUIDED PRACTICE

GEOMETRY In Exercises 1–4, match each triangle with all words that describe it.

A. Isosceles   B. Equiangular   C. Scalene   D. Obtuse

E. Equilateral   F. Right   G. Acute

1.
25°
35°
120°

2.
60°
60°
60°

3.
70°   25°
85°

4.
2   2
√8

PRACTICE AND PROBLEM SOLVING

DRAWING A DIAGRAM In Exercises 5–10, sketch a triangle that is an example of the indicated type. Then label it with appropriate angle measures and congruence tick marks.

5. Obtuse   **6.** Acute   **7.** Right scalene

8. Right isosceles   **9.** Acute isosceles   **10.** Obtuse scalene

In Exercises 11–19, classify the triangle according to its sides and angles.

11.

12.

13.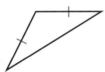

14.

15.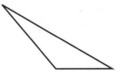

16.

17.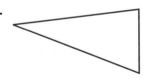

18.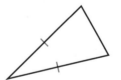

19.

DRAWING A DIAGRAM In Exercises 20–25, use a protractor to draw △*ABC* with the given angle measures. Then classify the triangle.

20. $m\angle A = 60°, m\angle B = 60°, m\angle C = 60°$ **21.** $m\angle A = 70°, m\angle B = 70°, m\angle C = 40°$

22. $m\angle A = 50°, m\angle B = 60°, m\angle C = 70°$ **23.** $m\angle A = 30°, m\angle B = 60°, m\angle C = 90°$

24. $m\angle A = 45°, m\angle B = 45°, m\angle C = 90°$ **25.** $m\angle A = 120°, m\angle B = 40°, m\angle C = 20°$

GEOMETRY In Exercises 26–29, classify the triangle according to its sides and angles.

26.

27.

28.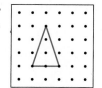

29.

30. REASONING An equiangular triangle is equilateral. Can a right triangle be equilateral? Explain your reasoning.

31. WRITING Can an equiangular triangle be obtuse? Explain.

32. ACTING IT OUT The figures at the right are made with popsicle sticks and fasteners. Is the triangle rigid or can you adjust its sticks to form a different shape of triangle? Is a rectangle rigid?

BICYCLING In Exercises 33 and 34, use the photo of the bicycle at the right.

33. Sketch the frame of the bicycle. Then label the frame with points and identify all of the triangles formed by the bicycle's frame.

34. MANUFACTURING Based on your answers to Exercise 32, why do you think triangles are used in bicycle construction instead of quadrilaterals?

 STANDARDIZED TEST PRACTICE

35. Which statement is *true*?

(A) An obtuse triangle must have two obtuse angles.

(B) An equiangular triangle must have three acute angles.

(C) An equilateral triangle can have one obtuse angle.

(D) An isosceles triangle must have one obtuse angle.

EXPLORATION AND EXTENSION

36. **BUILDING YOUR PROJECT** Design a food court for your mall. You should consider the paths that customers and employees will typically use and keep furniture and other obstacles out of these paths. Some examples of good work triangles are given below. Include at least one work triangle in your design. Classify your work triangle according to the sides and angles.

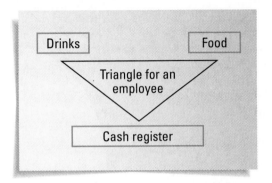

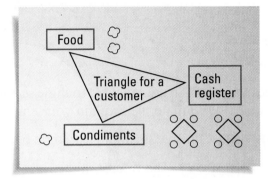

SPIRAL REVIEW

In Exercises 1–3, identify any symmetry of the figure. (10.4)

1.

2.

3.

In Exercises 4–9, solve the equation. (4.2, 7.2, 7.3, 9.1)

4. $2b - 2 = -2b$

5. $62p - 203 = 111 - 38p$

6. $2a + 4.04 = 16.08$

7. $\frac{1}{4}(3r - 1) = \frac{1}{4}$

8. $p^2 + 4 = 40$

9. $q - \frac{1}{2} = \frac{1}{3}$

In Exercises 10–14, rewrite the number in scientific notation. (6.8)

10. 2100

11. 0.00092

12. $16,000,000$

13. 0.00000046

14. 92.4×10^{18}

15. 0.0704

In Exercises 16–21, simplify the expression. (7.1, 7.2, 7.4, 7.5)

16. $\frac{1}{5} + \frac{2}{5}$

17. $\frac{4}{9} - \frac{2}{9}$

18. $\frac{4}{9} + \frac{1}{3}$

19. $\frac{4}{5} - \frac{3}{4}$

20. $\frac{3}{8} \times \frac{1}{2}$

21. $\frac{3}{10} \div \frac{9}{2}$

22. **GAMES** At an amusement park, each game costs $1.50 to play. You have a total of $7 to spend on the games to win stuffed animals. How many games can you play with your money? (9.6)

Take this test as you would take a test in class. The answers to the exercises are given in the back of the book.

GEOMETRY In Exercises 1–4, use the cube at the right. (10.1)

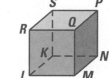

1. Name another point that lies in the same plane as M, N, and P.

2. Name two lines that are parallel to $\overleftrightarrow{SR}$.

3. Name the point of intersection of $\overleftrightarrow{SP}$ and $\overrightarrow{PQ}$.

4. Does the ray $\overrightarrow{NP}$ point up or down?

FAN In Exercises 5–8, use the photograph. (10.2)

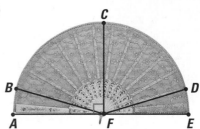

5. Name the right angles.

6. Name the acute angles.

7. Name the obtuse angles.

8. Name the straight angle.

In Exercises 9–12, use the figure at the right. Use the words *vertical* or *corresponding*. (10.3)

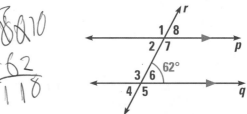

9. $\angle 1$ and $\angle 7$ are ? angles.

10. $\angle 1$ and $\angle 3$ are ? angles.

11. $\angle 2$ and $\angle 4$ are ? angles.

12. Find the measure of each angle.

MUSIC In Exercises 13–15, identify any symmetry. (10.4)

13.

14.

15.

In Exercises 16–19, classify the triangle by its sides and by its angles.

16.

17.

18.

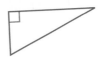

19.

20. **WRITING** If a triangle is obtuse, does it have to be scalene? Illustrate your answer with a sketch. (10.5)

Exploring Quadrilaterals

What you should learn:

Goal 1 How to identify quadrilaterals

Goal 2 How to identify quadrilaterals in real-life situations

Why you should learn it:

Being able to identify different types of quadrilaterals helps you communicate ideas about real-life situations.

A Chinese Tangram puzzle is a square that is cut into a smaller square, a parallelogram, and 5 triangles.

Goal 1 IDENTIFYING QUADRILATERALS

A quadrilateral is **convex** if a segment joining any two interior points lies completely within the quadrilateral.

There are many ways to classify convex quadrilaterals. Eight are shown below.

Parallelogram

Opposite sides are parallel.

Rectangle

Parallelogram with four right angles

Square

Rectangle with all sides congruent

Rhombus

Parallelogram with all sides congruent

Trapezoid

Exactly one pair of parallel sides

Isosceles Trapezoid

Trapezoid with nonparallel sides congruent

Kite

Neighboring sides (*not* opposite sides) are congruent.

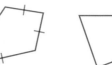

Scalene Quadrilateral

All sides have different lengths.

Example 1 Using Properties of Quadrilaterals

Find the values of x and y in the rhombus at the right.

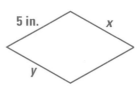

Solution

All 4 sides of a rhombus have the same length. So,

$x = 5$ in.   and $y = 5$ in.

This Venn diagram shows how the different quadrilaterals are related.

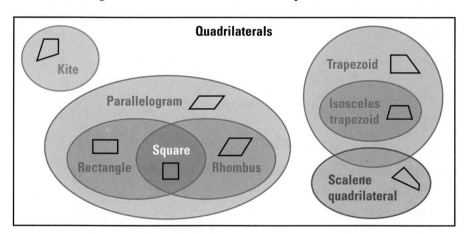

Quadrilaterals

Kite

Parallelogram

Rectangle | Square | Rhombus

Trapezoid

Isosceles trapezoid

Scalene quadrilateral

Example 2 **Classifying Quadrilaterals**

You decide to crop your favorite photo in different ways. Name all types of quadrilaterals that describe each shape.

REAL LIFE
Photography

A

B

C

Solution

a. Photo A appears to be a rectangle. It is also a parallelogram.

b. Photo B appears to be a square. This means that it is also a rectangle, a rhombus, and a parallelogram.

c. Photo C appears to be an isosceles trapezoid. This means that it is also a trapezoid.

GUIDED PRACTICE

1. Name all quadrilaterals that:

    a. have two pairs of parallel sides.   **b.** have no parallel sides.

    c. have exactly one pair of parallel sides.   **d.** have four congruent sides.

    e. have no congruent sides.   **f.** have at least one pair of congruent sides.

2. **WRITING** How can you tell whether a quadrilateral is convex or not convex? Draw examples of each.

3. **WRITING** Explain the difference between a kite and a rhombus.

4. **WRITING** Explain the difference between a square and a rectangle.

PRACTICE AND PROBLEM SOLVING

GEOMETRY In Exercises 5–12, identify the quadrilateral from its appearance. Use the name that *best* describes the quadrilateral.

5.    **6.** 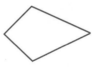   **7.**   **8.**

9.   **10.**   **11.** 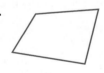   **12.**

USING LOGICAL REASONING In Exercises 13–16, complete the statement with *always*, *sometimes*, or *never*. Explain.

13. A quadrilateral is ? a parallelogram.   **14.** A rectangle is ? a rhombus.

15. A rhombus is ? a square.   **16.** A trapezoid is ? a convex quadrilateral.

GEOMETRY In Exercises 17–20, find the values of x and y.

17. Kite   **18.** Square   **19.** Rectangle   **20.** Isosceles trapezoid

x 5 m
y 11 m

y
x
10 cm

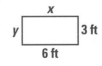
x
y 3 ft
6 ft

x 6 in.

SYMMETRY In Exercises 21–28, match the quadrilateral with the best description of its symmetry. You may list more than one description. Make a sketch to support your answers.

A. No symmetry
B. Exactly one line of symmetry
C. Exactly two lines of symmetry
D. Exactly three lines of symmetry
E. Exactly four lines of symmetry
F. Rotational symmetry

21. Parallelogram **22.** Rectangle **23.** Square **24.** Isosceles trapezoid

25. Trapezoid **26.** Rhombus **27.** Kite **28.** Scalene quadrilateral

BIRD FEEDER In Exercises 29 and 30, use the drawing of a bird feeder at the right.

29. Draw each piece of wood that is used to build the bird feeder. Label the dimensions.

30. Identify the shape of each piece of wood that you sketched in Exercise 29.

STANDARDIZED TEST PRACTICE

31. Which described figure is impossible to draw?

(A) A parallelogram with two pairs of congruent sides.

(B) A quadrilateral with one pair of congruent sides and another pair of parallel sides.

(C) A quadrilateral with no congruent sides.

(D) A trapezoid with four congruent sides.

EXPLORATION AND EXTENSION

PORTFOLIO

32. **BUILDING YOUR PROJECT** Draw walls to divide the mall into many stores. Use as many types of quadrilaterals and triangles as you can. Be sure to plan for stores of different sizes, including at least one large department store. Classify and label the shape of each store. Will customers have to enter the mall to shop there?

Polygons and Congruence

What you should learn:

Goal 1 How to recognize congruent polygons

Goal 2 How to identify regular polygons

Why you should learn it:

Congruent polygons can be used to design floor tiles.

This Moroccan mosaic is an example of the geometric tiling patterns found in Islamic art and architecture.

Goal 1 RECOGNIZING CONGRUENT POLYGONS

Two polygons are **congruent** if they are exactly the same size and shape. To decide whether two polygons are congruent, you can trace each on paper, cut one out, and try to move the cut polygon so that it lies exactly on top of the other polygon.

Example 1 Identifying Congruent Polygons

Which of the quadrilaterals are congruent?

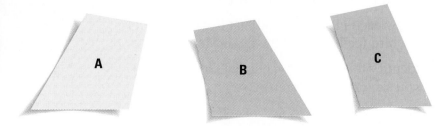

Solution

By flipping the quadrilateral over, you can make *A* exactly cover *B*. So, *A* and *B* are the same size and shape, and they must be congruent.

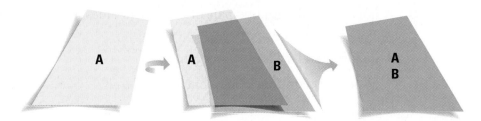

Next, try putting Quadrilateral *A* on top of Quadrilateral *C*. No matter how you turn it or flip it over, you cannot make it fit exactly on top of *C*. So, *A* and *C* are not congruent.

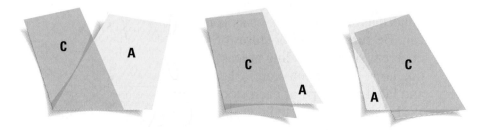

Goal 2 IDENTIFYING REGULAR POLYGONS

A polygon is **regular** if each of its sides has the same length *and* each of its angles has the same measure. Four examples are below.

| Regular triangle | Regular quadrilateral | Regular pentagon | Regular hexagon |

Example 2 Using Regular Polygons

In a regular pentagon, all angles have the same measure and all sides have the same length.

$m \angle B = m \angle A = 108°$

$BC = AB = 15$ ft

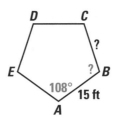

Example 3 Tiling with Regular Polygons

Which of the regular polygons above could you use to tile a floor with no gaps or overlapping tiles?

Solution

STRATEGY ACT IT OUT You can solve this problem experimentally by tracing several polygons of each shape and trying to fit the polygons together. After doing this, you can discover that regular triangles, quadrilaterals, and hexagons can be used as tiles, but the regular pentagons cannot be used.

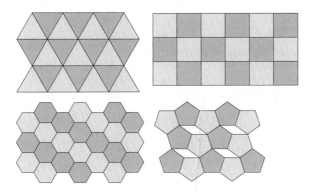

Real Life... Real Facts

Tiles from Spain
For over a thousand years castles and palaces in Spain have been decorated with ceramic tiles. These wall tiles from Spain repeat a single regular polygon, a square.

Tech Link

Investigation 10, Interactive Real-Life Investigations

ONGOING ASSESSMENT

Talk About It

1. Sketch several different ways to divide a regular triangle into congruent polygons.

10.7 Exercises

Extra Practice, page 733

GUIDED PRACTICE

1. **WRITING** Explain how you can tell whether two polygons are congruent.

2. What is another name for a regular triangle? What is another name for a regular quadrilateral?

3. In the figures below, two polygons are congruent. Which are they?

A.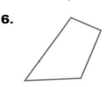

B.

C.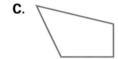

D.

4. **GEOMETRY** Name each polygon in Exercise 3. Is the polygon regular?

PRACTICE AND PROBLEM SOLVING

In Exercises 5–8, match the quadrilateral with a congruent quadrilateral.

A.   **B.**   **C.**   **D.**

5.   **6.**   **7.**   **8.**

9. **GEOMETRY** Use the words *congruent*, *equilateral*, *equiangular*, and *regular* to describe the polygons.

A.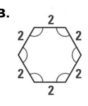
19   19   19

B.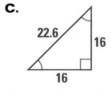
2   2   2   2   2

C.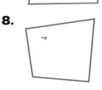
22.6   16   16

D.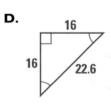
16   16   22.6

POLYGON In Exercises 10–13, use the regular hexagon shown below.

10. What is the measure of ∠ C?

11. What is the length of segment $\overline{EF}$?

12. Find the perimeter of the hexagon.

13. The sum of the measures of the angles of the hexagon is ? .

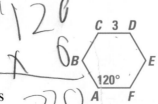

C 3 D
B
E
120°
A   F

490   **Chapter 10** *Geometry Concepts and Spatial Thinking*

14. WRITING Discuss the relationship between equilateral, equiangular, and regular. If a polygon is equilateral, must it be equiangular? Why?

15. FLOOR TILES Can you use regular heptagons to tile a floor with no gaps or overlapping tiles? Can you use regular octagons?

16. MAKING A CONJECTURE List examples of regular polygons that you can use to tile a floor without leaving gaps or overlaps. Next, list examples of regular polygons that you cannot use to tile a floor. Make a conjecture about when a regular polygon with *n* sides can be used to tile a floor.

PUZZLE In Exercises 17–19, use the figure at the right. The area of each polygon is given.

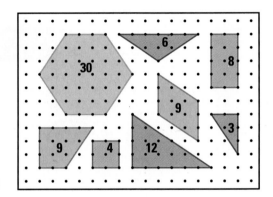

17. The eight polygons at the right can be rearranged to form a square. What is the area of the square? What are the dimensions of the square?

18. Which of the polygons are equilateral? Which are equiangular?

19. Copy the eight figures on dot paper and cut them out. Rearrange the figures to form a square. (*Hint:* Use the result of Exercise 17.)

STANDARDIZED TEST PRACTICE

20. A regular pentagon has a perimeter of 75 mm. What is the length of each side of the pentagon?

     A 12.50 mm   **B** 15.00 mm   **C** 15.50 mm   **D** 18.75 mm

EXPLORATION AND EXTENSION

PORTFOLIO

21. BUILDING YOUR PROJECT Most large department stores have separate areas for men's and women's clothing, cosmetics, shoes, linens, and other specialty items. Use polygons to separate one of your largest store areas into departments. Label each department. Identify all regular and congruent polygons.

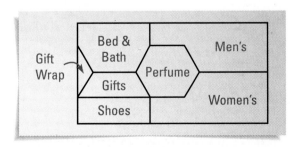

Exploring Angles of Polygons

In this investigation, you will look at patterns for the measures of angles of polygons.

Materials Needed
• paper
• protractor
• scissors

Part A POLYGON ANGLE MEASURES

1. Work in a group to complete the table. Use the procedure described in Example 2 on page 215.

Number of sides	Number of triangles	Sum of angle measures	Sketch of figure
3	1	1(180°) = 180°	
4	2	2(180°) = 360°	
5	?	?	
6	?	?	
7	?	?	?
8	?	?	?
9	?	?	?
10	?	?	?
n	?	?	—

2. Describe the pattern for the sum of the measures of the angles of a polygon.

3. What is $m \angle A$? Explain your reasoning.

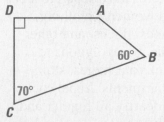

4. Trace the regular polygons on a sheet of paper. Use the result of Exercise 2 to predict the measure of each angle. Then use a protractor to check your result.

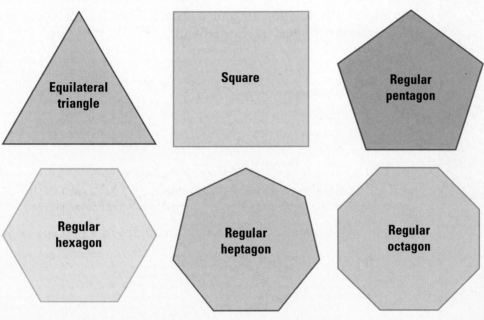

Equilateral triangle

Square

Regular pentagon

Regular hexagon

Regular heptagon

Regular octagon

NOW TRY THESE

5. Find the measure of each angle in a regular nonagon.

6. Use a protractor to draw a regular nonagon. Explain how you did it.

7. Find the measure of each angle in a regular decagon.

8. Use a protractor to draw a regular decagon. Explain how you did it.

10.8

Angles of Polygons

Goal 1 MEASURING EXTERIOR ANGLES

The angles of a polygon are called **interior angles**. Polygons also have **exterior angles**, as shown below.

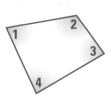

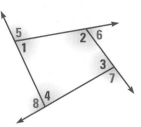

Here, $\angle 1$, $\angle 2$, $\angle 3$, and $\angle 4$ are *interior angles* of the polygon.

Here, $\angle 5$, $\angle 6$, $\angle 7$, and $\angle 8$ are *exterior angles* of the polygon.

The sum of the measures of the exterior angles of a polygon is 360°.

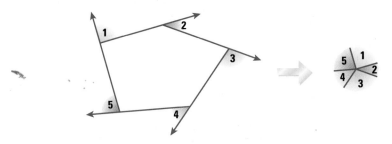

$$m \angle 1 + m \angle 2 + m \angle 3 + m \angle 4 + m \angle 5 = 360°$$

Example 1 Measuring Exterior Angles

Find the measure of $\angle 5$ in the pentagon at the right.

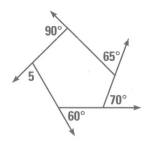

Solution

Notice that $\angle 5$ is an exterior angle. The sum of the measures of the exterior angles is 360°.

$$60° + 70° + 65° + 90° + m \angle 5 = 360°$$
$$285° + m \angle 5 = 360°$$
$$m \angle 5 = 75°$$

Goal 2 MEASURING THE ANGLES OF A POLYGON

The interior angles of a regular polygon are all congruent.

ANGLE MEASURES OF A POLYGON

Consider a polygon with n sides.

1. The sum of the interior angle measures is $(n - 2)(180°)$.
2. For a regular polygon, each interior angle measures
   $$\frac{(n - 2)(180°)}{n}.$$
3. The sum of the exterior angle measures is $360°$.
4. For a regular polygon, each exterior angle measures $\frac{360°}{n}$.

Example 2 — Finding Measures of Interior Angles

CONNECTION
Algebra

To find the measure of an interior angle of a regular pentagon, use the second formula above.

$$\text{Interior angle measure} = \frac{(n - 2)(180°)}{n}$$

$$= \frac{(5 - 2)(180°)}{5}$$

$$= \frac{3(180°)}{5}$$

$$= 108°$$

So, each interior angle has a measure of $108°$.

Example 3 — Finding Measures of Interior Angles

The sum of the measures of the interior angles of a triangle is $180°$.

$$5x + 9x + 4x = 180°$$

$$18x = 180°$$

$$x = 10°$$

So, the triangle has the following angle measures.

$m \angle A = 5x = 5(10°) = 50°$
$m \angle B = 4x = 4(10°) = 40°$
$m \angle C = 9x = 9(10°) = 90°$

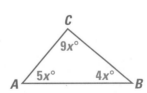

GUIDED PRACTICE

1. **DRAW A DIAGRAM** Draw a triangle with a 60° exterior angle.

2. **DRAW A DIAGRAM** Draw a quadrilateral with a 60° interior angle.

GEOMETRY In Exercises 3 and 4, find the measure of each labeled angle.

3. Hexagon (vertical line of symmetry)   4. Regular hexagon

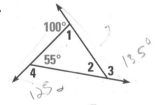

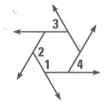

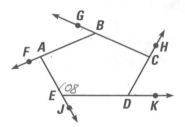

PRACTICE AND PROBLEM SOLVING

GEOMETRY In Exercises 5–7, use the pentagon at the right.

5. Name the interior angles of the pentagon. What is the sum of their measures?

6. What is the sum of the measures of the exterior angles?

7. If $m \angle ABG = 45°$, what is $m \angle ABC$?

GEOMETRY In Exercises 8–10, find the measures of the labeled angles.

8.
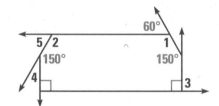

9.
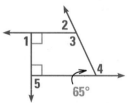

10.
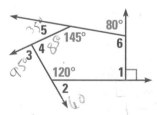

GEOMETRY In Exercises 11–13, find the measure of each interior and exterior angle of the regular polygon. Illustrate your results with a sketch.

11. Regular octagon   12. Regular decagon   13. Regular 12-gon

ALGEBRA In Exercises 14–17, find the measure of each interior angle.

14.
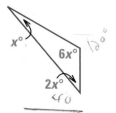

15.
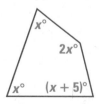

16.
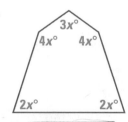

17.
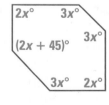

SUNROOM In Exercises 18–21, use the photo at the right. The ceiling meets the left wall of the sunroom at an angle of 117°.

18. Sketch the glass panes and describe their shapes.

19. Which panes appear to be congruent?

20. Find the angle measures of the top triangular glass pane.

21. Find the angle measures of the glass trapezoid.

22. **ERROR ANALYSIS** The polygon at the right has a vertical line of symmetry and exactly one of the angle measures is incorrect. Which measure is incorrect? What should it be?

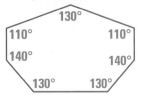

STANDARDIZED TEST PRACTICE

23. In the polygon given, find the value of *x*.

    A 55°   **B** 60°

    C 125°   **D** 235°

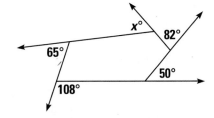

EXPLORATION AND EXTENSION

24. **KALEIDOSCOPE** To see how a kaleidoscope works, draw a line on a piece of paper. Tape two mirrors together and place them on the paper so the segment appears to form a hexagon. Notice that the angle between the two mirrors is 60°.

    a. Why are the mirrors placed at 60° to see the hexagon?

    b. What degree measure is needed to see an octagon?

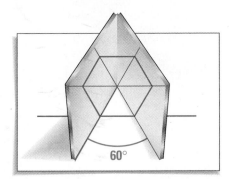

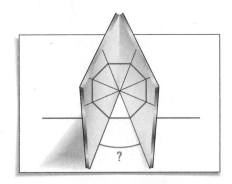

At the MALL

READ About It

The Mall of America, in Minneapolis-St. Paul, is the largest fully enclosed mall in the United States. It was built on 78 acres that were left vacant when Met Stadium was torn down.

The mall has four levels. The main hallway leading around each level is 3696 ft, or $\frac{7}{10}$ mi long.

Besides four major department stores, the mall contains more than 400 specialty stores and 14 movie theaters.

Each year more than 35 million consumers visit the Mall of America. Its great success is attributed to several key factors.

Its prosperity is mainly credited to the mall's location. Not only is the Mall of America situated within two miles of a major airport, but more than 28 million people live within one day's drive of the mall.

Another reason people are fascinated with this mall is because it has many unusual attractions, such as a 1.2 million gallon aquarium and a 7 acre indoor theme park complete with a roller coaster.

WRITE About It

1. About how far is it between Bloomingdale's and Macy's? Explain how you got your answer.

2. Name the polygons that are the outlines of the four major department stores. Are any congruent?

3. Copy the floor plan on a piece of paper. Trace a path you could walk from Bloomingdale's to Macy's that has three 90° turns and two 135° turns. Is this the shortest path between the two stores? Show your work.

4. Estimate the measures of the interior angles of Nordstrom. Explain how you got your estimate.

5. About what percent of the area of one level of the Mall of America is taken up by the theme park in the center? Explain.

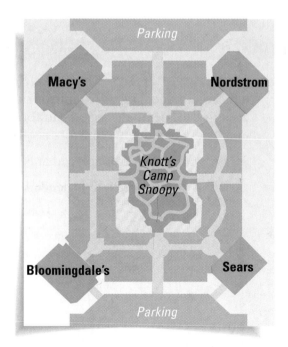

Measuring Angles

You can use a computer drawing program to discover properties of polygons.

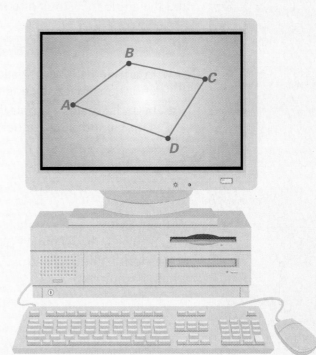

Exercises

1. Use a geometric drawing program to draw any quadrilateral. (It doesn't have to look like the one above.)

2. On the computer, select each angle and find its measure. Record your results in a table.

$m\angle A$	$m\angle B$	$m\angle C$	$m\angle D$
?	?	?	?

3. Add the four measures. What should the sum be? Is it? If not, is there a round-off error, or is something else wrong?

4. Select one of the vertices of the quadrilateral and move it. Measure all four angles again. Did all four change? Did the sum change?

5. Repeat Exercise 4 to create several different quadrilaterals. Do you get the same sum each time?

In Exercises 6–8, use a geometric drawing program to draw the indicated polygon. Measure each angle and find the sum of the measures. Is the sum equal to $(n - 2)(180°)$?

6. A nonregular pentagon

7. A nonregular hexagon

8. A nonregular octagon

What you should learn:

Goal 1 How to compare side lengths and angle measures of a triangle

Goal 2 How to find the angle measures of an isosceles triangle

Why you should learn it:

You can use angle measures and side lengths to analyze a house of cards.

Goal 1 ANGLES AND SIDES OF TRIANGLES

In this lesson you will study relationships between the side lengths and the angle measures of a triangle.

> **ANGLE AND SIDE RELATIONSHIPS**
>
> 1. In a triangle, the longest side is opposite the largest angle and the shortest side is opposite the smallest angle.
> 2. In an isosceles triangle, the angles opposite the sides of the same length have equal measures.

Example 1 Comparing Sides and Angles

Without using a ruler, state which side of the triangle at the right is longest and which is shortest.

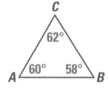

Solution

The largest angle is $\angle C$. So, the longest side is $\overline{AB}$.
The smallest angle is $\angle B$. So, the shortest side is $\overline{AC}$.

Example 2 Comparing Sides and Angles

Without using a ruler, state which side of the triangle is longest.

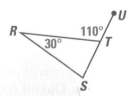

Solution

The angles $\angle STR$ and $\angle RTU$ are supplementary. So,

$$m\angle STR = 180° - m\angle RTU$$
$$= 180° - 110°$$
$$= 70°.$$

The sum of the angle measures of a triangle is 180°. So,

$$m\angle S = 180° - 30° - 70°$$
$$= 80°.$$

The largest angle is $\angle S$. So, the longest side is $\overline{RT}$.

Example 3 **Measuring Angles**

REAL LIFE
Games

You are building a house of cards. Each triangle formed by the cards has exactly one angle that measures 30°. What are the measures of the other two angles?

Solution

Each triangle has two sides formed by cards of the same size. So, each triangle is isosceles and has two angles, $\angle B$ and $\angle C$, that have the same measure. The sum of the measures of these two angles is

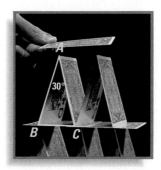

$$m \angle B + m \angle C = 180° - m \angle A$$
$$= 180° - 30°$$
$$= 150°.$$

Because $\angle B$ and $\angle C$ have the same measure, it follows that
$$m \angle B = m \angle C = \left(\frac{1}{2}\right)(150°) = 75°.$$

Example 4 **Analyzing an Isosceles Right Triangle**

Find the measures of the angles of any isosceles right triangle.

Solution

Begin by drawing an isosceles right triangle. Label the right angle $\angle P$. Label the other two angles $\angle Q$ and $\angle R$. The sum of the measures of these two angles is

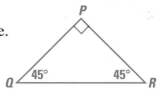

$$m \angle Q + m \angle R = 180° - m \angle P$$
$$= 180° - 90°$$
$$= 90°.$$

Because $\angle Q$ and $\angle R$ are opposite the sides that are the same length, they must have equal measures. So,
$$m \angle Q = m \angle R = \left(\frac{1}{2}\right)(90°) = 45°.$$

ONGOING ASSESSMENT

Talk About It
• • • • • • • • • • • • • • • • • • • •

The angles and sides of three triangles are listed below. Match the side lengths with the angle measures. Explain your reasoning.

A. 30°, 60°, 90°

B. 50°, 50°, 80°

C. 30°, 30°, 120°

1. 10.0, 10.0, 17.3

2. 5.00, 8.66, 10.00

3. 10.0, 10.0, 12.9

GUIDED PRACTICE

1. Describe the angle and side relationships of

   a. a scalene triangle.   **b.** an isosceles triangle.   **c.** a regular triangle.

2. **WRITING** In your own words, explain why an isosceles right triangle must have two 45° angles.

GEOMETRY In Exercises 3–6, identify the smallest angle, largest angle, shortest side, and longest side for each triangle.

3.

4.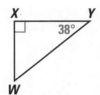

5.

6.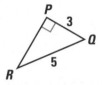

PRACTICE AND PROBLEM SOLVING

GEOMETRY In Exercises 7–10, name the triangle's shortest and longest sides.

7.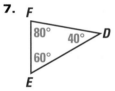

8.

9.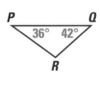

10.

In Exercises 11–14, name the smallest angle of the right triangle. Explain.

11.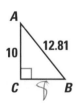

12.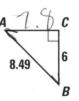

13.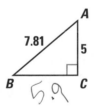

14.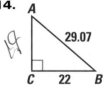

In Exercises 15–18, name the shortest and longest sides of the triangle. Explain.

15.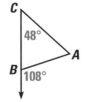

16.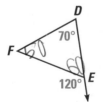

17.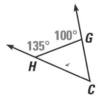

18.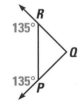

19. WRITING What is the longest side of a right triangle? Explain.

REASONING In Exercises 20–23, match the triangle's approximate side lengths with the triangle's angle measures. Explain your reasoning.

   A. 40°, 70°, 70°   **B.** 30°, 60°, 90°   **C.** 60°, 60°, 60°   **D.** 25°, 25°, 130°

20. 5, 5, 5   **21.** 5.0, 5.0, 9.1   **22.** 3.0, 5.2, 6.0   **23.** 5.0, 5.0, 3.4

WALKING In Exercises 24 and 25, use the following information.

You and a friend are on a walk, as shown at the right. From your point of view, the angle between your friend's house and the library is 55°. From your friend's point of view, the angle between your house and the library is 62°.

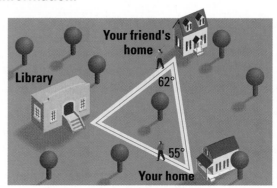

24. What is the third angle of the triangle?

25. Who has farther to walk to the library, you or your friend? Explain your reasoning.

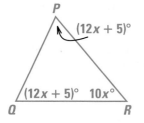

STANDARDIZED TEST PRACTICE

26. Order the sides of the triangles at the right from shortest to longest.

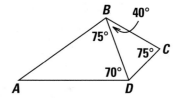

   Ⓐ $\overline{BC}, \overline{CD}, \overline{BD}, \overline{AB}, \overline{AD}$

   Ⓑ $\overline{CD}, \overline{BD}, \overline{BC}, \overline{AB}, \overline{AD}$

   Ⓒ $\overline{CD}, \overline{BC}, \overline{BD}, \overline{AD}, \overline{BD}$

   Ⓓ $\overline{CD}, \overline{BC}, \overline{BD}, \overline{AB}, \overline{AD}$

EXPLORATION AND EXTENSION

ALGEBRA In Exercises 27–29, solve for x. Then name the smallest angle, the largest angle, the shortest side, and the longest side of the triangle.

27.
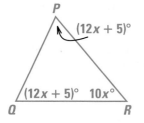

28.
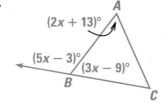

29.
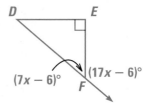

CHAPTER 10 *Summary*

WHAT **did you learn?**   WHY **did you learn it?**

Skills

10.1 Identify points, lines, and planes.
Use geometry figures to model objects in real life.

10.2 Classify angles and use a protractor to measure an angle.
Analyze reflections with mirrors.

10.3 Use a property of parallel lines.
Investigate parallel lines in real life.

10.4 Identify line symmetry and rotational symmetry.
Analyze symmetry found in nature.

10.5 Classify triangles by their sides and their angles.
Examine interior design methods, such as kitchen work triangles.

10.6 Classify quadrilaterals.
Use quadrilaterals to communicate ideas.

10.7 Recognize congruent polygons and regular polygons.
Use polygons to describe tiles.

10.8 Measure the interior and exterior angles of a polygon.
Analyze polygons used in architecture.

10.9 Compare side lengths and angle measures of a triangle.
Estimate unknown distances and angles.

Strategies

10.1–10.9 Use geometric diagrams to model and solve real-life problems.
Solve a wide variety of real-life problems.

Using Data

10.8 Use tables to solve problems.
Organize data and analyze geometric properties.

HOW **does it fit in the bigger picture of mathematics?**

The word *geo-metry* means "earth-measuring," and that describes geometry very well. In this chapter, you learned how to use geometry to measure line segments and angles.

You were also introduced to many geometric terms. Some are familiar: triangle, rectangle, line, plane, and so on. Many may be new: scalene, isosceles trapezoid, and exterior angle.

Your new mathematical vocabulary will help you communicate mathematics to others. However, *memorizing the meaning of mathematical terms is not nearly as important as being able to understand mathematical properties.*

VOCABULARY

- points (p. 460)
- line (p. 460)
- line segment (p. 460)
- ray (p. 460)
- plane (p. 460)
- congruent segments (p. 460)
- parallel (p. 461)
- intersection (p. 461)
- angle (p. 464)
- vertex (p. 464)
- measure (p. 464)
- congruent angles (p. 464)

- protractor (p. 464)
- acute angle (p. 465)
- right angle (p. 465)
- obtuse angle (p. 465)
- straight angle (p. 465)
- perpendicular (p. 465)
- complementary (p. 465)
- supplementary (p. 465)
- vertical angles (p. 470)
- corresponding angles (p. 470)
- line symmetry (p. 474)
- rotational symmetry (p. 475)

- scalene (p. 478)
- isosceles (p. 478)
- equilateral (p. 478)
- acute (p. 479)
- equiangular (p. 479)
- obtuse (p. 479)
- right (p. 479)
- convex (p. 484)
- congruent polygons (p. 488)
- regular (p. 489)
- interior angles (p. 494)
- exterior angles (p. 494)

10.1 EXPLORING POINTS, LINES, AND PLANES

1. Write two other names for the line $\overleftrightarrow{EG}$.

2. Name five line segments that have D as an endpoint.

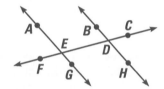

10.2 NAMING, MEASURING, AND DRAWING ANGLES

Example The protractor below shows that the measure of the angle is 35°. The angle is acute.

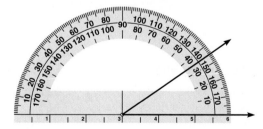

Use a protractor to measure each angle. Is each angle *acute*, *obtuse*, *right*, or *straight*?

3.

4.

10.3 EXPLORING PARALLEL LINES

Vertical angles are congruent. When two parallel lines are intersected by a third line, the corresponding angles are congruent.

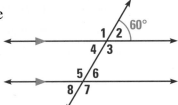

5. List each angle whose measure is 60°.

6. Find $m \angle 7$. Explain your reasoning.

10.4 SYMMETRY

To identify line symmetry, see if you can fold the figure in half so that the two halves coincide. To identify rotational symmetry, rotate the figure 180° or less and see if it coincides with itself.

Identify any symmetry of each figure.

7.
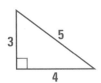

8.
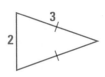

9.

10.5 EXPLORING TRIANGLES

To identify triangles by their sides, determine if the triangle is scalene, isosceles, or equilateral. To identify triangles by their angles, determine whether the triangle is acute, equiangular, obtuse, or right.

Example The triangle at the right is an obtuse triangle because one angle is greater than 90°.

Classify each triangle according to its sides and angles.

10.

11.

12.
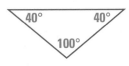

13.

14.
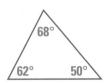

15.

10.6 EXPLORING QUADRILATERALS

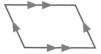   

| Parallelogram | Rectangle | Square | Trapezoid | Kite | Rhombus |

Classify each quadrilateral.

16.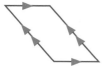

17.

10.7 POLYGONS AND CONGRUENCE

18. Draw a regular hexagon. Then divide it into three congruent quadrilaterals.

19. Draw a regular octagon. Then divide it into two congruent trapezoids and two congruent rectangles.

10.8 ANGLES OF POLYGONS

Example Find the measure of each labeled angle.

Solution
$m \angle 1 = 180° - 120° = 60°$
$m \angle 2 = 180° - 60° = 120°$
$m \angle 3 = 360° - (100° + 120° + 60°)$
$\qquad = 360° - 280°$
$\qquad = 80°$

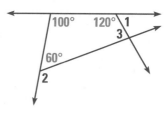

Find the measure of each interior and exterior angle of the polygon. Illustrate your results with a sketch.

20. Regular octagon

21. Regular pentagon

10.9 ANGLE AND SIDE RELATIONSHIPS

Order the sides of each triangle from the shortest to the longest.

22.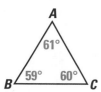

23.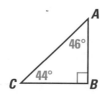

In Exercises 1–3, classify the triangle by its sides and by its angles.

1.

2.

3.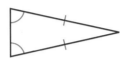

In Exercises 4 and 5, tell whether the statement is *true* or *false*.

4. A regular quadrilateral is a square.

5. The opposite sides of a kite are parallel.

PROTRACTOR **In Exercises 6–8, match the angle with its measure.**

A. 155°   **B.** 135°   **C.** 42°

6.   **7.**   **8.**

GEOMETRY **In Exercises 9–13, use the figure at the right.**

9. Give another name for $\overleftrightarrow{MP}$.

10. List the rays that have P as a beginning point.

11. List two pairs of vertical angles.

12. Is $\angle KML \cong \angle PSR$? Explain.

13. What is the measure of $\angle KML$?

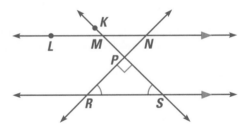

WRITING **In Exercises 14 and 15, find the measure of each interior angle of the polygon. Then identify any symmetry in the polygon.**

14. Regular pentagon

15. Regular hexagon

LASERS **In Exercises 16–18, use the diagram at the right, which shows a design for a laser TV.**

16. Describe the relationship between the three beams as they leave the lasers.

17. How many right angles are formed by each color of laser beam?

18. How many mirrors are parallel?

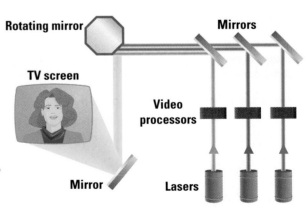

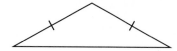

1. Which statement about $\overleftrightarrow{AB}$ is *false*?

A. $\overline{AC}$ lies on the line.

B. The line can be called $\overleftrightarrow{CB}$.

C. $\overrightarrow{DC}$ is the same as $\overrightarrow{DA}$.

D. $\overrightarrow{CB}$ is the same as $\overrightarrow{BC}$.

2. What type of angle is made by a clock's hands at 8:00 P.M.?

A. Acute   B. Right

C. Obtuse   D. Straight

3. Which statement about the figure below is *true*?

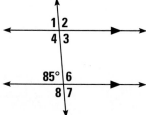

A. $\angle 1$ and $\angle 8$ are congruent.

B. $\angle 4$ and $\angle 6$ are corresponding angles.

C. The measure of $\angle 7$ is 85°.

D. $\angle 2$ and $\angle 3$ are vertical angles.

4. Which statement about the sand dollar is *true*?

A. It has no rotational symmetry.

B. It has a horizontal line of symmetry.

C. It coincides with itself after being rotated 90°.

D. It has a vertical line of symmetry.

5. Which best identifies the triangle?

A. Obtuse   B. Acute scalene

C. Acute   D. Obtuse isosceles

6. Which statement is *false*?

A. Some parallelograms are rectangles.

B. A scalene quadrilateral can be a kite.

C. All squares are rhombuses.

D. No trapezoid is a parallelogram.

7. Which word does *not* describe the polygons?

A. Equiangular   B. Regular

C. Equilateral   D. Congruent

8. Find the measures of all three angles of the triangle.

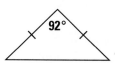

A. 44°, 44°, 92°

B. 45°, 45°, 92°

C. 15°, 73°, 92°

D. 44°, 92°, 92°

Congruence, Similarity, and Transformations

TECHNOLOGY

• **Interactive Real-Life
Investigations**

• **Middle School Tutorial
Software**

To find out more about space
exploration, go to:

http://www.mlmath.com

SPACE STATION This is an artist's rendering of the International Space
Station. A shuttle is shown docked with the station.

CHAPTER THEME
Space Exploration

CHAPTER PROJECT

Exploring the Space Station

PROJECT DESCRIPTION

The International Space Station is a cooperative effort among many countries. People can live at the space station while they do research in space. You will learn more about this space station and explore its design.

GETTING STARTED

Talking It Over

- What do you know about the space program? Have you ever watched the space shuttle take off? Would you like to travel in a spaceship someday?

- If you were designing a space station, what facilities would you include for eating, sleeping, recreation, research, and other activities? How would you provide power to the station?

Planning Your Project

- **Materials:** paper, pencils or pens

- Make a booklet out of several sheets of paper. Title your booklet "The International Space Station." Do research to find some facts about the space station. Put them in your booklet. As you complete the **BUILDING YOUR PROJECT** exercises throughout the chapter, add the results to your booklet.

BUILDING YOUR PROJECT

These are places throughout the chapter where you will work on your project.

11.1 Find the areas of some of the glass windows. *p. 515*

11.2 Examine the structure of one of the trusses. *p. 520*

11.4 Study the flags of some of the cooperating nations. *p. 529*

11.7 Design a solar panel. *p. 545*

11.9 Find the power produced by a solar array. *p. 555*

11.1

Area and Perimeter

What you should learn:

Goal ① How to find the areas of parallelograms and trapezoids

Goal ② How to use area and perimeter to solve real-life problems

Why you should learn it:

You can use area and perimeter to solve real-life problems, such as finding the area and perimeter of a miniature golf green.

Goal ① FINDING THE AREAS OF POLYGONS

The first diagram below shows the **height**, h, and **base**, b, of a parallelogram. The second diagram shows the **height**, h, and the two **bases**, b_1 and b_2, of a trapezoid. The variable b_1 is read "b sub 1."

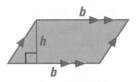 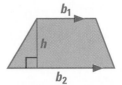

AREAS OF PARALLELOGRAMS AND TRAPEZOIDS

Parallelogram: Area $= bh$

Trapezoid: Area $= \frac{1}{2}(b_1 + b_2)h$

Example 1   Finding Polygon Areas

A trapezoid has been duplicated. Then the trapezoid and its duplicate have been arranged to form a parallelogram.

a. Find the area of the trapezoid.

b. Find the area of the parallelogram.

c. Compare the two areas.

Solution

a. Area $= \frac{1}{2}(b_1 + b_2)h$

$= \frac{1}{2} \cdot (2 + 4) \cdot 3$

$= 9$ square units

b. Area $= bh$

$= 6 \cdot 3$

$= 18$ square units

c. The parallelogram has twice the area of the trapezoid.

Example 2 Finding an Area

You are designing a miniature golf course. The plan for one putting green is shown at the right. Each square represents 1 ft². What is the total area of the green?

REAL LIFE
Miniature Golf

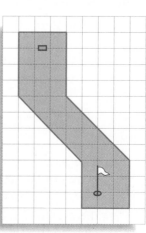

Solution

Divide the green into three smaller regions and find each area.

$$\text{Area of trapezoid} = \frac{1}{2}(b_1 + b_2)h$$

$$= \frac{1}{2} \cdot (4 + 7) \cdot 3$$

$$= 16.5 \text{ ft}^2$$

$$\text{Area of parallelogram} = bh$$

$$= 3 \cdot 4$$

$$= 12 \text{ ft}^2$$

$$\text{Area of triangle} = \frac{1}{2}bh$$

$$= \frac{1}{2} \cdot 3 \cdot 3$$

$$= 4.5 \text{ ft}^2$$

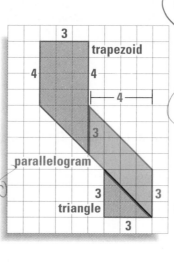

trapezoid

parallelogram

triangle

So, the total area of the green is $16.5 + 12 + 4.5 = 33 \text{ ft}^2$.

Example 3 Finding a Perimeter

You can find the perimeter of the golf green using the Pythagorean Theorem. The diagonal of a 1 ft-by-1 ft square is the hypotenuse of a right triangle with legs of length 1 ft. So, the length of each diagonal is $\sqrt{2}$ ft. To find the perimeter, start at the lower right corner of the green and move clockwise around the green.

$$P = 3 + 3 + \sqrt{2} + 3\sqrt{2} + 4 + 3 + 4 + 4\sqrt{2} + 3$$

$$= 20 + 8\sqrt{2}$$

$$\approx 31.3 \text{ ft}$$

ONGOING ASSESSMENT

Talk About It

1. Draw the golf green on graph paper. Then divide it into a rectangle, a parallelogram, and a square. Use these regions to find the total area. Does your result agree with that found in Example 2?

GUIDED PRACTICE

In Exercises 1–3, find the area and the perimeter of each figure.

1.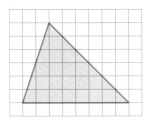

2.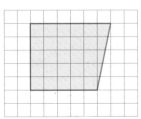

3.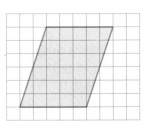

4. The parallelogram at the right has been cut and rearranged to form a rectangle. Find the perimeter and the area of each. Does rearranging change the area? Does it change the perimeter?

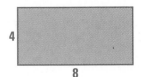

PRACTICE AND PROBLEM SOLVING

In Exercises 5 and 6, find the area of each figure. Describe two ways to find the area of the second figure.

5.

6.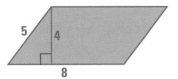

In Exercises 7 and 8, explain how the second figure can be used to find the area of the first. Then find the area and perimeter of each figure.

7.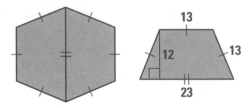

8.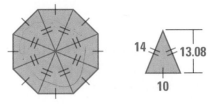

9. PICTURE FRAME The polygons at the right can be put together to form a picture frame.

   a. Find the area of each polygon.

   b. Sketch the picture frame.

   c. Find the area of the picture frame.

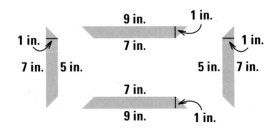

POLYGON PUZZLE In Exercises 10–12, use the figure at the right. Each small square of the grid has an area of 1 square unit.

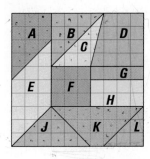

10. Name each type of polygon, *A* through *L*.

11. Find the area of each polygon.

12. Describe two ways to find the area of the entire figure. Then find the area.

DRAWING "EQUATIONS" In Exercises 13–16, make a sketch on dot paper to represent the "equation." Then find the area and perimeter of the final figure.

13. (2 Congruent Right Triangles) + (1 Square) = (1 Parallelogram)

14. (1 Trapezoid) + (1 Triangle) = (1 Parallelogram)

15. (1 Isosceles Triangle) + (1 Isosceles Trapezoid) = (1 Pentagon)

16. (2 Isosceles Trapezoids) + (1 Rectangle) = (1 Octagon)

STANDARDIZED TEST PRACTICE

In Questions 17 and 18, use the figure at the right.

17. What is the perimeter of the polygon?

 (**A**) 22 m   (**B**) 28 m

 (**C**) 32 m   (**D**) 36 m

18. What is the area of the polygon?

 (**A**) 24 m^2 (**B**) 36 m^2

 (**C**) 48 m^2 (**D**) 72 m^2

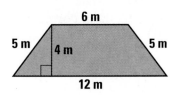

EXPLORATION AND EXTENSION

PORTFOLIO

19. BUILDING YOUR PROJECT The Cupola, shown at the right, gives astronauts on the International Space Station a wide view of what is outside. The Cupola has seven glass windows, six of which are identical trapezoids.

 a. Find the area of each trapezoid.

 b. Find the total area of all six glass trapezoids.

11.2

Exploring Congruence

What you should learn:

Goal ① How to determine whether two figures are congruent

Goal ② How to use congruence to solve real-life problems

Why you should learn it:

You can use congruence to solve real-life problems such as comparing the triangles used to make a kite.

Goal ① CONGRUENCE AND MEASURE

In Chapter 10, you were introduced to the idea of *congruence*.

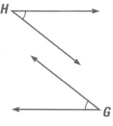

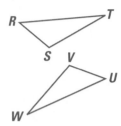

$$\overline{MN} \cong \overline{PQ}$$

Congruent line segments have the same length.

$$\angle H \cong \angle G$$

Congruent angles have the same measure.

$$\triangle RST \cong \triangle UVW$$

Congruent polygons have the same size and shape.

CONGRUENT POLYGONS

Two polygons are congruent if and only if all pairs of corresponding angles are congruent and all pairs of corresponding sides are congruent.

When two polygons are congruent, corresponding sides are congruent and corresponding angles are congruent.

Example 1 ▷ Corresponding Angles and Sides

Given that $\triangle ABC \cong \triangle DEF$, which angles are congruent? Which sides are congruent?

Solution

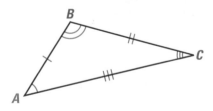

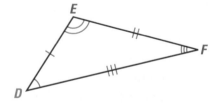

Corresponding Angles	Corresponding Sides
$\angle A \cong \angle D$	$\overline{AB} \cong \overline{DE}$
$\angle B \cong \angle E$	$\overline{BC} \cong \overline{EF}$
$\angle C \cong \angle F$	$\overline{AC} \cong \overline{DF}$

NEED TO KNOW

In congruent polygons, matching angles are called corresponding angles and matching sides are called corresponding sides. For example, when $\triangle QRS \cong \triangle XYZ$, the corresponding angles are $\angle Q$ and $\angle X$, $\angle R$ and $\angle Y$, and $\angle S$ and $\angle Z$.

Example 2 **Writing Congruence Statements**

Explain why the following triangles are congruent. Then write a
congruence statement about them.

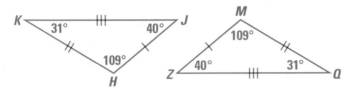

Solution

From the given angle measures, the following angles are congruent.

$\angle H \cong \angle M$ $\angle K \cong \angle Q$ $\angle J \cong \angle Z$ **Angles**

From the tick marks, you know the following sides are congruent.

$\overline{HJ} \cong \overline{MZ}$ $\overline{JK} \cong \overline{ZQ}$ $\overline{KH} \cong \overline{QM}$ **Sides**

All pairs of corresponding angles and sides are congruent, so the
triangles are congruent. You can write the congruence statement

$\triangle HJK \cong \triangle MZQ.$

Example 3 **Determining Congruence**

You are making a kite by attaching
the two triangular pieces at the right.
Are the two triangles congruent?
Explain your reasoning.

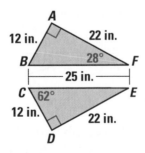

Solution

Use the fact that the sum of the angles of a triangle is $180°$. The two
unlabeled angles have the following measures.

$m\angle B = 180° - 90° - 28° = 62°$

$m\angle E = 180° - 90° - 62° = 28°$

Thus, you know that $\angle B \cong \angle C$, $\angle F \cong \angle E$, and $\angle A \cong \angle D$. The
corresponding sides are also congruent, so $\triangle BFA \cong \triangle CED.$

GUIDED PRACTICE

1. **WRITING** In your own words, explain what it means for two figures to be congruent. Give examples of congruent figures in real life.

In Exercises 2–4, write the congruence statement in words.

2. $\triangle ABC \cong \triangle DGH$

3. $\overline{AB} \cong \overline{DG}$

4. $\angle C \cong \angle H$

In Exercises 5–11, use the diagram below to complete the congruence statement.

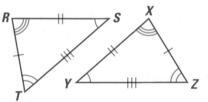

5. $\angle S \cong \angle\ \underline{?}$

6. $\overline{SR} \cong \underline{?}$

7. $\underline{?}\ \cong \angle X$

8. $\underline{?}\ \cong \overline{XZ}$

9. $\angle T \cong \underline{?}$

10. $\underline{?}\ \cong \overline{TS}$

11. Using the results of Exercises 5–10, complete the congruence statement: $\triangle SRT \cong \underline{?}$. Explain your reasoning.

In Exercises 12–15, decide whether the figures are congruent. Explain.

12.

13.

14.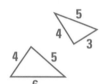

15.

PRACTICE AND PROBLEM SOLVING

In Exercises 16–21, use the fact that $\triangle BQR \cong \triangle KLM$ to complete the congruence statement.

16. $\angle B \cong \underline{?}$

17. $\overline{RB} \cong \underline{?}$

18. $\overline{ML} \cong \underline{?}$

19. $\angle R \cong \underline{?}$

20. $\angle L \cong \underline{?}$

21. $\overline{LK} \cong \underline{?}$

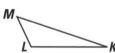

22. **DRAWING** Draw an obtuse triangle on cardboard. Cut the triangle out and trace two copies. Label the copies as $\triangle FGH$ and $\triangle MNP$. Write congruence statements about all corresponding parts of the triangles.

23. Which of these polygons are congruent?

A.   B.   C.   D.   E.

In Exercises 24–27, copy the figure on dot paper. Then divide it into two congruent parts. Give more than one answer, if possible.

24. 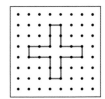 **25.** 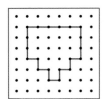 **26.** 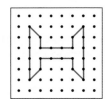 **27.**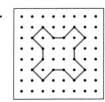

28. PHOTOGRAPHY Which of the pictures below are congruent? Explain how the pictures could have been created.

A.  **B.**  **C.**

COORDINATE GEOMETRY In Exercises 29–31, find the coordinates of the missing red point so that connecting all red points creates a figure congruent to the blue figure.

29. 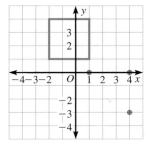 **30.** 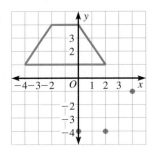 **31.**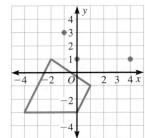

32. You cut a rectangular 3×5 index card into two triangles, as shown at the right. Explain how you know that the two pieces of the index card are congruent.

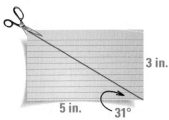

3 in.

5 in. 31°

33. REASONING For the isosceles triangle at the right, which one of the following congruence statements is true?

A. $\triangle XYZ \cong \triangle YXZ$ **B.** $\triangle XYZ \cong \triangle XZY$ **C.** $\triangle XYZ \cong \triangle ZYX$

34. REASONING Is there a type of triangle for which the following statements are both true? If so, sketch and describe such a triangle.

$$\triangle ABC \cong \triangle ACB \qquad \triangle ABC \cong \triangle BAC$$

35. In the diagram at the right, $\triangle ACE \cong \triangle RSN$.
Which statement is *false*?

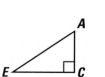

(A) $\overline{AE} \cong \overline{RN}$ **(B)** $\angle C \cong \angle S$

(C) $\angle A \cong \angle N$ **(D)** $\overline{CA} \cong \overline{SR}$

EXPLORATION AND EXTENSION

PORTFOLIO

36. **BUILDING YOUR PROJECT** In the International Space Station, *trusses* hold the solar panels far away from the rest of the station, to prevent the modules from casting shadows on the solar panels. Identify two pairs of congruent polygons in the truss pictured below.

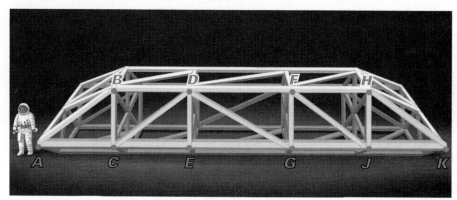

SPIRAL REVIEW

In Exercises 1–3, use graph paper to sketch a trapezoid that has the given measures. Then find its area. (11.1)

1. $b_1 = 6, b_2 = 12, h = 2$ **2.** $b_1 = 7, b_2 = 8, h = 4$ **3.** $b_1 = 1, b_2 = 9, h = 1$

In Exercises 4–7, rewrite the decimal as a simplified fraction. (6.6)

4. $0.\overline{1}$ **5.** $0.\overline{2}$ **6.** $0.\overline{3}$ **7.** $0.\overline{4}$

8. Use the results of Exercises 4–7 to describe a quick way to rewrite $\frac{n}{9}$ as a decimal. (6.6)

In Exercises 9–12, find the percent of increase or decrease. (8.6)

9. Before: $42.12   After: $40.18   **10.** Before: 3.6 lb   After: 7.6 lb

11. Before: 77.18 kg   After: 66.1 kg   **12.** Before: 4.4 ft   After: 6.3 ft

13. **PETS** You go to the pet store to start an aquarium of tropical fish. You purchase 2 angelfish for $2.89 each, 3 swordtails for $2.50 each, and a tank for $18.75. Write an expression that represents your total cost. Then simplify the expression to find out how much you spent. (1.4)

LAB 11.3

Properties of Reflections

COOPERATIVE LEARNING

In this investigation, you will explore properties of reflections.

Step ❶ Draw a large triangle on the left side of a piece of tracing paper. Label it △*MAT*.

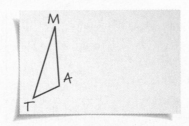

Step ❷ Fold the paper in half, as shown. Then trace the triangle and its labels in a new color.

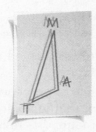

Step ❸ Unfold the paper. Draw three line segments that connect each vertex of the original triangle with the corresponding vertex of the new triangle.

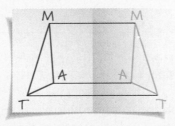

Materials Needed
- tracing paper
- colored pencils or pens
- ruler

1. Measure the distance between the crease in the paper and each of the six vertices.

2. What can you conclude about the relationship between the line segments and the crease in the paper?

NOW TRY THESE

3. Repeat the steps above using a different triangle. Is the conclusion you made in Exercise 2 also true for this triangle?

4. Do you think that the two triangles you made in Steps 1–3 above are congruent? Explain your reasoning.

What you should learn:

Goal **1** How to reflect a figure in a line

Goal **2** How to use properties of reflections to answer questions about real-life situations

Why you should learn it:

You can see examples of reflections in real life by looking at a mirror or the surface of a pond.

Line Reflections

Goal 1 REFLECTING FIGURES IN LINES

In the diagram below, $\triangle ABC$ is reflected in the line to produce a congruent image $\triangle A'B'C'$ on the other side of the line. This process is a **reflection**. The line is called a **reflection line**.

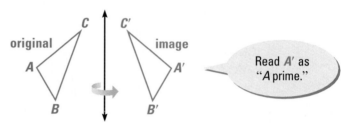

Read A' as "A prime."

PROPERTIES OF LINE REFLECTIONS

1. When a figure is reflected in a line, the image is congruent to the original figure.

2. A reflection line is perpendicular to each segment that joins an original point to its image. The reflection line divides each of these segments into two equal halves.

Example 1 Reflecting in a Coordinate Plane

Graph the triangle with vertices $R(1, 2)$, $S(3, 4)$, and $T(5, 1)$ in a coordinate plane. Reflect each point in the y-axis. Then compare $\triangle RST$ and its image.

Solution

Graph $\triangle RST$ and its image $\triangle R'S'T'$, as shown below. From the graph, you can see that the triangles are congruent. Their orientations, however, are different. This is comparable to the different orientations of your left and right hands.

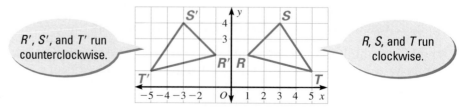

R', S', and T' run counterclockwise.

R, S, and T run clockwise.

You can use reflections to create figures that have line symmetry.

Example 2 Reflections and Line Symmetry

You work for a company that creates clothing patterns. The pattern shown below on the left is marked on a folded piece of cloth. When the cloth is cut and unfolded, you get the pieces shown on the right. Which pieces are reflections? Which piece has line symmetry?

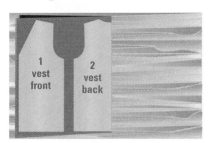

Solution

Piece 3 is a reflection of piece 1. Piece 2 has line symmetry because it had one edge lying along the fold.

Example 3 Finding a Pattern for a Reflection

You can use a *motion rule*, like $(x, y) \rightarrow (-x, y)$, to describe a reflection in a coordinate plane. The symbol $\rightarrow$ is read "goes to."

Reflection in *y*-axis

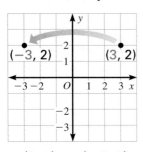

$$(3, 2) \rightarrow (-3, 2)$$

The *y*-coordinate is the same and the *x*-coordinate is the opposite. Describe this as
$$(x, y) \rightarrow (-x, y).$$

Reflection in *x*-axis

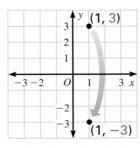

$$(1, 3) \rightarrow (1, -3)$$

The *x*-coordinate is the same and the *y*-coordinate is the opposite. Describe this as
$$(x, y) \rightarrow (x, -y).$$

ONGOING ASSESSMENT

Write About It
....

Find the coordinates of the images when the given point is reflected in the *x*-axis and in the *y*-axis.

1. (2, 4)

2. (−3, 5)

3. (−1, −3)

4. (2, −4)

GUIDED PRACTICE

In Exercises 1–4, copy the figure at the right on graph paper. Then draw the image of △LMN after the indicated reflection.

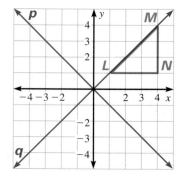

1. Reflect the triangle in the *x*-axis.

2. Reflect the triangle in the *y*-axis.

3. Reflect the triangle in line *p*.

4. Reflect the triangle in line *q*.

PRACTICE AND PROBLEM SOLVING

In Exercises 5 and 6, use the drawing at the right.

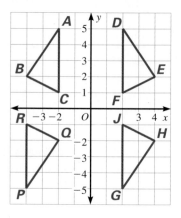

5. State whether the sentence is *true* or *false*.

   a. △*DEF* is the reflection of △*ABC* in the *y*-axis.

   b. △*DEF* is the reflection of △*GJH* in the *y*-axis.

   c. △*GHJ* is the reflection of △*PQR* in the *y*-axis.

6. Name the image after △*DEF* is reflected in the *x*-axis.

In Exercises 7 and 8, draw the reflection described by the motion rule. Tell what type of reflection happens.

7. $(-1, 3) \rightarrow (-1, -3)$

8. $(-5, -6) \rightarrow (5, -6)$

In Exercises 9–12, decide whether the red figure is a reflection of the blue figure in line *k*. If not, sketch the reflection of the blue figure.

9.

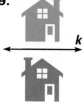

10.

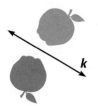

11.

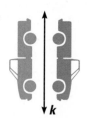

12.

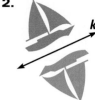

13. **WHAT DO YOU SEE?** When you look at yourself in a mirror, your right side appears to be on your left side. Is this also true when you look at a photo of yourself? Explain.

COORDINATE GEOMETRY In Exercises 14 and 15, graph △*ABC* in a coordinate plane. Then graph the image when △*ABC* is reflected in the *x*-axis and the image when △*ABC* is reflected in the *y*-axis.

14. $A(1, 3)$, $B(4, 1)$, $C(2, 0)$

15. $A(0, -1)$, $B(-2, -4)$, $C(2, -4)$

16. **ALPHABET REFLECTION** Which capital letters remain the same when reflected in a vertical line? Which capital letters remain the same when reflected in a horizontal line?

PLAYING POOL In Exercises 17 and 18, use the diagram at the right.

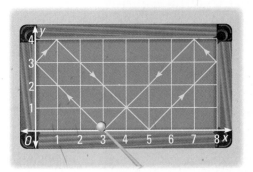

17. The ball is shot from the point (3, 0) and follows the path shown. Describe the line of reflection of the path.

18. Suppose you shoot the ball in the same direction from the point (1, 0). Sketch the path of the ball. Does the line of reflection change?

In Exercises 19–21, copy the figures on graph paper. Then draw the line that can be used to reflect the blue figure to the red figure.

19.
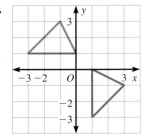

20.
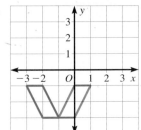

21.
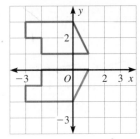

STANDARDIZED TEST PRACTICE

22. Use the figure at the right. Which motion rule describes the reflection from quadrilateral *ABCD* to quadrilateral *LMNP*?

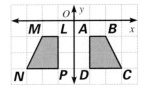

(**A**) $(x, y) \to (-x, -y)$

(**B**) $(x, y) \to (x, -y)$

(**C**) $(x, y) \to (-x, y)$

(**D**) $(x, y) \to (y, x)$

EXPLORATION AND EXTENSION

23. **SYMMETRICAL FACES** Find photographs in magazines or newspapers of faces that appear to have line symmetry and of faces that appear not to have line symmetry. Which type of photo is easier to find?

11.4

Rotations

What you should learn:

Goal 1 How to describe a rotation about a point

Goal 2 How to rotate a figure in a coordinate plane

Why you should learn it:

Rotation describes motion in real life, such as the turning of a windmill.

Goal 1 ROTATING FIGURES ABOUT POINTS

Reflection, which you studied in Lesson 11.3, is one type of **transformation**. **Rotation** about a point is another type of transformation. Three examples of rotation are shown below.

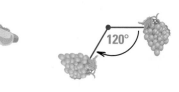

Clockwise rotation of 90°

Counterclockwise rotation of 60°

Clockwise rotation of 120°

Example 1 Finding an Angle of Rotation

The blue figure is rotated about the origin to become the red figure. Find the angle and direction of rotation.

Solution

STRATEGY **USE A GRAPH** Copy the diagram on graph paper. The direction of rotation from the blue figure to the red figure is clockwise. Follow the steps below to find the angle of rotation about the origin.

Step 1 Draw a line from a point in the blue figure to the origin.

Step 2 Draw a line from the origin to the point's image in the red figure.

Step 3 Use a protractor to measure the angle formed by the two lines.

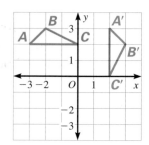

This transformation is a clockwise rotation of 90°.

Example 2 Finding a Pattern for a Rotation

Describe a motion rule for rotating a point in a coordinate plane 180° about the origin.

Solution

To begin, choose a few points and rotate them 180° about the origin.

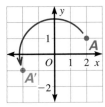 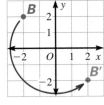 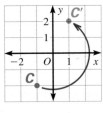

$$(2, 1) \rightarrow (-2, -1) \qquad (-2, 2) \rightarrow (2, -2) \qquad (-1, -2) \rightarrow (1, 2)$$

From these examples, you can see that both the *x*-coordinate and the *y*-coordinate get replaced by their opposites. So, the motion rule for rotating a point 180° about the origin is

$$(x, y) \rightarrow (-x, -y).$$

Rotations do not change the size or shape of an object. After a rotation, the image is always congruent to the original object.

LESSON INVESTIGATION

COOPERATIVE LEARNING

Investigating Reflections and Rotations

GROUP ACTIVITY Copy the quadrilateral *ABCD* on graph paper.

① Reflect *ABCD* in the *y*-axis.

② Then reflect the image from Step 1 in the *x*-axis.

③ Rotate *ABCD* 180° about the origin.

What do you notice? Write a general conjecture that describes a relationship between reflections and rotations.

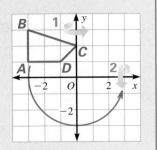

ONGOING ASSESSMENT

Write About It
....

1. Describe a motion rule for rotating a point in a coordinate plane 90° clockwise about the origin.

Extra Practice, page 735

GUIDED PRACTICE

In Exercises 1–4, the blue figure has been rotated to produce the red image. Estimate the angle and direction of the rotation.

1.

2.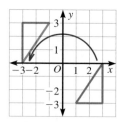

3.

4.

5. WRITING In Lesson 10.4, you studied rotational symmetry. Describe the relationship between rotations and rotational symmetry.

PRACTICE AND PROBLEM SOLVING

In Exercises 6–8, copy the diagram on graph paper. Find the angle of rotation about the origin.

6.

7.

8.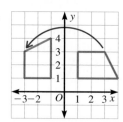

In Exercises 9–12, estimate the angle and direction of rotation.

9.

10.

11.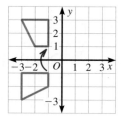

12.

In Exercises 13–15, use the figure at the right. $\triangle ABC$ is rotated 90° counterclockwise about the origin to produce $\triangle A'B'C'$.

13. Write the coordinates of A', B', and C'.

14. Which motion rule describes the rotation? Explain your reasoning.

A. $(x, y) \rightarrow (x, -y)$ **B.** $(x, y) \rightarrow (-x, y)$

C. $(x, y) \rightarrow (-y, x)$ **D.** $(x, y) \rightarrow (y, -x)$

15. Explain why $\triangle ABC \cong \triangle A'B'C'$.

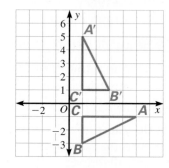

ACTING IT OUT In Exercises 16–18, trace the polygon and point *P*.
Rotate the tracing paper 90° clockwise about *P*. Trace the polygon again.

16.

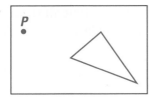

17.

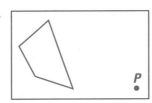

18.

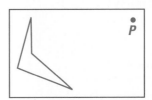

19. LUNAR ROTATION It takes about 14 days for the moon to be rotated
180° about Earth. About how many degrees does the moon rotate
about Earth per day?

In Exercises 20–23, name the image of the point, segment, or triangle.

20. 60° clockwise rotation of *D* about *E*

21. 60° clockwise rotation of $\overline{BC}$ about *E*

22. 60° counterclockwise rotation of △*ABC* about *C*

23. 180° rotation of $\overline{AC}$ about *C*

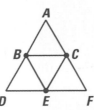

STANDARDIZED TEST PRACTICE

24. At the right, Figure *A* is rotated about the
origin to produce Figure *B*. What is the angle
of rotation?

    A 45°   **B** 60°   **C** 90°   **D** 180°

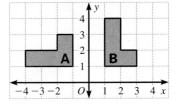

EXPLORATION AND EXTENSION

PORTFOLIO

25. BUILDING YOUR PROJECT Many countries have cooperated to build the
International Space Station. The flags below represent three of them.

United Kingdom   Switzerland   Sweden

a. Which flags have rotational symmetry? Find the angles of rotation.

b. Design a flag for the space station that has 180° rotation symmetry.

Translations

What you should learn:

Goal 1 How to translate a figure in a plane

Goal 2 How to represent translations in a coordinate plane

Why you should learn it:

You can use translations in the creation of computer graphics and animation.

A computer artist used translations to create this picture from a single photo of a skier.

Goal 1 TRANSLATING FIGURES IN A PLANE

A third type of transformation you will study is a **translation** (sometimes called a *slide*). When a figure is translated, each point of the figure is moved the same distance.

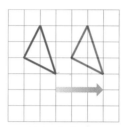

Translation:
3 units right

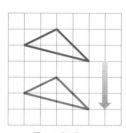

Translation:
3 units down

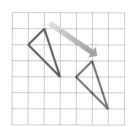

Translation:
3 units right and
2 units down

The image after a translation is congruent to the original and has the same orientation as the original.

Example 1 Drawing a Translation

In the diagram at the right, the arrow represents a translation. Write a verbal description of the translation. Then copy the figure on dot paper and perform the translation.

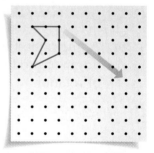

Solution

The arrow indicates a translation 5 units to the right and 4 units down.

Translate each vertex of the blue polygon by counting 5 units to the right and 4 units down. Connect the new points to draw the image polygon, shown in red.

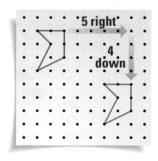

It doesn't matter in which direction you move first. In Example 1, moving 4 units down and then 5 units to the right gives you the same result.

Example 2 Translating in a Coordinate Plane

Graph the parallelogram with vertices $A(-4, 3)$, $B(-1, 4)$, $C(3, 3)$, and $D(0, 2)$. Use the following motion rule to translate each vertex.

$$(x, y) \rightarrow (x + 2, y - 5)$$

Finally, write a verbal description of the transformation.

Solution

Add 2 to each x-coordinate and subtract 5 from each y-coordinate.

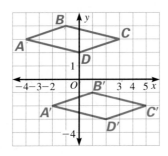

Original		Image
$A(-4, 3)$	$\rightarrow$	$A'(-2, -2)$
$B(-1, 4)$	$\rightarrow$	$B'(1, -1)$
$C(3, 3)$	$\rightarrow$	$C'(5, -2)$
$D(0, 2)$	$\rightarrow$	$D'(2, -3)$

Verbal Description: Each point moves 2 units to the right and 5 units down.

Example 3 Computer Animation

In computer graphics, translations are used to create patterns and animations. Describe the following translations of the creature shown at the right.

a. from A to B

b. from B to C

c. from C to D

Solution

a. The palm of the hand moves from $(3, 2)$ to $(5, 4)$. So, each point moves 2 units to the right and 2 units up.

b. The palm of the hand moves from $(5, 4)$ to $(8, 6)$. So, each point moves 3 units to the right and 2 units up.

c. The palm of the hand moves from $(8, 6)$ to $(9, 3)$. So, each point moves 1 unit to the right and 3 units down.

Tech Link

Investigation 11, Interactive Real-Life Investigations

ONGOING ASSESSMENT

Write About It

1. Write a motion rule for the translation in part (a) of Example 3.

2. Write a motion rule for the translation in part (b) of Example 3.

In Exercises 1–3, describe the translation verbally.

1.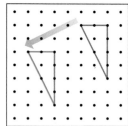

2.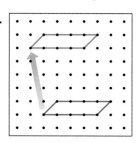

3.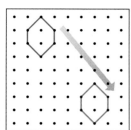

In Exercises 4–6, describe the transformation that maps the blue figure to the red figure.

4.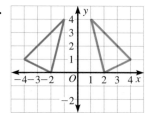

5.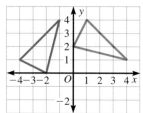

6.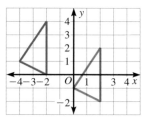

In Exercises 7–9, match the motion rule with a graph. Then describe the translation verbally.

A.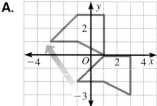

B.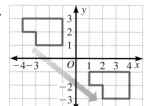

C.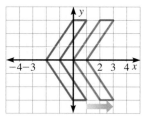

7. $(x, y) \rightarrow (x + 2, y)$

8. $(x, y) \rightarrow (x + 5, y - 4)$

9. $(x, y) \rightarrow (x - 2, y + 3)$

10. Graph the trapezoid whose vertices are $E(-2, 1)$, $F(-1, 3)$, $G(1, 3)$, and $H(4, 1)$. Then translate the trapezoid as indicated.

    a. 3 units to the left and 6 units down

    b. 4 units to the right and 3 units down

    c. 5 units to the right and 2 units up

11. Find the area of the original trapezoid in Exercise 10. Then find the area of each of the translated trapezoids. What do you notice?

In Exercises 12–14, copy the figure and translate it twice, as indicated by the arrows. Is the final image a translation of the original figure? If so, describe the single translation that will produce the final image.

12.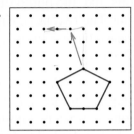

13.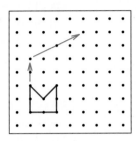

14.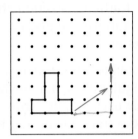

In Exercises 15–17, graph the triangle with vertices $A(0, 1)$, $B(3, 4)$, and $C(1, 5)$. Then graph the image of $\triangle ABC$ after it has been translated using the given motion rule. Finally, write a verbal description of the transformation.

15. $(x, y) \rightarrow (x, y + 7)$

16. $(x, y) \rightarrow (x + 2, y - 3)$

17. $(x, y) \rightarrow (x + 3, y + 4)$

DRIVING IN ALABAMA In Exercises 18 and 19, use the map shown at the right.

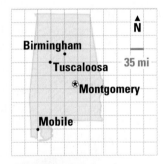

18. You leave Mobile and drive 35 mi east and 175 mi north. To what city do you drive?

19. You drive from Birmingham to Mobile. Describe the translation verbally.

 STANDARDIZED TEST PRACTICE

20. When the figure at the right is translated 3 units to the right and 5 units up, which point is *not* a vertex of the translated image?

 A $(1, 5)$ **B** $(2, 0)$

 C $(2, 3)$ **D** $(-1, 4)$

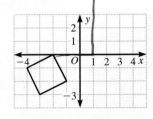

 EXPLORATION AND EXTENSION

21. **COMPUTER ANIMATION** You want to make an animation of a fish. Sketch the fish. Use a transformation (such as translation or rotation) to move the fish through the water, and draw the image. Use another transformation on this image to draw a new image. Continue until you have at least six images. Describe each transformation.

Looking at the Stars

READ About It

The Hubble Space Telescope orbits Earth. Its position above Earth's atmosphere gives a clear view of objects in space.

The Hubble's *solar arrays* are the two gold rectangular objects in the photo below. The Hubble uses its solar arrays to collect energy from the sun. This energy is used to power cameras and transmit information and images back to Earth.

The Hubble's cameras have taken many spectacular photographs, like the photo of a supernova shown below. The two large rings in the photo may be gases that are lit up by an unseen companion star.

The Hubble's cameras can be focused in any direction. However, they are not generally used to take photographs of objects within 50° of the sun, within 15° of the lighted side of Earth, or within 9° of the moon.

WRITE About It

1. Do you think the solar arrays of the Hubble are congruent? Explain your answer.

2. When the Hubble orbits Earth, what type of transformation is it undergoing?

3. Trace the two large rings in the supernova photo. Can you reflect one of the rings to get the other ring? Use a diagram in your answer.

4. Trace the two large rings again. Can you rotate one of the rings to get the other ring? Use a diagram in your answer.

5. Why do you think the Hubble's cameras do not generally take photographs of objects that appear within 50° of the sun?

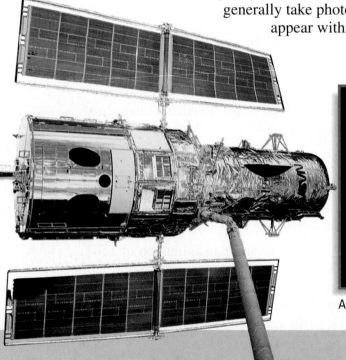

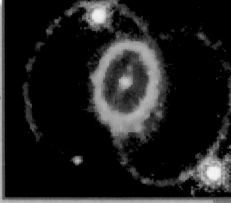

A supernova is an exploding star.

Take this test as you would take a test in class. The answers to the exercises are given in the back of the book.

In Exercises 1–4, use the congruent triangles at the right to complete the statement. (11.2)

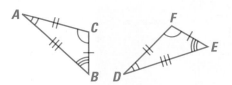

1. $\angle A \cong$ _?_

2. $\angle F \cong$ _?_

3. $\overline{AB} \cong$ _?_

4. _?_ $\cong \overline{DF}$

In Exercises 5–10, describe the transformation shown. (11.3–11.5)

5.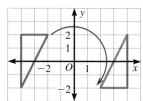

6.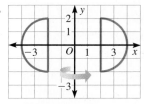

7.

8.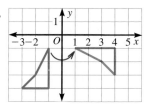

9.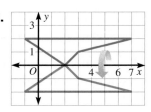

10.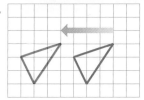

In Exercises 11–14, match the polygon with its area expression. (11.1)

A. $\frac{1}{2}$(Base)(Height) **B.** (Base)(Height) **C.** (Base)^2 **D.** $\frac{1}{2}$(Base 1 + Base 2)(Height)

11.

12.

13.

14.

AMUSEMENT PARK   In Exercises 15–17, use the amusement park ride shown. (11.4)

15. Find the angle of rotation from the red car to the orange car.

16. Find the angle of rotation from the red car to the yellow car.

17. Find the angle of rotation from the red car to the blue car.

11.6

Exploring Similarity

What you should learn:

Goal 1 How to recognize similar figures

Goal 2 How to use properties of similar figures

Why you should learn it:

You can use properties of similar figures to solve real-life problems, such as finding the height of a rocket launch tower.

Goal 1 RECOGNIZING SIMILAR FIGURES

Two objects are **similar** if they have the same shape. They do not have to be the same size.

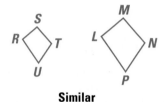

Similar

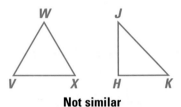

Not similar

PROPERTIES OF SIMILAR POLYGONS

1. Corresponding angles have the same measure.

2. The ratios of corresponding side lengths are equal.

The symbol $\sim$ means "is similar to." For the two similar quadrilaterals above, you can write $RSTU \sim LMNP$.

Example 1 Properties of Similarity

Given that $\triangle ABC \sim \triangle DEF$, write statements describing the relationships among their angles and sides.

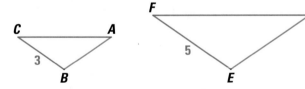

Solution

Corresponding angles have the same measure.

$$m\angle A = m\angle D \qquad m\angle B = m\angle E \qquad m\angle C = m\angle F$$

Ratios of corresponding side lengths are equal.

$$\frac{AB}{DE} = \frac{BC}{EF} = \frac{AC}{DF}$$

....

The common ratio of one polygon to a similar polygon is called the **scale factor** . In the triangles above, $BC = 3$ and $EF = 5$, so the scale factor of $\triangle ABC$ to $\triangle DEF$ is $\frac{3}{5}$.

Example 2 **Using Properties of Similar Triangles**

Given that $\triangle PQR \sim \triangle UTS$, find the lengths of $\overline{ST}$ and $\overline{TU}$.

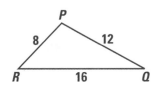 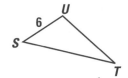

Solution

The triangles are similar, so the ratios of corresponding side lengths are equal. You can use these ratios to write proportions.

$$\frac{TU}{QP} = \frac{US}{PR} \qquad\qquad \frac{ST}{RQ} = \frac{US}{PR}$$

$$\frac{TU}{12} = \frac{6}{8} \qquad\qquad \frac{ST}{16} = \frac{6}{8}$$

$$12 \cdot \frac{TU}{12} = 12 \cdot \frac{6}{8} \qquad 16 \cdot \frac{ST}{16} = 16 \cdot \frac{6}{8}$$

$$TU = 9 \qquad\qquad ST = 12$$

Enlarging or reducing a figure proportionally is called a **dilation**. The image after a dilation is similar to the original figure.

Example 3 **Drawing a Dilation**

A dilation enlarges or reduces a polygon by a scale factor to create a similar image. For example, to dilate $\triangle ABC$ by a scale factor of 3, use the motion rule $(x, y) \rightarrow (3x, 3y)$ to form $\triangle A'B'C'$.

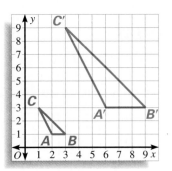

Original		Image
$A(2, 1)$	$\rightarrow$	$A'(6, 3)$
$B(3, 1)$	$\rightarrow$	$B'(9, 3)$
$C(1, 3)$	$\rightarrow$	$C'(3, 9)$

✔**Check:** The ratio of $A'B'$ to AB is $\frac{A'B'}{AB} = \frac{3}{1} = 3$, so the scale factor of the image to the original is 3.

ONGOING ASSESSMENT

Write About It

You dilate a figure that has the given dimensions. The image is 24 in. high. Find the width of the image.

1. 6 in. high × 7 in. wide

2. 8 in. high × 3 in. wide

11.6 Exercises

Extra Practice, page 735

GUIDED PRACTICE

1. **WRITING** In your own words, state what it means for two figures to be similar.

2. **REAL-LIFE SIMILARITY** Give some examples of similar figures in your classroom.

In Exercises 3 and 4, identify the two similar figures.

3. **A.** **B.** **C.**   4. **A.** **B.** **C.**

In Exercises 5–8, $\triangle HJG \sim \triangle KLM$, as shown at the right.

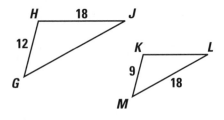

5. Write three equal ratios for $\triangle HJG$ and $\triangle KLM$.

6. Find the scale factor of $\triangle HJG$ to $\triangle KLM$.

7. Find the lengths of $\overline{KL}$ and $\overline{GJ}$.

8. Copy and complete the equation. $m\angle H = m\angle\underline{\ ?\ }$

PRACTICE AND PROBLEM SOLVING

In Exercises 9–12, quadrilaterals *QRST* and *WXYZ* are similar, as shown at the right.

 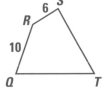

9. Write four equal ratios for $QRST$ and $WXYZ$.

10. Find the scale factor of $QRST$ to $WXYZ$.

11. Copy and complete the equation. $m\angle T = m\angle\underline{\ ?\ }$

12. Find the length of each segment.

    a. $\overline{QT}$ **b.** $\overline{ST}$ **c.** $\overline{XY}$

In Exercises 13–15, you are given a pair of similar figures. Solve for *x*.

13. 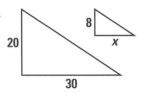   14.   15.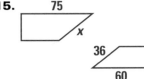

16. **DRAWING TRIANGLES** Draw two isosceles right triangles that are not congruent. Are the triangles similar? Explain.

538   **Chapter 11** *Congruence, Similarity, and Transformations*

LAUNCH TOWERS In Exercises 17 and 18, use the following information.

A 5 ft person is standing near a rocket launch tower, as shown at the right. The triangles formed by their shadows are similar. The person's shadow is 3 ft long and the tower's shadow is 240 ft long.

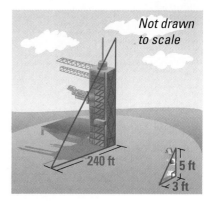

Not drawn to scale

240 ft

5 ft

3 ft

17. Explain why the ratio of the tower's height to the person's height is equal to the ratio of their shadows.

18. Find the height of the launch tower.

In Exercises 19–21, use the motion rule to draw a dilation of the figure. Find the scale factor of the image to the original.

19. $(x, y) \rightarrow (2x, 2y)$

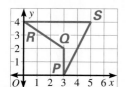

20. $(x, y) \rightarrow (3x, 3y)$

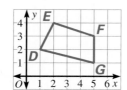

21. $(x, y) \rightarrow \left(\frac{1}{2}x, \frac{1}{2}y\right)$

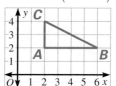

STANDARDIZED TEST PRACTICE

22. Which figure is not similar to any of the others?

Ⓐ   Ⓑ   Ⓒ   Ⓓ

EXPLORATION AND EXTENSION

23. **PAPER SIZES** In Europe and around the world, people use writing paper in International Standard sizes. Size A0 is larger than size A1, size A1 is larger than size A2, and so on. All of these sizes are similar rectangles. The basic size, A0, has dimensions 84.1 cm by 118.9 cm. The scale factor of each size to the next smaller size is $\sqrt{2}$.

a. Find the dimensions of A1, A2, A3, A4, and A5 sheets of paper.

b. Which size is closest to $8\frac{1}{2}$ in. by 11 in.? (1 in. = 2.54 cm)

c. Why do you think different sizes are made to be similar rectangles?

LAB 11.7

COOPERATIVE LEARNING

Using Properties of Similarity

Part **A** PLANNING A YEARBOOK

Materials Needed
- **paper**
- **pencil or pen**
- **ruler**

You are on the school yearbook staff. For class photos, you have decided to follow the page layout shown below.

1. Find the width of each photo. Explain your reasoning.

2. Find the height of each photo. Explain your reasoning.

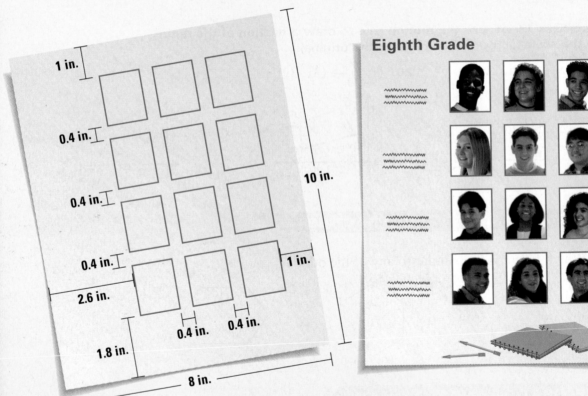

3. The original class photos you have for the yearbook are 5 in. wide by 7 in. high. Are these originals similar to the small photos that go in the yearbook? Explain your reasoning.

4. Which of the following is similar to the small photos in the yearbook? Explain.

   A. 5 in. by 6 in.

   B. 4 in. by 5 in.

   C. 4 in. by 6 in.

5. Suppose you dilate a photo that is 1.2 in. wide by 1.5 in. high. If the enlarged photo's width is 5 in., what is its height?

6. Suppose you dilate a photo that is 1.2 in. wide by 1.5 in. high. If the enlarged photo's height is 7 in., what is its width?

7. On a piece of paper, draw a rectangle that is 5 in. wide by 7 in. high. Show where to cut the rectangle so it is similar to a photo that is 1.2 in. wide by 1.5 in. high.

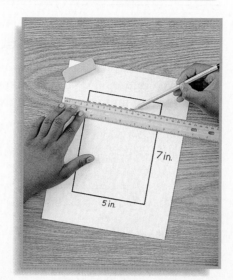

NOW TRY THESE

In Exercises 8–10, you have decided to redesign the yearbook pages so that you will not have to cut the 5 in.-by-7 in. original photos.

8. If you reduce each 5 in.-by-7 in. photo so that its width is 1.2 in., what will its height be?

9. If you reduce each 5 in.-by-7 in. photo so that its height is 1.5 in., what will its width be?

10. DRAWING A DIAGRAM Show how you will change the page layout so that you will not have to cut the original photos.

11.7

Problem Solving Using Similar Figures

What you should learn:

Goal 1 How to use similar figures to solve real-life problems

Goal 2 How to compare perimeters and areas of similar figures

Why you should learn it:

You can use properties of similar figures to solve real-life problems, such as finding the dimensions of a poster.

Goal 1 USING SIMILAR FIGURES

When two figures are similar, remember that corresponding angles are congruent and corresponding sides are proportional.

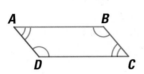 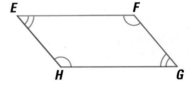

Corresponding Angles

$$\angle A \cong \angle E$$
$$\angle B \cong \angle F$$
$$\angle C \cong \angle G$$
$$\angle D \cong \angle H$$

Corresponding Sides

$$\frac{AB}{EF} = \frac{BC}{FG} = \frac{CD}{GH} = \frac{AD}{EH}$$

Example 1 Using Properties of Similar Figures

You are designing a poster to advertise the next meeting of the Space Club. You begin by sketching the design shown below at the left. The scale factor of the actual poster to your sketch is 4. Find the height and width of the actual poster.

Solution

You can use a verbal model to find the dimensions.

Verbal Model
$$\frac{\text{Poster height}}{\text{Sketch height}} = \frac{\text{Poster width}}{\text{Sketch width}} = \text{Scale factor}$$

Labels
Poster height $= h$	(inches)
Sketch height $= 7$	(inches)
Poster width $= w$	(inches)
Sketch width $= 5$	(inches)
Scale factor $= 4$	

Algebraic Models

$$\frac{h}{7} = 4 \qquad\qquad \frac{w}{5} = 4$$

$$7 \cdot \frac{h}{7} = 7 \cdot 4 \qquad 5 \cdot \frac{w}{5} = 5 \cdot 4$$

$$h = 28 \qquad\qquad w = 20$$

The poster has a height of 28 in. and a width of 20 in.

7 in.

5 in.

Example 2 › Comparing Perimeters

Find the perimeter of your sketch of the Space Club poster and the perimeter of the actual poster. Then find the ratio of the poster's perimeter to the sketch's perimeter. What can you conclude?

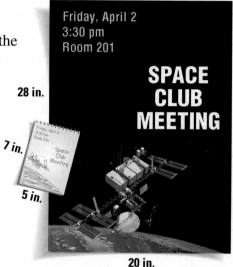

Friday, April 2
3:30 pm
Room 201

SPACE CLUB MEETING

28 in.

7 in.

5 in.

20 in.

Solution

$$\text{Perimeter of sketch} = 5 + 7 + 5 + 7$$
$$= 24 \text{ in.}$$

$$\text{Perimeter of poster} = 20 + 28 + 20 + 28$$
$$= 96 \text{ in.}$$

The ratio of the poster's perimeter to the sketch's perimeter is

$$\frac{\text{Perimeter of poster}}{\text{Perimeter of sketch}} = \frac{96 \text{ in.}}{24 \text{ in.}}$$
$$= 4.$$

The ratio of the perimeters, 4, is the same as the scale factor.

Example 3 › Comparing Areas

Find the area of your sketch of the poster and the area of the actual poster. Then find the ratio of the poster's area to the sketch's area. Compare this ratio to the scale factor.

Solution

$$\text{Area of sketch} = 5 \times 7$$
$$= 35 \text{ in.}^2$$

$$\text{Area of poster} = 20 \times 28$$
$$= 560 \text{ in.}^2$$

The ratio of the poster's area to the sketch's area is

$$\frac{\text{Area of poster}}{\text{Area of sketch}} = \frac{560 \text{ in.}^2}{35 \text{ in.}^2}$$
$$= 16.$$

The ratio of the areas, 16, is the square of the scale factor.

ONGOING ASSESSMENT

Talk About It
· · · · · · · · · · · · · · · · · · ·

Find the ratio of the area of the poster to the area of the sketch for the following scale factors.

1. Scale factor = 2

2. Scale factor = 3

3. Scale factor = 5

4. What can you conclude? Do your results agree with those of Example 3?

GUIDED PRACTICE

MODEL CAR In Exercises 1–5, you are designing a model car that is a scale replica of a full-sized car. The license plate on the car is 6 in. high and 12 in. wide. The model's license plate has a width of 1 in.

1. Find the height of the model's license plate.

2. Find the scale factor of the car to the model.

3. Find the perimeter and area of each license plate.

4. Find the ratio of the car plate's perimeter to the model plate's perimeter. Compare the result to the scale factor.

5. Find the ratio of the car plate's area to the model plate's area. How does this ratio compare to the scale factor?

Real Life...
Real Facts

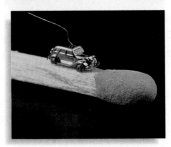

Compact Car The world's smallest running car is powered by a tiny electric motor. The car is shown driving on a match.

PRACTICE AND PROBLEM SOLVING

6. ESTIMATION A painting is 26 in. high. Use the reduction of the painting below to estimate the width of the actual painting.

7. SALAMANDERS The scale factor of an adult salamander to a baby salamander is 12. The adult is 90 cm long. How long is the baby?

8. KENTUCKY The state of Kentucky is about 420 mi wide. Use the map to estimate its height.

height

— 420 mi —

9. ESTIMATION The blueprint below is drawn with a scale factor of 1 in. to 16 ft. Estimate the perimeter and area of the actual room.

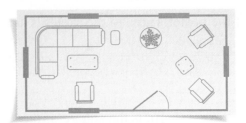

PAINTING In Exercises 10–15, use this photo of the painting *Keepers of the Secret*, by Julie Kramer Cole.

10. Measure the photo's height and width (in inches).

11. The actual painting is 16 in. wide. Find the scale factor of the painting to the photo.

12. Find the height of the actual painting.

13. Find the perimeter and area of the actual painting. Then find the perimeter and area of the photo.

14. Find the ratio of the painting's perimeter to the photo's perimeter. How does this ratio compare to the scale factor?

15. Find the ratio of the painting's area to the photo's area. Compare this ratio to the scale factor.

The painting has four owls. Two are clearly visible. How many do you see?

STANDARDIZED TEST PRACTICE

16. The two triangles at the right are similar. What is the value of *x*?

    Ⓐ 2   Ⓑ 3
    Ⓒ 5   Ⓓ 8

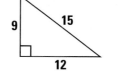

17. The two figures are similar. Find the area of the larger figure.

    Ⓐ 11 cm^2 Ⓑ 36 cm^2
    Ⓒ 81 cm^2 Ⓓ 162 cm^2

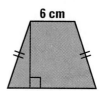

EXPLORATION AND EXTENSION

PORTFOLIO

18. **BUILDING YOUR PROJECT** Four of the International Space Station's solar panels are shown at the right.

    a. Find the area of each solar panel.

    b. You want to design a single solar panel whose area is the same as the total area of two of the panels at the right. Can you achieve this by doubling the length and width of one of the panels? Explain.

    c. Sketch your design for a new solar panel that has the desired area.

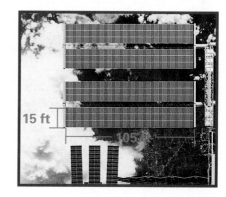

11.8

Trigonometric Ratios

What you should learn:

Goal 1 How to find trigonometric ratios

Goal 2 How to use the Pythagorean Theorem to find trigonometric ratios

Why you should learn it:

You can use trigonometric ratios to solve real-life problems, such as finding the height of a hot-air balloon.

Goal 1 FINDING TRIGONOMETRIC RATIOS

A **trigonometric ratio** is a ratio of the lengths of two sides of a right triangle. The three basic trigonometric ratios are **sine**, **cosine**, and **tangent**. These are abbreviated as *sin*, *cos*, and *tan*.

TRIGONOMETRIC RATIOS

$$\sin A = \frac{\text{side opposite } \angle A}{\text{hypotenuse}} = \frac{a}{c}$$

$$\cos A = \frac{\text{side adjacent to } \angle A}{\text{hypotenuse}} = \frac{b}{c}$$

$$\tan A = \frac{\text{side opposite } \angle A}{\text{side adjacent to } \angle A} = \frac{a}{b}$$

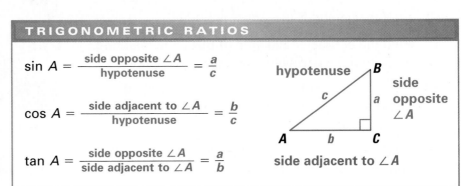

Because all right triangles that have the same measure for $\angle A$ are similar, the value of a trigonometric ratio depends only on the measure of $\angle A$. It does not depend on the triangle's size.

Example 1 Finding Trigonometric Ratios

For $\triangle PQR$, find the sine, cosine, and tangent of $\angle P$ and $\angle Q$.

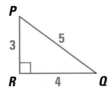

Solution

The length of the hypotenuse is 5.

For $\angle P$, the length of the opposite side is 4, and the length of the adjacent side is 3.

$$\sin P = \frac{\text{opposite}}{\text{hypotenuse}} = \frac{4}{5}$$

$$\cos P = \frac{\text{adjacent}}{\text{hypotenuse}} = \frac{3}{5}$$

$$\tan P = \frac{\text{opposite}}{\text{adjacent}} = \frac{4}{3}$$

For $\angle Q$, the length of the opposite side is 3, and the length of the adjacent side is 4.

$$\sin Q = \frac{\text{opposite}}{\text{hypotenuse}} = \frac{3}{5}$$

$$\cos Q = \frac{\text{adjacent}}{\text{hypotenuse}} = \frac{4}{5}$$

$$\tan Q = \frac{\text{opposite}}{\text{adjacent}} = \frac{3}{4}$$

TOOLBOX

Pythagorean Theorem, page 755

Example 2 Solving with the Pythagorean Theorem

You can use the triangle at the right to find the sine and cosine of 42°. First, use the Pythagorean Theorem to find the length, h, of the hypotenuse.

$$h^2 = 10^2 + 9^2 \qquad \text{Use the Pythagorean Theorem.}$$
$$h = \sqrt{181}$$
$$\approx 13.45$$

For the 42° angle, the opposite side has a length of 9, and the adjacent side has a length of 10.

$$\sin 42° = \frac{\text{opposite}}{\text{hypotenuse}} = \frac{9}{13.45} \approx 0.67$$

$$\cos 42° = \frac{\text{adjacent}}{\text{hypotenuse}} = \frac{10}{13.45} \approx 0.74$$

Example 3 Sine, Cosine, and Tangent of an Angle

Draw an isosceles right triangle. Then use the triangle to find the sine, cosine, and tangent of 45°.

Solution

All isosceles right triangles are similar, so you can draw one of any size. For example, use legs of length 1. Then find the length of the hypotenuse.

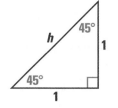

$$h^2 = 1^2 + 1^2 \qquad \text{Use the Pythagorean Theorem.}$$
$$h = \sqrt{2}$$
$$\approx 1.41$$

The opposite side and the adjacent side both have a length of 1.

$$\sin 45° = \frac{\text{opposite}}{\text{hypotenuse}} = \frac{1}{1.41} \approx 0.71$$

$$\cos 45° = \frac{\text{adjacent}}{\text{hypotenuse}} = \frac{1}{1.41} \approx 0.71$$

$$\tan 45° = \frac{\text{opposite}}{\text{adjacent}} = \frac{1}{1} = 1$$

ONGOING ASSESSMENT

Talk About It

Use the triangle in Example 2.

1. Find the sine and cosine of 48°.

2. Compare your results with the sine and cosine of 42°.

Extra Practice, page 736

GUIDED PRACTICE

In Exercises 1–3, match the trigonometric ratio with its definition.

A. $\dfrac{\text{Side opposite } \angle R}{\text{Hypotenuse}}$
B. $\dfrac{\text{Side opposite } \angle R}{\text{Side adjacent to } \angle R}$
C. $\dfrac{\text{Side adjacent to } \angle R}{\text{Hypotenuse}}$

1. $\tan R$
2. $\cos R$
3. $\sin R$

4. Use a protractor to draw a triangle with angle measures of 40°, 50°, and 90°. Measure the sides with a ruler. Then use your measurements to approximate the sine, cosine, and tangent of 40°.

5. Use a protractor to draw a 40°-50°-90° triangle that is larger than the one in Exercise 4. Measure the sides, then use your measurements to approximate the sine, cosine, and tangent of 40°. Do you get the same results as in Exercise 4?

In Exercises 6–11, use $\triangle XYZ$ **below to find the trigonometric ratio.**

6. $\sin X$
7. $\cos X$
8. $\tan X$
9. $\sin Y$
10. $\cos Y$
11. $\tan Y$

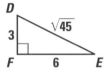

PRACTICE AND PROBLEM SOLVING

In Exercises 12–17, use $\triangle DEF$ **to find the trigonometric ratio.**

12. $\sin D$
13. $\cos D$
14. $\tan D$
15. $\sin E$
16. $\cos E$
17. $\tan E$

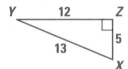

In Exercises 18–21, solve the triangle for its unlabeled angle and side. Then write six trigonometric ratios that can be formed with the triangle.

18.

19.

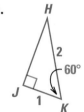

20.

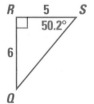

21.

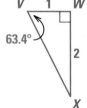

In Exercises 22 and 23, sketch a right triangle, $\triangle ABC$, **that has the given trigonometric ratios. Label each side with its length.**

22. $\tan A = \dfrac{15}{8}$, $\cos B = \dfrac{15}{17}$

23. $\sin A = \dfrac{2}{\sqrt{13}}$, $\cos A = \dfrac{3}{\sqrt{13}}$

In Exercises 24–26, use the right triangles at the right.

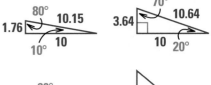

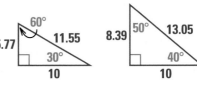

24. Copy and complete the table.

x	10°	20°	30°	40°	50°	60°	70°	80°
sin x	?	?	?	?	?	?	?	?
cos x	?	?	?	?	?	?	?	?

25. Describe the relationship between the sine and cosine values in the table.

26. From the table, guess which angle has the property that $\sin x = \cos x$. Draw a triangle that illustrates your answer. Explain your reasoning.

BALLOONING In Exercises 27–29, a balloon is released and travels straight upward. You are standing at point *A*, 20 m from the point of release of the balloon.

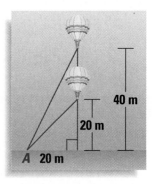

27. Write the tangent ratio for each height of the balloon shown in the diagram.

28. Does tan *A* *increase* or *decrease* as $m\angle A$ increases? Explain.

29. How high is the balloon when $\tan A = \frac{1}{2}$?

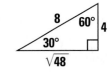

STANDARDIZED TEST PRACTICE

30. Use the figure shown. Which trigonometric ratio is *incorrect*?

(A) $\sin 30° = \dfrac{4}{8}$

(B) $\cos 60° = \dfrac{4}{8}$

(C) $\sin 60° = \dfrac{\sqrt{48}}{8}$

(D) $\tan 30° = \dfrac{\sqrt{48}}{8}$

EXPLORATION AND EXTENSION

In Exercises 31–34, the triangle shown is similar to one of the triangles used in Exercises 24–26. Write a proportion that allows you to solve for *x*. Then solve for *x*.

31.

32.

33.

34.

In Exercises 1–4, use the Pythagorean Theorem to solve for *x*. Round your result to two decimal places. (9.3)

1.

2.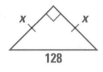

3.

4.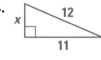

5. In $\triangle ABC$, $BC = 5$, $AC = 7$, and $AB = 10$. Which angle is smallest? Which angle is largest? **(10.9)**

In Exercises 6–9, you have a bag that contains 22 yellow marbles, 20 red marbles, and 14 green marbles. You choose 1 marble from the bag. What is the probability that it is the indicated color? (8.8)

6. Yellow   **7.** Red   **8.** Green   **9.** Red or Green

10. FUNDRAISING The science club raises money by washing cars for $5 per car. They wash 78 cars on Thursday, 85 on Friday, and 124 on Saturday. Write a verbal model that represents the total amount of money they raise. Use it to find how much money is raised. **(2.1)**

CAREER Interview

ROBOTICS ENGINEER

Larry Chao-Hsiung Li is a robotics engineer for NASA (the National Aeronautics and Space Administration). He works in a laboratory designing robots for use in current and future space missions.

Q What led you into this career?
In the summer between my junior and senior years of college, I started working for NASA as part of a cooperative education program with the NASA Johnson Space Center in Houston, TX. After I graduated, I started working there full time and I have been there ever since.

Q Do you use geometric reasoning in your work?
Yes. If we want a robot to move its arm to a certain spot, we have to change the x-, y-, and z-coordinates into angles of joint motor rotation and amounts of movement. This requires using sines, cosines, and many other trig functions.

Q What would you like to tell students about math or geometry?
If you want to work in a really fun job, you need to learn math! Math is really being used today!

Solving Right Triangles

Scientific calculators can evaluate trigonometric ratios.

Example 1

Use a calculator to find the sine, cosine, and tangent of 30°.

Solution

Calculator Keystrokes	Display
30 **SIN**	0.5
30 **COS**	0.8660254
30 **TAN**	0.5773503

Example 2

Use the triangle at the right to find the sine, cosine, and tangent of 30°. Compare your results with those in Example 1.

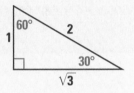

Solution

$$\sin 30° = \frac{\text{opposite}}{\text{hypotenuse}} = \frac{1}{2} = 0.5$$

$$\cos 30° = \frac{\text{adjacent}}{\text{hypotenuse}} = \frac{\sqrt{3}}{2} \approx 0.8660$$

$$\tan 30° = \frac{\text{opposite}}{\text{adjacent}} = \frac{1}{\sqrt{3}} \approx 0.5774$$

The values are the same as in Example 1.

Exercises

1. Use a calculator to find the sine, cosine, and tangent of 60°.

2. Use the triangle above to find the sine, cosine, and tangent of 60°. Compare your results with those in Exercise 1.

3. **DISCOVERING A TRIGONOMETRIC PROPERTY** Choose any acute angle, *A*. Use a scientific calculator to complete the table below. What do you notice? Make a conjecture about the sines and cosines of acute angles. Test your conjecture using a new acute angle.

$m \angle A$	$\sin A$	$(\sin A)^2$	$\cos A$	$(\cos A)^2$	$(\sin A)^2 + (\cos A)^2$
?	?	?	?	?	?

Problem Solving
Using Trigonometric Ratios

What you should learn:

Goal 1 How to use trigonometric ratios to solve right triangles

Goal 2 How to use trigonometric ratios to solve real-life problems

Why you should learn it:

You can use trigonometric ratios to solve real-life measurement problems, such as finding the altitude of the space shuttle.

Goal 1 SOLVING RIGHT TRIANGLES

In Lesson 9.3, you learned how to use the Pythagorean Theorem to solve a right triangle. You were given the lengths of two sides of the triangle, and were asked to find the length of the third side.

In this lesson, you will learn how to solve a right triangle when given only the length of one side and the measure of one acute angle.

Example 1 Solving a Right Triangle

a. Solve for a.

b. Solve for q.

CONNECTION
Algebra

Solution

a. Use the tangent of A.

$$\tan A = \frac{a}{b}$$ Use the definition of tangent.

$$\tan 40° = \frac{a}{12}$$ Substitute for A and b.

$$0.8391 \approx \frac{a}{12}$$ Use a calculator to find tan 40°.

$$12 \cdot (0.8391) \approx 12 \cdot \left(\frac{a}{12}\right)$$ Multiply each side by 12.

$$10.07 \approx a$$ Solution: a is by itself.

b. Use the cosine of P.

$$\cos P = \frac{q}{r}$$ Use the definition of cosine.

$$\cos 43° = \frac{q}{20}$$ Substitute for P and r.

$$0.7314 \approx \frac{q}{20}$$ Use a calculator to find cos 43°.

$$20 \cdot (0.7314) \approx 20 \cdot \left(\frac{q}{20}\right)$$ Multiply each side by 20.

$$14.63 \approx q$$ Solution: q is by itself.

CALCULATOR TIP

Instructions for finding trigonometric ratios using a calculator are given in Example 1 on page 551.

Goal 2 SOLVING REAL-LIFE PROBLEMS

Example 2 Using Trigonometric Ratios

You are operating a camera that is recording a space shuttle launch. Your camera is 2 mi from the launch pad. You are pointing the camera up at an angle of 60°. What is the altitude of the shuttle?

REAL LIFE
Space Shuttle

Solution

camera

STRATEGY **DRAW A DIAGRAM** A diagram like the one below is helpful for visualizing the problem.

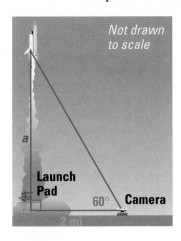

Not drawn to scale

Launch Pad

60° **Camera**

2 mi

Use the tangent of 60° to write an equation that you can solve for a, the shuttle's altitude.

$$\tan 60° = \frac{a}{2} \qquad \text{Use definition of tangent.}$$

$$1.732 \approx \frac{a}{2} \qquad \text{Use a calculator.}$$

$$2 \cdot 1.732 \approx a \qquad \text{Multiply each side by 2.}$$

$$3.464 \approx a \qquad \text{Solution: } a \text{ is by itself.}$$

The shuttle's altitude is about 3.5 mi.

NASA and the Air Force use over 100 cameras to track a space shuttle launch. Some cameras are only a few feet away from the shuttle, while others are as far as 50 miles away.

Example 3 Using Trigonometric Ratios

Find the length of the hypotenuse, x, of the right triangle shown.

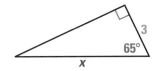

3

65°

x

Solution

Use the cosine of 65° to write an equation that you can solve for x.

$$\cos 65° = \frac{3}{x} \qquad \text{Use the definition of cosine.}$$

$$0.4226 \approx \frac{3}{x} \qquad \text{Use a calculator.}$$

$$x \cdot 0.4226 \approx 3 \qquad \text{Multiply each side by } x.$$

$$x \approx 7.099 \qquad \text{Divide each side by 0.4226.}$$

ONGOING ASSESSMENT

Write About It

1. When the camera angle is 30°, is the shuttle at half the altitude found in Example 2? Explain.

TECHNOLOGY In Exercises 1–9, use a scientific calculator, or refer to the *Table of Trigonometric Ratios* on page 766.

In Exercises 1–4, use the triangle at the right.

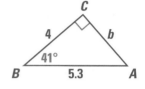

1. Explain how to use tan 41° to solve for *b*.

2. Explain how to use sin 41° to solve for *b*.

3. Explain how to use the Pythagorean Theorem to solve for *b*.

4. **OPEN-ENDED PROBLEM** Which of the methods in Exercises 1–3 do you prefer? Explain your reasoning.

In Exercises 5–8, find the value of the trigonometric ratio.

5. cos 33°   6. tan 74°

7. sin 44°   8. cos 80°

9. **FLAGPOLE** You stand 50 ft from the flagpole shown at the right. The angle from the point where you stand to the top of the flagpole is 40°. How tall is the flagpole?

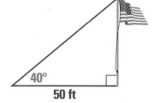

 TECHNOLOGY In Exercises 10–17, use a scientific calculator, or refer to the *Table of Trigonometric Ratios* on page 766.

In Exercises 10–13, find the length of the labeled side. Round your results to two decimal places.

10.
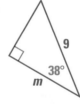

11.

12.
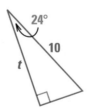

13.

In Exercises 14–17, solve the right triangle for all labeled sides and angles. Round your results to two decimal places.

14.

15.

16.
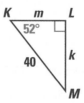

17.

TECHNOLOGY In Exercises 18–21, use a
scientific calculator, or refer to the *Table of
Trigonometric Ratios* on page 766.

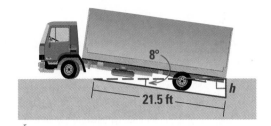

18. LOADING DOCK In the diagram at the right,
the angle of depression between the road
and the ramp is 8°. Find the height, h, of the
loading dock.

GIRAFFES In Exercises 19–21, use the following information.

You are 22 m from a mother giraffe and her baby.
The angle of elevation to the mother's head is 11°
and the angle to the baby's head is 5°.

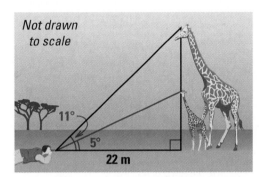

19. How tall is the mother?

20. How tall is the baby?

21. Find the difference between the heights of the
two giraffes.

STANDARDIZED TEST PRACTICE

22. Which equation can you use to find the length of the side labeled q?

A $\cos 36° = \dfrac{q}{5}$

B $\sin 36° = \dfrac{q}{5}$

C $\tan 36° = \dfrac{5}{q}$

D $\sin 36° = \dfrac{5}{q}$

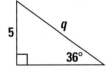

EXPLORATION AND EXTENSION

PORTFOLIO

23. BUILDING YOUR PROJECT The amount of power produced
by each of the space station's PVAs (solar arrays) depends
on the angle between the array and the sun's rays. When the
array makes an angle of $x°$ with the sun's rays, the power
(in kilowatts) is $P = 31 \cdot \sin x°$.

  a. Make a table showing the amount of power for several
  angles between 0° and 90°. What patterns do you see?

  b. In order to get at least 29 kW of power, what is the
  minimum angle necessary between the array and the
  sun's rays? Explain.

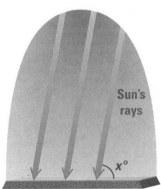

PVA (solar array)

WHAT did you learn?

WHY did you learn it?

Skills

11.1 Find the area and perimeter of a polygon.

Estimate the area and perimeter of regions with irregular shapes.

11.2 Determine whether two figures are congruent.

Compare pairs of triangles and polygons.

11.3 Reflect a figure in a line.

Understand patterns used in clothing manufacture.

11.4 Rotate a figure about a point.

Explore the rotation of the moon about Earth.

11.5 Translate a figure in a plane.

Analyze computer graphics and animation.

11.6 Recognize similar figures and apply their properties.

Use similar triangles to solve real-world problems.

11.7 Compare perimeters and areas of similar figures.

Use scale models of real-world objects.

11.8 Find trigonometric ratios.

Find the height of a hot-air balloon.

11.9 Use trigonometric ratios to solve right triangles.

Find the altitude of the space shuttle.

Strategies

11.1–11.9 Use geometric figures to model and solve real-life problems.

Solve a wide variety of real-life problems.

Using Data

11.1–11.9 Use tables and graphs to solve problems.

Organize data and solve problems.

HOW does it fit in the bigger picture of mathematics?

In this chapter, you learned that geometry is more than measuring. It is also about comparing figures to determine whether they are congruent or similar. For instance, if one figure can be translated, reflected, or rotated so that it fits exactly on top of another figure, then the two figures are congruent.

Knowing that figures are congruent or similar is important because it can save you time. For instance, if you have already measured the angles of one figure, you don't need to measure the angles of a figure that you know is similar (because the similar figure must have the same angle measures).

VOCABULARY

- height of parallelogram (p. 512)
- base of parallelogram (p. 512)
- height of trapezoid (p. 512)
- bases of trapezoid (p. 512)
- reflection (p. 522)
- reflection line (p. 522)

- transformation (p. 526)
- rotation (p. 526)
- translation (p. 530)
- similar (p. 536)
- scale factor (p. 536)

- dilation (p. 537)
- trigonometric ratio (p. 546)
- sine (p. 546)
- cosine (p. 546)
- tangent (p. 546)

11.1 AREA OF TRAPEZOIDS AND PARALLELOGRAMS

Examples Area of a Parallelogram

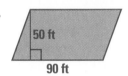

$$\text{Area} = bh$$
$$= 6 \cdot 4$$
$$= 24 \text{ in.}^2$$

6 in.
4 in.
6 in.

Area of a Trapezoid

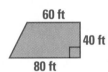

$$\text{Area} = \frac{1}{2}(b_1 + b_2)h$$
$$= \frac{1}{2}(5 + 8) \cdot 4$$
$$= 26 \text{ ft}^2$$

5 ft
4 ft
8 ft

In Exercises 1–3, find the area of the region.

1.

50 ft
90 ft

2.

60 ft
40 ft
80 ft

3.

90 ft
40 ft
120 ft

4. LANDSCAPING It costs 2.4 cents per square foot to fertilize grass. How much will it cost to fertilize the grass in each of the regions in Exercises 1–3?

11.2 CONGRUENT POLYGONS

Example $PQRS \cong EFGH$

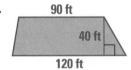

All pairs of corresponding angles are congruent.

$$\angle P \cong \angle E \qquad \angle Q \cong \angle F \qquad \angle R \cong \angle G \qquad \angle S \cong \angle H$$

All pairs of corresponding sides are congruent.

$$\overline{PQ} \cong \overline{EF} \qquad \overline{QR} \cong \overline{FG} \qquad \overline{RS} \cong \overline{GH} \qquad \overline{SP} \cong \overline{HE}$$

Use the fact that $\triangle ABC \cong \triangle NXV$ to complete the statement.

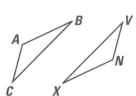

5. $\angle B \cong \underline{\ ?\ }$

6. $\overline{XV} \cong \underline{\ ?\ }$

7. $\overline{VN} \cong \underline{\ ?\ }$

8. $\angle V \cong \underline{\ ?\ }$

9. $\angle N \cong \underline{\ ?\ }$

10. $\overline{AB} \cong \underline{\ ?\ }$

11.3–11.6 TRANSFORMATIONS

Examples

Reflection in *y*-axis

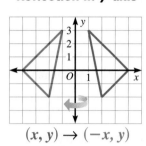

$$(x, y) \rightarrow (-x, y)$$

Rotation 90° counterclockwise

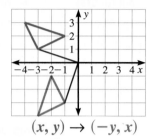

$$(x, y) \rightarrow (-y, x)$$

Translation 3 units right and 2 down

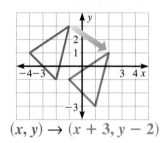

$$(x, y) \rightarrow (x + 3, y - 2)$$

Dilation with scale factor 2

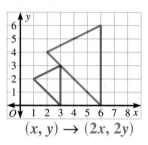

$$(x, y) \rightarrow (2x, 2y)$$

In Exercises 11–14, use the diagram at the right. State whether the sentence is *true* or *false*.

11. The green triangle is a translation of the red triangle 3 units to the left and 4 units down.

12. The blue triangle is a dilation of the red triangle by a scale factor of 2.

13. The orange triangle is a reflection of the red triangle in the *x*-axis.

14. The purple triangle is a rotation of the blue triangle 180° about the origin.

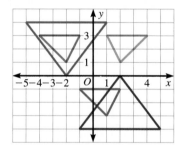

Copy the figure below on graph paper. Transform the figure using the motion rule. Then write a verbal description of the transformation.

15. $(x, y) \rightarrow (x - 3, y + 4)$

16. $(x, y) \rightarrow (0.5x, 0.5y)$

17. $(x, y) \rightarrow (-y, -x)$

18. $(x, y) \rightarrow (x + 2, y + 5)$

19. $(x, y) \rightarrow (-x, y)$

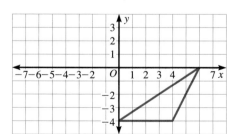

Example $KLMN \sim QRST$

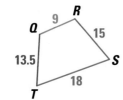

Corresponding angles have the same measure.

$$m \angle K = m \angle Q \qquad m \angle L = m \angle R$$
$$m \angle M = m \angle S \qquad m \angle N = m \angle T$$

The ratios of corresponding side lengths are equal.

$$\frac{QR}{KL} = \frac{RS}{LM} = \frac{ST}{MN} = \frac{TQ}{NK} = \frac{3}{2}$$

The scale factor of $QRST$ to $KLMN$ is $\frac{3}{2}$.

In Exercises 20–22, use the diagram, in which $\triangle UVW \sim \triangle XYZ$.

20. Find the scale factor of $\triangle UVW$ to $\triangle XYZ$.

21. Find the length of $\overline{UW}$.

22. Find the length of $\overline{YZ}$.

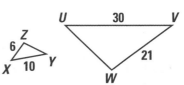

23. **PHOTOGRAPHY** The height of a photo is 6 in. and the width is 4 in. You have the photo enlarged. The height of the enlarged photo is 18 in. What is the width of the enlarged photo?

Example

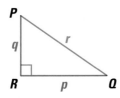

$$\sin Q = \frac{\text{side opposite } \angle Q}{\text{hypotenuse}} = \frac{q}{r}$$

$$\cos Q = \frac{\text{side adjacent to } \angle Q}{\text{hypotenuse}} = \frac{p}{r}$$

$$\tan Q = \frac{\text{side opposite } \angle Q}{\text{side adjacent to } \angle Q} = \frac{q}{p}$$

In Exercises 24 and 25, use the figure at the right.

24. Find $\sin A$, $\cos A$, and $\tan A$.

25. Find $\sin B$, $\cos B$, and $\tan B$.

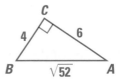

 In Exercises 26–28, use a scientific calculator or refer to the *Table of Trigonometric Ratios* on page 766. Find the value of *x*.

26.

27.

28.

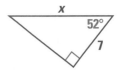

In Exercises 1–3, find the area and perimeter of the shaded region.

1.
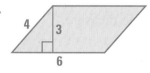

2.
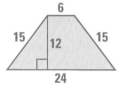

3.
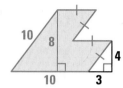

In Exercises 4–7, copy △MNP on graph paper. Then graph its image after the transformation indicated.

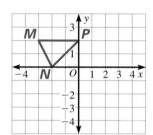

4. Reflection in the *y*-axis

5. Rotation 90° clockwise about the origin

6. $(x, y) \rightarrow (-x, -y)$

7. $(x, y) \rightarrow (x + 2, y - 3)$

In Exercises 8–10, describe the transformation of the blue lion to the red lion.

8.

9.

10.

In Exercises 11 and 12, use a scientific calculator or refer to the table on page 766. Use the diagram at the right.

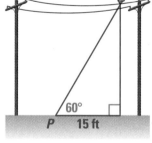

11. How high is the bird?

12. Find the distance between the bird and point *P*.

ART In Exercises 13 and 14, you are creating a small model of a sculpture that is 78 in. high and 24 in. wide.

13. You want the model to be 6 in. tall. How wide should it be?

14. What is the scale factor of the sculpture to the model?

In Exercises 15–19, use the triangles at the right.

15. Use a calculator to find tan 35°.

16. Use the result of Exercise 15 to find the length of $\overline{AC}$.

17. Use a calculator to find cos 35°.

18. Use the result of Exercise 17 to find the length of $\overline{EF}$.

19. Are △*ABC* and △*DEF* congruent? Explain.

For Questions 1 and 2, use the figure shown below.

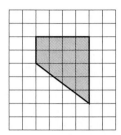

1. Find the area of the figure (in square units).

A 6   **B** 8

C 14   **D** 20

2. Find the perimeter of the figure.

A 5 units   **B** 12 units

C 14 units   **D** 16 units

3. What is the angle of rotation of the minute hand of a clock from 12:15 P.M. to 12:30 P.M.?

A 15°   **B** 45°

C 90°   **D** 180°

4. Which reflection describes the transformation from Figure *A* to Figure *B*?

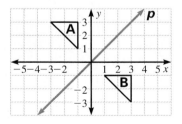

A in the *y*-axis

B in the *x*-axis

C in the line *p*

D none of the above

5. Use the fact that $\triangle ABC \cong \triangle DEF$. Which statement is false?

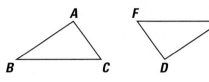

A $\overline{AC} \cong \overline{DF}$ **B** $\angle A \cong \angle D$

C $\overline{BC} \cong \overline{EF}$ **D** $\angle A \cong \angle E$

6. Which motion rule describes the translation from Figure *A* to Figure *B*?

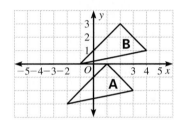

A $(x, y) \rightarrow (x + 1, y + 3)$

B $(x, y) \rightarrow (x + 3, y + 1)$

C $(x, y) \rightarrow (x - 1, y - 3)$

D $(x, y) \rightarrow (x - 3, y + 1)$

7. Which equation can be used to find the height, *h*, of the tree?

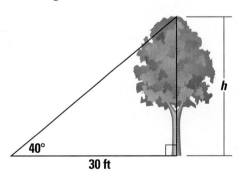

A $\sin 40° = \dfrac{h}{30}$ **B** $\cos 40° = \dfrac{h}{30}$

C $\tan 40° = \dfrac{h}{30}$ **D** $\sin 40° = \dfrac{30}{h}$

Measurements in Geometry

TECHNOLOGY

- **Interactive Real-Life Investigations**
- **Middle School Tutorial Software**

To find out more about model building, go to:

http://www.mlmath.com

HISTORY Models let us explore our architectural heritage.

CHAPTER THEME
Model Building

CHAPTER PROJECT

Making a Model Train

PROJECT DESCRIPTION

Model trains range from very small toys to scale models that people can actually ride. There are more than 400 clubs worldwide for model train enthusiasts. You can design and build your own model train.

GETTING STARTED

Talking It Over

- Have you ever had a model train? How big was it? Have you ever seen the model villages that people sometimes put around their trains?

- Imagine creating a model of a railroad train. Where would it travel? What would it carry? How many cars would it have? Think of a name and logo to put on your train.

Planning Your Project

- **Materials:** posterboard or heavy paper, tape or glue, paper, pencils or pens, colored pencils or markers

- You will build several model railroad cars. Use the method described in the **BUILDING YOUR PROJECT** exercise in Lesson 12.2 to make any other cars you think your train should have. You may construct scale railroad tracks and scenery to go with your train.

BUILDING YOUR PROJECT

These are places throughout the chapter where you will work on your project.

12.2 Construct four railroad cars. *p. 575*

12.3 Find the surface area of your cars. *p. 579*

12.4 Find the volume of the prism-shaped cars. *p. 584*

12.5 Find the volume of the cylindrical cars. *p. 589*

12.8 Find the scale factor of your model. *p. 605*

Exploring Diameter and Circumference

Materials Needed
- **can or paper towel tube**
- **ruler**
- **graph paper**
- **pencil**
- **marker**

You know that the *diameter* of a circle is a line segment that passes through the center of the circle and whose endpoints lie on the circle. But, *diameter* can also refer to the length of this segment. In this investigation, you will explore the relationship between the diameter and the circumference of a circle.

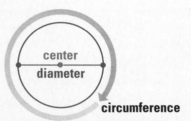

center
diameter
circumference

Part Ⓐ COMPARING DIAMETER AND CIRCUMFERENCE

Step ❶ Place a can on a piece of paper. Mark a point on both the rim of the can and on the paper at the spot where the can touches the paper.

Step ❷ Roll the can, without slipping, so it makes exactly one turn and mark the paper again.

Step ❸ Measure the distance between the marks. Then, measure the diameter of the can.

1. Find the ratio of the distance, *C*, to the diameter *d*.

2. Repeat this process three times. Measure as accurately as possible.

3. Which set of measures do you think is most accurate?

   The ratio $\dfrac{\text{Circumference}}{\text{Diameter}}$ is called π (pronounced "pie"). What is your experimental value of π?

Repeat the experiment in part (a) using a different can, paper towel tube, or other circular object. If possible, each person in your group should use an object with a different diameter. Record your results in a table.

4. What can you conclude about the ratio of the circumference of a circle to its diameter? Does the ratio depend on the size of the circle? Or is the ratio the same for all circles?

5. Write a formula that gives C, the circumference of a circle, in terms of its diameter, d.

$$\frac{C}{d} = ? \longrightarrow C = ? \cdot d$$

6. Use your formula to find the circumference of each circle.

a.

12 in.

b.
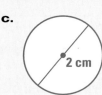
3 ft

c.
2 cm

NOW TRY THESE

7. Copy and complete the table.

d	1	2	3	4	5
C	?	?	?	?	?

8. Plot the data in the table in a coordinate plane. Describe the pattern.

9. If the diameter of a circle doubles, does the circumference double? Explain.

12.1

What you should learn:

Goal 1 How to find the circumference of a circle

Goal 2 How to find the area of a circle

Why you should learn it:

You can use the circumference and area of a circle to solve real-life problems, such as finding the circumference of a bicycle tire.

You can use the diameter of a camera lens to find its area.

Circle Relationships

Goal 1 THE CIRCUMFERENCE OF A CIRCLE

As shown at the right, the **diameter** of a circle is the distance across the circle through its **center**. The **radius** of a circle is the distance from the center to any point on the circle. The **circumference** of a circle is the distance around the circle.

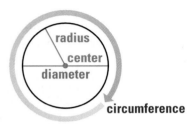

The ratio of the circumference of any circle to its diameter is approximately 3.14. This special number is denoted by the Greek letter *pi*, which is written as π. Pi is an irrational number. To two decimal places, $\pi \approx 3.14$.

THE CIRCUMFERENCE OF A CIRCLE

Let d be the diameter of a circle and let r be its radius. The circumference, C, of the circle is

$$C = \pi d \text{ or } C = 2\pi r.$$

Example 1 Finding the Circumference of a Circle

CONNECTION
Geometry

Bicycles are often classified by wheel diameter. A common diameter is 26 in. What is the circumference of this bicycle tire?

Solution

$\qquad C = \pi d$ Use the formula for circumference.

$\qquad \approx 3.14 \cdot 26$ Substitute for π and d.

$\qquad = 81.64$ Simplify.

The circumference is about 82 in.

Goal 2 FINDING THE AREA OF A CIRCLE

The circle below has a radius of 3 units.

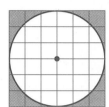

To estimate the area of the circle, you can reason that each blue corner region has an area of about 2 square units. Because the area of the square is 6^2, or 36, square units, you can reason that the area of the circle must be about $36 - 4(2)$, or 28, square units.

The following formula tells you that the exact area of the circle is 9π, or about 28.3, square units.

THE AREA OF A CIRCLE

Let r be the radius of a circle. The area, A, of the circle is

$$A = \pi r^2.$$

Example 2 **Finding the Area of a Circle**

The official United States Presidential Seal is shown at the right. The diameter of the seal is 4.75 in. Find the area of the Presidential Seal.

Solution

The radius is half of the diameter.

$$r = \frac{1}{2}(4.75)$$

$$= 2.375 \text{ in.}$$

Using this measurement, you can find the area of the seal.

$A = \pi r^2$ Use the formula for area of a circle.

$\approx 3.14 \cdot (2.375)^2$ Substitute for π and r.

≈ 17.7 Use a calculator.

The area of the seal is about 17.7 in.^{2}

STUDY TIP

If you are given the circumference or area, you can find the diameter or radius by solving $C = \pi d$ or $A = \pi r^2$.

ONGOING ASSESSMENT

Write About It

The circle has a diameter of 4 in. and it is divided into congruent parts. Find the area of the green portion. Show your work and explain your steps.

1.   2.

12.1 Exercises   **Extra Practice,** page 736

Extra Practice, page 736

GUIDED PRACTICE

GEOMETRY   In Exercises 1–4, use the figure at the right.

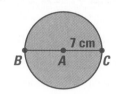

7 cm

B   A   C

1. Name the diameter.

2. Name a radius.

3. Find the circumference.

4. Find the area.

5. **EARTH**   Earth has a radius of about 4000 mi. Estimate our planet's circumference at the equator.

PRACTICE AND PROBLEM SOLVING

 TECHNOLOGY   In Exercises 6–9, find the circumference and area of the figure. Use 3.14 for π. Round your results to one decimal place.

6. $d = 5.8$ cm

7. $d = 12\frac{4}{5}$ in.

8. $r = 3$ cm

9. $r = 2$ in.

 TECHNOLOGY   In Exercises 10–13, find the radius and diameter of the figure. Use 3.14 for π. Round your results to one decimal place.

10. $C = 11$ in.

11. $A = 109$ in.^{2}

12. $A = 113.10$ cm^2

13. $C = 20$ in.

AREA MODELS   In Exercises 14–17, find the area of the shaded portion of the figure. Use 3.14 for π. Round your result to one decimal place.

14.

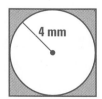

4 mm

15.

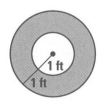

1 ft

1 ft

16.

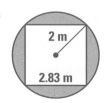

2 m

2.83 m

17.

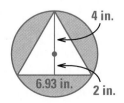

4 in.

6.93 in.

2 in.

PATTERNS In Exercises 18 and 19, create a table. Then describe the pattern.

18. Find the circumferences of circles whose radii are 1, 2, 3, 4, 5, and 6.

19. Find the areas of circles whose radii are 1, 2, 3, 4, 5, and 6.

20. REASONING If the diameter of a circle is doubled, will the area and circumference of the circle double? Explain your reasoning.

PIZZA In Exercises 21–23, a pizza with a 12 in. diameter is cut into pieces that each have an area of 14.14 in.^{2}

21. Find the area of the entire pizza.

22. How many pieces make up the pizza?

23. If the pizza is cut into 6 pieces, what is the area of each?

WASHINGTON, D.C. In Exercises 24–26, use the map to the right.

24. The road around Washington, D.C., is called the *Capital Beltway*. Estimate the length of a trip on the Beltway around the entire city.

25. Estimate the area inside the Beltway.

26. ESTIMATION About what percent of the region inside the Beltway is Washington, D.C.?

 STANDARDIZED TEST PRACTICE

In Exercises 27 and 28, the diameter of the circle is 5 in.

27. Find the circumference of the circle.

    (A) 31.400 in.   **(B)** 19.625 in.   **(C)** 15.700 in.   **(D)** 7.850 in.

28. Find the area of the circle.

    (A) 31.400 in.^{2} **(B)** 19.625 in.^{2} **(C)** 15.700 in.^{2} **(D)** 7.850 in.^{2}

EXPLORATION AND EXTENSION

29. PIE PUZZLE Can you cut a pie into eight congruent pieces using only three straight cuts? (You can rearrange the pieces after each cut.) If you can, show how.

Circumference and **Area** of a **Circle**

Many calculators have a special key for π. You can use this key to calculate the circumference and area of a circle.

CALCULATOR TIP

Your calculator approximates π to many decimal places. For example, your calculator may use 3.1415926536 for π.

Since the radius of the circle is 2.6 in., the diameter is 2(2.6), or 5.2 in.

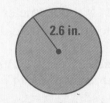

2.6 in.

$C = \pi d = \pi(5.2)$ **Use the circumference formula.**

$A = \pi r^2 = \pi(2.6)^2$ **Use the area formula.**

The keystrokes to find the circumference and area are below.

Keystrokes	Display	Conclusion
5.2 [×] [π] [=]	16.33628180	$C \approx 16.34$ in.
[π] [×] 2.6 [x²] [=]	21.23716634	$A \approx 21.24$ in.^{2}

Exercises

In Exercises 1–4, find the circumference and area of the indicated circle. Round your results to two decimal places.

1. $r = 1.7$ cm   **2.** $r = 5.5$ ft   **3.** $d = 3.9$ in.   **4.** $d = 10.4$ m

In Exercises 5 and 6, find the radius and diameter of the indicated circle. Round your results to two decimal places.

5. The circle has a circumference of 10 in.

6. The circle has an area of 6 m^2.

In Exercises 7–10, find the area of the blue portion of the circle. Round your result to two decimal places.

7.   **8.**   **9.**   **10.**

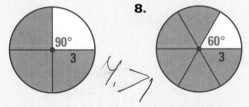

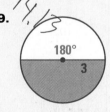

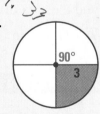

11. Which of the following is the best approximation of π? Explain your reasoning.

   A. 3.14   **B.** 3.1416   **C.** $\frac{22}{7}$ **D.** $\frac{355}{113}$

LAB
12.2

Exploring Nets

A net is a pattern that can be folded to form a solid object like a box or a pyramid. Follow the instructions below to make and fold a net.

Materials Needed
- **grid paper**
- **pencil**
- **ruler**
- **scissors**

Step 1 Draw the figure at the right on grid paper. Be sure to include the dashed lines.

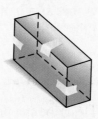

Cut on solid line.

Step 2 Cut on the solid line. Then fold on the dashed lines.

Step 3 Tape to form a box.

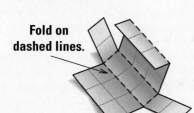

Fold on dashed lines.

NOW TRY THESE

1. In your group, draw and fold 3 other nets. The nets should form rectangular boxes of different sizes.

2. Draw a net that is made of 6 squares and can be folded into a rectangular box. Cut it out and fold it. What is the name of this type of rectangular box?

3. Does a net that forms a rectangular box have to have three pairs of congruent rectangles? Explain.

12.2

Polyhedrons and **Other Solids**

What you should learn:

Goal ① How to build and describe polyhedrons

Goal ② How to identify and draw solids

Why you should learn it:

A solid is 3-dimensional, but a computer screen is only 2-dimensional. You can represent a solid in 2 dimensions in many ways.

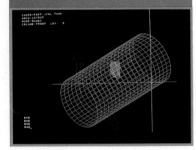

Goal ① DESCRIBING POLYHEDRONS

A **polyhedron** is a solid that is bounded by polygons, which are called **faces**. The segments where the faces meet are **edges**, and the points where the edges meet are **vertices**. Two common types of polyhedrons are **prisms** and **pyramids**.

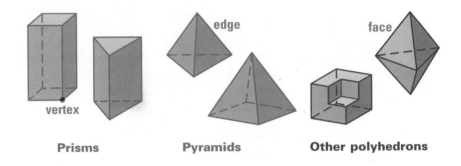

   Prisms   **Pyramids**   **Other polyhedrons**

A **net** is a pattern that can be folded to form a polyhedron or other solid.

Example 1   **Building Polyhedrons**

Describe the polyhedron that results from folding each net.

a. 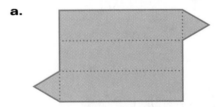   **b.**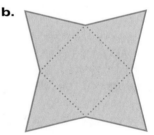

Solution

a. When the net is folded, it forms a prism. The prism has 5 faces, 9 edges, and 6 vertices.

b. When the net is folded, it forms a pyramid. The pyramid has 5 faces, 8 edges, and 5 vertices.

19. REASONING Sketch other nets that can be folded to form a cube. How many different nets are possible?

20. WRITING How are prisms and cylinders alike?

21. WRITING How are pyramids and cones alike?

GEOMETRY In Exercises 22–25, draw a front view, a side view, and a top view of the solid.

22.   23.   24.   25.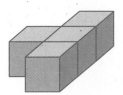

STANDARDIZED TEST PRACTICE

In Questions 26 and 27, use the polyhedron at the right.

26. Identify the polyhedron.

   A Prism   **B** Cone   **C** Pyramid   **D** Triangle

27. Identify the part of the polyhedron that is white.

   A Vertex   **B** Edge   **C** Face   **D** Wedge

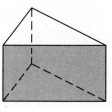

PORTFOLIO

EXPLORATION AND EXTENSION

28. BUILDING YOUR PROJECT In parts (a)–(c) you will make model railroad cars with the same dimensions as the ones shown at the right.

  a. Describe the shape of each car and tell whether each car is a polyhedron.

  b. On heavy paper or cardboard, draw a net of each car similar to the net shown in Example 1.

  c. Cut out the nets you drew in part (b) and tape or glue them together to make the cars. You may want to add windows, wheels, or other markings.

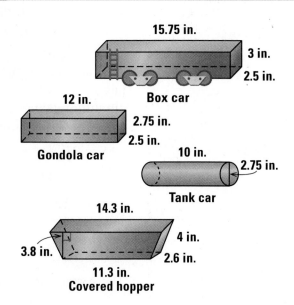

12.3

Exploring Surface Area of **Prisms** and **Cylinders**

What you should learn:

Goal 1 How to find the surface area of a prism and a cylinder

Goal 2 How to use surface area to answer questions about real life

Why you should learn it:

You can use surface area to answer questions about real life, such as finding the surface area of a building.

The artists Christo and Jean-Claude use surface areas of large objects to create works of art. Here, they have covered the Reichstag in Germany.

Goal 1 FINDING SURFACE AREA

The **surface area** of a polyhedron is the sum of the areas of its faces. For a prism or a cylinder, notice that you add the area of the vertical "sides" to the top and bottom areas.

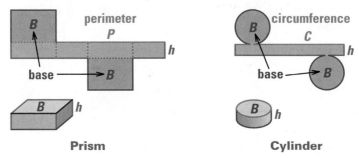

Prism   Cylinder

SURFACE AREA OF PRISM AND CYLINDER

Prism: The surface area is $S = 2B + Ph$, where B is the area of a base, P is the perimeter of a base, and h is the height of the prism.

Cylinder: The surface area is $S = 2B + Ch$, where B is the area of a base, C is the circumference of a base, and h is the height of the cylinder.

Example 1 Finding Surface Area

To find the surface area of the cylindrically shaped object at the right, first find the area of one base.

The radius of each base is 4 in. So, each base has an area of $B = \pi r^2$ or **16π in.**^{2} The circumference of each base is $C = 2\pi r$ or **8π in.**, and the height is $h = 6$ **in.**

$S = 2B + Ch$	Use the formula for surface area.
$= 2 \cdot (16\pi) + (8\pi) \cdot (6)$	Substitute for B, C, and h.
$= 32\pi + 48\pi$	Simplify.
$= 80\pi$	Simplify.
≈ 251.3	Use a calculator.

The surface area is about 251.3 in.^{2}

Example 2 — Comparing Surface Areas

The two cereal containers shown hold about the same amount of cereal.

You can compare the amount of material needed to make each container by comparing their surface areas.

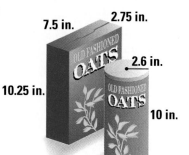

Tech Link

Investigation 12,
Interactive
Real-Life
Investigations

The area of each base of the prism is 7.5 · 2.75, or **20.6 in.**^{2} The perimeter of each base is 2 · 7.5 + 2 · 2.75, or **20.5 in.**

$$S = 2B + Ph \qquad \text{Surface area of a prism}$$
$$= 2 \cdot (20.6) + (20.5) \cdot (10.25) \qquad \text{Substitute.}$$
$$= 251.3 \text{ in.}^2 \qquad \text{Simplify.}$$

The area of each base of the cylinder is $\pi \cdot (2.6)^2$, or **21.2 in.**^{2} The circumference of each base is $2\pi \cdot (2.6)$, or **16.3 in.**

$$S = 2B + Ch \qquad \text{Surface area of a cylinder.}$$
$$\approx 2 \cdot (21.2) + (16.3) \cdot (10) \qquad \text{Substitute.}$$
$$= 205.4 \text{ in.}^2 \qquad \text{Simplify.}$$

The cylindrical package has less surface area, which implies that it uses less material.

Example 3 — Finding Surface Area

To find the surface area of the triangular prism at the right, first find the area and perimeter of each base. Each base is a right triangle whose area is

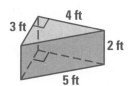

$$B = \frac{1}{2} \cdot 3 \cdot 4 = 6 \text{ ft}^2.$$

The perimeter of each base is 3 + 4 + 5, or **12 ft.**

$$S = 2B + Ph \qquad \text{Use the formula for surface area.}$$
$$= 2 \cdot 6 + 12 \cdot 2 \qquad \text{Substitute for } B, P, \text{ and } h.$$
$$= 36 \text{ ft}^2 \qquad \text{Simplify.}$$

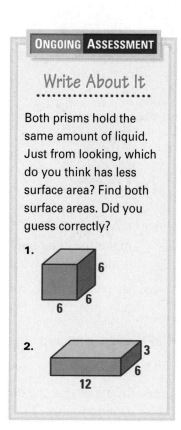

ONGOING ASSESSMENT

Write About It
••••••••••••••••••••

Both prisms hold the same amount of liquid. Just from looking, which do you think has less surface area? Find both surface areas. Did you guess correctly?

1.

2.

GUIDED PRACTICE

GEOMETRY In Exercises 1–4, use the following figures.

A.

B.

C.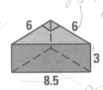

1. Identify each figure.

2. Find the surface area of Figure A.

3. Find the surface area of Figure B.

4. Find the surface area of Figure C.

PRACTICE AND PROBLEM SOLVING

GEOMETRY In Exercises 5–12, find the surface area of the solid.

5.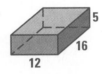

6.

7.

8.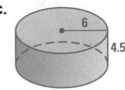

9.

10.

11.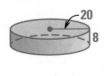

12.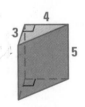

13. **MAKE A SKETCH** Draw a cube. Use dashed lines and shading to make the cube appear three dimensional. If each edge of the cube is 4 inches long, what is its surface area?

14. **GUESS, CHECK, AND REVISE** Draw a prism that has a surface area of 52 square units. (There is more than one correct answer.)

In Exercises 15 and 16, use the figure at the right.

15. Find the surface area of the large yellow cube.

16. Imagine that the cube is cut into eight congruent smaller cubes. Find the surface area of each. What is the total surface of the area of the eight cubes?

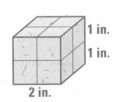

GIFT WRAPPING In Exercises 17 and 18, consider wrapping a present in a gift box that measures 45 cm by 27 cm by 6 cm.

17. **OPEN-ENDED PROBLEM** Which sheet of wrapping paper should you choose to wrap the gift? Explain your reasoning.

A.
67 cm

50 cm

B.
66 cm

52 cm

C.
102 cm

32 cm

18. **OPEN-ENDED PROBLEM** Describe the smallest rectangular piece of wrapping paper that could be used to wrap the box. Compare its area with the surface area of the box.

TOTEM POLES In Exercises 19 and 20, use the following.

A totem pole is to be carved out of a cylindrical log. The log is 22 ft long and has a diameter of 4 ft.

19. What is the surface area of the cylindrical log?

20. Will the surface area of the totem pole be greater than or less than the surface area of the log? Explain.

STANDARDIZED TEST PRACTICE

21. Which best estimates the surface area of a 12 oz beverage can?

   A 50 in.^{2} **B** 150 in.^{2} **C** 220 in.^{2} **D** 300 in.^{2}

22. Which best estimates the surface area of this book when closed?

   A 100 in.^{2} **B** 170 in.^{2} **C** 220 in.^{2} **D** 300 in.^{2}

23. Find the surface area of the polyhedron.

   A 240 in.^{2} **B** 245 in.^{2}

   C 310 in.^{2} **D** 324 in.^{2}

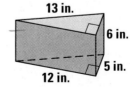

13 in.

6 in.

5 in.

12 in.

PORTFOLIO

EXPLORATION AND EXTENSION

24. **BUILDING YOUR PROJECT** Find the surface area of each of the cars you built in Exercise 28 of Lesson 12.2.

12.4

Exploring Volumes of Prisms

What you should learn:

Goal **1** How to find the volume of a prism

Goal **2** How to use the volume of a prism to solve real-life problems

Why you should learn it:

You can use the volume of a solid to solve real-life problems, such as designing a television studio.

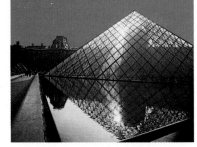

I.M. Pei designed this glass-enclosed volume as the entrance to the Louvre Museum. It brings natural light to the lower level.

Goal **1** **FINDING THE VOLUME OF A PRISM**

The **volume** of a solid is a measure of how much it will hold. The standard measures of volume are **cubic units** such as cubic inches, cubic centimeters, and cubic feet. Other measures of volume, such as liters and gallons, are discussed on page 587.

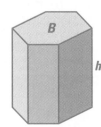

THE VOLUME OF A PRISM

1. The volume of a prism is the product of its height, h, and the area of its base, B. $V = Bh$
2. The volume of a rectangular prism (a prism whose sides are all rectangles) is the product of its length, l, its width, w, and its height, h. $V = lwh$.

The formula for the volume of a rectangular prism is a special case of the general formula. In a rectangular prism, each base has an area of $B = lw$. So, the volume is $V = Bh = lwh$.

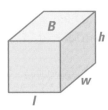

Example 1 Finding the Height of a Prism

Find the height of a trapezoidal prism with a base area of 18 m^2 and a volume of 252 m^3.

CONNECTION
Algebra

Solution

$V = Bh$	Use the volume formula.
$252 = 18 \cdot h$	Substitute for V and B.
$14 = h$	Divide each side by 18.

So, the prism has a height of 14 m.

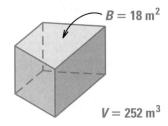

$B = 18\text{ m}^2$

$V = 252\text{ m}^3$

Example 2 Designing a Rectangular Room

You are designing a studio room for a talk show. You want room for an audience of 60 and 15 staff members and guests. A building code suggests that the room have about 480 ft^3 of air per person.

For each of the 75 people to have 480 ft^3 of air space, the room should have a volume of at least

$75 \cdot 480 = 36,000$ ft^3.

Typical room heights range between 7 and 12 ft. If the studio height is 12 ft, then the area of its base should be $36,000 \div 12$ or 3000 ft^2. One possible solution would be to have a base that is 60 ft by 50 ft, as shown at the right.

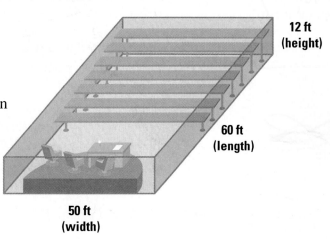

12 ft (height)

60 ft (length)

50 ft (width)

Example 3 Prisms with the Same Volume

How many different shapes of rectangular prisms can be formed with 64 cubes, each of which is one cubic inch?

Solution

You need to find all the ways that 64 can be factored into three positive integers. After trying different combinations, you can discover that there are 7 different ways, 6 of which are shown below. (The prism that is 1 by 1 by 64 is not shown.)

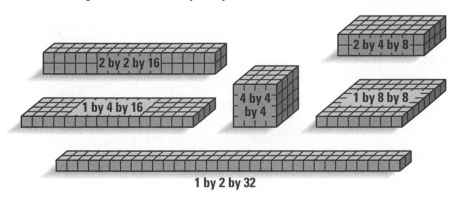

2 by 2 by 16

1 by 4 by 16

4 by 4 by 4

2 by 4 by 8

1 by 8 by 8

1 by 2 by 32

ONGOING ASSESSMENT

Talk About It

1. Work with a partner to sketch some other possible designs of the studio in Example 2. Describe advantages and disadvantages of each.

2. How does changing the height of the studio affect the amount of floor space?

Extra Practice, page 737

GUIDED PRACTICE

1. WRITING Which of these prisms have the same volume? Explain.

A.   B.   C.   D.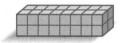

2. WRITING In your own words, state the formula for the volume of a rectangular prism.

GEOMETRY **In Exercises 3–6, state whether the figure is a prism. If the figure is a prism, find its volume.**

3.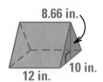
8.66 in. 12 in. 10 in.

4.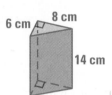
6 cm 8 cm 14 cm

5.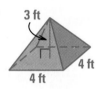
3 ft 4 ft 4 ft

6.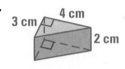
3 cm 4 cm 2 cm

In Exercises 7–10, state whether the figure is a prism. If it is, solve for *x*.

7. $V = 27 \text{ ft}^3$ **8.** $V = 16 \text{ ft}^3$ **9.** $V = 396 \text{ ft}^3$ **10.** $V = 125 \text{ in.}^3$

x

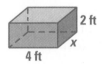
2 ft *x* 4 ft

x 12 ft 3 ft

3 in. *x*

PRACTICE AND PROBLEM SOLVING

MAKE A SKETCH **In Exercises 11 and 12, sketch and label the indicated rectangular prism. Then find its volume.**

11. Length: 2 in., Width: 3 in., Height: 5 in.   **12.** Length: 5 in., Width: 4 in., Height: 6 in.

CONTAINERS **In Exercises 13–16, find the volume of the prism.**

13.
10 in. 6 in. 2 in.

14.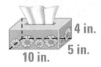
4 in. 10 in. 5 in.

15.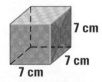
7 cm 7 cm 7 cm

16.
2 cm 7 cm 3 cm 1 cm

In Exercises 17–20, solve for x.

17. $V = 24$ in.^{3}
$B = 8$ in.^{2}

18. $V = 32$ cm^3

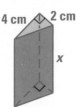

4 cm   2 cm

x

19. $V = 120$ cm^3

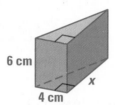

6 cm

x

4 cm

20. $V = 50$ ft^3
$B = 13.75$ ft^2

x

21. VISUALIZING SOLIDS How many different shapes of rectangular prisms can you build with 36 cubes, each of which is one cubic inch? Of these, which has the greatest surface area?

22. GEOMETRY Sketch a rectangular prism that is 2 by 3 by 4. Find its surface area, S, and volume, V.

  a. If you double one dimension, how do S and V change?

  b. If you double two dimensions, how do S and V change?

  c. If you double all three dimensions, how do S and V change?

DESIGNING A GREENHOUSE In Exercises 23 and 24, use the diagram of a greenhouse at the right.

23. About how much glass is used to create the greenhouse? (All sides, excluding the bottom, are made of glass.)

24. How many cubic feet of air does the greenhouse hold?

10 ft

9 ft

12 ft

25. SWIMMING Which pools hold the same amount of water?

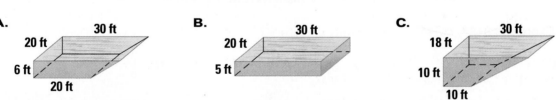

A.
30 ft
20 ft
6 ft
20 ft

B.
30 ft
20 ft
5 ft

C.
30 ft
18 ft
10 ft
10 ft

STANDARDIZED TEST PRACTICE

26. The volume of a cardboard box is 4608 in.^{3} The length of the box is 16 in. and the width is 16 in. What is the height of the box?

  A 16 in.   **B** 18 in.   **C** 20 in.   **D** 22 in.

27. Each side of a cube is 7 in. long. Find the volume of the cube.

  A 21 in.^{3} **B** 49 in.^{3} **C** 294 in.^{3} **D** 343 in.^{3}

NETS In Exercises 28–30, copy the net and use dashed lines to show how to fold the net to form a prism. Find the surface area and volume of the prism.

28.

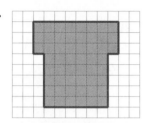

29.

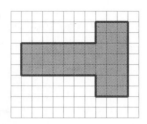

30.

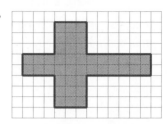

31. BUILDING YOUR PROJECT Which of the cars you made in Exercise 28 of Lesson 12.2 are shaped like prisms? Find the volume of each car.

SPIRAL REVIEW

In Exercises 1–3, find the surface area of the solid. (12.3)

1.

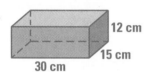

12 cm

15 cm

30 cm

2.

18 m

12 m   9 m

3.

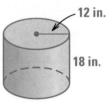

12 in.

18 in.

In Exercises 4–7, use Pascal's Triangle on page 391 to answer the question. (8.7, 8.8)

4. How many ways can you choose 3 people from a group of 6?

5. How many ways can you choose 4 birds from a flock of 5?

6. How many ways can you choose 3 animals from a herd of 7?

7. How many ways can you choose 2 goldfish from 5 goldfish?

In Exercises 8–13, solve the equation. (4.3, 4.5)

8. $4x + 3 = 2$

9. $2b + 5 = 7 - 5b$

10. $\frac{3}{8}r + 2 = \frac{7}{8}r$

11. $6 + 2y = 5y$

12. $5s - 4 = \frac{3}{2}s$

13. $42 + 3m = 4m$

In Exercises 14–19, solve the inequality. (9.6, 9.7)

14. $24 \le -2y$

15. $13z + 26 > 0$

16. $7 - 6t > 4t$

17. $2r - 5 < 5$

18. $-\frac{1}{2}p \ge \frac{11}{2}$

19. $\frac{1}{8}p \le -\frac{33}{4}$

20. WHALES The scale factor of a newborn blue whale to its mother is 1 to 4. The mother is 92 ft long. How long is the newborn? (11.7)

Take this test as you would take a test in class. The answers to the exercises are given in the back of the book.

In Exercises 1 and 2, find the circumference and area of the circle. (12.1)

In Exercises 3 and 4, find the area of the shaded region. (12.1)

1.

3 cm

2.
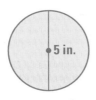
5 in.

3.

4 ft

4.

8 yd
6 yd
5 yd

In Exercises 5–9, match the name with a part of a solid at the right. (12.2)

5. Face   **6.** Vertex   **7.** Edge

8. Base   **9.** Lateral surface

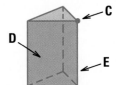
A   B   C   D   E

In Exercises 10–13, find the surface area of the solid. (12.3)

10. Diameter: 24 mm
Height: 2 mm

11. Diameter: 14 mm
Length: 49 mm

AA Battery

12.
0.5 cm
2.5 cm
5 cm
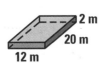

13. The disk is $\frac{1}{8}$ in. thick.

$3\frac{11}{16}$ in.
$3\frac{17}{32}$ in.

In Exercises 14–17, find the volume of the prism. (12.4)

14.

6 in.
4 in.
5 in.

15.
8 cm
13 cm
5 cm

16.
2 m
20 m
12 m

17.
4 in.
15 in.
14 in.
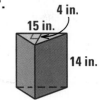

SCIENCE **In Exercises 18–20, use the following information.**

The Large Electron-Positron Collider can accelerate particles to nearly the speed of light. The collider is circular, with a diameter of 5.41 mi. **(12.1)**

18. Find the circumference of the collider.

19. Find the area of the land surrounded by the collider.

20. The collider's tunnel has a radius of 1.91 ft. What is the tunnel's circumference?

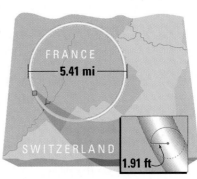
FRANCE
5.41 mi
SWITZERLAND
1.91 ft

Exploring Volumes of **Cylinders**

Why you should learn it:

You can use the volume of a cylinder to solve real-life problems, such as finding the volume of a ringette puck.

Ringette is a fast-paced sport similar to hockey. Players use a straight stick to shoot a cylindrical ring to score goals.

Goal 1 FINDING THE VOLUME OF A CYLINDER

You can find the volume of a cylinder in the same way you find the volume of a prism. That is, you multiply the height of the cylinder by the area of its base.

THE VOLUME OF A CYLINDER

The volume of a cylinder is the product of its height, h, and the area of its base, B.

$$V = Bh$$

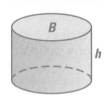

Example 1 **Finding Volumes of Cylinders**

Which cylinder has the greater volume?

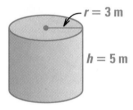

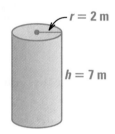

Solution

For the short cylinder, the area of the base is $B = 9\pi$. So, the volume is

$V = Bh$	Use the volume formula.
$= 9\pi \cdot 5$	Substitute.
$\approx 141.4 \text{ m}^3.$	Use a calculator.

For the tall cylinder, the area of the base is $B = 4\pi$. So, the volume is

$V = Bh$	Use the volume formula.
$= 4\pi \cdot 7$	Substitute.
$\approx 88.0 \text{ m}^3.$	Use a calculator.

The short cylinder has the greater volume.

Volume is usually measured in cubic units. There are, however, many other commonly used units for volume. Some examples are liters (L), gallons (gal), quarts (qt), and fluid ounces (fl oz). To compare volumes that are measured in different units, it helps to write both volumes with the same units. Here are some common conversions.

Tech Link

Investigation 12, Interactive Real-Life Investigations

$$1\ \text{L} = 33.8\ \text{fl oz} \qquad 1\ \text{gal} = 4\ \text{qt} \qquad 1\ \text{qt} = 32\ \text{fl oz}$$

Example 2 Comparing Volumes

You are shopping for spring water. The **2-liter** bottle costs $1.79 and the **6-pack** of 12 oz cans costs $1.99. Which is the greater volume? Which is the better buy?

Solution

For comparison, change the liters to ounces.

Bottle: $V = 2\ \text{L} \cdot 33.8\ \text{fl oz/L} = 67.6\ \text{fl oz}$

6-Pack: $V = 6\ \text{cans} \cdot 12.0\ \text{fl oz/can} = 72.0\ \text{fl oz}$

The 6-pack has the greater volume. A table can show you that the bottle is a slightly better buy.

Container	Volume	Price	Price for 1 fluid ounce
Bottle	67.6 fl oz	$1.79	$0.026
6-Pack	72.0 fl oz	$1.99	$0.028

Example 3 Finding the Height of a Cylinder

You can find the height of a cylinder if you know its volume and radius.

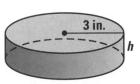

$V = 37.70\ \text{in.}^3$

$V = Bh$	Use the volume formula.
$37.70 = \pi \cdot 3^2 \cdot h$	Substitute for V and B.
$\dfrac{37.70}{\pi \cdot 9} = h$	Divide each side by 9π.
$1.33 \approx h$	Use a calculator.

So, the cylinder has a height of about 1.33 in.

ONGOING ASSESSMENT

Write About It
....

Use a ruler to help find the volume (in cubic inches) of a 12 fl oz beverage can. Then use your result to complete the following.

1. $1\ \text{fl oz} = ?\ \text{in.}^3$

2. $1\ \text{in.}^3 = ?\ \text{fl oz}$

3. How are the values related to each other?

GUIDED PRACTICE

GEOMETRY In Exercises 1–4, use the cylinder at the right.

1. Find the area of the base, B.

2. What is the height, h, of the cylinder?

3. State the formula for the volume of the cylinder.

4. Find the volume of the cylinder.

HOCKEY PUCK In Exercises 5 and 6, a hockey puck has a 3-inch diameter and a height of 1 in.

5. What is the area of its base?

6. What is the volume of the hockey puck?

PRACTICE AND PROBLEM SOLVING

INSTRUMENTS In Exercises 7–10, find the volume of the drum.

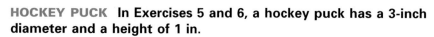

7. — 14 in. — $6\frac{1}{2}$ in.   **Snare drum**

8. — 20 in. —   24 in.   **Surdo drum**

9. ⊢14 in.⊣   28 in.   **Bass drum**

10. ⊢18 in.⊣   24 in.   **Djun Djun drum**

GEOMETRY In Exercises 11–14, find the height or the radius of the base.

11. $V = 37.7$ in.^{3}

2 in. h

12. $V = 197.9$ m^3

3 m h

13. $V = 290.5$ cm^3

r 8 cm

14. $V = 564.1$ ft^3

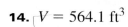

r 4 ft

REASONING In Exercises 15–18, the diameter of cylinder A is 6 in. and the height is 4 in. The diameter of cylinder B is 4 in. and the height is 6 in.

15. Without doing any calculations, do you think the volume of cylinder A is greater than, less than, or equal to the volume of cylinder B?

16. Sketch cylinder A and find its volume.

17. Sketch cylinder B and find its volume.

18. Does the cylinder with the greater volume also have the greater surface area? Explain.

RINGETTE In Exercises 19–21, use the following information.

Ringette, a sport similar to ice hockey, is played in Canada, Europe, and the northern United States. The object of the game is to shoot a rubber ring into a net. The volume of the ring is the volume of the cylinder with the outer diameter minus the volume of the cylinder with the inner diameter.

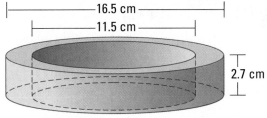

Not drawn to scale

19. Find the volume of the cylinder with the inner diameter.

20. Find the volume of the cylinder with the outer diameter.

21. Find the volume of the ring.

ENGINE SIZE In Exercises 22–25, use the following information.

A cylinder in a V8 engine has an inside diameter of 4.00 in. The height of the cylinder is 3.42 in.

22. What is the volume of the cylinder?

23. When the piston is fully extended, the height of the cylinder changes from 3.42 in. to 0.42 in. What is the volume at this point?

24. The change in the volume times the number of cylinders is the *size* of the engine in cubic inches. Find the size of the engine. (*Hint:* V8 means there are 8 cylinders.)

25. What is the size of the engine in liters? (*Hint:* 1 L = 61.02 in.^{3})

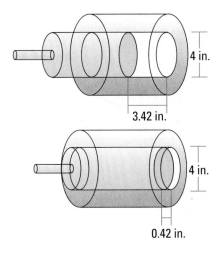

STANDARDIZED TEST PRACTICE

26. Which formula can you use to find the volume of a cylinder with radius, r, and height, h?

(**A**) $V = 2\pi rh$ (**B**) $V = \pi r^2$ (**C**) $V = \pi r^2 h$ (**D**) $V = 2\pi r^2 + 2\pi rh$

EXPLORATION AND EXTENSION

PORTFOLIO

27. BUILDING YOUR PROJECT Which of the cars you made in Exercise 28 of Lesson 12.2 are shaped like cylinders? Find the volume of each car.

Exploring Volume
of a Cone

In this investigation you will explore how radius and height affect the volume of a cone.

Materials Needed
- **thin cardboard**
- **compass**
- **scissors**
- **ruler**
- **unpopped popcorn**
- **paper clips**
- **pencil**
- **paper**

Part Ⓐ MAKING A CONE

Follow the steps below to make a cone.

Step ❶   Use a compass to draw a circle with a 4 in. radius on a piece of thin cardboard. Cut it out.

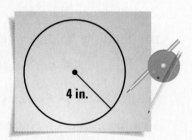

Step ❷   Draw a line segment from the edge of the circle to its center. Cut along the line segment.

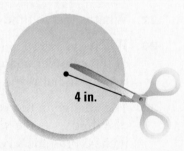

Step ❸   Overlap the cardboard to form an open cone. Secure the cardboard cone with a paper clip.

1. Use a ruler to measure the height h and radius r of the cone.

2. Use the height and radius to draw a right triangle as shown at the right. The hypotenuse should have a length of about 4 in. Why?

3. Use the Pythagorean Theorem to check that the sides of the right triangle have the correct relationship: $h^2 + r^2 = 4^2$.

4. Fill the cone you made with unpopped popcorn. Don't pile the corn above the rim of the cone. Count the number of pieces of corn you used.

5. Alter the size of the cone as shown below. Copy and complete the table. For each size, measure the height and the radius. Then fill the cone and count the number of pieces of corn.

Radius	Height	Pieces of corn	Sketch of the cone
?	?	?	
?	?	?	
?	?	?	

NOW TRY THESE

6. Which cone holds the most corn?

7. Can you make a different size cone that holds more corn than any shown above? If possible, then do it.

8. Describe how you would make a cone that holds as little corn as possible.

12.6

Exploring Volumes of **Pyramids** and **Cones**

What you should learn:

Goal 1 How to find the volume of a pyramid and a cone

Goal 2 How to find complicated volumes

Why you should learn it:

You can find volumes of real-life objects such as spacecraft.

Goal 1 VOLUMES OF PYRAMIDS AND CONES

To discover the volume of a pyramid, fill the pyramid with sand. Pour the sand into a prism that has the same base and height as the pyramid. The prism will be filled with exactly three pyramids of sand. This suggests that the pyramid has one third the volume of the prism. The same relationship is true of a cone and a cylinder.

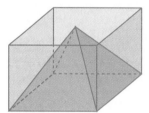 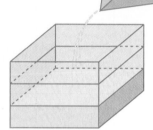

THE VOLUME OF A PYRAMID OR A CONE

The volume, V, of a pyramid or a cone is one third the product of its height, h, and the area of its base, B.

$$V = \frac{1}{3}Bh$$

Example 1 Finding a Volume

To find the volume of the pyramid, you need to know the area of the base. The area of the square base is $6 \cdot 6 = 36$ in.^{2}

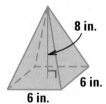

$V = \frac{1}{3}Bh$ Use the formula for volume of a pyramid.

$\quad = \frac{1}{3} \cdot 36 \cdot 8$ Substitute for *B* and *h*.

$\quad = 96$ Simplify.

The volume of the pyramid is 96 in.^{3}

Example 2 Finding a Complicated Volume

The U.S. sent nine manned Apollo spacecraft to the moon. Each spacecraft consisted of a command module and a service module, as shown at the right. Estimate the total volume of the spacecraft.

Solution

STRATEGY **SOLVE A SIMPLER PROBLEM** To find the total volume, first find the volume of each module.

Think of the command module as a cone.

Area of base of cone = $\pi r^2 = \pi(6.4)^2$
Height of cone = $26 - 15 = \mathbf{11}$ ft

$$V = \frac{1}{3}Bh \qquad \text{Use the formula for volume of a cone.}$$

$$= \frac{1}{3} \cdot \pi(6.4)^2 \cdot 11 \qquad \text{Substitute for } B \text{ and } h.$$

$$\approx 470 \text{ ft}^3 \qquad \text{Use a calculator.}$$

The volume of the command module is about 470 ft^3.

Think of the service module as a cylinder. The base of the cylinder is the same as the base of the cone.

$$V = Bh \qquad \text{Use the formula for volume of a cylinder.}$$

$$= \pi(6.4)^2 \cdot 15 \qquad \text{Substitute for } B \text{ and } h.$$

$$\approx 1930 \text{ ft}^3 \qquad \text{Use a calculator.}$$

The volume of the service module is about 1930 ft^3.

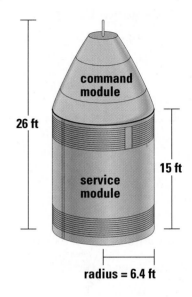

26 ft

command module

service module

15 ft

radius = 6.4 ft

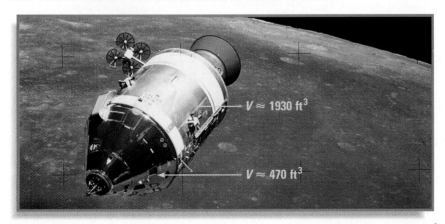

$V \approx 1930 \text{ ft}^3$

$V \approx 470 \text{ ft}^3$

The total volume of the spacecraft is about $1930 + 470 = 2400 \text{ ft}^3$.

ONGOING ASSESSMENT

Talk About It
. . . .

1. In Example 2, how accurate is the volume of the command module? Explain your reasoning.

2. Give dimensions of a rectangular room with about the same volume. Remember, the command module housed 3 astronauts.

12.6 Exercises   Extra Practice, page 737

Extra Practice, page 737

GUIDED PRACTICE

WRITING In Exercises 1 and 2, use the solids at the right.

1. How do the bases of cylinders and cones differ?

2. The cylinder and the cone have the same height and radius. Explain how their volumes compare.

GEOMETRY In Exercises 3 and 4, find the volume of the solid.

3.
   10 in.
   8 in.
   12 in.

4. 3 cm   10 cm

In Exercises 5–8, use the figure at the right.

5. What is the radius of the cone's base?

6. What is the height of the cone?

7. Find the volume of the cone.

8. Explain how to find the volume of the cone if its height is doubled. Then find it.

PRACTICE AND PROBLEM SOLVING

GEOMETRY In Exercises 9–16, find the volume of the solid.

9.
   20 cm
   12 cm
   15 cm

10.
    5 in.
    3 in.
    4 in.

11. 28 ft
    30 ft
    30 ft

12. 10 m
    7 m
    6 m

13.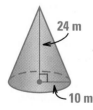
    24 m
    10 m

14.
    12 ft
    12 ft

15.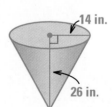
    14 in.
    26 in.

16.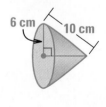
    6 cm   10 cm

GUESS, CHECK, AND REVISE In Exercises 17 and 18, draw the indicated figure. (There is more than one correct answer.)

17. A pyramid with a volume of 24 mm^3

18. A cone with a volume of 24π ft^3

GEOMETRY **In Exercises 19–21, find the volume of the solid.**

19.

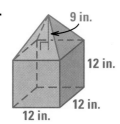

9 in.

12 in.

12 in.

12 in. 12 in.

20.

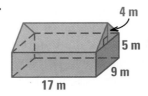

4 m

5 m

9 m

17 m

21.

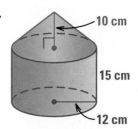

10 cm

15 cm

12 cm

22. **GRAIN** Suppose 35,000 m^3 of grain is in a cone-shaped pile. The radius of the pile is 40 m. Which of the following is the best estimate for the height of the pile?

A. 20 m   **B.** 40 m   **C.** 60 m

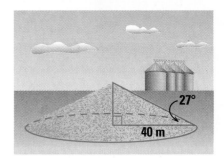

27°

40 m

23. **REASONING** Which has a greater effect on the volume of a cone, doubling the radius or doubling the height? Explain your reasoning.

24. Each solid has a height of 6 cm. Which solid has the greatest volume?

(A)

6 cm

(B)

6 cm

6 cm

(C)

6 cm

(D)

6 cm

6 cm

NETS **In Exercises 25 and 26, use the figure to make a paper cone.**

25. Trace a quarter and a dime to make a full-scale copy of the net on paper. Cut the net out. Then fold and tape the figure to form a cone.

26. Use a ruler to measure the height of the cone in centimeters. Then estimate the volume of the cone.

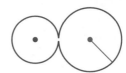

12.7

Exploring Volumes of Spheres

What you should learn:

Goal 1 How to find the volume of a sphere

Goal 2 How to use the volume of a sphere to solve real-life problems

Why you should learn it:

You can use the volume of a sphere to solve real-life problems, such as finding the volume of a natural gas storage tank.

Goal 1 FINDING VOLUMES OF SPHERES

To discover the volume of a sphere, imagine a sphere that is cut into two equal halves, called **hemispheres**. Fit a cone into one of the hemispheres as shown below. Fill the cone with sand and pour the sand into the hemisphere. The hemisphere is filled with *exactly* two cones of sand. A sphere is filled with four cones of sand.

The volume of a cone is $\frac{1}{3}Bh = \frac{1}{3}(\pi r^2)r$, so the volume of the sphere must be $4\left(\frac{1}{3}\pi r^3\right)$, or $\frac{4}{3}\pi r^3$.

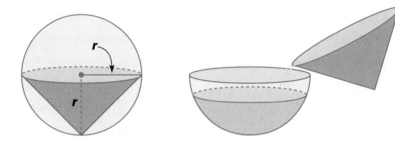

VOLUME OF A SPHERE

The volume of a sphere is four thirds the product of π and the cube of its radius, r.

$$V = \frac{4}{3}\pi r^3$$

Example 1 Finding the Volume of a Sphere

You want to measure the volume of a table tennis ball. The cylinder at the left is used in chemistry to measure volumes in cubic centimeters (1 cm³ is equal to 1 mL). Cut a small hole in a table tennis ball. Fill the ball with water and pour the water into the cylinder. About how high in the cylinder will the water come?

Solution

The radius of the table tennis ball is **1.9 cm**, so its volume is

$$V = \frac{4}{3}\pi r^3 \qquad \text{Use the formula for the volume of a sphere.}$$

$$= \frac{4}{3} \cdot \pi \cdot (1.9)^3 \qquad \text{Substitute for } r.$$

$$\approx 28.73 \text{ cm}^3. \qquad \text{Use a calculator.}$$

The water in the cylinder should be below the 29 mL mark.

Example 2 Comparing Volumes

REAL LIFE
Storage Tanks

You are designing a spherical storage tank for natural gas. The radius is 18 ft. How much gas will it hold? If you double the radius will the tank hold twice as much?

Solution

The volume of the tank is

$$V = \frac{4}{3}\pi r^3 = \frac{4}{3} \cdot \pi \cdot 18^3$$

$$\approx 24{,}429 \text{ ft}^3.$$

Doubling the radius gives a volume of

$$V = \frac{4}{3}\pi r^3 = \frac{4}{3} \cdot \pi \cdot 36^3$$

$$\approx 195{,}432 \text{ ft}^3.$$

36 ft

18 ft

This is 8 times the original volume, not twice the volume.

Example 3 Finding the Volume of a Shell

When you open a coconut, you find a core of sponge-like, white coconut meat. The shell seems to be a sphere with a diameter of 5.5 in. The hollow center has a radius of about 2 in.

To estimate the volume of coconut meat and shell, subtract the volume of the smaller sphere from the volume of the larger sphere.

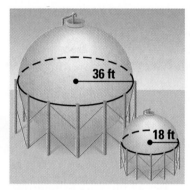

2 in.

├── 5.5 in. ──┤

Volume of larger sphere	Volume of smaller sphere
$V = \frac{4}{3}\pi r^3$	$V = \frac{4}{3}\pi r^3$
$\approx \frac{4}{3} \cdot 3.14 \cdot (2.75)^3$	$\approx \frac{4}{3} \cdot 3.14 \cdot 2^3$
$= 87.07 \text{ in.}^3$	$= 33.49 \text{ in.}^3$

The volume is about $87.07 - 33.49$, or about 53.6 in.^{3}

ONGOING ASSESSMENT

Write About It
• • • • • • • • • • • • • • • • •

1. In Example 2, suppose you are designing a spherical storage tank that is to contain 30,000 ft^3 of natural gas. Use the Guess, Check, and Revise strategy to find the radius of the tank.

12.7 Exercises

Extra Practice, page 737

GUIDED PRACTICE

SPHERE In Exercises 1–5, use the figure at the right.

1. Name a radius.

2. Is $\overline{AD}$ a radius? Explain.

3. Name a diameter. What is its measure?

4. What is one half of a sphere called?

5. Find the volume of the sphere.

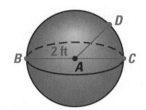

PRACTICE AND PROBLEM SOLVING

ATHLETIC EQUIPMENT In Exercises 6–13, find the volume of the ball.

6. $r = 1.5$ in.

7. $r = 12$ cm

8. $d = 8.6$ in.

9. $d = 1.68$ in.

10. $d = 0.5$ in.

11. $r = 11$ cm

12. $d = 8.25$ in.

13. $r = 1.25$ in.

In Exercises 14–17, find the volume of the orange portion of the figure.

14.

4
8
8
8

15.

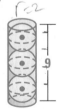

4.5

16.

r = 2
9

17.

6
20

18. **REASONING** Which is larger, the circumference or height of the cylinder in Exercise 16? Explain your reasoning.

GUESS, CHECK, AND REVISE In Exercises 19–22, find the radius of the sphere with the given volume.

19. 1436.76 cm^3 **20.** 659.58 ft^3 **21.** 32.52π cm^3 **22.** 2929.33π in.^{3}

The astronomy lab shown at the right allows people to learn about astronomy, mythology, earth science, and even biology through the use of its projection cylinders. This portable planetarium is dome-shaped with a diameter of 16 ft and can accommodate about 30 students.

23. If the lab were a complete sphere, what would its volume be?

24. Estimate the volume of the lab as constructed. Explain your reasoning.

25. PATTERNS What happens to the volume of a sphere when the radius doubles? Triples? Quadruples? Describe the pattern.

STANDARDIZED TEST PRACTICE

26. Which equation can you use to find the volume of the object's shell?

(A) $V = \frac{4}{3}\pi(10)^3 + \frac{4}{3}\pi(8)^3$

(B) $V = \frac{4}{3}\pi(18)^3$

(C) $V = \frac{4}{3}\pi(10)^3 - \frac{4}{3}\pi(8)^3$

(D) $V = \frac{4}{3}\pi(8)^3$

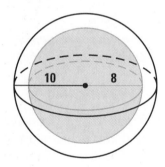

EXPLORATION AND EXTENSION

BASEBALL In Exercises 27 and 28, use the figure at the right, which shows the two pieces of a flattened baseball covering. The diameter of the blue circle is about the same as the diameter of the ball.

27. From the figure, which of the following is the correct formula for the surface area of a sphere? Explain your reasoning.

a. $S = 2\pi r^2$

b. $S = 3\pi r^2$

c. $S = 4\pi r^2$

d. $S = \frac{4}{3}\pi r^2$

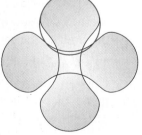

$\vdash d = 3 \text{ in.} \dashv$

28. Find the surface area of a baseball.

In Exercises 1–7, use the figure at the right. (10.1–10.3)

1. How are $\angle CDA$ and $\angle DEB$ related?

2. Which angle is congruent to $\angle GDE$?

3. Is $\overrightarrow{DA}$ a segment, a ray, or a line?

4. List two other names for $\overleftrightarrow{BH}$.

5. Is $\angle DEB$ acute, right, obtuse, or straight?

6. If $m\angle ADE = 60°$, what is $m\angle CDG$?

7. If $m\angle ADE = 60°$, what is $m\angle ADC$?

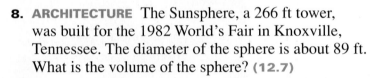

8. **ARCHITECTURE** The Sunsphere, a 266 ft tower, was built for the 1982 World's Fair in Knoxville, Tennessee. The diameter of the sphere is about 89 ft. What is the volume of the sphere? (12.7)

In Exercises 9–12, find the area of the indicated circle. (12.1)

9. $r = 8$ **10.** $r = 13$ **11.** $d = 8$ **12.** $d = 13$

In Exercises 13–16, write both solutions of the equation. (9.1)

13. $x^2 = 16$ **14.** $169 = y^2$

15. $121 = p^2$ **16.** $m^2 = \dfrac{25}{9}$

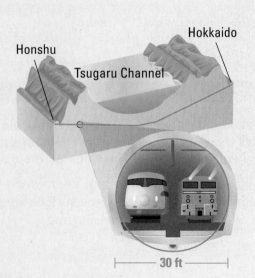

EARTH SCIENCE Connection   DESIGNING A TUNNEL

THE SEIKAN TUNNEL

Japan has an extensive railroad system, and its Seikan Tunnel is the longest in the world—33.1 mi! Large amounts of earth must be moved to dig a tunnel. What is the volume of the Seikan Tunnel?

To estimate the volume, think of the tunnel as a cylinder.

1. The base of the cylinder is the cross section you see in the diagram. Estimate the area of the base.

2. The length of the tunnel is 33.1 mi. Convert this length into feet. Remember that 1 mi = 5280 ft.

3. What is the approximate volume of the tunnel?

Beautiful
PHYSICS

READ About It

David Durlach is an unusual artist. One of his creations consists of a 15 in.-by-15 in. tray full of iron filings. Because of the pattern of electromagnets under the tray, the filings form 9 rows of 9 hemispheres. When Durlach puts a CD in his computer and flips a switch, the filings begin to 'dance' to music.

Durlach is also experimenting with magnets and *ferrofluid*, a liquid that is attracted to magnets. He doesn't want to spill any. A gallon costs $4500.

Companies hire Durlach to make advertising displays. He is currently working on a sign where words are formed by bubbles rising through fluid. To be readable, the sign will have to be 8 ft long, 6 ft high, and 2 ft deep. It won't be cheap to make. An aquarium of this size, even without the electronics, sells for $30,000.

WRITE About It

1. If each hemisphere of filings is $\frac{3}{4}$ in. high, estimate the total volume of iron filings on the tray. Explain how you got your answer.

2. How much would it cost to replace the iron filings with an equal volume of ferrofluid? $\left(1 \text{ in.}^3 = \frac{1}{231} \text{ gal}\right)$ Show your work.

3. Sketch the bubble sign. With glass on all sides, what is the surface area of the sign? Is your answer in square feet or cubic feet?

4. **OPEN-ENDED PROBLEM** Suppose you want to make a bubble sign that is similar to the one described above, but 12 ft long. Explain what "similar" means in this context. What are the new sign's dimensions?

5. **OPEN-ENDED PROBLEM** Estimate the cost of the sign you designed in Exercise 4. Explain how you got your estimate.

12.8

Exploring Similar Solids

What you should learn:

Goal 1 How to explore ratios of similar figures

Goal 2 How to use ratios of similar figures

Why you should learn it:

You can use ratios of similar figures to solve real-life problems, such as creating models.

Goal 1 EXPLORING MEASURES OF SIMILAR SOLIDS

Two solids are similar if they have the same shape and their corresponding lengths are proportional. Here are some examples.

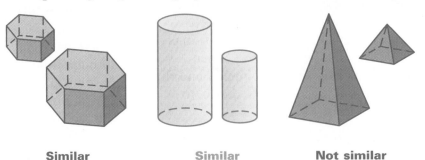

Similar   **Similar**   **Not similar**

LESSON INVESTIGATION

Investigating Ratios of Similar Solids

GROUP ACTIVITY Use wooden cubes to build cubes that have edge lengths of 1, 2, 3, 4, and 5 in. Find the surface areas and volumes of each cube. Compare the measure of each cube with the measure of the smallest cube. Copy and complete the table below. Describe the pattern for the ratios in your table.

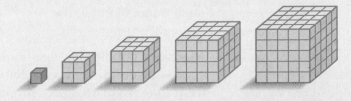

Edge length	New edge / Orig. edge	S (in.^{2})	New S / Orig. S	V (in.^{3})	New V / Orig. V
1 in.	$\frac{1}{1} = 1$	6	$\frac{6}{6} = 1$	1	$\frac{1}{1} = 1$
2 in.	$\frac{2}{1} = 2$	24	$\frac{24}{6} = 4$	8	$\frac{8}{1} = 8$
3 in.	?	?	?	?	?
4 in.	?	?	?	?	?
5 in.	?	?	?	?	?

There is an amazing relationship between measures of similar solids.

RATIOS OF MEASURES OF SIMILAR SOLIDS

1. If two solids are similar with a scale factor of k, then the ratio of their surface areas is k^2.

2. If two solids are similar with a scale factor of k, then the ratio of their volumes is k^3.

Example 1 Comparing Surface Areas and Volumes

You are building a scale model of a building. In your model a length of $\frac{1}{8}$ in. represents a length of 1 ft in the building.

a. What is the scale factor of the building to the model?

b. What is the ratio of the surface area of the building to the surface area of the model?

Solution

a. To find the scale factor, find the ratio of 1 ft to $\frac{1}{8}$ in.

$$\frac{1 \text{ ft}}{\frac{1}{8} \text{ in.}} = \frac{12 \text{ in.}}{\frac{1}{8} \text{ in.}} = 12 \cdot \left(\frac{8}{1}\right) = 96$$

The scale factor is 96.

b. Using a scale factor of 96, the building's surface area is 96^2 or 9216 times the model's surface area.

Example 2 Comparing Similar Solids

The solids are similar, so you can use a proportion to find x.

$$\frac{\text{Larger radius}}{\text{Smaller radius}} = \frac{\text{Larger height}}{\text{Smaller height}}$$

$$\frac{4}{2} = \frac{x}{3}$$

$$3 \cdot \frac{4}{2} = 3 \cdot \frac{x}{3}$$

$$6 = x$$

The larger cylinder is 6 cm high.

Real Life... Real Facts

REAL LIFE
Modeling

Japan
At Tobu World Square, the world's most famous buildings and monuments are precisely reproduced. The scale is always 1:25.

ONGOING ASSESSMENT

Write About It
....

In Example 1, a rectangular room in the model is 2 in. by 2 in. by 1 in.

1. Describe two different ways to find the surface area and volume of the actual room in the building.

GUIDED PRACTICE

REASONING In Exercises 1–3, decide whether the figures are similar. Explain.

1.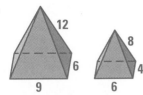

2.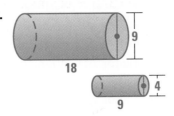

3.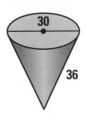

GEOMETRY In Exercises 4–7, use the similar prisms at the right.

4. Find the scale factor of Prism *A* to Prism *B*.

5. Find the surface area of Prism *B*.

6. Use a ratio of measures of similar solids to find the surface area of Prism *A*. Check your answer.

7. How are the two volumes related? Explain.

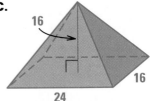

Prism *A*

Prism *B*

PRACTICE AND PROBLEM SOLVING

GEOMETRY In Exercises 8 and 9, match the solid with a similar solid.

8.

A.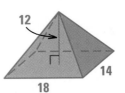

B.

C.

9.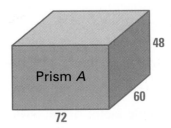

A.

B.

C.

In Exercises 10 and 11, the solids are similar. Solve for *x* and *y*.

10.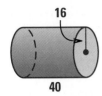

32.5 cm

30 cm

x

y

12 cm

11.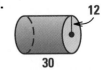

10 in.

8 in.

x

5 in.

y

30 in.

12. Copy and complete the table. The scale factor is the ratio of *A* to *B*.

Scale factor	Solid *A*			Solid *B*		
	Length	Surface area	Volume	Length	Surface area	Volume
3	15 ft	400 ft²	300 ft³	?	?	?
7.5	?	11,137.5 cm²	?	3 cm	?	162 cm³

MODEL TRAINS **In Exercises 13 and 14, use the following information.**

You are designing a model train station. In your model, a length of $\frac{1}{12}$ in. represents a length of 1 ft in the actual station.

13. Find the scale factor of the actual station to the model.

14. Find the ratio of the train station's volume to the model's volume.

LOGICAL REASONING **In Exercises 15–18, complete the statement using** *always*, *sometimes*, **or** *never*.

15. Two spheres are ? similar.

16. A cube is ? similar to a pyramid.

17. Two cones are ? similar.

18. A cylinder is ? similar to itself.

STANDARDIZED TEST PRACTICE

19. What is the ratio of the surface area of the small cube to the surface area of the large cube?

A $\frac{1}{9}$ **B** $\frac{1}{3}$ **C** 3 **D** 9

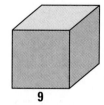

3   9

EXPLORATION AND EXTENSION

20. **BUILDING YOUR PROJECT** A real box car is 10 ft wide.

  a. Find the scale factor of your model train. Use the scale to find the other dimensions of an actual box car.

  b. Find the surface area and volume of the actual car.

  c. Refer to your portfolio for the surface area of your model car. Is the scale factor of your model the same as the ratio of the surface areas of the model and the real car? Explain.

WHAT did you learn?

WHY did you learn it?

Skills

12.1	Find the circumference and area of a circle.	Use circumference to describe objects such as a tire.
12.2	Identify and sketch polyhedrons and other solids.	Sketch real-life solids from different perspectives.
12.3	Find the surface area of a prism and a cylinder.	Use surface area to measure a container's material.
12.4	Find the volume of a prism.	Study different designs for a television studio.
12.5	Find the volume of a cylinder.	Decide which container is a better buy.
12.6	Find the volume of a pyramid and a cone.	Examine the living space of a spacecraft.
12.7	Find the volume of a sphere.	Analyze containers such as a natural gas tank.
12.8	Compare the surface areas and volumes of similar solids.	Analyze the scale model of a building.

Strategies

12.1–12.8	Model and solve real-life problems.	Solve a wide variety of real-world problems.

Using Data

12.1–12.8	Use tables and graphs to solve problems.	Organize data and solve problems.

HOW does it fit in the bigger picture of mathematics?

You also studied many different formulas. Some of these formulas are used often enough that you should memorize them. For instance,

The formula for the circumference of a circle is $C = \pi d$.

The formula for the area of a circle is $A = \pi r^2$.

This chapter helps build a sense of what surface area and volume are actually measuring. For instance,

Surface area is a measure of the material needed to cover the solid.

Volume is a measure of the material needed to fill the solid.

VOCABULARY

- diameter (p. 566)
- center (p. 566)
- radius (p. 566)
- circumference (p. 566)
- polyhedron (p. 572)

- faces (p. 572)
- edges (p. 572)
- vertices (p. 572)
- prisms (p. 572)
- pyramids (p. 572)

- net (p. 572)
- surface area (p. 576)
- volume (p. 580)
- cubic units (p. 580)
- hemispheres (p. 596)

12.1 CIRCLE RELATIONSHIPS

Find the circumference and area of each circle.

1.

14 in.

2.

12 cm

3.

11.2 m

12.2 POLYHEDRONS AND OTHER SOLIDS

A polyhedron is a solid that is bounded by polygons, which are called *faces*. The segments where the faces meet are *edges*, and the points where the edges meet are *vertices*.

Example ▷ The polyhedron that results from folding the net on the left is a cube with 6 faces, 12 edges, and 8 vertices.

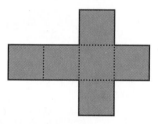

Describe the solids that result from folding each net. How many faces, vertices, and edges does each have?

4.
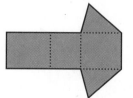

5.
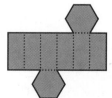

6.

12.3–12.6 EXPLORING SURFACE AREA AND VOLUME

Surface area of a prism:	$S = 2B + Ph$	Surface area of a cylinder: $S = 2B + Ch$
Volume of a prism:	$V = Bh$	Volume of a cylinder: $V = Bh$
Volume of a pyramid:	$V = \frac{1}{3}Bh$	Volume of a cone: $V = \frac{1}{3}\pi r^2 h$

Find the surface area of the solid.

7.

18 cm
12 cm
10 cm

8.
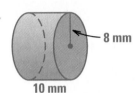
8 mm
10 mm

9.
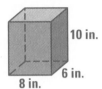
10 in.
6 in.
8 in.

Find the volume of the prism.

10.
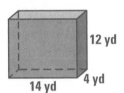
12 yd
4 yd
14 yd

11.

8 m
7 m
6 m

12.
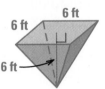
4 cm
9 cm
3 cm

Find the volume of the pyramid.

13.

8 mm
8 mm
24 mm

14.
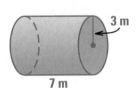
6 ft
6 ft
6 ft

15.

10 m
7.5 m
5 m

Find the volume of the cylinder.

16.

4 in. 1 in.

17.
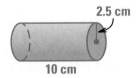
3 m
7 m

18.
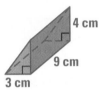
2.5 cm
10 cm

Find the volume of the cone.

19.

20 in.
45 in.

20.
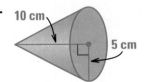
10 cm
5 cm

21.
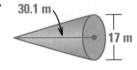
30.1 m
17 m

12.7 EXPLORING VOLUMES OF SPHERES

Volume of a sphere: $V = \frac{4}{3}\pi r^3$

Example

To find the volume of the sphere use the formula.

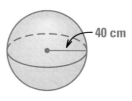
40 cm

$V = \frac{4}{3}\pi r^3$

$\approx \frac{4}{3}(3.14)(40)^3$

$= 267{,}946.67 \text{ cm}^3$

Find the volume of each sphere.

4.75

22.

2 in.

23.
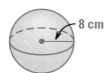
8 cm

24.

9.5 m

12.8 EXPLORING SIMILAR SOLIDS

To determine if two solids are similar, check their shape and size. If they have the same shape and their corresponding lengths are proportional, then the two solids are similar.

Example

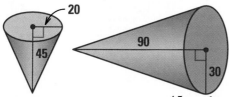
20
90
45
30

The solids above are not similar because $\frac{45}{90} = \frac{1}{2}$ and $\frac{20}{30} = \frac{2}{3}$, so the lengths are not proportional.

Use the solids at the right.

54 cm
18 cm

25. The cylinders are similar. Find the scale factor of the large cylinder to the smaller cylinder.

26. What is the radius of the small cylinder?

9 cm

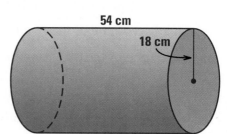

GEOMETRY   In Exercises 1–3, use the prism at the right.

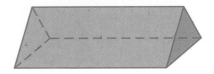

1. How many faces does the prism have?

2. How many vertices does the prism have?

3. How many edges does the prism have?

GEOMETRY   In Exercises 4–7, use the cylinder at the right.

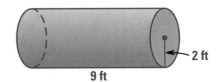

4. Find the circumference of one of the bases.

5. Find the area of one of the bases.

6. Find the surface area of the cylinder.

7. Find the volume of the cylinder.

In Exercises 8–11, find the indicated measure of the solid.

8. Volume

9. Volume

10. Surface area

11. Surface area

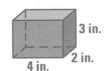

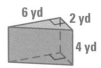

GEOMETRY   In Exercises 12–16, use the similar solids shown below. The area of Figure *A*'s base is $54\sqrt{3}$ ft².

12. Find the scale factor of Figure *A* to Figure *B*.

13. Find the surface area of Figure *A*.

14. Find the volume of Figure *A*.

15. Find the surface area of Figure *B*.

16. Find the volume of Figure *B*.

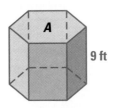

PIPES   In Exercises 17–19, use the diagram at the right.

17. What is the surface area of the manhole cover?

18. Approximate the volume of the manhole.

19. What is the volume of the 20 ft section of drainage pipe?

20. **MOON** The moon's diameter is about 2160 mi. What is the volume of the moon?

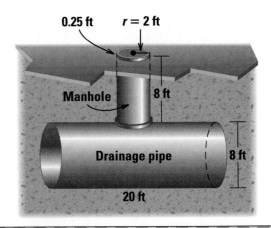

1. The diameter of a circle is 2.5 m. Approximate the area of the circle.

   (A) 4.9 m^2 (B) 7.9 m^2

   (C) 15.7 m^2 (D) 19.6 m^2

2. The radius of a circle is 2.5 m. Approximate the circumference of the circle.

   (A) 4.9 m   (B) 7.9 m

   (C) 15.7 m   (D) 19.6 m

3. What figure is formed by the net?

   (A) prism   (B) pyramid

   (C) cylinder (D) cone

4. Approximate the amount of frozen yogurt that can fit inside the waffle cone shown below.

   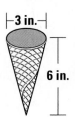

   (A) 14.1 in.^{3} (B) 18.8 in.^{2}

   (C) 42.4 in.^{2} (D) 56.5 in.^{3}

5. Approximate the volume of the sphere.

   (A) 65.4 ft^2 (B) 196.3 ft^3

   (C) 523.6 ft^3 (D) 1570.8 ft^2

6. Dan Sweeney designed two containers to hold fruit juice. Which statement is *false*? (The drawings are not drawn to scale.)

   (A) Both containers have about the same volume.

   (B) The cylindrical container uses more packaging.

   (C) They both hold about the same amount of fruit juice.

   (D) The surface area of the rectangular container is greater than the surface area of the cylindrical container.

7. The pyramids shown below are similar. What is the value of x?

   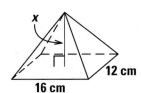

   (A) 4.4 cm   (B) 11.2 cm

   (C) 11.5 cm   (D) 22.9 cm

8. In the figure below, approximate the area of the shaded region.

   (A) 2.4 m   (B) 3.4 m

   (C) 4.2 m   (D) 4.3 m

Cumulative Review CHAPTERS 7–12

In Exercises 1–4, evaluate the expression. Then simplify. (7.1, 7.2, 7.4, 7.5)

1. $\frac{8}{6} + \frac{1}{3}$

2. $\frac{3}{4} \cdot \frac{8}{9}$

3. $\frac{7}{12} - \frac{5}{12}$

4. $\frac{12}{5} \div \frac{3}{5}$

In Exercises 5–8, solve the equation. (7.1, 7.2, 7.4, 7.5)

5. $y + \frac{3}{4} = \frac{1}{2}$

6. $\frac{1}{3}m = \frac{1}{6}$

7. $\frac{4}{5} = 8a$

8. $\frac{2}{7} = b - \frac{3}{2}$

 TECHNOLOGY In Exercises 9–12, use a calculator to evaluate the expression. Round your result to two decimal places. (7.1–7.5)

9. $\frac{31}{40} \cdot \frac{26}{51}$

10. $\frac{76}{55} + \frac{7}{35}$

11. $\frac{93}{95} - \frac{54}{73}$

12. $\frac{9}{92} \div \frac{26}{70}$

In Exercises 13–15, write the fraction that represents the portion of the figure's area that is blue. Then write the fraction as a percent. (7.6)

13.

14.

15.

JOB SECURITY In Exercises 16 and 17, use the circle graph. (7.7, 7.8)

16. Write each percent as a simplified fraction.

17. Five hundred people participated in the survey. How many people answered in each category?

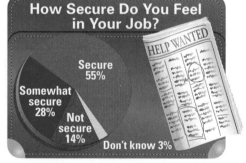
(Source: Deloitte and Touche Trade Survey)

In Exercises 18–20, write the verbal phrase as a rate or ratio. State whether it is a *rate* or a *ratio*. (8.1)

18. Five gallons used to drive one hundred mi.

19. Only 18 people out of 24 people attended.

20. Hooray, 99 chicks out of 100 chicks survived.

In Exercises 21–24, solve the proportion. (8.2)

21. $\frac{3}{4} = \frac{x}{32}$

22. $\frac{18}{5} = \frac{3}{y}$

23. $\frac{z}{6} = \frac{5}{9}$

24. $\frac{24}{w} = \frac{3}{5}$

In Exercises 25 and 26, use the table at the right that shows the number of points Tyrone "Muggsy" Bogues scored in each season in the National Basketball Association. (8.6)

Season	Points
1993–94	835
1994–95	862
1995–96	14
1996–97	522

25. Find the percent of increase in points from the 1993–94 season to the 1994–95 season.

26. In the 1995–96 basketball season, Bogues had a knee injury. Find the percent of decrease in points from the 1994–95 season to the 1995–96 season.

PROBABILITY In Exercises 27 and 28, you have 6 pencils and 3 pens. (8.7, 8.8)

27. How many different ways could you choose
one pencil and one pen?

28. If you randomly pick one writing instrument,
what is the probability that it is a pencil?

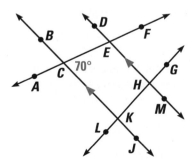

**In Exercises 29–31, solve the equation and state whether the solutions
are *rational* or *irrational*. (9.1, 9.2)**

29. $x^2 = 121$ **30.** $84 = y^2$ **31.** $-8 = m^2 - 17$

32. **TELEVISION** If you have a 25 in. diagonal television screen
and its width is 18.6 in., what is its height, h? **(9.4)**

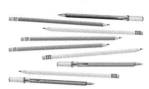

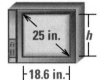 **TECHNOLOGY In Exercises 33–35, *a* and *b* are the lengths of the
legs of a right triangle, and *c* is the length of the hypotenuse. Find
the missing length. (9.3)**

33. $a = 7, b = 24$ **34.** $a = 5, c = 15$ **35.** $b = 13, c = 15$

**In Exercises 36–41, solve the inequality. Then graph the solution on a
number line. (9.5–9.7)**

36. $x + 14 \le 9$ **37.** $\frac{2}{3} < -4y$ **38.** $-17 \le -12n + 19$

39. $5(1 + 2p) < 13$ **40.** $2(7 - x) > 5x$ **41.** $3(5 + x) \le \frac{1}{4}(20 + 8x)$

**In Exercises 42–44, decide whether the triangle can have the given side
lengths. Explain. (9.3, 9.8)**

42.
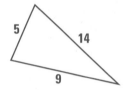

43.
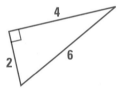

44.
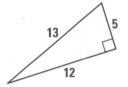

In Exercises 45–51, use the figure at the right. (10.1–10.3)

45. Write two other names for the line $\overleftrightarrow{EH}$.

46. Name five line segments that have C as an endpoint.

47. Write another name for $\overrightarrow{KH}$.

48. Name 2 pairs of vertical angles.

49. Name 2 pairs of congruent corresponding angles.

50. Name 2 pairs of noncongruent corresponding angles.

51. Name 4 angles whose measure is 70°.

In Exercises 52–54, use a protractor to measure the angle. Is it *acute,* *obtuse, right,* **or** *straight?* (10.2)

52.

53.

54.

In Exercises 55–57, find the values of *x* **and** *y.* (10.6)

55. Square

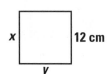

56. Rhombus

57. Rectangle

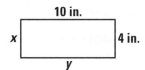

In Exercises 58–60, find the area and perimeter of the polygon. (11.1)

58.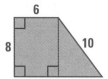

59.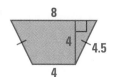

60.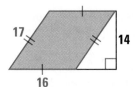

In Exercises 61–63, use the figure at the right, where △ABC is reflected in line *k.* (11.3)

61. Is △ *ABC* congruent to △ *A′B′C′*?

62. Is the length of $\overline{BB'}$ half the length of $\overline{CC'}$? Explain.

63. Is $\overline{CM} \cong \overline{MC'}$? Explain.

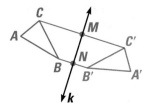

In Exercises 64 and 65, use the figure at the right, where △DEF is rotated about point *O.* (11.4)

64. Is △ *DEF* congruent to △ *D′E′F′*?

65. Is $\overline{DD'} = \overline{FF'}$? Explain.

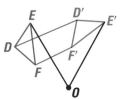

In Exercises 66–68, use the points *A*(2, 3), *B*(5, 3), *C*(4, 1), **and** *D*(1, 1). **Write the coordinates of the image of parallelogram** *ABCD* **after it has been translated using the given motion rule.** (11.5)

66. $(x, y) \rightarrow (x, y - 3)$

67. $(x, y) \rightarrow (x + 2, y)$

68. $(x, y) \rightarrow (x + 1, y + 2)$

QUILTS In Exercises 69–73, use the quilt shown below. The quilt is made from pieces that are each similar to the quilt. (11.6, 11.7)

69. Find the height of a rectangular piece.

70. Find the scale factor of the quilt to the piece.

71. Find the perimeter and area of the quilt and of the piece.

72. Find the ratio of the quilt's perimeter to the piece's perimeter. How does this ratio compare to the scale factor?

73. Find the ratio of the quilt's area to the piece's area. How does this ratio compare to the scale factor?

4 in.
24 in.
36 in.

INDIRECT MEASUREMENT In Exercises 74 and 75, you are measuring the width of the river shown in the diagram. To begin, you place stakes at points *A* and *B*. Then you measure $\overline{AB}$ and $\angle B$. (11.8)

74. Write the trigonometric ratio for the tangent of $\angle B$.

75. Find the width of the river.

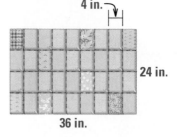
C
b ft
45°
B   60 ft   *A*

In Exercises 76–78, find the circumference and area of the circle. Round your results to two decimal places. (12.1)

76. $d = 12$ mm

77. $d = 3.4$ cm

78. $d = 9\frac{1}{4}$ in.

In Exercises 79–81, find the surface area and volume of the solid. Round your results to two decimal places. (12.3–12.5)

79.

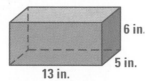
6 in.
5 in.
13 in.

80.

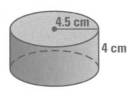
4.5 cm
4 cm

81.

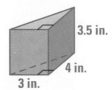
3.5 in.
4 in.
3 in.

In Exercises 82–84, find the volume of the solid. Round your result to two decimal places. (12.6, 12.7)

82.

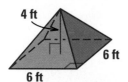
4 ft
6 ft
6 ft

83.

9.5 cm

84.

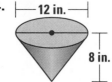
12 in.
8 in.

Exploring Linear Equations

CHICAGO, ILLINOIS

LOS ANGELES, CALIFORNIA

WASHINGTON, D.C.

TECHNOLOGY

- **Interactive Real-Life Investigations**
- **Middle School Tutorial Software**

To find out more about subways and public transportation, go to:

http://www.mlmath.com

CHAPTER THEME
Public Transportation

PORTFOLIO

CHAPTER **PROJECT**

Designing a Subway

PROJECT DESCRIPTION

Subways are underground train systems that can transport large numbers of people quickly. Designing a mass transit system takes careful planning. You will explore some of the factors that subway planners must consider. You will design a billboard to publicize your plans.

GETTING STARTED

Talking It Over

- Compare a subway with an above-ground train system. What are the advantages of each? What are the disadvantages?

- What factors do subway planners think about when deciding how much to charge passengers? How do you think planners decide what the fares should be?

Planning Your Project

- **Materials:** posterboard, paper, pencils or pens, colored pencils or markers

- Think of a name for your subway and use it in an advertising slogan. Write the slogan on your billboard. As you complete the **BUILDING YOUR PROJECT** exercises, add the results to your billboard.

BUILDING YOUR PROJECT

These are places throughout the chapter where you will work on your project.

13.1 Calculate travel distance. *p. 621*

13.2 Compare fare plans. *p. 625*

13.3 Plan seating and standing room. *p. 631*

13.4 Design station access. *p. 638*

13.7 Compare park-and-ride plans. *p. 655*

ALGEBRA CONNECTION

13.1

What you should learn:

Goal 1 How to find solutions of a linear equation with two variables

Goal 2 How to organize solutions of linear equations in real-life situations

Why you should learn it:

You can solve real-life problems, such as comparing Fahrenheit and Celsius temperature scales.

Linear Equations in Two Variables

Goal 1 **SOLUTIONS OF LINEAR EQUATIONS**

In this chapter, you will study **linear equations** in two variables. In a linear equation, variables occur only to the first power. For example, the following equations are linear.

$$y = 2x + 1 \qquad C = \pi d \qquad A = 1.06P$$

Equations such as $A = \pi r^2$ and $V = s^3$ are not linear.

In Lesson 3.8, you learned that (x, y) is a *solution* of an equation involving x and y if the equation is true when the values of x and y are substituted into the equation. Equations with two variables may have more than one solution. For example, here are three solutions of $y = x + 3$.

Equation	Solution (x, y)	Check by Substituting
$y = x + 3$	$(1, 4)$	$4 = 1 + 3$
$y = x + 3$	$(2, 5)$	$5 = 2 + 3$
$y = x + 3$	$(3, 6)$	$6 = 3 + 3$

To find a solution, choose a value for one of the variables, substitute it into the equation, and solve for the other variable.

Example 1 **Finding Solutions of Linear Equations**

List several solutions of $2x + y = 10$.

Solution

Begin by choosing values of x. Substitute each value into the equation and solve for y.

x-Value	Substitute for x	Solve for y	Solution
$x = 0$	$2(0) + y = 10$	$y = 10$	$(0, 10)$
$x = 1$	$2(1) + y = 10$	$y = 8$	$(1, 8)$
$x = 2$	$2(2) + y = 10$	$y = 6$	$(2, 6)$
$x = 3$	$2(3) + y = 10$	$y = 4$	$(3, 4)$
$x = 4$	$2(4) + y = 10$	$y = 2$	$(4, 2)$

You can organize your results in a table.

x	0	1	2	3	4
y	10	8	6	4	2

The table shows the value of y for each chosen value of x.

Example 2 Problem Solving: Organizing Solutions

The relationship between temperature measured in degrees Fahrenheit, F, and temperature measured in degrees Celsius, C, is given by the equation

$$F = \frac{9}{5}C + 32.$$

You are designing a poster to help people convert between the two temperature scales. Use some familiar temperatures.

a. Water freezes at 0°C and boils at 100°C. Convert these two temperatures to degrees Fahrenheit.

b. A comfortable room temperature is 68°F. Convert this temperature to degrees Celsius.

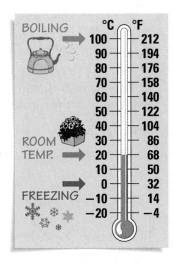

Solution

a. To convert from degrees Celsius to degrees Fahrenheit, use the formula above. Substitute the **freezing** and **boiling** values for C, and solve for F.

Freezing	**Boiling**	
$F = \frac{9}{5}C + 32$	$F = \frac{9}{5}C + 32$	**Write original equation.**
$F = \frac{9}{5} \cdot 0 + 32$	$F = \frac{9}{5} \cdot 100 + 32$	**Substitute for C.**
$F = 32$	$F = 212$	**Solution: F is by itself.**

Water freezes at 32°F and boils at 212°F.

b. To convert 68°F, substitute and solve for C.

$F = \frac{9}{5}C + 32$	**Write original equation.**
$68 = \frac{9}{5}C + 32$	**Substitute 68 for F.**
$36 = \frac{9}{5}C$	**Subtract 32 from each side.**
$\frac{5}{9} \cdot 36 = \frac{5}{9} \cdot \frac{9}{5}C$	**Multiply each side by $\frac{5}{9}$.**
$20 = C$	**Solution: C is by itself.**

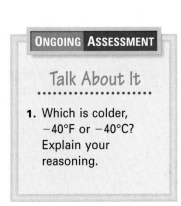

Talk About It
....

1. Which is colder, −40°F or −40°C? Explain your reasoning.

So, 20°C is a comfortable room temperature. The converted values found in parts (a) and (b) appear on the poster shown above.

GUIDED PRACTICE

1. Is the ordered pair a solution of $2x + 3y = 7$? Explain.

　　a. $(1, 2)$ 　　　**b.** $(2, 1)$ 　　　**c.** $(5, -1)$ 　　　**d.** $(4, -1)$

2. Tell whether the equation is linear. Explain.

　　a. $A = \pi r^2$ 　　**b.** $C = 2\pi r$ 　　**c.** $r + \dfrac{1}{2}t = 30$ 　　**d.** $100 - 6p = S$

In Exercises 3–6, copy and complete the table of values below to show solutions of the equation.

3. $y = x + 5$ 　　　**4.** $3x - 3 = y$

5. $y = 5x + 6$ 　　　**6.** $2x - y = 4$

x	−3	−2	−1	0	1	2	3
y	?	?	?	?	?	?	?

PRACTICE AND PROBLEM SOLVING

In Exercises 7–10, is the ordered pair a solution of $7x - y = 5$?

7. $(0, -5)$ 　　　**8.** $(2, 1)$ 　　　**9.** $(-1, 12)$ 　　　**10.** $\left(\dfrac{1}{2}, -\dfrac{3}{2}\right)$

In Exercises 11–14, copy and complete the table of values below to show solutions of the equation.

11. $y = x - 8$ 　　　**12.** $y = 2x + 4$

13. $4x + y = 20$ 　　　**14.** $6x - y = 18$

x	−3	−2	−1	0	1	2	3
y	?	?	?	?	?	?	?

In Exercises 15–18, find several solutions of the linear equation. Use a table of values to organize your results.

15. $x + y = 6$ 　　**16.** $x + 2y = 13$ 　　**17.** $6x + 2y = 24$ 　　**18.** $y = \dfrac{1}{3}x + 2$

In Exercises 19 and 20, write the sentence as a linear equation. Then list several solutions.

19. The difference of 6 times a number and 4 times another number is 12.

20. The sum of half a number and twice another number is 54.

GEOMETRY **In Exercises 21–24, match the linear equation with a figure. Then list several solutions.**

A. 　　**B.** 　　**C.** 　　**D.**

21. $x + y = 150$ 　　**22.** $x + y = 210$ 　　**23.** $x + y = 180$ 　　**24.** $x + y = 90$

UNIT CONVERSIONS In Exercises 25–27, use the equation $y = 2.54x$, which relates a centimeter measurement, y, to an inch measurement, x.

25. How long, in centimeters, is a 12 in. ruler?

26. How long, in inches, is a 100 cm ruler?

27. Use several values of x between 0 in. and 50 in. to make a table for converting between inches and centimeters.

28. WRITING How many solutions does a linear equation with two variables have? Explain your answer.

In Exercises 29 and 30, do you think the two equations have the same solutions? Explain your reasoning.

29. $3x + 5y = 16$
$12x + 20y = 64$

30. $9x - 2y = 18$
$18x - 4y = 30$

TRUCK SALES In Exercises 31 and 32, use the following information.

From 1991 through 1994, the number N (in millions) of trucks sold in the United States can be modeled by the linear equation $N = 0.76t + 2.6$, where $t = 1$ represents 1991, $t = 2$ represents 1992, and so on.

Tech Link

Investigation 13,
Interactive
Real-Life
Investigations

31. According to the model, how many trucks were sold in 1991?

32. According to the model, how many trucks were sold in 1994?

STANDARDIZED TEST PRACTICE

33. Which ordered pair is *not* a solution of the equation $3x + 2y = 9$?

(A) $(3, 0)$ **(B)** $(2, 3)$ **(C)** $(1, 3)$ **(D)** $(5, -3)$

34. Which linear equation does *not* represent the following statement?
The sum of twice one number and four times another number is 20.

(A) $2x + 4y = 20$ **(B)** $4y = -2x + 20$ **(C)** $0 = -2x + 4y + 20$ **(D)** $y = -\frac{1}{2}x + 5$

EXPLORATION AND EXTENSION

PORTFOLIO

35. BUILDING YOUR PROJECT Suppose that the cars in your subway can travel at a speed of 50 mi/h. The distance, d (in miles), that they can travel in t min is given by $d = 50 \times \frac{t}{60}$. Simplify this equation.

Then make a table of values to show how far a passenger will travel in 10, 20, 30, 40, and 50 min. Add this table to your billboard.

13.2

Exploring Graphs of Linear Equations

What you should learn:

Goal 1 How to use a table of values to sketch the graph of a linear equation

Goal 2 How to recognize graphs of horizontal and vertical lines

Why you should learn it:

You can use graphs of linear equations to help you recognize relationships between two variables, such as the relationship between the year and the number of members in a chess club.

Goal 1 GRAPHING LINEAR EQUATIONS

Solutions of linear equations are expressed as ordered pairs, so they can be graphed in a coordinate plane.

LESSON INVESTIGATION

Investigating Graphs of Linear Equations

GROUP ACTIVITY Find several solutions of the equation $y = 6 - x$. Use integer x-values from -3 to 5. Organize the nine solutions in a table of values. Then plot the solutions in a coordinate plane. What pattern do you notice about these graphed points?

As you may have discovered above, the graph of a linear equation is a line. In fact, this is why linear equations are called "linear"!

Example 1 Graphing a Linear Equation

Sketch the graph of $y = 2x - 2$.

Solution

STRATEGY **MAKE A LIST** Find solutions for several x-values. Express them as ordered pairs.

x-Value	Substitute	Solve for y	Solution
$x = -2$	$y = 2(-2) - 2$	$y = -6$	$(-2, -6)$
$x = -1$	$y = 2(-1) - 2$	$y = -4$	$(-1, -4)$
$x = 0$	$y = 2(0) - 2$	$y = -2$	$(0, -2)$
$x = 1$	$y = 2(1) - 2$	$y = 0$	$(1, 0)$
$x = 2$	$y = 2(2) - 2$	$y = 2$	$(2, 2)$

Plot the solutions in a coordinate plane. Then draw a line through the points. The line is the graph of the equation.

The arrowheads on the graph indicate that the line extends forever in both directions.

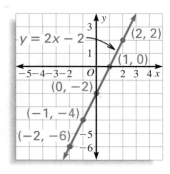

Some linear equations, such as

$$x = 3 \text{ and } y = 1,$$

have just one variable. All solutions
of $x = 3$ have the form $(3, y)$, and the
graph of this equation is a vertical line.
All solutions of $y = 1$ have the form
$(x, 1)$, and the graph is a horizontal line.

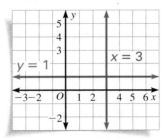

GRAPHS OF LINEAR EQUATIONS IN ONE VARIABLE

1. The graph of $x = a$ is a vertical line passing through $(a, 0)$.

2. The graph of $y = b$ is a horizontal line passing through $(0, b)$.

Example 2 **Plotting Data**

The memberships of two clubs, Club A and Club B, for 1991
through 1999 are shown in the table. In the table, 1 represents the
year 1991, 2 represents 1992, and so on. Plot the data and describe
the pattern.

Year	1	2	3	4	5	6	7	8	9
Club A	36	36	36	36	36	36	36	36	36
Club B	32	33	34	35	36	37	38	39	40

Solution

Plot the data for Club A in a
coordinate plane. The points
form a line, so the pattern is
linear.

Plot the data for Club B. These
data points form a line, so the
pattern for Club B is also linear.

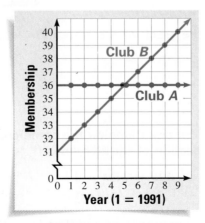

Write About It

1. At what point do
the two graphs in
Example 2 intersect?

2. Interpret this point
by completing the
sentence "Up until
1995, Club B had
fewer members than
Club A, but . . . "

For Club A, the line is horizontal because membership stayed the
same. For Club B, the line slopes up because membership grew.

13.2 Exercises

Extra Practice, page 738

GUIDED PRACTICE

1. WRITING Explain how to sketch the graph of an equation.

In Exercises 2–5, sketch the graph of the equation.

2. $y = 5$ **3.** $x = -4$ **4.** $y = 3x - 1$ **5.** $x + y = 8$

In Exercises 6–8, match the equation with the description of its graph.

A. Horizontal line   B. Vertical line   C. Slanted line

6. $2x + 3y = 8$ **7.** $y = 4$ **8.** $x = -2$

PRACTICE AND PROBLEM SOLVING

In Exercises 9–11, match the equation with its graph.

A. 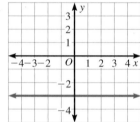   B. 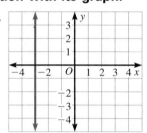   C.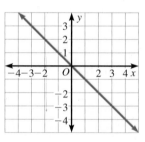

9. $y = -x$ **10.** $y = -3$ **11.** $x = -3$

DESCRIBING PATTERNS In Exercises 12 and 13, plot the points given in the table and explain whether the relationship between x and y is linear.

12.

x	−3	−2	−1	0	1	2	3
y	15	13	11	9	7	5	3

13.

x	−3	−2	−1	0	1	2	3
y	1	2	4	7	11	16	22

In Exercises 14–19, sketch the graph of the equation.

14. $y = x + 4$ **15.** $y = 2x - 6$ **16.** $y = -1$

17. $x = \dfrac{3}{2}$ **18.** $y = \dfrac{x}{3}$ **19.** $y = \dfrac{3}{2}x - 5$

In Exercises 20–22, graph both equations on the same coordinate plane. Then find the point of intersection of the two lines.

20. $x + y = -2$
    $y = x - 4$

21. $y = 6x + 14$
    $y = 8 + 3x$

22. $x = -5$
    $y = -4$

23. In the coordinate plane, the graphs of $x = 0$ and $y = 0$ have special names. What are these names?

24. GEOMETRY Sketch the graphs of these three equations on the same coordinate plane. Which two of the lines are parallel?

    a. $y = 2x + 3$ **b.** $y = x + 3$ **c.** $y = 2x - 1$

25. MAIL-ORDER SHOPPING The table shows the shipping charge for items purchased from a catalog, for the purchase of 1 to 6 items. Plot the data and describe the pattern. Is the pattern linear? Explain.

Number of items	1	2	3	4	5	6
Shipping charge	$2.19	$4.38	$6.57	$8.76	$10.95	$13.14

26. TEMPERATURE The average daily temperature of Oklahoma City (in degrees Fahrenheit) from January through August is given in the table. Decide how to write the data in ordered pairs so you can graph it. Then plot the data and describe the pattern. Is the pattern linear? Explain. (Source: *Statistical Abstract of the United States*)

Month	Jan.	Feb.	Mar.	Apr.	May	June	July	Aug.
Temperature	35.9	40.9	50.3	60.4	68.4	76.7	82.0	81.1

STANDARDIZED TEST PRACTICE

27. The graph of the equation $y = 5$ is ? .

    A a horizontal line   **B** a vertical line   **C** a slanted line   **D** not a line

28. The point (2, 5) lies on the graph of $y = cx + 1$. What is the value of c?

    A -2 **B** 0   **C** 1   **D** 2

EXPLORATION AND EXTENSION

PORTFOLIO

29. BUILDING YOUR PROJECT Users of your subway can either pay $1.25 per ride or buy a monthly pass for $25.00. Copy and complete the table. How many trips must a person make before the monthly pass becomes a better buy? Make a graph comparing rider costs with and without a pass. Add this to your billboard.

Number of rides	5	10	15	20	25	30	35
Cost with pass	$25.00	?	?	?	?	?	?
Cost without pass	$6.25	?	?	?	?	?	?

In Exercises 1–4, find the circumference and area of a circle with the given diameter or radius. Round your results to one decimal place. (12.1)

1. $d = 7$ ft
2. $d = 32$ in.
3. $r = 8$ cm
4. $r = 24$ yd

In Exercises 5–8, find the surface area and volume of the solid. (12.3–12.5)

5.
3 ft
3 ft
3 ft

6.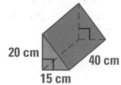
20 cm
40 cm
15 cm

7.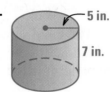
5 in.
7 in.

8.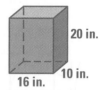
20 in.
16 in.
10 in.

In Exercises 9–11, find several solutions of the linear equation. Use a table of values to organize your results. (13.1)

9. $\frac{4}{5}x - 7 = y$
10. $-x - y = 12$
11. $6x - 8y = -4$

12. **BASKETBALL** In one season, Mia made 76% of the free throws she attempted. She made 19 free throws. How many did she attempt? (8.4)

CAREER Interview

DESIGN AND CONSTRUCTION MANAGER

Howard Haywood works for the Massachusetts Bay Transit Authority (MBTA), the oldest transit system in the United States. He is responsible for administering all MBTA construction, including tunnels, subway systems, rail systems, and bridges.

Q **What led you to this career?**
I began my career in general construction.

Q **What math do you use on your job?**
Basic math, algebra, geometry, and calculus. However, I feel that the most important math concepts I use are the problem solving skills such as the ability to decide what steps to take, what math operations to use, how to evaluate the results, and how to determine if the solution is reasonable.

Q **What would you like to tell students about school?**
When I was in fifth grade through junior high, I thought that I was a better reader than math student. Then one of my teachers explained to me that math is just like reading. It is a language that has logical steps and a logical progression. Once I tried to "read" math and comprehend it, I found it wasn't so hard.

Graphing Linear Equations

You can use a graphing calculator to graph equations. The example shows how to graph an equation on the TI-82 graphing calculator. The steps used with other graphing calculators are similar.

CALCULATOR TIP

The viewing window that you use in Step 1 is called the standard viewing window. Another way to get this window is to press ZOOM and select "6: ZStandard."

Example

Graph the line $y = 1.5x - 2$.

Solution

Step 1 Press WINDOW and enter the values shown for the viewing window. This gives the part of the coordinate plane that you will see on the screen.

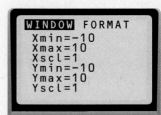

Step 2 Press Y= and enter the equation that you want to graph.

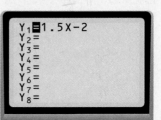

Step 3 Press GRAPH to graph the equation.

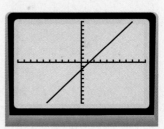

Exercises

In Exercises 1–4, graph the equation. Use the same viewing window that was used in the example.

1. $y = 2x - 3$ **2.** $y = 0.5x + 4$ **3.** $y = -x + 5$ **4.** $y = 0.75x - 2$

In Exercises 5 and 6, graph the equation using the given viewing window.

5. $y = 2x - 30$
   Xmin = -10 Ymin = -60
   Xmax = 10   Ymax = 10
   Xscl = 1   Yscl = 5

6. $y = -80x + 2000$
   Xmin = 0   Ymin = 0
   Xmax = 20   Ymax = 2100
   Xscl = 2   Yscl = 100

13.3 Exploring Intercepts of Graphs

What you should learn:

Goal 1 How to find intercepts of lines

Goal 2 How to use intercepts to sketch quick graphs

Why you should learn it:

You can use intercepts to solve real-life problems, such as finding the time and distance of a subway trip.

Goal 1 FINDING INTERCEPTS OF LINES

The **x-intercept** of a graph is the x-coordinate of the point where the graph crosses the x-axis. The **y-intercept** is the y-coordinate of the point where the graph crosses the y-axis. In the graph at the right, the x-intercept is **4** and the y-intercept is **−3**.

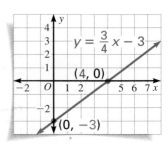

$y = \frac{3}{4}x - 3$

$(4, 0)$

$(0, -3)$

FINDING INTERCEPTS OF LINES

1. To find the x-intercept of a line, substitute $y = 0$ into the equation and solve for x.

2. To find the y-intercept of a line, substitute $x = 0$ into the equation and solve for y.

Example 1 Finding Intercepts of a Line

Find the intercepts of the graph of $y = \frac{3}{2}x - 3$.

Solution

First, find the x-intercept. Let $y = 0$ and solve for x.

$y = \frac{3}{2}x - 3$	Write original equation.
$0 = \frac{3}{2}x - 3$	Substitute 0 for y.
$3 = \frac{3}{2}x$	Add 3 to each side.
$2 = x$	Multiply each side by $\frac{2}{3}$.

The x-intercept is 2. The graph contains the point $(2, 0)$.

Next, find the y-intercept. Let $x = 0$ and solve for y.

$y = \frac{3}{2}x - 3$	Write original equation.
$y = \frac{3}{2}(0) - 3$	Substitute 0 for x.
$y = -3$	Solution: y is by itself.

The y-intercept is −3. The graph contains the point $(0, -3)$.

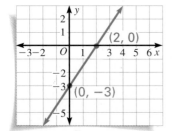

$(2, 0)$

$(0, -3)$

SKETCHING QUICK GRAPHS

To graph a line, you only need to know two points on the line.

SKETCHING A QUICK GRAPH OF A LINE

To sketch a quick graph of a linear equation, graph two solutions of the equation and draw a line through the points. You can use any two solutions, but the intercepts are often easy to find.

Example 2 **Sketching a Quick Graph**

You are riding the subway home. After x minutes, the number of miles from home, y, is given by $2x + 3y = 18$. Sketch the graph of this equation and interpret the intercepts.

REAL LIFE
Transportation

Solution

First, find the intercepts of the line.

To find the x-intercept, let $y = 0$ and solve for x.

$$2x + 3y = 18$$
$$2x + 3(0) = 18$$
$$2x = 18$$
$$x = 9$$

To find the y-intercept, let $x = 0$ and solve for y.

$$2x + 3y = 18$$
$$2(0) + 3y = 18$$
$$3y = 18$$
$$y = 6$$

The x-intercept is 9, so the point $(9, 0)$ is on the graph.

The y-intercept is 6, so the point $(0, 6)$ is on the graph.

Next, plot the intercepts and draw a line through them.

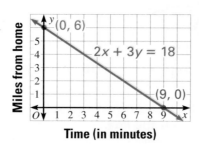

The y-intercept, **6**, means that you start the trip 6 mi from home.

The x-intercept, **9**, means that it takes you 9 min to get home.

ONGOING ASSESSMENT

Write About It

1. On a different subway trip home, y and x are related by the equation
$$y + \frac{3}{4}x = 12.$$

Sketch the graph of this equation and interpret the intercepts.

GUIDED PRACTICE

In Exercises 1–3, identify the intercepts of the graph.

1.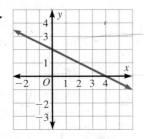

2.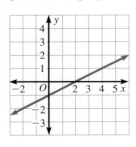

3.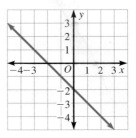

4. Find the x-intercept of $y = 2x - 1$. Explain each step.

5. Find the y-intercept of $5x + 3y = 9$. Explain each step.

In Exercises 6–9, find the intercepts of the line. Then sketch a quick graph.

6. $x + y = 5$ **7.** $x - y = 5$ **8.** $y = \frac{5}{4}x + 3$ **9.** $-7x + 3y = -21$

PRACTICE AND PROBLEM SOLVING

In Exercises 10–13, find the intercepts of the line.

10. $y = 4x + 4$ **11.** $y = -3x + 6$ **12.** $y = -\frac{2}{5}x - 2$ **13.** $y = \frac{5}{4}x - 5$

In Exercises 14–16, find the intercepts of the line given by the equation. Then match the equation with its graph.

A.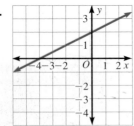

B.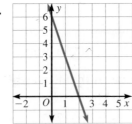

C.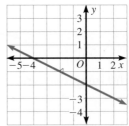

14. $y = \frac{1}{2}x + 2$ **15.** $y = -\frac{1}{2}x - 2$ **16.** $3x + y = 6$

In Exercises 17–24, sketch a quick graph of the line. Then create a table of values and compare the values with the points on the line.

17. $y = -3x + 6$ **18.** $y = 4x - 8$ **19.** $x - y = 1$ **20.** $x + y = -3$

21. $3x - 4y = 24$ **22.** $x + 5y = 5$ **23.** $y = -\frac{3}{2}x + 4$ **24.** $y = \frac{4}{3}x + 6$

TECHNOLOGY In Exercises 25 and 26, use a calculator to find the intercepts of the line. Round your results to two decimal places.

25. $y = -3.64x + 2.18$

26. $y = 1.85x - 14.302$

27. FUNDRAISING You and your friends are washing vehicles to raise money for a local charity organization. Working together, it takes you 10 min to wash a car and 15 min to wash a sport utility vehicle, minivan, or truck. The number of vehicles that you and your friends can wash in one hour is given by $10x + 15y = 60$. Sketch the graph of this equation. Interpret the intercepts.

28. BICYCLING You are riding your bike to school. After x minutes, the number of miles from school, y, is given by $y + \frac{1}{5}x = 2$. Sketch the graph of this equation and interpret the intercepts.

29. OPEN-ENDED PROBLEM Not every line has two distinct intercepts. Give two examples where the graph of a line has only one intercept.

 STANDARDIZED TEST PRACTICE

30. At which point does the graph of $y = 2x - 4$ cross the x-axis?

(A) $(0, -4)$ **(B)** $(0, 2)$ **(C)** $(2, 0)$ **(D)** $(-4, 0)$

31. Find the y-intercept of the line $y = 3x - 6$.

(A) -6 **(B)** -2 **(C)** 2 **(D)** 3

 EXPLORATION AND EXTENSION

PORTFOLIO

32. BUILDING YOUR PROJECT Suppose your engineer tells you that a standing passenger requires 4 ft^2 of floor space and a seated passenger requires 6 ft^2 of floor space. Each subway car in your system has a total of 400 ft^2 for passengers.

a. Graph the equation $4x + 6y = 400$.

b. Explain what each solution of the equation represents. What do the intercepts represent?

c. Decide which solution you will use in the design of your passenger car. Explain your choice and add the information to your billboard.

Cable Cars

READ About It

In addition to a large fleet of buses and streetcars, the San Francisco Municipal Railway still operates 40 historic cable cars. It costs $2.00 for each ride on a cable car. If you plan to ride often, however, you can buy a pass that covers an unlimited number of rides for one or more days. A three-day pass costs $10.

The cable cars are towed at a constant speed of 9.5 mi/h by underground cables made of steel. There are four cables in the city, with a total length of 56,900 ft. Each cable has to be replaced about three times a year. The four track brakes on a cable car wear out quickly because they are made of soft wood. The track brakes have to be replaced after about three days of use.

WRITE About It

1. You can use the equation $B = \frac{4}{3}d$ to estimate the number of track brakes, B, that a cable car needs for d days of operation. Explain what the equation means.

2. How would you change the equation from Exercise 1 to find the number of brakes needed by all of the cable cars for d days of operation?

3. The underground cable that your cable car uses has just been replaced. About how many track brakes will your car go through before the cable is replaced again? Write your answer as a sentence.

4. The equation $C = 2x$ represents the cost of riding a cable car x times. Graph the equation. What does the number 2 represent?

5. On the same coordinate plane as your graph from Exercise 4, graph the equation $C = 10$. This represents the cost of a three-day pass. Explain the significance of the point where the two lines intersect.

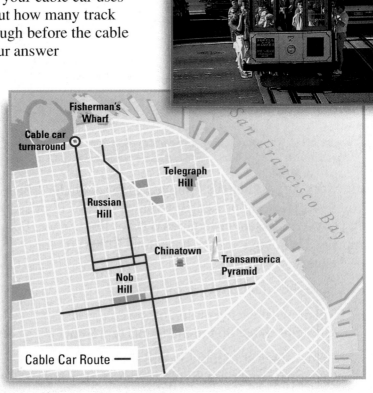

Fisherman's Wharf

Cable car turnaround

Telegraph Hill

Russian Hill

Chinatown

Transamerica Pyramid

Nob Hill

San Francisco Bay

Cable Car Route —

Exploring the Slope of a Line

On the geoboards shown below, the hypotenuse of each right triangle represents a line. You can use the length of the legs to describe the steepness of the line.

Materials Needed
- **geoboard**
- **rubber bands**

a. The line slopes up **2** units for each **3** units to the right.

b. The line slopes up **4** units for each **3** units to the right.

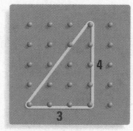

1. On your geoboard, make a line that slopes up 3 units for each 4 units to the right.

2. Look at the two lines shown above and the line you made in Exercise 1. Which of these three lines is the steepest?

3. Use the formula below to find the slope of each of the three lines in Exercise 2. Which line has the greatest slope?

$$Slope = \frac{\text{Number of units moved up}}{\text{Number of units moved to the right}}$$

4. Compare your answers to Exercises 2 and 3. What do you notice?

NOW TRY THESE

In Exercises 5–7, find the slope of each line.

5. The line slopes up 5 units for each 4 units to the right.

6. The line slopes up 4 units for each 5 units to the right.

7. The line slopes up 5 units for each 3 units to the right.

8. Which line in Exercises 5–7 is steepest? Which is least steep?

9. Which line in Exercises 5–7 has the greatest slope? Which has the smallest slope? Compare with your answers to Exercise 8.

13.4

Exploring Slope

What you should learn:

Goal 1 How to find the slope of a line

Goal 2 How to interpret the slope of a line

Why you should learn it:

You can use the slope of a line to solve real-life problems, such as describing the steepness of a hill or a staircase.

Goal 1 FINDING THE SLOPE OF A LINE

To find the slope of a line, choose two points (x_1, y_1) and (x_2, y_2) on the line. The **slope** of the line is the ratio of the *rise* (change in y) to the *run* (change in x).

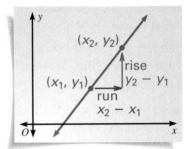

$$\text{Slope} = \frac{\text{Rise}}{\text{Run}} = \frac{y_2 - y_1}{x_2 - x_1}$$

The variable y_2 is read "y sub 2."

> **SLOPE OF A LINE**
>
> The slope m of the nonvertical line passing through the points (x_1, y_1) and (x_2, y_2) is $m = \dfrac{y_2 - y_1}{x_2 - x_1} = \dfrac{\text{Rise}}{\text{Run}}$.

Example 1 **Finding Slopes of Lines**

a. To find the slope of the line through $(1, 2)$ and $(3, 5)$, let $(1, 2)$ be (x_1, y_1), and let $(3, 5)$ be (x_2, y_2). Then the slope is

$$m = \frac{y_2 - y_1}{x_2 - x_1}$$

$$= \frac{5 - 2}{3 - 1}$$

$$= \frac{3}{2}.$$

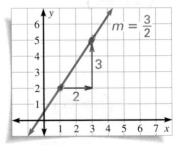

STUDY TIP

When you are using the formula for slope, it doesn't matter which point you represent with (x_1, y_1). In part (a) of Example 1, if you let $(3, 5)$ be (x_1, y_1), and let $(1, 2)$ be (x_2, y_2), you will obtain the same slope.

b. To find the slope of the line through $(-6, 5)$ and $(-3, 1)$, let $(-6, 5)$ be (x_1, y_1), and let $(-3, 1)$ be (x_2, y_2). Then the slope is

$$m = \frac{y_2 - y_1}{x_2 - x_1}$$

$$= \frac{1 - 5}{-3 - (-6)}$$

$$= \frac{-4}{3}$$

$$= -\frac{4}{3}.$$

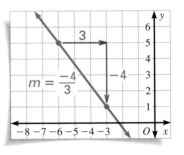

Goal 2 INTERPRETING SLOPE

Imagine that you are walking *to the right* on a line. A positive slope means you are walking uphill, a negative slope means you are walking downhill, and a zero slope means you are walking on level ground. (Slope is not defined for vertical lines.)

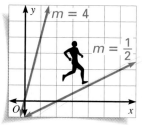

Positive slope

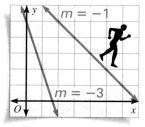

Negative slope

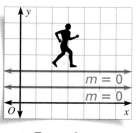

Zero slope

The slope of a line also tells you how steep the line is. A line with a slope of 4 is steeper than a line with a slope of $\frac{1}{2}$. Similarly, a line with a slope of -3 is steeper than a line with a slope of -1. If two lines have the same slope, then they are parallel.

Example 2 Comparing the Slopes of Two Lines

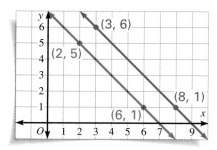

Find the slope of the **red line**.

$$m = \frac{y_2 - y_1}{x_2 - x_1}$$

$$= \frac{1 - 5}{6 - 2}$$

$$= \frac{-4}{4}$$

$$= -1$$

Find the slope of the **blue line**.

$$m = \frac{y_2 - y_1}{x_2 - x_1}$$

$$= \frac{1 - 6}{8 - 3}$$

$$= \frac{-5}{5}$$

$$= -1$$

Both lines have the same slope, $m = -1$. This means that they are parallel.

ONGOING ASSESSMENT

Write About It

A line includes the points $(-1, 1)$, $(0, 3)$, $(1, 5)$, $(2, 7)$, and $(3, 9)$.

1. Use two points to find the line's slope.

2. Use a different pair of points to find the line's slope.

3. Did you get the same result? Explain.

13.4 Exercises

GUIDED PRACTICE

In Exercises 1–3, find the slope of the line.

1.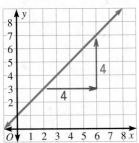

2.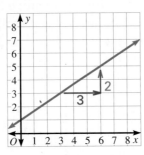

3.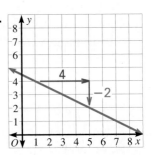

4. Find the slope of the line through $(-1, 3)$ and $(4, 2)$.

5. Sketch a line with a slope of 3 and another with a slope of 4. Which line is steeper?

PRACTICE AND PROBLEM SOLVING

In Exercises 6 and 7, the slopes of four lines are listed. Tell which of the lines is the steepest.

6. $m = \dfrac{5}{2}, m = 3, m = 0, m = 5$

7. $m = -1, m = -6, m = -4, m = -\dfrac{17}{4}$

In Exercises 8–10, find the slope of the line.

8.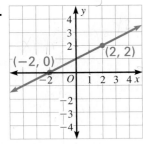

9.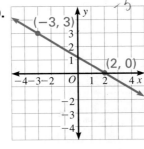

10.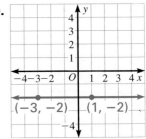

In Exercises 11–14, plot the points. Then find the slope of the line through the points.

11. $(2, 5), (0, 5)$ **12.** $(3, 4), (4, 3)$ **13.** $(1, -2), (-1, -6)$ **14.** $(0, -1), (1, -7)$

GEOMETRY In Exercises 15–18, find the slope of $\overleftrightarrow{AB}$ and the slope of $\overleftrightarrow{CD}$. Are the lines parallel? Explain.

15. $A(3, 3), B(1, -2), C(-4, 4), D(-3, -1)$ **16.** $A(1, 1), B(0, -2), C(-5, 1), D(-3, -2)$

17. $A(2, 3), B(0, -2), C(4, 3), D(6, 8)$ **18.** $A(-2, -2), B(2, 6), C(-1, -4), D(-5, 4)$

In Exercises 19–22, find the slope. (The figures may not be drawn to scale.)

19.

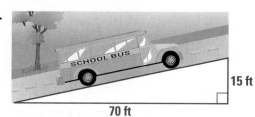

15 ft

70 ft

20.

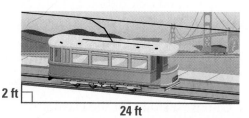

2 ft

24 ft

21.

40 m

180 m

22.

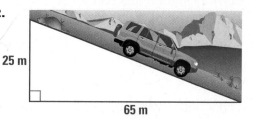

25 m

65 m

GEOMETRY In Exercises 23–25, find the slope of the hypotenuse. Use the Pythagorean Theorem, if necessary.

23.

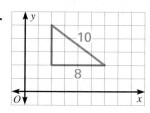

10

8

24.

(6, 5) $x_2 y_2$

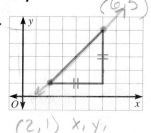

(2, 1) $x_1 y_1$

25.

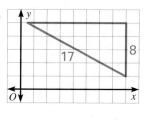

17

8

STAIRS In Exercises 26–28, find the slope of each set of stairs.

26.

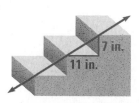

7 in.

11 in.

27.

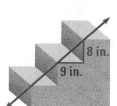

8 in.

9 in.

28.

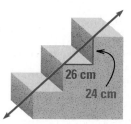

26 cm

24 cm

STANDARDIZED TEST PRACTICE

29. Find the slope of the line at the right.

Ⓐ −1   Ⓑ 1   Ⓒ 2   Ⓓ 4

30. Find the slope of the line passing through the points $(-3, 4)$ and $(2, -3)$.

Ⓐ $-\dfrac{7}{5}$ Ⓑ -1 Ⓒ $-\dfrac{5}{7}$ Ⓓ $\dfrac{1}{5}$

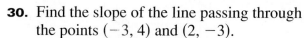

31. BUILDING YOUR PROJECT You need to plan an escalator to take passengers between a subway station and the street.

a. Find the slope of an escalator that has a vertical rise of 26 ft and a horizontal run of 50 ft.

b. Graph a line with a slope of 4 and a line with a slope of $\frac{1}{4}$. Do you think either of these would be a good slope for an escalator? Explain why or why not.

c. Choose a slope for the escalator that connects your subway station to street level. If the escalator has a vertical rise of 40 ft, what is its horizontal run?

d. Make a sketch of your escalator from part (c) and add it to your billboard.

Real Life...
Real Facts

Escalators The longest escalator in the London Underground has a length of 60 m, or 197 ft.

SPIRAL REVIEW

In Exercises 1–4, find the intercepts of the line. Then sketch a quick graph. (13.3)

1. $y = 4x + 12$ **2.** $y = -4x + 2$ **3.** $3y = 12 + 3x$ **4.** $2x + 3y = 6$

In Exercises 5–8, decide whether the number is *rational* or *irrational*. Explain. (9.2)

5. $\frac{2}{3}$ **6.** $\sqrt{7}$ **7.** 3.47 **8.** $\sqrt{\frac{64}{81}}$

In Exercises 9–12, find the least common multiple of the numbers. (6.4)

9. 24 and 36 **10.** 312 and 210 **11.** 111 and 55 **12.** 176 and 264

In Exercises 13–16, solve the percent equation. (8.4)

13. What is 18% of 32? **14.** 15 is 45% of what number?

15. 72 is what percent of 36? **16.** 17 is what percent of 40?

In Exercises 17–20, tell whether the numbers can be side lengths of a triangle. (9.8)

17. 12, 24, 30 **18.** 21, 26, 46

19. 13, 14, 29 **20.** 18, 18, 38

21. Use a scientific calculator or refer to the *Table of Trigonometric Ratios* on page 766. You are at an amusement park. You are 50 yd from the base of the observation tower. The angle of elevation to the top of the tower is 57°. How tall is the tower? (11.9)

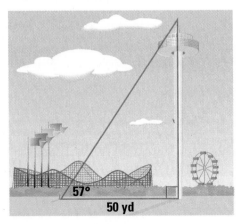

57°

50 yd

Take this test as you would take a test in class. The answers to the exercises are given in the back of the book.

MEASUREMENT In Exercises 1–3, use the equation $y = 28x$. The equation relates ounces, x, to grams, y. **(13.1)**

1. A sample of sodium chloride weighs 2 ounces. What is its measure in grams?

2. A notebook has a measure of 700 grams. What is its weight in ounces?

3. A rock has a measure of 1 kilogram (1000 grams). Does it weigh *more* or *less* than 1 pound (16 ounces)? Explain.

In Exercises 4–6, tell whether the ordered pair is a solution of the equation $3x + 4y = 28$. **(13.1)**

4. $(0, 7)$　　　　**5.** $\left(9, -\dfrac{1}{4}\right)$　　　　**6.** $(8, 1)$

In Exercises 7 and 8, use the equation $2x + 5y = 42$. **(13.2)**

7. Copy and complete the table at the right.

8. Use your table from Exercise 7 to sketch the graph of $2x + 5y = 42$.

x	1	6	11	16
y	?	?	?	?

In Exercises 9–11, find the intercepts of the line. **(13.3)**

9. $8x + 2y = 32$　　　　**10.** $4x + 5y = 20$　　　　**11.** $12x + 8y = 24$

In Exercises 12–15, find the slope of the line that passes through the points. **(13.4)**

12. $(2, 9), (4, 12)$　　**13.** $(5, 2), (3, 6)$　　**14.** $(7, -5), (-3, 2)$　　**15.** $(0, 7), (2, 10)$

16. Which of the lines in Exercises 12–15 are parallel? **(13.4)**

In Exercises 17–19, find the intercepts of the line given by the equation. Then match the equation with its graph. **(13.3)**

A.
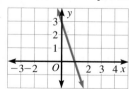

B.
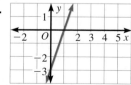

C.
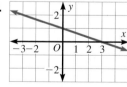

17. $y = 3x - 3$　　　　**18.** $3x + y = 3$　　　　**19.** $y = -\dfrac{1}{3}x + 1$

LAB 13.5

COOPERATIVE LEARNING

Exploring Slopes
and *y*-Intercepts

Part **A** COMPARING SLOPES OF LINES

Materials Needed
• **graphing calculator**

You can use a graphing calculator to discover properties of lines. Copy the table. Follow the directions below to complete the table.

Equation	$y = 2x - 3$	$y = 2x - 1$	$y = 2x + 3$
Coordinates of two points	(?, ?) (?, ?)	(?, ?) (?, ?)	(?, ?) (?, ?)
Slope	?	?	?

1. Graph the equation $y = 2x - 3$ on a graphing calculator. See page 627 for an explanation of how to use a graphing calculator to graph an equation. The graph should look similar to the one at the right.

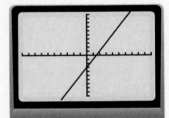

2. Press **TRACE**. You can use the ▶ and ◀ buttons to see the coordinates of different points on the line. Record the coordinates of two points. Round the coordinate values to the nearest hundredth.

3. Use the coordinates of the points to calculate the slope of the line. Round the result to the nearest integer. Record the slope in the table.

4. Repeat Exercises 1–3 for the equation $y = 2x - 1$.

5. Repeat Exercises 1–3 for the equation $y = 2x + 3$.

6. From the table, what do you notice about the slopes? How are they related to the equations? Write a conjecture that has the following form.

"The slope of the line $y = mx + b$ is . . . ."

Copy the table. Follow the directions below to complete the table.

Equation	$y = 2x + 3$	$y = -x + 3$	$y = \frac{1}{2}x + 3$
y-intercept	?	?	?

7. Enter the equations from the table in a graphing calculator, as shown at the right.

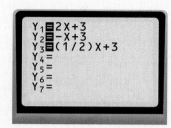

8. Graph the equations in the same viewing screen. The graphs should look similar to the ones shown at the right.

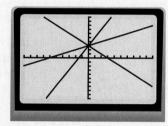

9. Use the calculator's trace feature to estimate the y-intercept of each line. How is the intercept related to each equation?

10. Use the results of Exercises 7–9 to write a conjecture about the y-intercept of the line $y = mx + b$.

NOW TRY THESE

In Exercises 11 and 12, use a graphing calculator to compare the graphs. What can you conclude?

11. $y = -x + 5$
$y = -x - 2$
$y = -x + 1$

12. $y = 2x - 4$
$y = x - 4$
$y = -\frac{1}{2}x - 4$

13. Without sketching the graph of $y = -x - 4$, find its slope and y-intercept. Then use a graphing calculator to check your answer.

13.5

The Slope-Intercept Form

What you should learn:

Goal 1 How to find the slope and *y*-intercept of a line from its equation

Goal 2 How to use the slope-intercept form to sketch a quick graph

Why you should learn it:

You can use the slope-intercept form of a line to solve real-life problems, such as finding the speed of a falling object.

Goal 1 USING THE SLOPE-INTERCEPT FORM

If the equation of a line is in the proper form, there is a quick way to find the line's slope and *y*-intercept. For instance, the line given by $y = 2x + 3$ has a slope of 2 and a *y*-intercept of 3.

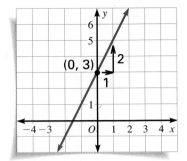

$$y = 2x + 3$$

Slope is 2.   *y*-intercept is 3.

THE SLOPE-INTERCEPT FORM OF THE EQUATION OF A LINE

The linear equation shown at the right is in **slope-intercept form**. The slope is *m*. The *y*-intercept is *b*.

$$y = mx + b$$

$$y = \square x + b$$

Example 1 Using the Slope-Intercept Form

Find the slope and *y*-intercept of each line.

a. $y = x - 4$ **b.** $y = -x + 2$

Solution

a. The line given by
$y = x - 4$
can be rewritten as
$y = 1x + (-4)$.

So, it has a slope of **1** and a *y*-intercept of **−4**.

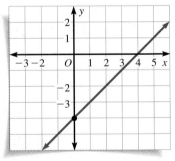

b. The line given by
$y = -x + 2$
can be rewritten as
$y = (-1)x + 2$.

So, it has a slope of **−1** and a *y*-intercept of **2**.

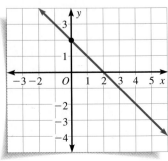

Example 2 Sketching a Quick Graph

To sketch a quick graph of $y = \frac{1}{2}x + 2$, follow these steps.

Step 1 The y-intercept is 2, so plot the point $(0, 2)$.

Step 2 The slope is $\frac{1}{2}$, so plot a second point by moving to the **right 2** units and **up 1** unit. Draw a line through the points.

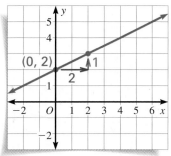

Step 3 You can check your result by plotting more points. To plot each new point, move **right 2** units and **up 1** unit.

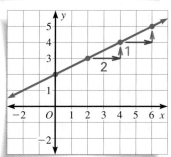

$y = -2x + 4$

Example 3 Sketching a Quick Graph

To sketch a quick graph of $2x + y = 4$, write the equation in slope-intercept form. Begin by solving the equation for y.

$$2x + y = 4 \qquad \text{Write original equation.}$$
$$y = 4 - 2x \qquad \text{Subtract 2x from each side.}$$
$$y = -2x + 4 \qquad \text{Rewrite in slope-intercept form.}$$

With the equation in slope-intercept form, you can see that the slope is -2 and the y-intercept is 4.

Since the y-intercept is 4, plot the point $(0, 4)$. The slope is -2, which equals $\frac{-2}{1}$. Plot a second point by moving to the **right 1** unit and **down 2** units. Draw a line through the points. You can check your line by drawing more points, as shown.

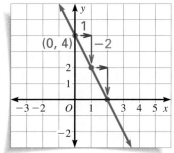

ONGOING ASSESSMENT

Talk About It

You are sketching a quick graph of a line with y-intercept $(0, 3)$. Explain how to find a second point on the line if the line has the given slope.

1. $m = \frac{2}{5}$

2. $m = 3$

3. $m = -\frac{2}{3}$

4. $m = 0$

1. **WRITING** Why do you think $y = mx + b$ is called the *slope-intercept form* of the equation of a line?

2. Explain how to write $3x + y = 5$ in slope-intercept form.

3. Which two of the equations below are equations of the line shown at the right?

   A. $y = 2x + 3$ **B.** $y = 2x - 3$ **C.** $y = -2x + 3$

   D. $y = -2x - 3$ **E.** $2x + y = 3$ **F.** $y - 2x = -3$

In Exercises 4–7, find the slope and *y*-intercept of the line. Then sketch a quick graph of the line.

4. $y = -4x + 5$ 5. $y = \frac{1}{4}x - 1$ 6. $-3x + y = 2$ 7. $2x + y = 8$

In Exercises 8–15, find the slope and *y*-intercept of the line. Then sketch a quick graph of the line.

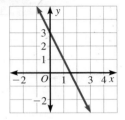

8. $y = x - 3$ 9. $y = -x + 3$ 10. $y = -\frac{2}{3}x + 2$ 11. $y = 3x$

12. $y - 4x = 5$ 13. $\frac{5}{2}x + y = 0$ 14. $2x + y = 1$ 15. $-2x + y = 3$

In Exercises 16–18, find the slope and *y*-intercept of the line. Then match the equation with its graph.

A. 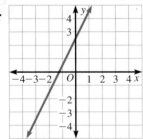   **B.** 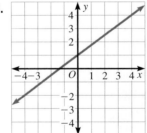   **C.**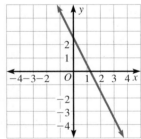

16. $y = -2x + \frac{5}{2}$ 17. $y = 2x + \frac{5}{2}$ 18. $y = \frac{3}{4}x + 1$

REASONING In Exercises 19 and 20, decide whether the statement is *true* or *false*. Explain your reasoning.

19. The line $y - 2x = 5$ has a slope of -2 and a y-intercept of 5.

20. The line $\frac{1}{4}x + y = 5$ has a slope of $-\frac{1}{4}$ and a y-intercept of 5.

PHYSICS **In Exercises 21 and 22, use the following information.**

An object is thrown straight down with an initial speed of 7 m/s. The speed of the object is given by the equation $y = 9.8x + 7$, where y represents the speed (in meters per second) and x represents the time (in seconds) after the object is released.

21. MAKING A TABLE Make a table showing the object's speed after 0, 1, 2, 3, and 4 s. How much does the speed increase every second?

22. Find the slope and y-intercept of the line $y = 9.8x + 7$. How is the slope related to the object's speed? How is the y-intercept related to the object's speed?

In Exercises 23–25, write the equation of the line in slope-intercept form.

23. 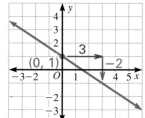   **24.** 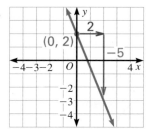   **25.**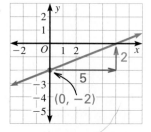

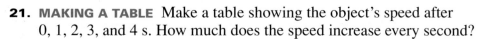

26. Which pair of points lie on the line $y = -\frac{1}{2}x + 3$?

   A $(4, 6), (-2, 3)$ **B** $(-2, 4), (4, 1)$ **C** $(2, 9), (-1, 3)$ **D** $(-1, 8), (3, 0)$

27. What is the slope of the line $-2x + y = \frac{1}{2}$?

   A -2 **B** $-\frac{1}{2}$ **C** $\frac{1}{2}$ **D** 2

EXPLORATION AND EXTENSION

28. TAXI FARES One taxi company's fare is given by the equation $y = 2.5x + 1.25$, where y represents the total fare (in dollars) and x represents the distance traveled (in miles).

  a. MAKING A TABLE Make a table of values showing what the fare will be after you ride 0, 1, 2, 3, 4, 5, and 6 mi.

  b. Graph the values in your table. How is the y-intercept related to the taxi fare? How is the slope related to the taxi fare?

Exploring Graphs of **Linear Equations**

In this investigation, you will work in small groups to collect and organize data.

Materials Needed
• graph paper
• measuring tape
• colored pencils or markers

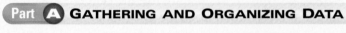

Part A GATHERING AND ORGANIZING DATA

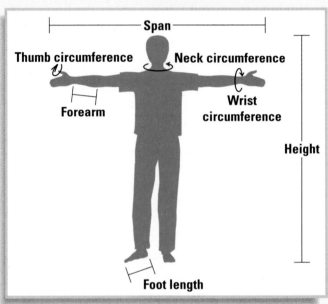

Span
Thumb circumference   Neck circumference
Forearm   Wrist circumference
Height
Foot length

1. Use a tape measure to take the measurements shown above (in inches). Use a table to record the data for each person in your group.

2. Copy your table and trade information with other groups. You need measurements for 8 to 12 people in all.

Measurement (in inches)	Person 1	Person 2
Span	?	?
Neck	?	?
Wrist	?	?
Thumb	?	?
Forearm	?	?
Foot	?	?
Height	?	?

3. For each person, write the following ordered pairs. Color the ordered pairs as shown.

   a. (Span, Height)   **b.** (Foot, Forearm)

   c. (Thumb, Wrist)   **d.** (Wrist, Neck)

4. Make a scatter plot of the points that your group collected. Use an entire sheet of graph paper and plot the points as accurately as possible. Make each point the same color as the ordered pair.

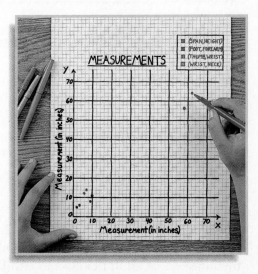

5. Describe any patterns you see in your scatter plot.

6. On your scatter plot, draw the lines $y = x$ and $y = 2x$.

   a. Which colors of ordered pairs tend to fall on or near the line $y = x$? What do these ordered pairs represent?

   b. Which colors of ordered pairs tend to fall on or near the line $y = 2x$? What do these ordered pairs represent?

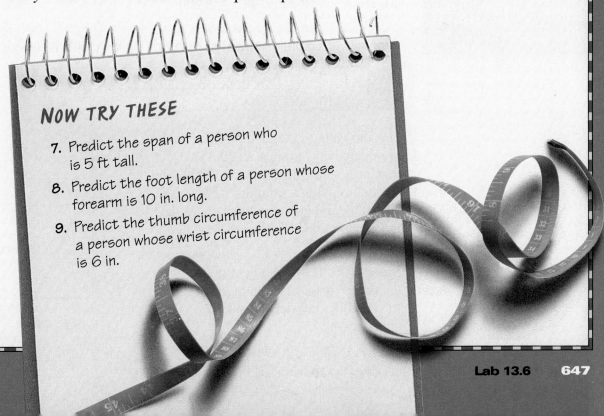

NOW TRY THESE

7. Predict the span of a person who is 5 ft tall.

8. Predict the foot length of a person whose forearm is 10 in. long.

9. Predict the thumb circumference of a person whose wrist circumference is 6 in.

Problem Solving with Linear Equations

What you should learn:

Goal 1 How to use graphs of linear equations to model real-life situations

Goal 2 How to use a scatter plot and a line of fit to make predictions from data

Why you should learn it:

You can use lines to model real-life data, such as the amount spent by tourists in Latin America.

Goal 1 USING GRAPHS OF LINEAR EQUATIONS

Throughout this chapter, you have studied several real-life situations that can be modeled with linear equations. Two quantities that can be modeled with a linear equation are said to have a **linear relationship**.

Example 1 Interpreting Linear Models

You are planning a dinner to raise $1200 for a volunteer fire department. You will charge $8 per adult and $4 per child. Write an equation that relates the numbers of adult tickets and child tickets you need to sell to meet your goal. Use a graph to analyze the situation.

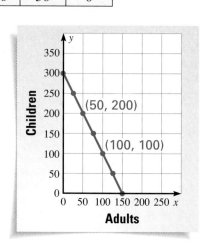
REAL LIFE
Ticket Prices

Solution

Write an algebraic model to represent the situation.

Verbal Model	$\$8 \cdot \dfrac{\text{Number}}{\text{of adults}} + \$4 \cdot \dfrac{\text{Number}}{\text{of children}} = \$1200$
Labels	Number of adults $= x$ Number of children $= y$
Algebraic Model	$8 \cdot x + 4 \cdot y = 1200$

One way to graph the equation is to first make a table of values.

x	0	25	50	75	100	125	150
y	300	250	200	150	100	50	0

Use the table to sketch a graph. There are many ways to raise $1200. For instance, since the point (50, 200) is on the line, it is a solution of the equation, and you could sell 50 adult tickets and 200 child tickets to meet your goal.

Since (100, 100) is on the line, another way to raise the money is to sell 100 adult tickets and 100 child tickets.

Example 2 **Using a Line of Fit**

The black points in this scatter plot show the population of Colorado from 1990 through 1995. The line of fit approximates the pattern of these data points. You can use the line to estimate the 1996 population, as shown.

The line appears to pass through the point (**1996, 3.85**), so you can estimate Colorado's 1996 population to be about 3.85 million.

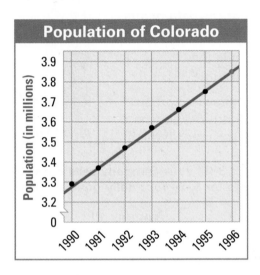

Population of Colorado

Colorado Population
The Colorado city with the most people is Denver. In 1994, Denver had a population of about 494,000.
(Source: U.S. Bureau of the Census)

Example 3 **Using a Scatter Plot**

The table shows the amount of money (in billions of dollars) spent by United States residents traveling in Latin America. Use a line of fit to estimate the amount spent in 1999.

Year	1991	1992	1993	1994	1995	1996
Amount	11.2	12.0	12.2	12.8	12.9	13.9

Solution

Make a scatter plot, as shown at the right. Since the relationship is almost linear, draw a line of fit.

Use the line of fit to estimate the amount spent in 1999. The line passes through the point (**1999, 15**). So, you can estimate that the amount spent in 1999 is about $15 billion.

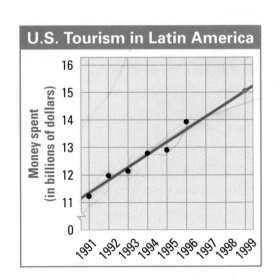

U.S. Tourism in Latin America

ONGOING ASSESSMENT

Talk About It
. . . .

Use the equation and graph in Example 1.

1. Find the *x*-intercept.

2. Find the *y*-intercept.

3. What do these numbers represent?

GUIDED PRACTICE

In Exercises 1 and 2, use the scatter plot, which shows the population of North Carolina in six different years. The line of fit approximates the pattern of the data points.
(Source: *Statistical Abstract of the United States*)

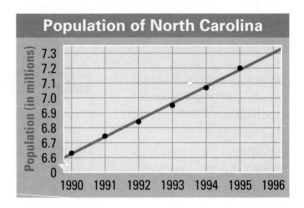

Population of North Carolina

1. In what year was the population 6.95 million?

2. An analyst used the data shown to predict a 1996 population of 7.4 million. Do you think the prediction was accurate? Explain.

RACKET SPORTS In Exercises 3–6, your company sells tennis rackets for $50 and racquetball rackets for $30. Your daily goal is $1800 in sales.

$$\$30 \cdot \begin{array}{c}\textbf{Number of}\\ \textbf{racquetball rackets}\end{array} + \$50 \cdot \begin{array}{c}\textbf{Number of}\\ \textbf{tennis rackets}\end{array} = \$1800$$

3. Write an algebraic model to represent the verbal model shown above.

4. Find several solutions of the algebraic model you wrote in Exercise 3. Organize the solutions in a table.

5. Sketch a graph of your data from Exercise 4.

6. Interpret the intercepts of the graph in terms of racket sales.

PRACTICE AND PROBLEM SOLVING

7. **CANS** From 1993 through 1996, the number of cans made from one pound of aluminum is shown in the graph at the right.

   a. Use the line of fit to estimate the number of cans made from one pound of aluminum in 1998.

   b. **OPEN-ENDED PROBLEM** Do you think the pattern described by the line will continue for 50 more years? Explain.

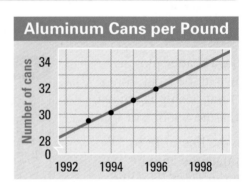

Aluminum Cans per Pound

8. **FLOWERS** Your class is selling flowers. Your profit is $1.50 on each carnation you sell and $3.00 on each rose. You want to raise $600.

   a. Write a verbal model and an algebraic model of the situation.

   b. Create a table of values and use it to graph the algebraic model.

   c. Interpret the intercepts of the graph in terms of flower sales.

9. CAULIFLOWER The table gives the average amount of cauliflower (in pounds) consumed by each American in five different years. Use a line of fit to estimate the amount for 1996.

Year	1990	1991	1992	1993	1994
Cauliflower	2.2	2.0	1.8	1.7	1.4

10. POTATOES The table gives the average amount of potatoes (in pounds) consumed by each American in four different years. Use a line of fit to estimate the amount for 1996.

Year	1991	1992	1993	1994
Potatoes	130	132	137	141

11. BASEBALL The table gives the number of people (in millions) who attended regular season American League baseball games from 1987 through 1993. Use a scatter plot to estimate the 1995 attendance.

Year	1987	1988	1989	1990	1991	1992	1993
Attendance	27.3	28.5	29.8	30.3	32.1	31.8	33.3

12. You weave wall hangings. You sell small ones for $20 and large ones for $40. Your goal is to make $800. Let x represent the number of small wall hangings you sell, and let y represent the number of large wall hangings you sell. Which equation models the situation?

A $40x + 20y = 800$ **B** $20x + 40y = 800$

C $800x - 40y = 20$ **D** $40 + 20y = 800x$

EXPLORATION AND EXTENSION

13. SUBWAY PUZZLE Hidden in the graph at the right are eight different cities in the United States that have subways. Make a copy of the puzzle or use tracing paper. Find as many of the cities as you can. For each city you find, draw a line through the centers of the letters in its name. Find the slope and y-intercept of the line for each city.

13.7

Graphs of Linear Inequalities

What you should learn:

Goal 1 How to check whether an ordered pair is a solution of a linear inequality

Goal 2 How to sketch the graph of a linear inequality

Why you should learn it:

You can use graphs of linear inequalities to solve real-life problems, such as analyzing strategies for running a marathon.

Goal 1 SOLUTIONS OF LINEAR INEQUALITIES

In this lesson, you will study **linear inequalities** in x and y. Here are some examples.

$$y < 2x \qquad y \le -3x + 4 \qquad y > x + 5 \qquad y \ge x - 3$$

An ordered pair (x, y) is a **solution of a linear inequality** if the inequality is true when the values of x and y are substituted into the inequality. For instance, $(1, 7)$ is a solution of $y > x + 5$ because $7 > 1 + 5$ is a true statement.

LESSON INVESTIGATION

COOPERATIVE LEARNING

Investigating Graphs of Linear Inequalities

GROUP ACTIVITY Sketch the graph of the line $y = x - 2$. Then draw several points above the line and below the line. Test each point and circle the ones that are solutions of the inequality $y > x - 2$. What do you notice?

In the investigation, you may have discovered that all solutions of $y > x - 2$ lie on the same side of the line $y = x - 2$. The inequality $y > x - 2$ is graphed below. The dashed line is the graph of the equation $y = x - 2$.

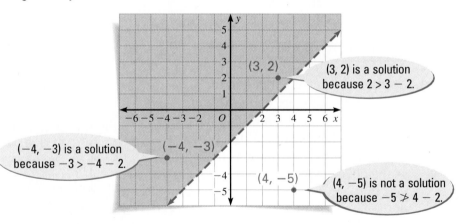

The shaded **half plane** represents all solutions of $y > x - 2$. In general, the graph of any linear inequality is a half plane.

The dashed line indicates that points on the line are *not* solutions. A solid line would indicate that points on the line *are* solutions.

GRAPH OF A LINEAR INEQUALITY

1. Replace the inequality symbol with "=" and graph the equation. Decide whether the line should be dashed (>, <) or solid (≥, ≤).
2. Test points above and below the line to decide which half plane to shade.

Example 1 **Graphing a Linear Inequality**

REAL LIFE
Fundraising

In Example 1 on page 648, the linear model $8x + 4y = 1200$ represented the different ways that you can sell \$8 adult tickets and \$4 child tickets to earn \$1200 at a fundraising dinner. Sketch the graph of $8x + 4y \geq 1200$.

Solution

First, graph the equation

$$8x + 4y = 1200.$$

Because the original inequality uses the symbol ≥, the line should be solid, not dashed.

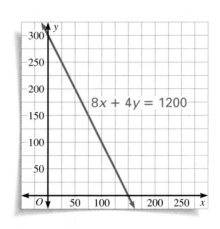

Choose the point (100, 50) below the line. It is not a solution because

$$8(100) + 4(50) = 1000 \neq 1200.$$

Choose the point (150, 200) above the line. It is a solution because

$$8(150) + 4(200) = 2000 \geq 1200.$$

Every point on or above the line represents a solution, so shade the half plane above the line.

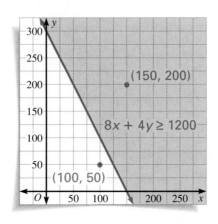

ONGOING ASSESSMENT

Talk About It
....

1. Discuss what the solutions of the inequality in Example 1 represent. If you sold the number of tickets represented by a solution, did you meet your fundraising goal?

GUIDED PRACTICE

In Exercises 1–4, use the graph of $y > 2x - 4$ at the right.

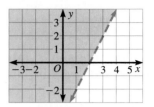

1. Is $(2, 3)$ a solution?

2. Is $(3, 2)$ a solution?

3. Name three other solutions of the inequality.

4. Find the slope and y-intercept of the dashed line.

In Exercises 5–8, does the inequality's graph use a solid or dashed line?

5. $x + y \geq 10$ **6.** $3x + 7y > 42$ **7.** $12x - 17y < 200$ **8.** $-9x + 20y \leq 150$

In Exercises 9–12, sketch the graph of the inequality.

9. $y \leq x + 3$ **10.** $y \geq \frac{1}{2}x - 1$ **11.** $x - y > 2$ **12.** $x > -2$

PRACTICE AND PROBLEM SOLVING

In Exercises 13–16, is the ordered pair a solution of $4x + 6y \leq 48$? Explain.

13. $(5, 5)$ **14.** $(10, -2)$ **15.** $(-2, 10)$ **16.** $(6, 4)$

In Exercises 17–19, match the inequality with its graph.

A. 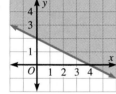   **B.** 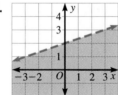   **C.**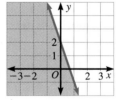

17. $y < \frac{1}{3}x + 2$ **18.** $-3x - y \geq -2$ **19.** $x + 2y \geq 4$

In Exercises 20–23, graph the inequality. Then list several solutions.

20. $y \leq \frac{1}{4}x + 1$ **21.** $y > -2x - 2$ **22.** $x + y < 25$ **23.** $4x + 3y \geq 9$

In Exercises 24 and 25, use the following statement.

The sum of twice a number and five times another number is less than 30.

24. Which of the following inequalities represents the sentence?

A. $7y < 30$ **B.** $2x + 5y < 30$ **C.** $2x + 5y > 30$ **D.** $2x + 5x < 30$

25. Graph the inequality from Exercise 24. Then list several solutions.

MARATHONS **In Exercises 26–29, use the following information.**

A marathon is a long-distance race that covers 26.2 mi. You are running in a marathon. To finish the marathon, you realize that you must walk part of the way. Let x represent the number of miles you walk and let y represent the number of miles you run.

26. You're not sure you can finish the marathon. Which of the following inequalities best describes your situation? Explain.

    A. $x + y > 26.2$ **B.** $x + y \geq 26.2$

    C. $x + y \leq 26.2$ **D.** $x + y < 26.2$

27. Sketch a graph of the correct inequality in Exercise 26.

28. Which of the inequalities in Exercise 26 best describes your situation if you are sure that you cannot finish the marathon?

29. **WRITING** Write a real-life interpretation of the other two inequalities in Exercise 26.

David Collins has run 14 marathons. He is blind, so he runs with a guide.

STANDARDIZED TEST PRACTICE

30. Which inequality matches the graph at the right?

    A $2x + y \geq 2$ **B** $2x - y \leq 2$

    C $-2x - y \geq 2$ **D** $-2x + y \geq 2$

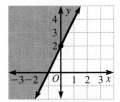

EXPLORATION AND EXTENSION

PORTFOLIO

31. **BUILDING YOUR PROJECT** There are parking lots at two locations where commuters can park to ride the subway into the city. Location A charges \$1/h for parking, and the subway fare from there is \$2.50. Location B charges \$1.25/h for parking, and the subway fare is \$1.50. If you park for h hours, the total cost for parking at and riding from each location is:

    Cost for location $A = h + 2.5$

    Cost for location $B = 1.25h + 1.5$

    Solve the inequality $h + 2.5 < 1.25h + 1.5$. Explain what the answer represents. Use the answer to write an advertisement for one of the parking lots.

13.8

The Distance and Midpoint Formulas

What you should learn:

Goal 1 How to find the distance between two points

Goal 2 How to find the midpoint of a line segment

Why you should learn it:

You can use the distance and midpoint formulas to solve real-life problems, such as finding a location for a telephone pole.

Goal 1 USING THE DISTANCE FORMULA

Suppose you are asked to find the distance between the points $A(1, 3)$ and $B(5, 6)$. How can you do it? One way is to draw a right triangle that has the line segment $\overline{AB}$ as its hypotenuse. You can find the length of $\overline{AB}$ as follows.

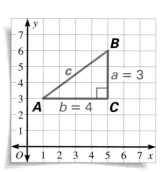

$c^2 = a^2 + b^2$	Use the Pythagorean Theorem.
$c^2 = 3^2 + 4^2$	Substitute for a and b.
$c^2 = 25$	Simplify.
$c = 5$	Choose the positive square root.

By performing this process with two general points (x_1, y_1) and (x_2, y_2), you can obtain the **Distance Formula**.

THE DISTANCE FORMULA

The distance, d, between the points (x_1, y_1) and (x_2, y_2) is

$$d = \sqrt{(x_2 - x_1)^2 + (y_2 - y_1)^2}.$$

Example 1 The Distance Between Two Points

Find the distance between $(1, 6)$ and $(5, 1)$.

Solution

$$d = \sqrt{(x_2 - x_1)^2 + (y_2 - y_1)^2}$$

$$= \sqrt{(5 - 1)^2 + (1 - 6)^2}$$

$$= \sqrt{4^2 + (-5)^2}$$

$$= \sqrt{41}$$

$$\approx 6.4$$

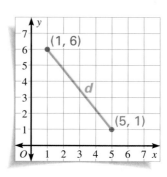

The distance between the points is about 6.4 units.

TOOLBOX

Square Roots and the Pythagorean Theorem, page 755

Goal 2 USING THE MIDPOINT FORMULA

The **midpoint** of a line segment $\overline{AB}$ is the point on the segment that is halfway between A and B.

LESSON INVESTIGATION

Investigating Midpoints

GROUP ACTIVITY Draw $\overline{AB}$ on graph paper. Find its midpoint. How is the midpoint's *x*-coordinate related to the *x*-coordinates of the two endpoints? How are the *y*-coordinates related?

  a. $A(1, 2)$, $B(5, 6)$ **b.** $A(0, 3)$, $B(6, 5)$ **c.** $A(2, 1)$, $B(-4, 3)$

In general, how can you find the coordinates of a midpoint?

Telephone Poles

Workers can locate the spot for a new utility pole by using a handheld computer with a GPS (Global Positioning System) receiver.

THE MIDPOINT FORMULA

The midpoint of the segment between (x_1, y_1) and (x_2, y_2) is

$$\left(\frac{x_1 + x_2}{2}, \frac{y_1 + y_2}{2} \right).$$

Example 2   Using the Midpoint Formula

You work for a telephone company. You want to find the coordinates of a telephone pole that will be halfway between two other poles, as shown at the right. Describe the location of the middle pole. (The units are in feet.)

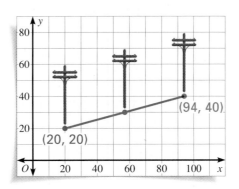

(94, 40)

(20, 20)

Solution

Let $(x_1, y_1) = (20, 20)$ and $(x_2, y_2) = (94, 40)$.

$$\text{Midpoint} = \left(\frac{x_1 + x_2}{2}, \frac{y_1 + y_2}{2} \right) \qquad \text{Use the Midpoint Formula.}$$

$$= \left(\frac{20 + 94}{2}, \frac{20 + 40}{2} \right) \qquad \text{Substitute for } x_1, x_2, y_1, \text{ and } y_2.$$

$$= (57, 30) \qquad \text{Simplify.}$$

The coordinates of the middle pole are $(57, 30)$.

ONGOING ASSESSMENT

Write About It

1. In Example 2, find the distance between the middle pole and each of the other poles.

2. Compare the two distances. Are they the same? Should they be the same? Explain.

13.8 Exercises

Extra Practice, page 739

GUIDED PRACTICE

In Exercises 1 and 2, find the distance between the points. Then find the midpoint of the segment that connects the points.

1. $(5, 4), (2, 0)$

2. $(-1, -3), (-1, -7)$

GEOMETRY **In Exercises 3 and 4, use the figure at the right.**

3. Find the perimeter of the polygon.

4. Show that the diagonals of the polygon have the same midpoint.

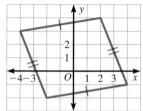

PRACTICE AND PROBLEM SOLVING

In Exercises 5–7, use the graph to estimate the distance between the points. Then use the Distance Formula to check your estimate.

5.
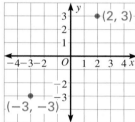

6.
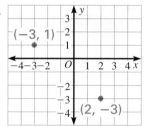

7.
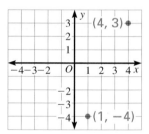

In Exercises 8–10, use the graph to estimate the midpoint of the segment. Then use the Midpoint Formula to check your estimate.

8.
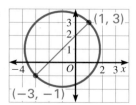

9.
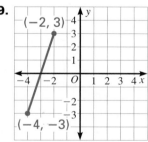

10.
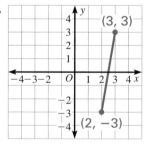

GEOMETRY **In Exercises 11–13, the labeled points are the endpoints of a diameter of the circle. Use the Midpoint Formula and the Distance Formula to find the center and the diameter of the circle.**

11.
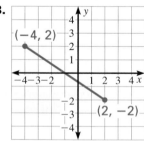

12.
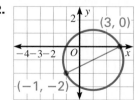

13.
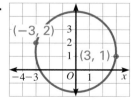

658   **Chapter 13** *Exploring Linear Equations*

In Exercises 14 and 15, the expression represents the distance between two points. What are the points?

14. $\sqrt{(5-3)^2 + (6-1)^2}$

15. $\sqrt{(0-4)^2 + (-8+2)^2}$

16. **UTILITIES** Two telephone poles are located at (10, 15) and (80, 55). Find the coordinates of a pole that will be halfway between them.

17. **PLANNING A TRIP** You live in Nashville, Tennessee, and are planning a trip to Wichita, Kansas. The latitude-longitude coordinates of each city are shown in the map at the right. You are planning a stop halfway between the two cities. Estimate the latitude-longitude coordinates of the halfway point.

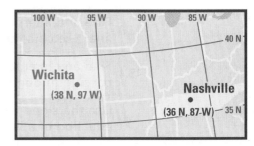

STANDARDIZED TEST PRACTICE

In Exercises 18 and 19, use the figure at the right.

18. Find the midpoint of the line segment.

   A (1, 2)   **B** $\left(-\dfrac{1}{2}, 0\right)$ **C** $\left(0, -\dfrac{1}{2}\right)$ **D** $\left(0, \dfrac{1}{2}\right)$

19. Which number best represents the distance between the points?

   A 6   **B** 7   **C** 8   **D** 9

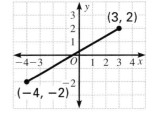

EXPLORATION AND EXTENSION

20. **COMMUNICATING ABOUT MATHEMATICS** Suppose you are walking along Columbus Avenue in San Francisco. You follow the route shown in red from the cable car turnaround to the Transamerica Pyramid. Find the midpoint of the route and explain how you found it. What landmark is closest to the midpoint? (For more information about the cable cars in San Francisco, see page 632.)

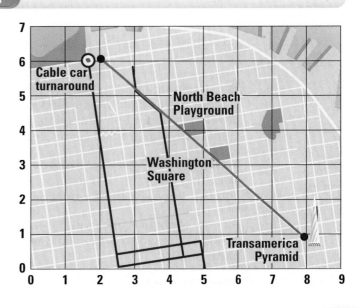

WHAT *did you learn?*

WHY *did you learn it?*

Skills	13.1	Find solutions of a linear equation in two variables.	Compare measurements that have different units.
	13.2	Use a table of values to graph a line. Graph horizontal and vertical lines.	Visualize the solutions of real-world linear equations.
	13.3	Find and interpret the intercepts of a line. Sketch a quick graph of the line.	Understand the real-life meaning of a graph.
	13.4	Find and interpret the slope of the line passing through two points.	Describe the steepness of a line, hill, or staircase.
	13.5	Use the slope-intercept form of the equation of a line to sketch a graph.	Sketch real-life graphs quickly, without plotting many points.
	13.6	Use a line of fit to model a linear relationship.	Recognize trends and make predictions.
	13.7	Sketch a graph of the solutions of a linear inequality.	Visualize limits in real-life situations.
	13.8	Find the distance between two points. Find the midpoint of a line segment.	Find distances and describe locations.
Strategies	13.1–13.2	Make a list.	Identify relationships between variables in real life.
	13.2–13.8	Use a graph.	Gain a visual understanding of real-life equations and inequalities.
Using Data	13.6	Draw a line of fit.	Use a scatter plot to make predictions.

HOW *does it fit in the bigger picture of mathematics?*

The combination of algebra (equations) and geometry (graphs) that you studied in this chapter is called *analytic geometry*. Analytic geometry was developed about 350 years ago, and it has proved to be a very useful way to study both algebra and geometry.

In this chapter, you saw that you can learn a lot about a linear equation by sketching its graph. For instance, from the graph you can find the intercepts and the slope—both of which have important real-life interpretations.

As you continue your study of mathematics, remember that the old saying "a picture is worth a thousand words" applies to algebra as well as to other parts of life.

VOCABULARY

- **linear equation** (p. 618)
- **x-intercept** (p. 628)
- **y-intercept** (p. 628)
- **slope** (p. 634)
- **slope-intercept form** (p. 642)
- **linear relationship** (p. 648)
- **linear inequality** (p. 652)
- **solution of a linear inequality** (p. 652)
- **half plane** (p. 652)
- **Distance Formula** (p. 656)
- **midpoint** (p. 657)

13.1 LINEAR EQUATIONS IN TWO VARIABLES

Example   You can find several solutions of $2x - y = 3$.

x-value	Substitute for x	Solve for y	Solution
$x = -1$	$2(-1) - y = 3$	$y = -5$	$(-1, -5)$
$x = 0$	$2(0) - y = 3$	$y = -3$	$(0, -3)$
$x = 1$	$2(1) - y = 3$	$y = -1$	$(1, -1)$
$x = 2$	$2(2) - y = 3$	$y = 1$	$(2, 1)$

You can organize your results in a table.

x	−1	0	1	2
y	−5	−3	−1	1

In Exercises 1–4, find several solutions of the linear equation. Use a table of values to organize your results.

[handwritten: y = 6x + 16]   *[handwritten: y = 3x − 8]*

1. $y = -4x + 6$
2. $6x + y = 16$
3. $3x - y = 8$
4. $y = 5x - 7$

5. **VALET PARKING** For parking cars, Amy earns $10 plus tips. She earns a $2 tip for each car she parks. You can model her income in dollars, y, by the equation $y = 2x + 10$, where x is the number of cars she parks. Make a table that shows her income when she parks from 5 to 10 cars.

13.2 EXPLORING GRAPHS OF LINEAR EQUATIONS

Example   Sketch the graph of $y = 3x - 4$.

Solution   First make a table of values.

x	y	Solution
0	−4	$(0, -4)$
1	−1	$(1, -1)$
2	2	$(2, 2)$

Then plot the ordered pairs and draw a line through the points.

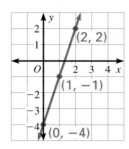

In Exercises 6–9, sketch the graph of the equation.

6. $y = 4x - 5$
7. $3x - y = 10$
8. $x = 2$
9. $y = -3$

13.3 EXPLORING INTERCEPTS OF GRAPHS

Example Find the *x*-intercept of the line $3x + 4y = 24$.

Solution To find the *x*-intercept, let $y = 0$ and solve for *x*.

$3x + 4y = 24$	Write original equation.
$3x + 4(0) = 24$	Substitute 0 for *y*.
$3x = 24$	Simplify.
$x = 8$	Divide both sides by 3.

The *x*-intercept is 8, so the point $(8, 0)$ is on the graph.

10. Find the *y*-intercept of $3x + 4y = 24$. Then sketch a quick graph by plotting the intercepts and drawing a line through them.

In Exercises 11–14, find the intercepts of the line. Then sketch a quick graph.

11. $5x - y = 10$ **12.** $y = -8x + 2$ **13.** $y = 4 + 3x$ **14.** $6x - 7 = -y$

13.4 EXPLORING SLOPE

Example Find the slope of the line through the points $(0, 1)$ and $(5, 4)$.

Solution Let $(0, 1)$ be (x_1, y_1) and let $(5, 4)$ be (x_2, y_2).

$$m = \frac{y_2 - y_1}{x_2 - x_1} = \frac{4 - 1}{5 - 0} = \frac{3}{5}$$

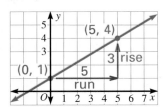

In Exercises 15–18, plot the line through the points and find its slope.

15. $(4, 9), (6, 3)$ **16.** $(1, 2), (8, 1)$ **17.** $(3, 5), (7, -2)$ **18.** $(-8, 6), (-1, -2)$

13.5 THE SLOPE-INTERCEPT FORM

Example Sketch a quick graph of the line $y = \frac{2}{5}x + 1$.

Solution The *y*-intercept is **1**, so plot the point $(0, 1)$.

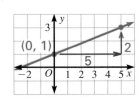

Since the slope is $\frac{2}{5}$, move to the **right 5** and **up 2** to plot a second point. Then draw a line through the two points.

In Exercises 19–22, find the slope and *y*-intercept. Then sketch the line.

19. $y = -3x - 5$ **20.** $y = 4 + 7x$ **21.** $9x + 3 = y$ **22.** $4x + y = 3$

13.6 PROBLEM SOLVING WITH LINEAR EQUATIONS

Example You want to buy tulips for $3 each and roses for $6 each. You have $60. You can use an algebraic model to find the assortments of tulips and roses you can buy.

Verbal Model $\$3 \cdot \dfrac{\text{Number}}{\text{of tulips}} + \$6 \cdot \dfrac{\text{Number}}{\text{of roses}} = \$60$

Labels Number of tulips $= x$
Number of roses $= y$

Some solutions are shown in the table below.

x	0	2	4	6
y	10	9	8	7

One solution is **6** tulips and **7** roses.

Algebraic Model $3x + 6y = 60$

23. You want to raise $600. You plan to sell subs for $3 each and pizzas for $4 each. Graph a linear equation and list several solutions.

13.7 GRAPHS OF LINEAR INEQUALITIES

Example Graph the inequality $y < 3x$.

Solution First graph the line $y = 3x$. Use a dashed line.

Since $6 \not< 3(0)$, the point $(0, 6)$ is not a solution of $y < 3x$. Shade the half plane that does not include $(0, 6)$.

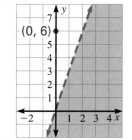

24. Graph $y < 8x - 12$. Is $(4, 10)$ a solution? Explain.

25. Graph $2x - y \geq -16$. Then list several solutions.

13.8 THE DISTANCE AND MIDPOINT FORMULAS

Example Find the distance between $(3, 4)$ and $(5, 8)$. Then find the midpoint of the segment that connects the two points.

Solution Distance $= \sqrt{(x_2 - x_1)^2 + (y_2 - y_1)^2}$

$= \sqrt{(5 - 3)^2 + (8 - 4)^2}$

$= \sqrt{20}$

The distance is $\sqrt{20}$ units.

Midpoint $= \left(\dfrac{x_1 + x_2}{2}, \dfrac{y_1 + y_2}{2} \right)$

$= \left(\dfrac{3 + 5}{2}, \dfrac{4 + 8}{2} \right)$

$= (4, 6)$

The midpoint is $(4, 6)$.

In Exercises 26–29, find the distance between the points. Then find the midpoint of the segment that connects the points.

26. $(5, 7), (8, 12)$ **27.** $(-2, 0), (1, 9)$ **28.** $(-3, 2), (6, 4)$ **29.** $(1, -7), (-5, -6)$

In Exercises 1–3, use the equation 2x + y = 6.

1. Complete the table of values at the right.

x	−3	−2	−1	0	1	2	3
y	?	?	?	?	?	?	?

2. Use your table of values to find the intercepts of the line.

3. Sketch a quick graph of the line.

In Exercises 4–7, tell whether the point is a solution of x + 3y = 16.

4. $(8, 3)$ **5.** $(1, 5)$ **6.** $(-2, 6)$ **7.** $(5, 3)$

In Exercises 8–10, plot the line through the points and find its slope.

8. $(3, 7)$ and $(2, 4)$ **9.** $(4, 6)$ and $(3, -2)$ **10.** $(1, 2)$ and $(-5, 4)$

11. Find the slope and y-intercept of $y = -2x + 4$. Then sketch the line.

In Exercises 12–14, sketch the line having the given intercepts.

12. x-intercept: -2
y-intercept: 3

13. x-intercept: 3
y-intercept: -4

14. x-intercept: 5
y-intercept: 7

In Exercises 15–17, write an equation of the line in slope-intercept form.

15.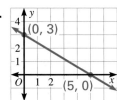

16.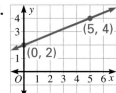

17.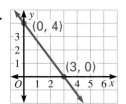

In Exercises 18–20, graph the inequality. Then list three solutions.

18. $y < 7x$ **19.** $y \geq 2x + 2$ **20.** $y > 5x - 7$

In Exercises 21–23, find the distance between the points. Then find the midpoint of the segment that connects the points.

21. $(-3, -2)$ and $(5, 6)$ **22.** $(1, 5)$ and $(8, 0)$ **23.** $(4, -9)$ and $(-1, -7)$

CARS **In Exercises 24 and 25, use the graph at the right. It shows the speed versus time of a car that accelerates from rest.**

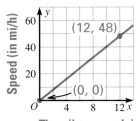

24. Let x represent the time (in seconds) and let y represent the speed (in miles per hour). Which of the following models is correct?

A. $y = 48x$ **B.** $y = 12x$ **C.** $y = 4x$

25. Use the graph to estimate the speed of the car after 8 s. Then use the model you chose in Exercise 24 to find the answer.

1. For 1990 through 1994, the amount A (in gallons) of skim milk consumed per person in the United States can be modeled by the linear equation

$$A = 0.17t + 2.6$$

where $t = 0$ represents 1990, $t = 1$ represents 1991, and so on. Which ordered pair is *not* described by the equation?

   Ⓐ (0, 2.77)   Ⓑ (2, 2.94)
   Ⓒ (3, 3.11)   Ⓓ (4, 3.28)

2. The table below shows the number of hits you had playing softball for each season from 1993 through 1997, where $t = 3$ represents 1993. Which linear equation represents the data?

t	3	4	5	6	7
N	21	25	29	33	37

   Ⓐ $N = 2t + 23$ Ⓑ $N = 3t + 12$
   Ⓒ $N = 4t + 9$ Ⓓ $N = 5t + 6$

3. Which statement is *false* about the graph of the following equation?

$$y = -\frac{1}{2}x + 3$$

   Ⓐ The line's x-intercept is 3.
   Ⓑ The line has a negative slope.
   Ⓒ The line's y-intercept is 3.
   Ⓓ The line has a slope of $-\frac{1}{2}$.

4. If you plot $(-1, 2)$ and $(3, -4)$ in a coordinate plane, about how far apart will the two points be?

   Ⓐ 4 units   Ⓑ 4.47 units
   Ⓒ 6.32 units   Ⓓ 7.21 units

In Questions 5–7, use the following information. Your class is selling oranges and apples to raise money for a field trip. Oranges sell for $6 per bag and apples sell for $5 per bag.

5. Your class wants to raise $900. Which linear equation represents the situation?

   Ⓐ $6x - 5y = 900$
   Ⓑ $6x + 5y = 900$
   Ⓒ $5x - 6y = 900$
   Ⓓ $5x + 6y = -900$

6. Your class sold 80 bags of oranges. How many bags of apples did your class sell if the earnings came to exactly $900?

   Ⓐ 84   Ⓑ 85
   Ⓒ 104   Ⓓ 820

7. Your class wants to earn at least $900. Which ordered pair represents the number of bags of oranges and apples your class can sell to meet the goal? The ordered pairs are of the form (oranges, apples).

   Ⓐ (30, 100)   Ⓑ (80, 65)
   Ⓒ (70, 95)   Ⓓ (90, 75)

8. What is the midpoint of the segment that connects the points (32.5, 96.5) and (29.3, 28.3)?

   Ⓐ (28.8, 64.5)
   Ⓑ (30.4, 62.9)
   Ⓒ (30.9, 62.4)
   Ⓓ (64.5, 28.8)

Exploring Data and Polynomials

TECHNOLOGY

- **Interactive Real-Life Investigations**
- **Middle School Tutorial Software**

To find out more about Galileo and scientific experiments, go to:

http://www.mlmath.com

CHAPTER THEME
Scientific Method

PORTFOLIO

CHAPTER PROJECT

Conducting an Experiment

PROJECT DESCRIPTION

Galileo, who lived around 1600, used observation and experimentation to understand natural occurrences. This approach is called the *scientific method*. Scientists test their ideas by doing experiments that can be duplicated by others. You will duplicate Galileo's "Inclined Plane" experiment, in which he investigated the speed of a falling object by rolling a ball down a ramp.

GETTING STARTED

Talking It Over

- In Galileo's time, how do you think it was possible to estimate the speed of a falling or rolling object?

- How would you measure the speed of a falling or rolling object today?

- Why do you think Galileo rolled a ball down a ramp instead of dropping it straight down?

Planning Your Project

- **Materials:** one 4 ft-by-8 ft foam core graphic arts board, utility knife, ruler, tape, marker, ball, stopwatch

- Cut the foam core board into four 1 ft-by-8 ft sections. Score and fold each piece in half lengthwise.

- Tape two pieces together.

- Mark the inside at 1 ft intervals.

- Put one end on the seat of a chair so the ramp is not steep.

BUILDING YOUR PROJECT

14.1 Conduct an experiment and find average times. *p. 671*

14.2 Display results in a stem-and-leaf plot. *p. 675*

14.3 Display results in a box-and-whisker plot. *p. 680*

14.4 Analyze results using matrices. *p. 685*

14.5 Use results to find an equation. *p. 691*

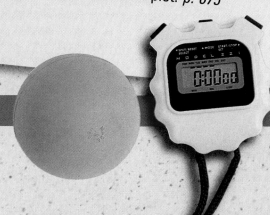

14.1

What you should learn:

Goal ❶ How to find measures of central tendency

Goal ❷ How to use measures of central tendency to solve real-life problems

Why you should learn it:

You can use measures of central tendency to solve real-life problems, such as describing the number of haircuts students get in a year.

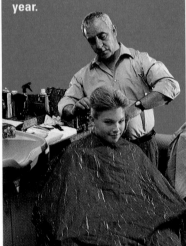

Goal ❶ MEASURES OF CENTRAL TENDENCY

A **measure of central tendency** is a single number that represents a set of numbers. Here are three common measures.

The **mean** or **average** is the sum of the numbers divided by how many numbers are in the set.

The **median** is the middle number (or the mean of the two middle numbers) when the numbers are written in order.

$$6, 8, 8, \mathbf{9}, 10, 12, 13 \qquad 2, 2, 4, \mathbf{6}, \mathbf{8}, 8, 9, 10$$

$$\textbf{median} \qquad \textbf{median} = \frac{6+8}{2} = 7$$

The **mode** is the number that occurs most often. The set 2, 5, 7, 8, and 9 has no mode. The set 5, 5, 6, 9, and 9 has two modes: 5 and 9.

Example 1 ⟩ Finding Measures of Central Tendency

Sixteen students were asked how many haircuts they got during the past year. The results are shown in the histogram. Find the mean, median, and mode of the data.

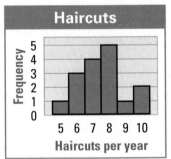

Haircuts

Solution

The histogram shows that the 16 numbers in the data set are 5, 6, 6, 6, 7, 7, 7, 7, 8, 8, 8, 8, 8, 9, 10, and 10.

$$\text{Mean} = \frac{5 + 6 + 6 + \cdots + 9 + 10 + 10}{16}$$

$$= \frac{120}{16}$$

$$= 7.5$$

If you write the numbers in order, the middle two numbers are 7 and 8. Average them to find the median.

$$\text{Median} = \frac{7+8}{2}$$

$$= 7.5$$

The mode is 8 because 8 occurs most frequently.

The three measures of central tendency for a group of numbers can be exactly the same, almost the same, or very different. Here are some examples.

	Data	Mean	Median	Mode
A	10, 10, 12, 12, 12, 13, 13, 14	12	12	12
B	10, 11, 12, 12, 12, 13, 13, 15	12.25	12	12
C	10, 10, 11, 12, 14, 20, 35, 40	19	13	10

In Group A, the mean, median, and mode are exactly the same. In Group B, the mean is close to the median and mode. In Group C, the mean is much higher than the median and mode.

Example 2 Interpreting Central Tendencies

The numbers of days of rain or snow per month in Boise, Idaho, and Lewiston, Idaho, are given in the table.

REAL LIFE
Weather

Which measure of central tendency would you use to describe the typical number of days of rain or snow per month in each city?

Month	J	F	M	A	M	J	J	A	S	O	N	D
Boise	12	11	10	8	9	7	2	2	3	7	10	12
Lewiston	13	9	10	8	10	10	4	4	4	9	10	11

Solution

The means, medians, and modes are shown in the table below.

	Mean	Median	Mode
Boise	7.75	8.5	—
Lewiston	8.5	9.5	10

Boise does not have a single mode because there is no number that occurs most often (2, 7, 10, and 12 each occur twice). So, the mode is not a good measure of the typical number of rain or snow days.

Either of the other two measures could be used as a typical number of rain or snow days. For instance, you could say that Boise has about 8 days of rain or snow per month and Lewiston has about 9 days.

GUIDED PRACTICE

1. Name the measure of central tendency associated with each phrase.

   a. middle **b.** most often **c.** average

In Exercises 2–5, use the histogram at the right.

2. Describe and order the data that is represented.

3. Find the mean of the numbers.

4. Find the median of the numbers.

5. Find the mode of the numbers.

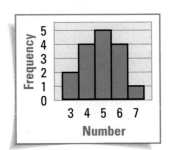

PRACTICE AND PROBLEM SOLVING

In Exercises 6–9, find the mean, median, and mode of the data.

6. 85, 86, 90, 90, 91, 92

7. 52.8, 53.6, 53.9, 54, 54.5, 54.8, 55.1

8. 34, 35, 36, 36, 37, 37, 38, 38, 39, 40

9. 55, 56, 57, 58, 59, 60, 60, 60, 62

In Exercises 10–12, use the line plot at the right.

10. How many numbers are represented in the line plot? List them in increasing order.

11. Find the mean, median, and mode of the numbers.

12. **OPEN-ENDED PROBLEM** Describe a real-life situation that can be represented by the line plot.

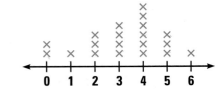

In Exercises 13–15, which measure of central tendency best represents the data? Explain your reasoning.

13. The salaries of 240 people in your neighborhood

14. The number of daily calories you consume for 30 days

15. The number of pairs of shoes owned by each person in your neighborhood

WILDLIFE PRESERVATION In Exercises 16–18, use the line graph, which shows the ages of the wolf population in a state park.

16. How many 3-year-old wolves are in the park?

17. Find the mean, median, and mode of the ages.

18. Which measure of central tendency best represents the age of the wolf population? Explain.

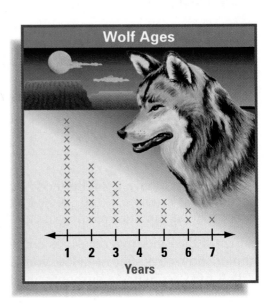

CHEMISTRY **In Exercises 19 and 20, use the following information.**

At a pool, you measure the pH level of the water for ten days. (The pH level of pure water is 7. Lower pH levels indicate that the water is acidic.)

pH Levels: 7.1, 6.9, 6.7, 6.5, 6.3, 6.9, 6.8, 6.5, 6.3, 6.1

19. Find the mean, median, and mode of the data.

20. Did the water tend to become more acidic or less acidic? On which of the 10 days was a chemical added to change the pH level?

OPEN-ENDED PROBLEMS **In Exercises 21 and 22, list six numbers that have the indicated measures of central tendency.**

21. The mean is 15, the median is 15, and the mode is 15.

22. The mean is 10, the median is 9, and the mode is 8.

23. **HOUSE PRICES** Explain the following statement in your own words. "In 1996, the median price of houses in Seattle, Washington, was $160,700." (Source: National Association of Realtors)

24. **TEST SCORES** On your first four tests of the grading period, you had scores of 95, 89, 91, and 93. What score must you get on your final test to raise your average to 93?

STANDARDIZED TEST PRACTICE

25. Find the mean, median, and mode of the data.

　　14, 10, 16, 11, 20, 19, 18, 16, 10, 16

　　A mean is 16; median is 16; mode is 16　　**B** mean is 16; median is 16; mode is 15

　　C mean is 15; median is 16; mode is 16　　**D** mean is 15; median is 15; mode is 16

EXPLORATION AND EXTENSION

PORTFOLIO

26. **BUILDING YOUR PROJECT** Use a stopwatch to find how long it takes a ball to reach the bottom of your ramp from four equally spaced heights, such as the 4 ft, 8 ft, 12 ft, and 16 ft marks. For each distance, roll the ball 10 times. What was the mean time for each distance?

14.2

Stem-and-Leaf Plots

What you should learn:

Goal 1 How to organize data with a stem-and-leaf plot

Goal 2 How to use two stem-and-leaf plots to compare sets of data

Why you should learn it:

You can use stem-and-leaf plots to help interpret real-life data, such as census data about urban population.

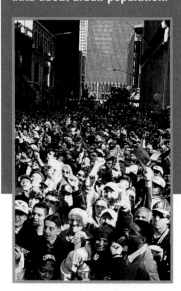

Goal 1 USING STEM-AND-LEAF PLOTS

A **stem-and-leaf plot** is a technique for ordering data in increasing or decreasing order.

Example 1 Making a Stem-and-Leaf Plot

Use a stem-and-leaf plot to order the following data.

Unordered Data: 5, 10, 14, 44, 32, 35, 14, 28, 8, 13, 11, 25, 30, 15, 20, 9, 29, 20, 23, 40, 19, 31, 32, 32, 43, 42, 25, 37, 11, 8, 4, 43, 7, 24

Solution

The numbers vary between 4 and 44, so you can let the *stem* represent the tens' digits and let the *leaves* represent the units' digits.

Begin by creating an unordered stem-and-leaf plot as shown below on the left. Then order the leaves to form an ordered stem-and-leaf plot as shown below on the right.

	Unordered Plot			**Ordered Plot**	
	4	4 0 3 2 3		4	0 2 3 3 4
	3	2 5 0 1 2 2 7		3	0 1 2 2 2 5 7
Stem	2	8 5 0 9 0 3 5 4	Leaf Stem	2	0 0 3 4 5 5 8 9	Leaf
	1	0 4 4 3 1 5 9 1		1	0 1 1 3 4 4 5 9
	0	5 8 9 8 4 7		0	4 5 7 8 8 9

Key: 4 | 3 represents 43   Key: 4 | 3 represents 43

You can use the ordered stem-and-leaf plot to order the data.

Ordered Data: 4, 5, 7, 8, 8, 9, 10, 11, 11, 13, 14, 14, 15, 19, 20, 20, 23, 24, 25, 25, 28, 29, 30, 31, 32, 32, 32, 35, 37, 40, 42, 43, 43, 44

When you make a stem-and-leaf plot, you should include a key that allows people to tell what the stem and leaves represent.

For instance, in Example 1, by knowing that 4 | 3 represents 43, you know that the stem represents the tens' digits and the leaves represent the units' digits.

A double stem-and-leaf plot can be used to compare two sets of data. You read to the left for one set of data and to the right for the other.

Example 2 **Comparing Two Sets of Data**

REAL LIFE
Social Studies

The data below show the percent of each state's population that is urban (lives in a city). Which group is more urban? (Source: U.S. Bureau of Census)

East

AL: 60%	IL: 85%	ME: 45%	NJ: 89%	SC: 55%
CT: 79%	IN: 65%	MI: 71%	NY: 84%	TN: 61%
DE: 73%	KY: 52%	MS: 47%	OH: 74%	VA: 69%
FL: 85%	MA: 84%	NC: 50%	PA: 69%	VT: 32%
GA: 63%	MD: 81%	NH: 51%	RI: 86%	WV: 36%

West

AK: 68%	HI: 89%	MN: 70%	NM: 73%	TX: 80%
AR: 54%	IA: 61%	MO: 69%	NV: 88%	UT: 87%
AZ: 88%	ID: 57%	MT: 53%	OK: 68%	WA: 76%
CA: 93%	KS: 69%	ND: 53%	OR: 71%	WI: 66%
CO: 82%	LA: 68%	NE: 66%	SD: 50%	WY: 65%

Solution

A double stem-and-leaf plot can help you answer the question. The leaves representing the western states point to the left of the stem. The leaves representing the eastern states point to the right of the stem. The western states tend to have more urban populations.

West		East
3	9	
9 8 8 7 2 0	8	1 4 4 5 5 6 9
6 3 1 0	7	1 3 4 9
9 9 8 8 8 6 6 5 1	6	0 1 3 5 9 9
7 4 3 3 0	5	0 1 2 5
	4	5 7
	3	2 6

0|7|1 **represents**
70% and 71%
urban populations

ONGOING ASSESSMENT

Write About It

1. Use the data in Example 2 to draw a double stem-and-leaf plot that represents the non-urban populations of the states.

2. Compare your plot to that in Example 2.

GUIDED PRACTICE

In Exercises 1 and 2, list the data represented by the stem-and-leaf plot.

1.
```
3 │ 1 2 4 4 6
2 │ 0 3 5 7
1 │ 0 1 5 5 6 9
0 │ 2 2 8
```
3 | 1 represents 31

2.
```
8 4 3 1 │ 7 │ 0 3 4 6
    5 5 0 │ 6 │ 1 4 7
  9 7 3 2 │ 5 │ 2 3 5 8 9
    4 2 0 │ 4 │ 3
```
8 | 7 | 0 represents 7.8 and 7.0

3. Use a stem-and-leaf plot to order the following set of data.

18, 6, 52, 41, 43, 8, 29, 24, 33, 30, 2, 55, 28, 32,
8, 21, 5, 2, 38, 10, 54, 65, 17, 29, 34, 50, 32, 1

PRACTICE AND PROBLEM SOLVING

In Exercises 4–6, list the data represented by the stem-and-leaf plot.
Then draw a histogram for the data.

4.
```
6 │ 4 6 6 8
5 │ 0 2 3
4 │ 1 8
3 │ 5 7 9
2 │ 0 1 1 3
```
6 | 4 represents 64

5.
```
12 │ 4 5 6 7
11 │ 0 3 8 8 9
10 │ 1 2 7
 9 │ 0 1
 8 │ 4 4 5 8
```
12 | 4 represents 124

6.
```
17 │ 2 3 4 6 8
16 │ 1 2 3 7
15 │ 1 9 9
14 │ 3 5 9
13 │ 5 6
```
17 | 2 represents 17.2

FINAL GRADES **In Exercises 7 and 8, use the set of data below, which lists the scores on a test for students.**

93, 84, 100, 92, 66, 89, 78, 52, 71, 85,
83, 95, 81, 80, 79, 67, 59, 90, 85, 77

7. Order the data in a stem-and-leaf plot.

8. Draw a histogram to represent the data.

9. INDIANAPOLIS 500 Winning speeds (in miles per hour) in the Indianapolis 500 are given below. Organize the data with an ordered stem-and-leaf plot. (Source: Indianapolis Motor Speedway)

1980 (143), 1981 (139), 1982 (162),
1983 (162), 1984 (164), 1985 (153),
1986 (171), 1987 (162), 1988 (145),
1989 (168), 1990 (186), 1991 (176),
1992 (134), 1993 (157), 1994 (161),
1995 (154), 1996 (148), 1997 (146)

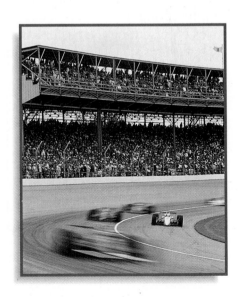

LIFE EXPECTANCY In Exercises 10 and 11, use the data below, which give the life expectancy in various countries of South Asia for 1970 and 1995.

Country	1970	1995	Country	1970	1995
Bangladesh	45	56	Mongolia	60	64
Bhutan	42	51	Myanmar	51	58
China	59	68	Nepal	42	54
India	48	60	Sri Lanka	64	72
Indonesia	47	63	Thailand	58	69

10. Order the data in a double stem-and-leaf plot.

11. **OPEN-ENDED PROBLEM** How does the double stem-and-leaf plot show that life expectancies are increasing in these countries?

POPULATION In Exercises 12 and 13, use the data below, which show the percent of each state's population that is between 5 and 17 years old.
(Source: U.S. Bureau of Census)

West					East				
AK: 23%	AR: 19%	AZ: 20%	CA:19%	CO: 19%	AL: 18%	CT: 17%	DE: 18%	FL: 17%	GA: 19%
HI: 18%	IA: 19%	ID: 22%	KS:20%	LA: 21%	IL: 19%	IN: 19%	KY: 18%	MA:17%	MD:18%
MN:20%	MO:19%	MT:21%	ND:20%	NE: 20%	ME:19%	MI: 19%	MS: 21%	NC: 18%	NH: 19%
NM:21%	NV: 18%	OK:20%	OR:19%	SD: 21%	NJ: 17%	NY: 18%	OH:19%	PA: 18%	RI: 17%
TX: 20%	UT: 25%	WA:19%	WI:20%	WY:22%	SC: 19%	TN: 18%	VA: 17%	VT: 19%	WV:17%

12. Order the data with a double stem-and-leaf plot.

13. Find the mean, median, and mode for each group of states.

14. What is the mean of the data in the stem-and-leaf plot?

   A 15   **B** 15.5   **C** 16   **D** 16.5

```
3 | 5
2 | 0 5 5
1 | 0 0 5 5
0 | 0 5
```

3 | 5 represents 35

EXPLORATION AND EXTENSION

PORTFOLIO

15. **BUILDING YOUR PROJECT** Gather each group's results from the experiment you did in Lesson 14.1. Make a stem-and-leaf plot summarizing the results for each distance the ball rolled.

14.3

Box-and-Whisker Plots

What you should learn:

Goal 1 How to organize data with a box-and-whisker plot

Goal 2 How to use box-and-whisker plots to interpret real-life data

Why you should learn it:

You can use box-and-whisker plots to help interpret real-life data, such as describing the age distribution in a state.

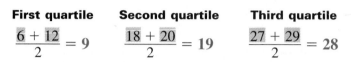

Goal 1 DRAWING BOX-AND-WHISKER PLOTS

The median (or **second quartile**) of an ordered collection of numbers roughly divides the collection into two halves. The **first quartile** is the median of the lower half, and the **third quartile** is the median of the upper half.

1, 5, 6, 12, 14, 18, 20, 26, 27, 29, 30, 31

First quartile
$$\frac{6 + 12}{2} = 9$$

Second quartile
$$\frac{18 + 20}{2} = 19$$

Third quartile
$$\frac{27 + 29}{2} = 28$$

A **box-and-whisker plot** of the data is shown below. It shows the least and greatest values, as well as the three quartiles. The plot places these values as they would be spaced on a number line.

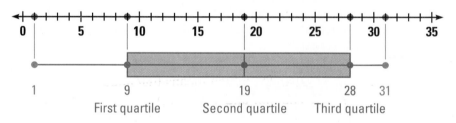

Example 1 Drawing a Box-and-Whisker Plot

Draw a box-and-whisker plot for the following data.

22, 65, 23, 19, 42, 62, 38, 29, 50, 46, 28, 36, 25, 40

Solution

Begin by writing the numbers in increasing order.

19, 22, 23, 25, 28, 29, 36, | 38, 40, 42, 46, 50, 62, 65

Lower half   **Upper half**

From this ordering, you can see that the first quartile is 25, the second quartile is 37, and the third quartile is 46. A box-and-whisker plot for the data is shown below.

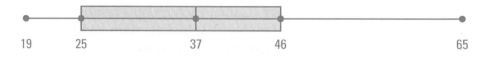

Example 2 Interpreting Box-and-Whisker Plots

The box-and-whisker plots below show the age distributions of Alaska's and Rhode Island's populations. What do the plots tell you about the two states? (Source: U.S. Bureau of Census)

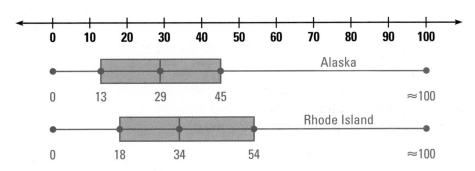

Solution

In Alaska, the median age is 29, which means that about 50% of the population is under 29. The box-and-whisker plot also tells you that 25% of the population is under 13 and 25% is over 45.

Rhode Island's population is older. In that state, about 50% of the population is under 34. The box-and-whisker plot also tells you that 25% of the population is under 18 and 25% is over 54.

Example 3 Interpreting Box-and-Whisker Plots

The box-and-whisker plots below show the age distributions in Utah and Florida. Which is which? Explain your reasoning.

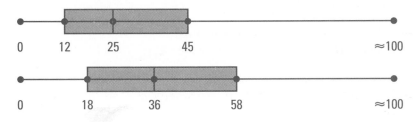

Solution

Because Florida has large retirement communities, it is reasonable to assume that the second plot represents Florida's population.

Tech Link

Investigation 14, Interactive Real-Life Investigations

ONGOING ASSESSMENT

Talk About It
....

Use the box-and-whisker plots on this page to complete each statement. Discuss your reasoning.

1. **?** % of Utah's population is under 25.

2. **?** % of Alaska's population is over 13.

3. **?** % of Florida's population is over 58.

GUIDED PRACTICE

In Exercises 1 and 2, use the box-and-whisker plot at the right.

6	21	34	44	56

1. Name the smallest and largest numbers.

2. Name the quartiles.

In Exercises 3 and 4, draw a box-and-whisker plot for the data.

3. 3, 4, 8, 10, 13, 17, 21, 26, 29, 31, 32, 36

4. 12, 52, 25, 61, 66, 15, 6, 46, 39, 54, 34, 50, 21, 56, 70, 40

PRACTICE AND PROBLEM SOLVING

In Exercises 5–8, use the box-and-whisker plot. There are 20 numbers in the collection, and each number is different.

5. Name the smallest and largest numbers.

6. Name the first, second, and third quartiles.

14	40	58	77	96

7. What percent of the numbers are less than 40?

8. What percent of the numbers are between 40 and 77?

In Exercises 9 and 10, draw a box-and-whisker plot of the data.

9. 26, 60, 36, 44, 62, 24, 29,
   50, 67, 72, 40, 41, 18, 39,
   64, 82, 41, 49, 32, 42

10. 78, 22, 29, 67, 10, 62, 50,
    72, 8, 63, 35, 80, 52, 3,
    60, 18, 65, 61, 15, 84

11. **ERROR ANALYSIS** The box-and-whisker plot at the right is supposed to represent the following data. There are three errors. What are they?

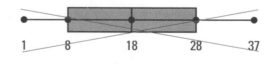

1	8	18	28	37

Data: 26, 10, 19, 34, 2, 5, 21, 12, 1, 39, 14, 30, 18, 37, 7, 24

SOCIAL STUDIES In Exercises 12 and 13, use the box-and-whisker plot, which shows the age distribution for Mississippi. (Source: U.S. Bureau of Census)

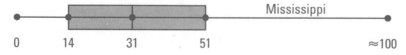

Mississippi

0	14	31	51	≈100

12. Write a description of Mississippi's population.

13. Compare Mississippi's population to the populations discussed on page 677.

14. BIOLOGY The table gives the average life span, in years, of certain animals. Create a box-and-whisker plot to represent the data.

Buffalo	20	Lion	13
Deer	20	Sheep	15
Goat	16	Wolf	14
Horse	25	Chimpanzee	55
Mouse	1	Elephant	60
Tiger	20	Hippopotamus	41
Cat	14	Monkey	28
Dog	16	Squirrel	7
Bear	25	Zebra	22

Real Life...
Real Facts

Galápagos Tortoise
The giant tortoises of the Galápagos Islands, Ecuador, can live more than 100 years. They can survive for up to a year without food or water.

STEREOS In Exercises 15 and 16, use the following data, which list the price in dollars of several stereo components.

Receivers	**CD Players**	**Cassette Decks**
165, 200, 380, 260,	170, 250, 270, 180,	200, 225, 150, 285,
180, 300, 460, 390,	140, 240, 195, 255,	260, 230, 295, 255,
445, 225, 325, 400,	160, 245, 200, 290,	290, 195, 265, 280
280, 360	230, 280	

15. Using the same scale, create a box-and-whisker plot for each stereo component.

16. WRITING What do the plots tell you about the prices of stereo components? Write your answer in paragraph form.

In Exercises 17–20, match the most reasonable box-and-whisker plot with the description. Explain your reasoning.

A. Season scores of a baseball team   **B. Weights in pounds of 4th-graders**

C. Scores on a 100-point test   **D. Ages in years in an algebra class**

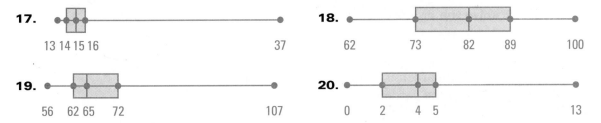

17.

13 14 15 16   37

18.

62   73   82   89   100

19.

56   62 65   72   107

20.

0   2   4 5   13

21. Find the third quartile of the data 15, 17, 25, 10, 21, 19, 8, 14, 23, 20, 16, 4, 19, 27, 24, 19.

Ⓐ 19   Ⓑ 21   Ⓒ 22   Ⓓ 23

22. Find the first quartile of the data 52, 48, 55, 42, 47, 45, 39, 51, 35, 43, 51, 46.

Ⓐ 35   Ⓑ 42.5   Ⓒ 43   Ⓓ 46.5

EXPLORATION AND EXTENSION

PORTFOLIO

23. BUILDING YOUR PROJECT Using the whole class's results, make a box-and-whisker plot for each distance that you timed in the experiment. Explain how the stem-and-leaf plots that you made in Lesson 14.2 helped you to make the box-and-whisker plots.

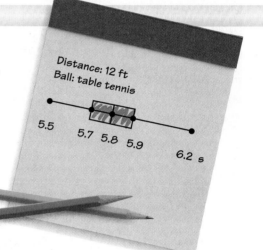

Distance: 12 ft
Ball: table tennis

SPIRAL REVIEW

In Exercises 1–8, use △*ABC* at the right. (11.8)

1. Find the length of the hypotenuse.

2. Find the area of the triangle.

3. Find sin A.

4. Find cos A.

5. Find tan A.

6. Find sin B.

7. Find cos B.

8. Find tan B.

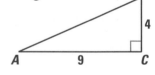

In Exercises 9–12, use the following data. (14.1, 14.2)

1.5, 1.6, 1.8, 1.8, 1.9, 2.3, 2.4, 2.4, 2.7, 2.7, 2.7, 3.0, 3.0, 3.1

9. What is the mean of the data?

10. What is the median of the data?

11. What is the mode of the data?

12. Create a stem-and-leaf plot for the data.

In Exercises 13–16, solve the proportion. (8.2)

13. $\dfrac{x}{13} = \dfrac{4}{12}$ **14.** $\dfrac{b}{6} = \dfrac{6}{16}$ **15.** $\dfrac{3}{2} = \dfrac{15}{r}$ **16.** $\dfrac{4}{s} = \dfrac{21}{18}$

17. You start a garden. The garden is a square with an area of 44.89 m^2. Find the dimensions of the garden. **(1.3)**

Box-and-Whisker Plots

Some graphing calculators can be used to sketch box-and-whisker plots. The following steps show how to use a Texas Instruments TI-82 to sketch the box-and-whisker plot shown at the right. The data for the plot is the same as that used in Example 1 on page 676.

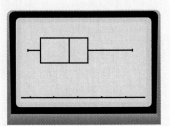

22, 65, 23, 19, 42, 62, 38, 29, 50, 46, 28, 36, 25, 40

TI-82 Keystrokes

To enter data in a list: [STAT] [ENTER] (Edit)

L1(1) = 22 [ENTER]   L1(3) = 23 [ENTER]

L1(2) = 65 [ENTER]   L1(4) = 19 [ENTER]

Repeat until all the data are entered.

To set boxplot: [2nd] STAT PLOT [ENTER] (Plot 1)

Then choose the following settings:

On, Type: ⊞— , Xlist: L1, Freq: 1, [ZOOM] 9

To find the minimum, first quartile, median, third quartile, and maximum:

[TRACE] and [◄] or [►].

Exercises

In Exercises 1–4, use a graphing calculator to sketch a box-and-whisker plot for the data.

1. 15, 19, 37, 15, 25, 33, 30, 27, 31, 37, 37, 14, 28, 34, 24, 25, 35, 18

2. 52, 79, 82, 56, 67, 69, 70, 73, 59, 64, 69, 72, 79, 58, 54, 60, 53, 67

3. 21, 24, 23, 26, 29, 23, 24, 25, 28, 28, 29, 24, 25, 27, 56, 42, 28, 24

4. 39, 52, 36, 45, 42, 43, 37, 43, 46, 42, 38, 34, 36, 45, 49, 34, 45, 48

OPEN-ENDED PROBLEMS In Exercises 5–7, create a collection of 16 numbers that corresponds to the box-and-whisker plot. Use a graphing calculator to confirm your answer.

5.
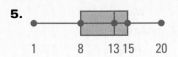

6.
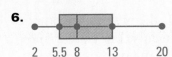

7.

Exploring Data and Matrices

What you should learn:

Goal 1 How to organize data with a matrix

Goal 2 How to add and subtract two matrices

Why you should learn it:

You can use matrices to organize real-life data, such as the income, expenses, and profit for a business, such as a flower shop or a café.

Goal 1 USING MATRICES

A **matrix** is a rectangular arrangement of numbers into rows and columns. For instance, the matrix

$$\begin{bmatrix} 2 & -4 & 5 \\ -3 & 1 & 0 \end{bmatrix}$$

has two rows and three columns. The numbers in the matrix are called **entries** .

In the above matrix, the entry in the second row and third column is 0. The entry in the first row and second column is -4.

The plural of *matrix* is *matrices*. Two matrices are **equal** if all of the entries in corresponding positions are equal.

$$\begin{bmatrix} -1 & \frac{3}{2} \\ \frac{1}{4} & 0 \end{bmatrix} = \begin{bmatrix} -1 & 1.5 \\ 0.25 & 0 \end{bmatrix} \qquad \begin{bmatrix} -3 & 2 \\ 4 & 1 \end{bmatrix} \neq \begin{bmatrix} 2 & -3 \\ 1 & 4 \end{bmatrix}$$

equal matrices **unequal matrices**

You can think of a matrix as a type of table that can be used to organize data.

Example 1 Writing a Table as a Matrix

You are opening two cafés. The income for each of the first four months (in hundreds of dollars) is shown in the table at the right. Write this table as a matrix. For Café 1, which month had the greatest income? For Café 2, which month had the greatest income?

Monthly Café Income (in hundreds of dollars)		
	Café 1	Café 2
April	142	209
May	158	213
June	162	206
July	178	198

Solution

The matrix representing the table has 4 rows and 2 columns.

For Café 1, the greatest income occurred in July. For Café 2, the greatest income occurred in May.

$$\begin{array}{c} \\ \text{April} \\ \text{May} \\ \text{June} \\ \text{July} \end{array} \begin{array}{cc} \text{Café} & \text{Café} \\ 1 & 2 \\ \begin{bmatrix} 142 & 209 \\ 158 & 213 \\ 162 & 206 \\ 178 & 198 \end{bmatrix} \end{array}$$

Goal 2 ADDING AND SUBTRACTING MATRICES

To **add** or **subtract** matrices, you simply add or subtract corresponding entries. You cannot add or subtract matrices that are different sizes. For instance, you cannot add a matrix that has 3 rows and 2 columns to a matrix that has 2 rows and 2 columns.

Example 2 Adding and Subtracting Matrices

a. $\begin{bmatrix} 3 & -2 \\ 0 & 4 \end{bmatrix} + \begin{bmatrix} 1 & 5 \\ -2 & 3 \end{bmatrix} = \begin{bmatrix} 3+1 & -2+5 \\ 0+(-2) & 4+3 \end{bmatrix} = \begin{bmatrix} 4 & 3 \\ -2 & 7 \end{bmatrix}$

b. $\begin{bmatrix} 3 & -2 \\ 0 & 4 \end{bmatrix} - \begin{bmatrix} 1 & 5 \\ -2 & 3 \end{bmatrix} = \begin{bmatrix} 3-1 & -2-5 \\ 0-(-2) & 4-3 \end{bmatrix} = \begin{bmatrix} 2 & -7 \\ 2 & 1 \end{bmatrix}$

Example 3 Subtracting Matrices

Expenses for the two cafés described in Example 1 are shown in the table below. Use subtraction of matrices to find the monthly profits for each café.

Monthly Café Expenses (in hundreds of dollars)

	Café 1	Café 2
April	139	205
May	153	206
June	158	201
July	172	190

Solution

To find the monthly profits, subtract the expense matrix from the income matrix.

Income   Expenses   Profit

$\begin{bmatrix} 142 & 209 \\ 158 & 213 \\ 162 & 206 \\ 178 & 198 \end{bmatrix} - \begin{bmatrix} 139 & 205 \\ 153 & 206 \\ 158 & 201 \\ 172 & 190 \end{bmatrix} = \begin{bmatrix} 3 & 4 \\ 5 & 7 \\ 4 & 5 \\ 6 & 8 \end{bmatrix}$

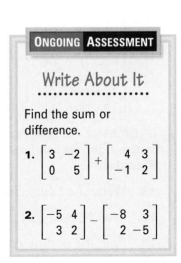

ONGOING ASSESSMENT

Write About It

Find the sum or difference.

1. $\begin{bmatrix} 3 & -2 \\ 0 & 5 \end{bmatrix} + \begin{bmatrix} 4 & 3 \\ -1 & 2 \end{bmatrix}$

2. $\begin{bmatrix} -5 & 4 \\ 3 & 2 \end{bmatrix} - \begin{bmatrix} -8 & 3 \\ 2 & -5 \end{bmatrix}$

GUIDED PRACTICE

In Exercises 1–3, use the matrix at the right.

1. How many rows and columns does the matrix have?

2. What is the entry in the first row and second column?

3. Describe the position of -4.

$$\begin{bmatrix} 2 & -5 \\ 0 & 3 \\ -4 & 1 \end{bmatrix}$$

4. Are the matrices at the right equal? Explain.

$$\begin{bmatrix} 0 & \frac{5}{4} & -1 \\ -\frac{8}{5} & 2 & 3 \end{bmatrix} \overset{?}{=} \begin{bmatrix} 0 & 1.25 & -1 \\ -1.6 & 2 & 3 \end{bmatrix}$$

In Exercises 5 and 6, find the matrix sum or difference.

5. $\begin{bmatrix} 2 & 3 & 0 \\ -3 & 0 & -1 \end{bmatrix} + \begin{bmatrix} -4 & 1 & -5 \\ -6 & 7 & 2 \end{bmatrix}$

6. $\begin{bmatrix} 2.1 & -1.5 \\ -3.5 & 6.4 \end{bmatrix} - \begin{bmatrix} 1.8 & 4.8 \\ -1.1 & -0.8 \end{bmatrix}$

PRACTICE AND PROBLEM SOLVING

In Exercises 7–14, find the sum and difference of the matrices.

7. $\begin{bmatrix} -2 & 3 \\ 1 & -5 \end{bmatrix}, \begin{bmatrix} -1 & 4 \\ -6 & 0 \end{bmatrix}$

8. $\begin{bmatrix} 5 & 2 \\ -2 & 7 \end{bmatrix}, \begin{bmatrix} -8 & 0 \\ -9 & 3 \end{bmatrix}$

9. $\begin{bmatrix} -4 & -5 & 2 \\ 0 & -9 & -3 \end{bmatrix}, \begin{bmatrix} -6 & 3 & 2 \\ 1 & -1 & 4 \end{bmatrix}$

10. $\begin{bmatrix} -4 & 4 \\ 5 & 3 \\ -6 & -2 \end{bmatrix}, \begin{bmatrix} 4 & 7 \\ 2 & -1 \\ -3 & -8 \end{bmatrix}$

11. $\begin{bmatrix} 3 & 5 & -6 \\ -4 & 0 & -6 \\ 4 & 8 & 1 \end{bmatrix}, \begin{bmatrix} -7 & 0 & 3 \\ -1 & -4 & 5 \\ 4 & -2 & 9 \end{bmatrix}$

12. $\begin{bmatrix} 4 & 2 & 8 \\ -2 & 6 & -1 \\ 7 & 9 & -1 \end{bmatrix}, \begin{bmatrix} 12 & -10 & -6 \\ -5 & 0 & 11 \\ -1 & 2 & 3 \end{bmatrix}$

13. $\begin{bmatrix} \frac{1}{3} & \frac{2}{3} & \frac{1}{3} \\ \frac{1}{4} & \frac{1}{4} & \frac{3}{4} \\ \frac{1}{5} & \frac{2}{5} & \frac{3}{5} \end{bmatrix}, \begin{bmatrix} \frac{2}{3} & \frac{2}{3} & \frac{1}{3} \\ \frac{3}{4} & \frac{1}{4} & \frac{1}{2} \\ \frac{1}{5} & \frac{3}{5} & \frac{1}{5} \end{bmatrix}$

14. $\begin{bmatrix} 4.1 & 2.5 & -2.3 \\ 6.8 & 0.4 & -7.3 \\ -4.8 & 4.7 & -5.0 \end{bmatrix}, \begin{bmatrix} -6.3 & 1.5 & 3.6 \\ 2.1 & 4.7 & -1.7 \\ 5.3 & 2.1 & 4.7 \end{bmatrix}$

GEOMETRY In Exercises 15–17, use the table at the right, which lists the sides of 4 different triangles.

15. Write the table as a matrix.

16. Which, if any, of the triangles are right?

17. Find the perimeter of each triangle.

	Side 1	Side 2	Side 3
Triangle 1	5	7	10
Triangle 2	9	12	15
Triangle 3	0.9	4	4.1
Triangle 4	5	6	9.2

PET STORE In Exercises 18–21, use the following information.

You are opening two pet stores. The income for each store (in thousands of dollars) for the first four months is shown in the left table and the expenses are shown in the right table.

Income		
	Store 1	Store 2
May	$32	$35
June	$35	$33
July	$30	$41
August	$37	$36

Expenses		
	Store 1	Store 2
May	$29	$30
June	$31	$29
July	$28	$35
August	$33	$31

18. Write each table as a matrix.

19. For each pet store, which month had the greatest income?

20. Find the monthly profits for each store.

21. Which store had a greater profit during the first four months?

MENTAL MATH In Exercises 22 and 23, find *a*, *b*, *c*, and *d*.

22. $\begin{bmatrix} 2a & b \\ c-3 & 2d \end{bmatrix} = \begin{bmatrix} -8 & 3 \\ 1 & -5 \end{bmatrix}$

23. $\begin{bmatrix} -4 & 6 \\ c-1 & -3d \end{bmatrix} = \begin{bmatrix} a+2 & 3b \\ 7 & 6c \end{bmatrix}$

STANDARDIZED TEST PRACTICE

24. Find the difference: $\begin{bmatrix} 3 & -2 \\ -1 & -6 \end{bmatrix} - \begin{bmatrix} 2 & 4 \\ -1 & 5 \end{bmatrix}$

(A) $\begin{bmatrix} 1 & 2 \\ -2 & -11 \end{bmatrix}$ **(B)** $\begin{bmatrix} 1 & -6 \\ 0 & -11 \end{bmatrix}$ **(C)** $\begin{bmatrix} -1 & 2 \\ 0 & -11 \end{bmatrix}$ **(D)** $\begin{bmatrix} 1 & 2 \\ 0 & -5 \end{bmatrix}$

EXPLORATION AND EXTENSION

PORTFOLIO

25. BUILDING YOUR PROJECT Use at least two group's results to complete the tables. Then write each table as a matrix. Subtract the matrices. What does the resulting matrix represent?

	16 ft	12 ft
Group 1	?	?
Group 2	?	?

	12 ft	8 ft
Group 1	?	?
Group 2	?	?

The Hardest 100

READ About It

An *ultrarace* is even longer than a marathon. A marathon is usually about 26 mi. Ultraraces range from 50 mi to 100 mi. The Hardrock 100 is one such race. Its 100 mi course loops through the San Juan Mountains in southwestern Colorado.

The Hardrock 100 is not for novices. The average elevation is over 11,000 ft. The race entry committee has set strict entrance requirements to ensure that candidates can endure running 100 mi at high elevations. Even so, 60 of the 99 people who started the race in 1997 did not finish.

WRITE About It

1997 Times (in h)	
30.6	37.4
30.6	37.8
32.3	37.8
32.7	38.8
33.7	39.5
33.7	40.2
34.9	40.2
35.3	40.4
35.9	40.4
36.7	40.6

1. Suppose the elevation is taken at each mile marker on the race. The low elevation is 7680 ft and the high elevation is 14,048 ft. Estimate the median elevation. Explain your answer.

2. What is the mean, median, and mode of the top 20 runners' times, shown at the left? Which best represents the data? Why?

3. Make a stem-and-leaf plot of the data. Include a key. What numbers did you pick to lie on the stem? Why?

4. Make a box-and-whisker plot of the data. Explain what measures you had to calculate to make the box-and-whisker plot.

5. The speeds of the fastest five runners in the Hardrock 100 in 1996 were 30.7, 30.9, 31.7, 31.9, and 32.6. Write a matrix comparing the five fastest times for 1996 and 1997.

Take this test as you would take a test in class. The answers to the exercises are given in the back of the book.

In Exercises 1–3, use the temperatures at the right. (14.1)

1. What is the mean of the data?

2. What is the median of the data?

3. What is the mode of the data?

80°, 81°, 82°,
83°, 85°, 87°,
87°, 89°, 89°,
87°, 84°, 81°

RAINFALL **In Exercises 4–6, use the table, which lists the normal monthly rainfall (in inches) in Miami and Jacksonville, Florida.** (14.2)

Month	J	F	M	A	M	J	J	A	S	O	N	D
Miami	2.0	2.1	2.4	2.9	6.2	9.3	5.7	7.6	7.6	5.6	2.7	1.8
Jacksonville	3.3	3.9	3.7	2.8	3.6	5.7	5.6	7.9	7.1	2.9	2.2	2.7

4. Create a double stem-and-leaf plot for the data above. Use the whole numbers for the stem and the tenths for the leaves.

5. Find the median rainfall for Miami.

6. Find the mean rainfall for Jacksonville.

TEMPERATURE **In Exercises 7–12, use the following temperatures (in degrees Fahrenheit), which are the record highs for May for the indicated cities.** (14.3)

Juneau, 82°; Phoenix, 113°; Denver, 96°; Washington, 99°;
Wichita, 100°; Boston, 95°; Detroit, 93°; Minneapolis, 96°;
Cleveland, 92°; Oklahoma City, 104°; El Paso, 104°; Spokane, 96°

7. Order the data from least to greatest.

8. Find the first quartile.

9. Find the second quartile.

10. Find the third quartile.

11. Draw a box-and-whisker plot of the data.

12. What percent of the data is above the first quartile?

In Exercises 13–15, use the box-and-whisker plot below. (14.3)

13. What is the third quartile?

14. What is the greatest number in the data?

15. What is the median of the data?

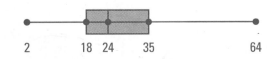

2   18 24   35   64

In Exercises 16–18, find the sum or difference. (14.4)

16. $\begin{bmatrix} 2 & 3 \\ 9 & 8 \end{bmatrix} + \begin{bmatrix} 6 & 2 \\ 11 & 0 \end{bmatrix}$

17. $\begin{bmatrix} 4 & 5 \\ 6 & 8 \end{bmatrix} - \begin{bmatrix} 1 & 3 \\ 8 & 21 \end{bmatrix}$

18. $\begin{bmatrix} 21 & 18 \\ 19 & 40 \end{bmatrix} - \begin{bmatrix} 20 & 6 \\ -4 & 16 \end{bmatrix}$

Exploring Polynomials

What you should learn:

Goal 1 How to identify polynomials and write them in standard form

Goal 2 How to use polynomials to solve real-life problems

Why you should learn it:

You can use polynomials to solve real-life problems, such as finding the time it takes for an amusement park ride to drop.

Goal 1 IDENTIFYING POLYNOMIALS

A **polynomial** is an expression that has one or more terms of the form ax^n where the coefficient a is any real number and the exponent n is a whole number. Polynomials are identified by the number of terms.

Type of polynomial	Number of terms	Example
Monomial	One	$3x^2$
Binomial	Two	$n + 4$
Trinomial	Three	$2y^2 + 4y - 5$

A polynomial is written in **standard form** if the powers of the variable decrease from left to right.

Example 1 ▷ Rewriting in Standard Form

Original Polynomial	**Rewrite in Standard Form.**
$3m + 4m^3 - 2m^2 + 5$	$4m^3 - 2m^2 + 3m + 5$

If two terms have the same variable, raised to the same power, they are called *like terms*. When you combine like terms of a polynomial (by adding their coefficients), you are *simplifying* the polynomial.

Example 2 ▷ Simplifying Polynomials

Simplify the polynomial and write the result in standard form.

a. $3x^2 - 4x + x^2 + 5x$ **b.** $5n^2 + 6 + 4n - 7$

NEED TO KNOW

The terms of a polynomial include minus signs.

For instance, the terms of $2x^2 - x + 4$ are $2x^2$, $-x$, and 4. The coefficient of x^2 is 2 and the coefficient of x is -1.

Solution

To simplify the polynomials, collect like terms, and add their coefficients.

a. $3x^2 - 4x + x^2 + 5x = 3x^2 + x^2 - 4x + 5x$
$$= (3 + 1)x^2 + (-4 + 5)x$$
$$= 4x^2 + x$$

b. $5n^2 + 6 + 4n - 7 = 5n^2 + 4n + 6 - 7$
$$= 5n^2 + 4n - 1$$

Goal 2 USING POLYNOMIALS IN REAL LIFE

When you drop a heavy object, does it fall at a constant speed or does it fall faster and faster the longer it is in the air? The answer is that it falls faster and faster.

Example 3 Using a Polynomial

You are riding the Giant Drop at Six Flags Great America Park in Illinois. You are in a car with three friends at the top of a 20-story tower. Suddenly the car drops. Your height h (in feet) after t seconds is given by

$$h = -16t^2 + 200.$$

Find your height when $t = 0, 1, 2, 3,$ and 3.5 s. How long does your ride last?

Solution

Time	Substitution	Height
$t = 0$	$h = -16(0)^2 + 200 = 0 + 200$	200
$t = 1$	$h = -16(1)^2 + 200 = -16 + 200$	184
$t = 2$	$h = -16(2)^2 + 200 = -64 + 200$	136
$t = 3$	$h = -16(3)^2 + 200 = -144 + 200$	56
$t = 3.5$	$h = -16(3.5)^2 + 200 = -196 + 200$	4

The ride lasts a little more than 3.5 s.

Example 4 Analyzing the Fall

How far does the car fall during each of the first 3 s?

Solution

Time	Distance
From $t = 0$ to $t = 1$	$200 - 184 = 16$ ft
From $t = 1$ to $t = 2$	$184 - 136 = 48$ ft
From $t = 2$ to $t = 3$	$136 - 56 = 80$ ft

Because it falls farther each second, you can see that it is falling faster and faster.

GUIDED PRACTICE

In Exercises 1–8, is the expression a polynomial? Explain.

1. $y + 1$

2. $3t^{-3}$

3. $4n^{-2} - 7$

4. 5

5. $3x^2 + x^{-1}$

6. $4s^3 - 8s^2 + 12$

7. $\sqrt{5}\,r^2 - \dfrac{1}{2}$

8. $2m^4 + m - 4$

In Exercises 9–11, write the polynomial in standard form. State its terms.

9. $4x - 2 + 3x^2$

10. $10 - 5r^3 + 4r$

11. $3p - 16p^2 - 12 + p^3$

In Exercises 12–14, simplify the polynomial. Then identify its type.

12. $t^2 + t - 5t + 2t^2$

13. $12 - 6x^3 + 5x^3 - 7$

14. $2n + 1 + 12n - 8$

PRACTICE AND PROBLEM SOLVING

In Exercises 15–18, is the expression a polynomial? If it is, state whether it is a *monomial*, a *binomial*, or a *trinomial*.

15. $\dfrac{1}{2}t^2 - 5t + 3$

16. $9n - \sqrt{2}\,n^3$

17. $6.2y^4$

18. $\dfrac{6}{x^2} - 3x^3$

LANGUAGE ARTS **In Exercises 19–22, match the term with a phrase.**

A. Three years

B. Having two modes

C. Single-color photo

D. Speak many languages

19. Polyglot

20. Monochrome

21. Bimodal

22. Triennium

In Exercises 23–28, write the polynomial in standard form and list its terms.

23. $14m - 10m^2 + 5m^3$

24. $6x^3 - x - 2x^2$

25. $5 - 11y - 8y^3$

26. $9z^2 - 7z + 3 - z^3$

27. $2 - t^4 + t^2 + t$

28. $w + 4w^2 - 3 + 15w^3$

In Exercises 29–38, simplify and write in standard form.

29. $y + 2y^2 - 3y$

30. $x^3 - 3x + 5x - x^3$ $2x^3 + 8x$

31. $8 - 4x^2 + 10x^2 - 11$

32. $x^2 + 7x + 10 + x^2 + 2x$

33. $2x^2 + 5x + 3 + 5x + 4$

34. $x^2 + 2x + 4 + 2x^2 + 4x + 6$

35. $15 + 7s^3 - 21 - 3s^2 + s^3$

36. $\dfrac{4}{3}m - 7 - \dfrac{2}{3}m + 8$

37. $1.1r^2 - 2.9r + 1.8r^2 + 3.3r$

-2.9

38. $-2(3p - 4p^3 + 6 - 9p)$

$-6p + 8p^3 - 12 + 18p$

BRIDGES **In Exercises 39–41, use the following information.**

You are standing on the Royal Gorge Bridge and accidentally drop your camera. The camera's height h (in feet above the river) after t seconds is modeled by

$$h = -16t^2 + 1053.$$

39. Copy and complete the table.

t	0	1	2	3	4	5	6	7	8	9
h	?	?	?	?	?	?	?	?	?	?

40. What is the camera's height after 4 s?

41. When will the camera hit the water?

STANDARDIZED TEST PRACTICE

42. Simplify the polynomial: $x^2 - 4x^3 + 5 - x + x^3 - 2x^2$.

$-3x^3 - x^2 - x + 5$

    A $-3x^3 + x^2 - x + 5$ **B** $-3x^3 - x^2 - x + 5$

    C $3x^3 + x^2 + x + 5$ **D** $3x^3 - x^2 - x + 5$

43. Write the polynomial in standard form: $4 + 5x^2 - 3x - 10x^3$.

    A $4 - 3x + 5x^2 - 10x^3$ **B** $-10x^3 + 5x^2 + 4 - 3x$

    C $-3x + 4 + 5x^2 - 10x^3$ **D** $-10x^3 + 5x^2 - 3x + 4$

EXPLORATION AND EXTENSION

PORTFOLIO

44. **BUILDING YOUR PROJECT** The distance that a rolling ball travels can be represented by $d = kt^2$, where d is distance, t is time, and k is some number.

  a. Choose one of the times it took the ball to roll the whole way down the ramp. Substitute the time and distance for t and d. Then solve for k.

  b. Using the k you found in part (a), substitute each of the other times recorded by your group and solve for d. Does the model $d = kt^2$ seem to represent your results? Explain.

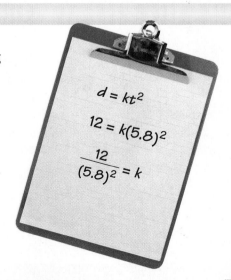

$d = kt^2$

$12 = k(5.8)^2$

$\dfrac{12}{(5.8)^2} = k$

LAB 14.6

COOPERATIVE LEARNING

Materials Needed
• algebra tiles

Exploring Polynomials

In this investigation, you will use algebra tiles like those below to represent polynomials.

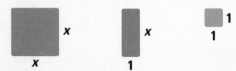

Part A EXPLORING POLYNOMIALS WITH ALGEBRA TILES

Algebra tiles can be used to represent polynomials. For instance, to represent the polynomial $2x^2 + 3x + 5$, use two large square tiles, three rectangular tiles, and 5 small square tiles.

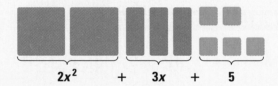

In Exercises 1–4, write the polynomial that is represented by the algebra tiles.

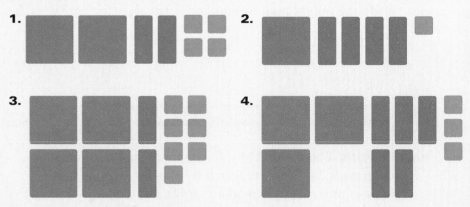

In Exercises 5–8, use algebra tiles to represent the polynomial. Sketch your result.

5. $3x^2 + 2x + 7$ **6.** $4x^2 + 5x + 3$

7. $x^2 + 6x + 4$ **8.** $5x^2 + 7x + 1$

You can use algebra tiles to model polynomial addition. For instance, the sum of $2x^2 + 3x + 3$ and $x^2 + x + 2$ is shown below.

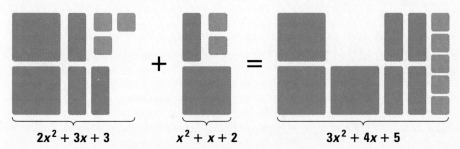

$2x^2 + 3x + 3$ $x^2 + x + 2$ $3x^2 + 4x + 5$

The combined group on the right represents $3x^2 + 4x + 5$. This polynomial is called the **sum** of the two original polynomials. It can be written as the polynomial equation

$$(2x^2 + 3x + 3) + (x^2 + x + 2) = 3x^2 + 4x + 5.$$

In Exercises 9–12, use algebra tiles to find the sum. Sketch your result.

9. $(3x^2 + 2x + 7) + (x^2 + x + 1)$

10. $(4x^2 + 5x + 3) + (2x^2 + 1)$

11. $(x^2 + 6x + 4) + (3x^2 + 2x)$

12. $(5x^2 + 7x + 1) + (4x + 3)$

NOW TRY THESE

In Exercises 13 and 14, write the polynomial equation suggested by the algebra tiles.

13.

14.

15. WRITING In your own words, explain how to add two polynomials.

14.6

Adding and Subtracting Polynomials

What you should learn:

Goal 1 How to add two or more polynomials

Goal 2 How to subtract two polynomials

Why you should learn it:

You can use polynomial subtraction to solve geometry problems, such as finding the area of a region.

Goal 1 ADDING POLYNOMIALS

You can **add** two polynomials by *combining like terms*. For instance, to add $2x^2 + 3x + 3$ and $x^2 + x + 2$, you can write the following.

$$(2x^2 + 3x + 3) + (x^2 + x + 2) = 2x^2 + 3x + 3 + x^2 + x + 2$$
$$= 2x^2 + x^2 + 3x + x + 3 + 2$$
$$= 3x^2 + 4x + 5$$

This technique is called the *horizontal format* for adding polynomials. You can also use a *vertical format*.

$$\begin{array}{l} 2x^2 + 3x + 3 \\ \underline{x^2 + \ x + 2} \\ 3x^2 + 4x + 5 \end{array}$$ Write each polynomial in standard form.
Line up like terms.
Add coefficients of like terms.

The **degree** of a polynomial is its largest exponent. *Any* two polynomials can be added. They do not have to have the same degree.

2nd-Degree Polynomial   **3rd-Degree Polynomial**

$$2n^2 - 5n + 3$$ $$-n^3 - 4n^2 + 7$$

Example 1 Adding Polynomials

Add the polynomials.

a. $(-n^3 + 2n^2 - n + 4) + (2n^3 + 3n + 6)$

b. $(x^3 + 5x^2 - 2x + 3) + (2x^2 + 4x - 5)$

Solution

You can use either a horizontal or vertical format. The vertical format is shown below.

Line up like terms.   Line up like terms.

a. $\begin{array}{l} -n^3 + 2n^2 - \ n + \ 4 \\ \underline{+ \ (2n^3 + \quad\quad 3n + \ 6)} \\ n^3 + 2n^2 + 2n + 10 \end{array}$

b. $\begin{array}{l} x^3 + 5x^2 - 2x + 3 \\ \underline{+ \quad\quad (2x^2 + 4x - 5)} \\ x^3 + 7x^2 + 2x - 2 \end{array}$

In part (a), the polynomial $2n^3 + 3n + 6$ is written with a blank space because there is no n^2 term.

STUDY TIP

When you use a vertical format to add polynomials, line up the like terms. Sometimes this means leaving a space.

To subtract two polynomials, you can use the Distributive Property. For instance, you can subtract $x^2 - x + 3$ from $3x^2 - x + 5$ as follows.

$$(3x^2 - x + 5) - (x^2 - x + 3) = 3x^2 - x + 5 - x^2 + x - 3$$
$$= 3x^2 - x^2 - x + x + 5 - 3$$
$$= 2x^2 + 2$$

A vertical format for this subtraction is shown below. Notice that the vertical format requires two steps.

$$
\begin{array}{r}
3x^2 - x + 5 \\
-(x^2 - x + 3) \\
\hline
\end{array}
$$
⟵ **Distribute.** ⟶
$$
\begin{array}{r}
3x^2 - x + 5 \\
-x^2 + x - 3 \\
\hline
2x^2 + 2
\end{array}
$$

Example 2 Subtracting Polynomials

Find an expression that represents the area of the blue region.

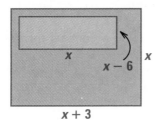

Solution

The area of the larger rectangle is

$$\text{Area} = x(x + 3) = x^2 + 3x.$$

The area of the smaller rectangle is

$$\text{Area} = x(x - 6) = x^2 - 6x.$$

To find the area of the blue region, subtract the area of the smaller rectangle from the area of the larger rectangle.

$$(x^2 + 3x) - (x^2 - 6x) = x^2 + 3x - x^2 + 6x$$
$$= x^2 - x^2 + 3x + 6x$$
$$= 9x$$

ONGOING ASSESSMENT

Write About It
••••••••••••••••••••

Solve each problem.
Show your work.

1. $(x^2 + 3x + 3) + (2x^2 - 2x + 4)$

2. $(3x^2 - x + 2) - (x^2 + 2x - 5)$

GUIDED PRACTICE

In Exercises 1 and 2, use a horizontal format to find the sum or difference.

1. $(3x^2 - 7x + 5) + (3x^2 - 10)$

2. $(n^2 + 8n - 7) - (-n^2 + 8n - 12)$

In Exercises 3 and 4, use a vertical format to find the sum or difference.

3. $\begin{aligned} 2y^3 + \ y^2 - 4y + 3 \\ + (y^3 - 5y^2 + 2y - 6) \end{aligned}$

4. $\begin{aligned} 2y^3 + \ y^2 - 4y + 3 \\ - (y^3 - 5y^2 + 2y - 6) \end{aligned}$

PRACTICE AND PROBLEM SOLVING

ERROR ANALYSIS In Exercises 5 and 6, find and correct the error.

5. $\begin{aligned} -4z^3 + z^2 \qquad + 7 \\ + \ (3z^3 \qquad - 6z - 5) \\ \hline -z^3 \ + z^2 + 6z + 2 \end{aligned}$

6. $\begin{aligned} 4x^3 + 3x^2 + 4x + 3 \\ - (2x^3 + x^2 + 2x + 1) \\ \hline 2x^3 + 4x^2 + 6x + 4 \end{aligned}$

In Exercises 7–10, add or subtract the polynomials. (Use a horizontal format.)

7. $(-x^2 + 9x - 5) + (6x^2 - 2x + 16)$

8. $(-8a^3 + a^2 + 17) + (6a^2 - 3a + 9)$

9. $(-b^3 + 4b^2 - 1) - (7b^3 + 4b^2 + 3)$

10. $(-5x^3 - 13x + 4) - (-3x^3 + x^2 + 10x - 9)$

In Exercises 11–14, add or subtract the polynomials. (Use a vertical format.)

11. $\begin{aligned} x^3 + 4x^2 - 9x + 2 \\ + (-2x^3 + 5x^2 + \ x - 6) \\ \hline \end{aligned}$

12. $\begin{aligned} 2n^4 + 2n^3 - \ n^2 - 4n + 6 \\ + (n^4 + 3n^3 - 3n^2 - 5n + 2) \\ \hline \end{aligned}$

13. $\begin{aligned} 3t^3 + 4t^2 + \ t - 5 \\ - (t^3 + 2t^2 - 9t + 1) \\ \hline \end{aligned}$

14. $\begin{aligned} x^4 + 3x^3 + \ x^2 + 2x + 5 \\ - (x^4 + 2x^3 + 3x^2 + 4x - 4) \\ \hline \end{aligned}$

In Exercises 15 and 16, perform the indicated operations.

15. $(2x^2 + 9x - 4) + (-8x^2 + 3x + 6) + (x^2 - 5x - 7)$

16. $(4x^2 + x - 17) - (x^2 - 15x + 7) - (-7x^2 + x + 6)$

GEOMETRY In Exercises 17 and 18, find the perimeter of the polygon. Then evaluate the perimeter when $x = 3$.

17.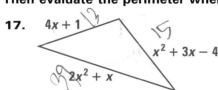

$4x + 1$

$x^2 + 3x - 4$

$2x^2 + x$

18. $2x^2 - 4x + 5$

$2x + 7$

$x^2 + 5$

$3x^2 - 2x - 4$

In Exercises 19 and 20, find an expression that represents the area of the blue region. Then evaluate the area when $x = 5$.

19.

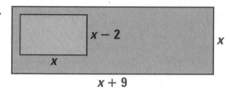

20.

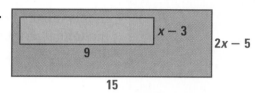

BUSINESS In Exercises 21–23, use the following information.

You spend $500 to start a small business selling a computer software program you wrote. Each program costs you $2.50 to package. You sell each program for $12.50.

Income $= 12.50x$ **Expense** $= 2.50x + 500$

21. Write a polynomial model for the profit you make selling x programs.

22. How much profit will you make if you sell 200 programs?

23. Will you make twice as much profit if you sell 400 programs? Explain.

STANDARDIZED TEST PRACTICE

24. Find the difference: $(2x^3 + 3x + 7) - (3x^3 - 2x^2 + 4x - 3)$.

- **A** $-x^3 - 2x^2 - x - 4$
- **B** $5x^3 - 2x^2 - 7x + 10$
- **C** $-x^3 + 2x^2 - x - 4$
- **D** $-x^3 + 2x^2 - x + 10$

EXPLORATION AND EXTENSION

25. COMMUNICATING ABOUT MATHEMATICS The expressions below show about how long it took, in minutes, for two runners to run x miles in the 1997 Hardrock 100.

Mark Hartell: $18.1x$
Joel Zucker: $28.4x$

a. Make a table of values showing how long it took each runner to go 20, 40, 60, and 80 mi.

b. How much longer did it take Zucker to go 80 mi than it took Hartell?

c. Subtract the first expression from the second. What does the resulting expression represent?

14.7 Multiplying Polynomials

What you should learn:

Goal 1 How to multiply a polynomial by a monomial

Goal 2 How to use polynomial multiplication to solve geometry problems

Why you should learn it:

You can use polynomial multiplication to solve geometry problems, such as finding the area of a region.

Goal 1 MULTIPLYING POLYNOMIALS

In this lesson, you will learn how to multiply a polynomial by a monomial. Example 1 reviews the types of polynomials that you already know how to multiply.

Example 1 Multiplying Polynomials

a. $2(3x + 5) = 6x + 10$ Distributive Property (Lesson 2.1)

b. $5(n - 3) = 5n - 15$ Distributive Property (Lesson 3.4)

c. $(y^2)(y^3) = y^5$ Property of Exponents (Lesson 6.7)

Each of the products in Example 1 is an example of multiplying a polynomial by a *monomial*. The general rule for finding this type of product is stated below.

> **MULTIPLYING A POLYNOMIAL BY A MONOMIAL**
>
> To multiply a polynomial by a monomial, multiply each term of the polynomial by the monomial.

Example 2 Multiplying a Polynomial by a Monomial

a. $3x(x^2 + 2x - 5) = 3x(x^2) + 3x(2x) - 3x(5)$ Distribute.

$= 3x^3 + 6x^2 - 15x$ Simplify.

b. $n^2(-2n^3 + 4n) = n^2(-2n^3) + n^2(4n)$ Distribute.

$= -2n^5 + 4n^3$ Simplify.

c. $2b^2(-4b^4 + b + 6) = 2b^2(-4b^4) + 2b^2(b) + 2b^2(6)$

$= -8b^6 + 2b^3 + 12b^2$

d. $-5y(3y^2 + y - 7) = -5y(3y^2) + (-5y)(y) - (-5y)(7)$

$= -15y^3 - 5y^2 + 35y$

STUDY TIP

One of the most common errors in algebra is to forget to "distribute negative signs."

Incorrect

$-x(2x^2 - 3x + 1)$

$= -2x^3 - 3x^2 + x$

Correct

$-x(2x^2 - 3x + 1)$

$= -2x^3 + 3x^2 - x$

Example 3 Using Polynomial Multiplication

The rectangle below is divided into five regions. Write an expression for the area of each region. Then write an expression for the area of the entire region.

CONNECTION
Geometry

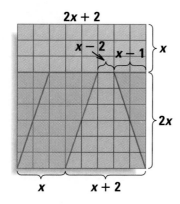

2x + 2

x − 2   x − 1   x

2x

x   x + 2

Solution

Polygon	Expression for area	Simplified
Rectangle	Area $= x(2x + 2)$	$2x^2 + 2x$
Parallelogram	Area $= x(2x)$	$2x^2$
Trapezoid	Area $= \frac{1}{2}(2x)[(x - 2) + (x + 2)]$	$2x^2$
Each triangle	Area $= \frac{1}{2}(2x)(x - 1)$	$x^2 - x$

To find an expression for the area of the entire region, you can add the expressions for the areas of the five regions.

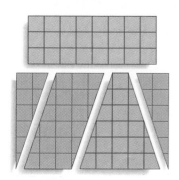

Area of rectangle	$2x^2 + 2x$
Area of parallelogram	$2x^2$
Area of trapezoid	$2x^2$
Area of triangle	$x^2 - x$
Area of triangle	$+ \ x^2 - x$
	$8x^2$

ONGOING ASSESSMENT

Talk About It
. . . .

1. The area of the entire region is also given by $3x(2x + 2) = 6x^2 + 6x$. Why?

2. Find a value of x that makes this expression equal to the expression found in Example 3.

3. Use the value of x to find the area of the entire region.

GUIDED PRACTICE

In Exercises 1 and 2, find the product.

1. $4n(2n^2 - 3n + 5)$

2. $-3y^2(y^2 + 2y - 5)$

GEOMETRY   In Exercises 3–7, use the figure at the right.

3. Write an expression for the area of each region.

4. Use the result of Exercise 3 to write an expression for the area of the entire region.

5. Write expressions for the length and width of the entire region.

6. Use the result of Exercise 5 to write an expression for the area of the entire region.

7. Compare the expressions obtained in Exercises 4 and 6.

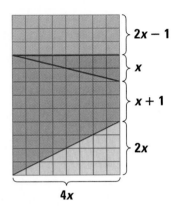

PRACTICE AND PROBLEM SOLVING

In Exercises 8–16, multiply.

8. $2y(y^2 + 1)$

9. $4x(x^2 - 2x - 1)$

10. $-2(3x^2 + 6x - 8)$

11. $8t^2(-6t - 5)$

12. $-b^4(8b^2 + 10b - 1)$

13. $2t(-4t^2 + 6t - 2)$

14. $y(-7y^3 + 8y - 4)$

15. $-4z(2z^5 - z^3 + 10)$

16. $n^3(-n^4 + n^3 - n^2 + n - 1)$

GEOMETRY   In Exercises 17–20, use the figure at the right.

17. Write an expression for the area of each region.

18. Use the result of Exercise 17 to write an expression for the area of the entire region.

19. Use the formula for the area of a rectangle to write an expression for the area of the entire region.

20. Compare the expressions obtained in Exercises 18 and 19.

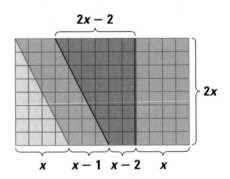

In Exercises 21 and 22, translate the verbal phrase to an algebraic expression. Then multiply.

21. The product of a number and one more than that number

22. The cube of a number times the difference of the number and 2

23. GARDENS Write an expression for the area of a garden plot that is twice as long as it is wide.

GEOMETRY In Exercises 24–27, use the rectangular prism
at the right.

24. Write an expression for the area of the base of
the prism.

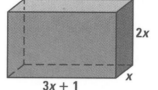

25. Write an expression for the volume of the prism.

26. Write an expression for the surface area of the prism.

27. The surface area of the prism is 216 square units. What is the
volume? Explain your reasoning.

ERROR ANALYSIS In Exercises 28–31, you are helping a friend. Your
friend's solution is given. What did your friend do wrong? What could you
say to help your friend avoid the error?

28. $3m(5m^3 + 7) = \cancel{15m^4 + 7}$

29. $4b(b^2 - 4) = \cancel{4b^2 - 16b}$

30. $7t^2(-t^3 + 3t^2 - 8t) = \cancel{7t^2(-t^3) + 7t^2(3t^2) - 7t^2(-8t)}$
$$= \cancel{-7t^5 + 21t^4 + 56t^3}$$

31. $-3x^3(2x^2 - 5x + 9) = \cancel{-3x^3(2x^2) - 3x^3(5x) + 3x^3(9)}$
$$= \cancel{-6x^5 - 15x^4 + 27x^3}$$

32. Multiply $5z(6 - 2z^2)$.

    (A) $30z - 2z^2$ (B) $30z - 10z^2$ (C) $30z - 10z^3$ (D) $30z + 10z^3$

33. Multiply $-t(4t^2 - 2t - 1)$.

    (A) $-4t^2 + 2t + t$ (B) $-5t^3 - 3t^2 + t$ (C) $4t^3 - 2t^2 - t$ (D) $-4t^3 + 2t^2 + t$

EXPLORATION AND EXTENSION

In Exercises 34–37, write the expression without using exponents.

34. 4^0 35. 2^{-1} 36. $3^3 \cdot 3^2$ 37. $5^{-1} \cdot 5^4$

In Exercises 38–41, use the Distributive Property to rewrite the
expression.

38. $2(6 + x)$ 39. $-3(t + 4)$ 40. $5(2x + 3)$ 41. $4(3x - 5)$

In Exercises 1–3, use the similar triangles at the right. (11.1)

1. Find the lengths of the hypotenuses of $\triangle ABC$ and $\triangle DEF$.

2. What is the scale factor of $\triangle DEF$ to $\triangle ABC$?

3. Find the area and perimeter of each triangle.

In Exercises 4–9, simplify. (7.4, 7.5)

4. $\dfrac{2}{3} + \dfrac{1}{6}$

5. $\dfrac{5}{8} - \dfrac{3}{4}$

6. $\dfrac{12}{15} \times \dfrac{2}{5}$

7. $-\dfrac{13}{21} \times \left(-\dfrac{4}{81}\right)$

8. $\dfrac{16}{21} \div \dfrac{4}{7}$

9. $\dfrac{6}{19} \div 2$

In Exercises 10–13, solve the inequality. (9.6)

10. $5y + 13 \geq 28$

11. $3 - 2r < 6$

12. $\dfrac{1}{2} < \dfrac{1}{4} - \dfrac{1}{3}s$

13. $4x + 3 \leq 2x$

In Exercises 14 and 15, add the polynomials. (14.6)

14. $(3x^2 + 2x + 1) + (x^2 + 2x + 3)$

15. $(6x^3 - x^2 + 2) + (3x^2 + 2)$

16. Find the volume of a can of tuna that has a radius of 4.2 cm and a height of 3.5 cm. (12.5)

HISTORY Connection

GALILEO

The Italian artist and inventor Galileo was one of the first thinkers to apply the scientific method. Before Galileo, people assumed that heavy objects fell faster than light objects.

This is a detail of a painting by Giuseppe Bezzuoli (1784–1855) depicting Galileo demonstrating his experiment with the inclined plane.

Using an inclined plane, Galileo showed that the distance an object falls depends only on the square of the time it has been falling, not on its weight.

Here is a table of times and distances for a ball rolling down an inclined plane:

t (s)	0	1	2	3	4
d (ft)	0	3	12	27	48

1. Write an equation of the form $d = kt^2$ that fits the data in the table. What is the value of k?

2. How many seconds would it take the ball to roll 1200 ft? Explain.

3. Drop a heavy and a light object at the same time. Do they land at the same time or at different times? Explain.

Exploring Binomial Multiplication

Materials Needed
• algebra tiles

You can represent the product of two binomials as follows.

Length = $2x + 1$

Width = $x + 3$

Area = (Length)(Width)

= $(2x + 1)(x + 3)$

The combined group represents the product $2x^2 + 7x + 3$. The result can be written as the polynomial equation

$$(2x + 1)(x + 3) = 2x^2 + 7x + 3.$$

In Exercises 1–6, write the polynomial equation that is modeled by the algebra tiles.

1.

2.

3.

4.

5.

6.

NOW TRY THESE

In Exercises 7–12, use algebra tiles to find the product. Sketch your result.

7. $2x(3x + 2)$

8. $x(4x + 3)$

9. $(x + 2)(3x + 1)$

10. $(x + 1)(4x + 3)$

11. $(x + 1)^2$

12. $(x + 2)^2$

More About Multiplying Polynomials

Goal 1 **MULTIPLYING TWO BINOMIALS**

In this lesson, you will learn how to use the Distributive Property and the FOIL method to multiply two binomials.

Example 1 **Multiplying Two Binomials**

Find the product of $(x + 1)$ and $(2x + 3)$.

Solution

Method 1 *Use a Horizontal Format.*

In the following solution, notice that the Distributive Property is used in the first step and in the second step.

$$(x + 1)(2x + 3) = (x + 1)(2x) + (x + 1)(3)$$
$$= (x)(2x) + (1)(2x) + (x)(3) + (1)(3)$$
$$= 2x^2 + 2x + 3x + 3$$
$$= 2x^2 + 5x + 3$$

Method 2 *Use a Vertical Format.*

$x + 1$	Write first binomial.
$2x + 3$	Write second binomial.
$3x + 3$	Multiply $x + 1$ by 3.
$2x^2 + 2x$	Multiply $x + 1$ by $2x$.
$2x^2 + 5x + 3$	Add $(3x + 3)$ and $(2x^2 + 2x)$.

With both methods, notice that you are multiplying the same quantities, and you get the same result.

Example 2 **The FOIL Method**

The horizontal format for multiplying binomials can be shortened, as follows.

First   Outer   Inner   Last

$$(3x + 5)(2x + 1) = 3x \cdot 2x + 3x \cdot 1 + 5 \cdot 2x + 5 \cdot 1$$
$$= 6x^2 + 3x + 10x + 5$$
$$= 6x^2 + 13x + 5$$

This shortcut is called the **FOIL** method because the products can be labeled as **F**irst, **O**uter, **I**nner, and **L**ast.

Example 3 Guess, Check, and Revise

REAL LIFE
Art

The area of the picture below, including the frame, is 80 in.² What are the dimensions of the frame?

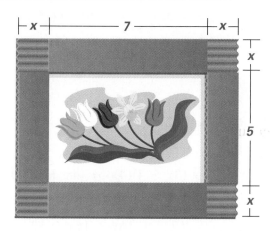

Solution

One way to solve the problem is to begin by writing a model for the total area.

Verbal Model   Area = Length · Width

Labels
Area = 80   (square inches)
Length = $2x + 7$ (inches)
Width = $2x + 5$ (inches)

Algebraic Model

$$80 = (2x + 7)(2x + 5)$$
$$= (2x + 7)(2x) + (2x + 7)(5)$$
$$= (2x)(2x) + (7)(2x) + (2x)(5) + (7)(5)$$
$$= 4x^2 + 14x + 10x + 35$$
$$= 4x^2 + 24x + 35$$

STRATEGY Using this model, you can use *Guess, Check, and Revise* to find the value of x for which $4x^2 + 24x + 35$ is equal to 80.

Let $x = 1$ $4(1)^2 + 24(1) + 35 = 4 + 24 + 35 = 63$ **too small**
Let $x = 2$ $4(2)^2 + 24(2) + 35 = 16 + 48 + 35 = 99$ **too big**
Let $x = 1.5$ $4(1.5)^2 + 24(1.5) + 35 = 9 + 36 + 35 = 80$ ✔

Because $x = 1.5$, the frame is 8 in. by 10 in.

ONGOING ASSESSMENT

Write About It
••••••••••••••••••••

Show all three methods for finding the product: horizontal format (showing all steps), vertical format, and FOIL.

1. $(2x + 3)(x + 4)$

2. $(3x + 5)(x + 2)$

In Exercises 1 and 2, use the Distributive Property to find the product. Explain each step.

1. $(x + 3)(3x + 2)$

2. $(2x + 1)(4x + 5)$

In Exercises 3–6, match the product with its equivalent expression.

A. $12x^2 + 15x + 3$ **B.** $12x^2 + 52x + 16$ **C.** $12x^2 + 32x + 16$ **D.** $12x^2 + 17x + 6$

3. $(4x + 3)(3x + 2)$ **4.** $(2x + 8)(6x + 2)$ **5.** $(12x + 3)(x + 1)$ **6.** $(6x + 4)(2x + 4)$

PRACTICE AND PROBLEM SOLVING

ERROR ANALYSIS In Exercises 7 and 8, find and correct the error.

7. $(x + 6)(2x + 5)$

$= (x + 6)(2x) + 5$

$= (x)(2x) + 6(2x) + 5$

$= 2x^2 + 12x + 5$

8. $(3x + 4)(4x + 3)$

$= (3x + 4)(4x) + (4x + 3)(4)$

$= 3x(4x) + 4(4x) + (4x)(4) + 3(4)$

$= 12x^2 + 16x + 16x + 12$

$= 12x^2 + 32x + 12$

In Exercises 9–17, find the product using the Distributive Property.

9. $(x + 3)(8x + 12)$

10. $(5x + 6)(x + 2)$

11. $(2x + 1)(9x + 7)$

12. $(4x + 5)(5x + 4)$

13. $(10x + 10)(2x + 2)$

14. $(3x + 8)(3x + 2)$

15. $(2x + 3)(4x + 1)$

16. $(2x + 4)(7x + 9)$

17. $(6x + 5)(3x + 5)$

In Exercises 18–23, multiply the binomials using a vertical format. Then check the result by using a horizontal format.

18. $3x + 2$
$\quad 6x + 8$

19. $9x + 6$
$\quad 3x + 1$

20. $\quad x + 10$
$\quad 4x + 15$

21. $5x + 1$
$\quad x + 7$

22. $6x + 1$
$\quad 6x + 1$

23. $3x + 10$
$\quad 10x + \; 3$

GEOMETRY In Exercises 24–26, find the area of the figure. Then evaluate the area when $x = 2$.

24.

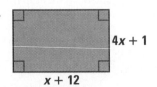

$4x + 1$

$x + 12$

25.

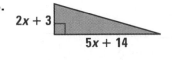

$2x + 3$

$5x + 14$

26.

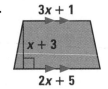

$3x + 1$

$x + 3$

$2x + 5$

27. MOSAICS You are designing a mosaic that is to have an area of 180 ft². The mosaic is a rectangle and is made up of rectangular enameled tiles that are each x ft by 1 ft. The mosaic is $(4x + 2)$ ft wide and $(7x + 4)$ ft high. Find the dimensions of the mosaic.

28. Multiply $(x + 15)$ by $(2x + 1)$. Then multiply $(2x + 1)$ by $(x + 15)$. What can you conclude? What property does this illustrate?

29. Multiply $2[(x + 3)(x + 5)]$. Then multiply $[2(x + 3)](x + 5)$. What property does this illustrate?

Real Life... **R**eal Facts

Mexican Art About 7.5 million stones make up the Juan O'Gorman mosaic found at Mexico's National Autonomous University. It depicts scenes from the history of Mexico.

STANDARDIZED TEST PRACTICE

30. Which expression does not represent the area of the parallelogram at the right?

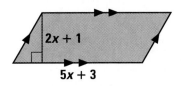

2x + 1

5x + 3

Ⓐ $(2x + 1)(5x + 3)$

Ⓑ $10x^2 + 11x + 3$

Ⓒ $10x^2 + 13x + 3$

Ⓓ All are valid expressions.

EXPLORATION AND EXTENSION

LOOKING FOR A PATTERN In Exercises 31–36, multiply.

31. $(x + 1)(x + 1)$

32. $(x + 2)(x + 2)$

33. $(x + 3)(x + 3)$

34. $(x + 4)(x + 4)$

35. $(x + 5)(x + 5)$

36. $(x + 6)(x + 6)$

$(x + k)(x + k)$
$x^2 + kx + kx + k^2$
$x^2 + 2kx + k^2$

37. WRITING Each of the products in Exercises 31–36 is an example of a "binomial pattern." Describe the pattern. Then use your description to find the product of $(x + 7)$ and $(x + 7)$. Use the Distributive Property to check your result.

WHAT *did you learn?*   **WHY** *did you learn it?*

Skills		WHAT did you learn?	WHY did you learn it?
Skills	14.1	Find the mean, median, and mode of a collection of numbers.	Describe measures of central tendency in data sets.
	14.2	Draw a stem-and-leaf plot.	Compare two sets of data visually.
	14.3	Draw a box-and-whisker plot.	Display the quartiles of a set of data visually.
	14.4	Add and subtract matrices.	Analyze mathematical information in table formats.
	14.5	Combine like terms in polynomials.	Simplify polynomial expressions.
	14.6	Add and subtract polynomials.	Find a variable expression for the area of a region.
	14.7	Multiply a polynomial by a monomial.	Simplify polynomial expressions, and prepare for multiplying binomials.
	14.8	Multiply two binomials.	Express the area of a rectangle in two different ways.
Strategies	14.1–14.8	Use problem solving strategies.	Solve a wide variety of real-life problems.
Using Data	14.1–14.4	Use stem-and-leaf plots, box-and-whisker plots, and matrices.	Organize data and solve problems.

HOW *does it fit in the bigger picture of mathematics?*

If someone asks you what you studied in math this year, what will you say? The goal of this textbook was to introduce you to two main parts of mathematics: algebra and geometry.

You learned that mathematics is not just a collection of formulas that need to be memorized. Instead, it is a language that can be used to model and solve real-life problems.

Of course, there is much more to algebra and geometry than is possible to put in this book. You can think of the 14 chapters in this book as "passports" to the realms of algebra and geometry that you might be studying in the next two or three years.

VOCABULARY

- measure of central tendency (p. 668)
- mean, or average (p. 668)
- median (p. 668)
- mode (p. 668)
- stem-and-leaf plot (p. 672)
- second quartile (p. 676)

- first quartile (p. 676)
- third quartile (p. 676)
- box-and-whisker plot (p. 676)
- matrix (p. 682)
- entries (p. 682)
- equal matrices (p. 682)

- add matrices (p. 683)
- subtract matrices (p. 683)
- polynomial (p. 688)
- standard form (p. 688)
- sum of polynomials (p. 693)
- add polynomials (p. 694)
- degree of a polynomial (p. 694)

14.1 MEASURES OF CENTRAL TENDENCY

Example Find the mean, median, and mode of 3, 4, 5, 5, 6, and 7.

Solution $\text{mean} = \dfrac{3 + 4 + 5 + 5 + 6 + 7}{6} = \dfrac{30}{6} = 5$ The sum of the numbers divided by how many numbers are in the set

$\text{median} = \dfrac{5 + 5}{2} = 5$ The middle number or the mean of the two middle numbers

$\text{mode} = 5$ The number that occurs most often

Find the mean, median, and mode of the data.

1. 6, 9, 3, 2, 5, 6, 4, 7, 5, 4, 8, 5, 5, 4, 3

2. 25, 20, 30, 22, 24, 23, 24, 28, 26, 29

3. 41, 44, 47, 40, 48, 49, 41, 45, 46, 42

4. 72, 73, 75, 77, 76, 79, 78, 71, 72, 77

14.2 STEM-AND-LEAF PLOTS

For each number in a stem-and-leaf plot, the last digit is a leaf.
The other digit (or digits) is the stem. Include a key with your plot.

Example

You can use a stem-and-leaf plot to order
43, 42, 56, 86, 65, 79, 43, 55, 72.

Ordered Data:
42, 43, 43, 55, 56, 65, 72, 79, 86

Stem	Leaves	
8	6	8|6 represents 86
7	2 9	
6	5	
5	5 6	
4	2 3 3	

Use a stem-and-leaf plot to order the data.

5. 5, 26, 48, 24, 32, 58, 51, 34, 26

6. 123, 158, 182, 147, 135, 165, 166

7. 61, 72, 31, 33, 35, 67, 71, 95, 99

8. 21, 29, 35, 47, 58, 62, 64, 36, 94, 77

14.3 BOX-AND-WHISKER PLOTS

The first and third quartiles of a data set are the medians of the lower and upper halves.

Example Draw a box-and-whisker plot of the data:
23, 84, 53, 63, 75, 29, 19, 38, 47, 57.

Solution 19, 23, **29**, 38, 47, 53, 57, **63**, 75, **84**   List the numbers in increasing order.

Plot the first number, the quartiles, and the last number, then draw a box.

Draw a box-and-whisker plot of the data.

9. 25, 27, 5, 8, 9, 12, 16, 18, 21, 22   **10.** 35, 67, 95, 100, 47, 82, 50, 0, 89, 71

14.4 EXPLORING DATA AND MATRICES

To add and subtract matrices, you add or subtract corresponding entries.

Examples   **Adding Matrices**   **Subtracting Matrices**

$$\begin{bmatrix} 3 & -4 \\ 5 & 2 \end{bmatrix} + \begin{bmatrix} 2 & 3 \\ 4 & -2 \end{bmatrix} = \begin{bmatrix} 5 & -1 \\ 9 & 0 \end{bmatrix} \qquad \begin{bmatrix} 3 & -4 \\ 5 & 2 \end{bmatrix} - \begin{bmatrix} 2 & 3 \\ 4 & -2 \end{bmatrix} = \begin{bmatrix} 1 & -7 \\ 1 & 4 \end{bmatrix}$$

Find the sum and difference of the matrices.

11. $\begin{bmatrix} 0 & -4 \\ 3 & 6 \end{bmatrix}, \begin{bmatrix} 8 & 7 \\ 4 & -6 \end{bmatrix}$ **12.** $\begin{bmatrix} 2 & -6 & 7 \\ 3 & 9 & -8 \end{bmatrix}, \begin{bmatrix} 1 & -3 & 6 \\ 2 & 9 & -5 \end{bmatrix}$

14.5 EXPLORING POLYNOMIALS

Example $4x + 3x^2 + 6x^3 - 4x^2 - 2x + 8$ Polynomial

$6x^3 - 4x^2 + 3x^2 + 4x - 2x + 8$ Rewrite in standard form.

$6x^3 - x^2 + 2x + 8$ Simplify.

Simplify the polynomial. Then state whether the result is a *monomial*, *binomial*, or *trinomial*.

13. $-10x - 7 + 3x + 7$ **14.** $4t^2 - 6t + t^2 + 9t$ **15.** $3x^4 - 8x^3 + 2x^2 + 5x^3$

16. $3s^2 - 4s + 2s^2 + 2s - 9$ **17.** $9 + 15r^3 - 7r^3 + 10$ **18.** $5m^2 + 4m^2 - 3m^2$

You can use similar methods to add or subtract polynomials. But, you need to distribute the minus sign when you subtract polynomials.

Example

$(-n^2 + 5n - 4) - (3n^2 - 4n + 3)$	Write original expression.
$(-n^2 + 5n - 4) - 3n^2 + 4n - 3$	Distribute the minus sign.
$-n^2 - 3n^2 + 5n + 4n - 4 - 3$	Combine like terms.
$-4n^2 + 9n - 7$	Simplify.

Add or subtract the polynomials.

19. $(6x^2 - 3x - 7) + (x^2 - 9)$

20. $(2x^3 - 4x^2 + x - 1) - (-7x^2 - x)$

21. $(4x^3 - 2x^2 - 5) - (-3x^3 + x^2 - 7)$

22. $(5x^2 - 2x + 9) + (8x^2 - 3x - 2)$

Example

$m(m^2 - 2m - 4)$	Write original expression.
$m(m^2) - m(2m) - m(4)$	Distribute.
$m^3 - 2m^2 - 4m$	Simplify.

Multiply.

23. $x(x^2 + x)$

24. $n^2(n^3 + 4)$

25. $x^2(3x + 7)$

26. $t^3(5t^2 + 5t - 3)$

You can use two methods to multiply two binomials.

Example

Distributive Property

		First Outside Inside Last (FOIL)
$(x + 1)(x + 3)$	Write original expression.	$(x + 1)(x + 3)$
$(x + 1)(x) + (x + 1)(3)$	Distribute or use FOIL.	$(x)(x) + (x)(3) + (1)(x) + (1)(3)$
$(x)(x) + (1)(x) + (x)(3) + (1)(3)$	Distribute again.	
$x^2 + x + 3x + 3$	Simplify.	$x^2 + 3x + x + 3$
$x^2 + 4x + 3$	Combine like terms.	$x^2 + 4x + 3$

Multiply using the Distributive Property or the FOIL method.

27. $(2z + 1)(6z + 5)$

28. $(4x + 3)(4x + 3)$

29. $(3p + 6)(p + 4)$

30. $(7x + 3)(x + 9)$

31. $(2s + 3)(8s + 7)$

32. $(x + 5)(3x + 9)$

In Exercises 1 and 2, use the table below showing the number of campers for the years 1986–1993. (Source: U.S. Bureau of Land Management)

Year	1986	1987	1988	1989	1990	1991	1992	1993
Campers (in millions)	95.2	195.3	178.7	173.6	165.4	196.3	181.5	162.7

1. Give the first, second, and third quartiles.   **2.** Create a box-and-whisker plot of the data.

In Exercises 3 and 4, find the mean, median, and mode of the data.

3. 77, 79, 84, 93, 93, 96, 99, 99, 99, 102   **4.** 22, 45, 67, 34, 23, 98, 65, 34, 32, 65, 74

5. Make a stem-and-leaf plot of the data in Exercise 4. $22, 23, 32, 34, 34, 45, 65, 65, 67,$ $74, 98$

In Exercises 6 and 7, find the sum or difference.

6. $\begin{bmatrix} 8 & 12 & 3 & -5 \\ 4 & 22 & 1 & 7 \end{bmatrix} + \begin{bmatrix} 6 & 2 & -7 & 2 \\ 9 & 14 & -4 & 9 \end{bmatrix}$ **7.** $\begin{bmatrix} 3 & 18 & 12 \\ 16 & 12 & 15 \end{bmatrix} - \begin{bmatrix} 1 & 8 & 4 \\ -21 & 0 & 6 \end{bmatrix}$

In Exercises 8–10, simplify the polynomial. Then state whether the result is a *monomial*, *binomial*, or *trinomial*.

8. $2p^2 - p^3 + p + 2p^3$ **9.** $3n^3 + 4 - n^2 - n^3$ **10.** $m^2 + 8m^2 - 5m^2 - 7m^2$

In Exercises 11 and 12, add or subtract the polynomials. Then simplify.

11. $(3x^2 + 2x + 5) + (7x^2 - 4x + 2)$ **12.** $(4p^3 + 6p - 4) - (p^3 - p^2 + 6p - 5)$

In Exercises 13–15, multiply the polynomials.

13. $2y(3y^2 + 2y + 1)$ **14.** $(3p + 1)(2p + 3)$ **15.** $(4x + 5)(x + 7)$

In Exercises 16 and 17, use the given information.

HOME REMODELING Your family plans to add a room to the house. The back wall and windows have the dimensions shown at the right.

16. Give an expression for the area of each window.

17. What is an expression for the area of wall that needs wallpaper?

[Diagram showing a wall with two windows, labeled: 2x + 1, 2x, 2x + 3, 2x, 2x, 8x]

In Exercises 18 and 19, the first matrix gives the numbers of dollars deposited into savings accounts at two different banks. The second matrix shows how much money is in each account after one year.

18. Write a matrix that shows the interest earned in each account.

19. Write a matrix that shows the percent of interest each account earned.

	Deposits		Balance After One Year	
	Bank 1	Bank 2	Bank 1	Bank 2
	100	150	108	164
	450	300	480	325
	600	1000	648	1100

Standardized Test Practice

1. The data below give ticket prices for different movie theaters. Which statement is *false*?

   $5.50, $5.50, $6.00, $5.75, $2.00, $6.25, $6.00, $3.75, $6.50, $5.75, $6.00, $1.00

   (A) The mean is $5.00.

   (B) The median is $5.75.

   (C) The mode is $5.50.

   (D) The most common price is $6.00.

2. The stem-and-leaf plot below shows the results of a survey that asked students to give the day of the month that they were born. Which statement is *false*?

   ```
   0 | 1 3 4 5 7 8 8
   1 | 0 2 3 4 4 4 4 5 6 9
   2 | 0 0 1 2 2 4 5 7
   3 | 1
   ```

   (A) More students were born on the 14th than on any other day.

   (B) The mean of the data is 15.

   (C) Twenty-five students were surveyed.

   (D) The median of the data is 4.

3. Which matrix represents the difference shown below?

   $$\begin{bmatrix} 1 & -5 \\ -4 & -3 \end{bmatrix} - \begin{bmatrix} -2 & 0 \\ -1 & 6 \end{bmatrix}$$

   (A) $\begin{bmatrix} 3 & -5 \\ -3 & -9 \end{bmatrix}$ **(B)** $\begin{bmatrix} -1 & -5 \\ -5 & 3 \end{bmatrix}$

   (C) $\begin{bmatrix} 3 & -5 \\ -5 & -3 \end{bmatrix}$ **(D)** $\begin{bmatrix} -1 & 5 \\ -3 & -9 \end{bmatrix}$

4. The box-and-whisker plot shows the number of words students can type in one minute. Which statement is *false*?

   ```
   15    20  23      29        35
   ```

   (A) The median number of words per minute is 23.

   (B) 50% of the students type fewer than 23 words per minute.

   (C) More students type between 23 and 29 words per minute than between 20 and 23 words per minute.

   (D) 25% of the students type more than 29 words per minute.

5. Simplify the expression $4n^2 - 3 + 4n + n^2 - 7n + 9$.

   (A) $4n^2 - 3n + 6$ **(B)** $5n^2 - 3n + 6$

   (C) $4n^2 - 11n + 12$ **(D)** $5n^2 + 3n + 6$

6. Which expression represents the perimeter of the triangle?

   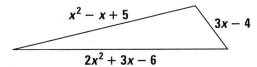

   (A) $2x^2 + x + 7$ **(B)** $2x^2 - x - 7$

   (C) $3x^2 + 6x - 5$ **(D)** $3x^2 + 5x - 5$

7. Which expression represents the area of the shaded region?

   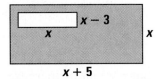

   (A) $2x$ **(B)** $8x$

   (C) $2x^2 + 2x$ **(D)** $2x^2 + 8x$

1. Evaluate $3 \times 4 + 7 \times (9 - 2)$.

   (A) 61   (B) 73

   (C) 126   (D) 231

2. Which expression is equivalent to $4(x - 3)$?

   (A) $4x - 3$ (B) $4x - 12$

   (C) $x - 12$ (D) none of these

3. Evaluate a^2b when $a = -3$ and $b = -2$.

   (A) -18 (B) -12

   (C) 12 (D) 18

4. Solve for k.

   $4k - 12 = 2k + 12$

   (A) 0 (B) 4

   (C) 12 (D) 24

5. You put the letters of the word GARGANTUAN into a hat. What is the probability you draw an A?

   (A) $\frac{1}{5}$ (B) $\frac{3}{10}$

   (C) $\frac{4}{10}$ (D) $\frac{3}{5}$

6. Which number is the greatest common factor of 36 and 24?

   (A) 2 (B) 6

   (C) 12 (D) 72

7. Divide $\frac{8}{12}$ by $\frac{4}{3}$.

   (A) $\frac{8}{9}$ (B) $\frac{4}{7}$

   (C) $\frac{1}{2}$ (D) $\frac{1}{6}$

8. 55 to 66 is what percent of increase?

   (A) 20%   (B) 55%

   (C) 83%   (D) 120%

9. Two legs of a right triangle are 6 units and 9 units long. What is the measure of the hypotenuse?

   (A) 117 units   (B) about 59 units

   (C) 15 units   (D) about 11 units

10. Each side of a regular pentagon is 3 units long. What is the perimeter?

    (A) 18 units   (B) 15 units

    (C) 12 units   (D) 9 units

11. The sides of a triangle are 3, 4, and 5 units long. What is the perimeter?

    (A) $7\frac{1}{2}$ units   (B) 12 units

    (C) 15 units   (D) 17 units

12. A circle has a radius of 8 units. What is the circumference?

    (A) 256 units   (B) 200.96 units

    (C) 50.24 units   (D) 25.12 units

13. What is the distance between the points $(-3, 2)$ and $(4, 6)$ on a coordinate plane?

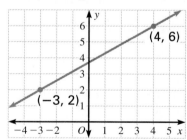

    (A) $\sqrt{11}$ units   (B) $\sqrt{17}$ units

    (C) $\sqrt{33}$ units   (D) $\sqrt{65}$ units

14. What is the median of the numbers 26, 9, 14, 22, 33, 15, 38, and 15?

    (A) 15   (B) 18.5

    (C) 21.5   (D) 29

Student Resources

Table of Contents

x^2

%

$\dfrac{a}{b}$

6   10

8

EXTRA PRACTICE

Use after Lesson 1.1, page 4

Describe a pattern for the sequence. Then list the next 3 numbers.

1. $-2, -5, -8, -11,$? , ? , ?

2. $0, 2, 5, 9,$? , ? , ?

3. $0, 1, 4, 9,$? , ? , ?

4. $99, 90, 81, 72,$? , ? , ?

5. $1, \frac{3}{2}, 2, \frac{5}{2},$? , ? , ?

6. $1, \frac{1}{2}, \frac{1}{3}, \frac{1}{4},$? , ? , ?

Use after Lesson 1.2, page 8

In Exercises 1–6, write a verbal description of the number sentence.

1. $132 - 16 = 116$ **2.** $24 + 12 = 36$ **3.** $42 \div 7 = 6$

4. $15 \cdot 5 = 75$ **5.** $16 / 8 = 2$ **6.** $12(6) = 72$

In Exercises 7–12, find the sum or difference.

7. $55 + 123$ **8.** $300 - 264$ **9.** $781 + 315$

10. $10.2 - 9.6$ **11.** $16.05 + 3.12 + 0.33$ **12.** $115.3 - 77.9$

In Exercises 13–18, find the product or quotient.

13. 18×9 **14.** $540 \div 36$ **15.** $(3.7)(4.9)$

16. $396 \div 18$ **17.** $5 \cdot \frac{4}{5}$ **18.** $5720 \div 65$

Use after Lesson 1.3, page 12

Write a verbal description of the number sentence.

1. $\sqrt{144} = 12$ **2.** $5^4 = 625$ **3.** $7^2 = 49$ **4.** $\sqrt{2.89} = 1.7$

Use after Lesson 1.4, page 18

Simplify the expression without using a calculator.

1. $3 + 14 \div 7$ **2.** $15 + 3 \times 5$ **3.** $3^2 - 10 \div 5$

4. $18 \div 2(9) \cdot 12$ **5.** $26 - 4(4) + 8$ **6.** $2[12 - (4 + 2) \div 3]$

7. $25 - 3^2 + 4 \cdot 5$ **8.** $6 \div (3 \times 2) \cdot 15$ **9.** $(8 + 2) \div 5 \cdot 10$

Use after Lesson 1.5, page 24

Evaluate the expression when $x = 3$.

1. $2 + x$ **2.** $21 \div x$ **3.** $11x$

4. $x \cdot 5x$ **5.** $2x^2 + 7$ **6.** $3x^2 \cdot 4x$

7. $(x + 5) 4$ **8.** $(x - 1) \div 8$ **9.** $(5 - x)^3$

Use after Lesson 1.6, page 28

The table shows the enrollments in Social Studies courses at Plainview High School for three years. Let P, W, and U represent the number of students in Psychology, World History, and U.S. History.

	Year		
Class	1994	1995	1996
Psychology	70	62	72
World History	82	80	55
U.S. History	98	93	88

1. Which subject has the highest enrollment every year?

2. In what year was the total enrollment in all three courses the highest?

3. For which year is it true that $U - 16 = W$?

4. For which year is $P - 17 = W$?

Use after Lesson 1.7, page 34

Decide whether the figure is a polygon. If it is, name it. If it is not, explain why not.

1.

2.

3.

Use after Lesson 1.8, page 40

Make a table showing your results.

1. Find the quotient of 132 and each of the first 4 natural numbers.

2. Find the product of 25 and each of the first 7 whole numbers.

3. Evaluate the fraction $\frac{n}{2}$ as a decimal for values of n from 1 through 8.

4. Calculate $\frac{n^2}{3}$ for the first 5 whole numbers.

Use after Lesson 2.1, page 54

Use the Distributive Property to rewrite the expression.

1. $3(2 + 5)$

2. $12(3 + 7)$

3. $2(x + 3)$

4. $15(y + 4)$

5. $4(z + 3)$

6. $a(2 + b)$

7. $x(y + z)$

8. $5(2 + 3 + 6)$

9. $10(a + b + c)$

Use after Lesson 2.2, page 58

Simplify the expression.

1. $4x + x$

2. $5b + 7b + 1$

3. $2z + 6z + 9$

4. $2a + 7b + 9a$

5. $7 + 3x + 7y + 4x$

6. $2a + 3 + 9b + 7a$

7. $2p + 3r + 3s + p$

8. $x + 2y + 4x + y + 3z$

9. $n^2 + n + 5n$

10. $4(a + 5) + 6a$

11. $5(x + 3) + x + 9$
$5x + 15 + x + 9$

12. $3(a + b) + 7(b + a)$
$3a + 3b + 7b + 7a$

Use after Lesson 2.3, page 62

In Exercises 1–4, write the equation as a question. Then solve it mentally.

1. $x + 2 = 10$ **2.** $6y = 54$ **3.** $z - 15 = 14$ **4.** $\dfrac{12}{n} = 4$

In Exercises 5–8, decide whether $r = 3$ is a solution of the equation. If it isn't, use mental math to find the solution.

5. $4r = 12$ **6.** $21 - r = 18$ **7.** $32 = 8r$ **8.** $5r + r = 18$

Use after Lesson 2.4, page 68

Solve the equation. Then check your solution.

1. $n + 25 = 48$ **2.** $x - 17 = 71$ **3.** $m - 23 = 43$

4. $410 = s - 208$ **5.** $17 + y = 94$ **6.** $t - 3.7 = 11.2$

7. $6.52 = w + 3.08$ **8.** $x + 12.5 = 17$ **9.** $y - 3.5 = 7.3$

Use after Lesson 2.5, page 74

Solve the equation. Check your solution.

1. $3x = 15$ **2.** $10y = 120$ **3.** $81 = 9z$ **4.** $7a = 42$

5. $\dfrac{b}{9} = 8$ **6.** $5 = \dfrac{c}{3}$ **7.** $\dfrac{d}{7} = 4$ **8.** $\dfrac{m}{5} = 10$

9. $6p = 13.2$ **10.** $9q = 23.4$ **11.** $\dfrac{v}{3.2} = 3$ **12.** $\dfrac{y}{15} = 3.2$

Use after Lesson 2.6, page 80

In Exercises 1–4, match the verbal phrase with its algebraic expression.

A. $10 - n$ **B.** $n - 10$ **C.** $10n$ **D.** $2n + 10$

1. 10 more than twice a number **2.** The difference of 10 and a number

3. 10 less than a number **4.** The product of a number and 10

In Exercises 5–10, translate the verbal phrase into an algebraic expression.

5. Six plus a number **6.** A number divided by 12

7. Eight times a number **8.** The quotient of a number and 12

9. Twelve less than a number **10.** Ten more than six times a number

Use after Lesson 2.7, page 84

Match the sentence with an equation.

A. $6n = 18$ **B.** $18 - n = 6$ **C.** $\dfrac{n}{6} = 18$ **D.** $18 = n + 6$

1. The difference of 18 and n is 6. **2.** The quotient of n and 6 is 18.

3. The product of n and 6 is 18. **4.** 18 is the sum of n and 6.

Use after Lesson 2.8, page 90

Consider the following question.

A CD player costs $195 including tax. You already have $45 saved, and you need to save the remaining amount. How much money will you need to save?

1. Write a verbal model that relates the amount of money needed, the amount already saved, and the amount you still need to save.

2. Assign labels to the three parts of your model.

3. Use the labels to translate your verbal model into an algebraic model.

4. Solve the algebraic model.

5. Answer the question, and evaluate your answer for reasonableness.

Use after Lesson 2.9, page 94

Solve the inequality.

1. $x + 5 < 18$ **2.** $y - 3 \geq 12$ **3.** $4z < 16$

4. $15 > c + 3$ **5.** $19 < y - 5$ **6.** $32 \leq 8t$

7. $\frac{x}{5} \leq 10$ **8.** $\frac{y}{2} > 200$ **9.** $\frac{z}{3.2} < 6.4$

Use after Lesson 3.1, page 106

In Exercises 1–6, compare the integers using the symbols < or >.

1. -2 ? 0 **2.** -2 ? -4 **3.** 3 ? -4

4. $\left|-2\right|$? -3 **5.** $\left|-5\right|$? $\left|-4\right|$ **6.** 0 ? $\left|-5\right|$

In Exercises 7–10, write the opposite and the absolute value of the integer.

7. -2 **8.** 5 **9.** -56 **10.** -7

Use after Lesson 3.2, page 112

Find the sum. Write your conclusion as an equation.

1. $3 + 10$ **2.** $-5 + (-4)$ **3.** $-11 + (-11)$

4. $6 + 17$ **5.** $-5 + 5$ **6.** $12 + (-18)$

7. $-19 + 12$ **8.** $22 + (-22)$ **9.** $12 + 0$

Use after Lesson 3.3, page 116

Find the sum. Write your conclusion as an equation.

1. $5 + (-2) + (-8)$ **2.** $-6 + (-2) + 9$ **3.** $5 + (-7) + (-8)$

4. $-16 + 14 + (-3)$ **5.** $-10 + 10 + (-2)$ **6.** $-10 + 6 + (-9)$

7. $-10 + (-7) + (-15)$ **8.** $6 + (-6) + (-4)$ **9.** $10 + (-2) + 12$

Use after Lesson 3.4, page 122

In Exercises 1–8, find the difference. Write your conclusion as an equation.

1. $3 - 7$ **2.** $-4 - (-3)$ **3.** $6 - (-8)$ **4.** $10 - (-2)$

5. $-23 - 2$ **6.** $12 - (-8)$ **7.** $14 - (-3)$ **8.** $16 - (-16)$

In Exercises 9–12, evaluate the expression when $a = 2$ and when $a = -2$.

9. $a - 3$ **10.** $3 - a$ **11.** $a - 2$ **12.** $6 - a$

Use after Lesson 3.5, page 128

In Exercises 1–8, find the product. Write your conclusion as an equation.

1. $6 \cdot 8$ **2.** $8(12)$ **3.** $-3 \cdot (-4)$ **4.** $-15 \cdot 3$

5. $10 \cdot (-7)$ **6.** $7 \cdot (-6)$ **7.** $(-3)(-8)$ **8.** $(0)(-20)$

In Exercises 9–12, simplify the expression.

9. $-8 \cdot (-y)$ **10.** $10 \cdot (-a)$ **11.** $(-11)(-x)$ **12.** $(-w) \cdot 13$

Use after Lesson 3.6, page 134

In Exercises 1–8, evaluate the expression. Check your result by multiplying.

1. $\dfrac{96}{3}$ **2.** $\dfrac{180}{4}$ **3.** $\dfrac{-512}{16}$ **4.** $-208 \div (-8)$

5. $288 \div (-16)$ **6.** $\dfrac{0}{-19}$ **7.** $0 \div 232$ **8.** $-1008 \div (-14)$

In Exercises 9–12, evaluate when $x = -3$, $y = 2$, and $z = -4$.

9. xz **10.** $\dfrac{-3y}{x}$ **11.** $\dfrac{xz}{y}$ **12.** $\dfrac{3z}{2xy}$

Use after Lesson 3.7, page 140

In Exercises 1–3, decide whether the value of the variable is a solution of the equation. If not, find the solution.

1. $x + 6 = 9, x = 3$ **2.** $y - 7 = -11, y = -4$ **3.** $-24 = -8c, c = -3$

In Exercises 4–15, solve the equation. Check your solution.

4. $a + 5 = 2$ **5.** $y - 6 = -3$ **6.** $x - 5 = 12$

7. $-20 = b - 8$ **8.** $c + 5 = -4$ **9.** $z - 4 = -12$

10. $-36 = 9d$ **11.** $-5f = -75$ **12.** $\dfrac{m}{-3} = -15$

13. $-24 = -8n$ **14.** $8p = -64$ **15.** $\dfrac{x}{2} = -14$

Use after Lesson 3.8, page 144

In Exercises 1–8, match the ordered pair with its corresponding point in the coordinate plane. Name the quadrant that contains the point.

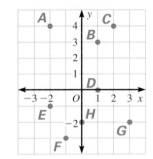

1. $(-2, 4)$ **2.** $(-2, -1)$

3. $(3, -2)$ **4.** $(-1, -3)$

5. $(1, 3)$ **6.** $(1, 0)$

7. $(2, 4)$ **8.** $(0, -2)$

In Exercises 9–12, plot the points on a single coordinate plane. Name the quadrant that contains the point.

9. $A(2, 1)$ **10.** $B(-2, 3)$ **11.** $C(0, 3)$ **12.** $D(-1, -5)$

Use after Lesson 4.1, page 160

In Exercises 1–6, solve the equation. Then check your solution.

1. $2x + 8 = 10$ **2.** $3x - 7 = 2$ **3.** $-2 = 3x + 1$

4. $\frac{m}{2} + 4 = 10$ **5.** $13 = 17 + \frac{n}{2}$ **6.** $\frac{x}{3} - 4 = -7$

In Exercises 7–10, write the sentence as an equation. Then solve it.

7. Two times a number, plus 3, is 13. **8.** Half of a number, plus 3, is 13.

9. The sum of 12 and $3y$ is 15. **10.** One fourth of a number, plus 3, is 8.

Use after Lesson 4.2, page 164

In Exercises 1 and 2, decide whether the given value is a solution of the equation. If not, find the solution.

1. $6x - x - 4 = 16; x = 4$ **2.** $5a - 2a - 3 = -21; a = -8$

In Exercises 3–11, solve the equation. Check your solution.

3. $4x + 5x = 18$ **4.** $3y + 2y - y = 20$ **5.** $32 = 7a - 2a + 3a$

6. $11m - 5m - 6 = 60$ **7.** $6b - 2b + 12 = -4$ **8.** $n - 7n - 6 = -36$

9. $12m - 3m + 6 = 42$ **10.** $\frac{4}{3}x - \frac{10}{3}x - 11 = 1$ **11.** $5z - 4(z + 2) = 2$

Use after Lesson 4.3, page 170

Solve the equation.

1. $3y - 12 = 18$ **2.** $2x + 11 = -29$ **3.** $-\frac{1}{2}z + 7 = -3$

4. $\frac{1}{3}m - 4 = 2$ **5.** $-4t + 6 = -10$ **6.** $18y - 6 = -30$

7. $-13t + 10 = -16$ **8.** $\frac{1}{10}y - 1 = 0$ **9.** $\frac{2}{3}x + \frac{1}{3}x - 6 = 1$

Use after Lesson 4.4, page 174

Solve the equation. Check your solution.

1. $3y + 2(y - 1) = 8$

2. $6 = 3z + 3(z - 6)$

3. $3(2 - s) = -9$

4. $16(q + 1) + 6q = -28$

5. $9(r - 4) + 18 = 0$

6. $12(x - 4) + 6x = 6$

7. $2(x + 7) = -26$

8. $-\frac{1}{7}(y - 11) = 2$

9. $16 = -\frac{1}{2}(p + 2)$

Use after Lesson 4.5, page 180

Solve the equation. Then check your solution.

1. $6x + 10 = 4x$

2. $8y + 12 = 4y - 4$

3. $-3z + 2 = -7z - 22$

4. $-5x + 12 = -3x$

5. $4(n - 1) = n + 11$

6. $-8x + 2 = -6x + 10$

7. $-16 - 8t = 7(t + 2)$

8. $5(x + 3) = 4(x - 4)$

9. $10(3m + 1) = 2(10m - 5)$

10. $8(x - 1) = 4x + 12$

11. $\frac{3}{2}z + 1 = 4 + \frac{5}{2}z$

12. $-15 - \frac{1}{9}r = \frac{8}{9}r + 7$

Use after Lesson 4.6, page 184

Use the following information.

At noon, the temperature in Wilmington, Delaware, is 88° and is decreasing at a rate of 2 degrees per hour. At the same time, the temperature in Bangor, Maine, is 73° and is increasing at a rate of 3 degrees per hour. When will the temperatures be the same?

1. Write a verbal model.

2. Assign labels to each part of the model.

3. Write an algebraic model.

4. Solve the algebraic model.

5. How long will it take for the temperatures to be the same?

6. At what time will the temperatures be the same?

Use after Lesson 4.7, page 190

 Use a calculator to solve the equation. Round your answers to two decimal places.

1. $4a + 6 = -4$

2. $12x + 2 = 14$

3. $26y - 4 = 26$

4. $13 - 12n = -7$

5. $6(2b - 4) = -12b + 14$

6. $22r - 4 = 5(7 - 2r)$

7. $2.4t + 42.6 = -9.2$

8. $0.25d - 11.6 = 2.45d$

9. $3.21(4.2y - 5.1) = 18.92$

Use after Lesson 4.8, page 194

Solve for *x* and find the dimensions of the polygon.

1. Rectangle

Perimeter: 64 units

Width: $5x + 2$

Length: $3x - 2$

2. Rectangle

Perimeter: 100 units

Width: $5x + 2$

Length: $2x + 6$

3. Square

Perimeter: 24 units

Side: $x - 2$

Use after Lesson 5.1, page 206

Use the pictograph at the right, which shows how many CDs were sold at the CD-Mart in January.

1. How many CDs in the category of country western were sold?

2. Approximately how many opera CDs were sold?

3. What was the total number of CDs sold in all categories?

CD Sales at CD-Mart

Pop rock	◉◉◉◉◉◉◉
Country western	◉◉◉◉◉
Hits of the 60's	◉◉◉◉
Classical	◉◉◉◉
Opera	◉◔

◉ = 10 CDs

Use after Lesson 5.2, page 210

Which type of bar graph would you use to represent the data? Explain.

1. The table shows the number of times that members of the Running Club ran in November.

Times per week	Number of members
0–9	7
10–19	7
20–29	2
30+	1

2. The table shows the number of endangered species in four categories in 1980 and 1993.

Category	1980	1993
Mammals	35	56
Birds	65	70
Reptiles	10	14
Fish	28	53

Use after Lesson 5.3, page 216

Use the line graph.

1. Name the units on the vertical axis.

2. Estimate the total amount of garbage per person per day in 1960.

3. Between which years did the amount of garbage stay about the same?

4. Approximate the increase in pounds of garbage from 1960 to 1990.

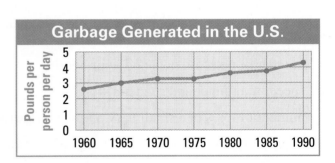

Garbage Generated in the U.S.

Use after Lesson 5.4, page 222

Choose a type of graph to represent the data. Explain why you chose that type, then draw the graph.

1. The total number of hurricanes recorded in the Atlantic basin by month from 1886–1986 is given below.

January:	0	February:	0	March:	1	April:	0
May:	3	June:	23	July:	33	August:	142
September:	182	October:	88	November:	21	December:	3

Use after Lesson 5.5, page 228

Use the bar graph at the right. The graph shows the number of items of trash collected on the banks of a river.

Trash Items Collected

1. If you look only at the length of the bar and ignore the scale on the vertical axis, how will you think the number of cigarette filters compares to the number of metal cans?

2. Use the scale on the vertical axis to estimate the number of cigarette filters and the number of metal cans.

3. Explain why this graph could be misleading.

4. Sketch a graph of the data that is not misleading.

Use after Lesson 5.6, page 232

1. The following data show the sum that results when a pair of dice is tossed 50 times. Organize the data in a line plot.

8	7	2	5	6	8	7	9	7	8
6	9	8	10	9	3	6	4	10	7
6	8	5	10	8	11	4	7	9	4
8	6	2	10	6	11	5	5	7	8
12	3	8	12	4	11	6	12	4	8

Use after Lesson 5.7, page 238

Decide whether a scatter plot relating the two quantities would tend to have a *positive*, *negative*, or *no correlation*.

1. number of pets you own and your height

2. speed of a runner and runner's weight

3. number of trees in a small park and the temperature on a sunny day

4. speed of typing and the number of pages typed

5. area of a soccer field and height of the grass

Use after Lesson 5.8, page 244

Find the probability that the spinner will land on the color.

1. Blue

2. Red

3. Green

4. Yellow

Use after Lesson 6.1, page 256

In Exercises 1–6, use the divisibility tests to determine whether the number is divisible by 2, 3, 4, 5, 6, 8, 9, and 10.

1. 945   **2.** 384   **3.** 2232

4. 51,840   **5.** 21,735   **6.** 7614

In Exercises 7–9, find the digit that makes the number divisible by 9.

7. 34,?21   **8.** 24,57?   **9.** 33,9?3

Use after Lesson 6.2, page 262

In Exercises 1–4, tell whether the number is prime or composite.

1. 16   **2.** 19   **3.** 36   **4.** 49

In Exercises 5–10, write the prime factorization of the number. Write your answer in exponent form.

5. 64   **6.** 120   **7.** 80

8. 84   **9.** 200   **10.** 60

Use after Lesson 6.3, page 268

Find the greatest common factor of the numbers.

1. 12, 20   **2.** 60, 130   **3.** 48, 96

4. 108, 198   **5.** 1004, 1040   **6.** 660, 1155

Use after Lesson 6.4, page 272

In Exercises 1–9, list the first several multiples of each number. Use the lists to find the least common multiple.

1. 5, 9   **2.** 8, 9   **3.** 9, 15

4. 10, 12   **5.** 12, 15   **6.** 12, 36

7. 4, 14   **8.** 16, 24   **9.** 5, 20

In Exercises 10–15, write the prime factorization of each expression. Use the results to find the least common multiple.

10. 5, 12   **11.** 20, 108   **12.** 145, 250

13. $7y, 21y^3$ **14.** $8m^2n, 64mn^2$ **15.** $9a^3b^5, 11a^2b^3$

Use after Lesson 6.5, page 276

Simplify the variable expression.

1. $\dfrac{3xy}{12x^2y}$ **2.** $\dfrac{5a^2b^3}{75a^4b^2}$ **3.** $\dfrac{33m^2n}{44mn^4}$

4. $\dfrac{7yz^3}{21y^2}$ **5.** $\dfrac{14p^2q^2}{35pq^5}$ **6.** $\dfrac{25x^3y^4}{125y^2}$

Use after Lesson 6.6, page 282

In Exercises 1–6, write the number as a fraction in simplest form.

1. -3

2. 0.30

3. 0.45

4. $1\frac{1}{5}$

5. $2\frac{3}{4}$

6. $-4\frac{3}{8}$

In Exercises 7–12, write the decimal as a fraction. Simplify the result.

7. 0.4

8. 0.28

9. 0.75

10. $0.\overline{27}$

11. $1.\overline{5}$

12. $2.\overline{18}$

Use after Lesson 6.7, page 286

Simplify the expression.

1. 2^{-3}

2. -4^{-2}

3. 24^0

4. x^{-3}

5. $5a^{-2}$

6. $6n^{-4}$

7. $3^0 \cdot 3^4$

8. $(-4)^{-2} \cdot (-4)^5$

9. $x^{14} \cdot x^{-12}$

10. $\dfrac{9^5}{9^3}$

11. $\dfrac{-7^3}{-7^5}$

12. $\dfrac{x^{12}}{x^9}$

Use after Lesson 6.8, page 290

In Exercises 1–4, write the number in scientific notation.

1. 4000

2. $253{,}000$

3. 0.28

4. $21{,}465{,}000$

In Exercises 5–8, write the number in decimal form.

5. 4.3×10^5

6. 6.70×10^{-4}

7. 7.2×10^6

8. 5.5×10^{-8}

Use after Lesson 6.9, page 296

Describe the pattern. Then list the next three terms in the sequence.

1. $0, 1, 3, 6, 10,$? , ? , ? , . . .

2. $0, 1, 4, 9, 16,$? , ? , ? , . . .

3. $12, 10, 6, 0, -8,$? , ? , ? , . . .

4. $2, -4, 8, -16, 32,$? , ? , ? , . . .

Use after Lesson 7.1, page 312

In Exercises 1–9, add or subtract. Then simplify.

1. $\dfrac{2}{5} + \dfrac{3}{5}$

2. $\dfrac{2}{10} + \dfrac{6}{10}$

3. $-\dfrac{2}{5} - \dfrac{3}{5}$

4. $\dfrac{-x}{7} - \dfrac{3x}{7}$

5. $\dfrac{12y}{8} - \dfrac{2y}{8}$

6. $1\frac{2}{5} + 3\frac{3}{5}$

7. $\dfrac{-2}{m} + \dfrac{3}{m}$

8. $\dfrac{1}{3x} - \dfrac{2}{3x}$

9. $\dfrac{2}{5x} - \dfrac{1}{5x}$

In Exercises 10–12, solve the equation. Then simplify.

10. $x + \dfrac{2}{5} = \dfrac{3}{5}$

11. $y - \dfrac{6}{10} = \dfrac{2}{10}$

12. $2x + \dfrac{2}{5} = \dfrac{4}{5}$

Use after Lesson 7.2, page 318

Find the sum or difference. Then simplify, if possible.

1. $\dfrac{7}{10} - \dfrac{2}{5}$

2. $\dfrac{2}{10} + \dfrac{6}{15}$

3. $\dfrac{-2}{8} - \dfrac{3}{12}$

4. $\dfrac{2}{15} + \dfrac{3}{5}$

5. $\dfrac{-2}{7} + \dfrac{1}{4}$

6. $\dfrac{2}{4} - \dfrac{3}{8} + \dfrac{3}{12}$

7. $\dfrac{a}{5} + \dfrac{a}{10}$

8. $\dfrac{-2}{z} + \dfrac{3}{2z}$

9. $\dfrac{2}{n} - \dfrac{1}{3n}$

Use after Lesson 7.3, page 322

Evaluate the expression.

1. $1.26 - 2.64$

2. $0.26 + 0.71$

3. $4.254 + 3.624$

4. $1.725 - 1.032$

5. $-0.021 + 4.269$

6. $5.79 + 3.27$

Use after Lesson 7.4, page 326

Multiply. Then simplify, if possible.

1. $\dfrac{1}{2} \cdot \dfrac{2}{5}$

2. $\dfrac{2}{6} \cdot \dfrac{-6}{7}$

3. $\dfrac{-2}{9} \cdot \dfrac{3}{4}$

4. $1\dfrac{7}{10} \cdot \dfrac{2}{5}$

5. $-2\dfrac{2}{10} \cdot \dfrac{6}{15}$

6. $\dfrac{-2}{8} \cdot \dfrac{3}{12} \cdot \dfrac{1}{2}$

7. $\dfrac{2x}{10} \cdot -\dfrac{2}{5}$

8. $2 \cdot \dfrac{5}{12}$

9. $8 \cdot \dfrac{3}{16}$

Use after Lesson 7.5, page 332

In Exercises 1–4, write the reciprocal.

1. $\dfrac{1}{5}$

2. $\dfrac{7}{y}$

3. $\dfrac{4x}{7}$

4. $-3\dfrac{1}{3}$

In Exercises 5–13, simplify the expression.

5. $\dfrac{5}{2} \div \dfrac{1}{2}$

6. $\dfrac{2}{6} \div \dfrac{-3}{6}$

7. $\dfrac{-4}{9} \div \dfrac{2}{3}$

8. $\dfrac{1}{2} \div 5$

9. $2 \div \dfrac{-7}{6}$

10. $\dfrac{-1}{3} \div \dfrac{-1}{4}$

11. $2\dfrac{1}{2} \div \dfrac{2}{5}$

12. $\dfrac{2}{5} \div 1\dfrac{1}{3}$

13. $\dfrac{-2}{x} \div \dfrac{3}{x}$

Use after Lesson 7.6, page 338

Write each portion as a percent.

1. $\dfrac{5}{20}$

2. $\dfrac{2}{40}$

3. $\dfrac{4}{50}$

4. $\dfrac{13}{25}$

5. $\dfrac{39}{60}$

6. $\dfrac{26}{40}$

7. $\dfrac{72}{120}$

8. $\dfrac{196}{400}$

Use after Lesson 7.7, page 342

In Exercises 1–4, rewrite the percent as a decimal.

1. 44% **2.** 15% **3.** 1.5% **4.** 125%

In Exercises 5–8, rewrite the decimal as a percent.

5. 0.5 **6.** 0.74 **7.** 0.3 **8.** 1.5

In Exercises 9–12, rewrite the percent as a fraction in simplest form.

9. 50% **10.** 65% **11.** 4% **12.** 250%

In Exercises 13–16, rewite the fraction as a percent.

13. $\dfrac{28}{32}$ **14.** $\dfrac{1}{400}$ **15.** $\dfrac{120}{32}$ **16.** $\dfrac{150}{50}$

Use after Lesson 7.8, page 346

Write the percent as a decimal. Then multiply to find the percent of the number.

1. 10% of 200 **2.** 23% of 250 **3.** 75% of 40 **4.** 150% of 6

5. 110% of 50 **6.** 200% of 26 **7.** 0.5% of 300 **8.** 2.5% of 80

Use after Lesson 7.9, page 352

The price of an item is given. Find the total cost of the item, including a 5% sales tax.

1. $4.25 **2.** $12.49 **3.** $80 **4.** $328.99

Use after Lesson 8.1, page 364

In Exercises 1–3, determine whether the quotient is a rate or a ratio.

1. $\dfrac{200 \text{ ft}}{10 \text{ s}}$ **2.** $\dfrac{9 \text{ committee members}}{10 \text{ committee members}}$ **3.** $\dfrac{210 \text{ points}}{7 \text{ games}}$

In Exercises 4–7, write the verbal phrase as a rate or a ratio. Explain why the phrase is a rate or a ratio.

4. walked 2 miles in 40 minutes **5.** 10 out of 12 users agree with the claim

6. washed 5 out of 8 windows **7.** wrote 3 pages in 45 minutes

Use after Lesson 8.2, page 370

Solve the proportion. Check your solution.

1. $\dfrac{x}{5} = \dfrac{14}{35}$ **2.** $\dfrac{z}{12} = \dfrac{3}{9}$ **3.** $\dfrac{5}{15} = \dfrac{y}{20}$

4. $\dfrac{6}{11} = \dfrac{n}{22}$ **5.** $\dfrac{2}{p} = \dfrac{3}{9}$ **6.** $\dfrac{5}{q} = \dfrac{12}{20}$

7. $\dfrac{8}{7} = \dfrac{64}{m}$ **8.** $\dfrac{2.5}{4} = \dfrac{3}{x}$ **9.** $\dfrac{9}{15} = \dfrac{12}{y}$

Use after Lesson 8.3, page 374

Use the following information. A speed of 50 mi/h is approximately equal to a speed of 80 km/h.

1. If you are traveling at 35 mi/h, how fast are you traveling in km/h?

2. If you are traveling at a speed of 110 km/h, what is your speed in miles per hour?

3. If the speed limit on a limited access highway is 55 mi/h, what is the speed limit in kilometers per hour?

Use after Lesson 8.4, page 378

In Exercises 1–3, solve the percent equation.

1. $\dfrac{10}{50} = \dfrac{p}{100}$

2. $\dfrac{a}{40} = \dfrac{35}{100}$

3. $\dfrac{9}{b} = \dfrac{12}{100}$

In Exercises 4–7, solve the percent equation. Round your answer to two decimal places if necessary.

4. 8 is what percent of 250?

5. What is 27 percent of 160?

6. What is 45% of 90?

7. 117 is 36% of what number?

Use after Lesson 8.5, page 384

Use the circle graph at the right. It shows the results of a survey of 4500 people about ways to get to work.

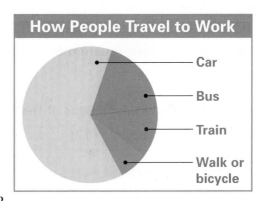

How People Travel to Work

- Car
- Bus
- Train
- Walk or bicycle

1. If 63% of the people drove a car to work, how many traveled to work by car?

2. If 315 people walked or rode a bicycle to work, what percent walked or biked to work?

3. If 12% of the people took a train to work, how many peole traveled to work by train?

4. The survey found that 810 people rode a bus to work. What percent of the people traveled to work by bus?

Use after Lesson 8.6, page 388

Decide whether the change is an *increase* or a *decrease* and find the percent.

1. Before: 15
After: 18

2. Before: 12
After: 15

3. Regular Price: $18.20
Sale Price: $16.80

4. Opening Price: $30.10
Closing Price: $31.20

Use after Lesson 8.7, page 394

1. A telephone area code consists of three digits. How many area codes can be formed if the first and last digits may *not* be zero, and the second digit *must* be zero or one?

2. The school menu offers a choice of meat consisting of beef, chicken, or fish, a choice of boiled rice or fried rice, and a choice of vegetable from corn, peas, beans, or broccoli. How many ways can you choose a meal of meat, rice, and a vegetable?

3. Your school offers sweatshirts with the school name. You can order either a hooded shirt or one without a hood. You may choose from red, navy blue, or white. How many choices do you have?

Use after Lesson 8.8, page 400

Use the spinners at the right.

Spinner 1 **Spinner 2**

1. What is the probability that spinner 1 will land on red?

2. What is the probability that spinner 2 will land on red?

3. What is the probability that both will land on red?

4. What is the probability that spinner 1 lands on red and spinner 2 lands on yellow?

Use after Lesson 9.1, page 412

In Exercises 1–4, write both square roots of the number.

1. 15   **2.** 32   **3.** 49   **4.** 169

In Exercises 5–8, write both solutions of the equation.

5. $z^2 = 36$ **6.** $x^2 = 121$ **7.** $t^2 = 32$ **8.** $n^2 + 2 = 51$

Use after Lesson 9.2, page 416

In Exercises 1–8, tell whether the number is rational or irrational. Explain your answers.

1. $\dfrac{13}{3}$ **2.** $\dfrac{-31}{17}$ **3.** $\sqrt{12}$ **4.** $-\sqrt{25}$

5. $\sqrt{169}$ **6.** $-\sqrt{\dfrac{49}{36}}$ **7.** $-\sqrt{\dfrac{5}{2}}$ **8.** $\sqrt{\dfrac{16}{25}}$

In Exercises 9–12, match the number with its graph.

9. $\sqrt{10}$ **10.** $-\sqrt{8}$ **11.** $\sqrt{0.81}$ **12.** $-\sqrt{\dfrac{9}{4}}$

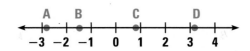

Use after Lesson 9.3, page 422

In Exercises 1–6, *a* and *b* are the lengths of the legs of a right triangle, and *c* is the length of the hypotenuse. Find the missing length. If necessary, use a calculator and round your answer to two decimal places.

1. $a = 6, c = 10$ **2.** $a = 5, b = 12$ **3.** $b = 24, c = 25$

4. $a = 6, b = 12$ **5.** $b = 28, c = 40$ **6.** $a = 9, b = 15$

In Exercises 7–9, find the length of the third side. If necessary, use a calculator and round your answer to two decimal places.

7.   **8.**    **9.**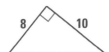

Use after Lesson 9.4, page 428

Find the perimeter and area of the figure.

1.   **2.**   **3.**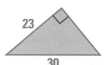

4. 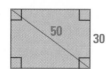   **5.**   **6.**

Use after Lesson 9.5, page 434

In Exercises 1–4, graph the inequality.

1. $x > 2$ **2.** $x < -1$ **3.** $x \geq -5$ **4.** $x \leq 3$

In Exercises 5–8, write the inequality represented by the graph.

5.
```
←──+──◇──+──+──+──+──→
   -3 -2 -1  0  1
```

6.
```
←──+──+──+──◆──+──+──→
   -7 -6 -5 -4 -3
```

7.
```
←──+──+──◆──+──+──→
   -1  0  1  2  3
```

8.
```
←──+──+──◇──+──+──→
    1  2  3  4  5
```

Use after Lesson 9.6, page 440

Solve the inequality. Then graph your solution.

1. $2x < 3$ **2.** $5y \geq 12$ **3.** $9 \leq \dfrac{x}{3}$

4. $-6a < -30$ **5.** $-4x > 4$ **6.** $-\dfrac{1}{3}p > 12$

7. $10 < \dfrac{n}{5}$ **8.** $\dfrac{2}{5}m \leq -8$ **9.** $-\dfrac{2}{3} < -\dfrac{1}{6}x$

EXTRA PRACTICE

Use after Lesson 9.7, page 444

Solve the inequality.

1. $8 \geq 5x + 10$

2. $25 + 2a > 7 + a$

3. $6x - 24 \leq 3$

4. $-2(x + 5) > 6$

5. $18 \leq 4(x + 2)$

6. $10 - x < 7x - 2$

Use after Lesson 9.8, page 448

Can the side lengths be correct? Explain.

1.

2.

3.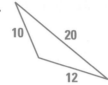

4.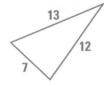

Use after Lesson 10.1, page 462

Use the diagram at the right.

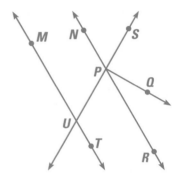

1. Write three other names for $\overleftrightarrow{SU}$.

2. Name three different line segments that lie on $\overleftrightarrow{NR}$.

3. Name five rays that have beginning point P.

4. Name two lines that appear parallel.

5. Name two pairs of lines that intersect.

6. Name a ray in the opposite direction of $\overrightarrow{PS}$.

Use after Lesson 10.2, page 466

Use the figure at the right.

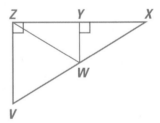

1. How many acute angles are in the figure? List them.

2. How many obtuse angles are in the figure? List them.

3. How many right angles are in the figure? List them.

4. If $\angle ZYW$ is supplementary to $\angle WYX$, then what is $m \angle ZYW$?

Use after Lesson 10.3, page 472

Use the figure at the right.

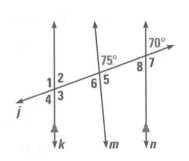

1. Explain why $\angle 4$ is not congruent to $\angle 6$.

2. List all numbered angles whose measure is $70°$.

3. List all numbered angles whose measure is $75°$.

4. List all numbered angles whose measure is $110°$.

5. Name two corresponding angles that have the same measure.

Use after Lesson 10.4, page 476

Copy the figure. Then shade one square so that the figure has the indicated symmetry.

1. Rotational

2. Line

3. Rotational

4. Line

Use after Lesson 10.5, page 480

Classify the triangle according to its sides and angles.

1.

2.

3.

4.

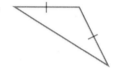

Use after Lesson 10.6, page 486

Find the values of *x* and *y*.

1. Square

12 in.

2. Rectangle

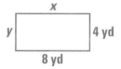

4 yd
8 yd

3. Isosceles trapezoid

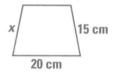

15 cm
20 cm

Use after Lesson 10.7, page 490

Use the words *congruent, equilateral, equiangular,* and *regular* to describe the polygons.

1.

2.

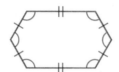

3.

Use after Lesson 10.8, page 496

Use the pentagon at the right.

1. Name the interior angles of the pentagon.

2. What is the sum of the measures of these angles?

3. Name the exterior angles of the pentagon.

4. What is the sum of the measures of these angles?

5. If $m \angle 3 = 105°$, then $m \angle 4 = $?

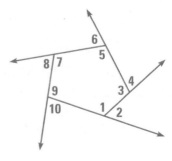

Use after Lesson 10.9, page 502

In Exercises 1–3, name the triangle's shortest and longest sides.

1.

2.

3.

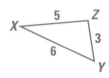

In Exercises 4–6, name the smallest angle of the triangle. Explain.

4.

5.

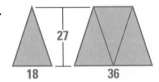

6.

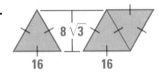

Use after Lesson 11.1, page 514

Find the area of each figure. Describe two ways to find the area of the second figure.

1.

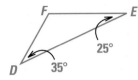

2.

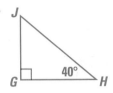

Use after Lesson 11.2, page 518

Use the fact that $\triangle ABC \cong \triangle DEF$ to complete the statement.

1. $\angle A \cong$ **?**   **2.** $AC =$ **?**

3. $DE =$ **?**   **4.** $\angle C \cong$ **?**

5. $\angle E \cong$ **?**   **6.** $EF =$ **?**

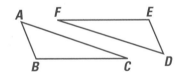

Use after Lesson 11.3, page 524

Use the triangle *XYZ* with coordinates *X*(−3, 4), *Y*(−1, 2) and *Z*(−4,1). Find the coordinates of the image after the indicated reflection.

1. Reflect about the *x*-axis.

2. Reflect about the *y*-axis.

3. Reflect about the *x*-axis, then about the *y*-axis.

4. Reflect about the *y*-axis, then about the *x*-axis.

5. Reflect about the *x*-axis, then again about the *x*-axis.

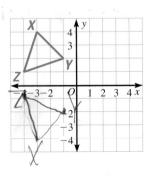

Use after Lesson 11.4, page 528

Copy the diagram on graph paper. Find the angle of rotation.

1.
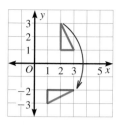

2.
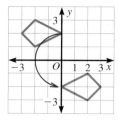

3.
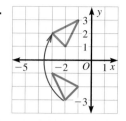

Use after Lesson 11.5, page 532

Match the graph with the motion rule that describes the translation. Then describe the translation verbally.

A.
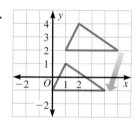

B.
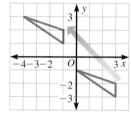

C.
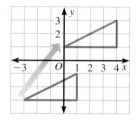

1. $(x, y) \rightarrow (x - 4, y + 4)$ **2.** $(x, y) \rightarrow (x - 1, y - 3)$ **3.** $(x, y) \rightarrow (x + 3, y + 4)$

Use after Lesson 11.6, page 538

Quadrilaterals *ABCD* and *PQRS*, shown at the right, are similar.

1. Write four equal ratios for *ABCD* and *PQRS*.

2. Find the scale factor of *ABCD* to *PQRS*.

3. Find the lengths *PS*, *PQ*, and *QR*.

Use after Lesson 11.7, page 544

Use the following information. The figure at the right is a scale drawing of the floor plan for a family room. The scale used is $\frac{1}{4}$ in. to 2 ft.

1. The width of the room on the floor plan is 1.5 in. What is the width of the room?

2. The length on the floor plan is 2 in. What is the length of the room?

3. The fireplace on your sketch measures $\frac{3}{4}$ in. What is the width of the fireplace in the room?

4. You want to arrange two sofas that measure 6 ft long and 3 ft deep. What dimensions will these be in the scale drawing?

fireplace

Use after Lesson 11.8, page 548

Use △ABC to find the trigonometric ratio.

1. $\sin A$ **2.** $\sin B$

3. $\cos A$ **4.** $\cos B$

5. $\tan A$ **6.** $\tan B$

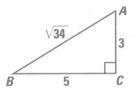

Use after Lesson 11.9, page 554

Solve the right triangle for all labeled sides and angles. Round your results to two decimal places.

1.   **2.**   **3.**

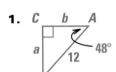 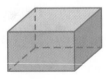 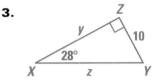

Use after Lesson 12.1, page 568

In Exercises 1–4, find the circumference and area of each circle. Use 3.14 for π. Round your result to one decimal place.

1. a circle with a radius of 7.5 in.   **2.** a circle with a diameter of 1 ft

3. a circle with a diameter of 6.2 cm   **4.** a circle with a radius of 2.2 yd

In Exercises 5–8, find the radius and diameter of each circle. Use 3.14 for π. Round your result to one decimal place.

5. a circle with an area of 735 in.^{2} **6.** a circle with a circumference of 57.8 cm

7. a circle with an area of 77 cm^2 **8.** a circle with a circumference of 17.3 ft

Use after Lesson 12.2, page 574

Identify the shape of the solid.

1.   **2.**   **3.**   **4.**

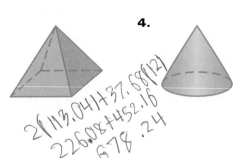

Use after Lesson 12.3, page 578

Find the surface area of the solid.

1.   **2.**   **3.**

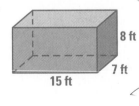 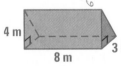 

Use after Lesson 12.4, page 582

Sketch and label the indicated regular prism. Then find its volume.

1. Length: 3 in., Width: 4 in., Height: 5 in. **2.** Length: 8 ft, Width: 6 ft, Height: 6 ft

Use after Lesson 12.5, page 588

Find the volume of the cylinder.

1.
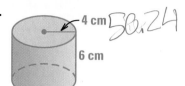
4 cm
6 cm
50.24

2.
78.5
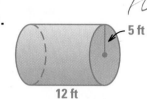
5 ft
12 ft

3.
200.96
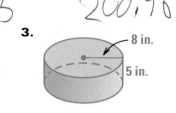
8 in.
5 in.

Use after Lesson 12.6, page 594

Find the volume of the pyramid or cone.

1.
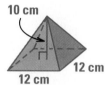
10 cm
12 cm
12 cm

2.
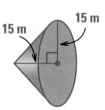
15 m
15 m

3.
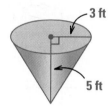
3 ft
5 ft

4.
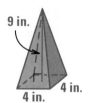
9 in.
4 in.
4 in.

Use after Lesson 12.7, page 598

Find the volume of the sphere with the given radius.

1. radius of 15 cm

2. radius of 6.3 ft

3. radius of 1.8 m

4. radius of 3.9 in.

Use after Lesson 12.8, page 604

The solids are similar. Solve for x and y.

1.
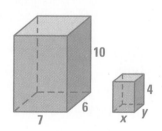
10
6
7
4
x y

2.
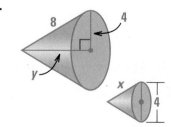
8
4
y
x
4

Use after Lesson 13.1, page 620

In Exercises 1–4, decide whether the ordered pair is a solution of $3x - y = 6$.

1. $(0, -6)$ **2.** $(2, 0)$ **3.** $(-2, 12)$ **4.** $(\frac{1}{3}, 5)$

5. Copy and complete the table of values at the right to show solutions of the equation $y = 4x - 6$.

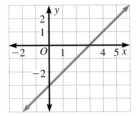

x	-2	-1	0	1	2
y	?	?	?	?	?

Use after Lesson 13.2, page 624

Match each equation with its graph.

A. 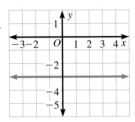   **B.** 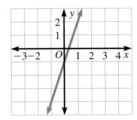   **C.**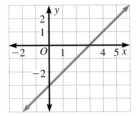

1. $y = 3x - 1$ **2.** $y = x - 3$ **3.** $y = -3$

Use after Lesson 13.3, page 630

In Exercises 1–3, identify the intercepts of the graph.

1. 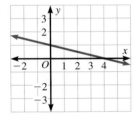   **2.** 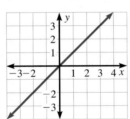   **3.**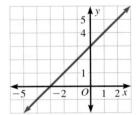

4. Find the x-intercept of $y = 2x + 2$.

5. Find the y-intercept of $3x + 5y = 15$.

Use after Lesson 13.4, page 636

In Exercises 1 and 2, the slopes of 4 lines are listed. Tell which of the lines is steepest.

1. $m = \frac{2}{3}, m = \frac{3}{4}, m = 0, m = 2$

2. $m = -2, m = -\frac{5}{3}, m = -4, m = -\frac{3}{2}$

In Exercises 3–8, plot the points. Then find the slope of the line through the points.

3. $(0, 3), (3, 1)$ **4.** $(2, 5), (5, 2)$ **5.** $(2, -1), (-3, 4)$

6. $(0, -2), (3, -1)$ **7.** $(-1, 0), (2, -2)$ **8.** $(-3, 0), (0, 3)$

Use after Lesson 13.5, page 644

Find the slope and *y*-intercept of the line. Then sketch a quick graph of the line.

1. $y = 2x + 5$

2. $y = -\frac{1}{2}x - 3$

3. $y = -2 + 3x$

4. $2y = -8x + 14$

5. $3x + 5y = 15$

6. $7x + 14y = 49$

Use after Lesson 13.6, page 650

Use the following information.

Your class is selling tickets for a talent show to raise money for computers. Tickets will cost \$3 for students and \$5 for adults. Your class wants to earn \$600 for the computers.

1. Write a verbal and an algebraic model of the situation.

2. Create a table of values and use it to graph the algebraic model.

3. If 125 student tickets are sold, how many adult tickets must be sold in order to earn \$600?

4. Interpret the intercepts of the graph in a real-life context.

Use after Lesson 13.7, page 654

In Exercises 1–4, is the ordered pair a solution of $2x - 3y > 12$? Explain.

1. $(0, 1)$

2. $(8, 2)$

3. $(2, -4)$

4. $(12, 2)$

In Exercises 5–7, match the inequality with its graph.

A.
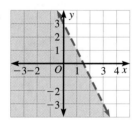

B.
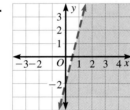

C.
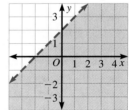

5. $4x - y > 2$

6. $2x + y < 3$

7. $-x + y < 2$

Use after Lesson 13.8, page 658

Use the graph to estimate the distance between the points. Then use the Distance Formula to check your estimate.

1.
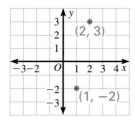

2.
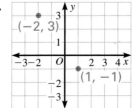

3.
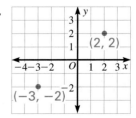

Use after Lesson 14.1, page 670

In Exercises 1–4, find the mean, median, and mode of the data.

1. 20, 22, 21, 24, 20, 19

2. 12, 8, 9, 11, 9, 8, 9, 8, 6, 12, 10, 8, 7

3. 46, 46, 48, 51, 51, 48, 43, 48, 42

4. 17.5, 18.8, 16.5, 19.3, 18, 18.2, 17

In Exercises 5–7, use the line plot at the right.

5. How many numbers are represented in the plot? List them in increasing order.

6. Find the mean, median, and mode of the numbers.

7. Describe a real-life situation that can be represented by the line plot.

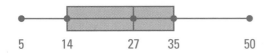

Use after Lesson 14.2, page 674

Use the stem-and-leaf plot.

1. List the data represented by the plot.

2. Draw a histogram for the data.

```
6 | 0 1 4 7
5 | 2 3 3 4 6 8
4 | 7 8 8
3 | 5
```

6 | 0 represents 60

Use after Lesson 14.3, page 678

Use the box-and-whisker plot. There are 20 numbers in the collection, and each number is different.

```
      5     14        27    35        50
```

1. Name the smallest and largest numbers.

2. Name the first, second, and third quartiles.

3. What percent of the numbers are less than 14?

4. What percent of the numbers are between 27 and 50?

5. What percent of the numbers are less than 35?

Use after Lesson 14.4, page 684

Find the sum and difference of the matrices.

1. $\begin{bmatrix} -1 & 2 \\ 3 & -5 \end{bmatrix}, \begin{bmatrix} -3 & 5 \\ 0 & 2 \end{bmatrix}$

2. $\begin{bmatrix} 4 & 2 \\ -1 & 7 \end{bmatrix}, \begin{bmatrix} -7 & 9 \\ -8 & 0 \end{bmatrix}$

3. $\begin{bmatrix} -1 & -3 & -2 \\ -2 & 7 & 4 \end{bmatrix}, \begin{bmatrix} 5 & 2 & -1 \\ -3 & -2 & 0 \end{bmatrix}$

4. $\begin{bmatrix} 2 & 4 & 6 \\ -1 & 5 & 1 \\ 6 & 8 & -1 \end{bmatrix}, \begin{bmatrix} 10 & -8 & 12 \\ -3 & 0 & 9 \\ -2 & 3 & 0 \end{bmatrix}$

Use after Lesson 14.5, page 690

In Exercises 1–3, write the polynomial in standard form and list its terms.

1. $2x - 3x^2 + 5x$

2. $2x^4 - x^2 + 3x$

3. $9 - 3z^2 + 6z - 12$

In Exercises 4–9, simplify and write in standard form.

4. $b + 4b^2 - 7b + 1$

5. $m^2 + 3m - 4 + 2m^2 - 5m + 5$

6. $n + 2n^2 - 2n + 5 - n^2$

7. $3 - 2p + 3p^3 - p^2 + 5p - 6$

8. $2.2x^2 - 3.5x + 2.5x^2 + 2.3x$

9. $\frac{4}{5}y + 6 - \frac{2}{5}y - 7$

Use after Lesson 14.6, page 696

Add or subtract the polynomials.

1. $(8a^2 - 3a - 3) + (-3a^2 + 4a - 7)$

2. $(3b^2 - 4b - 11) - (-b^2 - 2b + 1)$

3. $(m^3 - 3m^2 + 8m - 11) + (3m^3 + 2m^2 - 10m - 7)$

4. $(3n^4 - 3n^3 + 2n^2 - 16n - 11) + (-5n^4 + 2n^3 - 11n^2 + 10n - 7)$

5. $(3x^3 - 2x^2 + 5x - 11) - (-3x^3 + 11x^2 - 7x - 6)$

6. $(2y^4 - 11y^3 - 2y^2 + 5y - 11) - (-y^4 + 6y^3 + 11y^2 - 7y + 10)$

Use after Lesson 14.7, page 700

In Exercises 1–9, multiply.

1. $3x(x^2 - 1)$

2. $2a(a^2 + 3a + 2)$

3. $-3(4x^2 + 7x - 2)$

4. $3b^2(-5b - 8)$

5. $-y^3(2y^2 - 5y + 12)$

6. $4n(-2n^2 + 2n - 3)$

7. $m(-2m^3 - 7m + 15)$

8. $-5z(3z^4 - 2z^2 + 6)$

9. $a^4(-a^3 + a^2 - a + 1)$

In Exercises 10–12, suppose a rectangular prism has a base with dimensions *d* and 2*d* − 1, and a height 5*d*.

10. Write an expression for the area of the base of the prism.

11. Write an expression for the volume of the prism.

12. Write an expression for the surface area of the prism.

Use after Lesson 14.8, page 706

Find the product using the Distributive Property.

1. $(x + 2)(3x + 5)$

2. $(5x + 6)(x + 3)$

3. $(3x + 1)(2x + 3)$

4. $(2x + 5)(5x + 2)$

5. $(7x + 7)(3x + 3)$

6. $(4x + 3)(4x + 2)$

7. $(3x + 6)(4x + 7)$

8. $(2x + 5)(3x + 1)$

9. $(5x + 7)(3x + 9)$

Problem Solving Strategies

The ability to solve problems is an important part of mathematics. When you are solving a problem, organize your work by using the following four-step problem solving plan.

Step 1	**Understand the problem.** Read the problem carefully. Decide what information you are given and what you need to find.
Step 2	**Make a plan to solve the problem.** Choose a strategy. Decide if you will use a tool such as a calculator, a graph, or a spreadsheet.
Step 3	**Carry out the plan to solve the problem.** Use the strategy and tool(s) you have chosen. Do any calculations that are needed. Answer the question that the problem asks.
Step 4	**Check to see if your solution is reasonable.** Reread the problem and see if your answer agrees with the given information.

Example 1   Raoul bought some pencils for $.25 each and some erasers for $.40 each. If he spent $2.45 in all, how many of each did he buy?

Solution   *Step 1: Read and understand the problem.*
Notice that you are given the cost for each pencil, the cost for each eraser, and the total amount spent. You are asked to find the number of pencils and the number of erasers that Raoul bought.

Step 2: Choose a strategy to solve the problem.
It may appear at first that there is not enough information to solve the problem. Select the guess and check method as a problem solving strategy.

Step 3: Apply the guess and check method.
Guess how many pencils Raoul bought and see if the corresponding number of erasers is a whole number. For example, if he bought 3 pencils, then $0.25(3) + 0.4y = 2.45$; solving gives $y = 4.25$, which doesn't make sense in this situation because he cannot buy a portion of an eraser. By continuing to guess how many pencils he might have bought and testing each guess in the equation $0.25x + 0.40y = 2.45$, you will find that there is only one possible solution: $x = 5$ and $y = 3$. He bought 5 pencils and 3 erasers.

Step 4: Check your answer.
You can check your answer by putting the solutions into the equation and making sure that they make sense.

In Exercises 1–10, use the problem solving plan to solve the problem. A problem may contain information that is not needed or may not provide enough information to be solved. If there is not enough information, write *cannot be solved*.

1. May works 40 h a week at her usual hourly rate. When she works more than 40 h in a week, she is paid 50% more for each additional hour. One week May worked 48 h and was paid $936. Find her usual hourly rate.

2. A museum charges $8 per visit to nonmembers. Members pay a $25 membership fee and then $5 per visit. How many times must a person visit the museum for a membership to be less expensive than paying for each visit?

3. The Rogers family drove 140 mi on the interstate at an average speed of 56 mi/h. Then they spent 45 min at a restaurant having lunch and putting gas in the car. Finally, they completed their trip driving 57 mi through the country at an average speed of 30 mi/h. How long did their entire trip take?

4. Student tickets and general admission tickets were sold for the school play. The total amount of money collected was $1250. If 86 more student tickets than general admission tickets were sold, how many of each type of ticket was sold?

5. A customer handed a bank teller a check for $210 and asked for equal numbers of $20 bills and $10 bills. How many of each type of bill did the customer receive?

6. A regulation swimming pool is divided into eight lanes. Each lane in the pool is 50 m long and 2.4 m wide. The water in the pool is at least 1.2 m deep. If a person swims 12 laps from one end to the other in a regulation pool, how far did the person swim altogether?

7. A bunch of bananas weighs 2.5 lb and costs $1.70. Find the cost of a bunch that weighs 3.5 lb.

8. An electrician charges a basic service fee plus a labor charge for each hour of service. A 2 h job costs $74 and a 4 h job costs $118. Find the electrician's basic service fee.

9. In the National Hockey League, a team earns 2 points for a win, 1 point for a tie, and 0 points for a loss. In a recent season, the Detroit Red Wings played 82 games and earned 131 points. How many games did they win that season?

10. Sixty-four meters of fencing was needed to enclose a square garden. What is the area of the garden?

Problem Solving Strategies

In many problems, more than one strategy can be used to find the solution. You should be aware of many different problem solving strategies. If you are having difficulty solving a particular problem, try using another strategy to solve it. Here are some *problem solving strategies* that you may have used in previous mathematics courses:

1. Systematically guess and check until you find the solution.

2. Draw a diagram or a graph.

3. Use an equation or a formula.

4. Look for a pattern that can be extended.

5. Act out the situation to visualize it more easily.

6. Make a table or an organized list to keep track of your work or to be sure that you have included all the possibilities.

7. Try to break the problem into simpler parts that may be easier to solve than the original one.

8. Work backwards if you are given the result or final answer.

Example 1   **How many diagonals can be drawn in a polygon with 10 sides?**

Solution   One way to solve the problem is to look for a pattern. Draw a triangle, a quadrilateral, a pentagon, a hexagon, and a heptagon and see if one can be found.

Number of sides of polygon	3	4	5	6	7
Number of diagonals	0	2	5	9	14

Notice the pattern in the number of diagonals as the number of sides in the polygon increases. Each time the number of sides increases by one, the number of diagonals increases by one more then it had the previous time.

Number of diagonals

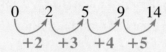

Continue the pattern to find the number of diagonals in a polygon with 10 sides.

Number of diagonals

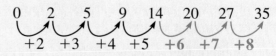

By extending the pattern you can predict that 35 diagonals can be drawn in a polygon with 10 sides.

Problem Solving Strategies

In Exercises 11–21, choose an appropriate problem solving strategy and solve the problem.

11. The perimeter of a rectangular yard is 140 ft and the area of the yard is 1200 ft^2. Find the dimensions of the yard.

12. At the school cafeteria, you can order a cheese pizza. Pepperoni, onions, and extra cheese toppings are available. If you can choose as many of these toppings as you like, how many different types of pizza can be ordered?

13. Suppose that there are twelve people in a group, and each person shakes hands with every other person. How many handshakes would there be altogether?

14. If the speed limit is increased by 10 km/h on a 120 km stretch of highway, the trip will take 10 min less. Find the original speed limit.

15. A test consists of 25 questions. For each question that is correctly answered, the student earns 4 points. For each point that is incorrectly answered, the student loses 1 point. A student received a score of 85 on the test. How many questions did the student answer correctly?

16. A graphic design consists of a triangular group of dots with one dot in the first row, three dots in the second row, five dots in the third row, seven dots in the fourth row, and so on. If there are 18 rows in the triangle, how many dots are there altogether?

17. The sum of the measures of the angles of a triangle is 180°. If one angle is a right angle and the ratio of the measures of the other two angles is 1:5, find the measures of all three angles of the triangle.

18. The numbers in each row, column, and diagonal of the square shown have the same sum. Each digit from 1 to 9 is used exactly once. Find the missing numbers of the square.

8	1	6
3	?	?
?	?	?

19. The sum of the measures of the angles of a quadrilateral is 360°. Suppose you are told that the angle measures of a certain quadrilateral are consecutive multiples of 10 (such as 10, 20, and 30). Show that this is impossible.

20. Suppose you use each of the digits 1 through 9 exactly once to form a 9-digit number. How many different numbers can be formed?

21. Robert has 485 min of music on CDs that he wants to tape to listen to in his portable stereo. When he goes to the store, he finds 45 min tapes, 60 min tapes, and 90 min tapes. If he wants to buy the same number of each kind of tape, how many of each will he need to buy? How much tape space will he have left over?

TOOLBOX

Fraction Concepts

Two fractions are **equivalent** if they represent the same number.

Example 1 Write $\frac{6}{9}$ in simplest form.

Solution $\frac{6}{9} = \frac{6 \div 3}{9 \div 3} = \frac{2}{3}$ Divide the numerator and denominator by 3.

Example 2 Find $\frac{3}{4}$ of 12.

Solution In this problem, the word "of" indicates multiplication.

$$\frac{3}{4} \times 12 = \frac{3 \times 12}{4} = \frac{36}{4} = 9$$

Example 3 What fraction of a dollar is 75 cents?

Solution The value of a dollar is 100 cents, so 75 cents is $\frac{75}{100}$ of a dollar.

$$\frac{75}{100} = \frac{75 \div 25}{100 \div 25} = \frac{3}{4}$$ Divide the numerator and denominator by 25.

In simplest form, 75 cents is $\frac{3}{4}$ of a dollar.

Example 4 Write $\frac{7}{25}$ as a decimal and as a percent.

Solution One way to write a fraction as a decimal is to rewrite the fraction with a denominator of 100.

$$\frac{7}{25} = \frac{7 \cdot 4}{25 \cdot 4} = \frac{28}{100}, \text{ or } 0.28$$

Percent means "per hundred."

Since $\frac{7}{25} = \frac{28}{100}$, $\frac{7}{25} = 28\%$.

PRACTICE AND PROBLEM SOLVING

In Exercises 1–5, write each fraction in simplest form.

1. $\frac{8}{10}$ **2.** $\frac{12}{20}$ **3.** $\frac{10}{15}$ **4.** $\frac{7}{14}$ **5.** $\frac{6}{24}$

In Exercises 6–10, find each number.

6. $\frac{1}{3}$ of 15   **7.** $\frac{7}{10}$ of 40   **8.** $\frac{5}{6}$ of 42   **9.** $\frac{1}{4}$ of 4   **10.** $\frac{4}{7}$ of 77

In Exercises 11–15, tell what fraction of a dollar each amount of money is. Write each fraction in simplest form.

11. 20 cents   **12.** 47 cents   **13.** 38 cents   **14.** 9 cents   **15.** 92 cents

In Exercises 16–20, write each number as a decimal and as a percent.

16. $\frac{3}{100}$ **17.** $\frac{11}{20}$ **18.** $\frac{3}{5}$ **19.** $\frac{17}{50}$ **20.** $\frac{1}{4}$

TOOLBOX

Add, Subtract, Multiply, and Divide Fractions

To add (or subtract) fractions with the same denominator, add (or subtract) the numerators and write the answer over the denominator. To add (or subtract) fractions with different denominators, rewrite the fractions so that they have the same denominator. Then add (or subtract) the resulting fractions.

Example 1   **Add or subtract the fractions.**

    a. $\dfrac{1}{8} + \dfrac{5}{8}$ **b.** $\dfrac{3}{4} - \dfrac{1}{6}$

Solution   **a.** $\dfrac{1}{8} + \dfrac{5}{8} = \dfrac{1+5}{8}$ **b.** $\dfrac{3}{4} - \dfrac{1}{6} = \dfrac{3 \cdot 3}{3 \cdot 4} - \dfrac{2 \cdot 1}{2 \cdot 6}$

$$= \dfrac{6}{8} \qquad\qquad\qquad\qquad\quad = \dfrac{9}{12} - \dfrac{2}{12}$$

$$= \dfrac{3}{4} \qquad\qquad\qquad\qquad\quad = \dfrac{7}{12}$$

To multiply fractions, multiply the numerators and denominators. To divide fractions, multiply by the reciprocal of the divisor.

Example 2   **Multiply or divide the fractions.**

    a. $1\dfrac{1}{2} \cdot \dfrac{5}{6}$ **b.** $2\dfrac{2}{3} \div \dfrac{4}{5}$

Solution   **a.** $1\dfrac{1}{2} \cdot \dfrac{5}{6} = \dfrac{3}{2} \cdot \dfrac{5}{6}$ **b.** $2\dfrac{2}{3} \div \dfrac{4}{5} = \dfrac{8}{3} \div \dfrac{4}{5}$

$$= \dfrac{3 \cdot 5}{2 \cdot 6} \qquad\qquad\qquad\quad = \dfrac{8}{3} \cdot \dfrac{5}{4}$$

$$= \dfrac{15}{12} \qquad\qquad\qquad\qquad = \dfrac{40}{12}$$

$$= 1\dfrac{1}{4} \qquad\qquad\qquad\qquad = 3\dfrac{1}{3}$$

PRACTICE AND PROBLEM SOLVING

In Exercises 1–12, add, subtract, multiply, or divide. Simplify if possible.

1. $\dfrac{1}{10} + \dfrac{7}{10}$ **2.** $\dfrac{3}{4} + \dfrac{2}{3}$ **3.** $\dfrac{5}{6} + \dfrac{4}{15}$ **4.** $\dfrac{4}{5} - \dfrac{1}{5}$

5. $\dfrac{8}{9} - \dfrac{5}{6}$ **6.** $1\dfrac{1}{8} - \dfrac{1}{6}$ **7.** $\dfrac{3}{4} \cdot \dfrac{2}{9}$ **8.** $\dfrac{3}{5} \cdot \dfrac{4}{11}$

9. $3\dfrac{1}{8} \cdot 3\dfrac{1}{5}$ **10.** $\dfrac{14}{15} \div \dfrac{2}{3}$ **11.** $\dfrac{3}{4} \div 6$ **12.** $5\dfrac{1}{7} \div 1\dfrac{1}{8}$

13. The Sabertooth football team won half of their games and lost one third of them. What fraction of the games resulted in a tie?

Add, Subtract, Multiply, and Divide Integers

A number line can be used to model the addition of integers. On a number line, adding a positive integer is represented by movement to the right and adding a negative integer is represented by movement to the left.

Example 1   **a.** $3 + (-5)$ **b.** $-2 + 3$

Solution   **a.** Start at **3**. Move **5** units to the left. You end at -2. So, $3 + (-5) = -2$.

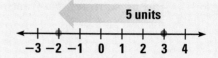

b. Start at -2. Move **3** units to the right. You end at **1**. So, $-2 + 3 = 1$.

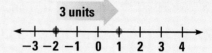

To subtract an integer, add its opposite.

Example 2   **a.** $4 - 8$ **b.** $1 - (-6)$

Solution   **a.** $4 - 8 = 4 + (-8)$ **b.** $1 - (-6) = 1 + 6$
$\qquad\qquad\quad = -4$ $\qquad\qquad\qquad\qquad = 7$

When multiplying or dividing integers, use the following rules.
The product or quotient of two integers with the same sign is positive.
The product or quotient of two integers with different signs is negative.

Example 3   **a.** $7(-5)$ **b.** $(-2)(-3)$ **c.** $-12 \div (-4)$ **d.** $\dfrac{9}{-3}$

Solution   **a.** $7(-5) = -35$ **b.** $(-2)(-3) = 6$ **c.** $-12 \div (-4) = 3$ **d.** $\dfrac{9}{-3} = -3$

PRACTICE AND PROBLEM SOLVING

In Exercises 1–12, add, subtract, multiply, or divide.

1. $-8 + (-1)$ **2.** $-5 + 5$ **3.** $6 + (-9)$ **4.** $3 - 7$

5. $-4 - (-4)$ **6.** $8 - (-2)$ **7.** $(-6)(-6)$ **8.** $-8 \cdot 0$

9. $4(-5)$ **10.** $-10 \div (-5)$ **11.** $\dfrac{18}{-3}$ **12.** $\dfrac{0}{-2}$

In Exercises 13 and 14, add, subtract, multiply, or divide to solve.

13. From noon until midnight, the temperature dropped 18°F. Find the average change in the temperature each hour during that period of time.

14. The melting point of ammonia is $-77.74°C$ and the boiling point of ammonia is $-33.35°C$. How much higher is the boiling point than the melting point?

Factors, Prime Factorization, and LCM

A *factor* of a whole number is a whole number that divides the first number evenly.

Example 1 **Find the factors of 24.**

Solution $24 \div 1 = 24$ $24 \div 3 = 8$ 1, 2, 3, 4, 6, 8, 12, and 24
$24 \div 2 = 12$ $24 \div 4 = 6$ are the factors of 24.

A whole number greater than 1 with exactly two factors, 1 and the number itself, is a *prime number*. To find the prime factorization of a whole number, write it as a product of prime numbers.

Example 2 **Find the prime factorization of 24.**

Solution $24 = 8 \cdot 3$ Factor out a prime number, 3.
$= 2 \cdot 2 \cdot 2 \cdot 3$ Factor the 8 into primes.
$= 2^3 \cdot 3$ $2^3 \cdot 3$ is the prime factorization of 24.

A number that is a multiple of two numbers is a called a *common multiple* of the numbers. Of all common multiples, the smallest is called the *least common multiple,* or *LCM.*

Example 3 **Find the least common multiple of 20 and 30.**

Solution *Multiples of 20: 20, 40, 60, 80, 100, 120, 140, . . .*
Multiples of 30: 30, 60, 90, 120, 150, 180, . . .
So, the least common multiple of 20 and 30 is 60.

PRACTICE AND PROBLEM SOLVING

In Exercises 1–8, find the factors of each number.

1. 27   2. 28   3. 15   4. 42

5. 30   6. 60   7. 55   8. 64

In Exercises 9–16, find the prime factorization of each number.

9. 4   10. 33   11. 45   12. 57

13. 32   14. 41   15. 72   16. 81

In Exercises 17–24, find the LCM of each pair of numbers.

17. 4 and 6   18. 6 and 15   19. 10 and 65   20. 6 and 17

21. 8 and 36   22. 14 and 21   23. 4 and 5   24. 7 and 13

25. Louisa has 50 identical ceramic tiles. In how many different ways can she arrange the tiles to form a rectangular surface? Explain your answer.

Exponents and Scientific Notation

A power is an expression such as 7^3. The number 7 is the *base*, and the number 3 is the *exponent*. The exponent tells the number of times the base is used as a factor: $7^3 = 7 \cdot 7 \cdot 7$.

Example 1 Evaluate each expression.

a. $(-2)^5$ **b.** 10^0 **c.** 10^{-2}

Solution **a.** $(-2)^5 = (-2)(-2)(-2)(-2)(-2)$

$\qquad\qquad\quad = -32$ Multiply the base together 5 times.

b. $10^0 = 1$ Any number raised to the zero power equals 1.

c. If n is a positive integer, then $10^{-n} = \dfrac{1}{10^n}$.

So, $10^{-2} = \dfrac{1}{10^2} = \dfrac{1}{100}$.

A number is written in scientific notation if it has the form $c \times 10^n$ where c is greater than or equal to 1 and less than 10. In each of the following examples, notice that the exponent of 10 is the number of places the decimal point is moved.

Example 2 Write each number in scientific notation.

a. 2751 **b.** 0.032

Solution **a.** $2751 = 2.751 \times 1000$ **b.** $0.032 = 3.2 \times \dfrac{1}{100}$

$\qquad\qquad\quad = 2.751 \times 10^3$ $\qquad\qquad = 3.2 \times 10^{-2}$

PRACTICE AND PROBLEM SOLVING

In Exercises 1–8, evaluate each expression.

1. 3^4 **2.** $(-6)^2$ **3.** 10^{-3} **4.** $(-10)^3$

5. 10^0 **6.** 10^4 **7.** 10^{-4} **8.** $(-10)^4$

In Exercises 9–16, write each number as a power of 10.

9. 10 **10.** 0.01 **11.** 1 **12.** 10,000

13. 0.00001 **14.** 1,000,000 **15.** 0.1 **16.** 0.0001

In Exercises 17–24, write each number in scientific notation.

17. 423,000 **18.** 0.0077 **19.** 0.000009 **20.** 457

21. 30,200,000 **22.** 0.00082 **23.** 0.00000025 **24.** 18.6

25. There are 8760 hours in a year. Write this number in scientific notation.

Solving One-Step Equations

When you solve an equation, your goal is to get the variable alone on one side.

Example 1 **Solve each equation.**

a. $a + 3 = 1$ **b.** $b - 7 = -4$ **c.** $-4x = -12$ **d.** $\frac{y}{3} = 5$

Solution To solve an addition equation, *subtract* the same number from both sides of the equation to get the variable alone on one side. To solve a subtraction equation, *add* the same number to both sides of the equation.

a. $a + 3 = 1$ **b.** $b - 7 = -4$

$a + 3 - 3 = 1 - 3$ $b - 7 + 7 = -4 + 7$

$a = -2$ $b = 3$

You can check a solution by substituting it into the original equation.

$a + 3 = 1$ $b - 7 = -4$

$-2 + 3 = 1 ✔$ $3 - 7 = -4 ✔$

To solve a multiplication equation, *divide* both sides of the equation by the same nonzero number to get the variable alone on one side. To solve a division equation, *multiply* both sides by the same nonzero number.

c. $-4x = -12$ **d.** $\frac{y}{3} = 5$

$\frac{-4x}{-4} = \frac{-12}{-4}$ $3 \cdot \frac{y}{3} = 3 \cdot 5$

$x = 3$ $y = 15$

PRACTICE AND PROBLEM SOLVING

In Exercises 1–16, solve the equation and check the solution.

1. $x + 3 = -5$ **2.** $y + 1.6 = 4$ **3.** $k + (-7) = 3$ **4.** $9 + z = 9$

5. $a - 1 = 8$ **6.** $b - 0.25 = 0.55$ **7.** $c - (-4) = 0$ **8.** $d - \frac{1}{2} = -2$

9. $7n = -35$ **10.** $-1.5t = -6$ **11.** $-6r = 4$ **12.** $15j = 0$

13. $x \div 4 = -4$ **14.** $\frac{m}{-0.6} = 5$ **15.** $\frac{s}{-10} = -2$ **16.** $w \div (-1) = 7.4$

In Exercise 17, choose the correct model and solve the problem.

17. Suppose you are driving at an average speed of 50 mi/h and travel 225 mi. Which of the following models will correctly determine your traveling time?

A. $50 + x = 225$ **B.** $50x = 225$ **C.** $225x = 50$

Solving Proportions

A *proportion* is an equation that states that two ratios are equal.
For example, $\frac{3}{4} = \frac{6}{8}$ is a proportion. To solve a proportion,
use the Cross Product Property:

$$\text{If } \frac{a}{b} = \frac{c}{d}, \text{ then } a \cdot d = b \cdot c.$$

Example 1 **Solve each proportion.**

a. $\frac{x}{15} = \frac{8}{20}$ b. $\frac{30}{18} = \frac{8}{y}$

Solution a. $\frac{x}{15} = \frac{8}{20}$

$20 \cdot x = 8 \cdot 15$ Use Cross Product Property.

$20x = 120$ Simplify.

$\frac{20x}{20} = \frac{120}{20}$ Divide both sides by 20.

$x = 6$ Solution: x is by itself.

Since the cross products of the proportion $\frac{6}{15} = \frac{8}{20}$
are equal, the solution is correct.

b. $\frac{30}{18} = \frac{8}{y}$

$30 \cdot y = 18 \cdot 8$ Use Cross Product Property.

$30y = 144$ Simplify.

$\frac{30y}{30} = \frac{144}{30}$ Divide both sides by 30.

$y = 4.8$ Solution: y is by itself.

PRACTICE AND PROBLEM SOLVING

In Exercises 1–8, solve each proportion.

1. $\frac{x}{18} = \frac{12}{27}$ 2. $\frac{44}{16} = \frac{y}{24}$ 3. $\frac{45}{a} = \frac{25}{48}$ 4. $\frac{40}{6} = \frac{2}{b}$

5. $\frac{n}{36} = \frac{48}{54}$ 6. $\frac{24}{6} = \frac{2}{k}$ 7. $\frac{2.5}{30} = \frac{z}{8}$ 8. $\frac{10}{m} = \frac{1.5}{6}$

In Exercises 9 and 10, write and solve a proportion to solve each problem.

9. If 5 lb of bananas cost \$3.45, find the cost of a 1.4 lb bunch of bananas.

10. On a map of Pennsylvania, 1 in. represents 10 mi. The distance from Harrisburg to Lancaster is about 36 mi. Find the map distance from Harrisburg to Lancaster.

TOOLBOX

Percents

The word **percent** means *per hundred*. A percent is often written using the percent symbol, %. The statement "*a* is *p* percent of *b*" can be expressed using the percent equation $\frac{a}{b} = \frac{p}{100}$.

Example 1　**a.** What percent of 24 is 9?

　　　　　b. What is 85% of 250?

　　　　　c. 56 is 32% of what number?

Solution　**a.** You want to find the percent, *p*.

$$\frac{9}{24} = \frac{p}{100} \qquad \text{Use the percent equation with } a = 9 \text{ and } b = 24.$$

$$24p = 900 \qquad \text{Use Cross Product Property.}$$

$$p = 37.5 \qquad \text{9 is 37.5% of 24.}$$

b. The word "of" in this problem indicates multiplication.

85% of 250 $\longrightarrow$ 0.85 × 250 = 212.5

So, 212.5 is 85% of 250.

c. You want to find the base, *b*.

$$\frac{56}{b} = \frac{32}{100} \qquad \text{Use the percent equation with } a = 56 \text{ and } p = 32.$$

$$32b = 5600 \qquad \text{Use Cross Product Property.}$$

$$b = 175 \qquad \text{56 is 32% of 175.}$$

PRACTICE AND PROBLEM SOLVING

In Exercises 1–10, solve the percent problem.

1. What is 42% of 200?

2. What percent of 16 is 14?

3. 72 is 45% of what number?

4. Find $33\frac{1}{3}\%$ of 21.

5. 8% of what number is 10?

6. 33 is what percent of 50?

7. 80 is 125% of what number?

8. What is 12.5% of 64?

9. What percent of 125 is 75?

10. What percent of 60 is 84?

In Exercises 11 and 12, use the percent equation to solve each problem.

11. Mary's score on her science quiz was 95%. If the quiz consisted of 40 questions, how many of the questions did Mary answer correctly?

12. The Washingtons deposited a sum of money in an account that paid 8% interest. After one year, the amount of interest earned was $200. How much money did they deposit in the account?

Areas

The area of a figure is a measure of how much surface is covered by the figure. Area is measured in *square units*.

Example 1   **Find the area of each figure.**

a.

b.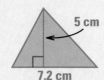

c.

Solution   **a.** Use the formula for the area of a rectangle.

$$\text{Area} = \textbf{length} \times \textbf{width}$$

$$= 8(7.5)$$

$$= 60 \text{ m}^2 \qquad \text{The units are square meters.}$$

b. Use the formula for the area of a triangle.

$$\text{Area} = \frac{1}{2}(\textbf{base})(\textbf{height})$$

$$= \frac{1}{2}(7.2)(5)$$

$$= 18 \text{ cm}^2 \qquad \text{Give the area in square centimeters.}$$

c. In a right triangle, the perpendicular sides can be used as the base and height.

$$\text{Area} = \frac{1}{2}(3)(4)$$

$$= 6 \text{ square units} \qquad \text{Use square units when no units are given.}$$

PRACTICE AND PROBLEM SOLVING

In Exercises 1–4, find the area of each figure.

1. a square with sides of length 7.5 ft

2. a rectangle with length 20 mm and width 18 mm

3. a right triangle with sides of lengths 5 cm, 12 cm, and 13 cm

4. a triangle with base 9 m and height 5 m

In Exercises 5 and 6, find the area of each figure by adding areas.

5.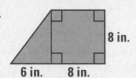

6.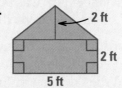

Square Roots and the Pythagorean Theorem

The positive square root of a positive number n is the number that when multiplied by itself is equal to n. For example, the square root of 16 is 4 because $4 \cdot 4 = 16$. This can be written as $\sqrt{16} = 4$.

Example 1 Evaluate each square root.

> **a.** $\sqrt{81}$ **b.** $\sqrt{0}$ **c.** $\sqrt{7}$

Solution **a.** $\sqrt{81} = 9$ since $9 \cdot 9 = 81$.

> **b.** $\sqrt{0} = 0$ since $0 \cdot 0 = 0$.

> **c.** Use a calculator. To two decimal places, $\sqrt{7} \approx 2.65$.

You can use the Pythagorean Theorem to find the lengths of the sides of right triangles. It states that the sum of the squares of the lengths of the legs, a and b, equals the square of the length of the hypotenuse, c.

$a^2 + b^2 = c^2$

Example 2 Find the length of the third side of the right triangle.

a.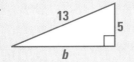

b.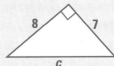

Solution **a.** $5^2 + b^2 = 13^2$

$$25 + b^2 = 169$$
$$b^2 = 144$$
$$b = \sqrt{144}$$
$$b = 12$$

b. $7^2 + 8^2 = c^2$

$$49 + 64 = c^2$$
$$113 = c^2$$
$$\sqrt{113} = c$$
$$10.63 \approx c$$

PRACTICE AND PROBLEM SOLVING

In Exercises 1–5, evaluate each square root. If necessary, round the result to two decimal places.

1. $\sqrt{9}$ **2.** $\sqrt{121}$ **3.** $\sqrt{72}$ **4.** $\sqrt{40}$ **5.** $\sqrt{324}$

In Exercises 6–11, a and b are the lengths of the legs of a right triangle, and c is the length of the hypotenuse. Find the unknown length. If necessary, round the result to two decimal places.

6. $a = 6, b = 8$ **7.** $a = 8, c = 17$ **8.** $a = 9, b = 12$

9. $b = 14, c = 16$ **10.** $a = 5, b = 5$ **11.** $a = 11, c = 20$

12. Marlene hiked 5 km east and then she went south. She ended about 8 km from her starting point. About how far did she hike south?

Surface Area and Volume

Example 1 **Find the surface area and volume of a rectangular prism with length 12 in., width 10 in., and height 5 in.**

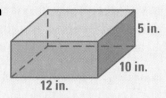

Solution The surface area of a prism is the sum of the areas of all the faces of the prism. Surface area is measured in *square units*. A rectangular prism has three pairs of identical rectangular faces.

$$\text{Surface area} = 2(12 \cdot 10) + 2(12 \cdot 5) + 2(10 \cdot 5)$$
$$= 240 + 120 + 100$$
$$= 460 \text{ in.}^2$$

The volume of a solid is a measure of how much it will hold and is measured in *cubic units*. The volume of a prism is calculated by multiplying the **area of the base** by the **height**.

$$\text{Volume} = \textbf{base} \times \textbf{height}$$
$$= (12 \cdot 10) \cdot 5$$
$$= 600 \text{ in.}^3$$

Example 2 **Find the surface area and volume of a cube with edges of length 5 cm.**

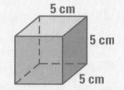

Solution A cube has six identical square faces. The area of each face is 5 cm · 5 cm or 25 cm^2.

$$\text{Surface area} = 25 + 25 + 25 + 25 + 25 + 25$$
$$= 150 \text{ cm}^2$$

$$\text{Volume} = \text{base} \times \text{height}$$
$$= (5 \cdot 5) \cdot 5$$
$$= 125 \text{ cm}^3$$

PRACTICE AND PROBLEM SOLVING

In Exercises 1–4, find the surface area and the volume.

1. a cube with edges of length 8 ft

2. a cube with edges of length 2.5 cm

3. a rectangular prism with length 8 mm, width 8 mm, and height 6 mm

4. a rectangular prism with length 12 in., width $4\frac{1}{2}$ in., and height 3 in.

In Exercises 5 and 6, solve each problem.

5. If the length of each edge of a cube is doubled, what happens to the surface area of the cube? Explain.

6. A gallon is about 231 in.^{3} Give the possible length, width, and height of a rectangular prism with a volume of about one gallon.

Triangles

Triangles can be classified by their sides and by their angles. Recall that in any triangle, the sum of the measures of the three angles is 180°.

Type of Triangle	Definition	Example
equilateral	All 3 sides have the same length.	All three sides are 2 cm long.
isosceles	At least 2 sides have the same length.	The lengths of the sides are 5 m, 5 m, and 4 m.
scalene	All sides have different lengths.	The lengths of the sides are 5 in., 6 in., and 7 in.
acute	All 3 angles are acute (between 0° and 90°).	The measures of the angles are 35°, 70°, and 75°.
right	One angle is a right angle (90°).	The measures of the angles are 30°, 60°, and 90°.
obtuse	One angle is an obtuse angle (between 90° and 180°).	The measures of the angles are 20°, 50°, and 110°.

Example 1 Classify the triangle according to its sides and angles.

a.   b.

Solution **a.** The red tick marks show that all three sides of the triangle are the same length. This means that the triangle is *equilateral*. The angles all appear to be acute, so the triangle is an *acute* triangle.

b. The red corner mark shows that one angle is a right angle, so the triangle is a *right* triangle. The triangle is also *scalene* because no two sides are the same length.

PRACTICE AND PROBLEM SOLVING

In Exercises 1–6, classify the triangle according to its sides and angles.

1.

2.

3.

4.

5.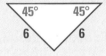

6.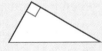

7. Explain why a triangle cannot have a right angle and an obtuse angle.

Translations

A **translation** slides every point of a figure the same distance in the same direction.

Example 1 Describe the translation of △*ABC* to triangle △*DEF*.

Solution △*ABC* is translated 4 units to the left and 2 units down.

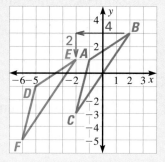

Example 2 Suppose △*ABC* in the diagram is translated 5 units up. Write the coordinates of the vertices of the translated triangle.

Solution Graph △*ABC* and the translation of △*ABC*. For each point on the translation of △*ABC*, the *y*-coordinate is 5 units greater than the original.

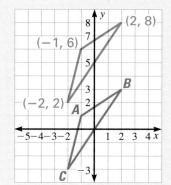

$$A(-1, 1) \longrightarrow (-1, 6)$$
$$B(2, 3) \longrightarrow (2, 8)$$
$$C(-2, -3) \longrightarrow (-2, 2)$$

PRACTICE AND PROBLEM SOLVING

In Exercises 1–3, describe the translation of △*ABC* to △*DEF*.

1.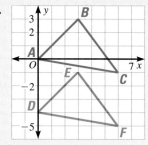

2.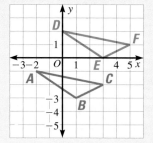

3.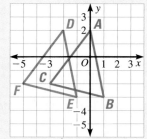

4. Use the diagram in Exercise 1. Find the coordinates of the vertices of triangle △*ABC* when it is translated 3 units to the right.

5. Use the diagram in Exercise 2. Find the coordinates of the vertices of △*ABC* when it is translated 1 unit to the left and 2 units up.

6. Use the diagram in Exercise 3. Find the coordinates of the vertices of △*ABC* when it is translated *x* units up (*x* > 0).

7. When a figure is translated, is the new figure the same shape as the original figure? Is it the same size?

TOOLBOX

Counting Methods

Example 1 — A restaurant offers three types of salads: a house salad, a Caesar salad, and a spinach salad. There are four types of salad dressing available: Italian, French, ranch, and fat-free vinaigrette. In how many different ways can a customer select a salad and a dressing?

Solution — You can use 3 different methods to solve the problem.

Method ❶ — Make a list and count the number of entries.

house & Italian	Caesar & Italian	spinach & Italian
house & French	Caesar & French	spinach & French
house & ranch	Caesar & ranch	spinach & ranch
house & vinaigrette	Caesar & vinaigrette	spinach & vinaigrette

The list shows that there are 12 different ways to select a salad and a dressing.

Method ❷ — Draw a *tree diagram* and count the number of "branches."

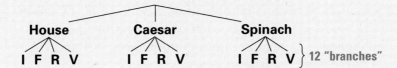

Method ❸ — Use the Counting Principle: If one item is to be selected from each of two or more sets, the total number of possible combinations is the product of the number of items in each set.

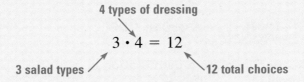

4 types of dressing

$$3 \cdot 4 = 12$$

3 salad types   12 total choices

PRACTICE AND PROBLEM SOLVING

1. Roberta has a gold necklace, a silver necklace, and a bead necklace. She has pearl earrings and hoop earrings. Make a list and a tree diagram to find the number of ways she can match her jewelry.

2. In how many ways can a true-false quiz with three questions be answered if each question must be marked true or false? Explain what method you used.

3. A code consists of a letter followed by one of the following odd digits: 1, 3, 5, 7. How many different codes are possible? Explain what method you used.

4. The Drama Club has 21 members: 3 freshmen, 5 sophomores, 7 juniors, and 6 seniors. In how many ways can a committee be formed with one representative from each class?

Permutations and Combinations

A **permutation** is an arrangement or listing of objects in which *order is important*. A **combination** is a collection of a set of objects in which *order is not important*.

Example 1
Eight runners compete in a race. In how many different orders can the runners cross the finish line?

Solution
This situation involves a permutation. The number of permutations of n objects is the product $n!$, called n factorial, and is calculated as $n \cdot (n - 1) \cdot (n - 2) \cdots \cdots 3 \cdot 2 \cdot 1$. In this problem there are eight runners. So,

$$8! = 8 \cdot 7 \cdot 6 \cdot 5 \cdot 4 \cdot 3 \cdot 2 \cdot 1$$
$$= 40{,}320$$

There are 40,320 ways the runners can cross the finish line.

Example 2
Five students are running for student council. In how many ways can two of them be elected to serve on the student council?

Solution
This situation involves a combination. Let A, B, C, D, and E represent the students. Make a list of the possible pairs of elected students. Remember, in a combination, AB and BA represent the same pair of students.

$$\text{AB} \quad \text{AC} \quad \text{AD} \quad \text{AE} \quad \text{BC}$$
$$\text{BD} \quad \text{BE} \quad \text{CD} \quad \text{CE} \quad \text{DE}$$

There are 10 ways that two students can be elected.

PRACTICE AND PROBLEM SOLVING

In Exercises 1–6, tell if the situation involves a permutation or a combination. Then solve the problem.

1. Five students are running for student council. In how many ways can three of them be elected to serve on the student council?

2. In how many ways can Troy choose two out of six cassettes to bring along for a walk?

3. The three music teachers at Central High School line up for a photograph. In how many ways can they do this?

4. Six swimmers are competing in a race. In how many ways can the swimmers be assigned to lanes in the pool?

5. There are eight people who work as cashiers at the Longview Hardware Store. In how many ways can two of them be assigned to work the evening shift?

6. Give a real-life example of a permutation and a real-life example of a combination.

TOOLBOX

Line Graphs

A **line graph** is a good way to represent sets of data that change over a given period of time.

Example 1 Draw a line graph to represent the data in the table. The data shows the number of days that rain or snow per month in Tokyo, Japan.

Month	J	F	M	A	M	J	J	A	S	O	N	D
Days of rain or snow in Tokyo	8	8	13	14	14	16	14	13	17	14	10	7

Solution

Include a title on the graph.

Draw evenly spaced horizontal and vertical grid lines.

Choose a reasonable scale.

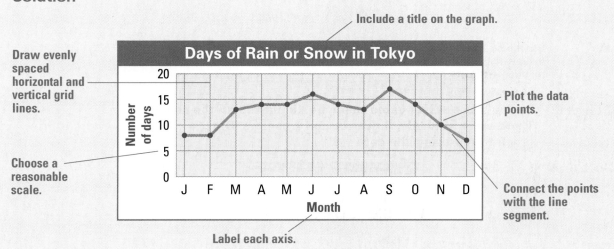

Plot the data points.

Connect the points with the line segment.

Label each axis.

PRACTICE AND PROBLEM SOLVING

1. Write a conclusion based on the graph in the example above.

2. The table below shows the different values of a company's stock price over the period of a year. Each price given represents the price of the stock on the first day of the month. Draw a line graph to represent the data. Write a conclusion based on your graph.

Month	J	F	M	A	M	J	J	A	S	O	N	D
Stock price	11	18	24	19	15	18	18	30	32	46	31	55

3. Use the data below and the data in Example 1 to draw a double line graph comparing the number of days of rain or snow in Tokyo and Sapporo, Japan. Write a conclusion based on your graph.

Month	J	F	M	A	M	J	J	A	S	O	N	D
Days of rain or snow in Sapporo	26	23	23	13	14	13	13	17	17	17	19	25

Circle Graphs

A circle graph is a good way to represent data as parts of a whole.

Example 1 **In the election for class president, Myra received 30% of the votes, Chou received 45%, Carlos received 15%, and Ginny received 10%. Draw a circle graph to represent the data.**

Solution The sum of all the percents is 100%, which will be represented by 360° of a circle. To find the measure of the angle for each part, rewrite the percent as a decimal and multiply by 360°.

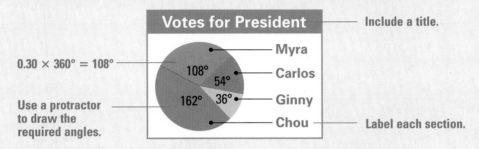

$0.30 \times 360° = 108°$

Use a protractor to draw the required angles.

Votes for President — Include a title.

Myra

Carlos

Ginny

Chou — Label each section.

Example 2 **During a basketball game there are 10 players on the court. There are 4 forwards, 4 guards, and 2 centers. Draw a circle graph to represent the data.**

Solution

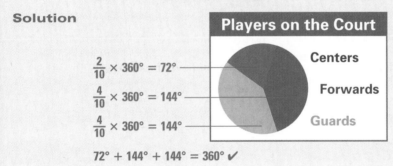

$\frac{2}{10} \times 360° = 72°$

$\frac{4}{10} \times 360° = 144°$

$\frac{4}{10} \times 360° = 144°$

Players on the Court

Centers

Forwards

Guards

$72° + 144° + 144° = 360°$ ✔

PRACTICE AND PROBLEM SOLVING

1. Air is 78% nitrogen and 21% oxygen. The rest is argon and other gases. Draw a circle graph to represent the data.

2. In the 1996 Summer Olympics, China won 16 gold medals, 22 silver medals, and 12 bronze medals. Draw a circle graph to represent the data.

3. Suppose that on a typical day you are in school 7 h and you sleep for 8 h. You do homework for 2 h and you work at a part-time job for 3 h. Draw a circle graph to represent this information. (Mark the remaining time as "Other.")

4. The sources of major league baseball revenue are as follows: ticket sales, 40%; television and radio, 35%; stadium revenue, 18%; licensing and other sources, 7%. Draw a circle graph to represent the data.

U.S. CUSTOMARY MEASURES

■ LENGTH

12 inches (in.) = 1 foot (ft)
3 feet = 1 yard (yd)
36 inches = 1 yard
5280 feet = 1 mile (mi)
1760 yards = 1 mile

■ CAPACITY

1 cup (c) = 8 fluid ounces (fl oz)
2 cups = 1 pint (pt)
2 pints = 1 quart (qt)
2 quarts = 1 half-gallon
4 quarts = 1 gallon (gal)

■ WEIGHT

16 ounces (oz) = 1 pound (lb)
2000 pounds = 1 ton

■ AREA

144 square inches $(in.^2)$ = 1 square foot (ft^2)
9 ft^2 = 1 square yard (yd^2)
640 acres = 1 square mile (mi^2)

■ VOLUME

1728 cubic inches $(in.^3)$ = 1 cubic foot (ft^3)
27 ft^3 = 1 cubic yard (yd^3)

■ TIME

60 seconds (s) = 1 minute (min)
3600 seconds = 1 hour (h)
60 minutes = 1 hour
24 hours = 1 day
7 days = 1 week

360 days = 1 business year
365 days = 1 year
366 days = 1 leap year
10 years = 1 decade
10 decades = 1 century = 100 years

■ CONVERTING MEASURES WITHIN THE U.S. CUSTOMARY SYSTEM

When you rewrite a measurement in another unit, you can use the relationships between the units.

STUDY TIP

To change 45 miles per hour to feet per second:

$$\frac{45 \text{ miles}}{\text{hour}} \times \frac{5280 \text{ feet}}{1 \text{ mile}} \times \frac{1 \text{ hour}}{3600 \text{ seconds}}$$

$$= \left(\frac{45 \times 5280}{3600}\right) \frac{\text{feet}}{\text{second}} = 66 \text{ ft/s}$$

STUDY TIP

To change 120 ounces per square inch to pounds per square foot:

$$\frac{120 \text{ oz}}{\text{in.}^2} \times \frac{144 \text{ in.}^2}{1 \text{ ft}^2} \times \frac{1 \text{ lb}}{16 \text{ oz}}$$

$$= \left(\frac{120 \times 144}{16}\right) \frac{\text{lb}}{\text{ft}^2} = 1080 \text{ lb/ft}^2$$

METRIC MEASURES

In the metric system, the units are related by powers of 10.

Table of Units				
PREFIX	POWER of 10	LENGTH	CAPACITY	MASS
kilo (k)	1000 units	kilometer	kiloliter*	kilogram
hecto (h)	100 units	hectometer*	hectoliter*	hectogram*
deka (da)	10 units	dekameter*	dekaliter*	dekagram*
	1 unit	meter	liter	gram
deci (d)	0.1 unit	decimeter*	deciliter*	decigram*
centi (c)	0.01 unit	centimeter	centiliter*	centigram*
milli (m)	0.001 unit	millimeter	milliliter	milligram
*These units are seldom used.				

■ **LENGTH**

10 millimeters (mm) = 1 centimeter (cm)
10 cm = 1 decimeter (dm)
100 cm = 1 meter (m)
1000 m = 1 kilometer (km)
100,000 cm = 1 km

■ **AREA**

100 square millimeters (mm^2) =
    1 square centimeter (cm^2)
10,000 cm^2 = 1 square meter (m^2)
1,000,000 m^2 = 1 square kilometer (km^2)

■ **CAPACITY**

1000 milliliters (mL) = 1 liter (L)
10 deciliters (dL) = 1 L

■ **MASS**

1000 milligrams (mg) = 1 gram (g)
1000 g = 1 kilogram (kg)

■ **VOLUME**

1,000,000 cubic centimeters (cm^3) =
    1 cubic meter (m^3)
1 cm^3 = 1 mL
1000 cm^3 = 1 L

■ **CONVERTING MEASURES WITHIN THE METRIC SYSTEM**

Use the relationships between units, which are shown in the table at the top of this page, to convert measures within the metric system.

STUDY TIP

When you rewrite a measurement using a smaller unit, you multiply.

0.24 m = ? cm

In the Table of Units, there are 2 steps from meters to centimeters, so multiply by 10^2, or 100.

0.24 m × 100 = 24 cm

STUDY TIP

When you rewrite a measurement using a larger unit, you divide.

3500 mg = ? kg

In the Table of Units, there are 6 steps from milligrams to kilograms, so divide by 10^6, or 1,000,000.

3500 mg ÷ 1,000,000 = 0.0035 kg

SQUARES AND SQUARE ROOTS

n	n^2	$\sqrt{n}$	n	n^2	$\sqrt{n}$	n	n^2	$\sqrt{n}$
1	1	1.000	33	1089	5.745	69	4761	8.307
2	4	1.414	34	1156	5.831	70	4900	8.367
3	9	1.732	35	1225	5.916	71	5041	8.426
4	16	2.000	36	1296	6.000	72	5184	8.485
5	25	2.236	37	1369	6.083	73	5329	8.544
6	36	2.449	38	1444	6.164	74	5476	8.602
7	49	2.646	39	1521	6.245	75	5625	8.660
8	64	2.828	40	1600	6.325	76	5776	8.718
9	81	3.000	41	1681	6.403	77	5929	8.775
10	100	3.162	42	1764	6.481	78	6084	8.832
11	121	3.317	43	1849	6.557	79	6241	8.888
12	144	3.464	44	1936	6.633	80	6400	8.944
13	169	3.606	45	2025	6.708	81	6561	9.000
14	196	3.742	46	2116	6.782	82	6724	9.055
15	225	3.873	47	2209	6.856	83	6889	9.110
16	256	4.000	48	2304	6.928	84	7056	9.165
17	289	4.123	49	2401	7.000	85	7225	9.220
18	324	4.243	50	2500	7.071	86	7396	9.274
19	361	4.359	51	2601	7.141	87	7569	9.327
20	400	4.472	52	2704	7.211	88	7744	9.381
21	441	4.583	53	2809	7.280	89	7921	9.434
22	484	4.690	54	2916	7.348	90	8100	9.487
23	529	4.796	55	3025	7.416	91	8281	9.539
24	576	4.899	56	3136	7.483	92	8464	9.592
25	625	5.000	57	3249	7.550	93	8649	9.644
26	676	5.099	58	3364	7.616	94	8836	9.695
27	729	5.196	59	3481	7.681	95	9025	9.747
28	784	5.292	60	3600	7.746	96	9216	9.798
29	841	5.385	61	3721	7.810	97	9409	9.849
30	900	5.477	62	3844	7.874	98	9604	9.899
31	961	5.568	63	3969	7.937	99	9801	9.950
32	1024	5.657	64	4096	8.000	100	10000	10.000
			65	4225	8.062			
			66	4356	8.124			
			67	4489	8.185			
			68	4624	8.246			

SQUARE ROOTS

TRIGONOMETRIC RATIOS

Angle	Sine	Cosine	Tangent
1°	0.0175	0.9998	0.0175
2°	0.0349	0.9994	0.0349
3°	0.0523	0.9986	0.0524
4°	0.0698	0.9976	0.0699
5°	0.0872	0.9962	0.0875
6°	0.1045	0.9945	0.1051
7°	0.1219	0.9925	0.1228
8°	0.1392	0.9903	0.1405
9°	0.1564	0.9877	0.1584
10°	0.1736	0.9848	0.1763
11°	0.1908	0.9816	0.1944
12°	0.2079	0.9781	0.2126
13°	0.2250	0.9744	0.2309
14°	0.2419	0.9703	0.2493
15°	0.2588	0.9659	0.2679
16°	0.2756	0.9613	0.2867
17°	0.2924	0.9563	0.3057
18°	0.3090	0.9511	0.3249
19°	0.3256	0.9455	0.3443
20°	0.3420	0.9397	0.3640
21°	0.3584	0.9336	0.3839
22°	0.3746	0.9272	0.4040
23°	0.3907	0.9205	0.4245
24°	0.4067	0.9135	0.4452
25°	0.4226	0.9063	0.4663
26°	0.4384	0.8988	0.4877
27°	0.4540	0.8910	0.5095
28°	0.4695	0.8829	0.5317
29°	0.4848	0.8746	0.5543
30°	0.5000	0.8660	0.5774
31°	0.5150	0.8572	0.6009
32°	0.5299	0.8480	0.6249
33°	0.5446	0.8387	0.6494
34°	0.5592	0.8290	0.6745
35°	0.5736	0.8192	0.7002
36°	0.5878	0.8090	0.7265
37°	0.6018	0.7986	0.7536
38°	0.6157	0.7880	0.7813
39°	0.6293	0.7771	0.8098
40°	0.6428	0.7660	0.8391
41°	0.6561	0.7547	0.8693
42°	0.6691	0.7431	0.9004
43°	0.6820	0.7314	0.9325
44°	0.6947	0.7193	0.9657
45°	0.7071	0.7071	1.0000

Angle	Sine	Cosine	Tangent
46°	0.7193	0.6947	1.0355
47°	0.7314	0.6820	1.0724
48°	0.7431	0.6691	1.1106
49°	0.7547	0.6561	1.1504
50°	0.7660	0.6428	1.1918
51°	0.7771	0.6293	1.2349
52°	0.7880	0.6157	1.2799
53°	0.7986	0.6018	1.3270
54°	0.8090	0.5878	1.3764
55°	0.8192	0.5736	1.4281
56°	0.8290	0.5592	1.4826
57°	0.8387	0.5446	1.5399
58°	0.8480	0.5299	1.6003
59°	0.8572	0.5150	1.6643
60°	0.8660	0.5000	1.7321
61°	0.8746	0.4848	1.8040
62°	0.8829	0.4695	1.8807
63°	0.8910	0.4540	1.9626
64°	0.8988	0.4384	2.0503
65°	0.9063	0.4226	2.1445
66°	0.9135	0.4067	2.2460
67°	0.9205	0.3907	2.3559
68°	0.9272	0.3746	2.4751
69°	0.9336	0.3584	2.6051
70°	0.9397	0.3420	2.7475
71°	0.9455	0.3256	2.9042
72°	0.9511	0.3090	3.0777
73°	0.9563	0.2924	3.2709
74°	0.9613	0.2756	3.4874
75°	0.9659	0.2588	3.7321
76°	0.9703	0.2419	4.0108
77°	0.9744	0.2250	4.3315
78°	0.9781	0.2079	4.7046
79°	0.9816	0.1908	5.1446
80°	0.9848	0.1736	5.6713
81°	0.9877	0.1564	6.3138
82°	0.9903	0.1392	7.1154
83°	0.9925	0.1219	8.1443
84°	0.9945	0.1045	9.5144
85°	0.9962	0.0872	11.4301
86°	0.9976	0.0698	14.3007
87°	0.9986	0.0523	19.0811
88°	0.9994	0.0349	28.6363
89°	0.9998	0.0175	57.2900

TRIGONOMETRIC RATIOS

SYMBOLS

■ ARITHMETIC AND ALGEBRA

$=$	Is equal to	a^0	1
$\neq$	Is not equal to	$(\,),\{\,\},[\,]$	Grouping symbols
$>$	Is greater than	5, or $+5$	Positive 5
$<$	Is less than	-5	Negative 5
$\geq$	Is greater than or equal to	$|a|$	Absolute value of a number a
$\leq$	Is less than or equal to		
$\approx$	Is approximately equal to	$\sqrt{a}$	Square root of a number a
ab $a(b)$ $a \cdot b$	a times b	$a:b$, or $\dfrac{a}{b}$	Ratio of a to b
a^n	A number a raised to the nth power	$P(A)$	Probability of the outcome A
a^{-n}	$\dfrac{1}{a^n}$	$n!$	n-factorial

■ GEOMETRY

(a, b)	Ordered Pair a, b
$\sim$	Is similar to
$\cong$	Is congruent to
$\triangle ABC$	Triangle ABC
$\overleftrightarrow{AB}$	Line AB
$\overline{AB}$	Segment AB
AB	Measure of segment AB
$\overrightarrow{AB}$	Ray AB
$\angle A$	Angle A
$m\angle A$	Measure of angle A
π	Pi

■ TRIGONOMETRY

$\sin A$	Sine of angle A
$\cos A$	Cosine of angle A
$\tan A$	Tangent of angle A

FORMULAS

■ **MISCELLANEOUS**

$d = rt$	Distance-rate-time formula (p. 23)
$F = \frac{9}{5}C + 32$	Temperature conversion to degrees in Fahrenheit (p. 127)
$C = \frac{5}{9}(F - 32)$	Temperature conversion to degrees in Celsius (p. 619)
$A = P(1 + r)^n$	The balance in a savings account (p. 348)
$d^2 = \frac{3}{2}h$	Distance to the horizon (p. 413)
$0 = -16t^2 + s$	Falling objects (p. 411)
$a^2 + b^2 = c^2$	Pythagorean Theorem (p. 420)

■ **PERIMETER**

$P = 4s$	Perimeter of a square (p. 11)
$P = 2(l + w)$	Perimeter of a rectangle (p. 21)
$C = \pi d$ or $C = 2\pi r$	Circumference of a circle (p. 566)

■ **AREA**

$A = s^2$	Area of a square (p. 10)
$A = lw$	Area of a rectangle (p. 7)
$A = bh$	Area of a parallelogram (p. 512)
$A = \frac{1}{2}bh$	Area of a triangle (p. 192)
$A = \frac{1}{2}h(b_1 + b_2)$	Area of a trapezoid (p. 512)
$A = \pi r^2$	Area of a circle (p. 567)

■ **SURFACE AREA**

$S = 6s^2$	Surface area of a cube (p. 13)
$S = 2B + Ph$	Surface area of a prism (p. 576)
$S = 2B + Ch$	Surface area of a cylinder (p. 576)
$S = 4\pi r^2$	Surface area of a sphere (p. 599)

■ **VOLUME**

$V = lwh$	Volume of a rectangular prism (p. 580)
$V = s^3$	Volume of a cube (p. 15)
$V = Bh$	Volume of a prism (p. 580)
$V = \pi r^2 h$	Volume of a cylinder (p. 586)
$V = \frac{1}{3}Bh$	Volume of a pyramid (p. 592)
$V = \frac{1}{3}\pi r^2 h$	Volume of a cone (p. 590)
$V = \frac{4}{3}\pi r^3$	Volume of a sphere (p. 596)

■ **COORDINATE GEOMETRY**

$m = \dfrac{y_2 - y_1}{x_2 - x_1}$	The slope of a line (p. 634)
$d = \sqrt{(x_2 - x_1)^2 + (y_2 - y_1)^2}$	The Distance Formula (p. 657)
$\text{Midpoint} = \left(\dfrac{x_1 + x_2}{2}, \dfrac{y_1 + y_2}{2}\right)$	The Midpoint Formula (p. 657)

absolute value (p. 105) The distance between a number and 0 on a number line. For example, $|3| = 3$, $|-3| = 3$, $|0| = 0$.

absolute value signs (p. 105) A pair of vertical rules that are used to indicate the absolute value of a number or expression between them, $|\ |$.

acute angle (p. 465) An angle whose measure is between $0°$ and $90°$.

acute triangle (p. 479) A triangle with three acute angles.

add matrices (p. 683) To find the sum of two matrices by adding the corresponding entries.

add polynomials (p. 694) To find the sum of two polynomials by combining their like terms.

Addition Property of Equality (p. 66) Adding the same number to each side of an equation produces an equivalent equation. If $a = b$, then $a + c = b + c$.

adjacent side *See* **cosine of an angle, sine of an angle, tangent of an angle**.

algebraic expression (p. 22) A collection of numbers, variables, operations, and grouping symbols. For example, $2(x + 3)$.

algebraic model (p. 23) An algebraic expression or equation used to represent a real-life situation.

angle (p. 464) A figure formed by two rays that begin at the same point. The rays are the *sides* of the angle and the point is the *vertex* of the angle.

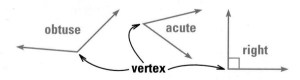

area (p. 7) A measure of how much surface is covered by a figure. Area is measured in square units.

Associative Property of Addition (p. 67) Changing the grouping of the addends does not change the sum. For example, $(a + b) + c = a + (b + c)$.

Associative Property of Multiplication (p. 67) Changing the grouping of the factors does not change the product. For example, $(ab)c = a(bc)$.

average (pp. 133, 668) The sum of a set of numbers divided by how many numbers are in the set. It is also called the *mean*.

axes (p. 142) The two real number lines that intersect at right angles to form a coordinate plane. The horizontal one is the x-axis and the vertical one is the y-axis.

bar graph (p. 208) A graph that organizes a collection of data by using horizontal or vertical bars to display how many times each event or number occurs in the collection.

base of a parallelogram (p. 512) A side of a parallelogram chosen so that it is perpendicular to the height of the parallelogram.

base of a percent (p. 376) The number from which a portion is to be found. In the percent equation $\frac{a}{b} = \frac{p}{100}$, the base is b.

base of a power (p. 10) The number or expression that is used as a factor in the repeated multiplication. For example, in the expression 4^6, 4 is the base.

bases of a trapezoid (p. 512) The two parallel sides of a trapezoid.

binomial (p. 688) A polynomial that has two terms.

box-and-whisker plot (p. 676) A graphical display that uses a box to represent the middle of a set of data and segments drawn to the extremes of both ends.

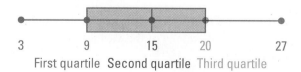

center of a circle (p. 566) The point inside a circle that is the same distance from all the points on the circle.

circle (p. 566) The set of all points in a plane that are the same distance from a given point called the center.

circle graph (p. 317) A graph that displays portions of data collections as parts of a circular region. The parts are often labeled using fractions or percents.

circumference (p. 566) The distance around a circle.

coefficient (p. 115) The numerical factor of an algebraic term. For example, in the term $3x^2$, the coefficient of x^2 is 3.

collect like terms (p. 56) A procedure to move like terms next to each other in an algebraic expression.

common factor (p. 266) A number that is a factor of two or more numbers. For example, 2 is a common factor of 4 and 6 because 2 is a factor of both 4 and 6.

common multiple (p. 270) A number that is a multiple of two or more natural numbers. For example, 60 is a common multiple of 5 and 6 because it is a multiple of both 5 and 6.

Commutative Property of Addition (p. 67) Changing the order of the addends does not change the sum. For example, $a + b = b + a$.

Commutative Property of Multiplication (p. 67) Changing the order of the factors does not change the product. For example, $ab = ba$.

complementary angles (p. 465) Two angles whose measures have a sum of 90°.

composite number (p. 260) A natural number that has three or more factors.

concave polygon *See* **nonconvex polygon**.

conditional equations (p. 60) Equations that are not true for all values of the variables they contain.

cone (p. 573) A solid that has a circular base, a vertex, and a lateral surface.

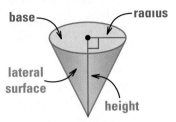

congruent angles (p. 464) Angles that have the same measure.

congruent polygons (p. 488) Two polygons that are exactly the same size and the same shape.

convex polygon (p. 484) A polygon is convex if a segment joining any two interior points lies completely within the polygon. *See also* **polygon**.

coordinate plane (p. 142) A plane formed by two real number lines called axes that intersect at a right angle; a plane used for locating a point whose coordinates are known.

coordinates (p. 142) An ordered pair of numbers that locate a point on a coordinate graph.

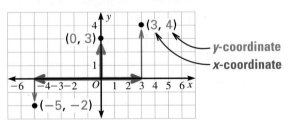

corresponding angles (p. 470) Angles that are in the same relative position when one line crosses two other lines. $\angle 1$ and $\angle 2$ are corresponding angles. $\angle 3$ and $\angle 4$ are also corresponding angles. *See also* **similar figures**.

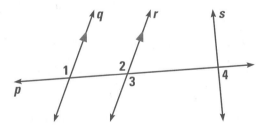

corresponding sides (p. 369) A pair of sides from two similar figures that are in the same relative position. *See also* **similar figures**.

cosine of an angle (p. 546) The cosine of an acute angle in a right triangle is the ratio of the length of the side adjacent to the acute angle to the length of the hypotenuse. For example, $\cos A = \dfrac{b}{c}$.

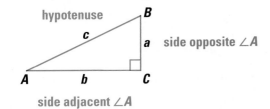

Counting Principle (p. 392) If one event can occur in m ways and another event can occur in n ways, then the two events can occur in mn ways.

Cross Product Property (p. 368) The cross products of a proportion are equal. If $\dfrac{a}{b} = \dfrac{c}{d}$, then $ad = bc$.

cube (p. 13) A rectangular prism whose six faces are congruent squares.

cubic units (p. 580) Standard measures of volume.

cylinder (p. 573) A solid figure with congruent circular bases that lie in parallel planes.

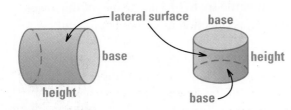

data (p. 26) The facts, or numbers, that describe something.

decagon (p. 32) A polygon with ten sides.

degree of a polynomial (p. 694) The largest exponent of a polynomial.

denominator (p. 6) The number or expression below the fraction bar in a fraction. 4 is the denominator of $\dfrac{x}{4}$.

diagonal (p. 33) A segment that connects two vertices of a polygon and is not a side.

diameter (p. 566) The distance across a circle through its center. The length of the diameter is twice the length of the radius.

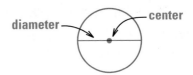

difference (pp. 6, 120) The result obtained when numbers or expressions are subtracted. The difference of a and b is $a - b$.

dimensions (p. 15) The measure of the magnitude or size of an object. For example, the dimensions of a rectangle are its length and its width.

discount (p. 383) The difference between the regular price and the sale price of an item.

discount percent (p. 383) The percent that a sale item is discounted. It is the ratio of the discount to the regular price of the item.

Distance Formula (p. 656) The distance, d, between the points (x_1, y_1) and (x_2, y_2) is $d = \sqrt{(x_2 - x_1)^2 + (y_2 - y_1)^2}$.

Distributive Property (p. 52) The product of a number and the sum of two numbers is equal to the sum of the two products. For example, $a(b + c) = ab + ac$ and $ab + ac = a(b + c)$.

divisible (p. 254) One natural number is divisible by another natural number if the second divides evenly into the first, that is, if there is a 0 remainder after division. For example, 84 is divisible by 2, since $84 \div 2$ leaves no remainder.

Division Property of Equality (p. 72) Dividing both sides of an equation by the same nonzero number produces an equivalent equation. If $a = b$, then $\dfrac{a}{c} = \dfrac{b}{c}$.

edge (p. 572) The segment formed when two faces of a solid figure meet. *See also* **polyhedron**.

endpoint (p. 460) The point at the end of a line segment or ray.

entries of a matrix (p. 682) The numbers in a matrix that are arranged in rows and columns.

equal matrices (p. 682) Two matrices are equal if all entries in corresponding positions are equal.

equation (p. 60) A statement that two expressions are equivalent. For example, $3 \times 9 = 27$ and $8 + x = 10$ are equations.

equiangular triangle (p. 479) A triangle in which all three angles have the same measure.

equilateral triangle (pp. 179, 478) A triangle in which all three sides have the same length.

equivalent equations (p. 60) Equations that have the same solutions.

equivalent expressions (p. 52) Expressions that have the same values when numbers are substituted for the variables.

equivalent fractions (p. 274) Fractions that have the same decimal form: $\frac{1}{2}, \frac{2}{4}, \frac{3}{6}$ are equivalent fractions because each is equal to 0.5.

evaluate an algebraic expression (p. 22) To find the value of an expression by replacing variables in an expression with numbers.

even number (p. 9) A whole number that is divisible by 2.

exponent (p. 10) A number or variable that represents the number of times the base is used as a factor. For example, in the expression 2^3, 3 is the exponent.

exterior angles (p. 494) Exterior angles are formed when the sides of a polygon are extended.

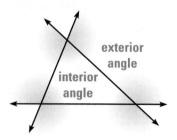

face (p. 572) The flat surface of a solid figure; one of the polygons that make up a polyhedron. *See also* **polyhedron**.

factored (p. 255) A natural number is factored when it is written as the product of two or more natural numbers.

factors (pp. 6, 255) Numbers or variable expressions that are multiplied. For example, 4 and x are the factors of $4x$.

Fibonacci Sequence (p. 41) An unending sequence such as 1, 1, 2, 3, 5, 8, 13, 21, . . . in which the first two terms are fixed and each other term is the sum of the two preceding terms.

first quartile (p. 676) The median of the lower half of a collection of ordered numbers.

FOIL method (p. 704) A method used to multiply two binomials in a single step. Find the sum of the products of the **F**irst terms, **O**uter terms, **I**nner terms, and **L**ast terms. For example, to find $(2x + 3)(x + 5)$, find

Outer: $(2x)(5)$ Inner: $(3)(x)$

$2x^2 + 10x + 3x + 15$

First: $(2x)(x)$ Last: $(3)(5)$

formula *See* **algebraic model**.

frequency distribution (p. 209) A way to organize data by displaying the number of items or events that occur in an interval.

general problem solving plan (p. 88) A series of steps that can be used to solve a real-life problem.

1. Write a verbal model.
2. Assign values to the labels.
3. Write an algebraic model.
4. Solve.
5. Answer.
6. Check.

geometry (p. 32) The study of shapes and their measures.

graph of a linear inequality (p. 653) The half plane that consists of all points on one side of the line that is the graph of the corresponding linear equation. For example, this is the graph of the inequality $y > 2x - 4$.

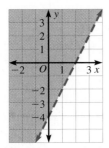

greatest common factor, GCF (p. 266) The largest common factor of two numbers or algebraic expressions. For example, $4a$ is the GCF of $20ab^2$ and $24a^2$.

grouping symbols (p. 17) Characters that are used to change the order of operations in an expression or to make an expression clearer. Parentheses ( ) and brackets [ ] are examples of grouping symbols.

half plane (p. 652) In a plane, the region on one side of a line.

height (p. 512) The perpendicular distance between parallel bases of a parallelogram, trapezoid, prism, or cylinder, or the distance from a vertex to an opposite side of a triangle, pyramid, or cone.

hemisphere (p. 596) One of the two halves of a sphere.

heptagon (p. 32) A polygon with seven sides.

hexagon (p. 32) A polygon with six sides.

histogram (p. 209) A bar graph in which the bars represent equally spaced intervals of numbers.

hypotenuse (p. 420) The side of a right triangle that is opposite the right angle. It is the longest side of a right triangle. *See also* **right triangle**.

identities (p. 60) Equations that are true for all values of the variable. For example, the identities $a + 0 = a$ and $a \cdot 1 = a$ are true for all numbers.

image (p. 522) The new figure formed by the transformation of a given figure.

inequalities (p. 92) Mathematical sentences that contain an inequality symbol.

inequality symbol (p. 92) One of the following symbols: $<$, $>$, $\leq$, $\geq$, or $\neq$.

integers (p. 104) The set of numbers $\ldots, -3, -2, -1, 0, 1, 2, 3, \ldots$

interior angle (p. 494) An angle of a polygon formed by two adjacent sides.

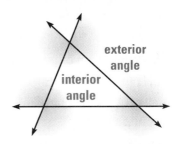

intersection of lines (p. 461) The set of points that are common to two or more lines.

inverse operations (p. 138) Operations that undo each other. For example, addition and subtraction are inverse operations, as are multiplication and division.

irrational number (p. 280) A real number that cannot be expressed as the quotient of two integers. For example, the square roots of numbers that are not perfect squares like 2, π, and nonterminating nonrepeating decimals like 0.1001000100001. . . are all irrational numbers.

isosceles trapezoid (p. 484) A trapezoid whose nonparallel sides have the same length.

isosceles triangle (pp. 421, 478) A triangle with at least two sides that have the same length.

kite (p. 484) A quadrilateral that has two pairs of neighboring sides of equal lengths.

least common denominator, LCD (p. 316) The least common denominator of two or more fractions is the least common multiple of their denominators.

least common multiple, LCM (p. 270) The least common multiple of two numbers or algebraic expressions is the smallest of their common multiples. $6a^2b$ is the LCM of $2ab$ and $3a^2$.

Left-to-Right Rule (p. 16) Operations having the same priority in an expression are evaluated from left to right.

leg of a right triangle (p. 420) Either of the sides of a right triangle that form the right angle. *See also* **right triangle**.

like fractions (p. 310) Fractions that have the same denominator.

like terms (p. 56) Two or more terms in an expression that have the same variables raised to the same powers.

line (p. 460) A straight path of points that extend forever in opposite directions.

line graph (p. 214) A graph that shows trends over intervals of time.

line plot (p. 230) A diagram showing the frequency of data on a number line.

line segment (p. 460) Part of a line consisting of two endpoints and all the points between them.

line symmetry (p. 474) A property of a figure that can be divided by a line into two parts, each of which is the mirror image of the other.

linear equation (p. 618) An equation in two variables whose graph is a straight line.

linear inequality (p. 652) An inequality in two variables for which the graph is a half plane above or below the corresponding linear equation.

linear relationship (p. 648) Two quantities that can be modeled with a linear equation.

matrix (p. 682) A rectangular array of numbers or data in rows and columns.

mean (pp. 133, 668) The sum of a set of numbers divided by how many numbers are in the set. It is also called the *average*.

measure of an angle, $m\angle$ (p. 464) The size of an angle. This can be estimated using a protractor. A common unit of angle measure is degrees.

measures of central tendency (p. 668) Numbers that can be used to represent a group of numbers. The mean, median, and mode of a distribution.

median (p. 668) The middle number (or the average of the two middle numbers) of a group of numbers listed in order.

midpoint (p. 657) The halfway point on a line segment.

mode (p. 668) The number that occurs most often in a given collection of numbers.

model (p. 7) Something that helps you visualize or understand an actual process or object.

monomial (p. 688) A polynomial with only one term; a variable, a number, or a product of variables and numbers.

multiple (p. 270) The product of a given number and any whole number greater than zero. For example, 8 is a multiple of 1, 2, 4, and 8.

Multiplication Property of Equality (p. 72) Multiplying both sides of an equation by the same nonzero number produces an equivalent equation. If $a = b$, then $ac = bc$.

n-gon (p. 32) A polygon with n sides.

natural numbers (p. 38) The set of numbers 1, 2, 3, 4, ...

negative correlation (p. 236) Data points on a scatter plot whose y-coordinates tend to decrease as the x-coordinates increase.

negative integer (p. 104) An integer that is less than 0.

negative slope (p. 635) A line in the coordinate plane has a negative slope if it slants downward as you move from left to right.

net (p. 572) A flat pattern that can be folded to form a solid.

no correlation (p. 236) Data points on a scatter plot for which no pattern exists among the x- and y-coordinates.

nonagon (p. 32) A polygon with nine sides.

nonconvex polygon (p. 484) A polygon that is not convex because one or more segments joining any two interior points does not lie completely within the polygon. *See also* **polygon**.

nonrepeating decimal (pp. 38, 281) A decimal that neither terminates nor repeats.

numerator (p. 6) The number or expression above the fraction bar in a fraction. x is the numerator of $\frac{x}{4}$.

numerical expression (p. 16) A collection of numbers, operations, and grouping symbols.

obtuse angle (p. 465) An angle that measures between 90° and 180°.

obtuse triangle (p. 479) A triangle with an obtuse angle.

octagon (p. 32) A polygon with eight sides.

odd number (p. 9) A whole number that is not divisible by 2. The numbers 1, 3, 5, 7, . . . are odd.

opposite side *See* **cosine of an angle, sine of an angle, tangent of an angle**.

opposites (p. 105) Two numbers that have the same absolute value but opposite signs; any two numbers whose sum is 0.

Order of Operations (p. 16) A procedure for evaluating an expression involving more than one operation.

1. First do operations that occur within grouping symbols.

2. Then evaluate powers.

3. Then do multiplications and divisions from left to right.

4. Finally, do additions and subtractions from left to right.

ordered pair (p. 142) A pair of numbers or coordinates used to locate a point in a coordinate plane. The solution of an equation or an inequality in two variables.

origin (p. 142) The point of intersection in the coordinate plane of the horizontal axis and the vertical axis. The point (0, 0).

outcome (p. 242) A possible result of an event. For example, obtaining heads is an outcome of tossing a coin.

parallel lines (p. 461) Lines in the same plane that do not intersect.
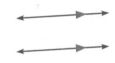

parallelogram (p. 484) A quadrilateral with opposite sides parallel.
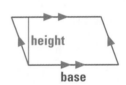

pentagon (p. 32) A polygon with five sides.

percent (p. 336) A way of expressing hundredths, that is, a fraction whose denominator is 100. *Percent* means "per hundred."

5% (5 percent) equals $\frac{5}{100}$.

percent equation (p. 376) The statement "a is p percent of b" is equivalent to the equation $\frac{a}{b} = \frac{p}{100}$.

percent of increase or decrease (p. 386) An indication of how much a quantity has increased or decreased.

perfect square (p. 11) A number whose square root can be written as an exact decimal.

perimeter of a polygon (p. 192) The distance around a figure; the sum of the lengths of the sides.

perpendicular lines (p. 465)
Two lines that meet at a right
angle.

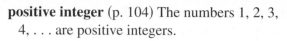

pi (p. 566) The number that is the
ratio of the circumference of a circle to its
diameter. It is represented by the Greek letter π
and is approximately equal to 3.1416.

pictograph (p. 204) A graph that organizes a
collection of data by using pictures in horizontal
or vertical rows to indicate how many times
each event or number occurs in the collection.

plane (p. 460) A flat surface that extends forever
in all directions.

plotting a point (pp. 104, 142) Locating a point
that corresponds to a number on a number line
or that corresponds to an ordered pair in the
coordinate plane.

point (p. 460) A dot that represents a location in a
plane or in a space.

polygon (p. 32) A closed figure whose sides are
straight line segments.

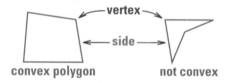

polyhedron (p. 572) A solid that is bounded by
polygons, which are called faces.

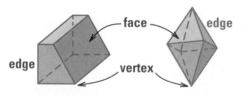

polynomial (p. 688) An expression that has one
or more terms of the form ax^n where a is any
real number and n is a whole number.

portion (p. 336) A fraction that compares the
measure of part of a quantity to the measure of
the whole quantity.

positive correlation (p. 236) Data points on a
scatter plot whose y-coordinates tend to increase
as the x-coordinates increase.

positive integer (p. 104) The numbers 1, 2, 3,
4, . . . are positive integers.

positive slope (p. 635) A line in the coordinate
plane has a positive slope if it slants upward as
you move from left to right.

possible outcomes (p. 242) All the different ways
an event can turn out.

power (p. 10) An expression such as 4^2 that has a
base (4) and an exponent (2).

prime factorization (p. 260) Expression of a
composite number as a product of prime factors.
The prime factorization of 18 is $2 \cdot 3 \cdot 3$.

prime number (p. 260) A natural number that
has exactly two factors, itself and 1. The
numbers 2, 3, 5, 7, 11, and 13 are examples of
prime numbers.

prism (p. 572) A polyhedron that has two
parallel, congruent faces called bases.

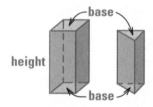

probability of an event (p. 242) A measure of the
likelihood that the event will occur.

product (p. 6) The result obtained when numbers
or expressions are multiplied. The product of
a and b is $a \cdot b$ or ab.

proportion (p. 368) An equation stating that two
ratios are equal. If a is to b as c is to d, then
$\frac{a}{b} = \frac{c}{d}$.

protractor (p. 464) A measuring device that can
be used to approximate the measure of an angle.

pyramid (p. 572) A space figure whose base is a
polygon and whose other faces are triangles that
share a common vertex.

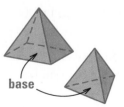

GLOSSARY

Pythagorean Theorem (p. 420) For any right triangle, the sum of the squares of the lengths of the legs, a and b, equals the square of the length of the hypotenuse, c.

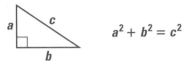

$$a^2 + b^2 = c^2$$

Pythagorean triple (p. 421) A set of three natural numbers that represent the lengths of the sides of a right triangle.

quadrants (p. 142) In the coordinate plane, the four parts into which the axes divide the plane.

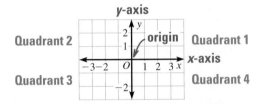

quadrilateral (p. 32) A polygon with four sides.

quotient (p. 6) The result obtained when numbers or expressions are divided. The quotient of a and b is $\frac{a}{b}$.

radical (p. 11) The square root symbol, $\sqrt{}$.

radius of a circle (p. 566) A segment that has the center as one endpoint and a point on the circle as the other endpoint.

rate (p. 362) The relationship $\frac{a}{b}$ of two quantities a and b that have different units of measure.

ratio (p. 363) The relationship $\frac{a}{b}$ of two quantities a and b that have the same unit of measure.

rational number (p. 280) A number that can be written as the quotient of two integers.

ray (p. 460) Part of a line that has one endpoint and extends forever in only one direction.

real numbers (p. 414) The set of all rational numbers and irrational numbers together.

reciprocal (p. 168) The reciprocal of a nonzero number a is $\frac{1}{a}$. The product of a number and its reciprocal is one.

rectangle (p. 484) A parallelogram that has four right angles.

rectangular prism (p. 580) A prism whose bases are rectangles.

reflection (p. 522) A transformation that flips a figure about a line onto its mirror image on the opposite side of the line.

reflection line (p. 522) In a reflection, a line that is perpendicular to and bisects each segment that joins an original point to its image.

regular polygon (p. 489) A polygon with each of its sides having the same length and each of its angles having the same measure.

repeating decimal (pp. 38, 281) A decimal in which a digit or group of digits repeats forever. Repeating digits are indicated by a bar.

$$0.3333\ldots = 0.\overline{3}$$
$$1.47474747\ldots = 1.\overline{47}$$

rhombus (p. 484) A parallelogram with four sides of equal length.

right angle (pp. 420, 465) An angle whose measure is $90°$.

right triangle (pp. 420, 479) A triangle that has a right angle.

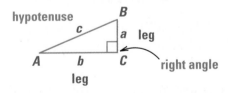

rotation (p. 526) A transformation that turns a figure a given angle and direction about a point.

rotational symmetry (p. 475) A figure has rotational symmetry if it coincides with itself after rotating $180°$ or less about a point.

round a number (p. 11) To replace a number by another one of approximately the same value that is easier to use.

scale factor (p. 536) In two similar polygons or two similar solids, the scale factor is the ratio of corresponding linear measures.

scalene quadrilateral (p. 484) A quadrilateral whose four sides all have different lengths.

scalene triangle (p. 478) A triangle whose three sides all have different lengths.

scatter plot (p. 236) The graph of a collection of ordered pairs of numbers (x, y).

scientific notation (p. 288) A short form of writing numbers whose absolute values are very large or very small. A number is written in scientific notation if it has the form $c \times 10^n$, where c is greater than or equal to 1 and less than 10, and where n is an integer.

second quartile (p. 676) The median of a collection of ordered numbers.

segment *See* **line segment**.

sequence (p. 3) An ordered list of numbers.

side of a polygon (p. 32) One of the straight line segments that make up the polygon.

similar figures (p. 536) Figures that have the same shape, but not necessarily the same size.

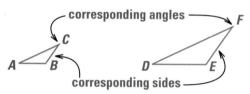

similar solids (p. 602) Solids that have the same shape with their corresponding lengths proportional.

similar triangles (p. 369) Two triangles that have the same angle measures.

simplest form (p. 274) A fraction is in simplest form if the numerator and denominator have no common factors.

simplify an expression (p. 56) To rewrite an algebraic expression so that there are no like terms.

simplifying a fraction (p. 274) To rewrite a fraction so that its numerator and denominator have no common factors.

simulation (p. 398) An experiment that models a real-life situation.

sine of an angle (p. 546) The sine of an acute angle in a right triangle is the ratio of the length of the side opposite the acute angle to the length of the hypotenuse. For example, $\sin A = \dfrac{a}{c}$.

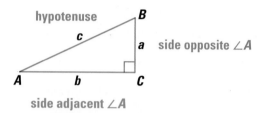

slope (p. 634) The ratio of the difference in y-coordinates to the difference in x-coordinates for any two points on the graph of a linear equation. Also defined as the *rise* over the *run*.

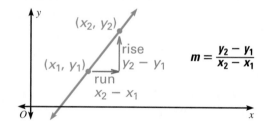

slope-intercept form of an equation (p. 642) A linear equation in x and y that has the form $y = mx + b$, where m is the slope of the line and b is the y-intercept.

solution (pp. 60, 92, 143, 652) A number (or ordered pair of numbers) that produces a true statement when substituted for the variable(s) in an equation or an inequality.

solving a right triangle (p. 421) Using the lengths of two sides of a right triangle to find the third side.

solving an equation (p. 60) Finding all the values of the variable that make the equation true.

solving an inequality (p. 92) Finding all the values of the variable that make the inequality true.

square (p. 484) A rectangle with four sides of equal length.

square root (p. 11) The number that when squared will produce the given number. Both 7 and −7 are square roots of 49, because $7^2 = 49$ and $(-7)^2 = 49$.

square root symbol *See* **radical**.

standard form of a polynomial (p. 688) A polynomial written so that the powers of the variable decrease from left to right.

statistics (p. 230) A branch of mathematics that organizes large collections of data in ways that can be used to understand trends and make predictions.

stem-and-leaf plot (p. 672) A method of organizing data in increasing or decreasing order.

straight angle (p. 465) An angle whose measure is 180°.

substitute (p. 22) To replace a variable in an expression by a number.

subtract matrices (p. 683) To find the difference of two matrices by finding the differences of the corresponding entries.

Subtraction Property of Equality (p. 66) Subtracting the same number from both sides of an equation produces an equivalent equation. If $a = b$, then $a - c = b - c$.

sum (p. 6) The result obtained when numbers or expressions are added. The sum of a and b is $a + b$.

supplementary angles (p. 465) Two angles whose measures have a sum of 180°.

surface area (p. 576) The sum of the areas of all the faces of a solid figure.

tangent of an angle (p. 546) The tangent of an acute angle in a right triangle is the ratio of the length of the side opposite the acute angle to the length of the side adjacent to that acute angle. For example, $\tan A = \frac{a}{b}$.

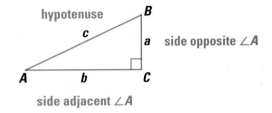

terminating decimal (pp. 38, 281) A decimal that contains a finite number of digits, for example, 0.5.

term (p. 22) A part of an expression that is separated by addition signs. In the expression $3x + (-2)$, the terms are $3x$ and -2.

third quartile (p. 676) The median of the upper half of a collection of ordered numbers.

time line (p. 205) A graph that shows the dates of several events.

transformation (p. 526) An operation such as a reflection (flip), rotation (turn), or translation (slide), that maps or moves a figure from an original position (preimage) to a new position (image).

translation (p. 530) A transformation that slides each point of a figure the same distance in a given direction.

trapezoid (p. 484) A quadrilateral with exactly one pair of parallel sides.

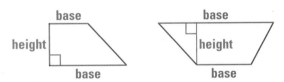

tree diagram (p. 260) A diagram that shows all the prime factors of a number or the possible outcomes of an event.

triangle (p. 32) A polygon with three sides.

Triangle Inequality (p. 446) The sum of the lengths of any two sides of a triangle is greater than the length of the third side of the triangle.

triangular prism (p. 577) A prism whose bases are triangles.

trigonometric ratio (p. 546) A ratio of the lengths of two sides of a right triangle; for example: sine, cosine, and tangent.

trinomial (p. 688) A polynomial that has only three terms.

two-step equation (p. 158) An equation whose solution involves two transformations.

value of an expression (p. 22) The number obtained after replacing each variable in the expression by a number and simplifying.

value of a variable (p. 22) A number that is represented by the variable.

variable (p. 22) A symbol, usually a letter, that is used to represent one or more numbers in an algebraic expression. For example, x is a variable in the expression $8x + 19$.

Venn Diagram (p. 485) A diagram that shows the relationships among sets of numbers or objects.

verbal model (p. 23) A phrase or sentence used to represent a real-life situation.

vertex (pp. 32, 464) The point at the corner of an angle, plane figure, or solid figure.

vertical angles (p. 470) Intersecting lines form two pairs of vertical angles. $\angle 1$ and $\angle 3$ are vertical angles. $\angle 2$ and $\angle 4$ are vertical angles.

vertices (p. 572) The plural of vertex.

volume (p. 580) The measure of the amount of space that an object occupies, or how much it will hold.

whole numbers (p. 38) Any of the numbers in the sequence 0, 1, 2, 3, 4, ...

x-coordinate (p. 142) The first number of an ordered pair; the position of the point relative to the horizontal axis.

x-intercept (p. 628) The x-coordinate of the point where a graph crosses the x-axis; the value of x when $y = 0$.

y-coordinate (p. 142) The second number of an ordered pair; the position of the point relative to the vertical axis.

y-intercept (p. 628) The y-coordinate of the point where a graph crosses the y-axis; the value of y when $x = 0$.

absolute value/valor absoluto (p. 105) Distancia entre un número y el 0 en una línea numérica. Por ejemplo: $|3| = 3$, $|-3| = 3$, $|0| = 0$.

absolute value signs/signos de valor absoluto (p. 105) Par de líneas verticales que se usan para indicar el valor absoluto del número o expresión que se coloca dentro de las mismas, $|\ |$.

acute angle/ángulo agudo (p. 465) Angulo que mide entre 0° y 90°.

acute triangle/triángulo agudo (p. 479) Triángulo con tres ángulos agudos.

add matrices/sumar matrices (p. 683) Hallar la suma de dos matrices sumando los elementos correspondientes.

add polynomials/sumar polinomios (p. 694) Hallar la suma de dos polinomios combinando sus términos semejantes.

Addition Property of Equality/Propiedad aditiva de la igualdad (p. 66) Si se suma el mismo número en cada lado de una ecuación se obtiene una ecuación equivalente. Si $a = b$, entonces $a + c = b + c$.

adjacent side/lado adyacente *Ver* **cosine/coseno, sine/seno, y tangent/tangente.**

algebraic expression/expresión algebraica (p. 22) Conjunto de números, variables, operaciones y símbolos de agrupamiento. Por ejemplo: $2(x + 3)$.

algebraic model/modelo algebraico (p. 23) Expresión o ecuación algebraica utilizada para representar una situación de la vida real.

angle/ángulo (p. 464) Figura formada por dos rayos que comienzan en el mismo punto. Los rayos son los *lados* del ángulo y el punto es el *vértice* del ángulo.

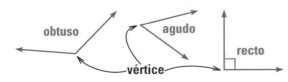

area/área (p. 7) Medida de la superficie cubierta por una figura. El área se mide en unidades cuadradas.

Associative Property of Addition/Propiedad asociativa de la adición (p. 67) Cambiar el agrupamiento de los sumandos no cambia el resultado de la suma. Por ejemplo, $(a + b) + c = a + (b + c)$.

Associative Property of Multiplication/ Propiedad asociativa de la multiplicación (p. 67) Cambiar el agrupamiento de los factores no cambia el producto. Por ejemplo, $(ab)c = a(bc)$.

average/promedio (pp. 133, 668) Suma de los números de un conjunto dividida entre la cantidad de números del conjunto. También se conoce como la *media*.

axes/ejes (p. 142) Dos líneas de números reales que se intersectan en un ángulo recto para formar un plano de coordenadas. La línea horizontal es el eje de las x y la línea vertical es el eje de las y.

bar graph/gráfico de barras (p. 208) Gráfico que organiza un conjunto de datos usando barras horizontales o verticales para mostrar cuántas veces cada hecho o número aparece en el conjunto.

base of a parallelogram/base de un paralelogramo (p. 512) Cualquier lado de un paralelogramo elegido de forma tal que sea perpendicular a la altura del paralelogramo.

base of a percent/base de un porcentaje (p. 376) Número del que se debe hallar una porción. Por ejemplo, en la ecuación porcentual $\dfrac{a}{b} = \dfrac{p}{100}$, la base es b.

base of a power/base de una potencia (p. 10) Número o expresión que se usa como factor en una multiplicación repetida. Por ejemplo, en la expresión 4^6, 4 es la base.

bases of a trapezoid/bases de un trapezoide
(p. 512) Los dos lados paralelos de un
trapezoide.

binomial/binomio (p. 688) Polinomio que tiene
dos términos.

box-and-whisker plot/gráfico de caja y costados
(p. 676) Gráfico que utiliza una caja para
representar el medio de un conjunto de datos y
segmentos dibujados hacia ambos extremos.

center of a circle/centro de un círculo (p. 566)
Punto interior a un círculo que está a la misma
distancia de todos los puntos del círculo.

circle/círculo (p. 566) Conjunto de todos los
puntos de un plano que están a la misma
distancia de un punto dado llamado centro.

circle graph/gráfica circular (p. 317) Gráfico
que representa ciertas partes de un conjunto de
datos como partes de una región circular. Con
frecuencia las porciones se denotan como
fracciones o porcentajes.

circumference/circunferencia (p. 566) Distancia
en torno a un círculo.

coefficient/coeficiente (p. 115) Factor numérico
de un término algebraico. Por ejemplo, en la
expresión $3x^2$ el coeficiente de x^2 es 3.

collect like terms/agrupar términos semejantes
(p. 56) Procedimiento para mover los términos
semejantes de las expresiones algebraicas y
ponerlos uno al lado del otro.

common factor/factor común (p. 266) Número
que es factor de dos o más números. Por
ejemplo, 2 es factor común de 4 y de 6 porque
2 es factor de 4 y también lo es de 6.

common multiple/común múltiplo (p. 270)
Número que es múltiplo de dos o más números
naturales. Por ejemplo, 60 es común múltiplo de
5 y de 6 porque 60 es múltiplo de 5 y también lo
es de 6.

**Commutative Property of Addition/Propiedad
conmutativa de la adición** (p. 67) Cambiar el
orden de los sumandos no cambia el resultado
de la suma. Por ejemplo, $a + b = b + a$.

**Commutative Property of Multiplication/
Propiedad conmutativa de la multiplicación**
(p. 67) Cambiar el orden de los factores no
cambia el resultado del producto. Por ejemplo,
$ab = ba$.

complementary angles/ángulos complementarios
(p. 465) Dos ángulos cuyas medidas suman 90°.

composite number/número compuesto (p. 260)
Número natural que tiene tres o más factores.

concave polygon/polígono cóncavo. *Ver*
nonconvex polygon/polígono no convexo.

conditional equations/ecuaciones condicionales
(p. 60) Ecuaciones que no se cumplen para
todos los valores de las variables que contienen.

cone/cono (p. 573) Sólido que tiene una base
circular, un vértice y una superficie lateral.

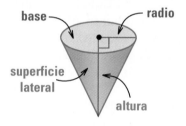

congruent angles/ángulos congruentes (p. 464)
Angulos que tienen la misma medida.

congruent polygons/polígonos congruentes
(p. 488) Dos polígonos que tienen exactamente
el mismo tamaño y la misma forma.

convex polygon/polígono convexo (p. 484)
Un polígono es convexo si un segmento que
une dos puntos interiores cualesquiera queda
completamente dentro del polígono. *Ver
también* **polygon/polígono.**

coordinate plane/plano de coordenadas (p. 142)
Plano formado por dos líneas de números reales
llamadas ejes que se intersectan en ángulo recto;
plano usado para ubicar un punto cuyas
coordenadas son conocidas.

coordinates/coordenadas (p. 142) Par ordenado de números que ubica un punto en un gráfico de coordenadas.

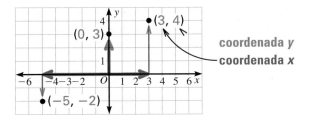

corresponding angles/ángulos correspondientes (p. 470) Angulos que están en la misma posición relativa cuando una línea cruza las otras dos líneas. Los ángulos 1 y 2 son ángulos correspondientes. Los ángulos 3 y 4 son también ángulos correspondientes. *Ver también* **similar figures/figuras semejantas.**

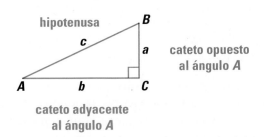

corresponding sides/lados correspondientes (p. 369) Par de lados de dos figuras semejantes que están en la misma posición relativa. *Ver también* **similar figures/figuras semejantes.**

cosine of an angle/coseno de un ángulo (p. 546) El coseno del ángulo agudo de un triángulo recto es el coeficiente entre la longitud del cateto adyacente al ángulo agudo y la longitud de la hipotenusa. Por ejemplo,

$$\text{coseno de } A = \frac{b}{c}.$$

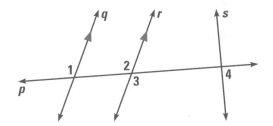

Counting Principle/Principio de conteo (p. 392) Si un acontecimiento puede ocurrir en *m* formas y otro acontecimiento puede ocurrir en *n* formas, ambos acontecimientos pueden ocurrir en *mn* formas.

Cross Product Property/Propiedad de los productos cruzados (p. 368) Los productos cruzados de una proporción son iguales.

$$\text{Si } \frac{a}{b} = \frac{c}{d}, \, ad = bc.$$

cube/cubo (p. 13) Prisma rectangular cuyas seis caras son cuadrados congruentes.

cubic units/unidades cúbicas (p. 580) Medidas estándar de volumen.

cylinder/cilindro (p. 573) Figura sólida con bases circulares congruentes que yace sobre planos paralelos.

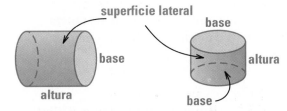

data/datos (p. 26) Hechos o números que describen algo.

decagon/decágono (p. 32) Polígono de diez lados.

degree of a polynomial/grado de un polinomio (p. 694) Mayor exponente del polinomio.

denominator/denominador (p. 6) Número o expresión situado debajo de la línea de una fracción en una fracción. 4 es el denominador de $\frac{x}{4}$.

diagonal/diagonal (p. 33) Segmento que conecta dos vértices de un polígono pero no es uno de sus lados.

diameter/diámetro (p. 566) Distancia a través de un círculo que pasa por su centro. La longitud del diámetro es el doble de la longitud del radio.

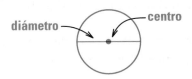

difference/diferencia (pp. 6, 120) Resultado obtenido cuando se restan números o expresiones. La diferencia entre a y b es $a - b$.

dimensions/dimensiones (p. 15) Medida de la magnitud o tamaño de un objeto. Por ejemplo, las dimensiones de un rectángulo son su longitud y su ancho.

discount/descuento (p. 383) Diferencia entre el precio habitual y el precio de venta de un artículo.

discount percent/porcentaje de descuento (p. 383) Porcentaje que se descuenta del precio de venta en una liquidación. Se trata del coeficiente entre el descuento y el precio habitual del artículo.

Distance Formula/Fórmula de distancia (p. 656) La distancia d entre los puntos (x_1, y_1) y (x_2, y_2) es
$$d = \sqrt{(x_2 - x_1)^2 + (y_2 - y_1)^2}.$$

Distributive Property/Propiedad distributiva (p. 52) El producto de un número por la suma de dos números es igual a la suma de los dos productos. Por ejemplo, $a(b + c) = ab + ac$ y $ab + ac = a(b + c)$.

divisible/divisible (p. 254) Un número natural es divisible por otro número natural si su cociente es exacto, es decir si el resto de la división es 0. Por ejemplo, 84 es divisible entre 2, porque $84 \div 2$ no deja ningún resto.

Division Property of Equality/Propiedad divisoria de la igualdad (p. 72) Si se dividen ambos lados de una ecuación entre el mismo número diferente de cero se obtiene una ecuación equivalente.

Si $a = b$, $\dfrac{a}{c} = \dfrac{b}{c}$.

edge/arista (p. 572) Segmento formado por la unión de dos caras de una figura sólida. *Ver también* **polyhedron/poliedro.**

endpoint/extremo (p. 460) Punto al extremo de un segmento de línea o rayo.

entries of a matrix/elementos de una matriz (p. 682) Números de una matriz que están dispuestos en filas y columnas.

equal matrices/matrices iguales (p. 682) Dos matrices son iguales si todos los elementos de las posiciones correspondientes son iguales.

equation/ecuación (p. 60) Aseveración de que dos expresiones son equivalentes. Por ejemplo, $3 \times 9 = 27$ y $8 + x = 10$ son ecuaciones.

equiangular triangle/triángulo equiangular (p. 479) Triángulo en el que los tres ángulos tienen la misma medida.

equilateral triangle/triángulo equilátero (pp. 179, 478) Triángulo que tiene tres lados de la misma longitud.

equivalent equations/ecuaciones equivalentes (p. 60) Ecuaciones que tienen las mismas soluciones.

equivalent expressions/expresiones equivalentes (p. 52) Expresiones que tienen los mismos valores cuando se sustituyen las variables por números.

equivalent fractions/fracciones equivalentes (p. 274) Fracciones que tienen la misma forma decimal; $\dfrac{1}{2}$, $\dfrac{2}{4}$ y $\dfrac{3}{6}$ son fracciones equivalentes porque todas son iguales a 0,5.

evaluate an algebraic expression/evaluar una expresión algebraica (p. 22) Hallar el valor de una expresión algebraica sustituyendo cada variable de la expresión por un número.

even number/número par (p. 9) Número entero que es divisible entre 2.

exponent/exponente (p. 10) Número o variable que representa el número de veces que se usa la base como factor. Por ejemplo, en la expresión 2^3, el exponente es 3.

exterior angles/ángulos exteriores (p. 494) Los ángulos exteriores se forman cuando se amplía los lados de un polígono.

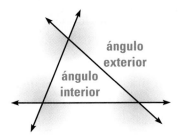

face/cara (p. 572) Superficie plana de una figura sólida; uno de los polígonos que compone un poliedro. *Ver también* **polyhedron/poliedro.**

factored/factorizado (p. 255) Un número natural está factorizado cuando está escrito como producto de dos o más números naturales.

factors/factores (pp. 6, 255) Números o expresiones variables que se multiplican. Por ejemplo, 4 y x son los factores de $4x$.

Fibonacci Sequence/secuencia de Fibonacci (p. 41) Secuencia interminable, como por ejemplo 1, 1, 2, 3, 4, 8, 13, 21, . . . , donde los dos primeros términos son fijos y los demás son la suma de los dos términos precedentes.

first quartile/primer cuartil (p. 676) Mediana de la mitad inferior de un conjunto de números ordenados.

FOIL method/método FOIL (p. 704) Método utilizado para multiplicar dos binomios en un sólo paso y que consiste en hallar la suma de los productos de los primeros términos (**First**), los términos exteriores (**Outer**), los términos interiores (**Inner**) y los últimos términos (**Last**). Por ejemplo, para hallar $(2x + 3)(x + 5)$, hallar:

Outer: $(2x)(5)$ **I**nner: $(3)(x)$

$$2x^2 + 10x + 3x + 15$$

First: $(2x)(x)$ **L**ast: $(3)(5)$

formula/fórmula *Ver* **algebraic model/modelo algebraico.**

frequency distribution/distribución de frecuencias (p. 209) Forma de organizar datos exhibiendo el número de artículos o acontecimientos que ocurren en un intervalo.

general problem solving plan/plan general para resolver problemas (p. 88) Serie de pasos que puede utilizarse para resolver un problema de la vida real:

1. Escribir un modelo verbal.

2. Asignar valores a las etiquetas.

3. Escribir un modelo algebraico.

4. Resolver.

5. Responder.

6. Verificar.

geometry/geometría (p. 32) Estudio de las formas y sus medidas.

graph of a linear inequality/gráfica de una desigualdad lineal (p. 653) Semiplano que consiste en todos los puntos de un lado de la línea que representa el gráfico de la ecuación lineal correspondiente. Por ejemplo, éste es el gráfico de la desigualdad $y > 2x - 4$.

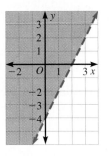

greatest common factor, GCF/mayor factor común (p. 266) Mayor factor común de dos números o expresiones algebraicas. Por ejemplo, $4a$ es el mayor factor común de $20ab^2$ y $24a^2$.

grouping symbols/símbolos de agrupamiento (p. 17) Caracteres que se usan para cambiar el orden de las operaciones de una expresión o para hacer que la expresión sea más clara. Ejemplo de símbolos de agrupamiento son los paréntesis curvos ( ) o rectos [ ].

half plane/semiplano (p. 652) En un plano, región situada a un lado de una línea.

height/altura (p. 512) Distancia perpendicular entre las bases paralelas de un paralelogramo, trapezoide, prisma o cilindro, o la distancia de un vértice a un lado opuesto de un triángulo, pirámide o cono.

hemisphere/hemisferio (p. 596) Una de las dos mitades de una esfera.

heptagon/heptágono (p. 32) Polígono de siete lados.

hexagon/hexágono (p. 32) Polígono de seis lados.

histogram/histograma (p. 209) Gráfica de barras en la que las barras representan intervalos de números igualmente espaciados.

hypotenuse/hipotenusa (p. 420) Lado de un triángulo recto que está opuesto al ángulo recto. Es el lado más largo de un triángulo recto. *Ver también* **right triangle/triángulo recto.**

identities/identidades (p. 60) Ecuaciones que se cumplen para todos los valores de la variable. Por ejemplo, las identidades $a + 0 = a$ y $a \cdot 1 = a$ se cumplen para todos los números.

image/imagen (p. 522) Nueva figura formada por la transformación de una figura dada.

inequalities/desigualdades (p. 92) Aseveraciones matemáticas que contienen un símbolo de desigualdad.

inequality symbol/símbolo de desigualdad (p. 92) Uno de los símbolos siguientes $<, >, \leq, \geq,$ o $\neq$.

integers/enteros (p. 104) Conjunto de números $\ldots, -3, -2, -1, 0, 1, 2, 3, \ldots$

interior angle/ángulo interior (p. 494) Angulo de un polígono formado por dos lados adyacentes.

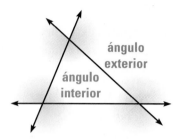

intersection of lines/intersección de líneas (p. 461) Conjunto de puntos que son comunes a dos o más líneas.

inverse operations/operaciones inversas (p. 138) Operaciones que se cancelan mutuamente. Por ejemplo, la adición y la sustracción son operaciones inversas, como también la multiplicación y la división.

irrational number/número irracional (p. 280) Número real que no puede ser expresado como cociente de dos enteros. Por ejemplo, las raíces cuadradas de los números que no son cuadrados perfectos, como 2, π y los decimales interminables que no se repiten como $0.1001000100001\ldots$ son todos números irracionales.

isosceles trapezoid/trapezoide isósceles (p. 484) Trapezoide cuyos lados no paralelos tienen la misma longitud.

isosceles triangle/triángulo isósceles (pp. 421, 478) Triángulo que tiene al menos dos lados de la misma longitud.

kite/cometa (p. 484) Cuadrilátero que tiene dos pares de lados consecutivos de la misma longitud.

least common denominator, LCD/mínimo común denominador (p. 316) El mínimo común denominador de dos o más fracciones es el mínimo común múltiplo de sus denominadores.

least common multiple, LCM/mínimo común múltiplo (p. 270) El mínimo común múltiplo de dos números o expresiones algebraicas es el más pequeño de sus múltiplos comunes. $6a^2b$ es el mínimo común múltiplo de $2ab$ y $3a^2$.

Left-to-Right Rule/regla de izquierda a derecha (p. 16) Las operaciones que tienen la misma prioridad en una expresión se evalúan de izquierda a derecha.

leg of a right triangle/cateto de un triángulo recto (p. 420) Cualquiera de los lados de un triángulo recto que forman el ángulo recto. *Ver también* **right angle/ángulo recto.**

like fractions/fracciones semejantes (p. 316) Fracciones que tienen el mismo denominador.

like terms/términos semejantes (p. 56) Dos o más términos de una expresión que tienen las mismas variables elevadas a las mismas potencias.

line/línea (p. 460) Secuencia recta de puntos que se extiende para siempre en direcciones opuestas.

line graph/gráfica de líneas (p. 214) Gráfica que muestra tendencias en función de intervalos de tiempo.

line plot/gráfica de líneas (p. 230) Diagrama que muestra la frecuencia de datos en una línea numérica.

line segment/segmento de línea (p. 460) Parte de una línea que consta de dos extremos y de todos los puntos situados entre ellos.

line symmetry/simetría lineal (p. 474) Propiedad de una figura que al dividirse en dos partes mediante una línea, cada una de las partes es la imagen especular de la otra.

linear equation/ecuación lineal (p. 618) Ecuación en dos variables cuya gráfica es una línea recta.

linear inequality/desigualdad lineal (p. 652) Desigualdad en dos variables para las cuales la gráfica es un semiplano arriba o abajo de la ecuación lineal correspondiente.

linear relationship/relación lineal (p. 648) Dos cantidades que pueden modelarse con una ecuación lineal.

matrix/matriz (p. 682) Arreglo rectangular de números o datos en filas y columnas.

mean/media (pp. 133, 668) Promedio de todos los números de un conjunto. Es la suma de los números dividida entre la cantidad de números. También se conoce como el *average/promedio.*

measure of an angle, $m\angle$/medida de un ángulo, $m\angle$ (p. 464) Tamaño de un ángulo. Puede estimarse usando un transportador. La unidad común para medir ángulos es el grado.

measures of central tendency/medidas de la tendencia central (p. 668) Números que pueden usarse para representar un grupo de números. Media, mediana y modo de una distribución.

median/mediana (p. 668) Número central (o promedio de los dos números centrales) de un grupo de números enumerados en orden.

midpoint/punto medio (p. 657) Punto situado en la mitad de un segmento de línea.

mode/modo (p. 668) Número que ocurre con mayor frecuencia en un conjunto dado de números.

model/modelo (p. 7) Algo que ayuda a visualizar o comprender un proceso u objeto real.

monomial/monomio (p. 688) Polinomio con un solo término; variable, número o producto de variables y números.

multiple/múltiplo (p. 270) Producto de un número dado y cualquier número entero mayor que cero. Por ejemplo, 8 es múltiplo de 1, 2, 4 y 8.

Multiplication Property of Equality/Propiedad multiplicativa de la igualdad (p. 72) Si se multiplican ambos lados de una ecuación por el mismo número se obtiene una ecuación equivalente. Si $a = b$, $ac = bc$.

***n*-gon/*n*-gono** (p. 32) Polígono de n lados.

natural numbers/números naturales (p. 38) Conjunto de números 1, 2, 3, 4, ...

negative correlation/correlación negativa
(p. 236) Puntos de datos de un gráfico de
dispersión cuyas coordenadas en el eje de las *y*
tienden a decrecer a medida que aumentan las
coordenadas en el eje de las *x*.

negative integer/entero negativo (p. 104)
Entero inferior a 0.

negative slope/inclinación negativa (p. 635)
Una línea del plano de coordenadas tiene
inclinación negativa si se inclina hacia abajo
de izquierda a derecha.

net/red (p. 572) Molde plano que puede plegarse
para formar un sólido. Por ejemplo, las redes
pueden plegarse de forma que se obtenga
un cubo.

no correlation/sin correlación (p. 236) Puntos
de datos de un gráfico de dispersión para los que
no existe un patrón entre las coordenadas *x* e *y*.

nonagon/nonágono (p. 32) Polígono de nueve
lados.

nonconvex polygon/polígono no convexo (p. 484)
Un polígono que no es convexo porque uno o más
segmentos que unen dos puntos interiores
cualesquiera no se sitúan completamente dentro
del polígono. *Ver* **polygon/polígono**.

nonrepeating decimal/decimal no periódico
(pp. 38, 281) Decimal que no termina ni se
repite.

numerator/numerador (p. 6) Número o
expresión situado encima de la línea de una
fracción. *x* es el numerador de $\frac{x}{4}$.

numerical expression/expresión numérica
(p. 16) Conjunto de números, operaciones y
símbolos de agrupamiento.

obtuse angle/ángulo obtuso (p. 465) Angulo que
mide entre 90° y 180°.

obtuse triangle/triángulo obtuso (p. 479)
Triángulo que tiene un ángulo obtuso.

octagon/octágono (p. 32) Polígono de ocho lados.

odd number/número impar (p. 9) Número
entero que no es divisible entre 2. Los números
1, 3, 5, 7, . . . son impares.

opposite side/lado opuesto *Ver* **cosine/coseno,
sine/seno, y tangent/tangente.**

opposites/opuestos (p. 105) Dos números que
tienen el mismo valor absoluto pero con signos
opuestos; dos números cualesquiera cuya suma
es 0.

Order of Operations/Orden de las operaciones
(p. 16) Procedimiento para evaluar las
expresiones que tienen más de una operación.

1. Primero realizar las operaciones dentro de
   los símbolos de agrupamiento.

2. Evaluar las potencias.

3. Multiplicar y dividir de izquierda a derecha.

4. Finalmente, sumar y restar de izquierda a
   derecha.

ordered pair/par ordenado (p. 142) Par de
números o coordenadas usados para ubicar un
punto en un plano de coordenadas. Solución de
una ecuación o de una desigualdad con dos
variables.

origin/origen (p. 142) Punto de intersección en
el plano de coordenadas entre el eje horizontal y
el eje vertical. El punto (0, 0).

outcome/resultado (p. 242) Posible resultado de
un acontecimiento. Por ejemplo, sacar "cara" es
un resultado de tirar al aire una moneda para ver
de qué lado cae.

parallel lines/líneas paralelas (p. 461) Líneas
del mismo plano que no se intersectan.

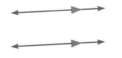

**parallelogram/
paralelogramo** (p. 484)
Cuadrilátero cuyos lados
opuestos son paralelos.

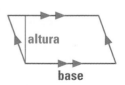

pentagon/pentágono (p. 32) Polígono de cinco
lados.

percent/porcentaje (p. 340) Una forma de expresar los centésimos; esto es, una fracción cuyo denominador es 100. *Porcentaje* significa "por cada cien".

5% (5 por ciento) es igual a $\frac{5}{100}$.

percent equation/ecuación porcentual (p. 376) El enunciado "*a* es un *p* por ciento de *b*" es equivalente a la ecuación $\frac{a}{b} = \frac{p}{100}$.

percent of increase or decrease/porcentaje de aumento o reducción (p. 386) Indicación de la magnitud del aumento o reducción de una cantidad.

perfect square/cuadrado perfecto (p. 11) Número cuya raíz cuadrada puede escribirse como un decimal exacto.

perimeter of a polygon/perímetro de un polígono (p. 192) Distancia en torno a una figura; suma de las longitudes de los lados.

perpendicular lines/ líneas perpendiculares (p. 465) Dos líneas que se cruzan en ángulo recto.

pi/pi (p. 566) Número que representa la relación entre la circunferencia de un círculo y su diámetro. Se denota con la letra griega π y es aproximadamente igual a 3.1416.

pictograph/pictografía (p. 204) Gráfica que organiza un conjunto de datos usando imágenes en hileras horizontales o verticales para indicar cuántas veces ocurre cada suceso o número en el conjunto.

plane/plano (p. 460) Superficie plana que se extiende para siempre en todas las direcciones.

plotting a point/representar un punto (pp. 104, 142) Ubicar un punto que corresponde a un número en una línea numérica o un punto que corresponde a un par ordenado en el plano de coordenadas.

point/punto (p. 460) Símbolo que representa un lugar en un plano o en un espacio.

polygon/polígono (p. 32) Figura cerrada cuyos lados son segmentos de recta.

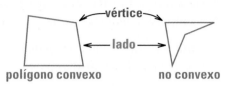

polyhedron/poliedro (p. 572) Sólido que está limitado por polígonos que se llaman caras.

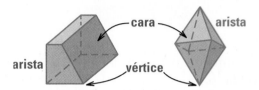

polynomial/polinomio (p. 688) Expresión que tiene uno o más términos de forma ax^n donde *a* es cualquier número real y *n* es un número entero.

portion/porción (p. 336) Fracción que compara la medida de parte de una cantidad con la medida de la cantidad total.

positive correlation/correlación positiva (p. 236) Puntos de datos en un gráfico de dispersión cuyas coordenadas en el eje de las *y* tienden a aumentar al aumentar las coordenadas en el eje de las *x*.

positive integer/entero positivo (p. 104) Los números 1, 2, 3, 4, . . . son enteros positivos.

positive slope/inclinación positiva (p. 635) Una línea del plano de coordenadas tiene inclinación positiva si se inclina hacia arriba de izquierda a derecha.

possible outcomes/resultados posibles (p. 242) Todas las formas diferentes en que puede resultar un suceso.

power/potencia (p. 10) Expresión tal como 4^2, que tiene una base y un exponente.

prime factorization/descomposición factorial (p. 260) Expresión de un número compuesto como producto de sus factores primos. La descomposición factorial de 18 es 2 · 3 · 3.

prime number/número primo (p. 260) Número natural que tiene exactamente dos factores, el mismo número y 1. Los números 2, 3, 5, 7, 11, 13, son ejemplos de números primos.

prism/prisma (p. 572) Poliedro con dos caras congruentes y paralelas llamadas bases.

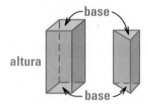

probability of an event/probabilidad de un evento (p. 242) Medición de la probabilidad de que el evento ocurra.

product/producto (p. 6) Resultado obtenido cuando se multiplican números o expresiones. El producto de a y b es $a \cdot b$ o ab.

proportion/proporción (p. 368) Ecuación que muestra que dos razones son iguales. Si a es a b como c es a d, entonces:

$$\frac{a}{b} = \frac{c}{d}.$$

protractor/transportador (p. 464) Instrumento de medición que puede usarse para aproximar la medición de un ángulo.

pyramid/pirámide (p. 572) Figura espacial cuya base es un polígono y cuyas demás caras son triángulos que comparten un vértice común.

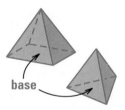

Pythagorean Theorem/teorema de Pitágoras (p. 420) En cualquier triángulo recto, la suma de los cuadrados de las longitudes de los catetos a y b es igual al cuadrado de la longitud de la hipotenusa c de modo que:

$$a^2 + b^2 = c^2$$

Pythagorean triple/terna pitagórica (p. 421) Conjunto de tres números naturales que representan los lados de un triángulo recto.

quadrants/cuadrante (p. 142) En el plano de coordenadas, las cuatro partes en que los ejes dividen el plano.

quadrilateral/cuadrilátero (p. 32) Polígono de cuatro lados.

quotient/cociente (p. 6) Resultado obtenido al dividir números o expresiones. El cociente de a y b es $\frac{a}{b}$.

radical/radical (p. 11) Símbolo de la raíz cuadrada, $\sqrt{}$.

radius of a circle/radio de un círculo (p. 566) Segmento cuyos extremos son el centro del círculo y un punto situado en el círculo.

rate/tasa (p. 362) Relación $\frac{a}{b}$ de dos cantidades a y b que se miden en unidades diferentes.

ratio/índice (p. 363) Relación $\frac{a}{b}$ de dos cantidades a y b que se miden en las mismas unidades.

rational number/número racional (p. 280) Número que puede escribirse como cociente de dos enteros.

ray/rayo (p. 460) Parte de una línea que comienza en un extremo y continúa para siempre en una única dirección.

real numbers/números reales (p. 414) Conjunto de todos los números racionales e irracionales.

reciprocal/recíproco (p. 168) El número recíproco de un número a diferente de cero es $\frac{1}{a}$. El producto de dos números recíprocos es 1.

rectangle/rectángulo (p. 484) Paralelogramo que tiene cuatro ángulos rectos.

rectangular prism/prisma rectangular (p. 580) Prisma cuyas bases son rectángulos.

reflection/reflexión (p. 522) Transformación que voltea una figura sobre una línea y que es su imagen especular en el lado opuesto de dicha línea.

reflection line/línea de reflexión (p. 522) En una reflexión, línea que es perpendicular y bisectriz de cada segmento que une un punto original con su imagen.

regular polygon/polígono regular (p. 489) Polígono en el que todos los lados tienen la misma longitud y todos los ángulos tienen la misma medida.

repeating decimal/decimal periódico (pp. 38, 281) Decimal en el que un dígito o grupo de dígitos se repiten para siempre. Los dígitos periódicos se indican con una barra.

$$0.3333 \ldots = 0.\overline{3}$$

$$1.47474747 \ldots = 1.\overline{47}$$

rhombus/rombo (p. 484) Paralelogramo con cuatro lados de la misma longitud.

right angle/ángulo recto (pp. 420, 465) Angulo que mide 90°.

right triangle/triángulo recto (pp. 420, 479) Triángulo con un ángulo recto.

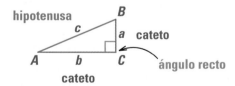

rotation/rotación (p. 526) Transformación que hace girar una figura en torno a punto con un cierto ángulo y en una cierta dirección.

rotational symmetry/simetría rotacional (p. 475) Una figura tiene simetría rotacional si coincide con sí misma luego de rotar 180 grados o menos en torno a un punto.

round a number/redondear un número (p. 11) Sustituir un número por otro de aproximadamente el mismo valor y que sea más fácil de usar.

scale factor/factor de escala (p. 536) En dos polígonos semejantes o dos sólidos semejantes el factor de escala es la razón entre las medidas lineales correspondientes.

scalene quadrilateral/cuadrilátero escaleno (p. 484) Cuadrilátero cuyos cuatro lados tienen longitudes diferentes.

scalene triangle/triángulo escaleno (p. 478) Triángulo cuyos tres lados tienen longitudes diferentes.

scatter plot/diagrama de dispersión (p. 236) Gráfica de un conjunto de pares ordenados de números (x, y).

scientific notation/notación científica (p. 288) Forma abreviada de escribir números cuyos valores absolutos son muy grandes o muy pequeños. Un número se escribe en notación científica si es de la forma $c \times 10^n$ donde c es mayor o igual que 1 y menor que 10 y donde n es un número entero.

second quartile/segundo cuartil (p. 676) Mediana de un conjunto de números ordenados.

segment/segmento *Ver* **line segment/segmento de línea**.

sequence/secuencia (p. 3) Listado ordenado de números.

side of a polygon/lado de un polígono (p. 32) Cada uno de los segmentos de recta que conforman el polígono.

similar figures/figuras semejantes (p. 536) Figuras que tienen la misma forma pero no necesariamente el mismo tamaño.

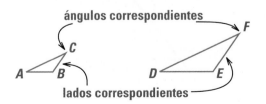

similar solids/sólidos semejantes (p. 602)
Sólidos que tienen la misma forma y cuyos lados correspondientes son proporcionales.

similar triangles/triángulos semejantes (p. 369)
Dos triángulos que tienen la misma medida de ángulo.

simplest form/forma más simple (p. 274) Una fracción está en su forma más simple si el numerador y el denominador no tienen factores en común.

simplify an expression/simplificar una expresión (p. 56) Reescribir una expresión algebraica de forma que no haya términos similares.

simplifying a fraction/simplificar una fracción (p. 274) Reescribir una fracción de forma tal que su numerador y su denominador no tengan factores en común.

simulation/simulación (p. 398) Experimento utilizado para modelar una situación de la vida real.

sine of an angle/seno de un ángulo (p. 546) El seno de un ángulo agudo en un triángulo recto es la razón entre la longitud del cateto opuesto al ángulo agudo y la longitud de la hipotenusa.

Por ejemplo, seno $A = \dfrac{a}{c}$.

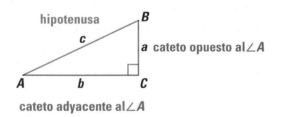

slope/inclinación (p. 634) Razón de la diferencia entre las coordenadas y la diferencia entre las coordenadas x de dos puntos cualesquiera del gráfico de una ecuación lineal. También se define como *elevación* del *recorrido*.

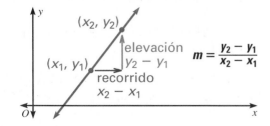

slope-intercept form of an equation/forma de inclinación e intersección de una ecuación (p. 642) Ecuación lineal en x e y de forma $y = mx + b$, donde m es la inclinación de la línea y b es la intersección del eje de las y.

solution/solución (pp. 60, 92, 143, 652) Número (o par ordenado de números) que genera una aseveración verdadera cuando se sustituyen las variables de una ecuación o de una desigualdad.

solving a right triangle/resolver un triángulo recto (p. 421) Hallar el tercer lado de un triángulo recto usando las longitudes de dos lados.

solving an equation/resolver una ecuación (p. 60) Hallar todos los valores de las variables que hacen que se cumpla la ecuación.

solving an inequality/resolver una desigualdad (p. 92) Hallar todos los valores de la variable que hacen que se cumpla la desigualdad.

square/cuadrado (p. 484) Rectángulo con cuatro lados de la misma longitud.

square root/raíz cuadrada (p. 11) Número que al ser elevado al cuadrado da como resultado el mismo número. 7 y -7 son raíces cuadradas de 49, porque $7^2 = 49$ y $(-7)^2 = 49$.

square root symbol/símbolo de raíz cuadrada
Ver **radical/radical.**

standard form of a polynomial/forma usual de un polinomio (p. 688) Polinomio escrito de tal forma que las potencias de la variable disminuyen de izquierda a derecha.

statistics/estadística (p. 230) Rama de la matemática que organiza grandes conjuntos de datos de forma que puedan usarse para comprender tendencias y hacer predicciones.

stem-and-leaf plot/gráfico de hojas y nervaduras (p. 672) Método de organizar datos en orden creciente o decreciente.

straight angle/ángulo llano (p. 465) Angulo que mide 180°

substitute/sustituir (p. 22) Reemplazar una variable de una expresión por un número.

subtract matrices/restar matrices (p. 683) Encontrar la diferencia de dos matrices hallando la diferencia de los elementos correspondientes.

Subtraction Property of Equality/Propiedad sustractiva de la igualdad (p. 66) Si se resta el mismo número de los dos lados de una ecuación se obtiene una ecuación equivalente. Si $a = b$, $a - c = b - c$.

sum/suma (p. 6) Resultado obtenido cuando se suman números o expresiones. La suma de a y b es $a + b$.

supplementary angles/ángulos suplementarios (p. 465) Dos ángulos cuyas medidas suman 180°.

surface area/área de la superficie (p. 576) Suma de las áreas de todas las caras de una figura sólida.

tangent of an angle/tangente de un ángulo (p. 546) La tangente del ángulo agudo de un triángulo recto es la razón entre la longitud del cateto opuesto al ángulo y la longitud del cateto adyacente al ángulo. Por ejemplo, tangente de $A = \dfrac{a}{b}$.

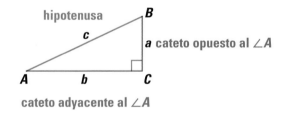

terminating decimal/decimal no periódico (pp. 38, 281) Decimal que contiene un número finito de dígitos, por ejemplo 0,5.

term/término (p. 22) Una parte de una expresión que está separada por signos de adición. En la expresión $3x + (-2)$, los términos son $3x$ y -2.

third quartile/tecer cuartil (p. 676) Mediana de la mitad superior de un cunjunto de números ordenados.

time line/línea temporal (p. 205) Gráfica que muestra las fechas de varios sucesos.

transformation/transformación (p. 526) Operación tal como una reflexión (inclinación), rotación (giro) o traslación (deslizamiento) que desplaza o mueve una figura desde una posición original (pre-imagen) a una nueva posición (imagen).

translation/traslación (p. 530) Transformación que desliza cada punto de una figura la misma distancia en una dirección dada.

trapezoid/trapezoide (p. 484) Cuadrilátero con exactamente un par de lados paralelos.

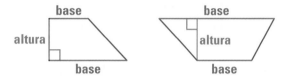

tree diagram/diagrama de árbol (p. 260) Diagrama que muestra todos los factores primos de un número o los resultados posibles de un suceso.

triangle/triángulo (p. 32) Polígono de tres lados.

Triangle Inequality/Desigualdad del triángulo (p. 446) La suma de las longitudes de dos lados cualesquiera de un triángulo es mayor que la longitud del tercer lado del triángulo.

triangular prism/prisma triangular (p. 577) Prisma cuyas bases son triángulos.

trigonometric ratio/razón trigonométrica (p. 546) Razón entre las longitudes de dos lados de un triángulo recto, por ejemplo: seno, coseno y tangente.

trinomial/trinomio (p. 688) Polinomio con solamente tres términos.

two-step equation/ecuación de dos pasos (p. 158) Ecuación cuya solución implica dos transformaciones.

value of an expression/valor de una expresión (p. 22) Número que se obtiene después de sustituir cada variable de la expresión por un número y simplificar.

value of a variable/valor de una variable (p. 22) Número que es representado por una variable.

variable/variable (p. 22) Símbolo, más generalmente letra, que se usa para representar uno o más números de una expresión algebraica. Por ejemplo, x es una variable en la expresión $8x + 19$.

Venn Diagram/diagrama de Venn (p. 485) Diagrama que muestra relaciones entre conjuntos de números u objetos.

verbal model/modelo verbal (p. 23) Frase o sentencia usada para representar una situación de la vida real.

vertex/vértice (pp. 32, 464) Punto ubicado en la esquina de un ángulo, una figura plana o una figura sólida.

vertical angles/ángulos verticales (p. 470) Líneas que se intersectan forman dos pares de ángulos verticales. Los ángulos 1 y 3 son ángulos verticales. Los ángulos 2 y 4 son ángulos verticales.

vertices/vértices (p. 464) Plural de "vértice".

volume/volumen (p. 580) Medida de la cantidad de espacio que ocupa un objeto o del espacio que contiene.

whole numbers/números enteros (p. 38) Cualquiera de los números de la secuencia $0, 1, 2, 3, 4, \ldots$.

x-coordinate/coordenada de las x (p. 142) Primer número de un par ordenado; posición de un punto en relación con el eje horizontal.

x-intercept/intercepción de las x (p. 628) Coordenada x del punto cuando una gráfica cruza el eje de las x; valor de x cuando $y = 0$.

y-coordinate/coordenada de las y (p. 142) Segundo número de un par ordenado; posición de un punto en relación con el eje vertical.

y-intercept/intercepción de las y (p. 628) Coordenada y del punto cuando una gráfica cruza el eje de las y; valor de y cuando $x = 0$.

TECHNOLOGY

Keystrokes for page 213

The following steps show the keystrokes for the TI-80, TI-81, and Casio fx-7700G that would be used for creating a histogram for the data given below.

Interval	54–55.9	56–57.9	58–59.9	60–61.9	62–63.9	64–65.9	66–67.9	68–69.9
Total	1	2	4	5	7	6	3	2

TI-80

| WINDOW |

$XMIN = 52$ $YMIN = -1$
$XMAX = 72$ $YMAX = 10$
$XSCL = 2$ $YSCL = 1$

| STAT | | ENTER | (Edit)

$L1(1) = 54$ $L2(1) = 1$ $L1(5) = 62$ $L2(5) = 7$
$L1(2) = 56$ $L2(2) = 2$ $L1(6) = 64$ $L2(6) = 6$
$L1(3) = 58$ $L2(3) = 4$ $L1(7) = 66$ $L2(7) = 3$
$L1(4) = 60$ $L2(4) = 5$ $L1(8) = 68$ $L2(8) = 2$

| 2nd | STAT PLOT | ENTER | (Plot 1)

Choose the following:

On, Type: [histogram], XL:L1, F:L2

| GRAPH |

TI-81

| RANGE |

$XMIN = 52$ $YMIN = -1$
$XMAX = 72$ $YMAX = 10$
$XSCL = 2$ $YSCL = 1$

| 2nd | STAT, cursor to DATA, | ENTER |

$x1 = 54$ $y1 = 1$ $x5 = 62$ $y5 = 7$
$x2 = 56$ $y2 = 2$ $x6 = 64$ $y6 = 6$
$x3 = 58$ $y3 = 4$ $x7 = 66$ $y7 = 3$
$x4 = 60$ $y4 = 5$ $x8 = 68$ $y8 = 2$

| 2nd | STAT, cursor to DRAW, | ENTER |

(Hist) | ENTER |

Casio fx-7700G

| Range |

$Xmin = 52$ $Ymin = -1$
$max = 72$ $max = 10$
$scl = 2$ $scl = 1$

| MODE | | × | (SD)
| MODE | | SHIFT | 3 (DRAW)
| SHIFT | Defm 8 | EXE |

54 | F3 | 1 | F1 | 62 | F3 | 7 | F1 |
56 | F3 | 2 | F1 | 64 | F3 | 6 | F1 |
58 | F3 | 4 | F1 | 66 | F3 | 3 | F1 |
60 | F3 | 5 | F1 | 68 | F3 | 2 | F1 |

| Graph | | EXE |

Keystrokes for page 627

The following steps show the keystrokes for the TI-80, TI-81, and Casio fx-7700G that would be used to sketch the graph of the equation $y = 1.5x - 2$.

TI-80

[WINDOW]

XMIN = −10
XMAX = 10
XSCL = 1
YMIN = −10
YMAX = 10
YSCL = 1
[Y=] 1.5 [X.T] [−] 2
:$Y_1 = 1.5X - 2$
:$Y_2 =$
:$Y_3 =$
:$Y_4 =$
[GRAPH]

TI-81

[RANGE]

Xmin = −10
Xmax = 10
Xscl = 1
Ymin = −10
Ymax = 10
Yscl = 1
[Y=] 1.5 [XIT] [−] 2
:$Y_1 = 1.5X - 2$
:$Y_2 =$
:$Y_3 =$
:$Y_4 =$
[GRAPH]

Casio fx-7700G

[Range]

Xmin = −10
  max = 10
  scl = 1
Ymin = −10
  max = 10
  scl = 1
[EXE] [Range]

 (Cls) [EXE]

 1.5 [X,θ,T] [−] 2

(Graph $y = 1.5x - 2$.)
[EXE]

Keystrokes for page 681

The following steps show the keystrokes for the TI-80 that would be used to sketch the box-and-whisker plot for the data on page 681.

TI-80

[WINDOW]

XMIN = 15   YMIN = 700

XMAX = 70   YMAX = 1000

XSCL = 1   YSCL = 50

[STAT] [ENTER] (Edit)

L1(1) = 22 [ENTER]   L1(8) = 29 [ENTER]
L1(2) = 65 [ENTER]   L1(9) = 50 [ENTER]
L1(3) = 23 [ENTER]   L1(10) = 46 [ENTER]
L1(4) = 19 [ENTER]   L1(11) = 28 [ENTER]
L1(5) = 42 [ENTER]   L1(12) = 36 [ENTER]
L1(6) = 62 [ENTER]   L1(13) = 25 [ENTER]
L1(7) = 38 [ENTER]   L1(14) = 40 [ENTER]

[2nd] STAT PLOT [ENTER] (Plot 1)

Choose the following:

On, Type: [box-and-whisker], XL:L1, F:1

[GRAPH]

To find the minimum, maximum, first quartile, median, and third quartile:

[TRACE] and [▶] or [◀]

A

Absolute value sign, 105

Absolute values, 104–107, 147

Acting it out, *See* Problem Solving Strategies.

Acute angle, 465

Acute triangle, 479

Addition, 6

  Associate Property of, 67

  on calculator, 114

  Commutative Property of, 67

  of decimals, 320–323, 356

  of fractions and mixed numbers, 310–319, 355

  of integers, 6, 110–117, 147, 148

  inverse of subtraction, 138–139

  of like terms, 56–59, 97, 115

  of matrices, 683–686

  patterns, 3–5, 41, 294, 297

  of polynomials, 692–697, 711

Addition equations

  modeling, 64–66, 108–109, 692–693

  solving, 64–69, 98, 149

Addition and Subtraction Properties of Equality, 66

Algebra

  connections, 22–25, 60–63, 138–141, 142–145, 158–161, 310–313, 442–445, 464–467, 494–497, 552–555, 580–584

  functions *See* Linear equations.

  inequalities, 92–95, 99, 432–433, 442–443, 446–447, 453, 652–655, 663

  inverse operations, 138–139

  and mental math, 60–63, 70, 113, 128, 134, 162, 286, 304, 332, 346

  properties, 52–55, 67, 68, 72, 115, 121, 172–175, 198, 368

  using formulas, 23, 33, 42, 44, 85, 127, 175, 192–193, 199, 215, 255, 348, 366, 411– 413, 420, 452, 492, 495, 512, 555, 557, 566, 567, 576, 580, 592, 596, 606, 619, 621, 634, 645,

656, 657, 663, 702

  writing equations, 23, 33, 35, 53, 61, 63, 67, 69, 73, 79, 82–87, 88–91, 99, 127, 133, 139, 159, 163, 169, 171, 173, 183–187, 189, 289, 372, 373, 376–379, 382, 411–412, 426–427, 439, 443, 513, 542, 577, 581, 593, 597, 619, 648, 657, 689, 705

  See also Addition, Algebraic expressions, Division, Equations, Formulas, Function, Integers, Multiplication, Polynomials, *and* Subtraction.

Algebra tiles, introduced, 50

  modeling addition, 64–65, 692–693

  modeling the Distributive Property, 52, 54

  modeling equations with variables on both sides, 177

  modeling expressions, 50–52, 54, 56

  modeling multiplication, 71, 703

  modeling two-step equations, 156–157

  writing and solving equations for, 65, 71

Algebraic expressions, defined, 22

  binomials, 688

  coefficients of 1 and –1, 115

  equivalent, 51, 52

  evaluating *See* Evaluating expressions.

  factoring, 261–263, 299

  finding greatest common factor, 267

  finding least common multiple, 271

  geometric to algebraic model, 57, 58

  like terms, 56, 115, 688

  modeling with algebra tiles, 50–52, 64–65, 71, 156–157, 177, 692–693, 703

  numerical, 16–19

  organizing using table of values, 57, 200, 618, 620, 623–625,

639, 645, 648

  parts of, 22, 115

  polynomials as, 688–691

  rewriting with the Distributive Property, 52–55, 97, 115, 121, 163, 172–175, 198, 694–697

  simplifying, 56–59, 97, 115, 121, 274–278, 284–287, 300, 301, 332, 612, 688–691, 694–701, 704–707, 710, 711

  terms, 56, 115

  unlike terms, 115

  value of, 22

  variable, 22–25, 267

  writing from verbal phrases, 23, 53, 59, 78–81, 86, 88–91, 98, 99, 181, 191

Algebraic factorization, 261–263, 299

Algebraic fractions, 274–278, 284–287, 300, 301

Algebraic model

  Distributive Property and, 52–55

  for proportions, 368

  for two-step, 156–157

  for variables on both sides, 177

  See also Algebra, writing equations.

Angles, defined, 464

  classifying, 464–467

  classifying triangles by, 479–481

  complementary, 164, 465

  congruent, 369, 464, 470–473

  corresponding, 369, 470–473, 516–520, 557

  drawing, 465–467

  exterior and interior, 494–497

  measures and side lengths of a triangle, 500–503, 507

  measuring, 464–467, 469, 492–493, 501, 505, 507, 508, 509

  naming, 464–467, 505

  of a polygon, 492–497, 499, 507, 508

  sides, 464

  straight, 465

  supplementary, 465

INDEX

trigonometric ratios for, 552–555

of a triangle, 164, 478–482, 500–503, 506, 507, 552–555

vertex, 464

vertical, 470

Applications

advertising, 235, 385, 601

air travel, 205, 206

altitude, 141

amusement parks, 408–409, 413, 423, 436, 437, 441, 535, 638

animal data, 544, 555, 584, 670, 679

architecture/construction, 35, 327, 373, 426, 428, 430, 458–459, 463, 467, 471, 477, 482, 487, 491, 581, 583, 597, 600

art/painting, 411, 447, 461

automobiles, 210, 435, 589

ballooning, 546, 549

baseball, 55, 194, 250, 598, 599, 651

basketball, 75, 85, 598, 626

beetles, 396, 401

bicycling, 95, 153, 423, 441, 445, 481, 566, 631

birds, 435

business, 49, 53, 55, 59, 61, 63, 69, 75, 81, 83, 87, 88, 130, 145, 165, 185, 250, 358, 389, 621

butterflies, 293, 325

carpentry, 327, 417, 431, 487

catering, 454

communications technology, 189, 191, 385, 387–388

computers, 210, 348, 375, 386, 397, 531, 533

conservation, 155, 161, 171, 181, 186, 195, 243, 257

consumer spending, 25, 55, 67, 69, 70, 79, 81, 227, 385, 390, 520, 587, 625

crafts, 269

dinosaurs, 113, 327

discount prices *See* Money.

diving, 105, 107, 238

driving, 420, 429, 463

earning or saving money *See* Money.

elections, 344, 345

electricity, 155, 161, 181, 317

energy conservation, 155, 161, 171, 181, 186, 195

engineering, 449

entertainment/media, 9, 25, 141, 180, 184, 204, 222, 225, 343, 379, 380, 441, 457

field trip, 1, 5, 9, 19, 25, 29

food and nutrition, 277, 287, 333, 334, 443, 445, 569, 597

football, 26–27, 112, 114, 117

fundraising, 141, 424, 441, 550, 631, 648, 653

games and puzzles, 482, 491, 501, 515, 525, 569

garden planning, 11, 169, 441, 557

gears, 273

golf, 116, 264, 513

health and fitness, 70, 233, 309, 327, 334, 339, 347, 374

hiking, 90

hobbies, 222, 228

house painting, 454

in-line skating, 75, 390

manufacturing, 481

menu planning, 394

model cars or trains, 544, 563, 575, 579, 584, 589, 605

money *See* Money.

music, 9, 468, 483

Olympics, 28, 135

origami, 476

packaging, 576, 577, 582

parks, 37, 426

pets, 222–223, 226

photography, 277, 477, 485, 519, 540–541, 559

population data, 171, 205, 211, 218–219, 220–221, 225, 245, 287, 290, 321, 343, 374, 384, 406, 650, 673, 675, 677, 678, 712

quilting, 414, 615

real estate, 439

recreation, 5

recipes, 313, 443

recycling, 202–203, 207, 211, 212, 217, 224, 226, 229, 231, 234

reporting, 103, 107, 113, 117, 135, 141

robots, 25

scale models, 372

space exploration, 23, 25, 123, 435, 511, 515, 520, 529, 534, 545, 553, 555, 593, 599

sports, 103, 107, 113, 117, 135, 136, 150, 233, 264, 423, 586, 589, 596, 598, 650, 686

subways, 616–617, 621, 625, 629, 631, 638, 655

talent show planning, 361, 365, 371, 375, 379, 385, 390, 395

television, 194, 239, 343, 358, 508, 613

temperature, 104, 111, 123, 127, 185, 237, 435, 619, 625, 687

test scoring, 90, 376, 379

tiling, 269, 417, 488, 489

track and field, 5, 28, 113, 311, 655, 686

travel and vacations, 1, 5, 9, 19, 25, 29, 328, 649

U.S. Congress, 214, 216

water resources, 347, 349, 353

weather, 364, 669, 687

zip codes, 457

See also Interdisciplinary connections, Projects, *and* Themes, Chapter.

Approximation

on a calculator, 11, 15, 167, 430, 431

of cube root, 15

of length using the Pythagorean Theorem, 420–423, 425–429, 452, 513, 547–549, 590–591, 656

of pi, 564–565

of square root, 11, 44, 430, 431

See also Estimation.

Area, introduced, 7

of circles, 567–569, 570, 606

of composite regions, 699–700

of irregular regions, 18, 30–31, 192–195, 233, 513

model for multiplication, 324, 326

models of fractions or percents, 318, 320, 323, 335–339

of parallelograms, 512–515, 557

and perimeter, 41, 70, 142, 144, 192–195, 365, 426, 512–515, 543, 545

ratios of similar figures, 543

of rectangles, 7, 20, 55, 70, 74, 75,

B

C

Cross-curricular exercises *See* Interdisciplinary connections.

Cross Product Property, 368

Cube, 13, 15, 285, 576–583

  faces, edges, vertices, 13

  finding dimensions given volume, 15

  nets for, 571, 607

  surface area of, 13, 576–579

  third power, 13, 15

  volume of, 15, 41, 285, 287, 580–583

Cube root, 15

Cubic numbers, 41, 294

Cubic units, 580

Cumulative Review, 152–153, 304–307, 456–457, 612–615

Curriculum connections *See* Applications, Interdisciplinary connections, *and* Projects.

Customary measurement, 763

Cylinder, defined, 573

  surface area of, 576–579, 608, 701

  volume of, 586–589, 608, 701

D

Data, defined, 26

  collection, 646–647, 667, 671, 675, 680, 685, 691 *See also* Probability *and* Survey.

  comparing using tables, 5, 21, 26–29, 31, 38–41, 129, 182, 200, 204–207, 209–210, 213, 215–223, 225, 232–235, 237–239, 243, 245, 250, 306, 327, 334, 357, 358, 492, 587, 612, 669, 712

  on a computer spreadsheet, 77, 189, 348

  organizing in line plot, 230–234, 240–241, 249, 397

  in probability experiments, 240–245, 397, 398–401

  representing proportional relationships *See* Scatter plot.

  range of, 681

  scale, 226–227

  See also Table to organize data.

Data analysis

  average, 133, 135, 668

  bar graph, 27–29, 70, 117, 130, 208–212, 220–221, 226, 228, 234, 247–249, 277, 387, 668

  box-and-whisker plot, 678–681, 710

  choosing an appropriate graph, 218–224, 235, 248, 306

  circle graph, 317, 319, 321, 323, 341, 345, 353, 358, 382, 385, 407, 457

  double bar graph, 27–29, 208

  evaluating measures of central tendency, 668–671, 709

  finding percent increase or decrease over time, 386–389

  frequency table, 209–210, 213

  histogram, 209–211, 213, 247, 668

  interpreting graphs, 9, 27, 45, 70, 85, 117, 130, 182, 186, 204–212, 214–217, 220, 223–231, 233–240, 247–249, 251, 317, 319, 321, 323, 341, 353, 382, 385, 407, 443, 457, 612, 647, 668, 672–681

  interpreting maps, 35, 339, 533, 659

  line graph, 27, 214–217, 227, 229, 248, 443

  line plot, 230–234, 240–241, 249, 397

  making a table, 21, 31, 40–41, 45, 54, 57, 81, 129, 182, 184, 189, 191, 200, 216, 348, 388, 413, 417, 443, 448, 492, 499, 549, 551, 591, 602, 605, 618, 620, 623–625, 639, 645, 646, 684, 685, 686, 691

  mean, median, and mode, 133, 668, 709

  misleading graph, 226–229, 249

  pictograph, 204, 206–207, 220–221, 226, 247, 248

  quartile, 676

  scatter plot, 236–239, 249, 647–649, 651

  stem-and-leaf plot, 672–675, 709

  tally, 209, 213

  time line, 205–207, 247

Decagon, 32

Decimals, introduced, 38

  adding and subtracting, 320–323, 356

  bar notation, 38, 45

  comparing and ordering, 414–417, 451

  fractions as, 38, 45, 281–283, 301, 320–323, 354, 356, 414–417, 451

  modeling, 281–282

  multiplying, 340, 376–379

  nonrepeating, 38, 281, 414, 416

  patterns in, 38, 41, 45

  and percent, 340–343, 354, 357, 376–379, 382–385

  plotting on a number line, 415–417, 451

  rational numbers and, 280–283, 301, 414–417, 451

  repeating, 38, 45, 281–283, 414

  rewriting as fractions, 274, 280–283, 301

  rounding, 167, 188, 320–323, 326

  terminating, 38, 281–283

  writing, 38

Decimal form and solving proportions, 376–379, 382–389

Decimal point, 288–292

Degrees

  in a circle, 345

  measured in angles, 464–473, 492–497, 499, 505, 507, 508

  in a polygon, 215, 491–497, 499

  of a polynomial, 694

  in a triangle, 164, 175, 215

Denominator, introduced, 6

  least common, 316

Dependent events, 399–401

Diagonal, 33

Diameter, 566

Difference, 6, 120

Dilations, 537, 541–545, 558

Discount, 383

Distance Formula, 44, 656, 663

Distributive Property, introduced, 52

  modeling with algebra tiles, 52, 54

  to multiply binomials, 698–707, 711

calculating sale bonus, 173

calculating tax, 190, 350, 352–353, 357, 379, 456

calculating tip in restaurant, 352

currency, 256, 263, 327, 329

finding best buy, 365, 383, 587

finding discounts, 346, 383–385

finding rate increases or decreases, 387–390

finding sales commission, 91

finding simple interest, 456

finding taxi fares, 645

graphing prices, 204, 206

graphing profits, 216

making change, 76

making purchases, 67, 69, 70, 79, 83, 128, 323

saving for a goal, 36

tracking income and expenses, 117, 683, 685

unit price, 362–365, 373

using exchange rates, 76, 81

wages, hourly or weekly, 36, 55, 59, 73, 77, 165, 228, 278, 331, 333, 334, 373, 669

See also Applications.

Monomial, 688

Multicultural connections, 14, 76, 258, 264, 337, 429, 484, 488, 489, 579, 667, 702

Multiples, defined, 270

common, 270

least common, 270–273, 300, 314–315, 317

modeling, 314–315

Multiplication

and division, inverse of, 138–139

of fractions and mixed numbers, 324–327, 356

of integers, 124–129, 148

of natural numbers, 6–7, 43

of polynomials, 698–707, 711

properties of, 67

solving inequalities using, 438–441, 453

Multiplication equations

modeling, 71, 73, 82–85, 255, 265, 703

solving, 72–75, 98, 158–161, 168–171

Multi-step equations

solving using the distributive property, 163–165, 172–175, 198

Multi-step inequalities, 442–445

N

n-gon, 32

Natural numbers, defined, 38

divisibility tests for, 254–257, 299

factors, 255–269

Need to Know, 16, 38, 56, 115, 120, 138, 168, 226, 230, 236, 243, 266, 311, 368, 410, 421, 470, 516, 517, 537, 688

Negative correlation, 236

Negative exponents, 284–292, 301

Negative integers, 104, 108–113

Negative slopes, 635

Net, 571–576, 584, 595

Nonagon, 32

Non-examples *See* Conjectures.

Non-proportional relationships

compared to proportional, 370, 373, 383, 389

Number line, introduced, 7

and absolute value, 105

box-and-whisker plot, 676–681, 710

common multiples on, 7, 8

decimals on, 415–417, 451

fractions on, 275, 313, 415–417, 451

inequalities on 432–436, 440, 442

integers on, 104–107, 112, 114, 116, 128, 134, 147, 148

irrational numbers on, 415–417, 425, 451

modeling probability, 242

multiplication on, 7, 8

Number patterns, 3–5, 10–13, 14, 39–41, 43, 294–297, 318, 388, 391, 393, 395, 623

See also Patterns.

Number sense, 4, 8, 9, 106, 123, 273, 389, 416, 449

Number Theory

composites and primes, 258–263

divisibility tests, 254–257, 299

factoring, 255–269, 299, 300

Goldbach's Conjecture, 263

multiples, 270–273, 300

Numbers

compared in Venn Diagram, 280, 298, 417, 450

composite, 260

cubic, 41

Fibonacci, 41

figurative, 296

irrational, 280–283, 414–417, 425, 451

natural, 38

perfect, 297

perfect square, 11

pi, 38, 564, 566

prime, 260

Pythagorean triples, 421

random, 240

rational, 280–283, 301

real, 414–417, 450, 451

in scientific notation, 288

triangular, 39, 296

twin prime, 263

whole vs. natural, 38

Numerator, introduced, 6

Numerical expression, defined, 16

evaluating, 16–19, 44

simplifying, 16–19, 44

O

Obtuse angle, 465

Obtuse triangle, 479

Octagon, 32, 194

Ongoing Assessment, *in every lesson, for example,* 23, 53, 127, 179, 215, 281, 331, 369, 433, 501, 523, 587, 643, 695

See also Talk About It *and* Write About it.

Open-ended problem, 28, 54, 58, 106, 113, 145, 185, 268, 297, 401, 430, 476, 477, 554, 579, 601, 631, 670, 675, 681

Operations, introduced, 6–9

order of, 16–19

selecting appropriate, 328, 333

Opposites, 105, 147

Order of Operations, introduced, 16

on a calculator, 16

and integers, 16–19, 44

Credits

Cover Image

Photography by Ralph Mercer

Stock Photography

v Giraudon/Art Resource (t); School Division, Houghton Mifflin Company (b); **vi** Gerd Ludwig/Woodfin Camp and Associates (t); Bob Daemmrich/Stock Boston (b); **vii** PhotoDisc, Inc. (t); Michael Newman/PhotoEdit (b); **viii** David Young-Wolff/PhotoEdit (t); Nancy Sheehan (b); **ix** Gary D. McMichael/Photo Researchers, Inc. (t); Jean Higgins/Unicorn Stock Photo (b); **x** Van Etten/Monkmeyer Press (t); Jeff Greenberg/New England Stock Photo (b); **xi** Comstock (t); Stephen Frisch/Stock Boston (b); **xii** Nicole Katano/Tony Stone Images/Chicago, Inc. (t); Karl Weatherly/Tony Stone Images/Chicago, Inc. (b); **xiii** Will McIntyre/Photo Researchers, Inc. (t); Michael Newman/PhotoEdit (b); **xiv** Michael Mancuso/Omni Photo Communications (t); Michael J. Howell/New England Stock Photo (b); **xv** Dana White/PhotoEdit (t); Alain Evrard/Photo-Researchers, Inc. (b); **xvi** NASA (t); Index Stock Photography (b); **xvii** Marc DeVille/Liaison International (t); James Mejuto (b); **xviii** David Weintraub/Photo Researchers, Inc. (t); Dennis Degnan/Westlight (b); **xix** Scala/Art Resource, NY (t); **xxi** Steve Vidler/Leo de Wys (tc); Pam Francis/Liaison International (tr); Kathleen Campbell/Tony Stone Images/Chicago, Inc. (cr); Japack/Leo de Wys (cl); Bob Daemmrich/Stock Boston (bl); Maslowski/Visuals Unlimited (br); **xxii** Stephanie Hollyman/Sygma (t); Michael Mancuso/Omni Photo Communication (cl); International Stock Photo (bl); Jeff Greenberg/Photo Researchers, Inc. (bc); **xxiii** David Young-Wolff/Tony Stone Images/Chicago, Inc.; **xxiv** John Lei/Omni Photo Communications (tl); Peter Menzel (cl); F. Rickard-Artdia/Agence Vandystadt/Photo Researchers, Inc.; **xxviii** Dan McCoy/Rainbow (tl); David Madison/Duomo (cl); Robert Aschenbrenner/Stock Boston (bl); **xxix** Andrea Booher/Tony Stone Images/Chicago, Inc.; **xxx** Gerd Ludwig/Woodfin Camp and Associates (b); Paul Conkiin/Uniphoto (tr); H. Schmeiser/Unicorn Stock Photo (tl); ; **1** Bob Daemmrich/Stock Boston; **2** Bob Daemmrich Photo, Inc.; **3** Tony Freeman/PhotoEdit; **5** Ian Howarth; **6** Bob Daemmrich Photo, Inc.; **10** Kevin Morris/Tony Stone Images/Chicago, Inc.; **13** Loren Santow/Tony Stone Images/Chicago, Inc.; **14** Museum of The History of Science, Oxford University; **20** Jeffrey Markowitz/Sygma; **21** School Division, Houghton Mifflin Company; **22** Carnegie Mellon University; **25** NASA; **26** William R. Sallaz/Duomo; **28** David Madison/The Image Bank; **31** School Division, Houghton Mifflin Company (b); **32** Dede Gilman/Unicorn Stock Photo; **34** PhotoDisc, Inc. (all); **35** Alex S. MacLean/Landslides; **36** NASA-Ames Research Center; **37** Adam Jones/Photo Researchers, Inc. (bl); Phyllis Picardi/Uniphoto Atlanta (br); **39** Steve Umland; **41** Renee Lynn/Tony Stone Images/Chicago, Inc.; **48** Michael Newman/PhotoEdit (tl); PhotoDisc, Inc.(tr); Bob Daemmrich/Tony Stone Images/Chicago, Inc. (b); **49** School Division, Houghton Mifflin Company; **51** School Division, Houghton Mifflin Company; **52** Mary Kate Denny/PhotoEdit; **55** M. Antman/Image Works; **59** Phyllis Picardi/Stock Boston; **61** John Foraste/Brown University; **65** School Division, Houghton Mifflin Company (l); **66** Robert W. Ginn/Uniphoto; **69** Scott Markewitz/FPG International; **73** David Young-Wolff/PhotoEdit; **75** Bob Daemmrich/Stock Boston; **76** Llewellyn/Uniphoto; **79** Mary Kate Denny/PhotoEdit; **81** National Baseball Hall of Fame Library, Cooperstown, N.Y.; **82** A. Pierce Bounds/Uniphoto; **85** Michael Newman/PhotoEdit; **87** Courtesy of Levi Strauss & Co. Archives, San Francisco, CA (cr); White/Packert/The Image Bank (l); **88** Jonathan Nourok/PhotoEdit; **89** Evan Agostini/Liaison International; **90** Dan McCoy/Rainbow; **92** Jeff Persons/Stock Boston; **95** Robert Aschenbrenner/Stock Boston; **99** School Division, Houghton Mifflin Company; **102** Ed Bock/The Stock Market (tr); David Young-Wolf/PhotoEdit (cl); Nancy Sheehan (b); **103** School Division, Houghton Mifflin Company; **104** Sylvester Allred/Visuals Unlimited (c); Bob Grant/Comstock (cl); **109** School Division, Houghton Mifflin Company; **110** David Young-Wolff/PhotoEdit; **111** Art Wolfe/Tony Stone Images/Chicago, Inc. (l, r); Art Wolfe, Inc. (c); **113** Jose Carrillo/PhotoEdit; **116** Ben Van Hook/Duomo; **118** Anthony Salamone/Houghton Mifflin Company; **122** Ken M. Johns/Photo Researchers, Inc.; **123** Liaison International; **125** School Division, Houghton Mifflin Company; **126** Science VU/Visual Impact; **127** Stephanie Hollyman/Sygma; **129** Helsinki University of Technology; **131** Don Mason (br); James Martin (background); **132** John Kelly/The Image Bank; **133** Russell R. Grundke/Unicorn Stock Photo; **135** Mike Powell/Allsport (t); School Division, Houghton Mifflin Company (b); **136** Jon Feingersh/The Stock Market; **141** Ira Wyman/Sygma; **150** Michael Newman/PhotoEdit;

Dan Feicht (br); **409** The Granger Collection, New York; **411** Robert Orduño; **413** Gayna Hoffman (t); Michael J. Howell/New England Stock Photo (b); **414** B. Daemmrich/Stock Boston; **419** School Division, Houghton Mifflin Company (b); **423** Betts Anderson-Loman/Unicorn Stock Photo; **424** Courtesy of Michael Amador/Texas Department of Transportation (br); **426** Alex S. MacLean/Landslides; **427** Dan Groshong/Bettmann; **428** Alex S. MacLean/Landslides; **430** Aurness/Woodfin Camp and Associates; **432** Stan Osolinski/FPG International; **435** Cliff Owen/Bettmann; **436** Steve Vidler/Leo de Wys; **437** Cedar Point Photo by Dan Feicht (b); Cedar Point Photo Courtesy of Sandusky Library (t); **438** B. Daemmrich/Image Works; **441** Elizabeth Holmes/Omni Photo Communications (t); Goodwyn/Monkmeyer Press (b); **442** Richard Nowitz/FPG International; **443** International Stock Photo; **445** Cedar Point Photo by Dan Feicht; **446** David Young-Wolff/PhotoEdit; **447** Jeff Greenberg/Photo Researchers, Inc.; **449** Cedar Point Photo by Dan Feicht; **458** Dana White/PhotoEdit (t); Bob Daemmrich/Stock Boston (cr); Alain Evrard/Photo Researchers, Inc. (bl); **459** PhotoDisc, Inc. (both); **461** Robert Brenner/PhotoEdit (c); Bill Cramer/Liaison International (r); **464** Manfred Kage/Peter Arnold, Inc. (c); **469** School Division, Houghton Mifflin Company; **471** Bruce Hands/Tony Stone Images/Chicago, Inc.; **474** Cabisco/Visuals Unlimited (l); PhotoDisc, Inc. (all others); **476** PhotoDisc, Inc. (all); **477** Uniphoto (tl); Superstock (tc); Kjellb. Sandved/Photo Researchers, Inc. (tr); **478** Sharon Green/The Stock Market; **481** Kermani/Liaison International; **483** School Division, Houghton Mifflin Company; **484** School Division, Houghton Mifflin Company; **485** John Lei/Omni Photo Communications (all); **488** Geophoto/Art Resource, NY; **489** Ulrike Welsch; **493** School Division, Houghton Mifflin Company (l); **494** Michael S. Thompson/Comstock; **495** PhotoDisc, Inc.; **497** Courtesy of Four Season Sunrooms; **498** Paul Chesley/Tony Stone Images/Chicago, Inc.; **500** M. Antman/Image Works; **501** Telegraph Colour Library/FPG International; **510** Index Stock Photography (tl); NASA (tr, b); **512** Rafael Macia/Photo Researchers, Inc.; **519** Elizabeth Zuckerman/PhotoEdit (all); **522** FourByFive, Inc.; **524** Bob Daemmrich/Image Works; **526** Michael Busselle/Tony Stone Images/Chicago, Inc.; **527** Gerben Oppermans/Tony Stone Images/Chicago, Inc.; **530** Omni Photo Communications; **534** NASA (bl); Dr. Christopher Burrows, ESA/STScI/NASA (br); **540** Nancy Sheehan/Houghton Mifflin Company (all); **541** Tony Freeman/PhotoEdit (cr); School Division, Houghton Mifflin Company (bl); **543** PhotoDisc, Inc.; **544** Denso Corporation; **545** Julie Kramer Cole (t); NASA (b); **546** Andrea Booher/Tony Stone Images/Chicago, Inc.; **550** Nash Baker/NASA; **553** NASA; **562** Michael Newman/PhotoEdit (t); Marc DeVille/Liaison International (b); **563** School Division, Houghton Mifflin Company (b); **565** School Division, Houghton Mifflin Company (b); **566** Yoav Levy/Phototake (cl); **568** PhotoDisc, Inc. (all); **569** Photodisc, Inc.; **571** School Division, Houghton Mifflin Company; **572** Rogers/Monkmeyer Press; **576** R. Bossu/Sygma (cl); **579** Morris/Stock Imagery; **580** Gian Berto Vanni/Art Resource; **586** Courtesy of Ringette Canada; **591** School Division, Houghton Mifflin Company (l); **592** Archive Photos; **593** NASA; **598** Photodisc, Inc. (all); **599** Courtesy of Learning Technologies, Inc. (both); **600** Randy Taylor/Sygma; **601** TechnoFrolics (cl); Lou Jones/Discover Magazine (r); **602** Ron McMillan/Liaison International; **603** Kaku Kurita/Liaison International (tr); **605** James Mejuto (tr); **616** David R. Frazier/Photo Researchers, Inc. (t); Mark Burnett/Photo Researchers, Inc. (cl); Dennis Degnan/Westlight (b); **617** School Division, Houghton Mifflin Company; **618** Janice Sheldon/Photo 20-20; **622** David Young-Wolff/Tony Stone Images/Chicago, Inc.; **625** A. Ramey/PhotoEdit; **626** Anthony Salamone/Houghton Mifflin Company; **631** Michael Heron/The Stock Market (t); Alison Wright/Image Works (b); **632** David Weintraub/Photo Researchers, Inc.; **635** Jose Carrillo/PhotoEdit; **638** Comstock; **639** Paul Conklin/Uniphoto; **641** School Division, Houghton Mifflin Company; **642** F. Rickard-Artdia/Agence Vandystadt/Photo Researchers, Inc.; **645** Richard Megna/Fundamental Photo; **647** School Division, Houghton Mifflin Company; **648** Eric A. Wessman/Viesti Associates, Inc.; **649** Jerry Driendl/FPG International; **652** David Madison/Duomo; **655** Courtesy of Team with a Vision/Massachusetts Association for the Blind (t); Paul Silverman/Fundamental Photo (b); **656** Elena Rooraid/PhotoEdit; **657** Courtesy of Trimble Navigation Limited, Sunnyvale, CA; **666** School Division, Houghton Mifflin Company (+); **668** Peter D. Byron/PhotoEdit; **671** Elena Rooraid/PhotoEdit (t); **672** Gish/Monkmeyer Press; **674** Duomo; **675** Tim Hauf/Visuals Unlimited; **676** B. Daemmrich/Stock Boston; **679** Ken Lucas/Visuals Unlimited; **680** School

Division, Houghton Mifflin Company; **682** David Young-Wolff/Tony Stone Images/Chicago, Inc.; **685** Elliott Smith/International Stock Photo; **686** Courtesy of Stan Jensen (all); **689** PhotoEdit; **691** Stock Imagery (t); School Division, Houghton Mifflin Company; **693** School Division, Houghton Mifflin Company; **697** Courtesy of Stan Jensen; **702** Scala/Art Resource, NY; **707** Cameramann/Image Works (t); School Division, Houghton Mifflin Company (b)

Illustrations

Eliot Bergman **107**; **114**
Steve Cowden **205**; **207**; **520**
All others: School Division, Houghton Mifflin Company

Technical Art

Burmar Technical Corporation

Assignment Photography

RMIP/Richard Haynes **xxiv**; **31** (t); **50**; **64** (all); **65** (r); **108**; **124**; **139**; **156**; **177** (t); **211**; **219** (t); **240**; **258**; **265** (t); **269** (b); **308** (br); **314** (both); **315** (t); **391**; **418** (all); **419** (t); **425** (both); **464** (l); **493** (r); **523**; **541** (t); **565** (t); **566** (b); **591** (r); **633**; **640**; **646**; **647**; **671** (b); **674** (t,b); **703**; **704**

Chapter 1

1.1 Exercises, pp. 4–5

1. *Sample answer:* Mathematics is the study of numbers, how they are related to each other, and how they can be used.   **3.** *Sample answer:* length or distance (meter, inch, mile, light-year); weight (ounce, kilogram, ton); temperature (degrees Fahrenheit or Celsius); time (seconds, days, millenia); speed (miles per hour, meters per second); area (square centimeters, square miles); volume (cubic inches, cubic feet, liters, cups, gallons); energy and power (watts, horsepower, calories)   **5.** Add two to the previous number; 9, 11, 13.   **7.** Add two, then three, then four, and so on; 15, 21, 28.   **9.** Increase the numerator and denominator each by one; $\frac{5}{6}, \frac{6}{7}, \frac{7}{8}$.   **11.** Add one and one half to the previous number; 8, $\frac{19}{2}$, 11.

13. Multiply the previous number by three; 162, 486, 1458.   **15.** Give the letter two letters after the previous letter; I, K, M.   **17.** Give the first letter in the alphabet followed by the first letter in the second half of the alphabet, then give the second letter of the alphabet followed by the second letter in the second half of the alphabet, and so on; C, P, D.   **19.** 50, 47, 44, 41, 38, 35
21.   **23.** You win.

25. They get smaller and smaller.   **27.** B

1.2 Exercises, pp. 8–9

1. addition, subtraction, multiplication, division   **5.** The product of 6 and 8 is 48.   **7.** The sum of 3 and 14 is 17.   **9.** The difference of 111 and 56 is 55.   **11.** The product of 2 and 54 is 108.
13. 682   **15.** 719   **17.** 213   **19.** 2.3   **21.** 1
23. $\frac{1}{3}$ **25.** 112   **27.** 17   **29.** 41.83
31. 50,076   **33.** 8   **35.** 2   **37.** 17.9
39. 131.8   **41.** $2 \times 4 = 8$ **43.** $3 \times 9 = 27$ or $9 \times 3 = 27$ **45.** 442 million   **47.** 315 million
49. 70   **51.** C

1.3 Exercises, pp. 12–13

1. base; exponent   **3.** 4   **5.** 9   **7.** 6 to the fourth power is 1296.   **9.** The square root of 1.21 is 1.1.

11. $12^2 = 144$ **13.** $3.4^3 = 39.304$ **15.** $3^6 =$ 729   **17.** 13   **19.** 10.82   **21.** 2.35   **23.** 8
25. 2.1   **27.** 81   **29.** $<$ **31.** $<$ **33.** 2^{10}
35. a. 22.5 ft   **b.** 90 ft   **c.** 56.25 ft^2 **d.** 7.5 ft
37. no   **39.** B

Spiral Review, p. 14

1. $\frac{1}{2}$ **3.** $\frac{3}{2}$ **5.** 0.5   **7.** 0.375   **9.** Each number is two more than the previous number; 10, 12, 14.
11. The numerators and denominators each increase by two when going from one number to the next; $\frac{9}{10}, \frac{11}{12}, \frac{13}{14}$.   **13. a.** \$8.25   **b.** \$1.75
15. 15.21

Using a Calculator, p. 15

1. Each edge must be about 4.64 ft long.

1.4 Exercises, pp. 18–19

3. a. 6   **b.** 24   **c.** 19   **5.** 9   **7.** 19   **9.** 29
11. 38   **13.** 8   **15.** −8   **17.** 42   **19.** 79
21. 2   **23.** about 19.33 $\left(19\frac{1}{3}\text{ or }\frac{58}{3}\right)$ **25.** 600
27. $2 \times 3 + 2^2 + 3 \times 4$; 22 square units
29. false; $(6 + 21) \div 3 = 9$ **31.** false; $(6 + 3^2) \div 3 = 5$ **33.** false; $7 + 7 \cdot (2 + 6) = 63$ **35.** $5 \times 0.5 + 3 \times 2.25 + 5.99$; \$15.24
37. C

Mid-Chapter Assessment, p. 20

1. *Sample answer:* Numbers can identify objects (phone numbers, barcode numbers, driver's license numbers), count objects (number of test questions, number of computers sold), put objects in order (the finishers in a race, the top producers of an item), or measure objects (distance, area, volume, speed, time, weight, energy).   **2.** Add three to the previous number; 15, 18, 21.
3. Subtract nine from the previous number; 54, 45, 36.   **4.** Give the squares of the counting numbers; 25, 36, 49.   **5.** Increase the denominator by one; $\frac{1}{6}, \frac{1}{7}, \frac{1}{8}$.
6.    **7.** **789**

8. The product of 22 and 4 is 88.   **9.** Four to the fifth power is 1024.   **10.** The square root of 289 is 17.   **11.** 48   **12.** 2112   **13.** 9   **14.** 390,625
15. 18.49   **16.** 16   **17.** 28.2   **18.** 4.36

19. 25 **20.** 64 **21.** 39 **22.** 8 **23.** 56
24. 3 **25.** $(21 - 8) \times 2 = 26$
26. $24 - 20 \div (4 + 6) = 22$
27. $24 - (12 - 4) \cdot 2 = 8$ **28.** 128,775 ft^2
29. about 19.6 ft **30.** about 137 ft

1.5 Exercises, pp. 24–25

1. An algebraic expression is a collection of numbers, variables, operations (such as addition or
division), and grouping symbols. **3.** n **5.** $4 + n$
7. 18 **9.** 9 **11.** 48 **13.** 57 **15.** 42 **17.** 25
19. 3 **21.** 5 **23.** 19 **25.** 84 **27.** 6 **29.** 125
31. 3 **33.** 4 **35.** 12 **37.** B **39.** C
41. 1500 ft **43.** 4 **45. a.** $6p + 2p$ **b.** $24
47. B

1.6 Exercises, pp. 28–29

1. *Sample answer:* You can use a list, table,
diagram, or graph. **3.** the United States
5. Russia **7.** *Sample answer:* A bar graph is
better.

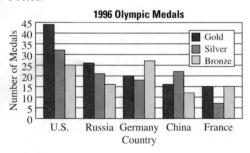
1996 Olympic Medals

9. 1988; 1980

11. Side Length	1	2	3	4	5	6	7
Perimeter (units)	4	8	12	16	20	24	28
Area (square units)	1	4	9	16	25	36	49

13. *Sample answer:* Cleveland: 50°F, Seattle:
53°F **15.** C

1.7 Exercises, pp. 34–35

1. *Sample answer:* A polygon is a figure formed
by line segments that are connected at their ends
so that they close in an area. **3.** 2 **5.** yes;
quadrilateral **7.** yes; hexagon **9.** No; this is
not a polygon because it does not have straight
sides that meet at vertices. **11.** yes; octagon
13. Area of triangle = Base $\times$ Height $\div$ 2
15. 64 in.^{2} **17.** yes; octagon **19.** yes;
pentagon **21.** yes; nonagon **23.** yes; pentagon
25. yes; hexagon **27.** *Sample answer:*
29. B

1. 85.2 **3.** 1.44 **5.** 16,807 **7. a.** 6×20
b. $6 \times 20 - 50$; $70 **9.** 4 **11.** 0 **13.** 2
15. $\dfrac{1}{2}$

1.8 Exercises, pp. 40–41

1. 0; 1 **3.**

n	1	2	3	4
$192 \div n$	192	96	64	48

5.

n	1	2	3	4	5	6	7	8	9
$\dfrac{n}{3}$	$0.\overline{3}$	$0.\overline{6}$	1.0	$1.\overline{3}$	$1.\overline{6}$	2.0	$2.\overline{3}$	$2.\overline{6}$	3.0

7.

n	1	2	3	4	5
$\dfrac{n}{n+1}$	0.5	$0.\overline{6}$	0.75	0.8	$0.8\overline{3}$

9. 18; 187; 1876; 18,765; 187,654; 1,876,543;
18,765,432 **11.** 111,111; 222,222; 333,333;
444,444; 555,555; 666,666; 777,777 **13.** 45
15. 64 **17.** C

Chapter 1 Review, pp. 43–45

1. Each number is 2 times the previous number;
32, 64. **3.** Each number is one half the previous
number; 12, 6. **5.** To get from one term to the
next, subtract 15, then subtract 14, then subtract
13, and so on; 51, 40. **7.** 113 **9.** 83 **11.** 300
13. 64 **15.** 512 **17.** 343 **19.** 20.52
21. 45.7 **23.** 13 **25.** 9 **27.** 3 **29.** 5
31. 25 **33.** 165 mi **35.** Maryland **37.** The
figure is not a polygon because it is not closed.
39. yes; pentagon

41.

n	1	2	3	4	5	6	7	8	9
$105 \times n$	105	210	315	420	525	630	735	840	945

Chapter 2

2.1 Exercises, pp. 54–55

1. First row: 6, 10, 24; second row: 6, 10, 24;
numerical examples result in the same answer.
3. a. true **b.** false; added instead of multiplied
c. false; $2 \cdot 11 = 22 \neq 21$ **5.** $6x + 4 =$
$2(3x + 2)$ **7.** $2x + 2$ **9.** $10x + 15$
11. $110 + 55 = 165$ **13.** $16z + 48$
15. $32 + 8q$ **17.** $ab + 4a$
19. $24 + 40 + 48 = 112$ **21.** $12s + 12t + 12w$
23. 158.7 **25.** $3(x + 6)$ **27. a.** Total Yearly
Pay = 12(employee 1's monthly salary +
employee 2's monthly salary + employee 3's
monthly salary) **b.** $55,200

2.2 Exercises, pp. 58–59

1. Like terms have the same variables raised to the same powers; $2x$ and $7x$. **3.** *Sample answer:* Any two values can be added in either order and the answer will be the same; $a + b = b + a$. **5.** yes; $4x$ **7.** no; not like terms **9.** $3a$ **11.** $9x + 9$ **13.** $7x + 2y$ **15.** $15p + 9q + 9$ **17.** $3a + 3b + 2c$ **19.** $2x^2$ **21.** $9y + 20$ **23.** $7x + 7y$ **25.** Add like terms first: $2x + 5x = 7x$; $7x + 3$. **27.** $5y + 8x$; 41 **29.** $9y + 2x$; 49 **31.** $12x + 6y$; 54 **33.** $2xy + x^2$; 24 **35.** $5x + 4, 6x + 5$; not equivalent **37.** $18x$; perimeter increases by 18 as x increases by 1. **39.** 5 h/day $\times$ 4 days **41.** B

2.3 Exercises, pp. 62–63

1. *Sample answer:* $2x = x + x$ **3.** Substitute the value of the variable into the equation. If the final step results in an identity, the value is the solution. If the final result is not an identity, the solution is incorrect. **5.** C **7.** A **9.** What number can you multiply by 7 to get 42?; 6 **11.** 9 divided by what number gives you 3?; 3 **13.** $z + 7 = 19$; 12 **15.** $\frac{w}{9} = 5$; 45 **17.** yes **19.** yes **21.** Yes; addition is commutative. **23.** No; division is not commutative. **25.** 21 **27.** 5 **29.** 7 **31.** 13 **33.** not an identity **35.** Let a be the weight for 1994; $a - 209.5 = 780.5$; 990. **37.** Let c be the weight for 1995; $c + 22 = 990$; 968.

2.4 Exercises, pp. 68–69

3. Subtract 24 from each side. **5.** Subtract 72 from each side. **7.** Associative Property of Multiplication **9.** Commutative Property of Addition **11.** 34; 34; 86 **13.** 62; 62; 49 **15.** 81 **17.** 139 **19.** 575 **21.** 138 **23.** 2.2 **25.** 13.35 **27.** Add 193 to each side of the equation. **29.** 380.61 **31.** 3.37 **33.** 8761 **35.** $x + 49 = 165$; 116 **37.** $y - 5.8 = 12.2$; 18 **39.** $189 = x + 137$; 52 **41.** 3050 ft **43.** $95.62 **45.** B

Mid-Chapter Assessment, p. 70

1. $5x + 15$ **2.** $2a + 4b + 8$ **3.** A, G **4.** B, F **5.** Distributive Property; $22.20 **6.** $12a$ **7.** $3x + 8$ **8.** $9x + 21$ **9.** $7x + 8$; 36 **10.** A, C **11.** perimeter $= 2x + 10$; area $= 3x + 6$ **12.** 13 **13.** 80 **14.** 14 **15.** 15 **16.** 23 **17.** 9 million **18.** 11 million

2.5 Exercises, pp. 74–75

1. When multiplying or dividing both sides of an equation by the same nonzero number, an equivalent equation or identity will result. **3.** Divide both sides by 6. **7.** The product of 3 and x is 21; 7. **9.** A number a divided by 3 is 3; 9. **11.** 12 **13.** 8 **15.** 24 **17.** 20 **19.** 9 **21.** 64 **23.** 1.3 **25.** 7.5 **27.** 44.4 **29.** 2070 **31.** 2 **33.** 55 **35.** 4992 **37.** 3591 **39.** 3 cm **41.** 8 km **43.** $4d = 100$; 25 **45.** $\frac{t}{6} = 10$; 60 **47.** Points per game $\cdot$ Number of games $=$ Total points scored **49.** 4.1 mi/day

Spiral Review, p. 76

1. 19 **3.** 28 **5.** 10 **7.** 9 **9.** $4r + 2$; 18 **11.** $6s + 3r$; 42 **13.** $3r^2 + 2s$; 58 **15.** $.51

2.6 Exercises, pp. 80–81

1. $t - 20°$ **3.** $1.00 + 0.10m$ **5.** B **7.** F **9.** A **11.** $\frac{n}{23}$ **13.** $9 + 10n$ **15.** $5n - 4$ **17.** $102n$ **19.** $\frac{n}{2 + m}$ **21.** $m + 4$ **23.** $6m$ **25.** $r - 2$ **27.** $\frac{s}{3}$ **29.** $a - 8$ **31.** $\frac{3}{4}a$, or $\frac{3a}{4}$ **33. a.** $7 + 3h$ **b.** $\frac{7 + 3h}{4}$, or $\frac{1}{4}(7 + 3h)$ **c.** $4 **35.** B

2.7 Exercises, pp. 84–86

1. equation; 16 **3.** equation; 9 **5.** $c - 21 = 84$; Addition Property of Equality **7.** C **9.** A **11.** B **13.** $d + 9 = 20$; 11; Subtraction Property of Equality **15.** $\frac{p}{12} = 4$; 48; Multiplication Property of Equality **17.** $5 = \frac{y}{45}$; 225; Multiplication Property of Equality **25.** 169 **27.** $24 = (w + 2)(w)$; 4 cm **29.** 95; total units sold last week $= 1000$; $\frac{190}{1000} = 19\%$; 19% of $500 = 95$ **31.** D

Spiral Review, p. 86

1. subtraction **3.** multiplication **5.** $5f$ **7.** $2g + 6$ **9.** $6s$ **11.** $4 + 5h$ **13.** 4 **15.** $\frac{2}{3}$ **17.** 10 **19.** 0 **21.** $26 per week

2.8 Exercises, pp. 90–91

1. D, A, F, C, B, E **3.** Sum of 4 tests + Fifth test score ≥ 460 points **5.** $363 + f \geq 460$ **7.** You need to score a 97 or higher to earn an A. **9.** yes **11.** Miles hiked $= 19$; Let $m =$ miles left to hike; Total trail length $= 29$ **13.** 10 miles

15. 10 mi is less than the total length of 29 mi and also less than the 19 mi you have hiked in two days. **17.** Base salary = $16,500; Commission = $\frac{1}{20}$($150,000) = $7500; Let y = yearly earnings. **19.** y = 24,000; $24,000 **21.** $161.50 **23.** C

2.9 Exercises, pp. 94–95

1. $>$ is greater than; $<$ is less than; $\geq$ is greater than or equal to; $\leq$ is less than or equal to.
3. yes **5.** yes **7.** $x \leq 3$ **9.** $14 < x$ **17.** $x < 6$
19. $y \leq 6$ **21.** $19 \geq s$ **23.** $9 > m$ **25.** $y \geq 4$
27. $y < 19.1$ **29.** $x \geq 88$ **31.** $a \leq 10.5$
33. $b - 7 < 24; b < 31$ **35.** $3y > 39; y > 13$
37. $15 \leq \frac{x}{5}; 75 \leq x$ **39.** The sum of d and 11 is less than 52. **41.** The product of 3 and h is less than or equal to 60. **43.** 17 is greater than the difference of c and 31. **45. a.** Hot Wheelers; 1.15 h **b.** Last place team's time − First place team's time < Minutes needed to place first; $85 - 69 < m$, where m = minutes needed to place first. Therefore, $m > 16$ minutes, which means that the last place team would have needed to complete the race course more than 16 minutes faster. **c.** Cruisin' Kids' time − Brave Bikers' time ≤ m minutes needed to tie or beat Brave Bikers. Therefore, $76 - 71 \leq m; m \geq 5$ minutes, which means that Cruisin' Kids would have needed to complete the course 5 or more minutes faster. **d.** 17.39 mi/h, or 0.29 mi/min

Chapter Review, pp. 97–99

1. $4x + 8$ **3.** $12m + 24$ **5.** $7d + 7f + 14$
7. $5g + 10h$ **9.** $17w$ **11.** $14 + 8v$
13. $14 + 6t + 2a$ **15.** 1 **17.** 2 **19.** 3 **21.** 4
23. 126 **25.** 56.11 **27.** $\frac{1}{4}$ **29.** 980
31. $s + 10$ **33.** $5 + w$ **35.** 192 ft **37.** 300
39. $120,000 **41.** $y < 16$ **43.** $k \geq 5$
45. $6 \geq t$ **47.** $1.77 < v$

Chapter 3

3.1 Exercises, pp. 106–107

1. all **3.** 1, 2, 3, 4 **5.** −1 **7.** −4 and 4, −3 and 3, −2 and 2, or −1 and 1 **9.** to the right of zero

11.
```
-4 -3 -2 -1  0  1  2  3  4
```

13.
```
-6 -5 -4 -3 -2 -1  0  1  2
```

15.
```
-8 -7 -6 -5 -4 -3 -2 -1  0
```

17. $<$ **19.** $>$ **21.** $>$ **23.** −1, 1 **25.** 3, 3
27. −20, 20 **29.** 100, 100 **31.** −250 **33.** 25
35. −17 **37.** −15 **39.** −6, −3, 0, 4, 5
41. −4, −2, −1, 0, 2 **43.** −5, −4, −2, 4, 6
45. 40 mi **47.** 75 mi **49.** 45 mi **51.** True; distance is positive. **53.** true; $6 > 4$ **55.** C

3.2 Exercises, pp. 112–113

1. 7 **3.** 2 **5.** a and d or b and c **7.** Rule 2; 8 and −11 are integers with different signs.
9. $11 + 15 = 26$ **11.** $-13 + (-13) = -26$
13. $10 + (-10) = 0$ **15.** $-13 + 13 = 0$
17. $13 + 0 = 13$ **19.** $0 + 15 = 15$
21. $2 + (-9) = -7$ **23.** $-16 + 12 = -4$ **25.** 6; 5; 4; 3; sums decrease by 1. **27.** −2; 0; 2; 4; sums increase by 2. **29.** D; −2; your sister owes you $2. **31.** C; 45; 45 yd line **33.** 3 **35.** −3
37. $x = 6, y = 1; x = 0; y = 7; x = 10, y = -3$
39. $x = -4, y = -4; x = 0, y = -8; x = -9, y = 1$
41. Jurassic **43.** Triassic **45.** D

3.3 Exercises, pp. 116–117

1.

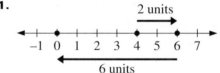

$4 + 2 + (-6) = 0$ **3.** $-3x, 5x, 7; 2x + 7$
5. $4 + (-5) + 6 = 5$ **7.** $-7 + 1 + (-8) = -14$
9. $-8 + 12 + (-1) = 3$
11. $-12 + (-4) + (-8) = -24$
13. $5 + (-6) + (-13) = -14$
15. $-7 + (-6) + 2 + (-7) = -18$
17. negative; $|-237| > |122 + 69|$
19. negative; $|-97 + (-213)| > |230|$ **21.** 93
23. −29 **25.** 117 **27.** Rocca and Stankowski
29. no; $6 + (-3) + (-4) + 8 = 7$ **31.** −$5
33. $3x + 9; 15$ **35.** $x; 2$ **37.** $3x; 6$ **39.** $25x; 50$ **41.** $10x + 8; 28$ **43.** $2x + (-5); -1$ **45.** D

Spiral Review, p. 118

1. 6 **3.** 55 **5.** 12 **7.** 3 **9.** $=$ **11.** $<$
13. 16 **15.** 20 **17.** 2 **19.** 10
21. $9x + 12x + 16x$, or $37x$; $166.50

3.4 Exercises, pp. 122–123

1. $5 - (-2) = 5 + 2 = 7$ **3.** all values of x; $3x - 12 = 3x + (-12)$ **5.** no values of x; $3x - 12 \neq 3x + 12$ **7.** $19 - 17 = 2$

9. $23 - (-8) = 31$　**11.** $-10 - 7 = -17$
13. $-5 - (-5) = 0$　**15.** $-5 - 5 = -10$
17. $0 - 27 = -27$　**19.** The $\boxed{\pm}$ key changes a number to its opposite; the $\boxed{-}$ key refers to the operation of subtraction.　**21.** $-4; 6$　**23.** $1; 11$
25. $7x + (-9x) + (-5); 7x, -9x, -5$
27. $4 + (-2n) + 4m; 4, -2n, 4m$　**29.** $6n + 4$
31. $10x + 10$　**33.** $6x$　**35.** $-26x - 13$
37. $-4y + 24$　**39.** $-11x$　**41.** $1080°; 204°;$
$265°; 288°$　**43.** $-125°$　**45.** $x = 3, y = 7$
47. $x = -5, y = -8$　**49.** -2　**51.** 19　**53.** C

3.5 Exercises, pp. 128–129

1. $3(-4); -12$　**3.** $4(-8); -32$　**5.** $(-4)^2$
7. $-4 \cdot (-6) = 24$　**9.** $5 \cdot (-11) = -55$
11. $(-7)(-9) = 63$　**13.** $(-1)(54) = -54$
15. negative　**17.** $-7x$　**19.** $14a$　**21.** -16
23. 2　**25.** $\$.79$　**27.** $-3c + r; \$.54; \$.92$
29. -3　**31.** -3　**33.** -6　**35.** 1.6　**37.** $100°C;$
$273.15K; -40°C; 233.15K$　**39.** -11

Mid-Chapter Assessment, p. 130

1.

```
 ←─●─┼─●─┼─┼─●─┼─┼─┼→
  -4 -3 -2 -1 0 1 2 3 4
```

2.

```
 ←─┼─┼─●─┼─●─┼─┼─┼─●→
  -4 -3 -2 -1 0 1 2 3 4
```

3.

```
 ←─┼─●─┼─┼─●─┼─●─┼─┼→
  -4 -3 -2 -1 0 1 2 3 4
```

4. $-7, 7$　**5.** $5, 5$　**6.** $-3, -2, 3, 4$　**7.** 8　**8.** 10
9. -5　**10.** $5 + (-7) = -2$　**11.** $-8 + (-1) = -9$
12. $-3 + 5 = 2$　**13.** $7 + (-7) = 0$
14. a. profit　**b.** $\$1718$　**15.** $6a - 6b; 24$
16. $4a - 2b; 20$　**17.** $9x + 2$　**18.** $5x - 6$
19. $2x$　**20.** $-12x - 6$　**21.** $6x + 12$　**22.** $11x$
23. -36　**24.** -56　**25.** 60　**26.** 18　**27.** -65
28. 3

3.6 Exercises. pp. 134–135

1. positive　**3.** negative　**5.** $3(-2) = -6$
7. positive　**9.** 27　**11.** -6　**13.** 0　**15.** 53
17. -98　**19.** -34　**21.** $-1; -2; -3; -4;$ quotients decrease by 1.　**23.** $0; 0; 0; 0;$ quotients are always 0.　**25.** 1　**27.** 1.5　**29.** -49　**31.** 48
33. -3 (eighths of a dollar)　**35.** 21　**37.** 1
39. -15　**43.** D

Spiral Review, p. 136

1. 12　**3.** 3　**5.** -32　**7.** -21　**9.** $3b = 4.20$
11. $32, -64, 128;$ each number (except the first) is the product of the preceding number and -2.

13. $-\dfrac{1}{8}, \dfrac{1}{16}, -\dfrac{1}{32};$ each number (except the first) is the quotient of the preceding number and -2.
15. 27　**17.** 9　**19.** 3
21. $[12 + 12(12) + 20 + 3\sqrt{4} \div 7] + 5(11) = 9^2$

Using a Calculator, p. 137

1. 0.38　**3.** -2.8　**5.** 2　**7.** About $1.9;$ parentheses indicate that addition comes before division.

3.7 Exercises, pp. 140–141

1. Adding the same number to both sides of an equation produces an equivalent equation. Subtracting the same number from both sides of an equation produces an equivalent equation. Multiplying both sides of an equation by the same number produces an equivalent equation. Dividing both sides of an equation by the same nonzero number produces an equivalent equation.
3. Subtraction Property; -14　**5.** Division Property; -7　**7.** yes　**9.** no; 4　**11.** yes
13. -13　**15.** -4　**17.** -12　**19.** 55　**21.** -80
23. 9　**25.** $x - 20 = -4; 16;$ the difference of 16 and 20 is -4.　**27.** $51 = -3a; -17;$ 51 is the product of -17 and -3.　**29.** -1217　**31.** -16
33. 1288　**35.** B　**37.** E　**39.** C　**41.** A;
$25,370$ ft　**43.** $P = 5n - (800 + 20 + 200 + 70)$
45. D

3.8 Exercises, pp. 144–145

1. Draw two lines that intersect at a right angle. Label the vertical line with a letter, usually y, and the horizontal line with another letter, usually x. Label points to the right and up from their intersection with positive numbers, and label points to the left and down from their intersection with negative numbers.　**3.** $(-4, 4); 2$
5. $(3.5, 2); 1$　**7.** $(-3, -2); 3$　**9.** $(2, -5); 4$
11. $J; 4$　**13.** $K;$ none　**15.** $N;$ none
17, 19, 21, 23.
17. 3
19. 1
21. none
23. 2

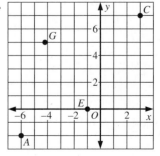

25. 20 units; 21 square units

31, 33, 35. Points lie on a line.
37. 4   **39.** 1   **41.** 34 pairs   **43.** No; when prices go up, sales usually go down.   **45.** B

Chapter 3 Review, pp. 147–149

1.

$$-5\ -4\ -3\ -2\ -1\ \ 0\ \ 1\ \ 2\ \ 3$$

3. $-3, 7$ **5.** sometimes   **7.** 1   **9.** Investment 1
11. 1   **13.** 24   **15.** -4 **17.** $n + (-9) = -21$;
-12 **19.** $\frac{n}{-15} = 3; -45$ **21.** 2   **23.** 28 units;
48 square units

Chapters 1–3 Cumulative Review, pp. 152–153

1. To get the next number, subtract 2 from the preceding number; 12, 10, 8.   **3.** To get the next number, add 2 to both the numerator and denominator of the preceding number; $\frac{9}{10}, \frac{11}{12}, \frac{13}{14}$.
5. To get the next letter, name the letter that is 3 positions earlier in the alphabet than the position of the preceding letter; N, K, H.
7. 65,536   **9.** 6.93   **11.** 11,441.56   **13.** 70
15. 280   **17.** -1 **19.** -8 **21.** 72   **23.** 13
25. No; not all sides are segments.   **27.** yes;
hexagon   **29.** $3x + 3y + 9$; 30   **31.** $2z + 6y$; 36
33. $8x + z + y$; 34   **35.** $10z - 9y - 25$; -1
37. $18x$; 54   **39.** $zy + 2z + |y|$; 40
41.

$$-4\ -3\ -2\ -1\ \ 0\ \ 1$$

43.   **45.** 15 mi/h

$$-4\ -3\ -2\ -1\ \ 0\ \ 1$$

51. 9   **53.** -8 **55.** 10   **57.** -96 **59.** $n < 1$
61. $x \geq 7$ **63.** $c > 2$ **65.** $q \leq 75$
67. $-12 = n + 9; -21$ **69.** $7n > 91; n > 13$
71. blue: $(-3, 3), (-1, 3), (-1, -1), (-3, -1)$;
12 units; green: $(-1, 4), (1, 4), (1, 2), (-1, 2)$;
8 units; yellow: $(-1, 2), (2, 2), (2, -1), (-1, -1)$;
12 units; red: $(2, 4), (5, 4), (5, -1), (2, -1)$;
16 units; area = 36 square units

Chapter 4

4.1 Exercises, pp. 160–161

1. Add 4 to each side.   **3.** Subtract 2 from each side.   **5.** B   **7.** A   **9.** 3   **11.** -1 **13.** -13
15. 8   **17.** -20 **19.** $3x + 7 = 34$; 9
21. $\frac{x}{4} - 2 = 5$; 28   **23.** $21 + 7x = -14; -5$
25. $3x + 17 = 38$; 7   **29.** $7\frac{1}{2}$ h   **31.** C

4.2 Exercises, pp. 164–165

1. First, combine like terms. Then subtract 8 from each side to isolate the x-term. Then divide each side by 2 to isolate x and give the solution.
3. First, combine like terms. Then subtract 11 from each side to isolate the x-term. Then divide each side by -8 to isolate x and give the solution.
5. no; $t = 4\frac{1}{2}$ **7.** 3   **9.** 2   **11.** -6 **13.** $-13\frac{1}{2}$
15. 8   **17.** 4   **19.** -1 **21.** -8
23. $4y - y - 5 = -29; -8$
25. $(5x + 15) + (x + 20) + (4x - 5) = 180$;
15   **27.** 26,667   **29.** C

Spiral Review, p. 166

1. 27   **3.** 3   **7.** $8x - 12$ **9.** 7   **11.** 2.6
13. 18   **15.** 8

Using a Calculator, p. 167

1. $x \approx 2.29$; the solution does not check exactly because it is an approximation.   **3.** $n = 1$; the solution is exact, so the check is exact.   **5.** $x = 7$; the solution is exact, so the check is exact.
7. $n \approx -2.78$; the solution does not check exactly because it is an approximation.   **9.** $b \approx 10.33$; the solution does not check exactly because it is an approximation.

4.3 Exercises, pp. 170–171

1. 3   **3.** $-\frac{1}{5}$ **5.** $\frac{1}{7}; \frac{1}{7}; -4$ **7.** 10   **9.** Rewrite the equation as $\frac{x}{3} = \frac{-15}{1}$ and cross multiply, or multiply each side by 3.   **11.** Divide each side by 9, or multiply each side by $\frac{1}{9}$.   **13.** 8   **15.** 64
17. $\frac{4}{3}$ **19.** -120 **21.** -36 **23.** 15   **25.** 2
27. 3.2   **29.** Alaska: about 607,000; Nebraska: about 1,652,000   **31.** C

4.4 Exercises, pp. 174–175

3. *Sample answer:* Multiply by 7 first. Otherwise, you have to deal with fractions like $-\frac{5}{7}$. **5.** The result of applying the Distributive Property to $2(x - 2)$ should have been $2x - 4$ instead of $2x - 2; 4$. **7.** Combining the like terms $-2x$ and $-4x$ should give $-6x$, not $-2x; -\frac{2}{3}$. **9.** 7 **11.** -5 **13.** 0 **15.** 65 **17.** -5 **19.** 6 **21.** $9(x + 3) = 63; 4$ **23.** $5(2x - 1) = 35; 4$ **25.** $(5x + 5) + 2(3x - 6) = 180; 17$ **27.** B

Mid-Chapter Assessment, p. 176

1. longest side (p): 7 cm; shortest side ($p - 4$): 3 cm; third side ($p - 1$): 6 cm

2. $\frac{1}{3}$ **3.** -21 **4.** -5 **5.** 7 **6.** -4 **7.** 3 **8.** 4
9. -1 **10.** 2 **11.** 5 **12.** -6 **13.** 4 **14.** 5
15. $2x + 3 = 21; 9$ **16.** $\frac{x}{4} - 3 = 1; 16$
17. $2x + x + 5 = 17; 4$ **18.** about 16,000 km
19. about 9000 km

4.5 Exercises, pp. 180–181

3. Left side; the coefficient of the x-term is greater on that side. **5.** Right side; the coefficient of the x-term is greater on that side.
7. 2 **9.** 2 **11.** 6 **13.** 1 **15.** 15 **17.** -6
19. 10 **21.** $x = 5; 24$ **23.** $4\frac{3}{4}$ **25.** B

27. The tortoise; the hare will catch up to the tortoise when the tortoise has run $20.1(0.25) = 5.025$ ft. The tortoise will already have crossed the finish line before the hare catches up. **29.** A

4.6 Exercises, pp. 184–185

3. $5 + 2\frac{1}{2}n = 11 + n; 4$ **5. a.** Bookstore cost: $35, $70, $105, $140, $175, $210, $245, $280, $315, $350; CD club cost: $75, $100, $125, $150, $175, $200, $225, $250, $275, $300; if you buy more than 5 CDs, it is cheaper to get them through the club. **b.** 5 **c.** Your friend is correct only if you intend to buy fewer than 5 CDs.

d.

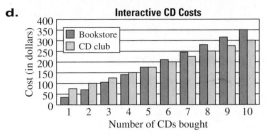

Interactive CD Costs

7. Original Santa Fe temperature $= 86°F$; Rate of decrease $= 3°F$/hour; Number of hours $= h$; Original Minot temperature $= 56°F$; Rate of increase $= 2°F$/hour **9.** 6 **11.** Substitute $h = 6$ into the algebraic model. **13.** 89 skateboards

Spiral Review, p. 186

1. 7 **3.** 2 **5.** 2 **7.** 4 **9.** $6x = 3; \frac{1}{2}$
11. $5x = 1 - x; \frac{1}{6}$ **13.** 17 **15.** $x \geq \frac{1}{2}$
17. $y > 3$ **19.** $r \geq 24$ **21.** 9 families

4.7 Exercises, pp. 190–191

1. A; calculators and computers use decimals in their calculations. **3.** The $=$ sign means an answer is exact, while the $\approx$ sign means an answer has been rounded. **5.** In going from the original equation to the second equation, the 2.8 and 3.9 should have been left unrounded; 5.47.
7. 1.67 **9.** -2.38 **11.** 5.06 **13.** -7.08
15. 2.77 **17.** -5.81 **19.** -1.00 **21.** $2.49

23.

Additional ounces	Calculations	Cost
1	$0.32 + 0.23(1) =$	$.55
2	$0.32 + 0.23(2) =$	$.78
3	$0.32 + 0.23(3) =$	$1.01
4	$0.32 + 0.23(4) =$	$1.24
5	$0.32 + 0.23(5) =$	$1.47
6	$0.32 + 0.23(6) =$	$1.70
7	$0.32 + 0.23(7) =$	$1.93
8	$0.32 + 0.23(8) =$	$2.16

You can have 7 additional ounces, for a total weight of 8 ounces.
25. Provider B **27.** C

4.8 Exercises, pp. 194–195

3. C; the perimeter of a rectangle is twice the length plus twice the width. **5.** B; the perimeter of a square is four times the length of a side.
7. 8 **9.** 80 in. **11.** $x = 3$; width $= 14$ units; length $= 15$ units **13.** 192 in.^{2}

15. $x = 5$; side $= 18$ units   **17.** $x = 8$; length $= 25$ units   **19.** 85 mi² **21.** D

Chapter 4 Review, pp. 197–199

1. 16   **3.** 2   **5.** 12   **7.** 4   **9.** 7   **11.** 6   **13.** 20
15. 11   **17.** –3   **19.** –2   **21.** You will catch up at 2:00 P.M.   **23.** 2.62   **25.** $x = 22$; each side $= 40$ in.

Chapter 5

5.1 Exercises, pp. 206–207

1. Tokyo, Sydney, London, New York, Toronto, Mexico City   **3.** 145 million

5.

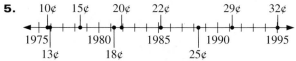

7. about 80 million   **9.** *Sample answer:* There would be half as many airplanes in each row.
11. 10 years   **13.** New Hampshire declared independence from Great Britain.

15.

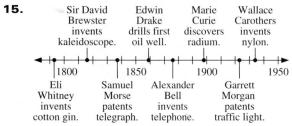

17. B

5.2 Exercises, pp. 210–211

1. Choose intervals and then tally the number of occurrences in each interval.   **3.** Owning a car; Being rich   **5.** simple bar graph; *sample answer:* Each category has one piece of data, so a simple bar graph is sufficient.   **9.** under 5 and 14–17
11. 14–17   **13.** No; the number of 14–17 year-olds, who will be in the 18–24 year-old group in 2010, is less than the 18–24 year-olds in 2005.   **15.** D

Spiral Review, p. 212

1. bar graph   **3.** about 7%   **5.** $\frac{3}{2}$ **7.** $-\frac{13}{2}$

Using a Graphing Calculator, p. 213

1.

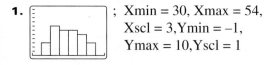 ; Xmin = 30, Xmax = 54, Xscl = 3, Ymin = –1, Ymax = 10, Yscl = 1

5.3 Exercises. pp. 216–217

1. 40   **3.** about 14   **5.** Each color represents a different region of the U.S.   **7.** the South

11.

13. *Sample answer:* The costs for public school are increasing at a slower rate. The change in each 3-year interval is smaller for the public schools. This results in a flatter line graph.   **15.** B

5.4 Exercises, pp. 222–224

1. 2.4   **3.** 426   **5.** *Sample answer:* bar graph, pictograph; choose one of these because the data fall into distinct categories.   **7.** *Sample answer:* bar graph, pictograph; the data fall into distinct categories.

9.

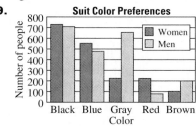

11. about 2.6 million   **13.** *Sample answer:* A line graph makes it easy to trace the changes in the number of players over time.   **15.** D

Spiral Review, p. 224

1. 27   **3.** 23   **5.** 30   **7.** –6   **9.** 10   **11.** 31
13. –12   **15.** 30   **17.** 13   **19.** 66   **21.** 4

Mid-Chapter Assessment, p. 225

1. line graph   **2.** apparel   **3.** restaurants
4. movies

5.

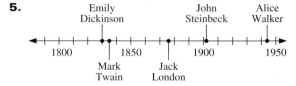

6.

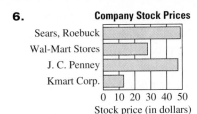

Company Stock Prices

Sample answer: A bar graph or pictograph would be appropriate, because the data fall into categories and you want to compare the totals.

7.

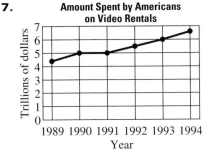

Amount Spent by Americans on Video Rentals

Sample answer: A line graph is appropriate because you want to display changes over time.
8. bar graph **9.** talking on the telephone
10. about 75 **11.** boredom

5.5 Exercises, pp. 228–229

3. There are more than twice as many drummers as saxophone players. **5.** Because of the break in the vertical axis, the graph exaggerates the difference between the number of drummers and the number of saxophone players. **7.** The hourly pay in mid-1996 looks about three times as large as in early 1995. **9.** The graph could be misleading because the vertical scale does not start at zero.
11. the graph on the right; sample answer: The top of the vertical axis is close to the highest point, which makes it appear that the data values are high.

5.6 Exercises, pp. 232–234

1. Sample answer: Statistics is a type of mathematics that involves organizing data. **3.** There are more younger squirrels than older squirrels.
5. Yes; you could have the ages on the line and then make an × for each person in the category.
7.

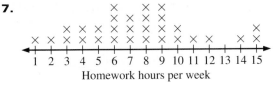

9. a. 4; 6 **b.** 3, 4, and 7; 347, 374, 437, 473, 734, and 743
11. **13.** C

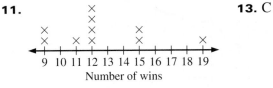

Spiral Review, p. 234

5. $\frac{1}{2}$ **7.** −1 **9.** 41 **11.** 112 in.^{2}

5.7 Exercises, pp. 238–239

1. negative correlation **7.** Positive correlation; in general, the more a student studies, the better his or her test scores should be. **9.** No correlation; the two attributes are not related.
11.

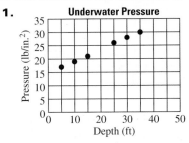

Underwater Pressure

13. about 23.5 lb/in.^{2} **15.** about 12 ft
19. 5, 4, 3, 2, 1 **21.** the data in Example 3; the data in Example 2

5.8 Exercises, pp. 244–245

1. It is equally likely that the event will occur or not occur. **3.** Sample answer: Yes; there is an 80% chance that it will rain. **5.** $\frac{3}{12}$ = 0.25
7. $\frac{1}{12}$ ≈ 0.083 **9.** 0.5 **13.** $\frac{1}{7}$ ≈ 0.14
17. one section red, four sections blue, three sections yellow, and two sections green
19. a. 0.38 **b.** 0.02 **c.** 0.4 **21.** Sample answer: No; the sample of people on one street does not accurately represent the entire population that will vote.

Chapter 5 Review, pp. 247–249

1. about 37.5 lb **3.** a simple bar graph
5. 4–6 year-olds **7.** about $8 billion

9.

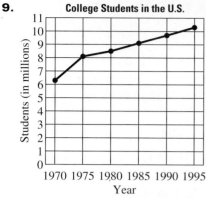

13.

15.

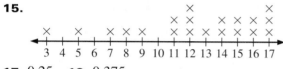

17. 0.25 **19.** 0.375

Chapter 6

6.1 Exercises, pp. 256–257

1. The smaller number can divide evenly into the larger number.   **3.** 1, 2, 3, 4, 6, 9, 12, 18, 36
5. false   **7.** true   **9.** all   **11.** 2, 3, 4, 6, 8
13. 2   **15.** none   **17.** 2, 5, or 8   **19.** 0 or 9
21. 4   **23.** $2 \cdot 3 \cdot 4 \cdot 5 \cdot 3 = 360$; the number $2 \cdot 3 \cdot 4 \cdot 5$ is divisible by 2, 3, 4, 5, and any product of those factors, such as 6, 8, and 10. But this number is not divisible by 9. However, $2 \cdot 3 \cdot 4 \cdot 5 \cdot 3$ *is* divisible by 9 because $3 \cdot 3$ is a factor. So, 360 is the smallest natural number divisible by 2, 3, 4, 5, 6, 8, and 9.   **25.** 1, 2, 3, 4, 6, 9, 12, 18, 36   **27.** 1, 3, 5, 9, 15, 45   **29.** 1, 2, 4, 5, 10, 20, 25, 50, 100   **31.** 1, 2, 3, 4, 6, 8, 12, 16, 24, 32, 48, 96   **33.** 4 or 5 ways; 80 times $1, 16 times $5, 8 times $10, 4 times $20, and possibly 40 times $2   **35.** 40 ft by 40 ft   **37.** If a number is divisible by 3 and the result after the division is not divisible by 3, then the original number is not divisible by 9.   **39. a.** Because 100 is divisible by 4, any multiple of 100 is also divisible by 4. So, only the last 2 digits of a number must be divisible by 4 for the entire number to be divisible by 4.

b. Because 1000 is divisible by 8, any multiple of 1000 is also divisible by 8. So, only the last 3 digits of a number must be divisible by 8 for the entire number to be divisible by 8.   **41.** yes
43. no   **41, 43.** Explanation: Let $a = 3x$ and $b = 3y$. Then $3x + 3y = 3(x + y)$, $3x - 3y = 3(x - y)$, $3x \cdot 3y = 3 \cdot 3 \cdot x \cdot y$, and $3x \div 3y = \frac{x}{y}$; only the last of the four expressions is not divisible by 3.

6.2 Exercises, pp. 262–263

1. **3.**

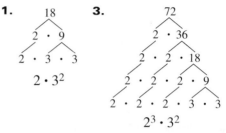

5. true   **7.** true   **9.** prime   **11.** composite;
$35 = 5 \cdot 7$ **13.** $2^2 \cdot 3 = 12$ **15.** $2^2 \cdot 3 \cdot 5 = 60$
17. $2^2 \cdot 3^2$ **19.** $2^2 \cdot 3 \cdot 7$ **21.** 2^5 **23.** $2^3 \cdot 3^2$
25. $(-1) \cdot 3 \cdot 3 \cdot 3$, $(-1) \cdot 3^3$ **27.** $3 \cdot 3 \cdot x \cdot x \cdot x$,
$3^2 \cdot x^3$ **29.** $2 \cdot 2 \cdot 2 \cdot a \cdot a \cdot a \cdot b \cdot b$, $2^3 \cdot a^3 \cdot b^2$
31. $(-1) \cdot 3 \cdot 3 \cdot 5 \cdot m \cdot n \cdot n \cdot n$,
$(-1) \cdot 3^2 \cdot 5 \cdot m \cdot n^3$ **33.** 120   **35.** −585
37. 1, 2, 4, 8   **39.** 1, 2, 4, 8, 16, 32   **41.** Yes; no; there is one new, additional factor each time the even number doubles. That new factor is the new number itself.   **43.** 17, 19; 29, 31; 41, 43; 59, 61; 71, 73   **45.** No; the number of students per group is a factor of the total number of students in the class, which therefore cannot be prime.   **47.** 500, $2^2 \cdot 5^3$; 1000, $2^3 \cdot 5^3$; 5000 = $2^3 \cdot 5^4$; 10,000 = $2^4 \cdot 5^4$; 100,000 = $2^5 \cdot 5^5$

Spiral Review, p. 264

1. divisible by 2, 3, 4, 6, 9   **3.** $\frac{1}{12}$ **5.** $\frac{1}{6}$
7. $3 \cdot 29$ **9.** $2^2 \cdot 19$ **11.** 6   **13.** −7
15. $-3 + (-2) = -5$; 5 under par

6.3 Exercises, pp. 268–269

1. 1, 2, 3, 6; 6   **3.** 1, 5; 5   **5.** 1   **7.** 4   **9.** 30
11. 72   **13.** 128   **19.** no   **21.** no   **23.** 15, 16; yes, GCF is 1.   **25.** 42, 26; no, GCF is 2.   **27.** 6
29. 13 cm lengths; Cut the reeds into 13 cm lengths. This is the longest possible length because it is the GCF of 39, 52, and 65.   **31.** true
33. $3x^2y$ **35.** $14s^3t^3$ **37.** D

6.4 Exercises, pp. 272–273

1. 4, 12, 24 **3.** 12 **5, 7.** LCM = 1800 **5.** C
7. A **9.** 3: 3, 6, 9, 12, 15, 18, 21; 7: 7, 14, 21; 21
11. 6: 6, 12, 18, 24; 8: 8, 16, 24; 24 **13.** 8: 8, 16,
24, 32, 40; 10: 10, 20, 30, 40; 40 **15.** 10: 10, 20,
30, 40, 50, 60, 70, 80, 90, 100, 110, 120, 130; 26:
26, 52, 78, 104, 130; 130 **17.** 3: 3, 6, 9, 12, 15,
18, 21, 24, 27, 30, 33, 36; 4: 4, 8, 12, 16, 20, 24,
28, 32, 36; 18: 18, 36; 36 **19.** 5: 5, 10, 15, 20;
10: 10, 20; 20: 20; 20 **21.** $90 = 2 \cdot 3^2 \cdot 5$; $108 =$
$2^2 \cdot 3^3$; LCM $= 2^2 \cdot 3^3 \cdot 5 = 540$ **23.** $125 = 5^3$;
$500 = 2^2 \cdot 5^3$; LCM $= 2^2 \cdot 5^3 = 500$ **25.** $135 =$
$3 \cdot 3 \cdot 3 \cdot 5$; $375 = 3 \cdot 5 \cdot 5 \cdot 5$; LCM $=$
$3^3 \cdot 5^3 = 3375$ **27.** $144 = 2^4 \cdot 3^2$; $162 = 2 \cdot 3^4$;
LCM $= 2^4 \cdot 3^4 = 1296$ **29.** $7s^2t = 7 \cdot s^2 \cdot t$;
$49st^2 = 7^2 \cdot s \cdot t^2$; LCM $= 7^2 \cdot s^2 \cdot t^2 = 49s^2t^2$
31. $3m^4n^4 = 3 \cdot m^4 \cdot n^4$; $7m^6n^2 = 7 \cdot m^6 \cdot n^2$;
LCM $= 3 \cdot 7 \cdot m^6 \cdot n^4 = 21m^6n^4$ **33.** The LCM
is the product of the two numbers; *sample
answers:* 12, 7: LCM = 84; 3, 11: LCM = 33.
35. 24 **37.** 6 **39.** 7 and 5 **41.** 1 and 36;
4 and 9; 4 and 36; 9 and 36; 36 and 36
43. 14 tiles **45.** 4:00 P.M. **47.** B

6.5 Exercises, pp. 276–277

1. $\frac{3}{9}, \frac{1}{3}$ **3.** $\frac{6}{12}, \frac{1}{2}$ **5.** $\frac{2}{3} = \frac{8}{12}; \frac{3}{4} = \frac{9}{12}; \frac{3}{4}$
7. 2; $\frac{7}{10}$ **9.** 3; $\frac{3}{14}$ **11.** 5; $\frac{2}{15}$ **13.** 18; $\frac{2}{3}$
15. $\frac{a}{4b}$ **17.** $\frac{1}{6z}$ **19.** $\frac{3z}{4}$ **21.** $\frac{2}{3pq}$
23. A fraction is in simplest form when its
numerator and denominator are relatively prime.
29. = **31.** > **33.** = **35.** < **37.** $\frac{3}{21}, \frac{1}{7}$
39. According to the graph, $\frac{7}{21}$ of food servings
should be fruits and vegetables. This simplifies to
$\frac{1}{3}$, which is exactly what your friend suggests.
41. B **43.** C

Spiral Review, p. 278

1. 18 **3.** 12 **5.** $x < 27$ **7.** $y \geq 15$
9.

; none

11. *Sample answers:* (2, 0), (1, 1) **13.** Club 1:
97.86 + 13.98d; Club 2: 95.94 + 15.99d

Mid-Chapter Assessment, p. 279

1. divisible by 2, 3, 5, 6, 10 **2.** divisible by 2, 4,
5, 8, 10 **3.** divisible by 12, 16, 17 **4.** 1, 2, 4, 7,
8, 14, 28, 56 **5.** $2^4 \cdot 5$ **6.** $2^2 \cdot 11$ **7.** $3 \cdot 5 \cdot 7$
8. 12 **9.** 3 **10.** 5 **11.** 65 **12.** 42 **13.** $18x^2$
14. $\frac{1}{5}$ **15.** $\frac{5}{34}$ **16.** $\frac{y}{3}$ **17.** 2; the length of the
square's sides is the LCM of the lengths of the
tile's sides. **18.** 28 **19.** Use three 14 in. boxes,
and seven 6 in. boxes. **20.** least common
multiple

6.6 Exercises, pp. 282–283

1. rational; $-\frac{3}{1}$ **3.** rational; $\frac{13}{5}$ **5.** rational; $\frac{4}{10}$
7. 0.75; $\frac{75}{100}, \frac{3}{4}$ **9.** 0.05; $\frac{5}{100}, \frac{1}{20}$ **11.** $\frac{5}{1}$ **13.** $\frac{1}{4}$
15. $\frac{7}{6}$ **17.** $-\frac{13}{8}$ **19.** 0.6; terminating
21. 2.8284…; nonrepeating **23.** $0.5\overline{3}$;
repeating **25.** 3.5; terminating **27.** $\frac{8}{10}, \frac{4}{5}$
29. $\frac{84}{100}, \frac{21}{25}$ **31.** $\frac{45}{99}, \frac{5}{11}$ **33.** $\frac{21}{9}, \frac{7}{3}$ **35.** E
37. C **39.** F **41.** Each term is $\frac{1}{11}$, or 0.09,
more than the previous term; $0.\overline{09}, 0.\overline{18}, 0.\overline{27}$,
$0.\overline{36}, 0.\overline{45}, 0.\overline{54}$. **43.** $\frac{1}{6}$ **45.** $3\frac{3}{5}$ in., $\frac{18}{5}$ in.,
3.6 in. **47.** $6\frac{2}{3}$ in., $\frac{20}{3}$ in., $6.\overline{6}$ in. **49.** D

6.7 Exercises, pp. 286–287

3. $\frac{1}{5^2}$ **5.** $\frac{1}{x^3}$ **7.** p^7 **9.** $\frac{m^6}{n^4}$ **11.** $\frac{1}{9}$ **13.** 1
15. $\frac{1}{t^4}$ **17.** $\frac{3}{s^2}$ **19.** 36 **21.** x^{15} **23.** 7
25. a^{12} **27.** 0.026 **29.** 5032.844 **31.** 3
33. 6 **35.** 16 **37.** = **39.** > **41.** $10^0, 10^1$,
$10^2, 10^3, 10^4, 10^5, 10^6$; increasing powers of 10
43. 4096 **45.** 10^{-5} **47.** C

6.8 Exercises, pp. 290–291

1. B **3.** −3 **5.** 0.0000087 **7.** 5×10^3
9. 4.1×10^{-4} **11.** 3.261×10^7
13. 1.2×10^{-8} **15.** 0.0057 **17.** 25,000
19. 62,000,000,000 **21.** 0.000000363 **23.** yes
25. no; 2.56×10^9 **27.** no; 7.91×10^{-2}
29. 4.96×10^6; 4,960,000 **31.** 1.8×10^{-6};
0.0000018 **33.** 1×10^9; 9 > 8
35. 4.704×10^{17} **37.** 1×10^{14} **39.** in order
from lightest to heaviest: Hydrogen: 8.375×10^{-5};
Helium: 1.664×10^{-4}; Nitrogen: 1.165×10^{-3};
Oxygen: 1.332×10^{-3}; Chlorine: 2.95×10^{-3}

Using a Calculator, p. 292

1. 2.268×10^7 **3.** 1.107×10^{-11}
5. 5.697×10^{10} **7.** 2.5×10^{-8}
9. The sequence of keystrokes shown does not account for order of operations, and therefore will not give the desired result. The $\boxed{EE}$ key, unlike the power key, is designed to compute using scientific notation.

6.9 Exercises, pp. 296–297

1. 3, 9, 19, 33, 51, 73 **3.** 2, 3, 4, 5, 6; each difference is one greater than the previous difference; 28, 36.

5.

n	1	2	3	4	5	6
$n^2 + 1$	2	5	10	17	26	37

7.

n	1	2	3	4	5	6
$2^n - 1$	1	2	4	8	16	32

9. 16, 22, 29; differences are consecutive numbers. **11.** −30, −48, −69; differences are −3, −6, −9, −12, and so on. **13.** $4\frac{1}{2}$

15. 45, 66;

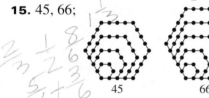

45   66

17. $1 + 2 + 5 \neq 10$, so 10 is not perfect; $1 + 2 + 3 + 4 + 6 \neq 12$, so 12 is not perfect.
19. 496 **21.** Add the previous three numbers together to get the next term; 44, 81, 149. **23.** B

Chapter 6 Review, pp. 299–301

1. divisible by 2, 3, 4, 5, 6, 9, 10 **3.** divisible by 5 **5.** yes **7.** 15 **9.** 1 **11.** 68 **13.** 52
15. $\frac{16}{3}$ **17.** $\frac{100x}{7}$ **19.** $0.6\overline{3}$ **21.** $\frac{4}{x^4}$ **23.** $15y^6$
25. 7.43×10^5 **27.** 1.203×10^6 **29.** 26, 37, 50 **31.** 0, −5, −11

Chapters 1–6 Cumulative Review, pp. 304–307

1. Add 7; 35, 42, 49. **3.** Skip 1 letter; I, K, M.
5. $2 \cdot 5 = 10$ **7.** 78,125 **9.** 9.17 **11.** 0.65
13. 4.22 **15.** 7 **17.** −180 **19.** 48
21. $x + 5 = 21$; 16 **23.** $4z = 32$; 8 **25.** Cost of palette + Total cost of tubes of paint = Money needed **27.** $\$5.70 + 8 \cdot \$2.70 = x$
29. $5.70 + 8 \cdot 2.70 = 27.30$ **31.** $y \cdot (-8) = -104$; 13 **33.** $x - 9 = -18$; −9

35. $7m > 147$; $m > 21$ **37.** 8, 0, 3, 9, 10, 6, 0
39. $5x + 5y + 5z$; 35 **41.** $-6x - 2y + 3z$; 19
43. $-7 + xz + xy$; −25 **45.** 4, 3, 2, 1; decreases by 1 **47.** 147, 126, 105, 84; decreases by 21
49. 8 units; 4 square units **51.** 12 units; 9 square units **53.** 4 **55.** 28 **57.** 12 **59.** 3 **61.** −0.9
63. $\frac{1}{2}$ **65.** 1.9 **67.** 0.8 **69.** Each category has two pieces of data, so a double bar graph is the best choice to represent the data.

71.

```
          ×
      × ×
      × ×
      × ×
      × ×       ×
      × × × ×
  × × × × × ×
  +--+--+--+--+--+
  0  1  2  3  4  5
```

73. Salary increases with years of service.
75. $\frac{1}{16}$ **77.** $\frac{1}{2}$ **79.** 5 **81.** 3 **83.** 3, 9
85. 2, 3, 5, 6, 9, 10 **87.** 7, 7^2; 49 **89.** $2 \cdot 3^3 \cdot 5$, $2 \cdot 3^2 \cdot 5^2$; 1350 **91.** $2 \cdot 3 \cdot x^2 \cdot y$, $2^3 \cdot x \cdot y^3$; $24x^2y^3$ **93.** 6; $\frac{1}{8}$ **95.** 5; $\frac{2}{3}$ **97.** 1 **99.** $\frac{1}{a^4}$
101. $\frac{4}{5a}$ **103.** $\frac{1}{3}$

Chapter 7

7.1 Exercises, pp. 312–313

1. $\frac{5}{6} - \frac{3}{6} = \frac{2}{6}$, or $\frac{1}{3}$ **5.** $\frac{1}{3}$ **7.** $\frac{-5}{4}$ **9.** $\frac{4y}{5}$ **11.** $\frac{-2}{3}$
13. $\frac{-7}{4t}$ **15.** $\frac{-3}{8x}$ **17.** $\frac{11}{8}$ **19.** $-\frac{4}{3}$ **21.** $\frac{2}{11}$ **23.** 1
25. 0.67 **27.** −0.38 **29.** $\frac{9}{2}, -\frac{11}{2}, \frac{5}{2}, -\frac{11}{2}$; the odd terms (first, third, and so on) decrease by $\frac{4}{2}$ each time, while all of the even terms equal $-\frac{11}{2}$; $\frac{1}{2}, -\frac{11}{2}, -\frac{3}{2}$ **31.** The student added the fractional parts incorrectly; $\frac{1}{3} + \frac{1}{3} = \frac{2}{3}$, so $3 + \frac{2}{3} = 3\frac{2}{3}$.
33. $\frac{6}{8} - \frac{5}{8} = \frac{1}{8}$ **35.** B

7.2 Exercises, pp. 318–319

1. $\frac{2}{3}, \frac{1}{2}; \frac{7}{6}$
3. $\frac{2}{5} + \frac{1}{3} = \frac{2 \cdot 3}{5 \cdot 3} + \frac{1 \cdot 5}{3 \cdot 5}$ LCD of 5 and 3 is 15.

$\qquad = \frac{6}{15} + \frac{5}{15}$ Rewrite as like fractions.

$\qquad = \frac{11}{15}$ Add like fractions.

5. $\dfrac{a}{2} - \dfrac{a}{3} = \dfrac{a \cdot 3}{2 \cdot 3} - \dfrac{a \cdot 2}{3 \cdot 2}$ LCD of 2 and 3 is 6.

$\qquad = \dfrac{3a}{6} - \dfrac{2a}{6}$ Rewrite as like fractions.

$\qquad = \dfrac{a}{6}$ Subtract like fractions.

7. $\dfrac{3}{4}$ **9.** $-\dfrac{13}{12}$ **11.** $-\dfrac{1}{3}$ **13.** $\dfrac{23}{40}$ **15.** $\dfrac{x}{2}$

17. $\dfrac{20 + 9x}{10x}$ **19.** $-\dfrac{10}{9t}$ **21.** $\dfrac{5}{3n}$ **23.** The numerators and denominators both increase by 1 each time, and the sign of the terms alternates between positive and negative. **25.** $\dfrac{7}{12}$ **27.** $7\dfrac{2}{3}$

29. $\dfrac{23}{50}$ **31.** $\dfrac{11}{100} + \dfrac{7}{25} + \dfrac{7}{25} + \dfrac{9}{50} + \dfrac{3}{20} =$
$\dfrac{11}{100} + \dfrac{28}{100} + \dfrac{28}{100} + \dfrac{18}{100} + \dfrac{15}{100} = \dfrac{100}{100} = 1$ **33.** C

7.3 Exercises, pp. 322–323

1. Write as rounded decimals; add decimals; round to two decimal places. **3.** $0.67; \dfrac{2}{3} = 0.6666\ldots,$ which is less than 0.67. **5.** 0.86 **7.** 1.64

9. $\dfrac{17}{36} + \dfrac{14}{25}; \dfrac{929}{900}$, or about 1.03 **15.** 1.48

17. \$1.50 **19.** 0.16 **21.** $3\dfrac{3}{4}$ min **23.** D

7.4 Exercises, pp. 326–327

3. 1 **5.** 4 **7.** $\dfrac{3}{6}$ by $\dfrac{6}{7}$; $\dfrac{3}{7}$ sq. units **9.** $\dfrac{3}{4}$ by $\dfrac{7}{8}$;
$\dfrac{21}{32}$ sq. units **11.** $-\dfrac{16}{27}$ **13.** $3\dfrac{1}{5}$ **15.** $11\dfrac{1}{2}$

17. $\dfrac{1}{9}$ **19.** $\dfrac{56y}{3}$ **21.** $\dfrac{a}{3}$ **23.** 2 in.^{2} **25.** 0.260

27. –3.354 **29.** $\dfrac{1}{4}; \dfrac{2}{3}; \dfrac{1}{6}$ **31.** $\dfrac{1}{5}; \dfrac{5}{8}; \dfrac{1}{8}$ **33.** 30 ft

35. 15 ft **37.** $\dfrac{12}{100}$, or $\dfrac{3}{25}$ **39.** $\dfrac{30}{100}$, or $\dfrac{3}{10}$

Spiral Review, p. 328

1. ÷ **3.** ÷ **5.** × **7.** $\dfrac{2}{3}$ **9.** 3 **11.** 14

13. 60 **15.** $\dfrac{3}{10}$ **17.** $\dfrac{3}{4}$ **19.** $\dfrac{3}{7}$

Mid-Chapter Assessment, p. 329

1. $\dfrac{4}{11}$ **2.** $\dfrac{2}{3}$ **3.** $\dfrac{27}{50}$ **4.** $\dfrac{2}{5}$ **5.** $-\dfrac{1}{2}$ **6.** $\dfrac{2}{5}$ **7.** $\dfrac{7}{5}$

8. $-\dfrac{12}{25}$ **9.** 0.90 **10.** $1.35x$ **11.** $0.14y$

12. 0.65 **13.** $15\dfrac{7}{15}$ in.; $12\dfrac{4}{5}$ in.^{2} **14.** $\dfrac{7}{16}$ sq.

units **15.** \$10 **16.** \$15; \$15 **17.** $\dfrac{8}{11}$ **18.** B

7.5 Exercises, pp. 332–333

1. 5 **3.** $\dfrac{1}{7}$ **5.** In the first step, you should multiply by $\dfrac{1}{3}$. This gives $\dfrac{5}{6} \cdot \dfrac{1}{3} = \dfrac{5 \cdot 1}{6 \cdot 3} = \dfrac{5}{18}$.

7. $\dfrac{3}{5}$ **9.** $\dfrac{2n}{9}$ **11.** 4 **13.** $\dfrac{5}{7a}$ **15.** In the first step, you should take the reciprocal of the divisor, not of the dividend. This gives $-\dfrac{3}{2} \cdot \dfrac{5}{3} = \dfrac{-3 \cdot 5}{2 \cdot 3} = -\dfrac{5}{2}$.
17. In the first step, you should multiply by 3. This gives $\dfrac{1}{3} \cdot \dfrac{3}{1} = \dfrac{3}{3} = 1$. **19.** $\dfrac{9}{2}$ **21.** $\dfrac{15}{2}$
23. $-\dfrac{18}{5}$ **25.** –7 **27.** $\dfrac{8}{15}$ **29.** $-\dfrac{x}{15}$ **31.** $\dfrac{4n}{5}$
33. $\dfrac{5}{6}$ **35.** $\dfrac{1}{12}$ **37.** $\dfrac{1}{20}$ **39.** 3; *sample:*
How many $2\dfrac{3}{4}$ are in 11? Although
$11 \div 2\dfrac{3}{4} = 4$, the fourth stop is not a rest.
41. 8; *sample answer:* I needed to know how many $\dfrac{3}{8}$ there are in 3. **43.** $\dfrac{7}{6}$ **45.** 1 **47.** D

Spiral Review, p. 334

1. 8; 12 units by 12 units **3.** 11.4; 11.4 units; 22.8 units; 16.8 units **5.** $\dfrac{19}{18}$ **7.** $-\dfrac{17}{40}$ **9.** $\dfrac{1}{3}$
11. $\dfrac{2}{3}$

7.6 Exercises, pp. 338–339

1. first row: 24%, 24 percent; second row: $\dfrac{83}{100}$, 83 percent; third row: $\dfrac{49}{100}$, 49% **3.** 45%
5. 36% **7.** 34% **9.** D; A **11.** 5% **13.** 28%
15. 45% **17.** 60% **23.** 50% **25.** 50%
27. Subtract the percent that is water from 100%.

7.7 Exercises, pp. 342–343

1. 0.6 **3.** 0.667 **5.** 36%, 0.36 **7.** 12%, 0.12
9. *Sample answer:* First remove the percent sign. Then divide by 100. 48% = 0.48 **11.** *Sample answer:* Multiply the decimal by 100 and add the percent sign. 0.045 = 4.5% **13.** 0.36 **15.** 1.15
17. 25% **19.** 70% **21.** $\dfrac{13}{25}$ **23.** $\dfrac{3}{50}$ **25.** $\dfrac{8}{5}$
27. $\dfrac{51}{50}$ **29.** 0.0625; 6.25% **31.** 0.7879; 78.79%
33. 1.625; 162.5% **35.** 3.3333; 333.33% **37.** >
39. = **41.** B **43.** D **47.** because people can have access to any or all of the media **49.** D

7.8 Exercises, pp. 346–347

1. *Sample answer:* First write the percent as a decimal. Then multiply the result by the number.
3. a. 4.8 **b.** 32 **c.** 32 **d.** 46 **5.** 0.8; 228
7. 3.4; 17 **9.** 2.5; 115 **11.** 0.065; 52 **13.** C; 72 **15.** B; 40 **19.** 24 **21.** 312 **23. a.** \$14
b. \$26 **25.** about 9.78 million mi^3 **27.** about 9.3×10^{18} gal **29.** D

Using a Computer, p. 348

3. $1603.57 **5.** $1469.33

7.9 Exercises, pp. 352–353

1. $20.93 **3.** $4.37 **5.** $4.84 **7.** $52
9. 23.2% **11.** 13.2% **13.** 6% **15.** 4%
17. 3.6% **19.** 2.4% **21.** 2% **23.** $370.13
25. $117.65 **27.** $40.30 **29.** $9.75
31. about 37,700 **33.** C

Chapter 7 Review, pp. 355–357

1. $\frac{2}{3}$ **3.** $\frac{5}{3}$ **5.** $\frac{w}{6}$ **7.** $1\frac{1}{3}$ **9.** $\frac{11}{18}$ **11.** $\frac{9+2w}{6}$
13. $\frac{3}{4}$ **15.** $-\frac{4a}{25}$ **17.** $\frac{9}{50}$ **19.** 0.65 **21.** 1.62
23. 0.24 **25.** $\frac{1}{12}$ **27.** $\frac{2}{33}$ **29.** $\frac{4}{39}$ **31.** 12
33. $\frac{4}{3}$ **35.** $\frac{9n}{5}$ **37.** 35% **39.** 20% **41.** 0.06
43. 88.9% **45.** 36 **47.** 54 **49.** Wyoming, Ohio, and Utah

Chapter 8

8.1 Exercises, pp. 364–365

1. The two quantities in a rate have different units; $3 per hour. The two quantities in a ratio have the same units, and it simplifies to a number without any units; $\frac{5 \text{ in.}}{10 \text{ in.}}$. **3.** ratio; $\frac{5}{2}$ **5.** rate; $9.33/lb **7.** $\frac{4}{9}, \frac{5}{9}, \frac{4}{5}, \frac{5}{4}, \frac{9}{5}, \frac{9}{4}$ **9.** ratio; $\frac{8}{9}$
11. rate; 22 points/game **13.** $\frac{4 \text{ doctors}}{5 \text{ doctors}}$; ratio; same units **15.** $\frac{1600 \text{ mi}}{3 \text{ days}}$; rate; different units
17. $\frac{24 \text{ in.}}{18 \text{ in.}} = \frac{4}{3}$ **19.** $\frac{120 \text{ s}}{300 \text{ s}} = \frac{2}{5}$ **21.** $\frac{640¢}{400¢} = \frac{8}{5}$
23. $\frac{200 \text{ cm}}{300 \text{ cm}} = \frac{2}{3}$ **25.** 1500 tickets/h
27. 10 apples is a better buy; $.179 < $.197.
29. 2 lb, 4 oz is a better buy; $.219 < $.230.
31. 41.2 mi/h **33.** $\frac{16}{9}; \frac{3}{4}$; perimeter **35.** $\frac{12}{17}; \frac{3}{8}$; perimeter **37.** B

8.2 Exercises, pp. 370–371

1. no; *sample answer:* $\frac{2000}{80,000} = 2.5\%$, $\frac{3000}{100,000} = 3\%$; $2.5\% < 3\%$ **3.** 1 **5.** 24 **7.** similar; $\frac{a}{d} = \frac{b}{e} = \frac{c}{f}$ **9.** True; cross products are equal.
11. True; cross products are equal. **13.** $\frac{4}{3}$
15. $1\frac{3}{7}$ **17.** 20 **19.** 18 **21.** $\frac{x}{6} = \frac{8}{9}; \frac{16}{3}$

23. $\frac{3}{8} = \frac{m}{24}$; 9 **25.** $\frac{5}{6} = \frac{12}{s}; \frac{72}{5}$ **27.** 23.33
29. 4 **31. a.** Canoe 1: 125 min; 2.08 h; Canoe 2: 133.3 min; 2.22 h **b.** Canoe 1: 9.6 mi/h; Canoe 2: 9 mi/h **c.** Canoe 1
33. $d = 4; f = 5$ **35.** $d = 1\frac{1}{10}, f = \frac{1}{2}$ **37.** B

8.3 Exercises, pp. 374–375

1.

3. $\frac{h}{5 \text{ ft}} = \frac{15 \text{ ft}}{3 \text{ ft}}$
5. 12
7. 160 beats/min
9. about 4 million
11. about $2000

13. Let a = actual width of amoeba; $\frac{25 \text{ mm}}{a} = \frac{100}{1}$.
15. 1024 pixels

8.4 Exercises, pp. 378–379

1. Simplify, then multiply both sides by 160.
3. 25; 80% **5.** Base is unknown; $b = 120$
7. 52 **9.** 5 **11.** 54.45 **13.** 55 **15.** 225%
17. 30 **19.** 68.85 **21.** 100 **23.** 33.33%
25. $\frac{a}{50} = \frac{24}{100}$ **27.** 5% **29.** about 35% **31.** B

Spiral Review, p. 380

1. 1 **3.** 2 **5.** $\frac{1}{2}$ **7.** 3 **9.** 12 **11.** 0.83
13. 2.06 **15.** rate; 7 points/quarter **17.** rate; 0.4 ft/s

Mid-Chapter Assessment, p. 381

1. rate; $5.\overline{5}$ m/s **2.** rate; 3 lures/fisherman
3. ratio; $\frac{14}{1}$ **4.** rate; 5 days/week **5.** similar; $\frac{a}{d} = \frac{b}{e} = \frac{c}{f}$ **6.** not similar **7.** true; 110 = 110
8. false; $750 \neq 700$ **9.** true; 175 = 175 **10.** 16
11. $\frac{27}{7}$ **12.** 25.92 **13.** 15 **14.** 6.3 **15.** 12
16. 24% **17.** 630 ft **18.** 13.5 **19.** 11.25

8.5 Exercises, pp. 384–385

1. a. $54.50 **b.** 30% **3.** 45 **5.** 1,000,000
7. $470(1.035) = $470(1 + 0.035)
9. 343 million **11.** 18.5% **13.** $85.60
15. Add the total income for all categories.
17. C

8.6 Exercises, pp. 388–389

1. 41.7% **3.** percent of increase; 11.4%

5. 20% increase   **7.** 20% decrease
9. 122% increase   **11.** 17.7% increase
13. 20.7% decrease   **15.** increases by 100%; 16, 32, 64   **17.** decreases by 80%; 25, 5, 1
19. *Sample answer:* Due to above normal precipitation, the summer corn crop yield was 15% greater than usual.   **21.** 60% increase; 60% decrease; 500; 300   **23.** true; $2x - x = x$, $\frac{x}{x} = 1 = 100\%$ **25.** false; $20\% \cdot 80 = 16$, $80 - 16 = 64$, $64 \neq 60$ **27.** 11.3%   **29.** 4.2%, 4%, 3.8%, 3.7%, 3.6%; the percent of increase gets smaller every year in Job 2.   **31.** D

Spiral Review, p. 390

1. $\frac{3}{8}$ **3.** $\frac{1}{4}$ **5.** 16   **7.** 6

9.

-4 -3 -2 -1 0 1 2 3 4

11. −1.01   **13.** 40   **15.** $12x + 20y$; −20
17. $71.\overline{1}$ **19.** 106.72

8.7 Exercises, pp. 394–395

1. 8   **3.** 72   **5.** 20; Let W = white rice, R = rice pilaf, B = baked potatoes, M = mashed potatoes, H = home fries, C = cole slaw, G = green beans, V = mixed vegetables, and S = salad. The 20 combinations are WC, WG, WV, WS, RC, RG, RV, RS, BC, BG, BV, BS, MC, MG, MV, MS, HC, HG, HV, HS.   **7.** A; each question is an event that can occur in 2 ways, so use the Counting Principle.   **9.** 35   **11.** 6   **13.** C

Using a Computer, p. 397

1. 100,000   **3.** 1.007%

8.8 Exercises, pp. 400–401

1. 10   **3.** $\frac{3}{10}$, or 0.3   **5.** $\frac{1}{4}$, or 0.25   **9.** $\frac{1}{20}$, or 0.05
11. $\frac{1}{100}$, or 0.01   **13.** $\frac{105}{676}$, or 0.155   **17.** $\frac{1}{40}$, or 0.025   **19.** $\frac{2 \cdot 4}{40}$, or 0.2   **21.** $\frac{3 \cdot 4}{40}$, or 0.3

Chapter 8 Review, pp. 403–405

1. $\frac{1500 \text{ mi}}{2 \text{ days}}$; rate   **3.** turkey; turkey = $1.25/lb, beef = $1.99/lb   **5.** 3.6   **7.** $\frac{80}{7}$ **9.** 10
11. 87.5%   **13.** 176   **15.** $8.25   **17.** 5% increase   **19.** No; there are 6 possible choices.

21. $\frac{1}{676}$, or 0.001

Chapter 9

9.1 Exercises, pp. 412–413

1. Since $2^2 = 4$ and $(-2)^2 = 4$, both 2 and −2 are solutions.   **3.** $\sqrt{5}$, $-\sqrt{5}$ or 2.24, −2.24   **5.** $\frac{5}{2}$, $-\frac{5}{2}$
7. $\sqrt{14}$, $-\sqrt{14}$ or 3.74, −3.74   **9.** 8, −8   **11.** 16, −16   **13.** 0.6, −0.6   **15.** 3, −3   **17.** 4.69, −4.69
19. 5, −5   **21.** 9, −9   **23.** 4.5   **25.** 5.6
27. $\sqrt{25} = x$; 5   **29.** $a^2 + 6 = 15$; 3, −3
31. 1.1 s   **33.** 6.7 mi   **35.** C

9.2 Exercises, pp. 416–417

1. *Sample answer:* A rational number can be expressed as a quotient of 2 integers.   **3. a.** rational; terminates   **b.** rational; repeats   **c.** irrational; neither repeats nor terminates   **5.** irrational
7. rational   **9.** rational; quotient of integers
11. Irrational; decimal neither repeats nor terminates.   **13.** Rational; decimal terminates.
15. Irrational; decimal neither repeats nor terminates.   **17.** Sometimes; both 5 and $\sqrt{5}$ are real numbers, but 5 is rational and $\sqrt{5}$ is irrational.
19. Never; all integers are rational numbers.
21. 3.414…; no   **23.** 6; yes   **25.** E   **27.** C
29. B
31. $<$ **33.** $<$ **35.** $-2\frac{1}{4}$, $-1\frac{1}{2}$, $-\frac{7}{8}$
37. −1.3, −0.75, −0.5   **39.** 25%, $\frac{1}{2}$, 0.75

9.3 Exercises, pp. 422–423

1. ; $m^2 + n^2 = t^2$ **3.** 9.2   **5.** never

7. sometimes   **9.** 13.04   **11.** 9   **13.** 9.98
15.   **17.** not possible   **19.** 8.49

21. 36   **23.** 8.9 ft, or 8 ft 11 in.   **25.** 5.7 ft, or 5 ft 8 in.   **27.**   **29.** C

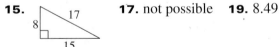

Spiral Review, p. 424

1. 5   **3.** 99.70   **5.** $x \geq 7$ **7.** $n > \frac{8}{5}$ **9.** 3
11. 2   **13.** no

9.4 Exercises, pp. 428–429

3. 29.21 m; 35 m^2 **5.** 53.24 in.; 69.72 in.^{2}
7. 90 mi; 180 mi^2 **9.** 8 ft; 4 ft^2 **11.** 6 ft
13. 147.56 ft   **15.** C

Using a Calculator, p. 430

1. 216 ft

Mid-Chapter Assessment, p. 431

1. 4, –4   **2.** 11, –11   **3.** 0.7, –0.7   **4.** 0.6, –0.6
5. 5.74 cm   **6.** 11 in.   **7.** $\sqrt{7}$, $-\sqrt{7}$ or 2.65,
–2.65   **8.** 7, –7   **9.** 1, –1   **10.** $\sqrt{13}$, $-\sqrt{13}$ or
3.61, –3.61   **11.** Irrational; decimal neither
repeats nor terminates.   **12.** Rational; $\sqrt{25}$ = 5,
an integer.   **13.** Irrational; decimal neither repeats nor terminates.   **14.** Rational; $\sqrt{0.25}$ =
0.5, a terminating decimal.   **15.** 12.37   **16.** 5
17. 90.51   **18.** 35.36   **19.** 21 in.   **20.** 70 in.
21. 210 in.^{2} **22.** false

9.5 Exercises, pp. 434–435

1. C   **3.** B   **5.** $x < 15$, $15 > x$ **7.** $x > -3$,
$-3 < x$ **9.** $x < -7$

11.

13.

15. $x \geq -5$ **17.** $x \leq -1$
19. $x > \sqrt{2}$;

21. $x < -\sqrt{3}$

23. $x \geq -1$

25. $17 < n$

27. $z > -9$

29. $-20 \geq x$; all real numbers less than or
equal to –20   **31.** $17 > s$; all real numbers less
than 17   **33.** D; the speed of the car is at first 0
and then increases to 48.71 mi/h.
35. $T \geq -459.7°F$ **37.** B; only the units are
graphed since each person is a "unit."   **39.** D

Spiral Review, p. 436

1. 400 ft   **3.** 10.1 ft
5. $2 > x$;

---

7. $13 \geq x$;

9. $2^3 \cdot 3^2 \cdot 5$ **11.** $3^3 \cdot 7$ **13.** $2^4 \cdot 23$

9.6 Exercises, pp. 440–441

1. $<$ **3.** $>$ **5.** yes   **7.** no   **9.** $b > 6$
11. $-25 < h$ **13.** Divide both sides by –0.4.
15. Reverse inequality when dividing by –4.
17. B   **19.** A

21. $n \geq \dfrac{5}{2}$;

23. $y > 36$;

25. $a < -\dfrac{1}{4}$;

27. $p \geq -10$;

29. $x \leq 3$;

31. $4 \geq m$;

33. $y \leq -10$;

35. $6 > x$;

37. $s \geq 400$; at least 400 sandwiches must be
sold.   **39.** at most 120 km   **41.** A

9.7 Exercises, pp. 444–445

1. $x \leq 5$;

$3x - 2 \leq 13$	Write original equation.
$3x - 2 + 2 \leq 13 + 2$	Add 2 to each side.
$3x \leq 15$	Simplify.
$\dfrac{3x}{3} \leq \dfrac{15}{3}$	Divide each side by 3.
$x \leq 5$	

3. when you multiply or divide each side of an
inequality by a negative number   **5.** $y \geq 3$;

7. Do not reverse inequality; $y < -\dfrac{2}{3}$.   **9.** never
11. always   **13.** C   **15.** B   **17.** $x > 3$
19. $a \geq -3$ **21.** $m \leq 4$ **23.** $x \geq -2$
25. $x \geq -3$ **27.** $n + (n + 1) + (n + 2) > 18$;
$n > 5$ **29.** $x \leq -4$ **31.** at least 7 oz   **35.** D

9.8 Exercises, pp. 448–449

1. A, C   **3.** no;

5. between 2 ft and 8 ft

7. between 4 cm and 36 cm   **9.** no; 8 + 5 = 13
11. yes; 5 + 5 > 5   **13.** yes   **15.** no   **17.** Yes;
the sum of each two sections appears longer than
the remaining section.   **19.** e **21.** c **23.** less
than 7.5 in.   **25.** 28 and 50   **27.** D

Chapter 9 Review, pp. 451–453

1. 13, –13   **3.** 3, –3
5. rational, irrational, rational;

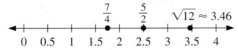

7. irrational, rational, rational;

9. 10.63   **11.** 7.62   **13.** 4 ft
15. $x > -3$;

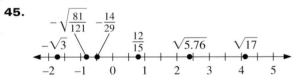

17. $-\dfrac{5}{2} < x$;

19. $x < \dfrac{16}{15}$;

21. yes   **23.** It is between 2 in. and 12 in.

Chapters 7–9 Cumulative Review, pp. 456–457

1. $\dfrac{6}{7}$ **3.** $\dfrac{5}{12}$ **5.** 1.53   **7.** –1.83   **9.** $\dfrac{25}{18}$
11. $28n$ **13.** 19.9 ft; 23.98 ft^2 **15.** 27 m; 35 m^2
17. 72%   **19.** 120%   **21.** $662.46   **23.** ratio;
5 to 3   **25.** rate; 42 m/s   **27.** 36   **29.** 34.375
31. 70%   **33.** 200   **35.** 150   **37.** 51   **39.** 9
41. 35% decrease   **43.** 200
45.

47. 17.49
49. $a < -5$;

51. $\dfrac{2}{3} \le m$;

53. yes   **55.** no

Chapter 10

10.1 Exercises, pp. 462–463

1. B   **3.** D   **5.** (1) $\overrightarrow{RS}$ (2) $\overleftrightarrow{AB}$ (3) $\overleftrightarrow{PQ}$
7. *Sample answer:* $\overleftrightarrow{CD}$, $\overleftrightarrow{CE}$, $\overleftrightarrow{DE}$, $\overleftrightarrow{DF}$

9. $\overrightarrow{EC}$, $\overrightarrow{EB}$, $\overrightarrow{EF}$, $\overrightarrow{EJ}$, $\overrightarrow{EH}$ **11.** *Sample answer:* $\overleftrightarrow{CF}$
and $\overleftrightarrow{AG}$, $\overleftrightarrow{BH}$ and $\overleftrightarrow{CF}$ **13.** Yes; they have the same
endpoints.   **15.** $3\dfrac{1}{2}$ **17.** $\overline{AB}$, $\overline{AC}$, $\overline{AD}$, $\overline{AE}$, $\overline{BC}$,
$\overline{CD}$, $\overline{DE}$, $\overline{BE}$ **19.** B, C, D, E   **21.** *Sample*
answer: $\overrightarrow{AB}$, $\overrightarrow{AC}$, $\overrightarrow{AD}$, $\overrightarrow{AE}$
23.   **25.**

27. $BD = 42$ ft, $DF = 42$ ft   **29.** No; the base
of a window on the side of the building is not
parallel to the base of a window on the front of
the building because parallel lines must be in the
same plane.   **31.** C

10.2 Exercises, pp. 466–467

1. X   **3.** $\angle X$, $\angle WXY$, $\angle YXW$, $\angle ZXW$ **5.** 90°;
right   **7.** about 70°; acute   **9.** 7; $\angle DAE$, $\angle ADE$,
$\angle CDE$, $\angle DCE$, $\angle BDC$, $\angle BCD$, $\angle CBD$
11. 90°   **13.** vertex: D; sides: $\overrightarrow{DC}$ and $\overrightarrow{DE}$;
naming the angle simply $\angle D$ could refer also to
$\angle BDC$ or $\angle ADE$.   **15.** 45°   **17.** supplementary
angles; $m\angle 1 + m\angle 4 = 180°$ **23.** about 100°
25. about 75°   **27.** straight   **29.** obtuse   **31.** A

Spiral Review, p. 468

1, 3.

5. $\overleftrightarrow{AB}$ and $\overleftrightarrow{CD}$, $\overleftrightarrow{AD}$ and $\overleftrightarrow{BC}$
7. 5.66   **9.** D   **11.** A
13. $\dfrac{7}{6}$ **15.** 6   **17.** $\dfrac{10 - 2y}{5y}$
19. $\dfrac{a}{10}$

10.3 Exercises, pp. 472–473

1. m and n **3.** $\angle 1$ and $\angle 5$, $\angle 2$ and $\angle 6$, $\angle 3$ and
$\angle 7$, $\angle 4$ and $\angle 8$ **5.** 55°; $\angle 4 \cong \angle 2$ because they
are vertical angles.   **7.** 45°, 135°, and 135°; the
45° angle will form vertical angles with another
angle. The 45° angles will be supplementary to
the two other angles.   **9.** Lines k and m are not
parallel.   **11.** $\angle 5$, $\angle 8$ **13.** $\angle 6$, $\angle 7$
15. *Sample answer:* $\angle 4$ and $\angle 12$ **17.** $\angle 3 \cong$
$\angle 4$ because they are vertical angles; $\angle 2 \cong \angle 3$ by
the corresponding angles property of parallel
lines; and $\angle 1 \cong \angle 2$ by the corresponding angles
property of parallel lines.
19. $\overleftrightarrow{KV}$, $\overleftrightarrow{MW}$, $\overleftrightarrow{QX}$, and $\overleftrightarrow{UY}$; $\overleftrightarrow{LM}$, $\overleftrightarrow{NQ}$, $\overleftrightarrow{RU}$, and $\overleftrightarrow{VZ}$

23. $m \angle 1 = m \angle 4 = 63°$; $m \angle 2 = m \angle 3 = 117°$, $m \angle 5 = m \angle 8 = 146°$, $m \angle 6 = m \angle 7 = 34°$ **25.** 6 angle measures: 25°, 65°, 90°, 115°, 155°, and 180°

10.4 Exercises, pp. 476–477

1. *Sample answer:* books, backs of chairs, light fixtures   **3.** vertical and horizontal line symmetry; rotational symmetry at 180°
5. horizontal line symmetry   **7.** vertical and horizontal lines of symmetry; rotational symmetry at 180°   **9.** no symmetry
15. 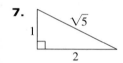   **17.**  or

19. yes; *sample answer:*

21. The butterfly has line symmetry along the length of its body.   **23.** BOX   **25.** OHIO   **27.** A

10.5 Exercises, pp. 480–481

1. C, D   **3.** C, G   **5.**

7.    **9.**

11. right scalene   **13.** obtuse isosceles
15. obtuse scalene   **17.** acute scalene
19. equiangular, acute   **21.** acute isosceles
23. right scalene   **25.** obtuse scalene
27. scalene right   **29.** obtuse scalene   **31.** No; the measure of each angle is 60°.   **33.** There are acute triangles and obtuse triangles.   **35.** B

Spiral Review, p. 482

1. vertical line symmetry   **3.** vertical and horizontal line symmetry; rotational symmetry at 180° in either direction   **5.** 3.14   **7.** $\frac{2}{3}$ **9.** $\frac{5}{6}$
11. 9.2×10^{-4} **13.** 4.6×10^{-7}
15. 7.04×10^{-2} **17.** $\frac{2}{9}$ **19.** $\frac{1}{20}$ **21.** $\frac{1}{15}$

Mid-Chapter Assessment, p. 483

1. Q **2.** any two of $\overleftrightarrow{KL}$, $\overleftrightarrow{MN}$, and $\overleftrightarrow{PQ}$ **3.** P
4. up   **5.** $\angle CFA$ and $\angle CFE$ **6.** $\angle BFA$, $\angle BFC$, $\angle CFD$, and $\angle DFE$ **7.** $\angle AFD$ and $\angle BFE$
8. $\angle AFE$ **9.** vertical   **10.** corresponding

11. corresponding   **12.** $m \angle 2 = m \angle 4 = m \angle 6 = m \angle 8 = 62°$; $m \angle 1 = m \angle 3 = m \angle 5 = m \angle 7 = 118°$ **13.** rotational symmetry; horizontal and vertical line symmetry
14. vertical line symmetry   **15.** horizontal line symmetry   **16.** obtuse scalene   **17.** equiangular, acute equilateral   **18.** right scalene   **19.** acute isosceles   **20.** no

10.6 Exercises, pp. 486–487

1. a. parallelogram, rectangle, square, rhombus
b. kite, some scalene quadrilaterals   **c.** trapezoid, isosceles trapezoid   **d.** rhombus, square
e. (non-isosceles) trapezoid, scalene quadrilateral
f. kite, parallelogram, rectangle, square, rhombus, isosceles trapezoid   **5.** trapezoid   **7.** square
9. rhombus   **11.** scalene quadrilateral
13. sometimes; *sample answer:* A rectangle is a parallelogram, but a trapezoid is not.   **15.** sometimes; *sample answer:* Only a rhombus with right angles is a square.   **17.** $x = 5$ m, $y = 11$ m
19. $x = 6$ ft, $y = 3$ ft
21. F; *sample answer:*   **23.** E, F; *sample answer:*

25. A; *sample answer:*   **27.** B; *sample answer:*

29. 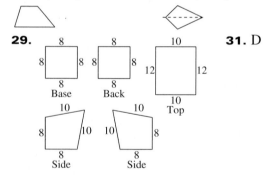   **31.** D

10.7 Exercises, pp. 490–491

1. *Sample answer:* They are congruent if they are exactly the same size and shape. If you could cut them out, you could match them up perfectly by laying one on top of the other.   **3.** A and D
5. B   **7.** A   **9.** A and B are both equiangular, equilateral, and regular. C and D are congruent to each other.   **11.** 3   **13.** 720°   **15.** no; no
17. 81 square units; 9 by 9
19. *Sample answer:*

10.8 Exercises, pp. 496–497

3. $m \angle 1 = 120°$, $m \angle 2 = 120°$, $m \angle 3 = 90°$, $m \angle 4 = 30°$, $m \angle 5 = 60°$ **5.** $\angle AED$, $\angle EDC$, $\angle DCB$, $\angle CBA$, $\angle BAE$; 540° **7.** 135° **9.** $m \angle 1 = 90°$, $m \angle 2 = 65°$, $m \angle 3 = 115°$, $m \angle 4 = 115°$, $m \angle 5 = 90°$ **11.** interior: 135°, exterior: 45° **13.** interior: 150°, exterior: 30° **15.** 71°, 71°, 76°, 142° **17.** 90°, 90°, 135°, 135°, 135°, 135° **19.** the triangles, the trapezoids, the tall rectangles, and the rectangles at the bottom of the photo **21.** 63°, 90°, 90°, and 117° **23.** A

Using a Computer, p. 499

3. The sum should be 360°. **7.** The sum is 720°; yes.

10.9 Exercises, pp. 502–503

1. a. All sides have different lengths, and all angles have different measures. **b.** Two sides have the same length, and the two angles opposite those sides have the same measure. **c.** All sides have the same length, and all angles have the same measures. **3.** smallest angle: $\angle B$, largest angle: $\angle C$, shortest side: $\overline{AC}$, longest side: $\overline{AB}$ **5.** smallest angle: $\angle F$, largest angle: $\angle D$, shortest side: $\overline{DE}$, longest side: $\overline{EF}$ **7.** shortest side: $\overline{EF}$, longest side: $\overline{DE}$ **9.** shortest side: $\overline{QR}$, longest side: $\overline{PQ}$ **11.** $\angle A$; opposite shortest side $\overline{CB}$, $CB = 8$ **13.** $\angle B$; opposite shortest side $\overline{AC}$, $AC = 5$ **15.** shortest: $\overline{AB}$, longest: $\overline{AC}$; $m \angle CBA = 72°$, and $m \angle A = 60°$ **17.** shortest: $\overline{GC}$, longest: $\overline{CH}$; $m \angle GHC = 45°$, $m \angle HGC = 80°$, and $m \angle C = 55°$, so $\angle GHC$ is the smallest angle and $\angle HGC$ is the largest. **19.** The side opposite the right angle; the measures of the non-right angles must total 90°, so they must both be less than 90°. The sides opposite them are shorter than the side opposite the right angle. **21.** D; two lengths are the same, so two angles will be the same. The different length is much greater than the other two lengths, so the angle opposite it will be much greater than the others. **23.** A; two lengths are the same, so two angles will be the same. The length that differs has less difference than in Exercise 21, so the angle opposite it will differ less from the others. **25.** You; you are opposite the larger of the two angles, so the side of the triangle that you are on will be longer.

Chapter 10 Review, pp. 505–507

1. $\overleftrightarrow{AG}$, $\overleftrightarrow{EA}$ **3.** 140°; obtuse **5.** $\angle 2$, $\angle 4$, $\angle 6$, $\angle 8$ **7.** vertical line symmetry; rotational symmetry at 72° and 144° in either direction **9.** horizontal and vertical lines of symmetry; rotational symmetry at 90° and 180° in either direction **11.** acute isosceles **13.** right scalene **15.** obtuse scalene **17.** trapezoid

19.  **23.** $\overline{AB}$, $\overline{BC}$, $\overline{AC}$

Chapter 11

11.1 Exercises, pp. 514–515

1. 24 square units; 22.8 units **3.** 30 square units; 22.65 units **5.** first figure: 72 square units; second figure: 144 square units; find the area of the parallelogram or find twice the area of the triangle. **7.** The area of the first figure is twice the area of the parallelogram in the second figure; first figure: 432 square units, 78 units; second figure: 216 square units, 62 units.

9. a. vertical: 6 in.^{2}; horizontal: 8 in.^{2} **c.** 28 in.^{2}

b.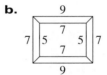

11. A: 10.5 square units; B: 8 square units; C: 6 square units; D: 14 square units; E: 15 square units; F: 9 square units; G: 4 square units; H: 8 square units; J: 9 square units; K: 12 square units; L: 4.5 square units **17.** B

11.2 Exercises, pp. 518–520

3. Line segment $\overline{AB}$ is congruent to line segment $\overline{DG}$. **5.** Y **7.** $\angle R$ **9.** $\angle Z$ **11.** $\triangle YXZ$; corresponding angles and sides are congruent: $\angle S \cong \angle Y$, $\angle R \cong \angle X$, $\angle T \cong \angle Z$, $\overline{SR} \cong \overline{YX}$, $\overline{RT} \cong \overline{XZ}$, and $\overline{ST} \cong \overline{YZ}$. **13.** Yes; the angles have the same measure. **15.** No; corresponding angles are congruent, but corresponding sides are not congruent. They have the same shape, but to be congruent they would also have to be the same size. **17.** $\overline{MK}$ **19.** $\angle M$ **21.** $\overline{QB}$ **23.** B and D; C and E

25. *Sample answer:*

27. *Sample answer:*

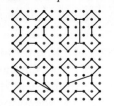

29. $(1, -3)$ **31.** $(2, 5)$ **33.** B **35.** C

Spiral Review, p. 520

1. 18 square units; *sample answer:*

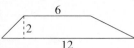

5. $\frac{2}{9}$ **7.** $\frac{4}{9}$ **9.** 4.61% decrease **11.** 14.4% decrease **13.** $2(2.89) + 3(2.50) + 18.75$; $32.03

11.3 Exercises, pp. 524–525

1.

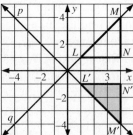

3.

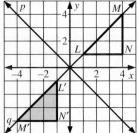

5. a. true **b.** false **c.** false

7.

reflection in the *x*-axis

9. no;

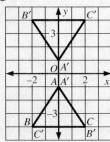

11. yes **13.** No; a photo does not reflect the image.

15.

17. The line of reflection is the vertical line through $x = 4$.

19.

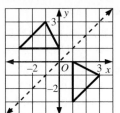

21.

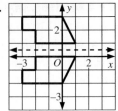

11.4 Exercises, pp. 528–529

1. about 115° counterclockwise **3.** about 100° counterclockwise **5.** *Sample answer:* If you can rotate a figure about its center point so that the figure and its image match up, then the figure has rotational symmetry.

7.

9. about 90° counterclockwise **11.** about 60° counterclockwise **13.** $A'(1, 5)$, $B'(3, 1)$, $C'(1, 1)$
15. *Sample answer:* After a rotation, the image is always congruent to the original object.

17.

19. about 13°
21. $\overline{CF}$
23. $\overline{FC}$

11.5 Exercises, pp. 532–533

1. Each point moves 4 units to the left and 2 units down. **3.** Each point moves 4 units to the right and 5 units down. **5.** clockwise rotation of 90° about the origin **7.** C; each point moves 2 units to the right. **9.** A; each point moves 2 units to the left and 3 units up. **11.** 8 square units; all of the translated trapezoids also have an area of 8 square units.

13. Yes; each point is translated 4 units to the right and 4 units up.

15. Each point is translated 7 units up. **17.** Each point is translated 3 units to the right and 4 units up. **19.** *Sample answer:* Drive 70 mi west and about 200 mi south.

Mid-Chapter Assessment, p. 535

1. $\angle D$ **2.** $\angle C$ **3.** $\overline{DE}$ **4.** $\overline{AC}$ **5.** $180°$ clockwise rotation about the origin
6. translation 5 units to the right and 2 units down
7. reflection in the y-axis **8.** $90°$ counter-clockwise rotation about the origin **9.** reflection in the x-axis **10.** translation 4 units to the left
11. B **12.** C **13.** A **14.** D **15.** $90°$
16. $135°$ **17.** $180°$

11.6 Exercises, 538–539

1. *Sample answer:* It means that they have the same shape, though they don't have to be the same size or have the same orientation.

3. A and C **5.** $\dfrac{HJ}{KL} = \dfrac{JG}{LM} = \dfrac{GH}{MK}$ **7.** $KL = 13.5$, $GJ = 24$ **9.** $\dfrac{QR}{WX} = \dfrac{RS}{XY} = \dfrac{ST}{YZ} = \dfrac{TQ}{ZW}$ **11.** Z
13. 12 **15.** 45

19.
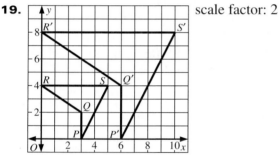
scale factor: 2

21. scale factor: $\dfrac{1}{2}$

11.7 Exercises, pp. 544–545

1. $\dfrac{1}{2}$ in. **3.** car: 36 in., 72 in.^{2}; model: 3 in., $\dfrac{1}{2}$ in.^{2}
5. 144; this is the square of the scale factor.
7. 7.5 cm **9.** about 100 ft; about 500 ft^2 **11.** 8
13. painting: 72 in., 320 in.^{2}; photo: 9 in., 5 in.^{2}
15. 64; this is the square of the scale factor.
17. C

11.8 Exercises, pp. 548–549

1. B **3.** A **5.** *Sample answer:* $\sin 40° \approx 0.64$, $\cos 40° \approx 0.77$, $\tan 40° \approx 0.84$ **7.** $\dfrac{5}{13} \approx 0.38$
9. $\dfrac{5}{13} \approx 0.38$ **11.** $\dfrac{5}{12} \approx 0.42$ **13.** $\dfrac{3}{\sqrt{45}} \approx 0.45$
15. $\dfrac{3}{\sqrt{45}} \approx 0.45$ **17.** $\dfrac{3}{6} = 0.5$ **19.** $m\angle H = 30°$, $JH = \sqrt{3}$; $\sin 60° = \dfrac{\sqrt{3}}{2} \approx 0.87$, $\cos 60° = \dfrac{1}{2} =$

0.5, $\tan 60° = \dfrac{\sqrt{3}}{1} \approx 1.73$, $\sin 30° = \dfrac{1}{2} = 0.5$, $\cos 30° = \dfrac{\sqrt{3}}{2} \approx 0.87$, $\tan 30° = \dfrac{1}{\sqrt{3}} \approx 0.58$
21. $m\angle X = 26.6°$, $VX = \sqrt{5}$; $\sin 26.6° = \dfrac{1}{\sqrt{5}} \approx$
0.45, $\cos 26.6° = \dfrac{2}{\sqrt{5}} \approx 0.89$, $\tan 26.6° = \dfrac{1}{2} =$
0.5, $\sin 63.4° = \dfrac{2}{\sqrt{5}} \approx 0.89$, $\cos 63.4° = \dfrac{1}{\sqrt{5}} \approx$
0.45, $\tan 63.4° = \dfrac{2}{1} = 2$ **25.** $\sin x =$
$\cos(90° - x)$ and $\cos x = \sin(90° - x)$
27. 20 m: 1; 40 m: 2 **29.** 10 m

Spiral Review, p. 550

1. 12.04 **3.** 13.50 **5.** smallest: $\angle A$; largest: $\angle C$
7. $\dfrac{5}{14}$ **9.** $\dfrac{17}{28}$

Using a Calculator, p. 551

1. $\sin 60° \approx 0.8660$, $\cos 60° \approx 0.5$,
$\tan 60° \approx 1.732$ **3.** $(\sin A)^2 + (\cos A)^2 = 1$

11.9 Exercises, pp. 554–555

1. $\tan B = \dfrac{b}{4}$; $b = 3.48$ **3.** $b^2 + 4^2 = (5.3)^2$;
$b = 3.48$ **5.** 0.8387 **7.** 0.6947 **9.** 42 ft
11. 11.23 **13.** 8.49 **15.** $m\angle G = 70°$,
$g \approx 14.10$, $h \approx 5.13$ **17.** $m\angle E = 23°$,
$d \approx 18.85$, $f \approx 20.47$ **19.** 4.28 m **21.** 2.36 m

Chapter 11 Review, pp. 557–559

1. 4500 ft^2 **3.** 4200 ft^2 **5.** $\angle X$ **7.** $\overline{CA}$
9. $\angle A$ **11.** false **13.** false **15.** Each point is translated 3 units to the left and 4 units up.
17. This is a reflection of the figure in the line $y = -x$. **19.** This is a reflection of the figure in the y-axis. **21.** 18 **23.** 12 in. **25.** $\sin B \approx$
0.83, $\cos B \approx 0.55$, $\tan B = 1.5$ **27.** 4.23

Chapter 12

12.1 Exercises, pp. 568–569

1. $\overline{BC}$ **3.** 44 cm **5.** about 25,120 mi
7. 40.2 in.; 128.6 in.^{2} **9.** 12.6 in.; 12.6 in.^{2}
11. 5.9 in., 11.8 in. **13.** 3.2 in., 6.4 in.
15. 9.4 ft^2 **17.** 29.5 in.^{2} **19.** 3.14, 12.56, 28.26, 50.24, 78.50, 113.04 **21.** 113.04 in.^{2}
23. 18.84 in.^{2} **25.** about 314 mi^2 **27.** C

Using a Calculator, p. 570

1. 10.68 cm, 9.08 cm^2 **3.** 12.25 in., 11.95 in.^{2}

5. 1.59 in., 3.18 in.　**7.** 21.21　**9.** 14.14
11. D; $\pi \approx 3.1415927$ and $\frac{355}{113} \approx 3.1415929$

12.2 Exercises, pp. 574–575

1. B　**3.** D　**5.** a: lateral surface; b: base
7. a: base or face; b: vertex; c: edge; d: face;
e: edge　**9.** prism　**11.** pyramid　**13.** pyramid
15. no　**17.** yes
19. 11;

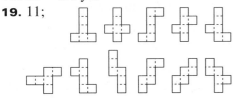

21. Both have 1 base and come to a point.
27. C

12.3 Exercises, pp. 578–579

1. prism; prism; cylinder　**3.** 144　**5.** 664
7. 40　**9.** 480　**11.** 3519　**13.** 96 in.^{2}
15. 24 in.^{2}　**17.** B　**19.** about 302 ft^2　**21.** A
23. A

12.4 Exercises, pp. 582–584

1. B, C; both have a volume of 36.　**3.** prism;
519.6 in.^{3}　**5.** not a prism; pyramid　**7.** prism;
3 ft　**9.** prism; 11 ft　**11.** 30 in.^{3}　**13.** 120 in.^{3}
15. 343 cm^3　**17.** 3 in.　**19.** 10 cm
21. 8: $1 \times 1 \times 36$, $1 \times 2 \times 18$, $1 \times 3 \times 12$,
$1 \times 4 \times 9$, $1 \times 6 \times 6$, $2 \times 2 \times 9$, $2 \times 3 \times 6$,
$3 \times 3 \times 4$; $1 \times 1 \times 36$　**23.** 330 ft^2
25. A and B　**27.** D

Spiral Review, p. 584

1. 1980 cm^2　**3.** 2262 in.^{2}　**5.** 5　**7.** 10　**9.** $\frac{2}{7}$
11. 2　**13.** 42　**15.** $z > -2$　**17.** $r < 5$
19. $p \le -66$

Mid-Chapter Assessment, p. 585

1. 18.85 cm, 28.27 cm^2　**2.** 15.71 in., 19.63 in.^{2}
3. 13.7 ft^2　**4.** 30.5 yd^2　**5.** D　**6.** C　**7.** E
8. B　**9.** A　**10.** 1055.58 mm^2
11. 2463.01 mm^2　**12.** 32.5 cm^2　**13.** 27.85 in.^{2}
14. 120 in.^{3}　**15.** 260 cm^3　**16.** 480 m^3
17. 420 in.^{3}　**18.** 17.00 mi　**19.** 22.99 mi^2
20. 12.00 ft

12.5 Exercises, pp. 588–589

1. 28.27 square units　**3.** $V = B \cdot h$　**5.** 7.07 in.^{2}
7. 1001 in.^{3}　**9.** 8621 in.^{3}　**11.** $h = 3$ in.

13. $r \approx 3.4$ cm　**15.** Volume A > Volume B
17. 75.40 in.^{3}　**19.** 280.4 cm^3　**21.** 296.9 cm^3
23. 5.28 in.^{3}　**25.** 4.94 L

12.6 Exercises, pp. 594–595

1. The cylinder has two bases.　**3.** 320 in.^{3}
5. 10　**7.** 1047　**9.** 1200 cm^3　**11.** 8400 ft^3
13. 2513 m^3　**15.** 5337 in.^{3}　**19.** 2160 in.^{3}
21. 8294 cm^3　**23.** Doubling the radius; when
the radius is squared, it increases the volume by a
factor of 4.

12.7 Exercises, pp. 598–599

1. $\overline{AC}$ or $\overline{AD}$ or $\overline{AB}$　**3.** $\overline{BC}$; 4 ft　**5.** 34 ft^3
7. 7238 cm^3　**9.** 2.48 in.^{3}　**11.** 5575 cm^3
13. 8.18 in.^{3}　**15.** 334　**17.** 302　**19.** 7 cm
21. 2.90 cm　**23.** 2145 ft^3　**25.** Volume
increases by factors of 8, 27, and 64; the factors
are of the form x^3, where x is 2, 3, 4, and so forth.

Spiral Review, p. 600

1. noncongruent corresponding angles　**3.** ray
5. obtuse　**7.** 120°　**9.** 201　**11.** 50　**13.** 4, −4
15. 11, −11

12.8 Exercises, pp. 604–605

1. similar; $\frac{9}{6} = \frac{6}{4} = \frac{12}{8}$　**3.** similar; $\frac{15}{5} = \frac{36}{12}$
5. 592　**7.** The ratio of the volumes is $\frac{6^3}{1}$, or
$\frac{216}{1}$.　**9.** C　**11.** $x = 1.7$ in., $y = 24$ in.
13. 144　**15.** always　**17.** sometimes　**19.** A

Chapter 12 Review, pp. 607–609

1. 44 in.; 154 in.^{2}　**3.** 35.2 m; 98.5 m^2
5. hexagonal prism; 8 faces, 12 vertices, 18 edges
7. 797 cm^2　**9.** 376 in.^{2}　**11.** 168 m^3
13. 512 mm^3　**15.** 125 m^3　**17.** 198 m^3
19. 18,850 in.^{3}　**21.** 2277 m^3　**23.** 2145 cm^3
25. 6

Chapters 7–12 Cumulative Review, pp. 612–615

1. $\frac{5}{3}$　**3.** $\frac{1}{6}$　**5.** $-\frac{1}{4}$　**7.** $\frac{1}{10}$　**9.** 0.40　**11.** 0.24
13. $\frac{1}{3}$; 33%　**15.** $\frac{10}{25}$; 40%　**17.** 275: secure,
15: don't know, 70: not secure, 140: somewhat
secure　**19.** $\frac{18}{24}$; ratio　**21.** 24　**23.** $\frac{10}{3}$
25. 3.2%　**27.** 18　**29.** 11, −11; rational
31. 3, −3; rational　**33.** $c = 25$　**35.** $a \approx 7.5$

37. $y < -\frac{1}{6}$;

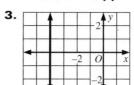

39. $p < \frac{4}{5}$;

41. $x \le -10$;

43. not possible; $2^2 + 4^2 < 6^2$ **45.** $\overleftrightarrow{EM}$, $\overleftrightarrow{HM}$
47. $\overrightarrow{KG}$ **49.** *Sample answer:* $\angle CKL$ and $\angle EHL$, $\angle FEH$ and $\angle ECK$ **51.** *Sample answer:* $\angle ECK$, $\angle BCA$, $\angle DEC$, $\angle FEH$ **53.** obtuse   **55.** $x = 12$ cm, $y = 12$ cm   **57.** $x = 4$ in., $y = 10$ in.
59. 24 square units, 21 units   **61.** yes   **63.** Yes; reflection preserves distance between corresponding points.   **65.** No; in a rotation, some points move farther than others.   **67.** $A'(4, 3)$, $B'(7, 3)$, $C'(6, 1)$, $D'(3, 1)$ **69.** 6 in.   **71.** quilt: 120 in., 864 in.^{2}; piece: 20 in., 24 in.^{2} **73.** 36; this is the square of the scale factor.   **75.** 60 ft
77. 10.68 cm, 9.08 cm^2 **79.** 346 in.^{2}, 390 in.^{3}
81. 54 in.^{2}, 21 in.^{3} **83.** 3591.36 cm^3

Chapter 13

13.1 Exercises, pp. 620–621

1. a. No; $2(1) + 3(2) = 8$.   **b.** Yes; $2(2) + 3(1) = 7$.   **c.** Yes; $2(5) + 3(-1) = 7$.
d. No; $2(4) + 3(-1) = 5$.

3.

x	-3	-2	-1	0	1	2	3
y	2	3	4	5	6	7	8

5.

x	-3	-2	-1	0	1	2	3
y	-9	-4	1	6	11	16	21

7. yes   **9.** no

11.

x	-3	-2	-1	0	1	2	3
y	-11	-10	-9	-8	-7	-6	-5

13.

x	-3	-2	-1	0	1	2	3
y	32	28	24	20	16	12	8

19. *Sample answer:* $6x - 4y = 12$; $(0, -3)$, $(2, 0)$, $(4, 3)$ **21.** B; *sample answer:* $(10, 140)$, $(30, 120)$, $(75, 75)$ $(80, 70)$ **23.** C; *sample answer:* $(20, 160)$, $(40, 140)$, $(60, 120)$, $(90, 90)$, $(100, 80)$ **25.** 30.48 cm   **29.** Yes; *sample answer:* If you divide both sides of the second equation by 4, the result is the first equation.
31. 3.36 million   **33.** B

13.2 Exercises, pp. 624–625

3.
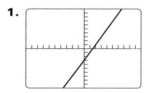
5.
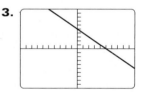

7. A   **9.** C   **11.** B   **13.** not linear

21.
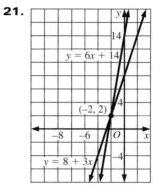

23. $x = 0$: the y-axis; $y = 0$: the x-axis
25. The pattern is linear because the data points form a line.   **27.** A

Spiral Review, p. 626

1. 22.0 ft; 38.5 ft^2 **3.** 50.3 cm; 201.1 cm^2
5. 54 ft^2; 27 ft^3 **7.** 377 in.^{2}; 550 in.^{3}

Using a Graphing Calculator, p. 627

1.
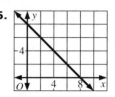
3.

13.3 Exercises, page 630–631

1. x-intercept: 4; y-intercept: 2   **3.** x-intercept: -2; y-intercept: -2

5. 3;

$5x + 3y = 9$	Write original equation.
$5(0) + 3y = 9$	Substitute 0 for x.
$3y = 9$	Divide each side by 3.
$y = 3$	

7. x-intercept: 5; y-intercept: -5

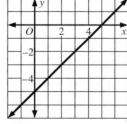

9. x-intercept: 3; y-intercept: -7

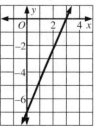

11. x-intercept: 2; y-intercept: 6
13. x-intercept: 4; y-intercept: -5 **15.** C
25. x-intercept: 0.60; y-intercept: 2.18

27.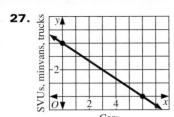

31. A

13.4 Exercises, pp. 636–637

1. 1   **3.** $-\dfrac{1}{2}$ **5.** the line with a slope of 4

7. $m = -6$ **9.** $-\dfrac{3}{5}$

11.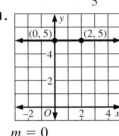

$m = 0$

13.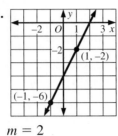

$m = 2$

15. slope of $\overleftrightarrow{AB} = \dfrac{5}{2}$; slope of $\overleftrightarrow{CD} = -5$; no; *sample answer:* They are not parallel because the slopes are different.   **17.** slope of $\overleftrightarrow{AB} = \dfrac{5}{2}$; slope of $\overleftrightarrow{CD} = \dfrac{5}{2}$; yes; *sample answer:* They are parallel because the slopes are the same.   **19.** $\dfrac{15}{70}$, or $\dfrac{3}{14}$

21. $\dfrac{40}{180}$, or $\dfrac{2}{9}$ **23.** $-\dfrac{3}{4}$ **25.** $-\dfrac{8}{15}$ **27.** $\dfrac{8}{9}$ **29.** A

Spiral Review, p. 638

1. *x*-intercept: -3; *y*-intercept: 12

3. *x*-intercept: -4; *y*-intercept: 4

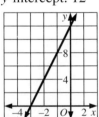   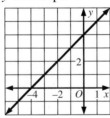

5. Rational; it is the ratio of integers.
7. Rational; decimal terminates.   **9.** 72
11. 6105   **13.** 5.76   **15.** 200%   **17.** yes
19. no   **21.** 77 yd

Mid-Chapter Assessment, p. 639

1. 56 g   **2.** 25 oz   **3.** more; *sample answer:* The rock weighs about 36 oz.   **4.** yes   **5.** no   **6.** yes

7.

x	1	6	11	16
y	8	6	4	2

8.

9. *x*-intercept: 4; *y*-intercept: 16   **10.** *x*-intercept: 5; *y*-intercept: 4   **11.** *x*-intercept: 2; *y*-intercept: 3

12. $\dfrac{3}{2}$ **13.** -2 **14.** $-\dfrac{7}{10}$ **15.** $\dfrac{3}{2}$ **16.** Ex. 12 and Ex. 15   **17.** B   **18.** A   **19.** C

13.5 Exercises, pp. 644–645

1. *Sample answer:* It contains the slope, m, and the *y*-intercept, b.   **3.** C, E

5. $m = \dfrac{1}{4}$; $b = -1$ **7.** $m = -2$; $b = 8$

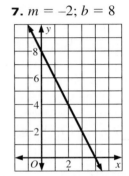

17. A   **19.** False; *sample answer:* The slope is 2.

21.

x	0	1	2	3	4
y	7	16.8	26.6	36.4	46.2

Every second, the speed increases by 9.8 m/s.

23. $y = -\dfrac{2}{3}x + 1$ **25.** $y = \dfrac{2}{5}x - 2$ **27.** D

13.6 Exercises, pp. 650–651

1. 1993   **3.** *Sample answer:* $30x + 50y = 1800$
7. a. about 33.5   **b.** *Sample answer:* Probably not; cans are very light now, and if they were much lighter, they might not be strong enough.

9. 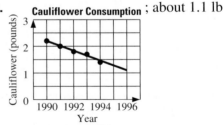 ; about 1.1 lb

11. about 35.2 million

13.7 Exercises, pp. 654–655

1. yes   **3.** *Sample answer:* $(1, 1)$, $(-2, 0)$, $(0, 3)$
5. solid   **7.** dashed

9.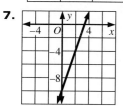

11.

13. No; $4(5) + 6(5) = 50$.   **15.** No; $4(-2) + 6(10) = 52$.   **17.** B   **19.** A

21. *Sample answer:* $(0, 0), (2, 3), \left(-\frac{1}{2}, 4\right), (3, -3)$

23. *Sample answer:* $(0, 3)$, $(2, 2.25)$, $(5, 5)$, $(-1, 7)$ **29.** *Sample answer:* A: You will be able to go farther than 26.2 mi.; B: You think you might be able to go farther than 26.2 mi.

13.8 Exercises, pp. 658–659

1. 5 units; $(3.5, 2)$ **3.** 22.9 units
5. about 7.8 units   **7.** about 7.6 units   **9.** $(-3, 0)$
11. $(-1, 1)$; 5.7 units   **13.** $(0, 1.5)$; 6.1 units
15. $(0, -8)$, $(4, -2)$ **17.** about (37 N, 92 W)
19. C

Chapter 13 Review, pp. 661–663

5.

x	5	6	7	8	9	10
y	20	22	24	26	28	30

7. 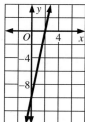   **9.**

11. *x*-intercept: 2; *y*-intercept: -10

13. *x*-intercept: $-\frac{4}{3}$; *y*-intercept: 4

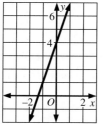

15. $m = -3$ **17.** $m = -\frac{7}{4}$ **19.** $m = -3$; $b = -5$
21. $m = 9$; $b = 3$ **23.** *Sample answer:* 100 subs and 75 pizzas

25. 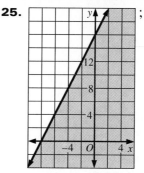 ; *sample answer:* $(0, 0)$, $(0, 4)$, $(4, 4)$, $(-6, -3)$

27. 9.5 units; $(-0.5, 4.5)$ **29.** 6.1 units; $(-2, -6.5)$

Chapter 14

14.1 Exercises, pp. 670–671

1. a. median   **b.** mode   **c.** mean   **3.** 4.875
5. 5   **7.** mean: 54.1, median: 54, mode: none
9. mean: $58.\overline{5}$, median: 59, mode: 60   **11.** mean: 3.2, median: 3.5, mode: 4   **17.** mean: about 2.64, median: 2, mode: 1   **19.** mean: 6.61, median: 6.6, modes: 6.3, 6.5, and 6.9   **21.** *Sample answer:* 7, 9, 15, 15, 17, 27   **23.** *Sample answer:* This means that half of the houses sold for less than \$160,700, and half sold for more.   **25.** C

14.2 Exercises, pp. 674–675

1. 2, 2, 8, 10, 11, 15, 15, 16, 19, 20, 23, 25, 27, 31, 32, 34, 34, 36

3.

6	5
5	0 2 4 5
4	1 3
3	0 2 2 3 4 8
2	1 4 8 9 9
1	0 7 8
0	1 2 2 5 6 8 8

6 | 5 represents 65

5. 84, 84, 85, 88, 90, 91, 101, 102, 107, 110, 113, 118, 118, 119, 124, 125, 126, 127

7.

10	0
9	0 2 3 5
8	0 1 3 4 5 5 9
7	1 7 8 9
6	6 7
5	2 9

10 | 0 represents 100

9.

```
18 | 6
17 | 1 6
16 | 1 2 2 2 4 8
15 | 3 4 7
14 | 3 5 6 8
13 | 4 9
```

18 | 6 represents 186 miles per hour

11. The values on the right (1995) tend to be significantly higher (representing older ages) than those on the left. **13.** West: mean: 20.2%, median: 20%, mode: 20%; East: mean: 18.2%, median: 18%, mode: 19%

14.3 Exercises, pp. 678–680

1. 6, 56 **3.**

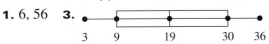

```
      3    9    19    30    36
```

5. 14, 96 **7.** 25%

9.

```
 18   34  41.5      61      82
```

11. The first quartile should be 8.5; the second quartile should be 18.5; the largest number should be 39. **13.** *Sample answer:* Mississippi's population is in the middle of the range of the states on page 677, with its quartiles falling between those of Alaska and Rhode Island.

15.

Receivers

```
 165   225   312.50   390   460
```

CD Players

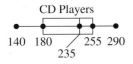

```
140  180      255  290
          235
```

Cassette Decks

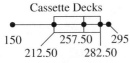

```
 150      257.50    295
     212.50  282.50
```

17. D; the students will all be about the same age, but the teacher will be significantly older.
19. B; this is about the right range. You would expect most of the students to be fairly similar in weight, with a smaller number considerably heavier. **21.** C

Spiral Review, p. 680

1. ≈9.85 **3.** ≈0.4061 **5.** ≈0.4444
7. ≈0.4061 **9.** 2.35 **11.** 2.7 **13.** $4\frac{1}{3}$ **15.** 10
17. 6.7 m on each side

Using a Graphing Calculator, p. 681

1.

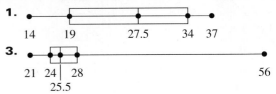

```
 14   19        27.5   34  37
```

3.

```
 21  24 | 28                           56
      25.5
```

5. *Sample answer:* 1, 3, 5, 7, 9, 10, 11, 12, 14, 14, 14, 15, 15, 17, 18, 20 **7.** *Sample answer:* 1, 1, 1, 4, 5, 6, 7, 8, 9, 10, 10, 12, 13, 13, 14, 16

14.4 Exercises, pp. 684–685

1. 3 rows, 2 columns **3.** third row and first column

5. $\begin{bmatrix} -2 & 4 & -5 \\ -9 & 7 & 1 \end{bmatrix}$ **7.** $\begin{bmatrix} -3 & 7 \\ -5 & -5 \end{bmatrix}, \begin{bmatrix} -1 & -1 \\ 7 & -5 \end{bmatrix}$

9. $\begin{bmatrix} -10 & -2 & 4 \\ 1 & -10 & 1 \end{bmatrix}, \begin{bmatrix} 2 & -8 & 0 \\ -1 & -8 & -7 \end{bmatrix}$

11. $\begin{bmatrix} -4 & 5 & -3 \\ -5 & -4 & -1 \\ 8 & 6 & 10 \end{bmatrix}, \begin{bmatrix} 10 & 5 & -9 \\ -3 & 4 & -11 \\ 0 & 10 & -8 \end{bmatrix}$

13. $\begin{bmatrix} 1 & \frac{4}{3} & \frac{2}{3} \\ 1 & \frac{1}{2} & \frac{5}{4} \\ \frac{2}{5} & 1 & \frac{4}{5} \end{bmatrix}, \begin{bmatrix} -\frac{1}{3} & 0 & 0 \\ -\frac{1}{2} & 0 & \frac{1}{4} \\ 0 & -\frac{1}{5} & \frac{2}{5} \end{bmatrix}$

17. Triangle 1: 22; Triangle 2: 36; Triangle 3: 9; Triangle 4: 20.2 **19.** Store 1: August, Store 2: July **21.** Store 2 **23.** $a = -6, b = 2, c = 8, d = -16$

Mid-Chapter Assessment, p. 687

1. about 84.58° **2.** 84.5° **3.** 87°
4. Jacksonville   Miami

```
              |  9 | 3
              |  8 |
          9 1 |  7 | 6 6
              |  6 | 2
          7 6 |  5 | 6 7
              |  4 |
      9 7 6 3 |  3 |
      9 8 7 2 |  2 | 0 1 4 7 9
              |  1 | 8
```

1 | 7 | 6 represents 7.1 and 7.6
5. 4.25 in. **6.** about 4.28 in. **7.** 82°, 92°, 93°, 95°, 96°, 96°, 96°, 99°, 100°, 104°, 104°, 113°
8. 94° **9.** 96° **10.** 102°

11.

82   94 96   102   113

12. 75%   **13.** 35   **14.** 64   **15.** 24

16. $\begin{bmatrix} 8 & 5 \\ 20 & 8 \end{bmatrix}$ **17.** $\begin{bmatrix} 3 & 2 \\ -2 & -13 \end{bmatrix}$ **18.** $\begin{bmatrix} 1 & 12 \\ 23 & 24 \end{bmatrix}$

14.5 Exercises, pp. 690–691

1. Yes; the exponents of the terms are 1 and 0, and the coefficients (1, 1) are real numbers.
3. No; one of the terms has a negative exponent.
5. No; one of the terms has a negative exponent.
7. Yes; the exponents of the terms are 2 and 0, and the coefficients $\left(\sqrt{5}, -\dfrac{1}{2}\right)$ are real numbers.
9. $3x^2 + 4x - 2$; $3x^2, 4x, -2$
11. $p^3 - 16p^2 + 3p - 12$; $p^3, -16p^2, 3p, -12$
13. $-x^3 + 5$; binomial   **15.** yes; trinomial
17. yes; monomial   **19.** D   **21.** B
23. $5m^3 - 10m^2 + 14m$; $5m^3, -10m^2, 14m$
25. $-8y^3 - 11y + 5$; $-8y^3, -11y, 5$
27. $-t^4 + t^2 + t + 2$; $-t^4, t^2, t, 2$ **29.** $2y^2 - 2y$
31. $6x^2 - 3$ **33.** $2x^2 + 10x + 7$
35. $8s^3 - 3s^2 - 6$ **37.** $2.9r^2 + 0.4r$ **39.** h: 1053, 1037, 989, 909, 797, 653, 477, 269, 29, –243
41. in a little more than 8 seconds   **43.** D

14.6 Exercises, pp. 696–697

1. $6x^2 - 7x - 5$ **3.** $3y^3 - 4y^2 - 2y - 3$ **5.** The term $-6z$ should have been added instead of subtracted; $-z^3 + z^2 - 6z + 2$.   **7.** $5x^2 + 7x + 11$
9. $-8b^3 - 4$ **11.** $-x^3 + 9x^2 - 8x - 4$
13. $2t^3 + 2t^2 + 10t - 6$ **15.** $-5x^2 + 7x - 5$
17. $3x^2 + 8x - 3$; 48   **19.** $11x$; 55
21. profit $= 12.50x - (2.50x + 500) = 10x - 500$
23. No; you will make \$3500, which is more than twice as much. This is because you don't have to spend any more to start the business when you sell 400 programs than you do when you sell 200 programs.

14.7 Exercises, pp. 700–701

1. $8n^3 - 12n^2 + 20n$ **3.** rectangle: $8x^2 - 4x$, small triangle: $2x^2$, large triangle: $4x^2$, trapezoid: $10x^2 + 4x$ **5.** $4x$ and $6x$ **7.** They are the same.
9. $4x^3 - 8x^2 - 4x$ **11.** $-48t^3 - 40t^2$
13. $-8t^3 + 12t^2 - 4t$ **15.** $-8z^6 + 4z^4 - 40z$
17. triangle: x^2, parallelogram: $2x^2 - 2x$, trapezoid: $3x^2 - 4x$, rectangle: $2x^2$ **19.** $8x^2 - 6x$
21. $x(x + 1) = x^2 + x$ **23.** $x \cdot 2x = 2x^2$
25. $6x^3 + 2x^2$

27. 180 cubic units; setting the expression for surface area equal to 216 gives $22x^2 + 6x = 216$, which is true when $x = 3$. Then you can substitute $x = 3$ into the volume expression $6x^3 + 2x^2$ and simplify.   **29.** The friend did not multiply $4b$ and b^2 correctly. The first term should be $4b^3$.
31. The friend did not distribute the minus sign over the last two terms of the polynomial.   **33.** D
35. $\dfrac{1}{2}$ **37.** 125   **39.** $-3t - 12$ **41.** $12x - 20$

Spiral Review, p. 702

1. ≈ 7.21; ≈ 10.82 **3.** area of $\triangle ABC =$ 12 square units; area of $\triangle DEF = 27$ square units; perimeter of $\triangle ABC \approx 17.21$; perimeter of $\triangle DEF \approx 25.82$ **5.** $-\dfrac{1}{8}$ **7.** $\dfrac{52}{1701}$ **9.** $\dfrac{3}{19}$
11. $r > -\dfrac{3}{2}$ **13.** $x \le -\dfrac{3}{2}$ **15.** $6x^3 + 2x^2 + 4$

14.8 Exercises, pp. 706–707

1. $(x + 3)(3x + 2)$
  $= (x + 3)(3x) + (x + 3)(2)$
  $= (x)(3x) + (3)(3x) + (x)(2) + (3)(2)$
  $= 3x^2 + 9x + 2x + 6$
  $= 3x^2 + 11x + 6$

3. D   **5.** A   **7.** The Distributive Property was carried out incorrectly in the first step. The binomial $(x + 6)$ also should have been multiplied by 5, and not just by $2x$. The answer should be $2x^2 + 17x + 30$.   **9.** $8x^2 + 36x + 36$
11. $18x^2 + 23x + 7$ **13.** $20x^2 + 40x + 20$
15. $8x^2 + 14x + 3$ **17.** $18x^2 + 45x + 25$
19. $27x^2 + 27x + 6$ **21.** $5x^2 + 36x + 7$
23. $30x^2 + 109x + 30$ **25.** $5x^2 + 21.5x + 21$; 84 square units   **27.** 10 ft by 18 ft
29. Associative Property of Multiplication

Chapter 14 Review, pp. 709–711

1. mean: about 5.07, median: 5, mode: 5
3. mean: 44.3, median: 44.5, mode: 41
5.

5	1 8
4	8
3	2 4
2	4 6 6
1	
0	5

  5 | 1 represents 51
ordered data: 5, 24, 26, 26, 32, 34, 48, 51, 58

7.

9	5 9
8	
7	1 2
6	1 7
5	
4	
3	1 3 5

9 | 5 represents 95

ordered data: 31, 33, 35, 61, 67, 71, 72, 95, 99

9.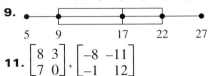

11. $\begin{bmatrix} 8 & 3 \\ 7 & 0 \end{bmatrix}, \begin{bmatrix} -8 & -11 \\ -1 & 12 \end{bmatrix}$

13. $-7x$; monomial **15.** $3x^4 - 3x^3 + 2x^2$; trinomial **17.** $8r^3 + 19$; binomial
19. $7x^2 - 3x - 16$ **21.** $7x^3 - 3x^2 + 2$
23. $x^3 + x^2$ **25.** $3x^3 + 7x^2$
27. $12z^2 + 16z + 5$ **29.** $3p^2 + 18p + 24$
31. $16s^2 + 38s + 21$

Extra Practice

p. 716

Lesson 1.1 1. $-14, -17, -20$ **3.** 16, 25, 36
5. $3, \frac{7}{2}, 4$ **Lesson 1.2 1.** The difference of 132 and 16 is 116. **3.** The quotient of 42 and 7 is 6.
5. The quotient of 16 and 8 is 2. **7.** 178
9. 1096 **11.** 19.5 **13.** 162 **15.** 18.13 **17.** 4
Lesson 1.3 1. The square root of 144 is 12.
3. The square of 7 is 49. **Lesson 1.4 1.** 5 **3.** 7
5. 18 **7.** 36 **9.** 20 **Lesson 1.5 1.** 5 **3.** 33
5. 25 **7.** 32 **9.** 8

p. 717

Lesson 1.6 1. U.S. History **3.** 1994
Lesson 1.7 1. Not a polygon; two sides are curved. **3.** pentagon **Lesson 1.8 1.** 132, 66, 44, 33 **3.** 0.5, 1, 1.5, 2, 2.5, 3, 3.5, 4
Lesson 2.1 1. $6 + 15$ **3.** $2x + 6$ **5.** $4z + 12$
7. $xy + xz$ **9.** $10a + 10b + 10c$
Lesson 2.2 1. $5x$ **3.** $8z + 9$ **5.** $7 + 7x + 7y$
7. $3p + 3r + 3s$ **9.** $n^2 + 6n$ **11.** $6x + 24$

p. 718

Lesson 2.3 1. What number plus 2 equals 10?; 8 **3.** What number minus 15 equals 14?; 29
5. yes **7.** no; $r = 4$ **Lesson 2.4 1.** 23 **3.** 66

5. 77 **7.** 3.44 **9.** 10.8 **Lesson 2.5 1.** 5
3. 9 **5.** 72 **7.** 28 **9.** 2.2 **11.** 9.6
Lesson 2.6 1. D **3.** B **5.** $6 + n$ **7.** $8n$
9. $n - 12$ **Lesson 2.7 1.** B **3.** A

p. 719

Lesson 2.8 1. Amount saved + Amount still needed to save = Total amount needed
3. $45 + x = 195$ **5.** You need to save another $150. This is reasonable, because $150 + 45 = 195$. **Lesson 2.9 1.** $x < 13$ **3.** $z < 4$
5. $y > 24$ **7.** $x \leq 50$ **9.** $z < 20.48$
Lesson 3.1 1. $<$ **3.** $>$ **5.** $>$ **7.** 2, 2 **9.** 56, 56 **Lesson 3.2 1.** 13 **3.** -22 **5.** 0 **7.** -7
9. 12 **Lesson 3.3 1.** -5 **3.** -10 **5.** -2
7. -32 **9.** 20

p. 720

Lesson 3.4 1. -4 **3.** 14 **5.** -25 **7.** 17
9. $-1, -5$ **11.** $0, -4$ **Lesson 3.5 1.** 48 **3.** 12
5. -70 **7.** 24 **9.** $8y$ **11.** $11x$
Lesson 3.6 1. 32 **3.** -32 **5.** -18 **7.** 0
9. 12 **11.** 6 **Lesson 3.7 1.** yes **3.** no; $c = 3$
5. 3 **7.** -12 **9.** -8 **11.** 15 **13.** 3 **15.** -28

p. 721

Lesson 3.8 1. A; 2 **3.** G; 4 **5.** B; 1 **7.** C; 1
9, 11. **9.** 1 **11.** none

Lesson 4.1 1. 1 **3.** -1 **5.** -8 **7.** 5 **9.** 1
Lesson 4.2 1. yes **3.** 2 **5.** 4 **7.** -4 **9.** 4
11. 10 **Lesson 4.3 1.** 10 **3.** 20 **5.** 4 **7.** 2
9. 7

p. 722

Lesson 4.4 1. 2 **3.** 5 **5.** 2 **7.** -20 **9.** -34
Lesson 4.5 1. -5 **3.** -6 **5.** 5 **7.** -2 **9.** -2
11. -3 **Lesson 4.6 1.** Wilmington temperature $- (2° \cdot$ Number of hours$) =$ Bangor temperature $+ (3° \cdot$ Number of hours$)$ **3.** $88 - 2h = 73 + 3h$
5. 3 hours **Lesson 4.7 1.** -2.5 **3.** 1.15
5. 1.58 **7.** -21.58 **9.** 2.62 **Lesson 4.8 1.** 4; 22×10 **3.** 8; 6×6

p. 723

Lesson 5.1 1. 50 **3.** about 210
Lesson 5.2 1. *Sample answer:* A bar graph helps

you compare how many club members run at each weekly rate. **Lesson 5.3 1.** pounds per person per day **3.** between 1970 and 1975

Lesson 5.4 1. *Sample answer:* I chose a bar graph. It demonstrates seasonal variation of weather patterns.

p. 724

Lesson 5.5 1. *Sample answer:* The graph makes it appear that 3 times as many cigarette filters as metal cans were collected. **3.** *Sample answer:* A viewer might conclude that the difference in magnitude between categories is greater than it actually is.

Lesson 5.6 1.

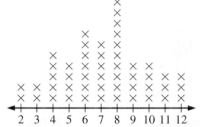

Lesson 5.7 1. no correlation **3.** negative **5.** no correlation **Lesson 5.8 1.** $\frac{1}{4}$ **3.** $\frac{1}{8}$

p. 725

Lesson 6.1 1. 3, 5, 9 **3.** 2, 3, 4, 6, 8, 9 **5.** 3, 5, 9 **7.** 8 **9.** 0, 9 **Lesson 6.2 1.** composite **3.** composite **5.** 2^6 **7.** $2^4 \cdot 5$ **9.** $2^3 \cdot 5^2$

Lesson 6.3 1. 4 **3.** 48 **5.** 4

Lesson 6.4 1. 45 **3.** 45 **5.** 60 **7.** 28 **9.** 20 **11.** 540 **13.** $21y^3$ **15.** $99a^3b^5$

Lesson 6.5 1. $\frac{1}{4x}$ **3.** $\frac{3m}{4n^3}$ **5.** $\frac{2p}{5q^3}$

p. 726

Lesson 6.6 1. $-\frac{3}{1}$ **3.** $\frac{9}{20}$ **5.** $\frac{11}{4}$ **7.** $\frac{2}{5}$ **9.** $\frac{3}{4}$ **11.** $\frac{14}{9}$ **Lesson 6.7 1.** $\frac{1}{8}$ **3.** 1 **5.** $\frac{5}{a^2}$ **7.** 81 **9.** x^2 **11.** $\frac{1}{49}$ **Lesson 6.8 1.** 4.00×10^3 **3.** 2.80×10^{-1} **5.** 430,000 **7.** 7,200,000

Lesson 6.9 1. 15, 21, 28 **3.** −18, −30, −44

Lesson 7.1 1. 1 **3.** −1 **5.** $\frac{5y}{4}$ **7.** $\frac{1}{m}$ **9.** $\frac{1}{5x}$ **11.** $\frac{4}{5}$

p. 727

Lesson 7.2 1. $\frac{3}{10}$ **3.** $-\frac{1}{2}$ **5.** $-\frac{1}{28}$ **7.** $\frac{3a}{10}$ **9.** $\frac{5}{3n}$ **Lesson 7.3 1.** −1.38 **3.** 7.878

5. 4.248 **Lesson 7.4 1.** $\frac{1}{5}$ **3.** $-\frac{1}{6}$ **5.** $-\frac{22}{25}$ **7.** $-\frac{2x}{25}$ **9.** $\frac{3}{2}$ **Lesson 7.5 1.** 5 **3.** $\frac{7}{4x}$ **5.** 5 **7.** $-\frac{2}{3}$ **9.** $-\frac{12}{7}$ **11.** $\frac{25}{4}$ **13.** $-\frac{2}{3}$

Lesson 7.6 1. 25% **3.** 8% **5.** 65% **7.** 60%

p. 728

Lesson 7.7 1. 0.44 **3.** 0.015 **5.** 50% **7.** 30% **9.** $\frac{1}{2}$ **11.** $\frac{1}{25}$ **13.** 87.5% **15.** 375%

Lesson 7.8 1. 20 **3.** 30 **5.** 55 **7.** 1.5
Lesson 7.9 1. $4.46 **3.** $84

Lesson 8.1 1. rate **3.** rate

5. $\frac{10 \text{ users}}{12 \text{ users}} = \frac{5}{6}$; ratio; same units

7. $\frac{3 \text{ pages}}{45 \text{ min}} = \frac{1 \text{ page}}{15 \text{ min}}$; rate; different units

Lesson 8.2 1. 2 **3.** $6.\overline{6}$ **5.** 6 **7.** 56 **9.** 20

p. 729

Lesson 8.3 1. 56 km/h **3.** 88 km/h
Lesson 8.4 1. 20% **3.** $b = 75$ **5.** 43.2 **7.** 325 **Lesson 8.5 1.** 2835 **3.** 540
Lesson 8.6 1. 20% increase **3.** 7.7% decrease

p. 730

Lesson 8.7 1. 162 **3.** 6 **Lesson 8.8 1.** $\frac{1}{2}$ **3.** $\frac{1}{8}$ **Lesson 9.1 1.** $\sqrt{15}, -\sqrt{15}$ **3.** 7, −7 **5.** 6, −6 **7.** $\sqrt{32}, -\sqrt{32}$

Lesson 9.2 1. rational **3.** irrational **5.** rational **7.** irrational **9.** D **11.** C

p. 731

Lesson 9.3 1. $b = 8$ **3.** $a = 7$ **5.** $a = 28.57$ **7.** 12.73 **9.** 12.81 **Lesson 9.4 1.** perimeter = 48 units, area = 96 square units **3.** perimeter = 72.26 units, area = 221.49 square units **5.** perimeter = 16 units, area = 16 square units
Lesson 9.5 1. ⟵―――○――⟶
0 1 2 3

3. ⟵―●――――⟶ **5.** $x > -2$ **7.** $x \geq 1$
−6 −5 −4 −3

Lesson 9.6 1. $x < 1.5$; ⟵――○―――⟶
0 1 2 3 4

3. $x \geq 27$; ⟵――●―――⟶
20 25 30 35 40

5. $x < -1$; ⟵―――○――⟶
−3 −2 −1 0 1

7. $n > 50$; ⟵――――○――⟶
30 40 50 60 70

9. $x < 4$;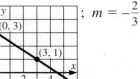

p. 732

Lesson 9.7 1. $x \le -\frac{2}{5}$ **3.** $x \le 4.5$ **5.** $x \ge 2.5$

Lesson 9.8 1. no **3.** yes **Lesson 10.1 1.** $\overleftrightarrow{SP}$, $\overleftrightarrow{PU}$, $\overleftrightarrow{US}$ **3.** $\overrightarrow{PN}$, $\overrightarrow{PS}$, $\overrightarrow{PQ}$, $\overrightarrow{PR}$, $\overrightarrow{PU}$ **5.** $\overleftrightarrow{SU}$ and $\overleftrightarrow{RN}$; $\overleftrightarrow{SU}$ and $\overleftrightarrow{MT}$ **Lesson 10.2 1.** 7: $\angle ZVW$, $\angle ZWV$, $\angle ZWY$, $\angle YWX$, $\angle YXW$, $\angle VZW$, $\angle WZY$ **3.** 3: $\angle VZX$, $\angle ZYW$, $\angle XYW$

Lesson 10.3 1. Line k is not parallel to line m. **3.** $\angle 6$ **5.** $\angle 3$, $\angle 7$ and $\angle 4$, $\angle 8$

p. 733

Lesson 10.4 1. **3.**

Lesson 10.5 1. acute, isosceles **3.** right, isosceles **Lesson 10.6 1.** $x = 12$ in., $y = 12$ in. **3.** $x = 15$ cm **Lesson 10.7 1.** equilateral, equiangular, and regular **3.** equilateral

Lesson 10.8 1. $\angle 1$, $\angle 3$, $\angle 5$, $\angle 7$, $\angle 9$ **3.** $\angle 2$, $\angle 4$, $\angle 6$, $\angle 8$, $\angle 10$ **5.** 75°

p. 734

Lesson 10.9 1. $\overline{AC}$, $\overline{AB}$ **3.** $\overline{JG}$, $\overline{JH}$ **5.** $\angle G$

Lesson 11.1 1. 243 square units, 729 square units; find the area of the trapezoid, or find 3 times the area of the triangle.

Lesson 11.2 1. $\angle D$ **3.** AB **5.** $\angle B$

Lesson 11.3 1. $X' = (-3, -4)$, $Y' = (-1, -2)$, $Z' = (-4, -1)$ **3.** $X' = (3, -4)$, $Y' = (1, -2)$, $Z' = (4, -1)$ **5.** $X' = (-3, 4)$, $Y' = (-1, 2)$, $Z' = (-4, 1)$

p. 735

Lesson 11.4 1. 90° clockwise **3.** 90° clockwise

Lesson 11.5 1. B **3.** C

Lesson 11.6 1. $\frac{AB}{PQ} = \frac{BC}{QR} = \frac{CD}{RS} = \frac{DA}{SP}$ **3.** $PS = 6$; $PQ = 2$; $QR = 9\frac{1}{3}$ **Lesson 11.7 1.** 12 ft **3.** 6 ft

p. 736

Lesson 11.8 1. $\frac{5}{\sqrt{34}}$ **3.** $\frac{3}{\sqrt{34}}$ **5.** $\frac{5}{3}$

Lesson 11.9 1. $m\angle B = 42°$; $a = 8.92$; $b = 8.03$ **3.** $m\angle Y = 62°$; $z = 21.30$; $y = 18.81$

Lesson 12.1 1. 47.1 in.; 176.6 in.^{2} **3.** 19.5 cm; 30.2 cm^2 **5.** 15.3 in., 30.6 in.

7. 5.0 cm; 10.0 cm **Lesson 12.2 1.** prism **3.** pyramid **Lesson 12.3 1.** 562 ft^2 **3.** 678.24 cm^2

p. 737

Lesson 12.4 1. 60 in.^{3} **Lesson 12.5 1.** 301.44 cm^3 **3.** 1004.8 in.^{3} **Lesson 12.6 1.** 480 cm^3 **3.** 47.1 ft^3 **Lesson 12.7 1.** 14,130 cm^3 **3.** 24.42 m^3 **Lesson 12.8 1.** $x = 2.8$; $y = 2.4$

p. 738

Lesson 13.1 1. yes **3.** no **5.** $-14, -10, -6, -2, 2$ **Lesson 13.2 1.** B **3.** A

Lesson 13.3 1. x-intercept: 4; y-intercept: 1 **3.** x-intercept: -3; y-intercept: 3 **5.** 3

Lesson 13.4 1. $m = 2$

3. 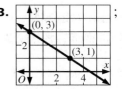 ; $m = -\frac{2}{3}$

5. 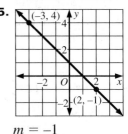 $m = -1$

7. 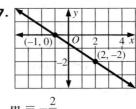 $m = -\frac{2}{3}$

p. 739

Lesson 13.5 1. $m = 2$; $b = 5$ **3.** $m = 3$; $b = -2$ **5.** $m = -\frac{3}{5}$; $b = 3$ **Lesson 13.6 1.** \$3 · Number of student tickets sold + \$5 · Number of adult tickets sold = \$600; $3s + 5a = 600$ **3.** 45 **Lesson 13.7 1.** no **3.** yes **5.** B **7.** C **Lesson 13.8 1.** $\sqrt{26}$ **3.** $\sqrt{41}$

p. 740

Lesson 14.1 1. 21, 20.5, 20 **3.** 47, 48, 48 **5.** 20; 0, 1, 1, 3, 3, 3, 4, 4, 4, 4, 4, 5, 5, 6, 6, 6, 7, 7, 7, 7 **Lesson 14.2 1.** 35, 47, 48, 48, 52, 53, 53, 54, 56, 58, 60, 61, 64, 67

Lesson 14.3 1. 5, 50 **3.** 25% **5.** 75%

Lesson 14.4 1. $\begin{bmatrix} -4 & 7 \\ 3 & -3 \end{bmatrix}$; $\begin{bmatrix} 2 & -3 \\ 3 & -7 \end{bmatrix}$ **3.** $\begin{bmatrix} 4 & -1 & -3 \\ -5 & 5 & 4 \end{bmatrix}$; $\begin{bmatrix} -6 & -5 & -1 \\ 1 & 9 & 4 \end{bmatrix}$

p. 741

Lesson 14.5 1. $-3x^2 + 7x$; $-3x^2$, $7x$
3. $-3z^2 + 6z - 3$; $-3z^2$, $6z$, -3 **5.** $3m^2 - 2m + 1$
7. $3p^3 - p^2 + 3p - 3$ **9.** $\frac{2}{5}y - 1$
Lesson 14.6 1. $5a^2 + a - 10$
3. $4m^3 - m^2 - 2m - 18$ **5.** $6x^3 - 13x^2 + 12x - 5$
Lesson 14.7 1. $3x^3 - 3x$ **3.** $-12x^2 - 21x + 6$
5. $-2y^5 + 5y^4 - 12y^3$ **7.** $-2m^4 - 7m^2 + 15m$
9. $-a^7 + a^6 - a^5 + a^4$ **11.** $10d^3 - 5d^2$
Lesson 14.8 1. $3x^2 + 11x + 10$
3. $6x^2 + 11x + 3$ **5.** $21x^2 + 42x + 21$
7. $12x^2 + 45x + 42$ **9.** $15x^2 + 66x + 63$

Toolbox

Problem Solving Strategies, pp. 742–745

1. $18/h **3.** 5 h 9 min **5.** 7 of each **7.** $2.38
9. cannot be solved **11.** 40 ft by 30 ft
13. 66 handshakes **15.** 22 questions **17.** 90°, 15°, and 75° **19.** $n + (n + 10) + (n + 20) + (n + 30) = 360$ implies $n = 75$; but 75 is not a multiple of 10. **21.** 3 of each; 100 min

Fraction Concepts, p. 746

1. $\frac{4}{5}$ **3.** $\frac{2}{3}$ **5.** $\frac{1}{4}$ **7.** 28 **9.** 1 **11.** $\frac{1}{5}$ **13.** $\frac{19}{50}$
15. $\frac{23}{25}$ **17.** 0.55; 55% **19.** 0.34; 34%

Add, Subtract, Multiply, and Divide Fractions, p. 747

1. $\frac{4}{5}$ **3.** $1\frac{1}{10}$ **5.** $\frac{1}{18}$ **7.** $\frac{1}{6}$ **9.** 10 **11.** $\frac{1}{8}$
13. $\frac{1}{6}$

Add, Subtract, Multiply, and Divide Integers, p. 748

1. -9 **3.** -3 **5.** 0 **7.** 36 **9.** -20 **11.** -6
13. $-1.5°$F

Factors, Prime Factorization, and LCM, p. 749

1. 1, 3, 9, 27 **3.** 1, 3, 5, 15 **5.** 1, 2, 3, 5, 6, 10, 15, 30 **7.** 1, 5, 11, 55 **9.** 2^2 **11.** $3^2 \cdot 5$
13. 2^5 **15.** $2^3 \cdot 3^2$ **17.** 12 **19.** 130 **21.** 72
23. 20 **25.** 3 ways: 50 by 1, 25 by 2, 10 by 5; the factors of 50 are 1, 2, 5, 10, 25, and 50.

Exponents and Scientific Notation, p. 750

1. 81 **3.** $\frac{1}{1000} = 0.001$ **5.** 1
7. $\frac{1}{10,000} = 0.0001$ **9.** 10^1 **11.** 10^0 **13.** 10^{-5}

15. 10^{-1} **17.** 4.23×10^5 **19.** 9×10^{-6}
21. 3.02×10^7 **23.** 2.5×10^{-7}
25. 8.76×10^3

Solving One-Step Equations, p. 751

1. -8 **3.** 10 **5.** 9 **7.** -4 **9.** -5 **11.** $-\frac{2}{3}$
13. -16 **15.** 20 **17.** B, 4.5 h

Solving Proportions, p. 752

1. 8 **3.** 86.4 **5.** 32 **7.** $\frac{2}{3}$ **9.** $.97

Percents, p. 753

1. 84 **3.** 160 **5.** 125 **7.** 64 **9.** 60%
11. 38 questions

Areas, p. 754

1. 56.25 ft^2 **3.** 30 cm^2 **5.** 88 in.^{2}

Pythagorean Theorem, p. 755

1. 3 **3.** 8.49 **5.** 18 **7.** $b = 15$ **9.** $a \approx 7.75$
11. $b \approx 16.70$

Surface Area and Volume, p. 756

1. 384 ft^2; 512 ft^3 **3.** 320 mm^2; 384 mm^3
5. The surface area is multiplied by 4, because each square face is 4 times as large.

Triangles, p. 757

1. scalene, obtuse **3.** equilateral, acute
5. isosceles, obtuse **7.** The sum of the measures of the three angles would be greater than 180°.

Translations, p. 758

1. 4 units down **3.** 2 units to the left **5.** A is translated to $(-3, 1)$, B to $(0, -1)$, and C to $(2, 0)$.
7. yes; yes

Counting Methods, p. 759

1. pearl earrings and gold necklace, pearl earrings and silver necklace, pearl earrings and bead necklace; hoop earrings and gold necklace, hoop earrings and silver necklace, hoop earrings and bead necklace

3. 104; the Counting Principle, $26 \cdot 4 = 104$

Permutations and Combinations, p. 760

1. combination; 10 ways **3.** permutation; 6 ways **5.** combination; 28 ways

Line Graphs, p. 761

3.

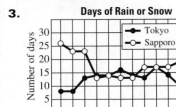

Days of Rain or Snow

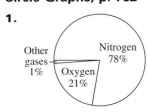

Circle Graphs, p. 762

1.

Other gases 1%

Nitrogen 78%

Oxygen 21%

3.

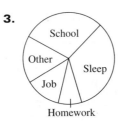

School

Other

Sleep

Job

Homework